Reader and Reviewer Comments

"I received your book in good shape. It is the Best Book on Stars ever written!...

Your book is the most complete of all books. It covers everybody. If I were a star, I couldn't wait to die just to get in your book!"

— Robert Allen Gray
(ELK VALLEY TIMES, Fayetteville, TN)

"This is a curious book.... In that 'The International Film Necrology' (published by Garland in 1981) does not provide information on causes of death, this book does have value, and it is, in a rather weird way, a fun book through which to browse."

— Anthony Slide
(CLASSIC IMAGES, Davenport, IA)

"As a film necrologist I want to say I found your book interesting and very informative; I would like to say also enjoyable reading, but how can one say they enjoy reading about deaths?"

— Billy H. Doyle (Valley Station, KY)

"I received the wonderful book 'Deaths of Noted Movie and TV Personalities' and it was exactly what I have been looking for for so many years....

The feature I like best, (yet so many chapters are great) is the feature telling how the stars died, such as with cancer, murder, heart attack. I have noticed over the years so many stars have died so young and I wondered just why.... I think they must lead a very fast life."

— James S. Harris (Dayton, OH)

"I correspond with a fellow N.E.A.S. member in Birmingham, England and he keeps quoting from (your book) so much that I think it must be very valuable, and so would like to have a copy...."

— Jane Fritz (Wheeling, WV)

"I have been waiting a very long time for someone to come out with this book! I truly love those old movie stars....

We can truly say that we had our heroes back there. I will never forget the fond memories that I have of them."

— T. Campbell (Washington, D.C.)

"I just today got your book...and enjoyed it very much. My dad called it a 'Dead' book; I thought that was kind of funny. Keep up the good work with your movie books. I sure do enjoy this first book I have bought of yours."

— Jesse Wayne Barker (Richmond, KY)

"Your revised edition of 'Deaths of Noted Movie and TV Personalities' has really impressed several members of my family and some friends. So far, I have given three copies as gifts. Enclosed is a check...for an additional copy."

— Ann Michalik (Dover, DE)

"I have received all of your editions of 'Deaths of Noted Movie and TV Personalities' and I've enjoyed them very much."

— Mrs. Lucy Jones (Sterling Heights, MI)

"I am in receipt of the 5th edition of your 'Deaths of Noted Movie and TV Personalities.' It is a wonderful book and most certainly reflects the enormous amount of research you put into the project.

As an author of movie-related books, I most certainly understand what goes into such a project. I have already found it to be a valuable tool in research and will recommend it to others. I wish you well and urge (strongly) to keep up the good work."

— Leon Smith (Bonsall, CA)

"I must tell you how much I appreciate the 5th edition of your 1991 book of stars, etc. It's beautiful and most informative;... I appreciate the work you put into it and I thank you."

— Frances Lucania (Woodhaven, NY)

"The latest 'Deaths of the Stars' arrived today — you've 'outdid' yourself with this one! It's well worth the money, and I'm going to recommend it to others I know...."

— Lucille Kaplan (Jackson Heights, NY)

"I recently purchased a copy of the 1992 'Final Curtain' and find it to be one of the most fascinating books of its kind...."

— Robert R. Young (Lansdale, PA)

"I just wanted to write and tell you how much I appreciate your book.... It has to be the most informative book in my library, and has helped me in my research.

I have obituaries on the stars going back to 1961, and have often wondered where they were laid to rest....

Thanks again for all the work and time spent on this book. I have looked for a long time to find this kind of book with the information I have been wanting."

— Rosalie Gunderson (Salt Lake City, UT)

"First of all, I think your book 'Final Curtain' is the most accurate and most interesting. It's about time a book like this came out. I refer to this as the 'cemetery bible'....

I am an actress, so hopefully someday I can be mentioned in your book, when that time comes."

— Michele Devulder (Orange, CA)

"Boy, am I glad to hear about you. I am also a movie and film buff....

I wrote to Bob Dorian—host of American Movie Classics—and guess what? I got your name and book title; called up and got your book within three days. Boy, was I surprised. I love the book and everything in it....

Mr. Jarvis, I wish you would print the photos of the deceased right next to the names, so that way I (would) know who they are....

I'm having a ball with your book 'Final Curtain.' If this book had been in any of my book stores, like Walden's or Books-a-Million, I would have gotten it a long time ago."

— Cathy Smith (Richmond, VA)

"I received my copy of 'Final Curtain' just this past week, and I must say that I am extremely pleased with your *accomplishment. You are to be congratulated for the great amount of effort and research this work must have entailed. As an avid movie fan, especially of those who were stars during Hollywood's Golden Age, I will treasure this book....*

I, for one, will be in the market for your next update!"

— Roger L. Belton (Longview, WA)

"I just bought your book 'Final Curtain' and I have to say it is the best reference book I have read in years. There is certainly nothing like it.

Many times you watch movies and you really wonder whatever happened to that person. Why don't we see them in any other movies? Your book tells you why. And more important, (it) tells you of the person's demise and age.

I was surprised to see that some of my favorite actors and actresses died tragically...

Please keep this book updated through the years. If Leonard Maltin can do it with home videos, you can, too...."

— Renee Grentus (Rochester Hills, MI)

"I commend you for your excellent book—so aptly titled! That picture on the front cover is so original! What a timely and interesting guide. Anyone who has written a book that includes David Hoffman and Maria Ouspenskaya gets an A+ from me.

I work at a military school and I am buying another copy of your book for the school library! My God, the research that you have done is unreal!...

Your book is worth $50. or more and I would have gladly paid (that) for it."

— Jim Dolce (Old Westbury, NY)

"About six weeks ago, I went into a Movie Bookstore here in Burbank (where I live). Looking around on a top shelf I saw two copies of 'Final Curtain.' I enjoyed it so much I told friends. They went in book stores in Glendale and Hollywood, but, believe it or not, the book was not in the stores there; ...they had to send away for it.

I am 87 years old and have lived in California since 1926. Have met many stars and have talked with them personally....

P.S. Get ready to write another book. We need you...."

— Anna Davis (Burbank, CA)

"A thousand thanks for your invaluable works! You see them on the screen (or tube), forever in their prime—you've grown up with them—they are somehow, friends!

And you wonder, are they still with us? What happened to them? Now, we are able to know....

Again—myriad thanks! Swell (monumental) job!"

— Tom Wolf (Phoenix, AZ)

"Thank you for your wonderful book, 'Final Curtain.' I am an actress in New York City....I visited Los Angeles for the first time last year and I found your book a wonderful tool for finding people.

I recently got interested in Ernie Kovacs and Susan Peters movies, and I never would have known what happened to them if it wasn't for your book. It enabled me to visit these people's graves, pray for them and honor them...."

— Sally Diumond Quine (New York, NY)

"I purchased the 1992 edition of your book and I must say I find it very helpful in locating graves of entertainment personalities. What the book lacks in biographical data is more than made up by your inclusion of specific grave locations. Most of the major books on the subject...fail to provide grave location. They stop at the cemetery name.

I hope you will be able to expand your specific interment locations in later issues....

Keep up the good work. I refer to your book often."

— David Lotz (Plano, TX)

"Thank you, thank you, thank you, thank you, and thank you again! It's not very often that a person who is as busy as you must be, will actually take the time to sit down and personally answer an inquiry. And I just want you to know I really appreciate it. (I'm the guy who writes articles on schlocker films.)...

As a matter of interest, I have been telling everyone I know, both writers and editors, of the wealth of information that can be found in 'Final Curtain.' My compliments; and once again, my thanks."

— Edward L. Mitchell (Oceanside, CA)

"What a great surprise and pleasure to find your book 'Final Curtain' under my Christmas tree!

I have been collecting autographs of movie/tv stars since I was 13 (I am 32 now) and have a collection of over 3,000. Because of this collection, I have also collected the obituary of every star since 1973. I have about 6,000 cut out of newspapers, magazines, Variety, and other sources. Your wonderful book has helped me in going back and dating many I didn't do when I was younger."

— Frankie Cifaldi (Memphis, TN)

"Bought your book 'Final Curtain' and I and my family and friends use it constantly. In fact, we use it so much, the poor book is starting to lose its pages."

— Stephen Pisha (Cedar Rapids, IA)

"I would like to thank you for your most informative book 'Final Curtain.' I purchased a copy for myself and a friend and have found it most useful. We collect grave photos as a hobby. It is also good exercise and gets us out in the fresh air!

Recently, my husband and I spent three days in California 'cemetery hopping' with your book."

— Ginny Michaels (Spring Valley, NY)

"I finally was able to purchase your revised and updated book, 'Final Curtain.' I must tell you how pleased I am with your book. Do not stop writing these books, they are really great. I noted that this book had many more pictures of the stars, which was great to see. Also your remembering Jeanette MacDonald was wonderful. I think you should write a book on some of the stars, remembering them as you did Jeanette. I truly enjoyed this.

I am now a member of the Jeanette MacDonald (fan) club, all due to you, as you advised me to get in touch with Clara Rhoades. I went to their Clanclave last June and had a grand time."

— Theresa Dombrowski (Cranford, NJ)

"I just picked up the latest edition of 'Final Curtain' and I wanted to congratulate you on a job well done. Such a project is obviously a labor of love and it shows in the meticulousness of your research. Every movie lover, film historian and cemetery buff should own a copy of this remarkable book."

— Robert Edwards (Burbank, CA)

[Many thanks to all who have written! — EGJ]

Ninth Edition

Final Curtain
Deaths of Noted Movie and Television Personalities

1912 – 1998

Everett G. Jarvis & Lois A. Johe

A Citadel Press Book • Published by Carol Publishing Group

Carol Publishing Group Edition, 1998

Ninth edition © 1998 by Everett G. Jarvis and Lois Johe
Eight previous editions © 1996, 1995, 1992, 1991, 1990, 1989, 1988, 1986 by the author

A Citadel Press Book
Published by Carol Publishing Group
Citadel Press is a registered trademark of Carol Communications, Inc.

Editorial, sales and distribution, rights and permissions inquiries should be addressed to
Carol Publishing Group, 120 Enterprise Avenue, Secaucus, N.J. 07094-1902

In Canada: Canadian Manda Group, One Atlantic Avenue, Suite 105, Toronto, Ontario M6K 3E7

Carol Publishing Group books may be purchased in bulk at special discounts for sales promotion,
fund-raising, or educational purposes. Special editions can be created to specifications.
For details, contact: Special Sales Department, Carol Publishing Group, 120 Enterprise Avenue, Secaucus, N.J. 07094-1902

Letters to the author should be sent to
Carol Publishing Group, 120 Enterprise Avenue, Secaucus, N.J. 07094-1902.
If a reply is requested, please enclose a stamped, self-addressed envelope, and allow 2 to 4 weeks.

Manufactured in the United States of America
10 9 8 7 6 5 4 3 2 1

Library of Congress Cataloging-in-Publication Data

Jarvis, Everett G., Lois A. Johe
    Final curtain : deaths of noted movie and television personalities /
    by Everett G. Jarvis and Lois Johe Ninth edition.
    p. cm.
    "A Citadel Press book."
    ISBN 0-8065-2058-2 (pbk.)
    1. Motion picture actors and actresses — Death.
    2. Television personalities — Death. I. Title.
PN1998.2.J37   1997
791.4'092'2—dc20   94-46368
[B]   CIP

This book was produced on an Apple Power Macintosh 7100/80av computer system
utilizing Adobe Systems PageMaker and Microsoft Excel software.
Fonts were selected from the Adobe Type Library,
and clip art was supplied by T/Maker's Click Art products.

Pictured on the title page: Nelson Eddy and Jeanette MacDonald in "Rose Marie" (M-G-M, 1936)

Dedication

To My Father-   *Everett Grant Jarvis*

Thank you for all of this! You touched many lives with your love of movies and music!

I love you Dad, your daughter,

Lois

My father was so appreciative of all the letters and correspondence he received from so many of you. He answered every one of them himself. He spent years of research for this wonderful book and devoted many hours perfecting it.

Everett Grant Jarvis's *Final Curtain* came on September 9, 1997, after a nine month battle with cancer. He was sixty-six years old. He was married to my mother Lillian, was the father of five and grandfather of twelve. He spent most of his life as an educator from elementary school to the college level. He had an extensive collection of 16mm films, and when we were young he would take us around to nursing homes and he would have "movie afternoons" for the residents. On occasion he would set up the projector and movie screen outside, and at dark we would have our friends over and have "movie night" outside.

I can still hear his laughter during the "Laurel and Hardy" films: I think they might have been his favorite at the time.

He was a very loving and caring person and will be greatly missed.

Besides the many librarians and cemetery employees who have assisted with this eleven-year research effort, there are many others who deserve special thanks for their most welcome contributions to this continuum:

Russell and Doris Anderson
    (*Madison Hts., MI*)
Michael R. Bahr (*Baltimore, MD*)
Roger L. Belton (*Longview, WA*)
Paul and Joy Bennett (*Stanley, VA*)
Matt Bohn (*Hemlock, MI*)
Hal J. Bonney, Jr. (*Norfolk, VA*)
Jerry W. Brown (*Anniston, AL*)
Eileen F. Calabrese (*Bedford Hills, NY*)
Art and Willetta Carrington
    (*Huntington Beach, CA*)
John J. Cashman (*Brooklyn, NY*)
Frankie Cifaldi (*Memphis, TN*)
Ed Colbert (*Los Angeles, CA*)
Raymond Combs (*Copiague, NY*)
Donald F. Deluccie (*Highland, CA*)
Michele Devulder (*Orange, CA*)
Daniel Timothy Dey (*Medford, NY*)
Carl Dolente (*Camden, NJ*)
Robert Edwards (*Burbank, CA*)
Chris & Melissa Ferguson (*Glen Allen, VA*)
Vivien Field (*Prescott, AZ*)
Frank Fife (*Elmira, NY*)
Sharon George (*Richmond, VA*)
Ann MacGregor Gibb (*New York, NY*)
David L. Graham (*Mt. Pleasant, TX*)
Robert Allen Gray (*Fayetteville, TN*)
Renee Grentus (*Rochester Hills, MI*)
Donald Hammarstrom (*Denver, CO*)
Matt Haestier (*Lincoln, England*)
Sherry B. Hansley (*Madison, CT*)
Harry B. Haymes (*Amherst, NH*)
Urwin E. Hendrix (*Lansing, MI*)
Lynn Hereford (*Austin, TX*)
Robert E. Herring (*Los Angeles, CA*)
Mark Holden (*Luton, Bedfordshire, U.K.*)
Jeff Holmes (*Euclid, OH*)
Terry Jeanson (*San Antonio, TX*)

Bernard Johnson (*Santa Monica, CA*)
Jeff Jourdan (*Boulder, CO*)
Joseph A. Lucia (*Fremont, CA*)
Lucille Kaplan (*Jackson Heights, NY*)
Jennifer Katz (*Berkeley, CA*)
Robert K. Klepper (*Pensacola, FL*)
Bill and LaVonne Lee (*Arlington, TX*)
David N. Lotz (*Plano, TX*)
Celia Lunn (*London, England*)
Peter W. Many, Jr. (*New Orleans, LA*)
Ginny Michaels (*Spring Valley, NY*)
Gerald Morales (*New Orleans, LA*)
Chuck Moran (*Whittier, CA*)
Joseph Morgan Neblett (*Brooklyn, NY*)
Glen Muir (*Bowie, MD*)
Steve and William Oster (*Orem, UT*)
James Robert Parish (*Studio City, CA*)
Barry A. Patraw (*Schaumburg, IL*)
Nicholas Patterson (*Pasadena, CA*)
Lucy and Perry Pickering (*Baltimore, MD*)
Charles Pierce (*N. Hollywood, CA*)
Robert Richards (*Dayton, OH*)
Mark H. Rowe (*Whittier, CA*)
Eleanor M. Rude (*New Haven, CT*)
Tom Hughes Sand (*Los Angeles, CA*)
Cindy Shank (*Hagerstown, MD*)
Anita Silverman (*Chesterland, OH*)
André Siscot (*Bruxelles, Belgium*)
Bryan Smith (*N. Hollywood, CA*)
Greg Smith (*Hollywood, CA*)
Scott L. Spencer (*Austin, TX*)
Mildred I. State (*Oceanside, CA*)
E. J. Stephens (*Pasadena, CA*)
George Sweeney (*Boone, NC*)
Stephen Urbaniak (*Roseville, MI*)
Robert White (*Asheboro, NC*)
B. Scott Wilson (*Richmond, IN*)
Tom Wolf (*Phoenix, AZ*)

Foreword

This new ninth edition of *FINAL CURTAIN: Deaths of Noted Movie and Television Personalities* includes deaths reported through August 31, 1998.

Thanks to you, the thousands of enthusiastic readers and owners of one or more of the eight previous editions of this work, the saga of this much-treasured memorial album continues with yet another update.

In addition to listing hundreds of new deaths, the author has concentrated her research efforts this time to filling-in missing or incomplete data—including ages, causes of death, places of death, original names, interment locations, relationships off-screen, and, of course, the latest Academy Award info. One new section of the book has also been added, making a total of eleven.

Determining who is still alive and what happened to those who are gone, have always been two of the most important objectives for compiling the data and statistics in this book. A third, and perhaps even more important goal, was to create an up-to-date, "all-inclusive" memorial record that endeavors to honor the memory of not only the more famous stars of film and television, but also the many lesser known supporting actors and actresses, directors, producers, screenwriters, stuntmen, musicians, studio heads, etc.

Regretfully, no single book of this type can ever be truly all-inclusive, for it would take many volumes of this size to list every deceased person who ever worked in the film and/or television industry.

Once again, the author and publisher would like to thank each of you for your continued interest in, and support of, this ongoing research effort. Without your participation, purchases and word-of-mouth advertising, no further updates would be possible. Do write and let us know if any of your favorites have been overlooked. The author would be especially grateful to hear from a family member who may be willing to reveal the exact location of a final resting place not already published herein. Send all such correspondence to the author via Carol Publishing Group, 120 Enterprise Avenue, Secaucus, New Jersey 07094-1902 or you may E-mail the author at finalcurtain@earthlink.net. If a reply is requested, please enclose a stamped, self-addressed envelope.

Out of respect for the honored dead and their families, this author would like to remind every reader to display their very best behavior while visiting any of the final resting places identified herein.

— *Lois A. Johe*

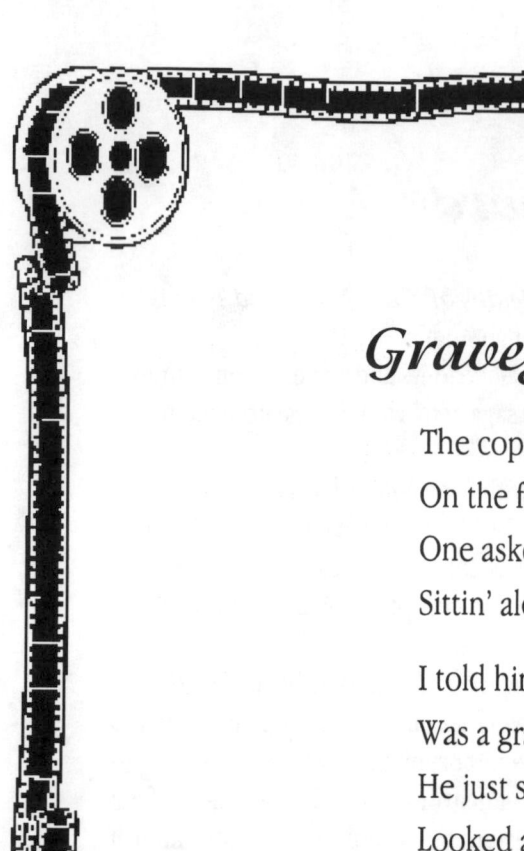

Graveyard Groupie

The cops found me sitting
On the floor of the tomb.
One asked me, "Whatcha doin'
Sittin' alone in this gloom?"

I told him that I
Was a graveyard groupie.
He just stood there and
Looked at me as though I was loopy.

I'm a Graveyard Groupie.
It's bigger than me.
I'm just looking for the graves
Of stars of stage, film and TV.

Clark Gable, Curly
And Lon Chaney, too;
Mel Blanc, Gracie Allen
And even Sabu.

— Scott L. Spencer
Austin, Texas

Features

■ Parts 1 and 2 each list more than 8,700 names of deceased movie and television personalities—first chronologically by Year of Death, then alphabetically by Last Name—*for easy reference.*

■ Key to Death List Symbols and Section Cross-Referencing:
- • a Bullet symbol in the left margin denotes new entries;
- \+ a Plus symbol on the left of the name indicates that a Specific Interment Location is identified in Parts 5 and 6;
- \# a Pound symbol on the left of the name indicates that an Original or Former Name is provided in Part 7;
- ★ a Black Star symbol following the name denotes a major Academy Award *winner* (see Part 10 for details);
- ☆ a White Star symbol following the name denotes a major Academy Award *nominee* (again, see Part 10 for details).

■ A Statistical Summary of Deaths (tabulated by Sex, Year, Age, and all major Causes of death) appears in Part 3.

■ A Directory of 232 Star Cemeteries—with addresses and current telephone numbers is provided in Part 4.

■ Dual listings of exact Interment Locations (now for more than 1,500 stars), arranged first by Last Name and then, as requested, by Interment Sites within each Cemetery, are provided in Parts 5 and 6.

■ Over 2,700 Original Birth (or Former) Names, for both living and deceased movie and television personalities, are identified in Part 7.

■ "Who is Related to Whom—Off Screen?" (in Part 8) identifies 2,000 spouses, children, siblings, and other relatives of film and television personalities *who are also in show-biz.*

■ Hollywood studio affiliations of 400 popular film stars of the mid-1930s are listed in Part 9.

■ A new chronological listing of Academy Award winners in six major categories, a new list of Multiple Oscar Winners, plus an alphabetical listing of all major Oscar winners and nominees, appears in Part 10.

NELSON EDDY

Contents

HEDY LAMARR

1

Deaths of
Movie and Television
Personalities
— by Year

Deaths of Movie and Television Personalities — by Year

YEAR	NAME	AGE	CAUSE and/or PLACE OF DEATH
1912	BOGGS, Francis	?	Murdered (shot at the Selig film studio by a disgruntled employee)
1913	GRAYBILL, Joseph	26	Spinal meningitis (in New York, NY)
• 1913	JASSET, Victorin	50	
1915	BOOTH, Elmer	32	Automobile accident (in Los Angeles, CA)
1915	+ BUNNY, John	51	Bright's disease (in Brooklyn, NY)
1915	KAUFMAN, Joseph	35	Pneumonia (in New York, NY)
1915	# PHILLIPS, Edwin R.	?	Pneumonia and other complications (in Coney Island Hospital, NY)
1915	RUSSELL, William	?	(Do not confuse with William Russell, d. 1929)
1915	WILDER, Marshall P.	56	Heart disease, aggravated by pneumonia (in St. Paul, MN)
1916	# AYRES, Sydney	37	After a long illness (in Oakland, CA)
1916	BRADLEY, Amanda	?	Automobile accident (in New York, NY)
1916	COTTON, Richard	?	Run over by an automobile (in Ephraim, WI)
1916	JOHNSON, Arthur V.	39	Died in Philadelphia, PA
1916	PETERS, Page E.	?	Drowned (at Hermosa Beach, CA)
1917	# Baby Sunshine	1	Run over by a truck (in Los Angeles, CA)
• 1917	BACH, Anna	82	Died in Chemmitz, Germany
1917	BERGMAN, Henri	?	Died in New York (Do not confuse with Henry Bergman, d. 1946)
1917	CAMPBELL, Eric	37	Automobile accident (in Los Angeles, CA)
1917	CHAMBERLIN, Riley C.	62	Died in New Rochelle, NY
1917	LaBADIE, Florence	29	Blood poisoning after being crushed when her car overturned (in NY)
1917	# MACE, Fred	38	Apoplexy (found dead in his room at the Hotel Astor in NYC)
1917	STANDING, Jack	31	Died in Los Angeles, CA
1918	BASSETT, Russell	71	Brain hemorrhage (in New York, NY)
1918	BINNS, George H.	?	Double pneumonia induced by influenza (in Glendale, CA)
1918	# BOARDMAN, True	36	Following a nervous breakdown (in Norwalk, CA)
1918	BREEN, Harry	?	Drowned in Lake Elsinore
1918	+ CASTLE, Vernon	30	Airplane crash (in Houston, TX)
1918	COLLINS, John Hancock	28	Pleural pneumonia following influenza (in New York, NY)
1918	COURTLEIGH, William Jr.	25	Pneumonia (in Philadelphia, PA)
1918	DEVERE, Margaret	22	Pneumonia (in New York, NY)
1918	FRANKLIN, Ruth Darling	22	Crushed by auto while waiting for a street car
1918	GONZALEZ, Myrtle	27	Heart disease and pneumonia (in Los Angeles, CA)
1918	GUNN, Charles E.	35	Spanish influenza (in Los Angeles, CA)
1918	# HARRON, Tessie	22	Spanish Influenza (in Los Angeles, CA)
1918	+ HELD, Anna	45	Pernicious anemia and bronchial pneumonia (in New York, NY)
1918	HILL, Dale P.	?	Spanish influenza
• 1918	KHOLODNAYA, Vera	?	Spanish influenza
1918	L'ESTRANGE, Julian	38	Spanish influenza (in New York, NY)
1918	LOCKWOOD, Harold A.	29	Spanish influenza (in New York, NY)
1918	# MAURICE, Mary "Mother"	73	Died in Port Carson, PA
1918	PEACOCK, Lillian	27	From previous filming injuries (in Los Angeles, CA)
1918	PEYTON, Lawrence R. "Larry"	23	Killed in action in France during World War I
1918	RITCHIE, Franklin	52	Crushed beneath his overturned automobile (in Los Angeles, CA)
1918	RITCHIE, Perry V.	30	Suicide (in Los Angeles, CA)
1918	RYCKMAN, Chester	21	Spanish influenza (in Fort Rosecrans, CA)
1918	SEELOS, Annette	27	Spanish influenza (in New York, NY)
1918	# SHEA, William J.	?	Heart attack (in Brooklyn, NY)
1918	TRASK, Wayland	31	Spanish influenza (in Los Angeles, CA)

Deaths of Movie and Television Personalities — by Year

YEAR	NAME	AGE	CAUSE and/or PLACE OF DEATH
1918	TURNER, Otis "Daddy"	55	Heart attack (in Hollywood, CA)
1918	VALE, Louise	?	Influenza (in Madison, WI)
1918	# WEBER, Rex	29	Spanish influenza (in Chicago, IL)
1918	WEST, William	?	Injuries from a fall (in New York, NY)
1918	WILLIAMS, John J.	62	Heart failure (in New York) Do not confuse w/John Williams, d. 1983
1919	ABELES, Edward	49	Pneumonia (in New York, NY)
• 1919	BACCANI, Ettore	?	Died in Rome, Italy
1919	DECKER, Kathryn Browne	?	Died in Columbo, Ceylon, while on a tour of the Orient
1919	+ DREW, Sidney	54	Uremic poisoning and heart disease (in New York, NY)
1919	GEBHARDT, George M.	39	Tuberculosis (in Switzerland)
1919	GILFETHER, Daniel	65	Kidney disease (in Long Beach, CA)
1919	GRIFFIN, Gerald	65	Died in Venice, CA
1919	LAMPTON, Dee	21	Appendicitis (in New York, NY)
1919	McCAULEY, Edna	?	Typhoid fever (in Rome, Italy)
1919	MONTAGUE, Frederick	55	Acute intestinal obstruction (in Los Angeles, CA)
1919	QUINN, James	35	Accidental (?) asphyxiation (gas) Do not confuse with Jimmie Quinn
1919	ROCK, Charles	53	Died in London, England
1919	ROGERS, Eugene	51	Found dead in bed of myocarditis and alcoholism (in Los Angeles)
1919	STOWELL, William H.	34	Killed in a train wreck (in Elizabethville, South Africa)
1919	WASHINGTON, Jesse	?	Drowned during a filming accident (in Newport, RI)
1920	FINLEY, Ned	50	Suicide (strychnine) in New York, NY
1920	# HARRON, Bobby	27	Accidentally shot (in New York, NY)
1920	+ LOCKLEAR, Omer	28	A plane crash filming accident (in Los Angeles, CA)
1920	# REID, Hal	46	
1920	SALTER, Harry	?	Natural causes (in a New Jersey hospital)
1920	SEYMOUR, Clarine	19	Surgical complications and pneumonia (in New York, NY)
1920	THOMAS, Olive	35	Suicide (mercury poisoning) in Paris, France
1921	# BROOKE, Van Dyke	62	Respiratory problems (in Saratoga Springs, NY)
1921	+ CARUSO, Enrico	48	Peritonitis (in Napoli, Italy)
1921	# GRIFFITH, Katherine	45	Died in Los Angeles, CA
1921	LAMBERT, Clara	?	
1921	# LYONS, Fred	?	After his car skidded and overturned
1921	+ RAPPE, Virginia	25	Ruptured bladder (in San Francisco, CA)
1921	RITCHIE, Billie	42	After a 2-yr. illness caused by a filming injury (in Los Angeles, CA)
• 1921	SAINT-SAENS, Camille	86	Died in his sleep (in Algiers, Algeria)
1921	# SEARLE, Kamuela C.	33	From injuries while filming "The Son of Tarzan" (in Los Angeles, CA)
• 1921	Severin-Mars	?	Heart ailment (in France)
1921	# TUCKER, George Loane	49	After a years' illness (in Los Angeles, CA)
1922	# AINSWORTH, Sidney	50	After an illness of several months (in Madison, WI)
• 1922	BACON, Frank	58	Heart attack (in Chicago, IL)
1922	# CLIFTON, Emma Bell	47	Heart attack (in Los Angeles, CA)
1922	# CONNELLY, Bobby	13	Bronchitis and an enlarged heart (in Lynbrook, NY)
1922	CROCKETT, John	?	Died in Los Angeles, CA
1922	HERNANDEZ, George F.	59	Died in Los Angeles, CA
1922	# MILLER, W. Christy	79	Died in Staten Island, NY
1922	#+ RUSSELL, Lillian	61	Complications after a fall onboard ship (in Pittsburgh, PA)
1922	#+ TAYLOR, William Desmond	45	Murdered (shot) in Los Angeles, CA
1922	# WILLIAMS, Bert	49	Pneumonia (in New York, NY)

Deaths of Movie and Television Personalities — by Year

YEAR	NAME	AGE	*CAUSE and/or PLACE OF DEATH*
1923	#+ BERNHARDT, Sarah	78	*Uremic poisoning/weak heart (in Paris, France)*
1923	KENT, Charles	70	*After being hospitalized (in Brooklyn, NY)*
1923	LONSDALE, Harry G.	?	*Died in England*
• 1923	LUBIN, Sigmund "Pop"	72	
1923	# MANSFIELD, Martha	23	*Burns when her dress accidentally ignited on location (San Antonio)*
• 1923	PALMER, Inda	70	*Skeleton found five months after her mysterious death*
1923	PATRICK, Jerome	40	*Heart disease (in New York)*
1923	# RALEIGH, Saba	57	
1923	+ REID, Wallace	31	*Drug addiction (in Los Angeles, CA)*
1923	STEVENS, Edwin	62	*Pleurisy (in Los Angeles, CA)*
1923	STRONG, Porter	44	*Heart attack in his hotel room (in New York City)*
1923	TOWNSEND, Anna	39	*After a brief illness (in Los Angeles, CA)*
1923	TURNER, Fred A.	64	
1924	ARMSTRONG, Billy	32	*Died in London, England*
1924	BRANDT, Charles	60	*Died in Philadelphia, PA*
1924	BROCK, Tony	?	*Auto accident while filming stunt in "The Great Circus Mystery" (NY)*
1924	+ HERBERT, Victor	65	*Heart attack (in Ireland)*
1924	INCE, Thomas H.	42	*Congestive heart failure (in Beverly Hills, CA)*
1924	# LESTER, Kate	65	*Burned as studio dressing room gas stove exploded (in England)*
1924	# LYTTON, L. Rogers	57	*Died in New York, NY*
1924	MOORE, Carlyle Sr.	49	*Suicide (in his Milford, NJ, home)*
1924	MUNRO, Douglas	?	*Double pneumonia (in Birmingham, England)*
1925	BARROWS, James O.	72	*Heart attack (in Hollywood, CA)*
1925	CULLINGTON, Margaret	34	*After a 6-month illness (in Hollywood, CA)*
1925	CUNEO, Lester	37	*Suicide (gunshot) after his wife filed for divorce (in Hollywood, CA)*
1925	EDWARDS, J. Gordon	57	*Pneumonia (in New York, NY)*
1925	FARRAR, Margaret	24	*After swallowing poison (in Los Angeles, CA)*
• 1925	FEUILLADE, Louis	52	*Complications from peritonitis (in Nice, France)*
1925	FIELD, George	46	*Tuberculosis (in Hollywood, CA)*
1925	HAMILTON, Jack "Shorty"	37	*Crushed after his car hit a steam shovel (in Hollywood, CA)*
1925	JAMES, Horace B.	72	*After a long illness (in Orange, NJ)*
1925	# LINDER, Max	45	*Suicided with his wife (cut wrists and took poison) in Paris, France*
1925	LYELL, Lottie	33	*Died in Sydney, Australia*
1925	# MARSH, Marguerite	33	*Bronchial pneumonia (in New York, NY)*
1925	McCABE, Harry	44	*After two operations (in Los Angeles, CA)*
1925	# McVEY, Lucille	35	*Respiratory illness (at her home in Hollywood, CA)*
1925	PAGET, Alfred	45	
1925	POWELL, David	39	*Pneumonia after a nervous breakdown (in a NY Sanitarium)*
1925	# RATTENBERRY, Harry	65	*Died at his home in Hollywood, CA*
1925	SANDOW, Eugene	58	*After a blood vessel in his brain burst (in London, England)*
• 1925	+ SATIE, Erik	59	*Cirrhosis of the liver (in Paris, France)*
1925	Teddy (dog)	14	*(In Mack Sennett comedies)*
1925	THOMPSON, Frederick A.	55	*Heart disease (in Hollywood, CA)*
1925	THURMAN, Mary	31	*Bronchial pneumonia (in New York, NY)*
1925	VOGEL, Henry	60	*Heart disease (in New York, NY)*
1925	WUNDERLEE, Frank	50	*Apoplexy attack (while dining at the Green Room Club in NYC)*
1926	# AVERY, Charles	53	*Suicide (in Hollywood, CA)*
1926	FORMAN, Tom	33	*Suicide (shot himself through the heart) in Venice, CA*
1926	# GRIFFITH, Harry	59	*Died in Pasadena, CA*
1926	HOLLINGSWORTH, Alfred	52	*After a brief illness (in Glendale, CA)*

• New entry. # Original name (Pt. 7). + Interment (Pt. 5).　　　5　　　☆ Oscar nominee, ★ Oscar winner (Pt. 10)

YEAR	NAME	AGE	CAUSE and/or PLACE OF DEATH
1926	#+ HOUDINI, Harry	52	Peritonitis from a ruptured appendix (in Detroit, MI)
1926	HUMPHREY, Paul	22	Premature explosion of dynamite while filming (in San Diego, CA)
1926	#+ LaMARR, Barbara	29	Over-dieting (in Altadena, CA)
1926	+ LAWRENCE, Lillian	66	Heart attack at the home of her daughter (in Beverly Hills, CA)
1926	LOUIS, Willard	40	After being ill with typhoid fever and pneumonia (in Glendale, CA)
1926	LYONS, Eddie	39	Died in Pasadena, CA
1926	NEWTON, Charles	?	
1926	QUIRK, William "Billy"	45	After a 2-yr. illness (at a rest home in Hollywood, CA)
1926	SHAW, Harold M.	47	Automobile accident (in Los Angeles, CA)
1926	#+ VALENTINO, Rudolph	31	Peritonitis from a perforated ulcer and ruptured appendix (in N.Y.)
1926	# WARD, Carrie	63	After a long illness (in Hollywood, CA)
1927	AUSTIN, Jere	51	Cancer (in Hollywood, CA)
• 1927	# BAGLEY, Don	?	Died in Salt Lake City, UT
• 1927	BAILY, George Donald	64	Died in Los Angeles, CA
1927	+ DUNCAN, Isadora	49	Strangled in her car by a scarf that caught in rear wheel (in France)
1927	HERBERT, Sidney	?	Died in Los Angeles, CA
• 1927	HOWARD, Helen	28	
1927	+ LEWIS, Tom	63	Following an operation for cancer (in New York, NY)
1927	+ LOEW, Marcus	57	Died in his sleep of heart failure (in Glen Cove, NY)
1927	MACK, Charles Emmett	27	When another car struck and overturned his car (in Riverside, CA)
1927	# MACK, Hughie	42	Heart disease (in Santa Monica, CA)
1927	+ MACK, Rose	61	Died in the Lenox Hill hospital in New York, NY
1927	McKIM, Robert	39	Cerebral hemorrhage (in Hollywood, CA)
1927	NICHOLS, George Sr.	62	Died at his home in Hollywood, CA
1927	+ REYNOLDS, Lynn	37	Suicide (gunshot) during a cocktail party in Los Angeles, CA
1927	+ WARNER, Sam	40	Sinus infection/brain abscess/pneumonia (in Los Angeles, CA)
1927	WILLIAMS, Cora	56	Heart trouble (in Los Angeles, CA)
1927	#+ WILLIAMS, Earle	47	Bronchial pneumonia (in Los Angeles, CA)
1928	BLINN, Holbrook	56	After falling from a horse (in Crota, NY)
1928	CARROLL, William A.	51	Cancer (in Glendale, CA)
1928	CLAIRE, Gertrude	75	Died in Los Angeles, CA
1928	CONNELLY, Edward J.	73	Influenza (in Hollywood, CA)
1928	CRANE, Ward	37	Pneumonia (in Saranac Lake, NY)
1928	CURRIER, Frank	71	Blood poisoning after car door was shut on a finger (in Hollywood)
1928	DOWLING, Joseph J.	80	After a 2-year illness (in Hollywood, CA)
1928	#+ FOY, Eddie Sr.	71	Heart disease (in Kansas City, MO)
1928	LINDSAY, James	59	Died in London, England
1928	McNAMARA, Ted	36	Pneumonia (in Ventura, CA)
1928	PLUMER, Lincoln	51	Heart disease (in Hollywood, CA)
1928	+ ROBERTS, Theodore	67	Uremic poisoning after a flu attack (in Los Angeles, CA)
1928	SEMON, Larry	39	Pneumonia (near Victorville, CA)
1928	SIEGMANN, George A.	45	Pernicious anemia (in Hollywood, CA)
1928	SIPPERLY, Ralph	37	Died in Bangor, ME
1928	STILLER, Mauritz	45	Pleurisy (in Stockholm, Sweden)
1928	+ THOMSON, Fred	38	After an operation for gall stones (in Los Angeles, CA)
1928	WHITNEY, Ralph	54	Injuries from a fall (in Los Angeles, CA)
1928	WILLIAMS, Clara	40	Following an operation (at her home in Los Angeles, CA)
1928	YEARSLEY, Ralph	31	Suicide (at his home in Hollywood, CA)
1929	BROCKWELL, Gladys	35	Peritonitis from car accident injuries (in Hollywood, CA)
1929	# BUTLER, Fred J.	61	Kidney trouble (in Los Angeles, CA)

Deaths of Movie and Television Personalities — by Year

YEAR	NAME	AGE	CAUSE and/or PLACE OF DEATH
1929	CAMP, Sheppard	47	*From injuries during filming of "Song of Flame" (in Hollywood, CA)*
1929	CORRIGAN, James	57	*General exhaustion (in Los Angeles, CA)*
1929	+ EAGELS, Jeanne ☆	35	*Alcohol and sleeping pills overdose (in New York, NY)*
1929	FARNUM, Dustin	53	*Kidney trouble (in New York, NY)*
1929	# HARVEY, Hank	80	*Died at his home in Culver City, CA*
1929	HITCHCOCK, Raymond	58	*Heart trouble (in Beverly Hills, CA)*
1929	HOLDING, Thomas	49	*Heart disease (in New York, NY)*
1929	LENI, Paul	44	*Blood poisoning from a neglected ulcerated tooth (in Hollywood, CA)*
1929	MAITLAND, Lauderdale	51	
1929	MALONEY, Leo D.	41	*Heart disease aggravated by alcoholism (in New York, NY)*
1929	# MASON, Dan	76	*Following an attack of pneumonia (in Baersville, NY)*
1929	McDERMOTT, Marc	47	*During gall bladder surgery (in Glendale, CA)*
1929	# RAMSEY, John Nelson	65	*Heart disease (in London, England)*
1929	# RICKARD, Tex	59	*Peritonitis following appendectomy (in Miami Beach, FL)*
1929	RUSSELL, Albert	37	*Pneumonia (in Beverly Hills, CA)*
1929	RUSSELL, William	42	*Pneumonia (in Beverly Hills) Do not confuse with W. Russell d. 1915*
1929	# STEINRUCK, Albert	57	*Died in Berlin, Germany*
1929	TITUS, Lydia Yeamans	63	*2 yrs. after a paralytic stroke (in a hospital in Glendale, CA)*
1929	WASHBURN, Alice	68	*Heart attack after an illness of several years (in Oshkosh, WI)*
• 1930	BAER, Thais	1	*Died in Painted Desert, AZ*
• 1930	BAINES, Beulah	25	*Died in Banning, CA*
1930	BLAISDELL, Charles "Big Bill"	56	*Heart attack (in Hollywood, CA)*
1930	#+ CHANEY, Lon Sr.	47	*Lung and throat cancer (in Los Angeles, CA)*
1930	COURTLEIGH, William Sr.	61	*Indigestion (in Rye, NY)*
1930	ELLIS, Diane	20	*Heart attack on her honeymoon (in Madras, India)*
1930	# HENDRICKS, Ben Sr.	67	*Died in Hollywood, CA*
1930	JONES, F. Richard "Dick"	36	*Bronchial pneumonia (in Hollywood, CA)*
1930	MELLISH, Fuller Jr.	35	*Cerebral hemorrhage (in Forest Hills, NY)*
1930	#+ NORMAND, Mabel	35	*Tuberculosis and pneumonia (in Monrovia, CA)*
1930	PENWARDEN, Duncan	50	*Died in Jackson Heights, NY*
1930	Petey ("Our Gang" dog)	7	*Arsenic poisoning (in Los Angeles, CA)*
1930	PHILLIPS, Tubby	45	*Automobile accident (in London, England)*
1930	# RANDOLPH, Anders	60	*Following a relapse after a recent operation (in Hollywood, CA)*
1930	SCHILDKRAUT, Rudolf	65	*Heart disease (in Los Angeles, CA)*
1930	+ SILLS, Milton	48	*Heart attack while playing tennis (in Santa Monica, CA)*
1930	TAYLOR, William H. "Billy"	101	*Died in Hollywood, CA*
1930	WILSON, Benjamin F.	54	*Heart ailment (in Glendale, CA)*
1931	+ ACORD, Art	39	*Suicide (arsenic) in Chihuahua, Mexico*
1931	AMES, Robert	33	*Bladder hemorrhage (in New York)*
1931	ARBUCKLE, Maclyn	68	*Cerebral hemorrhage (at his home in Waddington, NY)*
1931	ARNOLD, Cecile	?	*Influenza (in Hong Kong, China)*
• 1931	BAINBRIDGE, William	78	*Died in Los Angeles, CA*
1931	# BARRY, Tom	47	*Heart trouble (in Hollywood, CA)*
1931	#+ BEIDERBECKE, "Bix"	28	*Lobar pneumonia and edema of the brain (in Queens, NY)*
1931	# BENNETT, Joe	35	*Heart attack (in Amityville, NY)*
1931	BLAISDELL, William	?	*Died in Brooklyn, NY*
1931	CLARY, Charles	58	*Died in Los Angeles, CA*
1931	CONNELLY, Erwin	57	*Automobile accident (in Los Angeles, CA)*
1931	+ DePUTTI, Lya	31	*Pneumonia after operation to remove chicken bone from her throat*
1931	EDESON, Robert	63	*Hardening of the arteries (in Hollywood, CA)*
• 1931	FARNHAM, Joseph W. ★	?	*Heart attack*

• New entry.   # Original name (Pt. 7).   + Interment (Pt. 5).　　　　　7　　　　　☆ Oscar nominee, ★ Oscar winner (Pt. 10)

YEAR	NAME	AGE	CAUSE and/or PLACE OF DEATH
1931	+ FRANKLIN, Sidney (actor)	61	After a long illness (Do not confuse with director, d. 1972)
1931	# HATTON, Richard "Dick"	40	Traffic accident (in Los Angeles, CA)
1931	HAUPT, Ullrich	43	Accidentally shot on a deer hunting trip (near Santa Maria, CA)
1931	# KUWA, George K.	46	Died in Japan
1931	LAWRENCE, Eddy	?	Suicide (gas) in San Diego, CA
1931	McRAE, Duncan	49	Died in London, England (Do not confuse with Duncan Macrae)
1931	MILLARDE, Harry	45	Heart attack (in Queens, NY)
1931	MURNAU, F. W.	42	Automobile accident (in Santa Barbara, CA)
1931	+ NEILL, James	70	Heart trouble (in Glendale, CA)
1931	PAVLOVA, Anna	46	Pleurisy (in The Hague, Netherlands)
1931	PENROD, Alexander G.	?	Killed in a ship explosion while on location in the Antarctic
1931	PHILLIPS, Norman Sr.	38	Heart attack (in Culver City, CA)
1931	PICK, Lupu	45	Food poisoning (in Berlin, Germany)
1931	# POWER, F. Tyrone	62	Heart attack (in Hollywood, CA)
1931	#+ ROCKNE, Knute	43	Airplane crash (near Bazaar, KS)
1931	# RUBENS, Alma	33	Pneumonia (in Los Angeles, CA)
1931	SANTSCHI, Tom	51	High blood pressure (in Hollywood, CA)
1931	TERRY, Ethel Grey	48	After a year's illness (in Hollywood, CA)
1931	WESTMORE, George	52	Suicide (bichloride of mercury—which took 3 days to kill him)
1931	WILLIAMS, Robert	31	Peritonitis after an operation for appendicitis (in Hollywood, CA)
1931	+ WOLHEIM, Louis	50	Stomach cancer (in Los Angeles, CA)
1932	BAILEY, Oliver D.	55	Died in Long Lake Harrison, ME
1932	BENNETT, Belle	41	Following a long illness (in Los Angeles, CA)
1932	+ BERN, Paul	42	Suicide? Murdered? (gunshot) in Beverly Hills, CA
1932	# CROWELL, Josephine	?	Died in Amityville, NY
1932	# ENTWISTLE, Peg	24	Suicide (jumped off the "Hollywood" Hills sign)
1932	+ GILLETT, King	77	
1932	GRAN, Albert	70	Injuries from an automobile accident (in Los Angeles, CA)
1932	JEFFERSON, Thomas	76	Following a brief illness (in Hollywood, CA)
1932	# JENNINGS, S. E.	51	Died in Hollywood, CA
1932	# LEWIS, Walter P.	60	Died in New York, NY
1932	MATIESEN, Otto	58	Automobile accident (in Safford, AZ)
1932	MIDGLEY, Fannie	54	Died in Hollywood, CA
1932	NEVILLE, George	66	Died in New York, NY
1932	O'CONNER, Edward	70	Died in New York, NY
1932	OLIVER, Guy	54	After a long bout with cancer (in the Hollywood Hospital, CA)
1932	# OSBOURNE, Jefferson	61	Cerebral hemorrhage (in Hondo, CA)
1932	Rin Tin Tin (original dog)	16	
1932	+ SOUSA, John Philip	77	Heart attack (in Reading, PA)
1932	STEPPLING, John C.	62	After an extended illness (in Hollywood, CA)
1932	VALLIS, Robert "Bob"	?	After a long illness (in Brighton, England)
1932	WALLING, William "Will"	59	Died in Hollywood, CA
1932	+ ZIEGFELD, Florenz	63	Pleurisy and pneumonia (in Los Angeles, CA)
1933	# ADAMS, Jimmy	43	Heart attack (in Glendale, CA)
1933	ADOLFI, John G.	45	Cerebral hemorrhage (while on a hunting trip in Canada)
1933	#+ ADOREE, Renée	35	Tuberculosis (in Tujunga, CA)
1933	AITKEN, Frank "Spottiswoode"	64	After a lingering illness (in Los Angeles, CA)
1933	AMES, Gerald	51	Injuries from a fall (in London, England)
1933	#+ ARBUCKLE, Roscoe "Fatty"	46	Heart attack (in New York)
1933	BELL, Ruth	26	Suicide (poison) in Los Angeles, CA
1933	BIGGERS, Earl Derr	48	Heart attack (in Pasadena, CA)

Deaths of Movie and Television Personalities — by Year

YEAR	NAME	AGE	CAUSE and/or PLACE OF DEATH
1933	BURTON, Clarence	51	Heart attack (in Hollywood, CA)
1933	CORBETT, James J.	65	Cancer of the liver (in Bayside, NY)
1933	COURTRIGHT, William "Uncle Billy"	84	Died in Ione, CA
1933	# CRAIG, Richy Jr.	31	Heart failure after a long bout with cancer (in New York, NY)
1933	DALY, James L.	81	Heart trouble (in Philadelphia, PA)
1933	DILLON, Edward "Eddie"	53	Heart attack (in Hollywood, CA)
1933	DUNBAR, Helen	65	After a long illness (in Los Angeles, CA)
1933	DYER, William J. "Billy"	52	Died in Hollywood, CA
1933	# FREDERICI, Blanche	55	Heart attack enroute to a Christmas church service (in Visalia, CA)
1933	GORDON, Julia Swayne	54	After a long illness (in Columbus, OH)
1933	#+ GUINAN, Mary "Texas"	48	After an operation for colitis (in Vancouver, B.C., Canada)
1933	HALE, Louise Closser	60	Two strokes following an accident (in Los Angeles, CA)
1933	HALL-DAVIS, Lilian	32	Suicide (gas) in London, England
1933	HIERS, Walter	39	Pneumonia (in Los Angeles, CA)
1933	JARVIS, Jean	30	After a lingering illness (in Hollywood, CA)
1933	JARVIS, Laura E.	67	Injuries from a hit-and-run driver (in Downey, CA)
1933	KELLY, James T.	79	Do not confuse with James "Tiny" Kelly, d. 1964 (in New York, NY)
1933	#+ MARX, Samuel "Frenchie"	72	Heart and kidney failure (in Hollywood, CA)
1933	MATTOX, Martha	54	Heart ailment (in Sidney, NY)
1933	McKEEN, Snookums	8	Blood poisoning (in Los Angeles, CA)
1933	MORRIS, Lee	69	Died in Los Angeles, CA
1933	PASHA, Kalla	56	Died in Talmage, CA
1933	PAULIG, Albert	60	Heart trouble (in Berlin, Germany)
1933	#+ PICKFORD, Jack	36	Multiple neuritis (in Paris, France)
1933	ROBBINS, Roy "Skeeter Bill"	36	Killed by a truck while wiping snow from his car (in CA)
1933	# ROSCOE, Alan	45	Cancer (at a hospital in Hollywood, CA)
1933	STEWART, Roy	43	Heart attack (in Los Angeles, Ca.)
1933	# SULLIVAN, Pat	46	Pneumonia brought on by alcoholism (in New York, NY)
1933	#+ TORRENCE, Ernest	54	After an operation for gall stones (in New York, NY)
1933	TREVOR, Hugh	30	Three-weeks after an appendectomy (in Los Angeles, CA)
1934	ALLEN, Sam	73	Died in Los Angeles, CA
1934	BEAL, Frank	70	Died in Hollywood, CA
1934	BESSERER, Eugenie	64	Heart attack while planning her golden wedding anniversary (in L.A.)
1934	BILLINGS, George A.	63	Died in West Los Angeles, CA
1934	BROUGH, Mary	71	Heart ailment (in London, England)
1934	CHAUTARD, Emile	69	Organic trouble (in Westwood, CA)
1934	# CODY, Lew	50	Heart disease (in Beverly Hills, CA)
1934	#+ COLUMBO, Russ	26	Accidentally shot by a friend while examining a pistol (in Hollywood)
1934	CROCKETT, Charles B.	62	After a long illness (in Los Angeles, CA)
1934	+ DANE, Karl	47	Suicide (gunshot) in Los Angeles, CA
1934	DELL, Dorothy	19	Automobile accident (in Pasadena, CA)
1934	+ DILLON, John Francis	50	After suffering a heart attack at a dinner party (in Beverly Hills, CA)
1934	#+ DRESSLER, Marie ★	65	Cancer (in Santa Barbara, CA)
1934	FRANCIS, Alec B.	65	Following an emergency operation (in Hollywood, CA)
1934	# GREY, Robert H.	42	Died in Los Angeles, CA
1934	# HILL, George W.	40	Suicide (gunshot) in Venice, CA
1934	# LORRAINE, Harry	54	Died in London, England
1934	#+ MACK, Charles E.	46	Automobile accident (near Mesa, AZ) d.n.c. with C. Emmett Mack
1934	# MATTO, Sisto	39	Automobile accident (in Los Angeles, CA)
1934	PALLENBERG, Max	57	Airplane crash (near Karlovy Vary, Czechoslovakia)
1934	# PERCIVAL, Walter C.	46	Died of complications from an illness (in Hollywood, CA)
1934	PINERO, Arthur Wing	79	Died in London, England

Deaths of Movie and Television Personalities — by Year

YEAR	NAME	AGE	CAUSE and/or PLACE OF DEATH
1934	PLAYFAIR, Nigel	60	Died in London, England
1934	+ POLLARD, Harry	55	Cancer (in Pasadena, CA) Do not confuse with Harry "Snub" Pollard
1934	ROCCARDI, Albert	70	Died in Paris, France
1934	+ SHERMAN, Lowell J.	49	Pneumonia (in Hollywood, CA)
1934	SHOTWELL, Marie	54	Died in L.I., NY
1934	# SKELLY, Hal	42	Killed by a train in a grade crossing accident (in West Cornwall, CT)
1934	SUTHERLAND, Dick	51	Kidney disease (in Hollywood, CA)
1934	TASHMAN, Lilyan	33	Tumorous condition and/or cancer (in New York, NY)
1934	# TELLEGEN, Lou	52	Suicide (stabbed himself with a pair of scissors) in Los Angeles, CA
1934	#+ VIGO, Jean	29	Rheumatic septicemia
1934	# YORKE, Edith	66	Died in London, England
1934	+ YOUNG, Mary	77	Following a 3-month illness (in Los Angeles, CA)
• **1935**	BAILLET, Georges	86	Died in France
1935	BOLAND, Eddie	51	Heart attack (in Santa Monica, CA)
1935	BUNSTON, Herbert	61	Heart attack (in Los Angeles, CA)
1935	# COOGAN, Jack Sr.	55	Automobile accident (nr. San Diego, CA)
1935	DICKSON, W. K. Laurie	75	Died in Twickenham, England
1935	#+ DURKIN, Junior	19	Automobile accident (near San Diego, CA)
1935	GELDERT, Clarence	67	Heart attack (in Calabasas, CA)
1935	GRAHAM, Julia Ann	20	Suicide (gunshot) in Los Angeles, CA
1935	GRIEVES, Jack	33	Died in Burbank, CA
1935	HAMILTON, Lloyd	43	Following an operation for a stomach disorder (in Hollywood, CA)
1935	+ HARDY, Sam B.	52	After intestinal surgery (in Hollywood, CA)
1935	#+ HOPPER, De Wolf	77	Shortly after a radio broadcast (in Kansas City, MO)
1935	LANDAU, David	57	After a lingering illness (in Hollywood, CA)
1935	MURRAY, Tom	60	After a 1-year illness (in Hollywood, CA)
1935	NORTH, Wilfrid	82	After a brief illness (in Hollywood, CA)
1935	+ POST, Wiley	50	Airplane crash (near Barrow, Alaska)
1935	# ROBERTS, Edith	36	Died following the birth of a son (in Los Angeles, CA)
1935	#+ ROGERS, Will	55	Airplane crash (near Barrow, Alaska)
1935	RUSSELL, J. Gordon	52	Heart attack (in Los Angeles, CA)
1935	SALISBURY, Monroe	59	Skull fracture from a fall (in San Bernardino, CA)
1935	# SAXE, Templar	69	Died in Cincinnati, OH
1935	# SCHULTZ, Harry	52	After a lengthy illness (in Hollywood, CA)
1935	# STANHOPE, Adeline	82	Died in Los Angeles, CA
1935	SWAIN, Mack	59	Apparent heart attack (in Tacoma, WA)
1935	+ TODD, Thelma	30	Suicide? Murder? Accident? (carbon monoxide) in Santa Monica, CA
1935	TRAVERS, Richard C.	45	Pneumonia (in San Pedro, CA)
• 1935	WARDE, Frederick	84	
1935	WEBB, Millard	42	Intestinal ailment (in Los Angeles, CA)
1935	WESTCOTT, Gordon	31	After falling from his horse in a polo game (in Hollywood, CA)
1935	WHITE, Marjorie	27	Automobile accident (in Los Angeles, CA)
1936	ADAMS, Howard	27	Airplane crash (in Chicago, IL)
1936	ASHTON, Dorrit	63	Died in Los Angeles, CA
1936	BELL, Ralph W.	53	Pneumonia (in San Francisco, CA)
1936	BLOOD, Adele	50	Suicide (gunshot) in Yonkers, NY
1936	BOWERS, John	36	Suicide (walked into the surf off Malibu Beach)
1936	BRADBURY, James Jr.	41	Suicide (burns) in Los Angeles, CA
1936	+ BREESE, Edmund	64	Peritonitis (in New York, NY)
1936	BUCKLER, Hugh	64	Drowned with his son in a car accident (in Malibu Lake, CA)
1936	BUCKLER, John (Jack)	30	Drowned with his father in a car accident (in Malibu Lake, CA)

Deaths of Movie and Television Personalities — by Year

YEAR	NAME	AGE	CAUSE and/or PLACE OF DEATH
1936	# CHANEY, Norman "Chubby"	18	After an operation for a glandular ailment (in Baltimore, MD)
1936	CROSLAND, Alan	42	Injuries after a car wreck (in Los Angeles, CA)
1936	DARLING, Ida	60	After a long illness (in Hollywood, CA)
1936	#+ DAVENPORT, Alice	82	Died in Los Angeles, CA
1936	DAVIS, Edwards	64	After an illness of 2-years (in Hollywood, CA)
1936	DIONE, Rose	60	Died in Los Angeles, CA
1936	#+ GILBERT, John	38	Heart attack (in Los Angeles, CA)
1936	# HEGGIE, O. P.	59	Pneumonia (in Los Angeles, CA)
1936	HOWARD, Booth	47	Run down by a car (in Los Angeles, CA)
1936	+ HOWLAND, Jobyna	56	Heart attack (in Los Angeles, CA)
1936	INGERSOLL, William	75	Acute indigestion (in Los Angeles, CA)
1936	LAIDLAW, Roy	52	Heart attack (in Hollywood, CA)
1936	LARKIN, John	62	Pneumonia (in Los Angeles, CA)
1936	LIVESEY, Sam	63	Complications following surgery (in London, England)
1936	McCULLOUGH, Paul	52	Suicide after suffering a nervous breakdown (slit throat w/razor)
1936	MEIGHAN, Thomas	57	Lung cancer (in Great Neck, NY)
1936	MELLISH, Fuller Sr.	71	Heart attack (in New York, NY)
1936	#+ MILLER, Marilyn	37	Toxemia from a sinus infection (in New York, NY)
1936	MILLS, John Jr.	25	Tuberculosis (in Bellefontaine, OH)
1936	MURRAY, James	35	Drowned when he fell off a pier (in New York, NY)
1936	NORTHRUP, Harry S.	58	Died in Los Angeles, CA
1936	PAWLE, Lennox	63	Cerebral hemorrhage (at a hospital in Hollywood, CA)
1936	#+ PICKFORD, Lottie	41	Heart attack (in Brentwood, CA)
1936	# RICE, Frank	43	Nephritis and hepatitis (in Los Angeles, CA)
1936	ROBERTS, Stephen R.	41	Heart attack (in Beverly Hills, CA)
1936	#+ SALE, Chic	51	Pneumonia (in Los Angeles, CA)
1936	# SCHRECK, Max	57	Died in Munich, Germany
1936	+ SCHUMANN-HEINK, Ernestine	75	Leukemia (in Hollywood, CA)
1936	STUART, Iris	33	
1936	#+ THALBERG, Irving	37	Lobar pneumonia (in Santa Monica, CA)
1936	+ WALTHALL, Henry B.	58	Chronic illness (near Monrovia, CA)
1936	# WALTON, Fred	71	Pneumonia (in Los Angeles, CA)
1936	WYNN, Hugh	46	Heart attack
1936	YOUNG, Tammany	49	Died in his sleep of a heart attack (in Hollywood, CA)
1937	ABBOTT, Marion	69	Pneumonia (in Philadelphia, PA)
1937	# ABEL, Alfred	57	Died in Berlin, Germany
1937	+ ALEXANDER, Ross	29	Suicide (gunshot) in Los Angeles, CA
1937	# BARRIE, James	77	Pneumonia complicated by heart trouble (in London, England)
1937	BEAUMONT, Lucy	64	Died in New York, NY
1937	BLACKFORD, Mary	23	Results of an automobile accident (in Santa Monica, CA)
1937	BOLDER, Robert "Bobbie"	78	Died in Beverly Hills, CA
1937	+ BOLESLAWSKI, Richard	47	Apparent heart attack (in Hollywood, CA)
1937	BOOTH, Sydney Barton	60	Cerebral hemorrhage (in Stanford, CT)
1937	+ BURGESS, Helen	19	Lobar pneumonia (in Beverly Hills, CA)
1937	CAREWE, Arthur Edmund	42	Suicide (gunshot) in Santa Monica, CA
1937	CARR, William (actor/director)	69	Do not confuse with other actors of the same name (in Los Angeles)
1937	# CHASE, Colin	50	Paralysis attack (in Los Angeles, CA)
1937	#+ CLIVE, Colin	37	Tuberculosis complicated by alcoholism (in Los Angeles, CA)
1937	# DILLON, Jack	61	Pneumonia (in Los Angeles, CA)
1937	DONNELLY, James	71	Died in Hollywood, CA
1937	DUNN, Robert "Bobby"	45	Heart attack (in Hollywood, CA)
1937	+ EDWARDS, Snitz	75	Arthritis after a long illness (in Los Angeles, CA)

Deaths of Movie and Television Personalities — by Year

YEAR	NAME	AGE	CAUSE and/or PLACE OF DEATH
1937	#+ GERSHWIN, George	38	After surgery for a brain tumor (in Beverly Hills, CA)
1937	GLENDON, Jonathan Frank	49	Died in Hollywood, CA
1937	#+ HARLOW, Jean	26	Cerebral edema following uremic poisoning (in Hollywood, CA)
1937	HASSELL, George	55	Heart attack (in Chatsworth, CA)
1937	#+ HEALY, Ted	41	From injuries after a bar-room fight in Los Angeles, CA
1937	HEATHERLEY, Clifford	48	Died in London, England
1937	# INCE, Ralph W.	49	Automobile accident (in London, England)
1937	JENNINGS, De Witt	57	Heart attack (in Hollywood, CA)
1937	JOHNSON, Martin	52	Airplane crash (in Los Angeles, CA)
1937	LEWIS, Ralph	65	Injuries from an automobile accident (in Los Angeles, CA)
1937	LOSEE, Frank	81	Pulmonary embolism after an attack of arthritis (in Yonkers, NY)
1937	LOWELL, Helen	71	After a lingering illness (in Hollywood, CA)
1937	# MAILES, Charles H.	66	Died in Los Angeles, CA
1937	MARCUS, James A.	69	Heart attack (in Hollywood, CA)
1937	McCOY, Harry	43	Heart attack (in Hollywood, CA)
1937	# MULLER, Renate	30	Suicide (in Berlin, Germany)
1937	NEWALL, Guy	51	After a brief illness (in Hampstead, England)
1937	+ OWSLEY, Monroe	35	Heart attack (in Belmont, CA)
1937	PANZER, Paul	70	Heart trouble (in NYC) Do not confuse with Paul Wolfgang Panzer
1937	PERKINS, Osgood	45	Apparent heart attack after tonsilitis (in Washington, D.C.)
1937	PLAYTER, Wellington	57	Died in Oakland, CA
1937	+ POWELL, Richard	39	Fractured skull from an auto accident (in Hollywood, CA)
1937	# PREVOST, Marie	38	Acute alcoholism (in Los Angeles, CA)
1937	+ ROLAND, Ruth	45	Cancer (in Los Angeles, CA)
1937	ROSLEY, Adrian	47	Following a heart attack (in Hollywood, CA)
1937	SANDROCK, Adele	73	Died in Berlin, Germany
1937	SELLON, Charles	58	Cancer (in La Crescenta, CA)
1937	SHUBERT, Eddie	38	Heart attack watching a golf tournament (in Los Angeles, CA)
1937	SMITH, Clifford S.	51	Peritonitis following a ruptured appendix (in Hollywood, CA)
1937	STANDING, Guy	63	Following a heart attack (in Apple Valley, CA)
• 1937	STANLEY, Aileen	85	Died in Los Angeles, CA
1937	# TREE, Lady	72	After an operation from which she did not rally
1937	WATSON, Roy	61	Died in Hollywood, CA
1938	ACKERMAN, Walter	57	Died in Bishop, CA
1938	APFEL, Oscar	59	Heart attack (in Hollywood, CA)
1938	# BETZ, Matthew	56	After a long illness (in Los Angeles, CA)
1938	BLACK, Maurice	46	After an illness of 2-days (in Hollywood, CA)
1938	BLYSTONE, John G.	45	Heart attack (in Beverly Hills, CA)
1938	+ CHALIAPIN, Feodor Sr. "Felix"	65	Uremia (in Paris, France)
1938	CLARK, Harvey	52	Following a heart attack (in Hollywood, CA)
1938	COHL, Emil	81	Burns (after his beard caught fire from a candle)
1938	CRITTENDEN, Throckwood Dwight	59	Murdered (gunshot) in Los Angeles, CA
1938	DOUGHERTY, Virgil Jack	42	Suicide (carbon monoxide) in Hollywood, CA
1938	+ FACTOR, Max	61	Kidney and liver ailment (at his home in Beverly Hills, CA)
1938	#+ FREDERICK, Pauline (actress)	54	Asthma (in Los Angeles, CA) — Do not confuse with TV reporter
1938	FUREY, Barney	49	Liver ailment (in Los Angeles, CA)
1938	GARCIA, Allan	51	Died in Los Angeles, CA
1938	HENDRICKS, Ben Jr.	44	Died in Los Angeles, CA
1938	HILL, Thelma	32	Following a 3-month illness (in Culver City, CA)
1938	INCE, Richard	23	Died in Oakland, CA
1938	IRWIN, May	76	Bronchial pneumonia (in New York, NY)
1938	JANNEY, William "Bill"	34	After a short, serious setback while hospitalized (in New York, NY)

Deaths of Movie and Television Personalities — by Year

YEAR	NAME	AGE	CAUSE and/or PLACE OF DEATH
1938	KIMBALL, Edward M.	78	Died in Hollywood, CA
1938	KOHLER, Fred Sr.	49	Heart attack (in Los Angeles, CA)
1938	+ LAWRENCE, Florence	50	Suicide (mixture of cough syrup and ant paste) in Beverly Hills, CA
1938	LLOYD, Rollo	55	Died in Los Angeles, CA
1938	LONG, Jack	?	Motorcycle accident (in Los Angeles, CA)
1938	McCALL, William	58	Died in Hollywood, CA
1938	+ McWADE, Robert Jr.	55	Heart attack (in Culver City, CA)
1938	# MELIES, Georges	77	After a long illness (in Orly, France)
1938	# MONCRIES, Edward	78	Heart attack (in Hollywood, CA)
1938	MORENO, Thomas "Sky Ball"	43	Died in West Los Angeles, CA
1938	+ MYERS, Harry C.	52	Pneumonia (in Los Angeles, CA)
1938	#+ OLAND, Warner	57	Bronchial pneumonia (in Stockholm, Sweden)
1938	PINCHOT, Rosamond	33	Suicide (carbon monoxide poisoning) in Old Brookfield, NY
1938	ROBERTI, Lyda	29	Heart ailment (in Los Angeles, CA)
1938	RORKE, Mary	80	Died in London, England
1938	STEDMAN, Myrtle	48	Heart trouble (in Los Angeles, CA)
1938	STEWART, Richard	?	
1938	STRICKLAND, Helen	74	Died at Mt. Sinai Hospital in New York, NY
1938	# TEARLE, Conway	60	Heart attack (in Los Angeles, CA)
1938	# Toto the Clown	50	Died in New York, NY (Do not confuse with Toto, d. 1967)
1938	# WALLACE, May	61	Heart disease (in Los Angeles, CA)
1938	+ WHITE, Pearl	49	Cirrhosis of the liver (in Neuilly-Sur-Seine, France)
1938	WIENE, Robert	57	Cancer (in Paris, France)
1938	+ WOOLSEY, Robert	48	Kidney ailment (in Malibu Beach, CA)
1939	ANDERSON, Lawrence	45	Pneumonia (in London, England)
1939	ARBUCKLE, Andrew	55	Died in Los Angeles, CA
1939	BACKUS, George	81	Died in Merrick, NY
• 1939	BAKER, Daniel E.	78	Died in Englewood, NJ
1939	BORGATO, Agostino	67	Heart attack (in Hollywood, CA)
1939	+ BRADY, Alice ★	46	Cancer (in New York, NY)
1939	BROWN, Raymond "Ray"	58	After a long illness (in Los Angeles, CA)
1939	BRUNDAGE, Mathilde	67	Died in Long Beach, CA
1939	BURTIS, James	46	Died in California
1939	#+ FAIRBANKS, Douglas Sr.	56	Heart attack (in Santa Monica, CA)
1939	FAWCETT, George D.	77	Heart trouble (in Nantucket Island, MA)
1939	+ FRANKLIN, Rupert	77	Died in Los Angeles, CA
1939	FRAZIN, Gladys	37	Suicide (jumped from her apartment window) in New York, NY
1939	GILLINGWATER, Claude	69	Suicide (gunshot) in Beverly Hills, CA
1939	GIRARDOT, Etienne	83	After a brief illness (in Hollywood, CA)
1939	GLECKLER, Robert P.	49	Uremic poisoning (in North Hollywood, CA)
1939	GREET, Clare	67	Died in London, England
1939	+ GREY, Zane	64	Died at his home in Altadena, CA
1939	HARRON, John	36	Heart attack (in Seattle, WA)
• 1939	HOWARD, Sidney ★	48	Died in a tractor accident on his farm
1939	JARVIS, Sydney	58	Died in Hollywood, CA
1939	+ LAEMMLE, Carl Sr.	72	Heart attack (in Hollywood, CA)
1939	# LEONARD, Gus	83	After a long illness (in Los Angeles, CA)
1939	# MARSON, Aileen	26	Childbirth (in London, England)
1939	+ MERCER, Beryl	56	Following a major operation (in Santa Monica, CA)
1939	MEYERHOLD, Vsevolod	65	Tortured by Stalin's secret police on false charges of treason
1939	MILLER, Ranger Bill	61	Died in Los Angeles, CA
1939	MOORE, Owen	52	Heart attack (in Beverly Hills, CA)

• New entry. # Original name (Pt. 7). + Interment (Pt. 5). 13 ☆ Oscar nominee, ★ Oscar winner (Pt. 10)

Deaths of Movie and Television Personalities — by Year

YEAR	NAME	AGE	CAUSE and/or PLACE OF DEATH
1939	MUNDIN, Herbert	40	Fractured skull from auto accident (in Van Nuys, CA)
1939	# MURDOCK, Ann	48	Died in Lucerne, Switzerland
1939	+ NICHOLS, George Jr.	42	Automobile accident (in Los Angeles, CA)
1939	#+ PARROTT, James	46	Heart attack (in Hollywood, CA)
1939	RICKETTS, Thomas "Tom"	85	Pneumonia (in Hollywood, CA)
1939	# SELTEN, Morton	79	Died in London, England
1939	SHELBY, Margaret (Fillmore)	39	Chronic alcoholism
1939	SHINE, Wilfred	75	Died in Kingston, England
1939	#+ SMALLEY, Phillips	63	Died in Hollywood, CA
1939	# SMITH, Albert J.	44	Died in Hollywood, CA
1939	# STERLING, Ford	58	Thrombosis of veins and heart attack (in Los Angeles, CA)
1939	+ TEMPLETON, Fay	74	Died in San Francisco, CA
1939	THOMAS, Jameson	49	Tuberculosis (in Sierra Madre, CA)
1939	+ VERNON, Bobby	42	Heart attack (in Hollywood, CA)
1939	VIBART, Henry	75	Died in England
1939	WARE, Helen	61	Throat infection (in Carmel, CA)
1939	WEBER, Lois	56	After a long illness (in Los Angeles, CA)
1940	ADAIR, Jack	46	Died in Hollywood, CA
1940	ARNOLD, William R.	56	Streptococcus infection (in Hollywood, CA)
1940	ASHTON, Sylvia	60	Died in Los Angeles, CA
1940	ASKAM, Earl	41	After a heart attack while playing golf (in Los Angeles, CA)
1940	#+ AYRES, Agnes	42	Cerebral hemorrhage (while in a L.A. sanitarium for depression)
1940	+ BATES, Granville	58	Heart attack (in Hollywood, CA)
1940	BRADBURY, James Sr.	83	Died in Clifton, Staten Island, NY
1940	BURR, Eugene "Gene"	?	Pulmonary edema (in Los Angeles, CA)
1940	CALTHROP, Donald	52	After a heart attack (in London, England)
1940	# CAREWE, Edwin	56	Heart attack (in Los Angeles, CA)
1940	CECIL, Edward	52	Died in Los Angeles, CA
1940	CHADWICK, Helene	42	From injuries after a fall (in Los Angeles, CA)
1940	#+ CHASE, Charley	47	Heart attack (in Hollywood, CA)
1940	CHURCHILL, Berton	63	Uremic poisoning (in New York, NY)
1940	+ CLARK, Marguerite	53	Pneumonia after a cerebral hemorrhage (in New York, NY)
1940	# CLIVE, E. E.	60	Heart attack (in North Hollywood, CA)
1940	CONNOLLY, Walter	53	Stroke (in Beverly Hills, CA)
1940	# CRAIG, Blanche	74	Died in Los Angeles, CA
1940	DeGRASSE, Joseph	67	Heart attack (in Eagle Rock, CA)
1940	DWIRE, Earl	55	Died in Carmichael, CA
1940	+ FINCH, Flora	71	Streptococcus infection (in Hollywood, CA)
1940	+ FITZMAURICE, George	45	After a 2-month streptococcus infection (in Los Angeles, CA)
1940	# FRANEY, Billy	55	Influenza (in Hollywood, CA)
1940	# GORDON, C. Henry	57	Result of leg amputation (in Los Angeles, CA)
1940	GORDON, Maude Turner	71	Pneumonia (in Los Angeles, CA)
1940	GREEN, Fred E.	50	Injuries from an automobile accident (in San Mateo, CA)
1940	# GRIFFIN, Carlton E.	47	Heart attack (in Hollywood, CA)
1940	HACKATHORNE, George	44	After a long illness (in Hollywood, CA)
1940	# HALL, James	39	Cirrhosis of the liver (in Jersey City, NJ)
1940	HARLAN, Otis	75	Stroke (in Martinsville, IN)
1940	HART, Albert S.	65	After a long illness (in Hollywood, CA)
1940	JAUBERT, Maurice	40	Killed in action during World War 2 (in Azerailles, France)
1940	KEMP, Hal	36	Pneumonia after auto injuries (in Madera, CA)
1940	LAW, Walter	64	Died in Hollywood, CA
1940	LAWFORD, Ernest	69	Died in New York, NY

Deaths of Movie and Television Personalities — by Year

YEAR	NAME	AGE	CAUSE and/or PLACE OF DEATH
1940	LeSAINT, Edward J.	69	After a long illness (in Hollywood, CA)
1940	LESLIE, Lilie "Lila"	48	Died in Los Angeles, CA
1940	LUCAS, Wilfred	69	After an illness of 6-weeks (in Los Angeles, CA)
1940	MACKAYE, Dorothy	41	Injuries from an automobile accident (in San Fernando Valley, CA)
1940	McPHERSON, Quinton	68	Died in London, England
1940	# MEINS, Gus	45	Suicide (after arrest on morals charges) in La Crescenta, CA
1940	#+ MILLER, Walter C.	48	After collapsing on a Republic Pictures set (in Los Angeles, CA)
1940	#+ MIX, Tom	60	A broken neck after his car overturned (in Florence, AZ)
1940	MONG, William V.	65	After a 2-years' illness (in Studio City, CA)
1940	# MORGAN, Gene	48	Heart attack (in Santa Monica, CA)
1940	# MOSCOVITCH, Maurice	68	Following abdominal surgery (in Los Angeles, CA)
1940	+ MURRAY, J. Harold	49	After treatment for a kidney ailment (in Killingworth, CT)
1940	#+ OGLE, Charles	75	Died in Long Beach, CA
1940	# PEARCE, George C.	75	Died in Los Angeles, CA
1940	PERIOLAT, George	63	Suicide (arsenic) at his home in Los Angeles, CA
1940	RAND, John F.	67	Died in Hollywood, CA
1940	REGAS, George	50	Following an operation for a throat infection (in Los Angeles, CA)
1940	RICHMAN, Charles	75	After a brief illness (in a Bronx, NY nursing home)
1940	+ ROBERTS, Florence	79	After a brief illness (in Hollywood) Do not confuse with F.R., d. 1927
1940	# ROBERTS, Ralph Arthur	55	Died in Berlin, Germany
1940	SELBY, Norman "Kid McCoy"	66	Suicide (at a downtown hotel in Detroit, MI)
1940	# SIEGEL, Bernard	72	Heart attack (in Hollywood, CA)
1940	SPACEY, John Graham	44	Heart attack after attending a party (in Hollywood, CA)
1940	#+ STEVENS, Landers	63	Heart attack following appendectomy (in Hollywood, CA)
1940	STEWART, Athole	61	Died in Buckinghamshire, England
1940	STONE, Arthur	56	After a brief illness (in Hollywood, CA)
1940	SWICKARD, Joseph	74	After a long illness (in Hollywood, CA)
1940	+ TRAINOR, Leonard	61	Heart attack (in Los Angeles, CA)
1940	#+ TURPIN, Ben	65	Heart disease (in Santa Monica, CA)
1940	VANE, Denton	50	Heart attack (while walking in Union Hill, NJ)
1940	WALTERS, Hal	48	Killed by a German bomb during a WW2 air raid (in England)
1940	WARREN, E. Alyn	64	Died in Los Angeles, CA
1940	WARREN, Fred H.	60	Ruptured ulcer (in Hollywood, CA)
1940	WESTMORE, Monte	39	Heart condition after a tonsilectomy
1940	# WONG, Mary	25	Suicide (hanging) in Los Angeles, CA
1940	# WRAY, John	52	After a long illness (in Hollywood, CA)
1940	WRIGHT, Hugh E.	60	Died in Windsor, England
1940	YOUNG, Olive	33	Internal hemorrhages (in Bayonne, NJ)
1941	BACH, Reginald	54	Pneumonia (in New York, NY)
1941	+ BERGERE, Ramona	39	Died in Glendale, CA
1941	# BLACKTON, James Stuart Sr.	66	Fractured skull after being struck by a car (in Hollywood, CA)
1941	BLINN, Benjamin F.	68	Died in Hollywood, CA
1941	# CALVERT, E. H.	78	Died in Hollywood, CA
1941	# CARLE, Richard	69	Heart attack (in North Hollywood, CA)
1941	CAVEN, Allan	60	Died in Hollywood, CA
1941	CURRAN, Thomas A.	60	Pneumonia (in Hollywood, CA)
1941	# DeGREY, Sydney	55	
1941	DEXTER, Elliott	71	After several weeks illness (in Amityville, NY)
1941	#+ DOLLY, Jenny	48	Suicide (hanging) in Hollywood, CA
1941	# FAIRBROTHER, Sydney	69	Died in London, England
1941	# FIELDS, Stanley	57	Heart attack (in Los Angeles, CA)
1941	FITZGERALD, Cissy	68	Died in Ovingdean, England

YEAR	NAME	AGE	CAUSE and/or PLACE OF DEATH
1941	# FORREST, Alan	51	Died in Detroit, MI
1941	#+ GEHRIG, Lou	37	Amyotrophic lateral sclerosis (in New York, NY)
1941	GORDON, James	60	After an emergency operation (in Hollywood, CA)
1941	HARBEN, Hubert	63	Died in London, England
1941	HERSHELL, Mayall	78	Cerebral hemorrhage
1941	HOWARD, David	45	Heart ailment (in Hollywood, CA)
1941	KALIZ, Armand	48	Heart attack (in Beverly Hills, CA)
1941	# KING, Claude E.	62	Died in Los Angeles, CA
1941	LANG, Howard	64	Died in Hollywood, CA
1941	LEE, Auriol	?	Automobile accident (in Hutchison, KS)
1941	LLEWELLYN, Fewlass	55	Died in England
1941	MacDOWELL, Melbourne	84	Blood clot on the brain (in Decoto, CA)
1941	MANN, Margaret	72	Cancer (in Los Angeles, CA)
1941	MASON, William C. "Smiling Billy"	52	After a lengthy illness (in Orange, NJ)
1941	MAYALL, Hershell	78	Cerebral hemorrhage (in Detroit, MI)
1941	MEADE, Bill	?	Fell from a horse onto his sword while filming (in Hollywood, CA)
1941	+ MORGAN, Helen	41	Kidney and liver ailments (in Chicago, IL)
1941	MORRIS, Adrian	38	Died in Los Angeles, CA
1941	MURRAY, Charlie	69	Pneumonia (in Hollywood, CA)
1941	+ PADEREWSKI, Ignace	80	Pneumonia (in New York, NY)
1941	# PARKER, Barnett	54	Died in Los Angeles, CA
1941	#+ PENNER, Joe	35	Heart attack (in Philadelphia, PA)
1941	+ PORTER, Edwin S.	71	After a long illness (in New York, NY)
1941	PRATT, Purnell B.	54	Died in Hollywood, CA
1941	RAYNER, Minnie	72	Died in London, England
1941	ROBERTSHAW, Jerrold	74	Died in England
1941	RUTTMAN, Walther	54	Killed while filming a newsreel of the Eastern Front during W.W.2
1941	+ SCHERTZINGER, Victor ☆	52	Heart attack (in Hollywood, CA)
1941	#+ SHANNON, Peggy	32	Acute alcoholism and heart attack (in North Hollywood, CA)
1941	+ STEPHENSON, James ☆	53	Heart attack (in Pacific Palisades, CA)
1941	STONEHOUSE, Ruth	47	Died in Hollywood, CA
1941	TRUESDALE, Howard	80	Heart attack (in Los Angeles, CA)
1941	WALKER, Stuart	53	After a heart attack (at his home in Hollywood, CA)
1941	# WILSON, Clarence H.	64	Died in Hollywood, CA
1941	WORTHINGTON, William J.	68	Died in Beverly Hills, CA
1942	#+ BARRYMORE, John	60	Cardiac condition and other ailments (in Hollywood, CA)
1942	BRACEY, Sidney	64	After a brief illness (in Hollywood, CA)
1942	BRADY, Edward J.	53	Heart attack (in Hollywood, CA)
1942	CARLYLE, Richard	63	After a long illness (in San Fernando, CA)
1942	+ COHAN, George M.	64	Cancer of the lower intestine (in New York, NY)
1942	CORBIN, Virginia Lee	31	Heart disease (in Winfield, IL)
1942	COWL, George	64	Died in London, England
1942	+ CREWS, Laura Hope	62	After a month's illness (in New York, NY)
1942	#+ CRUZE, James	58	Heart ailment (in Hollywood, CA)
1942	CULLEY, Frederick	63	
1942	ELLSLER, Effie	87	Following a heart attack (in Hollywood, CA)
1942	FOWLER, Brenda	59	Following a short illness (in Los Angeles, CA)
1942	HAINES, Donald	24	
1942	# HALLARD, C. M.	75	Died in Surrey, England
1942	+ HAMILTON, Hale R.	62	Cerebral hemorrhage (in Los Angeles, CA)
1942	HAWTHORNE, David	54	Died in London, England
1942	HOLMES, Phillips	33	Air collision of two RCAF planes (near Armstrong, Ont., Canada)

Deaths of Movie and Television Personalities — by Year

YEAR	NAME		AGE	CAUSE and/or PLACE OF DEATH
1942	HORNE, James W.		60	Cerebral hemorrhage (in Hollywood, CA)
1942	#+ HOUSMAN, Arthur		52	Pneumonia (in Los Angeles, CA)
1942	# HUMPHREY, William		68	Coronary thrombosis (in Woodland Hills, CA)
1942	#+ JONES, Buck		52	Burned to death while trying to save others in a fire (in Boston, MA)
1942	#+ LOMBARD, Carole	☆	33	Airplane crash (southeast of Las Vegas, NV)
1942	LORD, Marion		59	After a long illness (in Hollywood, CA)
1942	LUPINO, Stanley		48	Died in London, England
1942	MacQUARRIE, Murdock		63	Died in Los Angeles, CA
1942	McFADDEN, Charles Ivor		55	Cerebral hemorrhage (in Los Angeles, CA)
1942	McINTOSH, Burr		79	Following a heart attack (in Hollywood, CA)
1942	MOFFAT, Margaret		49	Pneumonia (in Los Angeles, CA)
1942	MORTON, James C.		58	After a long illness (in Reseda, CA)
1942	NATHEAUX, Louis		44	Died in Los Angeles, CA
1942	#+ OLIVER, Edna May	☆	59	Intestinal disorder (in Hollywood, CA)
1942	OTTIANO, Rafaela		48	Heart attack (in Boston, MA)
1942	#+ ROBSON, May	☆	84	Neuritis (in Beverly Hills, CA)
1942	#+ ROSING, Bodil		63	Heart attack (in Hollywood, CA)
1942	RUBEN, J. Walter		43	Heart ailment (in Hollywood, CA)
1942	SEARS, Allan		55	After a long illness (in Los Angeles, CA)
1942	SKINNER, Otis		83	Uremic poisoning (at his home in New York, NY)
1942	# TEMPEST, Marie		78	After a long illness (in London, England)
1942	# THATCHER, Eva		80	Died in Los Angeles, CA
1942	# Tony (Tom Mix's horse)		33	
1942	# TUCKER, Richard (actor)		58	Heart attack (in Woodland Hills, CA) Do not confuse with singer
1942	VOGEDING, Fredrik		52	Following a heart attack (in Los Angeles, CA)
1942	#+ WEBER, Joe		74	After an illness of 2-months (in Van Nuys, CA)
1942	# WESTLEY, Helen		67	After a long illness (in Middlebush, NJ)
1942	WOODS, Arthur		38	Killed in action during World War 2
• **1943**	ANTOINE, Andre		85	
1943	ATCHLEY, Hooper		56	Suicide (gunshot) in Hollywood, CA
1943	# BACON, David		29	Murdered (stabbed) in Los Angeles, CA
• 1943	BAKER, Floyd		56	Died in Hollywood, CA
1943	BARLOW, Reginald		76	Died in Hollywood, CA
1943	BAUR, Harry		63	Died mysteriously after being interrogated by the Gestapo in Paris
1943	BELCHER, Charles M.		71	Died in Hollywood, CA
1943	BENNETT, Charles J.		51	Died in Hollywood (Do not confuse with Charles Bennett, d. 1995)
1943	+ BERNIE, Ben		52	After a lingering illness (in Hollywood, CA)
1943	BLEDSOE, Jules		44	Died in Hollywood, CA
1943	+ BOSWORTH, Hobart		76	Pneumonia (in Glendale, CA)
1943	BOTELER, Wade		52	Heart attack (in Hollywood, CA)
1943	BREAMER, Sylvia		45	Died in New York, NY
1943	# BROOKE, Tyler		52	Suicide (carbon monoxide in his car) in North Hollywood, CA
1943	BRUNETTE, Fritzi		53	Died in Hollywood, CA
1943	+ BYRON, Arthur		71	Heart attack after a long illness (in Hollywood, CA)
1943	CAMPEAU, Frank		79	Died in Woodland Hills, CA
1943	+ CHARTERS, Spencer		68	Suicide (pills and carbon monoxide) in Hollywood, CA
1943	COWLES, Jules		65	Died in Hollywood, CA
1943	# CUNNINGHAM, Joe		52	Coronary occlusion (in Los Angeles, CA)
1943	DeLEATH, Vaughn		42	Uremic poisoning and a heart condition
1943	ETHIER, Alphonse		68	Cancer (in Hollywood, CA)
1943	+ FRYE, Dwight		44	Heart attack (in Hollywood, CA)
1943	GUHL, George		67	Died in Los Angeles, CA

Deaths of Movie and Television Personalities — by Year

YEAR	NAME		AGE	CAUSE and/or PLACE OF DEATH
1943	+ HART, Lorenz		47	Pneumonia
1943	#+ HOWARD, Leslie	☆	50	In a passenger plane shot down by a Nazi fighter (in Bay of Biscay)
1943	IRVING, William J.		50	Died in Los Angeles, CA
1943	+ JULIAN, Rupert		54	Cerebral thrombosis (in Hollywood, CA)
1943	# JUNKERMANN, Hans		70	Died in Berlin, Germany
1943	LANGDON, Lillian		82	Died in Santa Monica, CA
1943	+ LOFTUS, Cecilia "Cissie"		66	Heart attack (in her New York City hotel room)
1943	# LOVE, Montagu		62	Died in Beverly Hills, CA
1943	#+ MARSHALL, Tully		78	Heart and lung ailment (in Encino, CA)
1943	+ McWADE, Edward		78	After a brief illness (in Hollywood, CA)
1943	# NARES, Owen		54	Died in Brecon, Wales
1943	O'CONNELL, Hugh		44	After a heart attack (in Hollywood, CA)
1943	OVERMAN, Lynne		55	Following two heart attacks (in Santa Monica, CA)
1943	PADDOCK, Charles		42	Airplane crash (near Sitaka, Alaska)
1943	# PRICE, Kate		70	After a long illness (in Woodland Hills, CA)
1943	+ RACHMANINOFF, Sergei		69	Cancer and pneumonia (in Beverly Hills, CA)
1943	#+ RAY, Charles		52	Throat infection from an infected tooth (in Hollywood, CA)
1943	+ REINHARDT, Max		70	Pneumonia following paralysis (in New York, NY)
1943	ROQUEMORE, Henry		55	Heart attack (at his home in Beverly Hills, CA)
1943	SAUM, Clifford		60	Died in Glendale, CA
1943	SHERIDAN, Frank		74	After a brief illness (in Hollywood, CA)
1943	# STANMORE, Frank		65	Died in England
1943	STRAUSS, William H.		58	After a heart attack (in Hollywood, Ca.)
1943	SWOR, Bert		65	Found dead in his Tulsa, Oklahoma hotel room
1943	# Tamara		?	Airplane crash (near Lisbon, Portugal)
1943	+ VEIDT, Conrad		50	Heart attack while playing golf (in Hollywood, CA)
1943	VEILLER, Bayard		74	After an illness of 2-months
1943	VonSEYFFERTITZ, Gustav		80	Died in Woodland Hills, CA
1943	+ WALLER, Thomas "Fats"		39	Influenza and bronchial pneumonia (in Kansas City, MO)
1943	WEST, Charles H.		57	Died in Los Angeles, CA
1943	WEST, Claudine		59	After a long illness (in Beverly Hills, CA)
1943	+ WOOLLCOTT, Alexander		56	Heart attack (while broadcasting at CBS in New York, NY)
1943	WRIGHT, Haidee		44	Died in London, England
1944	BAEKELAND, Léon Henri		80	Died in Los Angeles, CA
1944	BELLAMY, George		78	
1944	+ BENNETT, Richard		71	Heart attack (in Los Angeles, CA)
1944	BERESFORD, Harry		80	After a long illness (in Los Angeles, CA)
1944	# BRODY, Ann		59	Died in New York, NY
1944	BROOKS, Jesse Lee		50	Heart attack (in Hollywood, CA)
1944	#+ CARR, Nat		57	Died in Hollywood, CA
1944	+ COBB, Irvin S.		67	Died in New York, NY
1944	+ COLLIER, William Sr.		77	Pneumonia (in Beverly Hills, CA)
1944	#+ CREGAR, Laird		28	Following two heart attacks (in Los Angeles, CA)
1944	CROSMAN, Henrietta		83	Died in Pelham Manor, NY
1944	DILSON, John		53	Died in Ventura, CA
1944	#+ DINEHART, Alan Sr.		54	Heart attack (in Hollywood, CA)
1944	# EMERTON, Roy		51	Died in England
1944	FERGUSON, George S.		60	Died in Hollywood, CA
1944	# FISKE, Richard		29	Killed in action during World War 2 (in Bastogne, Belgium)
1944	FISKE, Robert L.		54	Congestive heart failure (in Sunland, CA)
1944	FRAZER, Robert W.		53	Leukemia (in Los Angeles, CA)
1944	# GERRON, Kurt		47	Executed (in Auschwitz, Germany)

YEAR	NAME	AGE	CAUSE and/or PLACE OF DEATH
1944	GOTT, Barbara	?	
1944	GOTTSCHALK, Ferdinand	75	*Died in London, England*
1944	HALLOR, Ray	44	*Automobile accident (near Palm Springs, CA)*
1944	HARRIS, Marion	38	*Burns in bed from a cigarette fire (in Hollywood, CA)*
1944	HARRIS, Mildred	42	*Pneumonia after an abdominal operation (in Hollywood, CA)*
1944	# HOFFMAN, Otto	65	*Lung cancer (in Woodland Hills, CA)*
1944	HOUSTON, George F.	46	*Heart attack (in Los Angeles, CA)*
1944	# JAMISON, Bud	50	*Heart attack (in Hollywood, CA)*
1944	KELLY, Lew	65	*Died in Los Angeles, CA*
1944	KENNEDY, Merna	35	*Following a heart attack (in Los Angeles, CA)*
1944	KING, Charles E.	54	*Pneumonia (in London, England)*
1944	KORFF, Arnold	73	*Heart ailment (in New York, NY)*
1944	LANGDON, Harry	60	*Cerebral hemorrhage (in Los Angeles, CA)*
1944	+ MacPHERSON, Aimee Semple	53	*Heart attack in her sleep*
1944	McNAMARA, Edward C.	57	*Heart attack (on a Hollywood-bound train near Boston)*
1944	McPHAIL, Douglas	30	*From the effects of poison (in Los Angeles, CA)*
1944	McRAE, Henry	68	*Heart attack (in Beverly Hills, CA)*
1944	# MILLER, Glenn	40	*Lost when his RAF plane disappeared while bound for Paris*
1944	# MORRISSEY, Betty	37	*Died in New York, NY*
1944	PAPE, Edward Lionel	77	*After a long illness (in Woodland Hills, CA)*
1944	PARSONS, Percy	66	*Died in England*
1944	PATON, Stuart	59	*Died in Woodland Hills, CA*
1944	#+ POWELL, Lee B.	36	*Killed in action in the S. Pacific, during W.W.II*
1944	PURCELL, Richard "Dick"	35	*Heart attack playing golf (in Hollywood, CA)*
1944	# RALPH, Jessie	79	*After a lingering illness (in Gloucester, MA)*
1944	ROWLANDS, Art	46	*Died in Hollywood, CA*
1944	RYAN, Joe	57	*Died in Los Angeles, CA*
1944	+ SEITZ, George B.	56	*Died in Hollywood, CA*
1944	+ SELWYN, Edgar	68	*After a cerebral hemorrhage (in Hollywood, CA)*
1944	+ SELZNICK, Myron	45	*Following an attack of portal thrombosis (in Santa Monica, CA)*
1944	SHARLAND, Reginald	57	*Died in Loma Linda, CA*
1944	# SHERRY, J. Barney	71	*Died in Philadelphia, PA*
1944	STANLEY, Edwin	64	*Died in Hollywood, CA*
1944	STUART, Donald	45	*Following a heart attack (in Hollywood, CA)*
1944	USHER, Guy	69	*After a brief illness (at his ranch in San Diego, CA)*
1944	#+ VanDYKE, W. S. "Woody" ☆	53	*After a 6-months' illness (in Brentwood, CA)*
1944	#+ VELEZ, Lupe	36	*Suicide (sleeping pills) in Beverly Hills, CA*
1944	# WEST, Pat	55	*Died in Hollywood, CA*
1944	YARDE, Margaret	65	*Died in London, England*
1945	AINLEY, Henry H.	66	*Died in London, England*
1945	+ ARMETTA, Henry	57	*Heart attack (in San Diego, CA)*
1945	BACQUE, André	65	*Died in Paris, France*
1945	BARBIER, George	83	*Heart attack (in Los Angeles, CA)*
1945	BARKER, Reginald	59	*Following a heart attack (in Los Angeles, CA)*
1945	BARROWS, Henry A.	69	*Died in Los Angeles, CA*
1945	+ BENCHLEY, Robert ★	56	*Cerebral hemorrhage (in New York, NY)*
1945	BLUM, Sammy	56	*Heart attack (in Hollywood, CA)*
1945	BRECKNER, Gary	49	*Automobile accident (in Redlands, CA)*
1945	# CASEY, Dolores	28	*Died in Hollywood, CA*
1945	CLYDE, David	60	*Died in San Fernando Valley, CA*
1945	CORRIGAN, D'Arcy	75	
1945	COSTELLO, Don	44	*Heart attack in his sleep (in Hollywood, CA)*

YEAR	NAME	AGE	CAUSE and/or PLACE OF DEATH
1945	CRAIG, Alec	60	After a long illness (in Glendale, CA)
1945	+ CRAVEN, Frank	70	Heart ailment (in Beverly Hills, CA)
1945	# CRIMMONS, Daniel "Dan"	82	Died in Los Angeles, CA
1945	DICKSON, Gloria	28	Asphyxiation from a fire (in Hollywood, CA)
1945	# DOUGLAS, Donald "Don"	40	Complications after appendectomy (in Los Angeles, CA)
1945	#+ EDWARDS, Gus	64	Cancer (in Los Angeles, CA)
1945	# ELMER, Billy	75	After a long illness (in Hollywood, CA)
1945	# EMERY, Gilbert	70	Died in Hollywood, CA
1945	EVANS, Charles	88	Died in Santa Monica, CA
1945	# FAIRBANKS, William	50	Lobar pneumonia (in Los Angeles, CA)
1945	FIELDING, Edward	65	Heart attack while mowing his lawn (in Beverly Hills, CA)
1945	FUNG, Willie	49	Coronary occlusion (in Los Angeles, CA)
1945	GRANACH, Alexander	54	Complications after surgery (in New York, NY)
1945	GREENE, Harrison	61	After a lingering illness (in Hollywood, CA)
1945	HARVEY, Forrester	65	Stroke (in Laguna Beach, CA)
1945	# HERNANDEZ, Anna	77	Pneumonia (in Los Angeles, CA)
1945	HOLMES, Ralph	56	Natural causes (in New York, NY)
1945	# HOPTON, Russell "Russ"	45	Found dead of an overdose of sleeping pills (in N. Hollywood, CA)
1945	HUTCHINS, Robert "Wheezer"	20	Killed in an Army training camp accident during World War 2
1945	KAYSSLER, Friedrich	71	Died in Leinmachnow, Germany
1945	#+ KERN, Jerome	60	Cerebral hemorrhage (in New York, NY)
1945	# LANE, Charles	76	Cancer (in Van Nuys, CA)
1945	LaRENO, Richard "Dick"	71	Died in Hollywood, CA
1945	#+ LAVERNE, Lucille	72	After being hospitalized for a broken hip (in Culver City, CA)
1945	LIEDTKE, Harry	64	Died in Bad-Sarrow-Pieskow, Germany
1945	LUCY, Arnold	80	Died in London, England
1945	MANDY, Jerry	52	Following a heart attack (in Hollywood, CA)
1945	+ MARION, George F. Sr.	85	Following a heart attack (in Carmel, CA)
1945	+ McCORMACK, John	61	Died at his home in Booterstown, Ireland
1945	# McGREGOR, Malcolm	52	Burns from smoking in bed (in Los Angeles, CA)
1945	# McKAY, George W. "Red"	60	Died in Hollywood, CA
1945	MUNIER, Ferdinand	55	After a heart attack (in Hollywood, CA)
1945	#+ NAZIMOVA, Alla	66	Coronary thrombosis (in Los Angeles, CA)
1945	# NORTH, Joe	71	Died in Woodland Hills, CA
1945	O'NEILL, Peggy	21	Suicide after a lover's quarrel (sleeping pills) in Beverly Hills, CA
1945	#+ RANDALL, Addison "Jack"	38	Fell to his death from a horse, while filming (in Canoga Park, CA)
1945	SANDRICH, Mark	44	Heart disease (at his home in Hollywood, CA)
1945	SAXON, Hugh A.	76	Died at his home in Beverly Hills, CA
1945	# SCHLETTOW, Hans Adelbert	57	Died in Berlin, Germany
1945	SHEEHAN, Winfield	62	Following abdominal surgery (in Hollywood, CA)
1945	SHY, Gus	51	After a long illness (in Hollywood, CA)
1945	# SIDNEY, George (actor)	69	After a long illness (in Hollywood, CA)
1945	SMILEY, Joseph W.	64	Died in New York
1945	VICTOR, Henry	46	Brain tumor (in Hollywood, CA)
1945	WALDMULLER, Lizzi	41	Killed during an air raid (in Vienna, Austria)
1945	# WESSELHOEFT, Eleanor	72	After a long illness (in Hollywood, CA)
1945	WHITE, J. Fisher	79	Died in England
1945	WU, Honorable	42	Died in Hollywood, CA
1945	# YOST, Herbert A.	65	Died in New York, NY
1946	# ALDEN, Mary	63	Died in Woodland Hills, CA
1946	# ARLISS, George ★	77	Bronchial trouble (in London, England)
1946	+ ATWILL, Lionel	61	Bronchial cancer and pneumonia (in Pacific Palisades, CA)

YEAR	NAME	AGE	CAUSE and/or PLACE OF DEATH
1946	AYLESWORTH, Arthur	61	Died in Los Angeles, CA
1946	+ BEERY, Noah Sr.	60	Heart attack (in Los Angeles, CA)
1946	BERGMAN, Henry	76	Heart attack (in Hollywood, CA) Do not confuse with Henri Bergman
1946	+ BOWES, Major Edward	71	Died at his summer home in Rumson, NJ
1946	BRECHER, Egon	66	After a heart attack (in Hollywood, CA)
1946	BROWER, Otto	50	Heart failure (in Hollywood, CA)
1946	BRUCE, Kate	87	
1946	BUCQUET, Harold S.	54	Died in Hollywood, CA
1946	+ BUSCH, Mae	55	After a 5-mo. illness (in a San Fernando Valley sanitarium)
1946	BUTTERWORTH, Charles	49	Automobile accident (Suicide?) in Los Angeles, CA
1946	CARR, Trem	54	After a heart attack (while vacationing in San Diego, CA)
1946	CARTER, Ben F.	35	(Do not confuse with musician Benny Carter)
1946	+ EMMETT, Fern (Roquemore)	50	Cancer (in Hollywood, CA)
1946	#+ FIELDS, W. C.	66	Violent hemorrhage, dropsy and other ailments (in Pasadena, CA)
1946	# GEARY, Bud	47	Injuries from an automobile crash (in Hollywood, CA)
1946	# GEORGE, Heinrich	53	During an appendectomy (in Sachsenhousen, Germany)
1946	GLEASON, Russell	37	Accidental fall from a 4th floor hotel window (in New York, NY)
1946	GORDON, Hal	52	Died in England
1946	#+ HART, William S.	83	Stroke (in Los Angeles, CA)
1946	+ HATTON, Rondo	51	Heart attack (in Beverly Hills, CA)
1946	HOPKINS, Sis		(See Rose Melville)
1946	HOWARD, Sydney	61	Died in London, England
1946	+ HURT, Marlin	40	Heart attack
1946	JAMES, Walter	60	Heart attack (in Gardena, CA)
1946	# KEATON, Joseph Sr.	78	Died in Hollywood, CA
1946	KELSO, Mayme	79	Heart attack (in South Pasadena, CA)
1946	# LARKIN, George	57	Died in New York, NY
1946	+ LEHRMAN, Henry	60	Following a heart attack (in Hollywood, CA)
1946	MacPHERSON, Jeanie	59	After a long illness (in Hollywood, CA)
1946	# MANDER, Miles	57	Heart attack (in Hollywood, CA)
1946	MANNING, Aileen	60	Died in Hollywood, CA
1946	MARIAN, Ferdinand	44	Automobile accident (near Durneck, Germany)
1946	MATTRAW, Scott	61	After a long illness (in Hollywood, CA)
1946	McDANIEL, Etta	55	Died in Los Angeles, CA
1946	+ MEEK, Donald	66	Acute leukemia and heart attack (in Los Angeles, CA)
1946	MELVILLE, Rose "Sis Hopkins"	73	Died at her home in Lake George, NY
1946	MERIVALE, Philip	65	Heart ailment (in Los Angeles, CA)
1946	MORRISON, Louis "Lou"	80	Died in CA
1946	NEILL, Roy William	59	After a heart attack (in London, England)
1946	# O'ROURKE, Brefni	57	Died in Ireland
1946	# OLDFIELD, Barney	68	Cerebral hemorrhage
1946	#+ PERRY, Antoinette	58	Heart attack (in New York, NY)
1946	PORCASI, Paul	66	After a long illness (in Hollywood, CA)
1946	# RAGLAND, John "Rags"	40	Uremia (in Los Angeles, CA)
1946	# RAIMU, Jules	62	Heart attack (in Neuilly-sur-Seine, France)
1946	RANKIN, Doris	66	Died in Washington, D.C.
1946	# ROYCE, Julian	76	Died in England
1946	ROYCE, Lionel	55	Heart attack in Manilla while entertaining troops with the U.S.O.
1946	#+ RUNYON, Damon	62	After a long bout with throat cancer (in New York, NY)
1946	SEMELS, Harry	58	Died in Los Angeles, CA
1946	SLEZAK, Leo	71	Died in Rottach-Ergen, Germany
1946	# ST. POLIS, John	72	Died in Los Angeles, CA
1946	STAMP-TAYLOR, Enid	41	Injuries from a fall (in London, England)

YEAR	NAME	AGE	CAUSE and/or PLACE OF DEATH
1946	SULLIVAN, William A. "Billy"	54	Died in Great Neck, NY
1946	#+ SUMMERVILLE, Slim	53	Stroke (in Laguna Beach, CA)
1946	#+ TAYLOR, Laurette (Cooney)	62	Coronary thrombosis after several weeks of illness (in New York, NY)
1946	TURNER, Florence	61	After a long illness (in Woodland Hills, CA)
1946	VanTASSELL, Marie	72	Died in Oakland, CA
1946	# VonBRINCKEN, Wilhelm	54	Following a ruptured artery (in Los Angeles, CA)
1946	+ WALDRON, Charles D.	71	After a long illness (in Hollywood, CA)
1946	WELLESLEY, Charles	71	Died at the Brunswick Home, Amityville, L.I., NY
1946	#+ WELLS, H. G.	80	Liver cancer (in London, England)
1946	# WELSH, William	76	Died in Los Angeles, CA
1946	+ YOUMANS, Vincent	47	Tuberculosis (in Denver, CO)
1947	ADAMS, Ernest S.	62	After a long illness (in Hollywood, CA)
1947	ADLON, Louis	40	Heart attack (in Los Angeles, CA)
1947	ALLEN, Alfred	80	Died in New York, NY
1947	#+ AMES, Adrienne	43	Cancer (in New York, NY)
1947	# ARLEDGE, John	41	Died in Hollywood, CA
1947	ASHE, Warren	44	Automobile accident (in Madison, CT)
1947	BAIRD, Stewart	66	Heart attack (in New York, NY)
1947	BARNETT, Chester A.	62	Pneumonia (in Jefferson City, MO)
1947	+ BING, Herman	57	Suicide (gunshot) in Los Angeles, CA
1947	#+ BORDEN, Olive	40	Stomach ailment (in Los Angeles, CA)
1947	BOWKER, Aldrich	71	Arteriosclerosis (in Los Angeles, CA)
1947	BRADLEY, Harry C.	78	Heart attack (in Hollywood, CA)
1947	BRAHAM, Lionel	68	Heart attack (in Hollywood, CA)
1947	+ CAREY, Harry ☆	67	Coronary thrombosis, attributed to a bee sting (in Brentwood, CA)
1947	+ CARLETON, William P.	73	Automobile accident (in Hollywood, CA)
1947	CARNEY, George	60	Died in England
1947	CLARK, John J.	69	Died in Hollywood, CA
1947	+ CORTHELL, Herbert	69	After a year's illness (in Hollywood, CA)
1947	DAVIDSON, William B.	59	Following an operation (in Santa Monica, CA)
1947	DEMPSEY, Thomas	79	After a long illness (in Hollywood, CA)
1947	+ DIGGES, Dudley	68	Stroke (in New York, NY)
1947	# FARLEY, Jim	65	Cancer (in a Pacolma, CA, sanitarium)
1947	FYFFE, Will	36	Fall from his hotel window (in St. Andrews, Scotland)
1947	GILBERT, Walter	60	Heart attack (in Brooklyn, NY)
1947	# GLEASON, Lucille	59	Heart attack (in Brentwood, CA)
1947	GREY, Gloria	38	Died in Hollywood, CA
1947	HALL, Winter	68	Died in London, England
1947	HALLIDAY, John	67	Heart ailment (in Honolulu, HI)
1947	HANRAY, Lawrence	73	Died in London, England
1947	+ HELLINGER, Mark	44	Heart attack (in Hollywood, CA)
1947	# HEWSTON, Alfred H.	66	Died in Los Angeles, CA
1947	HILLIARD, Ernest	57	Following a heart attack (in Santa Monica, CA)
1947	HILYARD, Norman	74	
1947	HOLMAN, Harry	73	After a heart attack at his home (in Hollywood, CA)
1947	HOMANS, Robert E.	72	Heart attack (in Los Angeles, CA)
1947	HURST, Brandon	80	Arteriosclerosis (in Burbank, CA)
1947	# INCE, John E.	68	Pneumonia (in Hollywood, CA)
1947	KELLY, John	46	
1947	#+ KERRIGAN, J. Warren	67	Bronchial pneumonia (in Balboa Island, CA)
1947	KING, Leslie	71	Died in Amityville, NY
1947	+ KOLKER, Henry	72	Injuries from a fall (in Los Angeles, CA)

Deaths of Movie and Television Personalities — by Year

YEAR	NAME	AGE	CAUSE and/or PLACE OF DEATH
1947	#+ LAWRENCE, William E. "Babe"	*51*	*Died in Hollywood, CA*
1947	LESSEY, George A.	*?*	*Died in Westbrook, CT*
1947	+ LOFT, Arthur	*49*	*Died in Los Angeles, CA*
1947	LORCH, Theodore A.	*74*	*After a long illness (in Hollywood, CA)*
1947	+ LUBITSCH, Ernst ☆	*55*	*Heart attack (in Los Angeles, CA)*
1947	#+ LUNCEFORD, Jimmy	*45*	*Died in Seaside, OR*
1947	MASON, LeRoy	*44*	*After a heart attack (while filming "California Firebrand") in L.A.*
1947	MAYNE, Eric	*80*	*Died in Hollywood, CA*
1947	# MERSON, Billy	*66*	*Died in London, England*
1947	+ MOORE, Grace ☆	*45*	*Airplane crash (in Kastrup, Denmark*
1947	+ NEGIN, Koliz	*60*	*Died in San Francisco, CA*
1947	NUGENT, J. C.	*72*	*Coronary thrombosis (at the Lambs Club in New York City)*
1947	#+ O'BRIEN, Tom	*55*	*Died in Los Angeles, CA*
1947	+ POTEL, Victor "Vic"	*57*	*Died in Hollywood, CA*
1947	#+ RANKIN, Arthur	*46*	*After a cerebral hemorrhage (in Hollywood, CA)*
1947	RAWLINS, Herbert	*?*	
1947	ROSS, Betty	*67*	*Died at her home in Hollywood, CA*
1947	SCHABLE, Robert	*74*	*Died in Hollywood, CA*
1947	# SOTHERN, Hugh	*65*	*After an illness of 2 years (in Hollywood, CA)*
1947	# STURGIS, Eddie	*66*	*Heart disease (in Los Angeles, CA)*
1947	TAGGART, Ben L.	*58*	*Died in Santa Monica, CA*
1947	+ TANGUAY, Eva	*68*	*Heart attack and cerebral hemorrhage (in Hollywood, CA)*
1947	+ TOLER, Sidney	*73*	*Died at his home in Beverly Hills, CA*
1947	VanBUREN, Mabel	*69*	*Pneumonia (in Hollywood, CA)*
1947	VonTRAPP, Baron Georg	*57*	
1947	WEBSTER, Ben	*82*	*Following an operation (in Hollywood, CA)*
1947	WELLS, Ted	*48*	*Heart attack*
1947	ZAHLER, Lee	*53*	
1948	AGAR, Jane	*59*	*Died in Lakewood, OH*
1948	AINSLEY, Norman	*67*	*After a year's illness (at a private sanitarium in Hollywood, CA)*
1948	# ARTAUD, Antonin	*52*	*Colon cancer (in Ivry-Sur-Seine, France)*
1948	BACON, Rod	*33*	*Died in Los Angeles, CA*
1948	BAGGOTT, King	*73*	*Cerebral thrombosis (in Los Angeles, CA)*
1948	# BANJAMIN, Gladys	*?*	
1948	+ BASKETT, James	*44*	*Heart ailment (in Los Angeles, CA)*
1948	BORLAND, Barlowe	*71*	*Died in Woodland Hills, CA*
1948	BRAITHWAITE, Lilian	*75*	*Heart attack (in London, England)*
1948	# BRITTON, Milt	*53*	*Heart attack (in New York, NY)*
1948	BROWN, Charles D.	*60*	*Heart ailment (in Hollywood, CA)*
1948	BROWNLEE, Frank	*73*	*Died in Los Angeles, CA*
1948	BRYANT, Charles	*67*	*Died in Mount Kisco, NY*
1948	BURNS, Harry	*63*	*Following a heart attack (in Santa Monica, CA)*
1948	+ CARROLL, Earl	*56*	*Airplane crash (in Mt. Carmel, PA)*
1948	CHANDLER, Eddie	*54*	*Do not confuse with actor Edward S. Chandler (in Los Angeles, CA)*
1948	CHAPMAN, Edythe	*85*	*Heart attack (in Glendale, CA)*
1948	# CODY, Bill Sr.	*57*	*After an illness of several months (in Santa Monica, CA)*
1948	COOLEY, James R.	*68*	*Died in Hollywood, CA*
1948	# D'ALBROOK, Sidney	*62*	*Heart attack (in Los Angeles, CA)*
1948	DeBRULIER, Nigel	*69*	*Died in London, England*
1948	EATON, Mary	*46*	*After a heart attack (in Hollywood, CA)*
1948	+ EISENSTEIN, Sergei	*50*	*Heart attack (in Moscow, Russia)*
1948	EVERTON, Paul	*79*	*Following a heart attack (in Calabasas, CA)*

• New entry. # Original name (Pt. 7). + Interment (Pt. 5).   23   ☆ Oscar nominee, ★ Oscar winner (Pt. 10)

Deaths of Movie and Television Personalities — by Year

YEAR		NAME	AGE	CAUSE and/or PLACE OF DEATH
1948		FAIR, Virginia	49	After a long illness (in Hollywood, CA)
1948		FEYDER, Jacques	54	After a long illness (in Rive-de-Frangins, France)
1948		FULLER, Leslie	58	Heart attack (in Margate, England)
1948		GALE, Marguerite H.	63	Died in Amsterdam, NY
1948		GORDON, Vera	61	Died in Beverly Hills, CA
1948	#+	GRIFFITH, D. W.	73	Massive cerebral hemorrhage (in Hollywood, CA)
1948		GRIFFITH, Linda Arvidson		(See Linda Arvidson)
1948	#	HACKETT, Karl	55	After a long illness (in Sawtelle, CA)
1948		HAMMERSTEIN, Elaine	50	Automobile collision (in Tijuana, Mexico)
1948		HINDS, Samuel S.	73	Pneumonia (in Pasadena, CA)
1948		HOLLIDAY, Frank Jr.	35	Suicide (hanged himself with a belt while in jail) in Hollywood, CA
1948		HYMER, Warren	42	After a long illness (alcoholism) in Los Angeles, CA
1948		JAMES, Gladden	56	Leukemia (in Hollywood, CA)
1948	+	KENNEDY, Edgar	58	Throat cancer (in Woodland Hills, CA)
1948	#	KIRK, Jack "Pappy"	53	Heart attack (in Alaska)
1948		KIRK, John	86	After a heart attack
1948	#	LANDI, Elissa	43	Cancer (in Kingston, NY)
1948	#+	LANDIS, Carole	29	Suicide (sleeping pills) in Brentwood Heights, CA
1948		LANG, Matheson	68	Died in Bridgeton, Barbados
1948	#+	LAUGHLIN, Billy "Froggy"	16	Motor scooter—truck accident (in Corvina, CA)
1948		LEHAR, Franz	78	Stomach cancer (in Austria)
1948		LEIGH, Frank	69	Died in Hollywood, CA
1948		LEYTON, George	84	Died in London, England
1948		LLOYD, Charles M.	78	Heart attack (in Hollywood, CA)
1948		LOUDEN, Thomas	73	After a stroke (in Hollywood, CA)
1948		LOVE, Robert	34	Suicide (5-story leap from his doctor's office) in Hollywood, CA
1948		MacGREGOR, Harman	70	Died in Marblehead, MA
1948		MACK, James T.	77	Died in Hollywood, CA
1948		MALLALIEU, Aubrey	74	Died in England
1948		MAXWELL, Edwin	62	Cerebral hemorrhage (in Falmouth, MA)
1948		MAYER, Ray	47	Heart attack (in Salt Lake City, UT)
1948		McCAREY, Ray	50	Died alone in his apartment (in Los Angeles, CA)
1948		MIKHOELS, Solomon	58	Murdered (run over by a truck) presumably on Stalin's orders
1948		MILLER, Edward G.	65	Died in Los Angeles, CA
1948	#	MORENO, Marguerite	77	Died in Touzac, France
1948		MOROSCO, Walter	49	Stroke (in Coronado, CA)
1948		NELSON, Anne	37	Died in Torrance, CA
1948	#+	NIBLO, Fred Sr.	74	Pneumonia (in New Orleans, LA)
1948	#+	NOLAN, Mary	42	Found dead at home (in Los Angeles, CA)
1948	#	NORWOOD, Eille	87	
1948	#	ORTES, Armand F.	68	Died in San Francisco, CA
1948	#	OSWALDA, Ossi	49	Died in Prague, Czechoslovakia
1948	#	PETRIE, Hay	53	Died in London, England
1948	#	RATCLIFFE, E. J.	85	Died in Los Angeles, CA
1948	#	RAZETTO, Stella	67	Died in Malibu, CA
1948		RICHMOND, Warner	53	Coronary thrombosis (in Los Angeles, CA)
1948		ROBERTSON, Willard	62	Died in Hollywood, CA
1948	#+	RUTH, Babe	53	Cancerous tumor (in New York, NY)
1948	#	SCHINDELL, Cy	41	After a long illness (in Van Nuys, CA)
1948	#	SELIG, William N.	84	Died in Hollywood, CA
1948	#	SELWYN, Clarissa	62	Died in West Hollywood, CA
1948	#+	SMITH, C. Aubrey	85	Double pneumonia (in Beverly Hills, CA)
1948		SODERLING, Walter	75	Died in Los Angeles, CA

Deaths of Movie and Television Personalities — by Year

YEAR	NAME		AGE	CAUSE and/or PLACE OF DEATH
1948	SOREL, George S.		48	Died in Hollywood, CA
1948	STEDMAN, Lincoln		41	Died in Los Angeles, CA
1948	#+ TAUBER, Richard		56	Complications after laryngitis (in a nursing home in London, England)
1948	+ TOLAND, Gregg		44	Coronary thrombosis (in Hollywood, CA)
1948	# WEGENER, Paul		74	Died in Berlin, Germany
1948	WHITE, Leo		68	Died in Hollywood, CA
1948	WHITTY, May	☆	82	Heart attack (in Beverly Hills, CA)
1948	# WILLIAM, Warren		52	Multiple myeloma and blood disease (in Encino, CA)
1948	WILSON, Charles Cahill		53	Esophagal hemorrhage
1949	ALLEN, Lester		58	Struck and killed by an automobile (in Hollywood, CA)
1949	# ARVIDSON, Linda		65	Died in New York, NY
1949	BACKER, Franklyn E.		72	Died in Suffern, NY
1949	BADET, Régina		73	Died in Bordeaux, France
1949	BARNES, George		59	Following an operation for cancer (in Hollywood, CA)
1949	+ BEERY, Wallace	★	64	Heart attack (in Beverly Hills, CA)
1949	BEERY, William C.		70	Died in Beverly Hills, CA
1949	BOHNEN, Roman		54	Heart attack (in Hollywood, CA)
1949	+ BRESSART, Felix		69	Leukemia (in Los Angeles, CA)
1949	BURNABY, Davy		68	Heart attack (in England)
1949	CAWTHORNE, Joseph		81	Stroke (in Beverly Hills, CA)
1949	CHESNEY, Arthur		67	Died in London, England
1949	CHRISTY, Ivan		61	After a heart attack (in Burbank, CA)
1949	#+ CLARK, Buddy		38	Airplane crash (in Beverly Hills, CA)
1949	+ CLIFTON, Elmer		59	Cerebral hemorrhage (in Hollywood, CA)
1949	COSGRAVE, Luke		86	Died in Woodland Hills, CA
1949	DAVENPORT, Harry		83	Heart attack (in Los Angeles, CA)
1949	DAVIS, Owen Jr.		42	Drowned after falling overboard from a sloop (in L.I. South, NY)
1949	DESMOND, William		71	Heart attack (in Los Angeles, CA)
1949	#+ DIX, Richard	☆	55	Acute cardiac collapse (in Los Angeles, CA)
1949	DRAYTON, Alfred		68	Died in London, England
1949	+ FLEMING, Victor	★	64	After a heart attack (in Cottonwood, AZ)
1949	# GIRARD, Joe		78	Died in Los Angeles, CA
1949	# GRAHAM, Morland		57	Heart attack (in London, England)
1949	# HART, Neal		70	Died in Woodland Hills, CA
1949	HAY, Will		60	Died in London, England
1949	# HODGSON, Leland		55	Heart attack at his home (in Hollywood, CA)
1949	#+ HOWARD, Willie		61	Pneumonia (in New York, NY)
1949	+ LEDBETTER, Huddie "Leadbelly"		60	Amyotrophic lateral sclerosis
1949	+ LEIBER, Fritz		67	Heart attack (in Pacific Palisades, CA)
1949	LLOYD, Frederick W.		69	Died in Hove, England
1949	LONG, Nick Jr.		43	Results of an automobile accident (in New York, NY)
1949	# MARRIOTT, Moore		64	Died in England
1949	McKENZIE, Robert B.		65	Heart attack (in Manunuck, RI)
1949	# MELESH, Alex		58	Died in Hollywood, CA
1949	MIDDLEMASS, Robert M.		64	Died in Los Angeles, CA
1949	MIDDLETON, Charles B.		69	Heart attack (in Los Angeles, CA)
1949	MIDGLEY, Florence		59	Died in Hollywood, CA
1949	MITCHELL, Geneva		42	Died in California
1949	+ MITCHELL, Margaret		46	Struck by a speeding automobile (in Atlanta, GA)
1949	# MORAN, George		67	After suffering a stroke (in Oakland, CA)
1949	#+ MORGAN, Frank	☆	59	Died at his home in Beverly Hills, CA
1949	# MORRIS, Philip		56	Died in Los Angeles, CA

Deaths of Movie and Television Personalities — by Year

YEAR	NAME		AGE	CAUSE and/or PLACE OF DEATH
1949	NORDEN, Cliff		26	Suicide (pills) in Hollywood, CA
1949	OAKMAN, Wheeler		59	Died in Van Nuys, CA
1949	OLCOTT, Sidney		76	After a long illness (in Hollywood, CA)
1949	+ OUSPENSKAYA, Maria	☆	73	Burned to death from a cigarette fire (in her Hollywood apartment)
1949	+ RAPF, Harry		67	Heart attack (in Manhattan, NY)
1949	# RAYMOND, Royal		33	Cancer (in Van Nuys, CA)
1949	# REYNOLDS, Craig		42	Motorcycle/car crash (in Los Angeles, CA)
1949	#+ RIPLEY, Robert L.		55	Heart attack (in New York, NY)
1949	+ ROBINSON, Bill "Bojangles"		71	Heart ailment (in New York, NY)
1949	+ SCHLESINGER, Leon		66	Viral infection (in Hollywood, CA)
1949	#+ SHEAN, Al		81	Died in New York, NY
1949	SPENCE, Ralph		60	Heart attack (in Woodland Hills, CA)
1949	STOTHART, Herbert		64	After an illness of several months (in Hollywood, CA)
1949	# TUCKER, Harland		?	Heart attack (in Los Angeles, CA)
1949	TYRELL, John E.		46	Died in Los Angeles, CA
1949	# VANBRUGH, Irene		76	Died in London, England
1949	# WAITE, Malcolm		56	Died in Los Angeles, CA
1949	WALKER, Johnnie		53	Coronary thrombosis (in New York, NY)
1949	WALLS, Tom		66	Died in Edwell, England
1949	WELLS, Marie		55	Suicide (sleeping pills) in Hollywood, CA
1949	# WHITE, Lee Roy "Lasses"		61	Died in Hollywood, CA
1949	+ WOOD, Sam	☆	66	Heart attack (in Hollywood, CA)
1949	WRIGHT, William		37	Cancer (in Ensenada, Mex.) Do not confuse with Will Wright d. 1962
1950	+ ALLGOOD, Sara	☆	66	Heart attack (in Woodland Hills, CA)
1950	APPLEBY, William C.		27	Coronary thrombosis (in North Hollywood, CA)
1950	ARLISS, Florence		79	Died in London, England
• 1950	BACON, Mabel		56	Cancer (in Los Angeles, CA)
• 1950	BAILEY, Edwin B.		77	Died in Santa Monica, CA
• 1950	BAKER, C. Graham		61	Died in Hollywood, CA
1950	# BANKS, Monty		52	Heart attack (in Italy)
1950	BELL, Henry "Hank"		58	Following a heart attack (in Hollywood, CA)
1950	BENNETT, Hugh		57	Coronary thrombosis (at his home in Malibu, CA)
1950	BENNETT, Mickey		35	Heart attack (in Hollywood, CA)
1950	BONIFACE, Symona		56	Died in Woodland Hills, CA
1950	# BORDEAUX, Joe		56	Died in Hollywood, CA
1950	BRISCOE, Lottie		69	Died in New York, NY
1950	BUCK, Frank		62	Pulmonary embolism (in Houston, TX)
1950	+ BURROUGHS, Edgar Rice		74	Heart ailment (in Encino, CA)
1950	# CABANNE, William C.		62	Heart attack (in Philadelphia, PA)
1950	CARLETON, George		65	Heart attack (in Hollywood, CA)
1950	CARTER, Monte		66	Died in San Francisco, CA
1950	CAVANAUGH, Hobart		53	Following major surgery (in Woodland Hills, CA)
1950	CLAYTON, Gilbert		89	Heart attack (in Los Angeles, CA)
1950	# CLAYTON, Marguerite B.		50	Injuries from an automobile accident (in Los Angeles, CA)
1950	# CLEMENTO, Steve		64	Cerebral hemorrhage (in Los Angeles, CA)
1950	COSTELLO, Maurice		73	Heart ailment (in Hollywood, CA)
1950	+ COWL, Jane		62	Cancer (in Santa Monica, CA)
1950	CULLINANI, Ralph		68	
1950	+ DAMROSCH, Walter		88	Died in New York, NY
1950	DAVIDSON, Max		75	After a long illness (in Woodland Hills, CA)
1950	DAWSON, Dorice		56	Heart attack (in Riverside, CA)
1950	+ DeCORDOBA, Pedro		68	Found dead of a heart attack (at his home in Sunland, CA)

Deaths of Movie and Television Personalities — by Year

YEAR	NAME		AGE	CAUSE and/or PLACE OF DEATH
1950	DeLaMOTTE, Marguerite		47	Cerebral thrombosis (in San Francisco, CA)
1950	DYALL, Franklin		76	Died in Worthing, England
1950	ELDRIDGE, Anna Mae		56	Heart attack (in Van Nuys, CA)
1950	EVANS, Jack		57	Heart attack (in Hollywood, CA)
1950	FELLOWES, Rockcliffe		65	Heart attack (in Los Angeles, CA)
1950	FRANCISCO, Betty		50	Heart attack at her ranch (in El Cerito, CA)
1950	+ FULTON, Maude		69	Died at the Motion Picture Country Home, CA
1950	GARWOOD, William		66	Coronary occlusion (in Los Angeles, CA)
1950	# GERRARD, Douglas		69	After being found unconscious on the street (in Hollywood, CA)
1950	#+ HALE, Alan Sr.		57	Liver ailment — virus infection (in Hollywood, CA)
1950	HICKMAN, Howard C.		69	Following a heart attack (in Los Angeles, CA)
1950	# HOLLES, Antony		49	Died in London, England
1950	HOLMES, Helen		58	Heart attack (in Burbank, CA)
1950	HOPKINS, Arthur		71	Heart ailment (in New York, NY)
1950	#+ HUSTON, Walter	★	66	Aneurysm (in Beverly Hills, CA)
1950	#+ INGRAM, Rex (Hitchcock)		57	Cerebral hemorrhage (in North Hollywood, CA)
1950	JACKSON, Warren		57	After his car collided with a truck (in Hollywood, CA)
1950	# JANNINGS, Emil	★	63	Cancer (in Wolfgangsee, Austria)
1950	+ JENNINGS, Humphrey		43	Accidentally fell off a cliff (on the greek island of Poros)
1950	#+ JOLSON, Al		64	Heart attack (in San Francisco, CA)
1950	# KAMPERS, Fritz		59	Died in Garmisch-Partenkirchen, Germany
1950	KEMPER, Charles		49	Injuries from an automobile crash (in Burbank, CA)
1950	KLOPFER, Eugen		64	Died in Wiesbaden, Germany
1950	# KRAHLY, Hanns		65	After a long illness (in Hollywood, CA)
1950	# LAMBERTI, Professor		58	After a long illness (in Hollywood, CA)
1950	LAUDER, Harry		79	Uremia (in Lenarkshire, Scotland)
1950	LEHR, Lew		54	Died at a sanitarium in Brookline, MA
1950	LINGHAM, Thomas J.		75	Died in Woodland Hills, CA
1950	LIPATTI, Dinu		33	
1950	+ LORD, Pauline		60	Heart trouble (in Alamogordo, NM)
1950	MARSHALL, Boyd		65	Died in Jackson Heights, NY
1950	METAXA, Georges		51	Heart ailment (in Monroe, LA)
1950	# MONTANA, Lewis "Bull"		62	Coronary thrombosis (in Los Angeles, CA)
1950	MORRISON, Arthur		71	Died in Los Angeles, CA
1950	NASH, Florence		60	Heart ailment (in Los Angeles, CA)
1950	+ NIJINSKY, Vaslav		62	Nephritis (in London, England)
1950	OBER, Robert		68	Died in New York
1950	OVERMAN, Jack		34	Following a heart attack (in Hollywood, CA)
1950	PATON, Charles		64	
1950	PATRICOLA, Tom		55	Following brain surgery (in Pasadena, CA)
1950	PEMBERTON, Brock		64	After a heart attack at his home (in New York, NY)
1950	PINE, Ed		46	Died at the Motion Picture Country Home, Woodland Hills, CA
1950	# POWELL, Russ		75	Arteriosclerosis (in Woodland Hills, CA)
1950	ROBINSON, Dewey		52	After a heart attack (in Las Vegas, NV)
1950	SELBIE, Evelyn		68	Heart ailment (in Hollywood, CA)
1950	+ SHAW, George Bernard		94	Bladder ailment and injuries from a fall (in Ayot St. Lawrence, Eng.)
1950	SMITH, "Whispering" Jack		51	Heart attack (in New York) Do not confuse with Jack Smith, d. 1989
1950	+ STAHL, John M.		63	Heart attack (in Hollywood, CA)
1950	STARR, Muriel		62	Heart attack (in New York, NY)
1950	# STOOPNAGLE, Col. Lemuel Q.		52	Died in Encino, CA
1950	# STUBBS, Harry		75	Heart attack (in Woodland Hills, CA)
1950	SWEENEY, Jack		61	Died in Hollywood, CA
1950	TILBURY, Zeffie		86	After a long illness (in Los Angeles, CA)

Deaths of Movie and Television Personalities — by Year

YEAR	NAME		AGE	CAUSE and/or PLACE OF DEATH
1950	WADSWORTH, William		77	*Died at Queens General Hospital in New York*
1950	# WINTHROP, Joy		86	*Died in Hollywood, CA*
1950	WRAY, Ted		41	*Following a heart attack (in Big Bear City, CA)*
1950	+ YULE, Joe		55	*Heart attack (in Hollywood, CA)*
1951	ALLEN, Harry R.		68	*Died in Los Angeles, CA*
1951	# ARTHUR, Johnny		68	*Heart disease (in Woodland Hills, CA)*
1951	ASH, Samuel Howard		67	*Died in Hollywood, CA*
1951	# AULT, Marie		81	*Died in London, England*
1951	AUSTIN, William		66	*Stroke*
1951	# AYE, Maryon		45	*Suicide (poison) in Hollywood, CA*
1951	BAILEY, Edward Lorenz		68	*Died in Lima, OH*
1951	BARKER, Bradley		68	*Died in New York, NY*
1951	+ BAXTER, Warner	★	58	*Pneumonia after lobotomy to ease pain (in Beverly Hills, CA)*
1951	BENEDICT, Kingsley		69	*Died in Woodland Hills, CA*
1951	# BENNETT, Billie		75	*Cerebral hemorrhage (in Los Angeles, CA)*
1951	# BERKES, John "Johnny"		54	*Died in Hollywood, CA*
1951	BOROS, Ferike		70	*Died in Hollywood, CA*
1951	#+ BRICE, Fanny		59	*Cerebral hemorrhage (in Beverly Hills, CA)*
1951	BROMBERG, J. Edward		47	*Heart attack (in London, England)*
1951	BROOKE, Clifford		79	*After being struck by a car (in Santa Monica, CA)*
1951	+ CHRISTIANS, Mady		51	*Cerebral hemorrhage (in South Norwalk, CT)*
1951	CHRISTIE, Al		69	*Heart attack (in Beverly Hills, CA)*
1951	COLEMAN, Charles C.		65	*Pulmonary embolism (in Woodland Hills, CA)*
1951	# COLLINS, Monty		52	*Heart attack (in North Hollywood, CA)*
1951	CONWAY, Jack (comedian/actor)		65	*Died in Forrest Hills, NY (Do not confuse with Jack Conway, d. 1952)*
1951	COSSART, Ernest		74	*Died in The Bronx, NY*
1951	+ DUCHIN, Eddie		41	*Leukemia (in New York, NY)*
1951	DUNN, Edward F. "Eddie"		55	*Cancer (in Hollywood, CA)*
1951	ELLIOTT, Robert		72	*Died in Los Angeles, CA*
1951	+ ERROL, Leon		70	*Heart attack (in Hollywood, CA)*
1951	FLAHERTY, Robert		67	*Heart attack (in Dummerston, VT)*
1951	# FORBES, Ralph		54	*Died at Montefiore Hospital in The Bronx, NY*
1951	GOWLAND, Gibson		79	*Died in London, England*
1951	HARCOURT, James		77	*Died in London, England*
1951	HART, Richard		35	*Heart attack (in New York, NY)*
1951	# HARTIGAN, Pat		69	*Coronary attack (in Los Angeles, CA)*
1951	HEYBURN, Weldon		46	*Died in Hollywood, CA*
1951	#+ HOLT, Jack		62	*Coronary thrombosis (in Los Angeles, CA)*
1951	# JOUVET, Louis		63	*Heart attack (in Paris, France)*
1951	KING, Joe		68	*Died in Woodland Hills, CA*
1951	LISTER, Francis		52	*Died in London, England*
1951	MacDONALD, Edmund		43	*Cerebral hemorrhage (in Los Angeles, CA)*
1951	MARIN, Edwin L.		50	*After a 3-week illness (in Hollywood, CA)*
1951	MAUDE, Cyril		88	*Died in Torquay, England*
1951	McGLYNN, Frank Sr.		84	*Died in Newburgh, NY*
1951	MELTON, Frank		43	*After a heart attack (in Hollywood, CA)*
1951	METHOT, Mayo		47	*Died in Portland, OR*
1951	# MONTEZ, Maria		33	*Heart seizure while bathing in her home (in Suresnes, France)*
1951	# NORMAN, Josephine		46	*Died in Roslyn, NY*
1951	# NOVELLO, Ivor		58	*Coronary thrombosis (in London, England)*
1951	O'MADIGAN, Isabel		78	*Died in Los Angeles, CA*
1951	# OVEY, George		80	*Died in Hollywood, CA*

• New entry.   # Original name (Pt. 7).   + Interment (Pt. 5).   28   ☆ Oscar nominee, ★ Oscar winner (Pt. 10)

Deaths of Movie and Television Personalities — by Year

YEAR	NAME		AGE	CAUSE and/or PLACE OF DEATH
1951	OWEN, Garry		48	Heart attack (in Hollywood, CA)
1951	PATTON, William "Bill"		57	Died in Los Angeles, CA
1951	# RAYMOND, Jack		49	Heart attack (in Santa Monica, CA) Do not confuse with British actor
1951	# RIDGES, Stanley		59	Died in Westbrook, CT
1951	# RIGBY, Edward		71	Died in London, England
1951	RODGERS, Walter		64	Following a stroke (in Los Angeles, CA)
1951	+ ROMBERG, Sigmund		64	Cerebral hemorrhage (in New York, NY)
1951	# ROSEN, Phil		63	Died in Hollywood, CA
1951	SHANNON, Ethel		53	Died in Hollywood, CA
1951	+ SIMON, S. Sylvan		41	Heart attack (in Beverly Hills, CA)
1951	SIMPSON, Ivan		76	Died in New York, NY
1951	# SINCLAIR, Arthur		68	Died in Belfast, Northern Ireland
1951	# STEERS, Larry		69	Died in Woodland Hills, CA
1951	TELL, Olive		56	Died in New York, NY
1951	# TORRENCE, David		87	Died in Scotland
1951	VISAROFF, Michael		58	Pneumonia (in Hollywood, CA)
1951	WAKEFIELD, Douglas		51	Died in London, England
1951	WALKER, Robert		32	Respiratory failure (Do not confuse with R. "Bob" Walker, d. 1954)
1951	WALLACE, Richard		57	Heart attack (in Los Angeles, CA)
1951	+ WARFIELD, David		84	Died in New York
1951	WEIGEL, Paul		83	Died in Germany
1951	WILLS, Drusilla		66	Died in London, England
1951	YARBOROUGH, Barton		51	Died in Hollywood, CA
1951	YOUNG, Clifton		34	Asphyxiation after falling asleep while smoking (in Los Angeles, CA)
1952	ABBEY, May		80	Fell or jumped from a building (in New York, NY)
1952	ABBOTT, Gypsy		57	Died in Hollywood, CA
1952	ADAIR, John		66	Died in New York
1952	ADAMS, Lionel		86	Died in New York, NY
1952	# BACHMANN, John		63	Heart attack (in Hollywood, CA)
1952	BACON, Allen		66	Died in Los Angeles, CA
1952	BAILEY, Albert		61	Suicide (in Hollywood, CA)
1952	BANKS, Leslie		61	Died in London, England
1952	BASSERMAN, Albert	☆	86	Heart attack (in Zurich, Switzerland)
1952	# BOND, Jack		52	Died in Hollywood, CA
1952	BRIGGS, Harlan		72	Cerebral thrombosis (in Woodland Hills, CA)
1952	+ BYRD, Ralph M. "Dick Tracy"		43	Heart attack (in Tarzana, CA)
1952	COLCORD, Mabel		80	Died in Los Angeles, CA
1952	CONWAY, Jack (actor/director)		65	Pulmonary infection (in Pacific Palisades, CA)
1952	#+ CROSBY, Dixie Lee		40	Cancer
1952	CURTIS, Dick		49	Died in Hollywood, CA
1952	DEAN, Julia		74	Died in Hollywood, CA
1952	# DeROACH, Charles		72	
1952	DUFKIN, Sam		61	Died in Hollywood, CA
1952	EDWARDS, Henry		70	Died in Chobham, England
1952	ELLIS, Edward		80	After 33 weeks of illness (in Hollywood, CA)
1952	EVANS, Herbert		68	Died in San Gabriel, CA
1952	FOX, William		73	Heart attack (in New York, NY)
1952	FRANCIS, Olin		59	Died in Hollywood, CA
1952	FRENCH, Charles K.		92	After a heart attack (in Hollywood, CA)
1952	#+ GARFIELD, John	☆	39	Heart attack (in New York, NY)
1952	GRANT, Lawrence		82	Died in Santa Barbara, CA
1952	# HARDING, Lyn		85	Died in London, England

• New entry. # Original name (Pt. 7). + Interment (Pt. 5). 29 ☆ Oscar nominee, ★ Oscar winner (Pt. 10)

Deaths of Movie and Television Personalities — by Year

YEAR	NAME		AGE	CAUSE and/or PLACE OF DEATH
1952	#+ HENDERSON, Fletch		54	Stroke (in New York, NY)
1952	+ HERBERT, Hugh		64	Heart attack (in North Hollywood, CA)
1952	#+ HOWARD, Jerome "Curly"		48	Following several strokes (in San Gabriel, CA)
1952	LaCAVA, Gregory	☆	59	Heart attack at his home (in Malibu Beach, CA)
1952	LAUGHTON, Edward "Eddie"		49	Pneumonia (in Hollywood, CA)
1952	#+ LAWRENCE, Gertrude		54	Cancer of the liver (in New York, NY)
1952	#+ LEE, Canada		45	Heart attack (in New York, NY)
1952	# LEE, Dixie		40	Cancer (in Holmby Hills, CA)
1952	#+ LINCOLN, Elmo		63	Heart attack (in Hollywood, CA)
1952	# LITTLE, Bozo		45	Heart ailment (in Los Angeles, CA)
1952	LONG, Walter		73	Heart attack (in Hollywood, CA)
1952	# LUFKIN, Sam		59	Uremia (in Los Angeles, CA)
1952	#+ MacDONALD, J. Farrell		77	Died in Hollywood, CA
1952	MAGRILL, George		52	Died in Los Angeles, CA
1952	MALA, Ray		46	Heart attack (in Hollywood, CA)
1952	MALATESTA, Fred		62	After a surgical operation (in Burbank, CA)
1952	MARKS, Willis		87	Died in Los Angeles, CA
1952	+ McDANIEL, Hattie	★	57	Breast cancer (in San Fernando Valley, CA)
1952	# McGOWAN, John P.		72	(Silent star/producer) Died in Hollywood, CA
1952	MITCHELL, Bruce		68	Anemia (in Hollywood, CA)
1952	# MORAN, Polly		68	Heart ailment (in Los Angeles, CA)
1952	MORLEY, Robert James	☆	60	Died in Hollywood, CA (Do not confuse with Robert Morley, d. 1992)
1952	PAWLEY, William		46	Died in New York
1952	#+ PETERS, Susan	☆	31	Bronchial pneumonia and chronic kidney infection (in Visalia, CA)
1952	# POFF, Lon		82	Died in Los Angeles, CA
1952	POST, Charles A. "Buddy"		55	Died in Los Angeles, CA
1952	PROSSER, Hugh		46	Automobile crash (near Gallup, NM)
1952	RADFORD, Basil		55	Heart attack (in London, England)
1952	REED, Barbara		85	
1952	# REED, George H.		85	Arteriosclerosis (in Woodland Hills, CA)
1952	RENOIR, Pierre		67	Uremic poisoning (in Paris, France)
1952	ROBER, Richard		46	Killed when his car went down an embankment due to fog (in CA)
1952	ROCHE, John C.		56	Cerebral thrombosis (in Hollywood, CA)
1952	SHEEHAN, John J., Jr.		61	Died in Hollywood, CA
1952	SHERMAN, Harry		67	After two surgical operations
1952	# SKIPWORTH, Alison		88	Died in New York, NY
1952	ST. CLAIR, Malcolm		55	Died in Pasadena, CA.
1952	STEWART, Blanche		?	Died in Los Angeles, CA
1952	STRANGE, Robert		70	Died in Hollywood, CA
1952	TAYLOR, Ray		63	Died in Hollywood, CA
1952	# WALDRON, Charles K.		37	Airplane crash (in Los Angeles, CA)
1952	WALES, Ethel		71	Died in Hollywood, CA
1952	WARD, Fannie		80	After suffering a cerebral hemorrhage (in Lennox Hill, NY)
1952	WARD, Lucille		72	Died in Dayton, OH
1952	WEST, Roland		65	Heart ailment (in Santa Monica, CA)
1952	YORK, Duke		49	Suicide (found shot to death at his home) in Hollywood, CA
1952	# ZEARS, Marjorie		41	Murdered in her bathroom (in Hollywood, CA)
1953	ADAIR, Jean		80	Died in New York
1953	#+ ADAMS, Maude		80	Heart attack (in Tannersville, NY)
1953	AUSTIN, Albert		71	After a long illness (in North Hollywood, CA)
1953	# BAILEY, Frankie		94	Died in Los Angeles, CA
1953	BARNARD, Ivor		66	Died in London, England

Deaths of Movie and Television Personalities — by Year

YEAR	NAME	AGE	CAUSE and/or PLACE OF DEATH
1953	+ BARNES, George S. ★	60	Heart attack (Do not confuse with George Barnes, d. 1949)
1953	BELMORE, Lionel	85	Died in Woodland Hills, CA
1953	BONN, Walter	64	Died in Hollywood, CA
1953	+ BORDONI, Irene	59	Died in New York, NY
1953	BRENEMAN, Mark L.	54	Heart attack
1953	#+ BRUCE, Nigel	58	Heart attack (in Santa Monica, CA)
1953	CLARK, Cliff	59	Heart attack (in Hollywood, CA)
1953	COOKE, Baldwin G. "Baldy"	65	Died in Los Angeles, CA
1953	# CRIPPS, Kernan	67	Died in CA
1953	# CURTIS, Alan	43	Following a kidney operation (in New York, NY)
1953	DAWSON, Frank	83	Died in Hollywood, CA
1953	DeGRASSE, Sam	78	Heart attack (in Hollywood, CA)
1953	DUNBAR, David	60	After a long illness (in Woodland Hills, CA)
1953	DUNDEE, Jimmie	52	Leukemia (in Woodland Hills, CA)
1953	+ FARNUM, William	76	Cancer (in Los Angeles, CA)
1953	# FINLAYSON, James	66	Heart attack (in Los Angeles, CA)
1953	FOO, Wing	43	Heart attack (in Los Angeles, CA)
1953	# FORD, Francis	71	After a long illness (in Los Angeles, CA)
1953	GALLAGHER, Raymond "Ray"	67	Heart attack (in Camarillo, CA)
1953	GRASSBY, Bertram	72	Died in Scottsdale, AZ
1953	GRIFFIN, Frank L.	63	Heart attack (in Hollywood, CA)
1953	# HALL, Porter	65	Heart attack (in Los Angeles, CA)
1953	HEPWORTH, Cecil M.	78	Died in Greenford, Middlesex, England
1953	HOYT, Arthur	79	After a long illness (in Woodland Hills, CA)
1953	HURST, Paul C.	64	Suicide (in Hollywood, CA)
1953	JOHNSON, Osa	58	Heart attack (in New York, NY)
1953	KEMP, Paul	54	Died in Bad Godesburg, West Germany
1953	# KENDALL, Cy	55	Died in Woodland Hills, CA
1953	KENT, Craufurd	72	After a short illness (in Los Angeles, CA)
1953	#+ Kiki	52	Natural causes (in Paris, France)
1953	LANE, Pat	53	Heart attack (in Beverly Hills, CA)
1953	+ LEBEDEFF, Ivan	53	Heart attack (in Hollywood, CA)
1953	# LESLIE, Gene	48	Died in Los Angeles, CA
1953	LOGAN, Stanley	67	Died in New York, NY
1953	LOVELL, Raymond	53	Died in London, England
1953	# LUTTRINGER, Al	74	Died in Hollywood, CA
1953	MANKIEWICZ, Herman J.	55	Uremic poisoning (in Hollywood, CA)
1953	# MARTIN, Chris-Pin	59	Heart attack (in Montebello, CA)
1953	McCORMACK, William M.	62	Following a heart attack (in Hollywood, CA)
1953	# McCORMICK, Merrill	61	Heart attack (in Hollywood, CA)
1953	# McINTYRE, Leila	70	After a long illness (in West Los Angeles, CA)
1953	MITCHELL, Millard	53	Lung cancer (in Santa Monica, CA)
1953	# NORTON, Edgar	84	Died in Woodland Hills, CA
1953	PAYNE, Edna	61	Liver ailment (in Los Angeles, CA)
1953	# PAYNE, Lou	77	Died in Woodland Hills, CA
1953	PHELPS, Lee	58	Died in Culver City, CA
1953	+ PROKOFIEV, Sergei	62	Cerebral hemorrhage (in Moscow, Russia)
1953	PUDOVKIN, Vsevolod	60	Natural causes (in Moscow, Russia)
1953	# PURDELL, Reginald	56	After a long illness (in London, England)
1953	RAWLINSON, Herbert	67	Lung cancer (in Woodland Hills, CA)
1953	# RAYMOND, Jack	66	Died in London, England (Do not confuse with U.S. actor)
1953	REIS, Irving	47	Following a cancer operation (in Woodland Hills, CA)
1953	# ROSE, Blanche	74	Died at her home in Hollywood, CA

YEAR	NAME		AGE	CAUSE and/or PLACE OF DEATH
1953	ROSENTHAL, Harry		52	*Heart attack (in Hollywood, CA)*
1953	+ ROSSON, Richard "Dick"		60	*Suicide (carbon monoxide poisoning) in Los Angeles, CA*
1953	SALTER, Thelma		44	*After a lingering illness (in Hollywood, CA)*
1953	# SANTLEY, Fred		64	*Died in Hollywood, CA*
1953	SARNO, Hector V.		73	*After a long illness (in Pasadena, CA)*
1953	SEDGWICK, Edward Jr.		60	*Following a heart attack (in North Hollywood, CA)*
1953	# SHEA, Mervin		52	*Died in Sacramento, CA*
1953	SPOOR, George K.		81	*Died in Chicago, IL*
1953	STEVENSON, Houseley		74	*Died at City of Hope Sanitarium, near Los Angeles, CA*
1953	# STOCKDALE, Carl		79	*Heart attack (in Woodland Hills, CA)*
1953	#+ STONE, Lewis ☆		74	*Heart attack (while chasing 3 teen-aged vandals) in Los Angeles, CA*
1953	# SYLVANI, Gladys		68	*After a long illness (in Alexandria, VA)*
1953	# TABLER, P. Dempsey		79	*Died in San Francisco, CA*
1953	TEARLE, Godfrey		68	*Died in London, England*
1953	+ THORPE, Jim		64	*Heart attack (in Lomita, CA)*
1953	VIERTEL, Berthold		68	*Heart ailment (in Vienna, Austria)*
1953	VIGNOLA, Robert G.		71	*Died in Hollywood, CA*
1953	WALLACE, Morgan		65	*Died in Tarzana, CA*
1953	+ WILLIAMS, Hank Sr.		29	*Heart attack from excessive drinking (in Oak Hill, WV)*
1953	WILSON, Dooley		59	*Died in Los Angeles, CA*
1953	YOUNG, Roland ☆		65	*Died at his home in New York, NY*
1954	ADAIR, Robert		54	*Died in London, England*
1954	AHLM, Philip E.		49	*Murdered (shot) in Hollywood, CA*
1954	BAGNI, John		43	*Heart attack (in Hollywood, CA)*
1954	BAILEY, Harry A.		74	*Died in Los Angeles, CA*
1954	#+ BARRYMORE, Lionel ★		76	*Heart attack (in Van Nuys, CA)*
1954	# BATES, Florence		65	*Heart attack (in Burbank, CA)*
1954	CAIN, Robert		67	*Died in New York, NY*
1954	# CARDWELL, James		32	*Suicide (gunshot) in Hollywood, CA*
1954	CARR, Geraldine		37	*Automobile accident (in Hollywood, CA)*
1954	CASS, Maurice		69	*Heart attack (in Hollywood, CA)*
1954	CLARK, Eddie		75	*Heart attack (in Hollywood, CA)*
1954	COLLINS, Lewis D.		55	*Heart attack (in Hollywood, CA)*
1954	CORDING, Harry		63	*Died in Sun Valley, CA*
1954	COXEN, Edward Albert		70	*Died in Hollywood, CA*
1954	# DEMAIN, Gordon		56	
1954	DIONNE, Emelie		20	*Epileptic seizure (in Canada)*
1954	DOWLING, Joan		26	*Found dead in a gas-filled room (in London, England)*
1954	EVANS, Evan		53	*Heart attack (in New York, NY)*
1954	GEBUEHR, Otto		76	*Heart attack (in Wiesbaden, West Germany)*
1954	# GEORGE, Gladys ☆		54	*Brain hemorrhage (in Los Angeles, CA)*
1954	# GLYNNE, Mary		56	*Died in London, England*
1954	GRAVINA, Cesare		96	*Died in Italy*
1954	#+ GREENSTREET, Sydney ☆		74	*After a long illness (in Los Angeles, CA)*
1954	HACKETT, Florence		72	*Died in New York, NY*
1954	HAMPTON, Louise		72	*Bronchial trouble (in London, England)*
1954	HAYS, Will H.		74	*Died in Sullivan, IN*
1954	HILL, Al		62	*(Do not confuse with stage actor of same name)*
1954	HILTON, James		54	*Cancer of the liver (in Long Beach, CA)*
1954	HOTELY, Mae		81	*Died in Coronado, CA*
1954	HOWARD, William K.		54	*Throat cancer (in Hollywood, CA)*
1954	# KEY, Kathleen		47	*Died in Woodland Hills, CA*

Deaths of Movie and Television Personalities — by Year

YEAR	NAME	AGE	CAUSE and/or PLACE OF DEATH
1954	KINNELL, Murray	65	Died in Santa Barbara, CA
1954	LLOYD, Art	58	Paralytic stroke (after filming the Bikini Atoll atom bomb test)
1954	# LOOS, Theodor	70	Died in Stuttgart, West Germany
1954	# LUCAN, Arthur	67	Heart attack (in Hull, England)
1954	LYTELL, Bert	69	Following surgery (in New York, NY)
1954	LYTELL, Wilfred	62	After an illness of several weeks (in Salem, NY)
1954	MacMILLAN, Violet	66	Died in Grand Rapids, MI
1954	MAY, Joe	73	After a long illness (in Hollywood, CA)
1954	McGUIRE, Tom	80	Died in Hollywood, CA
1954	MITCHELL, Julien	65	Died in London, England
1954	# NESBITT, Miriam	80	Died in Hollywood, CA
1954	+ OLSEN, Moroni	65	Found dead at home of a probable heart attack (in Los Angeles, CA)
1954	PAIGE, Mabel	74	Died in Van Nuys, CA
1954	PALLETTE, Eugene	65	Throat cancer (in Los Angeles, CA)
1954	PASCAL, Gabriel	60	After an illness of 3-weeks (in New York, NY)
1954	PAULSEN, Harald	59	Heart attack (in Hamburg, Germany)
1954	PERRY, Walter	85	Died in Los Angeles, CA
1954	PICHEL, Irving	63	Following a heart attack (in Hollywood, CA)
1954	# PRIOR, Herbert	87	Died in London, England
1954	+ RICE, Grantland ★	73	Following a heart attack (in New York)
1954	RICH, Lillian	53	Died at the Motion Picture Country Home, in Woodland Hills, CA
1954	ROBERTS, Leona	73	Died in Santa Monica, CA
1954	# ROBEY, George	85	Died in Saltdean, Sussex, England
1954	SAUNDERS, Jackie	61	Died in Palm Springs, CA
1954	SCARDON, Paul	75	Heart attack (in Fontana, CA)
1954	SCHUNZEL, Reinhold	68	Heart ailment (in Munich, Germany)
1954	#+ SELWYN, Ruth	49	After a long illness (in Hollywood, CA)
1954	SHANNON, Effie	87	Died in Bay Shore, L.I., NY
1954	SISSON, Vera	63	Overdose of barbiturates (in Carmel, CA)
1954	# Sojin	63	Died in Tokyo, Japan
1954	TRIMBLE, Lawrence	69	Died at the Motion Picture Country House in Ca.
1954	# TYLER, Tom	50	Heart attack after suffering crippling arthritis (in Hamtramck, MI)
1954	VAJDA, Ernest	67	Heart attack (in Woodland Hills, CA)
• 1954	# VERTOV, Dziga	58	Cancer
1954	WALKER, Robert "Bob"	65	(Do not confuse with actor Robert Walker, d. 1951)
1954	WEEKS, Barbara	47	Died in Los Angeles, CA
1954	WHITMAN, Ernest	61	Following a heart attack (in Hollywood, CA)
1955	+ AGEE, James	45	Heart attack (in New York, NY)
1955	AKED, Muriel	68	Died in Settle, England
1955	ARNHEIM, Gus	55	Heart attack (in Beverly Hills, CA)
1955	+ BACON, Lloyd	66	Cerebral hemorrhage (in Burbank, CA)
• 1955	BADGLEY, Frank C.	62	Died in Ottawa, Canada
1955	#+ BALL, Suzan (Long)	22	Cancer after knee surgery while filming in Sumatra (in Beverly Hills)
1955	#+ BARA, Theda (Brabin)	69	Abdominal cancer (in Los Angeles, CA)
1955	# BEECHER, Janet	70	Heart attack (in Washington, CT)
1955	BENGE, Wilson	80	Died in Hollywood, CA
1955	+ BERTRAND, Mary	73	Died in Woodland Hills, CA
1955	# BLACKLEY, Douglas	46	(See Robert Kent)
1955	BLACKWELL, Carlyle Sr.	71	Died in Miami Beach, FL
1955	BORDEN, Eddie	67	Died in Hollywood, CA
1955	+ BRUCKMAN, Clyde	60	Suicide (gunshot) in Santa Monica, CA
1955	BRYANT, Nana	67	Died in Hollywood, CA

Deaths of Movie and Television Personalities — by Year

YEAR	NAME		AGE	CAUSE and/or PLACE OF DEATH
1955	BURTON, George H.		55	Heart attack (in Los Angeles, CA)
1955	BUSSE, Henry		61	Heart attack (in Memphis, TN)
1955	CAMERON, Donald		66	Died in West Cornwall, CT
1955	# CAREWE, Ora		62	Died in Los Angeles, CA
1955	# CARVER, Lynn		45	Suicide (in New York, NY)
1955	CHEKHOV, Michael	☆	64	Died in Beverly Hills, CA
1955	# CLARENCE, O. B.		85	Died in Hove, England
1955	# COLLIER, Constance		77	Died in New York, NY
1955	# DAMPIER, Claude		75	Pneumonia (in London, England)
1955	#+ DANIELS, Victor		66	Cancer (in Ventura, CA)
1955	DARIEN, Frank Jr.		79	Died in Hollywood, CA
1955	DAVIES, Betty Ann		44	Complications after appendectomy (in Manchester, England)
1955	#+ DEAN, James	☆	24	Automobile accident (near Paso Robles, CA)
1955	+ DeMILLE, William C.		76	Died in Playa del Rey, CA
1955	DUDLEY, Robert Y.		80	Died in San Clemente, CA
1955	+ FRANCIS, Robert		25	Airplane crash (in Burbank, CA)
1955	FRIGANZA, Trixie		84	After being bedridden with arthritis (in Flintridge, CA)
1955	# GALLAGHER, Skeets		64	Following a heart attack (in Santa Monica, CA)
1955	GAYE, Howard		?	Died in London, England
1955	GILL, Basil		77	Died in Hove, England
1955	GODDEN, Jimmy		75	Died in England
1955	GOLDNER, Charles		54	Died in London, England
1955	GORCEY, Bernard		67	Injuries from an auto accident (in Hollywood, CA)
1955	GROVES, Frederick "Fred"		74	Died in London, England
1955	#+ HAMPDEN, Walter		75	Stroke (in Hollywood, CA)
1955	+ HARVEY, Paul (actor)		72	Coronary thrombosis (Do not confuse with radio commentator)
1955	+ HAYDEN, Harry		72	After a long illness (in West Los Angeles, CA)
1955	+ HODIAK, John		41	Coronary thrombosis (in Tarzana, CA)
1955	# HONEGGER, Arthur		63	Heart disease (in Paris, France)
1955	#+ HOWARD, Shemp		60	Coronary occlusion (in Hollywood, CA)
1955	HYTTEN, Olaf		67	After a heart attack (on the set of "Sir Walter Raleigh") in L.A.
1955	# JERROLD, Mary		77	Pneumonia (in London, England)
1955	JOYCE, Alice "Vitagraph Girl"		65	Heart ailment (in Hollywood, CA)
1955	KEATON, Myra		?	
1955	# KENT, Robert		46	
• 1955	+ KNAGGS, Skelton		43	Heart attack
1955	KNOTT, Lydia		88	Died in Woodland Hills, CA
1955	LEDERER, Gretchen		64	Died in Anaheim, CA
1955	LETONDAL, Henri		52	Heart attack (in Burbank, CA)
1955	LEVEY, Ethel		73	Heart attack (in New York, NY)
1955	# LORRAINE, Lillian		63	Died in New York, NY
1955	MARTINDEL, Edward B.		78	Heart attack (in Woodland Hills, CA)
1955	McGOWAN, Robert F.		72	Died in Santa Monica, CA
1955	McNAUGHTON, Charles		77	Died in London, England
1955	MILLER, Charles B.		64	Suicide (gunshot) due to unemployment and ill health (Hollywood)
1955	MILLICAN, James		45	After a brief illness (in Los Angeles, CA)
1955	#+ MIRANDA, Carmen		51	Heart attack (in Beverly Hills, CA)
1955	# Miroslava		29	Suicide (poison) in Mexico City, Mexico
1955	MOORE, Eva		85	Died in Maidenhead, England
1955	MOORE, Tom		70	Cancer (in Santa Monica, CA)
1955	MORRELL, George		82	After a long illness (in Hollywood, CA)
1955	#+ MUNSON, Ona		51	Suicide (sleeping pills) in New York, NY
1955	ODEMAR, Fritz		65	Cancer (in Munich, Germany)

YEAR	NAME		AGE	CAUSE and/or PLACE OF DEATH
1955	PARDAVE, Joaquin		54	Died in Mexico City, Mexico
1955	+ PARKER, Charlie "Bird"		34	Heart attack (in the New York apartment of a female friend)
1955	# PAYTON, Claude		72	Died in Los Angeles, CA
1955	+ PIERLOT, Francis		78	Heart ailment (in Hollywood, CA)
1955	POWERS, Tom		65	Heart ailment (in Hollywood, CA)
1955	PRICE, Stanley L.		55	Heart attack (in Hollywood, CA)
1955	RAY, Barbara		40	Leukemia (in Los Angeles, CA)
1955	RISKIN, Robert		58	After a long illness (in Beverly Hills, CA)
1955	ROSS, Anthony		46	Died in New York
1955	#+ SAKALL, S. Z. "Cuddles"		71	Heart attack (in Beverly Hills, CA)
1955	# SCHMITZ, Sybille		42	Suicide (pills) in Munich, Germany
1955	STANDING, Herbert Jr.		71	Died in New York, NY
1955	STANTON, Paul		70	Died in Los Angeles, CA
1955	STEELE, Vernon		72	Heart attack (in Los Angeles, Ca.)
1955	TATE, Reginald		58	Heart attack (in London, England)
1955	#+ THUNDERCLOUD, Chief (1st)		66	Cancer (Do not confuse with 2nd Chief Thundercloud, d. 1967)
1955	VAUGHAN, Dorothy		65	Cerebral hemorrhage (in Hollywood, CA)
1955	WHITE, Lew		52	Died in New York
1955	WILCOX, Robert		45	Heart attack (on a train near Rochester, NY)
1956	ACUFF, Eddie		48	Heart attack (in Hollywood, CA)
1956	# ADAMSON, James		59	Heart attack (in Los Angeles, CA)
1956	#+ ALLEN, Fred		62	Heart attack (in New York, NY)
1956	#+ ARNOLD, Edward		66	Cerebral hemorrhage (in Encino, CA)
1956	BACON, Faith		47	Suicide (in Chicago, IL)
1956	BACON, Jane		89	Died in Hollywood, CA
1956	BALLIN, Hugo		76	Died in Santa Monica, CA
1956	+ BANCROFT, George ☆		74	After a brief illness (in Santa Monica, CA)
1956	# BLINN, Genevieve		?	After a long illness (in Ross, CA)
1956	# BLYSTONE, Stanley		61	Heart attack (in Hollywood, CA)
1956	BOURNE, Hazel (Imboden)		?	After a 2-yr. illness (in Kansas City)
1956	BROWN, Clifford		25	Automobile accident (in Paris, France)
1956	+ BURNS, Bob "Bazooka"		64	After a 3-yr. illness (at his home in San Fernando Valley, CA)
1956	#+ CALHERN, Louis ☆		61	Heart attack, brought on by alcohol and medicine (in Tokyo, Japan)
1956	# CARVER, Louise		86	Died in Hollywood, CA
1956	CHARLOT, Andre		73	Complications after cancer surgery (in Woodland Hills, CA)
1956	# CLIFFORD, Jack		76	Died in New York, NY
1956	CLUTE, Chester		64	Heart attack (in Calabasas, CA)
1956	# CRAWFORD, Anne		35	Died in London, England
1956	CURTIS, Jack		75	(Do not confuse with the child actor or Jack B. Curtis)
1956	DINGLE, Charles W.		68	After an illness of several months (in Worcester, MA)
1956	# DORO, Marie		74	Heart ailment (in New York, NY)
1956	#+ DORSEY, Tommy		51	Choked while asleep (in Greenwich, CT)
1956	DOVZHENKO, Alexander		62	Heart attack (in Moscow, Russia)
1956	DRAPER, Ruth		72	Apparent heart attack (in New York)
1956	DUPONT, E. A.		64	After a long bout with cancer (in Hollywood, CA)
1956	EASON, Reeves "Breezy"		69	Heart attack (in Sherman Oaks, CA)
1956	ELLIOTT, John H.		80	Heart attack (in Los Angeles, CA)
1956	# EMERSON, John		84	After a long illness (in Pasadena, CA)
1956	+ GANZHORN, John W.		75	Died in Hollywood, CA
1956	+ GORDON, Huntly		59	Heart attack (in Van Nuys, CA)
1956	#+ GRAPEWIN, Charley		80	After a long illness (in Corona del Mar, CA)
1956	GRAY, Jack		76	After a long illness (in Woodland Hills, CA)

Deaths of Movie and Television Personalities — by Year

YEAR	NAME		AGE	CAUSE and/or PLACE OF DEATH
1956	GRIFFIN, Charles		67	*Died in Hollywood, CA*
1956	# HENDERSON, Del		73	*Died in Woodland Hills, CA*
1956	#+ HERBERT, Holmes		74	*Died in Hollywood, CA*
1956	+ HERSHOLT, Jean	★	69	*Cancer (in Beverly Hills, CA)*
1956	# HOEFLICH, Lucie		73	*Heart attack (in Berlin, Germany)*
1956	+ HOWARD, Kathleen		75	*Died in Hollywood, CA*
1956	INGRAHAM, Lloyd		81	*Pneumonia (in Woodland Hills, CA)*
1956	IRWIN, Bobby		42	*Died in Los Angeles, CA*
1956	KEARNS, Allen B.		61	*Died in Albany, NY*
1956	#+ KELLY, Paul		57	*Heart attack (in Los Angeles, CA)*
1956	# KERRY, Norman		66	*Died in Hollywood, CA*
1956	#+ KIBBEE, Guy		70	*Parkinson's disease (in East Islip, NY)*
1956	KORDA, Alexander		62	*Heart attack (in South Kensington, England)*
1956	KOSLOFF, Theodore		74	*Died in Los Angeles, CA*
1956	LEIGHTON, Lillian		81	*Died in Woodland Hills, CA*
1956	# LeMOYNE, Charles		76	*Died in Hollywood, CA*
1956	LEONARD, Marion		75	*Died in Woodland Hills, CA*
1956	+ LEWIS, Mitchell J.		76	*After a lengthy illness (in Woodland Hills, CA)*
1956	LEWIS, Vera		72	*Died at the Motion Picture Country Hospital near Los Angeles, CA*
1956	#+ LUGOSI, Bela		73	*Heart attack from an overdose of drugs (in Hollywood, CA)*
1956	+ MacARTHUR, Charles		60	*Internal hemorrhage after nephritis (in New York, NY)*
1956	MacDONALD, Katherine		62	*After a 30-month illness (in Santa Barbara, CA)*
1956	MACY, Jack		70	*Heart attack (in Wyoming)*
1956	MAKEHAM, Eliot		73	*Died in London, England*
1956	+ McWADE, Margaret		83	*Died in Los Angeles, CA*
1956	# MENJOU, Henri		64	*Died in Sawtelle, CA*
1956	MILTON, Robert D.		70	*After a long illness and hospitalization (in Woodland Hills, CA)*
1956	#+ MORGAN, Ralph		72	*After a 3-yr. illness (in New York, NY)*
1956	# NORTON, Barry		51	*Heart attack (in Hollywood, CA)*
1956	ORZAZEWSKI, Kasia		67	*Rheumatic heart disease (in Los Angeles, CA)*
1956	PROUTY, Jed		77	*After a brief illness (in New York, NY)*
1956	RASUMNY, Mikhail		65	*Died in Los Angeles, CA*
1956	# RICH, Freddie		58	*Paralysis after an accident (in Beverly Hills, CA)*
1956	RUB, Christian		69	*Died in Germany*
1956	RYAN, Tim		57	*Heart attack (in Hollywood, CA)*
1956	# SEYMOUR, Jane		56	*Died in New York, NY*
1956	SHADE, Jamesson		60	*Heart attack (in Hollywood, CA)*
1956	# SLAUGHTER, Tod		70	*Died in Derby, England*
1956	#+ STEPHENSON, Henry		85	*After a brief illness (in San Francisco, CA)*
1956	#+ SULLIVAN, Francis L.		53	*Died in New York, NY*
1956	TAPLEY, Rose		72	*Died at the Motion Picture Country Hospital in Woodland Hills, CA*
1956	+ TATUM, Art		46	*Uremia (in Los Angeles, CA)*
1956	TURNBULL, John		75	*Died in London, England*
1956	# VALK, Frederick		55	*Died in London, England*
1956	# VonMETER, Harry		85	*Died in Los Angeles, CA*
1956	WALKER, Hal		60	*Died in Tracy, CA*
1956	# WERBISECK, Gisela		81	*After a 3-year illness (in Hollywood, CA)*
1956	WIX, Florence E.		73	*Cancer (in Woodland Hills, CA)*
1956	WOOD, Freeman N.		59	*After a short illness (in Hollywood, CA)*
1956	# WORTH, Peggy		64	*Died in New York, NY*
1956	+ WYCHERLY, Margaret	☆	74	*Died in New York, NY*
1956	+ YOUNG, Victor	★	55	*Pneumonia (in Palm Springs, CA)*

Deaths of Movie and Television Personalities — by Year

YEAR	NAME		AGE	CAUSE and/or PLACE OF DEATH
1957	ABBOTT, Frank		77	*Died in Los Angeles, CA*
1957	ALDERSON, Erville		74	*Died in Glendale, CA*
1957	ASHER, Max		76	*Died in Hollywood, CA*
1957	AUERBACH, Arthur "Mr. Kitzel"		54	*Heart attack (in Van Nuys, CA)*
1957	AUSTIN, Lois		47	*Cachexia (in Hollywood, CA)*
1957	BAKER, Belle		60	*Heart attack (in Beverly Hills, CA)*
1957	BEDOYA, Alfonso		53	*Died in Mexico City, Mexico*
1957	BENNETT, Ray		62	*Heart attack (in Hollywood, CA)*
1957	# BEVAN, William "Billy"		60	*Died in Escondido, CA*
1957	# BINNEY, Faire		57	*Pneumonia (in Los Angeles, CA)*
1957	#+ BOGART, Humphrey	★	57	*Cancer of the esophagus (in Kolmby Hills, CA)*
1957	+ BRABIN, Charles J.		75	*Heart attack (in Santa Monica, CA)*
1957	BRIDGE, Alan "Al"		66	*Died in Los Angeles, CA*
1957	+ BROWN, John H. "Digger O'Dell"		53	*Following a heart attack (in Los Angeles, CA)*
1957	BUCHANAN, Jack		66	*Spinal arthritis (in London, England)*
1957	BURTON, Frederick		86	*After being hospitalized (in Woodland Hills, CA)*
1957	# CARR, Jane		48	
1957	CARTER, Louise		82	*After a 4-month illness (in Hollywood, CA)*
1957	# CLARKE, Robert "Buddy"		61	
1957	+ CLEVELAND, George		74	*Heart attack (in Burbank, CA)*
1957	COSTELLO, Helene		53	*Pneumonia, tuberculosis, narcotics (in Los Angeles, CA)*
1957	D'AMBRICOURT, Adrienne		69	*Heart attack after her car struck another car (in Hollywood, CA)*
1957	DALE, Dorothy (Hyman)		74	*Burned to death in her shack (in Hollywood, CA)*
1957	DALY, Mark		70	*Died in England*
1957	DEPP, Harry		70	*Died in Hollywood, CA*
1957	#+ DORSEY, Jimmy		53	*Cancer (in New York, NY)*
1957	# EYTHE, William		38	*Acute hepatitis (in Los Angeles, CA)*
1957	FAIR, Elinor		53	*Died in Seattle, WA*
1957	# FENTON, Frank		51	*Pulmonary embolism (in Los Angeles, CA)*
1957	FORD, Harrison		63	*Died in Calabasas, CA (Do not confuse with the younger actor)*
1957	GERSON, Paul		86	*Died in Hollywood, CA*
1957	GRIFFITH, Raymond		67	*Heart attack (while dining in Hollywood, CA)*
1957	HALLIGAN, William		72	*After a lingering illness (in Woodland Hills, CA)*
1957	#+ HARDY, Oliver		65	*Following a paralytic stroke (in North Hollywood, CA)*
1957	HAY, Mary		55	*Prolonged heart ailment (in Inverness, CA)*
1957	# HAYE, Helen		83	*Died in London, England*
1957	# HICKS, Russell		61	*Heart attack after a traffic accident (in Hollywood, CA)*
1957	#+ HULL, Josephine	★	71	*Cerebral hemorrhage (in New York, NY)*
1957	IRWIN, Boyd		76	*Died in Woodland Hills, CA*
1957	# JOHNSON, Katie		79	*Died in Elham, England*
1957	JOYCE, Peggy Hopkins		63	*Died in New York, NY*
1957	KING, Charles L. Sr.		58	*Died in Hollywood, CA*
1957	+ KORNGOLD, Erich Wolfgang		60	*The aftermath of a cerebral thrombosis (in North Hollywood, CA)*
1957	LAWRENCE, Gerald		84	*Died in England*
1957	# LINDER, Alfred		?	*Died in Hollywood, CA*
1957	#+ LOCKHART, Gene	☆	65	*Coronary thrombosis (in Santa Monica, CA)*
1957	LOFGREN, Marianne		47	*Died in Sweden*
1957	+ LYMAN, Abe		59	*Died in Los Angeles, CA*
1957	MacBRIDE, Donald		67	*After a long illness (in Los Angeles, CA)*
1957	#+ MAYER, Louis B.		72	*Leukemia (in Los Angeles, CA)*
1957	# MENZIES, William C.	★	60	*Died in Hollywood, CA*
1957	MITCHELL, Grant		82	*Following a stroke (in Los Angeles, CA)*
1957	MITCHELL, Rhea "Ginger"		52	*Found strangled to death (at her home in Los Angeles, CA)*

• New entry. # Original name (Pt. 7). + Interment (Pt. 5).

☆ Oscar nominee, ★ Oscar winner (Pt. 10)

Deaths of Movie and Television Personalities — by Year

YEAR	NAME	AGE	CAUSE and/or PLACE OF DEATH
1957	MURRAY, John T.	71	*Following a stroke (in Woodland Hills, CA)*
1957	# Musidora	68	*Died in Paris, France*
1957	O'NEILL, Jack	74	*Died in Hollywood, CA*
1957	# OPHULS, Max	54	*Two-months after a heart attack (in Hamburg, Germany)*
1957	ORLAMOND, William	89	*Died in Copenhagen, Denmark*
1957	PATHE, Charles	93	*Died in Monte Carlo, Monaco*
1957	# PERCY, Esme	69	*Died in Brighton, England*
1957	#+ PINZA, Ezio	65	*Following a series of strokes (in Stamford, CT)*
1957	# PONTO, Erich	71	*Died in Stuttgart, Germany*
1957	RAE, Jack	58	*Heart attack (in Hollywood, CA)*
1957	# RAHM, Knute	81	*Heart disease (in Los Angeles, CA)*
1957	RICH, Vivian	64	*Automobile accident (in Hollywood, CA)*
1957	ROBINSON, Inez Buck	67	
1957	ROLF, Erik	46	
1957	SCHAEFER, Ann	87	*Died in Los Angeles, CA*
1957	# SCHILLING, Gus	48	*Heart attack (in Hollywood, CA)*
1957	SEARS, Fred	44	*Heart attack (in Hollywood, CA)*
1957	+ SEBASTIAN, Dorothy	54	*Colon cancer (at the MPCH in Woodland Hills, CA)*
1957	SHANNON, Cora	88	*Cancer (in Woodland Hills, CA)*
1957	# SHEFFIELD, Reginald	56	*Died in Pacific Palisades, CA*
1957	SHORES, Byron L.	50	*Multiple sclerosis (in Kansas City, KS)*
1957	# SILVA, Simone	29	*Suicide (in London, England)*
1957	#+ SPARKS, Ned	73	*Intestinal block (in Victorville, CA)*
1957	ST. JOHN, Jane Lee	45	*After a long illness*
1957	# SULKY, Leo	82	*Died in CA*
1957	SWASEY, Bill	29	*Automobile accident*
1957	TABER, Richard	72	*Died in New York, NY*
1957	+ TALMADGE, Norma	64	*Cerebral stroke and pneumonia (in Las Vegas, NV)*
1957	# TERRY, Sheila	46	*Died in Los Angeles, CA*
1957	TOREN, Marta	30	*Rare brain disease (in Stockholm, Sweden)*
1957	+ TOSCANINI, Arturo	89	*Following a stroke (in Riverdale, NY)*
1957	# TWITCHELL, A. R. "Archie"	50	*Killed in a midair collision over Pacoima, CA*
1957	#+ TYLER, Judy	24	*Killed in an automobile crash (in Billy the Kid, WY)*
1957	VAUGHN, Hilda	60	*Died in Baltimore, MD*
1957	VINCENT, James	74	*After a long illness (in New York)*
1957	# VonSTROHEIM, Erich Sr. ☆	71	*Spinal cancer (in Maurepas, France)*
1957	WALDRIGE, Harold	50	*Died in New York, NY*
1957	+ WHALE, James	60	*After a fall in his empty swimming pool (in Hollywood, CA)*
1957	WHELAN, Tim	63	*Died in Beverly Hills, CA*
1957	# WHITLEY, Crane	57	*Died in Los Angeles, CA*
1957	WILLIAMS, Harcourt	77	*Died in London, England*
1957	WILTON, Eric	73	*Died in England*
1957	WING, Paul R.	65	*Following a heart attack (in Portsmouth, VA)*
1957	WITHERSPOON, Cora	67	*Died in Las Crusas, NM*
1957	YOUNG, Walter	79	*Pneumonia (in New York, NY)*
1958	# ADAMS, Sam	86	*Heart attack (in Beaufort, SC)*
1958	ANALLA, Isabel	37	*Cancer (in San Francisco, CA)*
1958	ARNAUD, Yvonne	65	*Died in London, England*
1958	BALLIN, Mabel	73	*Died in Santa Monica, CA*
1958	BARNETT, Griff	72	*Heart condition and pneumonia (in Hollywood, CA)*
1958	BEECROFT, Victor R.	71	*Died in Newport News, VA*
1958	+ BELL, Monta	66	*After a lengthy illness (in Hollywood, CA)*

Deaths of Movie and Television Personalities — by Year

YEAR	NAME		AGE	CAUSE and/or PLACE OF DEATH
1958	BENNETT, Barbara		52	*Heart attack (in Montreal, Canada)*
1958	BENTLEY, Robert		63	*Died in Benton Harbor, MI*
1958	BERKE, William		54	*Died in Hollywood, CA*
1958	BOSWELL, Martha (Lloyd)		53	*After a long illness (in Peekskill, NY)*
1958	BRENON, Herbert	☆	78	*Died in Hollywood, CA*
1958	# BRISSON, Carl		64	*Jaundice (in Copenhagen, Denmark)*
1958	# CAMERON, Rudolph "Rudy"		63	*Cerebral hemorrhage (in Los Angeles, CA)*
1958	CHAMBERS, J. Wheaton		69	*After a brief illness (in Hollywood, CA)*
1958	+ COHN, Harry		66	*Heart attack (in Phoenix, AZ)*
1958	COLLEANO, Bonar		34	*Automobile accident (in Birkenhead, England)*
1958	+ COLMAN, Ronald	★	67	*Following an operation for a lung infection (in Montecito, CA)*
1958	CROCKER, Harry		64	*Died in Beverly Hills, CA*
1958	DEBUCOURT, Jean		64	*Leukemia (in Mongeron, France)*
1958	DEVEREAUX, Jack		76	*Died in New York, NY*
1958	+ DONAT, Robert	★	53	*Asthma (in London, England)*
1958	DOONAN, Patric		33	*Suicide (by gassing himself) in London, England*
1958	DOUCET, Catherine		82	*Died in New York, NY*
1958	# DUGAN, Tom		69	*Automobile accident (in Redlands, CA)*
1958	EARLE, Dorothy		?	*Died in Los Angeles, CA*
1958	+ FOX, Wallace		63	*Died in Hollywood, CA*
1958	#+ FRISCO, Joe		68	*After a long illness (in Calabasas, CA)*
1958	GENTLE, Alice		69	*Died in Oakland, CA*
1958	#+ GOODWIN, Bill		47	*Heart attack (in Palm Springs, CA)*
1958	# GREEN, Harry		66	*Heart attack (in London, England)*
1958	GREIG, Robert		77	*Died in Hollywood, CA*
1958	GRIFFITH, Gordon		51	*Heart attack (in Hollywood, CA)*
1958	HACKETT, Raymond		55	*Cerebral hemorrhage (in Hollywood, CA)*
1958	HAGEN, Charles F.		96	*Died in Hollywood, CA*
1958	HALL, Thurston		75	*Heart attack (in Beverly Hills, CA)*
1958	HAMILTON, John		71	*Heart condition (in Hollywood) Do not confuse with J. H., d. 1985*
1958	HARMON, Pat		70	*Died in Riverside, CA*
1958	HARTMAN, Don		57	*Died in his sleep of apparent heart attack (in Palm Springs, CA)*
1958	# HAYES, Sam		53	*Heart attack preparing his morning news program (in San Diego, CA)*
1958	HEYES, Herbert		68	*Died in North Hollywood, CA*
1958	HINTON, Ed		30	*Airplane crash (on Catalina Island, CA)*
1958	HOLMES, Burton		88	*Died in Hollywood, CA*
1958	+ HUGHES, Lloyd		60	*Died in Los Angeles, CA*
1958	IMHOF, Roger		83	*Died in Hollywood, CA*
1958	# JAQUET, Frank		73	*Heart attack (in Los Angeles, CA)*
1958	# KATCH, Kurt		62	*During surgery for lung cancer (in Los Angeles, CA)*
1958	# KENNEDY, Fred		48	*A broken neck after falling from his horse during filming (in Louisiana)*
1958	KINGSFORD, Walter		75	*Heart attack (in North Hollywood, CA)*
1958	+ LASKY, Jesse L. Sr.		77	*Heart attack (in Beverly Hills, CA)*
1958	LEWIS, Sheldon		89	*Died in San Gabriel, CA*
1958	LOW, Jack		60	*After a 2-year illness (in Hollywood, CA)*
1958	LYNN, Emmett		61	*Heart attack (in Hollywood, CA)*
1958	MALLORY, Boots		45	*Died in Santa Monica, CA*
1958	MANKIEWICZ, Rose Stradner		45	*Found dead at the family summer home (in Bedford Village, NY)*
1958	MATHER, Aubrey		72	*After a long illness (in London, England)*
1958	McKENNA, Henry T.		64	*Heart attack (in Hollywood, CA)*
1958	NEILAN, Marshall		67	*Cancer (in Woodland Hills, CA)*
1958	+ NEUMANN, Kurt		50	*After emergency hospitalization (in Hollywood, CA)*
1958	# NORTON, Jack		69	*Respiratory ailment (in Saranac Lake, NY)*

• New entry. # Original name (Pt. 7). + Interment (Pt. 5).   39   ☆ Oscar nominee, ★ Oscar winner (Pt. 10)

Deaths of Movie and Television Personalities — by Year

YEAR	NAME	AGE	CAUSE and/or PLACE OF DEATH
1958	# OAKLAND, Vivien	63	*Died in Hollywood, CA*
1958	#+ OSBORN, Lyn	32	*Following brain surgery (in Los Angeles, CA)*
1958	+ PANGBORN, Franklin	65	*Died in Santa Monica, CA*
1958	#+ PANZER, Paul Wolfgang	86	*Died in Hollywood, CA (Do not confuse with Paul Panzer, d. 1937)*
1958	# Parkyakarkus	54	*Heart attack (in Los Angeles, CA)*
1958	PEARSON, Virginia	70	*Uremic poisoning (in Los Angeles, CA)*
1958	# PEIL, Edward Sr.	70	*Died in Hollywood, CA*
1958	#+ POWER, Tyrone	44	*Heart attack (in Madrid, Spain)*
1958	# PRATHER, Lee	67	*During surgery (in Los Angeles, CA)*
1958	+ PURVIANCE, Edna	63	*After a long illness (in Woodland Hills, CA)*
1958	QUARTERMAINE, Charles	80	*Died in England*
1958	RICKSON, Joe	77	*Died in Los Angeles, CA*
1958	RISDON, Elisabeth	71	*Brain hemorrhage (in Santa Monica, CA)*
1958	RODZINSKI, Artur	64	*Heart ailment*
1958	ROOKE, Irene	?	*Died in England*
1958	SCHUMANN-HEINK, Ferdinand	65	*Heart attack (in Los Angeles, CA)*
1958	SHORT, Lewis W.	83	*Died in Hollywood, CA*
1958	SNOW, Marguerite	68	*Kidney complications (in Hollywood, CA)*
1958	# SQUIRE, Ronald	72	*Died in London, England*
1958	STERLING, Larry	23	*A water-skiing accident (in Clear Lake, CA)*
1958	STRADNER, Rose	45	*Found dead in her summer house (in Bedford Village, NY)*
1958	+ TAYLOR, Estelle	58	*Cancer (in Los Angeles, CA)*
1958	TAYLOR, Sam	62	*Heart attack (in Santa Monica, CA)*
1958	#+ TODD, Mike	49	*Airplane crash (in Mount Zuni, NM)*
1958	#+ TWELVETREES, Helen	49	*Overdose of sleeping pills (in Harrisburg, PA)*
1958	VanZANDT, Philip	53	*Overdose of sleeping pills (in Hollywood, CA)*
1958	VARDEN, Evelyn	65	*Died in New York, NY*
1958	VERMILYEA, Harold	68	*Died in New York, NY*
1958	VILLARREAL, Julio	73	*Died in Mexico City, Mexico*
1958	# VonTWARDOWSKI, Hans	60	*Died in New York, NY*
• 1958	WAGNER, Fritz Arno	68	*Automobile accident*
1958	WALKER, Charlotte	80	*Died in Kerville, TX*
1958	#+ WARNER, H. B. ☆	82	*Died in Los Angeles, CA*
1958	+ WARNER, Harry M.	76	*Cerebral occlusion (in Bel Air, CA)*
1958	#+ WHITMAN, Gayne	68	*Heart attack (in Hollywood, CA)*
1958	WILLIAMS, Charles B.	59	*After a long illness (in Hollywood, CA)*
1958	WINTON, Jane	53	*Died in New York*
1958	WOOD, Victor	44	*Died in London, England*
1958	WUEST, Ida	74	*Died in Berlin, Germany*
1958	YOUNG, Noah	71	*Died in Los Angeles, CA*
1958	ZIMBALIST, Sam	57	*Heart attack (in Rome, Italy)*
1959	ADAMS, Kathryn	64	*Heart attack (in Hollywood, CA)*
1959	#+ Adrian	56	*Suicide (in New York)*
1959	AMBLER, Joss	59	*Died in England*
1959	#+ ANDRE, Gwili	51	*Burned to death when fire swept her apartment (in Venice, CA)*
1959	APPLEGATE, Hazel	73	*Died in Chicago, IL*
1959	ARCHAINBAUD, George	68	*Heart attack (in Beverly Hills, CA)*
1959	#+ BAER, Max Sr.	50	*Heart attack (in Hollywood, CA)*
1959	#+ BARRYMORE, Ethel ★	79	*Heart condition (in Beverly Hills, CA)*
1959	# BIRCH, Wyrley	75	
1959	BISHOP, William	42	*Cancer (in Malibu, CA)*
1959	BLAKENEY, Olive	56	*Died in Hollywood, CA*

Deaths of Movie and Television Personalities — by Year

YEAR	NAME		AGE	CAUSE and/or PLACE OF DEATH
1959	BLORE, Eric		71	Heart attack (in Hollywood, CA)
1959	BRODERICK, Helen		68	Died in Beverly Hills, CA
1959	BRYAN, Arthur Q.		60	Died in Hollywood, CA
1959	BYRON, Paul		68	Heart attack (in San Diego, CA)
1959	CARHART, Georgiana		93	
1959	CASTLE, Lillian		94	After a brief illness (in Los Angeles, CA)
1959	# CHESEBRO, George		70	Arteriosclerosis (in Hermosa Beach, CA)
1959	# CLARKE-SMITH, D. A.		71	Died in Withyam, England
1959	COLLINS, G. Pat		64	Cancer (in Los Angeles, CA)
1959	COMPTON, Walter		47	After a long illness
1959	CONKLIN, Charles "Heinie"		79	Died in Hollywood, CA
1959	# COOK, Joe		69	Died in Clinton Hollows, NY
1959	#+ COSTELLO, Lou		52	Heart attack (in Beverly Hills, CA)
1959	CREWS, Kay C.		58	Died in San Antonio, TX
1959	# CUMMINGS, Irving Sr.	☆	70	Heart attack (in Hollywood, CA)
1959	CUNNINGHAM, Cecil		70	Arteriosclerosis (in Woodland Hills, CA)
1959	# DAUBE, Belle		71	Died in Hollywood, CA
1959	# DEL MAR, Claire		57	Murdered (head and knife wounds) in her Carmel, CA home
1959	DELANEY, Charles		67	Died in Hollywood, CA
1959	#+ DeMILLE, Cecil B.	☆	77	Heart disease (in Los Angeles, CA)
1959	+ DOUGLAS, Paul		52	Heart attack (in Hollywood, CA)
1959	+ DUNCAN, Rosetta "Topsy"		58	Automobile accident (in Acero, IL)
1959	# EAGLE, Jimmy		52	Cirrhosis of the liver (in Los Angeles, CA)
1959	ELLIOTT, Lillian		83	Cerebral hemorrhage (in Hollywood, CA)
1959	#+ FLYNN, Errol		50	Heart attack (in Vancouver, B.C., Canada)
1959	# FOX, Harry		77	Died in Woodland Hills, CA
1959	FRANCIS, Noel		48	Died in Los Angeles, CA
1959	GAN, Chester		50	Died in San Francisco, CA
1959	GARAT, Henri		57	Heart attack (in Hyeres, France)
1959	GILBERT, Joe		56	Died in Hollywood, CA
1959	#+ GLEASON, James	☆	76	Asthma (in Woodland Hills, CA)
1959	GOULDING, Edmund		68	Died in Los Angeles, CA
1959	# GRANT, Tiny		45	
1959	#+ GRAY, Gilda		61	Heart attack after food poisoning (in Hollywood, CA)
1959	GREGG, Everley		60	Died in Beaconsfield, England
1959	#+ GWENN, Edmund	★	83	Died in Woodland Hills, CA
1959	HACKEL, A. W.		76	Heart attack (in Hollywood, CA)
1959	# HALE, Sonnie		57	Myelofibrosis (a blood disease) in London, England
1959	#+ HALL, Charlie		60	Died in North Hollywood, CA
• 1959	HALL, Lillian		63	Suicide (barbituate overdose) Do not confuse with L. Hall-Davis
1959	+ HALTON, Charles		83	Hepatitis (in Los Angeles, CA)
1959	#+ HOLIDAY, Billie		44	Liver ailment and cardiac failure (in New York, NY)
1959	#+ HOLLY, Buddy		22	Airplane crash (northwest of Mason City, IA)
1959	HOLMES, Taylor		87	Died in Hollywood, CA
1959	# HOWLIN, Olin		63	Died in Hollywood, CA
1959	HUBER, Harold		49	Died in New York, NY
1959	IVAN, Rosalind		75	After a brief illness (in New York, NY)
1959	KEANE, Edward		75	Died in Los Angeles, CA
1959	KELLY, Joe		57	Heart attack (in Los Angeles, CA)
1959	#+ KENDALL, Kay (Harrison)		32	Leukemia (in London, England)
1959	KRAUSS, Werner		75	Died in Vienna, Austria
1959	LANDOWSKA, Wanda		80	Died at her home in Lakeville, CT
1959	# LANE, Lupino "Nipper"		67	Died in London, England

Deaths of Movie and Television Personalities — by Year

YEAR	NAME	AGE	CAUSE and/or PLACE OF DEATH
1959	#+ LANZA, Mario	38	*Heart attack after suffering pneumonia and phlebitis (in Rome, Italy)*
1959	Lassie (original dog)	18	
1959	LEE, Duke R.	78	*Died in Los Angeles, CA*
1959	+ LITTLEFIELD, Lucien	64	*Died in Hollywood, CA*
1959	LONERGAN, Lester Jr.	65	*After a long illness (in New York, NY)*
1959	MacDONALD, Donald	61	*Died in New York, NY*
1959	MARTIN, Lock	?	
1959	MASON, Louis	71	*After a long illness (in Hollywood, CA)*
1959	McCOMB, Kate	87	*Died in New York, NY*
1959	McDONALD, Ray	34	*Died in New York, NY*
1959	McINTYRE, Hal	44	*Burns after falling asleep while smoking*
1959	# McKEE, Lafe	87	*Arteriosclerosis (in Temple City, CA)*
1959	+ McLAGLEN, Victor ★	72	*Congestive heart failure (in Newport Beach, CA)*
1959	# MERTON, John	58	*Heart attack (in Los Angeles, CA)*
1959	# MONTAGUE, Walter "Monte"	67	*Died in Burbank, CA*
1959	# MOORE, Clara	?	*Murdered*
1959	#+ MORRIS, Wayne	45	*Heart attack (aboard an aircraft carrier in the Pacific Ocean)*
1959	NORWORTH, Jack	80	*Stroke and heart ailment (in Laguna Beach, CA)*
1959	O'CONNOR, Frank (director/actor)	71	*After a long illness (in Hollywood, CA)*
1959	+ O'CONNOR, Una	78	*After a long illness (in New York, NY)*
1959	OSMOND, Hal	40	
1959	# PARIS, Manuel	65	*Congestive heart failure (in Woodland Hills, CA)*
1959	PARRISH, Helen	34	*Cancer (in Hollywood, CA)*
1959	+ PECKHAM, Francis Miles	66	*Died in New York, NY*
1959	PETERS, Ralph	56	*Died in Hollywood, CA*
1959	PHILIPE, Gerard	36	*Heart attack and liver cancer (in Paris, France)*
1959	PICKARD, Helena	59	*Died in Oxfordshire, England*
1959	# RAKER, Lorin	68	*Cancer (in Woodland Hills, CA)*
1959	REED, J. Theodore "Ted"	72	*Died in San Diego, CA*
1959	#+ REEVES, George "Superman"	45	*Apparent suicide (gunshot) in Beverly Hills, CA*
1959	#+ RICHARDSON, Jiles "Big Bopper"	28	*Airplane crash (along with Buddy Holly, near Mason City, IA)*
1959	RIEMANN, Johannes	72	*After a long illness (in Konstanz, West Germany)*
1959	ROSS, Thomas W.	86	*Died in Torrington, CT*
1959	SHANNON, Frank Connolly	83	*Died in Hollywood, CA*
1959	# SHUMWAY, Lee	75	
1959	SIMPSON, Russell	79	*Died in Hollywood, CA*
1959	SMITH, G. Albert	61	*After a brief illness (in New York, NY)*
1959	ST. MAUR, Adele	70	*Leukemia (in Sunnydale, CA)*
1959	STERLING, Richard	78	*Heart attack (in Douglaston, NY)*
1959	STOECKEL, Joe	65	*Circulatory ailment (in Munich, Germany)*
1959	+ STONE, Fred	85	*Heart attack after a 2-year illness (in North Hollywood, CA)*
1959	#+ STURGES, Preston	60	*Heart attack (at the Algonquin Hotel in New York, NY)*
1959	# SUNDMARK, Betty	45	*Died in New York*
1959	+ SWITZER, Carl "Alfalfa"	32	*Murdered (shot over a $50. debt) in Sepulveda, CA*
1959	#+ VALENS, Ritchie	17	*Airplane crash (along with Buddy Holly, near Mason City, IA)*
1959	# VIDAL, Henri	40	*Heart attack (in Paris, France)*
1959	+ VIDOR, Charles	58	*Apparent heart attack (in Vienna, Austria)*
1959	WAYNE, Robert "Duke"	55	*Following a heart attack (in San Antonio, TX)*
1959	WEBB, Harry	63	*Heart attack (in Hollywood, CA)*
1959	#+ WITHERS, Grant	54	*Suicide (sleeping pills) in North Hollywood, CA*
1960	+ ADAMS, Constance (DeMille)	67	*Died in Hollywood, CA*
1960	#+ ADLER, Buddy	51	*Lung cancer (in Hollywood, CA)*

• New entry. # Original name (Pt. 7). + Interment (Pt. 5).

☆ Oscar nominee, ★ Oscar winner (Pt. 10)

Deaths of Movie and Television Personalities — by Year

YEAR	NAME		AGE	CAUSE and/or PLACE OF DEATH
1960	ALBERS, Hans		67	Died in Munchen, Germany
• 1960	BACH, Rudi		?	Died in Buffalo, NY
1960	BAGGETT, Lynne		32	Overdose of barbiturates (in Hollywood, CA)
• 1960	BAKALEINIKOFF, Mischa		70	Died in Los Angeles, CA
1960	#+ BARRYMORE, Diana		38	Alcohol and sleeping pills overdose (in New York, NY)
1960	# BAUM, Vicki		64	After a brief illness (in Hollywood, CA)
1960	BJOERLING, Jussi		49	Heart attack (in Sweden)
1960	+ BOND, Ward		57	Heart attack (in Dallas, TX)
1960	#+ BROPHY, Ed		65	Died in Los Angeles, CA
1960	CATLETT, Walter		71	Stroke (in Calabasas, CA)
1960	CAVENDISH, David		69	Heart attack (in Hollywood, CA)
1960	#+ CLARK, Bobby		72	Heart attack (in New York, NY)
1960	# CLIVE, Henry		77	Lung cancer (in Hollywood, CA)
1960	+ COCHRAN, Eddie (singer)		21	Killed in a taxi crash (in Chippenham, England)
1960	# CODY, Emmett		40	
1960	CORBETT, Leonora		52	Died in Vleuten, Netherlands
1960	# CRAMER, Rychard		71	Laennec's cirrhosis (in Hollywood, CA)
1960	CRAVAT, Noel		49	After surgery (in Hollywood, CA)
1960	#+ CROMWELL, Richard		50	After a brief illness (in Hollywood, CA)
1960	CROSSLEY, Syd		75	Died in Troon, England
1960	CURLEY, Leo		82	Arteriosclerosis (in Woodland Hills, CA)
1960	+ DASTAGIR, Sheik		47	
1960	DUNCAN, Bud		77	Circulatory failure (in Los Angeles, CA)
1960	EBURNE, Maude		85	Died in Hollywood, CA
1960	+ EMERSON, Hope	☆	61	Liver ailment (in Hollywood, CA)
1960	+ FOWLER, Gene		70	Heart attack (in West Los Angeles, CA)
1960	#+ GABLE, Clark	★	59	Heart attack (in Hollywood, CA)
1960	# GALVANI, Dino		69	Died in London, England
1960	GAUGE, Alexander		46	Heart attack (in Woking, Surrey, England)
1960	+ GORDON, Leon		66	Heart ailment (in Hollywood, CA)
1960	+ GREEN, Alfred E.		71	Arthritis (in Hollywood, CA)
1960	GRIFFITH, William M.		62	Died in Hollywood, CA
1960	HAMILTON, Mahlon		77	Cancer (in Woodland Hills, CA)
1960	+ HAMMERSTEIN II, Oscar		65	Stomach cancer (in Doylestown, PA)
1960	HARBAUGH, Carl		73	Died in Hollywood, CA
1960	HAVER, Phyllis		61	Suicide (despondent over Mack Sennett's death) in Falls Village, CT
1960	HEYDT, Louis Jean		54	Heart attack (in Boston, MA)
1960	# HOEY, Dennis		67	Died in Palm Beach, FL
1960	JOHNSON, Emory		66	Critically burned when his bed caught fire (in San Mateo, CA)
1960	# KEITH, Ian		61	Died in New York, NY
1960	KRUGER, Alma		91	After a long illness (in Seattle, WA)
1960	# LaRUE, Frank H.		81	Died in Woodland Hills, CA
1960	LAWFORD, Betty		50	After a long illness (in New York, NY)
1960	+ LLOYD, Frank	★	74	Died in Santa Monica, CA
1960	LUND, Richard		75	Died in Sweden
1960	# LUTHER, Ann		67	Heart condition (in Hollywood, CA)
1960	LUTHER, Johnny		51	Drowned in a boating accident (in San Pedro, CA)
1960	# MATTHEWS, A. E. "Matty"		90	Heart attack in his sleep (in Bushey Heath, England)
1960	McLAUGHLIN, Gibb		76	Died in Los Angeles, CA
1960	METCALFE, James J.		53	Heart attack (in Northridge, CA)
1960	MILJAN, John		66	Died in Hollywood, CA
1960	MOORE, Matt		72	Died in Hollywood, CA
1960	# MUELLER, Wolfgang		36	Airplane crash (in Lostallo, Switzerland)

Deaths of Movie and Television Personalities — by Year

YEAR	NAME		AGE	CAUSE and/or PLACE OF DEATH
1960	NESBITT, John		49	Heart attack (in Carmel, CA)
1960	NICHOLS, Dudley		64	While hospitalized for cancer (in Hollywood, CA)
1960	O'SHEA, Oscar		78	Died in Hollywood, CA
1960	PARKE, Macdonald		68	Died in London, England
1960	PARKER, Edwin		59	Heart attack (in Sherman Oaks, CA)
1960	# PLUMB, E. Hay		77	Died in England
1960	# PORTEN, Henny		70	After a long illness (in Berlin, Germany)
1960	PURDY, Constance		75	Arteriosclerosis (in Los Angeles, CA)
1960	RATOFF, Gregory		63	Circulatory problems (in Solothurn, Switzerland)
1960	RELPH, George		72	Died in London, England
1960	ROSSON, Arthur H.		73	Died in Los Angeles, CA
1960	RUYSDAEL, Basil		72	Died in Hollywood, CA
1960	+ SCHWARTZ, Maurice		69	Heart attack (near Tel Aviv, Israel)
1960	SCOTT, Mark		45	Heart attack (in Burbank, CA)
1960	# SEASTROM, Victor		80	Died in Stockholm, Sweden
1960	#+ SENNETT, Mack		80	Heart attack (in Hollywood, CA)
1960	SMART, J. Scott		57	Died in Springfield, IL
1960	SPENCER, Douglas		50	Diabetic condition (in Hollywood, Ca.)
1960	#+ SULLAVAN, Margaret ☆		48	Suicide (sleeping pills) in New Haven, CT
1960	# TENBROOK, Harry		72	Lung cancer (in Woodland Hills, CA)
1960	THOMAS, John Charles		68	Intestinal cancer (in Apple Valley, CA)
1960	+ TIBBETT, Lawrence ☆		63	Following surgery for an old head injury (in New York, NY)
1960	# TIEDTKE, Jakob		85	Died in Berlin, Germany
1960	TREADWELL, Laura		81	Died in Hollywood, CA
1960	VENESS, Amy		84	Died in Saltdean, England
1960	WASHBURN, Bryant Jr.		?	
1960	WATKIN, Pierre		70	After a brief illness (in Hollywood, CA)
1960	WELCH, Joseph L.		69	Died in Hyannis, MA
1960	WESTON, Doris		42	Cancer (in New York, NY)
1960	WHITAKER, Charles "Slim"		66	Heart attack (in Los Angeles, CA)
• 1960	WILCOX, Harlow		60	
1960	WILLIAMS, Kathlyn		72	Died in Hollywood, CA
1960	WINDUST, Bretaigne		54	Died in New York
1960	WONTNER, Arthur		85	Died in London, England
1960	YOUNG, Clara Kimball		69	Died in Woodland Hills, CA
1960	+ ZUCCO, George		74	Pneumonia (at Monterey Sanitarium, S. San Gabriel, CA)
1961	ADAMS, Stella		78	
1961	AOKI, Tsuru		69	Acute peritonitis (in Tokyo, Japan)
• 1961	BACONNET, Georges		68	Died in Paris, France
• 1961	BAGLEY, Richard		41	After a long illness (in New York, NY)
1961	BANNISTER, Harry		71	After a long illness (in New York, NY)
1961	# BRADY, Fred		49	Heart failure (in Los Angeles, CA)
1961	BROWN, Wally		57	Died in Los Angeles, CA
1961	BURGESS, Dorothy		54	Died in Los Angeles, CA
1961	+ CARRILLO, Leo		80	Cancer (in Santa Monica, CA)
1961	CASON, John L.		43	Died in Los Angeles, CA
1961	#+ CHANDLER, Jeff ☆		42	Blood poisoning after spinal surgery (in Culver City, CA)
1961	CHARLESON, Mary		68	Died in Woodland Hills, CA
1961	+ CHATTERTON, Ruth ☆		67	After a brief illness (in Norwalk, CT)
1961	CLARK, Wallis		71	Died in Los Angeles, CA
1961	CLIFT, Denison		76	Heart ailment (in Hollywood, CA)
1961	# CLINE, Eddie		68	Died in Hollywood, CA

Deaths of Movie and Television Personalities — by Year

YEAR	NAME		AGE	CAUSE and/or PLACE OF DEATH
1961	#+ COBB, Ty		74	Prostate cancer and chronic heart disease (in Atlanta, GA)
1961	#+ COBURN, Charles	★	84	Heart ailment (in New York, NY)
1961	CODEE, Ann		70	Heart attack (in Hollywood, CA)
1961	COOK, Donald		60	Heart attack (in New Haven, CT)
1961	#+ COOPER, Gary	★	60	Cancer (in Hollywood, CA)
1961	CORBETT, Ben		69	Died in Hollywood, CA
1961	DALE, Esther		75	Died in Hollywood, CA
1961	#+ DAVIES, Marion		64	Cancer (in Hollywood, CA)
1961	+ DAVIS, Joan (Williams)		53	Heart attack (in Palm Springs, CA)
1961	DEL RUTH, Roy		66	Heart attack (in Sherman Oaks, CA)
1961	DUNCAN, William A.		80	Died in Hollywood, CA
1961	# ELDRIDGE, John		57	Heart attack (in Laguna Beach, CA)
1961	# ELLIOTT, Dick		75	Died in Burbank, CA
1961	+ FARNUM, Franklyn		85	Cancer (in Hollywood, CA)
1961	+ FAY, Frank		63	Died in Santa Monica, CA
1961	FERGUSON, Elsie		78	Died in New London, CT
1961	# FITZGERALD, Barry	★	72	After a long illness (in Dublin, Ireland)
1961	# FORMBY, George		56	Died in Preston, Lancashire, England
1961	+ FRENCH, George B.		78	Heart attack (in Hollywood, CA)
1961	FREY, Arno		60	Heart attack from a blood clot (in Los Angeles, CA)
1961	FULLER, Clem		52	Cancer (in Hollywood, CA)
1961	# GOODWIN, Ruby B.		57	Died in Hollywood, CA
1961	GREENWOOD, Winifred L.		69	Died in Woodland Hills, CA
1961	GRIBBON, Harry		76	After a long illness (in Los Angeles, CA)
1961	# GUARD, Kit		67	Cancer (in Hollywood, CA)
1961	GUILFOYLE, Paul		59	Heart attack (in Hollywood, CA)
1961	HANSEN, Juanita		64	Heart attack (in Hollywood, CA)
1961	+ HART, Moss		57	Heart attack (in Palm Springs, CA)
1961	HODGES, William C.		85	Died in Chardon, OH
1961	HOFFMAN, David		57	Died in Seattle, WA
1961	HOUSE, Billy		71	Heart attack (in Hollywood, CA)
1961	HOWELL, Alice		72	Died in Los Angeles, CA
1961	IRVING. George		87	Heart attack (in Hollywood, CA)
1961	JENNINGS, Al		97	Died in Tarzana, CA
1961	#+ JORDAN, Marion "Molly McGee"		64	Cancer (in Encino, CA)
1961	KEATING, Fred		64	Heart attack (in New York, NY)
1961	KELSEY, Fred A.		77	Died in Hollywood, CA
1961	KORDA, Zoltan		66	After a long illness (in Hollywood, CA)
1961	+ LAWRENCE, Walter Smith		59	Died in Palm Dale, CA
1961	LEE, Belinda		25	Automobile accident (in San Bernardino, CA)
1961	# LEE, Gwen		55	Died in Los Angeles, CA
1961	LIVESEY, Jack		60	Aneurysm (in Burbank, CA)
1961	LOMAS, Herbert		73	Died in Devonshire, England
1961	# LUPINO, Wallace		63	After a long illness (in Ashford, England)
1961	LYON, Frank		59	Died in Gardner, MA
1961	# MAITLAND, Ruth		81	Died in Dorking, England
1961	# MALYON, Eily		81	Cancer (in South Pasadena, CA)
1961	MARSHAL, Alan		52	Heart attack during live performance of "Sextette" (in Chicago, IL)
1961	#+ MARX, "Chico"		74	Heart attack (in Beverly Hills, CA)
1961	McLEOD, Gordon		71	
1961	McTURK, Joe		62	Heart attack (in Hollywood, CA)
1961	MELFORD, George		84	Heart attack (in Hollywood, CA)
1961	MELTON, James		57	Pneumonia (in New York, NY)

Deaths of Movie and Television Personalities — by Year

YEAR		NAME	AGE	CAUSE and/or PLACE OF DEATH
1961		MORAN, Lee	70	Heart ailment (in Woodland Hills, CA)
1961		MURPHY, Joseph J.	84	Died in San Jose, CA
1961	#+	NALDI, Nita	61	Died in New York, NY
1961		O'NEILL, Henry	69	Died in Hollywood, CA
1961		OSBORNE, Vivienne	64	Died in Los Angeles, CA
1961		PARNELL, James	38	Found dead in his automobile (in Hollywood, CA)
• 1961		PEARCE, Al	62	Complications from an ulcer operation
1961	#	POLO, Eddie	86	Heart attack at a restaurant (in Hollywood, CA)
1961		RAYMOND, Frances "Frankie"	92	Died in Hollywood, CA
1961		REED, Luther	73	After a long illness (in New York, NY)
1961	+	REYNOLDS, Adeline De Walt	98	Died in Los Angeles, CA
1961	#	RICHTER, Paul	65	Died in Vienna, Austria
1961		RING, Blanche	84	Died in Santa Monica, CA
1961		RIPLEY, Arthur	66	Cancer (in Los Angeles, CA)
1961		ROBERTS, John H.	76	Died in London, England
1961		ROOPE, Fay	68	Died in Port Jefferson, L.I., NY
• 1961		ROSS, Earle	73	
1961	+	RUSSELL, Gail (Moseley)	36	Found dead from alcohol overindulgence (in Los Angeles, CA)
1961	#	SANDFORD, Tiny	67	Died in Los Angeles, CA
1961		SCHOFIELD, Johnnie	71	Died in England
1961	#	SHEPLEY, Michael	53	Died in London, England
1961	#	SOLER, Domingo Jr.	59	Heart attack (in Acapulco, Mexico)
1961		STAINTON, Philip	53	Died in London, England
1961	+	STEWART, Anita	66	Heart attack (in Beverly Hills, CA)
1961		TAYLOR, Ferris	68	Heart attack (in Hollywood, Ca.)
1961		THESIGER, Ernest	81	Died in London, England
1961	#	TOURNEUR, Maurice	85	Injuries from a car accident (in Paris, France)
1961		TYLER, Harry	73	Cancer (in Hollywood, CA)
1961		VIVIAN, Percival	70	Arteriosclerosis (in Burbank, CA)
1961	#	VonWINTERSTEIN, Eduard	90	Died in East Berlin, Germany
1961	+	WALLING, Effie B.	81	Died in Berkeley, CA
1961	#	WALTON, Douglas	52	Died in New York
1961		WHITING, Jack	59	Died in New York
1961		WHITTELL, Josephine	73	After a long illness (in Hollywood, CA)
1961	#	WILLIAMS, Bramsby	91	Died in London, England
1961	#+	WONG, Anna May	54	Heart attack (in Santa Monica, CA)
1962		ALBERNI, Luis	74	Died in Hollywood, CA
1962		ALLEN, Joseph Jr.	44	Heart attack (in Patchogue, NY)
1962	+	ATES, Roscoe	70	Lung cancer (in Hollywood, CA)
1962		AUER, Florence	81	Died in New York, NY
• 1962		BACKUS, Lucia	88	Died in New York, NY
1962	#	BAILEY, William Norton	76	Died in Hollywood, CA (Do not confuse with Bill Bailey, d. 1978)
1962	+	BARRIS, Harry	57	Cancer (in Burbank, CA)
1962	+	BARTON, James	72	Heart attack (in Mineola, NY)
1962		BEAVERS, Louise "Beulah"	64	Heart attack (in Hollywood, CA)
1962	#+	BELL, Rex	58	Coronary occlusion (in Las Vegas, NV)
1962		BEST, Willie	45	Cancer (in Woodland Hills, CA)
1962	+	BLANDICK, Clara	81	Suicide (took pills and pulled a plastic bag over her head)
1962	+	BORZAGE, Frank ★	72	Cancer (in Hollywood, CA)
1962		BOULTON, Matthew	69	Died in London, England
1962		BRIGGS, Matt	79	
1962		BROOK-JONES, Elwyn	51	Died in Reading, England

• New entry. # Original name (Pt. 7). + Interment (Pt. 5).

46

☆ Oscar nominee, ★ Oscar winner (Pt. 10)

Deaths of Movie and Television Personalities — by Year

YEAR	NAME	AGE	CAUSE and/or PLACE OF DEATH
1962	+ BROWNING, Tod	82	*Following an operation for cancer (in Hollywood, CA)*
1962	# CANTOR, Ida	70	*Heart attack (in Beverly Hills, CA)*
1962	CAVENDER, Glen W.	77	*After a long illness (in Hollywood, CA)*
1962	# CAVENS, Fred	79	*Uremia (in Woodland Hills, CA)*
1962	CHRISTY, Ken	67	*Died in Hollywood, CA*
1962	CLIFFORD, Kathleen	74	*After a long illness (in Hollywood, CA)*
1962	CLYDE, Jean	73	*Died in Helensburgh, Scotland*
1962	CONLIN, Jimmy	77	*Cancer (in Encino, CA)*
1962	+ CRAWFORD, Jesse	66	*Stroke (in Los Angeles, CA)*
1962	#+ CURTIZ, Michael ★	73	*Cancer (in Hollywood, CA)*
1962	DAMON, Les	53	*Died in Hollywood, CA*
1962	# DANIEL, Billy	49	*Coronary attack (in Beverly Hills, CA)*
1962	# DILLON, Tom	66	*Died in Hollywood, CA*
1962	+ FAZENDA, Louise	66	*Cerebral hemorrhage (in Holmby Hills, CA)*
1962	FLAGSTAD, Kirsten	67	*Died in Oslo, Norway*
1962	GAWTHORNE, Peter	77	*Died in London, England*
1962	#+ GIBSON, Hoot	70	*Cancer (in Woodland Hills, CA)*
1962	HARDTMUTH, Paul	72	*Fall from his apartment building (in London, England)*
1962	HOBBES, Halliwell	84	*Heart attack (in Santa Monica, CA)*
1962	JENKS, Frank	60	*Cancer (in Hollywood, CA)*
1962	#+ JOHNSON, Chic	70	*Kidney ailment (in Las Vegas, NV)*
1962	KEARNS, Joseph	55	*Died in Los Angeles, CA*
1962	+ KOVACS, Ernie	42	*Automobile accident (in Beverly Hills, CA)*
1962	+ KREISLER, Fritz	86	*Following a heart attack*
1962	LANDERS, Lew	61	*Heart attack (in Palm Desert, CA)*
1962	+ LAUGHTON, Charles ★	63	*Following surgery for spinal cancer (in Hollywood, CA)*
1962	LEE, Florence	74	*Died in Hollywood, CA*
1962	+ LOVEJOY, Frank	48	*Heart attack (in New York, NY)*
1962	LUTHER, Lester	73	*Stroke (in Hollywood, CA)*
1962	LYNN, Ralph	81	*Died in London, England*
1962	# MACK, Cactus	62	*Heart attack (in Hollywood, CA)*
1962	# MacKENNA, Kenneth	63	*After a long bout with cancer (in Hollywood, CA)*
1962	MARRIOTT, Sandee	63	*Heart attack (in Hollywood, CA)*
1962	MASON, Reginald	80	*Died in Hermosa Beach, CA*
1962	McCARTHY, John P.	78	*Coronary thrombosis (in Pasadena, CA)*
1962	McCONNELL, Lulu	80	*Cancer (in Hollywood, CA)*
1962	McCORMICK, Myron	54	*Cancer (in New York, NY)*
1962	# McDANIEL, Sam "Deacon"	76	*Throat cancer (in Woodland Hills, CA)*
1962	MELLER, Raquel	74	
1962	MINCIOTTI, Esther	74	*Died in New York, NY*
1962	+ MITCHELL, Thomas ★	70	*Cancer (in Beverly Hills, CA)*
1962	#+ MONROE, Marilyn	36	*Suicide? (drug overdose) in Brentwood, CA*
1962	+ MOORE, Victor	86	*Heart attack (in East Islip, L.I., NY)*
1962	O'CONNOR, Robert Emmett	77	*Burns after his cigarette ignited his clothing (in Hollywood, CA)*
1962	ORTH, Frank	82	*Died in Hollywood, CA*
1962	PALANGE, Inez	73	*Died in Los Angeles, CA*
1962	# PARKER, Frank "Pinky"	70	*Heart attack (in Hollywood, CA)*
1962	# PAUL, Val	75	*Died in Hollywood, CA*
1962	# PEIL, Edward Jr.	54	*After a 2-year illness*
1962	PERRINS, Leslie	60	*Died in Esher, England*
1962	PERRY, Robert E. "Bob"	82	*Died in Hollywood, CA*
1962	PIGOTT, Tempe	78	*Died in Hollywood, CA*
1962	#+ POLLARD, Harry "Snub"	75	*Heart attack (in Burbank, CA) Do not confuse with Harry Pollard*

Deaths of Movie and Television Personalities — by Year

YEAR	NAME		AGE	CAUSE and/or PLACE OF DEATH
1962	REECE, Brian		48	*Bone disease (in London, England)*
1962	REISNER, Charles F. "Chuck"		75	*Following a heart attack (in La Jolla, CA)*
1962	# REYNOLDS, Vera		62	*Died in Woodland Hills, CA*
1962	RICHARDSON, Frankie		63	*Following a heart attack (in Philadelphia, PA)*
1962	RIDGELY, Cleo		68	*Died in Glendale, CA*
1962	ROBERTS, Evelyn		76	
1962	ROBINSON, Gertrude R.		70	*Died in Hollywood, CA*
1962	+ ROONEY, Pat, II		82	*Died in New York, NY*
1962	# SEGAR, Lucia		77	*Died in New York, NY*
1962	SHELDON, Jerome		71	*Died in Hollywood, CA (Do not confuse with Jerry Sheldon)*
1962	# SHELDON, Jerry		60	*Died in Hollywood, CA (Do not confuse with Jerome Sheldon)*
1962	SHIELD, Leroy		68	*Died in Fort Lauderdale, FL*
1962	SINCLAIR, Hugh		59	*Died in Slapton, England*
1962	+ SOKOLOFF, Vladimir		72	*Stroke (in Hollywood, CA)*
1962	SURATT, Valeska		79	*Died in Los Angeles, CA*
1962	#+ TOMACK, Sid		55	*Heart ailment (in Palm Springs, CA)*
1962	VAL, Paul		75	*Died in Hollywood, CA*
1962	VonBLOCK, Bela		73	*Died in Hollywood, CA*
1962	+ WALD, Jerry		51	*After three heart attacks (in Beverly Hills, CA)*
1962	WATSON, Lucile ☆		83	*Died in New York, NY*
1962	WHITEHEAD, John		89	*Died in Hollywood, CA*
1962	WILLIAMS, Guinn "Big Boy"		63	*Uremic poisoning (in Hollywood, CA)*
1962	WREN, Sam		65	*Died in Hollywood, CA*
1962	WRIGHT, Will		71	*Cancer (in Hollywood) Do not confuse with William Wright d. 1949*
1962	+ ZUCCO, Frances		30	*Throat cancer after an overdose of radiation therapy (in Los Angeles)*
1963	ARMENDARIZ, Pedro		51	*Suicide (gunshot) after suffering with lymph cancer (in Los Angeles)*
1963	ATKINSON, Frank		69	*Died in Pinner Hatch End, England*
1963	BAKER, Phil		67	*After a long illness (in Copenhagen, Denmark)*
1963	+ BARTHELMESS, Richard ☆		66	*Throat cancer (in Southampton, NY)*
1963	# BEVANS, Clem		83	*Died in Woodland Hills, CA*
1963	+ BLUE, Monte		73	*Coronary attack (in Milwaukee, WI)*
1963	+ BOLEY, May		81	*Cancer (in Hollywood, CA)*
1963	# BROOKE, Ralph		43	*Died in Hollywood, CA*
1963	BROWN, Rowland		62	*Heart attack (in Balboa Island, CA)*
1963	CAHN, Edward L.		64	*Died in New York, NY*
1963	CAMPBELL, Alan		58	*Died in West Hollywood, CA*
1963	+ CARSON, Jack		53	*Stomach cancer (in Encino, CA)*
1963	CASTIGLIONI, Iphigene		62	*After a long illness (in Hollywood, CA)*
1963	CAVANNA, Elise		61	*Cancer (in Hollywood, CA)*
1963	#+ CLINE, Patsy		30	*Airplane crash (in a forest near the Tennessee River)*
1963	+ COCTEAU, Jean		74	*Heart attack (in Milly-la-Foret, France)*
1963	# DANIELL, Henry		69	*Heart attack (in Santa Monica, CA)*
1963	DARMOND, Grace		65	*Bronchial pneumonia (in Los Angeles, CA)*
1963	+ DASTAGIR, Sabu			*(See under Sabu, below)*
1963	DAVIS, Boyd		77	*Heart attack (in Hollywood, CA)*
1963	DENT, Vernon		63	*Coronary thrombosis (in Hollywood, CA)*
1963	DeSOTO, Henry		75	
1963	DOLENZ, George		55	*Heart attack (in Hollywood, CA)*
1963	# DURYEA, George			*(See Tom Keene)*
1963	+ FARROW, John ☆		56	*Apparent heart attack (in Beverly Hills, CA)*
• 1963	# GARDNER, Ed		62	*Diseased liver*
1963	GASNIER, Louis J.		87	*Died in Hollywood, CA*

Deaths of Movie and Television Personalities — by Year

YEAR	NAME		AGE	CAUSE and/or PLACE OF DEATH
1963	GAXTON, William		70	After a long illness (in New York, NY)
1963	#+ GEORGE, Gorgeous		48	Heart attack (in Los Angeles, CA)
1963	GORDON, Mary		81	Died in Pasadena, CA
1963	# GRAY, Glen		63	Died in Plymouth, MA
1963	GREEN, Dorothy		71	Died in New York, NY
1963	GREENLEAF, Raymond		71	Died in Woodland Hills, CA
1963	#+ GRUNDGENS, Gustav		63	Suicide (in Manila, Philippine Islands)
1963	# HAMPTON, Grace		87	Died in Woodland Hills, CA
1963	HARVEY, Don C.		51	Heart attack (in Studio City, CA)
1963	# HAWLEY, Wanda		67	Died in Los Angeles, CA
1963	HAYLE, Grace		73	Died in Los Angeles, CA
1963	# HEARN, Edward "Eddie"		74	Died in Woodland Hills, CA
1963	HOPE, Vida		45	Automobile accident (in Chelmsford, England)
1963	HUDD, Walter		64	Died in London, England
1963	HUMBERT, George		81	
1963	JEAVES, Allan		78	Heart attack (in London, England)
1963	JONES, Gordon		52	Heart attack (in Tarzana, CA)
1963	# KEENE, Tom		67	Died in Woodland Hills, CA
1963	KING, Anita		74	Heart attack (in Hollywood, CA)
1963	KIRKWOOD, James Sr.		80	Died in Woodland Hills, CA
1963	KUPCINET, Karyn		22	Murdered (bound and strangled) in West Los Angeles, CA
1963	# L'ESTRANGE, Dick		73	Died in Burbank, CA
1963	LAIDLAW, Ethan		63	
1963	#+ LONDON, Tom		70	Died in North Hollywood, CA
1963	# LYNN, Sharon		58	Died in Hollywood, CA
1963	MACHATY, Gustav		63	After a lengthy illness (in Munich, Germany)
1963	# MALTBY, H. F.		82	Died in London, England
1963	MAXEY, Paul		54	Heart attack (in Pasadena, CA)
1963	+ MAXWELL, Elsa		80	Died in New York, NY
1963	+ MAYO, Frank		77	Heart attack (in Laguna Beach, CA)
1963	MEADER, George		75	
1963	MENAHAN, Jean		58	
1963	#+ MENJOU, Adolphe ☆		73	Chronic hepatitis (in Beverly Hills, CA)
1963	# MILLER, Max		68	Died in Brighton, England
1963	+ ODETS, Clifford		57	Cancer (in Los Angeles, CA)
1963	OFFERMAN, George Jr.		45	Died in New York, NY
1963	#+ OLSEN, Ole		71	Kidney ailment (in Albuquerque, NM)
1963	PHILLIPS, Mina		77	Heart ailment (in New Orleans, LA)
1963	#+ PIAF, Edith		47	Internal hemorrhage (in Plascassier, France)
1963	PIEL, Harry		71	Died in Munich, Germany
1963	PILOTTO, Camillo		73	Died in Rome, Italy
1963	+ PITTS, Zazu (Woodall)		65	Cancer (in Hollywood, CA)
1963	#+ POWELL, Dick		58	Cancer (in Hollywood, CA)
1963	READ, Barbara		45	
1963	RICHARDS, Grant		47	Leukemia (in Hollywood, CA)
1963	RIETTI, Victor		75	Heart ailment (in London, England)
1963	+ ROBARDS, Jason Sr.		70	Heart attack (in Sherman Oaks, CA)
1963	RUSSELL, Byron		79	After a brief illness (in New York)
1963	#+ Sabu		39	Heart attack (in Chatsworth, CA)
1963	SAMSON, Ivan		67	Died in London, England
1963	SANFORD, Ralph		64	Heart ailment (in Van Nuys, CA)
1963	# SAYLOR, Syd		67	Heart attack (in Hollywood, CA)
1963	# SCHARF, Herman "Boo-Boo"		61	Heart attack (in Hollywood, CA)

Deaths of Movie and Television Personalities — by Year

YEAR	NAME	AGE	CAUSE and/or PLACE OF DEATH
1963	# SHERIDAN, Dan	46	*Suicide (overdose of barbiturates) in Encino, CA*
1963	SIERRA, Margarita	27	*Following heart surgery (in Hollywood, CA)*
1963	SLOANE, Olive	66	*Died in London, England*
1963	# SMITH, Cyril	70	*Died in London, England*
1963	# ST. JOHN, Al "Fuzzy"	69	*Heart attack (in Vidalia, GA)*
1963	# STANDING, Wyndham	82	*Died in Los Angeles, CA*
1963	STRANDMARK, Erik	44	*Died in Trinidad, West Indies*
1963	# SUNSHINE, Marion	65	*Died in New York, NY*
1963	SUTTON, John	54	*Died in Cannes, France*
1963	#+ TUTTLE, Frank	70	*Heart attack (in Hollywood, CA)*
1963	# VINTON, Arthur	65	*Died in Guadalajara, Mexico*
1963	+ WAGNER, "Gorgeous" George	48	*Heart attack*
1963	WASHBURN, Bryant Sr.	74	*Heart attack (in Hollywood, CA)*
1963	#+ WASHINGTON, Dinah	39	*Overdose of sleeping pills (in Detroit, MI)*
1963	WEEMS, Ted	62	*Emphysema (in Tulsa, OK)*
1963	# WHEAT, Lawrence "Larry"	87	*Died in Los Angeles, CA*
1963	WILLS, Beverly	29	*Killed in a fire (in Palm Springs, CA)*
1963	#+ WOOLLEY, Monty ☆	74	*Kidney and heart ailment (in Albany, NY)*
1963	# WORTH, Constance	48	*Died in Australia*
1964	+ ALBERTSON, Frank	55	*Died in Santa Monica, CA*
1964	#+ ALLEN, Gracie	58	*Heart attack (in Los Angeles, CA)*
1964	# ANDERSON, Claire	68	*Died in Venice, CA*
1964	#+ ANKRUM, Morris	67	*Trichinosis (in Pasadena, CA)*
1964	AUGUST, Edwin	81	*Died in Hollywood, CA*
1964	AYLMER, David	31	*Suicide (in London, England)*
1964	BADGER, Clarence	84	*Following surgery (in Sydney, Australia)*
1964	+ BARRIER, Edgar	57	*Heart attack (in Hollywood, CA)*
1964	+ BENDIX, William ☆	58	*Lobar pneumonia and cancer (in Los Angeles, CA)*
1964	# BRENDEL, El	74	*Heart attack (in Hollywood, CA)*
1964	BROWN, Russ	72	*Died in Englewood, NJ*
1964	BURTON, Robert	69	*Lung cancer (in Woodland Hills, CA)*
1964	CAINE, Georgia	88	*Died in Hollywood, CA*
1964	#+ CANTOR, Eddie	72	*Heart attack (in Beverly Hills, CA)*
1964	CARD, Kathryn	70	*Heart attack (in Costa Mesa, CA)*
1964	CARPENTER, Paul	42	*Heart attack (in London, England)*
1964	CAVANAGH, Paul	68	*Heart attack (in London, England)*
1964	CHILDERS, Naomi	70	*After a long illness (in Hollywood, CA)*
1964	#+ COLE, Buddy	48	*Heart attack (in North Hollywood, CA)*
1964	COMPTON, Francis	79	*Died in Noroton, CT*
1964	CONROY, Frank	73	*Heart ailment (in Paramus, NJ)*
1964	+ COOKE, Sam	29	*Shot by motel manager while the actor was pursuing a girl (in L.A.)*
1964	DODD, Jimmie	54	*Heart ailment (in Honolulu, Hawaii)*
1964	# DODSWORTH, John	53	*Suicide (asphyxiation) in Los Angeles, CA*
1964	DUMKE, Ralph	64	*Died in Sherman Oaks, CA*
1964	EMERY, John	59	*Cancer (in New York, NY)*
1964	FILAURI, Antonio	74	*Emphysema (in San Gabriel, CA)*
1964	FORBES, Mary	84	*Heart attack (in Beaumont, CA)*
1964	GARGAN, Edward	63	*Died in New York, NY*
1964	GOETZKE, Bernhard	79	*Died in Berlin, Germany*
1964	GOSFIELD, Maurice	51	*After being hospitalized for diabetes (in Saronac Lake, NY)*
1964	# GUILFOYLE, James	72	*Heart attack (in Woodland Hills, CA)*
1964	HAINES, Rhea	69	*Died in Los Angeles, CA*

• New entry. # Original name (Pt. 7). + Interment (Pt. 5).   50   ☆ Oscar nominee, ★ Oscar winner (Pt. 10)

Deaths of Movie and Television Personalities — by Year

YEAR	NAME	AGE	CAUSE and/or PLACE OF DEATH
1964	HANEY, Carol	30	Pneumonia and diabetes (in Saddle River, NJ)
1964	HARDWICKE, Cedric	71	Throat and lung cancer (in New York, NY)
1964	HARE, F. Lumsden	89	Died in Hollywood, CA
1964	+ HEARN, Sam	75	Heart attack (in Los Angeles, CA)
1964	+ HECHT, Ben	70	Cerebral thrombosis (in New York, NY)
1964	HENLEY, Hobart	72	After a long illness (in Beverly Hills, CA)
1964	HEYWOOD, Herbert	83	Coronary thrombosis (in Van Nuys, CA)
1964	HODGINS, Earle	65	Heart attack (in Hollywood, CA)
1964	HOHL, Arthur	74	Died in Los Angeles, CA
1964	# HOWES, Reed	64	Died in Woodland Hills, CA
1964	HUDMAN, Wesley	47	Murdered (in Williams, AZ)
1964	# HULBERT, Claude	63	Bronchial pneumonia (in Sydney, Australia)
1964	JOY, Nicholas	79	After a long illness (in Philadelphia, PA)
1964	KEATING, Larry	67	Leukemia (in Hollywood, CA)
1964	KELLY, James "Tiny"	49	Heart ailment (in Hollywood) Do not confuse with James T. Kelly
1964	KERRIGAN, Joseph M.	76	Died in Hollywood, CA
1964	+ KILBRIDE, Percy	76	Brain injury from auto accident (in Los Angeles, CA)
1964	KOLB, Clarence	89	Stroke (in Los Angeles, CA)
1964	+ LADD, Alan	50	Accidental death (alcohol/drug mix) in Palm Springs, CA
1964	#+ LORRE, Peter	59	Stroke (in Hollywood, CA)
1964	MACK, Wilbur	91	Died in Hollywood, CA
1964	MADISON, Cleo	81	Heart attack (in Burbank, CA)
1964	MARLOWE, Frank	60	Heart attack (in Hollywood, CA)
1964	MARTIN, Edie	83	Died in London, England
1964	#+ MARX, "Harpo"	75	During heart surgery (in Hollywood, CA)
1964	MATE, Rudolph	66	Following several heart attacks (in Hollywood, CA)
1964	MAUR, Meinhart	73	
1964	# McLEOD, Norman Z.	65	After suffering a stroke (in Hollywood, CA)
1964	McSHANE, Kitty	65	Died in London, England
1964	+ MEREDITH, Charles	70	After a long illness (in Los Angeles, CA)
1964	MEREDITH, Cheerio	74	Died in Woodland Hills, CA
1964	MICHAEL, Gertrude	53	Died in Beverly Hills, CA
1964	MING, Moy Luke	101	Died in Grenada Hills, CA
1964	+ MONTEUX, Pierre	89	Died in Hancock, MI
1964	MOORE, Dennis	49	Died in New York, NY
1964	MOORE, Ida	81	
1964	# MORANTE, Milburn	76	Heart disease (in Pacoima, CA)
1964	# MORLAY, Gaby	67	Cancer (in Nice, France)
1964	MORTIMER, Charles	78	Died in London, England
1964	# MOSER, Hans	83	Cancer (in Vienna, Austria)
1964	MULCASTER, George H.	72	Died in England
1964	NEWFIELD, Sam	64	Cancer (in Hollywood, CA)
1964	# OLIVER, Vic	66	Died in Johannesburg, South Africa
1964	# OSBOURNE, Lennie "Bud"	82	Died in Hollywood, CA
1964	# PALMER, Patricia	69	Died in Hollywood, CA
1964	PAYSON, Blanche	83	Died in Hollywood, CA
1964	# PEARCE, Peggy	69	Died in Hollywood, CA
1964	PENNICK, Jack	68	After a year's illness (in Hollywood, CA)
1964	+ PORTER, Cole	71	Following surgery for a kidney stone (in Santa Monica, CA)
1964	# PRICE, Hal	77	
1964	QUIGLEY, Charles	58	Cirrhosis of the liver (in Los Angeles, CA)
1964	#+ REEVES, Jim	40	Airplane crash (near Nashville, TN)
1964	#+ RICHARDS, Addison	61	Heart attack (in Los Angeles, CA)

Deaths of Movie and Television Personalities — by Year

YEAR	NAME		AGE	CAUSE and/or PLACE OF DEATH
1964	RICHARDS, Gordon		70	Died in Hollywood, CA
1964	ROBERTSON, John Stuart		86	Died in Escondida, CA
1964	SADO, Keiji		38	Automobile accident (in Japan)
1964	+ SCHILDKRAUT, Joseph	★	67	Heart attack (in New York, NY)
1964	SCOTT, Harold		72	Died in London, England
1964	SEITER, William A.		72	Heart attack (at his home in Beverly Hills, CA)
1964	SHANNON, Harry		74	Died in Hollywood, CA
1964	# SHARP, Henry		76	Died in Brooklyn, NY
1964	SILETTI, Mario G.		59	Automobile accident (in Los Angeles, CA)
1964	SILVANI, Aldo		73	After a long illness (in Milan, Italy)
1964	STEVENS, Bert		59	Heart attack (in Hollywood, CA)
1964	STEVENS, Charles		71	Died in Hollywood, CA
1964	STRAYER, Frank R.		72	Cancer (in Hollywood, CA)
1964	+ TEAGARDEN, Jack		57	Pneumonia (in New Orleans, LA)
1964	TONG, Sammee		63	Suicide at his home (in Culver City, CA)
1964	TRAVERSE, Madlaine		88	Died in Cleveland, OH
1964	VanSLOAN, Edward		81	Died in San Francisco, CA
1964	VonELTZ, Theodore		70	After a long illness (in Woodland Hills, CA)
1964	WAGNER, William		79	Died in Hollywood, CA
1964	# WARWICK, Robert		85	Pulmonary embolism (in Hollywood, CA)
1964	WILCOX, Fred M.		59	Died at his home in Beverly Hills, CA
1964	WILSON, Whip		49	Heart attack (in Hollywood, CA)
1964	# WYNYARD, Diana	☆	58	Kidney ailment (in London, England)
1965	AMES, Jimmy		50	Heart attack (in Hollywood, CA)
1965	BACHER, William A.		67	Cerebral thrombosis
1965	+ BACON, Irving		71	Died in Hollywood, CA
1965	# BARBOUR, Dave		53	Hemorrhaged ulcer (in Malibu, CA)
1965	# BARNET, Boris		63	Suicide (despondent over his faltering career) in Riga, Lettonia
1965	BARRISCALE, Bessie		81	Died in Kentfield, CA
1965	+ BEATTY, Clyde		62	Cancer of the esophagus (in Ventura, CA)
1965	BECKWITH, Reginald		56	Died in Bourne End, England
1965	+ BENNETT, Constance		59	Cerebral hemorrhage (in Walston, NJ)
1965	# BENTLEY, Irene		61	Heart attack (in Palm Beach, FL)
1965	BERLIN, Abby		58	Heart attack in his sleep (in Hollywood, CA)
1965	+ BOLAND, Mary		83	Died in New York, NY
1965	+ BOW, Clara		60	Heart attack while watching a movie on TV (in West Los Angeles)
1965	BROWNE, Irene		72	Cancer (in London, England)
1965	# BUSTER, Budd		74	Heart attack (in Los Angeles, CA)
1965	# CARROLL, Nancy	☆	59	Heart attack (in New York, NY)
1965	CASEY, Kenneth		66	Heart ailment (in Newburgh, NY)
1965	CHANDET, Louis W.		81	After an illness of several years (in Burbank, CA)
1965	+ CHANDLER, Helen		59	After surgery for a bleeding ulcer (in Hollywood, CA)
1965	# CHAPLIN, Sydney		80	After a long illness (in Nice, France)
1965	# COCHRAN, Steve		48	Acute infectious edema of lung (off coast of Guatemala)
1965	#+ COLE, Nat "King"		45	Lung cancer (in Santa Monica, CA)
1965	+ COLLINS, Ray		75	Emphysema (in Santa Monica, CA)
1965	COLLINS, Russell		68	Heart attack (in West Hollywood, CA)
1965	# CORDY, Henry		57	Heart ailment (in New York, NY)
1965	CRAIG, Nell		73	Died in Hollywood, CA
1965	CRUZE, Mae		74	After a long illness (in Hollywood, CA)
1965	+ DANDRIDGE, Dorothy	☆	42	Overdose of Tofranil, an anti-depressant (in West Hollywood, CA)
1965	#+ DARNELL, Linda		43	Fire burns (in Chicago, IL)

Deaths of Movie and Television Personalities — by Year

YEAR	NAME		AGE	CAUSE and/or PLACE OF DEATH
1965	DAVIS, George		75	Cancer (in Woodland Hills, CA)
1965	DILLON, Tim		77	Died in Burbank, CA
1965	# DRESSER, Louise	☆	86	Intestinal obstruction (in Woodland Hills, CA)
1965	#+ DUMONT, Margaret		75	Heart attack (in Los Angeles, CA)
1965	# EDWARDS, Neely		75	Died in Woodland Hills, CA
1965	EDWARDS, Sarah		81	Died in Hollywood, CA
1965	# ELLIOTT, William "Wild Bill"		61	Cancer (in Las Vegas, NV)
1965	ENRIGHT, Ray		69	Heart attack after a long illness (in Hollywood, CA)
1965	ERWIN, June		47	Found dead in her home (in Carmichael, CA)
1965	FEIST, Felix E.		55	Cancer (in Encino, CA)
1965	# FETHERSTON, Eddie		68	Heart attack (in Yucca Valley, CA)
1965	# GARON, Pauline		63	Died in Canada
1965	GEORGE, Muriel		82	Died in London, England
1965	GEST, Inna		43	Hepatitis (in San Francisco, CA)
1965	GLASS, Gaston J.		66	Died in Santa Monica, CA
1965	GRANBY, Joseph		80	Cerebral hemorrhage (in Hollywood, CA)
1965	# GRIBBON, Eddie		75	Cancer (in North Hollywood, CA)
1965	# HALE, Creighton		83	Died in South Pasadena, CA
1965	HANSON, Lars		78	Died in Stockholm, Sweden
1965	# HARTE, Betty		81	Died in Sunland, CA
1965	HENDRIKSON, Anders		69	Died in Sweden
1965	#+ HOLLIDAY, Judy	★	41	Throat cancer (in New York, NY)
1965	HOOD, Joseph B. Sr.		69	Died in Philadelphia, PA
1965	HOWARD, Esther		72	Heart attack (in Hollywood, CA)
1965	HOWARD, Eugene		84	Died in New York, NY
1965	HOXIE, Jack		75	Died in Keyes, OK
1965	HUGHES, Gareth		71	Died in Woodland Hills, CA
1965	JOHNSON, Rita		52	Brain hemorrhage (in West Hollywood, CA)
1965	#+ JONES, Spike		53	Emphysema (in Beverly Hills, CA)
1965	JORDAN, Robert "Bobby"		42	Liver ailment (in Los Angeles, CA)
1965	+ KASSEL, Art		69	
1965	KENNEDY, Tom		81	Bone cancer (in Woodland Hills, CA)
1965	+ KILGALLEN, Dorothy		52	Accidental death? (Seconal and alcohol) in New York, NY
1965	# KULKY, Henry "Hank"		53	Heart attack (in Oceanside, CA)
1965	#+ LAUREL, Stan		74	Cerebral thrombosis (in Santa Monica, CA)
1965	# LEE, Johnny "Calhoun"		67	Heart attack (in Los Angeles, CA)
1965	# LIGON, Grover G.		79	Died in Hollywood, CA
1965	#+ LITTLE, Malcolm "Malcolm X"		39	Assassinated (shot) in the Audubon Ballroom in Harlem, NY
1965	LYNCH, Helen		64	Died in Miami Beach, FL
1965	+ MacDONALD, Jeanette Raymond		57	Heart attack (in Houston, TX)
1965	# MANTZ, Paul		61	When a makeshift aircraft crashed enroute to film set (in CA)
1965	MARION, Sid		65	Heart attack (in Hollywood, CA)
1965	# MAUGHAM, W. Somerset		91	Died in Nice, France
1965	#+ McDONALD, Marie		41	Accidental drug overdose (in Hidden Hills, CA)
1965	# MESSENGER, Buddy		55	Died in Hollywood, CA
1965	MEYER, Greta		82	Died in Los Angeles, CA
1965	MOFFATT, Graham		46	Heart attack (in Bath, England)
1965	MOWER, Jack		74	Died in Hollywood, CA
1965	# MUDIE, Leonard		81	Heart ailment (in Hollywood, CA)
1965	#+ MURRAY, Mae		75	Heart condition (in North Hollywood, CA)
1965	+ MURROW, Edward R.		57	Lung cancer (in Pawling, NY)
1965	+ NEWTON, Robert		50	Heart attack (in Beverly Hills, CA)
1965	#+ NICHOLS, Red		60	Heart attack (in Las Vegas, NV)

• New entry.   # Original name (Pt. 7).   + Interment (Pt. 5).

☆ Oscar nominee, ★ Oscar winner (Pt. 10)

Deaths of Movie and Television Personalities — by Year

YEAR	NAME		AGE	CAUSE and/or PLACE OF DEATH
1965	OWEN, Catherine Dale		62	Died in New York, NY
1965	PAYNE, Douglas		90	Died in England
1965	PERINAL, Georges		68	Died in London, England
1965	PETERS, Ann		45	Heart attack (in Paris, France)
1965	PHILLIPS, Edward N.		65	Killed by a car while crossing the street (in North Hollywood, CA)
• 1965	QUIMBY, Fred	★	79	Natural causes
1965	REICHER, Frank		89	Died in Playa del Rey, CA
1965	REID, Trevor		55	Died in London, England
1965	RENNIE, James		76	Died in New York, NY
1965	+ REYNOLDS, Quentin		62	Cancer (in Los Angeles, CA)
1965	#+ RITZ, Al		64	Heart attack (in New Orleans, LA)
1965	# ROME, Stewart		79	Died in Newbury, England
1965	SCHIPA, Tito		76	Heart attack (in New York, NY)
1965	#+ SCOTT, Zachary		51	Brain tumor (in Austin, TX)
1965	#+ SELZNICK, David O.		63	Acute coronary (in Hollywood, CA)
1965	SERDA, Julia		90	Died in Dresden, East Germany
1965	# SHUMWAY, Walter		80	Heart disease (in Woodland Hills, CA)
1965	# SLACK, Freddie		55	Heart attack (in Hollywood, CA)
1965	+ SLOANE, Everett		55	Suicide (sleeping pills) in Brentwood, CA
1965	STEINER, Elio		60	Died in Rome, Italy
1965	SWOR, John		82	Died in Dallas, Texas
1965	TANNEN, Julius		84	After suffering a stroke (in Hollywood, CA)
1965	TAYLOR, Forrest		80	Died in Garden Grove, CA
1965	#+ TRAVERS, Henry	☆	91	Arteriosclerosis (in Hollywood, CA)
1965	+ Trigger (Roy Rogers' horse)		33	Natural causes
1965	# VICTOR, Charles		69	Died in London, England
1965	WAGNER, Jack		68	Died in Hollywood, CA
1965	# WATSON, Bobby		77	Died in Hollywood, CA
1965	+ WATSON, Minor		75	Died in Alton, IL
1965	# WERNICKE, Otto		72	Died in Munich, Germany
1965	# WESSEL, Dick		51	Heart attack (in Studio City, CA)
1965	WILLIAMS, Mack		58	Heart attack (in Hollywood, CA)
1965	# WILSON, Tom		84	Died in Los Angeles, CA
1965	WOOD, Britt		70	After a 6-month illness (in Hollywood, CA)
1965	WRIGHT, Mack V.		69	Died in Boulder City, NV
1965	#+ X, Malcolm		39	(See Malcolm Little)
1965	YACONELLI, Frank		67	Lung cancer (in Los Angeles, CA)
1966	ALLENBY, Peggy		65	After a brief illness (in New York)
1966	ARLEN, Betty		62	Died in Los Angeles, CA
• 1966	BACUGALUPI, Louis		46	Died in Los Angeles, CA
• 1966	BAKALEINIKOFF, Constantin		68	Died in Hollywood, CA
1966	#+ BAKER, Art		68	Heart attack (in Los Angeles, CA)
1966	BEAUMONT, Harry	☆	78	Died in Santa Monica, CA
1966	+ BERG, Gertrude		66	Heart failure (in Beverly Hills, CA)
1966	# BLAKE, Al		89	Heart attack (in Los Angeles, CA)
1966	# BOYNE, Sunny		83	Died in Van Nuys, CA
1966	BRICE, Lew		72	Heart attack (in Hollywood, CA)
1966	#+ BRUCE, Lenny		40	Overdose of narcotics (in Hollywood, CA)
1966	BUNKER, Ralph		77	Stroke (in New York, NY)
1966	#+ BUSHMAN, Francis X.		83	Heart attack due to fall (in Pacific Palisades, CA)
1966	# CALHOUN, Alice		65	Cancer (in Los Angeles, CA)
1966	CAMPBELL, Colin		83	Cerebral hemorrhage (in Woodland Hills, CA)

Deaths of Movie and Television Personalities — by Year

YEAR	NAME		AGE	CAUSE and/or PLACE OF DEATH
1966	CASTLE, Don		47	*Found dead from overdose of medication (in Hollywood, CA)*
1966	CHALMERS, Thomas		82	*Died in Greenwich, CT*
1966	CHATTON, Sydney		48	*Coronary attack (in Berkeley, CA)*
1966	CLAYTON, Ethel		82	*Died in Oxnard, CA*
1966	+ CLIFT, Montgomery ☆		45	*Occlusive coronary artery disease (in New York, NY)*
1966	# COOMBE, Carol		55	*Died in London, England*
1966	CREHAN, Joseph		79	*Stroke (in Hollywood, CA)*
1966	DAWN, Isabel		62	*Pulmonary infection (in Woodland Hills, CA)*
1966	# DeCASALIS, Jeanne		70	*Died in London, England*
1966	#+ DISNEY, Walt		65	*Circulatory collapse after lung surgery (in Burbank, CA)*
1966	DODD, (Rev.) Neal		88	*After a long illness (in Burbank, CA)*
1966	# DOUGLASS, Kent		58	
1966	# DUNN, Bobby		74	*Heart attack (in Hollywood, CA)*
1966	DUNN, Emma		91	*Died in Los Angeles, CA*
1966	ENGLE, Billy		77	*Heart attack (in Hollywood, CA)*
1966	FAYE, Julia		72	*Cancer (in Santa Monica, CA)*
1966	FELTON, Verna		76	*Pulmonary embolism (in North Hollywood, CA)*
1966	#+ FLEMING, Eric		41	*Drowned in the Huallaga River while filming in Peru*
1966	# FORD, Wallace		68	*Heart ailment (in Woodland Hills, CA)*
1966	+ FRAWLEY, William		79	*Heart attack (in Los Angeles, CA)*
1966	FURTHMAN, Jules		78	*Stroke while vacationing (in Oxford, England)*
1966	GERAGHTY, Carmelita		65	*Died in New York, NY*
1966	GLASS, Everett		74	*Died in Los Angeles, CA*
1966	# GLORI, Enrico		64	*Died in Rome, Italy*
1966	GORSS, Saul		58	*Heart attack (in Los Angeles, CA)*
1966	HAADE, William		63	*Died in Los Angeles, CA*
1966	# HALE, Jonathan		74	*Suicide (gunshot) in Woodland Hills, CA*
1966	HALLIDAY, Gardner		56	*Suicide (sleeping pills) after suffering with cancer (in Hollywood, CA)*
1966	+ HARRIGAN, William		72	*Following surgery (in New York, NY)*
1966	HAYNES, Arthur		52	*Heart attack (in London, England)*
1966	HILL, Robert F.		79	*After a long illness (in Los Angeles, CA)*
1966	HILLIARD, Harry S.		?	*Complications after a fall (in St. Petersburg, FL)*
1966	#+ HOPPER, Hedda		75	*Double pneumonia and heart complications (in Los Angeles, CA)*
1966	JIMINEZ, Soledad		92	*Following a stroke (in Woodland Hills, CA)*
1966	JOHNSTON, Oliver		78	*Died in London, England*
1966	+ KANE, Helen		58	*After a 10-year bout with liver cancer (in Jackson Heights, NY)*
1966	#+ KEATON, Buster		70	*Lung cancer (in Woodland Hills, CA)*
1966	KEITH, Robert		68	*Died in Los Angeles, CA*
1966	# KELLY, Dorothy		51	*Died in a fire at her home in La Jolla, CA*
1966	KERN, James V.		57	*Pneumonia, after a short illness (in Encino, CA)*
1966	KIEPURA, Jan		64	*Heart ailment (in Harrison, NY)*
1966	# LAWSON, Wilfrid		66	*Heart attack (in London, England)*
1966	LEASE, Rex		64	*Found dead of a heart attack at his home (in Hollywood, CA)*
1966	MacKENZIE, Mary		44	*Automobile accident (in London, England)*
1966	+ MARSHALL, Herbert		75	*Heart attack (in Beverly Hills, CA)*
1966	MASON, Haddon		68	*Died in London, England*
1966	MATHER, Jack		58	*Heart attack (in Wauconda, IL)*
1966	# McDOWELL, Claire		88	*After a long illness (in Woodland Hills, CA)*
1966	MENKEN, Helen		63	*Heart attack (in New York, NY)*
1966	MERRILL, Frank		71	*Died in Hollywood, CA*
1966	MILLAR, Marjie		36	*Died in Los Angeles, CA*
1966	# MILOS, Milos		24	*Suicide (gunshot) in Los Angeles, CA*
1966	# MONTGOMERY, Douglass		57	*Died in Norwalk, CT*

• New entry. # Original name (Pt. 7). + Interment (Pt. 5).   55   ☆ Oscar nominee, ★ Oscar winner (Pt. 10)

Deaths of Movie and Television Personalities — by Year

YEAR	NAME		AGE	CAUSE and/or PLACE OF DEATH
1966	MORTON, Charles S.		59	Heart disease (in North Hollywood, CA)
1966	# NAGEL, Anne		53	Cancer (in Los Angeles, CA)
1966	NOVIS, Donald		60	After a brief illness
1966	O'BRIEN, Eugene		83	Bronchial pneumonia (in Los Angeles, CA)
1966	# O'MALLEY, Pat		75	Died while eating dinner at home (in Van Nuys, CA)
1966	#+ OWEN, Seena		71	After a brief illness (in Hollywood, CA)
1966	PAIVA, Nestor		61	Cancer (in Sherman Oaks, CA)
1966	PATTERSON, Elizabeth		91	Died in Los Angeles, CA
1966	PEACOCK, Kim		65	Heart attack (in Emsworth, England)
1966	PEARCE, Alice		46	Cancer (in Los Angeles, CA)
1966	PEARCE, Vera		69	Died in London, England
1966	PEARSON, Lloyd		68	Heart attack (in London, England)
1966	PETTINGELL, Frank		75	Died in London, England
1966	POMMER, Erich		77	Died in Hollywood, CA
1966	POWER, Hartley		71	After a long illness (in London, England)
1966	# RAMBOVA, Natacha		69	Dietary complications (in Pasadena, CA)
1966	REEVE, Ada		91	Cardiac arrest in her sleep (in London, England)
1966	RODRIGUEZ, Estelita		52	Died in Van Nuys, CA
1966	ROGERS, Rena		64	Died in Santa Monica, CA
1966	#+ ROPER, Jack		62	Throat cancer (in Woodland Hills, CA)
1966	+ ROSE, Billy		67	
1966	ROSEMOND, Clinton C.		82	Pneumonia and stroke (in Los Angeles, CA)
1966	ROSSEN, Robert	☆	57	After a long illness (in New York, NY)
1966	ROWAN, Donald W. "Don"		60	Cerebral hemorrhage (in Rocky Hill, CT)
1966	SHINER, Ronald		63	Died in London, England
1966	Shooting Star		76	Stroke (in Hollywood, CA)
1966	STEADMAN, Vera		66	Died in Long Beach, CA
1966	# STEELE, William "Bill"		76	Died in Los Angeles, CA
1966	# STEWART, Donald		54	After a long illness (in Chertsey, England)
1966	STEWART, Jack		51	Died in London, England
1966	# STOCKFIELD, Betty		61	Leukemia (in London, England)
1966	# STOKER, H. G.		81	Died in England
1966	TAYLOR, Deems		67	Stroke (in New York, NY)
1966	TAYLOR, Donald F.		47	Found dead at home from an overdose of seconal (in Hollywood, CA)
1966	#+ TERRELL, Kenneth		61	Arteriosclerosis (in Sherman Oaks, CA)
1966	#+ TUCKER, Sophie		82	Lung and kidney ailment (in New York, NY)
1966	UNDERWOOD, Loyal		73	Died in Los Angeles, CA
1966	# URECAL, Minerva		71	Heart attack (in Glendale, CA)
1966	# VINCENT, Sailor Billy		70	Heart attack (in Toluca Lake, CA)
1966	+ WALKER, June		61	After a 5-yr. illness (in Sherman Oaks, CA)
1966	# WATSON, Wylie		67	Died in Scotland
1966	WATTS, Charles		?	Cancer (in Nashville, TN)
1966	#+ WEBB, Clifton	☆	72	Heart attack (in Beverly Hills, CA)
1966	# WHEATCROFT, Stanhope		77	Heart attack (in Woodland Hills, CA)
1966	WHITLOCK, T. Lloyd		75	Died in Los Angeles, CA
1966	+ WHORF, Richard		60	Heart attack after hospitalization for an ulcer (in Santa Monica, CA)
1966	WILSON, Jack		49	Cerebral hemorrhage (in Los Angeles, CA)
1966	WOOD, Douglas		85	Died in Woodland Hills, CA
1966	#+ WYNN, Ed	☆	79	Cancer (in Los Angeles, CA)
1966	# YOWLACHIE, Chief		74	Pneumonia (in Los Angeles, CA)
1967	# AINLEY, Richard		56	Died in London, England
1967	# ALVARADO, Don		62	Cancer (in Los Angeles, CA)

YEAR	NAME		AGE	CAUSE and/or PLACE OF DEATH
1967	+ ANDREWS, LaVerne 'of Sisters'		51	Cancer and pneumonia (in Brentwood, CA)
1967	ANTRIM, Harry		71	Heart attack (in Hollywood, CA)
1967	# AUER, Mischa	☆	61	Heart attack (in Rome, Italy)
1967	# BAIRD, Cora		55	Died in New York, NY
1967	+ BICKFORD, Charles	☆	78	Emphysema (in Los Angeles, CA)
1967	# BIG TREE, Chief John		92	Died in Onondaga Indian Reservation, NY
1967	BROOKS, Pauline		54	Cancer (in Glendale, CA)
1967	BRUGGEMAN, George		62	Died in North Hollywood, CA
1967	#+ BURNETTE, Smiley		55	Leukemia (in Encino, CA)
1967	BURNS, Paul E.		86	Heart attack (in Van Nuys, CA)
1967	CADELL, Jean		83	Died in London, England
1967	CARNERA, Primo		60	Liver ailment (in Sequals, Italy)
1967	# CHANEY, Frances		78	Cerebral hemorrhage (in Sierra Madre, CA)
1967	CIOLLI, Augusta		65	Heart attack (in New York, NY)
1967	CLARK, Ivan-John		?	
1967	CLARK, Johnny		50	Heart attack (in Hollywood, CA)
1967	+ CLYDE, Andy		75	Heart attack in his sleep (in Hollywood, CA)
1967	# CONTI, Albert		79	Stroke (in Hollywood, CA)
1967	#+ CONWAY, Tom		63	Liver ailment (in Culver City, CA)
1967	COOLIDGE, Philip		58	Cancer (in Hollywood, CA)
1967	# CUNARD, Grace		73	After a long bout with cancer (in Woodland Hills, CA)
1967	CUNNINGHAM, Zamah		74	Died in New York, NY
1967	#+ DARWELL, Jane	★	87	Heart attack (in Woodland Hills, CA)
1967	#+ DENNY, Reginald		75	Stroke (in Surrey, England)
1967	DONATH, Ludwig		67	Leukemia (in New York, NY)
1967	DORLEAC, Francoise		25	After car skidded on wet road and burst into flames (Nice, France)
1967	#+ DUNN, James	★	65	Died in Santa Monica, CA
1967	DUVIVIER, Julien		71	After his car hit another car and tree (in Paris, France)
1967	#+ EDDY, Nelson		65	After suffering a stroke while performing on stage (in Miami Beach)
1967	EDWARDS, Edna Park		72	Died in Burbank, CA
1967	ELMAN, Mischa		76	Heart attack (in New York, NY)
1967	+ ERWIN, Stuart	☆	65	Heart attack (in Beverly Hills, CA)
1967	EVELYN, Judith		54	Cancer (in New York, NY)
1967	FARRAR, Geraldine		85	Died in Ridgefield, CT
1967	FLINT, Helen		69	Struck by a car while crossing the street (in Washington, D.C.)
1967	# FORTE, Joe		71	After a heart attack (in Hollywood, CA)
1967	# FREEMAN, Howard		68	After a brief illness (in New York, NY)
1967	GARDEN, Mary		92	Died in Aberdeen, Scotland
1967	# GLENNON, Bert	☆	72	Heart attack (in Sherman Oaks, CA)
1967	GRAF, Louis C.		77	Heart attack (in Hollywood, CA)
1967	#+ GUTHRIE, Woody		55	After a 13-yr. bout with Huntington's chorea (in Queens, NY)
1967	HACK, Herman		68	Heart attack (in Hollywood, CA)
1967	HACKETT, Hal		44	After a long illness (in New York, NY)
1967	HALLS, Ethel May		85	Died in Hollywood, CA
1967	HARKER, Gordon		81	After a long illness (in London, England)
1967	HARLAN, Kenneth D.		71	Aneurysm (in Sacramento, CA)
1967	HENCKLES, Paul		81	Died in Dusseldorf, Germany
1967	HESTERBERG, Trude		70	Died in Munich, Germany
1967	HINES, Harry		78	After suffering from emphysema (in Hollywood, CA)
1967	HOPPER, E. Mason		82	Died in Woodland Hills, CA
1967	HUME, Benita		61	Died in Egerton, England
1967	HUTH, Harold		75	After a long illness (in London, England)
1967	JACKSON, Thomas E.		81	Heart attack (in Hollywood, CA)

Deaths of Movie and Television Personalities — by Year

YEAR	NAME	AGE	CAUSE and/or PLACE OF DEATH
1967	KINGSTON, Winifred	73	*Died in La Jolla, CA*
1967	KORTMAN, Robert F.	79	*Cancer (in Long Beach, CA)*
1967	#+ LAHR, Bert	72	*Internal hemorrhage after pneumonia (in New York, NY)*
1967	LAKE, Alice	71	*Heart attack (in Paradise, CA)*
1967	# LATELL, Lyle	62	*Heart attack (in Hollywood, CA)*
1967	#+ LEIGH, Vivien ★	53	*Tuberculosis (in London, England)*
1967	# LITTLE, Billy	72	*Stroke (in Hollywood, CA)*
1967	LYNN, George M.	61	*Died in Los Angeles, CA*
1967	MacFADDEN, Gertrude "Mickey"	67	*Heart attack (in Hollywood, CA)*
1967	MacLEAN, Douglas	70	*Following a cerebral thrombosis (in Beverly Hills, CA)*
1967	# MACRAE, Duncan	61	*Died in Glasgow, Scotland (Do not confuse with Duncan McRae)*
1967	# MAERTENS, Willy	74	*Died in Hamburg, Germany*
1967	# MANN, Anthony	60	*Heart attack (in Berlin, Germany)*
1967	#+ MANSFIELD, Jayne	35	*Automobile accident (in New Orleans, LA)*
1967	MARCUSE, Theodore	47	*When his car struck a truck on a Hollywood freeway*
1967	# McCOY, Gertrude	77	*Died in Atlanta, GA*
1967	McGRATH, Frank	64	*Heart attack (in Beverly Hills, CA)*
1967	McKEEVER, Mike	27	*Brain injuries from an automobile accident (in Hollywood, CA)*
1967	McKENZIE, Eva B.	78	*Died in Hollywood, CA*
1967	McKINNEY, Nina Mae	54	*Died in New York, NY*
1967	McNAUGHTON, Harry	70	*Died in Amityville, NY*
1967	MILLS, John Sr.	78	*Died in Bellefontaine, OH*
1967	MOON, George	80	*Died in London, England*
1967	# MORAN, Frank	80	*Heart attack (in Hollywood, CA)*
1967	+ MORENO, Antonio	78	*After a long illness (in Beverly Hills, CA)*
1967	# MORGAN, Lee	64	*Heart disease (in Los Angeles, CA)*
1967	#+ MUNI, Paul ★	71	*Heart trouble (in Montecito, CA)*
1967	NESBIT, Evelyn (Thaw)	82	*Died at a nursing home in a Santa Monica, CA*
1967	+ NEWELL, William "Billy"	72	*Died in Hollywood, CA*
1967	NIELSEN, Hans	56	*Paralysis illness (in Berlin, Germany)*
1967	OVERTON, Frank	49	*Heart attack (in Pacific Palisades, CA)*
1967	PADDEN, Sarah	?	*Died in London, England*
1967	# PADULA, Vincent	66	*Peritonitis (in Glendale, CA)*
1967	PAYTON, Barbara	39	*Heart attack (in San Diego, CA)*
1967	PENDLETON, Nat	68	*Heart attack (in San Diego, CA)*
1967	PERRIN, Jack	71	*Heart attack (in Hollywood, CA)*
1967	# PETERS, House Sr.	87	*Died at M.P.C. Hospital, Woodland Hills, CA*
1967	PRUD'HOMME, Cameron	75	*After a long illness (at a hospital in Pompton Plains, NJ)*
1967	QUINN, Tony	67	*Died in London, England (Do not confuse with Anthony Quinn)*
1967	+ RAINS, Claude ☆	77	*Intestinal hemorrhage (in Laconia, NH)*
1967	RALSTON, Jobyna	62	*After a long illness (in Woodland Hills, CA)*
1967	# RAMBO, Dirk	25	*Burned to death in a car accident (in Los Angeles, CA)*
1967	+ RANDOLPH, Amanda	65	*Cerebral hemorrhage (in Durate, CA)*
1967	#+ RATHBONE, Basil ☆	75	*Heart attack (in New York, NY)*
1967	REDDING, Otis	26	*Airplane crash (near Madison, WI)*
1967	+ REED, Florence	86	*Died in East Islip, NY*
1967	#+ REEVES, Richard J.	54	*Cirrhosis of the liver (in Northridge, CA)*
1967	# REMY, Albert	54	*Heart attack (in Paris, France)*
1967	RHODES, Billy "Little Billy"	72	*Stroke (in Hollywood, CA)*
1967	RING, Cyril	74	*Died in Hollywood, CA*
1967	# RUMANN, Sig	82	*Heart attack (in Julian, NE)*
1967	SCHAEFER, Armand L.	69	*Died in Bridgeport, CA*
1967	SCHNEIDER, James	85	*Died in Hollywood, CA*

• New entry.   # Original name (Pt. 7).   + Interment (Pt. 5).   ☆ Oscar nominee, ★ Oscar winner (Pt. 10)

Deaths of Movie and Television Personalities — by Year

YEAR	NAME		AGE	CAUSE and/or PLACE OF DEATH
1967	SEYMOUR, Harry		77	Heart attack (in Hollywood, CA)
1967	# SHAIFFER, Howard "Tiny"		48	Died in Burbank, CA
1967	SHAW, Oscar		76	
1967	#+ SHERIDAN, Ann		51	Cancer (in San Fernando Valley, CA)
1967	# STONE, George E.		63	Following a paralytic stroke (in Woodland Hills, CA)
1967	+ TATUM, Reese "Goose"		45	
1967	THOMSON, Kenneth		68	Pulmonary emphysema and fibrosis (in Los Angeles, CA)
1967	THORBURN, June		36	Airplane crash (in Fernhurst, Sussex, England)
1967	# THUNDERCLOUD, Chief (2nd)		68	(Do not confuse with 1st Chief Thundercloud, d. 1955)
1967	# Toto		69	Died in Rome, Italy (Do not confuse with Toto the Clown, d. 1938)
1967	+ TRACY, Spencer	★	67	Heart attack (in Beverly Hills, CA)
1967	TRACY, William		49	Died in Hollywood, CA
1967	TREACY, Emerson		61	Injuries from a fall (in Woodland Hills, CA)
1967	+ TROWBRIDGE, Charles		85	Died in Los Angeles, CA
1967	TYNAN, Brandon		91	Died at Lynwood Nursing Home in New York, NY
1967	# VERNE, Kaaren		49	Heart attack (in Hollywood, CA)
1967	VOGEL, Rudolf		67	Died in Munich, Germany
1967	# WARD, Warwick		76	Died in London, England
1967	#+ WAXMAN, Franz		60	Cancer (in Los Angeles, CA)
1967	WEISBART, David		52	Stroke while playing golf (in Hollywood, CA)
1967	+ WESTMORE, Ernest		63	After a heart attack
1967	+ WHITEMAN, Paul		77	Heart attack (in Doylestown, PA)
1968	ABBOTT, Dorothy		48	Died in Los Angeles, CA
1968	#+ ADAMS, Nick	☆	35	Drug overdose (in Beverly Hills, CA)
1968	# ANDREWS, Lois		44	Lung cancer (in Encino, CA)
1968	ANSON, Laura		76	Died in Woodland Hills, CA
1968	ARNOLD, Phil		58	Heart attack (in Hollywood, CA)
1968	AYRES, Robert		54	Heart attack (in Hemel Hempstead, England)
1968	# BAGLEY, Sam		65	Heart attack (in Hollywood, CA)
1968	#+ BAINTER, Fay	★	76	After a long illness (in Beverly Hills, CA)
1968	# BAKER, Eddie		70	Emphysema (in Hollywood, CA)
1968	#+ BANKHEAD, Tallulah		66	Double pneumonia complicated by emphysema (in New York, NY)
1968	# BECKETT, Scotty		38	Following a serious beating (in Hollywood, CA)
1968	BELL, Rodney		52	
1968	+ BENADARET, Bea		62	Cancer (in Los Angeles, CA)
1968	BENEDICT, Brooks		63	
1968	BLACKTON, James Stuart Jr.		71	
1968	# BURKE, James		81	Heart attack (in Los Angeles, CA)
1968	CASSIDY, Ed		74	Died in Woodland Hills, CA
1968	#+ CASTLE, Nick		58	Heart attack (in Los Angeles, CA)
1968	CHAPLIN, Charles Jr.		42	Blood clot (in Hollywood, CA)
1968	+ CHESHIRE, Harry "Pappy"		76	
1968	#+ CLARK, Fred		54	Liver ailment (in Santa Monica, CA)
1968	+ COATES, Paul		47	Heart attack (in West Hollywood, CA)
1968	# COLLYER, June		60	Bronchial pneumonia (in Los Angeles, CA)
1968	+ COREY, Wendell		54	Liver ailment (in Woodland Hills, CA)
1968	COX, Morgan		68	Heart attack (in Hollywood, CA)
1968	# CURRIE, Finlay		90	Died in Gerrard's Cross, England
1968	D'ARRAST, Harry		71	
1968	DAVIDSON, John		81	Heart failure (in Los Angeles, CA) — Do not confuse with the singer
1968	DAVIS, Jack		?	
1968	# DEKKER, Albert		63	Found dead in his bath tub with S and M trappings (in Hollywood)

YEAR	NAME	AGE	CAUSE and/or PLACE OF DEATH
1968	# DICKERSON, Henry	61	Cerebral thrombosis (in Lynwood, CA)
1968	DRISCOLL, Bobby	31	Hardening of the arteries (in New York, NY)
1968	DUNN, Ralph	65	
1968	+ DURYEA, Dan	61	Cancer and heart attack (in Los Angeles, CA)
1968	EVANS, Douglas	64	Died in Hollywood, CA
1968	EVEREST, Barbara	77	Died in London, England
1968	+ FARRELL, Virginia	72	
1968	#+ FOLEY, Red	58	Acute pulmonary edema (in Fort Wayne, IN)
1968	# FRANCIS, Kay	65	Cancer (in New York, NY)
1968	# GARDNER, Helen	83	Died in Orlando, FL
1968	GEORGE, John	70	Emphysema (in Los Angeles, CA)
1968	#+ GISH, Dorothy	70	Bronchial pneumonia (in Rapallo, Italy)
1968	GOUGH, John	70	Cancer (in Hollywood, CA)
1968	GRANVILLE, Louise	73	Hong Kong flu after being hospitalized for asthma (in Hollywood, CA)
1968	# GUY-BLACHE, Alice	95	Natural causes (at her daughter's home in Mahwah, NJ)
1968	HAAS, Hugo	65	Asthmatic attack (in Vienna, Austria)
1968	HALL, Alexander ☆	74	Stroke (in San Francisco, CA)
1968	HALL, Juanita	66	Diabetic complications (in Bay Shore, NY)
1968	# HANCOCK, Tony	44	Suicide (overdose of sleeping pills) in Sydney, Australia
1968	# HARVEY, Lilian	61	Died in Antibes, France
1968	HEMSLEY, Estelle	70	After a brief illness (in Hollywood, CA)
1968	HOBBS, Jack	74	Died in Brighton, England
1968	INDRISANO, John "Johnny"	62	Apparent suicide (hanging) at his home in San Fernando Valley, CA
1968	KAHANAMOKU, Duke	77	After a heart attack at the Waikiki Yacht Club (in Honolulu, HI)
1968	KELLER, Helen	86	Died in Westport, CT
1968	KELLY, Kitty	66	Cancer (in Hollywood, CA)
1968	KELTON, Pert	60	Stroke
1968	KERR, Lorence "Larry"	?	
1968	+ KING, Martin Luther Jr.	39	Murdered (shot)
1968	LACKTEEN, Frank	73	Cerebral and respiratory illness (in Woodland Hills, CA)
1968	#+ LEONARD, Robert Z. ☆	78	Aneurysm (in Beverly Hills, CA)
1968	LEWIN, Albert	73	Pneumonia (in New York, NY)
1968	LEWIS, Cathy	50	Cancer (in Hollywood Hills, CA)
1968	LINDO, Olga	68	Died in London, England
1968	+ LINDSAY, Howard	78	Died in New York, NY
1968	LLOYD, Doris	68	"Strained" heart (in Santa Barbara, CA)
1968	# LORNE, Marion	80	Heart attack (in New York, NY)
1968	MacKAYE, Norman	62	After a brief illness
1968	# MARSH, Mae	72	Heart attack (in Hermosa Beach, CA)
1968	MASKELL, Virginia	31	Exposure and overdose of drugs (in Stoke Mandeville, England)
1968	+ MAYO, Archie	77	Cancer (in Guadalajara, Mexico)
1968	McDONALD, Francis J.	77	After a lengthy illness (in Hollywood, CA)
1968	# MEADE, Claire	84	Pneumonia (in Encino, CA)
1968	MEHAFFEY, Blanche	60	Died in Los Angeles, CA
1968	MOHR, Gerald	54	Heart attack (in Stockholm, Sweden)
1968	MORAN, Patsy	63	Died in Hollywood, CA
1968	MORAN, Percy	?	Died in England
1968	# MORENO, Dario	47	Cerebral hemorrhage (in Istanbul, Turkey)
1968	MORRIS, Margaret	64	(Do not confuse with choreographer of same name)
1968	# MORROW, Doretta	41	Cancer (in London, England)
1968	# MURAT, Jean	79	Coronary thrombosis (in Aix-en-Provence, France)
1968	# NOONAN, Tommy	45	After an operation for a malignant brain tumor (in Woodland Hills)
1968	#+ NOVARRO, Ramon	69	Murdered (bludgeoned) at his home in Hollywood Hills, CA

Deaths of Movie and Television Personalities — by Year

YEAR	NAME		AGE	CAUSE and/or PLACE OF DEATH
1968	#+ O'KEEFE, Dennis		60	Lung cancer (in Santa Monica, CA)
1968	# O'NEIL, Sally		57	Pneumonia (in Galesburg, IL)
1968	PETRIE, Howard A.		61	After a long illness (at a hospital in Keene, NH)
1968	+ PIERCE, Jack P.		79	Died in Hollywood, CA
1968	POST, Guy Bates		92	Died in Hollywood, CA
1968	# POWER, Paul		65	Died in Hollywood, CA
1968	PUIG, Eva G.		74	Diabetes and heart failure (in Panorama City, CA)
1968	REA, Mabel Lillian		36	Automobile accident (in Charlotte, NC)
1968	# RICE, Jack		75	Cancer (in Woodland Hills, CA)
1968	# RIDGELY, John		58	Heart ailment (in New York, NY)
1968	RIGA, Nadine		59	Cerebral hemorrhage (in Hollywood, CA)
1968	SALMONOVA, Lyda		79	Died in Prague, Czeckoslovakia
1968	SCARFIOTTI, Lodovico		34	Automobile crash (in Berchtesgaden, Germany)
1968	SCOBIE, James		?	
1968	SEATON, Scott		90	After a lengthy illness (in Hollywood, CA)
1968	#+ SEDDON, Margaret		95	Died in Philadelphia, PA
1968	SERVOSS, Mary		80	Heart ailment (at her home in Los Angeles, CA)
1968	# SHAW, C. Montague		83	Died in Woodland Hills, CA
1968	SHORT, Gertrude		66	After a brief illness (in Hollywood, CA)
1968	SKINNER, Frank		69	Cancer (in Los Angeles, CA)
1968	SMITH, Howard I.		74	Heart attack (in Hollywood, Ca.)
1968	#+ ST. DENIS, Ruth		90	Heart attack (in Hollywood, CA)
1968	#+ STAFFORD, Hanley		69	Heart attack (in Hollywood, Ca.)
1968	+ STROMBERG, Hunt		74	Massive stroke (in Santa Monica, CA)
1968	SUTHERLAND, Victor		79	Died in Los Angeles, CA
1968	SWANWICK, Peter		56	Died in London, England
1968	# SYDNEY, Basil		73	Pleurisy (in London, England)
1968	+ TALMAN, William		53	Cancer (in Encino, CA)
1968	# TONE, Franchot	☆	63	Lung cancer (in New York, NY)
1968	#+ TRACY, Lee	☆	70	Cancer of the liver (in Santa Monica, CA)
1968	#+ VALLI, Virginia (Farrell)		68	Following a stroke (in Palm Springs, CA)
1968	VAN, Gus		80	After two brain operations when hit by a car in Miami Beach, FL
1968	VonSTROHEIM, Erich Jr.		52	Cancer (in Woodland Hills, CA)
1968	WALKER, Helen		47	Cancer (in North Hollywood, CA)
1968	WATSON, Benjamin T. "Ben"		?	
1968	WEEKS, Marion		81	Died in New York
1968	WEIDLER, Virginia		41	Heart attack (in Los Angeles, CA)
1968	#+ WHEELER, Bert		72	Emphysema (in New York, NY)
1968	WIFSTRAND, Naima		78	Died in Stockholm, Sweden
1968	+ WILLARD, Jess		86	Cerebral hemorrhage (in Los Angeles, CA)
1968	# WITHERS, Isabel		72	Died in Hollywood, CA
1968	# WOODS, Harry L. Sr.		79	Uremia (in Los Angeles, CA)
1968	WRAY, Aloha		39	Died in Hollywood, CA
1969	AHEARNE, Tom		63	Influenza (in New York)
1969	# ALEXANDER, Ben		58	Natural causes (in Westchester, CA)
1969	ANDERSON, James "Jim"		48	Heart attack (in Billings, MT)
1969	ANDREWS, Stanley		77	Died in Los Angeles, CA
1969	BACCALONI, Salvatore		69	Following deterioration of a number of organs (in New York, NY)
• 1969	BADRAKHAN, Ahmed		59	Apoplexy attack (in Le Caire, Egypt)
• 1969	BAER, Arthur "Bugs"		84	Cancer (in New York, NY)
1969	# BANCROFT, Charles		57	Cancer (in Woodland Hills, CA)
1969	# BARCROFT, Roy		67	Cancer (in Woodland Hills, CA)

• New entry.   # Original name (Pt. 7).   + Interment (Pt. 5).   61   ☆ Oscar nominee, ★ Oscar winner (Pt. 10)

Deaths of Movie and Television Personalities — by Year

YEAR	NAME	AGE	CAUSE and/or PLACE OF DEATH
1969	BARZELL, Wolfe	71	Heart attack (in Acapulco, Mexico)
1969	#+ BATES, Barbara	43	Suicide (gas) in Denver, CO
1969	BEAL, Royal	68	Cancer (in Keene, NH)
1969	BELGADO, Maria	63	After a 3-week illness (in Hollywood, CA)
1969	# BENDER, Russell	59	Died in Woodland Hills, CA
1969	BENHAM, Harry	83	Died in Sarasota, FL
1969	BENNETT, Enid	74	Heart attack (in Malibu, CA)
1969	BERGER, Ludwig	77	Heart failure (in Schlagenbad, Germany)
1969	BIRCH, Paul	61	Died in Los Angeles, CA
1969	BLAKE, Madge	68	Heart attack (in Pasadena, CA)
1969	+ BOLES, John	73	Heart attack (in San Angelo, TX)
1969	# BOLGER, Robert "Bo"	32	Killed while skydiving (in Oceanside, CA)
1969	BONANOVA, Fortunio	73	Cerebral hemorrhage (in Woodland Hills, CA)
1969	BONUCCI, Alberto	49	Heart attack (in Rome, Italy)
1969	BRETHERTON, Howard	73	Died in San Diego, CA
1969	BUSH, Pauline	83	Pneumonia (in San Diego, CA)
1969	#+ CASTLE, Irene	75	Heart attack (in Eureka Springs, AR)
1969	CIANNELLI, Eduardo	81	Cancer (in Rome, Italy)
1969	+ COLLYER, Bud	61	Died in Greenwich, CT
1969	# COOLEY, Spade	58	Massive heart attack (in Oakland, CA)
1969	CORRIGAN, Lloyd	69	After a long illness (in Woodland Hills, CA)
1969	# COTTON, Billy	68	Heart attack (in London, England)
1969	+ CRANE, Richard	51	Heart attack (in San Fernando Valley, CA)
1969	# CRAWFORD, Howard Marion	55	An overdose of sleeping pills (in London, England)
1969	# D'ARCY, Roy	75	Died in Redlands, CA
1969	DALBY, Amy	81	Died in England
1969	DAVIS, Mildred	68	Heart attack (in Santa Monica, CA)
1969	DeAUBRY, Diane	79	Heart attack (in Santa Monica, CA)
1969	DELGADO, Maria	60	Died in Hollywood, CA
1969	DEUTSCH, Ernst	78	Heart attack (in Berlin, West Germany)
1969	+ DOWLING, Constance	49	Cardiac arrest (in Los Angeles, CA)
1969	# ENGLISH, John W.	66	Died in Hollywood, CA
1969	EVANS, Rex	66	Following surgery (in Glendale, CA)
1969	# FLEMING, Ian (actor)	80	Died in London, England (Do not confuse with the writer)
1969	+ FREEMAN, Young Frank	78	
1969	FREUND, Karl	79	Died in Santa Monica, CA
1969	#+ GARLAND, Judy ☆	47	Accidental drug overdose (in London, England)
1969	+ GOETZ, William	66	Cancer (in Holmby Hills, CA)
1969	#+ GORCEY, Leo	53	Liver ailment (in Oakland, CA)
1969	GRAFF, Wilton	65	Died in Pacific Palisades, CA
1969	GREEN, Kenneth	61	Heart attack while operating heavy equipment (in Hollywood, CA)
1969	# GREEN, Mitzi	48	Cancer (in Huntington Harbor, CA)
1969	# GURIE, Sigrid	58	Pulmonary embolism (in Mexico City, Mexico)
1969	+ HAYES, George "Gabby"	83	Heart ailment (in Burbank, CA)
1969	+ HENIE, Sonja	57	Leukemia (on a private plane bound for Oslo, Norway)
1969	HENNECKE, Clarence R.	74	After a brief illness (in Santa Monica, CA)
1969	HOLLIDAY, Marjorie	49	Brain hemorrhage (in Hollywood, CA)
1969	HUNT, Martita	68	Acute asthmatic bronchitis (in London, England)
1969	#+ HUNTER, Jeffrey	42	Head injuries from a fall at his home (in Van Nuys, CA)
1969	INGRAM, Jack	66	Heart attack (in Canoga Park, CA)
1969	+ INGRAM, Rex	73	Heart attack (in L.A.) — Do not confuse with Rex Ingram (Hitchcock)
1969	# IRWIN, Charles W.	81	Cancer (in Woodland Hills, CA)
1969	ITURBI, Amparo	70	Died in Beverly Hills, CA

Deaths of Movie and Television Personalities — by Year

YEAR	NAME		AGE	CAUSE and/or PLACE OF DEATH
1969	#+ JONES, Brian		25	Drowned while under the influence of liquor and drugs (in London)
1969	JUDELS, Charles		86	Died in Amsterdam, Netherlands
1969	KANE, Eddie		79	Heart attack (in Hollywood, CA)
1969	#+ KARLOFF, Boris		81	Respiratory ailment (in Midhurst, England)
1969	#+ LaROCQUE, Rod		70	Died in Beverly Hills, CA
1969	# LAWTON, Frank		64	Died in London, England
1969	#+ LOCHER, Felix		86	Died in Sherman Oaks, CA
1969	+ LOESSER, Frank		59	Lung cancer (in New York, NY)
1969	+ LOGAN, Ella		56	Cancer (in San Mateo, CA)
1969	LYDECKER, Howard		58	
1969	+ MacLANE, Barton		68	Double pneumonia (in Santa Monica, CA)
1969	MALLESON, Miles		80	Died in London, England
1969	#+ MARCIANO, Rocky		44	Airplane crash (near Des Moines, IA)
1969	# MASCHWITZ, Eric		68	Died in London, England
1969	MASTERS, Ruth		75	After a long illness (in Stamford, CT)
1969	+ McCAREY, Leo	★	70	Emphysema (in Santa Monica, CA)
1969	#+ McHUGH, Jimmy		74	Heart attack (in Beverly Hills, CA)
1969	# McNAUGHTON, Gus		85	Died in Castor, England
1969	+ McNEAR, Howard		63	After a long illness (in San Fernando Valley, CA)
1969	# MEREDYTH, Bess		?	After a long illness (in Woodland Hills, CA)
1969	MEYERS, Sidney		63	Died in New York, NY
1969	# MILLER, Martin		70	Heart attack (in Innsbruck, Austria)
1969	MINNER, Kathryn		77	Heart attack (in Van Nuys, CA)
1969	+ MORGAN, Russ		65	Cerebral hemorrhage (in Las Vegas, NV)
1969	# MORRIS, Johnny		83	Died in Hollywood, CA
1969	MORTON, Charles J.		70	Heart attack
1969	+ MOWBRAY, Alan		72	Heart attack (in Hollywood, CA)
1969	NEWBURG, Frank		83	Died at Motion Picture Country Hospital, Woodland Hills, CA
1969	# O'BRIEN, David "Dave"		57	Heart attack (on Catalina Island, CA)
1969	# OSCAR, Henry		78	Died in London, England
1969	#+ PEARSON, Drew		71	Died in Washington, D.C.
1969	PEPPER, Barbara		53	Coronary thrombosis (in Panorama City, CA)
1969	PORTMAN, Eric		66	Heart ailment (in St. Veep, England)
1969	REEVES, Michael		25	Suicide (sleeping pills) in London, England
1969	RENEVANT, George		74	After a long illness (in Guadalajara, Mexico)
1969	RITTER, Thelma	☆	63	Heart attack (in Forrest Hills, NY)
1969	RYAN, Dick		72	Cancer (in Burbank, CA)
1969	SANGER, Bert		75	Died in Blackpool, England
1969	# SEBRING, Jay		35	Murdered (in Los Angeles, CA)
1969	SETON, Bruce		60	After a long illness (in London, England)
1969	+ SHEA, Donald J. "Shorty"		36	Murdered (in Chatsworth, CA)
1969	SHERMAN, Fred E.		64	After suffering a stroke in 1962 (in Woodland Hills, CA)
1969	SIMON, Abe		56	Died in Queens, NY
1969	#+ SINGLETON, Catherine		65	Died in Fort Worth, TX
1969	SPEAR, Harry		47	Died in Hollywood, CA
1969	STANLEY, Forrest		80	Results of a fall (in Los Angeles, CA)
1969	# STANTON, Will		84	Bronchial pneumonia (in Santa Monica, CA)
1969	# STEPPAT, Ilse		52	Heart attack (in West Berlin, Germany)
1969	# SULLIVAN, Brian		49	Died in Lake Geneva, Switzerland
1969	SWARTHOUT, Gladys		64	Heart disease (at her villa in Florence, Italy)
1969	+ TALMADGE, Natalie		70	Died in Santa Monica, CA
1969	+ TATE, Sharon (Polanski)		26	Murdered by members of the Charles Manson cult (in Bel Air, CA)
1969	#+ TAYLOR, Robert		57	Lung cancer (in Santa Monica, CA)

• New entry. # Original name (Pt. 7). + Interment (Pt. 5).

☆ Oscar nominee, ★ Oscar winner (Pt. 10)

Deaths of Movie and Television Personalities — by Year

YEAR	NAME		AGE	CAUSE and/or PLACE OF DEATH
1969	TONG, Kam		62	*Died in Costa Mesa, CA*
1969	VanEYCK, Peter		55	*Died in Zurich, Switzerland*
1969	VARLEY, Beatrice		73	*Died in England*
1969	# VOGAN, Emmett		76	*Septicemia and pneumonia (in Woodland Hills, CA)*
1969	#+ VonSTERNBERG, Josef ☆		75	*Heart attack (in Hollywood, CA)*
1969	WALBURN, Raymond		81	*After a long illness (in New York, NY)*
1969	WHITE, Ruth		55	*Cancer (in Perth Amboy, NJ)*
1969	WHITNEY, Claire		79	*Died in Sylmar, CA*
1969	# WILLIAMS, Hugh		65	*Heart attack (in London, England)*
1969	+ WILLIAMS, Rhys		76	*After a brief illness (in Santa Monica, CA)*
1969	WILLIAMS, Spencer "Andy"		76	*Kidney ailment (in Los Angeles, CA)*
1969	WING, Dan		46	*Heart attack (in Fresno, CA)*
1969	# WINNINGER, Charles		84	*Died in Palm Springs, CA*
1969	YORK, Chick		83	
1970	AGUGLIA, Mimi		85	*Died in Woodland Hills, CA*
1970	AHERNE, Patrick		69	*Cancer (in Hollywood, CA)*
1970	# Aladdin		57	*Found dead at home of apparent heart attack (in Van Nuys, CA)*
1970	ALLEN, A. A.		?	*Found dead in a San Francisco hotel room*
1970	ALLEN, Dorothy		74	*After a brief illness (in New York, NY)*
1970	# ALLISTER, Claud		76	*Cancer (in Santa Barbara, CA)*
1970	BARRAT, Robert		78	*Died in Hollywood, CA*
1970	+ BEAUDINE, William Sr.		78	*Complications of uremic poisoning (in Canoga Park, CA)*
1970	+ BEGLEY, Ed ★		69	*Heart attack (in Hollywood, CA)*
1970	BLANCHARD, Mari		43	*Cancer (in Woodland Hills, CA)*
1970	BRODINE, Norbert		72	
1970	#+ BURKE, Billie ☆		84	*Died in Los Angeles, CA*
1970	CLARE, Mary		76	*Died in London, England*
1970	CRAIG, Carolyn		37	*Died in Los Angeles, CA*
1970	CURTIS, Willa Pearl		74	*Cerebral arteriosclerosis and diabetes (in Los Angeles, CA)*
1970	+ DARRELL, J. Stevan "Steve"		65	*Brain tumor (in Hollywood, CA)*
1970	# DAW, Evelyn		58	*Died in San Diego, CA*
1970	DIONNE, Marie		35	
1970	DIX, Dorothy		77	*Died in Los Angeles, CA*
1970	#+ DOLLY, Rosie		77	*Heart failure (in New York, NY)*
1970	# DOMINGUEZ, Joe		76	*Died in Woodland Hills, CA*
1970	DUNLAP, Scott		77	*Died in Los Angeles, CA*
1970	EATON, Jay		70	*Heart attack (in Hollywood, CA)*
1970	+ EDENS, Roger ★		64	*Cancer*
1970	EDWARDS, James		58	*Heart attack (in San Diego, CA)*
1970	# ELLIS, Patricia		49	*Cancer (in Kansas City, MO)*
1970	+ FARMER, Frances		55	*Cancer and heart attack (in Indianapolis, IN)*
1970	FLAHERTY, Pat J. Sr.		67	*Heart attack (in New York)*
1970	# FLYNN, Sean		29	*Missing in Cambodia (presumed dead)*
1970	+ FOSTER, Preston		69	*Following a heart attack (in La Jolla, CA)*
1970	FOULGER, Byron K.		69	*Heart condition (in Hollywood, CA)*
1970	FREDERICKS, Charles		50	*Heart attack (in Sherman Oaks, CA)*
1970	GARCIA, Henry		66	*After a long illness (in a hospital in San Antonio, TX)*
1970	# GERSTLE, Frank		54	*Cancer (in Santa Monica, CA)*
1970	GLAUM, Louise		70	*Pneumonia (in Los Angeles, CA)*
1970	GODFREY, Peter		70	*Cancer (in Hollywood, CA)*
1970	+ GRANT, Earl		39	*Automobile accident (near Lordsburg, NM)*
1970	# GRAVET, Fernand		64	*Myocardial infarction (in Paris, France)*

Deaths of Movie and Television Personalities — by Year

YEAR	NAME		AGE	CAUSE and/or PLACE OF DEATH
1970	GRAY, Lawrence		71	Died in Mexico City, Mexico
1970	GREENE, William		43	Heart attack (in Cleveland Heights, OH)
1970	GREENWOOD, Ethel		82	Heart attack (in Hollywood, CA)
1970	HALL, Geraldine		65	Heart attack while hospitalized (in Woodland Hills, CA)
1970	HANLEY, Jimmy		51	Cancer (in England)
1970	#+ HENDRIX, Jimi		27	Inhalation of vomit after barbiturate intoxication (in London, England)
1970	HERNANDEZ, Juan "Juano"		74	Cerebral hemorrhage (in San Juan, Puerto Rico)
1970	HINES, Johnny		73	Heart attack (in Los Angeles, CA)
1970	#+ HOPPER, William		55	Pneumonia (in Palm Springs, CA)
1970	HORNE, David		71	Died in London, England
1970	+ HORTON, Edward Everett		84	Cancer (in Encino, CA)
1970	HUGHES, Joseph Anthony		65	Acute alcohol and barbiturate mixture (in Pasadena, CA)
1970	JARVIS, Al		60	Heart attack (in Newport Beach, CA)
1970	# JENKS, Si		93	Heart disease (in Woodland Hills, CA)
1970	+ JOPLIN, Janis		27	Accidental drug overdose (heroin morphine) in Hollywood, CA
1970	+ KARNS, Roscoe		76	After being hospitalized (in Los Angeles, CA)
1970	# KEEN, Malcolm		82	Died in England
1970	KIBBEE, Milton		73	Died in Simi Valley, CA
1970	KORTNER, Fritz		78	Leukemia (in Munich, Germany)
1970	#+ LEE, Gypsy Rose		56	Cancer (in Los Angeles, CA)
1970	#+ LISTON, Sonny		38	Died in Las Vegas, NV
1970	#+ LOMBARDI, Vince		57	Cancer
1970	#+ LOUISE, Anita		55	Massive stroke (in West Los Angeles, CA)
1970	LULLI, Folco		58	Heart attack (in Rome, Italy)
1970	+ MARCH, Hal		49	Pneumonia and lung cancer (in Los Angeles, CA)
1970	MARLE, Arnold		81	Died in London, England
1970	# MAYO, Edna		76	Died in San Francisco, CA
1970	McGRAIL, Walter B.		70	Died in San Francisco, CA
1970	MODOT, Gaston		82	Died in Le Raincy, France
1970	MONTOYA, Alex P.		62	Congestive heart failure (in Los Angeles, CA)
1970	MOORE, Del		53	Apparent heart attack (at his home in Encino, CA)
1970	# MORRIS, Chester	☆	69	Overdose of barbiturates (in New Hope, PA)
1970	MUNSHIN, Jules		54	Heart attack (in New York, NY)
1970	NAGEL, Conrad		72	Found dead in his apartment (in New York, NY)
1970	NEILL, Richard R.		94	Died at Motion Picture Country Hospital, Woodland Hills, CA
1970	+ NEWMAN, Alfred	★	68	Emphysema and complications (in Hollywood, CA)
1970	# O'DONNELL, Cathy		44	Following a stroke (in Los Angeles, CA)
1970	# PATCH, Wally		82	Died in London, England
1970	PEABODY, Eddie		58	Cerebral thrombosis (in Covington, KY)
1970	+ PICCOLO, Brian		27	Cancer
1970	# PRICE, Nancy		90	Died in Worthing, England
1970	PYNE, Joe		45	Lung cancer (in Los Angeles, CA)
1970	+ RAMBEAU, Marjorie	☆	80	Died in Palm Springs, CA
1970	# REED, Carol		44	Cancer (Do not confuse with Carol Reed, d. 1976)
1970	REMARQUE, Erich Maria		72	Heart collapse (in Locarno, Switzerland)
1970	# RINDT, Jochen		28	Injuries from automobile crash (near Monza, Italy)
1970	RISS, Dan		60	Heart attack (at his home in Hollywood, CA)
1970	ROBLES, Rudy		60	Died in Manila, Philippine Islands
1970	+ RUGGLES, Charles		84	Cancer (in Santa Monica, CA)
1970	SAWYER, Laura		85	Died at a nursing home in a Matawan, NJ
1970	SHIELDS, Arthur		74	Emphysema (in Santa Barbara, CA)
1970	# SHRINER, Herb		51	Killed with his wife in a car crash (in Delray Beach, FL)
1970	SILVERA, Frank		56	Accidentally electrocuted in his home (in Pasadena, CA)

Deaths of Movie and Television Personalities — by Year

YEAR	NAME		AGE	CAUSE and/or PLACE OF DEATH
1970	SINCLAIR, Robert B.		65	Stabbed to death by a burglar (in his California home)
1970	SPITALNY, Phil		80	Cancer (in Miami Beach, FL)
1970	# STARR, Randy		39	Died in Los Angeles, CA
1970	#+ STEVENS, Inger		35	After an overdose of barbiturates (enroute to a Hollywood hospital)
1970	STEWART, Fred		63	Died at the Actors Studio in New York
1970	STRATTON, Chester		57	Died at his home in Los Angeles, CA
1970	SUDLOW, Joan		78	Results of a fall in back of her hillside home (in Laurel Canyon, CA)
1970	SUTTON, Paul		58	Muscular dystrophy (in Ferndale, MI)
1970	# Sylvie		87	Died in Compiegne, France
1970	TRYON, Glenn		70	Died in Los Angeles, CA
1970	#+ TUFTS, Sonny		57	Pneumonia (in Santa Monica, CA)
1970	# VERNON, Dorothy		94	Heart disease (in Grenada Hills, CA)
1970	VERNON, Wally		65	Killed by a hit-and-run driver (at a crosswalk in Van Nuys, CA)
1970	WAYNE, Naunton		69	Died in Surbiton, England
1970	WESTMAN, Nydia		68	Cancer (in Burbank, CA)
1970	#+ WESTMORE, Perc		65	Coronary occlusion
1970	+ WIERE, Sylvester		60	Kidney ailment (in Hidden Hills, CA)
1970	+ WYMARK, Patrick		44	Heart attack in his hotel room (in Melbourne, Australia)
1971	# ALBRIGHT, Hardie		67	Heart failure and pneumonia (in Mission Viejo, CA)
1971	ALLMAN, Duane		24	Motorcycle accident (in Macon, GA)
1971	#+ ANDERSON, G. M. "Broncho Billy"		88	Died in South Pasadena, CA
1971	# ANGELI, Pier		39	Suicide (overdose of barbiturates) in Beverly Hills, CA
1971	ANGOLD, Edit		76	After a long bout with cancer (in Hollywood, CA)
1971	#+ ARMSTRONG, Louis "Satchmo"		71	Heart ailment (in Queens, NY)
1971	# ARNOLD, Jessie		93	Heart attack (in Los Angeles, CA)
1971	BAIRD, Leah		88	Anemia, after a long illness (in Hollywood, CA)
• 1971	BAKER, Elsie		78	Heart attack (in Hollywood, CA)
1971	BIBERMAN, Herbert		71	Bone cancer (in New York, NY)
1971	BLAGOI, George		73	Died in Hollywood, CA
1971	# BOARDMAN, Virginia True		81	Heart attack (in Hollywood, CA)
1971	BOOTH, Helen		?	Died in England
1971	BOYD, Betty		63	
1971	BRADFORD, Marshall		74	Heart attack (in Hollywood, CA)
1971	# BRONSON, Betty		63	Pneumonia (in Pasadena, CA)
1971	BURNS, David		67	Heart attack (while performing on stage in Philadelphia, PA)
1971	+ BYINGTON, Spring ☆		84	Pneumonia (in Hollywood Hills, CA)
1971	# CARMINATI, Tullio		77	Stroke (in Rome, Italy)
1971	CARR, Georgia		46	Stroke (in Los Angeles, CA)
1971	+ CERF, Bennett		73	Heart attack
1971	# CHEATHAM, Jack		76	Heart failure (in La Mirada, CA)
1971	# COMINGORE, Dorothy		58	Cancer (in Stonington, CT)
1971	CONKLIN, Chester		83	Died in Woodland Hills, CA
1971	+ COOPER, Gladys ☆		82	Died in her sleep from pneumonia (in Henley-on-Thames, England)
1971	COSTELLO, William A.		73	Died in San José, CA
1971	# DALE, Charlie		90	Died in a Teaneck, N.J., nursing home
1971	# DALL, John ☆		52	Heart attack and pneumonia (in Beverly Hills, CA)
1971	#+ DANIELS, Bebe		70	Cerebral hemorrhage (in London, England)
1971	DARK, Christopher		51	Heart attack (in Hollywood, CA)
1971	# DARVI, Bella		42	Suicide (opened the gas jets on her apartment stove) in Monaco
1971	DILLON, Josephine		87	Died in Verdugo City, CA
1971	+ DISNEY, Roy		77	Cerebral hemorrhage (in Burbank, CA)
1971	#+ DUEL, Peter		31	Apparent suicide (gunshot) in Hollywood, CA

Deaths of Movie and Television Personalities — by Year

YEAR	NAME		AGE	CAUSE and/or PLACE OF DEATH
1971	# EAMES, Virginia			*(See Virginia True Boardman)*
1971	+ EDWARDS, Cliff "Ukelele Ike"		76	*Died in Hollywood, CA*
1971	# FARLEY, Dot		90	*Died in Woodland Hills, CA*
1971	+ FARRELL, Glenda		66	*Cancer (in New York, NY)*
1971	FEALY, Maude		90	*After being hospitalized (in Woodland Hills, CA)*
1971	FERGUSON, Al		83	*Died in Los Angeles, CA*
1971	#+ Fernandel		67	*Heart attack and lung cancer (in Paris, France)*
1971	FioRITO, Ted		70	*Heart attack (in Scottsdale, AZ)*
1971	+ FLIPPEN, Jay C.		72	*Aneurysm (in Hollywood, CA)*
1971	FUQUA, Charles		60	*Died in New Haven, CT*
1971	+ GILBERT, Billy		77	*Stroke (in North Hollywood, CA)*
1971	GILL, Tom		54	*Died in England*
1971	GLENN, Roy Sr.		56	*Apparent heart attack (in Los Angeles, CA)*
1971	# GOLDIN, Pat		68	*Heart attack (in Los Angeles, CA)*
1971	+ GOMEZ, Thomas	☆	65	*During a long coma after a car accident (in Santa Monica, CA)*
1971	# GOODE, Jack		63	*Acute infectious hepatitis (in New York, NY)*
1971	# GORDON, Robert		76	*Died in Victorville, CA*
1971	GREENE, Victor Hugo		76	*Died in Los Angeles, CA*
1971	# HATTON, Raymond		84	*Heart attack (in Palmdale, CA)*
1971	#+ HEFLIN, Van	★	60	*After a massive stroke while swimming (in Hollywood, CA)*
1971	+ HELTON, Percy		76	*Died in Hollywood, CA*
1971	HENRY, Robert "Buzz"		40	*Motorcycle accident (in Los Angeles, CA)*
1971	#+ HOLMAN, Libby "Peaches"		65	*Died in North Stamford, CT*
1971	HOLMES, Stuart		84	*Ruptured abdominal aortic (in Hollywood, CA)*
1971	# JACKSON, Selmer		82	*Heart disease (in Burbank, CA)*
1971	JARVIS, Robert C.		79	*Died in Bloomsbury, NJ*
1971	#+ JOHNSON, Tor		67	*Heart condition (in San Fernando, CA)*
1971	#+ JONES, Bobby		69	*Died in Atlanta, GA*
1971	# JONES, T. C.		50	*Cancer (in Duarte, CA)*
1971	KEENE, Richard		80	
1971	# KING, Dennis Sr.		73	*Heart condition (in New York, NY)*
1971	KIRKLAND, Muriel		68	*Emphysema and complications (in New York, NY)*
1971	LAVA, William B.		59	*Died in Los Angeles, CA*
• 1971	LENNART, Isobel	☆	56	*Automobile accident*
1971	+ LEWIS, Joe E.		69	*Liver and kidney ailments (in NYC) Do not confuse with the boxer*
1971	#+ LEWIS, Ted		80	*Heart attack (in New York, NY)*
1971	LIGHTNER, Winnie		69	*Heart attack (in Sherman Oaks, CA)*
1971	LLOYD, Gladys		74	*Stroke (in Culver City, CA)*
1971	LLOYD, Harold Jr. "Duke"		39	*Cerebral hemorrhage (in a sanitarium in North Hollywood, CA)*
1971	#+ LLOYD, Harold Sr.		77	*Cancer (in Glendale, CA)*
1971	LOCKWOOD, King		73	*Massive stroke (in Hollywood, CA)*
1971	+ LOMBARDO, Carmen		67	*Cancer (in North Miami, FL)*
1971	LONGDEN, John		70	*Died in London, England*
1971	+ LOWE, Edmund		81	*Lung cancer (in Woodland Hills, CA)*
1971	# LOWERY, Robert		57	*Heart attack (in Hollywood, CA)*
1971	# LUKAS, Paul	★	76	*Heart attack (in Tangier, Morocco)*
1971	#+ LYNN, Diana		45	*Brain hemorrhage (in Los Angeles, CA)*
1971	# MANN, Hank		84	*Died in South Pasadena, CA*
1971	MAYNARD, Kermit		68	*Heart attack (in North Hollywood, CA)*
1971	McGOWAN, Oliver F.		64	*Heart attack in his sleep (in Hollywood, CA)*
1971	McGUINN, Joseph Ford "Joe"		67	*Heart attack one week after surgery (in Hollywood, CA)*
1971	# McHUGH, Matt		76	*Heart attack (in Northridge, CA)*
1971	McMAHON, Horace		65	*Heart ailment*

• New entry. # Original name (Pt. 7). + Interment (Pt. 5).　　　　67　　　　☆ Oscar nominee, ★ Oscar winner (Pt. 10)

Deaths of Movie and Television Personalities — by Year

YEAR	NAME	AGE	CAUSE and/or PLACE OF DEATH
1971	MIDDLETON, Josephine	87	*Died in England*
1971	# MILLER, Flournoy E.	82	*Heart failure (in Hollywood, CA)*
1971	MOODY, Ralph	83	*Heart attack following surgery (in Burbank, CA)*
1971	+ MORRISON, Jim	27	*Heart attack in his bath tub (after heavy drinking) in Paris, France*
1971	#+ MURPHY, Audie	46	*Airplane crash (near Roanoke, VA)*
1971	O'CONNOR, Harry M.	98	*Pneumonia, complicated by cardiac trouble (in Woodland Hills, CA)*
1971	# O'NEAL, Anne	77	*Pancreatitis (in Woodland Hills, CA)*
1971	# PARKER, Cecil	73	*Died in Brighton, England*
1971	+ PENNINGTON, Ann	78	*Died in Manhattan, NY*
1971	PETERS, Werner	51	*Heart attack (in Wiesbaden, West Germany)*
1971	POLLACK, Ben	67	*Suicide (hanged himself in his bathroom) in Palm Springs, CA*
• 1971	+ POST, Edith Sedgwick	28	
1971	# RAFFERTY, Chips	62	*Heart attack (in Sydney, Australia)*
1971	# REDWING, Rodd	66	*Heart attack (while enroute by plane from London to Los Angeles)*
1971	REEVES, Kynaston	78	*Died in London, England*
1971	RENNIE, Michael	61	*Heart attack (in Harrogate, Yorkshire, England)*
1971	RIANO, Renie	71	*After a long illness (in Woodland Hills, CA)*
1971	ROACH, Bert	79	*Died in Los Angeles, CA*
1971	# ROBINSON, Frances	55	*Heart attack (in Hollywood, CA)*
1971	# ROMANOFF, Michael	81	*Heart failure (in Los Angeles, CA)*
1971	# ROSMER, Milton	90	*Died in Chesham, England*
1971	ROWLAND, Adele	88	*Died in Los Angeles, CA*
1971	ROYCE, Ruth	78	*Died in Los Angeles, CA*
1971	SAIS, Marin	81	*Cerebral arteriosclerosis (in Woodland Hills, CA)*
1971	# SANTLEY, Joseph	81	*Died in his West Los Angeles home*
1971	#+ SEDGWICK, Edie	28	*Acute barbitural intoxication (in Santa Barbara, CA)*
1971	SHAW, Denis	49	*Heart attack (in London, England)*
1971	SHEARER, Douglas	71	
1971	SHELTON, George	86	*Burns (in New York, NY)*
1971	+ SKOURAS, Spyros	78	*Died in Mamouroneck, NY*
1971	# Spivy	64	*Died at the Motion Picture Country Home in Woodland Hills, CA*
1971	+ STEINER, Max	83	*Died in Hollywood, CA*
1971	STERN, Bill	64	*Heart attack (in Rye, NY)*
1971	STREET, David	54	*Died in Los Angeles, CA*
1971	# TERRIS, Ellaline	100	*Died in London, England*
• 1971	TERRY, Paul	83	*Cancer (in Rye, NY)*
• 1971	THOMPSON, Bill	58	
1971	TSIANG, H. T.	71	*Died in Hollywood, CA*
1971	ULRIC, Lenore	78	*After several years of hospitalization (in Orangeburg, NY)*
1971	# VICKERS, Martha	46	*After a long illness (in Van Nuys, CA)*
1971	WAKEFIELD, Hugh	83	*Died in London, England*
1971	WALKER, Cheryl	49	*Cancer (in Los Angeles, CA)*
1971	WALKER, Nella	85	*Heart disease (in Los Angeles, CA)*
1971	#+ WALTHALL, Wallace	89	
1971	# WARREN, C. Denier	82	*Died in Torquay, England*
1971	WESTERFIELD, James	59	*Heart attack (in Woodland Hills, CA)*
1971	WILKERSON, Guy	72	*Cancer (in Hollywood, CA)*
1971	# WOLFF, Frank	43	*Suicide (slashed his throat with a safety razor) in Rome, Italy*
1971	WYNN, Nan	55	*Cancer (in Santa Monica, CA)*
1971	YOUNG, Carleton G.	64	*Cancer (in Hollywood, CA)*
1972	ADAMS, William Perry	85	*Died in New York*
1972	# ADAMSON, Victor	82	*Died in Hollywood, CA*

• New entry.   # Original name (Pt. 7).   + Interment (Pt. 5).   68   ☆ Oscar nominee, ★ Oscar winner (Pt. 10)

Deaths of Movie and Television Personalities — by Year

YEAR	NAME		AGE	CAUSE and/or PLACE OF DEATH
1972	ANDREWS, Tod		52	Heart attack (in Beverly Hills, CA)
1972	#+ AUSTIN, Gene		71	Cancer (in Palm Springs, CA)
1972	BAER, Mary		62	Died in Los Angeles, CA
1972	#+ BAGDASARIAN, Ross S.		52	Heart attack (in Beverly Hills, CA)
1972	BARLOW, Howard		80	Heart attack
1972	+ BLOCKER, Dan		43	Pulmonary embolus (in Inglewood, CA)
1972	# BLYTHE, Betty	★	78	Died in Woodland Hills, CA
1972	BOESEN, William		47	
1972	BOND, Lyle		54	Heart attack (in San Diego, CA)
1972	BORDEN, Eugene		75	
1972	BOURNE, William Payne		36	Suicide (gunshot) in Hollywood, CA
1972	+ BOYD, William "Hopalong Cassidy"		77	Parkinson's disease and heart failure (in South Laguna Beach, CA)
1972	BRADY, Pat		57	Heart attack while visiting friends in Green Mountain Falls, CO
1972	# BRITT, Elton		59	Died in Connellsville, PA
1972	BROWN, Harry Joe		78	Apparent heart attack (Do not confuse with Harry Brown, d. 1986)
1972	#+ CABOT, Bruce		68	Lung and throat cancer (in Woodland Hills, CA)
1972	# CAMPBELL, Webster		79	Heart attack (in Liberty, KS)
1972	CANNON, Esma		76	
1972	+ CARROLL, Leo G.		79	Cancer (in Hollywood, CA)
1972	# CHANDLER, Lane		73	Cardiovascular disease (in Hollywood, CA)
1972	#+ CHEVALIER, Maurice	☆	83	Heart attack after kidney surgery (in Paris, France)
1972	CLARKE, Gordon B.		65	After a heart attack (in New York, NY)
1972	#+ CLEMENTE, Roberto		38	Airplane crash (in San Juan, Puerto Rico)
1972	# COREY, Joseph		45	Heart attack (in Los Angeles, CA)
1972	+ CORRELL, Charles J. "Andy"		82	Heart attack (in Chicago, IL)
1972	#+ COWAN, Jerome		74	After a long illness (in Encino, CA)
1972	CRAIG, May		82	Died in Dublin, Ireland
1972	# CUTTING, Dick		59	Kidney disease and uremia (in Woodland Hills, CA)
1972	DALE, Margaret		92	Died in New York, NY
1972	DALTON, Dorothy		78	Died in Scarsdale, NY
1972	# DeWILDE, Brandon	☆	30	After his car skidded on wet pavement and hit a truck (in Denver)
1972	# DIETERLE, William	☆	79	Died in Ottobrunn, West Germany
1972	# DIXON, Denver		82	Heart attack (in Hollywood, CA)
1972	+ DONLEVY, Brian	☆	73	Throat cancer (in Woodland Hills, CA)
1972	DUNCAN, Evelyn		79	Died in Bellflower, CA
1972	# DUNCAN, Kenne		69	Stroke (in Hollywood, CA)
1972	# DUNHAM, Phil		87	Died in Los Angeles, CA
1972	EARLE, Edward		90	Died in Woodland Hills, CA
1972	FELDMAN, Andrea		?	Suicide (jumped from the 14th floor of 51 Fifth Ave, NY)
1972	FLEISCHER, Max		88	Arteriosclerosis (at the MPCH in Woodland Hills, CA)
1972	#+ FRANKLIN, Sidney (director)	☆	79	Heart attack (Do not confuse with silent film actor, d. 1931)
1972	#+ FRIML, Rudolph		92	Brain hemorrhage (at Hollywood Pres. Hosp. in Hollywood, CA)
1972	# GAAL, Franceska		68	Died in New York, NY
1972	GALLIAN, Ketti		58	Died in France
1972	GORDON, Colin		61	Died in Haslemere, England
1972	GOULDING, Alfred		76	Pneumonia (in Hollywood, CA)
1972	GREEN, Nigel		48	Overdose of sleeping pills at his home (in Brighton, England)
1972	GURIN, Ellen		24	Suicide, after a nervous depression (in Manhattan, NY)
1972	HAMMOND, Virginia		78	Died in Washington, D.C.
1972	HANNEN, Nicholas		91	Died in London, England
1972	+ HEATTER, Gabriel		82	Pneumonia (in Miami Beach, FL)
1972	# HEINZ, Gerard		68	Died in England
1972	#+ HOOVER, J. Edgar		77	Heart disease (in Washington, D.C.)

• New entry. # Original name (Pt. 7). + Interment (Pt. 5).   69   ☆ Oscar nominee, ★ Oscar winner (Pt. 10)

Deaths of Movie and Television Personalities — by Year

YEAR	NAME		AGE	CAUSE and/or PLACE OF DEATH
1972	# HOPKINS, Miriam	☆	69	Heart attack (in New York, NY)
1972	HUDSON, Rochelle		57	Found dead at her home (in Palm Desert, CA)
1972	+ IHNAT, Steve		37	Heart attack (in Cannes, France)
1972	+ JACKSON, Mahalia		60	Heart disease (in Evergreen Park, IL)
1972	JEWELL, Isabel		61	Heart attack (in Hollywood, CA)
1972	# JONES, Emrys		57	Heart attack (in Johannesburg, South Africa)
1972	KIKUME, Al		78	Heart attack (in Hollywood, CA)
1972	LANDIS, Jessie Royce		67	Cancer (in Danbury, CT)
1972	+ LANFIELD, Sidney		74	Heart attack (in Marina Del Rey, CA)
1972	LANG, Walter	☆	73	Kidney failure (in Palm Springs, CA)
1972	LANGLEY, Faith		43	Died in New York, NY
1972	# LANSING, Joi		42	Cancer (in Santa Monica, CA)
1972	# LAWFORD, (Lady) May		?	Died in Monterey Park, CA
1972	LEDERMAN, D. Ross		76	Kidney and heart condition (in Hollywood, CA)
1972	LEISEN, Mitchell		74	Coronary complications (in Woodland Hills, CA)
1972	+ LEVANT, Oscar		65	Heart attack (in Beverly Hills, CA)
1972	# LITEL, John		77	Died in Woodland Hills, CA
1972	# LYEL, Viola		71	Died in England
1972	MACK, Russell		79	Stroke (in New York, NY)
1972	#+ MAXWELL, Marilyn		49	High blood pressure and pulmonary ailment (in Beverly Hills, CA)
1972	# McDERMOTT, Hugh		63	Died in London, England
1972	# MOORE, Patti		71	Cancer (in Los Angeles, CA)
1972	MUIR, Gavin		64	After a brief illness (in Fort Lauderdale, FL)
1972	MUNRO, Janet		38	Choked to death while drinking tea (in London, England)
1972	NEAL, Tom		58	Lung cancer (in North Hollywood, CA)
1972	# NEDELL, Bernard		74	Died in Hollywood, CA
1972	NESMITH, Ottola		83	Died in Hollywood, CA
1972	# NIELSEN, Asta		89	Died in Copenhagen, Denmark
1972	#+ OWEN, Reginald		85	Heart attack (in Boise, ID)
1972	PARKER, Lew		64	Cancer (in New York, NY)
1972	#+ PARSONS, Louella (Martin)		91	Arteriosclerosis (in Santa Monica, CA)
1972	# PENA, Julio		60	Heart attack (in Marbella, Spain)
1972	PRAGER, Stanley		55	While on a business trip (in Hollywood, CA)
1972	# PRUD'HOMME, George		71	Brain tumor (in Los Angeles, CA)
1972	PURCELL, Irene		70	Died at her home in Racine, WI
1972	RANK, J. Arthur		83	Died in Winchester, England
1972	+ RICHMAN, Harry		77	Died in North Hollywood, CA
1972	+ ROACH, Hal Jr.		53	Pneumonia (in Santa Monica, CA)
1972	#+ ROBINSON, Jackie		53	Heart disease (in Stamford, CT)
1972	+ RUGGLES, Wesley	☆	82	After a stroke (in Santa Monica, CA)
1972	RUTHERFORD, Margaret	★	80	After breaking a hip in a fall (in Chalfont St. Peter, England)
1972	SANDE, Walter		65	Heart attack (while waiting for cab at O'Hare Airport in Chicago, IL)
1972	SANDERS, George	★	65	Suicide (overdose of barbiturates) in Casteldelfels, Spain
1972	#+ SCALA, Gia		38	Overdose of alcohol and medication (in Hollywood, CA)
1972	SCHULZ, Fritz		75	Died in Zurich, Switzerland
1972	SHELTON, John		54	Heart attack (in Sri Lanka, Ceylon)
1972	SHORT, Antrim		72	Emphysema (in Woodland Hills, CA)
1972	SLOMAN, Edward "Ted"		87	Died in Calabasas Park, CA
1972	TAMIROFF, Akim	☆	72	Died in Palm Springs, CA
1972	TASHLIN, Frank		59	Heart attack (in Beverly Hills, CA)
1972	# THORNDIKE, Russell		87	Died in London, England
1972	TOZERE, Frederic		71	Died in his New York apartment
1972	+ TRAUBEL, Helen		69	Heart attack (in Santa Monica, CA)

• New entry. # Original name (Pt. 7). + Interment (Pt. 5).

☆ Oscar nominee. ★ Oscar winner (Pt. 10)

Deaths of Movie and Television Personalities — by Year

YEAR	NAME	AGE	CAUSE and/or PLACE OF DEATH
1972	ULMER, Edgar G.	68	After a long illness (in Woodland Hills, CA)
1972	WALLINGTON, Jimmy	65	Died in Arlington, VA
1972	# WARWICK, John	67	Heart attack (in Sydney, Australia)
1972	#+ WEEDE, Robert	69	After several months in a hospital
1972	# WHITNEY, Peter	55	Heart attack (in Santa Barbara, CA)
1972	#+ WILSON, Marie	56	Cancer (in Hollywood Hills, CA)
1972	+ WINCHELL, Walter	74	Died in Los Angeles, CA
1972	# WINDSOR, Claire	75	Heart attack (in Los Angeles, CA)
1972	WOODWARD, Robert "Bob"	63	Heart attack (in Hollywood, CA)
1973	# ADRIAN, Max	70	Died in Wilford, England
1973	+ AKEMAN, David "Stringbean"	57	Shot to death by burglars in his home
1973	+ ARMSTRONG, Robert	76	Heart attack (in Santa Monica, CA)
1973	AVERY, Patricia	71	
1973	AVERY, Tol	58	Heart attack (in Los Angeles, CA)
1973	BACON, Walter Scott	82	Heart attack (in Hollywood, CA)
1973	# BANNER, John	62	Intestinal hemorrhage (in Vienna, Austria)
1973	# BARKER, Lex	53	Heart attack (in New York, NY)
1973	+ BAYLIS, Peter	63	
1973	BEAL, Scott	83	Cancer (in Hollywood, CA)
1973	BELL, James	81	
1973	BLACKMER, Sidney	79	Cancer (in New York, NY)
1973	# BLACKTON, Violet	60	
1973	BLAKE, Anne	43	Died in Los Angeles, CA
1973	BORG, Veda Ann	58	Cancer (in Hollywood, CA)
1973	#+ BOYD, Jim	77	
1973	BRADFORD, Lane	50	Following a massive cerebral hemorrhage (in Honolulu, Hawaii)
1973	BRADSHAW, Eunice	80	
1973	BREAKSTON, George P.	53	Died in Paris, France
1973	#+ BROWN, Joe E.	80	Cancer (in Brentwood, CA)
1973	+ BUCK, Pearl S.	80	Pleurisy (in Vermont)
1973	# BUTLER, Royal "Roy"	80	Died in Desert Hot Springs, CA
1973	CANE, Charles	74	Died in Woodland Hills, CA
1973	# CARNEY, Alan	63	Heart attack (at the Hollywood Park racetrack)
1973	# CARR, Mary K.	98	Died in Woodland Hills, CA
1973	CASTLE, Peggy	46	Cirrhosis of the liver and heart condition (in Hollywood, CA)
1973	# CHANEY, Lon Jr.	67	Heart attack, throat cancer, liver ailment (in San Clemente, CA)
1973	+ COOPER, Melville G.	76	Cancer (in Woodland Hills, CA)
1973	COOPER, Merian C.	79	Cancer (in Coronado, CA)
1973	#+ COWARD, Noel ★	73	Heart attack (in Port Maria, Jamaica)
1973	#+ COX, Wally	48	Heart attack (in Los Angeles, CA)
1973	COYNE, Jeanne	50	Died in Los Angeles, CA
1973	#+ CRANE, Norma	42	Cancer (in West Los Angeles, CA)
1973	+ CROCE, Jim	30	Airplane crash (on takeoff from Natchitoches Municipal airport, LA)
1973	DALLIMORE, Maurice	72	Laennec's cirrhosis (in Hollywood, CA)
1973	#+ DARIN, Bobby ☆	37	After heart surgery (in Hollywood, CA)
1973	# DeCORDOVA, Arturo	66	Heart attack (in Mexico City, Mexico)
1973	DeCORSIA, Ted	69	Heart attack (in Encino, CA)
1973	DELGADO, Roger	53	Automobile accident (in Turkey)
1973	DODD, Claire	64	Cancer (in Beverly Hills, CA)
1973	DOYLE, Maxine	58	Cancer (in Studio City, CA)
1973	# DUNN, Michael ☆	39	Congenital chondrodystrophy (dwarfism) in London, England
1973	ELLIS, Robert "Bobby"	40	Kidney failure following an operation (in Los Angeles, CA)

Deaths of Movie and Television Personalities — by Year

YEAR	NAME		AGE	CAUSE and/or PLACE OF DEATH
1973	ESSLER, Fred		77	*Cancer (in Woodland Hills, CA)*
1973	FIELD, Betty		55	*Stroke (in Hyannis, MA)*
1973	#+ FORD, John ★		78	*Cancer (in Palm Desert, CA)*
1973	FOSTER, Dudley		47	*Suicide (hanging) in London, England*
1973	FOXE, Earle A.		84	*Died in Los Angeles, CA*
1973	FRANCIS, Coleman		53	*Arteriosclerosis (in Hollywood, CA)*
1973	#+ FREED, Arthur		78	*Heart attack (in Bel Air, CA)*
1973	FRITSCH, Willy		72	*Heart attack (in Hamburg, Germany)*
1973	+ FULLER, Mary		85	*Massive pulmonary embolism (in Washington, D.C.)*
1973	# GERAY, Steven		75	*Died in Los Angeles, CA*
1973	#+ GOLDWYN, Samuel		91	*Cancer (in Beverly Hills, CA)*
1973	GOMBELL, Minna		80	*Cancer (in Santa Monica, CA)*
1973	#+ GRABLE, Betty		56	*Lung cancer (in Santa Monica, CA)*
1973	# GREAZA, Walter		76	*Died in New York, NY*
1973	GREEN, Abel		72	*Died in New York*
1973	GREENE, Billy M.		76	*Heart attack (in Los Angeles, CA)*
1973	# GREY, Olga		75	*Died in Los Angeles, CA*
1973	HACK, Signe		73	*Leukemia (in Hollywood, CA)*
1973	HACKETT, Lillian		76	*Cerebral hemorrhage (in Hollywood, CA)*
1973	# HAGNEY, Frank S.		79	*Died in Los Angeles, CA*
1973	+ HAINES, William		73	*Cancer (in Santa Monica, CA)*
1973	HARDIE, Russell		69	*Cancer (in Clarence, NY)*
1973	HARRIS, Stacy B.		54	*Heart attack (in Los Angeles, CA)*
1973	HARTMAN, Paul		69	*Heart attack (in Los Angeles, CA)*
1973	# HARVEY, Laurence ☆		45	*Stomach cancer (in London, England)*
1973	HAWKINS, Jack		62	*After cancer surgery (in London, England)*
1973	# HAYAKAWA, Sessue ☆		84	*Cerebral thrombosis and pneumonia (in Tokyo, Japan)*
1973	HENNING, Pat		62	*Died in Miami Beach, FL*
1973	#+ HOLDEN, Fay		77	*Cancer (in Woodland Hills, CA)*
1973	HOLLISTER, Alice		86	*Died in Costa Mesa, CA*
1973	# HOLT, Tim		54	*Brain cancer (in Shawnee, OK)*
1973	HUFF, Louise		77	*Died in New York, NY*
1973	# INGE, William		60	*Suicide (in Hollywood, CA)*
1973	JACOBS, Arthur P.		51	*Massive heart attack in his sleep (in Beverly Hills, CA)*
1973	# JEANS, Ursula		66	*Died near London, England*
1973	+ KELLAWAY, Cecil ☆		79	*Arteriosclerosis (in Beverly Hills, CA)*
1973	# KENNEDY, Douglas		58	*Cancer (in Kailua, Hawaii)*
1973	KLEMPERER, Otto		88	*Died in his sleep*
1973	KORNMAN, Mary		56	*Cancer (in Glendale, CA)*
1973	+ KRUPA, Gene		64	*Heart problems and leukemia (in Yonkers, NY)*
1973	#+ LAKE, Veronica		51	*Acute hepatitis (in Burlington, VT)*
1973	LANDIN, Hope		79	*After a short illness (in Hollywood, CA)*
1973	#+ LANE, Allan "Rocky"		69	*Bone marrow cancer (in Woodland Hills, CA)*
1973	#+ LEE, Bruce		32	*Acute cerebral edema after taking prescribed pain-killer (Hong Kong)*
1973	# LEE, Lila		71	*Stroke (in Saranac Lake, NY)*
1973	# LEONARD, Jack E.		62	*Diabetic complications after open-heart surgery (in New York, NY)*
1973	LORDE, Athena		58	*Cancer (in Van Nuys, CA)*
1973	MacGOWRAN, Jack		54	*After a bout with the flu (in his New York City hotel room)*
1973	MACKIN, Clara		?	*Died in Santa Monica, CA*
1973	+ MACREADY, George		63	*Emphysema (in Los Angeles, CA)*
1973	MAGNANI, Anna ★		64	*Pancreatic cancer (in Rome, Italy)*
1973	MARION, Frances		85	*Died in Los Angeles, CA*
1973	+ MAYNARD, Ken		77	*Died alone in his trailer of malnutrition (in Woodland Hills, CA)*

• New entry. # Original name (Pt. 7). + Interment (Pt. 5).   72   ☆ Oscar nominee, ★ Oscar winner (Pt. 10)

Deaths of Movie and Television Personalities — by Year

YEAR	NAME		AGE	CAUSE and/or PLACE OF DEATH
1973	# McLEOD, Tex		76	Heart attack (in Brighton, England)
1973	McVEY, Patrick		63	After being hospitalized (in New York, NY)
1973	# MELCHIOR, Lauritz		82	After gall bladder operation (in Santa Monica, CA)
1973	# MIDDLETON, Guy		64	Cancer (near London, England)
1973	MILLS, Frank		82	Arteriosclerosis (in Los Angeles, CA)
1973	MISHIMA, Masao		67	Heart ailment (in Tokyo, Japan)
1973	+ MONROE, Vaughn		62	Died in Stuart, FL
1973	MOORE, Cleo		44	Died in Inglewood, CA
1973	+ MORELAND, Mantan		72	Died in Hollywood, CA
1973	MORRISON, George "Pete"		81	Died in Los Angeles, CA
1973	#+ NAISH, J. Carrol ☆		73	Died in La Jolla, CA
1973	# O'SHEA, Michael		67	Heart attack (in Dallas, TX)
1973	+ ORY, Edward "Kid"		?	
1973	# PAXINOU, Katina ★		72	Cancer (in Athens, Greece)
1973	PERCY, Eileen		72	After a long bout with cancer (in Beverly Hills, CA)
1973	PICASSO, Pablo		91	Died in Mougins, France
1973	# PRICE, Dennis		58	Died in Guernsey, Channel Islands
1973	RANDOLPH, Isabel		82	Cancer (in Burbank, CA)
1973	RAYMOND, Cyril		76	Died in England
1973	REED, Donald		70	Died in Los Angeles, CA
1973	+ REID, Carl Benton		79	Died in Studio City, CA
1973	# RICHMOND, Kane		66	Died in Corona Del Mar, CA
1973	#+ ROBINSON, Edward G. ★		79	Cancer (in Hollywood, CA)
1973	# ROOSEVELT, Buddy		75	Died in Meeker, CO
1973	# ROQUEVERT, Noel		81	Heart attack (in Douarmenez, France)
1973	#+ RYAN, Irene		70	Stroke (in Santa Monica, CA)
1973	RYAN, Robert ☆		63	Lymphatic cancer (in New York, NY)
1973	+ SANDS, Diana		39	Cancer (in New York, NY)
1973	SEABURY, Ynez		64	Internal complications (at her home in Sherman Oaks, CA)
1973	SEDGWICK, Josie		75	Stroke (in Santa Monica, CA)
1973	#+ SHERMAN, Allan		48	Respiratory failure caused by emphysema (in Los Angeles, CA)
1973	+ SHUMAN, Roy		49	Heart attack (in New York, NY)
1973	# SIODMAK, Robert ☆		73	Heart attack (in Locarno, Switzerland)
1973	# SMITH, Art		73	Heart attack (in West Babylon, NY)
1973	STOSSEL, Ludwig		89	Died in Beverly Hills, CA
1973	#+ STRANGE, Glenn		74	Cancer (in Burbank, CA)
1973	# STUART, Nick		68	Cancer (in Biloxi, MS)
1973	# SUTHERLAND, Eddie		78	Cancer (in Palm Springs, CA)
1973	TAFT, Sara		80	Heart attack (in Los Angeles, CA)
1973	+ TALMADGE, Constance		75	Pneumonia (in Los Angeles, CA)
1973	TERHUNE, Max "Abibe"		82	Heart attack and stroke (in Cottonwood, AZ)
1973	+ TINDALL, Loren		51	Heart attack (in Hollywood, CA)
1973	TISSIER, Jean		76	Died in Granville, France
1973	+ TRUEX, Ernest		83	Heart attack (in Fallbrook, CA)
1973	VanROOTEN, Luis		66	Died in Chatham, MA
1973	# WESTMORE, Bud		55	Heart attack (in New York, NY)
1973	# WESTMORE, Wally		67	Stroke
1973	WILBUR, Crane		83	Following a stroke (in North Hollywood, CA)
1973	# WILLIAMS, Paul		33	Suicide (sang with "The Temptations")
1973	WOODBRIDGE, George		66	Died in London, England
1973	WORLOCK, Frederick		87	Cerebral ischemia after a long illness (in Woodland Hills, CA)
1974	#+ ABBOTT, Bud		78	Cancer (in Woodland Hills, CA)

• New entry.   # Original name (Pt. 7).   + Interment (Pt. 5).

☆ Oscar nominee, ★ Oscar winner (Pt. 10)

Deaths of Movie and Television Personalities — by Year

YEAR	NAME		AGE	CAUSE and/or PLACE OF DEATH
1974	#+ ACE, Jane		74	Died in Manhattan, NY
1974	ACOSTA, Rudolfo		53	Cancer (in Woodland Hills, CA)
1974	ALLEN, Barbara Jo "Vera Vague"		70	Died in Santa Barbara, CA
1974	#+ ARQUETTE, Cliff		69	Heart attack (in Burbank, CA)
1974	# ASH, Russell		63	Cancer (in Los Angeles, CA)
1974	AUSTIN, Richard		33	Automobile accident (in Hawthorne, CA)
• 1974	# Baby Lawrence		52	Cancer (in New York, NY)
• 1974	# Baby Ruth Jen		54	Cancer (in Culver City, CA)
1974	# BACLANOVA, Olga		78	Died in Vevey, Switzerland
1974	BARD, Ben		81	Cerebral thrombosis (in Los Angeles, CA)
1974	#+ BENNY, Jack		80	Pancreatic cancer (in Holmby Hills, CA)
1974	BERGERE, Ouida		88	Died in New York
1974	# BEST, Edna		74	After a long illness (in Geneva, Switzerland)
1974	BLACKWELL, Carlyle Jr.		61	After a 6-month illness (in Hollywood, CA)
1974	# BLOOM, Bobby		27	Murdered or suicide? (shot) in West Hollywood, CA
1974	+ BRADLEY, Truman		69	Died in Los Angeles, CA
1974	+ BRENNAN, Walter	★	80	Emphysema (in Oxnard, CA)
1974	+ BRITTON, Pamela		51	Brain tumor (in Arlington Heights, IL)
1974	# BROOK, Clive		87	Died in London, England
1974	BROWN, Helen "Mina"		58	Cancer (in Los Angeles, CA)
1974	+ BROWN, Johnny Mack		70	Cardiac condition (in Woodland Hills, CA)
1974	BRUCE, Betty		54	Cancer (in New York, NY)
1974	CAMPEAU, June Harrison		48	Cirrhosis of the liver
1974	CERVI, Gino		72	Pulmonary stroke (in Castiglione Bella Pescaia, Italy)
1974	CLAIRE, Helen		67	Died in Birmingham, AL
1974	COBB, Edmund F.		82	Heart attack (in Woodland Hills, CA)
1974	COLLINGE, Patricia	☆	81	Heart attack (in New York, NY)
1974	+ COMPSON, Betty		77	Died in Glendale, CA
1974	CONWAY, Curt		59	After suffering a massive heart attack (in Los Angeles, CA)
1974	# CORBETT, Mary		47	Died in New York, NY
1974	+ CORNELL, Katharine		81	Pneumonia after a long illness (in Vineyard Haven, MA)
1974	COX, Robert		79	Died in Phoenix, AZ
1974	COY, Walter		68	Died in Los Angeles, CA
1974	+ CRISP, Donald	★	93	After a series of strokes (in Van Nuys, CA)
1974	# CUSTER, Bob		76	Heart attack (in Torrance, CA)
1974	CUTTS, Patricia		48	Found dead at home from an overdose of pills (in London, England)
1974	# DARLING, Candy		25	Cancer and pneumonia (in New York)
1974	DARVAS, Lili		72	Died at her Manhattan home
1974	# DASH, Pauly		55	After cancer treatment (at a hospital in Miami, FL)
1974	# DAVIS, Rufe		66	Died in Torrance, CA
1974	DEARING, Edgar		81	Lung cancer (in Woodland Hills, CA)
1974	DeSICA, Vittorio	☆	73	Following lung cancer surgery (in Neuilly-sur-Seine, France)
1974	#+ DeWOLFE, Billy		67	Cancer and coronary thrombosis (in Los Angeles, CA)
1974	DREW, Ann		83	Died in a Miami nursing home
1974	DUMBRILLE, Douglas		85	Heart attack (in Woodland Hills, CA)
1974	#+ ELLINGTON, Duke		75	Lung cancer and pneumonia (in New York, NY)
1974	#+ ELLIOT, Cass		32	Heart attack, chronic obesity and exhaustion (in London, England)
1974	ELLIS, Robert Reel		82	Cardiac arrest (in Santa Monica, CA)
1974	#+ FLYNN, Joe		49	Accidental drowning (in Beverly Hills, CA)
1974	+ FONTANE, Tony		47	Cancer (in Canoga Park, CA)
1974	FOSTER, Lewis R.		75	Heart attack (in Tehachapi, CA)
1974	FRASER, Harry		84	Died in Pamona, CA
1974	GAUGUIN, Lorraine		50	Died when fire destroyed her home (in Los Angeles, CA)

Deaths of Movie and Television Personalities — by Year

YEAR	NAME	AGE	CAUSE and/or PLACE OF DEATH
1974	# GLENN, Raymond	76	Cardiac arrest in his sleep (in Torrance, CA)
1974	GORDON, Bert	76	After a long bout with cancer (in Duarte, CA)
1974	GORDON, Kitty	96	Died at a nursing home in Brentwood, NY
1974	# HADLEY, Reed	63	Heart attack (in Los Angeles, CA)
1974	HARLAN, Russell B.	70	Died in Newport Beach, CA
1974	# HAROLDE, Ralf	75	Pneumonia (in Santa Monica, CA)
1974	# HARRIS, Morris	59	Died in Syracuse, NY
1974	# HOLDREN, Judd	58	Suicide (gunshot) in West Los Angeles, CA
1974	#+ HUDSON, William	49	Laennec's cirrhosis (in Woodland Hills, CA)
1974	HUGO, Mauritz	65	Heart ailment (in Woodland Hills, CA)
1974	# HULL, Warren	71	Heart failure (in Waterbury, CT)
1974	+ HUNTLEY, Chet	61	Lung cancer (in Bozeman, MT)
1974	#+ HUROK, Sol	85	Apparent heart attack
1974	IMBODEN, David C.	87	Cardiac arrest in his sleep (in Kansas City, MO)
1974	# JAFFE, Carl	71	Died in London, England
1974	# JENKINS, Allen	74	Complications following surgery (in Santa Monica, CA)
1974	# JOHNSON, Chubby	71	Died in Hollywood, CA
1974	JUDGE, Arline	62	Heart attack at her home (in West Hollywood, CA)
1974	KINSOLVING, Lee	36	Died in Palm Beach, FL
1974	KNOX, Teddy	78	Died in England
1974	+ KRUGER, Otto	89	Stroke and cerebral vascular complications (in Woodland Hills, CA)
1974	#+ LANE, Rosemary	60	Diabetes and pulmonary obstruction (in Woodland Hills, CA)
1974	LARGAY, Raymond J. "Ray"	88	Pulmonary embolism (in Woodland Hills, CA)
1974	LEE, Raymond	64	Cancer (in Canoga Park, CA)
1974	# LESLEY, Carole	38	Overdose of barbiturates (in New Barnet, England)
1974	# LITVAK, Anatole ☆	72	Died in Neuilly-sur-Seine, France
1974	+ LONG, Richard	47	Heart ailment (in Los Angeles, CA)
1974	LONTOC, Leon	64	Died in Los Angeles, CA
1974	# LYONS, Cliff "Tex"	71	Died in Los Angeles, CA
1974	# MANN, Billy	?	Died in New York, NY
1974	MARCH, Eve	?	Cancer (in Hollywood, CA)
1974	#+ MASSEY, Ilona	63	Cancer (in Bethesda, MD)
1974	MOJICA, Don José	75	Complications after open-heart surgery (in Lima, Peru)
1974	#+ MOOREHEAD, Agnes ☆	67	Lung cancer (in Rochester, MN)
1974	MORRIS, Glenn	62	Cancer (in Palo Alto, CA)
1974	# MORRISON, James	86	Died in New York, NY
1974	MUMBY, Diana	51	Died in Westlake, CA
1974	# MURPHY, Edna	69	Died in Santa Monica, CA
1974	NAPIER, Russell	64	Died in London, England
1974	# NILSSON, Anna Q.	85	Heart attack (in Hemet, CA)
1974	NYE, Carroll	72	Heart attack and kidney failure (in North Hollywood, CA)
1974	# PAGE, Paul	70	Heart attack (in Hermosa Beach, CA)
1974	PARKER, Albert	87	Died in London, England (Do not confuse with Al Parker, d. 1992)
1974	PLATT, Edward C. "Ed"	58	Heart attack (in Santa Monica, CA)
1974	+ PROHASKA, Janos	52	Airplane crash (in Inyo County, CA)
1974	PRYOR, Roger	72	Heart attack (while visiting in Puerta Vallarta, Mexico)
1974	# RABAGLIATI, Alberto	67	Cerebral thrombosis (in Rome, Italy)
1974	REED, Billy	59	Heart attack (in New York, NY)
1974	REED, Maxwell	55	Died in England
1974	# REGAS, Pedro	92	Heart attack in his sleep (in Hollywood, CA)
1974	# REPP, Stafford	56	Heart attack (in Inglewood, CA)
1974	RICE, Florence	63	Lung cancer (in Honolulu, HI)
1974	RICHARDS, Paul E.	50	Cancer (in Los Angeles, CA)

• New entry. # Original name (Pt. 7). + Interment (Pt. 5).   75   ☆ Oscar nominee, ★ Oscar winner (Pt. 10)

YEAR	NAME	AGE	CAUSE and/or PLACE OF DEATH
1974	#+ RITTER, Tex	67	*Heart attack (in Nashville, TN)*
1974	+ ROBINSON, Edward G. Jr.	40	*Heart attack (found unconscious at his home in West Hollywood, CA)*
1974	# ROSAY, Françoise	82	*Complications after surgery (in Paris, France)*
1974	# ROUNESVILLE, Robert	60	*Heart attack (in New York, NY)*
1974	RUICK, Barbara	41	*Natural causes (in Reno, NV)*
1974	# SAGE, Willard	51	*Died in Sherman Oaks, CA*
1974	SAYRE, Jeffrey	73	*Murdered (shot) in Los Angeles, CA*
1974	SESSIONS, Almira	86	*From injuries after a fall (in Los Angeles, CA)*
1974	# SMITH, Gerald	77	*After a short illness (in Woodland Hills, CA)*
1974	SNEGOFF, Leonid	90	*Heart failure and arteriosclerosis (in Los Angeles, CA)*
1974	# SOMERSET, Pat	77	*Arterial hemorrhage (in Apple Valley, CA)*
1974	ST. CYR, Lillian "Red Wing"	100	*Died in New York, NY*
1974	ST. JOHN, Howard	68	*Heart attack (in New York, NY)*
1974	STRASSBERG, Morris	75	*Died in South Laguna Beach, CA*
1974	STRIKER, Joseph	74	*Died in St. Barnabas Hospital, Livingston, NJ*
1974	#+ SULLIVAN, Ed	72	*Cancer of the esophagus (in New York, NY)*
1974	SULLIVAN, Elliott (Elliot)	66	*Heart attack (while visiting in Los Angeles, CA)*
1974	+ SUTTON, Frank	50	*Heart attack (in Shreveport, LA)*
1974	TABBERT, William	53	*Apparent heart attack*
1974	TAYLOR, Alma	79	*Died in London, England*
1974	# VAGUE, Vera	70	*Died in Santa Barbara, CA*
1974	# VAN, Wally	93	*Died in Englewood, NJ*
1974	VENABLE, Reginald	48	*Heart attack (in Hollywood, Ca.)*
1974	+ WADSWORTH, Henry	72	*Died in New York, NY*
1974	WALDIS, Otto	68	*Heart attack (in Hollywood, CA)*
1974	# WENGRAF, John E.	76	*Died in Santa Barbara, CA*
1974	# WENTWORTH, Martha	84	*Died in Sherman Oaks, CA*
1974	# WHALEN, Michael	72	*Bronchial pneumonia (in Woodland Hills, CA)*
1974	WILCOX, Frank	66	*Died in Granada Hills, CA*
1974	# WING, Red	90	*Cardiac arrest in her sleep (in New York, NY)*
1974	YOUNGSON, Robert	56	*Died at St. Vincent's Hospital in New York*
1974	#+ YURKA, Blanche	87	*Arteriosclerosis (in New York, NY)*
1975	+ ARBUCKLE, Minta Durfee	85	*Congestive heart failure in Woodland Hills, CA*
1975	# ARNO, Sig	80	*Parkinson's disease (in Woodland Hills, CA)*
• 1975	BABOTCHKINE, Boris	71	*Died in Moscow, Russia*
• 1975	BAGDAD, William	54	*Died in Los Angeles, CA*
• 1975	BAHN, Roma	78	*Died in Bonn, Germany*
1975	# BAKER, Bob	73	*Pulmonary embolism (in Prescott, AZ)*
1975	BARAGREY, John	57	*Cerebral hemorrhage (in New York, NY)*
1975	# BARCLAY, Don	83	*Died in Palm Springs, CA*
1975	BARHARD, Lawrence "Slim"	71	*Apparent heart failure*
1975	BELLINI, Laura	73	
1975	#+ BLUE, Ben	73	*Died in Los Angeles, CA*
1975	# BLYDEN, Larry	49	*Automobile accident (while vacationing in Agadir, Morocco)*
1975	BORZAGE, Daniel "Danny"	78	*Died in Los Angeles, CA*
1975	# BRENT, Evelyn	75	*Heart attack (in Los Angeles, CA)*
1975	BROKAW, Charles	77	*Died in New York City*
1975	BROWN, Barbara	68	
1975	BUCHMAN, Sidney	73	*Cancer (in Cannes, France)*
1975	# CALLEIA, Joseph	78	*Died in Malta*
1975	#+ CALVIN, Henry	57	*Died in Dallas, TX*
1975	# CHEFEE, Jack	81	*Died in Hollywood, CA*

Deaths of Movie and Television Personalities — by Year

YEAR	NAME		AGE	CAUSE and/or PLACE OF DEATH
1975	COLMAN, Irene		60	Leukemia (in Santa Monica, CA)
1975	#+ CONTE, Richard		59	Heart attack and stroke (in Los Angeles, CA)
1975	COOPER, Clancy		68	Heart attack while driving his car near his home (in Hollywood, CA)
1975	COURTNEY, Inez		67	Died in Neptune, NJ
1975	CROSBY, Wade		70	After a grand mal seizure aboard a yacht (in Newport Beach, CA)
1975	+ CROSS, Milton		77	Apparent heart attack (in New York, NY)
1975	#+ DALEY, Cass		59	Neck pierced by glass in a fall at home (in Hollywood, CA)
1975	# DEL VAL, Jean		82	Heart attack (in Pacific Palisades, CA)
1975	DELEVANTI, Cyril		88	Lung cancer (in Hollywood, CA)
1975	DIERKES, John		69	Emphysema (in Hollywood, CA)
1975	#+ DORN, Philip		69	Heart attack (in Woodland Hills, CA)
1975	DOYLE, Patricia		60	Cancer (in Los Angeles, CA)
1975	+ DURFEE, Minta (Arbuckle)		85	Congestive heart failure (in Woodland Hills, CA)
1975	#+ FINE, Larry		72	Stroke (in Woodland Hills, CA)
1975	FRECHETTE, Mark		27	Crushed to death by a barbell while in jail
1975	# FRESNAY, Pierre		77	Respiratory ailment (in Neuilly-sur-Seine, France)
1975	#+ FRIZZELL, Lefty		47	After suffering a stroke (in Nashville, TN)
1975	GAINES, Richard H.		70	Heart attack (in North Hollywood, CA)
1975	+ GODOWSKY, Dagmar		78	Died in New York, NY
1975	GRAY, Alexander		73	Died in Los Angeles, CA
1975	# GREEN, Martyn		75	Blood infection (in Hollywood, CA)
1975	GREGSON, John		55	Apparent heart attack on a woodland stroll (in Porlock Weir, Eng.)
1975	# GRIFFIES, Ethel		97	Stroke (in London, England)
1975	GRIFFITH, Edward H.		86	Died in Los Angeles, CA
1975	HANSEN, William		64	After a lengthy illness (in Woodland Hills, CA)
1975	HARTNELL, William "Billy"		67	Died in London, England
1975	#+ HAYWARD, Susan	★	57	Brain tumor (in Beverly Hills, CA)
1975	+ HERRMANN, Bernard		64	Heart attack (in Hollywood, CA)
1975	#+ HOWARD, Moe		77	Lung cancer (in Hollywood, CA)
1975	HUNTER, Ian		75	Died in Northwood, England
1975	# JOHNSON, Kay		71	Died in Waterford, CT
1975	JUSTICE, James Robertson		70	Found dead in bed of apoplexy (in Winchester, Hampshire, England)
1975	KALICH, Jacob		82	Cancer (in Lake Mahopac, NY)
1975	KANE, Joseph		81	Heart attack (in Santa Monica, CA)
1975	KELLERMAN, Annette		87	Died in Southport, Australia
1975	LACHMAN, Harry		88	Heart attack (in Beverly Hills, CA)
1975	LANDIS, Cullen		77	Died in Bloomfield Hills, MI
1975	LARRIMORE, Francine		77	Pneumonia (in New York, NY)
1975	LEE, Rowland V.		84	Apparent heart attack at his home (in Palm Desert, CA)
1975	# LEE, Ruth		79	Cancer (in Woodland Hills, CA)
1975	LETTIERI, Al		47	After being hospitalized (in New York, NY)
1975	LEVEY, Jules		78	Apparent heart attack (on a street in Manhattan, NY)
1975	LOHR, Marie		84	Died in Brighton, England
1975	#+ LOPEZ, Vincent		76	Liver and pancreas failure (in Miami Beach, FL)
1975	# LOSCH, Tilly		70	Cancer (in Manhattan, NY)
1975	LUEDERS, Guenther		69	Cancer (in Duesseldorf, Germany)
1975	+ LUNDIGAN, William "Bill"		61	Lung and heart congestion (in Duarte, CA)
1975	#+ MABLEY, Jackie "Moms"		78	Heart attack (in White Plains, NY)
1975	# MADISON, Noel		77	Died in Fort Lauderdale, FL
1975	#+ MAIN, Marjorie	☆	85	Cancer (in Los Angeles, CA)
1975	#+ MARCH, Fredric	★	77	Cancer (in Los Angeles, CA)
1975	MARK, Michael		85	Heart failure (in Woodland Hills, CA)
1975	MARLOWE, Alan		40	Airplane crash

• New entry.   # Original name (Pt. 7).   + Interment (Pt. 5).   77   ☆ Oscar nominee, ★ Oscar winner (Pt. 10)

Deaths of Movie and Television Personalities — by Year

YEAR	NAME	AGE	CAUSE and/or PLACE OF DEATH
1975	+ MARSHALL, George E.	84	*Pneumonia (in Hollywood, CA)*
1975	# MASON, Buddy	71	*Died in Woodland Hills, CA*
1975	MATHIESON, Muir	64	*Died in Oxford, England*
1975	MATTHEWS, Lester	74	*Died in England*
1975	McFARLAND, Nan	58	*Cancer (in Stamford, CT)*
1975	# McGILL, Moyna	80	
1975	# McGIVER, John	61	*Heart attack (in West Fulton, NY)*
1975	McKINNEY, Florine	62	*Died in Woodland Hills, CA*
1975	# MERANDE, Doro	?	*Following a massive stroke (in Miami Beach, FL)*
1975	MEYER, Torben	90	*Bronchial pneumonia (in Hollywood, CA)*
1975	MORGAN, Ray	?	*Cancer (in Englewood, NJ)*
1975	MORRISON, Chester A.	52	*Died in Portland, OR*
1975	MORTON, Clive	71	*Died in London, England*
1975	MYLONG, John	82	*After a long illness (in Beverly Hills, CA)*
1975	#+ NELSON, Ozzie	69	*Cancer of the liver (in Hollywood, CA)*
1975	# NERVO, Jimmy	85	*Died in London, England*
1975	NIESEN, Gertrude	62	*Died in Kaiser-Permanente Hospital, Glendale, CA*
1975	# OLMSTEAD, Gertrude	70	*Died at her home in Beverly Hills, CA*
1975	#+ PARKS, Larry ☆	60	*Heart attack (in Studio City, CA)*
1975	PASOLINI, Pier Paolo	53	*Murdered (beaten) near Ostia, Italy*
1975	# PATTERSON, Hank	86	*Bronchial pneumonia (in Woodland Hills, CA)*
1975	PEERS, Joan	64	
1975	# PENN, Leonard	68	*Heart attack (in Los Angeles, CA)*
1975	PHILIPS, Mary	74	*Cancer (in Santa Monica, CA)*
1975	PIERSON, Arthur	73	*Died at St. John's Hospital in Santa Monica, CA*
1975	PUGLIA, Frank	83	*Died in South Pasadena, CA*
1975	RAY, Jack	58	*Died in Montclair, CA*
1975	# REYNOLDS, Peter	48	*Died in Australia*
1975	+ ROBERTS, Roy (actor)	69	*Died suddenly after complaining of back pain (in Los Angeles, CA)*
1975	# ROSS, Shirley	62	*Cancer (at a hospital in Menlo Park, CA)*
1975	# RYAN, Sheila	54	*Lung ailment (in Woodland Hills, CA)*
1975	SCHNEIDER, Stanley	45	*Heart attack in his hotel room (in New York, NY)*
1975	+ SERLING, Rod	50	*Complications after heart surgery (in Rochester, NY)*
1975	# SHIELDS, Frank	64	*Died in Los Angeles, CA*
1975	+ SHOSTAKOVICH, Dmitri	68	*After a 9-yr. battle with heart disease*
1975	# SIMON, Michel	80	*Pulmonary embolism (in Bry-sur-Marne, France)*
1975	# SISSLE, Noble	86	*Died in Tampa, FL*
1975	SLATER, John	58	*Heart attack (in London, England)*
1975	SOUSSANIN, Nicholas	66	*Cardiac arrest (in New York, NY)*
1975	+ STEVENS, George Sr. ★	70	*Heart attack (in Lancaster, CA)*
1975	STRAUSS, Robert ☆	61	*Complications following a stroke (in New York, NY)*
1975	# SULLY, Frank	67	*Died in Woodland Hills, CA*
1975	# TETLEY, Walter	60	*Died in Los Angeles, CA*
1975	# THIELE, William J.	85	*Died at the Motion Picture Country Home in Woodland Hills, CA*
1975	# TREACHER, Arthur	81	*Heart ailment (in Manhasset, NY)*
1975	+ TROTTER, John Scott	67	*Cancer (in Los Angeles, CA)*
1975	+ TUCKER, Richard (singer)	60	*Heart attack (Do not confuse with actor, d. 1942)*
1975	URE, Mary ☆	42	*Accidental mix of alcohol and tranquilizers (in London, England)*
1975	VERNO, Jerry	79	*Died in London, England*
1975	WAGNER, Max	73	*Heart attack (in West Los Angeles, CA)*
1975	WALKER, Lillian "Dimples"	87	*Died in Trinidad, West Indies (where she had a home)*
1975	WALKER, Walter "Wally"	74	*Stroke (in Woodland Hills, CA)*
1975	WARDE, Anthony	66	*Died in Hollywood, CA*

Deaths of Movie and Television Personalities — by Year

YEAR	NAME	AGE	CAUSE and/or PLACE OF DEATH
1975	WATTIS, Richard	62	Heart attack (in London, England)
1975	WEED, Leland T.	74	Stroke (in Prescott, AZ)
1975	#+ WELLMAN, William A. ☆	79	Leukemia (in Los Angeles, CA)
1975	# WEST, Billy	82	Heart attack (leaving Hollywood Park racetrack, CA)
1975	WHIPPER, Leigh	97	Cardiac arrest in her sleep (in Harlem, NY)
1975	+ WILLS, Bob	70	Bronchial pneumonia (in Ft. Worth, TX)
1975	# ZIMBALIST, Al	59	Heart attack (in Beverly Hills, CA)
1976	ALLYN, Alyce	?	While hospitalized (in Santa Monica, CA)
1976	ANDERSON, Warner	65	Cancer (in Santa Monica, CA)
1976	#+ ARLEN, Richard	75	Emphysema (in Hollywood, CA)
1976	# BADDELEY, Angela	71	Flu and bronchitis (in London, England)
• 1976	BADIA, Leopold	74	Died in New York, NY
1976	BAKER, Stanley	48	Complications after a lung cancer operation (in Malaga, Spain)
1976	BALLARD, Flo	33	Cardiac arrest from pills and alcohol (in Detroit, MI)
1976	BAXTER, Alan	67	Cancer (in Woodland Hills, CA)
1976	#+ BERKELEY, Busby	80	Heart attack (in Palm Springs, CA)
1976	+ BOSWELL, Connee	68	Stomach cancer (in New York, NY)
1976	# BRENT, Romney	74	Died in Mexico City, Mexico
1976	BROWNE, Lucile	69	Died in Los Angeles, CA
1976	BRUCE, David	60	Heart attack (in Hollywood, CA)
1976	BURTON, Martin	71	Cancer (in Santa Monica, CA)
1976	+ CAMBRIDGE, Godfrey	43	Heart attack (in Burbank, CA)
1976	#+ CASSIDY, Jack	49	Burned to death (in West Hollywood, CA)
1976	CAVENDISH, June	?	Leukemia (in Los Angeles, CA)
1976	#+ COBB, Lee J. ☆	64	Heart attack (in Woodland Hills, CA)
1976	COOPER, Miriam	83	Stroke (in Charlottesville, VA)
1976	# CORRIGAN, Ray "Crash"	74	Heart attack (in Brookings Harbor, OR)
1976	COUGHLIN, Kevin	30	Hit-and-run accident while cleaning his car windshield (in L.A., CA)
1976	CURZON, George	79	Died in London, England
1976	# DARRO, Frankie	58	Heart attack (in Huntington Beach, CA)
1976	DAVIES, Rupert	60	Cancer (in London, England)
1976	# DEVORE, Dorothy	77	Died in Woodland Hills, CA
1976	DEWITT, Alan "Boomie"	52	Heart attack (in Los Angeles, CA)
1976	# DOWLING, Eddie	81	Died in Smithfield, RI
1976	DUNN, Liam	59	Emphysema and other medical complications (in Granada Hills, CA)
1976	EVANS, Edith ☆	88	Heart attack after a brief illness (in Cranbrook, Kent, England)
1976	+ FAITH, Percy	67	Cancer (in Los Angeles, CA)
1976	FIELD, Walter	101	Died in Hollywood, CA
1976	# FITZGERALD, Walter	80	Died in London, England
1976	+ FLAVIN, James	69	Ruptured aorta (in Los Angeles, CA)
1976	#+ FORD, Paul	74	Died in Mineola, NY
1976	# FOSTER, Norman	76	Cancer (in Santa Monica, CA)
1976	FRANKLIN, Alberta	79	Died in Mountain View, CA
1976	# GABIN, Jean	72	Heart attack (in Neuilly-sur-Seine, France)
1976	#+ GOLDWYN, Frances Howard		(See Frances Howard)
1976	GOODLIFFE, Michael	61	Suicide leap while in a hospital (in London, England)
1976	GWYNN, Michael	59	Heart attack (in London, England)
1976	#+ HACKETT, Bobby	61	Died in Chatham, MA
1976	#+ HALOP, Billy	56	Heart attack in his sleep (in Brentwood, CA)
• 1976	HARRIS, Arlene	77	
1976	HENABERY, Joseph E.	88	Died in Woodland Hills, CA
1976	# HILDEBRAND, Hilde	78	Died in Berlin, Germany

Deaths of Movie and Television Personalities — by Year

YEAR	NAME		AGE	CAUSE and/or PLACE OF DEATH
1976	HOWARD, Frances		73	Heart attack after a lengthy illness (in Beverly Hills, CA)
1976	+ HOWE, James Wong		76	Cancer (in West Hollywood, CA)
1976	+ HUGHES, Howard		70	Stroke (on a chartered airplane from Acapulco to Texas)
1976	HUTCHESON, David		71	Died in Scotland
1976	# INESCORT, Frieda		74	Multiple sclerosis (in Woodland Hills, CA)
1976	JAMES, Sidney "Sid"		62	Cerebral hemorrhage (in Sunderland, England)
1976	+ JONES, Anissa "Buffy"		18	Lethal mix of Quaaludes and alcohol (in Oceanside, CA)
1976	KELLOGG, Ray		70	Cancer (in Ontario, CA)
1976	# KNIGHT, Fuzzy		74	Heart attack (in Hollywood, CA)
1976	+ KUHLMAN, Kathryn		63	Pulmonary hypertension after open-heart surgery
1976	+ LANG, Fritz		85	After a long illness (in Hollywood, CA)
1976	LEDERER, Charles		65	After a long illness (at UCLA Med. Ctr., CA)
1976	LEIBERT, Richard "Dick"		73	
1976	LEIGHTON, Margaret	☆	53	Multiple sclerosis (in Chichester, England)
1976	LERNER, Irving		67	Heart attack (in New York, NY)
1976	LESLIE, Gladys		77	Died in Boynton Beach, FL
1976	LIVESEY, Roger		69	Died in Watford, England
1976	# LOWRY, Judith		86	Apparent heart attack (in Greenwich Village, NY)
1976	MACK, Ted		71	
1976	MADDEN, Peter		71	Died in England
1976	MANNHEIM, Lucie		81	Died in Braunlage, West Germany
1976	MARTEL, Alphonse		85	
1976	MARTINI, Nino		72	Heart attack (in Verone, Italy)
1976	MASON, Sydney		70	Heart attack (in Los Angeles, CA)
1976	McBRIDE, Mary Margaret		77	Died in Los Angeles, CA
1976	McCALLUM, Neil		45	Brain hemorrhage (in Reading, England)
1976	# McDEVITT, Ruth		80	Died in Hollywood, CA
1976	#+ MERCER, Johnny		66	After surgery for a brain tumor (in Bel Air, CA)
1976	MERLO, Anthony "Tony"		88	Died in Woodland Hills, CA
1976	# MERVYN, William		64	Died in London, England
1976	MILLER, Ruby		86	Died in Chichester, England
1976	#+ MINEO, Sal	☆	37	Murdered (stabbed to death) in West Hollywood, CA
1976	# NASH, Mary		91	Died in Brentwood, CA
1976	NAUGHTON, Charlie		88	Died in London, England
1976	#+ NICHOLS, Barbara		47	Cancer of the liver (at Cedar Sinai Hospital in Los Angeles, CA)
1976	O'MALLEY, Rex		75	After a long illness (at the Mary Manning Walsh Home, NY)
1976	+ PIATIGORSKY, Gregor		73	Died in Los Angeles, CA
1976	PISU, Mario		66	Cerebral hemorrhage (in Castelli Romani, Italy)
1976	POLANSKI, Goury		83	Cancer (in Hollywood, CA)
1976	# PONS, Lily		77	Pancreatic cancer (in Dallas, TX)
1976	PRICKETT, Maudie		63	Uremic poisoning (in Pasadena, CA)
1976	RADD, Ronald		47	Brain hemorrhage (in Toronto, Canada)
1976	# RAEBURN, Frances		?	Heart failure (in Hollywood, CA)
1976	# RAMSEY-HILL, C. S.		84	Died in Van Nuys, CA
1976	# RASP, Fritz		85	Cancer (in Graefelfing, Germany)
1976	REDFIELD, William "Billy"		49	Respiratory ailment complicated by leukemia (in New York, NY)
1976	REED, Carol	★	69	Heart attack (in London) Do not confuse with Carol Reed, d. 1970
1976	# RICCI, Nora		50	Liver cancer (in Rome, Italy)
1976	RICHTER, Hans		87	Died in Locarno, Switzerland
1976	RIVERO, Julian		84	Died in Hollywood, CA
1976	#+ ROBESON, Paul		77	Cerebral vascular disorder (stroke) in Philadelphia, PA
1976	#+ ROSENBLOOM, "Slapsie" Maxie		71	Paget's disease (in South Pasadena, CA)
1976	# ROSS, Lenny		71	Cancer (in Los Angeles, CA)

• New entry. # Original name (Pt. 7). + Interment (Pt. 5).   80   ☆ Oscar nominee, ★ Oscar winner (Pt. 10)

Deaths of Movie and Television Personalities — by Year

YEAR	NAME	AGE	CAUSE and/or PLACE OF DEATH
1976	# ROTH, Gene	73	*Struck by a car (in Los Angeles, CA)*
1976	RUSKIN, Shimen	69	*Cancer (in Los Angeles, CA)*
1976	+ RUSSELL, Rosalind (Brisson) ☆	65	*Cancer complicated by arthritis (in Beverly Hills, CA)*
1976	SCOTT, Mabel Julienne	82	*Died at the Burlington Convalescent Hospital in Los Angeles, CA*
1976	SERVAIS, Jean	65	*Heart failure following surgery (in Paris, France)*
1976	SHELTON, Don	64	*Died in Los Angeles, CA*
1976	SHUTTA, Ethel	79	*Died at St. Clare's Hospital in New York*
1976	SIEBER, Rudolf	77	*Following a long illness*
1976	SILVA, David	58	*Thrombosis (in Mexico City, Mexico)*
1976	SILVERS, Sid	72	*Died in Los Angeles, CA*
1976	SIM, Alastair	75	*Cancer (in London, England)*
1976	# SKELTON, Georgia	54	*Suicide (gunshot) in Rancho Mirage, CA*
1976	# STUEWE, Hans	75	*Died in Berlin, Germany*
1976	# SUNBEAUTY, Olga	78	*Died in Italy*
1976	TANNEN, William	65	*After a 2-month hospitalization (in Woodland Hills, CA)*
1976	TEAL, Ray	74	*After a long illness (in Santa Monica, CA)*
1976	THOR, Larry	58	*Aneurysm (in Santa Monica, CA)*
1976	+ THORNDIKE, Sybil	93	*Heart attack (in London, England)*
1976	# VARCONI, Victor	85	*Heart attack (in Santa Barbara, CA)*
1976	# VESOTA, Bruno	54	*Heart attack (in Culver City, CA)*
1976	VISCONTI, Luchino	69	*Influenza/cardiac ailment (in Rome, Italy)*
1976	# VYE, Murvyn	62	*Heart attack (while vacationing in Pompano Beach, FL)*
1976	WELCH, Niles	81	*Died in Laguna Nigel, CA*
1976	+ ZUKOR, Adolph	103	*Died in Hollywood, CA*
1977	ABBOTT, Merriel	84	*Died in Chicago, IL*
1977	ADAMS, Stanley	62	*Suicide (gunshot) in Santa Monica, CA*
1977	ADDINSELL, Richard	73	*Died in London, England*
1977	+ ANDERSON, Eddie "Rochester"	71	*Heart attack (in Santa Barbara, CA)*
1977	# ASHLEY, Sylvia	73	*Cancer (in Los Angeles, CA)*
1977	ASTOR, Gertrude	90	*Stroke (in Woodland Hills, CA)*
1977	BACHELET, Jean	82	*Died in Cannes, France*
1977	BALDWIN, Walter	89	*Pneumonia (in Santa Monica, CA)*
1977	BARDETTE, Trevor	75	*Died in Los Angeles, CA*
1977	# BARNETT, Vince	75	*Heart ailment (in Encino, CA)*
1977	BARRETT, Edith	64	*Heart attack at a nursing home (in Albuquerque, NM)*
1977	BIBERMAN, Abner	68	*Died in San Diego, CA*
1977	# BOLES, Jim	63	*Apparent heart attack (in Sherman Oaks, CA)*
1977	BOUCHEY, Willis "Bill"	82	*Died in Burbank, CA*
1977	#+ BOYD, Stephen	48	*Heart attack (in Northridge, CA)*
1977	BREEDEN, John Norton	73	*Died in San Francisco, CA*
1977	BRENNEN, Claire	43	*Cancer (in Hollywood, CA)*
1977	# BROOKS, Geraldine	52	*Cancer (in Riverhead, NY)*
1977	+ CABOT, Sebastian	59	*Stroke (in Victoria, B.C., Canada)*
1977	#+ CALLAS, Maria	53	*Heart attack (in Paris, France)*
1977	+ CARLSON, Richard	65	*Cerebral hemorrhage (in Encino, CA)*
1977	CARSON, Charles	91	*Died in London, England*
1977	# CASTLE, William	63	*Heart attack (in Beverly Hills, CA)*
1977	#+ CHAPLIN, Charlie ☆	88	*Bronchitis (in Corsier-sur-vevey, Switzerland)*
1977	CHAPMAN, Edward	76	*Heart attack (in Brighton, England)*
1977	CHITTY, Erik	70	*Died in London, England*
1977	CLOUZOT, Henri Georges	70	*Heart attack (in Paris, France)*
1977	CONDON, Jackie	59	*Cancer (in Inglewood, CA)*

YEAR	NAME		AGE	CAUSE and/or PLACE OF DEATH
1977	# CORTEZ, Ricardo		77	*Died in New York, NY*
1977	#+ CRAWFORD, Joan	★	71	*Cancer and acute coronary occlusion (in New York, NY)*
1977	#+ CROSBY, Bing	★	73	*Heart attack (in Madrid, Spain)*
1977	DAVENPORT, Dorothy		81	*Died in Woodland Hills, CA*
1977	#+ DAVES, Delmar		73	*Died in La Jolla, CA*
1977	DECKERS, Eugene		60	
1977	DeHAVEN, Carter Sr.		90	*Died in Woodland Hills, CA*
1977	DELL, Claudia		67	*Died in Hollywood, CA*
1977	#+ DEVINE, Andy		71	*Leukemia and diabetic problems (in Orange, CA)*
1977	DUGGAN, Jan		95	*Died in Anaheim, CA*
1977	FERGUSON, Helen		76	*Died in Clearwater, FL*
1977	#+ FINCH, Peter	★	60	*Heart attack (in Beverly Hills, CA)*
1977	#+ FORD, Mary		52	*Complications of diabetes and pneumonia (in Arcadia, CA)*
1977	+ FOY, Bryon		82	*Following a series of heart attacks (in Los Angeles, CA)*
1977	# FRANCEN, Victor		89	*Died in Aix-en-Provence, France*
1977	FREND, Charles		68	*Cancer (in London, England)*
1977	GARBER, Jan		82	*Died in Shreveport, LA*
1977	GARDNER, Jack		77	*After a short illness (in Houston, TX)*
1977	+ GARNER, Erroll		53	*Emphysema and heart attack (in Los Angeles, CA)*
1977	GARNETT, Tay		83	*Leukemia*
1977	GATESON, Marjorie		86	*Pneumonia (in New York, NY)*
1977	GERING, Marion		73	*Died in New York, NY*
1977	# GIBSON, Helen		85	*Stroke and heart attack (in Roseburg, OR)*
1977	GRAVES, Ralph		77	*Heart attack (in Santa Barbara, CA)*
1977	GRIES, Tom		54	*Heart attack (in Santa Monica, CA)*
1977	# HAGEN, Jean	☆	54	*Throat cancer (in Woodland Hills, CA)*
1977	+ HAWKS, Howard	☆	81	*Died in his sleep following a fall and concussion (in Hollywood, CA)*
1977	# HAYES, Allison		47	*Blood poisoning (in La Jolla, CA)*
1977	# HAYES, Margaret		61	*Cancer complicated by hepatitis (in Miami Beach, FL)*
1977	HULL, Henry		86	*Died in Cornwall, England*
1977	HYAMS, Leila		72	*After a brief illness (in Bel Air, CA)*
1977	HYLAND, Diana		41	*Cancer (in Westwood, CA)*
1977	+ JOHNSON, Nunnally		80	*Pneumonia (in Los Angeles, CA)*
1977	LEWIS, Forrest		77	*Heart attack (in Burbank, CA)*
1977	LOCHARY, David		30	*Drug overdose (in New York, NY)*
1977	#+ LOMBARDO, Guy		75	*Respiratory, kidney and heart failure (in Houston, TX)*
1977	+ LUNT, Alfred	☆	84	*Cancer (in Chicago, IL)*
1977	MANN, George Kline		72	*Cancer (in Santa Monica, CA)*
1977	MARLOWE, Nora		62	*After a long illness (in Los Angeles, CA)*
1977	MARMONT, Percy		93	*Died in Denville Hall, England*
1977	#+ MARX, "Groucho"		86	*Pneumonia (in West Hollywood, CA)*
1977	#+ MARX, "Gummo"		84	*Lung cancer (in Palm Springs, CA)*
1977	+ MATTHEWS, Dorothy		54	*Stroke (in Los Angeles, CA)*
1977	McGANN, William H.		84	*Heart attack in his sleep (in Woodland Hills, CA)*
1977	McGINN, Walter		38	*After his car crashed into a parked truck (in Los Angeles, CA)*
1977	# McGOWAN, J. P. "Jack"		81	*(Screenplay writer) Died in Manhattan, NY*
1977	MELL, Joseph "Joe"		62	*Heart condition (in Los Angeles, CA)*
1977	MERRITT, George		86	*Died in London, England*
1977	# MIDDLETON, Robert		66	*Heart failure (in Encino, CA)*
1977	MOORE, Carlyle Jr.		67	*Died in Sun Valley, ID*
1977	# MOSTEL, Zero		62	*Cardiac disorder (in Philadelphia, PA)*
1977	+ MUSTIN, Burt		94	*Died in Glendale, CA*
1977	NICHOLLS, Anthony		69	*Died in London, England*

Deaths of Movie and Television Personalities — by Year

YEAR	NAME	AGE	CAUSE and/or PLACE OF DEATH
1977	PELT, Timothy "Tim"	39	Automobile accident (in Pacific Palisades, CA)
1977	PERKINS, Voltaire	80	Apparent heart attack (in Los Angeles, CA)
1977	# PETROVA, Olga	91	Died in Clearwater, FL
1977	# POTTER, H. C.	73	After a brief illness (in New York, NY)
1977	#+ PRESLEY, Elvis	42	Cardiac arrhythmia (possibly due to drug abuse) in Memphis, TN
1977	# PRINTEMPS, Yvonne	81	Complications after fracturing her thighbone (in Paris, France)
1977	#+ PRINZE, Freddie	22	Suicide (gunshot) in Hollywood, CA
1977	RATTIGAN, Terence	66	Bone marrow cancer (in London, England)
1977	# RAY, Ted	67	Died in London, England
1977	#+ REED, Alan	69	After a long illness (in St. Vincent's hosp., West Los Angeles, CA)
1977	RISSONI, Giuditta	80	Died in Rome, Italy
1977	#+ RITCHARD, Cyril	80	Cardiac arrest (in Chicago, IL)
1977	RIVERS, Victor	29	Injuries from performing a stunt (in Los Angeles, CA)
1977	ROSSELLINI, Roberto	71	Heart attack (in Rome, Italy)
1977	# SHINDO, Eitaro	78	Heart failure (in Tokyo, Japan)
1977	# STARK, Pauline	76	Died in Santa Monica, CA
1977	# STEVENS, Onslow	74	Murdered (while in a convalescent home) in Van Nuys, CA
1977	STEWART, Sophie	69	Died in London, England
1977	#+ STOKOWSKI, Leopold	95	Coronary attack (in Nether Wallop, Hampshire, England)
1977	TANAKA, Kinuyo	67	Cerebral tumor (in Tokyo, Japan)
1977	TETZEL, Joan	56	Cancer (in Sussex, England)
1977	THURSBY, David	88	Died in Hollywood, CA
1977	TOURNEUR, Jacques	73	Died in Bergerac, France
1977	TRUMAN, Ralph	77	Died in Ipswich, England
1977	VALLIN, Richard "Rick"	57	Died in Los Angeles, CA
1977	VanSICKEL, Dale	69	After a lengthy illness (at his home in Newport Beach, CA)
1977	+ VanZANT, Ronnie	28	Airplane crash (in Mississippi)
1977	# VIDOR, Florence	82	Died in Pacific Palisades, CA
1977	+ WALLER, Eddy C.	88	Stroke (in Los Angeles, CA)
1977	+ WATERS, Ethel ☆	80	Heart ailment (in Chatsworth, CA)
1977	WILCOX, Herbert	85	Following a long illness (in London, England)
1978	+ ACKER, Jean (Valentino)	85	Died in Los Angeles, CA
1978	ADAMS, Claire	78	Died in Melbourne, Australia
1978	ADLER, Jay	82	After a long illness (in Woodland Hills, CA)
1978	AHN, Philip	66	Lung cancer (in Los Angeles, CA)
1978	+ ALLWYN, Astrid	68	Cancer (in Los Angeles, CA)
• 1978	AMES, Vic	52	Automobile accident (in Nashville, TN)
1978	BACCHIOCCHI, Norman	34	
• 1978	BACQUE, Jean	54	Died in France
1978	BAILEY, Bill	66	Died in Phila. PA (Do not confuse with any of the 3 William Bailey's)
1978	BARCENA, Catalina	82	Died in Madrid, Spain
1978	#+ BARRIE, Wendy	65	After a long illness (in Englewood, NJ)
1978	BATES, Michael	57	Cancer (in Cambridge, England)
1978	#+ BERGEN, Edgar	75	Heart attack (in Las Vegas, NV)
1978	BETZ, Carl	56	Lung cancer (in Los Angeles, CA)
1978	BINYON, Claude	72	Died in Glendale, CA
1978	# BLAKE, Marie	81	Died in Woodland Hills, CA
1978	BOHN, Merritt F.	73	Pneumonia following a stroke (in Torrence, CA)
1978	BOND, Johnny	63	Died in Burbank, CA
1978	BONOMO, Joe	75	Kidney ailment and pneumonia (in Hollywood, CA)
1978	BOURBON, Diana	77	Cancer (in Los Angeles, CA)
1978	+ BOYER, Charles ☆	78	Suicide (overdose of Seconal 2 days after his wife died) in AZ

Deaths of Movie and Television Personalities — by Year

YEAR	NAME		AGE	CAUSE and/or PLACE OF DEATH
1978	BROWN, Barry		27	Suicide at home (self-inflicted wounds) in Silver Lake, CA
1978	BRYANT, Marie		58	Cancer (in Los Angeles, CA)
1978	BUSHMAN, Ralph		74	Respiratory failure (in Los Angeles, CA)
1978	+ CARTER, Maybelle		69	Died in Nickelsville, VA
1978	CAZALE, John		42	Cancer (in New York, NY)
1978	CHASE, Ilka		72	Internal hemorrhage from a fall (in Mexico City, Mexico)
1978	CLARK, Roger W.		69	Stroke (in Los Angeles, CA)
1978	COMPTON, Fay		84	Died in London, England
1978	COOGAN, Robert		53	Died in Los Angeles, CA
1978	+ CRANE, Bob		48	Murdered (skull crushed by a blow while sleeping) in Scottsdale, AZ
• 1978	+ CULLY, Zara		86	Died in Los Angeles, CA
1978	+ DAILEY, Dan	☆	62	Anemia (in Hollywood, CA)
1978	DALY, James		59	Heart attack (in Nyack, NY) — Do not confuse with James L. Daly
1978	# DAUPHIN, Claude		75	Intestinal occlusion (in Paris, France)
1978	# DAVID, Thayer		51	Heart attack (in New York, NY)
1978	DAY, Josette		63	Died in Paris, France
1978	DOUGLAS, Tom		82	Heart attack (in Cuernavaca, Mexico)
1978	DOWNS, Cathy		52	Died in Los Angeles, CA
1978	DRURY, Norma		?	
1978	#+ EILERS, Sally		69	Heart attack (in Woodland Hills, CA)
1978	+ ETTING, Ruth		81	After a long illness (in Colorado Springs, CO)
1978	# FENTON, Leslie C.		76	Died in Montecito, CA
1978	FERGUSON, Frank		78	Cancer (in Los Angeles, CA)
1978	#+ FIELDS, Totie		48	Apparent heart failure (in Las Vegas, NV)
1978	+ FONTAINE, Frank		58	Heart attack (in Spokane, WA)
1978	GAGE, Ben		62	Died in Los Angeles, CA
1978	GARMES, Lee	★	80	Died in Los Angeles, CA
1978	#+ GEER, Will		76	Respiratory arrest (in Los Angeles, CA)
1978	+ GELLER, Bruce		47	Airplane crash (in Los Angeles, CA)
1978	GENN, Leo	☆	72	Heart attack (in London, England)
1978	GILBERT, Lou		69	Apparent heart attack (in Reseda, CA)
1978	GIRDLER, William		30	Helicopter crash (in Santa Cruz, Philippine Islands)
1978	GIVNEY, Kathryn		80	Died in Hollywood, CA
• 1978	GOFF, Norris "Abner"		72	Stroke
1978	GRAVERS, Steve		56	Lung cancer (in Studio City, CA)
1978	GREENE, Angela		55	Stroke (in Los Angeles, CA)
1978	# GREENWOOD, Charlotte		84	Died in Beverly Hills, CA
1978	# HANDWORTH, Octavia		90	Died in Hemet, CA
1978	HARRINGTON, Kate		74	Following a stroke (in New York, NY)
1978	# HASSE, O. E.		75	Died in a hospital (in West Berlin, Germany)
1978	HENDERSON, Douglas "Doug"		58	Suicide (carbon monoxide) in Studio City, CA
1978	HOMOLKA, Oscar	☆	79	Died in Sussex, England
1978	# HORVATH, Charles		57	Died in Woodland Hills, CA
1978	HULBERT, Jack		69	Died in London, England
1978	JOLLEY, L. Stanford		78	Died in Woodland Hills, CA
1978	L'HERBIER, Marcel		91	Cardiac arrest in his sleep (in Paris, France)
1978	# LINGEN, Theo		75	Died in Vienna, Austria
1978	# LOCKHART, Kathleen		83	After a long illness (in Los Angeles, CA)
1978	MacDONALD, Wallace		87	Died in Santa Barbara, CA
1978	MALONEY, James J. "Jim"		63	Died in Los Angeles, CA
1978	MARDEN, Adrienne		69	Massive heart attack (in Los Angeles, CA)
1978	# MARLY, Florence		59	Heart attack (in Glendale, CA)
1978	MATRAY, Ernst		87	Heart attack (in Los Angeles, CA)

Deaths of Movie and Television Personalities — by Year

YEAR	NAME		AGE	CAUSE and/or PLACE OF DEATH
1978	#+ McCOY, Tim		86	Heart attack (in Fort Huachuca, AZ)
1978	McGRATH, Paul		74	Cardiac arrest in his sleep (in London, England)
1978	McGUIRE, Kathryn		73	Pancreatic cancer (in Los Angeles, CA)
1978	McKINNEY, Mira		?	
1978	McLAGLEN, Clifford		86	Undisclosed causes (in Huddersfield, Yorkshire, England)
1978	McNAMARA, Maggie		48	Suicide (overdose of pills) in New York, NY
1978	# MILLER, Lorraine		49	Died in Los Angeles, CA
1978	MONTGOMERY, Goodee		72	After a brief illness (in Hollywood, CA)
1978	MOON, Keith		31	Found dead from an overdose of heminevrin (in London, England)
1978	# MORELL, André		69	After a long illness (in London, England)
1978	Morris (the original TV cat)		17	
1978	MORRISON, Ann		62	Cancer (in Woodland Hills, CA)
1978	MURPHY, Maurice		65	Died in Los Angeles, CA
1978	MYRTILE, Odette		80	Stroke (at a hospital in Doylestown, PA)
1978	# NEWMAN, Scott		28	Apparent accidental overdose of Valium and alcohol
1978	# NOBLE, Ray		70	Cancer (in London, England)
1978	#+ OAKIE, Jack	☆	74	Aortic aneurysm (in Northridge, CA)
1978	+ PATERSON, Pat		67	Cancer (in Phoenix, AZ)
1978	+ PERFECT, Rose		82	Died in Hollywood, CA
1978	# PHIPPS, Sally		67	Died at Long Island College Hospital, NY
1978	PICKLES, Wilfrid		73	Died in Brighton, England
1978	# POLLARD, Daphne		87	Died in Los Angeles, CA
1978	PORTER, Dick		45	Heart attack (in Sedalia, MO)
1978	PRETTY, Arline		84	Died in Hollywood, CA
1978	+ PRIMA, Louis		66	Pneumonia (in New Orleans, LA)
1978	RICHARDS, Cully		68	Cancer (in Los Angeles, CA)
1978	ROBERTS, Lenore		47	Cancer (in Los Angeles, CA)
1978	#+ ROBERTS, Lynne (Mary Hart)		58	An intracranial hemorrhage
1978	ROBSON, Mark		64	Heart attack (in London, England)
1978	SANO, Shuji		66	Died in Japan
1978	# SCHOENHALS, Albrecht		90	Died in Baden-Baden, West Germany
1978	SHAW, Robert	☆	53	Heart attack (near Tourmakeady, Ireland)
1978	# SHAW, Susan		49	Died in Middlesex, England
1978	#+ SHAY, Dorothy		57	Following a massive stroke (in Santa Monica, CA)
1978	SHOEMAKER, Ann		87	Cancer (in Hollywood, CA)
1978	SMITH, Queenie		70	Cancer (in Burbank, CA)
1978	# STANTON, Harry		76	Heart disease (in Los Angeles, CA)
1978	# STUART, John		81	Cardiac arrest in his sleep (in London, England)
1978	SWENSON, Karl		70	Apparent heart attack (while visiting relatives in Torrington, CT)
1978	THORDSEN, Kelly		61	Cancer (in Sun Valley, CA)
1978	TOZZI, Fausto		57	Emphysema (in Rome, Italy)
1978	# TREVOR, Austin		80	Died in London, England
1978	#+ TUNNEY, Gene		80	Blood poisoning (in Greenwich, CT)
1978	UNSWORTH, Geoffrey	★	64	Heart attack (in London, England)
1978	VENUTI, Joe		81	Died in Seattle, WA
1978	# WALLACE, Regina		86	Stroke (in Englewood, N.J.)
1978	+ WARNER, Jack L.		86	Pulmonary edema (in Los Angeles, CA)
1978	WILLS, Chill	☆	75	Cancer (in Encino, CA)
1978	WONG, Joe		75	Heart condition (in Los Angeles, CA)
1978	#+ WOOD, Ed		54	Heart attack brought on by acute alcoholism (in Los Angeles, CA)
1978	WOOD, Peggy	☆	86	Cerebral hemorrhage (in Stamford, CT)
1978	#+ YOUNG, Gig	★	64	Suicide (gunshot) after shooting his 5th wife (in New York, NY)

Deaths of Movie and Television Personalities — by Year

YEAR	NAME	AGE	CAUSE and/or PLACE OF DEATH
1979	ADAM, Ronald	83	*Died in London, England*
1979	# ADLER, Celia	88	*Died in The Bronx, NY*
1979	ALLBRITTON, Louise	58	*Cancer*
1979	ARVAN, Jan	66	*Heart attack (in Los Angeles, CA)*
1979	ARZNER, Dorothy	82	*Pneumonia (in La Quinta, CA)*
1979	# AYLMER, Felix	90	*Died in a nursing home in Sussex, England*
1979	# BLETCHER, Billy	84	*After a long illness (in Los Angeles, CA)*
1979	#+ BLONDELL, Joan ☆	73	*Leukemia (in Santa Monica, CA)*
1979	BOURNEUF, Philip	71	*Found dead in his Santa Monica apartment*
1979	BOWMAN, Lee	64	*Heart attack (in Brentwood, CA)*
1979	# BRENT, George	75	*Emphysema (in Solana Beach, CA)*
1979	#+ BUCHANAN, Edgar	76	*After brain tumor surgery (in Palm Desert, CA)*
1979	# BUTLER, David	84	*Ruptured diverticulum, peritonitis and heart failure (in Arcadia, CA)*
1979	BUTTERWORTH, Peter	60	*Heart attack (in Coventry, England)*
1979	CARLETON, Claire	66	*Cancer (in Northridge, CA)*
1979	# CARR, Joe "Fingers"	69	*Automobile accident (in Camarillo, CA)*
1979	+ CARROLL, John	71	*Leukemia (in Hollywood, CA)*
1979	CARSON, Robert	69	*Stroke (in Atascadero, CA)*
1979	+ CASSIDY, Ted "Lurch"	46	*During heart surgery (in Los Angeles, CA)*
1979	CHANDLER, Joan	55	*Died in New York, NY*
1979	+ CHARLES, Lewis	73	*Lung cancer (in Los Angeles, CA)*
1979	COSTELLO, Delores	73	*Emphysema (in Fallbrook, CA)*
1979	CRAIG, Edith	71	*After a long illness (Do not confuse with the English actress)*
1979	# CROCKETT, Dick	63	*Cancer (in Los Angeles, CA)*
1979	# CROMWELL, John	91	*Pulmonary embolism (in Santa Barbara, CA)*
1979	DAVIS, Karl "Killer"	72	*Died in Chicago, IL*
1979	DeHAVEN, Carter Jr.	68	*After a brief illness (in Encino, CA)*
1979	DIGNAM, Basil	74	*Died in England*
1979	DIONNE, Oliva	71	*Died in North Bay, Ontario, Canada*
1979	DONALD, Peter	60	*Cancer of the stomach and throat*
1979	#+ DVORAK, Ann	67	*Died in Honolulu, Hawaii*
1979	EBERLE, Ray	60	*Heart attack (in Douglasville, GA)*
1979	+ FIEDLER, Arthur	84	*Heart failure*
1979	# FIELDS, Gracie	81	*After a hospital stay for bronchial pneumonia (in Capri, Italy)*
1979	#+ FLATT, Lester	64	*Heart attack (in Nashville, TN)*
1979	FLEISCHER, Dave	84	*Stroke (in Woodland Hills, CA)*
1979	# FORAN, Dick	69	*Blood disorder (in Panorama City, CA)*
1979	+ GALENTO, Tony "Twoton"	69	*Heart attack (in Livingston, NJ)*
1979	GARGAN, William ☆	73	*Heart attack (in San Diego, CA)*
1979	GILBERT, Jody	62	*Following an automobile accident (in Sherman Oaks, CA)*
1979	GRAHAM, Fred	61	*Died in Scottsdale, AZ*
1979	# GRENFELL, Joyce	69	*Cancer (in London, England)*
1979	# GRIFFITH, Corinne	84	*Cardiac arrest (in Santa Monica, CA)*
1979	#+ HALEY, Jack	80	*Heart attack (in Los Angeles, CA)*
1979	#+ HALL, Jon	64	*Suicide after bladder cancer surgery (gunshot) in Sherman Oaks, CA*
1979	HARE, J. Robertson	87	*Died in London, England*
1979	+ HEISLER, Stuart R.	82	*Died in San Diego, CA*
1979	# Hilo Hattie	78	*Cancer following a stroke (in Honolulu, HI)*
1979	HOCH, Winton C.	73	*Effects of a stroke*
1979	+ HODGE, Al	66	*Heart failure from chronic bronchitis and emphysema (in New York)*
1979	#+ HOOD, Darla	47	*Died in North Hollywood, CA*
1979	HUNNICUTT, Arthur ☆	68	*Cancer (in Woodland Hills, CA)*
1979	#+ HUTTON, Jim	45	*Cancer of the liver (in Los Angeles, CA)*

Deaths of Movie and Television Personalities — by Year

YEAR	NAME	AGE	CAUSE and/or PLACE OF DEATH
1979	# JASON, Leigh	74	After a long illness (in Woodland Hills, CA)
1979	# JENNINGS, Claudia	29	Head-on collision with a truck on Pacific Coast Hwy. (in Malibu, CA)
1979	KADAR, Jan	61	Heart attack after being hospitalized (in Los Angeles, CA)
1979	KARNES, Robert	62	Heart failure (in Sherman Oaks, CA)
1979	# KASZNAR, Kurt	65	Cancer (in Santa Monica, CA)
1979	+ KELLY, Emmett	80	Heart attack (in Sarasota, FL)
1979	#+ KENTON, Stan	66	Stroke (in Hollywood, CA)
1979	KENYON, Doris	81	Cardiac arrest in her sleep (in Beverly Hills, CA)
1979	+ KILIAN, Victor	81	Killed by burglars (in his Hollywood, CA, apartment)
1979	LACEY, Catherine	75	Died in London, England
1979	LAEMMLE, Carl Jr.	71	Stroke after a 16-yr. battle with multiple sclerosis (in Beverly Hills)
1979	LaPLANCHE, Rosemary	54	Cancer (in Glendale, CA)
1979	LEHMANN, Beatrix	76	Died in London, England
1979	# LEONETTI, Tommy	50	Cancer (in Houston, TX)
1979	+ LYON, Ben	78	Heart attack (aboard "Queen Elizabeth 2" in the Pacific Ocean)
1979	MANNI, Ettore	52	Accidental gun shot (in Rome, Italy)
1979	# MARQUET, Mary	84	Heart attack resulting from a fall (in Paris, France)
1979	#+ MARX, "Zeppo"	78	Cancer (in Palm Springs, CA)
1979	#+ MASON, Shirley (Lanfield)	78	Cancer (in Los Angeles, CA)
1979	MAUDE, Margery	90	Died in Cleveland, OH
1979	McCONNELL, Gladys	71	Died in Los Angeles, CA
1979	McCOY, Van	38	Heart attack
1979	# MILLER, Carl	85	Died in Honolulu, Hawaii
1979	MITCHELL, Belle	90	After a long illness (in Woodland Hills, CA)
1979	MITCHELL, Yvonne	53	Cancer (in London, England)
1979	MULHALL, Jack	87	Congestive heart failure (in Woodland Hills, CA)
1979	MULLEN, Barbara	64	Heart attack (in London, England)
1979	# MURRAY, Bobby	80	Died in Nashua, NH
1979	MUSE, Clarence	90	Cerebral hemorrhage (in Perris, CA)
1979	NASH, June	68	Died in Hampton Bays, L.I., NY
1979	# NAZZARI, Amedeo	71	Cardiac arrest (in Rome, Italy)
1979	NELSON, Billy	75	Following a heart attack (in Los Angeles, CA)
1979	NOVAES, Guiomar	84	
1979	O'BRIEN-MOORE, Erin	77	Cancer (in Woodland Hills, CA)
1979	+ O'HARA, Barry J.	53	Injuries from a car accident (in Woodland Hills, CA)
1979	# O'HARA, Shirley	68	Cancer (in Hollywood, CA)
1979	#+ OBERON, Merle ☆	68	Stroke (in Los Angeles, CA)
1979	ORCHARD, Julian	49	After a brief illness (in London, England)
1979	PARNELL, Emory	85	Heart attack (in Woodland Hills, CA)
1979	# PETERSON, Dorothy	78	Died in Los Angeles, CA
1979	#+ PICKFORD, Mary ★	86	Cerebral hemorrhage (in Santa Monica, CA)
1979	PIOUS, Minerva	75	
1979	PIPER, Frederick	77	Died in London, England
1979	# POHLMANN, Eric	66	Died in Bad Reichenhall, Germany
1979	PREJEAN, Albert	85	Heart attack (in Paris, France)
1979	PRENTISS, Eleanor	67	Died in New York, NY
1979	RAINE, Jack	82	Died in South Laguna, CA
1979	#+ RAND, Sally	75	Heart failure (in Glendora, CA)
1979	# RAY, Nicholas	67	Lung cancer (in New York, NY)
1979	RENOIR, Jean ☆	84	Parkinson's disease (in Beverly Hills, CA)
1979	RHODES, Marjorie	76	Died in Hove, Sussex, England
1979	+ RIPPERTON, Minnie	31	Cancer
1979	+ RODGERS, Richard	77	

YEAR		NAME		AGE	CAUSE and/or PLACE OF DEATH
1979		ROONEY, Pat, III		70	*Died in Lake Blaisdell, NH*
1979		ROSE, Jane		66	*Cancer (in Studio City, CA)*
1979		ROTA, Nino		68	*Cerebral thrombosis (in Rome, Italy)*
1979		SAVILLE, Victor		82	*Died in London, England*
1979		SEATON, George	☆	68	*Cancer (in Beverly Hills, CA)*
1979	#+	SEBERG, Jean		40	*Suicide (drug overdose) found dead in her car in Paris, France*
1979		SHEAR, Barry		56	*Cancer (in New York, NY)*
1979	+	SHEEN, (Bishop) Fulton J.		84	*Heart trouble (in New York, NY)*
1979		SHUMLIN, Herman E.		80	*Heart failure complicated by emphysema (in New York, NY)*
1979	+	SKINNER, Cornelia Otis		78	*Cerebral hemorrhage (in New York, NY)*
1979		SMITH, Pete	★	86	*Suicide (jumped from the roof of a nursing home) in Santa Monica*
1979	#+	SOO, Jack		63	*Cancer of the esophagus (in Los Angeles, CA)*
1979		STANDING, Joan		75	*Cancer (in Houston, TX)*
1979		SUMMERS, Hope		78	*Heart failure (in Woodland Hills, CA)*
1979		TAFLER, Sydney		63	*Cancer (in London, England)*
1979		TALIAFERRO, Mabel		89	*Died in Honolulu, Hawaii*
1979		TEMPLETON, Olive		96	*Died in Manhattan, NY*
1979	+	TIOMKIN, Dimitri	★	80	*Cardiac arrest in his sleep (in London, England)*
1979	#	URZI, Saro		66	*Heart attack (in San Giuseppe Vesuviano, Italy)*
1979	+	VANCE, Vivian		66	*Cancer (in Belvedere, CA)*
1979		VICIOUS, Sid		21	*Overdose of heroin*
1979	+	WAGENHEIM, Charles		83	*Murdered (bludgeoned) in Hollywood, CA*
1979	#+	WAYNE, John	★	72	*Lung and stomach cancer (in Santa Monica, CA)*
1979	#	WESSON, Dick		59	*Suicide (gunshot) in Costa Mesa, CA*
1979		WHITLEY, Ray		77	*While on a fishing trip (in Mexico)*
1979		WILDING, Michael		66	*Injuries from a fall (at his home in Chichester, England)*
1979	#+	ZANUCK, Darryl F.		77	*Pulmonary embolism aggravated by pneumonia (in Hollywood, CA)*
1980	#	ALDERSON, Floyd Taliaferro		84	*Pneumonia after suffering a stroke (in Mt. Sheridan, WY)*
1980	#+	AVERY, Tex		71	*Cancer (in Burbank, CA)*
• 1980		BABB, Kroger		85	*Heart attack complicated by diabetes (in Palm Springs, CA)*
• 1980		BAILEN, Maurice		78	*Died in Maywood, IL*
• 1980		BAILEY, Jack		72	*Complications of pneumonia (in Santa Monica, CA)*
1980		BAILEY, Raymond		75	*Heart attack (in Irvine, CA)*
1980		BAKER, Frank		86	*Died in Woodland Hills, CA*
1980	#	BARR, Leonard		77	*After suffering a stroke*
1980		BARRIE, John		62	*After a long illness (in York, England)*
1980	#+	BARRY, Don "Red"		69	*Suicide (gunshot) after a scuffle with his estranged wife (in H'wood)*
1980		BAVA, Mario		66	*Heart attack (in Rome, Italy)*
1980		BEATON, Cecil		78	
1980		BECKLEY, Tony		50	*Cancer (in Los Angeles, CA)*
1980		BELL, David Scott		22	*Murdered (shot) in North Hollywood, CA*
1980		BLISS, Lela		84	*Died in Woodland Hills, CA*
1980	#	BONELLI, Richard		91	*Died in Los Angeles, CA*
1980	+	BONHAM, John		32	*Choked to death after drinking 40 shots of vodka*
1980	#+	BRASSELLE, Keefe		57	*Cirrhosis of the liver (in Downey, CA)*
1980	#	BRITTON, Barbara		59	*Cancer (in New York, NY)*
1980		BURKE, Kathleen		66	*Died in Chicago, IL*
1980	#	CARROLL, Dee		54	*Following corrective surgery after a stroke (in Burbank, CA)*
1980		CHAMPION, Gower		60	*Waldenstrom's disease (in New York, NY)*
1980		COURTNEIDGE, Cicely		87	*Died in London, England*
• 1980	#	CRASH, Darby		22	*Probable suicide (from a massive heroin overdose)*
1980		CRAWFORD, Kathryn		72	*Cancer (in Pasadena, CA)*

Deaths of Movie and Television Personalities — by Year

YEAR	NAME		AGE	CAUSE and/or PLACE OF DEATH
1980	d'USSEAU, Armand		63	Stomach cancer (in New York, NY)
1980	# DAGOVER, Lil		82	Died in Munich, West Germany
1980	+ DASSIN, Joseph "Joe"		42	Heart attack (in Papeete, Tahiti)
1980	DEUTSCH, Adolph	★	82	Died in Palm Desert, CA
1980	# DORR, Harry		87	Pneumonia (in Los Angeles, CA)
1980	DRAGONETTE, Jessica		75	Heart attack (in New York City)
1980	#+ DURANTE, Jimmy		86	Pneumonitis (in Santa Monica, CA)
1980	EMERY, Katherine		73	Pulmonary embolism (in Portland, ME)
1980	EMNEY, Fred		79	Died in Bognor Regis, England
1980	FADDEN, Tom		84	Died in Vero Beach, FL
1980	# FAIRE, Virginia Brown		75	Died at a hospital in Laguna Beach, CA
1980	FAYE, Herbie		81	Died in Las Vegas, NV
1980	FITZPATRICK, James A.		78	Stroke (in Cathedral City, CA)
1980	FLINT, Sam		98	Died in Woodland Hills, CA
1980	FOX, Virgil		68	Cancer
1980	FROMAN, Jane		71	Cardiac arrest in her sleep
1980	FULLER, Frances		73	Died in New York, NY
1980	+ GARDINER, Reginald		77	Heart attack and pneumonia (in Westwood, CA)
1980	GOOLDEN, Richard		86	Died in London, England
1980	GRIFFITH, Hugh	★	67	Died in London, England
1980	# HAMMOND, Kay		71	Following a heart attack (in Brighton, England)
1980	#+ HAYMES, Dick		64	Lung cancer (in Los Angeles, CA)
1980	# HENRY, Charlotte		65	Brain tumor (in La Jolla, CA)
1980	# HENRY, Tom		?	Died in Los Angeles, CA
1980	+ HITCHCOCK, Alfred	☆	80	Heart attack (in Beverly Hills, CA)
1980	HOLTZ, Lou		87	Following open-heart surgery (in Los Angeles, CA)
1980	# HOSKINS, Allen "Farina"		59	Cancer (in Oakland, CA)
1980	# HOUSTON, Renée		77	Died in London, England
1980	HOYOS, Rudolfo Sr.		83	Results of a fall (in Los Angeles, CA)
1980	+ ITURBI, José		84	Heart attack (in Hollywood, CA)
1980	# JACQUES, Hattie		56	Heart attack (in London, England)
1980	JANNEY, Leon		63	Cancer (in Guadalajara, Mexico)
1980	#+ JANSSEN, David		48	Died of a massive heart attack at his home (in Malibu, CA)
1980	JOYCE, Yootha		53	Cirrhosis of the liver (in London, England)
1980	# KALLMAN, Dick		46	Murdered (in his Manhattan, NY, apartment)
1980	KAMINSKA, Ida	☆	80	Heart attack (in New York, NY)
1980	KAUFMAN, Boris	★	74	Cancer (at Hollywood Presbyterian Hospital in Hollywood, CA)
1980	KENTON, Erle C.		83	Parkinson's disease and emphysema (in Glendale, CA)
1980	+ KORJUS, Miliza	☆	73	Heart attack (in Culver City, CA)
1980	+ KOSTELANETZ, Andre		79	Heart attack after pneumonia (in Haiti)
1980	LAKE, Florence		75	Died in Woodland Hills, CA
1980	LANGTON, Paul		66	Heart attack (in Burbank, CA)
1980	+ LAUCK, Chester H. "Lum"		79	After a brief illness (in Hot Springs, AR)
1980	LAURIE, John		83	Emphysema and a lung ailment (in Chalfont St. Peter, England)
1980	LEE, Chingwah		78	Died in San Francisco, CA
1980	+ LENNON, John		40	Murdered (shot) in New York, NY
1980	LESSER, Sol	★	90	Cardiac arrest in his sleep (in Hollywood, CA)
1980	# LEVENE, Sam		74	Heart attack (in New York, NY)
1980	#+ LEVENSON, Sam		68	
1980	LEVIN, Henry		70	Heart attack on the final day of filming (in Glendale, CA)
1980	LODEN, Barbara		48	Cancer (in New York, NY)
1980	LONDON, Jean "Babe"		79	
1980	# LOVELY, Louise		83	Died in Hobart, Australia

Deaths of Movie and Television Personalities — by Year

YEAR	NAME		AGE	CAUSE and/or PLACE OF DEATH
1980	MANNING, Knox		76	Died in Woodland Hills, CA
1980	+ MARTIN, Strother		61	Heart attack (in Thousand Oaks, CA)
1980	# MASON, Mary		69	Cancer (in New York, NY)
1980	MAX, Edwin "Ed"		71	Died in Los Angeles, CA
1980	MAY, Alyce		65	Heart attack (in Rosa Rito Beach, Baja, Mexico)
1980	# MAY, Mia		96	After a brief illness (in Los Angeles, CA)
1980	McCARTY, Mary		56	Died in Westwood, CA
1980	McDONALD, Frank		80	Died in Oxnard, CA
1980	# McGRAW, Charles		66	After falling thru a glass shower door at home (in Studio City, CA)
1980	#+ McQUEEN, Steve ☆		50	Heart attack after cancer surgery (in Juarez, Mexico)
1980	# MEDFORD, Kay ☆		59	Heart attack (in Manhattan, NY)
1980	# MEREDITH, Iris		64	Died in Los Angeles, CA
1980	#+ MILESTONE, Lewis ★		84	Following abdominal surgery (in Los Angeles, CA)
1980	MONTOVANI, Annunzio		75	
1980	+ MYERS, Carmel		79	After a heart attack (in Los Angeles, CA)
1980	NEWELL, David (actor)		75	Died in Los Angeles, CA
1980	+ NOLAN, Bob		72	Heart attack (in Newport Beach, CA)
1980	NUGENT, Elliott		80	Died in his sleep (in New York, NY)
1980	O'NEIL, Barbara ☆		69	Died in Cos Cob, CT
1980	O'SHEA, Daniel T.		75	
1980	OWEN, Malcolm		24	Overdose of heroin
1980	#+ OWENS, Jesse		66	Lung cancer (in Tucson, AZ)
1980	# PAGLIERO, Marcello		73	Cancer (in Paris, France)
1980	+ PAL, George		72	Heart attack (in Beverly Hills, CA)
1980	PARSONS, Milton		75	
1980	# PATRICK, Gail		69	Leukemia (in Hollywood, CA)
1980	PHILLIPS, Dorothy		90	Pneumonia (in Woodland Hills, CA)
1980	PHILLPOTTS, Ambrosine		68	Died in Ascot, England
1980	PHIPPS, Nicholas		66	Died in London, England
1980	POE, James ★		58	Heart attack (at his home in Malibu, CA)
1980	#+ RAFT, George		85	Leukemia (in Los Angeles, CA)
1980	+ RANDOLPH, Lillian		65	Cancer (in Arcadia, CA)
1980	REED, Marshall J.		62	Massive hemorrhage after suffering a brain tumor (in Los Angeles)
1980	# RENALDO, Duncan "Cisco Kid"		76	Lung cancer (in Goleta, CA)
1980	ROBBINS, Gale		57	Lung cancer (in Tarzana, CA)
1980	+ ROBERTS, Rachel ☆		53	Suicide (acute barbiturate intoxication) in Los Angeles, CA
1980	#+ ROTH, Lillian		69	Stroke (in New York, NY)
1980	+ SANDERS, (Col.) Harland		90	Leukemia and pneumonia (in Louisville, KY)
1980	SANDRINI, Luis "Felipe"		75	Cerebral hemorrhage (in Buenos Aires, Argentina)
1980	SCHARY, Dore		74	Cancer (in New York, NY)
1980	SCHRAMM, Karla		88	Died in Los Angeles, CA
1980	SELBY, Sarah		73	Died in Los Angeles, CA
1980	+ SELLERS, Peter ☆		54	Heart attack (in London, England)
1980	SELTZER, Daniel		47	Heart attack (in New York, NY)
1980	SEN YUNG, Victor		65	Apparent victim of a gas leak at his home in North Hollywood, CA
1980	+ SHARPE, David H.		70	Parkinson's disease (in Altadena, CA)
1980	# SHERMAN, Mary		93	Died in Santa Monica, CA
1980	# SILVA, Mario		79	
1980	#+ SILVERHEELS, Jay "Tonto"		62	Complications from pneumonia (in Woodland Hills, CA)
1980	# SINATRA, Ray		76	Intestinal problems (in Las Vegas, NV)
1980	STEPANEK, Karel		80	Died in Los Angeles, CA
1980	STOLOFF, Morris W. ★		85	Died in Woodland Hills, CA
1980	+ STONE, Milburn		75	Heart attack (in La Jolla, CA)

• New entry. # Original name (Pt. 7). + Interment (Pt. 5). 90 ☆ Oscar nominee, ★ Oscar winner (Pt. 10)

Deaths of Movie and Television Personalities — by Year

YEAR	NAME		AGE	CAUSE and/or PLACE OF DEATH
1980	#+ STRATTEN, Dorothy		20	Murdered (shot by her husband) in West Los Angeles, CA
1980	# STRONG, Leonard		71	Died in Glendale, CA
1980	STRONG, Michael		55	Cancer (in Los Angeles, CA)
1980	# SYLVIA, Gaby		60	Cerebral hemorrhage (in Chamalieres, France)
1980	# TAMBERLANI, Carlo		81	Died in Subiaco, Italy
1980	TANNEN, Charles D.		65	Heart attack (while vacationing in San Bernardino, CA)
1980	#+ THOMAS, Billy "Buckwheat"		49	Heart attack (in Los Angeles, CA)
1980	TOBIAS, George		78	Cancer (in Los Angeles, CA)
1980	TRIESAULT, Ivan		79	Heart failure (in Los Angeles, CA)
1980	# TSCHECHOWA, Olga		83	Died in Munich, Germany
1980	VALLI, Romolo		54	Automobile accident (in Rome, Italy)
1980	#+ VAN, Bobby		49	After surgery to remove a brain tumor (in Los Angeles, CA)
1980	# WALES, Wally		83	Pneumonia, after suffering a stroke (in Sheridan, WY)
1980	WALKER, Ray W.		76	Heart failure (in Los Angeles, CA)
1980	WARDE, Harlan		63	
1980	WATTS, Queenie		52	Cancer (in London, England)
1980	#+ WEST, Mae		88	Complications following a stroke (in Hollywood, CA)
1980	WINTLE, Julian		67	Stroke (in Brighton, England)
1980	WOODRUFF, Eleanor		89	Cardiac arrest in her sleep
1981	+ ALBERTSON, Jack	★	74	Cancer (in Hollywood Hills, CA)
1981	ALEXANDER, Katherine		79	Died in Florida
1981	+ ANDERS, Glenn		92	Died in Englewood, NJ
1981	#+ ASTAIRE, Adele		82	Stroke (in Phoenix, AZ)
1981	ASTHER, Nils		84	Died in Stockholm, Sweden
• 1981	BAGNOLD, Enid		91	Died in St. John's Wood, England
• 1981	BAILEY, James		31	Died in Punene, HI
• 1981	BALTZELL, Deborah		25	Heart attack
1981	BARTON, Charles T.		79	After two heart attacks (in Burbank, CA)
1981	+ BEARD, Matthew "Stymie" Jr.		56	Stroke (in Los Angeles, CA)
• 1981	BEDFORD, Barbara		78	
1981	BERNHARDT, Curtis (Kurt)		81	Apoplexy attack (in Pacific Palisades, CA)
1981	# BONDI, Beulah	☆	88	Pulmonary complications (in Woodland Hills, CA)
1981	+ BOONE, Richard		63	Throat cancer (in St. Augustine, FL)
1981	#+ BOWLING, Alice		54	Skin disease
1981	BYRNE, Eddie		70	Died in Dublin, Ireland
1981	#+ CARMICHAEL, Hoagy		82	Heart attack (in Rancho Mirage, CA)
1981	CASTLETON, Barbara		85	Died in Boca Raton, FL
• 1981	CHAPIN, Harry		38	Automobile accident
1981	#+ CHAYEFSKY, Paddy		58	Cancer (in Manhattan, NY)
1981	# CLAIR, René		82	Cardiac arrest in her sleep (in Neuilly-sur-Seine, France)
1981	CLEMENTS, Stanley		55	Emphysema (in Pacoima, CA)
1981	CONWAY, Morgan		81	Died in Livingston, NJ
1981	COOK, Billy Boy		?	
1981	COOPER, Dulcie		77	After a lengthy illness (in New York, NY)
1981	#+ DAVIS, Jim		65	Following surgery for a perforated ulcer (in Northridge, CA)
1981	DeBANZIE, Brenda		66	Following surgery on a non-malignant tumor (in Sussex, England)
1981	DeKOVA, Frank		71	Found dead in his home from a heart attack (in Sepulveda, CA)
1981	DIXON, Jean (actress)		84	After a long illness (in New York, NY)
1981	# DOUGLAS, Melvyn	★	80	Pneumonia and cardiac complications (in New York, NY)
1981	DRAYTON, Noel		68	
1981	#+ DWAN, Alan		96	Heart failure (in Woodland Hills, CA)
1981	EBERLY, Bob		65	After 4 heart attacks from cancer chemotherapy

Deaths of Movie and Television Personalities — by Year

YEAR	NAME		AGE	CAUSE and/or PLACE OF DEATH
1981	# ELSOM, Isobel		87	*Died in Woodland Hills, CA*
1981	ENGEL, Roy		67	*Meningitis (in Burbank, CA)*
1981	FORAN, Mary		61	*Died in Los Angeles, CA*
1981	# FRANCIS, Sandra		47	*Results of a motorcycle accident (in Santa Monica, CA)*
1981	FRIEDHOFER, Hugo	★	80	*While hospitalized after a fall at his home (in Los Angeles, CA)*
1981	GAFNI, Miklos		57	*Massive heart attack (at Kennedy Airport, NY)*
1981	GANCE, Abel		92	*Lung ailment (in Paris, France)*
1981	# GARRALAGA, Martin		85	*Died in Woodland Hills, CA*
1981	# GEORGE "Chief" Dan	☆	82	*Died in Vancouver, Canada*
• 1981	GIANELLO, Nino		?	
1981	GODDARD, Alf		83	*Died in England*
1981	#+ GRAHAME, Gloria	★	57	*Cancer (in Manhattan, NY)*
1981	GRAY, Mack		75	*Following a prolonged illness (in Los Angeles, CA)*
1981	GREENE, Stanley N.		70	*After a long illness (in New York, NY)*
1981	# HADEN, Sara		82	*Died in Woodland Hills, CA*
1981	HALE, Richard		87	*Cardiac arrest in his sleep (in Northridge, CA)*
1981	HALL, Ella		85	*Died in Canoga Park, CA*
1981	+ HARBURG, E. Y.		84	*Killed in an automobile crash (in Hollywood, CA)*
1981	#+ HARDING, Ann	☆	79	*After an illness of several months (in Sherman Oaks, CA)*
1981	HARRIS, Robert H.		72	*Died in Brentwood, CA (Do not confuse with British actor)*
1981	#+ HAYDEN, Russell "Lucky"		68	*Viral pneumonia (in Palm Springs, Ca.)*
1981	+ HEAD, Edith		82	*Undisclosed causes (in Los Angeles, CA)*
1981	# HEMING, Violet		86	*Died in New York, NY*
1981	#+ HENDRIX, Wanda		52	*Double pneumonia (in Burbank, CA)*
1981	HOERBIGER, Paul		87	*Died in Vienna, Austria*
1981	#+ HOLDEN, William	★	63	*Blood loss after head was cut in a fall (in Santa Monica, CA)*
1981	HOVEN, Adrian		57	*Heart attack (in Tegernsee, West Germany)*
1981	+ JESSEL, George		83	*Heart attack (in Los Angeles, CA)*
1981	JOHNSON, Brad		56	*Died in Burbank, CA*
1981	JONES, Barry		87	*Died in England*
1981	JOSLYN, Allyn		75	*Cardiac failure (in Woodland Hills, CA)*
1981	KEANE, Robert Emmett		96	*Died in Hollywood, CA*
1981	KEATON, Louise		78	*Cancer (in Van Nuys, CA)*
1981	#+ KELLY, Patsy		71	*Cancer (in Woodland Hills, CA)*
1981	KNAPP, Evelyn		72	*Died in West Hollywood, CA*
1981	KNOPF, Edwin H.		82	*Apoplexy attack (in Brentwood, CA)*
1981	KRASKER, Robert		67	*Died in London, England*
1981	#+ LANE, Lola		75	*Inflammation of the arteries (in Santa Barbara, CA)*
1981	# LEANDER, Zarah		74	*Died near Stockholm, Sweden*
1981	LEE, Bernard		73	*Cancer (in London, England)*
1981	# LENYA, Lotte	☆	83	*Died in New York, NY*
1981	#+ LINDSAY, Margaret		70	*Emphysema (in Los Angeles, CA)*
1981	LOOS, Anita		93	*Heart attack (in Manhattan, NY)*
1981	# LORRAINE, Louise		79	*After a long illness (in New York, NY)*
1981	#+ LOUIS, Joe "Brown Bomber"		66	*Cardiac arrest (in Las Vegas, NV)*
1981	LUDDEN, Allen		63	*Cancer (in Los Angeles, CA)*
1981	MARKEY, Enid		83	*Heart attack (in Bay Shore, NY)*
1981	MARKHAM, Dewey "Pigmeat"		77	*Stroke (in New York, NY)*
1981	# MARSH, Garry		78	*Heart attack (in London, England)*
1981	#+ MARTIN, Ross		61	*Heart attack playing tennis (in Poway, CA)*
1981	MATTHEWS, Jessie		74	*Cancer (in London, England)*
1981	MAXWELL, Jenny		39	*Shot to death outside her condo by possible robbers (in Los Angeles)*
1981	McCULLOUGH, Philo		90	*Died in Burbank, CA*

Deaths of Movie and Television Personalities — by Year

YEAR		NAME		AGE	CAUSE and/or PLACE OF DEATH
1981		McHUGH, Frank		82	After a brief illness (in Greenwich, CT)
1981	#	MEGOWAN, Don		59	Throat cancer (in Panorama City, CA)
1981		MILLER, Ruth		78	Died in Santa Monica, CA
1981	#+	MONTGOMERY, Robert	☆	77	Cancer (in New York, NY)
1981		MORE, Unity		86	Died in London, England
1981	#	NEY, Marie		86	Died in London, England
1981		O'CONNELL, Arthur	☆	73	Alzheimer's disease (in Woodland Hills, CA)
1981		PALMER, Maria		57	Cancer (in Los Angeles, CA)
1981	#	PATRICK, Nigel		68	Cancer (at a hospital in London, England)
1981		PONSELLE, Rosa		84	
1981		PRACK, Rudolf		77	Died in Vienna, Austria
1981		RIGON, Paolo		22	Injuries from a filming accident (in Cortina d'Ampezzo, Italy)
1981		ROCHELLE, Claire		72	Cancer (in La Jolla, CA)
1981		ROULEAU, Raymond		77	Died in Paris, France
1981	#	RUSSELL, Don		54	Heart attack (in Miami Beach, FL)
1981	+	SAGAL, Boris		58	Injuries from a helicopter crash (in Portland, OR)
1981	#	SANTELL, Alfred		86	After a lengthy illness and several strokes (in Salinas, CA)
1981	#+	SCOTT, Hazel		61	Cancer (in New York, NY)
1981	#	SHERWOOD, Bobby		65	Cancer (in Auburn, MA)
1981		SHIMODA, Yuki		58	Emphysema (in Los Angeles, CA)
1981	#+	SMITH, Joseph		96	Died in Englewood, NJ
1981		SPADARO, Umberto		77	Cancer (in Rome, Italy)
1981	#	TALMADGE, Richard		88	Cancer (in Carmel, CA)
1981		TAUROG, Norman	★	82	After a long illness (in Rancho Mirage, CA)
1981	#	THATCHER, Torin		76	Cancer (in Thousand Oaks, CA)
1981		THOMAS, David		73	Died in New York, NY
1981	+	THOMAS, Lowell		89	Heart attack (in Pawling, NY)
1981	#+	Vera-Ellen		55	Cancer (in Los Angeles, CA)
1981		VonZELL, Harry		75	Cancer (in Woodland Hills, CA)
1981		VOSKOVEC, George		76	Died in Pear Blossom, CA
1981		WALSH, George		92	Complications from pneumonia (in Pomona, CA)
1981	#	WALSH, Raoul		93	Apparent heart attack (in Simi Valley, CA)
1981		WARBURTON, John		78	Cancer (in Sherman Oaks, CA)
1981	#+	WARREN, Harry (songwriter)	★	87	Lung cancer (at Cedars-Sinai Med. Ctr. in Los Angeles, CA)
1981	#+	WILSON, Edith		83	Cerebral hemorrhage (in Chcago, IL)
1981	#+	WOOD, Natalie	☆	43	Accidental drowning (off Catalina Island, CA)
1981	+	WYLER, William	★	79	Heart attack (in Beverly Hills, CA)
1982	+	ACE, Goodman		83	
1982		ALBERTSON, Mabel		81	Complications from numerous illnesses (in Santa Monica, CA)
1982	+	ALEXANDER, John		85	
1982		ASKEY, Arthur		82	After amputation of a leg (in London, England)
1982	#	ASLAN, Gregoire		74	Heart attack (in England)
1982		Baby Early		76	Emphysema (in Dover, NJ)
1982	#	BADEL, Alan		58	Heart attack (in Chichester, England)
1982		BAKER, Lenny		37	Cancer (in Hallandale, FL)
1982		BAKER, Russell F.		66	After a brief illness (in White Plains, NY)
1982		BAKER, Sam		56	Heart attack at a restaurant (in Boston, MA)
1982		BALDWIN, Bill		69	Cancer (in Hollywood, CA)
1982		BAYNE, Beverly		87	Heart attack (in Scottsdale, AZ)
1982		BEAUMONT, Hugh		72	Apparent heart attack (in Munich, Germany)
1982	+	BELUSHI, John		33	After speedballing a mix of cocaine and heroin (in Hollywood, CA)
1982		BENET, Brenda		36	Suicide (gunshot) in West Los Angeles, CA

Deaths of Movie and Television Personalities — by Year

YEAR	NAME	AGE	CAUSE and/or PLACE OF DEATH
1982	BENNETT, Marjorie	87	Cancer (in Hollywood, CA)
1982	+ BERGMAN, Ingrid ★	67	Breast cancer (in London, England)
1982	BISHOP, Ronald	59	After a brief illness (in Manhattan, NY)
1982	BLAKE, Larry J.	68	Died in Los Angeles, CA
1982	+ BLOCH, Ray	79	Heart attack (in Miami, FL)
1982	BLUE, David	41	Heart attack while jogging (in Greenwich Village, NY)
1982	BOND, Rudy	66	Heart attack (in Denver, CO)
1982	BRAHM, John	89	Heart attack in his sleep at home (in Malibu, CA)
1982	BREEDING, Larry	36	Killed when his car struck a pole (in Hollywood, CA)
1982	+ BRODERICK, James	55	Cancer (in New Haven, CT)
1982	BROWN, Joseph	59	Died in Mexico City, Mexico
1982	# BRUCE, Virginia	72	Cancer (in Woodland Hills, CA)
1982	BRUCK, Bella	70	Heart attack (in Hollywood, CA)
1982	+ BUONO, Victor	44	Heart attack (in Apple Valley, CA)
1982	CALVE, Olga	82	Bronchial pneumonia (in Santa Paula, CA)
1982	CAROL, Sue		(See Sue Carol Ladd)
1982	CARSON, Wayne	55	After a long illness (in New York, NY)
1982	CAVALCANTI, Alberto	85	After a long illness (in Paris, France)
1982	CHEN, Renee Shinn	6	Killed by helicopter rotor while filming
1982	CHRISTI, Frank	52	Shot to death at his home (in Hollywood Hills, CA)
1982	CHURCHILL, Sarah	67	Cirrhosis of the liver (in London, England)
1982	# CONRIED, Hans	64	Heart ailment (in Burbank, CA) body donated to medical science
1982	COOTE, Robert	73	Heart attack (in New York, NY)
1982	CORBETT, Harry H.	57	Heart attack (in Hastings, England)
1982	CULLEN, Fred	48	Heart attack
1982	# CUMMINGS, Sandy	68	Pneumonia while hospitalized for another illness (in San Diego, CA)
1982	+ DANTINE, Helmut	63	Massive coronary (in Beverly Hills, CA)
1982	DAVIS, Herbert H.	52	Died in New York, NY
1982	# DEVEAU, Jack	47	Cancer (in New York, NY)
1982	DILLAWAY, Donald P.	78	After a long illness
1982	DIX, Constance	60	Died in New York, NY
1982	DONNELLY, Ruth	86	Died in New York, NY
1982	#+ DRAKE, Tom	64	Lung cancer (in Hollywood, CA)
1982	DUKE, E. L. Tony	48	Heart attack (in Burbank, CA)
1982	+ DUNNE, Dominique	23	Strangled by her boyfriend (in Los Angeles, CA)
1982	ETHRIDGE, Ella	88	Died in Woodland Hills, CA
1982	FASSBINDER, Rainer Werner	36	Lethal combination of cocaine and sleeping pills (in Munich, Ger.)
1982	+ FELDMAN, Marty	48	Heart attack (in Mexico City, Mexico)
1982	FITZGERALD, Neil	90	Died in Princeton, NJ
1982	#+ FONDA, Henry ★	77	Heart failure and prostate cancer (in Los Angeles, CA)
1982	FORMAN, Joey	53	Complications from pulmonary fibrosis (in West Hollywood, CA)
1982	FORSTER, Peter	62	Died in Brentwood, CA
1982	FOX, Virginia (Zanuck)	79	Complications from stroke and emphysema (in Palm Springs, CA)
1982	GARROWAY, Dave	69	Apparent suicide (gunshot) in Swarthmore, PA
1982	GORDON, Steve	44	Heart attack (in New York, NY)
1982	GORIN, Igor	80	
1982	+ GOSDEN, Freeman "Amos"	83	Heart failure (in Los Angeles, CA)
1982	+ GOULD, Glenn	50	Massive stroke (in Toronto, Canada)
1982	GRAHAME, Margot	70	Respiratory failure from chronic bronchitis (in London, England)
1982	HAMPTON, Hope	84	Heart attack (in New York, NY)
1982	HESSEL, Edith Bell	58	Alzheimer's disease and exposure
1982	HOLLOWAY, Stanley ☆	91	Died in Little Hampton, England
1982	HOWELL, Lottice	84	Died in Greensboro, AL

Deaths of Movie and Television Personalities — by Year

YEAR	NAME		AGE	CAUSE and/or PLACE OF DEATH
1982	HOXIE, Al		80	Died in Redlands, CA
1982	JOHNSON, Celia		73	Stroke (in Nettlebed, England)
1982	JOHNSON, Dan		38	Undisclosed causes (in New York, NY)
1982	+ JORY, Victor		79	Apparent heart attack (in Santa Monica, CA)
1982	+ JURGENS, Curt		69	Heart attack (in Vienna, Austria)
1982	# KELLJAN, Robert		52	After a long bout with cancer (in Los Angeles, CA)
1982	+ KELLY, Grace	★	52	Brain hemorrhage after a car crash (in Monaco)
1982	+ KING, Henry	☆	86	Died in his sleep at home (in Toluca Lake, CA)
1982	KING, Mollie		86	Following a stroke (in Fort Lauderdale, FL)
1982	KLINGER, Ruth S.		59	Heart attack in her sleep (in Great Neck, NY)
1982	KYDD, Sam		67	Respiratory ailment (in London, England)
1982	+ LADD, Sue Carol		73	Complications of heart attack (in Hollywood, CA)
1982	+ LAMAS, Fernando		67	Cancer (in Los Angeles, CA)
1982	LANE, Richard		83	Died in Newport Beach, CA
1982	LEE, My-ca Dinh		7	Killed by helicopter rotor while filming
1982	LEE, Will		74	Heart attack (in New York, NY)
1982	+ LEMBECK, Harvey		59	Heart attack (in Los Angeles, CA)
1982	LEWIS, Ronald		54	Suicide (sleeping pills) Do not confuse with R. "Raan" Lewis, d. 1995
1982	LITTLER, Susan		33	Cancer (in London, England)
1982	LOWE, Arthur		67	Following a stroke (in Birmingham, England)
1982	LUCAS, Nick		84	Following a stroke
1982	LUDWIG, Edward		83	Stroke while hospitalized (in Santa Monica, CA)
1982	+ LYNDE, Paul		55	Prostate cancer and heart attack (in Beverly Hills, CA)
1982	- MAGEE, Patrick		58	Heart attack (in London, England)
1982	#+ MARLOWE, Hugh		71	Heart attack (in Manhattan, NY)
1982	MERCHANT, Vivien	☆	53	Jaundice and hemorrhage caused by alcoholism (in London, Eng.)
1982	+ MILLS, Harry F.		68	Following a tumor operation
1982	# MINER, Tony		82	Heart attack (in New York, NY)
1982	MIRANDA, Isa		77	Infected bone fracture (in Rome, Italy)
1982	+ MONK, Thelonius		64	Following a stroke (in Weehawken, NJ)
1982	MORAN, Dolores		56	Died in Woodland Hills, CA
1982	MORE, Kenneth		67	Parkinson's disease (in London, England)
1982	+ MORROW, Vic		50	Killed in a filming accident (in Sangus Desert, CA)
1982	MULLANEY, Jack		51	Stroke (in Hollywood, CA)
1982	NESBITT, Cathleen		93	Cardiac arrest in her sleep (in Chelsea, England)
1982	NOVELLO, Jay		78	Died in North Hollywood, CA
1982	NUTT, Rev. Grady		47	Airplane crash
1982	OATES, Warren		53	Heart attack (in Los Angeles, CA)
1982	+ OBER, Philip		80	Heart failure (in Mexico City, Mexico)
1982	+ PATRICK, Lee (Wood)		76	Heart seizure (in Laguna Hills, CA)
1982	PATTON, Mary		66	Cancer (in Santa Monica, CA)
1982	PHILBROOK, James		58	Died in Los Angeles, CA
1982	# PHILLIPS, Barney		68	After a brief illness (in Los Angeles, CA)
1982	PICKMAN, Kathryn		60	Cancer
1982	+ POWELL, Eleanor		69	Cancer (in Beverly Hills, CA)
1982	PURSELL, Robert		26	Apparent suicide (hung himself from a tree) in Levittown, PA
1982	REVILLE, Alma (Hitchcock)		82	After a long illness (in Bel Air, CA)
1982	+ ROBBINS, Marty		57	Heart attack (in Nashville, TN)
1982	+ ROSS, Joe E.		67	Apparent heart attack (in Burbank, CA)
1982	+ RUBINSTEIN, Artur		95	Cardiac arrest in his sleep (in Geneva, Switzerland)
1982	RUTHERFORD, Jack "Buffalo Bill"		89	Died in Tucson, AZ
1982	SAKATA, Harold		56	Cancer (in Honolulu, HI)
1982	# SAWYER, Joe		80	Liver cancer (in Ashland, OR)

• New entry. # Original name (Pt. 7). + Interment (Pt. 5).

95

☆ Oscar nominee, ★ Oscar winner (Pt. 10)

Deaths of Movie and Television Personalities — by Year

YEAR	NAME	AGE	CAUSE and/or PLACE OF DEATH
1982	#+ SCHNEIDER, Romy	43	Found dead of cardiac arrest (at her apartment in Paris, France)
1982	SCHREIBER, Elsa (Shdanoff)	81	Heart failure (in Los Angeles, CA)
1982	SEDAN, Rolfe	86	Died in Santa Monica, CA
1982	SEKA, Ron	48	Heart attack (in Hollywood, CA)
1982	+ SHAW, Reta	69	Died in Encino, CA
1982	# SHAW, Wini	72	Died in New York, NY
1982	SHELDON, Gene	75	Heart attack
1982	SHIMURA, Takashi	76	Emphysema (in Tokyo, Japan)
1982	SNOWDEN, Leigh	51	Cancer (in Los Angeles, CA)
1982	STANLEY, Louise	66	Died in Cocoa Beach, FL
1982	#+ STRASBERG, Lee ☆	80	Heart attack (in New York, NY)
1982	# TATI, Jacques	74	Pulmonary embolism (in Paris, France)
1982	TAYLOR, John	61	Heart attack (in Geneva, Switzerland)
1982	THEARD, Sam	78	Died in Los Angeles, CA
1982	THOMA, Michael	55	Cancer (in Hollywood, CA)
1982	TOBIN, Dan	72	After a lengthy illness (in Santa Monica, CA)
1982	TULLY, Tom ☆	74	Complications after a long bout with cancer (in Newport Beach, CA)
1982	VARELA, Nina	83	Died in Hollywood, CA
1982	VESTOFF, Virginia	42	After a long illness (in New York, NY)
1982	VIDOR, King ☆	89	Heart ailment (in Pablo Robles, CA)
1982	WAKELY, Jimmy	68	Heart failure (in Mission Hills, CA)
1982	WALKER, Betty	54	Cancer (in Manhattan, NY)
1982	WALTERS, Charles ☆	70	Lung cancer (in Malibu, CA)
1982	WEBB, Alan	75	Died in Sussex, England
1982	+ WEBB, Jack	62	Heart attack (in West Hollywood, CA)
1982	WEBB, Roy	94	Heart attack
1982	WHITNEY, John Hay "Jock"	77	After a long illness (in Manhasset, NY)
1982	WILSON, Don	81	Stroke
1982	+ ZANUCK, Virginia Fox	83	Emphysema and stroke (in Santa Monica, CA)
1983	ALDRICH, Robert	65	Kidney failure (in Los Angeles, CA)
1983	ALEXANDROV, Grigori	80	Died in Moscow, Russia
1983	# ARNE, Peter	62	Murdered (battered to death) in London, England
1983	AURIC, Georges	84	Died in Paris, France
• 1983	BACKUS, Georgia	83	Died in Sun City, CA
1983	BAILEY, Robert	71	Died in Lancaster, CA
• 1983	BAIM, Gary L.	36	Heart attack (in Los Angeles, CA)
• 1983	BAKER, Barbara	49	Heart attack (in New York, NY)
1983	+ BALANCHINE, George	79	Creutzfeld-Jakob disease (in New York, NY)
1983	BIERNE, Michael	46	Died in Johnson City, NY
1983	BILON, Michael "E. T."	35	Complications from pneumonia (in Youngstown, OH)
1983	# BLAIR, Randy	32	Cardiac and respiratory arrest while playing a charity basketball game
1983	# BLAKE, Eubie	100	Died in Brooklyn, NY
1983	BRANDON, Peter	57	Apparent heart attack after jogging
1983	BRAY, Robert	65	Heart attack (in Bishop, CA)
1983	BRENGEL, George	69	Cancer (in Cincinnati, OH)
1983	BRYANT, Hazel	44	Heart attack
1983	BUNUEL, Luis	83	Cirrhosis of the liver (in Mexico City, Mexico)
1983	CAINE, Joan-Ellen	57	Cancer (in Van Nuys, CA)
1983	# CAMERON, Rod	73	Cancer (in Gainesville, GA)
1983	#+ CANOVA, Judy	66	Cancer (in Hollywood, CA)
1983	+ CARPENTER, Karen	32	Heart attack caused by anorexia nervosa (in Downey, CA)
1983	CHECCO, Jessie	85	Died in Sherman Oaks, CA

Deaths of Movie and Television Personalities — by Year

YEAR	NAME		AGE	CAUSE and/or PLACE OF DEATH
1983	CHRISTIAN, Robert		42	*Cancer (in New York, NY)*
1983	CHRISTOPHER, Richard		37	*Cancer (in New York, NY)*
1983	CLARK, Kendall		70	*Cancer (in Vero Beach, FL)*
1983	CLAYTON, Jan		66	*Cancer (in West Hollywood, CA)*
1983	COFFIELD, Peter		37	*After a long illness (in New York, NY)*
1983	CONRAD, Michael		58	*Stomach cancer (in Los Angeles, CA)*
1983	COSTELLO, Anthony		42	*After a long illness (in Hollywood, CA)*
1983	# CRABBE, Larry "Buster"		75	*Heart attack (in Scottsdale, AZ)*
1983	+ CUKOR, George	★	83	*Heart failure (in Los Angeles, CA)*
1983	# CUMMINS, Dorothy		80	
1983	+ D'ORSAY, Fifi		79	*Cancer (in Woodland Hills, CA)*
1983	# DALIO, Marcel		83	*Found dead in his home (in Paris, France)*
1983	DANA, Leora		60	*Cancer (in New York, NY)*
1983	DARNAY, Toni		61	*Lung cancer (in New York, NY)*
1983	DAVIS, Johnny "Scat"		73	*Heart attack (in Pecos, TX)*
1983	deFUNES, Louis		68	*Heart attack (in Nantes, France)*
1983	# DEL RIO, Dolores		77	*Heart attack (in Newport Beach, CA)*
1983	DEMAREST, William	☆	91	*After a long illness (in Palm Springs, CA)*
1983	+ DEMPSEY, Jack		87	*After an illness of several years (in New York, NY)*
1983	DIETZ, Howard		86	*Died in New York, NY*
1983	DRISCOLL, Robert Miller		55	*Died in Hollywood, CA*
1983	DUNN, Josephine		76	*Cancer (in Thousand Oaks, CA)*
1983	# ELLIOTT, William D.		49	*Died in L.A. (Do not confuse with William "Wild Bill" Elliott, d. 1965)*
1983	EMERSON, Faye		65	*Stomach cancer (in Deyva, Spain)*
1983	EMERY, Dick		65	*Bronchial pneumonia (in London, England)*
1983	EVANS, Madge		73	*Cancer (in Oakland, NJ)*
1983	FARMER, Richard		67	*Cancer (in Glendale, CA)*
1983	#+ FIX, Paul		82	*Kidney failure (in Santa Monica, CA)*
1983	#+ FONTANNE, Lynn	☆	95	*Pneumonia (in Genesee Depot, WI)*
1983	# FOY, Eddie Jr.		78	*Pancreatic cancer*
1983	FRANZ, Eduard		81	*After a long illness (in Los Angeles, CA)*
1983	FUJIKAWA, Jerry		71	*Heart disease (in Los Angeles, CA)*
1983	GARGAN, Mary Elizabeth		76	*Lung cancer (in Rancho La Costa, CA)*
1983	+ GEORGE, Christopher		54	*Heart attack (in Los Angeles, CA)*
1983	+ GERSHWIN, Ira		86	*Died in Beverly Hills, CA*
1983	GODFREY, Arthur		79	*Pneumonia and emphysema (in New York, NY)*
1983	GOODWIN, Robert L.		55	*Died in Los Angeles, CA*
1983	GORDON, Gavin		82	*Cerebral thrombosis (in Canoga Park, CA)*
1983	GUFFEY, Burnett		78	*After a brief illness (in Goleta, CA)*
1983	#+ HACKETT, Joan		49	*Cancer (in Encino, CA)*
1983	HAYTER, James		75	*Died in Spain*
1983	HENDERSON, Jack E.		88	*Died in Woodland Hills, CA*
• 1983	HINES, Earl		77	*Heart attack*
1983	HOYOS, Rudolfo Jr.		68	*Cerebral hemorrhage (in Los Angeles, CA)*
1983	HUGHES, Arthur		89	*Pneumonia (in New York, NY)*
1983	JAMES, Harry		67	*Lymphatic cancer (in Las Vegas, NV)*
1983	JONAH, Dolly		53	*After a long illness*
1983	+ JONES, Carolyn	☆	54	*Cancer (in Los Angeles, CA)*
1983	+ KAPER, Bronislau		81	*Cancer (in Hollywood, CA)*
1983	KELLIN, Mike		61	*Lung cancer (in Nyack, NY)*
1983	KINSER, Patrick		30	*Pulmonary failure (in Los Angeles, CA)*
1983	KLEIN, Adelaide		82	*Brain tumor (in New York, NY)*
1983	KULLMAN, Charles		80	*Heart attack (in New Haven, CT)*

Deaths of Movie and Television Personalities — by Year

YEAR	NAME		AGE	CAUSE and/or PLACE OF DEATH
1983	LANCASTER, Robert		70	Died in Lancaster, CA
1983	LeBOUVIER, Jean		62	Died in Van Nuys, CA
1983	LeMESURIER, John		71	Abdominal illness (in Ramsgate, England)
1983	+ LIBERACE, George		71	Leukemia and heart disease
1983	#+ LIVINGSTONE, Mary		77	Heart attack in her sleep (in Los Angeles, CA)
1983	LLEWELLYN, Richard		76	Heart attack
1983	LOGAN, Jacqueline		78	Died in Melbourne, FL
1983	LOO, Richard		80	Died in Los Angeles, CA
1983	MACE, Paul		33	Killed in a traffic accident (in Los Angeles, CA)
1983	MADDEN, Donald		49	Died in Central Islip, NY
1983	MANULIS, Katherine Bard		66	
1983	MARTIN, Freddy		76	After a series of strokes
1983	MASSENGALE, Joseph		66	Suicide (gunshot) in Burbank, CA
1983	+ MASSEY, Raymond ☆		86	Pneumonia (in Los Angeles, CA)
1983	# McHUGH, Jack		69	Heart attack (in Las Vegas, NV)
1983	MICHAELS, Loretta R.		45	Cancer (in Boston, MA)
1983	MOORE, Kathryn		96	Died in Woodland Hills, CA
1983	MOSQUINI, Marie		84	Died in Los Angeles, CA
1983	NAPIER, Diana		76	
1983	+ NIVEN, David ★		73	Amyotrophic lateral sclerosis (in Chateau d'Oex, Switzerland)
1983	NIXON, Marion		78	Complications following open-heart surgery (in Los Angeles, CA)
1983	NORRIS, Kenneth		34	Injuries from a fall (in New York, NY)
1983	#+ O'BRIEN, Pat		83	Massive heart attack
1983	O'BRIEN, Richard		65	Cancer
1983	O'MOORE, Patrick		74	Following surgery (in Van Nuys, CA)
1983	OAKLAND, Simon		61	After a long illness (in Cathedral City, CA)
1983	# PAGE, Gale		72	Lung cancer (in Santa Monica, CA)
1983	PELISH, Thelma		55	Died in Woodland Hills, CA
1983	+ PEREIRA, Hal		78	Died in Los Angeles, CA
1983	# PICKENS, Slim		64	Pneumonia and brain tumor (in Modesto, CA)
1983	+ PULEO, Johnny		75	Respiratory failure (in Washington, D.C.)
1983	RAPHAELSON, Samson		87	Died in Manhattan, NY
1983	+ REYNOLDS, Frank		59	Viral hepatitis
1983	RICHARDSON, James G.		37	Injuries from a fall while skiing (in Rock Creek, CA)
1983	+ RICHARDSON, Ralph ☆		80	
1983	RONET, Maurice		55	Cancer (in Paris, France)
1983	ROUNDS, David		53	Cancer (in Lomontville, NY)
1983	ROYLE, Selena		78	After a brief illness (in Guadalajara, Mexico)
1983	RUTTENBERG, Joseph		93	Died in Los Angeles, CA
1983	#+ SAMPLES, Junior		56	Heart attack (in Cummings, GA)
1983	SAVITCH, Jessica		35	Automobile accident
1983	SHAYNE, Tamara		80	Following a heart attack (in Los Angeles, CA)
1983	#+ SHEARER, Norma ★		82	Bronchial pneumonia (in Woodland Hills, CA)
1983	SKOLSKY, Sidney		78	Parkinson's disease (in Hollywood, CA)
1983	SLEEPER, Martha		72	Heart attack (in Beaufort, NC)
1983	SLEZAK, Walter		80	Suicide (gunshot) in Flower Hill, NY
1983	SOMACK, Jack		64	Heart attack (in Hollywood, CA)
1983	SPACE, Arthur		74	Cancer (in Hollywood, CA)
1983	SPAIN, Fay		50	Cancer (in Los Angeles, CA)
1983	STEEN, Malcolm H. "Mike"		55	After a brief illness (in New York, NY)
1983	STRUDWICK, Shepperd		75	Cancer (in Manhattan, NY)
1983	# SWANSON, Gloria ☆		84	Following heart surgery (in New York, NY)
1983	TAYLOR, Vaughn		72	Massive cerebral hemorrhage (in Los Angeles, CA)

• New entry. # Original name (Pt. 7). + Interment (Pt. 5).   98   ☆ Oscar nominee, ★ Oscar winner (Pt. 10)

Deaths of Movie and Television Personalities — by Year

YEAR	NAME	AGE	CAUSE and/or PLACE OF DEATH
1983	+ TINCHER, Fay	99	Natural causes (in Brooklyn, NY)
1983	TORS, Ivan	67	Massive heart attack (in Matto Grosso, Brazil)
1983	TRAUBE, Shepard	76	Cancer (in Manhattan, NY)
1983	VALERIE, Joan	68	Automobile accident (in Long Beach, CA)
1983	VICTOR, Dee	57	After a long illness (in Greenwich Village, NY)
1983	# VITTE, Ray	33	Stopped breathing after forcible police arrest (in Los Angeles, CA)
1983	+ VIVYAN, John	67	Heart failure (in Santa Monica, CA)
1983	WALLGREN, Gunn	69	After a long illness (in Stockholm, Sweden)
• 1983	+ WALTON, William	80	Heart failure (at his home on the Italian island of Ischia)
• 1983	WARD, Penelope Dudley	67	
1983	WARREN, Flip	69	Died in Hollywood, CA
1983	#+ WEAVER, Doodles	71	Apparent suicide (gunshot) in Burbank, CA
• 1983	WEBB, Rita	77	
1983	WHITE, Alice	78	Stroke (in Los Angeles, CA)
1983	WHITNEY, Michael	52	After a heart attack in a restaurant (in New York, NY)
1983	WILDER, Marie	53	
1983	WILLIAMS, John	80	Following an aneurysm (Do not confuse with John J. Williams)
1983	+ WILLIAMS, Tennessee	71	After choking on a plastic bottle cap (in Manhattan, NY)
1983	+ WILSON, Dennis	39	Drowned (in Marina Del Rey, CA)
1983	WOOD, Cindi	52	After a long illness (in Malibu, CA)
1983	WOODS, Maurice	45	Cancer (in New York, NY)
1984	ADLER, Luther	81	Died in Kutztown, PA
1984	AGNEW, Robert "Bobby"	84	Kidney failure (in Palm Springs, CA)
1984	ALLEN, Chet	44	Suicide (in Columbus, OH)
1984	ANDRE, E. J.	76	Cancer (in Hollywood, CA)
1984	AUERBACH, Leon	48	Died in London, England
1984	BARRY, Jack	66	Heart attack while jogging (in New York, NY)
1984	+ BASEHART, Richard	70	Stroke (in Los Angeles, CA)
1984	#+ BASIE, William "Count"	79	Pancreatic cancer (in Hollywood, FL)
1984	BENEDICT, Richard	64	Heart attack (in Studio City, CA)
1984	BENSON, Lucille	69	Cancer (in Scottsboro, AL)
1984	BOND, Sudie	56	Respiratory ailment (in New York, NY)
1984	BONNEY, Gail	83	Died in Los Angeles, CA
1984	BOYLAN, Mary	70	After a long illness (in New York, NY)
1984	+ BRISSON, Frederick	71	After suffering a stroke (in New York, NY)
1984	BULL, Peter	72	Heart attack (in London, England)
1984	BURKE, Walter	75	Emphysema (in Woodland Hills, CA)
1984	BURTON, Margaret	60	Heart attack (in Hove, England)
1984	#+ BURTON, Richard ☆	58	Cerebral hemorrhage (in Nyon, Switzerland)
1984	CAGNEY, Jeanne	65	Lung cancer (in Newport Beach, CA)
1984	+ CAPOTE, Truman	59	Died in his sleep (drug and alcohol mix) in Bel Air, CA
1984	+ CARPENTER, Ken	84	After a brief illness (in Santa Monica, CA)
1984	CHAMBERLIN, Howland	73	Complications of lung and liver disease (in Los Angeles, CA)
1984	+ COOGAN, Jackie	69	Heart ailment (in Santa Monica, CA)
1984	COOK, Clyde	92	Died in his sleep (in Carpinteria, CA)
1984	COOPER, Edwin	89	Died in Danbury, CT
1984	CULVER, Roland	83	Heart attack (in Henley-on-Thames, England)
1984	CUMMINGS, Ruth Sinclair	90	Died in Woodland Hills, CA
1984	DALTON, Doris	82	Cardiac arrest (in Prout's Neck, ME)
1984	DAWSON, Ronald	81	Pneumonia (in Silver Spring, MD)
1984	DEACON, Richard	62	Heart attack (in Los Angeles, CA)
1984	+ DELMAR, Kenny	73	Died at a hospital in Stamford, CT

Deaths of Movie and Television Personalities — by Year

YEAR	NAME	AGE	CAUSE and/or PLACE OF DEATH
1984	DEMILLE, Cecilia (Harper)	75	After a brief illness (in Hollywood, CA)
1984	DEXTER, Alan	65	Heart attack (in Oxnard, CA)
1984	DORS, Diana	52	After two operations for ovarian cancer (in Windsor, England)
1984	DUPREZ, June	66	Died in London, England
1984	DURANT, Jack	78	Cancer (in Miami, FL)
1984	EARLE, Merie	95	Uremic poisoning after colon cancer surgery (in Glendale, CA)
1984	FLOWERS, Bess	85	Died in Woodland Hills, CA
1984	FOREMAN, Carl	69	Brain cancer (in Beverly Hills, CA)
1984	FOX, John	60	Died in Los Angeles, CA
1984	GALLO, Mario	61	Died in Ontario, CA
1984	GARNER, Peggy Ann	52	Cancer (in Woodland Hills, CA)
1984 #+	GAYE, Marvin	44	Murdered (shot by his father) in Los Angeles, CA
1984 #+	GAYNOR, Janet ★	77	Pneumonia (in Palm Springs, CA)
1984	GIVOT, George	81	Died in Palm Springs, CA
1984	GLASS, Ned	78	After a lengthy illness (in Encino, CA)
1984	GOODRICH, Frances	93	
1984	GORCEY, David	63	Diabetic coma (in Los Angeles, CA)
1984	GOUGH, Lloyd	77	Aortic aneurysm (in Sherman Oaks, CA)
1984 #	GRANT, Shauna	20	Suicide (gunshot) in Palm Springs, CA
1984	GREEN, Gilbert	68	Complications after an illness (in Tarzana, CA)
1984	GUNEY, Yilmaz	47	Stomach cancer (in Paris, France)
1984 #	HAMILTON, Neil	85	Complications from asthma (in Escondido, CA)
1984	HARGREAVES, Christine	43	Brain hemorrhage (in London, England)
1984	HASKIN, Byron ☆	84	Lung cancer (in Santa Barbara, CA)
1984 +	HELLMAN, Lillian	79	Heart disease (in Martha's Vineyard, MA)
1984	HENDRY, Ian	53	Heart attack (in London, England)
1984	HEXUM, Jon-Erik	26	Accidentally shot himself (in Beverly Hills, CA)
1984	HOLLANDER, Adam	19	Struck by car while riding a bicycle (in Albuquerque, NM)
1984	HOLLIDAY, Bill	49	Apparent heart attack (in Sidell, CA)
1984	HOLMES, Billy	56	Cancer
1984	HOWLETT, Noel	82	Died in London, England
1984 +	HUMBERSTONE, Bruce H.	80	Stomach cancer and pneumonia (in Hollywood, CA)
1984	HUTTON, Ina Ray	65	
1984 +	JAFFE, Sam ☆	93	Cancer and heart attack (in Beverly Hills, CA)
1984	JENKINS, Gordon	73	Amyotrophic lateral sclerosis (in Los Angeles, CA)
1984	JOHNSON, E. Lamont	29	Died in Marina Del Rey, CA
1984	JOHNSON, Sunny	30	Cerebral hemorrhage (in Los Angeles, CA)
1984	JORDAN, John Duffield	81	
1984	KADLER, Karen (Hartford)	50	Cancer (in Los Angeles, CA)
1984	KARAS, Anton	78	Cancer (in Vienna, Austria)
1984	KAST, Pierre	63	Heart attack (on an airplane from Rome to Paris)
1984 +	KAUFMAN, Andy	35	Lung cancer (in Los Angeles, CA)
1984 +	KEIGHLEY, William	94	Pulmonary embolism (in New York, NY)
• 1984	KENDAL, Jennifer	50	
1984	KING, Walter Woolf	84	Heart attack (in Beverly Hills, CA)
1984	KINGSLEY, Susan	37	Died when her car was struck head-on by another (in Athens, Greece)
1984	KRASNA, Norman ★	74	Heart attack
1984 #+	LaRUE, Jack	83	Heart attack (in Santa Monica, CA)
1984	LAU, Wesley	63	Heart failure (in Los Angeles, CA)
1984 +	LAWFORD, Peter	61	Cardiac arrest, liver and kidney disease (in Los Angeles, CA)
1984	LeCLAIR, Lucille	62	Diabetic infection (in Miami, FL)
1984 #	LEEDS, Andrea ☆	70	Cancer (in Palm Springs, CA)
1984	LITTLE, Ann	93	Died in Los Angeles, CA

Deaths of Movie and Television Personalities — by Year

YEAR	NAME		AGE	CAUSE and/or PLACE OF DEATH
1984	LOEB, Tony		76	Cancer
1984	LONG, Avon		73	Cancer (in New York, NY)
1984	# LOSEY, Joseph		75	Died in London, England
1984	MAPES, Ted		82	After a brief illness (in Burbank, CA)
1984	MARLEY, John	☆	77	Following open-heart surgery (in Los Angeles, CA)
1984	+ MARLOWE, June		81	Died in Burbank, CA
1984	MARTIN, D'urville		45	Heart attack (in Los Angeles, CA)
1984	MASON, James	☆	75	Massive heart attack (in Vevey, Switzerland)
1984	+ MASSEY, Edith		65	Cancer (in Los Angeles, CA)
1984	MATTHEWS, George		73	Heart disease
1984	MAY, Doris		82	Heart failure (in Camarillo, CA)
1984	McAVOY, May		82	Died in Sherman Oaks, CA
1984	McINTYRE, Christine		69	After a brief illness (in Northridge, CA)
1984	McMURRAY, Richard		68	Lung cancer (in Burbank, CA)
1984	MERCER, Jack		74	After a brief illness (in New York, NY)
1984	# MERMAN, Ethel		75	Results of a brain tumor (in Manhattan, NY)
1984	MIDDLETON, Ray		77	Heart attack (in Panorama City, CA)
1984	#+ MINTER, Mary Miles		82	Heart failure (in Santa Monica, CA)
1984	MOORE, Robert (director)		56	After a brief illness (in New York, NY)
1984	# MORECAMBE, Eric		58	Heart disease (in Cheltenham, England)
1984	MYLES, Mary		93	Congestive heart failure (in Los Angeles, CA)
1984	PARFREY, Woodrow		61	Heart attack (in Los Angeles, CA)
1984	PEARCE, Muriel		85	After a long illness (in Natick, MA)
1984	PECKINPAH, Sam		59	Following several heart attacks (in Inglewood, CA)
1984	PEEPLES, Dennis		50	Heart attack
1984	PEERCE, Jan		80	Pneumonia and coma (in New York, NY)
1984	+ PIDGEON, Walter	☆	87	Series of strokes (in Santa Monica, CA)
1984	+ POWELL, William	☆	91	Cardiac arrest in his sleep (in Palm Springs, CA)
1984	PREISSER, June		61	Automobile collision (in Boca Raton, FL)
1984	RAISCH, William		79	Lung cancer (in Santa Monica, CA)
1984	RANDALL, Sue		49	Cancer of the lungs and larynx (in Philadelphia, PA)
1984	+ RENICK, Ruth		91	Died in Hollywood, CA
1984	+ RIORDAN, Marjorie (Schlaff)		63	
1984	+ ROBSON, Flora	☆	82	Undisclosed causes (in Brighton, England)
1984	# ROCK, Joe		93	After a brief illness (in Sherman Oaks, CA)
1984	ROSSITER, Leonard		57	Apparent heart attack (in London, England)
1984	ROTHA, Paul		76	Died in Wallingford, England
1984	ROWLAND, Henry		70	Died in Northridge, CA
1984	+ RYAN, Edmond		79	Heart attack (in Louisville, KY)
1984	SALVIO, Robert		45	Complications from A.I.D.S. (in New York, NY)
1984	+ SANDS, Billy		73	Lung cancer (in Los Angeles, CA)
1984	SHARP, Anthony		69	Died in London, England
1984	SHIELDS, John Webster		34	Cancer (in Modesto, CA)
1984	SINCLAIR, Gordon		83	Died in Toronto, Canada
1984	STAUDTE, Wolfgang		77	Heart attack (in Zigarski, Slovenia)
1984	TAYLOR, Lance Sr.		69	Heart attack (in Los Angeles, CA)
1984	+ TRUFFAUT, François		52	Brain cancer (in Neuilly-sur-Seine, France)
1984	+ TUBB, Ernest		70	Emphysema (in Nashville, TN)
1984	VanDYKE, Truman		86	Heart failure (in Los Angeles, CA)
1984	VEAZIE, Carol Eberts		89	Cardiac arrest in her sleep (in Carmel, CA)
1984	VERNAC, Denise		66	Died in Paris, France
1984	#+ VonERICH, David		25	
1984	WAGGNER, George		90	Natural causes (in Hollywood, CA)

• New entry. # Original name (Pt. 7). + Interment (Pt. 5).

101

☆ Oscar nominee, ★ Oscar winner (Pt. 10)

Deaths of Movie and Television Personalities — by Year

YEAR	NAME	AGE	CAUSE and/or PLACE OF DEATH
1984	WARING, Fred	84	Stroke
1984	WEBSTER, Paul Francis	77	Parkinson's disease (in Beverly Hills, CA)
1984	#+ WEISSMULLER, Johnny	79	Heart disease and cerebral thrombosis (in Acapulco, Mexico)
1984	# WERNER, Oskar ☆	61	Heart attack (in Marbourg, Germany)
1984	+ WEST, Brooks	67	Cerebral hemorrhage (in Los Angeles, CA)
1984	WHITING, Napoleon	75	Heart attack (in Los Angeles, CA)
1984	WILCOXON, Henry	78	Congestive heart failure (in Los Angeles, CA)
1984	# WILLSON, Meredith	82	Heart failure (in Santa Monica, CA)
1984	#+ WINWOOD, Estelle	101	Heart failure (in Woodland Hills, CA)
1985	ADDAMS, Dawn	55	Cancer
• 1985	ALDRICH, David	54	After a long illness
1985	ANDEN, Matthew	42	After a lengthy illness (in New York)
1985	ANDERSON, Edward	70	
1985	#+ ANDREWS, Edward	70	Heart attack (in Pacific Palisades, CA)
1985	ANKERS, Evelyn	67	Cancer (in Haiku, Hawaii)
• 1985	BADIE, Jean	78	Died in Nice, France
1985	#+ BAKER, Kenny	72	Heart attack (in Solvang, CA)
1985	BARNEY, Jay	72	Cancer (in Philadelphia, PA)
1985	BARR, Patrick	77	Died in London, England
1985	BATE, Tom	85	Died in New York, NY
1985	BAUER, Charita	62	Following a long illness (in New York, NY)
1985	BAXTER, Anne ★	62	Stroke (in New York, NY)
1985	BERLE, Jack	80	After a long illness (in Woodland Hills, CA)
1985	BLACK, Dorothy	85	Died in London, England
1985	# BLAKE, Arthur	70	Heart attack (in Fort Lauderdale, FL)
1985	BOULTING, John	71	Cancer (in Sunningdale, England)
1985	#+ BRADY, Scott	60	Respiratory failure
1985	BRAMBELL, Wilfrid	72	Cancer (in London, England)
1985	BRIGGS, Charles	53	Died in Boswell, GA
1985	+ BROOKS, Louise	78	Heart attack
1985	#+ BRYNNER, Yul ★	65	Lung cancer (in New York, NY)
1985	BULOFF, Joseph	85	After a long illness (in Manhattan, NY)
1985	BURGE, James C.	41	Respiratory failure (pneumonia) in New York, NY
1985	# BURROWS, Abe	74	After a long illness (in New York, NY)
1985	# BUZZELL, Eddie	89	Died in Los Angeles, CA
1985	CAMPBELL, Kay	80	Injuries from automobile accident (in Greenwich, CT)
1985	CAMPOS, Rafael	49	Stomach cancer (in Woodland Hills, CA)
1985	CARIDEO, Eddie	72	Died in Hollywood, CA
1985	CARTER, Lynne	60	Pneumonia complicated by A.I.D.S. (in New York, NY)
1985	CHANDLER, George L.	82	Alzheimer's disease (in Hollywood, CA)
1985	# CLAIRE, Ina	95	Lingering effects of a stroke (in San Francisco, CA)
1985	CLARKE, Philip Norman	81	Died in Dothan, AL
1985	CLUTE, Sidney	69	Cancer (in Los Angeles, CA)
1985	+ COLASANTO, Nicholas "Coach"	61	Heart ailment (in Studio City, CA)
1985	COLE, Lester	81	Heart attack (in San Francisco, CA)
1985	#+ CRAIG, James	73	Lung cancer (in Santa Ana, CA)
1985	CROTHERS, Joel	44	Cancer (in Los Angeles, CA)
1985	# CURTIS, Jackie	38	Drug overdose (in New York, NY)
1985	DAVIS, Rick	71	Heart failure (in Los Angeles, CA)
1985	DAWSON, Kurt	43	Complications from cancer
1985	+ DESMOND, Johnny	65	Cancer (in Los Angeles, CA)
1985	+ DIAMOND, Selma	64	Cancer (in Los Angeles, CA)

Deaths of Movie and Television Personalities — by Year

YEAR	NAME	AGE	CAUSE and/or PLACE OF DEATH
1985	DOWNEY, Morton Sr.	83	Effects of a stroke (in Palm Beach, FL)
1985	DYALL, Valentine	75	Died in London, England
1985	# EARLES, Harry	83	Died in Sarasota, FL
1985	ELLSWORTH, Stephen R.	77	Heart failure (in Paterson, NJ)
1985	ENGLE, Darleen	48	Cancer (in Santa Monica, CA)
1985	ERVIN, (Senator) Sam	88	Kidney failure after gall bladder surgery
1985	EVANS, Clifford	73	Died in Wales
1985	#+ FAYLEN, Frank	79	After a long illness (in Burbank, CA)
1985	# FETCHIT, Stepin	83	Pneumonia and heart failure (in Woodland Hills, CA)
1985	FEURY, Peggy	?	Automobile accident (in Los Angeles, CA)
1985	FLEISCHER, Louis	94	Died in Woodland Hills, CA
1985	FOSTER, Alan	80	Cancer (in Los Angeles, CA)
1985	# FOSTER, Phil	71	Heart attack (in Rancho Mirage, CA)
1985	# FRAZEE, Jane	67	Pneumonia following a stroke (in Newport Beach, CA)
1985	GANTRY, Donald	52	Cancer (in New York, NY)
1985	GERASIMOV, Sergei	79	Heart attack (in Moscow, Russia)
1985	GILMAN, Sam	70	Cancer (in North Hollywood, CA)
1985	GORDON, Noele	61	Cancer (in Birmingham, England)
1985	# GORDON, Ruth ★	88	Stroke (in Edgartown, MA)
1985	+ GOUDAL, Jetta	86	After a long illness (in Los Angeles, CA)
1985	# GRANT, Kirby	74	Automobile accident (in Titusville, FL)
1985	GREENE, Richard	66	Cardiac arrest after a fall (in Norfolk, England)
1985	GREENFIELD, Calvin "Rusty"	58	Lung cancer (in Santa Monica, CA)
1985	GREENWAY, Tom	75	Heart attack (in Los Angeles, CA)
1985	# HALE, Georgia	79	Died in Hollywood, CA
1985	HALL, Grayson ☆	58	Cancer (in New York, NY)
1985	HAMILTON, John	?	Heart attack (Do not confuse with John Hamilton, d. 1958)
1985	+ HAMILTON, Margaret	83	Heart attack (in Salisbury, CO)
1985	HANEY, David	44	Heart attack (in Studio City, CA)
1985	HARVEY, Harry Sr.	84	Died in Sylmar, CA
1985	+ HATHAWAY, Henry ☆	86	Heart attack after pneumonia (in Los Angeles, CA)
1985	HAUSER, Gayelord	89	Complications from pneumonia
1985	HAYDN, Richard	80	Heart attack (in Los Angeles, CA)
1985	# HAYWARD, Louis	76	Lung cancer (in Palm Springs, CA)
1985	+ HECHT, Harold	77	Cancer (in Beverly Hills, CA)
1985	# HENDERSON, Dickie	62	Cancer (in London, England)
1985	HIBBS, Jesse	79	Alzheimer's disease (in Ojai, CA)
1985	HILLPOT, William A.	79	Pneumonia (in New York, NY)
1985	#+ HUDSON, Rock ☆	59	Complications from A.I.D.S. (in Beverly Hills, CA)
1985	HUFFMAN, David	40	Murdered (stabbed to death) at his home in Balboa Island, CA
1985	JEANS, Isabel	93	Died in London, England
1985	JONES, Tyrone	29	Automobile accident (in Los Angeles, CA)
1985	# JOY, Leatrice	91	Pernicious anemia (in Riverdale, NY)
1985	# KARLSON, Phil	77	Cancer (in Los Angeles, CA)
1985	+ KATZ, Mickey	75	Natural causes
1985	KENIN, Alexa	23	Undisclosed causes (in New York)
1985	KEYSER, Andy	33	Cancer (in Santa Monica, CA)
1985	KING, Wayne	84	
1985	+ KYSER, Kay	79	Heart attack (in Chapel Hill, NC)
1985	LALLY, Michael Sr.	82	Died in Woodland Hills, CA
1985	LATCHAW, Paul	38	Complications from A.I.D.S. (in New York, NY)
• 1985	LEMAIRE, Charles ★	87	Died in his sleep
1985	# LeROY, Hal	71	Following heart surgery (in Hackensack, NJ)

Deaths of Movie and Television Personalities — by Year

YEAR		NAME		AGE	CAUSE and/or PLACE OF DEATH
1985		LEWIS, Jarma		54	*Heart attack in her sleep (in Los Angeles, CA)*
1985		LINTON, Mark		28	*Heart failure and pneumonia (in New York, NY)*
1985		LIST, Eugene		66	*Found dead at home (in New York, NY)*
1985		LIVINGSTON, Margaret		89	*Died in Warrington, PA*
1985		LODGE, John Davis		82	*Heart attack (in New York, NY)*
1985		LONDON, George		64	*Following a heart attack*
1985		MacLAREN, Mary		85	*Double pneumonia (in Los Angeles, CA)*
1985		MacVEIGH, Earle		74	*Cancer (in Los Angeles, CA)*
1985	#+	Margo (Margo Albert)		68	*After a long illness (in Pacific Palisades, CA)*
1985	+	MARIS, Roger		51	*Lymphatic cancer*
1985	+	MARTIN, Marion		76	*Cardiac arrest in her sleep (in Santa Monica, CA)*
1985		MASONER, Gene		41	*A.I.D.S. (in New York, NY)*
1985		MATHESON, Murray		73	*Heart failure (in Woodland Hills, CA)*
1985		MAYER, Kenneth M. "Ken"		66	*Died in North Hollywood, CA*
1985		MEMMOLI, George T.		46	*Heart failure (in Los Angeles, CA)*
1985		MICHAELIDES, George		66	*Complications after heart surgery (in Los Angeles, CA)*
1985	+	MILLER, Marvin		72	*Heart attack (in Santa Monica, CA)*
1985		NASH, Clarence "Donald Duck"		80	*Leukemia (in Burbank, CA)*
1985	#+	NELSON, Rick		45	*Airplane crash (near DeKalb, TX) traces of cocaine found in his body*
1985		NOLAN, James		69	*Lung cancer (in Woodland Hills, CA)*
1985	+	NOLAN, Lloyd		83	*Lung cancer (in Los Angeles, CA)*
1985	+	O'BRIEN, Edmond	★	69	*Alzheimer's disease after suffering heart problems (in Inglewood, CA)*
1985		O'BRIEN, George		85	*Following a stroke (in Broken Arrow, CA)*
1985		O'BRIEN, Kenneth		49	*Cancer (in Los Angeles, CA)*
1985		O'MALLEY, J. Pat		80	*Heart condition (in CA) Do not confuse with Pat O'Malley, d. 1966*
1985		OLSON, Johnny ("Come on down")		75	*Brain hemorrhage*
1985		ORMANDY, Eugene		85	
1985		PARKER, Dennis		38	*After a brief illness (in New York, NY)*
1985		PARRY, Harvey		85	*Heart attack (in Sherman Oaks, CA)*
1985		PEARY, Harold "Gildersleeve"		76	*Heart attack (in Torrance, CA)*
1985		PURCELL, Noel		84	*Died in Dublin, Ireland*
1985		READICK, Robert		59	*Automobile accident (in Trenton, NJ)*
1985		REDGRAVE, Michael	☆	77	*Parkinson's disease (in Denham, England)*
1985		REESE, Sammy Pharr		55	*Massive stroke (in Montgomery, AL)*
1985	+	RIDDLE, Nelson		64	*Cardiac and kidney failure (in Los Angeles, CA)*
1985	#+	RITZ, Jimmy		81	*Heart failure (in Los Angeles, CA)*
1985		ROBBINS, Randall		45	*After a long illness (in New York, NY)*
1985		ROSS, Jane		50	*During surgery for cancer (in Los Angeles, CA)*
1985		RYAN, Kathleen		63	*Died in Dublin, Ireland*
1985		RYSKIND, Morrie		89	*Apparent stroke (in Washington, D.C.)*
1985	#	SAPPINGTON, Fay		78	*After a long illness (in New York, NY)*
1985	#	SARONY, Leslie		88	*Died in London, England*
1985	+	SAVALAS, George		60	*Leukemia (in Westwood, CA)*
1985		SAVILLE, Ruth		92	*Died in Los Angeles, CA*
• 1985		SCHOEN, Margarethe		89	
1985		SCOURBY, Alexander		71	*Died in Boston, MA*
1985	#	SHAUGHNESSY, Mickey		64	*Lung cancer (in Cape May Courthouse, NJ)*
1985		SHERMAN, Ransom		87	*Died in Henderson, NV*
1985		SHUE, Larry		38	*Airplane crash (in Weyers Cave, VA)*
1985	#+	SIGNORET, Simone	★	64	*Pancreatic cancer (in Auteuil-Anthouillet, France)*
1985	#+	SILVERS, Phil		73	*Heart attack (in Century City, CA)*
1985		SIMPSON, Mickey		72	*Heart attack (in Northridge, CA)*
1985		SMITH, Kent		78	*Congestive heart failure (in Woodland Hills, CA)*

Deaths of Movie and Television Personalities — by Year

YEAR	NAME		AGE	CAUSE and/or PLACE OF DEATH
1985	SMITH, Muriel		61	Died in Richmond, VA
1985	SMITH, Samantha		13	Airplane crash after filming in England (in Auburn-Lewiston, ME)
1985	SOLON, Ewen		62	Died in Addlestone, England
1985	# SONDERGAARD, Gale	★	86	After a long illness (in Woodland Hills, CA)
1985	SPIEGEL, Sam		84	After surgery (while vacationing in Ile-Saint-Martin, Antilles)
1985	SPOLIANSKY, Mischa		86	Died in London, England
1985	STOLL, George		79	After a brief illness (in Monterey, CA)
1985	STORER, Conrad L.		55	Cancer (in Burbank, CA)
1985	STRETTON, Ellen		71	Pneumonia (in New York, NY)
1985	STROUD, Claude		78	Throat cancer (in Santa Monica, CA)
1985	SWEET, Dolph		64	Cancer (in Tarzana, CA)
1985	# TERRY, Tex		82	Died in Terre Haute, IN
1985	TRUBSHAWE, Michael		80	Died in England
1985	WAYNE, Carol		42	Drowned (in Nanzanillo, Mexico)
1985	# WELLES, Orson	☆	70	Heart attack (in Los Angeles, CA)
1985	WELSH, John		70	Cancer (in London, England)
1985	WEST, Madge		93	Cardiac arrest in her sleep (in Memphis, TN)
1985	WESTMORE, Frank		62	After treatment for a cardiac condition
1985	WESTON, Steve		45	Results of a fall from the roof of his home (in Toronto, Canada)
1985	WHITE, Jules J.		84	Alzheimer's disease (in Van Nuys, CA)
1985	WILLIAMS, Grant		54	Peritonitis (in Los Angeles, CA)
1985	WILLIAMS, Tex		68	Cancer (in Newhall, CA)
1985	WORMS, Robert A. III		52	Heart failure (in Hollywood, CA)
1985	ZIMBALIST, Efrem Sr.		95	
1986	# ACKLES, Kenneth		70	Stroke (in Pasadena, TX)
1986	AHERNE, Brian	☆	83	Heart failure (in Venice, FL)
1986	#+ ALDA, Robert		72	Effects of a stroke (in Los Angeles, CA)
1986	AMY, George J.		86	After a long illness (in Los Angeles, CA)
1986	ANDREWS, Ann		95	
1986	+ ANGEL, Heather		76	Cancer (in Santa Barbara, CA)
1986	ARLEN, Harold		81	Died in Manhattan, NY
1986	+ ARMSTRONG, Herbert W.		93	Died in his sleep
1986	#+ ARNAZ, Desi		69	Lung cancer (in Del Mar, CA)
1986	ATWATER, Edith		74	Cancer (in Los Angeles, CA)
1986	BADDELEY, Hermione	☆	79	Cerebral thrombosis (in Los Angeles, CA)
1986	BAEHR, Nicholas E.		61	Cancer
1986	+ BAER, Jacob "Buddy"		71	Died in Los Angeles, CA
1986	BAKER, Hylda		78	Died in Lancashire, England
1986	BAKER-BERGEN, Stuart		40	Complications from A.I.D.S. (in New Orleans, LA)
1986	BANDY, Way		45	A.I.D.S.
1986	BASELEON, Michael		61	Died in Lenox, MA
1986	BECHER, John C.		71	Cancer (in Hollywood, CA)
1986	BERGNER, Elizabeth	☆	85	After a long illness (in London, England)
1986	+ BERNARDI, Herschel		62	Heart attack (in Los Angeles, CA)
1986	# BJÖRNSTRAND, Gunnar		77	After a long illness (in Stockholm, Sweden)
1986	BONNELL, Lee		67	Heart attack (in Santa Monica, CA)
1986	BREMEN, Lennie		71	Died in Hollywood, CA
1986	BRIGGS, Donald P.		75	Cancer (in Woodland Hills, CA)
1986	BRODUS, Tex		81	Massive stroke (in Woodland Hills, CA)
1986	BROOKE, Walter		71	Emphysema
1986	BROWN, Harry		69	Emphysema (in Los Angeles) Do not confuse with Harry Joe Brown
1986	BRYAN, Ken		32	An A.I.D.S.-related illness (in Walnut Creek, CA)

• New entry. # Original name (Pt. 7). + Interment (Pt. 5).

105

☆ Oscar nominee, ★ Oscar winner (Pt. 10)

Deaths of Movie and Television Personalities — by Year

YEAR	NAME		AGE	CAUSE and/or PLACE OF DEATH
1986	# BUBBLES, John W.		84	Cerebral hemorrhage (in Los Angeles, CA)
1986	CABOT, Susan		59	Beaten to death in her home (in Los Angeles, CA)
1986	CAESAR, Adolph		52	Heart attack (in Los Angeles, CA)
1986	+ CAGNEY, James ★		86	Diabetes, heart and lung problems (in Stanfordville, NY)
1986	CALDWELL, Don		51	A.I.D.S. (in Sherman Oaks, CA)
1986	CAMPBELL, Muriel		75	Died in Warren, CT
1986	+ CANTY, Marietta		80	
1986	# CANUTT, Yakima		90	Cardiac arrest in her sleep (in North Hollywood, CA)
1986	CAREY, Denis		77	Died in London, England
1986	CARMEL, Roger		53	Drug overdose (in Hollywood, CA)
1986	CASE, Allen		51	Heart attack (in Truckee, CA)
1986	CHAPMAN, Ted		63	Natural causes (in Studio City, CA)
1986	CHILDRESS, Alvin		78	Parkinson's disease, diabetes, pneumonia (in Inglewood, CA)
1986	CLARK, Mamo		72	Cancer (in Panorama City, CA)
1986	COHEN, Myron		83	Died in New York, NY
1986	COLERIDGE, Sylvia		76	Died in London, England
1986	# COLONNA, Jerry		82	Kidney failure (in Woodland Hills, CA)
1986	COOPER, Edna Mae		85	Died in Woodland Hills, CA
1986	COURTOT, Marguerite		88	Died in Long Beach, CA
1986	CRAIG, Helen		74	Cardiac arrest in her sleep (in New York, NY)
1986	#+ CRAWFORD, Broderick ★		74	Series of strokes (in Rancho Mirage, CA)
1986	+ CROTHERS, Benjamin "Scatman"		76	Lung cancer (in Van Nuys, CA)
1986	CUNNINGHAM, Sarah		67	Asthmatic attack (in Los Angeles, CA)
1986	# DAINTY, Billy		59	Died in Shackleford, England
1986	DaSILVA, Howard		76	Lymphatic cancer (in Ossining, NY)
1986	DEERING, Olive		67	Cancer (in New York, NY)
1986	DeRUE, Carmen		78	Heart attack (in North Hollywood, CA)
1986	DOMINIQUE, Laurien		29	Embolism (in San Francisco, CA)
1986	DRIVAS, Robert		50	Died in New York, NY
1986	+ DUNCAN, Vivian "Little Eva"		84	Alzheimer's disease (in Los Angeles, CA)
1986	ECCLES, Donald		77	Automobile crash (in Sussex, England)
1986	EDWARDS, Guy		51	Heart attack (in Los Angeles, CA0
1986	# ERICKSON, Leif		72	Cancer (in Pensacola, FL)
1986	FARR, Derek		74	Cancer (in London, England)
1986	FERNANDEZ, Emilio		82	Heart attack (in Mexico City, Mexico)
1986	FRANCIS, Ivor		68	Died in Sherman Oaks, CA
1986	+ FREDERICK, Freddie Burke		65	Ventricular arrhythmia due to myocardial infarction
• 1986	FREES, Paul		66	Heart failure
1986	GABEL, Martin		73	Heart attack (in New York, NY)
1986	GIBNEY, Louise		90	Died in Santa Maria, CA
1986	GILLMORE, Margalo		88	Died in New York, NY
1986	GILMORE, Virginia		66	Emphysema (in Santa Barbara, CA)
1986	+ GOODMAN, Benny		77	Heart attack (in Manhattan, NY)
1986	#+ GRANT, Cary ☆		82	Massive stroke (in Davenport, IA)
1986	GREGG, Virginia		70	Cancer (in Encino, CA)
1986	HALOP, Florence		63	Cancer (in Los Angeles, CA)
1986	HAMILTON, Murray		63	Lung cancer (in Washington, D.C.)
• 1986	+ HATLEY, T. Marvin ☆		81	Cancer
1986	# HAYDEN, Sterling		70	Cancer (in Sanjalito, CA)
1986	HAYNES, Hilda		72	Died in New York, NY
1986	+ HEIDT, Horace		85	Pneumonia and heart trouble (in Los Angeles, CA)
1986	HELPMANN, Robert		76	After a long illness (in Sydney, Australia)
1986	HERBERT, Tim		71	Heart attack (in Los Angeles, CA)

Deaths of Movie and Television Personalities — by Year

YEAR	NAME		AGE	CAUSE and/or PLACE OF DEATH
1986	HEWITT, Alan		71	Cancer (in New York, NY)
1986	HICKMAN, Bill		65	Cancer (in Indio, CA)
1986	HIGBE, Mary Jane		70	Stroke
1986	HOFFMAN, Beth Webb		89	Died in Studio City, CA
1986	HURST, B. D.		91	
1986	JAMES, Claire		65	
1986	# JEROME, Suzie		26	Cut wrists and exposure (in Cornwall, England)
1986	JONES, Darby		76	Cancer (in Los Angeles, CA)
1986	JOYCE, Anna		74	Died in Hialeah, FL
• 1986	JUTRA, Claude		56	Suicide after Alzheimer's (drowned himself in the St. Lawrence River)
1986	# KAY, Beatrice		79	After suffering several strokes (in North Hollywood, CA)
1986	KEAN, Betty		69	After a brief illness (in Hollywood, CA)
1986	KEENAN, Paul		30	A.I.D.S. (in Boston, MA)
1986	KING, Dennis Jr.		?	Heart attack
1986	#+ KNIGHT, Ted		62	After surgery for a urinary tract growth (in Pacific Palisades, CA)
1986	LAMBERT, Douglas		50	A.I.D.S. (in London, England)
1986	#+ LANCHESTER, Elsa	☆	84	Bronchial pneumonia (in Woodland Hills, CA)
1986	LANDIS, Joseph P.		67	Cancer
1986	LEE, Carl		52	Died in New York, NY
1986	LEONE, Johnny		71	Cerebral thrombosis (in Rome, Italy)
1986	LERNER, Alan Jay		67	Lung cancer (in New York, NY)
1986	LEWIS, Buddy		62	Apparent heart attack
1986	LOOS, Anne		70	After a long illness (in Los Angeles, CA)
1986	LOPEZ, J. Victor		39	A.I.D.S. (in Los Angeles, CA)
1986	LORMER, Jon		80	Died in Burbank, CA
1986	# LOVE, Bessie	☆	87	Undisclosed causes (in London, England)
1986	# LYS, Lya		78	Heart ailment (in Newport Beach, CA)
1986	# MACK, Helen		72	Cancer (in Beverly Hills, CA)
1986	MacLAUGHLIN, Don		79	After a brief illnes (in Goshen, CT)
1986	MacRAE, Gordon		65	Cancer of the mouth and jaw (in Lincoln, NE)
• 1986	MATHEWS, Beau		29	A.I.D.S.
1986	McCARTHY, Frank		74	Cancer (in Woodland Hills, CA)
1986	McINTIRE, Tim		42	Heart failure (in Los Angeles, CA)
1986	McKENNA, Siobhan		63	Heart attack and lung cancer (in Dublin, Ireland)
1986	McKENZIE, Ida Mae		75	Died in Los Angeles, CA
1986	McLAUGHLIN, Don		79	After a brief illness
• 1986	MEADOWS, Robert		29	After a brief illness
1986	MEARS, Martha		78	Complications from Alzheimer's disease
1986	+ MERKEL, Una	☆	82	Died in Los Angeles, CA
1986	# MILLAND, Ray	★	81	Cancer (in Torrance, CA)
1986	MILLER, Court		34	Complications from A.I.D.S. (in Portland, ME)
1986	+ MINNELLI, Vincente	★	83	Emphysema and pneumonia (in Beverly Hills, CA)
1986	MOLLISON, Clifford		89	Undisclosed causes (in Cyprus)
1986	MORRIS, Rolland "Rusty"		63	Cancer (in Los Angeles, CA)
1986	NAZARRO, Ray		83	Died in Los Angeles, CA
1986	# NEAGLE, Anna		81	Exhaustion (in England)
1986	+ NELSON, Frank		75	Cancer
1986	# NICHOLS, Dandy		78	Arthritis complications (in London, England)
1986	#+ PALMER, Lilli		71	Cancer and heart attack (in Los Angeles, CA)
1986	PALMER, Norman		65	After a long illness (in Duarte, CA)
1986	PARIS, Jerry		60	Complications from a brain tumor (in Los Angeles, CA)
1986	PENDER, Stephen		35	Complications from A.I.D.S. (in Los Angeles, CA)
1986	# PERKINS, Marlin		81	Lymphatic cancer

• New entry. # Original name (Pt. 7). + Interment (Pt. 5).　　　107　　　☆ Oscar nominee, ★ Oscar winner (Pt. 10)

Deaths of Movie and Television Personalities — by Year

YEAR	NAME		AGE	CAUSE and/or PLACE OF DEATH
1986	# PHOENIX, Pat		62	Lung cancer (in Manchester, England)
1986	POOLE, Roy		62	Died in Mount Kisco, NY
1986	PREMINGER, Otto	☆	79	Cancer (in Manhattan, NY)
1986	PROACH, Henry		66	
1986	#+ REED, Donna	★	64	Pancreatic cancer (in Beverly Hills, CA)
1986	#+ RITZ, Harry		78	Cancer (in San Diego, CA)
1986	ROBINS, Barry		41	After a long illness (in Los Angeles, CA)
1986	ROBINSON, Bartlett "Bart"		73	After a long bout with cancer (in Fallbrook, CA)
1986	RUBIN, Benny		86	Heart attack after surgery (in Los Angeles, CA)
1986	SCHUSTER, Harold D.		83	Died in Westlake Village, CA
1986	SCOTT, Ken		58	Emphysema and heart failure (in Los Angeles, CA)
1986	# SIMPSON, Bill		54	After a long illness (in Mauchline, Scotland)
1986	SMITH, Justin		66	Complications from A.I.D.S. (in Santa Monica, CA)
1986	#+ SMITH, Kate		79	After a long bout with diabetes and heart problems (in Raleigh, NC)
1986	STARRETT, Charles		82	Cancer (in Borrego Springs, CA)
1986	STEPHENS, Harvey		85	Died in Laguna Hills, CA
1986	STEVENS, Paul		65	Pneumonia (in New York, NY)
1986	STEVENSON, Robert (director)		81	After a long illness (in Santa Barbara, CA)
1986	STEWART, Paul		77	Heart attack (in Los Angeles, CA)
1986	STOCK, Nigel		66	Heart attack (in London, England)
1986	STONE, Sidney		83	Heart failure (in New York, NY)
1986	STUCKER, Stephen		36	Complications from A.I.D.S. (in Hollywood, CA)
1986	SWEET, Blanche		90	Stroke (in Manhattan, NY)
1986	TARKOVSKY, Andrei		54	Lung cancer (in Neilly-sur-Seine, France)
1986	TEITEL, Carol		62	Complications after a car accident (in Camden, NJ)
1986	TRACY, Steve		34	Complications from A.I.D.S. (in Tampa, FL)
1986	+ TUCKER, Forrest		71	Throat cancer
1986	TUCKER, Lorenzo		79	Cancer (in Hollywood, CA)
1986	+ TUTTLE, Lurene		79	Died in Encino, CA
1986	#+ VALLEE, Rudy		84	Heart attack and cancer (in North Hollywood, CA)
1986	VanDYKE, Willard		79	Heart attack (while driving from N.M. to MA.) in Jackson, TN
1986	VIGRAN, Herbert		76	Cancer (in Los Angeles, CA)
1986	+ WALLIS, Hal B.		88	Cardiac arrest in his sleep (in Rancho Mirage, CA)
1986	WARNER, Gertrude		68	Cancer (in Los Angeles, CA)
1986	WARNERS, Robert		29	After a long illness (in New York, NY)
1986	WHEEL, Patricia		61	After a long illness (in New York, NY)
1986	WIECK, Dorothea		78	Died in Berlin, Germany
1986	WILSON, Margery		89	Cardiac arrest in her sleep (in Alhambra, CA)
1986	WILSON, Teddy		73	Following intestinal surgery (in New Britain, CT)
1986	WINDSOR, Marie		64	
1986	#+ WYNN, Keenan		70	Cancer (in Brentwood, CA)
1986	YALE, Joseph		36	Complications from A.I.D.S. (in Palm Springs, CA)
1986	# ZAREMBA, Jack		77	Heart attack (in Newport Beach, CA)
1987	ABEL, Walter		88	Heart attack (in Essex, CT)
1987	ADAMS, Peter		69	Cancer (in Beverly Hills, CA)
1987	ALDERMAN, John		53	Apparent heart attack (in Hollywood, CA)
1987	ALLEGRET, Yves		79	Heart attack (in France)
1987	ALLEN, Irving		82	After a long illness (in Encino, CA)
1987	ALLEN, Vera		89	Heart failure (at a retirement home in Croton-on-Hudson, NY)
1987	ARLISS, Leslie		86	Died in London, England
1987	# ARNAUD, Georges		69	Died in Barcelona, Spain
1987	#+ ASTAIRE, Fred	☆	88	Pneumonia (in Los Angeles, CA)

• New entry. # Original name (Pt. 7). + Interment (Pt. 5).

☆ Oscar nominee, ★ Oscar winner (Pt. 10)

Deaths of Movie and Television Personalities — by Year

YEAR	NAME	AGE	CAUSE and/or PLACE OF DEATH
1987	#+ ASTOR, Mary ★	81	Emphysema (in Los Angeles, CA)
1987	ATTAWAY, Ruth	77	Injuries from a fire in her apartment
1987	AVRAKIAN, Aram	61	Heart failure
1987	BAILEY, Sherwood "Spud"	64	Cancer (in Newport Beach, CA)
1987	# BAIRD, Bill	82	Died in New York, NY
1987	# BASS, Alfie	66	Heart attack (in London, England)
1987	BAUERSMITH, Paula	78	Cancer (in New York, NY)
1987	BELLIN, Olga	54	Cancer (in New York, NY)
1987	BENNET, Spencer Gordon	94	Died in Santa Monica, CA
1987	BERMAN, Dr. Edgar	68	
1987	BISSELL, Patrick	30	Overdose of cocaine, codeine, methadone (in Hoboken, NJ)
1987	# BLAKELY, Colin	56	Leukemia (in England)
1987	BLAKELY, Gene	66	Bone cancer (in Creston, IA)
1987	BLASETTI, Alessandro	86	Heart attack (in Rome, Italy)
1987	BOLAND, Joseph S.	83	Heart attack (in Newington, CT)
1987	#+ BOLGER, Ray	83	Gall bladder cancer (in Los Angeles, CA)
1987	BOOKER, Bernice Ingalls	91	
1987	BRANNUM, Hugh	77	Cancer (in East Stroudsburg, PA)
1987	BRESSAN, Arthur J. Jr.	44	A.I.D.S. (in New York, NY)
1987	+ BROWN, Clarence ☆	97	Kidney failure (in Santa Monica, CA)
1987	BRUCK, Karl	81	Cancer (in Los Angeles, CA)
1987	BURNELL, Peter	44	Died in Chicago, IL
1987	BUTTERFIELD, Paul	44	Died in North Hollywood, CA
1987	CAMERON, Donald A.	61	Died in Philadelphia, PA
1987	CAMPBELL, Archie	72	Renal and heart failure (in Knoxville, TN)
1987	CARROLL, Madeleine	81	Pancreatic cancer (in Marbella, Spain)
1987	# CARUSO, Enrico Jr.	82	Following a heart attack (in Jacksonville, FL)
1987	CASPARY, Vera	87	Died in New York, NY)
1987	CHARLES, Anthony	42	Heart attack (in Burbank, CA)
1987	CHRISTY, Ann	82	Heart attack (in Vernon, TX)
1987	CLARKE, Raymond	47	A.I.D.S. (in Toronto, Canada)
1987	COCO, James	56	Heart attack (in New York, NY)
1987	COE, Peter	58	Killed when his car collided with a van (in Byfleet, England)
1987	# COLLIER, Patience	76	Died in London, England
1987	COLLIER, William "Buster" Jr.	86	Cardiac arrest from arteriosclerosis (in San Francisco, CA)
1987	COOPER, Olive	94	Pneumonia (in Los Angeles, CA)
1987	COSTELLO, Carole	48	Stroke
1987	# CULVER, Calvin	43	Pulmonary infection (in Inverness, FL)
1987	DAMON, Cathryn	56	Cancer (in Los Angeles, CA)
1987	# DANA, Viola	90	Heart failure (in Woodland Hills, CA)
1987	DANDRIDGE, Ruby	87	Died in Los Angeles, CA
1987	DAWSON, Hal K.	90	Stroke (in Loma Linda, CA)
1987	DEMPSTER, Hugh	86	Heart failure (in Chicago, IL)
1987	DOBSON, James	67	Heart attack
1987	# DONOVAN, Casey	43	Pulmonary infection
1987	DONOVAN, King	69	Cancer
1987	DUNN, Clara Whips	90	Congestive heart failure (in Atlanta, GA)
1987	DuPRE, Jacqueline	42	Multiple sclerosis (in London, England)
1987	+ EGAN, Richard	65	Prostate cancer (in Santa Monica, CA)
1987	EVANS, Wilbur W.	81	Died in Elmer, NJ
1987	FAULKNER, Ralph B.	95	After a brief illness (in Burbank, CA)
1987	+ FLYNT, Althea Leasure	33	Drowned in her bathtub after getting high on heroin
1987	FONG, Benson	70	Following a stroke (in Los Angeles, CA)

Deaths of Movie and Television Personalities — by Year

YEAR	NAME		AGE	CAUSE and/or PLACE OF DEATH
1987	# FOSSE, Bob	★	60	Massive heart attack (in Washington, D.C.)
1987	FRANCIS, Raymond		76	Died in London, England
1987	FRANJU, Georges		75	Undisclosed causes (in Paris, France)
1987	# FRASER, Bill		79	Emphysema (in Hertfordshire, England)
1987	FREGONESE, Hugo		78	Heart attack (in Buenos Aires, Argentina)
1987	FROHLICH, Gustav		85	Following surgery (in Lugano, Switzerland)
1987	GEARY, John		47	Apparent heart attack (while driving) in Fall River, MA
1987	GERAGHTY, Maurice		78	Died in Palm Springs, CA
1987	GESSNER, Adrienne		90	Died in Vienna, Austria
1987	GIBSON, Wynne		82	Stroke (in Laguna Miguel, CA)
1987	+ GINGOLD, Hermione		89	Pneumonia and cardiac disease (in New York, NY)
1987	+ GLEASON, Jackie	☆	71	Cancer of the liver and colon (in Fort Lauderdale, FL)
1987	+ GREENE, Lorne		72	Pneumonia following ulcer surgery (in Santa Monica, CA)
1987	GREENWOOD, Joan		65	Heart attack (in London, England)
1987	HAMMER, Irene Wicker		86	
1987	HANDL, Irene		85	Died in London, England
1987	+ HARTMAN, Elizabeth	☆	45	Suicide (jumped from her 5th-floor apartment) in Pittsburgh, PA
1987	HAYES, Bernadine		75	Heart attack (in Los Angeles, CA)
1987	HAYNES, Lloyd		52	Lung cancer (in Coronado, CA)
1987	#+ HAYWORTH, Rita		68	Alzheimer's disease (in New York, NY)
1987	HEIFETZ, Jascha		86	Following brain surgery after a fall (in Los Angeles, CA)
1987	#+ HERMAN, Woody		74	Congestive heart failure and emphysema (in Los Angeles, CA)
1987	HOLCOMBE, Harry		80	Died in Valencia, CA
1987	HONRI, Baynham		83	
1987	+ HUSTON, John	★	81	Complications from emphysema and pneumonia (in Middletown, RI)
1987	# HUTTON, Marion		67	Cancer (in Kirkland, WA)
1987	ILINSKY, Igor		85	Died in Moscow, Russia
1987	JAMESON, Joyce		55	Undisclosed causes (in Burbank, CA)
1987	# JARRETT, Art		81	Pneumonia
1987	JEFFRIES, Lang		55	Cancer (in Huntington Beach, CA)
1987	#+ KAYE, Danny		74	Heart failure due to hepatitis (in Los Angeles, CA)
1987	+ KAYE, Nora (Ross)		67	Cancer (in Santa Monica, CA)
1987	KAYE, Sammy		77	
1987	KELLER, Harry		73	Heart complications (in Los Angeles, CA)
1987	KENNEDY, Madge		96	Respiratory failure (in Woodland Hills, CA)
1987	KEZER, Glenn B.		63	Cancer (in Okemah, OK)
1987	KIDD, Jonathan (Kurt Richards)		73	After surgery for an aorta aneurysm (in Los Angeles, CA)
1987	KNIGHT, Esmond		80	Died in Egypt
1987	# KNIGHT, June		74	Complications after a stroke (in Los Angeles, CA)
1987	#+ LAKE, Arthur "Dagwood"		81	Heart attack (in Indian Wells, CA)
1987	LEARN, Betsy		98	Died in Burbank, CA
1987	+ LeROY, Mervyn	☆	86	Heart failure and Alzheimer's disease (in Beverly Hills, CA)
1987	LESCOULIE, Jack		75	Colon cancer (in Los Angeles, CA)
1987	LEVINE, Joseph E.		81	After a brief illness (in Greenwich, CT)
1987	#+ LIBERACE, Walter "Lee"		67	Complications from A.I.D.S. (in Palm Springs, CA)
1987	LONERGAN, Lenore		59	Cancer (in Stuart, FL)
1987	LUBOFF, Norman		70	Cancer (in Bynam, NC)
1987	# LUCE, Clare Boothe		84	Cancer (Do not confuse with Claire Luce, d. 1989)
1987	LUDLAM, Charles		44	Pneumonia complicated by A.I.D.S. (in New York, NY)
1987	MacGIBBON, Harriet		81	After suffering from pulmonary and heart problems (in Beverly Hills)
1987	MACKAY, Fulton		64	Undisclosed causes (in London, England)
1987	MAGNOTTA, Vic		43	Drowned during filming of a car stunt (in Hoboken, NJ)
1987	+ MAMOULIAN, Rouben		90	Cardiac arrest in his sleep (in Woodland Hills, CA)

• New entry.   # Original name (Pt. 7).   + Interment (Pt. 5).

110

☆ Oscar nominee, ★ Oscar winner (Pt. 10)

Deaths of Movie and Television Personalities — by Year

YEAR	NAME	AGE	CAUSE and/or PLACE OF DEATH
1987	MANGER, Winifred Brison	94	*Following a long illness*
1987	MANN, Jerry	77	*After a series of strokes that left him an invalid (in Los Angeles, CA)*
1987	MARQUAND, Richard	49	*Stroke (in London, England)*
1987	+ MARTIN, Dean Paul Jr.	35	*Crash of his F-4C Phantom-II jet on a training flight (in CA)*
1987	MARTIN, Vivian	95	*After a long illness (in New York, NY)*
1987	+ MARVIN, Lee ★	63	*Heart attack (in Tucson, AZ)*
1987	McKAY, Scott	71	*Kidney failure (in New York, NY)*
1987	McKENZIE, Ella	82	*Died in Hollywood, CA*
1987	MEYER, Dorothy	62	*Cancer (in Los Angeles, CA)*
1987	+ MEYER, Emile G.	76	*Alzheimer's disease (in Covington, LA)*
1987	MINOR, Michael	46	*A.I.D.S.*
1987	MONTGOMERY, Earl	65	*Heart attack and leukemia (in Los Angeles, CA)*
1987	MORGAN, Elizabeth	84	*After a stroke (in New York, NY)*
1987	#+ NEGRI, Pola	87	*Brain tumor, complicated by pneumonia (in San Antonio, TX)*
1987	NELSON, Ralph	71	*Cancer (in Santa Monica, CA)*
1987	O'BRIEN, Eloise Taylor	84	
1987	# O'DAY, Molly	64	*Cancer*
1987	O'PHELAN, Sean	33	*Cancer (in Minneapolis, MN)*
1987	OBOLER, Arch	78	*Stroke (in Westlake Village, CA)*
1987	ONDRA, Anny	84	*Cerebral thrombosis (in Hamburg, Germany)*
1987	# ORLANDO, Don	75	*Heart attack while playing golf (in Glendale, CA)*
1987	PAGE, Geraldine ★	62	*Heart attack (in New York, NY)*
1987	# PAIGE, Robert	76	*Heart attack (in San Clemente, CA)*
1987	#+ PAM, Anita	77	*Died in Los Angeles, CA*
1987	PATRICK, Dorothy	65	*Cancer and heart attack (in Los Angeles, CA)*
1987	+ PELLER, Clara	86	*Died in her sleep (at her home in Chicago, IL)*
1987	POLK, David	55	*Cancer (in Los Angeles, CA)*
1987	# PRESTON, Robert	68	*Lung cancer (in Santa Barbara, CA)*
1987	PRICE, Kenny	?	
1987	# QUALEN, John	87	*Heart failure (in Torrance, CA)*
1987	REED, T. Michael	42	*Complications from A.I.D.S.*
1987	+ REY, Alejandro	57	*Cancer (in Los Angeles, CA)*
1987	RHODES, Grandon	82	*After a long illness (in Encino, CA)*
1987	+ RICE, Adnia	64	*Cancer*
1987	#+ RICH, Buddy	69	*Heart attack (during brain tumor surgery)*
1987	+ RORKE, Hayden	76	*Cancer (in Toluka Lake, CA)*
1987	ROSE, William	67	*After a lengthy illness (in Jersey, England)*
1987	ROUSE, Russell	74	*Heart failure after a cerebral thrombosis (in Santa Monica, CA)*
1987	ROWAN, Dan	65	*Lymphatic cancer (in Englewood, FL)*
1987	SALT, Waldo	72	*Cancer (in Los Angeles, CA)*
1987	SAMPSON, Will	53	*Following a heart-lung transplant (in Houston, TX)*
1987	SANDERS, Denis	58	*Heart attack in his sleep (in San Diego, CA)*
1987	SANTORO, Dean	49	*Undisclosed causes (in Sherman Oaks, CA)*
1987	#+ SCOTT, Randolph	89	*Cardiac arrest in his sleep (in Los Angeles, CA)*
1987	SECREST, James	51	*Lymphoma of the brain (in New York, NY)*
1987	SEGOVIA, Andres	94	*Heart failure*
1987	# SHAWLEE, Joan	61	*Cancer (in Hollywood, CA)*
1987	#+ SHAWN, Dick	63	*Apparent heart attack (while appearing on stage) in San Diego, CA*
1987	# SIRK, Douglas	86	*Cancer (in Lugano, Switzerland)*
1987	SLATER, Patrick Scott	42	*A.I.D.S. (in New York, NY)*
1987	STRYKER, Christopher	27	*A.I.D.S. (in New York, NY)*
1987	SULLIVAN, Maxine	75	*A seizure brought on by pneumonia (in The Bronx, NY)*
1987	SUNDBERG, Clinton	81	*Heart failure (in Santa Monica, CA)*

YEAR	NAME		AGE	CAUSE and/or PLACE OF DEATH
1987	SUSSKIND, David		66	*Heart attack (in New York, NY)*
1987	SUTHERLAND, Esther		54	*Heart attack (in Los Angeles, CA)*
1987	#+ TAYLOR, Kent		80	*Following several heart operations (in Woodland Hills, CA)*
1987	TEASDALE, Verree		80	*Died in Beverly Hills, CA*
1987	# TERRY, Alice (Alice Ingram)		88	*Pneumonia (in Burbank, CA)*
1987	THATCHER, Heather		90	*Died in Hiddington, England*
1987	TOMLIN, Pinky		80	*Heart attack*
1987	+ TORRES, Raquel		78	*Heart attack (in Malibu, CA)*
1987	TRAEGER, Kim Patrick		36	*Heart attack (in Lakewood, CA)*
1987	# TRAEGER, Rick		74	*Apparent heart attack two days after his son died (in Lakewood, CA)*
1987	TROUGHTON, Patrick		67	*Heart attack (in Columbus, GA)*
1987	TURNER, Jerry		60	*Throat cancer (in Baltimore, MD)*
1987	VALENTY, Lili		86	*Died in Hollywood, CA*
1987	VERNON, Jackie		62	*Apparent heart attack (in Hollywood, CA)*
1987	#+ VonERICH, Michael		23	
1987	VonTRAPP, Marie Augusta		82	*Congestive heart failure*
1987	+ WARHOL, Andy		59	*Cardiac arrest during gall bladder surgery (in New York, NY)*
1987	WATT, Harry		80	*Died in London, England*
1987	WEISENBORN, Gordon		64	*Died in Chicago, IL*
1987	WHITE, Ward		60	*Cancer (in West Palm Beach, FL)*
1987	WIARD, William		59	*Lung cancer (in Pacific Palisades, CA)*
1987	WILLIAMS, Emlyn		81	*Following cancer surgery (in London, England)*
1987	WILSON, Earl		79	*After a long illness (in Los Angeles, CA)*
1988	AAMES, Angela		32	*Died in West Hills, CA*
1988	ADAMS, Dorothy		88	*Died in Woodland Hills, CA*
1988	ARAGON, Jesse		32	*Motorcycle accident (in Los Angeles, CA)*
1988	ARUNDELL, Dennis		90	*Died in London, England*
1988	ASHBY, Hal	★	59	*Liver cancer (in Malibu, CA)*
1988	ASHCROFT, Ronnie		65	*After a long illness (in Sylmar, CT)*
1988	AUCLAIR, Michel		65	*Cerebral hemorrhage (in Saint-Paul-en-Foret, France)*
1988	# BAKER, Chet		59	*Fall from a 2nd floor window (in Amsterdam)*
1988	BALLARD, Lucien		84	*Bicycle accident (in Rancho Mirage, CA)*
1988	BARNETT, Nate		48	*Heart attack (in New York, NY)*
1988	BARNETT, Sanford H.	★	79	*Following a stroke (in Oxnard, CA)*
1988	+ BARSI, Judith		10	*Murdered (shot by her father) in Los Angeles, CA*
1988	BELASCO, Leon		86	*Complications after a stroke (in Orange, CA)*
1988	+ BESSER, Joe		80	*Found dead of a heart attack in his home (in Los Angeles, CA)*
1988	BONNER, Margerie		83	*Following a stroke (in Los Angeles, CA)*
1988	# BOSWELL, Vet		77	*Died in Peekskill, NY*
1988	BOW, Simmy		65	*Complications after a stroke (in Los Angeles, CA)*
1988	BROADBENT, George		83	*Died in Laguna Hills, CA*
1988	BROWN, Alfredine "Alfie"		56	*Heart failure from kidney disease (in Baltimore, MD)*
1988	BROX, Patricia (Gerstenzang)		?	
1988	BRYANT, Margot		90	*Died in Manchester, England*
1988	BUTTERFIELD, Billy		71	*Died in North Palm Beach, FL*
1988	CAGNEY, William J.		82	*Heart attack (in Newport Beach, CA)*
1988	CAMP, Wilson		74	*Cancer (in Tarzana, CA)*
1988	CAPPELLANO, Francesca (Piazza)		92	*Pneumonia (in Los Angeles, CA)*
1988	CAREY, Olive (Golden)		92	*Died in Carpinteria, CA*
1988	#+ CARRADINE, John		82	*Heart attack after strenuous stair climbing (in Milan, Italy)*
1988	CASTELLANO, Richard	☆	55	*Heart failure (in North Bergen, NJ)*
1988	# CHANDLER, Chick		83	*Died in Laguna Beach, CA*

Deaths of Movie and Television Personalities — by Year

YEAR	NAME	AGE	CAUSE and/or PLACE OF DEATH
1988	CHANDLER, Jim	65	Lung cancer (in San Francisco, CA)
1988	CHODOROV, Edward	84	Died in New York, NY
1988	CLEMENTS, John	77	
1988	CLEWES, Howard	75	
1988	CODY, William "Wild Bill"	75	Died in Denver, CO
1988	COHEN, Nat	82	After 3 heart attacks (in London, England)
1988	COLLINS, Brent	46	Apparent heart attack (in New York)
1988	COLMAN, Ben	81	Septicemia (in Tarzana, CA)
1988	CONDOS, Nick	73	Died in Los Angeles, CA
1988	CONNELLY, Christopher	47	Stomach cancer (in Burbank, CA)
1988	CONNOR, Whitfield	71	Complications following surgery (in Norwalk, CT)
1988	COOK, Nathan	38	Allergic reaction to penicillin (in Los Angeles, CA)
1988	COOPER, Dorothy Jordan	82	
1988	CORTLAND, Nicholas	47	A.I.D.S. (in New York, NY)
1988	CRUICKSHANK, Andrew	80	Heart attack (in London, England)
1988	CURTIS, Billy	79	Heart attack (in Dayton, OH)
1988	CUTHBERTSON, Allan	67	Died in London, England
1988	DANIELS, William "Billy"	73	Stomach cancer (in Los Angeles, CA)
1988	DAWN, Hazel	98	Died in New York, NY
1988	#+ DAY, Dennis	71	Amyotrophic lateral sclerosis (in Brentwood, CA)
1988	DEAN, Priscilla	91	As a result of a fall (in Leonia, NJ)
1988	DEENE, Lally	68	Died in Santa Monica, CA
1988	DeKOVEN, Roger	81	Cancer (in New York, NY)
1988	DELL, Gabriel	68	Leukemia (in North Hollywood, CA)
1988	DELVANDO, Amapola	78	Died in Lake View Terrace, CA
1988	DENTLER, Mary Ann	96	Stroke (in Kingston, NY)
1988	dePAUL, Gene Vincent	68	Brain tumor (in Northridge, CA)
1988	DEPEW, Joseph D.	76	Died in Escondido, CA
1988	DeSALES, Francis	76	Cancer (in Van Nuys, CA)
1988	# DIAMOND, I. A. L.	67	Multiple myeloma (a form of cancer) in Beverly Hills, CA
1988	#+ Divine	42	Heart disease (in Hollywood, CA)
1988	DOHERTY, Charla	41	Cancer (in Calabasas, CA)
1988	# DONNELL, Jeff	66	Apparent heart attack (in Hollywood, CA)
1988	DONOVAN, Warde	72	Died in Los Angeles, CA
1988	DRU, Jason	58	Emphysema-induced heart failure (in Van Nuys, CA)
1988	DUGGAN, Andrew	64	Cancer (in Westwood, CA)
1988	DUGGAN, Elizabeth	56	Cancer
1988	EDWARDS, Gloria	43	Cancer (in Los Angeles, CA)
1988	# EDWARDS, Jimmy	68	Bronchial pneumonia (Do not confuse with James Edwards, d. 1970)
1988	EGOROV, Youri	33	Complications of A.I.D.S. (in Amsterdam, Netherlands)
1988	# ELDRIDGE, Florence	86	Heart attack (in Santa Barbara, CA)
1988	EMERY, Mary	91	Died in Los Angeles, CA
1988	FARLEY, Morgan	90	Died in San Pedro, CA
1988	# FARMER, Virginia	90	Died in Long Beach, CA
1988	FARRELL, Jack	52	Cancer (in Los Angeles, CA)
1988	FENNELLY, Parker	96	Died in Peekskill, NY
1988	FIDLER, Jimmie	89	
1988	FLETCHER, Bramwell	84	Died in Westmoreland, NH
1988	# FLOWERS, Wayland	48	Cancer (in Los Angeles, CA)
1988	FOLSEY, George	90	Cerebral hemorrhage (in Santa Monica, CA)
1988	FORD, Ross	65	Cardiac arrest (in Hollywood, CA)
1988	FOULGER, Dorothy Adams	88	
1988	FRANK, Melvin	75	Complications following open-heart surgery (in Los Angeles, CA)

Deaths of Movie and Television Personalities — by Year

YEAR	NAME	AGE	CAUSE and/or PLACE OF DEATH
1988	FREY, Leonard ☆	49	A.I.D.S. (in New York, NY)
1988	FRIEBUS, Florida	79	Died in Laguna Miguel, CA
1988	# FROEBE, Gert	75	Heart attack (in Munich, Germany)
1988	GAUTHIER, Suzanne	61	Cancer (in Hollywood, CA)
1988	GEISE, Tanya "Sugar"	71	After a brief illness (in Hollywood, CA)
1988	+ GIBB, Andy	30	Heart inflammation caused by a virus (in Oxford, England)
1988	GIBBS, Alan R.	47	Cancer (in Los Angeles, CA)
1988	GOODMAN, Lee	64	Tuberculosis (in New York, NY)
1988	GORMAN, Bobby	59	Following a long illness (in Los Angeles, CA)
1988	GRAHAM, Sheilah	84	Congestive heart failure (in West Palm Beach, FL)
1988	GRANDIN, Ethel	94	Died in Woodland Hills, CA
1988	+ GRANVILLE, Bonita (Wrather) ☆	65	Cancer (in Santa Monica, CA)
1988	HAHN, Paul	67	After a short illness (in Hollywood, CA)
1988	HARRIS, Fox	52	Lung cancer (in Los Angeles, CA)
1988	HAWTREY, Charles	72	Heart attack caused by arterial disease (in Walmer, England)
1988	HAYES, William S.	29	A.I.D.S. (in Wayland, MA)
1988	HENDERSON, Jo	54	Automobile accident (in Pamona, NY)
1988	HENDLEY, Janet Stover	55	Cancer (in Vorhees, NJ)
1988	HIGGINS, Colin	47	A.I.D.S. (in Beverly Hills, CA)
1988	HILLAIRE, Marcel	79	Complications following surgery (in Los Angeles, CA)
1988	HINTERMANN, Carlo	64	Automobile accident (in Catania, Italy)
1988	HOLLAND, Anthony	60	Suicide (after suffering from A.I.D.S.) in New York, NY
1988	HOLMES, John C.	43	Encephalitis as a result of A.I.D.S. (in Los Angeles, CA)
1988	HOPE, Harry	62	Heart attack after playing in a basketball game (in Hollywood, CA)
1988	HOPPER, Jerry	81	After suffering from heart problems (in San Clemente, CA)
1988	# HOUSEMAN, John ★	86	Spinal cancer (in Los Angeles, CA)
1988	HOWARD, Trevor ☆	71	Influenza, bronchitis and jaundice (in Bushey, England)
1988	HUBBARD, John	65	Died in Camarillo, CA
• 1988	HUFFMAN, Gregory	35	A.I.D.S.
1988	JACOBSON, Henrietta	82	Died in New York, NY
1988	JEFFREY, Howard	53	A.I.D.S. (in Los Angeles, CA)
1988	JONES, Duane	51	Undisclosed causes (in Mineola, NY)
1988	JORDAN, Dorothy (Cooper)	82	Died in Los Angeles, CA
1988	+ JORDAN, Jim "Fibber McGee"	91	Blood clot in brain (from a fall) in Los Angeles, CA
1988	KINNEAR, Roy	54	After falling from his horse during filming (in Madrid, Spain)
1988	KJELLIN, Alf	68	Heart attack (in Los Angeles, CA)
1988	KOSTER, Henry	83	After a long illness (in Camarillo, CA)
• 1988	L'AMOUR, Louis	80	Died in Los Angeles, CA
1988	LARSON, Eric	83	After a lengthy illness (in Flintridge, CA)
1988	+ LASKY, Jesse L. Jr.	77	Cancer (in London, England)
1988	# LATZ, Elaine	71	
1988	LEIGH, George	78	Heart disease and diabetes (in Culver City, CA)
1988	LIGHT, Ann Rork	79	
1988	LINDSAY, Phillip	64	Pneumonia (in New York, NY)
1988	# LIVINGSTON, Robert (Bob)	79	Emphysema (in Tarzana, CA)
1988	LLOYD, Paul Francis (Jimmy)	69	Liver disease (in Medford, OR)
1988	# LODER, John	90	Died in Selbourne, England
1988	LOEWE, Frederick	86	Heart failure (in Palm Springs, CA)
1988	LOGAN, Joshua ☆	79	Supranuclear palsy (in New York, NY)
1988	LOW, Carl	71	Cancer (in Nyack, NY)
1988	LOWRY, Margerie Bonner	83	After suffering a stroke
1988	LUMMIS, Dayton	84	Died in Santa Monica, CA
1988	LYNN, Mara	60	Cancer (in The Bahamas)

Deaths of Movie and Television Personalities — by Year

YEAR	NAME		AGE	CAUSE and/or PLACE OF DEATH
1988	MANSFIELD, Marian		83	Emphysema (in La Jolla, CA)
1988	+ MARAVICH, Pete		40	
1988	MARICLE, Leona		81	Apparent heart attack (in New York, NY)
1988	MARTIN-HARVEY, Muriel		97	Died in Northwood, England
1988	MAURA, Luis		38	A.I.D.S. (in Los Angeles, CA)
1988	McCRACKEN, James		61	Following two strokes
1988	McGUIRE, Tucker		75	Died in London, Canada
1988	# MEEKER, Ralph		67	Heart attack (in Los Angeles, CA)
1988	MEGLIN, Ethel		98	
1988	MILLER, Joan		78	Died in London, England
1988	# MINTZ, Eli		83	Pneumonia (in Point Pleasant, NJ)
1988	MITCHELL, Ewing Young		77	Following a stroke (in La Jolla, CA)
1988	MITRY, Jean		83	Cancer (in La Garenne-Colombes, France)
1988	MOBERLY, Robert		49	A.I.D.S. (in Los Angeles, CA)
1988	# MOORE, Colleen		87	Following a long illness (in Paso Robles, CA)
1988	MORGAN, Boyd F. "Red"		72	Heart attack (in Tarzana, CA)
1988	MORRIS, Mary		72	Undisclosed causes (in Aigle, Switzerland)
1988	MURPHY, Timothy Patrick		29	A.I.D.S. (in Sherman Oaks, CA)
1988	MURRAY, Ken		85	Died in Burbank, CA
1988	# NAPIER, Alan		85	After a stroke (in Santa Monica, CA)
1988	NELSON, Christine		60	Lung cancer (in Los Angeles, CA)
1988	#+ Nico		49	Cerebral hemorrhage from a bicycle fall (in Ibiza, Spain)
1988	NILES, Ken		82	
1988	NISSEN, Greta		82	Parkinson's disease (in Montecito, CA)
1988	NORDEN, Christine		63	Chest infection after heart surgery (in London, England)
1988	NOVAK, Eva		90	Pneumonia (in Woodland Hills, CA)
1988	+ O'ROURKE, Heather		12	Septic shock, congenital bowel narrowing (in San Diego, CA)
1988	# OLIVER, Sy		77	Died in New York, NY
1988	OLIVER, Virgil		72	Died in Baton Rouge, LA
1988	+ ORBISON, Roy		52	Heart attack (in Hendersonville, TN)
1988	OSBORN, Paul		86	Died in New York, NY
1988	PAWLEY, Edward		84	Died in Charlottesville, VA
1988	PINERO, Miguel		41	Cirrhosis of the liver (in New York, NY)
1988	PRESSBURGER, Emeric		85	Bronchial pneumonia (in England)
1988	QUINN, Louis		73	After a brief illness (in Los Angeles, CA)
1988	RAAB, Kurt		46	A.I.D.S. (in Hamburg, Germany)
1988	RAINES, Ella		66	Throat cancer (in Sherman Oaks, CA)
1988	# RAMAGE, Cecil		93	Cardiac arrest in his sleep (in Scotland)
1988	RAMSEY, Anne	☆	59	Throat cancer (in Los Angeles, CA)
1988	RAWLINS, Lester		63	Heart attack (in New York, NY)
1988	REARDON, John		58	Pneumonia
1988	# RHODES, Billie		93	Died in Los Angeles, CA
1988	# RICH, Irene		96	Heart failure (in Santa Barbara, CA)
1988	RILEY, Jay Flash		72	Died in Los Angeles, CA
1988	+ ROBERSON, Chuck		69	Cancer (in Bakersfield, CA)
1988	ROBERTSON, Hugh A.		55	Cancer (in Los Angeles, CA)
1988	+ ROBINSON, Dar Allen		39	Motorcycle accident (in Page, AZ)
1988	ROBINSON, Max		49	A.I.D.S.
1988	ROGELL, Albert S.		86	Cancer and diabetes (in Los Angeles, CA)
1988	ROSE, George		68	Murdered by his son (in Rio Plata, Dominican Republic)
1988	# ROSS, Lanny		82	Following two strokes (in New York, NY)
1988	ROSSON, Harold "Hal"		93	Cardiac arrest in his sleep (in Palm Beach, FL)
1988	# ROWE, Fanny		75	Died in London, England

Deaths of Movie and Television Personalities — by Year

YEAR	NAME	AGE	CAUSE and/or PLACE OF DEATH
1988	SCOTT, Timothy	32	Complications from A.I.D.S. (Do not confuse with T. Scott, d. 1995)
1988	SEYMOUR, Anne	79	Heart failure and respiratory complications (in Los Angeles, CA)
1988	# SHAW, Victoria	53	Asthma (in Sydney, Australia)
1988	SHER, Jack	75	After a brief illness (in Beverly Hills, CA)
1988	SHOLOMIR, Jack	57	Heart attack (in Miami Beach, FL)
1988	SILVA, Trinidad Jr.	38	Traffic accident (in Whittier, CA)
1988	SMITH, Charles "Dizzy"	67	Apparent heart attack (in Burbank, CA)
1988	SMITH, Tucker	52	Cancer of the neck and jaw (in Los Angeles, CA)
1988	SOFAER, Abraham	91	Congestive heart failure (in Woodland Hills, CA)
1988	+ SPERLING, Milton	76	After a long illness (in Beverly Hills, CA)
1988	ST. JOHN, Adela Rogers	94	Died in Arroyo Grande, CA
1988	STAVRIDIS, Nicos	77	Heart failure (in Greece)
1988	#+ STEELE, Bob	82	Heart failure after a long illness (in Burbank, CA)
1988	STOPPA, Paolo	81	Leukemia (in Rome, Italy)
1988	# TERRY, Don	86	Stroke (in Oceanside, CA)
1988	THOMPKINS, Toney	33	A.I.D.S. (in Los Angeles, CA)
1988	TREVELYAN, John	83	
1988	VEHR, Bill	48	A.I.D.S. (in New York, NY)
1988	VonSTROHEIM, Valerie	91	
1988	WARREN, Jerry	65	Lung cancer (in Escondito, CA)
1988	WASHBOURNE, Mona	84	Undisclosed causes (in London, England)
1988	WASHINGTON, Vernon	64	Died in Woodland Hills, CA
1988	WHITE, John Sylvester	68	Pancreatic cancer (in Waikiki, HI)
1988	WILLES, Jean	65	Liver cancer (in Van Nuys, CA)
1988	WILLIAMS, Kenneth	62	Heart attack (in London, England)
1988	WILLMAN, Noel	70	Heart attack (in New York, NY)
1988	WILSON, Lois	93	Pneumonia (in Reno, NV)
1988	WYCKOFF, Michael	69	After a stroke (in Madrid, Spain)
1989	AILEY, Alvin	58	Dyscrasia (a blood disorder) in New York
1989	ALEXANDER, Richard	86	Pulmonary edema (in Woodland Hills, CA)
1989	ALLISON, Fran	81	Complications of a blood disorder (in Sherman Oaks, CA)
1989	ALLISON, May	98	Respiratory failure (in Bratenahl, OH)
1989	ANDREWS, Harry	77	Viral infection complicated by asthma (in Sussex, England)
1989	ANDREWS, Nancy	68	Heart attack (in Queens, NY)
1989	# ANTHONY, Rick	60	
1989	ARLEN, Roxanne (Shafer)	57	Cancer (in London, England)
1989	ARTHUR, Lee	49	Cancer (in Houston, TX)
• 1989	BAC, André	83	Heart attack (in Paris, France)
• 1989	BACKHAUS, Helmuth M.	68	Died in Germany
1989	#+ BACKUS, Jim "Mr. Magoo"	76	Pneumonia and Parkinson's disease (in Santa Monica, CA)
1989	BAILEY, John (actor)	73	Undisclosed causes (in London, England)
1989	#+ BALL, Lucille	77	Ruptured aorta after heart surgery (in Los Angeles, CA)
1989	BANZHAF, Peter G.	57	Arrhythmia (in Milwaukee, WI)
1989	# BARI, Lynn	73	After a long illness (in Santa Barbara, CA)
1989	BARRIER, Ernestine	81	Died in Long Beach, CA
1989	BARRY, Joan	87	Died in Marbella, Spain
1989	BASTIN, Charles A.	68	Cardiopulmonary arrest (in Los Angeles, CA)
1989	BAUM, Bobby	62	Following a brief illness (in Los Angeles, CA)
1989	+ BAVIER, Frances "Aunt Bee"	86	Heart disease and cancer (in Siler City, NC)
1989	BAZLEN, Brigid	44	Died in Seattle, WA
1989	BEAM, Alvin	61	Cardiopulmonary arrest (in New York, NY)
1989	BENSON, Joe	73	Cancer (in Thousand Oaks, CA)

Deaths of Movie and Television Personalities — by Year

YEAR	NAME		AGE	CAUSE and/or PLACE OF DEATH
1989	#+ BERLIN, Irving		101	Heart attack in his sleep (in New York, NY)
1989	BERNAU, Christopher		49	Died in New York, NY
1989	# BLAKE, Amanda "Miss Kitty"		60	A.I.D.S.-related complications (in Sacramento, CA)
1989	#+ BLANC, Mel		81	Heart disease (in Los Angeles, CA)
1989	BLEYER, Archie		79	Died in Sheboygan, WI
1989	BLIER, Bernard		73	Cancer (in Saint-Cloud, France)
1989	BLOOM, George		95	Died in Woodland Hills, CA
1989	BOND, Raleigh		54	Lymphoma (in Los Angeles, CA)
1989	BOUISE, Jean		60	Lung cancer (in Lyon, France)
1989	BRIGHT, John		81	Stroke (in Panorama City, CA)
1989	BRISTER, John Tyler		38	A.I.D.S. (in Minneapolis, MN)
1989	BROCK, Heinie		89	Emphysema (in Canoga Park, CA)
1989	BROOKNER, Howard		34	A.I.D.S.
1989	BROTHERSON, Eric		78	Died in New York, NY
1989	BROWN, Tally		64	After suffering a stroke (in New York, NY)
1989	BRUMER, Martin		28	Automobile accident (in Los Angeles, CA)
1989	BRYANT, John		72	Cancer (in Hollywood, CA)
1989	BUCK, David		53	Cancer (in England)
1989	BUETEL, Jack		74	After a long illness (in Portland, OR)
1989	BURKS, Rick		26	Automobile accident (in Hollywood, CA)
1989	BUTRICK, Merritt		29	A.I.D.S. (in Los Angeles, CA)
1989	CARMINE, Michael		30	Heart failure (in New York, NY)
1989	+ CASSAVETES, John ☆		59	Cirrhosis of the liver (in Los Angeles, CA)
1989	CAVALLARO, Carmen		76	Cancer (in Columbus, OH)
1989	CAYATTE, André		80	Died in Paris, France
1989	CHALLEE, William		84	Alzheimer's disease (in Woodland Hills, CA)
1989	CHANDLER, Marjorie Grossel		71	Cancer (in Santa Monica, CA)
1989	CHAPMAN, Graham		48	Spinal cancer (in Maidstone, England)
1989	CHERRILL, Christine		71	Died in Kensington, England
1989	CHIARI, Mario		79	After a long illness (in Rome, Italy)
1989	CHING, William		75	Congestive heart failure (in Tustin, CA)
1989	CHRISTIE, Audrey		79	Emphysema (in West Hollywood, CA)
1989	CIRO, Steve		46	Died in New York, NY
1989	CLARK, Dort		71	Diabetes and cancer (in Wellington, KS)
1989	CLARKE, T. E. B.		81	Died in Surrey, England
1989	COLEY, Thomas		75	Heart attack (in New York, NY)
1989	COLIN, Jean		83	Died in London, England
1989	COONAN, Sheila M.		66	Liver disease (in New York, NY)
1989	CORTEZ, Mildred		72	Cardiac arrest (in Hollywood, CA)
1989	COSTA, Bob		66	Died in Honolulu, HI
1989	COULOURIS, George		85	Heart attack (in London, England)
1989	COVAN, Willie		92	Died in Los Angeles, CA
1989	CROSBY, Lindsay		51	Suicide (gunshot) in Los Angeles, CA
1989	CUMMINGS, Jack		84	Heart attack (in Los Angeles, CA)
1989	D'AMICO, Teresa Tirelli		81	Brain tumor
1989	DaCOSTA, Morton		74	Heart failure (in Redding, CT)
1989	DALI, Salvador		84	Heart failure and pneumonia (in Figueras, Spain)
1989	DALRYMPLE, Ian		85	Died in London, England
1989	#+ DAVIS, Bette ★		81	Breast cancer (in Neuilly-sur-Seine, France)
1989	DeCARLO, Vinnie		54	Heart attack (in Milan, Italy)
1989	DeSANTIS, Joe		80	Congestive heart failure (in Provo, UT)
1989	DIFFRING, Anton		70	Died in Chateauneuf-de-Grasse, France
1989	DIGNAM, Mark		80	Cardiac arrest in his sleep (in London, England)

Deaths of Movie and Television Personalities — by Year

YEAR	NAME	AGE	CAUSE and/or PLACE OF DEATH
1989	DITTMAN, Dean Gus	57	Heart failure (in Los Angeles, CA)
1989	DRAKE, Dona	69	Cancer (in Mexico City, Mexico)
1989	DRANE, Gary	46	Died in New York, NY
1989	DRINKWATER, Terry	53	Cancer (in Malibu, CA)
1989	DRYHURST, Edward	84	Died in London, England
1989	DuMAURIER, Daphne	81	After a brief illness (in Cornwall, England)
1989	DURANTE, Vito	64	A.I.D.S. (in New York, NY)
1989	EAMES, John Matthew	64	Died in New York, NY
1989	EVANS, Maurice	87	Cancer (in Brighton, England)
1989	EVANS, Peter	38	Complications of A.I.D.S. (in Los Angeles, CA)
1989	FAIN, Sammy	87	Heart attack (in Los Angeles, CA)
1989	FARRELL, Timothy (Sperl)	66	Heart condition (in Santa Monica, CA)
1989	FIELD, Ron	55	Neurological impairment due to brain lesions (in New York, NY)
1989	FINLEY, Evelyn	73	Heart attack (in Big Bear City, CA)
1989	FORREST, William H.	86	Heart attack (in Santa Monica, CA)
1989	FRENCH, Norma	47	Lymphoma (in Toronto, Canada)
1989	FRENCH, Victor	54	Lung cancer (in Sherman Oaks, CA)
1989	FROME, Milton	78	Heart failure (in Woodland Hills, CA)
1989	GARDE, Betty	84	Died in Hollywood, CA
1989	GARDNER, Hy	80	Pneumonia (in Miami, FL)
1989	GEER, Lenny	75	Heart failure (in Topega Canyon, CA)
1989	GENTRY, Britt Nilsson	46	Cancer (in Los Angeles, CA)
1989	GERRINGER, Robert	63	After a series of strokes
1989	GIFFORD, Alan	78	Died in Scotland
1989	GIMPEL, Jakob	82	Died in Los Angeles, CA
1989	# GLAUDI, Hap	77	Cancer
1989	GREEN, John	80	Pulmonary edema (in Beverly Hills, CA)
1989	GRIFFIN, Bessie	67	Cancer (in Culver City, CA)
1989	GUIGLEY, Robert	76	Died in Los Angeles, CA
1989	HAIG, Jack	76	Cancer (in London, England)
1989	HALLIWELL, Leslie	59	Abdominal cancer
1989	HALSTED, Fred	47	Overdose of barbiturates
1989	HAMBLEN, Stuart	80	Brain cancer (in Santa Monica, CA)
1989	HARRIGAN, Nedda	89	Lung cancer (in New York, NY)
1989	HAYES, Grace	93	Heart attack (in Las Vegas, NV)
1989	HAYMER, Johnny	69	Cancer (in Los Angeles, CA)
1989	HENSHAW, Wandalie	54	Parkinson's disease (in Petoskey, MI)
1989	HERBERT, Pitt	74	Amyotrophic lateral sclerosis
1989	HESLER, G. Christian	33	A.I.D.S. (in Carmel, IN)
1989	HEYWOOD, Eddie	73	Parkinson's and Alzheimer's disease (in North Miami, FL)
1989	HOFFMAN, Abbie	52	Suicide (massive drug overdose)
1989	HOLT, Jason	39	A.I.D.S. (in New York, NY)
1989	HORNEZ, André	84	Died in Le-Perreux-sur-Marne, France
1989	#+ HOROWITZ, Vladimir	85	Heart attack (in New York, NY)
1989	HOULE, Daniel	41	A.I.D.S. (in Los Angeles, CA)
• 1989	HOVEY, Tim	44	Drug overdose
1989	# HOWARD, Mary	76	After a brief illness (in Santa Monica, CA)
1989	HURLOCK, Madeline (Sherwood)	89	Died in Los Angeles, CA
1989	# IMMEDIATO, Al	72	Cancer
1989	INGRAM, Bill	69	
1989	IVENS, Joris	90	Heart attack (in Paris, France)
1989	JAFFE, Allen	60	After a long illness (in Woodland Hills, CA)
1989	JONES, Reed	35	Liver cancer (in Sherman Oaks, CA)

Deaths of Movie and Television Personalities — by Year

YEAR	NAME	AGE	CAUSE and/or PLACE OF DEATH
1989	JORGENSEN, Christine (George)	62	Cancer of the bladder
1989	KAYE-MARTIN, Edward	50	Lymphoma
1989	KENNER, Warren	64	Heart attack (in New Orleans, LA)
1989	KIRKWOOD, James Jr.	64	Cancer (in Manhattan, NY)
1989	KRAMER, Mandel J.	72	Died in Delray Beach, FL
1989	KREEL, Kenneth	48	A.I.D.S.
1989	LAMPKIN, Charles	76	Heart attack (in San José, CA)
1989	LeBORG, Reginald	86	Heart attack (in Los Angeles, CA)
1989	# LEE, Billy	60	Heart failure (in Beaumont, CA)
1989	LEE, Brian	36	Pneumonia (in Los Angeles, CA)
1989	LEONE, Sergio	60	Heart attack (in Rome, Italy)
1989	+ LERNER, Sam	86	Cancer (in Los Angeles, CA)
1989	LeVEQUE, Edward	92	Died in Los Angeles, CA
1989	LEVINE, Nathan	89	Heart attack (in Woodland Hills, CA)
1989	# LILLIE, Beatrice	94	Died in Henley-On-Thames, England
1989	LION, Margo	90	Died in Annecy-Le-Vieux, France
1989	LOW, Warren	83	Following a long illness (in Woodland Hills, CA)
1989	LUCE, Claire	88	Died in New York (Do not confuse with Clare Booth Luce, d. 1987)
1989	LUCKHAM, Cyril	81	Died in London, England
1989	MACCARI, Ruggero	70	Died in Rome, Italy
1989	# MACK, Marion	86	Heart failure (in Costa Mesa, CA)
1989	MADDEN, Jeanne	73	Heart trouble
1989	MAGUIRE, Kathleen	64	Cancer (in New York, NY)
1989	# MAHONEY, Jock	70	Heart attack following an auto accident (in Washington, D.C.)
1989	MANES, Gina	96	Died in Toulouse, France
1989	MANGANO, Silvano	59	Heart attack following a tumor operation (in Madrid, Spain)
1989	MARCH, Alex	68	Heart failure (in Los Angeles, CA)
1989	MARQUISS, Ralph E. Jr.	34	Adrenal cancer
1989	# MARSH, Tiger Joe	78	Heart attack (in Chicago, IL)
1989	MARSHALL, Andrew 3rd	52	Cancer (in Los Angeles, CA)
1989	MATSUDA, Yusaku	40	Bladder cancer (in Tokyo, Japan)
1989	MATUSZAK, John	38	Heart failure from drug overdose (in Burbank, CA)
1989	McANALLY, Ray	63	Died in County Wicklow, Ireland
1989	McGUIRE, Jon Brandon	34	Liver failure (in North Hollywood, CA)
1989	McMILLAN, Kenneth	56	Liver disease (in Santa Monica, CA)
1989	MEILLON, John	55	Died in Sydney, Australia
1989	MELVILLE, Sam	52	Heart attack
1989	MEYERS, Timothy	44	A.I.D.S. (in New York, NY)
1989	MILANOV, Zinka	83	Stroke
1989	MILLS, Herbert	77	
1989	MILTON, Billy	83	Cardiac arrest in his sleep (in Northwood, England)
1989	MORGAN, Mary	81	
1989	MORGAN, Rex	67	Parkinson's disease (in Fairfax, VA)
1989	MORIN, Alberto	86	Stroke (in Burbank, CA)
1989	# MORRISON, Ernie	76	Cancer (in Lynwood, CA)
1989	MOSS, Arnold	80	Lung cancer (in New York, NY)
1989	MOWER, Margaret	93	
1989	# MUELLER, Cookie	40	A.I.D.S. (in New York, NY)
1989	# MURRAY-MAZWI, Mark	52	Heart attack (in Los Angeles, CA)
1989	NEIDORF, Ross Lee	34	A.I.D.S. (in Miami, FL)
1989	+ NEWMAN, Lionel	73	Cardiac arrest (in Los Angeles, CA)
1989	NIGHTINGALE, Earl	68	After heart surgery
1989	O'DAVOREN, Vesey	100	Died in Los Angeles, CA

Deaths of Movie and Television Personalities — by Year

YEAR	NAME		AGE	CAUSE and/or PLACE OF DEATH
1989	O'DAY, Nell		79	*Cardiac arrest in her sleep (in Los Angeles, CA)*
1989	# O'HANLON, George		76	*Stroke (in Burbank, CA)*
1989	+ OLIVIER, Laurence	★	82	*Died in his sleep (in London, England)*
1989	OSTRICHE, Muriel		93	*Cardiac arrest in her sleep (in St. Petersburg, FL)*
1989	OSWALD, Gerd		72	*Cancer (in Los Angeles, CA)*
1989	OZERAY, Madeleine		78	*Cancer (in Paris, France)*
1989	PASS, Lenny		37	*Died in New York, NY*
1989	PAULSON, Al		67	*Heart failure*
1989	PAYNE, John		77	*Congestive heart failure (in Malibu, CA)*
1989	PERRIN, Vic		73	*Cancer (in Los Angeles, CA)*
1989	POMPEII, James S.		51	*After a long illness (in New York, NY)*
1989	POST, William Jr.		88	*Pulmonary embolism (in Oklahoma City, OK)*
1989	# PRINGLE, Aileen		94	*Died in New York, NY*
1989	QUAYLE, Anthony	☆	76	*Cancer (in London, England)*
1989	QUERTERMOUS, Charlie		41	*Cancer (in Hollywood, CA)*
1989	QUINE, Richard		68	*Suicide (shot himself) at his home in Los Angeles, CA*
1989	+ RADNER, Gilda		42	*Ovarian cancer (in Los Angeles, CA)*
1989	REID, Vivian		95	*Natural causes*
1989	+ ROBINSON, Sugar Ray		67	*Heart and Alzheimer's disease and diabetes*
1989	ROOS, Joanna		88	*Ruptured aorta (in Princeton, NJ)*
1989	ROUD, Richard		59	*Heart attack*
1989	ROZAKIS, Gregory		46	*A.I.D.S. (in Brooklyn, NY)*
1989	SAUERS, Patricia		49	*Complications from diabetes (in CA)*
1989	SAYER, Philip		42	*Abdominal cancer (in London, England)*
1989	+ SCHAEFFER, Rebecca		21	*Murdered (shot) in Los Angeles, CA*
1989	+ SCHAFFNER, Franklin J.	★	69	*Cancer (in Santa Monica, CA)*
1989	SCHAKNE, Robert		63	*Cancer*
1989	SCHORR, William W.		88	*Respiratory failure (in Los Angeles, CA)*
1989	# SERATO, Massimo		73	*Heart attack (in Rome, Italy)*
1989	SHELLEY, Dave		58	*Lung complications after heart surgery (in Woodland Hills, CA)*
1989	SHENAR, Paul		53	*A.I.D.S. (in West Hollywood, CA)*
1989	SHERMAN, Connie		72	*Respiratory failure (in Pittsburgh, PA)*
1989	SHERMAN, Hiram		81	*Following a stroke (in Springfield, IL)*
1989	SHERWOOD, Lydia		82	*Died in London, England*
1989	SHIRLEY, Bill		68	*Lung cancer (in Los Angeles, CA)*
1989	SILVER, Joe		66	*Liver cancer*
1989	SILVERMAN, Mark		36	*A.I.D.S. (in New York, NY)*
1989	SLATE, Jack		80	*Heart attack (in Los Angeles, CA)*
1989	SMITH, Jack		57	*A.I.D.S. (Do not confuse with "Whispering" Jack Smith, d. 1950)*
1989	SORM, Evald		57	
1989	SPINELL, Joe		51	*Heart attack (in New York, NY)*
1989	SPITZ, Hank		84	
1989	SQUIRE, William		72	*Undisclosed causes (in London, England)*
1989	STARRETT, Jack		52	*Kidney failure (in Sherman Oaks, CA)*
1989	STEVENS, Robert		68	*Heart attack (in Westport, CT)*
1989	STOUT, Bill		62	*Cardiac arrest (in Los Angeles, CA)*
1989	SUNDIN, Michael		28	*Undisclosed causes (in Newcastle, England)*
1989	SYDNOR, Earl L.		81	*Lung cancer (in New York, NY)*
1989	TAFOYA, Alfonso		60	*Massive heart attack (in Pasadena, CA)*
1989	TERRIS, Norma		87	*After a brief illness (in Lyme, CT)*
1989	THOMAS, Ann		75	*Lung cancer (in New Rochelle, NY)*
1989	THOMAS, Frank M.		100	*Cardiac arrest in his sleep*
1989	THOMAS, Madoline		99	*Cardiac arrest in her sleep (in Weston-Super-Mare, England)*

• New entry.   # Original name (Pt. 7).   + Interment (Pt. 5).   120   ☆ Oscar nominee, ★ Oscar winner (Pt. 10)

Deaths of Movie and Television Personalities — by Year

YEAR	NAME		AGE	CAUSE and/or PLACE OF DEATH
1989	THOR, Dan		34	A.I.D.S. (in Los Angeles, CA)
1989	THORPE-BATES, Peggy		75	Undisclosed causes (in London, England)
1989	TIRELLI, Teresa		81	Brain tumor (in Northridge, CA)
1989	TRAVIS, Richard		76	
1989	TRAYLOR, William		60	After a long illness (in Los Angeles, CA)
1989	TREEN, Mary		82	Cancer (in Newport Beach, CA)
1989	TREGOE, William L.		67	Cardiac arrest (in Los Angeles, CA)
1989	TUCKER, Julius L.		92	
1989	TUCKER, Tommy		86	
1989	+ VanCLEEF, Lee		64	Heart attack (in Oxnard, CA)
1989	VANEL, Charles		96	Heart attack (in Cannes, France)
1989	VARDEN, Norma		90	Heart failure (in Santa Barbara, CA)
1989	VAUGHAN, Skeeter		66	Heart attack
1989	+ VINCENT, Romo		80	Died in Los Angeles, CA
1989	VonCZIFFRA, Geza		88	Died in Diessen, Germany
1989	VonKARAJAN, Herbert		81	Heart failure (in Anif, Austria)
1989	VOORHEES, Donald		85	Pneumonia
1989	WATSON, Douglass		68	Heart attack (in AZ)
1989	WEAVER, Carl Earl		36	A.I.D.S. (in New York, NY)
1989	WEBBER, Robert		64	Amyotrophic lateral sclerosis
1989	WEST, Lockwood		83	Cancer (in Brighton, England)
1989	WETMORE, Joan		77	Cancer (in New York, NY)
1989	WHITE, Chrissie		94	Died in London, England
1989	WHITLEY, Keith		33	Alcohol poisoning
1989	#+ WILDE, Cornel ☆		74	Leukemia (in Los Angeles, CA)
1989	WILLIAMS, Clark		83	Died in Carmel, CA
1989	#+ WILLIAMS, Guy		65	Heart attack (in Buenos Aires, Argentina)
1989	WILLINGER, Laszlo		80	
1989	# WILLIS, Matt		75	Died in Fredericksburg, VA
1989	WILSON, Trey		40	Cerebral hemorrhage (in New York, NY)
1989	WINCKLER, Robert		62	Stomach cancer (in Woodland Hills, CA)
1989	WINTERS, Roland		84	Stroke (in Englewood, NJ)
1989	WONG, Iris		68	Died in Honolulu, HI
1989	WOODBURY, Joan		73	Respiratory failure (in Desert Hot Springs, CA)
1989	WOOLAND, Norman		83	Following several strokes (in Staplehurst, England)
1989	WRIGHT, Ben		74	Heart failure after heart surgery (in Burbank, CA)
1989	ZAVATTINA, Cesare		86	Cerebral hemorrhage (in Rome, Italy)
1989	ZEMAN, Karel		78	Died in Gottwaldov, Czechoslovakia
1990	ABERNATHY, Ralph		64	
1990	ALEX, Robert		30	Gunshot wounds during a robbery at his home (in Silver Lake, CA)
1990	ALINDER, Dallas		58	Heart failure following a liver transplant
1990	ALLAN, Elizabeth		80	Died in London, England
1990	APPLEBY, Dorothy		84	Died in Long Island, NY
1990	#+ ARDEN, Eve ☆		83	Heart failure and cancer (in Los Angeles, CA)
1990	#+ BAILEY, Pearl		72	Heart failure following surgery to replace a knee (in Philadelphia, PA)
1990	BAILEY, William H.		72	Died in Camden, NJ (Do not confuse with actor Bill Bailey, d. 1978)
1990	BALFOUR, Katharine		69	
1990	BALIN, Ina		52	Pulmonary hypertension and cancer (in New Haven, CT)
1990	BANEY, Joan Blazer		55	Brain tumor
1990	BARA, Nina		66	Cancer (in Glendale, CA)
1990	BARKER, Eric L.		78	Died in Faverham, England
1990	BARRY, J. J.		58	Bronchial complications (in Huntington Station, NY)

Deaths of Movie and Television Personalities — by Year

YEAR	NAME	AGE	CAUSE and/or PLACE OF DEATH
1990	BARTLETT, Scott	47	Complications from a kidney and liver transplant (in San Francisco)
1990	BARTON, Larry	80	Following a stroke (in Encino, CA)
1990	# BATORS, Stiv	40	After being hit by a car (in Paris, France)
1990	BAXLEY, Barbara	63	Apparent heart attack (in New York, NY)
1990	BEAGLE, Edward H.	46	Natural causes (in Culver City, CA)
1990	BELL, David	53	After a long illness (Do not confuse with David Scott Bell, d. 1980)
1990	BELLAMY, Madge	89	Heart failure (in Ontario, Canada)
1990	BENNER, Richard	47	A.I.D.S. (in Toronto, Canada)
1990	BENNETT, Jill	59	Suicide (in London, England)
1990	BENNETT, Joan	80	Cardiac arrest (in White Plains, NY)
1990	BERGHOF, Herbert	81	Heart ailment (in New York, NY)
1990	+ BERNSTEIN, Leonard	72	Complications from lung cancer and emphysema (in New York, NY)
1990	BERTO, Juliet	42	Breast cancer (in Breur-Jouy, France))
1990	BINGO, Joe	65	Complications from a staph infection
1990	BINNS, Edward	74	Heart attack (in Brewster, NY)
1990	BLAKEY, Art	71	Lung cancer
1990	BLOCK, Eva Sully	88	Heart failure
1990	+ BOCK-LEADER, Deborah Lyn	38	
1990	BRADDELL, Maurice	89	Died in England
1990	BRANDON, Henry	77	Apparent heart attack (in Hollywood, CA)
1990	# BRAUER, Tiny	82	Heart condition (in Sepulveda, CA)
1990	BRAUNBERGER, Pierre	85	Died in Paris, France
1990	BRAY, Stephen	33	Died in Dallas, TX
1990	BREM, Beppo	84	Heart failure (in Munich, Germany)
1990	BRIGGS, Richard R.	71	After a short illness
1990	BRODKIN, Herbert	77	Aneurysm (in New York, NY)
1990	BROWN, Karl	93	Kidney failure (in Woodland Hills, CA)
1990	# BROWN, Tom	75	Cancer (in Woodland Hills, CA)
1990	BUNNAGE, Avis	67	After a brief illness (in London, England)
1990	BURNS, Stephan	35	A.I.D.S. (in Santa Barbara, CA)
1990	BURRUD, Bill	65	Heart attack while swimming in the ocean (in Los Angeles, CA)
1990	CALLOWAY, Northern J.	41	After being taken to a psychiatric hospital (in Westchester Cty, NY)
1990	# Capucine	57	Suicide plunge from her 8th floor apartment (in Lausanne, Switz.)
1990	CAREY, Mary Jane	66	Died in Pasadena, CA
1990	CARISTI, Vincent	42	Cancer (in New York, NY)
1990	CARPENTER, Charles	77	Heart attack (in Oxnard, CA)
1990	CARRERAS, James	81	Cerebral hemorrhage (in Henley-on-Thames, England)
1990	# CARSON, Sunset "Kit"	67	Heart attack (in Reno, NV)
• 1990	CASON, Barbara	61	Heart attack
1990	CASSON, Ann	74	Died in London, England
1990	CASTLE, Lee	75	Heart attack
1990	CATHEY, Dalton	44	A.I.D.S. (in Los Angeles, CA)
1990	CHAFFEY, Don	72	Heart disease (in Kawau Island, New Zealand)
1990	# CHAMPLIN, Irene	59	After a long illness (in Greenwich, CT)
1990	CHARLESON, Ian	40	A.I.D.S. (Septicemia) in London, England
1990	CHENAL, Pierre	86	Heart attack (in La-Garenne-Columbe, France)
1990	# CHRISTY, June	64	Complications of kidney failure (in Sherman Oaks, CA)
1990	# CHRYSIS, International	38	Cancer (in New York, NY)
1990	CLAIRE, Ludi	70	After a long illness
1990	CLANCY, Tom	67	Stomach cancer (in Cork, Ireland)
1990	CLARK, Dee	52	
1990	CLEMENT, Marc R.	39	Automobile accident (in Atlanta, GA)
1990	CLOCHE, Maurice	82	Parkinson's disease (in Bordeaux, France)

Deaths of Movie and Television Personalities — by Year

YEAR	NAME		AGE	CAUSE and/or PLACE OF DEATH
1990	COFFIN, Tristram "Tris"		80	Lung cancer (in Santa Monica, CA)
1990	CONDOS, Steve		71	Heart attack (in Lyon, France)
1990	+ CONIGLIARO, Tony		45	Pneumonia and kidney failure
1990	COOK, Roderick		58	Died in Los Angeles, CA
1990	COPLAND, Aaron	★	90	Complications of 2 strokes and respiratory problems (in NY)
1990	CORBUCCI, Sergio		62	Heart attack (in Rome, Italy)
1990	CUGAT, Xavier		90	Heart failure due to arterial sclerosis (in Barcelona, Spain)
1990	# CULLEN, Bill		70	Heart failure from lung cancer (in Bel Air, CA)
1990	+ CUMMINGS, Robert "Bob"		80	Parkinson's disease, kidney failure and pneumonia (in W'land Hills)
1990	CURRIN, Jay C.		34	Injuries from a 55-foot fall while filming (in Malibu, CA)
1990	d'USSEAU, Arnaud		73	After surgery
1990	DAVIS, Patrick "Grampy"		87	Heart attack (in Upland, CA)
1990	+ DAVIS, Sammy Jr.		64	Throat cancer (in Beverly Hills, CA)
1990	# DEANE, Palmer		56	A.I.D.S. (in New York, NY)
1990	DeGRUNWALD, Dimitri		76	Died in Hove, England
1990	DEMY, Jacques		59	Leukemia (in Paris, France)
1990	DENNY, Joe		61	Respiratory failure (in Fontana, CA)
1990	DeTREAUX, Tamara "E.T."		31	Respiratory and heart problems (in Hollywood, CA)
1990	DeVEGA, José Jr.		56	A.I.D.S. (in Westwood, CA)
1990	DeVITO, Julia		85	
1990	DeWITT, Lew		53	Intestinal disorder
1990	DRAKE, Fabia		86	Died in London, England
1990	DRAPER, Don		62	A.I.D.S. (in Los Angeles, CA)
1990	DUFF, Howard		72	Heart attack (in Santa Barbara, CA)
1990	DUNN, Patricia		60	Lung cancer
1990	DUNN, Peter		68	Heart attack (in Willcox, AZ)
1990	#+ DUNNE, Irene	☆	88	Heart failure (in Los Angeles, CA)
1990	DUX, Pierre		82	Died in Paris, France
1990	EASTERLING, Gary Lamont		38	Died in Los Angeles, CA
1990	EDDY, Helen Jerome		92	Heart failure (in Alhambra, CA)
1990	EDWARDS, Douglas		73	Cancer of the bladder
1990	# EICHELBERGER, Ethyl		45	Suicide (cut wrists) in Staten Island, NY
1990	EMERSON, Elsie Mae		86	Complications from strokes (in Burbank, CA)
1990	ENRIQUEZ, Rene		58	Pancreatic cancer (in Tarzana, CA)
1990	Erté		97	After a brief illness (in Paris, France)
1990	ESMOND, Jill		82	Died in Wimbledon, England
1990	FABRIZI, Aldo		84	Heart attack (in Rome, Italy)
1990	+ FARRELL, Charles "Charlie"		89	Cardiac arrest (in Palm Springs, CA)
1990	FIELD, Irene		59	
1990	FLAUM, Mayer		89	Pneumonia (in Los Angeles, CA)
1990	FLETCHER, Jack		68	Heart failure (in Los Angeles, CA)
1990	FLUELLEN, Joel		82	Apparent suicide (gunshot) in Los Angeles, CA
1990	FOGERTY, Tom		48	Tuberculosis-related respiratory failure (in Scottsdale, AZ)
1990	FONTANA, Arlene		54	Cancer (in New York, NY)
1990	FRANCHI, Sergio		64	Brain cancer (in Stonington, NY)
1990	FRANCK, Edward A.		70	Pneumonia (in New York, NY)
1990	FRANK, Ben		56	Heart attack (in Los Angeles, CA)
1990	FREDERICK, Pauline (TV news)		84	Heart attack (Do not confuse with actress Pauline Frederick, d. 1938)
1990	FRENCH, Valerie		59	Leukemia (in New York, NY)
1990	GAMBARELLI, Maria		89	Cerebral hemorrhage (in Huntington, NY)
1990	#+ GARBO, Greta	☆	84	Undisclosed causes (in New York, NY)
1990	#+ GARDNER, Ava	☆	67	Pneumonia and heart attack (in Kensington, England)
1990	GATLIFF, Frank		62	Died in London, England

Deaths of Movie and Television Personalities — by Year

YEAR	NAME	AGE	CAUSE and/or PLACE OF DEATH
1990	# GILFORD, Jack ☆	81	Stomach cancer (in New York, NY)
1990	GLIDDON, John	92	
1990	# GODDARD, Paulette ☆	84	Heart failure (in Porto Rosco, Switzerland)
1990	GODSELL, Vanda	70	
1990	GORDON, Dexter ☆	67	Kidney failure and cancer of the larynx (in Philadelphia, PA)
1990	GOULDING, Ray	68	Kidney failure (in Manhasset, NY)
1990	# GRAZIANO, Rocky	68	Cardiopulmonary failure (in New York, NY)
1990	GREGORY, Charles "Mr. Music"	89	Pneumonia
1990	HAINES, Richard	43	After surgery for a brain tumor (in Johannesburg, South Africa)
1990	HAKINS, Dick	87	Died in Sherman Oaks, CA
1990	+ HALE, Alan Jr.	71	Cancer of the thymus (in Los Angeles, CA)
1990	HALL, Stuart	86	Complications from lung surgery (in Woodland Hills, CA)
1990	# HAMER, Rusty	42	Suicide (gunshot) in De Ridder, LA
1990	+ HAMMER, Armand	92	
1990	HARDY, Ian Dudley	79	Killed in a storm (in London, England)
1990	HARDY, Joseph	71	Died in New York, NY
1990	HARMON, Tom	70	Heart attack (in Los Angeles, CA)
1990	+ HARRIS, Robin	36	Found dead in his hotel room (in Chicago, IL)
1990	HARRISON, Rex	82	Pancreatic cancer (in Manhattan, NY)
1990	HARVUOT, Clifford	77	Pancreatic cancer (in The Netherlands)
1990	HENSON, Basil	71	Stroke (in Sevenoaks, England)
1990	HENSON, Jim	53	Streptococcus pneumonia and heart attack (in New York, NY)
1990	# HERNDON, Bill	54	A.I.D.S. (in New York, NY)
1990	HILL, Ken	49	A.I.D.S. (in Los Angeles, CA)
1990	HOLE, William J. Jr.	71	Respiratory failure (in Woodland Hills, CA)
1990	HUNTLEY, Raymond	86	Undisclosed causes (in Westminster, England)
1990	IBBS, Ronald	74	Cancer (in San Antonio, TX)
1990	IDEN, Rosalind	82	
1990	+ IRELAND, Jill	54	Breast and lung cancer (in Malibu, CA)
1990	IRVING, Richard	73	After heart surgery (in San Diego, CA)
1990	JACKSON, Freda	82	Undisclosed causes (in London, England)
1990	JACKSON, Gordon	66	Cancer (in London, England)
1990	JAMES, Jessica	60	Cancer (in Los Angeles, CA)
1990	JANSSEN, Werner	91	
1990	JARAY, Hans	83	Heart failure (in Vienna, Austria)
1990	JARVIS, Scott	48	A.I.D.S. (in New York, NY)
1990	# JONES, Candy	64	Cancer
1990	KASHA, Lawrence	57	Brain cancer (in Los Angeles, CA)
1990	KATZKA, Gabriel	58	Heart attack (in Los Angeles, CA)
1990	KENDRICK, Henry	56	Emphysema and pneumonia (in AZ)
1990	KENNEDY, Arthur ☆	75	Brain tumor (in Branford, CT)
1990	# KERMACK, Paul	57	Heart attack (in Glasgow, Scotland)
1990	KIELY, Pat	59	After a long illness
1990	KIRK, Lisa	62	Lung cancer (in New York, NY)
1990	KRUEGER, Michael	39	Cancer (in Milwaukee, WI)
1990	KULUVA, Will	78	Pulmonary embolism
1990	LAMONT, Estelle	82	Respiratory failure (in Woodland Hills, CA)
1990	LANSON, Snooky	76	
1990	LaRUE, Bart	57	Heart failure (in Sweetwater, TX)
1990	LAUTER, Harry	76	Heart failure (in Ojai, CA)
1990	LAWRENCE, Keith	39	Pneumonia (in Los Angeles, CA)
1990	LEACOCK, Philip	73	Collapsed lungs (in London, England)
1990	LEBERMAN, Joseph	85	Cancer (in New York, NY)

Deaths of Movie and Television Personalities — by Year

YEAR	NAME	AGE	CAUSE and/or PLACE OF DEATH
1990	LEE, Larry	48	A.I.D.S.
1990	LEGATT, Alison	86	
1990	LEHMANN, Carla	73	Died in England
1990	LEIGH, Megan	26	Apparent suicide
1990	LEWIS, Elliott	73	Cardiac arrest (in Newport Beach, CA)
1990	+ LOCKER, Frances	79	
1990	# LOCKWOOD, Alexander	88	Died in Los Angeles, CA
1990	LOCKWOOD, Margaret	73	Complications of obesity (in London, England)
1990	LOCKWOOD, Paul	51	Heart disease
1990	# LOSS, Joe	80	Kidney failure
1990	LUCAS, Gail	37	Viral hemorrhagic pneumonia (in Cleveland, OH)
1990	LUND, Art	75	Liver cancer (in Salt Lake City, UT)
1990	LYNCH, Ken	79	Viral infection (in Burbank, CA)
1990	MACKAILL, Dorothy	87	Kidney failure (in Honolulu, HI)
1990	MARGLISS, Frances	76	Heart attack
1990	MARQUARD, Yvonne Peattie	73	Heart attack in her sleep (in Los Angeles, CA)
1990	MARR, Alice	89	Died in Woodland Hills, CA
1990	MARSH, Lois R.	74	After a long illness
1990	MARSTON, Merlin	45	Non-Hodgkins lymphoma (in Los Angeles, CA)
1990	MARTIN, Kiel	46	Cardiovascular collapse caused by lung cancer (in Rancho Mirage)
1990	+ MARTIN, Mary	76	Cancer (in Rancho Mirage, CA)
1990	MAXWELL, James	33	A.I.D.S.
1990	# MAZURKI, Mike	82	After a long illness (in Glendale, CA)
1990	McBEAN, Angus	86	
1990	# McCRAY, Helen Mary "Honey"	83	
1990	McCREA, Joel	84	Pulmonary complications (in Woodland Hills, CA)
1990	McGIVENEY, Maura	51	Liver disease (in Sherman Oaks, CA)
1990	McPHILLIPS, Hugh	70	Injuries from an automobile accident (in Sherman Oaks, CA)
1990	MENDENHALL, Jim	62	Brain cancer
1990	MERIVALE, John	72	Pneumonia (in London, England)
1990	MERRILL, Gary	74	Cancer (in Falmouth, ME)
1990	METCALFE, Gordon	43	A.I.D.S. (in Los Angeles, CA)
1990	MILLER, Barbara	68	After a brain tumor operation (in London, England)
1990	MINOTIS, Alexis	90	Stroke (in Athens, Greece)
1990	# MORAN, Jackie	67	Cancer (in Greenfield, MA)
1990	# MORAN, Lois	81	Cancer (in Sedona, AZ)
1990	MORRIS, Jack Julius	87	Cardiac arrest in his sleep (in Sherman Oaks, CA)
1990	MULLINS, Ted	50	Heart attack
1990	MURDOCH, Richard B.	83	Apparent heart attack (in Walton Heath, England)
1990	MURRAY, Mary Phillips	68	Cancer
1990	MYDLAND, Brent	37	Overdose of morphine and cocaine
1990	NADEL, Arthur H.	68	Diabetes (in Los Angeles, CA)
1990	NAPOLEAN, Phil	89	
1990	NATWICK, Grim	100	Pneumonia and heart disease (in Santa Monica, CA)
1990	NELSON, Herbert	76	Heart attack (in Englewood, NJ)
1990	# NESBITT, Frank M.	48	Cancer (in Upper Marlboro, MD)
1990	NORTH, Edmund	79	Complications after surgery (in Santa Monica, CA)
1990	NOVAK, Jane	94	Complications caused by a stroke (in Woodland Hills, CA)
1990	NOVELLI, Santo Alex	73	Died in Philadelphia, PA
1990	# OLIVER, Susan	53	Cancer (in Woodland Hills, CA)
1990	# PAGE, Jean	95	Died in Los Angeles, CA
1990	PALEY, William S.	89	Apparent heart attack brought on by pneumonia
1990	PALK, Anna	48	Cancer (in London, England)

• New entry. # Original name (Pt. 7). + Interment (Pt. 5).   125   ☆ Oscar nominee, ★ Oscar winner (Pt. 10)

Deaths of Movie and Television Personalities — by Year

YEAR	NAME	AGE	CAUSE and/or PLACE OF DEATH
1990	PAN, Hermes	80	*Apparent stroke (in Beverly Hills, CA)*
1990	PARADJANOV, Sergei	66	*Cancer (in Yerevan, Armenia)*
1990	PARKER, Ed	59	*Following a heart attack*
1990	PIPPIN, Nick	35	*A.I.D.S. (in New York, NY)*
1990	PITOEFF, Sacha	70	*Heart failure (in Paris, France)*
1990	POND, Barbara	?	*Lung cancer*
1990	POWELL, Michael	84	*Cancer (in Avening, England)*
1990	QUILLAN, Eddie	83	*Cancer (in Burbank, CA)*
1990	# RAFFETTO, Michael	91	*Natural causes (in Berkeley, CA)*
1990	RAPPAPORT, David	38	*Apparent suicide (gunshot) in Laurel Canyon, CA*
1990	RAY, Johnnie (pop singer)	63	*Liver failure (Do not confuse with actor Johnny Ray, d. 1927)*
1990	REED, Gavin	59	*Respiratory failure (in Portland, ME)*
1990	REEVE, Scott	38	*A.I.D.S.*
1990	REVERE, Anne ★	87	*Pneumonia (in Locust Valley, NY)*
1990	REYNOLDS, Helen Fortescu	65	
1990	REYNOLDS, Jack	83	*Heart attack in his sleep (in Escondido, CA)*
1990	+ RHODES, Erik	84	*Pneumonia (in Oklahoma City, OK)*
1990	RICE, Felix	46	*A.I.D.S. (in Key West, FL)*
1990	RITT, Martin ☆	76	*Cardiac disease (in Santa Monica, CA)*
1990	ROLFING, Tom	40	*An A.I.D.S.-related illness (in New York, NY)*
1990	+ ROSE, David (pianist/composer)	80	*Heart disease (in Burbank, CA) Do not confuse with David E. Rose*
1990	ROSEN, Al	80	
1990	ROSS, Betsy King	66	
1990	ROSS, Frank	85	*After brain surgery (in Los Angeles, CA)*
1990	ROSSIF, Frédéric	67	*Heart attack (in Paris, France)*
1990	RUSINOW, Irving	75	*Cancer (in Washington, D.C.)*
1990	RUSSELL, Craig	42	*A.I.D.S. (in Toronto, Canada)*
1990	SACHS, Leonard	82	*Kidney failure (in London, England)*
1990	SALCIDO, Michael A.	39	*Liver failure (in Van Nuys, CA)*
1990	SALMI, Albert	62	*Suicide after murdering his wife (gunshot) in Spokane, WA*
1990	Sandy (original "Annie" dog)	16	*Died in his sleep*
1990	SANSBERRY, Hope	94	*Heart attack in her sleep (in Laguna Hills, CA)*
1990	SCHNUR, Jerome	66	*Melanoma (skin cancer)*
1990	SCHUMM, Hans	93	*Heart failure (in Los Angeles, CA)*
1990	SEALES, Franklyn	37	*A.I.D.S. (in Brooklyn, NY)*
1990	SEEGAR, Sara	76	*Cerebral hemorrhage (in Langhorne, PA)*
1990	SELZNICK, Irene	83	*Breast cancer*
1990	SEYLER, Athene	101	*Died in London, England*
1990	SEYRIG, Delphine	58	*Lung cancer (in Paris, France)*
1990	SHANNON, Del	50	*Suicide (in Santa Clarita, CA)*
1990	SHANNON, Paul	80	*Cancer*
1990	SHAW, Steve	25	*Injuries from an automobile accident (in Los Angeles, CA)*
1990	SHAWLEY, Robert	63	*Pneumonia (in Westwood, CA)*
1990	SHERWOOD, Bill	38	*A.I.D.S. (in New York, NY)*
1990	SLOANE, Doreen	56	*Cancer (in Liverpool, England)*
1990	SOMMER, Bert	42	*Liver failure (in Albany, NY)*
1990	SOUTHARD, Stephen	30	*A.I.D.S. (in Sherman Oaks, CA)*
1990	SPEWACK, Bella	91	*Died in New York, NY*
1990	# SPITALNY, Evelyn	79	
1990	# ST. JACQUES, Raymond	60	*Lymphatic cancer (in Los Angeles, CA)*
1990	STALKER, John	67	
1990	# STANLEY, Helene	62	*Died in Los Angeles, CA*
1990	#+ STANWYCK, Barbara ☆	82	*Congestive heart failure (in Santa Monica, CA)*

• New entry. # Original name (Pt. 7). + Interment (Pt. 5).   126   ☆ Oscar nominee, ★ Oscar winner (Pt. 10)

Deaths of Movie and Television Personalities — by Year

YEAR	NAME		AGE	CAUSE and/or PLACE OF DEATH
1990	STARR, Jimmy		86	Died in Phoenix, AZ
1990	STEBER, Eleanor		76	Congestive heart failure (in Langhorne, PA)
1990	STUSSY, Jan		68	Cancer
1990	TARRON, Elsie		87	Heart failure
1990	+ TAYBACK, Vic "Mel"		60	Heart attack (in Glendale, CA)
1990	# Terry-Thomas		78	Parkinson's disease (in Godalming, England)
1990	TESSIER, Robert		56	Cancer (in Lowell, MA)
1990	# THOMPSON, Carlos		67	Suicide (gunshot) in Buenos Aires, Argentina
1990	TOGNAZZI, Ugo		68	Cerebral hemorrhage (in Rome, Italy)
1990	TRAUBERG, Leonid		88	Died in Moscow, Russia
1990	TRENKER, Luis		97	After a long illness (in Bolzano, Italy)
1990	TUPPER, Loretta		84	Cancer (in New York, NY)
1990	UNGER, Bertil		69	Liver disease (in Hollywood, CA)
1990	VanHEUSEN, Jimmy		77	After a long illness (in Rancho Mirage, CA)
1990	VAUGHAN, Sarah		66	Lung cancer (in Los Angeles, CA)
1990	+ VAUGHAN, Stevie Ray		35	Helicopter crash
1990	VEJAR, Rudolph L.		57	Respiratory failure (in Burbank, CA)
1990	WALL, Max		82	Died in Westminster, England
1990	# WALLACE, Jean		66	After an internal hemorrhage (in Hollywood, CA)
1990	WARREN, Betty		83	Died in London, England
1990	WARREN, Charles Marquis		77	Following surgery for a heart aneurysm (in West Hills, CA)
1990	WATERS, Elsie		95	Died in London, England
1990	WATTS, Jr., Leroy		72	Died in Northfield, NJ
1990	WAYNE, Johnny		72	Cancer
1990	WEBB, Robert D.		87	Following a long illness
1990	WEBER, Karl		74	Congestive feart failure (in Boston, MA)
1990	WHEELER, Jerry B.		44	A.I.D.S. (in Los Angeles, CA)
1990	WHITE, David		74	Heart attack after being run over by an auto (in Hollywood, CA)
1990	WHITE, Larry		74	Heart attack
1990	WILLIAMS, Brenda		43	Cancer
1990	WILLOCK, Dave		81	Complications following a stroke (in Woodland Hills, CA)
1990	WILSON, Josephine		86	Heart attack (in London, England)
1990	WITTENBERG, Marguerite N.		77	Cancer (in Culver City, CA)
1990	WITTENBERG, Paul B.		63	Cancer (in Mission Hills, CA)
1990	WOOD, George		56	Diabetes (in New Orleans, LA)
1990	WURSCHMIDT, Sigrid		37	Metastasized breast cancer (in San Francisco, CA)
1990	WYNNE, Paul		47	A.I.D.S.
1991	+ ACKERMAN, Harry		78	Pulmonary failure (in Burbank, CA)
1991	ACKERMAN, Jack		59	Brain tumor (in Los Angeles, CA)
1991	# ADRIAN, Louis		93	Died in Lakeport, CA
1991	AGMON, Ami		43	After a long bout with cancer
1991	+ ALLEN, Irwin	★	75	After suffering a heart attack (in Santa Monica, CA)
1991	ALLEN, Ronald		56	Lung cancer (in Reading, England)
1991	# ANDOR, Lotte Palfi		87	After an illness (in New York, NY)
1991	# ANDOR, Paul		90	After a long illness (in Berlin, Germany)
1991	ARAVINDAM, Govindan		55	Heart attack (in Trivandrum, India)
1991	ARKIN, David		49	Died in Los Angeles, CA
1991	ARNOLD, Monroe		64	After a heart attack
1991	ARRAU, Claudio		88	Complications after surgery for intestinal blockage (in Austria)
1991	#+ ARTHUR, Jean	☆	89	Heart failure following a paralyzing stroke (in Carmel, CA)
1991	# ASHCROFT, Peggy	★	83	After suffering a stroke (in Croydon, England)
1991	ASHE, Martin		80	Respiratory failure (in Woodland Hills, CA)

Deaths of Movie and Television Personalities — by Year

YEAR	NAME		AGE	CAUSE and/or PLACE OF DEATH
1991	ASHMAN, Howard	★	40	*Complications from A.I.D.S. (in New York, NY)*
1991	AUBUCHON, Jacques		67	*Heart failure (in Woodland Hills, CA)*
1991	+ AUDLEY, Eleanor		86	*Respiratory failure (in North Hollywood, CA)*
1991	AXTHELM, Pete		47	*Liver failure*
1991	BAKER, Terence		52	*Died in London, England*
1991	BALL, William		60	*Died in Los Angeles, CA*
1991	#+ BANKY, Vilma		90	*After a 10-yr. illness (at a nursing home in Los Angeles, CA)*
1991	BAREFIELD, Eddie		81	*Heart attack (in New York, NY)*
1991	BARNET, Charlie		77	*Alzheimer's disease and pneumonia*
1991	BARTELL, Eddie		83	*Aneurysm (in Los Angeles, CA)*
1991	BARTELME, Joe		61	*Cancer*
1991	BARUCH, André		83	
1991	BATCHELOR, Joy		77	*After a long illness (in London, England)*
1991	BATES, Ralph		50	*Cancer (in London, England)*
1991	BEDDOE, Don		102	*Died in Texas*
1991	BELL, Hal		65	*After suffering a stroke (in Glendale, CA)*
1991	+ BELLAMY, Ralph	★	87	*Respiratory infection (in Santa Monica, CA)*
1991	BENNETT, Matt		52	*Brain tumor (in Lexington, KY)*
1991	BERNSTEIN, Sam		80	*Died in Los Angeles, CA*
1991	BERTI, Dehl		70	*Heart attack (in Los Angeles, CA)*
1991	BINDER, Maurice		72	*Lung cancer (in London, England)*
1991	BLAKE, Katharine		62	*Died in England*
1991	BLATT, Edward A.		88	*Heart attack (in Los Angeles, CA)*
1991	BOARDMAN, Eleanor		93	*Died in Santa Barbara, CA*
1991	BOIS, Curt		90	*Died in Berlin, Germany*
1991	BOND, Lilian		83	*Heart attack (in Reseda, CA)*
1991	# BOOTH, Edwina		86	*Heart failure (in Long Beach, CA)*
1991	# BOSTWICK, Dorothy Davis		?	*Cardiac arrest*
1991	BOTTCHER, Ron		50	*A.I.D.S.*
1991	BOVASSO, Julie		61	*Cancer (in New York, NY)*
1991	BOWEN, Joe		56	*Heart attack (in Los Angeles, CA)*
1991	BOX, Muriel		85	*Died in London, England*
1991	BROCK, Stanley		59	*Heart attack (in Los Angeles, CA)*
1991	BROIDY, Steve		86	*Following a heart attack (in Los Angeles, CA)*
1991	# BROWN, Reno		70	*Cancer (in Reno, NV)*
1991	+ BROWNE, Coral		77	*Breast cancer (in Los Angeles, CA)*
1991	BRUNNER, Howard		51	*A.I.D.S. (in Marietta, GA)*
1991	BUSCH, Niven		88	*Heart failure (in San Francisco, CA)*
1991	BUSH, Warren V.		65	*Cardiac arrest (in Los Angeles, CA)*
1991	BUTLER, Tim		36	*A.I.D.S.*
1991	CAHAN, George M.		72	*Pneumonia (in Woodland Hills, CA)*
1991	CANTOR, Michael (Max)		32	*Died in New York, NY*
1991	+ CAPRA, Frank	★	94	*Died in his sleep of natural causes (in Los Angeles, CA)*
1991	CARLIN, Thomas A.		62	*Heart failure (in New Rochelle, NY)*
1991	CARR, Eric		41	*Complications from cancer (in Manhattan, NY)*
1991	CASSIDY, Tom		41	*A.I.D.S.*
1991	+ CAULFIELD, Joan		69	*After surgery for cancer (in Los Angeles, CA)*
1991	CHABEAU, Ray Edgar		49	
1991	CHAMBERS, Kathy L.		41	*Cancer*
1991	CHAPLIN, Oona		66	*Following cancer surgery (in Corsier-sur-Vevey, Switzerland)*
1991	CHAPMAN, Ben		83	*Heart and kidney failure (in Orange, CA)*
1991	CHIARI, Walter		67	*Heart attack (in Milan, Italy)*
1991	CHRISTMAS, Jason		49	*Killed outside a NY comedy club by robbers*

• New entry. # Original name (Pt. 7). + Interment (Pt. 5). 128 ☆ Oscar nominee, ★ Oscar winner (Pt. 10)

Deaths of Movie and Television Personalities — by Year

YEAR	NAME		AGE	CAUSE and/or PLACE OF DEATH
1991	CHURCHILL, Donald		60	*Apparent heart attack (in Fuengirola, Spain)*
1991	# CLAYTON, Buck		80	*Died in New York, NY*
1991	CLEVELAND, James		59	*Respiratory problems and heart failure*
1991	COBB, Dita		68	*After a long illness*
1991	CODY, Iron Eyes		84	
1991	COLVIG, Vance		72	*Cancer (in Hollywood, CA)*
1991	COLVIN, Michael		41	*After suffering a head injury on a film set*
1991	+ CONVY, Bert		56	*Cancer (brain tumor) in Los Angeles, CA*
1991	# COOK, Cookie		77	*Kidney failure (in New York, NY)*
1991	COPPOLA, Carmine ★		80	*After suffering a stroke (in Los Angeles, CA)*
1991	COSTON, Ann Sorg		62	*After a short illness (in Roaring Brook Lake, NY)*
1991	# CRAVEN, Eddie		?	*After an illness*
1991	CRAVENS, Kathryn		92	*Cancer (in Burkett, TX)*
1991	+ CROSBY, Dennis		56	*Suicide (gunshot) in Novato, CA)*
1991	# CURTIS, Ken		74	*Died in Fresno, CA*
1991	# DALE, Bobby		92	*Myocardial infarction (in Woodland Hills, CA)*
1991	# DALY, John		77	*Cardiac arrest (in Johannesburg, South Africa)*
1991	+ DAVIS, Brad		41	*Complications from A.I.D.S. (in Los Angeles, CA)*
1991	DAVIS, Jerome L.		73	*Stroke (in Los Angeles, CA)*
1991	#+ DAVIS, Miles		65	*Pneumonia, respiratory failure and a stroke (in Los Angeles, CA)*
1991	DeACUTIS, William		33	*Brain lymphoma (in Los Angeles, CA)*
1991	DEMPSTER, Carol		89	*After a long illness (in La Jolla, CA)*
1991	DEUTSCH, David		65	*Kidney failure (in London, England)*
1991	# DEVLIN, J. G.		84	*Died in Belfast, Ireland*
1991	DEWHURST, Colleen		67	*Cancer (in South Salem, NY)*
1991	DHIEGH, Khigh		75	*Kidney and heart disease (in Mesa, AZ)*
1991	DONN, Lee		96	*Stroke (in Los Angeles, CA)*
1991	DOYLE, Roz		49	*Breast cancer (in Hampstead, England)*
1991	+ DOZIER, William		83	*Stroke (in Los Angeles, CA)*
1991	DRAKE, Oliver		88	*After a long illness (in Las Vegas, NV)*
1991	DUBBINS, Don		62	
1991	# DUNBAR, Dixie		72	*After a series of heart attacks (in Miami, FL)*
1991	DUNNOCK, Mildred ☆		90	*Died in Oak Bluffs, Martha's Vineyard, MA*
1991	+ DUROCHER, Leo		86	*Natural causes (in Palm Springs, CA)*
1991	DYER-BENNETT, Richard		73	
1991	ECKHARDT, John		82	*Heart failure*
1991	EDWARDS, George		67	*Cancer (in Sherman Oaks, CA)*
1991	ELKINS, Lenore		77	*Heart failure*
1991	ELLIS, Karl		41	*A.I.D.S. (in Grand Junction, CO)*
1991	EMR, Roland Jon		45	*Murdered (shot in his car) in Los Angeles, CA*
1991	# EPSTEIN, Jerry		69	*Causes unreported (in London, England)*
1991	EVANS, John Morgan		49	*After a long illness (in Los Angeles, CA)*
1991	FALAT, Stephen J.		34	*After a long illness (in New York, NY)*
1991	FAYE, Frances		71	*Following a series of strokes (in Los Angeles, CA)*
1991	FELDMAN, Phil		69	*Cancer (in Los Angeles, CA)*
1991	FIELD, Filip J.		67	*Heart failure*
1991	FISHELSON, Stanley		66	*Natural causes*
1991	FLORANCE, Sheila		75	*Cancer (in Melbourne, Australia)*
1991	# FONTEYN, Margot		71	*Cancer*
1991	# FORD, "Tennessee" Ernie		72	*Liver disease (in Reston, VA)*
1991	FORD, Lloyd		79	*Ventricular fibrillation (in Woodland Hills, CA)*
1991	#+ FOXX, Redd		68	*Heart attack during rehearsal for new TV show (in Hollywood, CA)*
1991	FRANCESCATTI, Zino		89	

Deaths of Movie and Television Personalities — by Year

YEAR	NAME		AGE	CAUSE and/or PLACE OF DEATH
1991	# FRANCIS, Wilma		73	Complications after lung surgery
1991	# FRANCISCUS, James		57	Emphysema (in Hollywood, CA)
1991	FREEMAN, Dexter		53	A.I.D.S.
1991	FREEMAN, Everett		79	Renal failure (in Westwood, CA)
1991	# FURST, Anton	★	47	Suicide (jumped from 8th level of parking garage) in Hollywood, CA
1991	GAILLARD, Slim		74	Cancer (in London, England)
1991	GAINSBOURG, Serge		62	Heart trouble (in Paris, France)
1991	GERRY, Toni		65	Bone cancer (in Los Angeles, CA)
1991	GETZ, Stan		64	After a 5-year battle with liver cancer (in Los Angeles, CA)
1991	GIBSON, Marc		51	Apparent heart attack after a workout
1991	GILBERT, Joan		84	
1991	GILLIES, Carol		50	Cancer (in London, England)
1991	+ GOBEL, George		71	Complications after arterial leg surgery (in Encino, CA)
1991	GOLDEN, Murray		79	Complications after a stroke (in Encino, CA)
1991	GOLDRICH, Bert		84	
1991	# GRAHAM, Bill		60	Helicopter crash (in Sonoma County, CA)
1991	GRAHAM, Martha		96	Pneumonia and cardiac arrest (in New York, NY)
1991	GRANGE, Red		87	
1991	GREEN, Lee		72	Automobile accident (in Baja, Mexico)
1991	GREENE, Graham		86	Leukemia (in Vevey, Switzerland)
1991	GREENSPAN, David		68	Lung cancer
1991	GUTHRIE, A. B. Jr.		90	
1991	GUZMAN, Pato		57	After a brief illness (in Santiago, Chile)
1991	HAGERTY, Michael		39	A.I.D.S. (in New York, NY)
1991	HALL, Ed		60	Cancer (in Providence, RI)
1991	HALL, Kevin Peter		35	Pneumonia (in Hollywood, CA)
1991	HAMILTON, Frank		66	Prostate cancer (in Los Angeles, CA)
1991	HARDIN, Ken		62	Cancer
1991	HARRIS, Cassandra		39	Ovarian cancer (in Los Angeles, CA)
1991	HARRIS, Lou		85	Heart attack (in Woodland Hills, CA)
1991	HARRIS, Ted		52	Cancer (in Los Angeles, CA)
1991	HAULMAN, Bob		49	Apparent heart attack
1991	HAYDON, Tom		53	Cancer (in Sydney, Australia)
1991	HAYES, Christopher		?	Heart attack (in Hollywood, CA)
1991	HEATH, Gordon		72	After a long illness (in Paris, France)
1991	HOLDEN, Gloria		82	
1991	HORRALL, Craig		?	A.I.D.S. (in New York, NY)
1991	HOUSTON, Donald		67	Undisclosed causes (in Coimbra, Portugal)
1991	HOWDEN, Victoria		27	Suicide (gunshot)
1991	# HOYT, John		86	Lung cancer (in Santa Cruz, CA)
1991	HUDDLESTON, Floyd	☆	73	Following a heart attack (in Los Angeles, CA)
1991	HURWITZ, Leo		81	
1991	HUTCHENRIDER, C. B.		83	
1991	HYDE-WHITE, Wilfrid		87	Congestive heart failure (in Woodland Hills, CA)
1991	IMAI, Tadashi		79	Cerebral hemorrhage (in Tokyo, Japan)
1991	#+ JACKSON, Mary Ann		68	
1991	JAFFA, Max		79	
1991	JAGGER, Dean	★	87	Influenza and heart attack (in Los Angeles, CA)
1991	JEFFRIES, Peter		62	Following open-heart surgery (in San Francisco, CA)
1991	JOHANSEN, Gunnar		85	Liver cancer
1991	JORDAN, Gerry		45	A.I.D.S.
1991	KAUFMAN, Robert	☆	60	Heart attack (in Beverly Hills, CA)
1991	KAYE, Sylvia Fine		78	Emphysema (in New York, NY)

• New entry. # Original name (Pt. 7). + Interment (Pt. 5).   130   ☆ Oscar nominee, ★ Oscar winner (Pt. 10)

Deaths of Movie and Television Personalities — by Year

YEAR	NAME	AGE	CAUSE and/or PLACE OF DEATH
1991	KELLEY, Edward (Barry)	82	Congestive heart failure (in Woodland Hills, CA)
1991	KEMPFF, Wilhelm	95	Parkinson's disease
1991	KERMAN, Sheppard	62	Lung cancer (in Manhasset, NY)
1991	+ KERT, Larry	60	A.I.D.S. (in New York, NY)
1991	KIKER, Douglas	61	Heart attack
1991	# KILIAN, Pauline	83	Complications from diabetes (in Peacham, VT)
1991	KINGHAM, Bernard	65	A stroke related to spinal cancer (in Amersham, England)
1991	KINSKI, Klaus	65	Found dead of a heart attack (at his home in Lagunitas, CA)
1991	KOBAL, John	51	Pneumonia
1991	KOLB, Glenn	39	A.I.D.S.
1991	KREBS, Nita	85	Apparent heart attack
1991	KROEGER, Berry	78	Kidney failure (in Los Angeles, CA)
1991	KULP, Nancy	69	Cancer of the jaw (in Palm Desert, CA)
1991	LACEY, Ronald	55	Cancer (in London, England)
1991	+ LAIRD, Jack	69	Cancer (in Los Angeles, CA)
1991	LAMONT, Deni	59	Lung cancer
1991	LANDERS, Hal	63	After being hospitalized for cancer treatment (in Los Angeles, CA)
1991	#+ LANDON, Michael	54	Cancer of the liver and pancreas (in Malibu, CA)
1991	LANGAN, Glenn	73	Complications from cancer (in Los Angeles, CA)
1991	LANHAM, Roy	68	Cancer
1991	LANIN, Howard	93	Pneumonia
1991	LaVERE, Jane	87	Heart problems (in Woodland Hills, CA)
1991	LAWRENCE, Mark (producer)	70	Prostate cancer (in Boston) Do not confuse with actor Marc Lawrence
1991	LAWRENCE, Mary	73	Respiratory failure following pneumonia (in Santa Monica, CA)
1991	LEAMING, Jim	72	After a long illness
1991	LEAN, David	83	After a long illness (in London, England)
1991	LEFÈVRE, René	93	Cancer (in Poissy, France)
1991	LeGALLIENNE, Eva	92	Heart failure
1991	LEIGHTON, Merrill	51	Automobile accident
1991	LENSKY, Leib	82	Liver cancer (in New York, NY)
1991	LESLIE, Bob	64	Undisclosed causes (in Los Angeles, CA)
1991	# LEWIS, Robert Q.	71	Emphysema (in Los Angeles, CA)
1991	LOMBARDI, Paul Michael	31	A.I.D.S. (in Los Angeles, CA)
1991	LOTT, Lawrence	40	A.I.D.S.
1991	LOURIE, Eugene	89	Heart failure and complications from strokes (in Woodland Hills, CA)
1991	LOVE, Edward M.	43	A.I.D.S. (in New York, NY)
1991	LOVE, Geoff	73	Undisclosed causes (in London, England)
1991	LOWENSTEIN, Lynn Gendron	30	An inoperable brain tumor
1991	+ LUKE, Keye	86	After a stroke (in Hollywood, CA)
1991	MacDONALD, James	84	Heart failure (in Glendale, CA)
1991	MacMAHON, Aline ☆	92	Pneumonia (in New York, NY)
1991	#+ MacMURRAY, Fred	83	Pneumonia and cancer (in Santa Monica, CA)
1991	MAIBAUM, Richard	81	After a short illness (in Santa Monica, CA)
1991	# MANN, Daniel	79	Heart failure (in Los Angeles, CA)
1991	MARKHAM, Marcella	68	Breast cancer (in New York, NY)
1991	MARKLE, Fletcher	70	Heart failure (in Los Angeles, CA)
1991	MARLOWE, Louis J.	85	Kidney failure (in Laguna Hills, CA)
1991	MAROFF, Robert	57	
1991	MARRERO, Ralph	33	Automobile accident (in Albuquerque, NM)
1991	MARSHALL, Robert H.	67	After a brief illness
1991	+ MASSEY, Curt	81	Undisclosed causes (in Rancho Mirage, CA)
1991	McCALLION, James	72	Heart attack (in Van Nuys, CA)
1991	McCOY, Jack	72	

Deaths of Movie and Television Personalities — by Year

YEAR	NAME	AGE	CAUSE and/or PLACE OF DEATH
1991	McCULLOUGH, Stephen N.	48	Pulmonary hypertension
1991	McINTIRE, John Herrick	83	Emphysema and cancer (in Pasadena, CA)
1991	McLAUGHLIN, Emily	61	Cancer (in Los Angeles, CA)
1991	# MERCURY, Freddie	45	A.I.D.S.
1991	MILES, Bernard	83	Died in Knaresborough, England
1991	# MILFORD, Gene ★	89	Pneumonia (in Santa Monica, CA)
1991	MILLIGAN, Andy	62	A.I.D.S. (in Los Angeles, CA)
1991	MITCHELL, Frank	84	Cardiac arrest (in North Hollywood, CA)
1991	MONDO, Peggy	50	Heart attack (in Los Angeles, CA)
1991	MONICA, Maria A. G.	92	Died in Las Vegas, NV
1991	MONTALBAN, Carlos	87	Heart failure (in New York, NY)
1991	#+ MONTAND, Yves	70	Heart attack following a stroke (in Senlis, France)
1991	MOORCROFT, Judy	58	
1991	# MOORE, Eleanor	84	Complications from emphysema (in Santa Monica, CA)
1991	MORALI, Jacques	44	A.I.D.S.
1991	MORGAN, George J.	77	Cancer (in Canoga Park, CA)
1991	# MURRAY, Arthur	95	Pneumonia
1991	MUSILLI, John	55	Cancer (in Kinnelon, NJ)
1991	# NALDER, Reggie	80	Bone cancer (in Santa Monica, CA)
1991	NEWMAN, Thomas	60	Heart attack (in Los Angeles, CA)
1991	NICHOLSON, Thomas D.	68	Cancer
1991	NORTH, Alex ☆	81	Pancreatic cancer (in Pacific Palisades, CA)
1991	NUTE, Don	56	A.I.D.S. (in New York, NY)
1991	O'CONNOR, Kevin	56	Cancer (in New York, NY)
1991	OCKO, Daniel	78	Respiratory failure (in Argentina)
1991	PADILLA, Ruben Dario Sr.	81	Cancer (in San Diego, CA)
1991	PAGANO, Ronald F.	37	After a long illness (in Los Angeles, CA)
1991	PALMER, John	75	After a short illness
1991	# PARIS, Freddie	63	Cancer (in Sydney, Australia)
1991	PASTERNAK, Joe	89	Parkinson's disease and other ailments (in Beverly Hills, CA)
1991	PATTISON, Arthur	60	Cancer
1991	PERTWEE, Michael	74	Undisclosed causes (in London, England)
1991	PIAZZA, Ben	58	Cancer (in Sherman Oaks, CA)
1991	PIERCE, Webb	69	Pancreatic cancer
1991	POPKIN, Harry M.	85	Cancer (in Santa Monica, CA)
1991	POWERS, Tim	34	A.I.D.S. (in New York, NY)
1991	PRATT, James C.	86	Pneumonia (in Los Angeles, CA)
1991	PRICE, Gilbert	48	Found dead of diabetic coma (in Vienna, Austria)
1991	PRIM, Suzy	95	Suicide (in Boulogne-Billancourt, France)
1991	# PROVENZA, Sal	45	Lymphoma (in New York, NY)
1991	RAGNI, Gerome	48	Cancer (in New York, NY)
1991	RAPF, Matthew	71	After an attack of the flu
1991	RASCEL, Renato	78	Heart failure (in Rome, Italy)
1991	RASULALA, Thalmus	55	Heart attack after suffering from leukemia (in Albuquerque, NM)
1991	# RAY, Aldo	64	Complications from throat cancer and pneumonia (in San Francisco)
1991	READING, Bertice	58	Stroke (in London, England)
1991	REASONER, Harry	68	Complications and pneumonia after brain clot surgery
1991	REILLY, Howard	79	After a coronary bypass operation
1991	Rellys	85	Died in Marseille, France
1991	REMICK, Lee	55	Kidney and lung cancer (in Brentwood, CA)
1991	RENICK, Ralph	62	Hepatitis and liver cancer
1991	RICHARDSON, Tony ★	63	A.I.D.S. (in Los Angeles, CA)
1991	RODDENBERRY, Gene	70	Cardiac arrest from a massive blood clot (in Santa Monica, CA)

Deaths of Movie and Television Personalities — by Year

YEAR	NAME	AGE	CAUSE and/or PLACE OF DEATH
1991	# ROGERS, Jean	74	Following surgery (in Sherman Oaks, CA)
1991	ROGOT, Peter	37	Apparent heart attack
1991	ROMAN, Paul Reid	55	Cancer (in Los Angeles, CA)
1991	ROMANCE, Viviane	82	Cancer (in Nice, France)
1991	ROOSEVELT, James	83	Complications from a stroke and Parkinson's disease (in CA)
1991	ROSENBLATT, Martin	74	Heart attack (in New York, NY)
1991	ROSQUI, Tom	62	Cancer (in Los Angeles, CA)
1991	# ROSSITTO, Angelo	83	Complications from surgery (in Los Angeles, CA)
1991	RUDOLPH, Oscar	79	Following a stroke (in Encino, CA)
1991	RUFFIN, David	50	Apparent drug overdose
1991	RUSSELL, John	70	Died in Los Angeles, CA
1991	SCHAEFFER, Elizabeth	42	Cerebral hemorrhage
1991	SCHAFER, Natalie	90	Cancer (in Los Angeles, CA)
1991	# SCOTT, Daniel Simon	71	Alzheimer's disease (in Alamitos, CA)
1991	SCOTT, Dennis	51	After a long illness
1991	SEDGWICK, Eileen	93	Died in Hollywood, CA
1991	SERKIN, Rudolph	88	Cancer
1991	# SEUSS, Dr.	87	Respiratory and kidney problems
1991	SHERMAN, George	82	Heart and kidney failure (in Los Angeles, CA)
1991	SHUMAN, Mort	52	Cancer of the liver (in London, England)
1991	SIEGEL, Don	78	After a long bout with cancer (in Nipoma, CA)
1991	SILVER, Dave	72	Heart attack
1991	SMITH, Burleigh	70	Cancer
1991	SMITH, Ray	55	
1991	SOBEK, Allan	46	A.I.D.S. (in New York, NY)
1991	SONNTAG, Jack	77	After a long illness (in Santa Barbara, CA)
1991	# SOUTHERN, Jeri	64	Pneumonia
1991	STEIN, Robert M.	40	Lung cancer (in Los Angeles, CA)
1991	STEVENS, Fran	72	Cancer (in The Bronx, NY)
1991	STEVENS, Mort	62	Pancreatic cancer (in Encino, CA)
1991	STIERLE, Edward	23	A.I.D.S.
1991	STROHM, Walter Clarence	86	Heart failure
1991	SUBOTSKY, Milton	70	Heart disease (in London, England)
1991	SULLIVAN, Marie Madeline	80	After a brief illness (in Ojai, CA)
1991	TALLICHET, Margaret (Wyler)	77	Cancer (in Indio, CA)
1991	# THOMAS, Danny	79	After a heart attack (in Los Angeles, CA)
1991	THOMAS, Wilfrid	87	
1991	# THORPE, Richard	95	Died in Palm Springs, CA
1991	+ TIERNEY, Gene ☆	70	Emphysema (in Houston, TX)
1991	TOOMEY, Regis	93	Heart attack (in Woodland Hills, CA)
1991	# TRYON, Tom	65	Stomach cancer (in Los Angeles, CA)
1991	TUCKER, Lem	52	Liver failure
1991	TULLY, Lee	61	Cancer (in Englewood, NJ)
1991	VANOFF, Nick	61	Cardiac arrest
1991	+ VAUGHN, Billy	72	Cancer
1991	# VINCENT, Chuck	51	Heart attack after a bout with pneumonia (in Key West, FL)
1991	# VITTO, G. L.	69	Heart attack
1991	#+ VonERICH, Chris	21	
1991	WALTERS, Casey	75	After an illness brought on by a stroke
1991	WALTERS, Thorley	78	Undisclosed causes (in London, England)
1991	# WARFIELD, Marjorie	88	Pneumonia (in Los Angeles, CA)
1991	WEBSTER, Byron	58	A.I.D.S. (in Sherman Oaks, CA)
1991	WEIST, Dwight	81	Heart attack (in Block Island, RI)

• New entry. # Original name (Pt. 7). + Interment (Pt. 5).   133   ☆ Oscar nominee, ★ Oscar winner (Pt. 10)

YEAR	NAME		AGE	CAUSE and/or PLACE OF DEATH
1991	# WEST, Dottie		58	Complications after an automobile accident
1991	WHEATLEY, Alan		84	Heart attack (in London, England)
1991	WHEDON, John Ogden		86	Pneumonia (in Redford, OR)
1991	WHITE, Carol		47	Overdose of drugs and alcohol (in London, England)
1991	WILSHIN, Sunday		86	Undisclosed causes (in Chemsford, England)
1991	WILSON, Richard		75	Pancreatic cancer (in Santa Monica, CA)
1991	WILSON, Stu		87	Died in Los Angeles, CA
1991	WILSON, Theodore R.		47	Stroke (in Los Angeles, CA)
1991	WINSLOW, Dick		75	Complications from diabetes (in Los Angeles, CA)
1991	WINTERS, Bernie		58	Cancer (in London, England)
1991	WORSLEY, Wallace Jr.		82	Heart failure
1991	YATES, Sterling		65	Cerebral hemorrhage
1991	YELLEN, Jack		98	Died in Springville, NY
1991	ZAMPA, Luigi		86	After a long illness (in Rome, Italy)
1991	ZORNOW, Edith		72	Cancer (in New York, NY)
1991	ZWICKLER, Phil		36	Complications from A.I.D.S. (in New York, NY)
1992	ABRAHAMS, Gary		48	A.I.D.S.
1992	+ ACUFF, Roy		89	Congestive heart failure
1992	ADES, Daniel		59	Causes unreported (in Los Angeles, CA)
1992	ADLER, Stella		91	Died in her sleep of heart failure (in Los Angeles, CA)
1992	# AHERNE, Gladys		?	After a brief illness
1992	AIKEN, Bill		34	After a 1-year bout with cancer
1992	ALEXANDER, Tom		29	A.I.D.S. (in Hollywood, CA)
1992	ALISON, Dorothy		66	Causes unreported (in London, England)
1992	ALLEN, Peter	★	48	An A.I.D.S.-related illness (in San Diego, CA)
1992	ALLMAN, Elvia		87	Pneumonia (in Santa Monica, CA)
1992	ALMENDROS, Nestor	★	61	Lymphoma (in New York)
1992	ALZADO, Lyle		43	After suffering brain cancer (in Portland, OR)
1992	AMYES, Julian		74	Causes unreported (in London, England)
1992	# ANDERS, Laurie		70	Cancer (in Tarzana, CA)
1992	ANDERSON, John		69	Heart attack
1992	# ANDERSON, Judith	☆	93	Pneumonia after suffering a brain tumor
1992	# ANDREWS, Dana		83	Congestive heart failure and pneumonia (in Los Alamitos, CA)
1992	ANDREWS, Thomas		37	A.I.D.S.
1992	ARDENT, Keith		38	A.I.D.S.
1992	# Arletty		94	Died in Paris, France
1992	ARNOLD, Jack		75	Arteriosclerosis (in Woodland Hills, CA)
1992	ASIMOV, Isaac		72	Heart and kidney failure (in New York, NY)
1992	ATTERBURY, Malcolm		85	Died in Beverly Hills, CA
1992	AUDLEY, Maxine		69	Heart attack (in London, England)
1992	# BABBITT, Art		85	Kidney failure (in Los Angeles, CA)
1992	BABIN, Vitya Vronsky		82	After a long illness
1992	BAIR, Ron		62	Cancer
1992	BAKER, Albie		75	Heart attack (in Los Angeles, CA)
1992	BAKER, Dorothy Helen		78	Died in Los Angeles, CA
1992	# BARBER, Red		84	Intestinal disorder
1992	# BARTHOLOMEW, Freddie		67	Emphysema and heart failure (in Sarasota, FL)
1992	BEATTY, Robert		82	Pneumonia (in London, England)
1992	BEAUCHAMP, Clem		94	Natural causes
1992	BENEDEK, Laslo		87	After a lengthy hospital stay (in New York, NY)
1992	BERKELEY, George		70	Heart attack (in Glendale, CA)
1992	BEYERS, Bill		37	A.I.D.S. (in Los Angeles, CA)

Deaths of Movie and Television Personalities — by Year

YEAR	NAME		AGE	CAUSE and/or PLACE OF DEATH
1992	BLACKWOOD, Christian		50	*Lung cancer (in New York, NY)*
1992	# BLAIRE, Sallie		68	*Liver failure*
1992	BLATTNER, Robert		40	*Airplane crash*
1992	BLETCHER, Arline		99	*Cardiac arrest in her sleep (in Los Angeles, CA)*
1992	# BOOTH, Shirley	★	94	*Cardiac arrest in her sleep (in Chatham, MA)*
1992	BOTAS, Juan Suarez		34	*A.I.D.S. (in New York, NY)*
1992	BOXER, Warren Neal		34	*A.I.D.S. (in Los Angeles, CA)*
1992	+ BRAND, Neville		71	*Emphysema (in Sacramento, CA)*
1992	BRENNER, Glenn		44	*Cerebral hemorrhage from a malignant brain tumor*
1992	BRIGHT, David		49	*Automobile accident*
1992	BRODIE, Steve		72	*Cancer (in West Hills, CA)*
1992	# BROOKS, Beverley		63	*Stroke (in Nice, France)*
1992	BROOKS, Richard	☆	79	*Congestive heart failure (in Beverly Hills, CA)*
1992	# BROWN, Georgia		57	*Infection after surgery for an intestinal blockage (in London, England)*
1992	BROWN, James		72	*Lung cancer (in Woodland Hills, CA)*
1992	# BROWN, Lucille E.		74	*After a long illness (in Buffalo, NY)*
1992	BRUNI, Peter		60	*Heart failure (in Hollywood, CA)*
1992	BRYAN, William Donald Sr.		74	*Cancer*
1992	BURKE, Alan		69	*Emphysema*
1992	CADY, Frank		74	*Complications following heart surgery*
1992	# CALLENDER, Red		76	*Thyroid cancer (in Saugus, CA)*
1992	CARISI, Johnny		70	*Complications from heart surgery*
1992	CARNOVSKY, Morris		94	*Natural causes (in Easton, CT)*
1992	# CARROL, Regina		49	*Cancer (in St. George, UT)*
1992	CARROLL, David		41	*A.I.D.S. (in New York, NY)*
1992	CARTER, Beverly		51	*Cancer*
1992	CASCELLA, John J.		45	*Found dead in his car of apparent heart attack*
1992	CASSELL, W. Barry Jr.		74	*Pneumonia*
1992	CATTANI, Rico		64	*Respiratory disease from a chronic heart condition (in Los Angeles)*
1992	CHALIAPIN, Feodor Jr.		87	*After a brief illness (in Rome, Italy)*
1992	CHRISTI, Panos		54	*Complications from A.I.D.S. (in Los Angeles, CA)*
1992	CHRISTY, Howard		79	*After a long illness (in Oak View, CA)*
1992	# CLARKE, Mae		81	*Cancer (in Woodland Hills, CA)*
1992	CLATWORTHY, William	☆	80	*After a brief illness*
1992	CLORE, Leon		73	*Cancer (in London, England)*
1992	# COLBY, Anita		77	*Lung disease (in New York, NY)*
1992	COLES, Charles "Honi"		81	*Died in his sleep of lung cancer*
1992	COLLOFF, Roger		46	*Cancer*
1992	COMBS, Frederick		57	*A.I.D.S. (in Los Angeles, CA)*
1992	#+ CONNORS, Chuck		71	*Lung cancer (in Los Angeles, CA)*
1992	COOPER, Ralph		?	*Cancer (in New York, NY)*
1992	CORBETT, Ruth (Thom)		78	*After a long illness (in Los Angeles, CA)*
1992	# CORDAY, Rita		68	*Complications of diabetes after gall bladder surgery (in CA)*
1992	COTTLE, Graham D.		51	*Congestive heart failure (in Los Angeles, CA)*
1992	CRISTALDI, Franco	★	68	*Heart attack (in Monte Carlo, Monaco)*
1992	CRONIN, Laurel		53	*Cancer (in Chicago, IL)*
1992	# CUEVAS, Joey		34	*A.I.D.S. (in Naples, FL)*
1992	DANOVA, Cesare		66	*Heart attack (in Los Angeles, CA)*
1992	DANTON, Ray		61	*After suffering from kidney disease (in Los Angeles, CA)*
1992	+ DARBY, Ken	★	82	*Died in Sherman Oaks, CA*
1992	# DAVIS, Jackie		78	*Respiratory failure (in Santa Monica, CA)*
1992	DEA, Marie		72	*Heart attack (in Paris, France)*
1992	# DEHNER, John		76	*Emphysema and diabetes (in Santa Barbara, CA)*

Deaths of Movie and Television Personalities — by Year

YEAR	NAME		AGE	CAUSE and/or PLACE OF DEATH
1992	DELAUDER, Doug		38	A.I.D.S. (in New York, NY)
1992	DeLAURENTIIS, Luigi		75	After a 3-year illness (in Rome, Italy)
1992	DELERUE, Georges	★	67	After a brief illness (in Los Angeles, CA)
1992	DEMAZIS, Orane		87	Died in Boulogne-Billancourt, France
1992	#+ DENNIS, Sandy	★	54	Ovarian cancer (at her home in Westport, CT)
1992	DERR, Richard		74	Pancreatic cancer and heart failure (in Santa Monica, CA)
1992	DEUTSCH, Helen		85	Heart attack in her sleep (in New York)
1992	#+ DIETRICH, Marlene	☆	90	Heart attack (in Paris, France)
1992	+ DINEHART, Alan Jr.		74	Emphysema (in Van Nuys, CA)
1992	DIXON, Adèle		83	Bronchial pneumonia (in Manchester, England)
1992	DIXON, Joan		61	Heart disease (in Los Angeles, CA)
1992	DOWELL, Clifton		44	A.I.D.S.
1992	# DRAKE, Alfred		77	Heart failure after a long bout with cancer (in New York, NY)
1992	DUBMAN, Laura		69	Kidney failure (in New York)
1992	DUELL, Randall	☆	89	Stroke
1992	DUFINE, Herbert		61	Heart condition
1992	DUNBAR, Dorothy		90	Died in Seattle, WA
1992	DUNNE, Philip		84	Cancer (in Malibu, CA)
1992	EISLER, David		36	Pneumonia
1992	ELLERBE, Harry		91	Died in Atlanta, GA
1992	ELLIOTT, Denholm	☆	70	AIDS-related tuberculosis (in Ibiza, Spain)
1992	ENRIGHT, Dan		74	After a brief illness
1992	EPHRON, Henry		81	Died in Los Angeles, CA
1992	EPPER, John		86	Prostate cancer (in Newhall, CA)
1992	# EPSTEIN, David S.		73	Heart attack (in Greenwich, CT)
1992	# Esmeralda		65	Diabetes and complications (in Mexico City, Mexico)
1992	FAYE, Marty		70	Heart attack
1992	FELLOWS, Arthur		74	Cancer (in Century City, CA)
1992	FENNELL, Willie		72	Apparent heart attack (in Sydney, Australia)
1992	# FERRER, José	★	80	After a brief illness (in Coral Gables, FL)
1992	# FIELD, Virginia		74	Cancer (in Palm Desert, CA)
1992	FIELDING, Sol Baer		83	Following a long illness (in Reseda, CA)
1992	FOREMAN, John C.		67	Heart attack (in Beverly Hills, CA)
1992	# FRANCHI, Franco		70	Hemorrhage (in a hospital in Rome, Italy)
1992	# FRANKOVICH, Mike	★	82	Pneumonia and Alzheimer's disease (in Los Angeles, CA)
1992	FRASER, June Joyce Lewis		75	Complications of pneumonia (in Englewood, NJ)
1992	FRASER, Tom		60	Heart failure after exercising at his gym (in Los Angeles, CA)
1992	FROMMER, Ben		78	Died in Burbank, CA
1992	# GARDENIA, Vincent	☆	71	Found dead in his hotel room of a heart attack (in Philadelphia, PA)
1992	# GAUDIO, Joe		79	Cancer
1992	GEIL, Joe "Corky"		64	After a brief illness (in Long Beach, CA)
1992	GEORGE, Joseph L.		65	Cancer (in Agawam, MA)
1992	# GERSON, Jeanne		87	Cancer and pneumonia (in Laguna Hills, CA)
1992	GILL, Ray		42	A.I.D.S.
1992	# GIOVALE, Franco		44	After a car accident (in Capalbio, Italy)
1992	GIOVANNITTI, Len		71	Heart disease (in New York, NY)
1992	GLIONA, Michael		45	Liver failure (in Los Angeles, CA)
1992	+ GOODSON, Mark		77	Cancer (in Los Angeles, CA)
1992	GOODWIN, Thomas Jr.		51	Prostate cancer (in Washington, D.C.)
1992	GREGORY, Mercedes		56	Cancer (in New York, NY)
1992	GRIFFIN, Rodney		46	A.I.D.S.
1992	HALEY, Alex		70	Heart attack
1992	HAMMOND, Ruth		96	Cardiac arrest in her sleep (in Englewood, NJ)

• New entry. # Original name (Pt. 7). + Interment (Pt. 5).   136   ☆ Oscar nominee, ★ Oscar winner (Pt. 10)

Deaths of Movie and Television Personalities — by Year

YEAR	NAME		AGE	CAUSE and/or PLACE OF DEATH
1992	+ HANCOCK, John		51	Found dead of a heart attack (in Los Angeles, CA)
1992	HANNES, Art		72	Respiratory failure
1992	HARRIS, William E.		37	Stabbed when he interrupted a burglary (in Playa Del Rey, CA)
1992	HARTOG, Simon		52	Leukemia (in London, England)
1992	HARVEY, Rudy		60	Kidney failure after a series of strokes
1992	HAYS, Mickey		20	Progeria (a rare aging disorder)
1992	HEIDER, Frederick		75	
1992	HELD, Martin		83	
1992	#+ HENREID, Paul		84	Pneumonia after a stroke (in Santa Monica, CA)
1992	HERBERT, Percy		72	Heart attack
1992	HERZBERGER, Jack L.		75	Following heart surgery (in Downey, CA)
1992	#+ HILL, Benny		67	Heart ailment (in London, England)
1992	HOFF, Louise		69	After a brief illness (in Bethlehem, PA)
1992	HOLLOWAY, Sterling		87	Cardiac arrest (in Los Angeles, CA)
1992	HOVING, Jane Pickens		83	Heart failure
1992	HOWERD, Frankie		70	Apparent heart attack (in London, England)
1992	#+ HUDNET, Bill		47	Liver disease
1992	HUNT, Richard		40	A.I.D.S. (in New York, NY)
1992	HYDE, Jacquelyn		61	Died in Woodland Hills, CA
1992	IRELAND, John	☆	78	Leukemia (in Santa Barbara, CA)
1992	ISING, Rudolf "Rudy"	★	88	Died in Newport Beach, CA
1992	JABARA, Paul	★	44	Lymphoma from A.I.D.S. (in Los Angeles, CA)
1992	JACKSON, Felix		90	Congestive heart failure
1992	JACOBS, Everett "Jake"		68	Cancer
1992	JAFFE, Henry		85	Died in Beverly Hills, CA
1992	JAMES, Ralph		67	Died in Los Angeles, CA
1992	JONES, Allan		84	Lung cancer (in New York, NY)
1992	# JONES, Charlotte		76	Heart disease
1992	JONSON, Kevin Joe		74	Cancer
1992	KANE, Dennis		69	Cancer (in Great Neck, NY)
1992	KANE, Paul		?	Heart attack
1992	KELLY, Jack		65	After suffering a stroke (in Huntington Beach, CA)
1992	KELLY, Paula		72	After a long illness (in Costa Mesa, CA)
1992	KENDRICKS, Eddie		52	Lung cancer
1992	#+ KENNY, Herbert C.		77	Cancer
1992	# KING, Michael		69	Died in Tarzana, CA
1992	KINISON, Sam		38	Internal injuries following a car crash (in Needles, CA)
1992	KINNEY, Jack		82	Died in Glendale, CA
1992	KIRSTEN, Dorothy		82	Complications from a stroke and Alzheimer's disease (in L.A., CA)
1992	KOPLIN, Merton Y.		71	
1992	KRAMER, Sy		59	Cancer (in Los Angeles, CA)
1992	KRAMER, Tim		34	A.I.D.S.
1992	KRUGMAN, Lou		78	Cancer (in Burbank, CA)
1992	KUSELL, Maurice L.		89	Pneumonia (in Los Angeles, CA)
1992	# LANDIS, David		42	A.I.D.S. (in Los Angeles, CA)
1992	LANDIS, Walter James		65	After a long illness (in Glendale, CA)
1992	# LANTZ, Gracie		88	Spinal cancer (in Burbank, CA)
1992	LAWRENCE, John		60	Heart attack (in Los Angeles, CA)
1992	LEAMING, Chet		66	After a brief illness (in New York, NY)
1992	LECLERC, Ginette		79	Cancer (in Paris, France)
1992	LEDERMAN, Victoria Kellem		52	Amyloidosis
1992	LEE, Irving Allen		43	A.I.D.S. (in New York, NY)
1992	# LEE, Vanessa		71	Causes unreported (in London, England)

Deaths of Movie and Television Personalities — by Year

YEAR	NAME	AGE	CAUSE and/or PLACE OF DEATH
1992	+ LEHRMAN, Oscar S.	73	Prostate cancer
1992	LEVY, Franklin R.	43	Pulmonary embolism (in Southington, CT)
1992	LEWIS, David	83	After a short illness (in New York, NY)
1992	LIDDELL, Laura	83	Following a series of heart problems (in London, England)
1992	LISS, Ted	72	Heart attack (in Chicago, IL)
1992	LITTLE, Cleavon	53	Colon cancer (in Sherman Oaks, CA)
1992	LORENTZ, Pare	86	Heart failure (in Armonk, NY)
1992	LOWENSTEIN, Cary Scott	30	A.I.D.S. (in Boca Raton, FL)
1992	LUND, John	81	Found dead in his home; heart trouble (in Coldwater Canyon, CA)
1992	MacGRATH, Leueen	77	Complications after a stroke (in London, England)
1992	MAGERMAN, Les	46	A.I.D.S.
1992	# MARSHALL, Brenda	77	Throat cancer (in Palm Springs, CA)
1992	# MARTON, Andrew	87	Pneumonia (in Santa Monica, CA)
1992	+ MARX, Samuel	90	Congestive heart failure (Do not confuse with Samuel Marx, d. 1933)
1992	MAXWELL, Paul	70	Undisclosed causes (in London, England)
1992	MAYS, Wendell	72	Cancer (in Santa Monica, CA)
1992	McBATH, James H.	69	Heart attack
1992	McCARTHY, Julia	64	Cancer (in London, England)
1992	McCULLERS, Edward	64	Heart attack
1992	McEDWARD, Jack	94	Died in Los Angeles, CA
1992	McGILL, Shaun	30	A.I.D.S.
1992	# MELL, Marisa	53	Cancer of the thyroid (in Vienna, Austria)
1992	MERRILL, Joan	74	Stroke and Alzheimer's disease (in New York, NY)
1992	MILLER, David	82	Cancer (in Los Angeles, CA)
1992	MILLER, Hope	63	Breast cancer (in New York, NY)
1992	MILLER, Roger	56	Cancer (in Los Angeles, CA)
1992	MILSTEIN, Nathan	88	Heart attack
1992	MITCHELL, Chuck	64	Cirrhosis of the liver (in Hollywood, CA)
1992	MITCHELL, Coleman	48	After a sudden illness
1992	MOLINARI, Antoinette	63	Kidney failure (in Burbank, CA)
1992	MOORE, Brian	59	Congestive heart failure (in Hollywood, CA)
1992	MORLEY, Robert	84	After suffering a stroke (Do not confuse with Robert Morley, d. 1952)
1992	MORRISON, Barbara	84	Heart failure (in Woodland Hills, CA)
1992	MUELLER, William A. ☆	92	Natural causes
1992	MUNRO, Nan	87	Died in London, England
1992	MURPHY, George	89	Leukemia (in Palm Beach, FL)
1992	MYHERS, John	70	Pneumonia (in Los Angeles, CA)
1992	NABBIE, Jim	72	After double bypass heart surgery
1992	# NAISMITH, Laurence	83	After a short illness (in Southport, Australia)
1992	NAUGHTON, Bill	81	Died in England
1992	NELSON, Ruth	87	Cancer complicated by a stroke and pneumonia (in Manhattan, NY)
1992	NIGRO, Robert	45	A.I.D.S.
1992	NOVELLO, Roselle	95	Died in Los Angeles, CA
1992	O'DONNELL, Gene	81	Lung cancer (in Woodland Hills, CA)
1992	# O'NEAL, Frederick	86	After a long illness (in New York, NY)
1992	O'TOOLE, Ollie	79	After a long illness (in Los Angeles, CA)
1992	OGAWA, Shinsuke	56	
1992	OLIVER, David	30	A.I.D.S. (in Los Angeles, CA)
1992	# ORLOFF, Thelma	76	Kidney failure (in Los Angeles, CA)
1992	OULTON, Brian	84	Died in London, England
1992	PARKER, Al	40	A.I.D.S. (Do not confuse with Albert Parker, d. 1974)
1992	PARKS, Bert	77	Lung cancer (in La Jolla, CA)
1992	PARSONS, Lindsley Sr.	87	Heart failure (in Burbank, CA)

Deaths of Movie and Television Personalities — by Year

YEAR	NAME	AGE	CAUSE and/or PLACE OF DEATH
1992	PASCAL, Jean-Claude	64	Following surgery for stomach cancer (in Paris, France)
1992	PASTOR, Guy	55	Heart attack
1992	PECK, Ed	75	Heart attack (in Los Angeles, CA)
1992	PENDRELL, Ernest	?	Cancer (in New York, NY)
1992	+ PERKINS, Anthony ☆	60	Complications from A.I.D.S. (at his home in Hollywood, CA)
1992	PETERS, Lennie	59	
1992	# PETTYJOHN, Angelique	48	Cancer (in Las Vegas, NV)
1992	PEYTON, Rev. Patrick	83	Renal failure
1992	PICON, Molly	94	Died in her sleep following Alzheimer's disease (in Lancaster, PA)
1992	POIRET, Jean	65	Heart attack (in Suresnes, France)
1992	+ PORCARO, Jeff	38	After an apparent allergic reaction to pesticides
1992	PRENTICE, Keith	52	Cancer (in Kettering, OH)
1992	PRESTON, Wayde	62	Cancer (in Lovelock, NV)
1992	RACKMIL, Milton R.	89	Stroke
1992	RALSTON, Howard	?	After a brief illness (in Los Angeles, CA)
1992	RAMOS, Lou	51	After a brief illness (in New York, NY)
1992	RAWLINGS, Richard Sr.	75	After a brief illness (in Los Angeles, CA)
1992	RAY, Harry Milton	45	Stroke
1992	RAY, Satyajit ★	70	Heart ailment (in Calcutta, India)
1992	READE, Charles A.	82	After a 2-year hospitalization for a stroke (in Sangus, MA)
1992	#+ REED, Robert	59	Colon lymphoma and A.I.D.S. (in Pasadena, CA)
1992	REED, Vernon William Sr.	73	After a long illness (in Burlington, VT)
1992	REESE, Robert	66	Heart attack (in Los Angeles, CA)
1992	REMME, John	56	A.I.D.S. (in New York, NY)
1992	# Renie ★	90	Natural causes
1992	RICHARDS, Lloyd	89	Pneumonia (in Wales)
1992	RILEY, Alice Mary	51	Cancer (in Concord, CA)
1992	RILEY, Larry	39	A.I.D.S. complications (in Burbank, CA)
1992	# RINALDO, Fred	78	Complications after an operation for a broken hip (in Los Angeles)
1992	RINI, David	40	Brain cancer (in Cleveland, OH)
1992	RIO, Joan Maloney	57	Cancer
1992	+ ROACH, Hal Sr. ★	100	Pneumonia (in Bel Air, CA)
1992	ROBBINS, Duke	71	Pneumonia (in Duarte, CA)
1992	+ ROBBINS, Fred	73	Lymphoma
1992	ROBBINS, Michael	62	Died in London, England
1992	ROBERTS, Howard	62	Prostate cancer
1992	ROBERTS, Meade	61	Congestive heart failure (in New York, NY)
1992	ROBINSON, Cardew	75	Following a bowel infection (in Boethampton, England)
1992	ROSE, David E. (producer)	96	Died in Phoenix, AZ (Do not confuse with the pianist/composer)
1992	ROSENBERG, Mark	44	Heart attack (in Stanton, TX)
1992	ROSENBERGER, James	84	Pneumonia
• 1992	+ ROSS, Margery Jane	72	
1992	RUBENSTEIN, Phil	51	Heart attack (in Los Angeles, CA)
1992	# RUSSELL, Andy	72	Complications from a stroke
1992	SACHA, Kenny	39	A.I.D.S. (in Hollywood, CA)
1992	SACHS, Scotty	39	Murdered (multiple gunshot wounds) in Los Angeles, CA
1992	SALE, Virginia (Wren)	92	Heart failure (in Woodland Hills, CA)
1992	SAMUEL, Andrew	82	Died in Colton, CA
1992	SANDERSON, Joan	79	After a lengthy illness (in Norwich, England)
1992	SATZ, Wayne	47	Found dead in his home
1992	SCHWARTZ, Sammy	86	Heart attack
1992	SEAY, James	78	Died in Capitol Beach, CA
1992	SEGAL, Vivienne	95	Heart failure (in Beverly Hills, CA)

• New entry. # Original name (Pt. 7). + Interment (Pt. 5).

☆ Oscar nominee, ★ Oscar winner (Pt. 10)

Deaths of Movie and Television Personalities — by Year

YEAR	NAME		AGE	CAUSE and/or PLACE OF DEATH
1992	SERPE, Ralph B.		81	Cancer (in Tarzana, CA)
1992	SEVAREID, Eric		79	Stomach cancer
1992	# SHAYNE, Robert		92	Lung cancer (in Woodland Hills, CA)
1992	SHELDON, Richard		59	Cancer (in Montecito, CA)
1992	SHORR, Lester	★	85	Cancer (in Los Angeles, CA)
1992	SIMON, Robert F.		83	Heart attack (in Tarzana, CA)
1992	SINCLAIR, Ronald		68	Respiratory failure (in Woodland Hills, CA)
1992	SLYTER, Fred		56	After a long illness (in Los Angeles, CA)
1992	SMITH, Jacqueline		?	After a lengthy illness
1992	# SOUEZ, Ina		89	Stroke
1992	SPENCER, Herbert	☆	87	Died in Culver City, CA
1992	STAFFORD, Grace		88	
1992	STEEL, Pippa		44	Cancer (in London, England)
1992	STEPHENSON, Skip		54	Following an apparent heart attack
1992	# STOREY, June		73	Cancer (in Vista, CA)
1992	STRAIT, Ralph		56	Heart attack (in New York, NY)
1992	STRANGE, Bill		62	Cancer
1992	STURGES, John	☆	82	Heart attack and emphysema (at his home in San Luis Obispo, CA)
1992	SULLIVAN, Larry		46	Stroke
1992	# Superman		54	Slain in combat with "Doomsday"
1992	SWEENEY, Bob		73	Cancer (in Westlake Village, CA)
1992	SYMS, Sylvia		74	Apparent heart attack (while performing on stage in London, England)
1992	TALTON, Alix		72	After a long battle with lung cancer (in Burbank, CA)
1992	TARLOW, Florence		70	Cancer (in New York, NY)
1992	TAVARES, Albert		39	A.I.D.S.
1992	THACKER, Jim		64	Stroke
1992	# THOMAS, Ted		88	Heart attack (in Van Nuys, CA)
1992	# THOMPSON, Marshall		66	Congestive heart failure (in Royal Oak, MI)
1992	TINDALL, Hilary		54	Cancer (in Selbourne, England)
1992	TIPPET, Clark		37	A.I.D.S.
1992	# TODD, Christopher		30	A.I.D.S. (in New York, NY)
1992	TOUCHSTONE, John		59	Cirrhosis of the liver (in Sherman Oaks, CA)
1992	TRACE, Christopher		59	Cancer (in London, England)
1992	# TREE, Dorothy		85	Heart failure (in Englewood, NJ)
1992	TROP, Jack Dunn		92	Respiratory infection (in Miami, FL)
1992	TUNBERG, Karl		83	Died in London, England
1992	TURNER, Teddy		75	Died in Horsforth, England
1992	VARSI, Diane	☆	54	Respiratory problems and Lyme disease (in Los Angeles, CA)
1992	VENTURA, Charlie		75	Lung cancer
1992	VINE, Sam		69	Cancer
1992	VonZERNECK, Peter		84	Complications after surgery (in Burbank, CA)
1992	WAGNER, Roger		78	Cancer
1992	WALKER, Bill		95	Cancer (in Woodland Hills, CA)
1992	# WALKER, Nancy		69	Following a 2-year battle with lung cancer (in Studio City, CA)
1992	WALKER, William Arlen		74	Died in Lancaster, CA
1992	WALLACK, Roy Homer		64	Pneumonia (in Van Nuys, CA)
1992	WEAVER, Jackson		72	Heart and kidney failure
1992	+ WELK, Lawrence		89	Pneumonia
1992	+ WELLS, Mary		49	After a long bout with cancer
1992	WHALEY, Jim		44	Heart attack
1992	WHITE, Glenn		42	A.I.D.S.
1992	# WILLIAMS, Bill		77	Complications of a brain tumor (in Burbank, CA)
1992	WILLIAMS, Tony		64	

Deaths of Movie and Television Personalities — by Year

YEAR	NAME		AGE	CAUSE and/or PLACE OF DEATH
1992	WOLFE, Ian		95	Cardiac arrest in his sleep (in Los Angeles, CA)
1992	# WOOLERY, Ade		82	Cancer (in Santa Monica, CA)
1992	#+ WORDEN, Hank		91	Died in his sleep of natural causes (at his Brentwood, CA, home)
1992	WYATT, Allan Sr.		72	Cancer (in Burbank, CA)
1992	WYLER, Jorie		61	After a brief illness (in New York, NY)
1992	YARMY, Dick		59	Lung cancer (in Studio City, CA)
1992	YEVSTIGNEEV, Yevgeny		66	Cardio-vascular problems (in London, England)
1992	+ YORK, Dick		63	Emphysema and degenerative spinal condition (Grand Rapids, MI)
1992	YOUNG, Jack Haydn		81	Neurological illness
1993	ADLER, Clyde		67	After a long illness (in Petasky, Michigan)
1993	AGUILAR, Thomas J.		41	A.I.D.S. (in Honolulu, Hawaii)
1993	+ AIDMAN, Charles		68	Cancer (in Beverly Hills, CA)
1993	ALLEN, Adrianne		86	After suffering from cancer (in Montreux, Switzerland)
1993	# ALLEY, Paul		87	Died in Winter Park, Florida
1993	#+ AMECHE, Don ★		85	Prostate cancer (at his son's home in Scottsdale, AZ)
1993	+ AMES, Leon		91	Complications after a stroke (Laguna Beach, CA)
1993	ANDERSON, Marian		96	Congestive heart failure following a stroke
1993	ANTHONY, Joseph		80	Died in Hyannis, MA
1993	ARDOLINO, Emile ★		50	Complications from A.I.D.S. (in Bel-Air, CA)
1993	+ ASHE, Arthur		49	A.I.D.S.-related pneumonia (at a New York hospital)
1993	BAKER, Howard		61	Cancer (in Hale, Cheshire, England)
1993	BAKEWELL, Billy		85	Leukemia (in Los Angeles, CA)
1993	BALLARD, Lucinda ☆		87	Cancer
1993	BARCLIFT, Edgar Nelson		76	After a lengthy illness (in Los Angeles, CA)
1993	BARRON, Lee		78	Respiratory failure (in Omaha, Nebraska)
1993	BARROW, Bernard		65	Lung cancer (at Lennox Hill Hospital in NY)
1993	BATTLE, Edwin Louis		33	Stroke (in Toronto, Canada)
1993	BECK, John		83	Cancer (in Woodland Hills, CA)
1993	BECKER, Robert		47	Car accident (in Santa Clarita, CA)
1993	BELLAVER, Harry		88	Pneumonia (in a Nyack, NY, hospital)
1993	BERRY, Eric		80	Cancer (in Laguna Beach, CA)
1993	BERTHELSON, Larry		60	Died in Santa Barbara, CA
1993	BISHOP, Wesdon		60	Liver ailment (in Nashville, TN)
1993	BISSELL, Jennifer Raine		60	Heart ailment (in Los Angeles, CA)
1993	BITTNER, Jack		76	Heart attack (in New York)
1993	+ BIXBY, Bill		59	Prostate cancer (in his Century City, CA, home)
1993	BJORLING, Rolf		64	
1993	# BOOTS, Tubby		59	After a blood clot traveled to his lungs
1993	BOZYK, Reizl		79	Died at St. Vincent's Hosp. Med. Ctr., New York, NY
1993	BRADEN, Bernard		76	Heart attack (in London, England)
1993	BRAFA, Tony		72	Heart attack (in Los Angeles, CA)
1993	BRANDA, Richard		57	Colon cancer (in Los Angeles, CA)
1993	# BRANDT, Buzz		60	Heart failure
1993	BRIAN, David		82	Cancer and heart failure (in Sherman Oaks, CA)
1993	BRIDGES, James ☆		57	Intestinal cancer (in Los Angeles, CA)
1993	BROCCO, Peter		89	Heart attack (in Los Angeles, CA)
1993	BROWN, Richard "Dick"		68	Cancer (in Los Angeles, CA)
1993	BROX, Lorayne (Hall)		94	Unreported causes (in Los Angeles, CA)
1993	BRUSATI, Franco		66	Leukemia (in Rome, Italy)
1993	BULLOCK, Burdette III		38	Cancer
1993	BURDETT, Winston		79	After a long illness (in Rome, Italy)
1993	BURKS, Stephen		36	Undisclosed causes (in Los Angeles, CA)

• New entry.   # Original name (Pt. 7).   + Interment (Pt. 5).   141   ☆ Oscar nominee,   ★ Oscar winner (Pt. 10)

Deaths of Movie and Television Personalities — by Year

YEAR	NAME	AGE	CAUSE and/or PLACE OF DEATH
1993	#+ BURR, Raymond	76	*Cancer of the liver (in Sonoma County, CA)*
1993	BUTLER, John	74	*Cancer (in New York)*
1993	BYRD, William D.	27	*Heart failure (in Inglewood, CA)*
1993	+ CAHN, Sammy ★	79	*Congestive heart failure (in Los Angeles, CA)*
1993	CAINE, Howard	67	*Heart attack (in Los Angeles, CA)*
1993	CALLEN, Michael	38	*A.I.D.S. (in Los Angeles, CA)*
1993	+ CAMPANELLA, Roy	71	*After a heart attack (in Woodland Hills, CA)*
1993	# Cantinflas	81	*Lung cancer (in Mexico City, Mexico)*
1993	CARLON, Fran	80	*Cancer (at her home in Manhattan, NY)*
1993	CARROLL, Janice	61	*Cancer (in San Fernando Valley, CA)*
1993	CHECCHI, Robert J.	67	*After suffering a stroke (in Los Angeles, CA)*
1993	CHURCH, Sandie	32	*A.I.D.S.*
1993	CINCOTTA, Carmine	41	*Hodgkin's disease (in New York)*
1993	CLAYWORTH, June	80	*Lymphoma (in Calabasas, CA)*
1993	COLLARD, Cyril	35	*A.I.D.S. (in Paris, France)*
1993	COLLINS, Albert	61	*Cancer*
1993	CONN, Billy	75	*Pneumonia (in Pittsburgh, PA)*
1993	CONNOR, Kenneth	77	*Cancer (in London, England)*
1993	CONSTANTINE, Eddie	75	*Heart attack (in Wiesbaden, Germany)*
1993	CORBETT, Glenn	59	*Lung cancer (in San Antonio, TX)*
1993	# CORDAY, Josephine Rich	79	*Heart and kidney failure (in Los Angeles, CA)*
1993	COREY, Dorian	56	*A.I.D.S. (in a New York hospital)*
1993	CORT, William	53	*Cancer (in Los Angeles, CA)*
1993	CORY, Ken	51	*A.I.D.S. (in New York, NY)*
1993	COVINGTON, Fred	65	*Cancer (at a hospital in Marietta, GA)*
1993	CROSBY, Bob	79	*Cancer (in La Jolla, CA)*
1993	CUSACK, Cyril	82	*Motor neuron disease (at his home in London, England)*
1993	D'ORSA, Lonnie	96	*Died in Beverly Hills, CA*
1993	DAUGHERTY, Herschel	82	*Pneumonia (in Encinitas, CA)*
1993	DAVENPORT, John	62	*Diabetes*
1993	DAVID, Mack	81	*Died in a hospital in Rancho Mirage, CA*
1993	DAVIS, Robert	76	*Emphysema (in Beverly Hills, CA)*
1993	+ DeFORE, Don	80	*Cardiac arrest (in Santa Monica, CA)*
1993	DeGROOT, Katherine Hynes	88	*Complications from a stroke (in Englewood, NJ)*
1993	DeMILLE, Agnes	88	*Stroke and heart failure in her sleep (at her home in Manhattan, NY)*
1993	#+ DeRITA, Joe	83	*Pneumonia (in Woodland Hills, CA)*
1993	# DESMOND, Florence	87	*Unreported causes (in Guildford, England)*
1993	DONALD, James	76	*Stomach cancer (at his home in Wiltshire, England)*
1993	DORR, John	48	*A.I.D.S. (in Los Angeles, CA)*
1993	DOUGLAS, Gordon	85	*Cancer (in Los Angeles, CA)*
1993	DOUGLAS, Hugh	78	*Heart attack (in Los Angeles, CA)*
1993	# DOUGLAS, Steve	55	*Heart attack (during a studio recording session)*
1993	DREIFUSS, Arthur	85	*After a bout with the flu (in Studio City, CA)*
1993	DREW, Larry	73	*After a long illness (in London, England)*
1993	DUFFY, John Paul	42	*Apparent suicide (in West Hollywood, CA)*
1993	DUNCAN, Mary (Sanford)	98	*Natural causes (in Palm Beach, FL)*
1993	EARLE, Don (TV sportscaster)	64	
1993	ECKSTINE, Billy	78	*Cardiac arrest after suffering a stroke (in Pittsburgh, PA)*
1993	# ELLISON, James	83	*After breaking his neck in a fall (in Montecito, CA)*
1993	ENGLUND, Kenneth	78	*A recurring illness (in Woodland Hills, CA)*
1993	FALCO, Louis	50	*A.I.D.S. (in New York)*
1993	+ FELD, Fritz	93	*After a lengthy illness (in Santa Monica, CA)*
1993	+ FELLINI, Federico ★	73	*After suffering a stroke and heart attack (in Rome, Italy)*

• New entry. # Original name (Pt. 7). + Interment (Pt. 5). 142 ☆ Oscar nominee, ★ Oscar winner (Pt. 10)

Deaths of Movie and Television Personalities — by Year

YEAR	NAME		AGE	CAUSE and/or PLACE OF DEATH
1993	FITZSIMMONS, Bob		53	Heart attack (after collapsing in a NY restaurant)
1993	FORD, Constance		69	Cancer (in New York, NY)
1993	FOX, William J.		95	Died in Fillmore, CA
1993	FROST, Terry		86	Heart failure (in Los Angeles, Ca)
1993	FUCCELLO, Tom		55	A.I.D.S. (at a convalescent home in Van Nuys, CA)
1993	FUCHS, Daniel	★	84	Heart failure (in Los Angeles, CA)
1993	GARRETT, Joy		47	Liver failure (in Los Angeles, CA)
1993	GARVARENTZ, George		61	Heart failure (in Aubagne, France)
1993	GENTRY, Minnie L.		77	Lung cancer (in New York, NY)
1993	GEORGE, George L.	★	85	Heart failure (in New York, NY)
1993	GIBBINS, Duncan		41	Burns while trying to rescue a cat from a fire (in Malibu, CA)
1993	# GILLESPIE, Dizzy		75	Died in his sleep of pancreatic cancer (in Englewood, NJ)
1993	+ GISH, Lillian	☆	99	Cerebral hemorrhage and heart failure (in New York, NY)
1993	GOLDSTEIN, Elayne		59	Cancer
1993	GORDON, Michael S.		83	Cardiac arrest in his sleep while hospitalized (in Century City, CA)
1993	GORI, Mario Cecchi		73	Apparent heart attack (in Rome, Italy)
1993	GRANGER, John		69	Cerebral hemmorhage (in Doylestown, PA)
1993	# GRANGER, Stewart		80	Prostate and bone cancer (in Santa Monica, CA)
1993	GREGORY, Dennis		40	Pneumonia (in East Meadow, NY)
1993	# GREY, Nan		75	Heart failure at her home (in San Diego, CA)
1993	GRUNDY, Bill		69	Died in Cheshire, England
1993	GUNN, Moses		64	Complications of asthma (in Guilford, CT)
1993	# GWYNNE, Fred "Herman Munster"		66	Pancreatic cancer (in Taneytown, MD)
1993	HAMMER, Alvin		78	Died in New York, NY
1993	HAMMER, Peter		54	Cancer (in New York)
1993	HARVEY, Rick		43	Kidney failure (in Memphis, TN)
1993	HAWORTH, Ted	★	76	Heart failure (in Sundance, UT)
1993	+ HAYES, Helen	★	92	Congestive heart failure (in Nyack, NY)
1993	HEARST, William Randolph Jr.		85	Heart attack (in New York)
1993	#+ HEPBURN, Audrey	★	63	Colon cancer (in Tolochenaz, Switzerland)
1993	HEYES, Douglas		73	Congestive heart failure (in Beverly Hills, CA)
1993	HIBBERT, Dora		77	Following a brief illness (in New York, NY)
1993	HILL, Jacqueline		68	Cancer (in London, England)
1993	HILL, Martin		80	Cancer (in Sherman Oaks, CA)
1993	HOGAN, Paul (of WMAQ-TV)		48	Apparent heart attack (Do not confuse with the actor)
1993	HOLLAND, John		85	Respiratory failure and pneumonia (in Woodland Hills, CA)
1993	HONDA, Ishiro		81	Died in Tokyo, Japan
1993	HOPKINS, Speed	☆	44	Viral infection (in Sparks, MD)
1993	HOUSTON, David		57	Brain aneurysm
1993	HOWARD, Cy		77	Heart failure (in Los Angeles, CA)
1993	# HOWELL, Wayne		72	Unreported causes (in Pompano Beach, FL)
1993	HUBER, Gusti		78	Heart failure (in Mount Kisco, NY)
1993	HUNT, Frances		77	Complications following a stroke
1993	INGLIS, Brian		76	Died in London, England
1993	INNOCENT, Harold		60	After a short illness (in London, England)
1993	JACOBSON, Arthur		92	Died in Woodland Hills, CA
1993	JARVIS, Patience		56	Melanoma
1993	JENSEN, Lenore Kingston		79	Cancer (in Van Nuys, CA)
1993	JOHANN, Zita		89	Pneumonia (in Nyack Hospital, Nyack, NY)
1993	+ JONES, Ken		54	Cancer (in Los Angeles, CA)
1993	# JORDAN, Richard		56	Brain tumor (at his home in Los Angles, CA)
1993	JURIST, Ed		76	Died in Los Angeles, CA
1993	KANIN, Michael		83	Died in Los Angeles, CA

Deaths of Movie and Television Personalities — by Year

YEAR	NAME		AGE	CAUSE and/or PLACE OF DEATH
1993	KARAS, Barry		49	Leukemia (in Boston, MA)
1993	KARIN, Rita		73	Following a bout with pneumonia (in New York)
1993	KEANE, Joe		69	Cancer (in Woodland Hills, CA)
1993	KEEGAN, Terry		59	Suicide (near Kingman, Arizona)
1993	+ KEELER, Ruby		83	Cancer (in Rancho Mirage, CA)
1993	KIBBEE, Lois		71	Brain tumor (at Sloane-Kettering Cancer Ctr., NY)
1993	KING, Jean		76	Heart attack (in North Hollywood, CA)
1993	KINGSTON, Lenore (Jensen)		79	Cancer (in Van Nuys, CA)
1993	KLOS, Elmar	★	83	Cause unreported (in Prague, Czechoslovakia)
1993	# KNIGHT, Bob		72	Heart attack (in New York)
1993	KRAFT, David		35	Crohn's disease (in Los Angeles, CA)
1993	KULLER, Sid Charles		83	Colon cancer (in Sherman Oaks, CA)
1993	LAMONT, Charles		98	Pneumonia (in Woodland Hills, CA)
1993	LANDAU, Ely A.		73	Complications following a stroke (in Los Angeles, CA)
1993	LANDAU, Richard		79	Complications after surgery (in Century City, CA)
1993	LANE, David T.		52	Brain cancer (in Dallas, TX)
1993	# LANTEAU, William		70	Complications after heart surgery (in Los Angeles, CA)
1993	LAZARUS, Irma		80	Cancer (in Cincinnati, OH)
1993	LEDOUX, Fernand		96	Unreported causes (in Villerville, France)
1993	+ LEE, Brandon		27	Hit with a .44-caliber bullet in a filming accident (in Wilmington, NC)
1993	# LEE, Pinky		85	Heart attack (in Viejo, CA)
1993	LEETCH, Thomas		60	Leukemia (in Sherman Oaks, CA)
1993	LEHMAN, Gladys Collins		101	Pneumonia (in Newport Beach, CA)
1993	LeMASSENA, William		76	Lung cancer
1993	LEONTOVICH, Eugenie		93	Cardiac arrest and pneumonia (in Los Angeles, CA)
1993	LEOPOLD, Douglas		49	A.I.D.S.
1993	# LEWIS, Edwina		42	Heart attack (in Augusta, MI)
1993	LEWIS, Marlo		77	Heart failure (in Los Angeles, CA)
1993	LINDQUIST, Dan		65	Pneumonia (in Burbank, CA)
1993	LOMBARDO, Lebert J.		88	Emphysema (in Fort Meyers, FL)
• 1993	LOMBARDO, Victor		82	Asthma
1993	LONDON, Roy		50	Lymphoma (in Los Angeles, CA)
1993	#+ LOY, Myrna	★	88	During surgery, after a lengthy illness (in New York)
1993	LYNN, Jack		67	Leukemia (in Albuquerque, NM)
1993	MACK, Wayne		68	Cancer (in New Orleans, LA)
1993	MACKENDRICK, Alexander		81	Pneumonia (in Los Angeles, CA)
1993	MAGALOFF, Nikita		80	After a long illness
1993	MALVERN, Paul		91	Died in Los Angeles, CA
1993	MANKIEWICZ, Francis		69	Cancer (in Montreal, Canada)
1993	# MANKIEWICZ, Joseph L.	★	83	Heart failure (in Bedford, NY)
1993	MANOS, Gloria		69	Cancer (in Reno, NV)
1993	MARGOLIN, Janet		50	Ovarian cancer (in Los Angeles, CA)
1993	MARLAND, Douglas		58	Complications following abdominal surgery (in Norwalk, CT)
1993	MARTINEZ, José "Tun Tun"		61	Following surgery for intestinal blockage (in Mexico)
1993	McBEE, Keith W.		66	Cancer complicated by other illnesses
1993	McCLEOD, Mercer		86	Heart failure (in New York)
1993	+ McFARLAND, George "Spanky"		64	Unknown causes (at a hospital in Grapevine, TX)
1993	McNEIL, Claudia		77	Complications from diabetes (in Englewood, NJ)
1993	MEISER, Edith		95	Heart attack (at Roosevelt Hospital in New York)
1993	MILLHOLLIN, James		77	Cancer (in Biloxi, MS)
1993	MONTI, Carlotta		86	After a long illness (in Woodland Hills, CA)
1993	# MOORE, Garry		78	Emphysema (at his home on Hilton Head Island, SC)
1993	MOORE, Irving		74	Heart attack (in Sherman Oaks, CA)

Deaths of Movie and Television Personalities — by Year

YEAR	NAME		AGE	CAUSE and/or PLACE OF DEATH
1993	MORGAN, Edward P.		82	Cancer
1993	MORK, Erik		67	Died in Copenhagen, Denmark
1993	MORRISON, Harold		62	Died in Springfield, MO
1993	MORRISON, Michael D.		33	Accidental overdose of alcohol and illegal drugs
1993	MORROW, Jeff		86	After a long illness (in Canoga Park, CA)
1993	MORSE, Carleton		91	Died in Sacramento, CA
1993	MURPHY, Richard		81	Stroke (in Los Angeles, CA)
1993	MYERS, Stanley		63	Cancer (in London, England)
1993	+ NEGULESCO, Jean		93	Heart failure (in Marbella, Spain)
1993	NELSON, Kenneth		60	An A.I.D.S.-related illness (in London, England)
1993	NEWMAN, Walter Brown ☆		77	Cancer (at his home in Sherman Oaks, CA)
1993	NIGH, Jane		68	Stroke (in Los Angeles, CA)
1993	#+ NIXON, Pat		81	Lung cancer
1993	NORMAN, Lester		81	Heart failure (in London, England)
1993	+ NUREYEV, Rudolph		54	Cardiac complications from A.I.D.S. (in Paris, France)
1993	NUSSBAUM, Raphael		61	Cancer (in Burbank, CA)
1993	NYBY, Christian ☆		80	Cardiac arrest in his sleep (in Temecula, CA)
1993	+ O'CONNELL, Helen (Devol)		73	Cancer (at a hospice in San Diego, CA)
1993	O'HARA, Patrick J.		55	After a lengthy illness (in Burbank, CA)
1993	OCHS, Saul P.		82	Unreported causes (in North Hollywood, CA)
1993	PALEY, Irving		77	Heart attack (in Los Angeles, CA)
1993	# PARHAM, Ernie		64	After a long illness (in Glen Falls, NY)
1993	PARKER, Cecilia		79	Died in Ventura, CA
1993	PARKIN, Leonard		64	Cancer of the spine (in England)
1993	PEALE, (Rev.) Norman Vincent		95	Following a stroke (at his farm in Pawling, NY)
1993	PEARDON, Patricia		69	Pneumonia (at St. Luke's Hospital in Manhattan, NY)
1993	# PEPPER, Buddy		70	Heart failure
1993	+ PEPPLE, Sydney Chester		83	Died at Scripps Ocean View Hospital, Encinitas, CA
1993	PEREDES, Daniel		46	A.I.D.S. (in Los Angeles, CA)
1993	PHELPS, Donald		61	A.I.D.S. (in West Hollywood, CA)
1993	+ PHILBIN, Mary		90	Complications from Alzheimer's disease (in Huntington Beach, CA)
1993	PHILLIPS, Linn III		45	Heart attack (in Denver, Colorado)
1993	+ PHOENIX, River		23	Acute multiple drug intoxication (at a niteclub in West Hollywood, CA)
1993	PIERCE, Edward		77	Natural causes (in Jamesport, NY)
1993	PLAGE, Dieter		57	Died in an airplane filming accident in the Sumatra rain forest
1993	POLK, Lee		69	Leukemia
1993	PREVIN, Steve		68	Unreported causes (in Palm Desert, CA)
1993	+ PRICE, Vincent		82	Lung cancer (at his home in Hollywood Hills, CA)
1993	PRIESTLY, Jack		66	Unreported causes (at his home in Los Angeles, CA)
1993	# RA, Sun		79	Circulatory problems after a series of strokes
1993	RAMSEY, Gordon		63	Cancer (at his home in New York, NY)
1993	RANDOLPH, Donald		87	Pneumonia (in Los Angeles, CA)
1993	# RAY, René		81	Unreported causes (in Jersey, the Channel Islands)
1993	REED, Taylor		60	Heart attack (in New York)
1993	REID, Kate		62	Cancer (in Stratford, Ontario)
1993	REINHEART, Alice		83	Died in Avon, CT
1993	REVIER, Dorothy		89	Died at Queen of Angels–Hollywood Pres. Med. Ctr., CA
1993	RIVERS, Al		65	Cancer
1993	ROBERTS, Davis		76	Emphysema (in Chicago, IL)
1993	ROGERS, Will Jr.		81	Apparent suicide (gunshot) in Tubac, AZ
1993	ROLFE, Sam ☆		69	Heart attack while playing tennis (in Los Angeles, CA)
1993	RYU, Chishu		88	Cancer (in Yokohama, Japan)
1993	SABATINO, Anthony		48	A.I.D.S. (in Los Angeles, CA)

Deaths of Movie and Television Personalities — by Year

YEAR	NAME		AGE	CAUSE and/or PLACE OF DEATH
1993	SALANT, Richard "Dick"		78	*Heart failure (while giving a speech)*
1993	SALE, Richard		80	*After suffering two strokes (in Los Angeles, CA)*
1993	SALKIN, Leo	☆	80	*Congestive heart failure (in Burbank, CA)*
1993	SALMON, Scott		51	*After an auto accident (in Northridge, CA)*
1993	SARGENT, Thornton		90	*Died in Rancho Palos Verdes, CA*
1993	SAUTER, Carl		44	*Undisclosed causes (in Los Angeles, CA)*
1993	SCHAFFEL, Hal		78	*Undisclosed causes*
1993	SCHMIECHEN, Richard		45	*A.I.D.S. (in Los Angeles, CA)*
1993	SCHNEIDER, Abe		87	*Pneumonia and Alzheimer's disease complications*
1993	SCHNEIDER, Alexander		84	*Heart disease (in New York)*
1993	SCHOENBRUN, Michael		54	*Pancreatic cancer (in Tarzana, CA)*
1993	SCORSESE, Luciano Charles		80	*After a long illness (in New York)*
1993	+ SEYMOUR, Dan		78	*Following a stroke (in Santa Monica, CA)*
1993	SHARAFF, Irene	★	83	*Congestive heart failure (in New York)*
1993	SHARITS, Paul		50	*Heart attack (in Buffalo, NY)*
1993	SHARKEY, Ray		40	*A.I.D.S. (at a hospital in Brooklyn, NY)*
1993	SHEARER, Jacqueline		46	*Colon cancer (at her home in Cambridge, MA)*
1993	SHEPARD, Bob		76	*Heart attack (on a visit to Manhattan, NY)*
1993	SHIELDS, Pat		70	*Found dead in his car (in Death Valley)*
1993	# SHIRLEY, Anne	☆	74	*Lung cancer after a long illness (in Los Angeles, CA)*
1993	SIDNEY, Sid		?	*Parkinson's disease*
1993	SIEGRIST, Jeremy		20	*Killed in a hiking accident (in Topanga Canyon Mountains, CA)*
1993	SMANEY, June		71	*An apparent suicide (in Los Angeles, CA)*
1993	# SMITH, Alexis		72	*Cancer (at Cedars-Sinai Med. Ctr. in Los Angeles, CA)*
1993	ST. JOSEPH, Ellis		82	*Cancer (in Beverly Hills, CA)*
1993	STEADMAN, John		83	*Pneumonia (in Montrose, CA)*
1993	# STEN, Anna		85	*Cardiac arrest (at her home in Manhattan, NY)*
1993	STEVENS, Dudley		57	*A.I.D.S. (in Hove, England)*
1993	STEWART, Bill		67	*Heart attack (at a London airport, after filming in Madeira)*
1993	STORRS, Tim		43	*Found dead in his apartment after a fall*
1993	STRIVELLI, Jerry		61	*Heart attack (in New York)*
1993	STRONG, Robert B.		87	*Cardiac arrest in his sleep (in Burbank, CA)*
1993	SULLIVAN, Jeremiah		58	*An A.I.D.S.-related illness (in Hollywood, CA)*
• 1993	SUNDSTROM, Mark		36	*A.I.D.S.*
• 1993	SWENSON, Swen		63	*A.I.D.S.*
1993	SYRON, Brian		58	*Leukemia (in Sydney, Australia)*
1993	TARLETON, Diane R.		51	*Breast cancer (at her home in Manhattan, NY)*
1993	THOMAS, Gerald		72	*Died in Beaconsfield, England*
1993	THOR, Jerome		69	*Cardiac arrest (in Westwood, CA)*
1993	TIPPING, Tim "Tip"		34	*While re-enacting a sky-diving accident for TV (in Alnwick, England)*
1993	TODD, Ann		82	*After a stroke (at a hospital in London, England)*
1993	TOMLINSON, Kate		96	*Died in New Jersey, cause unreported*
1993	TRUSCOTT, John	★	57	*During emergency heart surgery (in Melbourne, Australia)*
1993	# TWITTY, Conway		59	*Surgery complications after a stomach aneurysm (Springfield, MO)*
1993	VALLI, June		64	*Cancer*
1993	VALVANO, Jim		45	*After a 1-year bout with cancer (in Durham, NC)*
1993	+ VENABLE, Evelyn		80	*Cancer (in Post Falls, Idaho)*
1993	VILLECHAIZE, Herve "Tatoo"		50	*Suicide (gunshot) at his home in North Hollywood, CA*
1993	#+ VonERICH, Kerry		33	
1993	WALTON, Gladys (Herbel)		90	*Cancer (at a nursing home in Morro Bay, CA)*
1993	WANAMAKER, Sam		74	*After a 5-yr. bout with cancer (in London, England)*
1993	WARING, Richard		82	*Natural causes*
1993	WARREN, Joseph		77	*Respiratory failure (at Village Nursing Home, NY)*

• New entry. # Original name (Pt. 7). + Interment (Pt. 5).　　　146　　　☆ Oscar nominee, ★ Oscar winner (Pt. 10)

Deaths of Movie and Television Personalities — by Year

YEAR	NAME	AGE	CAUSE and/or PLACE OF DEATH
1993	WARRISS, Ben	83	*Died in Twickenham, England*
1993	WATERS, Chuck	70	*Died in Saginaw, Michigan*
1993	WEBB, Richard	77	*Suicide (gunshot) after suffering a long illness (in Van Nuys, CA)*
1993	WEEDIN, Harfield	77	*Undisclosed causes (in Boise, ID)*
1993	WELLES, Gwen	42	*Cancer (at her home in Santa Monica, CA)*
1993	WELLINGTON, Valerie	33	*Brain aneurysm (in Maywood, IL)*
1993	# WELSH, Ronnie	52	*Brain cancer (in New York)*
1993	+ WHELAN, Arleen (Cagney)	78	*Following a stroke (in Orange County, CA)*
1993	WHELAN, Kenneth	72	*Died in New York*
1993	WILBERN, George E.	77	*Emphysema (in Los Angeles, CA)*
1993	WILEY, Jan (Greene)	82	*Cancer (in Rancho Palos Verdes, CA)*
1993	WILKINSON, Kate	76	*Bone cancer (in New York)*
1993	WILSON, Lester	51	*Heart attack (in Los Angeles, CA)*
1993	WOLF, Harry L.	85	*Died at Cedars-Sinai Hospital in Los Angeles, CA*
1993	WONDER, Tommy	78	*Complications from an ulcer (in New York City)*
1993	WRIGHTSON, Earl	77	*Heart failure (in E. Norwich, CT)*
1993	YOUNG, Marvin	90	*Natural causes (in Los Angeles, CA)*
1993	# YOUNG, Skip "Wally"	63	*Found dead of a heart attack (at his CA home)*
1993	#+ ZAPPA, Frank	52	*Prostate cancer (in Los Angeles, CA)*
1994	# ADRIAN, Iris	81	*Complications from earthquake injuries (in Northridge, CA)*
1994	+ AKINS, Claude	67	*Cancer (in Altadena, CA)*
1994	ALBIN, Andy	86	*After a long illness (in Woodland Hills, CA)*
1994	ALDRIDGE, Michael	73	*Died in London, England*
1994	ANDERSON, Herbert	77	*Died in his sleep 2-months after a stroke (in Palm Springs, CA)*
1994	ANDERSON, Lindsay	71	*Heart attack after swimming at a friend's pool (in Nice, France)*
1994	+ AUBREY, James T.	75	*Heart attack (at UCLA Med. Ctr. emergency room)*
1994	# BAKER, Benny	87	*Died at MPTF Hospital in Woodland Hills, CA*
1994	BARRAULT, Jean-Louis	83	*Died in his sleep of apparent heart attack (in Paris, France)*
1994	# BARTLETT, Richard	70	*Complications of diabetes (in Havre de Grace, MD)*
1994	# BASQUETTE, Lina	87	*Cancer (at her home in Wheeling, WV)*
1994	BEERY, Noah Jr.	81	*After surgery for bleeding in his brain (nr. Tehachapi, CA)*
1994	BELLIN, Steve	43	*A.I.D.S. complications (in Los Angeles, CA)*
1994	BERNARDI, Jack	85	*Heart attack (in Los Angeles, CA)*
1994	BLACKBURN, Royce	69	*Cancer (in New Ipswich, NH)*
1994	BLACKTON, Jay S.	84	*Heart attack (in Los Angeles, CA)*
1994	BONDARCHUK, Sergei	74	*Cardio-vascular disease (in Moscow, Russia)*
1994	+ BOOKE, Sorrell "Boss Hogg"	64	*Colon cancer (in Sherman Oaks, CA)*
1994	BOOTH, Jim	48	*Cancer (in Wellington, New Zealand)*
1994	BORLAND, Carroll	79	*Pneumonia (in Arlington, VA)*
1994	BOYLAN, John	82	*Lung cancer and pneumonia (at his home in Bellevue, Wash.)*
1994	BRAZZI, Rossano	78	*Viral infection (in Rome, Italy)*
1994	BRONSTON, Samuel	85	*After a brief illness (in Sacramento, CA)*
1994	BULGAKOVA, Maya	62	*Automobile accident (in Russia)*
1994	BUTLER, Chris ☆	42	*A.I.D.S. complications (in Los Angeles, CA)*
1994	BUTTRAM, Pat	78	*Kidney failure (at UCLA Medical Center)*
1994	# CALLOWAY, Cab	86	*Pneumonia following a stroke (in Hockessin, DE)*
1994	#+ CANDY, John	43	*Heart attack in his sleep (on location in Durango, Mexico)*
1994	+ CAREY, Macdonald	81	*Cancer (in his Beverly Hills, CA, home)*
1994	+ CAREY, Timothy	65	*After suffering a stroke (at Cedars-Sinai Med. Ctr. in L.A.)*
1994	CARMET, Jean •	73	*Heart failure (at his home in Sèvres, France)*
1994	CARROLL, Bob	76	*After a long illness (at a hospital in Manhasset, L.I., NY)*
1994	CARSON, Ken	79	*Amyotrophic lateral sclerosis (in Jacksonville, FL)*

• New entry. # Original name (Pt. 7). + Interment (Pt. 5).   147   ☆ Oscar nominee, ★ Oscar winner (Pt. 10)

Deaths of Movie and Television Personalities — by Year

YEAR	NAME	AGE	CAUSE and/or PLACE OF DEATH
1994	CARTER, Janis	80	Heart attack (in Durham, NC)
1994	CARTIER, Rudolph	90	Died in his sleep (in London, England)
1994	# CHANDLER, Janet	78	Heart failure after a stroke (at UCLA Med. Ctr., CA)
1994	# Christian-Jaque	89	Heart attack (in Boulogne-Billancourt, France)
1994	CLAVELL, James	69	Stroke after suffering from cancer (at home in Vevey, Switzerland)
1994	+ COBAIN, Kurt	27	Suicide (gunshot) while high on heroin and valium
1994	COCHRAN, Ron	81	After a short illness (in Florida)
1994	COLLINS, Christopher	44	After a brief illness (in Ventura, CA)
1994	# COLLINS, Dorothy	67	Heart failure (at her home in Watervliet, NY)
1994	+ CONRAD, William	73	Heart attack (at the Medical Center of North Hollywood, CA)
1994	CONWELL, John	72	Cancer (at his home in Santa Barbara, CA)
1994	CORVO, Phil	67	After a long illness (in Los Angeles, CA)
1994	COSSART, Valerie (Livingston)	87	Pneumonia (in New York)
1994	+ COTTEN, Joseph	88	Pneumonia (at his home in Westwood, CA)
1994	CRAVAT, Nick	82	Lung cancer (in Woodland Hills, CA)
1994	CUNY, Alain	85	Died at the Cochin Hospital in Paris, France
1994	CURRY, John	44	A.I.D.S.-related heart attack (at his home in England)
1994	CUSHING, Peter	81	Cancer (in a Canterbury hospice, England)
1994	# DALE, Virginia	77	Complications of emphysema (in Burbank, CA)
1994	#+ DAMITA, Lili	92	Alzheimer's disease (in Palm Beach, FL)
1994	DANO, Royal "Ted" Jr.	47	Liver failure (in Santa Monica, CA)
1994	DANO, Royal Sr.	71	Pulmonary fibrosis (at his home in Santa Monica, CA)
1994	DAVIES, Richard	80	Heart attack (in Weaverville, CA)
1994	# DAVIS, Battle	42	Non-Hodgkins lymphoma
1994	DENGEL, Jake	61	Cancer (at Group One Hospice in Sherman Oaks, CA)
1994	DENNY, C. Patterson	46	Cancer (in Glenbrook, IL)
1994	DEVINE, Jerry	85	Died in Santa Barbara, CA
1994	DODSON, Jack	63	Heart failure after a year of failing health (in Encino, CA)
1994	DONALDSON, Norma	68	Cancer (at Cedars-Sinai Med. Ctr. in Los Angeles, CA)
1994	DOUCETTE, John	73	Cancer (at his home in Cabazon, CA)
1994	DOUGLAS, Jack	72	Cancer (in Los Angeles, CA)
1994	DOWNS, Johnny "Our Gang"	80	Cancer (at his home in Coronado, CA)
1994	DRAKE, Charles	79	After a lengthy illness (at his home in East Lyme, CT)
1994	# DUFF-GRIFFIN, William	54	Prostate cancer (at the Manhattan home of his companion)
1994	DUKE, Edward	50	Cancer (in London, England)
1994	DULO, Jane	75	After cardiac surgery (at Cedars-Sinai Med. Ctr. in Los Angeles)
1994	# DUNFEE, Nora	78	After a brief illness (in Manhattan, NY)
1994	EMHARDT, Robert	80	Heart attack (at his home in Ojai, CA)
1994	EWART, John	66	Cancer (in Sydney, Australia)
1994	# EWELL, Tom	85	After a long series of illnesses (in Woodland Hills, CA)
1994	FABRI, Zoltan	77	Heart attack at his home (in Budapest, Hungary)
1994	FEDDERSON, Donald	81	After a series of heart problems (at Cedars-Sinai Hosp. in L.A.)
1994	FINK, Agnes	74	Died in Germany
1994	FIRKUSNY, Rudolf	82	Cancer (in New York)
1994	FOX, George S.	89	Congestive heart failure (in Los Angeles, CA)
1994	FRANKEL, Daniel	91	Natural causes (in Winchester, NH)
1994	FREDERICK, Lynne	39	Found dead in bed, apparently of natural causes (in Los Angeles)
1994	FREED, Bert	74	Heart attack (while on vacation in British Columbia)
1994	FRYD, Joseph	89	Following a stroke (in Rome, Italy)
1994	# FURNESS, Betty	78	Stomach cancer (at Sloan-Kettering Memorial Hospital, NY)
1994	FUSCO, Nelly	85	Cancer (at St. Francis Hosp. in Poughkeepsie, NY)
1994	GARFIELD, David	51	Heart attack (in Los Angeles, CA)
1994	GIBBERSON, William	74	Effects of a stroke (in New York)

Deaths of Movie and Television Personalities — by Year

YEAR	NAME		AGE	CAUSE and/or PLACE OF DEATH
1994	GIFFORD, Frances		72	*Emphysema (in Pasadena, CA)*
1994	GILLETTE, Ruth		89	*Cancer (in Los Angeles, CA)*
1994	GILLIAT, Sidney		85	*Leukemia at his home (in Wiltshire, England)*
1994	GRAF, William N.		82	*Heart failure complicated by pneumonia (in Los Angeles, CA)*
1994	GRAY, Nadia		70	*Stroke (at New York Hospital in Manhattan)*
1994	GRIGAS, John		71	*Heart attack*
1994	HACKES, Peter		69	*Heart attack (in Washington, D.C.)*
1994	HARP, Bill		70	*Heart attack (in Hollywood, CA)*
1994	HARPER, Pat (TV anchor)		59	*Heart attack at her home (in Capiliera, Spain)*
1994	HARRIS, Chris		51	*Apparent heart attack at his home (in Newbury Park, CA)*
1994	HARRISON, Joan		83	*Died in London, England*
1994	HARTLEY, Neil		78	*Heart failure (at his home in Los Angeles, CA)*
1994	HAWKINS, Corwin		29	*Pneumonia (in Los Angeles, CA)*
1994	HAYDON, Julie		84	*Abdominal cancer (in LaCrosse, WI)*
1994	HAYMAN, Lillian		72	*Heart attack at her home (in Hollis, NY)*
1994	HAYNES, Tiger		79	*Cardiac arrest (at St. Vincent's Hospital in New York, NY)*
1994	HAZEN, Joseph		96	*Died in his sleep at home (in Boca Raton, FL)*
1994	HEFLIN, Frances		71	*Lung cancer (in New York, NY)*
1994	# HIATT, Ruth		88	*Congestive heart failure (in Montrose, CA)*
1994	HICKS, Bill		32	*Pancreatic cancer (in Little Rock, AR)*
1994	HILL, James		75	*Undisclosed causes (in London, England)*
1994	HOLLAND, Joseph		84	*Heart failure (in Santa Fe, N.M.)*
1994	HOREN, Robert		68	*Cancer (in New York)*
1994	HORNER, Harry	★	84	*Pneumonia (at his home in Pacific Palisades, CA)*
1994	HUGO, Laurence		76	*Alzheimer's disease (in Charlottesville, VA)*
1994	+ HUMANN, Helena Enize		52	*After a long illness (in Dallas, Texas)*
1994	HURST, Margaret		75	*Heart failure (at Sherman Oaks Med. Ctr., CA)*
1994	# HUTTON, Robert		73	*Died in Kingston, NY*
1994	JARMAN, Derek		52	*Complications of A.I.D.S. (in London, England)*
1994	JOBIM, Antonio Carlos		67	*Heart failure after minor surgery (in New York City)*
1994	#+ JULIA, Raul		54	*Complications of a stroke (at a hospital in Manhasset, NY)*
1994	# KABIBBLE, Ish		86	*Respiratory failure due to emphysema (Joshua Tree, CA)*
1994	KEATS, Steven		48	*Suicide (found dead in his apartment) in Manhattan, NY*
1994	# KERR, Stu		66	*After 8-yr. battle with bone marrow cancer (in Balt., MD)*
1994	KOSCINA, Sylva		61	*Cancer complicated by heart problems (in Rome, Italy)*
1994	KOSLECK, Martin		89	*After abdominal surgery (in Santa Monica, CA)*
1994	KOSTAL, Irwin	★	83	*Heart attack (in Studio City, CA)*
1994	KRIM, Arthur		84	*After a long illness (at his home in New York City)*
1994	#+ LANCASTER, Burt		80	*Heart attack after suffering a stroke (at his condo in Los Angeles, CA)*
1994	LANGTON, David		82	*Heart attack (at Stratford-on-Avon, England)*
1994	# LANSING, Robert		66	*Cancer (at Calgary Hospice in the Bronx, NY)*
1994	+ LANTZ, Walter	★	93	*Heart attack (in Burbank, CA)*
1994	LAYTON, Joe		64	*After an extended illness (in Key West, FL)*
1994	LEONARD, Bill		78	*Stroke (at Laurel Regional Hospital in Laurel, MD)*
1994	LOCCHI, Pino		69	*After suffering two strokes (in Rome, Italy)*
1994	LUXFORD, Nola (Dolberg)		99	*Died at a convalescent home in Pasadena, CA*
1994	LYNCH, Christopher		73	*Heart attack (at his home in Worchestershire, England)*
1994	LYNN, Donald		54	*A.I.D.S. complications (at his home in Manhattan, NY)*
1994	MANCINI, Henry	★	70	*Complications from liver and pancreatic cancer (in Los Angeles, CA)*
1994	MARTIN, Richard		75	*Leukemia (at Hoag Mem. Hospital, Newport Beach, CA)*
1994	+ MASINA, Giulietta (Fellini)		74	*Lung cancer (at the Columbus Clinic in Rome, Italy)*
1994	MAYS, Joe		45	*A.I.D.S. complications (in Little Rock, AR)*
1994	McCALL, Barbara "Bobbie"		50	*After a 3-yr. bout with cancer (in Beverly Hills, CA)*

Deaths of Movie and Television Personalities — by Year

YEAR	NAME		AGE	CAUSE and/or PLACE OF DEATH
1994	McHUGH, Burke		77	*Heart failure and pnemonia (at Falmouth Hosp., MA)*
1994	McLIAM, John		76	*Chronic bronchitis, Parkinson's disease and melanoma (in L.A.)*
1994	McMANUS, Mark		59	*Pneumonia (in Glasgow, Scotland)*
1994	#+ McNALLY, Stephen		82	*Heart failure (at his home in Beverly Hills, CA)*
1994	McRAE, Carmen		74	*Following a stroke (at her home in Beverly Hills, CA)*
1994	MEISNER, Gunter		66	*Heart failure (in Berlin, Germany)*
1994	# MERCOURI, Melina		68	*Complications of lung cancer (at a New York hospital)*
1994	+ MITCHELL, Cameron		75	*Lung cancer (at his home in Pacific Palisades, CA)*
1994	MITTY, Nomi		54	*Cancer (at her home in Los Angeles, CA)*
1994	MONKS, James		81	*Cancer (at St. Luke's-Roosevelt Hospital in New York City)*
1994	# MORGAN, Dennis		85	*Heart failure (at a hospital in Fresno, CA)*
1994	# MORGAN, Henry		79	*Lung cancer (at his home in Manhattan, NY)*
1994	MORRILL, Priscilla		67	*Kidney infection (in Los Angeles, CA)*
1994	MORRIS, Anita		50	*Cancer (at her home in Los Angeles, CA)*
1994	+ NATWICK, Mildred ☆		89	*Cancer (at her home in Manhattan, NY)*
1994	#+ NELSON, Harriet		85	*Congestive heart failure (at her home in Laguna Beach, CA)*
1994	+ NELSON, Nels P.		76	
1994	NEWINGTON, Peter		71	
1994	#+ NILSSON, Harry		52	*Following a heart attack (in Agoura Hills, CA)*
1994	NOBLE, Leighton		82	*Died in Victoria, Canada*
1994	NOVOTNA, Jarmila		86	*Natural causes (at her home in Manhattan, NY)*
1994	# O'HARE, Brad		43	*Complications of A.I.D.S. (in Manhattan, NY)*
1994	O'NEAL, Patrick		66	*Respiratory failure, tuberculosis and cancer (in Manhattan, NY)*
1994	ORMONT, David		79	*Heart attack (at his home in West Hollywood, CA)*
1994	# OSBORNE, John ★		65	*Heart attack (at a hospital in Shropshire, England)*
1994	OSIRIS, Wanda "Wandissima"		89	*Cardiac arrest (at her home in Milan, Italy)*
1994	OTT, Dennis C.		36	*A.I.D.S. (in Los Angeles, CA)*
1994	+ PEPPARD, George		65	*Pneumonia (at UCLA Medical Center, CA)*
1994	PERILLI, Ivo		92	*After suffering a stroke (in Rome, Italy)*
1994	PETERKOCH, Lydia		29	*Automobile accident (in Los Angeles, CA)*
1994	PETERS, Michael		46	*Complications from A.I.D.S. (in Los Angeles, CA) (not orchestra leader)*
1994	# POTAMKIN, Luba		73	*Alzheimer's disease (at her home in Miami, FL)*
1994	POTTER, Dennis		59	*Pancreatic and liver cancer (in Gloucestershire, England)*
1994	POZZI, Moana		33	*Liver cancer (in Lyon, France)*
1994	RALSTON, Esther		91	*After a short illness (in Ventura, CA)*
1994	RAMBO, Dack		53	*A.I.D.S. (in Delano, CA)*
1994	RAWSON, Ron		76	*Cancer (at his home in Cohasset, MA)*
1994	#+ RAYE, Martha		78	*After a stroke and circulatory problems (in Los Angeles, CA)*
1994	RECTOR, Richard		69	*After a brief illness (in San Rafael, CA)*
1994	REINHARDT, Gottfried		80	*Pancreatic cancer (in Los Angeles, CA)*
1994	# REY, Fernando		76	*Bladder cancer (in Madrid, Spain)*
1994	RIGGS, Marlon		37	*A.I.D.S. complications (in Oakland, CA)*
1994	RODNEY, Red		66	*Lung cancer (in Boynton Beach, FL)*
1994	ROEBLING, Paul		60	*While vacationing on a Navajo Indian reservation in Arizona*
1994	ROGERS, Milton "Shorty"		70	*Undisclosed causes (in Van Nuys, CA)*
1994	# ROLAND, Gilbert "Cisco Kid"		88	*Cancer (at his home in Beverly Hills, CA)*
1994	+ ROMERO, Cesar		86	*Complications from bronchitis and pneumonia (Santa Monica, CA)*
1994	RUEHMANN, Heinz		92	*Died in Berg, Germany*
1994	SABLON, Jean		87	*After a 3-yr. illness (at Clinica Hosp. in Cannes-la-Bocca, France)*
1994	SACKS, Amy Jill		39	*Complications from lupus (in Philadelphia, PA)*
1994	SADOFF, Fred		68	*A.I.D.S. complications (in Los Angeles, CA)*
1994	SALTER, Hans J.		98	*Cardiac arrest in his sleep (in Los Angeles, CA)*
1994	SALTZMAN, Harry		78	*Died at the American Hospital in Neuilly-Sur-Seine, France*

Deaths of Movie and Television Personalities — by Year

YEAR	NAME		AGE	CAUSE and/or PLACE OF DEATH
1994	# SARGENT, Dick		64	*Prostate cancer (at Cedars-Sinai Med. Ctr. in Los Angeles, CA)*
1994	#+ SAVALAS, Telly "Kojak"	☆	70	*Died in his sleep of prostate cancer (in Universal City, CA)*
1994	SCANLAN, John		73	*Congestive heart failure (at his home in Closter, NJ)*
1994	SCARFIOTTI, Ferdinando	★	53	*After a brief illness (in Los Angeles, CA)*
1994	SCHNEIDER, Harold		55	*Heart attack*
1994	SCOTT, Terry		67	*Cancer (in Godalming, England)*
1994	# SHARKEY, Jack		91	*Respiratory arrest (at a hospital in Beverly, MA)*
1994	SHELTON, Anne		66	*Apparent heart attack (at her home in Herstmonceux, Eng.)*
1994	SHILTS, Randy		42	*A.I.D.S. (in Guerneville, CA)*
1994	#+ SHORE, Dinah		76	*Cancer (at her home in Beverly Hills, CA)*
1994	SILVANI, Jole		84	*Died in her hometown of Trieste, Italy*
1994	SIMEK, Vasek		66	*Heart attack while playing at the Croatian Nat. Theatre (in Zagreb)*
1994	SIMMS, Ginny		81	*Heart attack (at Desert Hosp. in Palm Springs, CA)*
1994	# SIMMS, Hilda		75	*Pancreatic cancer (in Buffalo, NY)*
1994	SKALA, Lilia	☆	90s	*Died at her home in Bay Shore, NY*
1994	+ SMITH, Hal		77	*Apparent heart attack (at his home in Santa Monica, CA)*
1994	SOMES, Michael		77	*Brain tumor (in London, England)*
1994	SOULE, Olan		84	*Lung cancer (at his daughter's home in Corona, CA)*
1994	SPIVAK, Laurence		93	*Congestive heart failure (in Washington, D.C.)*
1994	ST. JUST, Maria		?	*Heart failure from severe rheumatoid arthritis (in London, England)*
1994	+ STANDER, Lionel		86	*Lung cancer (at his home in Brentwood, CA)*
1994	STANLEY, Anita		88	
1994	# STEVENS, K. T.		74	*Lung cancer (at her home in Brentwood, CA)*
1994	STEWART, Dennis		46	*Heart problems and swelling of the brain*
1994	STONE, Ezra "Henry Aldrich"		76	*Automobile accident (near Perth Amboy, NJ)*
1994	STRODE, Woody		80	*Died in his sleep after long bout with cancer (Glendora, CA)*
1994	STYNE, Jule		88	*After open-heart surgery (at Mt. Sinai Med. Ctr., NY)*
1994	SULLIVAN, Barry		81	*After a chronic respiratory ailment (Sherman Oaks, CA)*
1994	SWACKHAMER, E. W.		67	*Ruptured aortic aneurysm (in Berlin, Germany)*
1994	+ SWIFT, Paul "Eggman"		60	*A.I.D.S. (at Francis Scott Key Med. Ctr., Baltimore, MD)*
1994	TANDY, Jessica	★	85	*Ovarian cancer (at her home in Easton, CT)*
1994	# TAYLOR, Dub		87	*Congestive heart failure (at Westlake Med. Ctr., L.A., CA)*
1994	TEALE, Leonard		72	*Heart attack (in Sydney, Australia)*
1994	TEAS, William Ellis		80	*Died at Fort Miley Veterans Hospital in San Francisco, CA*
1994	TESSARI, Duccio		67	*Cancer (in Rome, Italy)*
1994	THRING, Frank Jr.		68	*Cancer (in Melbourne, Australia)*
1994	THURSTON, Ted		77	*Stomach cancer (in East Hampton, NY)*
1994	TRAVERS, Bill		72	*Died in his sleep (at his home in Dorking, England)*
1994	TROISI, Massimo		41	*Heart attack (in Ostia, near Rome, Italy)*
1994	TROY, Louise		60	*Breast cancer (at her home in Manhattan, NY)*
1994	TRUEMAN, Paula		96	*Died in New York Hospital*
1994	VANCE, Danitra		35	*Breast cancer (at her grandfather's home in Markham, IL)*
1994	VAWTER, Ron		45	*A.I.D.S.-related heart attack (on a plane bound to NY)*
1994	VILLARD, Tom		40	*Pneumonia complicated by A.I.D.S. (at a hosp. in Los Angeles, CA)*
1994	VOLONTE, Gian Maria		61	*Heart attack (in Florina, Greece)*
1994	WALKER, Sydney		73	*After a brief bout with cancer (in San Francisco, CA)*
1994	WASHINGTON, Fredi		91	
1994	WELLS, Frank		62	*Helicopter crash (in central Nevada)*
1994	WICKS, Mark Randall		43	*A.I.D.S. complications (in Los Angeles, CA)*
1994	WIGGINS, James		30	*A.I.D.S. (in Goldsboro, NC)*
1994	WILLIAMS, Marion		66	*Vascular disease (in Philadelphia, PA)*
1994	WILSON, Billy		59	*Complications from A.I.D.S. (in New York)*
1994	WOLFBERG, Dennis		48	*After a 2-yr. battle with melanoma (in Culver City, CA)*

• New entry. # Original name (Pt. 7). + Interment (Pt. 5). 151 ☆ Oscar nominee, ★ Oscar winner (Pt. 10)

Deaths of Movie and Television Personalities — by Year

YEAR	NAME	AGE	CAUSE and/or PLACE OF DEATH
1994	WOOLF, Charles	67	*Cancer (in Sherman Oaks, CA)*
1994	YOUNG, Terence	79	*Heart attack (at a hospital in Cannes, France)*
1994	ZAMORA, Pedro	22	*Neurological complications from A.I.D.S. (in Miami, FL)*
1994	# ZANE, Bartine	96	*Heart attack (in Burbank, CA)*
1994	# ZETTERLING, Mai	68	*Cancer (in London, England)*
1994	ZUKOR, Eugene	97	*Died at his home in Beverly Hills, CA*
1995	ABBOTT, George	107	*Stroke (at his home in Miami Beach, FL)*
1995	ADAMSON, Al	66	*Found murdered and buried under his house (in Indio, CA)*
1995	# ALDRIDGE, Kay (Tucker)	77	*Heart attack (in Camden, ME)*
1995	ALLEN, Dennis	55	*Lung cancer (in Kansas City, Missouri)*
1995	ALLEN, Randy	38	*A.I.D.S.*
1995	+ ANDREWS, Maxine 'of Sisters'	79	*Heart attack (while vacationing in Hyannis, Cape Cod, MA)*
1995	# ARNOLD, Danny	70	*Heart failure (in Los Angeles, CA)*
1995	# AUDLEY, Michael	82	*Died at his home in New Orleans, LA*
1995	AVILES, Rick	41	*Heart failure (in Los Angeles, CA)*
1995	AZITO, Tony	46	*A.I.D.S.*
1995	BAILEY, William	84	*Died in San Francisco, CA (Do not confuse with Bill Bailey, d. 1978)*
1995	BAKER, Tommie	70	
1995	BEGELMAN, David	73	*Apparent suicide (gunshot) in a Los Angeles hotel room*
1995	BENNETT, Charles	95	*Natural causes (Do not confuse with Charles J. Bennett, d. 1943)*
1995	# BENSON, Court	80	*Heart failure (in Mount Kisco, NY)*
1995	BERNSTEIN, Rick	51	*Pancreatic cancer (at his home in Los Angeles, CA)*
1995	BLACKBURN, Clarice	74	*Cancer (in New York, NY)*
1995	BLACKWELL, Charles	65	*Stomach cancer (in New York, NY)*
1995	BLAINE, Vivian	74	*Congestive heart failure and pneumonia (at a NYC hospital)*
1995	BLAIR, Frank	79	*Died on Hilton Head Island, S.C.*
1995	# BLANE, Ralph ☆	81	*After battling Parkinson's disease (in Broken Arrow, OK)*
1995	BLASI, Silverio	73	*Undisclosed causes (in Rome, Italy)*
1995	BLAUSTEIN, Julian	82	*Cancer (in Beverly Hills, CA)*
1995	# BOLT, Robert ★	70	*Heart problems (at home nr. Petersfield, Hampshire, Eng.)*
1995	BORBONI, Paola	95	*After suffering a stroke (in Bodio Lomnago, Varese)*
1995	BORSOS, Phillip	41	*Leukemia (in Vancouver, B.C.)*
1995	BRESLO, Robert Paul	37	*Complications of A.I.D.S. (at New York Hosp. in Manhattan)*
1995	BRETT, Jeremy	59	*Died in his sleep of heart failure (at his London home)*
1995	BRIGGS, Fred	63	*Cancer (in Boston, MA)*
1995	BRINEGAR, Paul	77	*Emphysema (in Los Angeles, CA)*
1995	BROCK, Alan	85	*Died at his home in Hastings-On-Hudson, NY*
1995	BROCKETT, Don	65	*Apparent heart attack (in Shadyside, PA)*
1995	BROOKS, Phyllis (Macdonald)	80	*Died in Cape Neddick, ME*
1995	CALLAGHAN, Jack	64	*Heart attack (in Charlotte, N.C.)*
1995	CAMPBELL, Mifflin James	89	*Cancer (in Indianapolis, IN)*
1995	CAREW, Peter	73	*Heart attack (at his home in Paramus, NJ)*
1995	CARRARO, Tino	84	*Cardiac arrest (in a Milan, Italy, hospital)*
1995	CASH, Rosalind	56	*Cancer (at Cedars-Sinai Med. Ctr. in Los Angeles, CA)*
1995	CHERKASSKY, Shura	84	*Respiratory complications (in London, England)*
1995	CHEROT, Lewis	26	*Automobile accident (in Los Angeles, CA)*
1995	CLAYTON, Jack	73	*After a short illness (at a hosp. in Slough, Berkshire, Eng.)*
1995	COLE, David	32	*A.I.D.S.*
1995	COLON, Alex	53	*After an extended illness (in Los Angeles, CA)*
1995	COOK, Elisha Jr.	91	*After suffering a stroke (in Big Pine, CA)*
1995	COOK, Peter	57	*Gastro-intestinal hemorrhage (at a hospital in Hampstead, England)*
1995	CORRIGAN, Douglas "Wrong Way"	88	*Died in Orange, CA*

• New entry. # Original name (Pt. 7). + Interment (Pt. 5).   152   ☆ Oscar nominee, ★ Oscar winner (Pt. 10)

Deaths of Movie and Television Personalities — by Year

YEAR	NAME	AGE	CAUSE and/or PLACE OF DEATH
1995	CORSAUT, Aneta	62	*Cancer (in Studio City, CA)*
1995	# COSELL, Howard	77	*A heart embolism (at NYU Hospital in New York)*
1995	CRAVEN, John	79	*Following a brief illness (in Salt Point, NY)*
1995	#+ CROGHAN, Joe	74	*Cancer (at Manor Care Ruxton, Baltimore, MD)*
1995	+ CROSBY, Gary	62	*Complications of lung cancer (at St. Jos. Med Ctr, Burbank, CA)*
1995	CULLINGHAM, Mark	53	*Complications of A.I.D.S. (in Los Angeles, CA)*
1995	DARDEN, Severn	65	*Heart failure (at his home in Santa Fe, N.M.)*
• 1995	DeLACY, Philippe	78	*Heart attack*
1995	DELANEY, Bessie	104	*Died in her sleep*
1995	DeMILLE, Katherine (Quinn)	83	*Alzheimer's disease (in Tucson, AZ)*
1995	DENNER, Charles	69	*Cancer (in Dreux, France)*
1995	DILLARD, William	83	*Complications from lupus and pneumonia (in Manhattan)*
1995	DOYLE, Mary	63	*Lung cancer (in New York)*
1995	EAGLE, White	43	*A.I.D.S. (in Sioux Falls, S.D.)*
1995	EDDINGTON, Paul	68	*After suffering a rare form of skin cancer (in London, Eng.)*
1995	EGAN, Eddie	65	*Cancer*
1995	EISENSTAEDT, Alfred	96	*Natural causes*
1995	+ ELGART, Les	77	*Heart attack (in Dallas, TX)*
1995	# ENDFIELD, Cy	80	*Stroke (in Shipston-on-Tour, England)*
1995	# ERGAS, Joseph	72	*Diabetes (in New York)*
1995	ESTABROOK, Ted	76	*Died in New York*
• 1995	EVERHART, Scott	36	*A.I.D.S.*
1995	FABRIZI, Franco	79	*Cancer (in Cortemaggiore, Italy)*
1995	FARRAR, David	87	*Died in South Africa*
1995	FINCH, Nigel	45	*An A.I.D.S.-related illness (at his home in London, Eng.)*
1995	FINNEY, Jack	84	*Pneumonia (in Greenbrae, CA)*
1995	FLACK, Tim	?	*After a long battle with A.I.D.S. (in Los Angeles, CA)*
1995	FLANDERS, Ed	60	*Suicide (shot himself in the head) in Denny, CA*
1995	FLEETWOOD, Susan	51	*After a 10-yr. bout with cancer (in Salisbury, England)*
1995	FORD, Derek	62	*Heart attack (in Bromly, Kent, England)*
1995	FORRISTAL, John	37	*Automobile accident (in Colorado)*
1995	FRANK, Richard Edward	42	*Complications of A.I.D.S. (in Los Angeles, CA)*
1995	# FRANKLIN, Melvin	52	*Heart failure after a series of seizures (in Los Angeles, CA)*
1995	#+ FRELENG, Friz	89	*Natural causes (in Hollywood, CA)*
1995	+ GABOR, Eva	74	*Complications of pneumonia (at Cedars-Sinai Med. Ctr. in L.A.)*
1995	#+ GARCIA, Jerry	53	*Heart attack (at Serenity Knolls drug treatment center in CA)*
1995	#+ GAZZO, Michael V. ☆	71	*Complications from a stroke (in Los Angeles, CA)*
1995	GEE, Kevin John	40	*Pneumonia (in New York City)*
1995	GIANNETI, Alfredo	71	*After suffering a stroke (in Rome, Italy)*
1995	GIBBENS, Vince	46	*Apparent heart attack (in Milwaukee, WI)*
1995	GODUNOV, Alexander	45	*Natural causes (found dead in his West Hollywood, CA, home)*
1995	GONZALES, Pancho	67	
1995	#+ GORDON, Gale	89	*Cancer (at Redwood Terrace Health Ctr. in Escondido, CA)*
1995	+ GOTTLIEB, Conrad I.	77	*Congestive heart failure (at J. Hopkins Hosp. in Balt., MD)*
1995	GRANGER, Dorothy	83	*Cancer (at her home in Los Angeles, CA)*
1995	GRAYSON, Arlene	45	*Bone cancer (at her home in Los Angeles, CA)*
1995	GREENE, John L.	82	*Died at UCLA Med. Ctr. in Los Angeles, CA*
• 1995	GREY, Lita (Chaplin)	87	
1995	GRIMSBY, Roger	66	*Lung cancer (at Lenox Hill Hospital, NYC)*
1995	+ GRINKOV, Sergei	28	*Massive heart attack while ice skating (in Lake Placid, NY)*
1995	GRUENBERG, Leonard S.	83	*Natural causes (at his home in Rancho Mirage, CA)*
1995	# GUARDINO, Harry	69	*Lung cancer (in Palm Springs, CA)*
1995	HACKETT, Albert	95	*Pneumonia (at St. Lukes-Roosevelt Hosp. in Manhattan, NY)*

YEAR	NAME	AGE	CAUSE and/or PLACE OF DEATH
1995	HAMILTON, Anthony	42	A.I.D.S. pneumonia
1995	HANSEN, Larry	42	A.I.D.S.
1995	+ HARRIS, Phil	91	Heart failure (at his home in Rancho Mirage, CA)
1995	HARRIS, Robert	95	After a brief illness (in Denville Hall, England)
1995	HARRISON, Henry M. Jr. (Rev.)	67	Stroke (in Pineville, N.C.)
1995	HEALY, David	64	Following a heart operation (in London, England)
1995	HELMORE, Tom	91	Died in Longboat Key, FL
1995	# HERRIOT, James	78	Prostate cancer (at his home in Thirsk, England)
1995	HERSHMAN, Robert	41	A.I.D.S. (in Santa Monica, CA)
1995	HIVELY, Jack B.	85	After a brief illness (at his home in Hollywood, CA)
1995	HODGES, Gill	80	
1995	# HOON, Shannon	28	Drug overdose (on a tour bus in New Orleans, LA)
1995	HORDERN, Michael	83	After a long illness (at an Oxford, England, hospital)
1995	HORNUNG, Richard	45	Complications from A.I.D.S. (in Los Angeles, CA)
1995	HOWARD, John	82	Heart failure (at his home in Santa Rosa, CA)
1995	HUGHES, Lillian H.	73	Cancer (at her Charlestown Retire. Ctr. home in Balt., MD)
1995	HURD, Hugh	70	Complications of hypertension and kidney failure (in NY)
1995	HURWITZ, Harry	57	Heart failure (in Los Angeles, CA)
1995	+ HYMAN, Phyllis	45	Suicide (pills) found unconscious in her NYC apt.
1995	IPPOLITO, Joseph A.	39	Kidney failure (in Santa Monica, CA)
1995	#+ IVES, Burl	85	Mouth cancer and congestive heart failure (in Anacortes, WA)
1995	# JACK, Wolfman	57	Heart attack (at his home in Belvidere, N.C.)
1995	JAMES, Edward	86	Heart failure (in Escondido, CA)
1995	JEAKINS, Dorothy ☆	81	Alzheimer's and Parkinson's diseases (in Santa Barbara, CA)
1995	JURGENS, Dick	85	Cancer (in Sacramento, CA)
1995	KAIDANOVSKY, Alexander	49	Heart attack (in Moscow)
1995	KALKIN, Gary	44	Complications from A.I.D.S. (at his home in L.A., CA)
1995	KAROL, Darcie	37	Breast cancer (in Boston, MA)
1995	KAYE, Toni	49	Cancer (in Los Angeles, CA)
1995	KELLIN, Sally Moffet	63	Lung cancer (in Nyack, NY)
1995	+ KELLY, Nancy ☆	73	Complications of diabetes (at her home in Bel Air, CA)
1995	KETCHUM, Larry	49	Heart attack (in Sierra Vista, AZ)
1995	KHEIFITS, Iosif	89	Died in St. Petersburg, Russia
1995	# KINGSLEY, Sidney	88	Stroke (at his home in Oakland, N.J.)
1995	+ KIRBY, George	71	Parkinson's disease (at a nursing home in Las Vegas, NV)
1995	# KNOWLES, Patric	84	Cerebral hemorrhage (in Los Angeles, CA)
1995	KNOX, Alexander	88	Bone cancer (at an infirmary in Northumberland, Eng.)
1995	KOCH, Howard ★	93	Pneumonia (in Kingston, NY) Do not confuse with producer
1995	KRAMEROV, Savelly	60	Cancer (in San Francisco, CA)
1995	# LANE, Priscilla	76	After a brief illness (in an Andover, MA, nursing home)
1995	LANE, Ziggy	75	Congestive heart failure (at his home in Miami, FL)
1995	# LAWRENCE, Bruno	54	Lung cancer (at his home on New Zealand's North Island)
1995	# LAWRENCE, Rhoda	71	Pulmonary fibrosis (in Sherman Oaks, CA)
1995	LESTER, Jerry	85	Complications of Alzheimer's disease (in Miami, FL)
1995	#+ LEWIS, Ronald "Raan"	39	Complications from A.I.D.S. (Do not confuse with R. Lewis, d. 1982)
1995	# LINDFORS, Viveca	74	Complications from rheumatoid arthritis (in Uppsala, Sweden)
1995	LISTYEV, Vladislav	?	Assassinated (at his home in Moscow)
1995	LOCKE, Katherine	85	Brain tumor (at her home in Thousand Oaks, CA)
1995	LORIMER, Louise	97	Following an extended illness (in Newton, MA)
1995	# LOY, Nanni	69	Heart attack (while vacationing in Fregene nr. Rome, Italy)
1995	LUBIN, Arthur	96	Six months after a stroke (in a Glendale, CA, nursing home)
1995	LUKAS, Karl	75	Died in Agoura Hills, CA
1995	LUPINO, Ida	77	Colon cancer following a stroke (at her home in Burbank, CA)

Deaths of Movie and Television Personalities — by Year

YEAR	NAME		AGE	*CAUSE and/or PLACE OF DEATH*
1995	# LYNN, Jeffrey		89	*Stroke (at St. Joseph's Hospital in Burbank, CA)*
1995	LYON, Milton		72	*Natural causes (at his home in Princeton, NJ)*
1995	MALEY, Alan	★	64	*Heart attack (at his Belvedere, CA, home)*
1995	# MALLE, Louis		63	*Lymphoma complications (at his home in Beverly Hills, CA)*
1995	+ MANTLE, Mickey		63	*Cancer following a liver transplant (in Dallas, TX)*
1995	MARCH, Donald		53	*Complications from A.I.D.S.*
1995	#+ MARTIN, Dean		78	*Acute respiratory failure (at his home in Beverly Hills, CA)*
1995	# MARTIN, Ernest H.		75	*Liver cancer (at his home in Los Angeles, CA)*
1995	MATHEWS, Carmen Sylva		84	*Natural causes (at her farm in W. Redding, CT)*
1995	MAYA, Frank		45	*Heart failure due to complications of A.I.D.S. (in NYC)*
1995	MAYER, Seymour R.		86	*Heart failure (in New York City)*
1995	+ McCLURE, Doug		59	*Lung cancer (at his home in Sherman Oaks, CA)*
1995	McCOY, Dan		37	*Complications of A.I.D.S. (at Roosevelt Hosp. in Manhattan)*
1995	McDANIEL, Keith		38	*Complications of A.I.D.S. (in Los Angeles, CA)*
1995	McHUGH, Dorothy		87	*Stroke*
1995	McLEAN, David		73	*Lung cancer (at UCLA Med. Ctr. in Los Angeles, CA)*
1995	#+ McQUEEN, "Butterfly"		84	*Burns (while lighting a kerosene heater at her home in Augusta, GA)*
1995	MEDINA, James		33	*A.I.D.S.*
1995	MEGNA, John		42	*A.I.D.S. (in Los Angeles, CA)*
1995	MEIGHAN, Howard S.		88	*Cardiac arrest (at New York Hospital in Manhattan)*
1995	MELTZER, Lewis		84	*Pneumonia (at his home in Albuquerque, N.M.)*
1995	MILLER, Patsy Ruth		91	*Heart failure (at her home in Palm Desert, CA)*
1995	MOFFET, Sally		63	*Lung cancer (in Nyack, NY)*
1995	+ MONTGOMERY, Elizabeth		62	*Cancer after surgery to remove a tumor (Beverly Hills, CA)*
1995	MORRIS, Charlotte		75	*Multiple medical problems (at NY Hosp.–Cornell Med. Ctr.)*
1995	MOSES, Gilbert		52	*Multiple myeloma (in New York)*
1995	MUIR, Esther		92	*Natural causes (in Mount Kisco, NY)*
1995	MYERS, William		74	*Pneumonia (in New York City)*
1995	NEVAREZ, Aramando		44	*Complications of A.I.D.S. (in Los Angeles, CA)*
1995	NEWMAN, Joseph		86	*Lymphoma (in Washington, D.C.)*
1995	NIJHOFF, Loudi		94	*Died in Amsterdam, Holland*
1995	O'CONNOR, Hugh		33	*Suicide (gunshot) after 16 yrs. of drug abuse (in Los Angeles)*
1995	O'SHEA, Tessie		82	*Congestive heart failure (in Leesburg, FL)*
1995	OKADA, Eiji		75	*Died in Japan*
1995	OLIVER, Gordon		84	*Emphysema (at Cedars-Sinai Med. Ctr. in Los Angeles)*
1995	OLLE, Andrew		47	*Brain tumor (after collapsing in his Sydney, Australia home)*
1995	PAICH, Martin "Marty" Louis		70	*Cancer (at his Santa Ynez, CA, home)*
1995	PARRISH, Robert	★	79	*Died at Southampton Hospital on Long Island, NY*
1995	PERRY, Frank		65	*Prostate cancer (at Mem. Sloan-Kettering Cancer Ctr. in NY)*
1995	PETTIT, Tom		64	*Complications after surgery to repair a ruptured aorta (in NYC)*
1995	PLEASENCE, Donald		75	*After surgery to replace a heart valve (at home in France)*
1995	PORTER, Eric		67	*Colon cancer (at a hospital in north London, England)*
1995	POTTER, Allan M.		75	*Cancer (in Stuart, FL)*
1995	PRECHT, Andrew		34	*Cause unreported (in Grenada)*
1995	REDENBACHER, Orville		88	*Drowned in his whirlpool spa after heart attack (Coronado, CA)*
1995	RICH, Charlie		62	*Acute pulmonary embolism (in Hammond, LA)*
1995	# RICHARDSON, Ron		43	*Complications from A.I.D.S. (in a Bronxville, NY, hospital)*
1995	RIGGS, Bobby		77	*Prostate cancer (at his home in Leucadia, CA)*
1995	# ROBIN, Dany		68	*Died in a fire (at her home in Paris, France)*
1995	ROBINSON, Darren		28	*Cardiac arrest during a bout with the flu*
1995	ROCCA, Daniela		57	*Heart failure (at a rest home in Milo, Sicily)*
1995	#+ ROGERS, Ginger		83	*Diabetic coma (at her home in Rancho Mirage, CA)*
1995	ROKER, Roxie		66	*Undisclosed causes (in Brooklyn, NY)*

Deaths of Movie and Television Personalities — by Year

YEAR	NAME		AGE	CAUSE and/or PLACE OF DEATH
1995	# ROMAGNOLI, Margaret		73	Died in Mount Auburn hospital in Cambridge, MA
1995	ROSENBLUM, Ralph		69	Heart failure (at his home in Manhattan)
1995	ROSS, Bob		52	Cancer (at his home in Orlando, FL)
1995	ROSS, Gordon		65	Cancer (at his home in Studio City, CA)
1995	ROTH, David		72	Leukemia (in Leonia, NJ)
1995	ROZSA, Miklos	★	88	Pneumonia following a stroke (at Good Sam. Hosp. in L.A.)
1995	RUSHTON, Donald		70	Died in Indianapolis, IN
1995	RUSHTON, Matthew		43	Complications of A.I.D.S. (in Los Angeles, CA)
• 1995	RYDER, Richard		53	A.I.D.S.
1995	#+ SANDERS, Al		54	Lung cancer (at Johns Hopkins Hosp., Baltimore, MD)
1995	SANTI, Lionello "Nello"		77	After a long illness (in Rome, Italy)
1995	SCALI, John A.		77	Heart failure (in Washington, D.C.)
1995	SCHULMAN, Edward L.		79	Heart disease (at his daughter's home in Detroit, MI)
1995	SCOTT, Timothy		57	Lung cancer (in Los Angeles) Do not confuse with T. Scott, d. 1988
1995	SHULMAN, Irving		82	Alzheimer's disease (in Sherman Oaks, CA)
1995	# SINCLAIR, Madge		57	Leukemia (in Los Angeles, CA)
1995	# SMITH, John		63	Cirrhosis and heart problems (at his home in L.A., CA)
1995	SMITH, Michael C.		34	Died in Stoughton, MA)
1995	SONBERT, Warren		46	Complications of A.I.D.S. (in Los Angeles, CA)
1995	SOUTHERN, Terry		71	Emphysema (in New York, NY)
1995	SPENCE, Irven "Irv"		86	Heart attack (in Dallas, TX)
1995	STARK, Wilbur		83	Cancer (at New York Hospital in Manhattan)
• 1995	STEFANO, Joey		27	Drug overdose
1995	STEPHENS, Robert		64	After a liver and kidney transplant (in London, England)
1995	STEWART, Samuel Douglas		75	Parkinson's disease (at the Motion Picture Hospital)
1995	STONE, Christopher		55	Heart attack
1995	STONEBURNER, Sam		66	Esophageal cancer (at his Manhattan home)
1995	SUGHRUE, John		67	Lung cancer (in New York)
1995	SULLIVAN, Joseph H.		67	After suffering a heart attack (at his Baltimore, MD, home)
1995	SUTTER, Linda		54	Brain cancer (in Cambridge, MA)
1995	# SUTTON, Grady		89	Natural causes (in Woodland Hills, CA)
1995	SWAYZE, John Cameron		89	Natural causes (at his home in Sarasota, FL)
1995	TAGLIAVINI, Ferruccio		81	Respiratory problems after a long illness (in Reggio Emilia, Italy)
1995	# THOMAS, Rachel		90	After a fall and long illness (at Cardiff Hosp. in London, Eng.)
1995	TOBIN, Genevieve		93	Died at Las Encinas Hospital in Pasadena, CA
1995	TORNBERG, Jeff		43	Complications of A.I.D.S. (in Los Angeles, CA)
1995	TOTTEN, Robert		57	Heart attack (at his home in Sherman Oaks, CA)
1995	# TOWNSEND, Claire		43	Cancer (at her parents' home in Los Angeles, CA)
1995	TOWNSEND, Dallas		76	Injuries from a fall (at Montclair, N.J., Community Hospital)
1995	# TURNER, Lana		75	After a long battle with throat cancer (in Century City, CA)
1995	VanEYSSEN, John		73	Cancer (at a hospital in London, England)
1995	VENUTA, Benay		84	Lung cancer (at her home in Manhattan)
1995	WALKER, Junior		57	Cancer
1995	WALLACH, Ira	☆	83	Complications following a stroke (in New York City)
1995	WARD, Janet		70	Comp. from a heart attack (at Mt. Sinai Med. Ctr. in NYC)
1995	+ WARNER, Jack M.		79	Cancer (at Cedars-Sinai Med. Ctr. in Los Angeles, CA)
1995	WARRILOW, David		60	Complications of A.I.D.S. (in New York City)
1995	WATERMAN, Willard		80	Bone marrow disease (at his home in Burlingame, CA)
1995	# WAYNE, David		81	After a long bout with lung cancer (in Los Angeles, CA)
1995	WELSH, Patricia		79	Pneumonia (in Green Valley, AZ)
1995	# WHITE, Slappy		74	Heart attack (at his home in Brigantine, N.J.)
1995	#+ WICKES, Mary		85	Complications from surgery (at UCLA Med. Ctr. in Los Angeles)
1995	# WILDER, Honeychile		76	Cancer (at Mem. Sloan-Kettering Cancer Ctr., NY)

Deaths of Movie and Television Personalities — by Year

YEAR	NAME		AGE	CAUSE and/or PLACE OF DEATH
1995	WILLIAMS, Frances E.		89	*Complications from a stroke (in Los Angeles, CA)*
1995	WILLINGHAM, Calder		72	*Lung cancer (at a hospital in Laconia, N.H.)*
1995	WOODMAN, William		63	*Cardiac arrest (in New York)*
1995	WRIGHT, Eric "Easy-E"		31	*A.I.D.S.*
1995	YOUNG, Donald Jr.		63	*Coronary artery disease (at his home in Los Angeles, CA)*
1995	YOUNGERMAN, Joseph C.		89	*Complications from a stroke (at Cedars-Sinai Med. Ctr. in L.A.)*
• **1996**	ABBOTT, John		90	*After a long illness (in Los Angeles, CA)*
• 1996	ADAIR, Peter		53	*A.I.D.S.-related illness (in San Francisco, CA)*
1996	ALEA, Tomas Gutierrez		69	*Lung cancer (in Havana, Cuba)*
• 1996	ALLEN, Mel		83	*After a long illness (at his home in Greenwich, CT)*
• 1996	ALTON, John ★		94	*After hip replacement surgery (in Santa Monica, CA)*
1996	AMOS, Beth		80	*Died in Toronto, Canada while attending a theatre*
• 1996	+ AMSTERDAM, Morey		87	*Heart attack (at Cedars-Sinai Hospital in Los Angeles, CA)*
• 1996	ANDERS, Luana		57	*Breast cancer (in Mar Vista, CA)*
1996	ANDERSON, Thomas Charles		90	*After a long illness following a stroke (in Englewood, NJ)*
1996	ANDREWS, Norma		66	*An Aneurysm (at Tarzana Hospital in Tarzana, CA)*
1996	ANGUS, Robert		74	*Pneumonia (in Fountain Valley, CA)*
• 1996	# Annabella		86	*Heart attack (in Paris, France)*
• 1996	ATSUMI, Kiyoshi		68	*Lung cancer (in Japan)*
• 1996	AYERS, Lew ☆		88	*Died in his sleep at his home in Los Angeles, CA*
• 1996	BALL, Deedie		79	*Heart attack playing piano in a stage play (in San Luis Obispo, CA)*
1996	# BALSAM, Martin ★		76	*Heart attack (found dead in a hotel room in Rome, Italy)*
1996	BASS, Saul ★		75	*Non-Hodgkin's lymphoma (at Cedars-Sinai Med. Ctr. in L.A., CA)*
• 1996	BAXTER, Jane		87	*Stomach cancer (in London, England)*
1996	BAXTER, Les		73	*Heart attack due to kidney failure (in Newport Beach, CA)*
1996	BEACH, Scott		65	*Died in San Francisco, CA*
1996	BECKER, Sandy		74	*Heart attack*
• 1996	BECKERMAN, Barry		53	*Cancer (in Los Angeles, CA)*
• 1996	+ BERADINO, John		79	*Cancer (at his home in Los Angeles, CA)*
• 1996	BERMAN, Pandro S.		91	*Congestive heart failure (at his home in Beverly Hills, CA)*
• 1996	BERNAL, Ishmael		58	*Heart attack (in Manila, Philippine Islands)*
• 1996	BERNARD, Jason		58	*Apparent heart attack while driving (in Hollywood, CA)*
• 1996	BERTINO, Albert		84	*Died in Los Angeles, CA*
• 1996	BESCH, Bibi		56	*Cancer (in Los Angeles, CA)*
• 1996	+ BESSELL, Ted		57	*Aortic aneurysm (at UCLA Med Ctr., Los Angeles, CA)*
• 1996	BILLIG, Steve S.		66	*Killed by a robber/carjacker*
1996	#+ BISSELL, Whit		86	*Died in Woodland Hills, CA*
1996	BLACKWOOD, Caroline		64	*Cancer (in New York)*
1996	BOMBECK, Erma		69	*Complications from a kidney transplant (in San Francisco, CA)*
1996	BONNER, Priscilla		97	*Died in Los Angeles, CA*
1996	BOWEN, Roger		63	*Heart attack (while vacationing in Marathon, FL)*
1996	BREMER, Lucille		79	*Heart attack (in San Diego, CA)*
• 1996	BROCCOLI, Albert R. "Cubby"		87	*A year after heart bypass surgery (at his home in Beverly Hills, CA)*
• 1996	BRODSKY, Stanley		45	*Complications from A.I.D.S. (in Los Angeles, CA)*
1996	BROWN, Terry James		48	*Lupus (in Los Angeles, CA)*
1996	#+ BURNS, George		100	*Died at his home in Beverly Hills, CA*
• 1996	BYERS, Bill		69	*After a 10-yr. battle with cancer (at his home in Malibu, CA)*
1996	CAMMELL, Donald		57	*Suicide (gunshot) at his home in Hollywood Hills, CA*
• 1996	CAMPBELL, Bruce Post		64	*Massive cerebral hemorrhage (in La Crosse, WI)*
• 1996	CARLSON, June		72	*Aneurysm (in San Clemente, CA)*
1996	CASARES, Maria		74	*Died at her country home in La Vergnes, France*
• 1996	CHANCELLOR, John		68	*After a long bout with stomach cancer (at his home in Princeton, NJ)*

• New entry.　# Original name (Pt. 7).　+ Interment (Pt. 5).　　　　157　　　　☆ Oscar nominee,　★ Oscar winner (Pt. 10)

Deaths of Movie and Television Personalities — by Year

YEAR		NAME		AGE	CAUSE and/or PLACE OF DEATH
•	1996	CHANDLER, Martin Pat "Patsy"		84	*Aneurysm (at his home in East Meadow, L.I., NY)*
•	1996	CHERRILL, Virginia (Martini)		88	*Unreported causes (at a hospital in Santa Barbara, CA)*
•	1996	CHRISTINE, Virginia		76	*Heart complications at her home (in Los Angeles, CA)*
•	1996	# CLARK, Garrett Cameron		33	*Automobile accident (in Los Angeles, CA)*
•	1996	CLARK, Lillian		70	*Cancer (at her home in New York, NY)*
	1996	CLEMENT, Rene	★	82	*Following heart trouble (in Monte Carlo, France)*
	1996	COHN, Joseph Judson		100	*Died in his sleep (at his home in Beverly Hills, CA)*
•	1996	# COLBERT, Claudette	★	92	*Stroke (at her home in Barbados)*
•	1996	COMBS, Ray		40	*Suicide in anguish over a pending divorce (hanging) in Glendale, CA*
•	1996	COSTA, Johnny		74	*Leukemia (in Oakmont, PA)*
•	1996	COX, Winston H. "Tony"		55	*Heart attack (during a workout at a Manhattan health club, NY)*
•	1996	CRAWFORD, Paul		71	*Cancer (in New Orleans, LA)*
•	1996	CULHANE, Shamus		87	*Congestive heart failure (in New York)*
•	1996	CULLEN, Eric		31	*Following surgery (at a hospital in Glasgow, Scotland)*
	1996	CUMMINGS, Irving Jr.		77	*Cancer (in Van Nuys, CA)*
	1996	D'ARCY, Alexander		87	*Heart failure (at his home in West Hollywood, CA)*
•	1996	DANON, Jack		64	*Lung cancer and emphysema (in Burbank, CA)*
•	1996	DAVID, Saul		74	*Complications of congestive heart failure (in Culver City, CA)*
•	1996	DAVIS, Fred		74	*After suffering a stroke (at a hospital in Toronto, Canada)*
•	1996	#+ DAVIS, Philip K.		32	*Died at his home in Baltimore, MD*
•	1996	DAWSON, Thomas H.		82	*Natural causes (in Palm Desert, CA)*
	1996	DECKARD, James		58	*Brain cancer (in Garden Grove, CA)*
•	1996	DelRUBIO, Eadie		?	*Cancer (in Los Angeles, CA)*
•	1996	DeSANTIS, Pasquale	★	69	*Heart attack while working on location (in Ukraine)*
•	1996	DILIAN, Irasema		71	*Heart attack (at her home in Ceprano, Italy)*
•	1996	DOVE, Ulysses		49	*A.I.D.S. (in New York, NY)*
•	1996	DRU, Joanne		73	*Lymphedema (in Beverly Hills, CA)*
•	1996	EASTHOUSE, Richard		35	*A.I.D.S. complications (in New York, NY)*
•	1996	EDELMAN, Herb		62	*Emphysema (at M.P. & T. Hospital in Woodland Hills, CA)*
	1996	#+ EDWARDS, Vince		67	*Pancreatic cancer (in Los Angeles, CA)*
•	1996	ELDER, Lonne 3rd	☆	69	*After a chronic illness (in Los Angeles, CA)*
	1996	EVERSON, William K.		67	*Prostate cancer (in New York)*
	1996	FABREGAS, Manolo		75	*After suffering a heart attack (in Mexico City)*
•	1996	FIELD, Lisabeth		72	*Heart disease (at her home in Hollywood Hills, CA)*
•	1996	# FINN, Lila		86	*Died in Santa Monica, CA*
•	1996	FITCH, Louise		81	*Natural causes (at her home in Venice, CA)*
•	1996	+ FITZGERALD, Ella		78	*Complications of diabetes (at her home in Beverly Hills, CA)*
•	1996	FLEMING, James F.		81	*Died in Princeton, NJ*
•	1996	FOREMAN, Jack P.		71	*Heart attack (at his home in Brentwood, CA)*
•	1996	# FORTE, Chet		60	*Heart attack (at his home in San Diego, CA)*
•	1996	FOX, Michael		75	*Pneumonia (in Woodland Hills) Do not confuse with Michael J. Fox*
•	1996	FRANEY, Pierre		75	*Stroke (at a hospital in Southampton, NY)*
•	1996	FRANKEL, Mark		34	*Injuries from a motorcycle accident (in London, England)*
•	1996	FRIEDMAN, Stephen		59	*Multiple myeloma (at his home in Brentwood, CA)*
	1996	FULCI, Lucio		68	*After a long battle with diabetes (at his home in Rome, Italy)*
•	1996	+ GARSON, Greer	★	92	*Heart failure (at Presbyterian Hospital in Dallas, TX)*
•	1996	GATES, Larry		81	*Died in Sharon, CT*
•	1996	GOLDFARB, Howard		55	*Heart failure after open-heart surgery (at Holy Cross Hosp. in L.A.)*
•	1996	GOOD, John		77	*Lung cancer (in Los Angeles, CA)*
•	1996	GOODMAN, Miles		47	*After suffering a heart attack (at his home in Los Angeles, CA)*
•	1996	GOTTLIEB, Lawrence		64	*Apparent heart failure (at his home in Newport, CA)*
	1996	GOULD, Morton		82	*Died in Orlando, FL*
	1996	# GRANGIER, Gilles		85	*Died in Suresnes, France*

• New entry.   # Original name (Pt. 7).   + Interment (Pt. 5).   158   ☆ Oscar nominee, ★ Oscar winner (Pt. 10)

Deaths of Movie and Television Personalities — by Year

YEAR	NAME		AGE	CAUSE and/or PLACE OF DEATH
1996	# GRAY, Barry		80	Complications from back surgery (at a hospital in Manhattan, NY)
1996	GREEN, Joseph		96	After suffering from emphysema
1996	GREENBERG, Harold		66	Pancreatic cancer (in Montreal, Quebec, Canada)
1996	GREY, Denise		99	Died in Paris, France
1996	GROSS, Marjorie		40	Ovarian cancer (at Cedars-Sinai Med. Ctr. in Los Angeles, CA)
1996	GROVES, William "Bill"		74	Lung cancer (at his home in Morongo Valley, CA)
1996	GUESS, Alvaleta		36	Breast cancer (in Manhattan, NY)
1996	HALIDAY, Bryant		68	Stroke (in Paris, France)
1996	HAN-HSIANG, Li		70	Heart problems (at a hospital in Beijing, China)
1996	HAREN, Christian		61	A.I.D.S. (in San Francisco, CA)
1996	HARGREAVES, John		50	After a long illness (in Sydney, Australia)
1996	HARVEY, Harold A. "Herk"		71	Died in Lawrence, Kansas
1996	HEINEMAN, George		78	Natural causes (in New York, NY)
1996	# HELM, Brigitte		88	Heart failure (in Ascona, Switzerland)
1996	HEMINGWAY, Margaux		41	Suicide (phenobarbital overdose) in her Santa Monica, CA, apartment
1996	HEYMAN, Barton		59	Heart failure (at his home in Manhattan, NY)
1996	# HILL, Dana		32	Following a diabetic coma and stroke (in Burbank, CA)
1996	HILL, Ralston		69	While in rehearsal at the Paper Mill Playhouse (in NJ)
1996	HOLDEN, Gloria (Hoyt)		73	Cardiac arrest (in Redlands, CA)
1996	HOLLYWOOD, Daniel Lawrence		82	Kidney failure (at his home in Orlando, FL)
1996	HORN, Camilla		93	Died at a home for senior citizens (in Gilching, Germany)
1996	HOWARD, Ronald		78	
1996	#+ HUNTER, Ross	☆	75	Cancer (in Century City, CA)
1996	HUTIN, Jean-Pierre		64	Died in Paris, France
1996	HYSON, Dorothy		81	Died in London, England
1996	IVERS, Irving		57	Complications following surgery to remove his spleen (in Toronto)
1996	JOELSON, Ben		70	Died in Los Angeles, CA
1996	+ JOHNSON, Ben	★	77	Apparent heart attack (in Mesa, AZ)
1996	JOHNSTON, Johnny		80	Heart failure (in Cape Coral, FL)
1996	KARAYN, Jim		64	Died in Washington, D.C.
1996	KATZ, Oscar		82	After a bout with pneumonia (at his home in Los Angeles, CA)
1996	KATZMAN, Leonard		69	Apparent heart attack (at his home in Malibu, CA)
1996	#+ KELLY, Gene	★	83	Died in his sleep after suffering 2 strokes in 2 yrs. (in Beverly Hills)
1996	KIESLOWSKI, Krzysztof	☆	54	Heart attack after suffering with A.I.D.S. (in Warsaw, Poland)
1996	KIMBROUGH, Clinton		63	Pneumonia (in Ada, OK)
1996	KINDLE, Tom		47	Complications of A.I.D.S. (in Los Angeles, CA)
1996	KING, Alyce (Clarke)		80	Chronic bronchial asthma (in Los Angeles, CA)
1996	KING, Paul Donaldson	☆	69	Cancer (at his home in Newport Beach, CA)
1996	KITCHELL, Alma		103	Died at her home in Sarasota, FL
1996	KOBAYASHI, Masaki		80	Cardiac arrest (at his home in Tokyo, Japan)
1996	KOREMIN, Walter Michael		69	Following an embolism (at Johns Hopkins Hosp. in Baltimore, MD)
1996	# LaCENTRA, Peg		86	Heart attack (at her home in Los Angeles, CA)
1996	LAMMERS, Paul		74	Cancer (at his home in Washington, CT)
1996	#+ LAMOUR, Dorothy (Howard)		81	Died at her home in Los Angeles, CA
1996	LANG, Jennings		81	Pneumonia (at Manor Care nursing home in Palm Desert, CA)
1996	LaPLANTE, Laura		91	Died at the Motion Picture Country Home in Woodland Hills, CA
1996	+ LARSEN, William		67	Heart attack (found dead at his home in Houston, TX)
1996	# LaRUE, Lash		78	Died at Providence St. Joseph Med. Ctr. in Burbank, CA
1996	LEDER, Paul		70	Lung cancer (at his home in Los Angeles, CA)
1996	LEEDS, Peter		79	Cancer
1996	#+ LeFEVRE, Bill		75	Congestive heart failure (at his home in Shrewsbury, PA)
1996	LEI, Chao		68	Pneumonia (in Hong Kong, China)
1996	LEIGH, Norman		66	Cancer (in New York, NY)

Deaths of Movie and Television Personalities — by Year

YEAR	NAME	AGE	CAUSE and/or PLACE OF DEATH
• 1996	LEISER, Erwin	73	*Died in Zurich, Switzerland*
• 1996	LENARD, Mark	68	*Multiple myeloma (at NYU Hospital in Manhattan, NY)*
• 1996	LENOX, John Thomas	50	*Massive heart attack (at his home in Los Angeles, CA)*
1996	LEVIN, Irving H.	74	*Cancer (at his home in Brentwood, CA)*
1996	LEWIN, Albert E.	79	*Heart failure (at USC Health Center, CA)*
1996 #	LEWIS, Henry	63	*Heart attack (at his home in Manhattan)*
• 1996	LIDINGTON, Bruce Howard	46	
• 1996	LIST, Shelly	55	*Cancer (at her apartment in Manhattan, NY)*
1996	LUDMIR, Joseph (Pepe)	64	*Heart attack (in Woodland Hills, CA)*
1996 #+	MADISON, Guy	74	*Emphysema (at Desert Hospital Hospice in Palm Springs, CA)*
1996	MANLEY, Walter	?	*Apparent asthma attack (in New York)*
• 1996	MANSON, Eddy Lawrence	77	*Congestive heart failure (in Los Angeles, CA)*
• 1996	MASON, Pamela	80	*Heart failure in her sleep (at her home in Beverly Hills, CA)*
• 1996	MASTERSON, Paul C.	78	*Cancer (at South Coast Med. Ctr. in Laguna Beach, CA)*
• 1996	MASTROIANNI, Marcello ☆	72	*Pancreatic cancer (at his home in Paris, France)*
• 1996	MASTROIANNI, Ruggero	67	*Heart attack (at his summer home in Torvaianica, Italy)*
• 1996	MATAS, Alfredo	76	*Lung cancer (in Barcelona, Spain)*
• 1996	MATEOS, Julian	57	*Lung cancer (in Madrid, Spain)*
• 1996	MATHIS, Lee	44	*Complications of A.I.D.S. (in New York, NY)*
• 1996	MATTHEWS, Billy	76	*Aortal aneurysm (in London, England)*
1996	MAXWELL, Larry	43	*Leukemia (at his home in Laurelville, OH)*
1996	McCREA, Dusty Iron Wing	55	*Diabetes (in Hondo, N.M.)*
1996	McDERMOTT, Tom	83	*Complications of prostate cancer (at Beth Israel hosp. in NY)*
1996	McLEAN, Barbara ★	92	*Died in Newport Beach, CA*
1996 +	MEADOWS, Audrey	71	*Lung cancer (at Cedars-Sinai Med. Ctr. in Los Angeles, CA)*
• 1996	MEES, Tom	46	*Accidentally drowned in his neighbor's pool (in Southington, CT)*
• 1996 #+	MIRANDA, Willy	70	*Lung cancer (at Good Samaritan Hosp. in Baltimore, MD)*
• 1996	MONROE, Bill	84	*After suffering a stroke (in Springfield, TN)*
• 1996	MORRIS, Greg	61	*After a 2-yr. battle with brain cancer (at his home in Las Vegas, NV)*
1996	MORRIS, Richard	72	*Cancer (in Los Angeles, CA)*
• 1996	MORRIS, Wolfe	71	
• 1996	MUIR, Jean	85	*Natural causes (at a nursing home in Mesa, AZ)*
1996	MUSTARD, Jim	51	*Bone cancer and A.I.D.S. (in Baltimore, MD)*
• 1996	MYEROVICH, Alvin	89	*Heart failure (at a retirement home in Manchester Township, NJ)*
• 1996	NEISE, George N.	79	*Natural causes (at his home in Hollywood, CA)*
• 1996	NELSON, Gene	76	*Cancer (in Los Angeles, CA)*
1996	NGOR, Dr. Haing S. ★	55	*Murdered (shot) outside his home in Los Angeles, CA*
• 1996	NORMAN, Connie	47	*Complications of A.I.D.S.*
1996	O'BRIEN, Liam ☆	83	*Heart failure (at his home in Los Angeles, CA)*
1996	O'CONNELL, David J.	79	*Chronic lung disease (in Santa Monica, CA)*
1996	O'DONNELL, Lynn	43	*Ovarian cancer (in San Francisco, CA)*
• 1996	O'HARA, Jack	39	*Airplane crash (TWA Flight 800, off Long Island, NY)*
1996 #	OPATOSHU, David	78	*After a long illness (in Los Angeles, CA)*
• 1996	PANOZZO, John	47	*Gastrointestinal hemorrhage*
• 1996	PAPP, Frank	?	*Cancer (in New York, NY)*
1996	PASCAL, Christine	42	*Suicide after suffering depression (jumped out window in Paris)*
1996	PATTEN, Luana	57	*Lung cancer (in Long Beach, CA)*
1996 #	PEARL, Minnie	83	*Following a stroke (in Nashville, TN)*
• 1996	PERRY, Joan (Cohn)	85	*Emphysema (at her home in Montecito, CA)*
• 1996	PERTWEE, Jon	76	*Undisclosed causes (in New York, NY)*
• 1996	PETERSON, Arthur	83	*Alzheimer's disease (in Pasadena, CA)*
1996	PISTILLI, Luigi	66	*Suicide at his home before appearing on stage (in Milan, Italy)*
• 1996	PIVNICK, Marlene	59	*Cancer (at her home in Encino, CA)*

Deaths of Movie and Television Personalities — by Year

	YEAR	NAME		AGE	CAUSE and/or PLACE OF DEATH
•	1996	PRINCE, William		83	*Unreported causes (at Phelps Memorial Hosp. in Tarrytown, NY)*
•	1996	PROWSE, Juliet		59	*Pancreatic cancer (at her home in Holmby Hills, CA)*
•	1996	PUTTERMAN, William Zev		67	*Cancer (in Tucson, AZ)*
•	1996	RADASKY, Michael J.		43	*Automobile accident (in Texas)*
•	1996	RANDALL, Dick		70	*Heart failure after a series of strokes (in London, England)*
	1996	# REGAN, Phil		89	*Died in Santa Barbara, CA*
•	1996	REID, Beryl		76	*In London, England*
•	1996	REID, Don		85	*Lymphoma (at his home in Harrison, NY)*
•	1996	RENE, Norman		45	*Complications from A.I.D.S. (in Manhattan, NY)*
	1996	# RETTIG, Tommy		54	*Cancer (at his home in Marina Del Rey, CA)*
	1996	REVUELTAS, Rosaura		85	*Lung cancer (at her home in Cuernavaca, Mexico)*
	1996	RICHARDS, E. Claude		72	*Leukemia (at the VA Hospital in The Bronx, NY)*
	1996	RICHARDSON, Don		77	*Heart failure (in Los Angeles, CA)*
•	1996	RIVERS, Jerry		68	*Cancer (at a hospital in Hermitage, TN)*
	1996	# ROARKE, Adam		58	*Heart attack (at his home in Euless, TX)*
	1996	ROCKETT, Norman		84	*Heart failure (in Los Angeles, CA)*
•	1996	ROLLINS, Howard E. Jr. ☆		46	*Complications from lymphoma (in New York, NY)*
	1996	ROSATTI, Gregory Joseph		43	*Complications of A.I.D.S. (in Sherman Oaks, CA)*
•	1996	ROVERE, Luigi		88	*Heart attack (in Rome, Italy)*
•	1996	ROZELLE, Pete		70	*Brain cancer*
•	1996	RUSHTON, Willie		59	*Complications from diabetes and heart surgery (in London, Eng.)*
•	1996	SACKS, David Michael		79	*Heart failure (in Pleasanton, CA)*
•	1996	SAGAN, Carl		62	*Pneumonia after a 2-yr. bout with bone marrow disease (in Seattle)*
•	1996	SCHNEIDER, Magda		87	*Heart disease (in Schoenau, Germany)*
•	1996	SCOTTI, Vito		78	*Died at the Motion Picture and TV Hosp. in Woodland Hills, CA*
•	1996	SECOLSKY, Herman		73	*Complications from lung cancer (in Palm Beach, FL)*
•	1996	+ SENECA, Joe		82	*Asthma and heart attack (in New York, NY)*
•	1996	SHAFTEL, Josef		76	*After a 3-yr. battle with multiple myeloma (in London, England)*
•	1996	+ SHAKUR, Tupac "2-Pac"		25	*Cardiopulmonary arrest from a drive-by shooting (in Las Vegas, NV)*
•	1996	SHANLEY, Lila		86	*Heart failure (at St. John's Hosp. in Santa Monica, CA)*
•	1996	SHIMA, Keiji		68	*Acute respiratory failure (in Japan)*
	1996	SILLIPHANT, Stirling ★		78	*Prostate cancer (in Bangkok, Thailand)*
	1996	# SIMPSON, Don		52	*Heart failure due to drug abuse (at his home in Bel-Air, CA)*
•	1996	SIMPSON, Sloan		80	*After an illness (in Dallas, TX)*
	1996	SNYDER, Jimmy "The Greek"		76	*Heart failure (at a hospital in Las Vegas, NV)*
	1996	SOSNICK, Harry		89	*After a long illness (at Calvary Hospital in New York)*
	1996	STAMENKOVIC, Stan		39	*Head injuries from a fall in his home (in Titova Uzice, Serbia)*
•	1996	STANLEY, Alvah W., Jr.		56	*Heart attack (at his home in Los Angeles, CA)*
•	1996	STEADMAN, Kenneth Keith		27	*Killed in a dune buggy accident on the set (40 mi. east of L.A.)*
•	1996	STEPHENS, Phil		89	*Cardiac arrest at his home*
	1996	STEVENS, Chuck		64	*Massive heart attack (in Las Vegas, NV)*
	1996	STEVENSON, McLean		66	*Heart attack (at a hospital in Los Angeles, CA)*
•	1996	STORKE, William F.		73	*Cancer (at his home in Manhattan, NY)*
•	1996	SULLIVAN, Daniel Webster		65	*Cancer (at his Amelia Island, FL)*
	1996	SULLIVAN, Fred G. Jr.		50	*Heart failure (in Saranac Lake, NY)*
•	1996	TAK-HING, Kwan		91	*Pancreatic cancer (in Hong Kong, China)*
	1996	TAKEMITSU, Toru		65	*Pneumonia while undergoing cancer treatments (in Tokyo, Japan)*
	1996	# TALBOT, Lyle		94	*Natural causes (at his home in San Francisco, CA)*
•	1996	TESICH, Steve ★		53	*Heart attack (while vacationing in Nova Scotia, Canada)*
•	1996	# Tiny Tim		66	*Heart attack while singing on stage (in Minneapolis, MN)*
•	1996	+ TODISCO, Mario		46	*Cancer*
•	1996	TOUMANOVA, Tamara		77	*After a brief illness (at Santa Monica Hospital, CA)*
	1996	# UYS, Jamie		74	*Heart attack (at his home in Johannesburg, South Africa)*

• New entry. # Original name (Pt. 7). + Interment (Pt. 5). 161 ☆ Oscar nominee, ★ Oscar winner (Pt. 10)

Deaths of Movie and Television Personalities — by Year

	YEAR	NAME		AGE	CAUSE and/or PLACE OF DEATH
•	1996	VanFLEET, Jo	★	76	Died at Jamaica Hosp. in Queens, NY
•	1996	VARNO, Roland		88	Heart attack after a brief illness (in Lancaster, CA)
•	1996	VERNON, Harvey		69	Heart failure (at his home in Sun Valley, CA)
•	1996	VOUYOUKLAKI, Aliki		63	Cancer (in Athens, Greece)
•	1996	WALKER, Keith A.		61	Following a short battle with cancer (in Franklin, TN)
•	1996	WEEKS, Clair		84	Cancer (in Los Angeles, CA)
	1996	WEI, Lo		76	Heart failure (in a Hong Kong hospital)
•	1996	WELLS, William G.		73	Aortic disection due to artherosclerosis (in Sydney, Australia)
	1996	# WESTON, Jack		71	After a 6 yr. bout with lymphoma (at Lenox Hill Hosp. in New York)
•	1996	WESTON, Paul		84	Natural causes (at St. John's Hospital in Santa Monica, CA)
•	1996	WILLIAMS, Palmer		79	Prostate cancer
•	1996	WILLIMAN, Earl		80	Natural causes (at his home in Santa Maria, CA)
•	1996	WOOD, Forrest Benjamin		76	Unreported causes (in Los Angeles, CA)
•	1996	YODER, Alma Kitchell		103	Died in Sarasota, FL
•	1996	YOUNG, Faron		64	Suicide (gunshot) after prostate surgery (in Nashville, TN)
•	**1997**	ABBOTT, Bud Jr.		57	Apparent heart attack (in Valencia, CA)
•	1997	+ ADDINGTON, John		44	Heart attack (at his home in Dallas, TX)
•	1997	ADDY, Wesley		83	Died in New York, NY
•	1997	AGUILAR, Luis		79	Heart attack in Mexico City
•	1997	ALLAND, William		81	Died in Long Beach, CA of heart disease
•	1997	# AMES, Francine		75	Heart failure in Sarasota, FL
•	1997	ANDERSON, Ernie		73	Cancer (at his home in Los Angeles, CA)
•	1997	ANDERSON, Scott		35	Brain cancer in Los Angeles, CA
•	1997	ASHLEY, John		62	Heart attack on the film set of "Scarred City" in NY
•	1997	AUSTIN, Laurence		74	Shot to death in the lobby of his Los Angeles silent movie theatre
•	1997	AVERBACK, Hy		76	Died following open heart surgery in Los Angles, CA
•	1997	AYRES, Lew		88	Died in Los Angeles
•	1997	BAHAM, Ron		33	AIDS
•	1997	# BARBARA		67	Respiratory problems at the American Hospital in Paris, London
•	1997	BEAL, John		87	Complications from a stroke (in Santa Cruz, CA)
•	1997	Bebe (Flipper)		40	Died at the Miami Sea-quarium
•	1997	BELL, Bob		75	Died in Lake San Marcos, CA
•	1997	BELL, Marion		78	Died in Culver City, CA of natural causes
•	1997	BEST, Marjorie O.	★	94	Died at her home in Toluca Lake, CA of heart failure
•	1997	BEXLEY, Donald T.		87	Died in Hampton, VA of heart and kidney failure
•	1997	BEYER, Edward		64	Following open heart surgery in Los Angeles, CA
•	1997	BLACKSTONE, Harry		62	Pancreatic cancer at Loma Linda U. Medical Center in CA
•	1997	# BLAIR, Joan		93	After a brief illlness (in Culver City, CA)
•	1997	BLANE, Sally		87	Died in Palm Springs, CA
•	1997	BRADLEY, David		77	Died at Cedars-Sinai Medical Center in Los Angeles, CA
•	1997	BRAM, Rose		92	Natural causes in Los Angeles, CA
•	1997	BRAUN, Michael		60	Heart failure (at his home in New York City)
•	1997	BROWN, Mary Jane		80	Died of cancer at Gilchrist Center in Baltimore, MD
•	1997	BRUNER, Wallace		66	Died of liver cancer in Indianapolis, Indian
•	1997	BURNETT, Murray		86	Died of congestive heart failur in New York City, NY
•	1997	CAJAFA, Gianni		82	Embolism in a Milan, Rome Hospital
•	1997	CARLIN, Brenda		57	Liver cancer in Santa Monica, CA
•	1997	CARLSON, Violet		97	Died of natural causes in Los Angeles, CA
•	1997	CAROW, Heiner		67	Cause undisclosed (in Berlin, Germany)
•	1997	CARPENTER, Thelma		77	Found dead of natural causes (in her Manhattan apartment, NY)
•	1997	CARPENTER, Thelma		75	Heart attack in her Manhattan, NY apartment
•	1997	CARR, Carole		68	

• New entry.   # Original name (Pt. 7).   + Interment (Pt. 5).   162   ☆ Oscar nominee, ★ Oscar winner (Pt. 10)

Deaths of Movie and Television Personalities — by Year

	YEAR	NAME		AGE	CAUSE and/or PLACE OF DEATH
•	1997	CARR, Harriette "Hedy" Williams		91	Heart failure at her son's home in New Orleans, LA
•	1997	CASELOTTI, Adriana		80	Cancer (at her home in Los Angeles, CA.)
•	1997	CHAMBERLAIN, Jennifer Holt		76	Cancer at home in Dorset, England
•	1997	CHAPLIN, Saul	★	85	At Cedars-Sinai Medical Ctr., Los Angeles, CA after a fall
•	1997	CLARKE, Shirley		78	In Boston, MA after a long illness
•	1997	# CLASTER, Nancy "Miss Nancy"		82	Colon cancer (at her Cross Keys condominium in Baltimore, MD)
•	1997	CLOUSE, Robert		68	Complications of kidney failure (at his home in Ashland, OR)
•	1997	COMPTON, Joyce		90	Died in Los Angeles, CA
•	1997	# CORNETT, Barbara		86	Natural causes (in Ojai Valley Hospital - Ojai, CA)
•	1997	CORTEZ, Stanley	☆	92	Died of a heart attact in Los Angeles, CA
•	1997	COUSTEAU, Jacques		87	Died at his home in Paris of a respiratory infection
•	1997	COWLES, Chandler		79	Heart attack (in New York , NY)
•	1997	COYTE, Kenneth		64	After a brief illness (in London, England)
•	1997	CRANHAM, Tom		63	Died of cancer in Houston, TX
•	1997	DANIEL, Eliot	☆	89	Cancer in Placerville, CA
•	1997	DANON, Marcello		?	Undisclosed cause (in Rome, Italy)
•	1997	DARRACH, Jr., Henry Bradford		76	heart attack in Los Angeles, CA
•	1997	DAVIS, Gail		71	Cancer (in Burbank, CA)
•	1997	DELFINO, Frank J.		86	Complications from bone marrow cancer (in San Diego, CA)
•	1997	DENVER, John		53	Died in a plane crash in CA, he was piloting the plane
•	1997	DeSANTIS, Giuseppe		80	After a heart attack in Eugenio Hospital-Rome, Italy
•	1997	DEWINDT, Hal		72	Cancer at UCLA Medical Center in Los Angeles, CA
•	1997	DISNEY, Lillian		98	Died from complications of a stroke at her home in Los Angeles, CA
•	1997	DORRIS, Michael		52	Suicide in a motel in Concord, NH
•	1997	DOVE, Billie		97	Died of pneumonia
•	1997	DOWELL, George Brendan		87	Cancer (at Gilchrist Hospice in Towson, MD)
•	1997	DOYLE, David		67	Heart attack
•	1997	EASTMAN, Ronald William		60	
•	1997	EBERT, Joyce		64	Cancer at a Southport, Conn. rest home
•	1997	ENO, Terry		50	Liver cancer in Manhattan, NY
•	1997	ESSEX, Harry		86	Heart failure (at Cedars-Sinai Med. Ctr. in Los Angeles, CA)
•	1997	EVANS, Barry		53	Murdered at his home in England
•	1997	FARLEY, Chris		33	
•	1997	FARREN, Jack		75	Complications following heart surgery in Surger, LA
•	1997	FAYE, Joey		87	Died of a heart attack at his home in Englewood, NJ
•	1997	FAYED, Dodi		42	Car accident in Paris with Princess Diana
•	1997	FENNEMAN, George		77	Emphysema at his home in Los Angeles, CA
•	1997	FERRERI, Marco		68	Heart attack (in Paris, France)
•	1997	FIGUEROA, Gabriel	☆	90	Stroke in Mexico City, Mexico
•	1997	FISCHER, Wayne		39	A.I.D.S. (in Manhattan, NY)
•	1997	FORE, Edith		81	Died in Camden, NJ
•	1997	# FOSTER, Frances		73	Cerebral hemorrhage in Fairfax, VA
•	1997	FRANCOVICH, Allan		56	Heart failure going though US Customs in Houston, TX
•	1997	FULLER, Samuel		86	Natural causes in Hollywood Hills, CA
•	1997	GABOR, Magda		78	Kidney failer at Eisenhower Medical Center in Rancho Mirage, CA
•	1997	GAYNES, Lloyd H.		68	Pancreatic cancer at home in Hollywood, CA
•	1997	GEVA, Tamara		91	Died at her home in Manhattan, NY
•	1997	GILL, David		69	Heart attack in Huntingdon, England
•	1997	GLOOR, Kurt		54	Suicide in Zurich, Switzerland
•	1997	GLOVER, Brian		63	Died of complications from a brain tumor
•	1997	GOKHLE, Kamalbai		97	Died in Pune City
•	1997	GRANGER, Percy		51	Cardiac arrest (in New York City, NY)
•	1997	GUETARY, Georges		82	Heart attack in Mougins, France

Deaths of Movie and Television Personalities — by Year

YEAR	NAME		AGE	CAUSE and/or PLACE OF DEATH
1997	GUILAROFF, Sydney		89	*Died of pneumonia in Los Angeles, CA*
1997	HALLAHAN, Charles		54	*Died of a heart attack driving his car in Los Angeles, CA*
1997	HANLEY, Eddie		91	*After a long illness (in Los Angeles, CA)*
1997	HARE, Will		81	*Heart attack in NY*
1997	HARTMAN, Maureen		53	*Cancer at home in Harrison, NY*
1997	HARVEY, Rita Morley		69	*Died of cancer in Simsbury, Conn*
1997	HELLER, Franklin M.		86	*Emphysema in North Branford, Conn.*
1997	HICKEY, William	☆	69	*Died in New York, NY from complications of emphysema*
1997	HOFFMAN, Joseph		88	*Heart disease in Los Angeles, CA*
1997	HORNBERGER, H. Richard		73	*Died in Portland, Maine of leukemia*
1997	HU, King		65	*After heart surgery (in Taipei, Taiwan)*
1997	ITAMI, Juzo		64	*Suicide (jumped from 8 story roof top) in Tokyo, Japan*
1997	JACKSON, Enid		43	*Brain aneurysm in Las Vegas, NV*
1997	JAECKEL, Richard	☆	70	*Died of cancer in Woodland Hills, CA*
1997	JAFFE, Leo		88	*After a long illness at home in New York City, NY*
1997	JAMES, Dennis		79	*Cancer in Palm Springs, CA*
1997	JARRICO, Paul	☆	82	*Died in a car accident in Los Angeles, CA*
1997	JEWELL, Stuart		84	*Died of colon cancer in Costa Mesa, CA*
1997	KAJITA, Alvin T.		55	*Lung cancer at Good Samaritan Hospital in Los Angeles, CA*
1997	KAYE, Stubby		79	*Died at his home in Los Rancho Mirage, CA of lung cancer*
1997	KEAREY, Antony		77	
1997	KEITH, Brian		75	*Died at his home in Malibu, CA of a self-inflicted gun shot wound*
1997	KENNEDY, Adam		75	*Heart attack at home in Kent, Conn.*
1997	KINGSLEY, Dorothy		87	*Died of a heart ailment in Monterey, CA*
1997	KLAP, Hans		52	*Heart attack (at International Film Festival in Rotterdam, Netherlands)*
1997	KOMACK, James		67	*Died of heart failure in Los Angeles, CA*
1997	KULLE, Jarl		70	*Died of bone cancer at his home in Stockholm, Sweden*
1997	KURALT, Charles		62	*Died in NY Hospital-Cornell Medical Ctr. of heart failure*
1997	LAMBERT, Paul		74	*Cancer at St. John's Hospital in Santa Monica, CA*
1997	LANE, Burton		84	*Died in New York, N.Y.*
1997	LATTANZI, Tina		99	*After a brief illness at home in Milan, Italy*
1997	LAUNDER, Frank		91	*Cause unreported (at Princess Grace Hospital in Monaco)*
1997	LAUZON, Jean-Claude		43	*Plane crash in Northern Quebec, Canada*
1997	LAWRENCE, Rosina		84	*Died at Mt. Sinai Hospital Ctr. in New York City, NY*
1997	LEE, Terry H.		75	*Natural causes at home in Naples, FL*
1997	LENARD, Kay		?	*Natural causes (in Portland, OR)*
1997	# LEONARD, Sheldon		89	*Natural causes (at his home in Beverly Hills, CA)*
1997	LEWENSTEIN, Oscar		80	*Died in Brighton, England*
1997	LEWIS, Abby		87	*Died of natural causes in her Greenwich Village Apt. NY City, NY*
1997	LEWIS, Robert		88	*Heart Attack*
1997	LINDLEY, Audra		79	*Died of complicatins from leukemia in Los Angeles, CA*
1997	LISTER, Eve		83	*Died in England*
1997	LOHMANN, Dietrick		54	*Leukemia at City of Hope Medical Ctr. in Duarte, CA*
1997	LOMBARDI, Joe		74	*Bronchial pneumonia in London*
1997	LOUIS, Jean	★	89	*Natural causes at his Palm Springs, CA home*
1997	LUCAS, Isabelle Harriet		69	
1997	MACINTOSH, Alex		71	
1997	MANNIX, Daniel Pratt		85	*After a long illness (at his home in Malvern, PA)*
1997	# MARCHAL , Georges		77	*In Maurens, France*
1997	MARTINELLI, Enzo		89	*Natural causes (in Jackson, TN)*
1997	MASON, Richard		78	*Throat cancer in Rome*
1997	MATEOS, Gabriel Figueroa	☆	90	*Stroke in Mexico City, Mexico*
1997	MATEOS, Julian		57	*Lung cancer in Madrid, Spain*

Deaths of Movie and Television Personalities — by Year

YEAR	NAME		AGE	CAUSE and/or PLACE OF DEATH
1997	MATHER, George E.		77	Heart attack at home in North Hollywood, CA
1997	MAY, Brian		63	Heart attack in Australia
1997	MAY, Jack		75	
1997	MCBRIDE, Elizabeth	☆	42	Cancer at home in Santa Fe, NM
1997	McLEOD, Catherine		75	Pneumonia (at Encino-Tarzana Medical Center in CA)
1997	MEISNER, Sanford		91	Natural causes (at his home in Sherman Oaks, CA)
1997	# MEREDITH, Burgess	☆	88	At his home in Malibu, CA
1997	MICHENER, James A.		90	Renal failure at home in Austin, TX from kidney problems
1997	MIFUNE, Toshiro		77	Died of organ failure at a Tokyo hospital
1997	MILMO, Emilio Azcarraga		66	Cancer in Miami, FL
1997	MIRO, Pilar		57	Heart attack at home in Madrid, Spain
1997	MITCHUM, Robert	☆	79	Died at his home in CA from emphysema and lung cancer
1997	+ MOORE, Jack "Alvy"		75	Heart failure at his home in Palm Desert, CA
1997	MOORE, Joanna		63	Died of lung cancer in Indian Wells, CA
1997	MORAN, Grace E.		79	Died in her sleep at her son's home in Catonsville, MD
1997	MORTON, Howard		71	Stroke at St. Joseph's Hospital in Burbank, CA
1997	MOSS, Carlton		88	Died in Los Angeles, CA
1997	MULHARE, Edward		74	Lung Cancer in Los Angeles, CA
1997	NEWI, George		62	Heart attack while on vacation in Norway
1997	NINCHI, Ave		83	Died at her home in Trieste, Italy of diabetes
1997	O'BRIEN, Robert H.		93	
1997	O'HERLIHY, Michael		69	Died in his sleep in Ireland
1997	OLIVER, Maurine		93	Natural causes at Marycrest Manor Culver City
1997	PAULSEN, Pat		69	Colon and Brain cancer in Mexico
1997	PETRIE, George O.		85	Lymphoma in Los Angeles, CA
1997	PHILLIPS, Mirian		98	Died at Actors' Equity Home in NJ of Alzheimer's disease
1997	POLIER, Dan A.		78	Heart failure (in Palm Desert, CA)
1997	PORTER, Don		84	Natural causes in Los Angeles, CA
1997	PRESCOTT, Eleanor		50	Heart failure (in Bayside, NY)
1997	+ PYLE, Denver		77	Lung cancer at Providence St. Joseph Medical Ctr., Burbank, CA
1997	RAWLINS, John		94	Pneumonia in Arcadia, CA
1997	# REYNOLDS, Marjorie		76	Congestive heart failure (in Manhattam Beach, CA)
1997	RICE, Joan		66	
1997	RIDGELY, Robert		65	Cancer at his home in Toluca Lake, CA
1997	ROBBINS, Harold		81	Respiratory failure at Desert Hospital in Palm Springs, CA
1997	ROKER, Roxie		66	Died in Los Angeles, CA
1997	RYAN, William Emmett III		70	After a long illness (in Point Marion, PA)
1997	SALKIND, Alexander		76	Leukemia (at the American Hospital in Paris, France)
1997	SARNOFF, Robert W.		78	Cancer (in New York, NY)
1997	SAUDEK, Robert		85	Heart ailment (at Johns Hopkins Hospital in Baltimore, MD)
1997	SCHAEFER, George		76	After a long illness
1997	SCORSESE, Catherine		84	Complications from Alzheimer's disease (in New York, NY)
1997	SELZNICK, L. Jeffery		64	Heart attack during a business meeting in Los Angeles, CA
1997	SEYMOUR, John D.		?	
1997	SHELTON, Reid		72	Died of a Stroke in Protland, Ore.
1997	+ SKELTON, Red		84	After a long illness at Eisenhower Med. Ctr. Rancho Mirage, CA
1997	SLATTERY, Richard X.		72	Following a stroke (in Woodland Hills, CA)
1997	SOLARES, Gilberto Martinez		90	Heart attack (in Mexico City, Mexico)
1997	SPIELMANN, Fritz (Fred)		90	Natural causes in NY
1997	SPILLER, Cyreld		89	Brookline, Mass following a brief illness
1997	STEELE, Daron		51	Died of a brain tumor in Los Angeles, CA
1997	# STEINER, Arthur H.		82	Heart failure
1997	+ STEWART, James (Jimmy)	★	89	Died at his home in Beverly Hills, CA from a lung blood clot

• New entry. # Original name (Pt. 7). + Interment (Pt. 5).

☆ Oscar nominee, ★ Oscar winner (Pt. 10)

Deaths of Movie and Television Personalities — by Year

YEAR	NAME		AGE	CAUSE and/or PLACE OF DEATH
1997	STEWART, Larry		67	*Bacterial Infection and heart failure (in Van Nuys, CA)*
1997	STILL, Frank		79	*Heart attack (at his home in Laguna Beach, CA)*
1997	STONE, Jon		65	*Amyotrophic lateral sclerosis (in New York, NY)*
1997	STREHLER, Giorgio		76	*Died of a heart attact in Lugano, Switzerland*
1997	STROKA, Michael		58	*Cancer in West Hollywood, CA*
1997	SUGIMURA, Haruko		91	*Cancer at a Tokyo, Japan hospital*
1997	SUMMERS, Jill		86	
1997	TANAKA, Tomoyuki		86	*Stroke (at a hospital in Tokyo, Japan)*
1997	TAPPS, Georgie		85	*Died at Providence St. Joseph Medical Center in Burbank, CA*
1997	TAPS, Jonie		89	*Natural causes in Santa Fe, NM*
1997	TARTIKOFF, Brandon		48	*UCLA Medical Ctr. after Treatment for Hodgkins disease*
1997	TATELMAN, Harry		82	*After a brief illness in Los Angeles, CA*
1997	TEDESCO, Tommy		67	*Lung cancer at home in Northridge, CA*
1997	TOKATYAN, LEON		73	*Natural causes in Los Angeles, CA*
1997	TOPOR, Roland		59	*Cerebral hemorrhage/aneurysm in Paris*
1997	# TREE, Joanne		73	*After a long illness in New York City, NY*
1997	USHIYAMA, Junichi		67	*Liver disease in Tokyo, Japan*
1997	UTTAL, Ivan E.		66	*Died of complications from AIDS at his home in New Orleans, LA*
1997	VALE, Eugene		81	*Natural causes at home in Los Angeles, CA*
1997	VERNON, Richard		72	*Parkinsons disease in London, England*
1997	VERSACE, Gianni		50	*Murdered at his home in South Miami Beach, FL*
1997	VOLPI, Franco		75	*Cancer (at a clinic in Rome, Italy)*
1997	WARBECK, David		55	*Cancer in London*
1997	WARCICK, Richard		52	*AIDS*
1997	WEBSTER, Charles D.		73	*Died at his home in Ashland, OR after a prolonged illness*
1997	WECHSLER, Bert		64	*Died of cancer in New York*
1997	#+ WHITE, Jesse		79	*Heart attack after surgery (at Cedars Sinai Med. Ctr. in Los Angeles, CA)*
1997	WIDERBERG, Bo		66	*Unspecified long illness (at a hospital in Angelholm, Sweden)*
1997	WILDERBERG, Bo	☆	66	*After a long illness in Angelholm, Sweden*
1997	#+ WILLIAMS, Harriette "Hedy" (Carr)		91	*Heart failure (at her son's home in New Orleans, LA)*
1997	WILLIAMS, Ronald Clive		68	
1997	WILLIAMS, Vince		39	*Cancer (in Englewood, NJ)*
1997	WILLS, Mary Lillain	☆	82	*Died in Sedona, AZ*
1997	WILSON, Dennis Main		73	
1997	WINBLAD, Marjorie King		86	*Heart failure at Mercy Medical Center in Baltimore, MD*
1997	WOOD, Duncan		71	
1997	YOUNGSTEIN, Max E.		84	*Died in Los Angeles, CA*
1997	ZINNEMANN, Fred	★	89	*Natural causes (at his home in London, England)*
1997	ZINNEMANN, Renee Bartlett		88	*Natural causes in London*
1997	ZUCKERT, Bill		76	*Pneunonia in Woodland Hills, CA*
1998	ABBOTT, Philip		73	*Cancer in Los Angeles, CA*
1998	ALVAREZ, Santiago		78	*Lung infection and Parkinson's disease in Havana, Cuba*
1998	BABBS, Dorothy		71	*Complications from heart surgery in Thousand Oaks, CA*
1998	BAGLEY, Ben		64	*Complications of Emphysema in New York*
1998	BARNES, Binnie		95	*Natural causes in his Beverly Hills, CA home*
1998	BARNES, Walter "Piggy"		79	*Complications from diabetes in Calif.*
1998	BARRY, Jr., Philip		74	*Cancer in Lenox Hill Hospital, New York City, NY*
1998	# BARTOK, Eva		69	*After a long illness at St. Charles Hospital in London*
1998	BEECHMAN, Laurie		43	*Ovarian cancer at home in White Plains, NY*
1998	BIXBY, Jerome		75	*Complications after heart bypass surgery in San Bernardino, CA*
1998	BONO, Sonny		62	*Skiing Accident at Heavenly Ski Resort in S. Lake Tahoe, CA*
1998	BRAGAGLIA, Carlo Ludovico		103	*Following surgery for broken hip in a Rome hospital*

• New entry. # Original name (Pt. 7). + Interment (Pt. 5).

☆ Oscar nominee, ★ Oscar winner (Pt. 10)

Deaths of Movie and Television Personalities — by Year

YEAR	NAME		AGE	CAUSE and/or PLACE OF DEATH
• 1998	BRIDGES, Lloyd		85	*Natural causes in his Los Angeles, CA home*
• 1998	CHALKER, Harold "Curly"		66	*Cancer related brain tumor*
• 1998	CHRISTOPHER, Keith		40	*From complications of AIDS*
• 1998	COLEMAN, Shepard		74	*Died in Warwick, NY*
• 1998	CONRAD, Charles		88	
• 1998	COWAN, Kenneth		35	*Died in the China Airlines Airbus crash in Taipei, Taiwan*
• 1998	CROSS, Beverley		66	*At his home in London*
• 1998	D'ANDREA, Tom		88	*Died in Southport Square, FLA.*
• 1998	DAUMAN, Anatole		73	*Heart attack at his Paris home*
• 1998	DELPRETE, Duilio		61	*After a long illnes in a Rome, Italy Hospital*
• 1998	# DEREK, John		71	*Catastrophic problem with- aorta and heart in Santa Maria, CA*
• 1998	DEVANEY, Frank		58	*Cancer in Burbank, CA*
• 1998	DORE, Robert E.		44	*From a blood infection at Holy Cross Hosp. in Silver Spring, MD*
• 1998	DOWNS, Frederic		81	*Died in Los Angeles, CA*
• 1998	DUNCAN, Todd		95	*Of a heart condition at his home in Washington, DC*
• 1998	DUNN, Linwood	★	93	*Natural causes in Burbank, CA*
• 1998	ELISCU, Edward		96	*Died of natural causes in Newtown, Conn.*
• 1998	EVANS, Gene		75	*Natural causes in Jackson, Tenn.*
• 1998	# FAYE, Alice		83	*Cancer at Eisenhower Medical Center in Rancho Mirage, CA*
• 1998	FOWLER, JR., Gene	★	80	*Died of natural causes in Los Angeles, CA*
• 1998	FOWLEY, Douglas V.		86	*Natural causes in Woodland Hills, CA*
• 1998	FRANCHINA, Sandro		58	*Cancer in Paris*
• 1998	FRANCIOSA, Massimo		73	*Heart attack at his home in Rome, Italy*
• 1998	FRANCO, Ricardo		48	*Heart failure in Madrid, Spain*
• 1998	FRANKEL, Kenneth		56	*Brain tumor at his home in Los Angeles, CA*
• 1998	FRIENDLY, Fred		82	*Died after a series of Strokes at his New York home*
• 1998	GANG, Martin		96	*After a long illness in Santa Monica, CA*
• 1998	GARY, John		65	*Cancer at Baylor Hospital in Dallas, TX*
• 1998	# GORA, Claudio		84	*Heart failure at his home near Rome, Italy*
• 1998	GREENFIELD, WIlliam E.		68	*Riverdale, N.Y.*
• 1998	+ HARTMAN, Phil		49	*Murdered by his wife at his home in Encino, CA*
• 1998	HAYNES, Joy Hatton		64	*Cancer at her home in Manhattan, NY*
• 1998	HERRING, Sue		49	*Cancer at Tarzana Medical Center*
• 1998	HERTHUM, Harold		69	*Heart attack in Baton Rouge, LA*
• 1998	HOPKINS, John		67	*Died in Woodland Hills, CA*
• 1998	HUTCHINSON, Josephine		94	*Died in New York*
• 1998	# JONES, Grandpa		84	*Died after a series of strokes in Nashville, Tenn.*
• 1998	KAISER, Sharon Lee		56	*Cancer in California*
• 1998	KAMPEN, Irene		75	*Breast cancer at her Oceanside, CA home*
• 1998	KHAMBATTA, Persis		49	*Heart attack in Bombay, India*
• 1998	# KINLEY, Edwin		82	*Heart failure in New York City, NY*
• 1998	# KORVIN, Charles		90	*Died at Lenox Hill Hospital in Manhattan, NY*
• 1998	LANG, Charles	★	96	*Pneumonia in Santa Monica, CA*
• 1998	LEEDS, Phil		82	*Pneumonia at Cedars-Sinai Medical Center in Los Angeles, CA*
• 1998	LEWIS, Shari		65	*Cancer at Cedars-Sinai Medical Center in Los Angeles, CA*
• 1998	LORD, Jack		77	*At his home in Honolulu, Hawaii of heart failure*
• 1998	MAHER, Joseph		64	*Brain tumor at his home in Los Angeles, CA*
• 1998	MANKOWITZ, Wolf		73	*Died in Dublin, Ireland of cancer*
• 1998	MARSHALL, Everett G.		88	*After a brief illness at his home in Mount Kisco*
• 1998	MASSEY, Daniel		64	*After a long illness at a London Hospital*
• 1998	MASTERS, George		61	*Heart failure in Los Angeles, CA*
• 1998	MATTINGLY, Hedley		83	*Cancer in Encino, CA*
• 1998	# MAYNE, Ferdinand (Ferdy)		81	*Parkinson's disease in London*

• New entry. # Original name (Pt. 7). + Interment (Pt. 5).   167   ☆ Oscar nominee, ★ Oscar winner (Pt. 10)

Deaths of Movie and Television Personalities — by Year

YEAR	NAME	AGE	CAUSE and/or PLACE OF DEATH
• 1998	MERRILL, Bob ☆	77	*Suicide in front of his Beverly Hills, CA home*
• 1998	MERRITT, Theresa	75	*Skin cancer in the Bronx, NY*
• 1998	MILHAUPT, Charles	48	*AIDS at his home in Manhattan, NY*
• 1998	MONAHAN, John Paul 'Jay'	42	*Cancer*
• 1998	# MONTANA, Montie	87	*After a series of strokes in Los Angeles, CA*
• 1998	NARDINO, Gary	62	*Stroke at Cedars-Sinai Medical Center in Los Angeles, CA*
• 1998	NEWEY, Murray	45	*Suicide at his home in Auckland, New Zealand*
• 1998	NOLAN, Jeanette ☆	86	*Stroke in Los Angeles, CA*
• 1998	NORDEN, Joseph	84	*Long illness, Motion Picture & T.V. Hosp., Woodland Hills, CA*
• 1998	NORIS, Assia	85	*After a brief illness at a hospital in San Remo, Italy*
• 1998	NORMAN, Maidie	85	*Lung cancer in San Jose, CA*
• 1998	O'CONNOR, Kendall	90	*Natural causes at his home in Burbank, CA*
• 1998	O'NEIL, Thomas F.	82	*Heart failure at his home in Greenwich, Conn.*
• 1998	+ O'SULLIVAN, Maureen	87	*Heart attack in Scottsdale Memorial Hospital In Phoenix, AZ*
• 1998	PAGE, Ken	69	*Cancer in Toronto, Canada*
• 1998	PALCA, Alfred	78	*Cancer in New York*
• 1998	PALMIERI, Dominic	58	*Cancer at his home in Florida*
• 1998	PETERSEN, Don	70	*Lung and liver disease in Pittsfield, MA*
• 1998	PETERSON, Louis	76	*Lung cancer at his home in Manhattan, NY*
• 1998	PHILLIPS, Webster	83	*Cancer at Cedars-Sinai Medical Center in Los Angeles, CA*
• 1998	PRESTON, William	77	*After a brief illness in New York*
• 1998	QUESTEL, Mae	89	*At her home in Manhattan, NY*
• 1998	RABB, Ellis	67	*Heart failure in Tennessee*
• 1998	RAYMOND, Gene	89	*Pneumonia in Los Angeles, CA*
• 1998	REGEN, Stuart	39	*Cancer, U. of Southern CA/Kenneth Norris, Jr. Cancer Center*
• 1998	RENFRO, V. Buddy	61	*Cancer at his farm near Shepherdstown, W.VA*
• 1998	# ROBBINS, Jerome ★	79	*Stroke at his home in Manhattan, NY*
• 1998	ROGERS, Roy	86	*Congestive heart failur in his sleep in Apple Valley, CA*
• 1998	ROSS, Sam	86	*Heart failure in Laguna Beach, CA*
• 1998	ROWAN, Roy	78	*Heart failure in Los Angeles, CA*
• 1998	RUSSELL, Bob	90	*In a Hospital near his Sarasota, Fla. home*
• 1998	RYSANEK, Leonie	71	*Bone cancer in Vienna*
• 1998	SANDERS, Steve	45	*Self-inflicted gunshot wound to the head in Cape Coral, FLA*
• 1998	SAPERSTEIN, Henry G.	80	*Cancer in Beverly Hills, CA*
• 1998	SCHAMONI, Ulrich	58	*Died in Berlin, Germany*
• 1998	SELINGER, Dennis	77	*Cancer in London*
• 1998	SESSA, Alejandro	60	*Heart failure in Buenos Aires, Argentine*
• 1998	SIMMONS, Ed	78	*Cardiac arrest at Cedars-Sinai Med. Ctr. in Los Angeles, CA*
• 1998	SINATRA, Frank		*Heart attack at Cedars-Sinai Med. Ctr. in Los Angeles, CA*
• 1998	+ SITKA, Emil	83	*Following a stroke in Camarillo, CA*
• 1998	# SMITH, "Buffalo Bob"	80	*Lung cancer in a Hospital in Hendersonville, N.C.*
• 1998	# SQUIRES, Dorothy	83	*Cancer in Llwynpia, Wales*
• 1998	STANGERUP, Henrik	60	
• 1998	STEVENS, Leslie	74	*After emergency angioplasty in Los Angeles, CA*
• 1998	STICKNEY, Dorothy	101	*At her home in New York City, NY*
• 1998	STONE, Martin	83	*Heart attack in Washington, DC*
• 1998	STOTTER, Don	69	*Heart failure at his home in Hollywood, Fla.*
• 1998	TILLMAN, Harrel Gordon	73	*Cancer in Houston, TX*
• 1998	TROMBERG, Sheldon	68	*Heart attack in Richmond, CA*
• 1998	TRUEX, Sylvia Field	97	*Died at a nursing home in Falbrook-San Diego, CA*
• 1998	TUERCK, George N.	91	*In Weymouth, MA*
• 1998	VANSELOW, Robert A.	79	*Heart related illness in Los Angeles, CA*
• 1998	WALSH, J.T.	54	*Died of a heart attack in La Mesa, CA*

• New entry. # Original name (Pt. 7). + Interment (Pt. 5).　　　　168　　　　☆ Oscar nominee, ★ Oscar winner (Pt. 10)

Deaths of Movie and Television Personalities — by Year

YEAR	NAME	AGE	CAUSE and/or PLACE OF DEATH
• 1998	WASSERMAN, Steven M.	45	*Killed in a sailing accident off Los Angeles, CA*
• 1998	WAYNE, Gus	77	*Heart failure at a Lakeland, Fla. Hospital*
• 1998	WAYNE, Olive Brasno	80	*Heart failure at a Lakeland, Fla. Hospital*
• 1998	WEST, Paul	86	*Pneumonia at his home in San Anselmo, CA*
• 1998	WESTCOTT, Helen	70	*Cancer at Stevens Hospital in Edmunds, WA*
• 1998	WILBER, Carey	81	*Cancer in Seattle, WA*
• 1998	WILCOX-SMITH, Tamara	57	*Heart failure in Los Angeles, CA*
• 1998	WILLIAMS, Mark	38	*Respiratory failure at Kaiser Hosp. in Panorama City, CA*
• 1998	WILSON, Carl D.	51	*Lung cancer in Los Angeles, CA*
• 1998	WOLFF, Albert H.	95	*Died in Mason, Ohio*
• 1998	WORTH, Marvin	72	*Complications frome Bronchioloalar carcinoma*
• 1998	WRIGHT, George	77	*Died in California*
• 1998	WYNETTE, Tammy	55	*Blood clot in her lungs at her Nashville, Tenn. home*
• 1998	YOUNG, Robert	91	*Respiratory failure at his home in Westlake Village, CA*
• 1998	YOUNGMAN, Henny	91	*Complications from flu at Mt. Sinai Hosp. in New York City, NY*

GUY MADISON

2

Deaths of
Movie and Television
Personalities
— by Name

Deaths of Movie and Television Personalities — by Name

YEAR	NAME		AGE	CAUSE and/or PLACE OF DEATH
	A			
1988	AAMES, Angela		32	Died in West Hills, CA
1952	ABBEY, May		80	Fell or jumped from a building (in New York, NY)
1974	#+ ABBOTT, Bud		78	Cancer (in Woodland Hills, CA)
• 1997	ABBOTT, Bud Jr.		57	Apparent heart attack (in Valencia, CA)
1968	ABBOTT, Dorothy		48	Died in Los Angeles, CA
1957	ABBOTT, Frank		77	Died in Los Angeles, CA
1995	ABBOTT, George		107	Stroke (at his home in Miami Beach, FL)
1952	ABBOTT, Gypsy		57	Died in Hollywood, CA
• 1996	ABBOTT, John		90	After a long illness (in Los Angeles, CA)
1937	ABBOTT, Marion		69	Pneumonia (in Philadelphia, PA)
1977	ABBOTT, Merriel		84	Died in Chicago, IL
• 1998	ABBOTT, Philip		73	Cancer in Los Angeles, CA
1937	# ABEL, Alfred		57	Died in Berlin, Germany
1987	ABEL, Walter		88	Heart attack (in Essex, CT)
1919	ABELES, Edward		49	Pneumonia (in New York, NY)
1990	ABERNATHY, Ralph		64	
1992	ABRAHAMS, Gary		48	A.I.D.S.
1982	+ ACE, Goodman		83	
1974	#+ ACE, Jane		74	Died in Manhattan, NY
1978	+ ACKER, Jean (Valentino)		85	Died in Los Angeles, CA
1991	+ ACKERMAN, Harry		78	Pulmonary failure (in Burbank, CA)
1991	ACKERMAN, Jack		59	Brain tumor (in Los Angeles, CA)
1938	ACKERMAN, Walter		57	Died in Bishop, CA
1986	# ACKLES, Kenneth		70	Stroke (in Pasadena, TX)
1931	+ ACORD, Art		39	Suicide (arsenic) in Chihuahua, Mexico
1974	ACOSTA, Rudolfo		53	Cancer (in Woodland Hills, CA)
1956	ACUFF, Eddie		48	Heart attack (in Hollywood, CA)
1992	+ ACUFF, Roy		89	Congestive heart failure
1940	ADAIR, Jack		46	Died in Hollywood, CA
1953	ADAIR, Jean		80	Died in New York
1952	ADAIR, John		66	Died in New York
• 1996	ADAIR, Peter		53	A.I.D.S.-related illness (in San Francisco, CA)
1954	ADAIR, Robert		54	Died in London, England
1979	ADAM, Ronald		83	Died in London, England
1978	ADAMS, Claire		78	Died in Melbourne, Australia
1960	+ ADAMS, Constance (DeMille)		67	Died in Hollywood, CA
1988	ADAMS, Dorothy		88	Died in Woodland Hills, CA
1947	ADAMS, Ernest S.		62	After a long illness (in Hollywood, CA)
1936	ADAMS, Howard		27	Airplane crash (in Chicago, IL)
1933	# ADAMS, Jimmy		43	Heart attack (in Glendale, CA)
1959	ADAMS, Kathryn		64	Heart attack (in Hollywood, CA)
1952	ADAMS, Lionel		86	Died in New York, NY
1953	#+ ADAMS, Maude		80	Heart attack (in Tannersville, NY)
1968	#+ ADAMS, Nick	☆	35	Drug overdose (in Beverly Hills, CA)
1987	ADAMS, Peter		69	Cancer (in Beverly Hills, CA)
1958	# ADAMS, Sam		86	Heart attack (in Beaufort, SC)
1977	ADAMS, Stanley		62	Suicide (gunshot) in Santa Monica, CA
1961	ADAMS, Stella		78	
1972	ADAMS, William Perry		85	Died in New York
1995	ADAMSON, Al		66	Found murdered and buried under his house (in Indio, CA)
1956	# ADAMSON, James		59	Heart attack (in Los Angeles, CA)
1972	# ADAMSON, Victor		82	Died in Hollywood, CA

• New entry. # Original name (Pt. 7). + Interment (Pt. 5).   173   ☆ Oscar nominee, ★ Oscar winner (Pt. 10)

Deaths of Movie and Television Personalities — by Name

YEAR	NAME		AGE	CAUSE and/or PLACE OF DEATH
1985	ADDAMS, Dawn		55	*Cancer*
• 1997	+ ADDINGTON, John		44	*Heart attack (at his home in Dallas, TX)*
1977	ADDINSELL, Richard		73	*Died in London, England*
• 1997	ADDY, Wesley		83	*Died in New York, NY*
1992	ADES, Daniel		59	*Causes unreported (in Los Angeles, CA)*
1960	#+ ADLER, Buddy		51	*Lung cancer (in Hollywood, CA)*
1979	# ADLER, Celia		88	*Died in The Bronx, NY*
1993	ADLER, Clyde		67	*After a long illness (in Petasky, Michigan)*
1978	ADLER, Jay		82	*After a long illness (in Woodland Hills, CA)*
1984	ADLER, Luther		81	*Died in Kutztown, PA*
1992	ADLER, Stella		91	*Died in her sleep of heart failure (in Los Angeles, CA)*
1947	ADLON, Louis		40	*Heart attack (in Los Angeles, CA)*
1933	ADOLFI, John G.		45	*Cerebral hemorrhage (while on a hunting trip in Canada)*
1933	#+ ADOREE, Renée		35	*Tuberculosis (in Tujunga, CA)*
1959	#+ Adrian		56	*Suicide (in New York)*
1994	# ADRIAN, Iris		81	*Complications from earthquake injuries (in Northridge, CA)*
1991	# ADRIAN, Louis		93	*Died in Lakeport, CA*
1973	# ADRIAN, Max		70	*Died in Wilford, England*
1948	AGAR, Jane		59	*Died in Lakewood, OH*
1955	+ AGEE, James		45	*Heart attack (in New York, NY)*
1991	AGMON, Ami		43	*After a long bout with cancer*
1984	AGNEW, Robert "Bobby"		84	*Kidney failure (in Palm Springs, CA)*
1970	AGUGLIA, Mimi		85	*Died in Woodland Hills, CA*
• 1997	AGUILAR, Luis		79	*Heart attack in Mexico City*
1993	AGUILAR, Thomas J.		41	*A.I.D.S. (in Honolulu, Hawaii)*
1969	AHEARNE, Tom		63	*Influenza (in New York)*
1986	AHERNE, Brian	☆	83	*Heart failure (in Venice, FL)*
1992	# AHERNE, Gladys		?	*After a brief illness*
1970	AHERNE, Patrick		69	*Cancer (in Hollywood, CA)*
1954	AHLM, Philip E.		49	*Murdered (shot) in Hollywood, CA*
1978	AHN, Philip		66	*Lung cancer (in Los Angeles, CA)*
1993	+ AIDMAN, Charles		68	*Cancer (in Beverly Hills, CA)*
1992	AIKEN, Bill		34	*After a 1-year bout with cancer*
1989	AILEY, Alvin		58	*Dyscrasia (a blood disorder) in New York*
1945	AINLEY, Henry H.		66	*Died in London, England*
1967	# AINLEY, Richard		56	*Died in London, England*
1948	AINSLEY, Norman		67	*After a year's illness (at a private sanitarium in Hollywood, CA)*
1922	# AINSWORTH, Sidney		50	*After an illness of several months (in Madison, WI)*
1933	AITKEN, Frank "Spottiswoode"		64	*After a lingering illness (in Los Angeles, CA)*
1955	AKED, Muriel		68	*Died in Settle, England*
1973	+ AKEMAN, David "Stringbean"		57	*Shot to death by burglars in his home*
1994	+ AKINS, Claude		67	*Cancer (in Altadena, CA)*
1970	# Aladdin		57	*Found dead at home of apparent heart attack (in Van Nuys, CA)*
1962	ALBERNI, Luis		74	*Died in Hollywood, CA*
1960	ALBERS, Hans		67	*Died in Munchen, Germany*
1964	+ ALBERTSON, Frank		55	*Died in Santa Monica, CA*
1981	+ ALBERTSON, Jack	★	74	*Cancer (in Hollywood Hills, CA)*
1982	ALBERTSON, Mabel		81	*Complications from numerous illnesses (in Santa Monica, CA)*
1994	ALBIN, Andy		86	*After a long illness (in Woodland Hills, CA)*
1971	# ALBRIGHT, Hardie		67	*Heart failure and pneumonia (in Mission Viejo, CA)*
1986	#+ ALDA, Robert		72	*Effects of a stroke (in Los Angeles, CA)*
1946	# ALDEN, Mary		63	*Died in Woodland Hills, CA*
1987	ALDERMAN, John		53	*Apparent heart attack (in Hollywood, CA)*

Deaths of Movie and Television Personalities — by Name

YEAR	NAME		AGE	CAUSE and/or PLACE OF DEATH
1957	ALDERSON, Erville		74	Died in Glendale, CA
1980	# ALDERSON, Floyd Taliaferro		84	Pneumonia after suffering a stroke (in Mt. Sheridan, WY)
• 1985	ALDRICH, David		54	After a long illness
1983	ALDRICH, Robert		65	Kidney failure (in Los Angeles, CA)
1995	# ALDRIDGE, Kay (Tucker)		77	Heart attack (in Camden, ME)
1994	ALDRIDGE, Michael		73	Died in London, England
1996	ALEA, Tomas Gutierrez		69	Lung cancer (in Havana, Cuba)
1990	ALEX, Robert		30	Gunshot wounds during a robbery at his home (in Silver Lake, CA)
1969	# ALEXANDER, Ben		58	Natural causes (in Westchester, CA)
1982	+ ALEXANDER, John		85	
1981	ALEXANDER, Katherine		79	Died in Florida
1989	ALEXANDER, Richard		86	Pulmonary edema (in Woodland Hills, CA)
1937	+ ALEXANDER, Ross		29	Suicide (gunshot) in Los Angeles, CA
1992	ALEXANDER, Tom		29	A.I.D.S. (in Hollywood, CA)
1983	ALEXANDROV, Grigori		80	Died in Moscow, Russia
1990	ALINDER, Dallas		58	Heart failure following a liver transplant
1992	ALISON, Dorothy		66	Causes unreported (in London, England)
1990	ALLAN, Elizabeth		80	Died in London, England
• 1997	ALLAND, William		81	Died in Long Beach, CA of heart disease
1979	ALLBRITTON, Louise		58	Cancer
1987	ALLEGRET, Yves		79	Heart attack (in France)
1970	ALLEN, A. A.		?	Found dead in a San Francisco hotel room
1993	ALLEN, Adrianne		86	After suffering from cancer (in Montreux, Switzerland)
1947	ALLEN, Alfred		80	Died in New York, NY
1974	ALLEN, Barbara Jo "Vera Vague"		70	Died in Santa Barbara, CA
1984	ALLEN, Chet		44	Suicide (in Columbus, OH)
1995	ALLEN, Dennis		55	Lung cancer (in Kansas City, Missouri)
1970	ALLEN, Dorothy		74	After a brief illness (in New York, NY)
1956	#+ ALLEN, Fred		62	Heart attack (in New York, NY)
1964	#+ ALLEN, Gracie		58	Heart attack (in Los Angeles, CA)
1951	ALLEN, Harry R.		68	Died in Los Angeles, CA
1987	ALLEN, Irving		82	After a long illness (in Encino, CA)
1991	+ ALLEN, Irwin	★	75	After suffering a heart attack (in Santa Monica, CA)
1962	ALLEN, Joseph Jr.		44	Heart attack (in Patchogue, NY)
1949	ALLEN, Lester		58	Struck and killed by an automobile (in Hollywood, CA)
• 1996	ALLEN, Mel		83	After a long illness (at his home in Greenwich, CT)
1992	ALLEN, Peter	★	48	An A.I.D.S.-related illness (in San Diego, CA)
1995	ALLEN, Randy		38	A.I.D.S.
1991	ALLEN, Ronald		56	Lung cancer (in Reading, England)
1934	ALLEN, Sam		73	Died in Los Angeles, CA
1987	ALLEN, Vera		89	Heart failure (at a retirement home in Croton-on-Hudson, NY)
1966	ALLENBY, Peggy		65	After a brief illness (in New York)
1993	# ALLEY, Paul		87	Died in Winter Park, Florida
1950	+ ALLGOOD, Sara	☆	66	Heart attack (in Woodland Hills, CA)
1989	ALLISON, Fran		81	Complications of a blood disorder (in Sherman Oaks, CA)
1989	ALLISON, May		98	Respiratory failure (in Bratenahl, OH)
1970	# ALLISTER, Claud		76	Cancer (in Santa Barbara, CA)
1971	ALLMAN, Duane		24	Motorcycle accident (in Macon, GA)
1992	ALLMAN, Elvia		87	Pneumonia (in Santa Monica, CA)
1978	+ ALLWYN, Astrid		68	Cancer (in Los Angeles, CA)
1976	ALLYN, Alyce		?	While hospitalized (in Santa Monica, CA)
1992	ALMENDROS, Nestor	★	61	Lymphoma (in New York)
• 1996	ALTON, John	★	94	After hip replacement surgery (in Santa Monica, CA)

• New entry. # Original name (Pt. 7). + Interment (Pt. 5).   175   ☆ Oscar nominee, ★ Oscar winner (Pt. 10)

Deaths of Movie and Television Personalities — by Name

YEAR	NAME		AGE	CAUSE and/or PLACE OF DEATH
1967	# ALVARADO, Don		62	Cancer (in Los Angeles, CA)
1998	ALVAREZ, Santiago		78	Lung infection and Parkinson's disease in Havana, Cuba
1992	ALZADO, Lyle		43	After suffering brain cancer (in Portland, OR)
1959	AMBLER, Joss		59	Died in England
1993	#+ AMECHE, Don ★		85	Prostate cancer (at his son's home in Scottsdale, AZ)
1947	#+ AMES, Adrienne		43	Cancer (in New York, NY)
1997	# AMES, Francine		75	Heart failure in Sarasota, FL
1933	AMES, Gerald		51	Injuries from a fall (in London, England)
1965	AMES, Jimmy		50	Heart attack (in Hollywood, CA)
1993	+ AMES, Leon		91	Complications after a stroke (Laguna Beach, CA)
1931	AMES, Robert		33	Bladder hemorrhage (in New York)
1978	AMES, Vic		52	Automobile accident (in Nashville, TN)
1996	AMOS, Beth		80	Died in Toronto, Canada while attending a theatre
1996	+ AMSTERDAM, Morey		87	Heart attack (at Cedars-Sinai Hospital in Los Angeles, CA)
1986	AMY, George J.		86	After a long illness (in Los Angeles, CA)
1992	AMYES, Julian		74	Causes unreported (in London, England)
1958	ANALLA, Isabel		37	Cancer (in San Francisco, CA)
1985	ANDEN, Matthew		42	After a lengthy illness (in New York)
1981	+ ANDERS, Glenn		92	Died in Englewood, NJ
1992	# ANDERS, Laurie		70	Cancer (in Tarzana, CA)
1996	ANDERS, Luana		57	Breast cancer (in Mar Vista, CA)
1964	# ANDERSON, Claire		68	Died in Venice, CA
1977	+ ANDERSON, Eddie "Rochester"		71	Heart attack (in Santa Barbara, CA)
1985	ANDERSON, Edward		70	
1997	ANDERSON, Ernie		73	Cancer (at his home in Los Angeles, CA)
1971	#+ ANDERSON, G. M. "Broncho Billy"		88	Died in South Pasadena, CA
1994	ANDERSON, Herbert		77	Died in his sleep 2-months after a stroke (in Palm Springs, CA)
1969	ANDERSON, James "Jim"		48	Heart attack (in Billings, MT)
1992	ANDERSON, John		69	Heart attack
1992	# ANDERSON, Judith ☆		93	Pneumonia after suffering a brain tumor
1939	ANDERSON, Lawrence		45	Pneumonia (in London, England)
1994	ANDERSON, Lindsay		71	Heart attack after swimming at a friend's pool (in Nice, France)
1993	ANDERSON, Marian		96	Congestive heart failure following a stroke
1997	ANDERSON, Scott		35	Brain cancer in Los Angeles, CA
1996	ANDERSON, Thomas Charles		90	After a long illness following a stroke (in Englewood, NJ)
1976	ANDERSON, Warner		65	Cancer (in Santa Monica, CA)
1991	# ANDOR, Lotte Palfi		87	After an illness (in New York, NY)
1991	# ANDOR, Paul		90	After a long illness (in Berlin, Germany)
1984	ANDRE, E. J.		76	Cancer (in Hollywood, CA)
1959	#+ ANDRE, Gwili		51	Burned to death when fire swept her apartment (in Venice, CA)
1986	ANDREWS, Ann		95	
1992	# ANDREWS, Dana		83	Congestive heart failure and pneumonia (in Los Alamitos, CA)
1985	#+ ANDREWS, Edward		70	Heart attack (in Pacific Palisades, CA)
1989	ANDREWS, Harry		77	Viral infection complicated by asthma (in Sussex, England)
1967	+ ANDREWS, LaVerne 'of Sisters'		51	Cancer and pneumonia (in Brentwood, CA)
1968	# ANDREWS, Lois		44	Lung cancer (in Encino, CA)
1995	+ ANDREWS, Maxine 'of Sisters'		79	Heart attack (while vacationing in Hyannis, Cape Cod, MA)
1989	ANDREWS, Nancy		68	Heart attack (in Queens, NY)
1996	ANDREWS, Norma		66	An Aneurysm (at Tarzana Hospital in Tarzana, CA)
1969	ANDREWS, Stanley		77	Died in Los Angeles, CA
1992	ANDREWS, Thomas		37	A.I.D.S.
1972	ANDREWS, Tod		52	Heart attack (in Beverly Hills, CA)
1986	+ ANGEL, Heather		76	Cancer (in Santa Barbara, CA)

• New entry.   # Original name (Pt. 7).   + Interment (Pt. 5).   176   ☆ Oscar nominee, ★ Oscar winner (Pt. 10)

Deaths of Movie and Television Personalities — by Name

YEAR	NAME	AGE	CAUSE and/or PLACE OF DEATH
1971	# ANGELI, Pier	39	Suicide (overdose of barbiturates) in Beverly Hills, CA
1971	ANGOLD, Edit	76	After a long bout with cancer (in Hollywood, CA)
1996	ANGUS, Robert	74	Pneumonia (in Fountain Valley, CA)
1985	ANKERS, Evelyn	67	Cancer (in Haiku, Hawaii)
1964	#+ ANKRUM, Morris	67	Trichinosis (in Pasadena, CA)
• 1996	# Annabella	86	Heart attack (in Paris, France)
1968	ANSON, Laura	76	Died in Woodland Hills, CA
1993	ANTHONY, Joseph	80	Died in Hyannis, MA
1989	# ANTHONY, Rick	60	
• 1943	ANTOINE, Andre	85	
1967	ANTRIM, Harry	71	Heart attack (in Hollywood, CA)
1961	AOKI, Tsuru	69	Acute peritonitis (in Tokyo, Japan)
1938	APFEL, Oscar	59	Heart attack (in Hollywood, CA)
1990	APPLEBY, Dorothy	84	Died in Long Island, NY
1950	APPLEBY, William C.	27	Coronary thrombosis (in North Hollywood, CA)
1959	APPLEGATE, Hazel	73	Died in Chicago, IL
1988	ARAGON, Jesse	32	Motorcycle accident (in Los Angeles, CA)
1991	ARAVINDAM, Govindan	55	Heart attack (in Trivandrum, India)
1939	ARBUCKLE, Andrew	55	Died in Los Angeles, CA
1931	ARBUCKLE, Maclyn	68	Cerebral hemorrhage (at his home in Waddington, NY)
1975	+ ARBUCKLE, Minta Durfee	85	Congestive heart failure in Woodland Hills, CA
1933	#+ ARBUCKLE, Roscoe "Fatty"	46	Heart attack (in New York)
1959	ARCHAINBAUD, George	68	Heart attack (in Beverly Hills, CA)
1990	#+ ARDEN, Eve ☆	83	Heart failure and cancer (in Los Angeles, CA)
1992	ARDENT, Keith	38	A.I.D.S.
1993	ARDOLINO, Emile ★	50	Complications from A.I.D.S. (in Bel-Air, CA)
1991	ARKIN, David	49	Died in Los Angeles, CA
1947	# ARLEDGE, John	41	Died in Hollywood, CA
1966	ARLEN, Betty	62	Died in Los Angeles, CA
1986	ARLEN, Harold	81	Died in Manhattan, NY
1976	#+ ARLEN, Richard	75	Emphysema (in Hollywood, CA)
1989	ARLEN, Roxanne (Shafer)	57	Cancer (in London, England)
1992	# Arletty	94	Died in Paris, France
1950	ARLISS, Florence	79	Died in London, England
1946	# ARLISS, George ★	77	Bronchial trouble (in London, England)
1987	ARLISS, Leslie	86	Died in London, England
1963	ARMENDARIZ, Pedro	51	Suicide (gunshot) after suffering with lymph cancer (in Los Angeles)
1945	+ ARMETTA, Henry	57	Heart attack (in San Diego, CA)
1924	ARMSTRONG, Billy	32	Died in London, England
1986	+ ARMSTRONG, Herbert W.	93	Died in his sleep
1971	#+ ARMSTRONG, Louis "Satchmo"	71	Heart ailment (in Queens, NY)
1973	+ ARMSTRONG, Robert	76	Heart attack (in Santa Monica, CA)
1987	# ARNAUD, Georges	69	Died in Barcelona, Spain
1958	ARNAUD, Yvonne	65	Died in London, England
1986	#+ ARNAZ, Desi	69	Lung cancer (in Del Mar, CA)
1983	# ARNE, Peter	62	Murdered (battered to death) in London, England
1955	ARNHEIM, Gus	55	Heart attack (in Beverly Hills, CA)
1975	# ARNO, Sig	80	Parkinson's disease (in Woodland Hills, CA)
1931	ARNOLD, Cecile	?	Influenza (in Hong Kong, China)
1995	# ARNOLD, Danny	70	Heart failure (in Los Angeles, CA)
1956	#+ ARNOLD, Edward	66	Cerebral hemorrhage (in Encino, CA)
1992	ARNOLD, Jack	75	Arteriosclerosis (in Woodland Hills, CA)
1971	# ARNOLD, Jessie	93	Heart attack (in Los Angeles, CA)

Deaths of Movie and Television Personalities — by Name

YEAR	NAME		AGE	CAUSE and/or PLACE OF DEATH
1991	ARNOLD, Monroe		64	*After a heart attack*
1968	ARNOLD, Phil		58	*Heart attack (in Hollywood, CA)*
1940	ARNOLD, William R.		56	*Streptococcus infection (in Hollywood, CA)*
1974	#+ ARQUETTE, Cliff		69	*Heart attack (in Burbank, CA)*
1991	ARRAU, Claudio		88	*Complications after surgery for intestinal blockage (in Austria)*
1948	# ARTAUD, Antonin		52	*Colon cancer (in Ivry-Sur-Seine, France)*
1991	#+ ARTHUR, Jean	☆	89	*Heart failure following a paralyzing stroke (in Carmel, CA)*
1951	# ARTHUR, Johnny		68	*Heart disease (in Woodland Hills, CA)*
1989	ARTHUR, Lee		49	*Cancer (in Houston, TX)*
1988	ARUNDELL, Dennis		90	*Died in London, England*
1979	ARVAN, Jan		66	*Heart attack (in Los Angeles, CA)*
1949	# ARVIDSON, Linda		65	*Died in New York, NY*
1979	ARZNER, Dorothy		82	*Pneumonia (in La Quinta, CA)*
1974	# ASH, Russell		63	*Cancer (in Los Angeles, CA)*
1951	ASH, Samuel Howard		67	*Died in Hollywood, CA*
1988	ASHBY, Hal	★	59	*Liver cancer (in Malibu, CA)*
1991	# ASHCROFT, Peggy	★	83	*After suffering a stroke (in Croydon, England)*
1988	ASHCROFT, Ronnie		65	*After a long illness (in Sylmar, CT)*
1993	+ ASHE, Arthur		49	*A.I.D.S.-related pneumonia (at a New York hospital)*
1991	ASHE, Martin		80	*Respiratory failure (in Woodland Hills, CA)*
1947	ASHE, Warren		44	*Automobile accident (in Madison, CT)*
1957	ASHER, Max		76	*Died in Hollywood, CA*
• 1997	ASHLEY, John		62	*Heart attack on the film set of "Scarred City" in NY*
1977	# ASHLEY, Sylvia		73	*Cancer (in Los Angeles, CA)*
1991	ASHMAN, Howard	★	40	*Complications from A.I.D.S. (in New York, NY)*
1936	ASHTON, Dorrit		63	*Died in Los Angeles, CA*
1940	ASHTON, Sylvia		60	*Died in Los Angeles, CA*
1992	ASIMOV, Isaac		72	*Heart and kidney failure (in New York, NY)*
1940	ASKAM, Earl		41	*After a heart attack while playing golf (in Los Angeles, CA)*
1982	ASKEY, Arthur		82	*After amputation of a leg (in London, England)*
1982	# ASLAN, Gregoire		74	*Heart attack (in England)*
1981	#+ ASTAIRE, Adele		82	*Stroke (in Phoenix, AZ)*
1987	#+ ASTAIRE, Fred	☆	88	*Pneumonia (in Los Angeles, CA)*
1981	ASTHER, Nils		84	*Died in Stockholm, Sweden*
1977	ASTOR, Gertrude		90	*Stroke (in Woodland Hills, CA)*
1987	#+ ASTOR, Mary	★	81	*Emphysema (in Los Angeles, CA)*
1943	ATCHLEY, Hooper		56	*Suicide (gunshot) in Hollywood, CA*
1962	+ ATES, Roscoe		70	*Lung cancer (in Hollywood, CA)*
1963	ATKINSON, Frank		69	*Died in Pinner Hatch End, England*
• 1996	ATSUMI, Kiyoshi		68	*Lung cancer (in Japan)*
1987	ATTAWAY, Ruth		77	*Injuries from a fire in her apartment*
1992	ATTERBURY, Malcolm		85	*Died in Beverly Hills, CA*
1986	ATWATER, Edith		74	*Cancer (in Los Angeles, CA)*
1946	+ ATWILL, Lionel		61	*Bronchial cancer and pneumonia (in Pacific Palisades, CA)*
1994	+ AUBREY, James T.		75	*Heart attack (at UCLA Med. Ctr. emergency room)*
1991	AUBUCHON, Jacques		67	*Heart failure (in Woodland Hills, CA)*
1988	AUCLAIR, Michel		65	*Cerebral hemorrhage (in Saint-Paul-en-Foret, France)*
1991	+ AUDLEY, Eleanor		86	*Respiratory failure (in North Hollywood, CA)*
1992	AUDLEY, Maxine		69	*Heart attack (in London, England)*
1995	# AUDLEY, Michael		82	*Died at his home in New Orleans, LA*
1962	AUER, Florence		81	*Died in New York, NY*
1967	# AUER, Mischa	☆	61	*Heart attack (in Rome, Italy)*
1957	AUERBACH, Arthur "Mr. Kitzel"		54	*Heart attack (in Van Nuys, CA)*

• New entry. # Original name (Pt. 7). + Interment (Pt. 5).   178   ☆ Oscar nominee, ★ Oscar winner (Pt. 10)

Deaths of Movie and Television Personalities — by Name

YEAR	NAME	AGE	CAUSE and/or PLACE OF DEATH
1984	AUERBACH, Leon	48	Died in London, England
1964	AUGUST, Edwin	81	Died in Hollywood, CA
1951	# AULT, Marie	81	Died in London, England
1983	AURIC, Georges	84	Died in Paris, France
1953	AUSTIN, Albert	71	After a long illness (in North Hollywood, CA)
1972	#+ AUSTIN, Gene	71	Cancer (in Palm Springs, CA)
1927	AUSTIN, Jere	51	Cancer (in Hollywood, CA)
• 1997	AUSTIN, Laurence	74	Shot to death in the lobby of his Los Angeles silent movie theatre
1957	AUSTIN, Lois	47	Cachexia (in Hollywood, CA)
1974	AUSTIN, Richard	33	Automobile accident (in Hawthorne, CA)
1951	AUSTIN, William	66	Stroke
• 1997	AVERBACK, Hy	76	Died following open heart surgery in Los Angles, CA
1926	# AVERY, Charles	53	Suicide (in Hollywood, CA)
1973	AVERY, Patricia	71	
1980	#+ AVERY, Tex	71	Cancer (in Burbank, CA)
1973	AVERY, Tol	58	Heart attack (in Los Angeles, CA)
1995	AVILES, Rick	41	Heart failure (in Los Angeles, CA)
• 1987	AVRAKIAN, Aram	61	Heart failure
1991	AXTHELM, Pete	47	Liver failure
1951	# AYE, Maryon	45	Suicide (poison) in Hollywood, CA
• 1996	AYERS, Lew ☆	88	Died in his sleep at his home in Los Angeles, CA
1946	AYLESWORTH, Arthur	61	Died in Los Angeles, CA
1964	AYLMER, David	31	Suicide (in London, England)
1979	# AYLMER, Felix	90	Died in a nursing home in Sussex, England
1940	#+ AYRES, Agnes	42	Cerebral hemorrhage (while in a L.A. sanitarium for depression)
• 1997	AYRES, Lew	88	Died in Los Angeles
1968	AYRES, Robert	54	Heart attack (in Hemel Hempstead, England)
1916	# AYRES, Sydney	37	After a long illness (in Oakland, CA)
• 1995	AZITO, Tony	46	A.I.D.S.
	B		
• 1980	BABB, Kroger	85	Heart attack complicated by diabetes (in Palm Springs, CA)
1992	# BABBITT, Art	85	Kidney failure (in Los Angeles, CA)
• 1998	BABBS, Dorothy	71	Complications from heart surgery in Thousand Oaks, CA
1992	BABIN, Vitya Vronsky	82	After a long illness
• 1975	BABOTCHKINE, Boris	71	Died in Moscow, Russia
• 1982	Baby Early	76	Emphysema (in Dover, NJ)
• 1974	# Baby Lawrence	52	Cancer (in New York, NY)
• 1974	# Baby Ruth Jen	54	Cancer (in Culver City, CA)
• 1917	# Baby Sunshine	1	Run over by a truck (in Los Angeles, CA)
• 1989	BAC, André	83	Heart attack (in Paris, France)
1969	BACCALONI, Salvatore	69	Following deterioration of a number of organs (in New York, NY)
• 1919	BACCANI, Ettore	?	Died in Rome, Italy
1978	BACCHIOCCHI, Norman	34	
• 1917	BACH, Anna	82	Died in Chemmitz, Germany
1941	BACH, Reginald	54	Pneumonia (in New York, NY)
• 1960	BACH, Rudi	?	Died in Buffalo, NY
• 1977	BACHELET, Jean	82	Died in Cannes, France
• 1965	BACHER, William A.	67	Cerebral thrombosis
• 1952	# BACHMANN, John	63	Heart attack (in Hollywood, CA)
• 1949	BACKER, Franklyn E.	72	Died in Suffern, NY
• 1989	BACKHAUS, Helmuth M.	68	Died in Germany
• 1939	BACKUS, George	81	Died in Merrick, NY
• 1983	BACKUS, Georgia	83	Died in Sun City, CA

• New entry. # Original name (Pt. 7). + Interment (Pt. 5).   179   ☆ Oscar nominee, ★ Oscar winner (Pt. 10)

Deaths of Movie and Television Personalities — by Name

YEAR	NAME	AGE	CAUSE and/or PLACE OF DEATH
1989	#+ BACKUS, Jim "Mr. Magoo"	76	Pneumonia and Parkinson's disease (in Santa Monica, CA)
• 1962	BACKUS, Lucia	88	Died in New York, NY
1974	# BACLANOVA, Olga	78	Died in Vevey, Switzerland
• 1952	BACON, Allen	66	Died in Los Angeles, CA
1943	# BACON, David	29	Murdered (stabbed) in Los Angeles, CA
• 1956	BACON, Faith	47	Suicide (in Chicago, IL)
• 1922	BACON, Frank	58	Heart attack (in Chicago, IL)
1965	+ BACON, Irving	71	Died in Hollywood, CA
• 1956	BACON, Jane	89	Died in Hollywood, CA
1955	+ BACON, Lloyd	66	Cerebral hemorrhage (in Burbank, CA)
• 1950	BACON, Mabel	56	Cancer (in Los Angeles, CA)
1948	BACON, Rod	33	Died in Los Angeles, CA
• 1973	BACON, Walter Scott	82	Heart attack (in Hollywood, CA)
• 1961	BACONNET, Georges	68	Died in Paris, France
• 1945	BACQUE, André	65	Died in Paris, France
• 1978	BACQUE, Jean	54	Died in France
• 1966	BACUGALUPI, Louis	46	Died in Los Angeles, CA
1976	# BADDELEY, Angela	71	Flu and bronchitis (in London, England)
1986	BADDELEY, Hermione ☆	79	Cerebral thrombosis (in Los Angeles, CA)
1982	# BADEL, Alan	58	Heart attack (in Chichester, England)
• 1949	BADET, Régina	73	Died in Bordeaux, France
1964	BADGER, Clarence	84	Following surgery (in Sydney, Australia)
• 1955	BADGLEY, Frank C.	62	Died in Ottawa, Canada
• 1976	BADIA, Leopold	74	Died in New York, NY
• 1985	BADIE, Jean	78	Died in Nice, France
• 1969	BADRAKHAN, Ahmed	59	Apoplexy attack (in Le Caire, Egypt)
• 1986	BAEHR, Nicholas E.	61	Cancer
• 1944	BAEKELAND, Léon Henri	80	Died in Los Angeles, CA
• 1969	BAER, Arthur "Bugs"	84	Cancer (in New York, NY)
1986	+ BAER, Jacob "Buddy"	71	Died in Los Angeles, CA
• 1972	BAER, Mary	62	Died in Los Angeles, CA
1959	#+ BAER, Max Sr.	50	Heart attack (in Hollywood, CA)
• 1930	BAER, Thais	1	Died in Painted Desert, AZ
• 1975	BAGDAD, William	54	Died in Los Angeles, CA
1972	#+ BAGDASARIAN, Ross S.	52	Heart attack (in Beverly Hills, CA)
1960	BAGGETT, Lynne	32	Overdose of barbiturates (in Hollywood, CA)
1948	BAGGOTT, King	73	Cerebral thrombosis (in Los Angeles, CA)
• 1998	BAGLEY, Ben	64	Complications of Emphysema in New York
• 1927	# BAGLEY, Don	?	Died in Salt Lake City, UT
• 1961	BAGLEY, Richard	41	After a long illness (in New York, NY)
• 1968	# BAGLEY, Sam	65	Heart attack (in Hollywood, CA)
1954	BAGNI, John	43	Heart attack (in Hollywood, CA)
1981	BAGNOLD, Enid	91	Died in St. John's Wood, England
• 1997	BAHAM, Ron	33	AIDS
• 1975	BAHN, Roma	78	Died in Bonn, Germany
• 1980	BAILEN, Maurice	78	Died in Maywood, IL
• 1952	BAILEY, Albert	61	Suicide (in Hollywood, CA)
1978	BAILEY, Bill	66	Died in Phila. PA (Do not confuse with any of the 3 William Bailey's)
• 1951	BAILEY, Edward Lorenz	68	Died in Lima, OH
• 1950	BAILEY, Edwin B.	77	Died in Santa Monica, CA
• 1953	# BAILEY, Frankie	94	Died in Los Angeles, CA
• 1954	BAILEY, Harry A.	74	Died in Los Angeles, CA
• 1980	BAILEY, Jack	72	Complications of pneumonia (in Santa Monica, CA)

Deaths of Movie and Television Personalities — by Name

YEAR		NAME		AGE	CAUSE and/or PLACE OF DEATH
•	1981	BAILEY, James		31	*Died in Punene, HI*
	1989	BAILEY, John (actor)		73	*Undisclosed causes (in London, England)*
•	1932	BAILEY, Oliver D.		55	*Died in Long Lake Harrison, ME*
	1990	#+ BAILEY, Pearl		72	*Heart failure following surgery to replace a knee (in Philadelphia, PA)*
	1980	BAILEY, Raymond		75	*Heart attack (in Irvine, CA)*
	1983	BAILEY, Robert		71	*Died in Lancaster, CA*
	1987	BAILEY, Sherwood "Spud"		64	*Cancer (in Newport Beach, CA)*
	1995	BAILEY, William		84	*Died in San Francisco, CA (Do not confuse with Bill Bailey, d. 1978)*
	1990	BAILEY, William H.		72	*Died in Camden, NJ (Do not confuse with actor Bill Bailey, d. 1978)*
	1962	# BAILEY, William Norton		76	*Died in Hollywood, CA (Do not confuse with Bill Bailey, d. 1978)*
•	1935	BAILLET, Georges		86	*Died in France*
•	1927	BAILY, George Donald		64	*Died in Los Angeles, CA*
•	1983	BAIM, Gary L.		36	*Heart attack (in Los Angeles, CA)*
•	1931	BAINBRIDGE, William		78	*Died in Los Angeles, CA*
•	1930	BAINES, Beulah		25	*Died in Banning, CA*
	1968	#+ BAINTER, Fay	★	76	*After a long illness (in Beverly Hills, CA)*
	1992	BAIR, Ron		62	*Cancer*
	1987	# BAIRD, Bill		82	*Died in New York, NY*
•	1967	# BAIRD, Cora		55	*Died in New York, NY*
	1971	BAIRD, Leah		88	*Anemia, after a long illness (in Hollywood, CA)*
	1947	BAIRD, Stewart		66	*Heart attack (in New York, NY)*
•	1966	BAKALEINIKOFF, Constantin		68	*Died in Hollywood, CA*
•	1960	BAKALEINIKOFF, Mischa		70	*Died in Los Angeles, CA*
•	1992	BAKER, Albie		75	*Heart attack (in Los Angeles, CA)*
	1966	#+ BAKER, Art		68	*Heart attack (in Los Angeles, CA)*
•	1983	BAKER, Barbara		49	*Heart attack (in New York, NY)*
	1957	BAKER, Belle		60	*Heart attack (in Beverly Hills, CA)*
	1994	# BAKER, Benny		87	*Died at MPTF Hospital in Woodland Hills, CA*
	1975	# BAKER, Bob		73	*Pulmonary embolism (in Prescott, AZ)*
•	1950	BAKER, C. Graham		61	*Died in Hollywood, CA*
	1988	# BAKER, Chet		59	*Fall from a 2nd floor window (in Amsterdam)*
•	1939	BAKER, Daniel E.		78	*Died in Englewood, NJ*
	1992	BAKER, Dorothy Helen		78	*Died in Los Angeles, CA*
	1968	# BAKER, Eddie		70	*Emphysema (in Hollywood, CA)*
•	1971	BAKER, Elsie		78	*Heart attack (in Hollywood, CA)*
•	1943	BAKER, Floyd		56	*Died in Hollywood, CA*
	1980	BAKER, Frank		86	*Died in Woodland Hills, CA*
	1993	BAKER, Howard		61	*Cancer (in Hale, Cheshire, England)*
	1986	BAKER, Hylda		78	*Died in Lancashire, England*
	1985	#+ BAKER, Kenny		72	*Heart attack (in Solvang, CA)*
	1982	BAKER, Lenny		37	*Cancer (in Hallandale, FL)*
	1963	BAKER, Phil		67	*After a long illness (in Copenhagen, Denmark)*
	1982	BAKER, Russell F.		66	*After a brief illness (in White Plains, NY)*
	1982	BAKER, Sam		56	*Heart attack at a restaurant (in Boston, MA)*
	1976	BAKER, Stanley		48	*Complications after a lung cancer operation (in Malaga, Spain)*
	1991	BAKER, Terence		52	*Died in London, England*
	1995	BAKER, Tommie		70	
	1986	BAKER-BERGEN, Stuart		40	*Complications from A.I.D.S. (in New Orleans, LA)*
	1993	BAKEWELL, Billy		85	*Leukemia (in Los Angeles, CA)*
	1983	+ BALANCHINE, George		79	*Creutzfeld-Jakob disease (in New York, NY)*
	1982	BALDWIN, Bill		69	*Cancer (in Hollywood, CA)*
	1977	BALDWIN, Walter		89	*Pneumonia (in Santa Monica, CA)*
	1990	BALFOUR, Katharine		69	

Deaths of Movie and Television Personalities — by Name

	YEAR	NAME		AGE	CAUSE and/or PLACE OF DEATH
	1990	BALIN, Ina		52	Pulmonary hypertension and cancer (in New Haven, CT)
•	1996	BALL, Deedie		79	Heart attack playing piano in a stage play (in San Luis Obispo, CA)
	1989	#+ BALL, Lucille		77	Ruptured aorta after heart surgery (in Los Angeles, CA)
	1955	#+ BALL, Suzan (Long)		22	Cancer after knee surgery while filming in Sumatra (in Beverly Hills)
	1991	BALL, William		60	Died in Los Angeles, CA
	1976	BALLARD, Flo		33	Cardiac arrest from pills and alcohol (in Detroit, MI)
	1988	BALLARD, Lucien		84	Bicycle accident (in Rancho Mirage, CA)
	1993	BALLARD, Lucinda	☆	87	Cancer
	1956	BALLIN, Hugo		76	Died in Santa Monica, CA
	1958	BALLIN, Mabel		73	Died in Santa Monica, CA
	1996	# BALSAM, Martin	★	76	Heart attack (found dead in a hotel room in Rome, Italy)
•	1981	BALTZELL, Deborah		25	Heart attack
	1969	# BANCROFT, Charles		57	Cancer (in Woodland Hills, CA)
	1956	+ BANCROFT, George	☆	74	After a brief illness (in Santa Monica, CA)
	1986	BANDY, Way		45	A.I.D.S.
	1990	BANEY, Joan Blazer		55	Brain tumor
	1948	# BANJAMIN, Gladys		?	
	1968	#+ BANKHEAD, Tallulah		66	Double pneumonia complicated by emphysema (in New York, NY)
	1952	BANKS, Leslie		61	Died in London, England
	1950	# BANKS, Monty		52	Heart attack (in Italy)
	1991	#+ BANKY, Vilma		90	After a 10-yr. illness (at a nursing home in Los Angeles, CA)
	1973	# BANNER, John		62	Intestinal hemorrhage (in Vienna, Austria)
	1961	BANNISTER, Harry		71	After a long illness (in New York, NY)
	1989	BANZHAF, Peter G.		57	Arrhythmia (in Milwaukee, WI)
	1990	BARA, Nina		66	Cancer (in Glendale, CA)
	1955	#+ BARA, Theda (Brabin)		69	Abdominal cancer (in Los Angeles, CA)
	1975	BARAGREY, John		57	Cerebral hemorrhage (in New York, NY)
•	1997	# BARBARA		67	Respiratory problems at the American Hospital in Paris, London
	1992	# BARBER, Red		84	Intestinal disorder
	1945	BARBIER, George		83	Heart attack (in Los Angeles, CA)
	1965	# BARBOUR, Dave		53	Hemorrhaged ulcer (in Malibu, CA)
	1978	BARCENA, Catalina		82	Died in Madrid, Spain
	1975	# BARCLAY, Don		83	Died in Palm Springs, CA
	1993	BARCLIFT, Edgar Nelson		76	After a lengthy illness (in Los Angeles, CA)
	1969	# BARCROFT, Roy		67	Cancer (in Woodland Hills, CA)
	1974	BARD, Ben		81	Cerebral thrombosis (in Los Angeles, CA)
	1977	BARDETTE, Trevor		75	Died in Los Angeles, CA
	1991	BAREFIELD, Eddie		81	Heart attack (in New York, NY)
	1975	BARHARD, Lawrence "Slim"		71	Apparent heart failure
	1989	# BARI, Lynn		73	After a long illness (in Santa Barbara, CA)
	1951	BARKER, Bradley		68	Died in New York, NY
	1990	BARKER, Eric L.		78	Died in Faverham, England
	1973	# BARKER, Lex		53	Heart attack (in New York, NY)
	1945	BARKER, Reginald		59	Following a heart attack (in Los Angeles, CA)
	1972	BARLOW, Howard		80	Heart attack
	1943	BARLOW, Reginald		76	Died in Hollywood, CA
	1953	BARNARD, Ivor		66	Died in London, England
•	1998	BARNES, Binnie		95	Natural causes in his Beverly Hills, CA home
	1949	BARNES, George		59	Following an operation for cancer (in Hollywood, CA)
•	1953	+ BARNES, George S.	★	60	Heart attack (Do not confuse with George Barnes, d. 1949)
•	1998	BARNES, Walter "Piggy"		79	Complications from diabetes in Calif.
	1965	# BARNET, Boris		63	Suicide (despondent over his faltering career) in Riga, Lettonia
	1991	BARNET, Charlie		77	Alzheimer's disease and pneumonia

Deaths of Movie and Television Personalities — by Name

YEAR	NAME		AGE	CAUSE and/or PLACE OF DEATH
1947	BARNETT, Chester A.		62	Pneumonia (in Jefferson City, MO)
1958	BARNETT, Griff		72	Heart condition and pneumonia (in Hollywood, CA)
1988	BARNETT, Nate		48	Heart attack (in New York, NY)
1988	BARNETT, Sanford H.	★	79	Following a stroke (in Oxnard, CA)
1977	# BARNETT, Vince		75	Heart ailment (in Encino, CA)
1985	BARNEY, Jay		72	Cancer (in Philadelphia, PA)
1980	# BARR, Leonard		77	After suffering a stroke
1985	BARR, Patrick		77	Died in London, England
1970	BARRAT, Robert		78	Died in Hollywood, CA
1994	BARRAULT, Jean-Louis		83	Died in his sleep of apparent heart attack (in Paris, France)
1977	BARRETT, Edith		64	Heart attack at a nursing home (in Albuquerque, NM)
1937	# BARRIE, James		77	Pneumonia complicated by heart trouble (in London, England)
1980	BARRIE, John		62	After a long illness (in York, England)
1978	#+ BARRIE, Wendy		65	After a long illness (in Englewood, NJ)
1964	+ BARRIER, Edgar		57	Heart attack (in Hollywood, CA)
1989	BARRIER, Ernestine		81	Died in Long Beach, CA
1962	+ BARRIS, Harry		57	Cancer (in Burbank, CA)
1965	BARRISCALE, Bessie		81	Died in Kentfield, CA
1993	BARRON, Lee		78	Respiratory failure (in Omaha, Nebraska)
1993	BARROW, Bernard		65	Lung cancer (at Lennox Hill Hospital in NY)
1945	BARROWS, Henry A.		69	Died in Los Angeles, CA
1925	BARROWS, James O.		72	Heart attack (in Hollywood, CA)
1980	#+ BARRY, Don "Red"		69	Suicide (gunshot) after a scuffle with his estranged wife (in H'wood)
1990	BARRY, J. J.		58	Bronchial complications (in Huntington Station, NY)
1984	BARRY, Jack		66	Heart attack while jogging (in New York, NY)
1989	BARRY, Joan		87	Died in Marbella, Spain
1998	BARRY, Jr., Philip		74	Cancer in Lenox Hill Hospital, New York City, NY
1931	# BARRY, Tom		47	Heart trouble (in Hollywood, CA)
1960	#+ BARRYMORE, Diana		38	Alcohol and sleeping pills overdose (in New York, NY)
1959	#+ BARRYMORE, Ethel	★	79	Heart condition (in Beverly Hills, CA)
1942	#+ BARRYMORE, John		60	Cardiac condition and other ailments (in Hollywood, CA)
1954	#+ BARRYMORE, Lionel	★	76	Heart attack (in Van Nuys, CA)
1988	+ BARSI, Judith		10	Murdered (shot by her father) in Los Angeles, CA
1991	BARTELL, Eddie		83	Aneurysm (in Los Angeles, CA)
1991	BARTELME, Joe		61	Cancer
1963	+ BARTHELMESS, Richard	☆	66	Throat cancer (in Southampton, NY)
1992	# BARTHOLOMEW, Freddie		67	Emphysema and heart failure (in Sarasota, FL)
1994	# BARTLETT, Richard		70	Complications of diabetes (in Havre de Grace, MD)
1990	BARTLETT, Scott		47	Complications from a kidney and liver transplant (in San Francisco)
1998	# BARTOK, Eva		69	After a long illness at St. Charles Hospital in London
1981	BARTON, Charles T.		79	After two heart attacks (in Burbank, CA)
1962	+ BARTON, James		72	Heart attack (in Mineola, NY)
1990	BARTON, Larry		80	Following a stroke (in Encino, CA)
1991	BARUCH, André		83	
1969	BARZELL, Wolfe		71	Heart attack (in Acapulco, Mexico)
1984	+ BASEHART, Richard		70	Stroke (in Los Angeles, CA)
1986	BASELEON, Michael		61	Died in Lenox, MA
1984	#+ BASIE, William "Count"		79	Pancreatic cancer (in Hollywood, FL)
1948	+ BASKETT, James		44	Heart ailment (in Los Angeles, CA)
1994	# BASQUETTE, Lina		87	Cancer (at her home in Wheeling, WV)
1987	# BASS, Alfie		66	Heart attack (in London, England)
1996	BASS, Saul	★	75	Non-Hodgkin's lymphoma (at Cedars-Sinai Med. Ctr. in L.A., CA)
1952	BASSERMAN, Albert	☆	86	Heart attack (in Zurich, Switzerland)

Deaths of Movie and Television Personalities — by Name

YEAR	NAME		AGE	CAUSE and/or PLACE OF DEATH
1918	BASSETT, Russell		71	Brain hemorrhage (in New York, NY)
1989	BASTIN, Charles A.		68	Cardiopulmonary arrest (in Los Angeles, CA)
1991	BATCHELOR, Joy		77	After a long illness (in London, England)
1985	BATE, Tom		85	Died in New York, NY
1969	#+ BATES, Barbara		43	Suicide (gas) in Denver, CO
1954	# BATES, Florence		65	Heart attack (in Burbank, CA)
1940	+ BATES, Granville		58	Heart attack (in Hollywood, CA)
1978	BATES, Michael		57	Cancer (in Cambridge, England)
1991	BATES, Ralph		50	Cancer (in London, England)
1990	# BATORS, Stiv		40	After being hit by a car (in Paris, France)
1993	BATTLE, Edwin Louis		33	Stroke (in Toronto, Canada)
1985	BAUER, Charita		62	Following a long illness (in New York, NY)
1987	BAUERSMITH, Paula		78	Cancer (in New York, NY)
1989	BAUM, Bobby		62	Following a brief illness (in Los Angeles, CA)
1960	# BAUM, Vicki		64	After a brief illness (in Hollywood, CA)
1943	BAUR, Harry		63	Died mysteriously after being interrogated by the Gestapo in Paris
1980	BAVA, Mario		66	Heart attack (in Rome, Italy)
1989	+ BAVIER, Frances "Aunt Bee"		86	Heart disease and cancer (in Siler City, NC)
1990	BAXLEY, Barbara		63	Apparent heart attack (in New York, NY)
1976	BAXTER, Alan		67	Cancer (in Woodland Hills, CA)
1985	BAXTER, Anne	★	62	Stroke (in New York, NY)
• 1996	BAXTER, Jane		87	Stomach cancer (in London, England)
1996	BAXTER, Les		73	Heart attack due to kidney failure (in Newport Beach, CA)
1951	+ BAXTER, Warner	★	58	Pneumonia after lobotomy to ease pain (in Beverly Hills, CA)
1973	+ BAYLIS, Peter		63	
1982	BAYNE, Beverly		87	Heart attack (in Scottsdale, AZ)
1989	BAZLEN, Brigid		44	Died in Seattle, WA
1996	BEACH, Scott		65	Died in San Francisco, CA
1990	BEAGLE, Edward H.		46	Natural causes (in Culver City, CA)
1934	BEAL, Frank		70	Died in Hollywood, CA
• 1997	BEAL, John		87	Complications from a stroke (in Santa Cruz, CA)
1969	BEAL, Royal		68	Cancer (in Keene, NH)
1973	BEAL, Scott		83	Cancer (in Hollywood, CA)
1989	BEAM, Alvin		61	Cardiopulmonary arrest (in New York, NY)
1981	+ BEARD, Matthew "Stymie" Jr.		56	Stroke (in Los Angeles, CA)
1980	BEATON, Cecil		78	
1965	+ BEATTY, Clyde		62	Cancer of the esophagus (in Ventura, CA)
1992	BEATTY, Robert		82	Pneumonia (in London, England)
1992	BEAUCHAMP, Clem		94	Natural causes
1970	+ BEAUDINE, William Sr.		78	Complications of uremic poisoning (in Canoga Park, CA)
1966	BEAUMONT, Harry	☆	78	Died in Santa Monica, CA
1982	BEAUMONT, Hugh		72	Apparent heart attack (in Munich, Germany)
1937	BEAUMONT, Lucy		64	Died in New York, NY
1962	BEAVERS, Louise "Beulah"		64	Heart attack (in Hollywood, CA)
• 1997	Bebe (Flipper)		40	Died at the Miami Sea-quarium
1986	BECHER, John C.		71	Cancer (in Hollywood, CA)
1993	BECK, John		83	Cancer (in Woodland Hills, CA)
1993	BECKER, Robert		47	Car accident (in Santa Clarita, CA)
1996	BECKER, Sandy		74	Heart attack
• 1996	BECKERMAN, Barry		53	Cancer (in Los Angeles, CA)
1968	# BECKETT, Scotty		38	Following a serious beating (in Hollywood, CA)
1980	BECKLEY, Tony		50	Cancer (in Los Angeles, CA)
1965	BECKWITH, Reginald		56	Died in Bourne End, England

• New entry.   # Original name (Pt. 7).   + Interment (Pt. 5).

☆ Oscar nominee,   ★ Oscar winner (Pt. 10)

Deaths of Movie and Television Personalities — by Name

YEAR	NAME	AGE	CAUSE and/or PLACE OF DEATH
1991	BEDDOE, Don	102	*Died in Texas*
• 1981	BEDFORD, Barbara	78	
1957	BEDOYA, Alfonso	53	*Died in Mexico City, Mexico*
1955	# BEECHER, Janet	70	*Heart attack (in Washington, CT)*
• 1998	BEECHMAN, Laurie	43	*Ovarian cancer at home in White Plains, NY*
1958	BEECROFT, Victor R.	71	*Died in Newport News, VA*
1994	BEERY, Noah Jr.	81	*After surgery for bleeding in his brain (nr. Tehachapi, CA)*
1946	+ BEERY, Noah Sr.	60	*Heart attack (in Los Angeles, CA)*
1949	+ BEERY, Wallace ★	64	*Heart attack (in Beverly Hills, CA)*
1949	BEERY, William C.	70	*Died in Beverly Hills, CA*
1995	BEGELMAN, David	73	*Apparent suicide (gunshot) in a Los Angeles hotel room*
1970	+ BEGLEY, Ed ★	69	*Heart attack (in Hollywood, CA)*
1931	#+ BEIDERBECKE, "Bix"	28	*Lobar pneumonia and edema of the brain (in Queens, NY)*
1988	BELASCO, Leon	86	*Complications after a stroke (in Orange, CA)*
1943	BELCHER, Charles M.	71	*Died in Hollywood, CA*
1969	BELGADO, Maria	63	*After a 3-week illness (in Hollywood, CA)*
• 1997	BELL, Bob	75	*Died in Lake San Marcos, CA*
1990	BELL, David	53	*After a long illness (Do not confuse with David Scott Bell, d. 1980)*
1980	BELL, David Scott	22	*Murdered (shot) in North Hollywood, CA*
1991	BELL, Hal	65	*After suffering a stroke (in Glendale, CA)*
1950	BELL, Henry "Hank"	58	*Following a heart attack (in Hollywood, CA)*
1973	BELL, James	81	
• 1997	BELL, Marion	78	*Died in Culver City, CA of natural causes*
1958	+ BELL, Monta	66	*After a lengthy illness (in Hollywood, CA)*
1936	BELL, Ralph W.	53	*Pneumonia (in San Francisco, CA)*
1962	#+ BELL, Rex	58	*Coronary occlusion (in Las Vegas, NV)*
1968	BELL, Rodney	52	
1933	BELL, Ruth	26	*Suicide (poison) in Los Angeles, CA*
1944	BELLAMY, George	78	
1990	BELLAMY, Madge	89	*Heart failure (in Ontario, Canada)*
1991	+ BELLAMY, Ralph ★	87	*Respiratory infection (in Santa Monica, CA)*
1993	BELLAVER, Harry	88	*Pneumonia (in a Nyack, NY, hospital)*
1987	BELLIN, Olga	54	*Cancer (in New York, NY)*
1994	BELLIN, Steve	43	*A.I.D.S. complications (in Los Angeles, CA)*
1975	BELLINI, Laura	73	
1953	BELMORE, Lionel	85	*Died in Woodland Hills, CA*
1982	+ BELUSHI, John	33	*After speedballing a mix of cocaine and heroin (in Hollywood, CA)*
1968	+ BENADARET, Bea	62	*Cancer (in Los Angeles, CA)*
1945	+ BENCHLEY, Robert ★	56	*Cerebral hemorrhage (in New York, NY)*
1969	# BENDER, Russell	59	*Died in Woodland Hills, CA*
1964	+ BENDIX, William ☆	58	*Lobar pneumonia and cancer (in Los Angeles, CA)*
1992	BENEDEK, Laslo	87	*After a lengthy hospital stay (in New York, NY)*
1968	BENEDICT, Brooks	63	
1951	BENEDICT, Kingsley	69	*Died in Woodland Hills, CA*
1984	BENEDICT, Richard	64	*Heart attack (in Studio City, CA)*
1982	BENET, Brenda	36	*Suicide (gunshot) in West Los Angeles, CA*
1955	BENGE, Wilson	80	*Died in Hollywood, CA*
1969	BENHAM, Harry	83	*Died in Sarasota, FL*
1990	BENNER, Richard	47	*A.I.D.S. (in Toronto, Canada)*
1987	BENNET, Spencer Gordon	94	*Died in Santa Monica, CA*
1958	BENNETT, Barbara	52	*Heart attack (in Montreal, Canada)*
1932	BENNETT, Belle	41	*Following a long illness (in Los Angeles, CA)*
1951	# BENNETT, Billie	75	*Cerebral hemorrhage (in Los Angeles, CA)*

Deaths of Movie and Television Personalities — by Name

YEAR	NAME	AGE	CAUSE and/or PLACE OF DEATH
1995	BENNETT, Charles	95	Natural causes (Do not confuse with Charles J. Bennett, d. 1943)
1943	BENNETT, Charles J.	51	Died in Hollywood (Do not confuse with Charles Bennett, d. 1995)
1965	+ BENNETT, Constance	59	Cerebral hemorrhage (in Walston, NJ)
1969	BENNETT, Enid	74	Heart attack (in Malibu, CA)
1950	BENNETT, Hugh	57	Coronary thrombosis (at his home in Malibu, CA)
1990	BENNETT, Jill	59	Suicide (in London, England)
1990	BENNETT, Joan	80	Cardiac arrest (in White Plains, NY)
1931	# BENNETT, Joe	35	Heart attack (in Amityville, NY)
1982	BENNETT, Marjorie	87	Cancer (in Hollywood, CA)
1991	BENNETT, Matt	52	Brain tumor (in Lexington, KY)
1950	BENNETT, Mickey	35	Heart attack (in Hollywood, CA)
1957	BENNETT, Ray	62	Heart attack (in Hollywood, CA)
1944	+ BENNETT, Richard	71	Heart attack (in Los Angeles, CA)
1974	#+ BENNY, Jack	80	Pancreatic cancer (in Holmby Hills, CA)
1995	# BENSON, Court	80	Heart failure (in Mount Kisco, NY)
1989	BENSON, Joe	73	Cancer (in Thousand Oaks, CA)
1984	BENSON, Lucille	69	Cancer (in Scottsboro, AL)
1965	# BENTLEY, Irene	61	Heart attack (in Palm Beach, FL)
1958	BENTLEY, Robert	63	Died in Benton Harbor, MI
1996	+ BERADINO, John	79	Cancer (at his home in Los Angeles, CA)
1944	BERESFORD, Harry	80	After a long illness (in Los Angeles, CA)
1966	+ BERG, Gertrude	66	Heart failure (in Beverly Hills, CA)
1978	#+ BERGEN, Edgar	75	Heart attack (in Las Vegas, NV)
1969	BERGER, Ludwig	77	Heart failure (in Schlagenbad, Germany)
1974	BERGERE, Ouida	88	Died in New York
1941	+ BERGERE, Ramona	39	Died in Glendale, CA
1990	BERGHOF, Herbert	81	Heart ailment (in New York, NY)
1917	BERGMAN, Henri	?	Died in New York (Do not confuse with Henry Bergman, d. 1946)
1946	BERGMAN, Henry	76	Heart attack (in Hollywood, CA) Do not confuse with Henri Bergman
1982	+ BERGMAN, Ingrid ★	67	Breast cancer (in London, England)
1986	BERGNER, Elizabeth ☆	85	After a long illness (in London, England)
1958	BERKE, William	54	Died in Hollywood, CA
1976	#+ BERKELEY, Busby	80	Heart attack (in Palm Springs, CA)
1992	BERKELEY, George	70	Heart attack (in Glendale, CA)
1951	# BERKES, John "Johnny"	54	Died in Hollywood, CA
1985	BERLE, Jack	80	After a long illness (in Woodland Hills, CA)
1965	BERLIN, Abby	58	Heart attack in his sleep (in Hollywood, CA)
1989	#+ BERLIN, Irving	101	Heart attack in his sleep (in New York, NY)
1987	BERMAN, Dr. Edgar	68	
1996	BERMAN, Pandro S.	91	Congestive heart failure (at his home in Beverly Hills, CA)
1932	+ BERN, Paul	42	Suicide? Murdered? (gunshot) in Beverly Hills, CA
1996	BERNAL, Ishmael	58	Heart attack (in Manila, Philippine Islands)
1996	BERNARD, Jason	58	Apparent heart attack while driving (in Hollywood, CA)
1986	+ BERNARDI, Herschel	62	Heart attack (in Los Angeles, CA)
1994	BERNARDI, Jack	85	Heart attack (in Los Angeles, CA)
1989	BERNAU, Christopher	49	Died in New York, NY
1981	BERNHARDT, Curtis (Kurt)	81	Apoplexy attack (in Pacific Palisades, CA)
1923	#+ BERNHARDT, Sarah	78	Uremic poisoning/weak heart (in Paris, France)
1943	+ BERNIE, Ben	52	After a lingering illness (in Hollywood, CA)
1990	+ BERNSTEIN, Leonard	72	Complications from lung cancer and emphysema (in New York, NY)
1995	BERNSTEIN, Rick	51	Pancreatic cancer (at his home in Los Angeles, CA)
1991	BERNSTEIN, Sam	80	Died in Los Angeles, CA
1993	BERRY, Eric	80	Cancer (in Laguna Beach, CA)

Deaths of Movie and Television Personalities — by Name

YEAR	NAME		AGE	CAUSE and/or PLACE OF DEATH
1993	BERTHELSON, Larry		60	Died in Santa Barbara, CA
1991	BERTI, Dehl		70	Heart attack (in Los Angeles, CA)
• 1996	BERTINO, Albert		84	Died in Los Angeles, CA
1990	BERTO, Juliet		42	Breast cancer (in Breur-Jouy, France))
1955	+ BERTRAND, Mary		73	Died in Woodland Hills, CA
• 1996	BESCH, Bibi		56	Cancer (in Los Angeles, CA)
• 1996	+ BESSELL, Ted		57	Aortic aneurysm (at UCLA Med Ctr., Los Angeles, CA)
1988	+ BESSER, Joe		80	Found dead of a heart attack in his home (in Los Angeles, CA)
1934	BESSERER, Eugenie		64	Heart attack while planning her golden wedding anniversary (in L.A.)
1974	# BEST, Edna		74	After a long illness (in Geneva, Switzerland)
• 1997	BEST, Marjorie O.	★	94	Died at her home in Toluca Lake, CA of heart failure
1962	BEST, Willie		45	Cancer (in Woodland Hills, CA)
1978	BETZ, Carl		56	Lung cancer (in Los Angeles, CA)
1938	# BETZ, Matthew		56	After a long illness (in Los Angeles, CA)
1957	# BEVAN, William "Billy"		60	Died in Escondido, CA
1963	# BEVANS, Clem		83	Died in Woodland Hills, CA
• 1997	BEXLEY, Donald T.		87	Died in Hampton, VA of heart and kidney failure
• 1997	BEYER, Edward		64	Following open heart surgery in Los Angeles, CA
1992	BEYERS, Bill		37	A.I.D.S. (in Los Angeles, CA)
1977	BIBERMAN, Abner		68	Died in San Diego, CA
1971	BIBERMAN, Herbert		71	Bone cancer (in New York, NY)
1967	+ BICKFORD, Charles	☆	78	Emphysema (in Los Angeles, CA)
1983	BIERNE, Michael		46	Died in Johnson City, NY
1967	# BIG TREE, Chief John		92	Died in Onondaga Indian Reservation, NY
1933	BIGGERS, Earl Derr		48	Heart attack (in Pasadena, CA)
• 1996	BILLIG, Steve S.		66	Killed by a robber/carjacker
1934	BILLINGS, George A.		63	Died in West Los Angeles, CA
1983	BILON, Michael "E. T."		35	Complications from pneumonia (in Youngstown, OH)
1991	BINDER, Maurice		72	Lung cancer (in London, England)
1947	+ BING, Herman		57	Suicide (gunshot) in Los Angeles, CA
1990	BINGO, Joe		65	Complications from a staph infection
1957	# BINNEY, Faire		57	Pneumonia (in Los Angeles, CA)
1990	BINNS, Edward		74	Heart attack (in Brewster, NY)
1918	BINNS, George H.		?	Double pneumonia induced by influenza (in Glendale, CA)
1978	BINYON, Claude		72	Died in Glendale, CA
1969	BIRCH, Paul		61	Died in Los Angeles, CA
1959	# BIRCH, Wyrley		75	
1982	BISHOP, Ronald		59	After a brief illness (in Manhattan, NY)
1993	BISHOP, Wesdon		60	Liver ailment (in Nashville, TN)
1959	BISHOP, William		42	Cancer (in Malibu, CA)
1993	BISSELL, Jennifer Raine		60	Heart ailment (in Los Angeles, CA)
1987	BISSELL, Patrick		30	Overdose of cocaine, codeine, methadone (in Hoboken, NJ)
1996	#+ BISSELL, Whit		86	Died in Woodland Hills, CA
1993	BITTNER, Jack		76	Heart attack (in New York)
1993	+ BIXBY, Bill		59	Prostate cancer (in his Century City, CA, home)
• 1998	BIXBY, Jerome		75	Complications after heart bypass surgery in San Bernardino, CA
1960	BJOERLING, Jussi		49	Heart attack (in Sweden)
1993	BJORLING, Rolf		64	
1986	# BJÖRNSTRAND, Gunnar		77	After a long illness (in Stockholm, Sweden)
1985	BLACK, Dorothy		85	Died in London, England
1938	BLACK, Maurice		46	After an illness of 2-days (in Hollywood, CA)
1995	BLACKBURN, Clarice		74	Cancer (in New York, NY)
1994	BLACKBURN, Royce		69	Cancer (in New Ipswich, NH)

• New entry.   # Original name (Pt. 7).   + Interment (Pt. 5).

187

☆ Oscar nominee, ★ Oscar winner (Pt. 10)

YEAR	NAME	AGE	CAUSE and/or PLACE OF DEATH
1937	BLACKFORD, Mary	23	Results of an automobile accident (in Santa Monica, CA)
1955	# BLACKLEY, Douglas	46	(See Robert Kent)
1973	BLACKMER, Sidney	79	Cancer (in New York, NY)
• 1997	BLACKSTONE, Harry	62	Pancreatic cancer at Loma Linda U. Medical Center in CA
1968	BLACKTON, James Stuart Jr.	71	
1941	# BLACKTON, James Stuart Sr.	66	Fractured skull after being struck by a car (in Hollywood, CA)
1994	BLACKTON, Jay S.	84	Heart attack (in Los Angeles, CA)
1973	# BLACKTON, Violet	60	
1974	BLACKWELL, Carlyle Jr.	61	After a 6-month illness (in Hollywood, CA)
1955	BLACKWELL, Carlyle Sr.	71	Died in Miami Beach, FL
1995	BLACKWELL, Charles	65	Stomach cancer (in New York, NY)
1996	BLACKWOOD, Caroline	64	Cancer (in New York)
1992	BLACKWOOD, Christian	50	Lung cancer (in New York, NY)
1971	BLAGOI, George	73	Died in Hollywood, CA
1995	BLAINE, Vivian	74	Congestive heart failure and pneumonia (at a NYC hospital)
1995	BLAIR, Frank	79	Died on Hilton Head Island, S.C.
• 1997	# BLAIR, Joan	93	After a brief illlness (in Culver City, CA)
1983	# BLAIR, Randy	32	Cardiac and respiratory arrest while playing a charity basketball game
1992	# BLAIRE, Sallie	68	Liver failure
1930	BLAISDELL, Charles "Big Bill"	56	Heart attack (in Hollywood, CA)
1931	BLAISDELL, William	?	Died in Brooklyn, NY
1966	# BLAKE, Al	89	Heart attack (in Los Angeles, CA)
1989	# BLAKE, Amanda "Miss Kitty"	60	A.I.D.S.-related complications (in Sacramento, CA)
1973	BLAKE, Anne	43	Died in Los Angeles, CA
1985	# BLAKE, Arthur	70	Heart attack (in Fort Lauderdale, FL)
1983	# BLAKE, Eubie	100	Died in Brooklyn, NY
1991	BLAKE, Katharine	62	Died in England
1982	BLAKE, Larry J.	68	Died in Los Angeles, CA
1969	BLAKE, Madge	68	Heart attack (in Pasadena, CA)
1978	# BLAKE, Marie	81	Died in Woodland Hills, CA
1987	# BLAKELY, Colin	56	Leukemia (in England)
1987	BLAKELY, Gene	66	Bone cancer (in Creston, IA)
1959	BLAKENEY, Olive	56	Died in Hollywood, CA
1990	BLAKEY, Art	71	Lung cancer
1989	#+ BLANC, Mel	81	Heart disease (in Los Angeles, CA)
1970	BLANCHARD, Mari	43	Cancer (in Woodland Hills, CA)
1962	+ BLANDICK, Clara	81	Suicide (took pills and pulled a plastic bag over her head)
1995	# BLANE, Ralph ☆	81	After battling Parkinson's disease (in Broken Arrow, OK)
• 1997	BLANE, Sally	87	Died in Palm Springs, CA
1987	BLASETTI, Alessandro	86	Heart attack (in Rome, Italy)
1995	BLASI, Silverio	73	Undisclosed causes (in Rome, Italy)
1991	BLATT, Edward A.	88	Heart attack (in Los Angeles, CA)
1992	BLATTNER, Robert	40	Airplane crash
1995	BLAUSTEIN, Julian	82	Cancer (in Beverly Hills, CA)
1943	BLEDSOE, Jules	44	Died in Hollywood, CA
1992	BLETCHER, Arline	99	Cardiac arrest in her sleep (in Los Angeles, CA)
1979	# BLETCHER, Billy	84	After a long illness (in Los Angeles, CA)
1989	BLEYER, Archie	79	Died in Sheboygan, WI
1989	BLIER, Bernard	73	Cancer (in Saint-Cloud, France)
1941	BLINN, Benjamin F.	68	Died in Hollywood, CA
1956	# BLINN, Genevieve	?	After a long illness (in Ross, CA)
1928	BLINN, Holbrook	56	After falling from a horse (in Crota, NY)
1980	BLISS, Lela	84	Died in Woodland Hills, CA

Deaths of Movie and Television Personalities — by Name

YEAR	NAME		AGE	CAUSE and/or PLACE OF DEATH
1982	+ BLOCH, Ray		79	Heart attack (in Miami, FL)
1990	BLOCK, Eva Sully		88	Heart failure
1972	+ BLOCKER, Dan		43	Pulmonary embolus (in Inglewood, CA)
1979	#+ BLONDELL, Joan	☆	73	Leukemia (in Santa Monica, CA)
1936	BLOOD, Adele		50	Suicide (gunshot) in Yonkers, NY
1974	# BLOOM, Bobby		27	Murdered or suicide? (shot) in West Hollywood, CA
1989	BLOOM, George		95	Died in Woodland Hills, CA
1959	BLORE, Eric		71	Heart attack (in Hollywood, CA)
1975	#+ BLUE, Ben		73	Died in Los Angeles, CA
1982	BLUE, David		41	Heart attack while jogging (in Greenwich Village, NY)
1963	+ BLUE, Monte		73	Coronary attack (in Milwaukee, WI)
1945	BLUM, Sammy		56	Heart attack (in Hollywood, CA)
1975	# BLYDEN, Larry		49	Automobile accident (while vacationing in Agadir, Morocco)
1938	BLYSTONE, John G.		45	Heart attack (in Beverly Hills, CA)
1956	# BLYSTONE, Stanley		61	Heart attack (in Hollywood, CA)
1972	# BLYTHE, Betty	★	78	Died in Woodland Hills, CA
1991	BOARDMAN, Eleanor		93	Died in Santa Barbara, CA
1918	# BOARDMAN, True		36	Following a nervous breakdown (in Norwalk, CA)
1971	# BOARDMAN, Virginia True		81	Heart attack (in Hollywood, CA)
1990	+ BOCK-LEADER, Deborah Lyn		38	
1972	BOESEN, William		47	
1957	#+ BOGART, Humphrey	★	57	Cancer of the esophagus (in Kolmby Hills, CA)
1912	BOGGS, Francis		?	Murdered (shot at the Selig film studio by a disgruntled employee)
1978	BOHN, Merritt F.		73	Pneumonia following a stroke (in Torrence, CA)
1949	BOHNEN, Roman		54	Heart attack (in Hollywood, CA)
1991	BOIS, Curt		90	Died in Berlin, Germany
1935	BOLAND, Eddie		51	Heart attack (in Santa Monica, CA)
1987	BOLAND, Joseph S.		83	Heart attack (in Newington, CT)
1965	+ BOLAND, Mary		83	Died in New York, NY
1937	BOLDER, Robert "Bobbie"		78	Died in Beverly Hills, CA
1977	# BOLES, Jim		63	Apparent heart attack (in Sherman Oaks, CA)
1969	+ BOLES, John		73	Heart attack (in San Angelo, TX)
1937	+ BOLESLAWSKI, Richard		47	Apparent heart attack (in Hollywood, CA)
1963	+ BOLEY, May		81	Cancer (in Hollywood, CA)
1987	#+ BOLGER, Ray		83	Gall bladder cancer (in Los Angeles, CA)
1969	# BOLGER, Robert "Bo"		32	Killed while skydiving (in Oceanside, CA)
1995	# BOLT, Robert	★	70	Heart problems (at home nr. Petersfield, Hampshire, Eng.)
1996	BOMBECK, Erma		69	Complications from a kidney transplant (in San Francisco, CA)
1969	BONANOVA, Fortunio		73	Cerebral hemorrhage (in Woodland Hills, CA)
1952	# BOND, Jack		52	Died in Hollywood, CA
1978	BOND, Johnny		63	Died in Burbank, CA
1991	BOND, Lilian		83	Heart attack (in Reseda, CA)
1972	BOND, Lyle		54	Heart attack (in San Diego, CA)
1989	BOND, Raleigh		54	Lymphoma (in Los Angeles, CA)
1982	BOND, Rudy		66	Heart attack (in Denver, CO)
1984	BOND, Sudie		56	Respiratory ailment (in New York, NY)
1960	+ BOND, Ward		57	Heart attack (in Dallas, TX)
1994	BONDARCHUK, Sergei		74	Cardio-vascular disease (in Moscow, Russia)
1981	# BONDI, Beulah	☆	88	Pulmonary complications (in Woodland Hills, CA)
1980	# BONELLI, Richard		91	Died in Los Angeles, CA
1980	+ BONHAM, John		32	Choked to death after drinking 40 shots of vodka
1950	BONIFACE, Symona		56	Died in Woodland Hills, CA
1953	BONN, Walter		64	Died in Hollywood, CA

• New entry.   # Original name (Pt. 7).   + Interment (Pt. 5).   189   ☆ Oscar nominee,   ★ Oscar winner (Pt. 10)

YEAR	NAME	AGE	CAUSE and/or PLACE OF DEATH
1986	BONNELL, Lee	67	Heart attack (in Santa Monica, CA)
1988	BONNER, Margerie	83	Following a stroke (in Los Angeles, CA)
1996	BONNER, Priscilla	97	Died in Los Angeles, CA
1984	BONNEY, Gail	83	Died in Los Angeles, CA
1998	BONO, Sonny	62	Skiing Accident at Heavenly Ski Resort in S. Lake Tahoe, CA
1978	BONOMO, Joe	75	Kidney ailment and pneumonia (in Hollywood, CA)
1969	BONUCCI, Alberto	49	Heart attack (in Rome, Italy)
1994	+ BOOKE, Sorrell "Boss Hogg"	64	Colon cancer (in Sherman Oaks, CA)
1987	BOOKER, Bernice Ingalls	91	
1981	+ BOONE, Richard	63	Throat cancer (in St. Augustine, FL)
1991	# BOOTH, Edwina	86	Heart failure (in Long Beach, CA)
1915	BOOTH, Elmer	32	Automobile accident (in Los Angeles, CA)
1971	BOOTH, Helen	?	Died in England
1994	BOOTH, Jim	48	Cancer (in Wellington, New Zealand)
1992	# BOOTH, Shirley ★	94	Cardiac arrest in her sleep (in Chatham, MA)
1937	BOOTH, Sydney Barton	60	Cerebral hemorrhage (in Stanford, CT)
1993	# BOOTS, Tubby	59	After a blood clot traveled to his lungs
1995	BORBONI, Paola	95	After suffering a stroke (in Bodio Lomnago, Varese)
1950	# BORDEAUX, Joe	56	Died in Hollywood, CA
1955	BORDEN, Eddie	67	Died in Hollywood, CA
1972	BORDEN, Eugene	75	
1947	#+ BORDEN, Olive	40	Stomach ailment (in Los Angeles, CA)
1953	+ BORDONI, Irene	59	Died in New York, NY
1973	BORG, Veda Ann	58	Cancer (in Hollywood, CA)
1939	BORGATO, Agostino	67	Heart attack (in Hollywood, CA)
1948	BORLAND, Barlowe	71	Died in Woodland Hills, CA
1994	BORLAND, Carroll	79	Pneumonia (in Arlington, VA)
1951	BOROS, Ferike	70	Died in Hollywood, CA
1995	BORSOS, Phillip	41	Leukemia (in Vancouver, B.C.)
1975	BORZAGE, Daniel "Danny"	78	Died in Los Angeles, CA
1962	+ BORZAGE, Frank ★	72	Cancer (in Hollywood, CA)
1991	# BOSTWICK, Dorothy Davis	?	Cardiac arrest
1976	+ BOSWELL, Connee	68	Stomach cancer (in New York, NY)
1958	BOSWELL, Martha (Lloyd)	53	After a long illness (in Peekskill, NY)
1988	# BOSWELL, Vet	77	Died in Peekskill, NY
1943	+ BOSWORTH, Hobart	76	Pneumonia (in Glendale, CA)
1992	BOTAS, Juan Suarez	34	A.I.D.S. (in New York, NY)
1943	BOTELER, Wade	52	Heart attack (in Hollywood, CA)
1991	BOTTCHER, Ron	50	A.I.D.S.
1977	BOUCHEY, Willis "Bill"	82	Died in Burbank, CA
1989	BOUISE, Jean	60	Lung cancer (in Lyon, France)
1985	BOULTING, John	71	Cancer (in Sunningdale, England)
1962	BOULTON, Matthew	69	Died in London, England
1978	BOURBON, Diana	77	Cancer (in Los Angeles, CA)
1956	BOURNE, Hazel (Imboden)	?	After a 2-yr. illness (in Kansas City)
1972	BOURNE, William Payne	36	Suicide (gunshot) in Hollywood, CA
1979	BOURNEUF, Philip	71	Found dead in his Santa Monica apartment
1991	BOVASSO, Julie	61	Cancer (in New York, NY)
1965	+ BOW, Clara	60	Heart attack while watching a movie on TV (in West Los Angeles)
1988	BOW, Simmy	65	Complications after a stroke (in Los Angeles, CA)
1991	BOWEN, Joe	56	Heart attack (in Los Angeles, CA)
1996	BOWEN, Roger	63	Heart attack (while vacationing in Marathon, FL)
1936	BOWERS, John	36	Suicide (walked into the surf off Malibu Beach)

Deaths of Movie and Television Personalities — by Name

YEAR	NAME		AGE	CAUSE and/or PLACE OF DEATH
1946	+ BOWES, Major Edward		71	*Died at his summer home in Rumson, NJ*
1947	BOWKER, Aldrich		71	*Arteriosclerosis (in Los Angeles, CA)*
1981	#+ BOWLING, Alice		54	*Skin disease*
1979	BOWMAN, Lee		64	*Heart attack (in Brentwood, CA)*
1991	BOX, Muriel		85	*Died in London, England*
1992	BOXER, Warren Neal		34	*A.I.D.S. (in Los Angeles, CA)*
1971	BOYD, Betty		63	
1973	#+ BOYD, Jim		77	
1977	#+ BOYD, Stephen		48	*Heart attack (in Northridge, CA)*
1972	+ BOYD, William "Hopalong Cassidy"		77	*Parkinson's disease and heart failure (in South Laguna Beach, CA)*
1978	+ BOYER, Charles	☆	78	*Suicide (overdose of Seconal 2 days after his wife died) in AZ*
1994	BOYLAN, John		82	*Lung cancer and pneumonia (at his home in Bellevue, Wash.)*
1984	BOYLAN, Mary		70	*After a long illness (in New York, NY)*
1966	# BOYNE, Sunny		83	*Died in Van Nuys, CA*
1993	BOZYK, Reizl		79	*Died at St. Vincent's Hosp. Med. Ctr., New York, NY*
1957	+ BRABIN, Charles J.		75	*Heart attack (in Santa Monica, CA)*
1942	BRACEY, Sidney		64	*After a brief illness (in Hollywood, CA)*
1936	BRADBURY, James Jr.		41	*Suicide (burns) in Los Angeles, CA*
1940	BRADBURY, James Sr.		83	*Died in Clifton, Staten Island, NY*
1990	BRADDELL, Maurice		89	*Died in England*
1993	BRADEN, Bernard		76	*Heart attack (in London, England)*
1973	BRADFORD, Lane		50	*Following a massive cerebral hemorrhage (in Honolulu, Hawaii)*
1971	BRADFORD, Marshall		74	*Heart attack (in Hollywood, CA)*
1916	BRADLEY, Amanda		?	*Automobile accident (in New York, NY)*
• 1997	BRADLEY, David		77	*Died at Cedars-Sinai Medical Center in Los Angeles, CA*
1947	BRADLEY, Harry C.		78	*Heart attack (in Hollywood, CA)*
1974	+ BRADLEY, Truman		69	*Died in Los Angeles, CA*
1973	BRADSHAW, Eunice		80	
1939	+ BRADY, Alice	★	46	*Cancer (in New York, NY)*
1942	BRADY, Edward J.		53	*Heart attack (in Hollywood, CA)*
1961	# BRADY, Fred		49	*Heart failure (in Los Angeles, CA)*
1972	BRADY, Pat		57	*Heart attack while visiting friends in Green Mountain Falls, CO*
1985	#+ BRADY, Scott		60	*Respiratory failure*
1993	BRAFA, Tony		72	*Heart attack (in Los Angeles, CA)*
• 1998	BRAGAGLIA, Carlo Ludovico		103	*Following surgery for broken hip in a Rome hospital*
1947	BRAHAM, Lionel		68	*Heart attack (in Hollywood, CA)*
1982	BRAHM, John		89	*Heart attack in his sleep at home (in Malibu, CA)*
1948	BRAITHWAITE, Lilian		75	*Heart attack (in London, England)*
• 1997	BRAM, Rose		92	*Natural causes in Los Angeles, CA*
1985	BRAMBELL, Wilfrid		72	*Cancer (in London, England)*
1992	+ BRAND, Neville		71	*Emphysema (in Sacramento, CA)*
1993	BRANDA, Richard		57	*Colon cancer (in Los Angeles, CA)*
1990	BRANDON, Henry		77	*Apparent heart attack (in Hollywood, CA)*
1983	BRANDON, Peter		57	*Apparent heart attack after jogging*
1993	# BRANDT, Buzz		60	*Heart failure*
1924	BRANDT, Charles		60	*Died in Philadelphia, PA*
1987	BRANNUM, Hugh		77	*Cancer (in East Stroudsburg, PA)*
1980	#+ BRASSELLE, Keefe		57	*Cirrhosis of the liver (in Downey, CA)*
1990	# BRAUER, Tiny		82	*Heart condition (in Sepulveda, CA)*
• 1997	BRAUN, Michael		60	*Heart failure (at his home in New York City)*
1990	BRAUNBERGER, Pierre		85	*Died in Paris, France*
1983	BRAY, Robert		65	*Heart attack (in Bishop, CA)*
1990	BRAY, Stephen		33	*Died in Dallas, TX*

YEAR	NAME		AGE	CAUSE and/or PLACE OF DEATH
1994	BRAZZI, Rossano		78	*Viral infection (in Rome, Italy)*
1973	BREAKSTON, George P.		53	*Died in Paris, France*
1943	BREAMER, Sylvia		45	*Died in New York, NY*
1946	BRECHER, Egon		66	*After a heart attack (in Hollywood, CA)*
1945	BRECKNER, Gary		49	*Automobile accident (in Redlands, CA)*
1977	BREEDEN, John Norton		73	*Died in San Francisco, CA*
1982	BREEDING, Larry		36	*Killed when his car struck a pole (in Hollywood, CA)*
1918	BREEN, Harry		?	*Drowned in Lake Elsinore*
1936	+ BREESE, Edmund		64	*Peritonitis (in New York, NY)*
1990	BREM, Beppo		84	*Heart failure (in Munich, Germany)*
1986	BREMEN, Lennie		71	*Died in Hollywood, CA*
1996	BREMER, Lucille		79	*Heart attack (in San Diego, CA)*
1964	# BRENDEL, El		74	*Heart attack (in Hollywood, CA)*
1953	BRENEMAN, Mark L.		54	*Heart attack*
1983	BRENGEL, George		69	*Cancer (in Cincinnati, OH)*
1974	+ BRENNAN, Walter	★	80	*Emphysema (in Oxnard, CA)*
1977	BRENNEN, Claire		43	*Cancer (in Hollywood, CA)*
1992	BRENNER, Glenn		44	*Cerebral hemorrhage from a malignant brain tumor*
1958	BRENON, Herbert	☆	78	*Died in Hollywood, CA*
1975	# BRENT, Evelyn		75	*Heart attack (in Los Angeles, CA)*
1979	# BRENT, George		75	*Emphysema (in Solana Beach, CA)*
1976	# BRENT, Romney		74	*Died in Mexico City, Mexico*
1995	BRESLO, Robert Paul		37	*Complications of A.I.D.S. (at New York Hosp. in Manhattan)*
1987	BRESSAN, Arthur J. Jr.		44	*A.I.D.S. (in New York, NY)*
1949	+ BRESSART, Felix		69	*Leukemia (in Los Angeles, CA)*
1969	BRETHERTON, Howard		73	*Died in San Diego, CA*
1995	BRETT, Jeremy		59	*Died in his sleep of heart failure (at his London home)*
1993	BRIAN, David		82	*Cancer and heart failure (in Sherman Oaks, CA)*
1951	#+ BRICE, Fanny		59	*Cerebral hemorrhage (in Beverly Hills, CA)*
1966	BRICE, Lew		72	*Heart attack (in Hollywood, CA)*
1957	BRIDGE, Alan "Al"		66	*Died in Los Angeles, CA*
1993	BRIDGES, James	☆	57	*Intestinal cancer (in Los Angeles, CA)*
• 1998	BRIDGES, Lloyd		85	*Natural causes in his Los Angeles, CA home*
1985	BRIGGS, Charles		53	*Died in Boswell, GA*
1986	BRIGGS, Donald P.		75	*Cancer (in Woodland Hills, CA)*
1995	BRIGGS, Fred		63	*Cancer (in Boston, MA)*
1952	BRIGGS, Harlan		72	*Cerebral thrombosis (in Woodland Hills, CA)*
1962	BRIGGS, Matt		79	
1990	BRIGGS, Richard R.		71	*After a short illness*
1992	BRIGHT, David		49	*Automobile accident*
1989	BRIGHT, John		81	*Stroke (in Panorama City, CA)*
1995	BRINEGAR, Paul		77	*Emphysema (in Los Angeles, CA)*
1950	BRISCOE, Lottie		69	*Died in New York, NY*
1958	# BRISSON, Carl		64	*Jaundice (in Copenhagen, Denmark)*
1984	+ BRISSON, Frederick		71	*After suffering a stroke (in New York, NY)*
1989	BRISTER, John Tyler		38	*A.I.D.S. (in Minneapolis, MN)*
1972	# BRITT, Elton		59	*Died in Connellsville, PA*
1980	# BRITTON, Barbara		59	*Cancer (in New York, NY)*
1948	# BRITTON, Milt		53	*Heart attack (in New York, NY)*
1974	+ BRITTON, Pamela		51	*Brain tumor (in Arlington Heights, IL)*
1988	BROADBENT, George		83	*Died in Laguna Hills, CA*
1993	BROCCO, Peter		89	*Heart attack (in Los Angeles, CA)*
• 1996	BROCCOLI, Albert R. "Cubby"		87	*A year after heart bypass surgery (at his home in Beverly Hills, CA)*

Deaths of Movie and Television Personalities — by Name

YEAR	NAME		AGE	CAUSE and/or PLACE OF DEATH
1995	BROCK, Alan		85	*Died at his home in Hastings-On-Hudson, NY*
1989	BROCK, Heinie		89	*Emphysema (in Canoga Park, CA)*
1991	BROCK, Stanley		59	*Heart attack (in Los Angeles, CA)*
1924	BROCK, Tony		?	*Auto accident while filming stunt in "The Great Circus Mystery" (NY)*
1995	BROCKETT, Don		65	*Apparent heart attack (in Shadyside, PA)*
1929	BROCKWELL, Gladys		35	*Peritonitis from car accident injuries (in Hollywood, CA)*
1959	BRODERICK, Helen		68	*Died in Beverly Hills, CA*
1982	+ BRODERICK, James		55	*Cancer (in New Haven, CT)*
1992	BRODIE, Steve		72	*Cancer (in West Hills, CA)*
• 1970	BRODINE, Norbert		72	
1990	BRODKIN, Herbert		77	*Aneurysm (in New York, NY)*
• 1996	BRODSKY, Stanley		45	*Complications from A.I.D.S. (in Los Angeles, CA)*
1986	BRODUS, Tex		81	*Massive stroke (in Woodland Hills, CA)*
1944	# BRODY, Ann		59	*Died in New York, NY*
1991	BROIDY, Steve		86	*Following a heart attack (in Los Angeles, CA)*
1975	BROKAW, Charles		77	*Died in New York City*
1951	BROMBERG, J. Edward		47	*Heart attack (in London, England)*
1971	# BRONSON, Betty		63	*Pneumonia (in Pasadena, CA)*
1994	BRONSTON, Samuel		85	*After a brief illness (in Sacramento, CA)*
1974	# BROOK, Clive		87	*Died in London, England*
1962	BROOK-JONES, Elwyn		51	*Died in Reading, England*
1951	BROOKE, Clifford		79	*After being struck by a car (in Santa Monica, CA)*
1963	# BROOKE, Ralph		43	*Died in Hollywood, CA*
1943	# BROOKE, Tyler		52	*Suicide (carbon monoxide in his car) in North Hollywood, CA*
1921	# BROOKE, Van Dyke		62	*Respiratory problems (in Saratoga Springs, NY)*
1986	BROOKE, Walter		71	*Emphysema*
1989	BROOKNER, Howard		34	*A.I.D.S.*
1992	# BROOKS, Beverley		63	*Stroke (in Nice, France)*
1977	# BROOKS, Geraldine		52	*Cancer (in Riverhead, NY)*
1944	BROOKS, Jesse Lee		50	*Heart attack (in Hollywood, CA)*
1985	+ BROOKS, Louise		78	*Heart attack*
1967	BROOKS, Pauline		54	*Cancer (in Glendale, CA)*
1995	BROOKS, Phyllis (Macdonald)		80	*Died in Cape Neddick, ME*
1992	BROOKS, Richard	☆	79	*Congestive heart failure (in Beverly Hills, CA)*
1960	#+ BROPHY, Ed		65	*Died in Los Angeles, CA*
1989	BROTHERSON, Eric		78	*Died in New York, NY*
1934	BROUGH, Mary		71	*Heart ailment (in London, England)*
1946	BROWER, Otto		50	*Heart failure (in Hollywood, CA)*
1988	BROWN, Alfredine "Alfie"		56	*Heart failure from kidney disease (in Baltimore, MD)*
1975	BROWN, Barbara		68	
1978	BROWN, Barry		27	*Suicide at home (self-inflicted wounds) in Silver Lake, CA*
1948	BROWN, Charles D.		60	*Heart ailment (in Hollywood, CA)*
1987	+ BROWN, Clarence	☆	97	*Kidney failure (in Santa Monica, CA)*
1956	BROWN, Clifford		25	*Automobile accident (in Paris, France)*
1992	# BROWN, Georgia		57	*Infection after surgery for an intestinal blockage (in London, England)*
1986	BROWN, Harry		69	*Emphysema (in Los Angeles) Do not confuse with Harry Joe Brown*
1972	BROWN, Harry Joe		78	*Apparent heart attack (Do not confuse with Harry Brown, d. 1986)*
1974	BROWN, Helen "Mina"		58	*Cancer (in Los Angeles, CA)*
1992	BROWN, James		72	*Lung cancer (in Woodland Hills, CA)*
1973	#+ BROWN, Joe E.		80	*Cancer (in Brentwood, CA)*
1957	+ BROWN, John H. "Digger O'Dell"		53	*Following a heart attack (in Los Angeles, CA)*
1974	+ BROWN, Johnny Mack		70	*Cardiac condition (in Woodland Hills, CA)*
1982	BROWN, Joseph		59	*Died in Mexico City, Mexico*

Deaths of Movie and Television Personalities — by Name

YEAR	NAME	AGE	CAUSE and/or PLACE OF DEATH
1990	BROWN, Karl	93	*Kidney failure (in Woodland Hills, CA)*
1992	# BROWN, Lucille E.	74	*After a long illness (in Buffalo, NY)*
• 1997	BROWN, Mary Jane	80	*Died of cancer at Gilchrist Center in Baltimore, MD*
1939	BROWN, Raymond "Ray"	58	*After a long illness (in Los Angeles, CA)*
1991	# BROWN, Reno	70	*Cancer (in Reno, NV)*
1993	BROWN, Richard "Dick"	68	*Cancer (in Los Angeles, CA)*
1963	BROWN, Rowland	62	*Heart attack (in Balboa Island, CA)*
1964	BROWN, Russ	72	*Died in Englewood, NJ*
1989	BROWN, Tally	64	*After suffering a stroke (in New York, NY)*
1996	BROWN, Terry James	48	*Lupus (in Los Angeles, CA)*
1990	# BROWN, Tom	75	*Cancer (in Woodland Hills, CA)*
1961	BROWN, Wally	57	*Died in Los Angeles, CA*
1991	+ BROWNE, Coral	77	*Breast cancer (in Los Angeles, CA)*
1965	BROWNE, Irene	72	*Cancer (in London, England)*
1976	BROWNE, Lucile	69	*Died in Los Angeles, CA*
1962	+ BROWNING, Tod	82	*Following an operation for cancer (in Hollywood, CA)*
1948	BROWNLEE, Frank	73	*Died in Los Angeles, CA*
1993	BROX, Lorayne (Hall)	94	*Unreported causes (in Los Angeles, CA)*
1988	BROX, Patricia (Gerstenzang)	?	
1974	BRUCE, Betty	54	*Cancer (in New York, NY)*
1976	BRUCE, David	60	*Heart attack (in Hollywood, CA)*
1946	BRUCE, Kate	87	
1966	#+ BRUCE, Lenny	40	*Overdose of narcotics (in Hollywood, CA)*
1953	#+ BRUCE, Nigel	58	*Heart attack (in Santa Monica, CA)*
1982	# BRUCE, Virginia	72	*Cancer (in Woodland Hills, CA)*
1982	BRUCK, Bella	70	*Heart attack (in Hollywood, CA)*
1987	BRUCK, Karl	81	*Cancer (in Los Angeles, CA)*
1955	+ BRUCKMAN, Clyde	60	*Suicide (gunshot) in Santa Monica, CA*
1967	BRUGGEMAN, George	62	*Died in North Hollywood, CA*
1989	BRUMER, Martin	28	*Automobile accident (in Los Angeles, CA)*
1939	BRUNDAGE, Mathilde	67	*Died in Long Beach, CA*
• 1997	BRUNER, Wallace	66	*Died of liver cancer in Indianapolis, Indian*
1943	BRUNETTE, Fritzi	53	*Died in Hollywood, CA*
1992	BRUNI, Peter	60	*Heart failure (in Hollywood, CA)*
1991	BRUNNER, Howard	51	*A.I.D.S. (in Marietta, GA)*
1993	BRUSATI, Franco	66	*Leukemia (in Rome, Italy)*
1959	BRYAN, Arthur Q.	60	*Died in Hollywood, CA*
1986	BRYAN, Ken	32	*An A.I.D.S.-related illness (in Walnut Creek, CA)*
1992	BRYAN, William Donald Sr.	74	*Cancer*
1948	BRYANT, Charles	67	*Died in Mount Kisco, NY*
1983	BRYANT, Hazel	44	*Heart attack*
1989	BRYANT, John	72	*Cancer (in Hollywood, CA)*
1988	BRYANT, Margot	90	*Died in Manchester, England*
1978	BRYANT, Marie	58	*Cancer (in Los Angeles, CA)*
1955	BRYANT, Nana	67	*Died in Hollywood, CA*
1985	#+ BRYNNER, Yul ★	65	*Lung cancer (in New York, NY)*
1986	# BUBBLES, John W.	84	*Cerebral hemorrhage (in Los Angeles, CA)*
1979	#+ BUCHANAN, Edgar	76	*After brain tumor surgery (in Palm Desert, CA)*
1957	BUCHANAN, Jack	66	*Spinal arthritis (in London, England)*
1975	BUCHMAN, Sidney	73	*Cancer (in Cannes, France)*
1989	BUCK, David	53	*Cancer (in England)*
1950	BUCK, Frank	62	*Pulmonary embolism (in Houston, TX)*
1973	+ BUCK, Pearl S.	80	*Pleurisy (in Vermont)*

Deaths of Movie and Television Personalities — by Name

YEAR	NAME		AGE	CAUSE and/or PLACE OF DEATH
1936	BUCKLER, Hugh		64	Drowned with his son in a car accident (in Malibu Lake, CA)
1936	BUCKLER, John (Jack)		30	Drowned with his father in a car accident (in Malibu Lake, CA)
1946	BUCQUET, Harold S.		54	Died in Hollywood, CA
1989	BUETEL, Jack		74	After a long illness (in Portland, OR)
1994	BULGAKOVA, Maya		62	Automobile accident (in Russia)
1984	BULL, Peter		72	Heart attack (in London, England)
1993	BULLOCK, Burdette III		38	Cancer
1985	BULOFF, Joseph		85	After a long illness (in Manhattan, NY)
1966	BUNKER, Ralph		77	Stroke (in New York, NY)
1990	BUNNAGE, Avis		67	After a brief illness (in London, England)
1915	+ BUNNY, John		51	Bright's disease (in Brooklyn, NY)
1935	BUNSTON, Herbert		61	Heart attack (in Los Angeles, CA)
1983	BUNUEL, Luis		83	Cirrhosis of the liver (in Mexico City, Mexico)
1982	+ BUONO, Victor		44	Heart attack (in Apple Valley, CA)
1993	BURDETT, Winston		79	After a long illness (in Rome, Italy)
1985	BURGE, James C.		41	Respiratory failure (pneumonia) in New York, NY
1961	BURGESS, Dorothy		54	Died in Los Angeles, CA
1937	+ BURGESS, Helen		19	Lobar pneumonia (in Beverly Hills, CA)
1992	BURKE, Alan		69	Emphysema
1970	#+ BURKE, Billie ☆		84	Died in Los Angeles, CA
1968	# BURKE, James		81	Heart attack (in Los Angeles, CA)
1980	BURKE, Kathleen		66	Died in Chicago, IL
1984	BURKE, Walter		75	Emphysema (in Woodland Hills, CA)
1989	BURKS, Rick		26	Automobile accident (in Hollywood, CA)
1993	BURKS, Stephen		36	Undisclosed causes (in Los Angeles, CA)
1949	BURNABY, Davy		68	Heart attack (in England)
1987	BURNELL, Peter		44	Died in Chicago, IL
1997	BURNETT, Murray		86	Died of congestive heart failur in New York City, NY
1967	#+ BURNETTE, Smiley		55	Leukemia (in Encino, CA)
1956	+ BURNS, Bob "Bazooka"		64	After a 3-yr. illness (at his home in San Fernando Valley, CA)
1971	BURNS, David		67	Heart attack (while performing on stage in Philadelphia, PA)
1996	#+ BURNS, George		100	Died at his home in Beverly Hills, CA
1948	BURNS, Harry		63	Following a heart attack (in Santa Monica, CA)
1967	BURNS, Paul E.		86	Heart attack (in Van Nuys, CA)
1990	BURNS, Stephan		35	A.I.D.S. (in Santa Barbara, CA)
1940	BURR, Eugene "Gene"		?	Pulmonary edema (in Los Angeles, CA)
1993	#+ BURR, Raymond		76	Cancer of the liver (in Sonoma County, CA)
1950	+ BURROUGHS, Edgar Rice		74	Heart ailment (in Encino, CA)
1985	# BURROWS, Abe		74	After a long illness (in New York, NY)
1990	BURRUD, Bill		65	Heart attack while swimming in the ocean (in Los Angeles, CA)
1939	BURTIS, James		46	Died in California
1933	BURTON, Clarence		51	Heart attack (in Hollywood, CA)
1957	BURTON, Frederick		86	After being hospitalized (in Woodland Hills, CA)
1955	BURTON, George H.		55	Heart attack (in Los Angeles, CA)
1984	BURTON, Margaret		60	Heart attack (in Hove, England)
1976	BURTON, Martin		71	Cancer (in Santa Monica, CA)
1984	#+ BURTON, Richard ☆		58	Cerebral hemorrhage (in Nyon, Switzerland)
1964	BURTON, Robert		69	Lung cancer (in Woodland Hills, CA)
1946	+ BUSCH, Mae		55	After a 5-mo. illness (in a San Fernando Valley sanitarium)
1991	BUSCH, Niven		88	Heart failure (in San Francisco, CA)
1969	BUSH, Pauline		83	Pneumonia (in San Diego, CA)
1991	BUSH, Warren V.		65	Cardiac arrest (in Los Angeles, CA)
1966	#+ BUSHMAN, Francis X.		83	Heart attack due to fall (in Pacific Palisades, CA)

Deaths of Movie and Television Personalities — by Name

YEAR	NAME		AGE	*CAUSE and/or PLACE OF DEATH*
1978	BUSHMAN, Ralph		74	*Respiratory failure (in Los Angeles, CA)*
1955	BUSSE, Henry		61	*Heart attack (in Memphis, TN)*
1965	# BUSTER, Budd		74	*Heart attack (in Los Angeles, CA)*
1994	BUTLER, Chris ☆		42	*A.I.D.S. complications (in Los Angeles, CA)*
1979	# BUTLER, David		84	*Ruptured diverticulum, peritonitis and heart failure (in Arcadia, CA)*
1929	# BUTLER, Fred J.		61	*Kidney trouble (in Los Angeles, CA)*
1993	BUTLER, John		74	*Cancer (in New York)*
1973	# BUTLER, Royal "Roy"		80	*Died in Desert Hot Springs, CA*
1991	BUTLER, Tim		36	*A.I.D.S.*
1989	BUTRICK, Merritt		29	*A.I.D.S. (in Los Angeles, CA)*
1988	BUTTERFIELD, Billy		71	*Died in North Palm Beach, FL*
1987	BUTTERFIELD, Paul		44	*Died in North Hollywood, CA*
1946	BUTTERWORTH, Charles		49	*Automobile accident (Suicide?) in Los Angeles, CA*
1979	BUTTERWORTH, Peter		60	*Heart attack (in Coventry, England)*
1994	BUTTRAM, Pat		78	*Kidney failure (at UCLA Medical Center)*
1985	# BUZZELL, Eddie		89	*Died in Los Angeles, CA*
• 1996	BYERS, Bill		69	*After a 10-yr. battle with cancer (at his home in Malibu, CA)*
1971	+ BYINGTON, Spring ☆		84	*Pneumonia (in Hollywood Hills, CA)*
1952	+ BYRD, Ralph M. "Dick Tracy"		43	*Heart attack (in Tarzana, CA)*
1993	BYRD, William D.		27	*Heart failure (in Inglewood, CA)*
1981	BYRNE, Eddie		70	*Died in Dublin, Ireland*
1943	+ BYRON, Arthur		71	*Heart attack after a long illness (in Hollywood, CA)*
1959	BYRON, Paul		68	*Heart attack (in San Diego, CA)*
	C			
1950	# CABANNE, William C.		62	*Heart attack (in Philadelphia, PA)*
1972	#+ CABOT, Bruce		68	*Lung and throat cancer (in Woodland Hills, CA)*
1977	+ CABOT, Sebastian		59	*Stroke (in Victoria, B.C., Canada)*
1986	CABOT, Susan		59	*Beaten to death in her home (in Los Angeles, CA)*
1967	CADELL, Jean		83	*Died in London, England*
1992	CADY, Frank		74	*Complications following heart surgery*
1986	CAESAR, Adolph		52	*Heart attack (in Los Angeles, CA)*
1986	+ CAGNEY, James ★		86	*Diabetes, heart and lung problems (in Stanfordville, NY)*
1984	CAGNEY, Jeanne		65	*Lung cancer (in Newport Beach, CA)*
1988	CAGNEY, William J.		82	*Heart attack (in Newport Beach, CA)*
1991	CAHAN, George M.		72	*Pneumonia (in Woodland Hills, CA)*
1963	CAHN, Edward L.		64	*Died in New York, NY*
1993	+ CAHN, Sammy ★		79	*Congestive heart failure (in Los Angeles, CA)*
1954	CAIN, Robert		67	*Died in New York, NY*
1964	CAINE, Georgia		88	*Died in Hollywood, CA*
1993	CAINE, Howard		67	*Heart attack (in Los Angeles, CA)*
1983	CAINE, Joan-Ellen		57	*Cancer (in Van Nuys, CA)*
• 1997	CAJAFA, Gianni		82	*Embolism in a Milan, Rome Hospital*
1986	CALDWELL, Don		51	*A.I.D.S. (in Sherman Oaks, CA)*
1956	#+ CALHERN, Louis ☆		61	*Heart attack, brought on by alcohol and medicine (in Tokyo, Japan)*
1966	# CALHOUN, Alice		65	*Cancer (in Los Angeles, CA)*
1995	CALLAGHAN, Jack		64	*Heart attack (in Charlotte, N.C.)*
1977	#+ CALLAS, Maria		53	*Heart attack (in Paris, France)*
1975	# CALLEIA, Joseph		78	*Died in Malta*
1993	CALLEN, Michael		38	*A.I.D.S. (in Los Angeles, CA)*
1992	# CALLENDER, Red		76	*Thyroid cancer (in Saugus, CA)*
1994	# CALLOWAY, Cab		86	*Pneumonia following a stroke (in Hockessin, DE)*
1990	CALLOWAY, Northern J.		41	*After being taken to a psychiatric hospital (in Westchester Cty, NY)*
1940	CALTHROP, Donald		52	*After a heart attack (in London, England)*

Deaths of Movie and Television Personalities — by Name

YEAR	NAME		AGE	CAUSE and/or PLACE OF DEATH
1982	CALVE, Olga		82	Bronchial pneumonia (in Santa Paula, CA)
1941	# CALVERT, E. H.		78	Died in Hollywood, CA
1975	#+ CALVIN, Henry		57	Died in Dallas, TX
1976	+ CAMBRIDGE, Godfrey		43	Heart attack (in Burbank, CA)
1955	CAMERON, Donald		66	Died in West Cornwall, CT
1987	CAMERON, Donald A.		61	Died in Philadelphia, PA
1983	# CAMERON, Rod		73	Cancer (in Gainesville, GA)
1958	# CAMERON, Rudolph "Rudy"		63	Cerebral hemorrhage (in Los Angeles, CA)
1996	CAMMELL, Donald		57	Suicide (gunshot) at his home in Hollywood Hills, CA
1929	CAMP, Sheppard		47	From injuries during filming of "Song of Flame" (in Hollywood, CA)
1988	CAMP, Wilson		74	Cancer (in Tarzana, CA)
1993	+ CAMPANELLA, Roy		71	After a heart attack (in Woodland Hills, CA)
1963	CAMPBELL, Alan		58	Died in West Hollywood, CA
1987	CAMPBELL, Archie		72	Renal and heart failure (in Knoxville, TN)
1996	CAMPBELL, Bruce Post		64	Massive cerebral hemorrhage (in La Crosse, WI)
1966	CAMPBELL, Colin		83	Cerebral hemorrhage (in Woodland Hills, CA)
1917	CAMPBELL, Eric		37	Automobile accident (in Los Angeles, CA)
1985	CAMPBELL, Kay		80	Injuries from automobile accident (in Greenwich, CT)
1995	CAMPBELL, Mifflin James		89	Cancer (in Indianapolis, IN)
1986	CAMPBELL, Muriel		75	Died in Warren, CT
1972	# CAMPBELL, Webster		79	Heart attack (in Liberty, KS)
1943	CAMPEAU, Frank		79	Died in Woodland Hills, CA
1974	CAMPEAU, June Harrison		48	Cirrhosis of the liver
1985	CAMPOS, Rafael		49	Stomach cancer (in Woodland Hills, CA)
1994	#+ CANDY, John		43	Heart attack in his sleep (on location in Durango, Mexico)
1973	CANE, Charles		74	Died in Woodland Hills, CA
1972	CANNON, Esma		76	
1983	#+ CANOVA, Judy		66	Cancer (in Hollywood, CA)
1993	# Cantinflas		81	Lung cancer (in Mexico City, Mexico)
1964	#+ CANTOR, Eddie		72	Heart attack (in Beverly Hills, CA)
1962	# CANTOR, Ida		70	Heart attack (in Beverly Hills, CA)
1991	CANTOR, Michael (Max)		32	Died in New York, NY
1986	+ CANTY, Marietta		80	
1986	# CANUTT, Yakima		90	Cardiac arrest in her sleep (in North Hollywood, CA)
1984	+ CAPOTE, Truman		59	Died in his sleep (drug and alcohol mix) in Bel Air, CA
1988	CAPPELLANO, Francesca (Piazza)		92	Pneumonia (in Los Angeles, CA)
1991	+ CAPRA, Frank	★	94	Died in his sleep of natural causes (in Los Angeles, CA)
1990	# Capucine		57	Suicide plunge from her 8th floor apartment (in Lausanne, Switz.)
1964	CARD, Kathryn		70	Heart attack (in Costa Mesa, CA)
1954	# CARDWELL, James		32	Suicide (gunshot) in Hollywood, CA
1995	CAREW, Peter		73	Heart attack (at his home in Paramus, NJ)
1937	CAREWE, Arthur Edmund		42	Suicide (gunshot) in Santa Monica, CA
1940	# CAREWE, Edwin		56	Heart attack (in Los Angeles, CA)
1955	# CAREWE, Ora		62	Died in Los Angeles, CA
1986	CAREY, Denis		77	Died in London, England
1947	+ CAREY, Harry	☆	67	Coronary thrombosis, attributed to a bee sting (in Brentwood, CA)
1994	+ CAREY, Macdonald		81	Cancer (in his Beverly Hills, CA, home)
1990	CAREY, Mary Jane		66	Died in Pasadena, CA
1988	CAREY, Olive (Golden)		92	Died in Carpinteria, CA
1994	+ CAREY, Timothy		65	After suffering a stroke (at Cedars-Sinai Med. Ctr. in L.A.)
1959	CARHART, Georgiana		93	
1985	CARIDEO, Eddie		72	Died in Hollywood, CA
1992	CARISI, Johnny		70	Complications from heart surgery

Deaths of Movie and Television Personalities — by Name

	YEAR	NAME	AGE	CAUSE and/or PLACE OF DEATH
	1990	CARISTI, Vincent	42	*Cancer (in New York, NY)*
	1941	# CARLE, Richard	69	*Heart attack (in North Hollywood, CA)*
	1979	CARLETON, Claire	66	*Cancer (in Northridge, CA)*
	1950	CARLETON, George	65	*Heart attack (in Hollywood, CA)*
	1947	+ CARLETON, William P.	73	*Automobile accident (in Hollywood, CA)*
•	1997	CARLIN, Brenda	57	*Liver cancer in Santa Monica, CA*
	1991	CARLIN, Thomas A.	62	*Heart failure (in New Rochelle, NY)*
	1993	CARLON, Fran	80	*Cancer (at her home in Manhattan, NY)*
•	1996	CARLSON, June	72	*Aneurysm (in San Clemente, CA)*
	1977	+ CARLSON, Richard	65	*Cerebral hemorrhage (in Encino, CA)*
•	1997	CARLSON, Violet	97	*Died of natural causes in Los Angeles, CA*
	1942	CARLYLE, Richard	63	*After a long illness (in San Fernando, CA)*
	1986	CARMEL, Roger	53	*Drug overdose (in Hollywood, CA)*
	1994	CARMET, Jean	73	*Heart failure (at his home in Sèvres, France)*
	1981	#+ CARMICHAEL, Hoagy	82	*Heart attack (in Rancho Mirage, CA)*
	1971	# CARMINATI, Tullio	77	*Stroke (in Rome, Italy)*
	1989	CARMINE, Michael	30	*Heart failure (in New York, NY)*
	1967	CARNERA, Primo	60	*Liver ailment (in Sequals, Italy)*
	1973	# CARNEY, Alan	63	*Heart attack (at the Hollywood Park racetrack)*
	1947	CARNEY, George	60	*Died in England*
	1992	CARNOVSKY, Morris	94	*Natural causes (in Easton, CT)*
	1982	CAROL, Sue		*(See Sue Carol Ladd)*
•	1997	CAROW, Heiner	67	*Cause undisclosed (in Berlin, Germany)*
	1990	CARPENTER, Charles	77	*Heart attack (in Oxnard, CA)*
	1983	+ CARPENTER, Karen	32	*Heart attack caused by anorexia nervosa (in Downey, CA)*
	1984	+ CARPENTER, Ken	84	*After a brief illness (in Santa Monica, CA)*
	1964	CARPENTER, Paul	42	*Heart attack (in London, England)*
•	1997	CARPENTER, Thelma	77	*Found dead of natural causes (in her Manhattan apartment, NY)*
•	1997	CARPENTER, Thelma	75	*Heart attack in her Manhattan, NY apartment*
•	1997	CARR, Carole	68	
	1991	CARR, Eric	41	*Complications from cancer (in Manhattan, NY)*
	1971	CARR, Georgia	46	*Stroke (in Los Angeles, CA)*
	1954	CARR, Geraldine	37	*Automobile accident (in Hollywood, CA)*
•	1997	CARR, Harriette "Hedy" Williams	91	*Heart failure at her son's home in New Orleans, LA*
	1957	# CARR, Jane	48	
	1979	# CARR, Joe "Fingers"	69	*Automobile accident (in Camarillo, CA)*
	1973	# CARR, Mary K.	98	*Died in Woodland Hills, CA*
	1944	#+ CARR, Nat	57	*Died in Hollywood, CA*
	1946	CARR, Trem	54	*After a heart attack (while vacationing in San Diego, CA)*
	1937	CARR, William (actor/director)	69	*Do not confuse with other actors of the same name (in Los Angeles)*
	1988	#+ CARRADINE, John	82	*Heart attack after strenuous stair climbing (in Milan, Italy)*
	1995	CARRARO, Tino	84	*Cardiac arrest (in a Milan, Italy, hospital)*
	1990	CARRERAS, James	81	*Cerebral hemorrhage (in Henley-on-Thames, England)*
	1961	+ CARRILLO, Leo	80	*Cancer (in Santa Monica, CA)*
	1992	# CARROL, Regina	49	*Cancer (in St. George, UT)*
	1994	CARROLL, Bob	76	*After a long illness (at a hospital in Manhasset, L.I., NY)*
	1992	CARROLL, David	41	*A.I.D.S. (in New York, NY)*
	1980	# CARROLL, Dee	54	*Following corrective surgery after a stroke (in Burbank, CA)*
	1948	+ CARROLL, Earl	56	*Airplane crash (in Mt. Carmel, PA)*
	1993	CARROLL, Janice	61	*Cancer (in San Fernando Valley, CA)*
	1979	+ CARROLL, John	71	*Leukemia (in Hollywood, CA)*
	1972	+ CARROLL, Leo G.	79	*Cancer (in Hollywood, CA)*
	1987	CARROLL, Madeleine	81	*Pancreatic cancer (in Marbella, Spain)*

Deaths of Movie and Television Personalities — by Name

YEAR	NAME		AGE	CAUSE and/or PLACE OF DEATH
1965	# CARROLL, Nancy	☆	59	Heart attack (in New York, NY)
1928	CARROLL, William A.		51	Cancer (in Glendale, CA)
1977	CARSON, Charles		91	Died in London, England
1963	+ CARSON, Jack		53	Stomach cancer (in Encino, CA)
1994	CARSON, Ken		79	Amyotrophic lateral sclerosis (in Jacksonville, FL)
1979	CARSON, Robert		69	Stroke (in Atascadero, CA)
1990	# CARSON, Sunset "Kit"		67	Heart attack (in Reno, NV)
1982	CARSON, Wayne		55	After a long illness (in New York, NY)
1946	CARTER, Ben F.		35	(Do not confuse with musician Benny Carter)
1992	CARTER, Beverly		51	Cancer
1994	CARTER, Janis		80	Heart attack (in Durham, NC)
1957	CARTER, Louise		82	After a 4-month illness (in Hollywood, CA)
1985	CARTER, Lynne		60	Pneumonia complicated by A.I.D.S. (in New York, NY)
1978	+ CARTER, Maybelle		69	Died in Nickelsville, VA
1950	CARTER, Monte		66	Died in San Francisco, CA
1994	CARTIER, Rudolph		90	Died in his sleep (in London, England)
1921	+ CARUSO, Enrico		48	Peritonitis (in Napoli, Italy)
1987	# CARUSO, Enrico Jr.		82	Following a heart attack (in Jacksonville, FL)
1956	# CARVER, Louise		86	Died in Hollywood, CA
1955	# CARVER, Lynn		45	Suicide (in New York, NY)
• 1996	CASARES, Maria		74	Died at her country home in La Vergnes, France
1992	CASCELLA, John J.		45	Found dead in his car of apparent heart attack
1986	CASE, Allen		51	Heart attack (in Truckee, CA)
• 1997	CASELOTTI, Adriana		80	Cancer (at her home in Los Angeles, CA.)
1945	# CASEY, Dolores		28	Died in Hollywood, CA
1965	CASEY, Kenneth		66	Heart ailment (in Newburgh, NY)
1995	CASH, Rosalind		56	Cancer (at Cedars-Sinai Med. Ctr. in Los Angeles, CA)
• 1990	CASON, Barbara		61	Heart attack
1961	CASON, John L.		43	Died in Los Angeles, CA
1987	CASPARY, Vera		87	Died in New York, NY
1954	CASS, Maurice		69	Heart attack (in Hollywood, CA)
1989	+ CASSAVETES, John	☆	59	Cirrhosis of the liver (in Los Angeles, CA)
1992	CASSELL, W. Barry Jr.		74	Pneumonia
1968	CASSIDY, Ed		74	Died in Woodland Hills, CA
1976	#+ CASSIDY, Jack		49	Burned to death (in West Hollywood, CA)
1979	+ CASSIDY, Ted "Lurch"		46	During heart surgery (in Los Angeles, CA)
1991	CASSIDY, Tom		41	A.I.D.S.
1990	CASSON, Ann		74	Died in London, England
1988	CASTELLANO, Richard	☆	55	Heart failure (in North Bergen, NJ)
1963	CASTIGLIONI, Iphigene		62	After a long illness (in Hollywood, CA)
1966	CASTLE, Don		47	Found dead from overdose of medication (in Hollywood, CA)
1969	#+ CASTLE, Irene		75	Heart attack (in Eureka Springs, AR)
1990	CASTLE, Lee		75	Heart attack
1959	CASTLE, Lillian		94	After a brief illness (in Los Angeles, CA)
1968	#+ CASTLE, Nick		58	Heart attack (in Los Angeles, CA)
1973	CASTLE, Peggy		46	Cirrhosis of the liver and heart condition (in Hollywood, CA)
1918	+ CASTLE, Vernon		30	Airplane crash (in Houston, TX)
1977	# CASTLE, William		63	Heart attack (in Beverly Hills, CA)
1981	CASTLETON, Barbara		85	Died in Boca Raton, FL
1990	CATHEY, Dalton		44	A.I.D.S. (in Los Angeles, CA)
1960	CATLETT, Walter		71	Stroke (in Calabasas, CA)
1992	CATTANI, Rico		64	Respiratory disease from a chronic heart condition (in Los Angeles)
1991	+ CAULFIELD, Joan		69	After surgery for cancer (in Los Angeles, CA)

Deaths of Movie and Television Personalities — by Name

	YEAR	NAME		AGE	CAUSE and/or PLACE OF DEATH
	1982	CAVALCANTI, Alberto		85	*After a long illness (in Paris, France)*
	1989	CAVALLARO, Carmen		76	*Cancer (in Columbus, OH)*
	1964	CAVANAGH, Paul		68	*Heart attack (in London, England)*
	1950	CAVANAUGH, Hobart		53	*Following major surgery (in Woodland Hills, CA)*
	1963	CAVANNA, Elise		61	*Cancer (in Hollywood, CA)*
	1941	CAVEN, Allan		60	*Died in Hollywood, CA*
	1962	CAVENDER, Glen W.		77	*After a long illness (in Hollywood, CA)*
	1960	CAVENDISH, David		69	*Heart attack (in Hollywood, CA)*
	1976	CAVENDISH, June		?	*Leukemia (in Los Angeles, CA)*
	1962	# CAVENS, Fred		79	*Uremia (in Woodland Hills, CA)*
	1949	CAWTHORNE, Joseph		81	*Stroke (in Beverly Hills, CA)*
	1989	CAYATTE, André		80	*Died in Paris, France*
	1978	CAZALE, John		42	*Cancer (in New York, NY)*
	1940	CECIL, Edward		52	*Died in Los Angeles, CA*
	1971	+ CERF, Bennett		73	*Heart attack*
	1974	CERVI, Gino		72	*Pulmonary stroke (in Castiglione Bella Pescaia, Italy)*
	1991	CHABEAU, Ray Edgar		49	
	1940	CHADWICK, Helene		42	*From injuries after a fall (in Los Angeles, CA)*
	1990	CHAFFEY, Don		72	*Heart disease (in Kawau Island, New Zealand)*
	1992	CHALIAPIN, Feodor Jr.		87	*After a brief illness (in Rome, Italy)*
	1938	+ CHALIAPIN, Feodor Sr. "Felix"		65	*Uremia (in Paris, France)*
•	1998	CHALKER, Harold "Curly"		66	*Cancer related brain tumor*
	1989	CHALLEE, William		84	*Alzheimer's disease (in Woodland Hills, CA)*
	1966	CHALMERS, Thomas		82	*Died in Greenwich, CT*
•	1997	CHAMBERLAIN, Jennifer Holt		76	*Cancer at home in Dorset, England*
	1984	CHAMBERLIN, Howland		73	*Complications of lung and liver disease (in Los Angeles, CA)*
	1917	CHAMBERLIN, Riley C.		62	*Died in New Rochelle, NY*
	1958	CHAMBERS, J. Wheaton		69	*After a brief illness (in Hollywood, CA)*
	1991	CHAMBERS, Kathy L.		41	*Cancer*
	1980	CHAMPION, Gower		60	*Waldenstrom's disease (in New York, NY)*
	1990	# CHAMPLIN, Irene		59	*After a long illness (in Greenwich, CT)*
•	1996	CHANCELLOR, John		68	*After a long bout with stomach cancer (at his home in Princeton, NJ)*
	1965	CHANDET, Louis W.		81	*After an illness of several years (in Burbank, CA)*
	1988	# CHANDLER, Chick		83	*Died in Laguna Beach, CA*
	1948	CHANDLER, Eddie		54	*Do not confuse with actor Edward S. Chandler (in Los Angeles, CA)*
	1985	CHANDLER, George L.		82	*Alzheimer's disease (in Hollywood, CA)*
	1965	+ CHANDLER, Helen		59	*After surgery for a bleeding ulcer (in Hollywood, CA)*
	1994	# CHANDLER, Janet		78	*Heart failure after a stroke (at UCLA Med. Ctr., CA)*
	1961	#+ CHANDLER, Jeff	☆	42	*Blood poisoning after spinal surgery (in Culver City, CA)*
	1988	CHANDLER, Jim		65	*Lung cancer (in San Francisco, CA)*
	1979	CHANDLER, Joan		55	*Died in New York, NY*
	1972	# CHANDLER, Lane		73	*Cardiovascular disease (in Hollywood, CA)*
	1989	CHANDLER, Marjorie Grossel		71	*Cancer (in Santa Monica, CA)*
•	1996	CHANDLER, Martin Pat "Patsy"		84	*Aneurysm (at his home in East Meadow, L.I., NY)*
	1967	# CHANEY, Frances		78	*Cerebral hemorrhage (in Sierra Madre, CA)*
	1973	# CHANEY, Lon Jr.		67	*Heart attack, throat cancer, liver ailment (in San Clemente, CA)*
	1930	#+ CHANEY, Lon Sr.		47	*Lung and throat cancer (in Los Angeles, CA)*
	1936	# CHANEY, Norman "Chubby"		18	*After an operation for a glandular ailment (in Baltimore, MD)*
•	1981	CHAPIN, Harry		38	*Automobile accident*
	1968	CHAPLIN, Charles Jr.		42	*Blood clot (in Hollywood, CA)*
	1977	#+ CHAPLIN, Charlie	☆	88	*Bronchitis (in Corsier-sur-vevey, Switzerland)*
	1991	CHAPLIN, Oona		66	*Following cancer surgery (in Corsier-sur-Vevey, Switzerland)*
•	1997	CHAPLIN, Saul	★	85	*At Cedars-Sinai Medical Ctr., Los Angeles, CA after a fall*

• New entry. # Original name (Pt. 7). + Interment (Pt. 5).　　　　200　　　　☆ Oscar nominee, ★ Oscar winner (Pt. 10)

Deaths of Movie and Television Personalities — by Name

YEAR	NAME	AGE	CAUSE and/or PLACE OF DEATH
1965	# CHAPLIN, Sydney	80	*After a long illness (in Nice, France)*
1991	CHAPMAN, Ben	83	*Heart and kidney failure (in Orange, CA)*
1977	CHAPMAN, Edward	76	*Heart attack (in Brighton, England)*
1948	CHAPMAN, Edythe	85	*Heart attack (in Glendale, CA)*
1989	CHAPMAN, Graham	48	*Spinal cancer (in Maidstone, England)*
1986	CHAPMAN, Ted	63	*Natural causes (in Studio City, CA)*
1987	CHARLES, Anthony	42	*Heart attack (in Burbank, CA)*
1979	+ CHARLES, Lewis	73	*Lung cancer (in Los Angeles, CA)*
1990	CHARLESON, Ian	40	*A.I.D.S. (Septicemia) in London, England*
1961	CHARLESON, Mary	68	*Died in Woodland Hills, CA*
1956	CHARLOT, Andre	73	*Complications after cancer surgery (in Woodland Hills, CA)*
1943	+ CHARTERS, Spencer	68	*Suicide (pills and carbon monoxide) in Hollywood, CA*
1940	#+ CHASE, Charley	47	*Heart attack (in Hollywood, CA)*
1937	# CHASE, Colin	50	*Paralysis attack (in Los Angeles, CA)*
1978	CHASE, Ilka	72	*Internal hemorrhage from a fall (in Mexico City, Mexico)*
1961	+ CHATTERTON, Ruth ☆	67	*After a brief illness (in Norwalk, CT)*
1966	CHATTON, Sydney	48	*Coronary attack (in Berkeley, CA)*
1934	CHAUTARD, Emile	69	*Organic trouble (in Westwood, CA)*
1981	#+ CHAYEFSKY, Paddy	58	*Cancer (in Manhattan, NY)*
1971	# CHEATHAM, Jack	76	*Heart failure (in La Mirada, CA)*
1993	CHECCHI, Robert J.	67	*After suffering a stroke (in Los Angeles, CA)*
1983	CHECCO, Jessie	85	*Died in Sherman Oaks, CA*
1975	# CHEFEE, Jack	81	*Died in Hollywood, CA*
1955	CHEKHOV, Michael ☆	64	*Died in Beverly Hills, CA*
1982	CHEN, Renee Shinn	6	*Killed by helicopter rotor while filming*
1990	CHENAL, Pierre	86	*Heart attack (in La-Garenne-Columbe, France)*
1995	CHERKASSKY, Shura	84	*Respiratory complications (in London, England)*
1995	CHEROT, Lewis	26	*Automobile accident (in Los Angeles, CA)*
1989	CHERRILL, Christine	71	*Died in Kensington, England*
• 1996	CHERRILL, Virginia (Martini)	88	*Unreported causes (at a hospital in Santa Barbara, CA)*
1959	# CHESEBRO, George	70	*Arteriosclerosis (in Hermosa Beach, CA)*
1968	+ CHESHIRE, Harry "Pappy"	76	
1949	CHESNEY, Arthur	67	*Died in London, England*
1972	#+ CHEVALIER, Maurice ☆	83	*Heart attack after kidney surgery (in Paris, France)*
1989	CHIARI, Mario	79	*After a long illness (in Rome, Italy)*
1991	CHIARI, Walter	67	*Heart attack (in Milan, Italy)*
1964	CHILDERS, Naomi	70	*After a long illness (in Hollywood, CA)*
1986	CHILDRESS, Alvin	78	*Parkinson's disease, diabetes, pneumonia (in Inglewood, CA)*
1989	CHING, William	75	*Congestive heart failure (in Tustin, CA)*
1977	CHITTY, Erik	70	*Died in London, England*
1988	CHODOROV, Edward	84	*Died in New York, NY*
1982	CHRISTI, Frank	52	*Shot to death at his home (in Hollywood Hills, CA)*
1992	CHRISTI, Panos	54	*Complications from A.I.D.S. (in Los Angeles, CA)*
1983	CHRISTIAN, Robert	42	*Cancer (in New York, NY)*
1994	# Christian-Jaque	89	*Heart attack (in Boulogne-Billancourt, France)*
1951	+ CHRISTIANS, Mady	51	*Cerebral hemorrhage (in South Norwalk, CT)*
1951	CHRISTIE, Al	69	*Heart attack (in Beverly Hills, CA)*
1989	CHRISTIE, Audrey	79	*Emphysema (in West Hollywood, CA)*
• 1996	CHRISTINE, Virginia	76	*Heart complications at her home (in Los Angeles, CA)*
1991	CHRISTMAS, Jason	49	*Killed outside a NY comedy club by robbers*
• 1998	CHRISTOPHER, Keith	40	*From complications of AIDS*
1983	CHRISTOPHER, Richard	37	*Cancer (in New York, NY)*
1987	CHRISTY, Ann	82	*Heart attack (in Vernon, TX)*

Deaths of Movie and Television Personalities — by Name

YEAR	NAME		AGE	CAUSE and/or PLACE OF DEATH
1992	CHRISTY, Howard		79	After a long illness (in Oak View, CA)
1949	CHRISTY, Ivan		61	After a heart attack (in Burbank, CA)
1990	# CHRISTY, June		64	Complications of kidney failure (in Sherman Oaks, CA)
1962	CHRISTY, Ken		67	Died in Hollywood, CA
1990	# CHRYSIS, International		38	Cancer (in New York, NY)
• 1993	CHURCH, Sandie		32	A.I.D.S.
1940	CHURCHILL, Berton		63	Uremic poisoning (in New York, NY)
1991	CHURCHILL, Donald		60	Apparent heart attack (in Fuengirola, Spain)
1982	CHURCHILL, Sarah		67	Cirrhosis of the liver (in London, England)
1969	CIANNELLI, Eduardo		81	Cancer (in Rome, Italy)
1993	CINCOTTA, Carmine		41	Hodgkin's disease (in New York)
1967	CIOLLI, Augusta		65	Heart attack (in New York, NY)
1989	CIRO, Steve		46	Died in New York, NY
1981	# CLAIR, René		82	Cardiac arrest in her sleep (in Neuilly-sur-Seine, France)
1928	CLAIRE, Gertrude		75	Died in Los Angeles, CA
1974	CLAIRE, Helen		67	Died in Birmingham, AL
1985	# CLAIRE, Ina		95	Lingering effects of a stroke (in San Francisco, CA)
1990	CLAIRE, Ludi		70	After a long illness
1990	CLANCY, Tom		67	Stomach cancer (in Cork, Ireland)
1970	CLARE, Mary		76	Died in London, England
1955	# CLARENCE, O. B.		85	Died in Hove, England
1960	#+ CLARK, Bobby		72	Heart attack (in New York, NY)
1949	#+ CLARK, Buddy		38	Airplane crash (in Beverly Hills, CA)
1953	CLARK, Cliff		59	Heart attack (in Hollywood, CA)
1990	CLARK, Dee		52	
1989	CLARK, Dort		71	Diabetes and cancer (in Wellington, KS)
1954	CLARK, Eddie		75	Heart attack (in Hollywood, CA)
1968	#+ CLARK, Fred		54	Liver ailment (in Santa Monica, CA)
• 1996	# CLARK, Garrett Cameron		33	Automobile accident (in Los Angeles, CA)
1938	CLARK, Harvey		52	Following a heart attack (in Hollywood, CA)
1967	CLARK, Ivan-John		?	
1947	CLARK, John J.		69	Died in Hollywood, CA
1967	CLARK, Johnny		50	Heart attack (in Hollywood, CA)
1983	CLARK, Kendall		70	Cancer (in Vero Beach, FL)
• 1996	CLARK, Lillian		70	Cancer (at her home in New York, NY)
1986	CLARK, Mamo		72	Cancer (in Panorama City, CA)
1940	+ CLARK, Marguerite		53	Pneumonia after a cerebral hemorrhage (in New York, NY)
1978	CLARK, Roger W.		69	Stroke (in Los Angeles, CA)
1961	CLARK, Wallis		71	Died in Los Angeles, CA
1972	CLARKE, Gordon B.		65	After a heart attack (in New York, NY)
1992	# CLARKE, Mae		81	Cancer (in Woodland Hills, CA)
1985	CLARKE, Philip Norman		81	Died in Dothan, AL
1987	CLARKE, Raymond		47	A.I.D.S. (in Toronto, Canada)
1957	# CLARKE, Robert "Buddy"		61	
• 1997	CLARKE, Shirley		78	In Boston, MA after a long illness
1989	CLARKE, T. E. B.		81	Died in Surrey, England
1959	# CLARKE-SMITH, D. A.		71	Died in Withyam, England
1931	CLARY, Charles		58	Died in Los Angeles, CA
• 1997	# CLASTER, Nancy "Miss Nancy"		82	Colon cancer (at her Cross Keys condominium in Baltimore, MD)
1992	CLATWORTHY, William	☆	80	After a brief illness
1994	CLAVELL, James		69	Stroke after suffering from cancer (at home in Vevey, Switzerland)
1991	# CLAYTON, Buck		80	Died in New York, NY
1966	CLAYTON, Ethel		82	Died in Oxnard, CA

Deaths of Movie and Television Personalities — by Name

YEAR	NAME		AGE	CAUSE and/or PLACE OF DEATH
1950	CLAYTON, Gilbert		89	Heart attack (in Los Angeles, CA)
1995	CLAYTON, Jack		73	After a short illness (at a hosp. in Slough, Berkshire, Eng.)
1983	CLAYTON, Jan		66	Cancer (in West Hollywood, CA)
1950	# CLAYTON, Marguerite B.		50	Injuries from an automobile accident (in Los Angeles, CA)
1993	CLAYWORTH, June		80	Lymphoma (in Calabasas, CA)
1990	CLEMENT, Marc R.		39	Automobile accident (in Atlanta, GA)
1996	CLEMENT, Rene	★	82	Following heart trouble (in Monte Carlo, France)
1972	#+ CLEMENTE, Roberto		38	Airplane crash (in San Juan, Puerto Rico)
1950	# CLEMENTO, Steve		64	Cerebral hemorrhage (in Los Angeles, CA)
1988	CLEMENTS, John		77	
1981	CLEMENTS, Stanley		55	Emphysema (in Pacoima, CA)
1957	+ CLEVELAND, George		74	Heart attack (in Burbank, CA)
1991	CLEVELAND, James		59	Respiratory problems and heart failure
1988	CLEWES, Howard		75	
1956	# CLIFFORD, Jack		76	Died in New York, NY
1962	CLIFFORD, Kathleen		74	After a long illness (in Hollywood, CA)
1961	CLIFT, Denison		76	Heart ailment (in Hollywood, CA)
1966	+ CLIFT, Montgomery	☆	45	Occlusive coronary artery disease (in New York, NY)
1949	+ CLIFTON, Elmer		59	Cerebral hemorrhage (in Hollywood, CA)
1922	# CLIFTON, Emma Bell		47	Heart attack (in Los Angeles, CA)
1961	# CLINE, Eddie		68	Died in Hollywood, CA
1963	#+ CLINE, Patsy		30	Airplane crash (in a forest near the Tennessee River)
1937	#+ CLIVE, Colin		37	Tuberculosis complicated by alcoholism (in Los Angeles, CA)
1940	# CLIVE, E. E.		60	Heart attack (in North Hollywood, CA)
1960	# CLIVE, Henry		77	Lung cancer (in Hollywood, CA)
1990	CLOCHE, Maurice		82	Parkinson's disease (in Bordeaux, France)
1992	CLORE, Leon		73	Cancer (in London, England)
1997	CLOUSE, Robert		68	Complications of kidney failure (at his home in Ashland, OR)
1977	CLOUZOT, Henri Georges		70	Heart attack (in Paris, France)
1956	CLUTE, Chester		64	Heart attack (in Calabasas, CA)
1985	CLUTE, Sidney		69	Cancer (in Los Angeles, CA)
1967	+ CLYDE, Andy		75	Heart attack in his sleep (in Hollywood, CA)
1945	CLYDE, David		60	Died in San Fernando Valley, CA
1962	CLYDE, Jean		73	Died in Helensburgh, Scotland
1968	+ COATES, Paul		47	Heart attack (in West Hollywood, CA)
1994	+ COBAIN, Kurt		27	Suicide (gunshot) while high on heroin and valium
1991	COBB, Dita		68	After a long illness
1974	COBB, Edmund F.		82	Heart attack (in Woodland Hills, CA)
1944	+ COBB, Irvin S.		67	Died in New York, NY
1976	#+ COBB, Lee J.	☆	64	Heart attack (in Woodland Hills, CA)
1961	#+ COBB, Ty		74	Prostate cancer and chronic heart disease (in Atlanta, GA)
1961	#+ COBURN, Charles	★	84	Heart ailment (in New York, NY)
1960	+ COCHRAN, Eddie (singer)		21	Killed in a taxi crash (in Chippenham, England)
1994	COCHRAN, Ron		81	After a short illness (in Florida)
1965	# COCHRAN, Steve		48	Acute infectious edema of lung (off coast of Guatemala)
1987	COCO, James		56	Heart attack (in New York, NY)
1963	+ COCTEAU, Jean		74	Heart attack (in Milly-la-Foret, France)
1961	CODEE, Ann		70	Heart attack (in Hollywood, CA)
1948	# CODY, Bill Sr.		57	After an illness of several months (in Santa Monica, CA)
1960	# CODY, Emmett		40	
1991	CODY, Iron Eyes		84	
1934	# CODY, Lew		50	Heart disease (in Beverly Hills, CA)
1988	CODY, William "Wild Bill"		75	Died in Denver, CO

Deaths of Movie and Television Personalities — by Name

	YEAR	NAME		AGE	CAUSE and/or PLACE OF DEATH
	1987	COE, Peter		58	Killed when his car collided with a van (in Byfleet, England)
	1983	COFFIELD, Peter		37	After a long illness (in New York, NY)
	1990	COFFIN, Tristram "Tris"		80	Lung cancer (in Santa Monica, CA)
	1942	+ COHAN, George M.		64	Cancer of the lower intestine (in New York, NY)
	1986	COHEN, Myron		83	Died in New York, NY
	1988	COHEN, Nat		82	After 3 heart attacks (in London, England)
	1938	COHL, Emil		81	Burns (after his beard caught fire from a candle)
	1958	+ COHN, Harry		66	Heart attack (in Phoenix, AZ)
	1996	COHN, Joseph Judson		100	Died in his sleep (at his home in Beverly Hills, CA)
	1985	+ COLASANTO, Nicholas "Coach"		61	Heart ailment (in Studio City, CA)
•	1996	# COLBERT, Claudette ★		92	Stroke (at her home in Barbados)
	1992	# COLBY, Anita		77	Lung disease (in New York, NY)
	1952	COLCORD, Mabel		80	Died in Los Angeles, CA
	1964	#+ COLE, Buddy		48	Heart attack (in North Hollywood, CA)
•	1995	COLE, David		32	A.I.D.S.
	1985	COLE, Lester		81	Heart attack (in San Francisco, CA)
	1965	#+ COLE, Nat "King"		45	Lung cancer (in Santa Monica, CA)
	1951	COLEMAN, Charles C.		65	Pulmonary embolism (in Woodland Hills, CA)
•	1998	COLEMAN, Shepard		74	Died in Warwick, NY
	1986	COLERIDGE, Sylvia		76	Died in London, England
	1992	COLES, Charles "Honi"		81	Died in his sleep of lung cancer
	1989	COLEY, Thomas		75	Heart attack (in New York, NY)
	1989	COLIN, Jean		83	Died in London, England
	1993	COLLARD, Cyril		35	A.I.D.S. (in Paris, France)
	1958	COLLEANO, Bonar		34	Automobile accident (in Birkenhead, England)
	1955	# COLLIER, Constance		77	Died in New York, NY
	1987	# COLLIER, Patience		76	Died in London, England
	1987	COLLIER, William "Buster" Jr.		86	Cardiac arrest from arteriosclerosis (in San Francisco, CA)
	1944	+ COLLIER, William Sr.		77	Pneumonia (in Beverly Hills, CA)
	1974	COLLINGE, Patricia ☆		81	Heart attack (in New York, NY)
•	1993	COLLINS, Albert		61	Cancer
	1988	COLLINS, Brent		46	Apparent heart attack (in New York)
	1994	COLLINS, Christopher		44	After a brief illness (in Ventura, CA)
	1994	# COLLINS, Dorothy		67	Heart failure (at her home in Watervliet, NY)
	1959	COLLINS, G. Pat		64	Cancer (in Los Angeles, CA)
	1918	COLLINS, John Hancock		28	Pleural pneumonia following influenza (in New York, NY)
	1954	COLLINS, Lewis D.		55	Heart attack (in Hollywood, CA)
	1951	# COLLINS, Monty		52	Heart attack (in North Hollywood, CA)
	1965	+ COLLINS, Ray		75	Emphysema (in Santa Monica, CA)
	1965	COLLINS, Russell		68	Heart attack (in West Hollywood, CA)
	1992	COLLOFF, Roger		46	Cancer
	1969	+ COLLYER, Bud		61	Died in Greenwich, CT
	1968	# COLLYER, June		60	Bronchial pneumonia (in Los Angeles, CA)
	1988	COLMAN, Ben		81	Septicemia (in Tarzana, CA)
	1975	COLMAN, Irene		60	Leukemia (in Santa Monica, CA)
	1958	+ COLMAN, Ronald ★		67	Following an operation for a lung infection (in Montecito, CA)
	1995	COLON, Alex		53	After an extended illness (in Los Angeles, CA)
	1986	# COLONNA, Jerry		82	Kidney failure (in Woodland Hills, CA)
	1934	#+ COLUMBO, Russ		26	Accidentally shot by a friend while examining a pistol (in Hollywood)
	1991	COLVIG, Vance		72	Cancer (in Hollywood, CA)
	1991	COLVIN, Michael		41	After suffering a head injury on a film set
	1992	COMBS, Frederick		57	A.I.D.S. (in Los Angeles, CA)
•	1996	COMBS, Ray		40	Suicide in anguish over a pending divorce (hanging) in Glendale, CA

Deaths of Movie and Television Personalities — by Name

YEAR	NAME	AGE	CAUSE and/or PLACE OF DEATH
1971	# COMINGORE, Dorothy	58	Cancer (in Stonington, CT)
1974	+ COMPSON, Betty	77	Died in Glendale, CA
1978	COMPTON, Fay	84	Died in London, England
1964	COMPTON, Francis	79	Died in Noroton, CT
• 1997	COMPTON, Joyce	90	Died in Los Angeles, CA
1959	COMPTON, Walter	47	After a long illness
1977	CONDON, Jackie	59	Cancer (in Inglewood, CA)
1988	CONDOS, Nick	73	Died in Los Angeles, CA
1990	CONDOS, Steve	71	Heart attack (in Lyon, France)
1990	+ CONIGLIARO, Tony	45	Pneumonia and kidney failure
1959	CONKLIN, Charles "Heinie"	79	Died in Hollywood, CA
1971	CONKLIN, Chester	83	Died in Woodland Hills, CA
1962	CONLIN, Jimmy	77	Cancer (in Encino, CA)
1993	CONN, Billy	75	Pneumonia (in Pittsburgh, PA)
1922	# CONNELLY, Bobby	13	Bronchitis and an enlarged heart (in Lynbrook, NY)
1988	CONNELLY, Christopher	47	Stomach cancer (in Burbank, CA)
1928	CONNELLY, Edward J.	73	Influenza (in Hollywood, CA)
1931	CONNELLY, Erwin	57	Automobile accident (in Los Angeles, CA)
1940	CONNOLLY, Walter	53	Stroke (in Beverly Hills, CA)
1993	CONNOR, Kenneth	77	Cancer (in London, England)
1988	CONNOR, Whitfield	71	Complications following surgery (in Norwalk, CT)
1992	#+ CONNORS, Chuck	71	Lung cancer (in Los Angeles, CA)
• 1998	CONRAD, Charles	88	
1983	CONRAD, Michael	58	Stomach cancer (in Los Angeles, CA)
1994	+ CONRAD, William	73	Heart attack (at the Medical Center of North Hollywood, CA)
1982	# CONRIED, Hans	64	Heart ailment (in Burbank, CA) body donated to medical science
1964	CONROY, Frank	73	Heart ailment (in Paramus, NJ)
1993	CONSTANTINE, Eddie	75	Heart attack (in Wiesbaden, Germany)
1975	#+ CONTE, Richard	59	Heart attack and stroke (in Los Angeles, CA)
1967	# CONTI, Albert	79	Stroke (in Hollywood, CA)
1991	+ CONVY, Bert	56	Cancer (brain tumor) in Los Angeles, CA
1974	CONWAY, Curt	59	After suffering a massive heart attack (in Los Angeles, CA)
1952	CONWAY, Jack (actor/director)	65	Pulmonary infection (in Pacific Palisades, CA)
1951	CONWAY, Jack (comedian/actor)	65	Died in Forrest Hills, NY (Do not confuse with Jack Conway, d. 1952)
1981	CONWAY, Morgan	81	Died in Livingston, NJ
1967	#+ CONWAY, Tom	63	Liver ailment (in Culver City, CA)
1994	CONWELL, John	72	Cancer (at his home in Santa Barbara, CA)
1935	# COOGAN, Jack Sr.	55	Automobile accident (nr. San Diego, CA)
1984	+ COOGAN, Jackie	69	Heart ailment (in Santa Monica, CA)
1978	COOGAN, Robert	53	Died in Los Angeles, CA
1981	COOK, Billy Boy	?	
1984	COOK, Clyde	92	Died in his sleep (in Carpinteria, CA)
1991	# COOK, Cookie	77	Kidney failure (in New York, NY)
1961	COOK, Donald	60	Heart attack (in New Haven, CT)
1995	COOK, Elisha Jr.	91	After suffering a stroke (in Big Pine, CA)
1959	# COOK, Joe	69	Died in Clinton Hollows, NY
1988	COOK, Nathan	38	Allergic reaction to penicillin (in Los Angeles, CA)
1995	COOK, Peter	57	Gastro-intestinal hemorrhage (at a hospital in Hampstead, England)
1990	COOK, Roderick	58	Died in Los Angeles, CA
1953	COOKE, Baldwin G. "Baldy"	65	Died in Los Angeles, CA
1964	+ COOKE, Sam	29	Shot by motel manager while the actor was pursuing a girl (in L.A.)
1948	COOLEY, James R.	68	Died in Hollywood, CA
1969	# COOLEY, Spade	58	Massive heart attack (in Oakland, CA)

• New entry. # Original name (Pt. 7). + Interment (Pt. 5).   205   ☆ Oscar nominee, ★ Oscar winner (Pt. 10)

YEAR	NAME		AGE	CAUSE and/or PLACE OF DEATH
1967	COOLIDGE, Philip		58	*Cancer (in Hollywood, CA)*
1966	# COOMBE, Carol		55	*Died in London, England*
1989	COONAN, Sheila M.		66	*Liver disease (in New York, NY)*
1975	COOPER, Clancy		68	*Heart attack while driving his car near his home (in Hollywood, CA)*
1988	COOPER, Dorothy Jordan		82	
1981	COOPER, Dulcie		77	*After a lengthy illness (in New York, NY)*
1986	COOPER, Edna Mae		85	*Died in Woodland Hills, CA*
1984	COOPER, Edwin		89	*Died in Danbury, CT*
1961	#+ COOPER, Gary ★		60	*Cancer (in Hollywood, CA)*
1971	+ COOPER, Gladys ☆		82	*Died in her sleep from pneumonia (in Henley-on-Thames, England)*
1973	+ COOPER, Melville G.		76	*Cancer (in Woodland Hills, CA)*
1973	COOPER, Merian C.		79	*Cancer (in Coronado, CA)*
1976	COOPER, Miriam		83	*Stroke (in Charlottesville, VA)*
1987	COOPER, Olive		94	*Pneumonia (in Los Angeles, CA)*
1992	COOPER, Ralph		?	*Cancer (in New York, NY)*
1982	COOTE, Robert		73	*Heart attack (in New York, NY)*
1990	COPLAND, Aaron ★		90	*Complications of 2 strokes and respiratory problems (in NY)*
1991	COPPOLA, Carmine ★		80	*After suffering a stroke (in Los Angeles, CA)*
1961	CORBETT, Ben		69	*Died in Hollywood, CA*
1993	CORBETT, Glenn		59	*Lung cancer (in San Antonio, TX)*
1982	CORBETT, Harry H.		57	*Heart attack (in Hastings, England)*
1933	CORBETT, James J.		65	*Cancer of the liver (in Bayside, NY)*
1960	CORBETT, Leonora		52	*Died in Vleuten, Netherlands*
1974	# CORBETT, Mary		47	*Died in New York, NY*
1992	CORBETT, Ruth (Thom)		78	*After a long illness (in Los Angeles, CA)*
1942	CORBIN, Virginia Lee		31	*Heart disease (in Winfield, IL)*
1990	CORBUCCI, Sergio		62	*Heart attack (in Rome, Italy)*
1993	# CORDAY, Josephine Rich		79	*Heart and kidney failure (in Los Angeles, CA)*
1992	# CORDAY, Rita		68	*Complications of diabetes after gall bladder surgery (in CA)*
1954	CORDING, Harry		63	*Died in Sun Valley, CA*
1965	# CORDY, Henry		57	*Heart ailment (in New York, NY)*
1993	COREY, Dorian		56	*A.I.D.S. (in a New York hospital)*
1972	# COREY, Joseph		45	*Heart attack (in Los Angeles, CA)*
1968	+ COREY, Wendell		54	*Liver ailment (in Woodland Hills, CA)*
1974	+ CORNELL, Katharine		81	*Pneumonia after a long illness (in Vineyard Haven, MA)*
• 1997	# CORNETT, Barbara		86	*Natural causes (in Ojai Valley Hospital - Ojai, CA)*
1972	+ CORRELL, Charles J. "Andy"		82	*Heart attack (in Chicago, IL)*
1945	CORRIGAN, D'Arcy		75	
1995	CORRIGAN, Douglas "Wrong Way"		88	*Died in Orange, CA*
1929	CORRIGAN, James		57	*General exhaustion (in Los Angeles, CA)*
1969	CORRIGAN, Lloyd		69	*After a long illness (in Woodland Hills, CA)*
1976	# CORRIGAN, Ray "Crash"		74	*Heart attack (in Brookings Harbor, OR)*
1995	CORSAUT, Aneta		62	*Cancer (in Studio City, CA)*
1993	CORT, William		53	*Cancer (in Los Angeles, CA)*
1989	CORTEZ, Mildred		72	*Cardiac arrest (in Hollywood, CA)*
1977	# CORTEZ, Ricardo		77	*Died in New York, NY*
• 1997	CORTEZ, Stanley ☆		92	*Died of a heart attack in Los Angeles, CA*
1947	+ CORTHELL, Herbert		69	*After a year's illness (in Hollywood, CA)*
1988	CORTLAND, Nicholas		47	*A.I.D.S. (in New York, NY)*
1994	CORVO, Phil		67	*After a long illness (in Los Angeles, CA)*
1993	CORY, Ken		51	*A.I.D.S. (in New York, NY)*
1995	# COSELL, Howard		77	*A heart embolism (at NYU Hospital in New York)*
1949	COSGRAVE, Luke		86	*Died in Woodland Hills, CA*

Deaths of Movie and Television Personalities — by Name

YEAR		NAME	AGE	CAUSE and/or PLACE OF DEATH
1951		COSSART, Ernest	74	Died in The Bronx, NY
1994		COSSART, Valerie (Livingston)	87	Pneumonia (in New York)
1989		COSTA, Bob	66	Died in Honolulu, HI
• 1996		COSTA, Johnny	74	Leukemia (in Oakmont, PA)
1983		COSTELLO, Anthony	42	After a long illness (in Hollywood, CA)
1987		COSTELLO, Carole	48	Stroke
1979		COSTELLO, Delores	73	Emphysema (in Fallbrook, CA)
1945		COSTELLO, Don	44	Heart attack in his sleep (in Hollywood, CA)
1957		COSTELLO, Helene	53	Pneumonia, tuberculosis, narcotics (in Los Angeles, CA)
1959	#+	COSTELLO, Lou	52	Heart attack (in Beverly Hills, CA)
1950		COSTELLO, Maurice	73	Heart ailment (in Hollywood, CA)
1971		COSTELLO, William A.	73	Died in San José, CA
1991		COSTON, Ann Sorg	62	After a short illness (in Roaring Brook Lake, NY)
1994	+	COTTEN, Joseph	88	Pneumonia (at his home in Westwood, CA)
1992		COTTLE, Graham D.	51	Congestive heart failure (in Los Angeles, CA)
1969	#	COTTON, Billy	68	Heart attack (in London, England)
1916		COTTON, Richard	?	Run over by an automobile (in Ephraim, WI)
1976		COUGHLIN, Kevin	30	Hit-and-run accident while cleaning his car windshield (in L.A., CA)
1989		COULOURIS, George	85	Heart attack (in London, England)
1918		COURTLEIGH, William Jr.	25	Pneumonia (in Philadelphia, PA)
1930		COURTLEIGH, William Sr.	61	Indigestion (in Rye, NY)
1980		COURTNEIDGE, Cicely	87	Died in London, England
1975		COURTNEY, Inez	67	Died in Neptune, NJ
1986		COURTOT, Marguerite	88	Died in Long Beach, CA
1933		COURTRIGHT, William "Uncle Billy"	84	Died in Ione, CA
• 1997		COUSTEAU, Jacques	87	Died at his home in Paris of a respiratory infection
1989		COVAN, Willie	92	Died in Los Angeles, CA
1993		COVINGTON, Fred	65	Cancer (at a hospital in Marietta, GA)
1972	#+	COWAN, Jerome	74	After a long illness (in Encino, CA)
• 1998		COWAN, Kenneth	35	Died in the China Airlines Airbus crash in Taipei, Taiwan
1973	#+	COWARD, Noel ★	73	Heart attack (in Port Maria, Jamaica)
1942		COWL, George	64	Died in London, England
1950	+	COWL, Jane	62	Cancer (in Santa Monica, CA)
• 1997		COWLES, Chandler	79	Heart attack (in New York , NY)
1943		COWLES, Jules	65	Died in Hollywood, CA
1968		COX, Morgan	68	Heart attack (in Hollywood, CA)
1974		COX, Robert	79	Died in Phoenix, AZ
1973	#+	COX, Wally	48	Heart attack (in Los Angeles, CA)
• 1996		COX, Winston H. "Tony"	55	Heart attack (during a workout at a Manhattan health club, NY)
1954		COXEN, Edward Albert	70	Died in Hollywood, CA
1974		COY, Walter	68	Died in Los Angeles, CA
1973		COYNE, Jeanne	50	Died in Los Angeles, CA
• 1997		COYTE, Kenneth	64	After a brief illness (in London, England)
1983	#	CRABBE, Larry "Buster"	75	Heart attack (in Scottsdale, AZ)
1945		CRAIG, Alec	60	After a long illness (in Glendale, CA)
1940	#	CRAIG, Blanche	74	Died in Los Angeles, CA
1970		CRAIG, Carolyn	37	Died in Los Angeles, CA
1979		CRAIG, Edith	71	After a long illness (Do not confuse with the English actress)
1986		CRAIG, Helen	74	Cardiac arrest in her sleep (in New York, NY)
1985	#+	CRAIG, James	73	Lung cancer (in Santa Ana, CA)
1972		CRAIG, May	82	Died in Dublin, Ireland
1965		CRAIG, Nell	73	Died in Hollywood, CA
1933	#	CRAIG, Richy Jr.	31	Heart failure after a long bout with cancer (in New York, NY)

Deaths of Movie and Television Personalities — by Name

YEAR	NAME	AGE	CAUSE and/or PLACE OF DEATH
1960	# CRAMER, Rychard	71	Laennec's cirrhosis (in Hollywood, CA)
1978	+ CRANE, Bob	48	Murdered (skull crushed by a blow while sleeping) in Scottsdale, AZ
1973	#+ CRANE, Norma	42	Cancer (in West Los Angeles, CA)
1969	+ CRANE, Richard	51	Heart attack (in San Fernando Valley, CA)
1928	CRANE, Ward	37	Pneumonia (in Saranac Lake, NY)
• 1997	CRANHAM, Tom	63	Died of cancer in Houston, TX
• 1980	# CRASH, Darby	22	Probable suicide (from a massive heroin overdose)
1994	CRAVAT, Nick	82	Lung cancer (in Woodland Hills, CA)
1960	CRAVAT, Noel	49	After surgery (in Hollywood, CA)
1991	# CRAVEN, Eddie	?	After an illness
1945	+ CRAVEN, Frank	70	Heart ailment (in Beverly Hills, CA)
1995	CRAVEN, John	79	Following a brief illness (in Salt Point, NY)
1991	CRAVENS, Kathryn	92	Cancer (in Burkett, TX)
1956	# CRAWFORD, Anne	35	Died in London, England
1986	#+ CRAWFORD, Broderick ★	74	Series of strokes (in Rancho Mirage, CA)
1969	# CRAWFORD, Howard Marion	55	An overdose of sleeping pills (in London, England)
1962	+ CRAWFORD, Jesse	66	Stroke (in Los Angeles, CA)
1977	#+ CRAWFORD, Joan ★	71	Cancer and acute coronary occlusion (in New York, NY)
1980	CRAWFORD, Kathryn	72	Cancer (in Pasadena, CA)
• 1996	CRAWFORD, Paul	71	Cancer (in New Orleans, LA)
1944	#+ CREGAR, Laird	28	Following two heart attacks (in Los Angeles, CA)
1966	CREHAN, Joseph	79	Stroke (in Hollywood, CA)
1959	CREWS, Kay C.	58	Died in San Antonio, TX
1942	+ CREWS, Laura Hope	62	After a month's illness (in New York, NY)
1945	# CRIMMONS, Daniel "Dan"	82	Died in Los Angeles, CA
1953	# CRIPPS, Kernan	67	Died in CA
1974	+ CRISP, Donald ★	93	After a series of strokes (in Van Nuys, CA)
1992	CRISTALDI, Franco ★	68	Heart attack (in Monte Carlo, Monaco)
1938	CRITTENDEN, Throckwood Dwight	59	Murdered (gunshot) in Los Angeles, CA
1973	+ CROCE, Jim	30	Airplane crash (on takeoff from Natchitoches Municipal airport, LA)
1958	CROCKER, Harry	64	Died in Beverly Hills, CA
1934	CROCKETT, Charles B.	62	After a long illness (in Los Angeles, CA)
1979	# CROCKETT, Dick	63	Cancer (in Los Angeles, CA)
1922	CROCKETT, John	?	Died in Los Angeles, CA
1995	#+ CROGHAN, Joe	74	Cancer (at Manor Care Ruxton, Baltimore, MD)
1979	# CROMWELL, John	91	Pulmonary embolism (in Santa Barbara, CA)
1960	#+ CROMWELL, Richard	50	After a brief illness (in Hollywood, CA)
1992	CRONIN, Laurel	53	Cancer (in Chicago, IL)
1977	#+ CROSBY, Bing ★	73	Heart attack (in Madrid, Spain)
1993	CROSBY, Bob	79	Cancer (in La Jolla, CA)
1991	+ CROSBY, Dennis	56	Suicide (gunshot) in Novato, CA
1952	#+ CROSBY, Dixie Lee	40	Cancer
1995	+ CROSBY, Gary	62	Complications of lung cancer (at St. Jos. Med Ctr, Burbank, CA)
1989	CROSBY, Lindsay	51	Suicide (gunshot) in Los Angeles, CA
1975	CROSBY, Wade	70	After a grand mal seizure aboard a yacht (in Newport Beach, CA)
1936	CROSLAND, Alan	42	Injuries after a car wreck (in Los Angeles, CA)
1944	CROSMAN, Henrietta	83	Died in Pelham Manor, NY
• 1998	CROSS, Beverley	66	At his home in London
1975	+ CROSS, Milton	77	Apparent heart attack (in New York, NY)
1960	CROSSLEY, Syd	75	Died in Troon, England
1986	+ CROTHERS, Benjamin "Scatman"	76	Lung cancer (in Van Nuys, CA)
1985	CROTHERS, Joel	44	Cancer (in Los Angeles, CA)
1932	# CROWELL, Josephine	?	Died in Amityville, NY

Deaths of Movie and Television Personalities — by Name

YEAR	NAME		AGE	CAUSE and/or PLACE OF DEATH
1988	CRUICKSHANK, Andrew		80	Heart attack (in London, England)
1942	#+ CRUZE, James		58	Heart ailment (in Hollywood, CA)
1965	CRUZE, Mae		74	After a long illness (in Hollywood, CA)
1992	# CUEVAS, Joey		34	A.I.D.S. (in Naples, FL)
1990	CUGAT, Xavier		90	Heart failure due to arterial sclerosis (in Barcelona, Spain)
1983	+ CUKOR, George	★	83	Heart failure (in Los Angeles, CA)
1996	CULHANE, Shamus		87	Congestive heart failure (in New York)
1990	# CULLEN, Bill		70	Heart failure from lung cancer (in Bel Air, CA)
• 1996	CULLEN, Eric		31	Following surgery (at a hospital in Glasgow, Scotland)
1982	CULLEN, Fred		48	Heart attack
1942	CULLEY, Frederick		63	
1950	CULLINANI, Ralph		68	
1995	CULLINGHAM, Mark		53	Complications of A.I.D.S. (in Los Angeles, CA)
1925	CULLINGTON, Margaret		34	After a 6-month illness (in Hollywood, CA)
• 1978	+ CULLY, Zara		86	Died in Los Angeles, CA
1987	# CULVER, Calvin		43	Pulmonary infection (in Inverness, FL)
1984	CULVER, Roland		83	Heart attack (in Henley-on-Thames, England)
1996	CUMMINGS, Irving Jr.		77	Cancer (in Van Nuys, CA)
1959	# CUMMINGS, Irving Sr.	☆	70	Heart attack (in Hollywood, CA)
1989	CUMMINGS, Jack		84	Heart attack (in Los Angeles, CA)
1990	+ CUMMINGS, Robert "Bob"		80	Parkinson's disease, kidney failure and pneumonia (in W'land Hills)
1984	CUMMINGS, Ruth Sinclair		90	Died in Woodland Hills, CA
1982	# CUMMINGS, Sandy		68	Pneumonia while hospitalized for another illness (in San Diego, CA)
1983	# CUMMINS, Dorothy		80	
1967	# CUNARD, Grace		73	After a long bout with cancer (in Woodland Hills, CA)
1925	CUNEO, Lester		37	Suicide (gunshot) after his wife filed for divorce (in Hollywood, CA)
1959	CUNNINGHAM, Cecil		70	Arteriosclerosis (in Woodland Hills, CA)
1943	# CUNNINGHAM, Joe		52	Coronary occlusion (in Los Angeles, CA)
1986	CUNNINGHAM, Sarah		67	Asthmatic attack (in Los Angeles, CA)
1967	CUNNINGHAM, Zamah		74	Died in New York, NY
1994	CUNY, Alain		85	Died at the Cochin Hospital in Paris, France
1960	CURLEY, Leo		82	Arteriosclerosis (in Woodland Hills, CA)
1941	CURRAN, Thomas A.		60	Pneumonia (in Hollywood, CA)
1968	# CURRIE, Finlay		90	Died in Gerrard's Cross, England
1928	CURRIER, Frank		71	Blood poisoning after car door was shut on a finger (in Hollywood)
1990	CURRIN, Jay C.		34	Injuries from a 55-foot fall while filming (in Malibu, CA)
1994	CURRY, John		44	A.I.D.S.-related heart attack (at his home in England)
1953	# CURTIS, Alan		43	Following a kidney operation (in New York, NY)
1988	CURTIS, Billy		79	Heart attack (in Dayton, OH)
1952	CURTIS, Dick		49	Died in Hollywood, CA
1956	CURTIS, Jack		75	(Do not confuse with the child actor or Jack B. Curtis)
1985	# CURTIS, Jackie		38	Drug overdose (in New York, NY)
1991	# CURTIS, Ken		74	Died in Fresno, CA
1970	CURTIS, Willa Pearl		74	Cerebral arteriosclerosis and diabetes (in Los Angeles, CA)
1962	#+ CURTIZ, Michael	★	73	Cancer (in Hollywood, CA)
1976	CURZON, George		79	Died in London, England
1993	CUSACK, Cyril		82	Motor neuron disease (at his home in London, England)
1994	CUSHING, Peter		81	Cancer (in a Canterbury hospice, England)
1974	# CUSTER, Bob		76	Heart attack (in Torrance, CA)
1988	CUTHBERTSON, Allan		67	Died in London, England
1972	# CUTTING, Dick		59	Kidney disease and uremia (in Woodland Hills, CA)
1974	CUTTS, Patricia		48	Found dead at home from an overdose of pills (in London, England)

• New entry.   # Original name (Pt. 7).   + Interment (Pt. 5).   209   ☆ Oscar nominee, ★ Oscar winner (Pt. 10)

YEAR	NAME	AGE	CAUSE and/or PLACE OF DEATH

D

1948	# D'ALBROOK, Sidney	62	Heart attack (in Los Angeles, CA)
1957	D'AMBRICOURT, Adrienne	69	Heart attack after her car struck another car (in Hollywood, CA)
1989	D'AMICO, Teresa Tirelli	81	Brain tumor
• 1998	D'ANDREA, Tom	88	Died in Southport Square, FLA.
1996	D'ARCY, Alexander	87	Heart failure (at his home in West Hollywood, CA)
1969	# D'ARCY, Roy	75	Died in Redlands, CA
1968	D'ARRAST, Harry	71	
1993	D'ORSA, Lonnie	96	Died in Beverly Hills, CA
1983	+ D'ORSAY, Fifi	79	Cancer (in Woodland Hills, CA)
• 1980	d'USSEAU, Armand	63	Stomach cancer (in New York, NY)
1990	d'USSEAU, Arnaud	73	After surgery
1989	DaCOSTA, Morton	74	Heart failure (in Redding, CT)
1980	# DAGOVER, Lil	82	Died in Munich, West Germany
1978	+ DAILEY, Dan ☆	62	Anemia (in Hollywood, CA)
1986	# DAINTY, Billy	59	Died in Shackleford, England
1969	DALBY, Amy	81	Died in England
1991	# DALE, Bobby	92	Myocardial infarction (in Woodland Hills, CA)
1971	# DALE, Charlie	90	Died in a Teaneck, N.J., nursing home
1957	DALE, Dorothy (Hyman)	74	Burned to death in her shack (in Hollywood, CA)
1961	DALE, Esther	75	Died in Hollywood, CA
1972	DALE, Margaret	92	Died in New York, NY
1994	# DALE, Virginia	77	Complications of emphysema (in Burbank, CA)
1975	#+ DALEY, Cass	59	Neck pierced by glass in a fall at home (in Hollywood, CA)
1989	DALI, Salvador	84	Heart failure and pneumonia (in Figueras, Spain)
1983	# DALIO, Marcel	83	Found dead in his home (in Paris, France)
1971	# DALL, John ☆	52	Heart attack and pneumonia (in Beverly Hills, CA)
1973	DALLIMORE, Maurice	72	Laennec's cirrhosis (in Hollywood, CA)
1989	DALRYMPLE, Ian	85	Died in London, England
1984	DALTON, Doris	82	Cardiac arrest (in Prout's Neck, ME)
1972	DALTON, Dorothy	78	Died in Scarsdale, NY
1978	DALY, James	59	Heart attack (in Nyack, NY) — Do not confuse with James L. Daly
1933	DALY, James L.	81	Heart trouble (in Philadelphia, PA)
1991	# DALY, John	77	Cardiac arrest (in Johannesburg, South Africa)
1957	DALY, Mark	70	Died in England
1994	#+ DAMITA, Lili	92	Alzheimer's disease (in Palm Beach, FL)
1987	DAMON, Cathryn	56	Cancer (in Los Angeles, CA)
1962	DAMON, Les	53	Died in Hollywood, CA
1955	# DAMPIER, Claude	75	Pneumonia (in London, England)
1950	+ DAMROSCH, Walter	88	Died in New York, NY
1983	DANA, Leora	60	Cancer (in New York, NY)
1987	# DANA, Viola	90	Heart failure (in Woodland Hills, CA)
1965	+ DANDRIDGE, Dorothy ☆	42	Overdose of Tofranil, an anti-depressant (in West Hollywood, CA)
1987	DANDRIDGE, Ruby	87	Died in Los Angeles, CA
1934	+ DANE, Karl	47	Suicide (gunshot) in Los Angeles, CA
1962	# DANIEL, Billy	49	Coronary attack (in Beverly Hills, CA)
• 1997	DANIEL, Eliot ☆	89	Cancer in Placerville, CA
1963	# DANIELL, Henry	69	Heart attack (in Santa Monica, CA)
1971	#+ DANIELS, Bebe	70	Cerebral hemorrhage (in London, England)
1955	#+ DANIELS, Victor	66	Cancer (in Ventura, CA)
1988	DANIELS, William "Billy"	73	Stomach cancer (in Los Angeles, CA)
1994	DANO, Royal "Ted" Jr.	47	Liver failure (in Santa Monica, CA)
1994	DANO, Royal Sr.	71	Pulmonary fibrosis (at his home in Santa Monica, CA)

Deaths of Movie and Television Personalities — by Name

YEAR	NAME	AGE	CAUSE and/or PLACE OF DEATH
• 1996	DANON, Jack	64	Lung cancer and emphysema (in Burbank, CA)
• 1997	DANON, Marcello	?	Undisclosed cause (in Rome, Italy)
1992	DANOVA, Cesare	66	Heart attack (in Los Angeles, CA)
1982	+ DANTINE, Helmut	63	Massive coronary (in Beverly Hills, CA)
1992	DANTON, Ray	61	After suffering from kidney disease (in Los Angeles, CA)
1992	+ DARBY, Ken ★	82	Died in Sherman Oaks, CA
1995	DARDEN, Scvcrn	65	Heart failure (at his home in Santa Fe, N.M.)
1955	DARIEN, Frank Jr.	79	Died in Hollywood, CA
1973	#+ DARIN, Bobby ☆	37	After heart surgery (in Hollywood, CA)
1971	DARK, Christopher	51	Heart attack (in Hollywood, CA)
1974	# DARLING, Candy	25	Cancer and pneumonia (in New York)
1936	DARLING, Ida	60	After a long illness (in Hollywood, CA)
1963	DARMOND, Grace	65	Bronchial pneumonia (in Los Angeles, CA)
1983	DARNAY, Toni	61	Lung cancer (in New York, NY)
1965	#+ DARNELL, Linda	43	Fire burns (in Chicago, IL)
• 1997	DARRACH, Jr., Henry Bradford	76	heart attack in Los Angeles, CA
1970	+ DARRELL, J. Stevan "Steve"	65	Brain tumor (in Hollywood, CA)
1976	# DARRO, Frankie	58	Heart attack (in Huntington Beach, CA)
1974	DARVAS, Lili	72	Died at her Manhattan home
1971	# DARVI, Bella	42	Suicide (opened the gas jets on her apartment stove) in Monaco
1967	#+ DARWELL, Jane ★	87	Heart attack (in Woodland Hills, CA)
1974	# DASH, Pauly	55	After cancer treatment (at a hospital in Miami, FL)
1986	DaSILVA, Howard	76	Lymphatic cancer (in Ossining, NY)
1980	+ DASSIN, Joseph "Joe"	42	Heart attack (in Papeete, Tahiti)
1963	+ DASTAGIR, Sabu		(See under Sabu, below)
1960	+ DASTAGIR, Sheik	47	
1959	# DAUBE, Belle	71	Died in Hollywood, CA
1993	DAUGHERTY, Herschel	82	Pneumonia (in Encinitas, CA)
• 1998	DAUMAN, Anatole	73	Heart attack at his Paris home
1978	# DAUPHIN, Claude	75	Intestinal occlusion (in Paris, France)
1936	#+ DAVENPORT, Alice	82	Died in Los Angeles, CA
1977	DAVENPORT, Dorothy	81	Died in Woodland Hills, CA
1949	DAVENPORT, Harry	83	Heart attack (in Los Angeles, CA)
1993	DAVENPORT, John	62	Diabetes
1977	#+ DAVES, Delmar	73	Died in La Jolla, CA
1993	DAVID, Mack	81	Died in a hospital in Rancho Mirage, CA
• 1996	DAVID, Saul	74	Complications of congestive heart failure (in Culver City, CA)
1978	# DAVID, Thayer	51	Heart attack (in New York, NY)
1968	DAVIDSON, John	81	Heart failure (in Los Angeles, CA) — Do not confuse with the singer
1950	DAVIDSON, Max	75	After a long illness (in Woodland Hills, CA)
1947	DAVIDSON, William B.	59	Following an operation (in Santa Monica, CA)
1955	DAVIES, Betty Ann	44	Complications after appendectomy (in Manchester, England)
1961	#+ DAVIES, Marion	64	Cancer (in Hollywood, CA)
1994	DAVIES, Richard	80	Heart attack (in Weaverville, CA)
1976	DAVIES, Rupert	60	Cancer (in London, England)
1994	# DAVIS, Battle	42	Non-Hodgkins lymphoma
1989	#+ DAVIS, Bette ★	81	Breast cancer (in Neuilly-sur-Seine, France)
1963	DAVIS, Boyd	77	Heart attack (in Hollywood, CA)
1991	+ DAVIS, Brad	41	Complications from A.I.D.S. (in Los Angeles, CA)
1936	DAVIS, Edwards	64	After an illness of 2-years (in Hollywood, CA)
• 1996	DAVIS, Fred	74	After suffering a stroke (at a hospital in Toronto, Canada)
• 1997	DAVIS, Gail	71	Cancer (in Burbank, CA)
1965	DAVIS, George	75	Cancer (in Woodland Hills, CA)

Deaths of Movie and Television Personalities — by Name

YEAR	NAME	AGE	CAUSE and/or PLACE OF DEATH
1982	DAVIS, Herbert H.	52	Died in New York, NY
1968	DAVIS, Jack	?	
1992	# DAVIS, Jackie	78	Respiratory failure (in Santa Monica, CA)
1991	DAVIS, Jerome L.	73	Stroke (in Los Angeles, CA)
1981	#+ DAVIS, Jim	65	Following surgery for a perforated ulcer (in Northridge, CA)
1961	+ DAVIS, Joan (Williams)	53	Heart attack (in Palm Springs, CA)
1983	DAVIS, Johnny "Scat"	73	Heart attack (in Pecos, TX)
1979	DAVIS, Karl "Killer"	72	Died in Chicago, IL
1969	DAVIS, Mildred	68	Heart attack (in Santa Monica, CA)
1991	#+ DAVIS, Miles	65	Pneumonia, respiratory failure and a stroke (in Los Angeles, CA)
1949	DAVIS, Owen Jr.	42	Drowned after falling overboard from a sloop (in L.I. South, NY)
1990	DAVIS, Patrick "Grampy"	87	Heart attack (in Upland, CA)
• 1996	#+ DAVIS, Philip K.	32	Died at his home in Baltimore, MD
1985	DAVIS, Rick	71	Heart failure (in Los Angeles, CA)
1993	DAVIS, Robert	76	Emphysema (in Beverly Hills, CA)
1974	# DAVIS, Rufe	66	Died in Torrance, CA
1990	+ DAVIS, Sammy Jr.	64	Throat cancer (in Beverly Hills, CA)
1970	# DAW, Evelyn	58	Died in San Diego, CA
1988	DAWN, Hazel	98	Died in New York, NY
1966	DAWN, Isabel	62	Pulmonary infection (in Woodland Hills, CA)
1950	DAWSON, Dorice	56	Heart attack (in Riverside, CA)
1953	DAWSON, Frank	83	Died in Hollywood, CA
1987	DAWSON, Hal K.	90	Stroke (in Loma Linda, CA)
1985	DAWSON, Kurt	43	Complications from cancer
1984	DAWSON, Ronald	81	Pneumonia (in Silver Spring, MD)
• 1996	DAWSON, Thomas H.	82	Natural causes (in Palm Desert, CA)
1988	#+ DAY, Dennis	71	Amyotrophic lateral sclerosis (in Brentwood, CA)
1978	DAY, Josette	63	Died in Paris, France
1992	DEA, Marie	72	Heart attack (in Paris, France)
1984	DEACON, Richard	62	Heart attack (in Los Angeles, CA)
1991	DeACUTIS, William	33	Brain lymphoma (in Los Angeles, CA)
1955	#+ DEAN, James ☆	24	Automobile accident (near Paso Robles, CA)
1952	DEAN, Julia	74	Died in Hollywood, CA
1988	DEAN, Priscilla	91	As a result of a fall (in Leonia, NJ)
1990	# DEANE, Palmer	56	A.I.D.S. (in New York, NY)
1974	DEARING, Edgar	81	Lung cancer (in Woodland Hills, CA)
1969	DeAUBRY, Diane	79	Heart attack (in Santa Monica, CA)
1981	DeBANZIE, Brenda	66	Following surgery on a non-malignant tumor (in Sussex, England)
1948	DeBRULIER, Nigel	69	Died in London, England
1958	DEBUCOURT, Jean	64	Leukemia (in Mongeron, France)
1989	DeCARLO, Vinnie	54	Heart attack (in Milan, Italy)
1966	# DeCASALIS, Jeanne	70	Died in London, England
1996	DECKARD, James	58	Brain cancer (in Garden Grove, CA)
1919	DECKER, Kathryn Browne	?	Died in Columbo, Ceylon, while on a tour of the Orient
1977	DECKERS, Eugene	60	
1950	+ DeCORDOBA, Pedro	68	Found dead of a heart attack (at his home in Sunland, CA)
1973	# DeCORDOVA, Arturo	66	Heart attack (in Mexico City, Mexico)
1973	DeCORSIA, Ted	69	Heart attack (in Encino, CA)
1988	DEENE, Lally	68	Died in Santa Monica, CA
1986	DEERING, Olive	67	Cancer (in New York, NY)
1993	+ DeFORE, Don	80	Cardiac arrest (in Santa Monica, CA)
1983	deFUNES, Louis	68	Heart attack (in Nantes, France)
1940	DeGRASSE, Joseph	67	Heart attack (in Eagle Rock, CA)

• New entry. # Original name (Pt. 7). + Interment (Pt. 5).

☆ Oscar nominee, ★ Oscar winner (Pt. 10)

Deaths of Movie and Television Personalities — by Name

YEAR	NAME		AGE	CAUSE and/or PLACE OF DEATH
1953	DeGRASSE, Sam		78	Heart attack (in Hollywood, CA)
1941	# DeGREY, Sydney		55	
1993	DeGROOT, Katherine Hynes		88	Complications from a stroke (in Englewood, NJ)
1990	DeGRUNWALD, Dimitri		76	Died in Hove, England
1979	DeHAVEN, Carter Jr.		68	After a brief illness (in Encino, CA)
1977	DeHAVEN, Carter Sr.		90	Died in Woodland Hills, CA
1992	# DEHNER, John		76	Emphysema and diabetes (in Santa Barbara, CA)
1968	# DEKKER, Albert		63	Found dead in his bath tub with S and M trappings (in Hollywood)
1981	DeKOVA, Frank		71	Found dead in his home from a heart attack (in Sepulveda, CA)
1988	DeKOVEN, Roger		81	Cancer (in New York, NY)
1959	# DEL MAR, Claire		57	Murdered (head and knife wounds) in her Carmel, CA home
1983	# DEL RIO, Dolores		77	Heart attack (in Newport Beach, CA)
1961	DEL RUTH, Roy		66	Heart attack (in Sherman Oaks, CA)
1975	# DEL VAL, Jean		82	Heart attack (in Pacific Palisades, CA)
• 1995	DeLACY, Philippe		78	Heart attack
1950	DeLaMOTTE, Marguerite		47	Cerebral thrombosis (in San Francisco, CA)
1995	DELANEY, Bessie		104	Died in her sleep
1959	DELANEY, Charles		67	Died in Hollywood, CA
1992	DELAUDER, Doug		38	A.I.D.S. (in New York, NY)
1992	DeLAURENTIIS, Luigi		75	After a 3-year illness (in Rome, Italy)
1943	DeLEATH, Vaughn		42	Uremic poisoning and a heart condition
1992	DELERUE, Georges	★	67	After a brief illness (in Los Angeles, CA)
1975	DELEVANTI, Cyril		88	Lung cancer (in Hollywood, CA)
• 1997	DELFINO, Frank J.		86	Complications from bone marrow cancer (in San Diego, CA)
1969	DELGADO, Maria		60	Died in Hollywood, CA
1973	DELGADO, Roger		53	Automobile accident (in Turkey)
1977	DELL, Claudia		67	Died in Hollywood, CA
1934	DELL, Dorothy		19	Automobile accident (in Pasadena, CA)
1988	DELL, Gabriel		68	Leukemia (in North Hollywood, CA)
1984	+ DELMAR, Kenny		73	Died at a hospital in Stamford, CT
• 1998	DELPRETE, Duilio		61	After a long illnes in a Rome, Italy Hospital
• 1996	DelRUBIO, Eadie		?	Cancer (in Los Angeles, CA)
1988	DELVANDO, Amapola		78	Died in Lake View Terrace, CA
1954	# DEMAIN, Gordon		56	
1983	DEMAREST, William	☆	91	After a long illness (in Palm Springs, CA)
1992	DEMAZIS, Orane		87	Died in Boulogne-Billancourt, France
1993	DeMILLE, Agnes		88	Stroke and heart failure in her sleep (at her home in Manhattan, NY)
1959	#+ DeMILLE, Cecil B.	☆	77	Heart disease (in Los Angeles, CA)
1984	DEMILLE, Cecilia (Harper)		75	After a brief illness (in Hollywood, CA)
1995	DeMILLE, Katherine (Quinn)		83	Alzheimer's disease (in Tucson, AZ)
1955	+ DeMILLE, William C.		76	Died in Playa del Rey, CA
1983	+ DEMPSEY, Jack		87	After an illness of several years (in New York, NY)
1947	DEMPSEY, Thomas		79	After a long illness (in Hollywood, CA)
1991	DEMPSTER, Carol		89	After a long illness (in La Jolla, CA)
1987	DEMPSTER, Hugh		86	Heart failure (in Chicago, IL)
1990	DEMY, Jacques		59	Leukemia (in Paris, France)
1994	DENGEL, Jake		61	Cancer (at Group One Hospice in Sherman Oaks, CA)
1995	DENNER, Charles		69	Cancer (in Dreux, France)
1992	#+ DENNIS, Sandy	★	54	Ovarian cancer (at her home in Westport, CT)
1994	DENNY, C. Patterson		46	Cancer (in Glenbrook, IL)
1990	DENNY, Joe		61	Respiratory failure (in Fontana, CA)
1967	#+ DENNY, Reginald		75	Stroke (in Surrey, England)
1963	DENT, Vernon		63	Coronary thrombosis (in Hollywood, CA)

Deaths of Movie and Television Personalities — by Name

YEAR	NAME		AGE	CAUSE and/or PLACE OF DEATH
1988	DENTLER, Mary Ann		96	Stroke (in Kingston, NY)
• 1997	DENVER, John		53	Died in a plane crash in CA, he was piloting the plane
1988	dePAUL, Gene Vincent		68	Brain tumor (in Northridge, CA)
1988	DEPEW, Joseph D.		76	Died in Escondido, CA
1957	DEPP, Harry		70	Died in Hollywood, CA
1931	+ DePUTTI, Lya		31	Pneumonia after operation to remove chicken bone from her throat
• 1998	# DEREK, John		71	Catastrophic problem with- aorta and heart in Santa Maria, CA
1993	#+ DeRITA, Joe		83	Pneumonia (in Woodland Hills, CA)
1952	# DeROACH, Charles		72	
1992	DERR, Richard		74	Pancreatic cancer and heart failure (in Santa Monica, CA)
1986	DeRUE, Carmen		78	Heart attack (in North Hollywood, CA)
1988	DeSALES, Francis		76	Cancer (in Van Nuys, CA)
• 1997	DeSANTIS, Giuseppe		80	After a heart attack in Eugenio Hospital-Rome, Italy
1989	DeSANTIS, Joe		80	Congestive heart failure (in Provo, UT)
• 1996	DeSANTIS, Pasquale	★	69	Heart attack while working on location (in Ukraine)
1974	DeSICA, Vittorio	☆	73	Following lung cancer surgery (in Neuilly-sur-Seine, France)
1993	# DESMOND, Florence		87	Unreported causes (in Guildford, England)
1985	+ DESMOND, Johnny		65	Cancer (in Los Angeles, CA)
1949	DESMOND, William		71	Heart attack (in Los Angeles, CA)
1963	DeSOTO, Henry		75	
1990	DeTREAUX, Tamara "E.T."		31	Respiratory and heart problems (in Hollywood, CA)
1980	DEUTSCH, Adolph	★	82	Died in Palm Desert, CA
1991	DEUTSCH, David		65	Kidney failure (in London, England)
1969	DEUTSCH, Ernst		78	Heart attack (in Berlin, West Germany)
1992	DEUTSCH, Helen		85	Heart attack in her sleep (in New York)
• 1998	DEVANEY, Frank		58	Cancer in Burbank, CA
1982	# DEVEAU, Jack		47	Cancer (in New York, NY)
1990	DeVEGA, José Jr.		56	A.I.D.S. (in Westwood, CA)
1918	DEVERE, Margaret		22	Pneumonia (in New York, NY)
1958	DEVEREAUX, Jack		76	Died in New York, NY
1977	#+ DEVINE, Andy		71	Leukemia and diabetic problems (in Orange, CA)
1994	DEVINE, Jerry		85	Died in Santa Barbara, CA
1990	DeVITO, Julia		85	
1991	# DEVLIN, J. G.		84	Died in Belfast, Ireland
1976	# DEVORE, Dorothy		77	Died in Woodland Hills, CA
1991	DEWHURST, Colleen		67	Cancer (in South Salem, NY)
1972	# DeWILDE, Brandon	☆	30	After his car skidded on wet pavement and hit a truck (in Denver)
• 1997	DEWINDT, Hal		72	Cancer at UCLA Medical Center in Los Angeles, CA
1976	DEWITT, Alan "Boomie"		52	Heart attack (in Los Angeles, CA)
1990	DeWITT, Lew		53	Intestinal disorder
1974	#+ DeWOLFE, Billy		67	Cancer and coronary thrombosis (in Los Angeles, CA)
1984	DEXTER, Alan		65	Heart attack (in Oxnard, CA)
1941	DEXTER, Elliott		71	After several weeks illness (in Amityville, NY)
1991	DHIEGH, Khigh		75	Kidney and heart disease (in Mesa, AZ)
1988	# DIAMOND, I. A. L.		67	Multiple myeloma (a form of cancer) in Beverly Hills, CA
1985	+ DIAMOND, Selma		64	Cancer (in Los Angeles, CA)
1968	# DICKERSON, Henry		61	Cerebral thrombosis (in Lynwood, CA)
1945	DICKSON, Gloria		28	Asphyxiation from a fire (in Hollywood, CA)
1935	DICKSON, W. K. Laurie		75	Died in Twickenham, England
1975	DIERKES, John		69	Emphysema (in Hollywood, CA)
1972	# DIETERLE, William	☆	79	Died in Ottobrunn, West Germany
1992	#+ DIETRICH, Marlene	☆	90	Heart attack (in Paris, France)
1983	DIETZ, Howard		86	Died in New York, NY

Deaths of Movie and Television Personalities — by Name

YEAR		NAME		AGE	CAUSE and/or PLACE OF DEATH
1989		DIFFRING, Anton		70	Died in Chateauneuf-de-Grasse, France
1947	+	DIGGES, Dudley		68	Stroke (in New York, NY)
1979		DIGNAM, Basil		74	Died in England
1989		DIGNAM, Mark		80	Cardiac arrest in his sleep (in London, England)
1996		DILIAN, Irasema		71	Heart attack (at her home in Ceprano, Italy)
1995		DILLARD, William		83	Complications from lupus and pneumonia (in Manhattan)
1982		DILLAWAY, Donald P.		78	After a long illness
1933		DILLON, Edward "Eddie"		53	Heart attack (in Hollywood, CA)
1937	#	DILLON, Jack		61	Pneumonia (in Los Angeles, CA)
1934	+	DILLON, John Francis		50	After suffering a heart attack at a dinner party (in Beverly Hills, CA)
1971		DILLON, Josephine		87	Died in Verdugo City, CA
1965		DILLON, Tim		77	Died in Burbank, CA
1962	#	DILLON, Tom		66	Died in Hollywood, CA
1944		DILSON, John		53	Died in Ventura, CA
1992	+	DINEHART, Alan Jr.		74	Emphysema (in Van Nuys, CA)
1944	#+	DINEHART, Alan Sr.		54	Heart attack (in Hollywood, CA)
1956		DINGLE, Charles W.		68	After an illness of several months (in Worcester, MA)
1936		DIONE, Rose		60	Died in Los Angeles, CA
1954		DIONNE, Emelie		20	Epileptic seizure (in Canada)
1970		DIONNE, Marie		35	
1979		DIONNE, Oliva		71	Died in North Bay, Ontario, Canada
1997		DISNEY, Lillian		98	Died from complications of a stroke at her home in Los Angeles, CA
1971	+	DISNEY, Roy		77	Cerebral hemorrhage (in Burbank, CA)
1966	#+	DISNEY, Walt		65	Circulatory collapse after lung surgery (in Burbank, CA)
1989		DITTMAN, Dean Gus		57	Heart failure (in Los Angeles, CA)
1988	#+	Divine		42	Heart disease (in Hollywood, CA)
1982		DIX, Constance		60	Died in New York, NY
1970		DIX, Dorothy		77	Died in Los Angeles, CA
1949	#+	DIX, Richard ☆		55	Acute cardiac collapse (in Los Angeles, CA)
1992		DIXON, Adèle		83	Bronchial pneumonia (in Manchester, England)
1972	#	DIXON, Denver		82	Heart attack (in Hollywood, CA)
1981		DIXON, Jean (actress)		84	After a long illness (in New York, NY)
1992		DIXON, Joan		61	Heart disease (in Los Angeles, CA)
1987		DOBSON, James		67	Heart attack
1966		DODD, (Rev.) Neal		88	After a long illness (in Burbank, CA)
1973		DODD, Claire		64	Cancer (in Beverly Hills, CA)
1964		DODD, Jimmie		54	Heart ailment (in Honolulu, Hawaii)
1994		DODSON, Jack		63	Heart failure after a year of failing health (in Encino, CA)
1964	#	DODSWORTH, John		53	Suicide (asphyxiation) in Los Angeles, CA
1988		DOHERTY, Charla		41	Cancer (in Calabasas, CA)
1963		DOLENZ, George		55	Heart attack (in Hollywood, CA)
1941	#+	DOLLY, Jenny		48	Suicide (hanging) in Hollywood, CA
1970	#+	DOLLY, Rosie		77	Heart failure (in New York, NY)
1970	#	DOMINGUEZ, Joe		76	Died in Woodland Hills, CA
1986		DOMINIQUE, Laurien		29	Embolism (in San Francisco, CA)
1993		DONALD, James		76	Stomach cancer (at his home in Wiltshire, England)
1979		DONALD, Peter		60	Cancer of the stomach and throat
1994		DONALDSON, Norma		68	Cancer (at Cedars-Sinai Med. Ctr. in Los Angeles, CA)
1958	+	DONAT, Robert ★		53	Asthma (in London, England)
1967		DONATH, Ludwig		67	Leukemia (in New York, NY)
1972	+	DONLEVY, Brian ☆		73	Throat cancer (in Woodland Hills, CA)
1991		DONN, Lee		96	Stroke (in Los Angeles, CA)
1988	#	DONNELL, Jeff		66	Apparent heart attack (in Hollywood, CA)

Deaths of Movie and Television Personalities — by Name

YEAR		NAME	AGE	CAUSE and/or PLACE OF DEATH
1937		DONNELLY, James	71	*Died in Hollywood, CA*
1982		DONNELLY, Ruth	86	*Died in New York, NY*
1987	#	DONOVAN, Casey	43	*Pulmonary infection*
1987		DONOVAN, King	69	*Cancer*
1988		DONOVAN, Warde	72	*Died in Los Angeles, CA*
1958		DOONAN, Patric	33	*Suicide (by gassing himself) in London, England*
• 1998		DORE, Robert E.	44	*From a blood infection at Holy Cross Hosp. in Silver Spring, MD*
1967		DORLEAC, Francoise	25	*After car skidded on wet road and burst into flames (Nice, France)*
1975	#+	DORN, Philip	69	*Heart attack (in Woodland Hills, CA)*
1956	#	DORO, Marie	74	*Heart ailment (in New York, NY)*
1980	#	DORR, Harry	87	*Pneumonia (in Los Angeles, CA)*
1993		DORR, John	48	*A.I.D.S. (in Los Angeles, CA)*
• 1997		DORRIS, Michael	52	*Suicide in a motel in Concord, NH*
1984		DORS, Diana	52	*After two operations for ovarian cancer (in Windsor, England)*
1957	#+	DORSEY, Jimmy	53	*Cancer (in New York, NY)*
1956	#+	DORSEY, Tommy	51	*Choked while asleep (in Greenwich, CT)*
1958		DOUCET, Catherine	82	*Died in New York, NY*
1994		DOUCETTE, John	73	*Cancer (at his home in Cabazon, CA)*
1938		DOUGHERTY, Virgil Jack	42	*Suicide (carbon monoxide) in Hollywood, CA*
1945	#	DOUGLAS, Donald "Don"	40	*Complications after appendectomy (in Los Angeles, CA)*
1993		DOUGLAS, Gordon	85	*Cancer (in Los Angeles, CA)*
1993		DOUGLAS, Hugh	78	*Heart attack (in Los Angeles, CA)*
1994		DOUGLAS, Jack	72	*Cancer (in Los Angeles, CA)*
1981	# DOUGLAS, Melvyn ★			80	*Pneumonia and cardiac complications (in New York, NY)*
1959	+	DOUGLAS, Paul	52	*Heart attack (in Hollywood, CA)*
1993	#	DOUGLAS, Steve	55	*Heart attack (during a studio recording session)*
1978		DOUGLAS, Tom	82	*Heart attack (in Cuernavaca, Mexico)*
1966	#	DOUGLASS, Kent	58	
• 1997		DOVE, Billie	97	*Died of pneumonia*
• 1996		DOVE, Ulysses	49	*A.I.D.S. (in New York, NY)*
1956		DOVZHENKO, Alexander	62	*Heart attack (in Moscow, Russia)*
1992		DOWELL, Clifton	44	*A.I.D.S.*
• 1997		DOWELL, George Brendan	87	*Cancer (at Gilchrist Hospice in Towson, MD)*
1969	+	DOWLING, Constance	49	*Cardiac arrest (in Los Angeles, CA)*
1976	#	DOWLING, Eddie	81	*Died in Smithfield, RI*
1954		DOWLING, Joan	26	*Found dead in a gas-filled room (in London, England)*
1928		DOWLING, Joseph J.	80	*After a 2-year illness (in Hollywood, CA)*
1985		DOWNEY, Morton Sr.	83	*Effects of a stroke (in Palm Beach, FL)*
1978		DOWNS, Cathy	52	*Died in Los Angeles, CA*
• 1998		DOWNS, Frederic	81	*Died in Los Angeles, CA*
1994		DOWNS, Johnny "Our Gang"	80	*Cancer (at his home in Coronado, CA)*
• 1997		DOYLE, David	67	*Heart attack*
1995		DOYLE, Mary	63	*Lung cancer (in New York)*
1973		DOYLE, Maxine	58	*Cancer (in Studio City, CA)*
1975		DOYLE, Patricia	60	*Cancer (in Los Angeles, CA)*
1991		DOYLE, Roz	49	*Breast cancer (in Hampstead, England)*
1991	+	DOZIER, William	83	*Stroke (in Los Angeles, CA)*
1980		DRAGONETTE, Jessica	75	*Heart attack (in New York City)*
1992	#	DRAKE, Alfred	77	*Heart failure after a long bout with cancer (in New York, NY)*
1994		DRAKE, Charles	79	*After a lengthy illness (at his home in East Lyme, CT)*
1989		DRAKE, Dona	69	*Cancer (in Mexico City, Mexico)*
1990		DRAKE, Fabia	86	*Died in London, England*
1991		DRAKE, Oliver	88	*After a long illness (in Las Vegas, NV)*

Deaths of Movie and Television Personalities — by Name

YEAR	NAME		AGE	CAUSE and/or PLACE OF DEATH
1982	#+ DRAKE, Tom		64	Lung cancer (in Hollywood, CA)
1989	DRANE, Gary		46	Died in New York, NY
1990	DRAPER, Don		62	A.I.D.S. (in Los Angeles, CA)
1956	DRAPER, Ruth		72	Apparent heart attack (in New York)
1949	DRAYTON, Alfred		68	Died in London, England
1981	DRAYTON, Noel		68	
1993	DREIFUSS, Arthur		85	After a bout with the flu (in Studio City, CA)
1965	# DRESSER, Louise	☆	86	Intestinal obstruction (in Woodland Hills, CA)
1934	#+ DRESSLER, Marie	★	65	Cancer (in Santa Barbara, CA)
1974	DREW, Ann		83	Died in a Miami nursing home
1993	DREW, Larry		73	After a long illness (in London, England)
1919	+ DREW, Sidney		54	Uremic poisoning and heart disease (in New York, NY)
1989	DRINKWATER, Terry		53	Cancer (in Malibu, CA)
1968	DRISCOLL, Bobby		31	Hardening of the arteries (in New York, NY)
1983	DRISCOLL, Robert Miller		55	Died in Hollywood, CA
1986	DRIVAS, Robert		50	Died in New York, NY
1988	DRU, Jason		58	Emphysema-induced heart failure (in Van Nuys, CA)
• 1996	DRU, Joanne		73	Lymphedema (in Beverly Hills, CA)
1978	DRURY, Norma		?	
1989	DRYHURST, Edward		84	Died in London, England
• 1991	DUBBINS, Don		62	
1992	DUBMAN, Laura		69	Kidney failure (in New York)
1951	+ DUCHIN, Eddie		41	Leukemia (in New York, NY)
1955	DUDLEY, Robert Y.		80	Died in San Clemente, CA
1971	#+ DUEL, Peter		31	Apparent suicide (gunshot) in Hollywood, CA
1992	DUELL, Randall	☆	89	Stroke
1990	DUFF, Howard		72	Heart attack (in Santa Barbara, CA)
1994	# DUFF-GRIFFIN, William		54	Prostate cancer (at the Manhattan home of his companion)
1993	DUFFY, John Paul		42	Apparent suicide (in West Hollywood, CA)
1992	DUFINE, Herbert		61	Heart condition
1952	DUFKIN, Sam		61	Died in Hollywood, CA
1958	# DUGAN, Tom		69	Automobile accident (in Redlands, CA)
1988	DUGGAN, Andrew		64	Cancer (in Westwood, CA)
• 1988	DUGGAN, Elizabeth		56	Cancer
1977	DUGGAN, Jan		95	Died in Anaheim, CA
1982	DUKE, E. L. Tony		48	Heart attack (in Burbank, CA)
1994	DUKE, Edward		50	Cancer (in London, England)
1994	DULO, Jane		75	After cardiac surgery (at Cedars-Sinai Med. Ctr. in Los Angeles)
1989	DuMAURIER, Daphne		81	After a brief illness (in Cornwall, England)
1974	DUMBRILLE, Douglas		85	Heart attack (in Woodland Hills, CA)
1964	DUMKE, Ralph		64	Died in Sherman Oaks, CA
1965	#+ DUMONT, Margaret		75	Heart attack (in Los Angeles, CA)
1953	DUNBAR, David		60	After a long illness (in Woodland Hills, CA)
1991	# DUNBAR, Dixie		72	After a series of heart attacks (in Miami, FL)
1992	DUNBAR, Dorothy		90	Died in Seattle, WA
1933	DUNBAR, Helen		65	After a long illness (in Los Angeles, CA)
1960	DUNCAN, Bud		77	Circulatory failure (in Los Angeles, CA)
1972	DUNCAN, Evelyn		79	Died in Bellflower, CA
1927	+ DUNCAN, Isadora		49	Strangled in her car by a scarf that caught in rear wheel (in France)
1972	# DUNCAN, Kenne		69	Stroke (in Hollywood, CA)
1993	DUNCAN, Mary (Sanford)		98	Natural causes (in Palm Beach, FL)
1959	+ DUNCAN, Rosetta "Topsy"		58	Automobile accident (in Acero, IL)
• 1998	DUNCAN, Todd		95	Of a heart condition at his home in Washington, DC

• New entry.   # Original name (Pt. 7).   + Interment (Pt. 5).   217   ☆ Oscar nominee, ★ Oscar winner (Pt. 10)

YEAR	NAME		AGE	CAUSE and/or PLACE OF DEATH
1986	+ DUNCAN, Vivian "Little Eva"		84	*Alzheimer's disease (in Los Angeles, CA)*
1961	DUNCAN, William A.		80	*Died in Hollywood, CA*
1953	DUNDEE, Jimmie		52	*Leukemia (in Woodland Hills, CA)*
1994	# DUNFEE, Nora		78	*After a brief illness (in Manhattan, NY)*
1972	# DUNHAM, Phil		87	*Died in Los Angeles, CA*
1970	DUNLAP, Scott		77	*Died in Los Angeles, CA*
1966	# DUNN, Bobby		74	*Heart attack (in Hollywood, CA)*
1987	DUNN, Clara Whips		90	*Congestive heart failure (in Atlanta, GA)*
1951	DUNN, Edward F. "Eddie"		55	*Cancer (in Hollywood, CA)*
1966	DUNN, Emma		91	*Died in Los Angeles, CA*
1967	#+ DUNN, James ★		65	*Died in Santa Monica, CA*
1983	DUNN, Josephine		76	*Cancer (in Thousand Oaks, CA)*
1976	DUNN, Liam		59	*Emphysema and other medical complications (in Granada Hills, CA)*
• 1998	DUNN, Linwood ★		93	*Natural causes in Burbank, CA*
1973	# DUNN, Michael ☆		39	*Congenital chondrodystrophy (dwarfism) in London, England*
1990	DUNN, Patricia		60	*Lung cancer*
1990	DUNN, Peter		68	*Heart attack (in Willcox, AZ)*
1968	DUNN, Ralph		65	
1937	DUNN, Robert "Bobby"		45	*Heart attack (in Hollywood, CA)*
1982	+ DUNNE, Dominique		23	*Strangled by her boyfriend (in Los Angeles, CA)*
1990	#+ DUNNE, Irene ☆		88	*Heart failure (in Los Angeles, CA)*
1992	DUNNE, Philip		84	*Cancer (in Malibu, CA)*
1991	DUNNOCK, Mildred ☆		90	*Died in Oak Bluffs, Martha's Vineyard, MA*
1956	DUPONT, E. A.		64	*After a long bout with cancer (in Hollywood, CA)*
1987	DuPRE, Jacqueline		42	*Multiple sclerosis (in London, England)*
1984	DUPREZ, June		66	*Died in London, England*
1984	DURANT, Jack		78	*Cancer (in Miami, FL)*
1980	#+ DURANTE, Jimmy		86	*Pneumonitis (in Santa Monica, CA)*
1989	DURANTE, Vito		64	*A.I.D.S. (in New York, NY)*
1975	+ DURFEE, Minta (Arbuckle)		85	*Congestive heart failure (in Woodland Hills, CA)*
1935	#+ DURKIN, Junior		19	*Automobile accident (near San Diego, CA)*
1991	+ DUROCHER, Leo		86	*Natural causes (in Palm Springs, CA)*
1968	+ DURYEA, Dan		61	*Cancer and heart attack (in Los Angeles, CA)*
1963	# DURYEA, George			*(See Tom Keene)*
1967	DUVIVIER, Julien		71	*After his car hit another car and tree (in Paris, France)*
1990	DUX, Pierre		82	*Died in Paris, France*
1979	#+ DVORAK, Ann		67	*Died in Honolulu, Hawaii*
1981	#+ DWAN, Alan		96	*Heart failure (in Woodland Hills, CA)*
1940	DWIRE, Earl		55	*Died in Carmichael, CA*
1950	DYALL, Franklin		76	*Died in Worthing, England*
1985	DYALL, Valentine		75	*Died in London, England*
1933	DYER, William J. "Billy"		52	*Died in Hollywood, CA*
1991	DYER-BENNETT, Richard		73	
	E			
1929	+ EAGELS, Jeanne ☆		35	*Alcohol and sleeping pills overdose (in New York, NY)*
1959	# EAGLE, Jimmy		52	*Cirrhosis of the liver (in Los Angeles, CA)*
1995	EAGLE, White		43	*A.I.D.S. (in Sioux Falls, S.D.)*
1989	EAMES, John Matthew		64	*Died in New York, NY*
1971	# EAMES, Virginia			*(See Virginia True Boardman)*
1993	EARLE, Don (TV sportscaster)		64	
1958	EARLE, Dorothy		?	*Died in Los Angeles, CA*
1972	EARLE, Edward		90	*Died in Woodland Hills, CA*
1984	EARLE, Merie		95	*Uremic poisoning after colon cancer surgery (in Glendale, CA)*

Deaths of Movie and Television Personalities — by Name

YEAR	NAME	AGE	CAUSE and/or PLACE OF DEATH
1985	# EARLES, Harry	83	Died in Sarasota, FL
1956	EASON, Reeves "Breezy"	69	Heart attack (in Sherman Oaks, CA)
1990	EASTERLING, Gary Lamont	38	Died in Los Angeles, CA
• 1996	EASTHOUSE, Richard	35	A.I.D.S. complications (in New York, NY)
• 1997	EASTMAN, Ronald William	60	
1970	EATON, Jay	70	Heart attack (in Hollywood, CA)
1948	EATON, Mary	46	After a heart attack (in Hollywood, CA)
1979	EBERLE, Ray	60	Heart attack (in Douglasville, GA)
1981	EBERLY, Bob	65	After 4 heart attacks from cancer chemotherapy
• 1997	EBERT, Joyce	64	Cancer at a Southport, Conn. rest home
1960	EBURNE, Maude	85	Died in Hollywood, CA
1986	ECCLES, Donald	77	Automobile crash (in Sussex, England)
1991	ECKHARDT, John	82	Heart failure
1993	ECKSTINE, Billy	78	Cardiac arrest after suffering a stroke (in Pittsburgh, PA)
1995	EDDINGTON, Paul	68	After suffering a rare form of skin cancer (in London, Eng.)
1990	EDDY, Helen Jerome	92	Heart failure (in Alhambra, CA)
1967	#+ EDDY, Nelson	65	After suffering a stroke while performing on stage (in Miami Beach)
• 1996	EDELMAN, Herb	62	Emphysema (at M.P. & T. Hospital in Woodland Hills, CA)
1970	+ EDENS, Roger ★	64	Cancer
1931	EDESON, Robert	63	Hardening of the arteries (in Hollywood, CA)
1971	+ EDWARDS, Cliff "Ukelele Ike"	76	Died in Hollywood, CA
1990	EDWARDS, Douglas	73	Cancer of the bladder
1967	EDWARDS, Edna Park	72	Died in Burbank, CA
1991	EDWARDS, George	67	Cancer (in Sherman Oaks, CA)
1988	EDWARDS, Gloria	43	Cancer (in Los Angeles, CA)
1945	#+ EDWARDS, Gus	64	Cancer (in Los Angeles, CA)
1986	EDWARDS, Guy	51	Heart attack (in Los Angeles, CA0
1952	EDWARDS, Henry	70	Died in Chobham, England
1925	EDWARDS, J. Gordon	57	Pneumonia (in New York, NY)
1970	EDWARDS, James	58	Heart attack (in San Diego, CA)
1988	# EDWARDS, Jimmy	68	Bronchial pneumonia (Do not confuse with James Edwards, d. 1970)
1965	# EDWARDS, Neely	75	Died in Woodland Hills, CA
1965	EDWARDS, Sarah	81	Died in Hollywood, CA
1937	+ EDWARDS, Snitz	75	Arthritis after a long illness (in Los Angeles, CA)
1996	#+ EDWARDS, Vince	67	Pancreatic cancer (in Los Angeles, CA)
1995	EGAN, Eddie	65	Cancer
1987	+ EGAN, Richard	65	Prostate cancer (in Santa Monica, CA)
1988	EGOROV, Youri	33	Complications of A.I.D.S. (in Amsterdam, Netherlands)
1990	# EICHELBERGER, Ethyl	45	Suicide (cut wrists) in Staten Island, NY
1978	#+ EILERS, Sally	69	Heart attack (in Woodland Hills, CA)
1995	EISENSTAEDT, Alfred	96	Natural causes
1948	+ EISENSTEIN, Sergei	50	Heart attack (in Moscow, Russia)
1992	EISLER, David	36	Pneumonia
• 1996	ELDER, Lonne 3rd ☆	69	After a chronic illness (in Los Angeles, CA)
1950	ELDRIDGE, Anna Mae	56	Heart attack (in Van Nuys, CA)
1988	# ELDRIDGE, Florence	86	Heart attack (in Santa Barbara, CA)
1961	# ELDRIDGE, John	57	Heart attack (in Laguna Beach, CA)
1995	+ ELGART, Les	77	Heart attack (in Dallas, TX)
• 1998	ELISCU, Edward	96	Died of natural causes in Newtown, Conn.
1991	ELKINS, Lenore	77	Heart failure
1992	ELLERBE, Harry	91	Died in Atlanta, GA
1974	#+ ELLINGTON, Duke	75	Lung cancer and pneumonia (in New York, NY)
1974	#+ ELLIOT, Cass	32	Heart attack, chronic obesity and exhaustion (in London, England)

• New entry. # Original name (Pt. 7). + Interment (Pt. 5).   219   ☆ Oscar nominee, ★ Oscar winner (Pt. 10)

Deaths of Movie and Television Personalities — by Name

YEAR	NAME	AGE	CAUSE and/or PLACE OF DEATH
1992	ELLIOTT, Denholm ☆	70	AIDS-related tuberculosis (in Ibiza, Spain)
1961	# ELLIOTT, Dick	75	Died in Burbank, CA
1956	ELLIOTT, John H.	80	Heart attack (in Los Angeles, CA)
1959	ELLIOTT, Lillian	83	Cerebral hemorrhage (in Hollywood, CA)
1951	ELLIOTT, Robert	72	Died in Los Angeles, CA
1965	# ELLIOTT, William "Wild Bill"	61	Cancer (in Las Vegas, NV)
1983	# ELLIOTT, William D.	49	Died in L.A. (Do not confuse with William "Wild Bill" Elliott, d. 1965)
1930	ELLIS, Diane	20	Heart attack on her honeymoon (in Madras, India)
1952	ELLIS, Edward	80	After 33 weeks of illness (in Hollywood, CA)
1991	ELLIS, Karl	41	A.I.D.S. (in Grand Junction, CO)
1970	# ELLIS, Patricia	49	Cancer (in Kansas City, MO)
1973	ELLIS, Robert "Bobby"	40	Kidney failure following an operation (in Los Angeles, CA)
1974	ELLIS, Robert Reel	82	Cardiac arrest (in Santa Monica, CA)
1993	# ELLISON, James	83	After breaking his neck in a fall (in Montecito, CA)
1942	ELLSLER, Effie	87	Following a heart attack (in Hollywood, CA)
1985	ELLSWORTH, Stephen R.	77	Heart failure (in Paterson, NJ)
1967	ELMAN, Mischa	76	Heart attack (in New York, NY)
1945	# ELMER, Billy	75	After a long illness (in Hollywood, CA)
1981	# ELSOM, Isobel	87	Died in Woodland Hills, CA
1990	EMERSON, Elsie Mae	86	Complications from strokes (in Burbank, CA)
1983	EMERSON, Faye	65	Stomach cancer (in Deyva, Spain)
1960	+ EMERSON, Hope ☆	61	Liver ailment (in Hollywood, CA)
1956	# EMERSON, John	84	After a long illness (in Pasadena, CA)
1944	# EMERTON, Roy	51	Died in England
1983	EMERY, Dick	65	Bronchial pneumonia (in London, England)
1945	# EMERY, Gilbert	70	Died in Hollywood, CA
1964	EMERY, John	59	Cancer (in New York, NY)
1980	EMERY, Katherine	73	Pulmonary embolism (in Portland, ME)
1988	EMERY, Mary	91	Died in Los Angeles, CA
1994	EMHARDT, Robert	80	Heart attack (at his home in Ojai, CA)
1946	+ EMMETT, Fern (Roquemore)	50	Cancer (in Hollywood, CA)
1980	EMNEY, Fred	79	Died in Bognor Regis, England
1991	EMR, Roland Jon	45	Murdered (shot in his car) in Los Angeles, CA
1995	# ENDFIELD, Cy	80	Stroke (in Shipston-on-Tour, England)
1981	ENGEL, Roy	67	Meningitis (in Burbank, CA)
1966	ENGLE, Billy	77	Heart attack (in Hollywood, CA)
1985	ENGLE, Darleen	48	Cancer (in Santa Monica, CA)
1969	# ENGLISH, John W.	66	Died in Hollywood, CA
1993	ENGLUND, Kenneth	78	A recurring illness (in Woodland Hills, CA)
• 1997	ENO, Terry	50	Liver cancer in Manhattan, NY
1992	ENRIGHT, Dan	74	After a brief illness
1965	ENRIGHT, Ray	69	Heart attack after a long illness (in Hollywood, CA)
1990	ENRIQUEZ, Rene	58	Pancreatic cancer (in Tarzana, CA)
1932	# ENTWISTLE, Peg	24	Suicide (jumped off the "Hollywood" Hills sign)
1992	EPHRON, Henry	81	Died in Los Angeles, CA
1992	EPPER, John	86	Prostate cancer (in Newhall, CA)
1992	# EPSTEIN, David S.	73	Heart attack (in Greenwich, CT)
1991	# EPSTEIN, Jerry	69	Causes unreported (in London, England)
1995	# ERGAS, Joseph	72	Diabetes (in New York)
1986	# ERICKSON, Leif	72	Cancer (in Pensacola, FL)
1951	+ ERROL, Leon	70	Heart attack (in Hollywood, CA)
1990	Erté	97	After a brief illness (in Paris, France)
1985	ERVIN, (Senator) Sam	88	Kidney failure after gall bladder surgery

Deaths of Movie and Television Personalities — by Name

YEAR	NAME	AGE	CAUSE and/or PLACE OF DEATH
1965	ERWIN, June	47	Found dead in her home (in Carmichael, CA)
1967	+ ERWIN, Stuart ☆	65	Heart attack (in Beverly Hills, CA)
1992	# Esmeralda	65	Diabetes and complications (in Mexico City, Mexico)
1990	ESMOND, Jill	82	Died in Wimbledon, England
• 1997	ESSEX, Harry	86	Heart failure (at Cedars-Sinai Med. Ctr. in Los Angeles, CA)
1973	ESSLER, Fred	77	Cancer (in Woodland Hills, CA)
1995	ESTABROOK, Ted	76	Died in New York
1943	ETHIER, Alphonse	68	Cancer (in Hollywood, CA)
1982	ETHRIDGE, Ella	88	Died in Woodland Hills, CA
1978	+ ETTING, Ruth	81	After a long illness (in Colorado Springs, CO)
• 1997	EVANS, Barry	53	Murdered at his home in England
1945	EVANS, Charles	88	Died in Santa Monica, CA
1985	EVANS, Clifford	73	Died in Wales
1968	EVANS, Douglas	64	Died in Hollywood, CA
1976	EVANS, Edith ☆	88	Heart attack after a brief illness (in Cranbrook, Kent, England)
1954	EVANS, Evan	53	Heart attack (in New York, NY)
• 1998	EVANS, Gene	75	Natural causes in Jackson, Tenn.
1952	EVANS, Herbert	68	Died in San Gabriel, CA
1950	EVANS, Jack	57	Heart attack (in Hollywood, CA)
1991	EVANS, John Morgan	49	After a long illness (in Los Angeles, CA)
1983	EVANS, Madge	73	Cancer (in Oakland, NJ)
1989	EVANS, Maurice	87	Cancer (in Brighton, England)
1989	EVANS, Peter	38	Complications of A.I.D.S. (in Los Angeles, CA)
1969	EVANS, Rex	66	Following surgery (in Glendale, CA)
1987	EVANS, Wilbur W.	81	Died in Elmer, NJ
1967	EVELYN, Judith	54	Cancer (in New York, NY)
1968	EVEREST, Barbara	77	Died in London, England
• 1995	EVERHART, Scott	36	A.I.D.S.
1996	EVERSON, William K.	67	Prostate cancer (in New York)
1948	EVERTON, Paul	79	Following a heart attack (in Calabasas, CA)
1994	EWART, John	66	Cancer (in Sydney, Australia)
1994	# EWELL, Tom	85	After a long series of illnesses (in Woodland Hills, CA)
1957	# EYTHE, William	38	Acute hepatitis (in Los Angeles, CA)
	F		
1996	FABREGAS, Manolo	75	After suffering a heart attack (in Mexico City)
1994	FABRI, Zoltan	77	Heart attack at his home (in Budapest, Hungary)
1990	FABRIZI, Aldo	84	Heart attack (in Rome, Italy)
1995	FABRIZI, Franco	79	Cancer (in Cortemaggiore, Italy)
1938	+ FACTOR, Max	61	Kidney and liver ailment (at his home in Beverly Hills, CA)
1980	FADDEN, Tom	84	Died in Vero Beach, FL
1989	FAIN, Sammy	87	Heart attack (in Los Angeles, CA)
1957	FAIR, Elinor	53	Died in Seattle, WA
1948	FAIR, Virginia	49	After a long illness (in Hollywood, CA)
1939	#+ FAIRBANKS, Douglas Sr.	56	Heart attack (in Santa Monica, CA)
1945	# FAIRBANKS, William	50	Lobar pneumonia (in Los Angeles, CA)
1941	# FAIRBROTHER, Sydney	69	Died in London, England
1980	# FAIRE, Virginia Brown	75	Died at a hospital in Laguna Beach, CA
1976	+ FAITH, Percy	67	Cancer (in Los Angeles, CA)
1991	FALAT, Stephen J.	34	After a long illness (in New York, NY)
1993	FALCO, Louis	50	A.I.D.S. (in New York)
• 1997	FARLEY, Chris	33	
1971	# FARLEY, Dot	90	Died in Woodland Hills, CA
1947	# FARLEY, Jim	65	Cancer (in a Pacolma, CA, sanitarium)

Deaths of Movie and Television Personalities — by Name

YEAR	NAME	AGE	CAUSE and/or PLACE OF DEATH
1988	FARLEY, Morgan	90	Died in San Pedro, CA
1970	+ FARMER, Frances	55	Cancer and heart attack (in Indianapolis, IN)
1983	FARMER, Richard	67	Cancer (in Glendale, CA)
1988	# FARMER, Virginia	90	Died in Long Beach, CA
• 1931	FARNHAM, Joseph W. ★	?	Heart attack
1929	FARNUM, Dustin	53	Kidney trouble (in New York, NY)
1961	+ FARNUM, Franklyn	85	Cancer (in Hollywood, CA)
1953	+ FARNUM, William	76	Cancer (in Los Angeles, CA)
1986	FARR, Derek	74	Cancer (in London, England)
1995	FARRAR, David	87	Died in South Africa
1967	FARRAR, Geraldine	85	Died in Ridgefield, CT
1925	FARRAR, Margaret	24	After swallowing poison (in Los Angeles, CA)
1990	+ FARRELL, Charles "Charlie"	89	Cardiac arrest (in Palm Springs, CA)
1971	+ FARRELL, Glenda	66	Cancer (in New York, NY)
1988	FARRELL, Jack	52	Cancer (in Los Angeles, CA)
1989	FARRELL, Timothy (Sperl)	66	Heart condition (in Santa Monica, CA)
1968	+ FARRELL, Virginia	72	
• 1997	FARREN, Jack	75	Complications following heart surgery in Surger, LA
1963	+ FARROW, John ☆	56	Apparent heart attack (in Beverly Hills, CA)
1982	FASSBINDER, Rainer Werner	36	Lethal combination of cocaine and sleeping pills (in Munich, Ger.)
1987	FAULKNER, Ralph B.	95	After a brief illness (in Burbank, CA)
1939	FAWCETT, George D.	77	Heart trouble (in Nantucket Island, MA)
1961	+ FAY, Frank	63	Died in Santa Monica, CA
• 1998	# FAYE, Alice	83	Cancer at Eisenhower Medical Center in Rancho Mirage, CA
1991	FAYE, Frances	71	Following a series of strokes (in Los Angeles, CA)
1980	FAYE, Herbie	81	Died in Las Vegas, NV
• 1997	FAYE, Joey	87	Died of a heart attack at his home in Englewood, NJ
1966	FAYE, Julia	72	Cancer (in Santa Monica, CA)
1992	FAYE, Marty	70	Heart attack
• 1997	FAYED, Dodi	42	Car accident in Paris with Princess Diana
1985	#+ FAYLEN, Frank	79	After a long illness (in Burbank, CA)
1962	+ FAZENDA, Louise	66	Cerebral hemorrhage (in Holmby Hills, CA)
1971	FEALY, Maude	90	After being hospitalized (in Woodland Hills, CA)
1994	FEDDERSON, Donald	81	After a series of heart problems (at Cedars-Sinai Hosp. in L.A.)
1965	FEIST, Felix E.	55	Cancer (in Encino, CA)
1993	+ FELD, Fritz	93	After a lengthy illness (in Santa Monica, CA)
1972	FELDMAN, Andrea	?	Suicide (jumped from the 14th floor of 51 Fifth Ave, NY)
1982	+ FELDMAN, Marty	48	Heart attack (in Mexico City, Mexico)
1991	FELDMAN, Phil	69	Cancer (in Los Angeles, CA)
1993	+ FELLINI, Federico ★	73	After suffering a stroke and heart attack (in Rome, Italy)
1950	FELLOWES, Rockcliffe	65	Heart attack (in Los Angeles, CA)
1992	FELLOWS, Arthur	74	Cancer (in Century City, CA)
1966	FELTON, Verna	76	Pulmonary embolism (in North Hollywood, CA)
1992	FENNELL, Willie	72	Apparent heart attack (in Sydney, Australia)
1988	FENNELLY, Parker	96	Died in Peekskill, NY
• 1997	FENNEMAN, George	77	Emphysema at his home in Los Angeles, CA
1957	# FENTON, Frank	51	Pulmonary embolism (in Los Angeles, CA)
1978	# FENTON, Leslie C.	76	Died in Montecito, CA
1971	FERGUSON, Al	83	Died in Los Angeles, CA
1961	FERGUSON, Elsie	78	Died in New London, CT
1978	FERGUSON, Frank	78	Cancer (in Los Angeles, CA)
1944	FERGUSON, George S.	60	Died in Hollywood, CA
1977	FERGUSON, Helen	76	Died in Clearwater, FL

Deaths of Movie and Television Personalities — by Name

YEAR	NAME		AGE	CAUSE and/or PLACE OF DEATH
1971	#+ Fernandel		67	Heart attack and lung cancer (in Paris, France)
1986	FERNANDEZ, Emilio		82	Heart attack (in Mexico City, Mexico)
1992	# FERRER, José	★	80	After a brief illness (in Coral Gables, FL)
• 1997	FERRERI, Marco		68	Heart attack (in Paris, France)
1985	# FETCHIT, Stepin		83	Pneumonia and heart failure (in Woodland Hills, CA)
1965	# FETHERSTON, Eddie		68	Heart attack (in Yucca Valley, CA)
• 1925	FEUILLADE, Louis		52	Complications from peritonitis (in Nice, France)
1985	FEURY, Peggy		?	Automobile accident (in Los Angeles, CA)
1948	FEYDER, Jacques		54	After a long illness (in Rive-de-Frangins, France)
1988	FIDLER, Jimmie		89	
1979	+ FIEDLER, Arthur		84	Heart failure
1973	FIELD, Betty		55	Stroke (in Hyannis, MA)
1991	FIELD, Filip J.		67	Heart failure
1925	FIELD, George		46	Tuberculosis (in Hollywood, CA)
1990	FIELD, Irene		59	
• 1996	FIELD, Lisabeth		72	Heart disease (at her home in Hollywood Hills, CA)
1989	FIELD, Ron		55	Neurological impairment due to brain lesions (in New York, NY)
1992	# FIELD, Virginia		74	Cancer (in Palm Desert, CA)
1976	FIELD, Walter		101	Died in Hollywood, CA
1945	FIELDING, Edward		65	Heart attack while mowing his lawn (in Beverly Hills, CA)
1992	FIELDING, Sol Baer		83	Following a long illness (in Reseda, CA)
1979	# FIELDS, Gracie		81	After a hospital stay for bronchial pneumonia (in Capri, Italy)
1941	# FIELDS, Stanley		57	Heart attack (in Los Angeles, CA)
1978	#+ FIELDS, Totie		48	Apparent heart failure (in Las Vegas, NV)
1946	#+ FIELDS, W. C.		66	Violent hemorrhage, dropsy and other ailments (in Pasadena, CA)
• 1997	FIGUEROA, Gabriel	☆	90	Stroke in Mexico City, Mexico
1964	FILAURI, Antonio		74	Emphysema (in San Gabriel, CA)
1940	+ FINCH, Flora		71	Streptococcus infection (in Hollywood, CA)
1995	FINCH, Nigel		45	An A.I.D.S.-related illness (at his home in London, Eng.)
1977	#+ FINCH, Peter	★	60	Heart attack (in Beverly Hills, CA)
1975	#+ FINE, Larry		72	Stroke (in Woodland Hills, CA)
1994	FINK, Agnes		74	Died in Germany
1953	# FINLAYSON, James		66	Heart attack (in Los Angeles, CA)
1989	FINLEY, Evelyn		73	Heart attack (in Big Bear City, CA)
1920	FINLEY, Ned		50	Suicide (strychnine) in New York, NY
• 1996	# FINN, Lila		86	Died in Santa Monica, CA
1995	FINNEY, Jack		84	Pneumonia (in Greenbrae, CA)
1971	FioRITO, Ted		70	Heart attack (in Scottsdale, AZ)
1994	FIRKUSNY, Rudolf		82	Cancer (in New York)
• 1997	FISCHER, Wayne		39	A.I.D.S. (in Manhattan, NY)
1991	FISHELSON, Stanley		66	Natural causes
1944	# FISKE, Richard		29	Killed in action during World War 2 (in Bastogne, Belgium)
1944	FISKE, Robert L.		54	Congestive heart failure (in Sunland, CA)
• 1996	FITCH, Louise		81	Natural causes (at her home in Venice, CA)
1961	# FITZGERALD, Barry	★	72	After a long illness (in Dublin, Ireland)
1941	FITZGERALD, Cissy		68	Died in Ovingdean, England
• 1996	+ FITZGERALD, Ella		78	Complications of diabetes (at her home in Beverly Hills, CA)
1982	FITZGERALD, Neil		90	Died in Princeton, NJ
1976	# FITZGERALD, Walter		80	Died in London, England
1940	+ FITZMAURICE, George		45	After a 2-month streptococcus infection (in Los Angeles, CA)
1980	FITZPATRICK, James A.		78	Stroke (in Cathedral City, CA)
1993	FITZSIMMONS, Bob		53	Heart attack (after collapsing in a NY restaurant)
1983	#+ FIX, Paul		82	Kidney failure (in Santa Monica, CA)

• New entry. # Original name (Pt. 7). + Interment (Pt. 5).   223   ☆ Oscar nominee, ★ Oscar winner (Pt. 10)

Deaths of Movie and Television Personalities — by Name

YEAR	NAME		AGE	CAUSE and/or PLACE OF DEATH
1995	FLACK, Tim		?	After a long battle with A.I.D.S. (in Los Angeles, CA)
1962	FLAGSTAD, Kirsten		67	Died in Oslo, Norway
1970	FLAHERTY, Pat J. Sr.		67	Heart attack (in New York)
1951	FLAHERTY, Robert		67	Heart attack (in Dummerston, VT)
1995	FLANDERS, Ed		60	Suicide (shot himself in the head) in Denny, CA
1979	#+ FLATT, Lester		64	Heart attack (in Nashville, TN)
1990	FLAUM, Mayer		89	Pneumonia (in Los Angeles, CA)
1976	+ FLAVIN, James		69	Ruptured aorta (in Los Angeles, CA)
1995	FLEETWOOD, Susan		51	After a 10-yr. bout with cancer (in Salisbury, England)
1979	FLEISCHER, Dave		84	Stroke (in Woodland Hills, CA)
1985	FLEISCHER, Louis		94	Died in Woodland Hills, CA
• 1972	FLEISCHER, Max		88	Arteriosclerosis (at the MPCH in Woodland Hills, CA)
1966	#+ FLEMING, Eric		41	Drowned in the Huallaga River while filming in Peru
1969	# FLEMING, Ian (actor)		80	Died in London, England (Do not confuse with the writer)
• 1996	FLEMING, James F.		81	Died in Princeton, NJ
1949	+ FLEMING, Victor	★	64	After a heart attack (in Cottonwood, AZ)
1988	FLETCHER, Bramwell		84	Died in Westmoreland, NH
1990	FLETCHER, Jack		68	Heart failure (in Los Angeles, CA)
1967	FLINT, Helen		69	Struck by a car while crossing the street (in Washington, D.C.)
1980	FLINT, Sam		98	Died in Woodland Hills, CA
1971	+ FLIPPEN, Jay C.		72	Aneurysm (in Hollywood, CA)
1991	FLORANCE, Sheila		75	Cancer (in Melbourne, Australia)
1984	FLOWERS, Bess		85	Died in Woodland Hills, CA
1988	# FLOWERS, Wayland		48	Cancer (in Los Angeles, CA)
1990	FLUELLEN, Joel		82	Apparent suicide (gunshot) in Los Angeles, CA
1959	#+ FLYNN, Errol		50	Heart attack (in Vancouver, B.C., Canada)
1974	#+ FLYNN, Joe		49	Accidental drowning (in Beverly Hills, CA)
1970	# FLYNN, Sean		29	Missing in Cambodia (presumed dead)
• 1987	+ FLYNT, Althea Leasure		33	Drowned in her bathtub after getting high on heroin
1990	FOGERTY, Tom		48	Tuberculosis-related respiratory failure (in Scottsdale, AZ)
1968	#+ FOLEY, Red		58	Acute pulmonary edema (in Fort Wayne, IN)
1988	FOLSEY, George		90	Cerebral hemorrhage (in Santa Monica, CA)
1982	#+ FONDA, Henry	★	77	Heart failure and prostate cancer (in Los Angeles, CA)
1987	FONG, Benson		70	Following a stroke (in Los Angeles, CA)
1978	+ FONTAINE, Frank		58	Heart attack (in Spokane, WA)
1990	FONTANA, Arlene		54	Cancer (in New York, NY)
1974	+ FONTANE, Tony		47	Cancer (in Canoga Park, CA)
1983	#+ FONTANNE, Lynn	☆	95	Pneumonia (in Genesee Depot, WI)
1991	# FONTEYN, Margot		71	Cancer
1953	FOO, Wing		43	Heart attack (in Los Angeles, CA)
1979	# FORAN, Dick		69	Blood disorder (in Panorama City, CA)
1981	FORAN, Mary		61	Died in Los Angeles, CA
1964	FORBES, Mary		84	Heart attack (in Beaumont, CA)
1951	# FORBES, Ralph		54	Died at Montefiore Hospital in The Bronx, NY
1991	# FORD, "Tennessee" Ernie		72	Liver disease (in Reston, VA)
1993	FORD, Constance		69	Cancer (in New York, NY)
1995	FORD, Derek		62	Heart attack (in Bromly, Kent, England)
1953	# FORD, Francis		71	After a long illness (in Los Angeles, CA)
1957	FORD, Harrison		63	Died in Calabasas, CA (Do not confuse with the younger actor)
1973	#+ FORD, John	★	78	Cancer (in Palm Desert, CA)
1991	FORD, Lloyd		79	Ventricular fibrillation (in Woodland Hills, CA)
1977	#+ FORD, Mary		52	Complications of diabetes and pneumonia (in Arcadia, CA)
1976	#+ FORD, Paul		74	Died in Mineola, NY

Deaths of Movie and Television Personalities — by Name

YEAR	NAME	AGE	CAUSE and/or PLACE OF DEATH
1988	FORD, Ross	65	Cardiac arrest (in Hollywood, CA)
1966	# FORD, Wallace	68	Heart ailment (in Woodland Hills, CA)
• 1997	FORE, Edith	81	Died in Camden, NJ
1984	FOREMAN, Carl	69	Brain cancer (in Beverly Hills, CA)
1996	FOREMAN, Jack P.	71	Heart attack (at his home in Brentwood, CA)
1992	FOREMAN, John C.	67	Heart attack (in Beverly Hills, CA)
1982	FORMAN, Joey	53	Complications from pulmonary fibrosis (in West Hollywood, CA)
1926	FORMAN, Tom	33	Suicide (shot himself through the heart) in Venice, CA
1961	# FORMBY, George	56	Died in Preston, Lancashire, England
1941	# FORREST, Alan	51	Died in Detroit, MI
1989	FORREST, William H.	86	Heart attack (in Santa Monica, CA)
1995	FORRISTAL, John	37	Automobile accident (in Colorado)
1982	FORSTER, Peter	62	Died in Brentwood, CA
• 1996	# FORTE, Chet	60	Heart attack (at his home in San Diego, CA)
1967	# FORTE, Joe	71	After a heart attack (in Hollywood, CA)
1987	# FOSSE, Bob ★	60	Massive heart attack (in Washington, D.C.)
1985	FOSTER, Alan	80	Cancer (in Los Angeles, CA)
1973	FOSTER, Dudley	47	Suicide (hanging) in London, England
• 1997	# FOSTER, Frances	73	Cerebral hemorrhage in Fairfax, VA
1974	FOSTER, Lewis R.	75	Heart attack (in Tehachapi, CA)
1976	# FOSTER, Norman	76	Cancer (in Santa Monica, CA)
1985	# FOSTER, Phil	71	Heart attack (in Rancho Mirage, CA)
1970	+ FOSTER, Preston	69	Following a heart attack (in La Jolla, CA)
1970	FOULGER, Byron K.	69	Heart condition (in Hollywood, CA)
1988	FOULGER, Dorothy Adams	88	
1942	FOWLER, Brenda	59	Following a short illness (in Los Angeles, CA)
1960	+ FOWLER, Gene	70	Heart attack (in West Los Angeles, CA)
• 1998	FOWLER, JR., Gene ★	80	Died of natural causes in Los Angeles, CA
• 1998	FOWLEY, Douglas V.	86	Natural causes in Woodland Hills, CA
1994	FOX, George S.	89	Congestive heart failure (in Los Angeles, CA)
1959	# FOX, Harry	77	Died in Woodland Hills, CA
1984	FOX, John	60	Died in Los Angeles, CA
• 1996	FOX, Michael	75	Pneumonia (in Woodland Hills) Do not confuse with Michael J. Fox
1980	FOX, Virgil	68	Cancer
1982	FOX, Virginia (Zanuck)	79	Complications from stroke and emphysema (in Palm Springs, CA)
1958	+ FOX, Wallace	63	Died in Hollywood, CA
1952	FOX, William	73	Heart attack (in New York, NY)
1993	FOX, William J.	95	Died in Fillmore, CA
1973	FOXE, Earle A.	84	Died in Los Angeles, CA
1991	#+ FOXX, Redd	68	Heart attack during rehearsal for new TV show (in Hollywood, CA)
1977	+ FOY, Bryon	82	Following a series of heart attacks (in Los Angeles, CA)
1983	# FOY, Eddie Jr.	78	Pancreatic cancer
1928	#+ FOY, Eddie Sr.	71	Heart disease (in Kansas City, MO)
1977	# FRANCEN, Victor	89	Died in Aix-en-Provence, France
1991	FRANCESCATTI, Zino	89	
1992	# FRANCHI, Franco	70	Hemorrhage (in a hospital in Rome, Italy)
1990	FRANCHI, Sergio	64	Brain cancer (in Stonington, NY)
• 1998	FRANCHINA, Sandro	58	Cancer in Paris
• 1998	FRANCIOSA, Massimo	73	Heart attack at his home in Rome, Italy
1934	FRANCIS, Alec B.	65	Following an emergency operation (in Hollywood, CA)
1973	FRANCIS, Coleman	53	Arteriosclerosis (in Hollywood, CA)
1986	FRANCIS, Ivor	68	Died in Sherman Oaks, CA
1968	# FRANCIS, Kay	65	Cancer (in New York, NY)

Deaths of Movie and Television Personalities — by Name

YEAR	NAME	AGE	CAUSE and/or PLACE OF DEATH
1959	FRANCIS, Noel	48	Died in Los Angeles, CA
1952	FRANCIS, Olin	59	Died in Hollywood, CA
1987	FRANCIS, Raymond	76	Died in London, England
1955	+ FRANCIS, Robert	25	Airplane crash (in Burbank, CA)
1981	# FRANCIS, Sandra	47	Results of a motorcycle accident (in Santa Monica, CA)
1991	# FRANCIS, Wilma	73	Complications after lung surgery
1950	FRANCISCO, Betty	50	Heart attack at her ranch (in El Cerito, CA)
1991	# FRANCISCUS, James	57	Emphysema (in Hollywood, CA)
1990	FRANCK, Edward A.	70	Pneumonia (in New York, NY)
• 1998	FRANCO, Ricardo	48	Heart failure in Madrid, Spain
• 1997	FRANCOVICH, Allan	56	Heart failure going though US Customs in Houston, TX
1940	# FRANEY, Billy	55	Influenza (in Hollywood, CA)
• 1996	FRANEY, Pierre	75	Stroke (at a hospital in Southampton, NY)
1987	FRANJU, Georges	75	Undisclosed causes (in Paris, France)
1990	FRANK, Ben	56	Heart attack (in Los Angeles, CA)
1988	FRANK, Melvin	75	Complications following open-heart surgery (in Los Angeles, CA)
1995	FRANK, Richard Edward	42	Complications of A.I.D.S. (in Los Angeles, CA)
1994	FRANKEL, Daniel	91	Natural causes (in Winchester, NH)
• 1998	FRANKEL, Kenneth	56	Brain tumor at his home in Los Angeles, CA
• 1996	FRANKEL, Mark	34	Injuries from a motorcycle accident (in London, England)
1976	FRANKLIN, Alberta	79	Died in Mountain View, CA
1995	# FRANKLIN, Melvin	52	Heart failure after a series of seizures (in Los Angeles, CA)
1939	+ FRANKLIN, Rupert	77	Died in Los Angeles, CA
1918	FRANKLIN, Ruth Darling	22	Crushed by auto while waiting for a street car
1931	+ FRANKLIN, Sidney (actor)	61	After a long illness (Do not confuse with director, d. 1972)
1972	#+ FRANKLIN, Sidney (director) ☆	79	Heart attack (Do not confuse with silent film actor, d. 1931)
1992	# FRANKOVICH, Mike ★	82	Pneumonia and Alzheimer's disease (in Los Angeles, CA)
1983	FRANZ, Eduard	81	After a long illness (in Los Angeles, CA)
1987	# FRASER, Bill	79	Emphysema (in Hertfordshire, England)
1974	FRASER, Harry	84	Died in Pamona, CA
1992	FRASER, June Joyce Lewis	75	Complications of pneumonia (in Englewood, NJ)
1992	FRASER, Tom	60	Heart failure after exercising at his gym (in Los Angeles, CA)
1966	+ FRAWLEY, William	79	Heart attack (in Los Angeles, CA)
1985	# FRAZEE, Jane	67	Pneumonia following a stroke (in Newport Beach, CA)
1944	FRAZER, Robert W.	53	Leukemia (in Los Angeles, CA)
1939	FRAZIN, Gladys	37	Suicide (jumped from her apartment window) in New York, NY
1975	FRECHETTE, Mark	27	Crushed to death by a barbell while in jail
1933	# FREDERICI, Blanche	55	Heart attack enroute to a Christmas church service (in Visalia, CA)
1986	+ FREDERICK, Freddie Burke	65	Ventricular arrhythmia due to myocardial infarction
1994	FREDERICK, Lynne	39	Found dead in bed, apparently of natural causes (in Los Angeles)
1990	FREDERICK, Pauline (TV news)	84	Heart attack (Do not confuse with actress Pauline Frederick, d. 1938)
1938	#+ FREDERICK, Pauline (actress)	54	Asthma (in Los Angeles, CA) — Do not confuse with TV reporter
1970	FREDERICKS, Charles	50	Heart attack (in Sherman Oaks, CA)
1973	#+ FREED, Arthur	78	Heart attack (in Bel Air, CA)
1994	FREED, Bert	74	Heart attack (while on vacation in British Columbia)
• 1991	FREEMAN, Dexter	53	A.I.D.S.
1991	FREEMAN, Everett	79	Renal failure (in Westwood, CA)
1967	# FREEMAN, Howard	68	After a brief illness (in New York, NY)
1969	+ FREEMAN, Young Frank	78	
• 1986	FREES, Paul	66	Heart failure
1987	FREGONESE, Hugo	78	Heart attack (in Buenos Aires, Argentina)
1995	#+ FRELENG, Friz	89	Natural causes (in Hollywood, CA)
1952	FRENCH, Charles K.	92	After a heart attack (in Hollywood, CA)

Deaths of Movie and Television Personalities — by Name

YEAR	NAME		AGE	CAUSE and/or PLACE OF DEATH
1961	+ FRENCH, George B.		78	*Heart attack (in Hollywood, CA)*
1989	FRENCH, Norma		47	*Lymphoma (in Toronto, Canada)*
1990	FRENCH, Valerie		59	*Leukemia (in New York, NY)*
1989	FRENCH, Victor		54	*Lung cancer (in Sherman Oaks, CA)*
1977	FREND, Charles		68	*Cancer (in London, England)*
1975	# FRESNAY, Pierre		77	*Respiratory ailment (in Neuilly-sur-Seine, France)*
1969	FREUND, Karl		79	*Died in Santa Monica, CA*
1961	FREY, Arno		60	*Heart attack from a blood clot (in Los Angeles, CA)*
1988	FREY, Leonard ☆		49	*A.I.D.S. (in New York, NY)*
1988	FRIEBUS, Florida		79	*Died in Laguna Miguel, CA*
1981	FRIEDHOFER, Hugo ★		80	*While hospitalized after a fall at his home (in Los Angeles, CA)*
1996	FRIEDMAN, Stephen		59	*Multiple myeloma (at his home in Brentwood, CA)*
1998	FRIENDLY, Fred		82	*Died after a series of Strokes at his New York home*
1955	FRIGANZA, Trixie		84	*After being bedridden with arthritis (in Flintridge, CA)*
1972	#+ FRIML, Rudolph		92	*Brain hemorrhage (at Hollywood Pres. Hosp. in Hollywood, CA)*
1958	#+ FRISCO, Joe		68	*After a long illness (in Calabasas, CA)*
1973	FRITSCH, Willy		72	*Heart attack (in Hamburg, Germany)*
1975	#+ FRIZZELL, Lefty		47	*After suffering a stroke (in Nashville, TN)*
1988	# FROEBE, Gert		75	*Heart attack (in Munich, Germany)*
1987	FROHLICH, Gustav		85	*Following surgery (in Lugano, Switzerland)*
1980	FROMAN, Jane		71	*Cardiac arrest in her sleep*
1989	FROME, Milton		78	*Heart failure (in Woodland Hills, CA)*
1992	FROMMER, Ben		78	*Died in Burbank, CA*
1993	FROST, Terry		86	*Heart failure (in Los Angeles, Ca)*
1994	FRYD, Joseph		89	*Following a stroke (in Rome, Italy)*
1943	+ FRYE, Dwight		44	*Heart attack (in Hollywood, CA)*
1993	FUCCELLO, Tom		55	*A.I.D.S. (at a convalescent home in Van Nuys, CA)*
1993	FUCHS, Daniel ★		84	*Heart failure (in Los Angeles, CA)*
1983	FUJIKAWA, Jerry		71	*Heart disease (in Los Angeles, CA)*
1996	FULCI, Lucio		68	*After a long battle with diabetes (at his home in Rome, Italy)*
1961	FULLER, Clem		52	*Cancer (in Hollywood, CA)*
1980	FULLER, Frances		73	*Died in New York, NY*
1948	FULLER, Leslie		58	*Heart attack (in Margate, England)*
1973	+ FULLER, Mary		85	*Massive pulmonary embolism (in Washington, D.C.)*
1997	FULLER, Samuel		86	*Natural causes in Hollywood Hills, CA*
1950	+ FULTON, Maude		69	*Died at the Motion Picture Country Home, CA*
1945	FUNG, Willie		49	*Coronary occlusion (in Los Angeles, CA)*
1971	FUQUA, Charles		60	*Died in New Haven, CT*
1938	FUREY, Barney		49	*Liver ailment (in Los Angeles, CA)*
1994	# FURNESS, Betty		78	*Stomach cancer (at Sloan-Kettering Memorial Hospital, NY)*
1991	# FURST, Anton ★		47	*Suicide (jumped from 8th level of parking garage) in Hollywood, CA*
1966	FURTHMAN, Jules		78	*Stroke while vacationing (in Oxford, England)*
1994	FUSCO, Nelly		85	*Cancer (at St. Francis Hosp. in Poughkeepsie, NY)*
1947	FYFFE, Will		36	*Fall from his hotel window (in St. Andrews, Scotland)*

G

YEAR	NAME		AGE	CAUSE and/or PLACE OF DEATH
1972	# GAAL, Franceska		68	*Died in New York, NY*
1986	GABEL, Martin		73	*Heart attack (in New York, NY)*
1976	# GABIN, Jean		72	*Heart attack (in Neuilly-sur-Seine, France)*
1960	#+ GABLE, Clark ★		59	*Heart attack (in Hollywood, CA)*
1995	+ GABOR, Eva		74	*Complications of pneumonia (at Cedars-Sinai Med. Ctr. in L.A.)*
1997	GABOR, Magda		78	*Kidney failer at Eisenhower Medical Center in Rancho Mirage, CA*
1981	GAFNI, Miklos		57	*Massive heart attack (at Kennedy Airport, NY)*
1978	GAGE, Ben		62	*Died in Los Angeles, CA*

Deaths of Movie and Television Personalities — by Name

YEAR	NAME	AGE	CAUSE and/or PLACE OF DEATH
1991	GAILLARD, Slim	74	Cancer (in London, England)
1975	GAINES, Richard H.	70	Heart attack (in North Hollywood, CA)
1991	GAINSBOURG, Serge	62	Heart trouble (in Paris, France)
1948	GALE, Marguerite H.	63	Died in Amsterdam, NY
1979	+ GALENTO, Tony "Twoton"	69	Heart attack (in Livingston, NJ)
1953	GALLAGHER, Raymond "Ray"	67	Heart attack (in Camarillo, CA)
1955	# GALLAGHER, Skeets	64	Following a heart attack (in Santa Monica, CA)
1972	GALLIAN, Ketti	58	Died in France
1984	GALLO, Mario	61	Died in Ontario, CA
1960	# GALVANI, Dino	69	Died in London, England
1990	GAMBARELLI, Maria	89	Cerebral hemorrhage (in Huntington, NY)
1959	GAN, Chester	50	Died in San Francisco, CA
1981	GANCE, Abel	92	Lung ailment (in Paris, France)
1998	GANG, Martin	96	After a long illness in Santa Monica, CA
1985	GANTRY, Donald	52	Cancer (in New York, NY)
1956	+ GANZHORN, John W.	75	Died in Hollywood, CA
1959	GARAT, Henri	57	Heart attack (in Hyeres, France)
1977	GARBER, Jan	82	Died in Shreveport, LA
1990	#+ GARBO, Greta ☆	84	Undisclosed causes (in New York, NY)
1938	GARCIA, Allan	51	Died in Los Angeles, CA
1970	GARCIA, Henry	66	After a long illness (in a hospital in San Antonio, TX)
1995	#+ GARCIA, Jerry	53	Heart attack (at Serenity Knolls drug treatment center in CA)
1989	GARDE, Betty	84	Died in Hollywood, CA
1967	GARDEN, Mary	92	Died in Aberdeen, Scotland
1992	# GARDENIA, Vincent ☆	71	Found dead in his hotel room of a heart attack (in Philadelphia, PA)
1980	+ GARDINER, Reginald	77	Heart attack and pneumonia (in Westwood, CA)
1990	#+ GARDNER, Ava ☆	67	Pneumonia and heart attack (in Kensington, England)
1963	# GARDNER, Ed	62	Diseased liver
1968	# GARDNER, Helen	83	Died in Orlando, FL
1989	GARDNER, Hy	80	Pneumonia (in Miami, FL)
1977	GARDNER, Jack	77	After a short illness (in Houston, TX)
1994	GARFIELD, David	51	Heart attack (in Los Angeles, CA)
1952	#+ GARFIELD, John ☆	39	Heart attack (in New York, NY)
1964	GARGAN, Edward	63	Died in New York, NY
1983	GARGAN, Mary Elizabeth	76	Lung cancer (in Rancho La Costa, CA)
1979	GARGAN, William ☆	73	Heart attack (in San Diego, CA)
1969	#+ GARLAND, Judy ☆	47	Accidental drug overdose (in London, England)
1978	GARMES, Lee ★	80	Died in Los Angeles, CA
1977	+ GARNER, Erroll	53	Emphysema and heart attack (in Los Angeles, CA)
1984	GARNER, Peggy Ann	52	Cancer (in Woodland Hills, CA)
1977	GARNETT, Tay	83	Leukemia
1965	# GARON, Pauline	63	Died in Canada
1981	# GARRALAGA, Martin	85	Died in Woodland Hills, CA
1993	GARRETT, Joy	47	Liver failure (in Los Angeles, CA)
1982	GARROWAY, Dave	69	Apparent suicide (gunshot) in Swarthmore, PA
1996	+ GARSON, Greer ★	92	Heart failure (at Presbyterian Hospital in Dallas, TX)
1993	GARVARENTZ, George	61	Heart failure (in Aubagne, France)
1950	GARWOOD, William	66	Coronary occlusion (in Los Angeles, CA)
1998	GARY, John	65	Cancer at Baylor Hospital in Dallas, TX
1963	GASNIER, Louis J.	87	Died in Hollywood, CA
1996	GATES, Larry	81	Died in Sharon, CT
1977	GATESON, Marjorie	86	Pneumonia (in New York, NY)
1990	GATLIFF, Frank	62	Died in London, England

• New entry.   # Original name (Pt. 7).   + Interment (Pt. 5).

☆ Oscar nominee,   ★ Oscar winner (Pt. 10)

YEAR	NAME		AGE	CAUSE and/or PLACE OF DEATH
1992	# GAUDIO, Joe		79	Cancer
1960	GAUGE, Alexander		46	Heart attack (in Woking, Surrey, England)
1974	GAUGUIN, Lorraine		50	Died when fire destroyed her home (in Los Angeles, CA)
1988	GAUTHIER, Suzanne		61	Cancer (in Hollywood, CA)
1962	GAWTHORNE, Peter		77	Died in London, England
1963	GAXTON, William		70	After a long illness (in New York, NY)
1955	GAYE, Howard		?	Died in London, England
1984	#+ GAYE, Marvin		44	Murdered (shot by his father) in Los Angeles, CA
• 1997	GAYNES, Lloyd H.		68	Pancreatic cancer at home in Hollywood, CA
1984	#+ GAYNOR, Janet	★	77	Pneumonia (in Palm Springs, CA)
1995	#+ GAZZO, Michael V.	☆	71	Complications from a stroke (in Los Angeles, CA)
1946	# GEARY, Bud		47	Injuries from an automobile crash (in Hollywood, CA)
1987	GEARY, John		47	Apparent heart attack (while driving) in Fall River, MA
1919	GEBHARDT, George M.		39	Tuberculosis (in Switzerland)
1954	GEBUEHR, Otto		76	Heart attack (in Wiesbaden, West Germany)
1995	GEE, Kevin John		40	Pneumonia (in New York City)
1989	GEER, Lenny		75	Heart failure (in Topega Canyon, CA)
1978	#+ GEER, Will		76	Respiratory arrest (in Los Angeles, CA)
1941	#+ GEHRIG, Lou		37	Amyotrophic lateral sclerosis (in New York, NY)
1992	GEIL, Joe "Corky"		64	After a brief illness (in Long Beach, CA)
1988	GEISE, Tanya "Sugar"		71	After a brief illness (in Hollywood, CA)
1935	GELDERT, Clarence		67	Heart attack (in Calabasas, CA)
1978	+ GELLER, Bruce		47	Airplane crash (in Los Angeles, CA)
1978	GENN, Leo	☆	72	Heart attack (in London, England)
1958	GENTLE, Alice		69	Died in Oakland, CA
1989	GENTRY, Britt Nilsson		46	Cancer (in Los Angeles, CA)
1993	GENTRY, Minnie L.		77	Lung cancer (in New York, NY)
1981	# GEORGE "Chief" Dan	☆	82	Died in Vancouver, Canada
1983	+ GEORGE, Christopher		54	Heart attack (in Los Angeles, CA)
1993	GEORGE, George L.	★	85	Heart failure (in New York, NY)
1954	# GEORGE, Gladys	☆	54	Brain hemorrhage (in Los Angeles, CA)
1963	#+ GEORGE, Gorgeous		48	Heart attack (in Los Angeles, CA)
1946	# GEORGE, Heinrich		53	During an appendectomy (in Sachsenhousen, Germany)
1968	GEORGE, John		70	Emphysema (in Los Angeles, CA)
1992	GEORGE, Joseph L.		65	Cancer (in Agawam, MA)
1965	GEORGE, Muriel		82	Died in London, England
1966	GERAGHTY, Carmelita		65	Died in New York, NY
1987	GERAGHTY, Maurice		78	Died in Palm Springs, CA
1985	GERASIMOV, Sergei		79	Heart attack (in Moscow, Russia)
1973	# GERAY, Steven		75	Died in Los Angeles, CA
1977	GERING, Marion		73	Died in New York, NY
1950	# GERRARD, Douglas		69	After being found unconscious on the street (in Hollywood, CA)
1989	GERRINGER, Robert		63	After a series of strokes
1944	# GERRON, Kurt		47	Executed (in Auschwitz, Germany)
1991	GERRY, Toni		65	Bone cancer (in Los Angeles, CA)
1937	#+ GERSHWIN, George		38	After surgery for a brain tumor (in Beverly Hills, CA)
1983	+ GERSHWIN, Ira		86	Died in Beverly Hills, CA
1992	# GERSON, Jeanne		87	Cancer and pneumonia (in Laguna Hills, CA)
1957	GERSON, Paul		86	Died in Hollywood, CA
1970	# GERSTLE, Frank		54	Cancer (in Santa Monica, CA)
1987	GESSNER, Adrienne		90	Died in Vienna, Austria
1965	GEST, Inna		43	Hepatitis (in San Francisco, CA)
1991	GETZ, Stan		64	After a 5-year battle with liver cancer (in Los Angeles, CA)

Deaths of Movie and Television Personalities — by Name

YEAR	NAME	AGE	CAUSE and/or PLACE OF DEATH
• 1997	GEVA, Tamara	91	Died at her home in Manhattan, NY
• 1981	GIANELLO, Nino	?	
1995	GIANNETI, Alfredo	71	After suffering a stroke (in Rome, Italy)
1988	+ GIBB, Andy	30	Heart inflammation caused by a virus (in Oxford, England)
1995	GIBBENS, Vince	46	Apparent heart attack (in Milwaukee, WI)
1994	GIBBERSON, William	74	Effects of a stroke (in New York)
1993	GIBBINS, Duncan	41	Burns while trying to rescue a cat from a fire (in Malibu, CA)
1988	GIBBS, Alan R.	47	Cancer (in Los Angeles, CA)
1986	GIBNEY, Louise	90	Died in Santa Maria, CA
1977	# GIBSON, Helen	85	Stroke and heart attack (in Roseburg, OR)
1962	#+ GIBSON, Hoot	70	Cancer (in Woodland Hills, CA)
1991	GIBSON, Marc	51	Apparent heart attack after a workout
1987	GIBSON, Wynne	82	Stroke (in Laguna Miguel, CA)
1989	GIFFORD, Alan	78	Died in Scotland
1994	GIFFORD, Frances	72	Emphysema (in Pasadena, CA)
1971	+ GILBERT, Billy	77	Stroke (in North Hollywood, CA)
1991	GILBERT, Joan	84	
1979	GILBERT, Jody	62	Following an automobile accident (in Sherman Oaks, CA)
1959	GILBERT, Joe	56	Died in Hollywood, CA
1936	#+ GILBERT, John	38	Heart attack (in Los Angeles, CA)
1978	GILBERT, Lou	69	Apparent heart attack (in Reseda, CA)
1947	GILBERT, Walter	60	Heart attack (in Brooklyn, NY)
1919	GILFETHER, Daniel	65	Kidney disease (in Long Beach, CA)
1990	# GILFORD, Jack ☆	81	Stomach cancer (in New York, NY)
1955	GILL, Basil	77	Died in Hove, England
• 1997	GILL, David	69	Heart attack in Huntingdon, England
1992	GILL, Ray	42	A.I.D.S.
1971	GILL, Tom	54	Died in England
1993	# GILLESPIE, Dizzy	75	Died in his sleep of pancreatic cancer (in Englewood, NJ)
1932	+ GILLETT, King	77	
1994	GILLETTE, Ruth	89	Cancer (in Los Angeles, CA)
1994	GILLIAT, Sidney	85	Leukemia at his home (in Wiltshire, England)
1991	GILLIES, Carol	50	Cancer (in London, England)
1939	GILLINGWATER, Claude	69	Suicide (gunshot) in Beverly Hills, CA
1986	GILLMORE, Margalo	88	Died in New York, NY
1985	GILMAN, Sam	70	Cancer (in North Hollywood, CA)
1986	GILMORE, Virginia	66	Emphysema (in Santa Barbara, CA)
1989	GIMPEL, Jakob	82	Died in Los Angeles, CA
1987	+ GINGOLD, Hermione	89	Pneumonia and cardiac disease (in New York, NY)
1992	# GIOVALE, Franco	44	After a car accident (in Capalbio, Italy)
1992	GIOVANNITTI, Len	71	Heart disease (in New York, NY)
1949	# GIRARD, Joe	78	Died in Los Angeles, CA
1939	GIRARDOT, Etienne	83	After a brief illness (in Hollywood, CA)
1978	GIRDLER, William	30	Helicopter crash (in Santa Cruz, Philippine Islands)
1968	#+ GISH, Dorothy	70	Bronchial pneumonia (in Rapallo, Italy)
1993	+ GISH, Lillian ☆	99	Cerebral hemorrhage and heart failure (in New York, NY)
1978	GIVNEY, Kathryn	80	Died in Hollywood, CA
1984	GIVOT, George	81	Died in Palm Springs, CA
1966	GLASS, Everett	74	Died in Los Angeles, CA
1965	GLASS, Gaston J.	66	Died in Santa Monica, CA
1984	GLASS, Ned	78	After a lengthy illness (in Encino, CA)
1989	# GLAUDI, Hap	77	Cancer
1970	GLAUM, Louise	70	Pneumonia (in Los Angeles, CA)

Deaths of Movie and Television Personalities — by Name

YEAR	NAME	AGE	CAUSE and/or PLACE OF DEATH
1987	+ GLEASON, Jackie ☆	71	Cancer of the liver and colon (in Fort Lauderdale, FL)
1959	#+ GLEASON, James ☆	76	Asthma (in Woodland Hills, CA)
1947	# GLEASON, Lucille	59	Heart attack (in Brentwood, CA)
1946	GLEASON, Russell	37	Accidental fall from a 4th floor hotel window (in New York, NY)
1939	GLECKLER, Robert P.	49	Uremic poisoning (in North Hollywood, CA)
1937	GLENDON, Jonathan Frank	49	Died in Hollywood, CA
1974	# GLENN, Raymond	76	Cardiac arrest in his sleep (in Torrance, CA)
1971	GLENN, Roy Sr.	56	Apparent heart attack (in Los Angeles, CA)
1967	# GLENNON, Bert ☆	72	Heart attack (in Sherman Oaks, CA)
1990	GLIDDON, John	92	
1992	GLIONA, Michael	45	Liver failure (in Los Angeles, CA)
1997	GLOOR, Kurt	54	Suicide in Zurich, Switzerland
1966	# GLORI, Enrico	64	Died in Rome, Italy
1997	GLOVER, Brian	63	Died of complications from a brain tumor
1954	# GLYNNE, Mary	56	Died in London, England
1991	+ GOBEL, George	71	Complications after arterial leg surgery (in Encino, CA)
1981	GODDARD, Alf	83	Died in England
1990	# GODDARD, Paulette ☆	84	Heart failure (in Porto Rosco, Switzerland)
1955	GODDEN, Jimmy	75	Died in England
1983	GODFREY, Arthur	79	Pneumonia and emphysema (in New York, NY)
1970	GODFREY, Peter	70	Cancer (in Hollywood, CA)
1975	+ GODOWSKY, Dagmar	78	Died in New York, NY
1990	GODSELL, Vanda	70	
1995	GODUNOV, Alexander	45	Natural causes (found dead in his West Hollywood, CA, home)
1969	+ GOETZ, William	66	Cancer (in Holmby Hills, CA)
1964	GOETZKE, Bernhard	79	Died in Berlin, Germany
1978	GOFF, Norris "Abner"	72	Stroke
1997	GOKHLE, Kamalbai	97	Died in Pune City
1991	GOLDEN, Murray	79	Complications after a stroke (in Encino, CA)
1996	GOLDFARB, Howard	55	Heart failure after open-heart surgery (at Holy Cross Hosp. in L.A.)
1971	# GOLDIN, Pat	68	Heart attack (in Los Angeles, CA)
1955	GOLDNER, Charles	54	Died in London, England
1991	GOLDRICH, Bert	84	
1993	GOLDSTEIN, Elayne	59	Cancer
1976	#+ GOLDWYN, Frances Howard		(See Frances Howard)
1973	#+ GOLDWYN, Samuel	91	Cancer (in Beverly Hills, CA)
1973	GOMBELL, Minna	80	Cancer (in Santa Monica, CA)
1971	+ GOMEZ, Thomas ☆	65	During a long coma after a car accident (in Santa Monica, CA)
1995	GONZALES, Pancho	67	
1918	GONZALEZ, Myrtle	27	Heart disease and pneumonia (in Los Angeles, CA)
1996	GOOD, John	77	Lung cancer (in Los Angeles, CA)
1971	# GOODE, Jack	63	Acute infectious hepatitis (in New York, NY)
1976	GOODLIFFE, Michael	61	Suicide leap while in a hospital (in London, England)
1986	+ GOODMAN, Benny	77	Heart attack (in Manhattan, NY)
1988	GOODMAN, Lee	64	Tuberculosis (in New York, NY)
1996	GOODMAN, Miles	47	After suffering a heart attack (at his home in Los Angeles, CA)
1984	GOODRICH, Frances	93	
1992	+ GOODSON, Mark	77	Cancer (in Los Angeles, CA)
1958	#+ GOODWIN, Bill	47	Heart attack (in Palm Springs, CA)
1983	GOODWIN, Robert L.	55	Died in Los Angeles, CA
1961	# GOODWIN, Ruby B.	57	Died in Hollywood, CA
1992	GOODWIN, Thomas Jr.	51	Prostate cancer (in Washington, D.C.)
1980	GOOLDEN, Richard	86	Died in London, England

• New entry. # Original name (Pt. 7). + Interment (Pt. 5).   231   ☆ Oscar nominee, ★ Oscar winner (Pt. 10)

Deaths of Movie and Television Personalities — by Name

YEAR	NAME	AGE	CAUSE and/or PLACE OF DEATH
1998	# GORA, Claudio	84	Heart failure at his home near Rome, Italy
1955	GORCEY, Bernard	67	Injuries from an auto accident (in Hollywood, CA)
1984	GORCEY, David	63	Diabetic coma (in Los Angeles, CA)
1969	#+ GORCEY, Leo	53	Liver ailment (in Oakland, CA)
1974	GORDON, Bert	76	After a long bout with cancer (in Duarte, CA)
1940	# GORDON, C. Henry	57	Result of leg amputation (in Los Angeles, CA)
1972	GORDON, Colin	61	Died in Haslemere, England
1990	GORDON, Dexter ☆	67	Kidney failure and cancer of the larynx (in Philadelphia, PA)
1995	#+ GORDON, Gale	89	Cancer (at Redwood Terrace Health Ctr. in Escondido, CA)
1983	GORDON, Gavin	82	Cerebral thrombosis (in Canoga Park, CA)
1946	GORDON, Hal	52	Died in England
1956	+ GORDON, Huntly	59	Heart attack (in Van Nuys, CA)
1941	GORDON, James	60	After an emergency operation (in Hollywood, CA)
1933	GORDON, Julia Swayne	54	After a long illness (in Columbus, OH)
1974	GORDON, Kitty	96	Died at a nursing home in Brentwood, NY
1960	+ GORDON, Leon	66	Heart ailment (in Hollywood, CA)
1963	GORDON, Mary	81	Died in Pasadena, CA
1940	GORDON, Maude Turner	71	Pneumonia (in Los Angeles, CA)
1993	GORDON, Michael S.	83	Cardiac arrest in his sleep while hospitalized (in Century City, CA)
1985	GORDON, Noele	61	Cancer (in Birmingham, England)
1971	# GORDON, Robert	76	Died in Victorville, CA
1985	# GORDON, Ruth ★	88	Stroke (in Edgartown, MA)
1982	GORDON, Steve	44	Heart attack (in New York, NY)
1948	GORDON, Vera	61	Died in Beverly Hills, CA
1993	GORI, Mario Cecchi	73	Apparent heart attack (in Rome, Italy)
1982	GORIN, Igor	80	
1988	GORMAN, Bobby	59	Following a long illness (in Los Angeles, CA)
1966	GORSS, Saul	58	Heart attack (in Los Angeles, CA)
1982	+ GOSDEN, Freeman "Amos"	83	Heart failure (in Los Angeles, CA)
1964	GOSFIELD, Maurice	51	After being hospitalized for diabetes (in Saronac Lake, NY)
1944	GOTT, Barbara	?	
1995	+ GOTTLIEB, Conrad I.	77	Congestive heart failure (at J. Hopkins Hosp. in Balt., MD)
1996	GOTTLIEB, Lawrence	64	Apparent heart failure (at his home in Newport, CA)
1944	GOTTSCHALK, Ferdinand	75	Died in London, England
1985	+ GOUDAL, Jetta	86	After a long illness (in Los Angeles, CA)
1968	GOUGH, John	70	Cancer (in Hollywood, CA)
1984	GOUGH, Lloyd	77	Aortic aneurysm (in Sherman Oaks, CA)
1982	+ GOULD, Glenn	50	Massive stroke (in Toronto, Canada)
1996	GOULD, Morton	82	Died in Orlando, FL
1972	GOULDING, Alfred	76	Pneumonia (in Hollywood, CA)
1959	GOULDING, Edmund	68	Died in Los Angeles, CA
1990	GOULDING, Ray	68	Kidney failure (in Manhasset, NY)
1951	GOWLAND, Gibson	79	Died in London, England
1973	#+ GRABLE, Betty	56	Lung cancer (in Santa Monica, CA)
1967	GRAF, Louis C.	77	Heart attack (in Hollywood, CA)
1994	GRAF, William N.	82	Heart failure complicated by pneumonia (in Los Angeles, CA)
1969	GRAFF, Wilton	65	Died in Pacific Palisades, CA
1991	# GRAHAM, Bill	60	Helicopter crash (in Sonoma County, CA)
1979	GRAHAM, Fred	61	Died in Scottsdale, AZ
1935	GRAHAM, Julia Ann	20	Suicide (gunshot) in Los Angeles, CA
1991	GRAHAM, Martha	96	Pneumonia and cardiac arrest (in New York, NY)
1949	# GRAHAM, Morland	57	Heart attack (in London, England)
1988	GRAHAM, Sheilah	84	Congestive heart failure (in West Palm Beach, FL)

Deaths of Movie and Television Personalities — by Name

YEAR	NAME	AGE	CAUSE and/or PLACE OF DEATH
1981	#+ GRAHAME, Gloria ★	57	Cancer (in Manhattan, NY)
1982	GRAHAME, Margot	70	Respiratory failure from chronic bronchitis (in London, England)
1932	GRAN, Albert	70	Injuries from an automobile accident (in Los Angeles, CA)
1945	GRANACH, Alexander	54	Complications after surgery (in New York, NY)
1965	GRANBY, Joseph	80	Cerebral hemorrhage (in Hollywood, CA)
1988	GRANDIN, Ethel	94	Died in Woodland Hills, CA
1991	GRANGE, Red	87	
1995	GRANGER, Dorothy	83	Cancer (at her home in Los Angeles, CA)
1993	GRANGER, John	69	Cerebral hemmorhage (in Doylestown, PA)
1997	GRANGER, Percy	51	Cardiac arrest (in New York City, NY)
1993	# GRANGER, Stewart	80	Prostate and bone cancer (in Santa Monica, CA)
1996	# GRANGIER, Gilles	85	Died in Suresnes, France
1986	#+ GRANT, Cary ☆	82	Massive stroke (in Davenport, IA)
1970	+ GRANT, Earl	39	Automobile accident (near Lordsburg, NM)
1985	# GRANT, Kirby	74	Automobile accident (in Titusville, FL)
1952	GRANT, Lawrence	82	Died in Santa Barbara, CA
1984	# GRANT, Shauna	20	Suicide (gunshot) in Palm Springs, CA
1959	# GRANT, Tiny	45	
1988	+ GRANVILLE, Bonita (Wrather) ☆	65	Cancer (in Santa Monica, CA)
1968	GRANVILLE, Louise	73	Hong Kong flu after being hospitalized for asthma (in Hollywood, CA)
1956	#+ GRAPEWIN, Charley	80	After a long illness (in Corona del Mar, CA)
1953	GRASSBY, Bertram	72	Died in Scottsdale, AZ
1978	GRAVERS, Steve	56	Lung cancer (in Studio City, CA)
1977	GRAVES, Ralph	77	Heart attack (in Santa Barbara, CA)
1970	# GRAVET, Fernand	64	Myocardial infarction (in Paris, France)
1954	GRAVINA, Cesare	96	Died in Italy
1975	GRAY, Alexander	73	Died in Los Angeles, CA
1996	# GRAY, Barry	80	Complications from back surgery (at a hospital in Manhattan, NY)
1959	#+ GRAY, Gilda	61	Heart attack after food poisoning (in Hollywood, CA)
1963	# GRAY, Glen	63	Died in Plymouth, MA
1956	GRAY, Jack	76	After a long illness (in Woodland Hills, CA)
1970	GRAY, Lawrence	71	Died in Mexico City, Mexico
1981	GRAY, Mack	75	Following a prolonged illness (in Los Angeles, CA)
1994	GRAY, Nadia	70	Stroke (at New York Hospital in Manhattan)
1913	GRAYBILL, Joseph	26	Spinal meningitis (in New York, NY)
1995	GRAYSON, Arlene	45	Bone cancer (at her home in Los Angeles, CA)
1990	# GRAZIANO, Rocky	68	Cardiopulmonary failure (in New York, NY)
1973	# GREAZA, Walter	76	Died in New York, NY
1973	GREEN, Abel	72	Died in New York
1960	+ GREEN, Alfred E.	71	Arthritis (in Hollywood, CA)
1963	GREEN, Dorothy	71	Died in New York, NY
1940	GREEN, Fred E.	50	Injuries from an automobile accident (in San Mateo, CA)
1984	GREEN, Gilbert	68	Complications after an illness (in Tarzana, CA)
1958	# GREEN, Harry	66	Heart attack (in London, England)
1989	GREEN, John	80	Pulmonary edema (in Beverly Hills, CA)
1996	GREEN, Joseph	96	After suffering from emphysema
1969	GREEN, Kenneth	61	Heart attack while operating heavy equipment (in Hollywood, CA)
1991	GREEN, Lee	72	Automobile accident (in Baja, Mexico)
1975	# GREEN, Martyn	75	Blood infection (in Hollywood, CA)
1969	# GREEN, Mitzi	48	Cancer (in Huntington Harbor, CA)
1972	GREEN, Nigel	48	Overdose of sleeping pills at his home (in Brighton, England)
1996	GREENBERG, Harold	66	Pancreatic cancer (in Montreal, Quebec, Canada)
1978	GREENE, Angela	55	Stroke (in Los Angeles, CA)

Deaths of Movie and Television Personalities — by Name

YEAR		NAME		AGE	CAUSE and/or PLACE OF DEATH
1973		GREENE, Billy M.		76	Heart attack (in Los Angeles, CA)
1991		GREENE, Graham		86	Leukemia (in Vevey, Switzerland)
1945		GREENE, Harrison		61	After a lingering illness (in Hollywood, CA)
1995		GREENE, John L.		82	Died at UCLA Med. Ctr. in Los Angeles, CA
1987	+	GREENE, Lorne		72	Pneumonia following ulcer surgery (in Santa Monica, CA)
1985		GREENE, Richard		66	Cardiac arrest after a fall (in Norfolk, England)
1981		GREENE, Stanley N.		70	After a long illness (in New York, NY)
1971		GREENE, Victor Hugo		76	Died in Los Angeles, CA
1970		GREENE, William		43	Heart attack (in Cleveland Heights, OH)
1985		GREENFIELD, Calvin "Rusty"		58	Lung cancer (in Santa Monica, CA)
1998		GREENFIELD, William E.		68	Riverdale, N.Y.
1963		GREENLEAF, Raymond		71	Died in Woodland Hills, CA
1991		GREENSPAN, David		68	Lung cancer
1954	#+	GREENSTREET, Sydney ☆		74	After a long illness (in Los Angeles, CA)
1985		GREENWAY, Tom		75	Heart attack (in Los Angeles, CA)
1978	#	GREENWOOD, Charlotte		84	Died in Beverly Hills, CA
1970		GREENWOOD, Ethel		82	Heart attack (in Hollywood, CA)
1987		GREENWOOD, Joan		65	Heart attack (in London, England)
1961		GREENWOOD, Winifred L.		69	Died in Woodland Hills, CA
1939		GREET, Clare		67	Died in London, England
1959		GREGG, Everley		60	Died in Beaconsfield, England
1986		GREGG, Virginia		70	Cancer (in Encino, CA)
1990		GREGORY, Charles "Mr. Music"		89	Pneumonia
1993		GREGORY, Dennis		40	Pneumonia (in East Meadow, NY)
1992		GREGORY, Mercedes		56	Cancer (in New York, NY)
1975		GREGSON, John		55	Apparent heart attack on a woodland stroll (in Porlock Weir, Eng.)
1958		GREIG, Robert		77	Died in Hollywood, CA
1979	#	GRENFELL, Joyce		69	Cancer (in London, England)
1996		GREY, Denise		99	Died in Paris, France
1947		GREY, Gloria		38	Died in Hollywood, CA
1995		GREY, Lita (Chaplin)		87	
1993	#	GREY, Nan		75	Heart failure at her home (in San Diego, CA)
1973	#	GREY, Olga		75	Died in Los Angeles, CA
1934	#	GREY, Robert H.		42	Died in Los Angeles, CA
1939	+	GREY, Zane		64	Died at his home in Altadena, CA
1965	#	GRIBBON, Eddie		75	Cancer (in North Hollywood, CA)
1961		GRIBBON, Harry		76	After a long illness (in Los Angeles, CA)
1977		GRIES, Tom		54	Heart attack (in Santa Monica, CA)
1935		GRIEVES, Jack		33	Died in Burbank, CA
1975	#	GRIFFIES, Ethel		97	Stroke (in London, England)
1989		GRIFFIN, Bessie		67	Cancer (in Culver City, CA)
1940	#	GRIFFIN, Carlton E.		47	Heart attack (in Hollywood, CA)
1956		GRIFFIN, Charles		67	Died in Hollywood, CA
1953		GRIFFIN, Frank L.		63	Heart attack (in Hollywood, CA)
1919		GRIFFIN, Gerald		65	Died in Venice, CA
1992		GRIFFIN, Rodney		46	A.I.D.S.
1979	#	GRIFFITH, Corinne		84	Cardiac arrest (in Santa Monica, CA)
1948	#+	GRIFFITH, D. W.		73	Massive cerebral hemorrhage (in Hollywood, CA)
1975		GRIFFITH, Edward H.		86	Died in Los Angeles, CA
1958		GRIFFITH, Gordon		51	Heart attack (in Hollywood, CA)
1926	#	GRIFFITH, Harry		59	Died in Pasadena, CA
1980		GRIFFITH, Hugh ★		67	Died in London, England
1921	#	GRIFFITH, Katherine		45	Died in Los Angeles, CA

Deaths of Movie and Television Personalities — by Name

YEAR	NAME	AGE	CAUSE and/or PLACE OF DEATH
1948	GRIFFITH, Linda Arvidson		(See Linda Arvidson)
1957	GRIFFITH, Raymond	67	Heart attack (while dining in Hollywood, CA)
1960	GRIFFITH, William M.	62	Died in Hollywood, CA
1994	GRIGAS, John	71	Heart attack
1995	GRIMSBY, Roger	66	Lung cancer (at Lenox Hill Hospital, NYC)
1995	+ GRINKOV, Sergei	28	Massive heart attack while ice skating (in Lake Placid, NY)
• 1996	GROSS, Marjorie	40	Ovarian cancer (at Cedars-Sinai Med. Ctr. in Los Angeles, CA)
1955	GROVES, Frederick "Fred"	74	Died in London, England
1996	GROVES, William "Bill"	74	Lung cancer (at his home in Morongo Valley, CA)
1995	GRUENBERG, Leonard S.	83	Natural causes (at his home in Rancho Mirage, CA)
1963	#+ GRUNDGENS, Gustav	63	Suicide (in Manila, Philippine Islands)
1993	GRUNDY, Bill	69	Died in Cheshire, England
1961	# GUARD, Kit	67	Cancer (in Hollywood, CA)
1995	# GUARDINO, Harry	69	Lung cancer (in Palm Springs, CA)
• 1996	GUESS, Alvaleta	36	Breast cancer (in Manhattan, NY)
• 1997	GUETARY, Georges	82	Heart attack in Mougins, France
1983	GUFFEY, Burnett	78	After a brief illness (in Goleta, CA)
1943	GUHL, George	67	Died in Los Angeles, CA
1989	GUIGLEY, Robert	76	Died in Los Angeles, CA
• 1997	GUILAROFF, Sydney	89	Died of pneumonia in Los Angeles, CA
1964	# GUILFOYLE, James	72	Heart attack (in Woodland Hills, CA)
1961	GUILFOYLE, Paul	59	Heart attack (in Hollywood, CA)
1933	#+ GUINAN, Mary "Texas"	48	After an operation for colitis (in Vancouver, B.C., Canada)
1984	GUNEY, Yilmaz	47	Stomach cancer (in Paris, France)
1918	GUNN, Charles E.	35	Spanish influenza (in Los Angeles, CA)
1993	GUNN, Moses	64	Complications of asthma (in Guilford, CT)
1969	# GURIE, Sigrid	58	Pulmonary embolism (in Mexico City, Mexico)
1972	GURIN, Ellen	24	Suicide, after a nervous depression (in Manhattan, NY)
1991	GUTHRIE, A. B. Jr.	90	
1967	#+ GUTHRIE, Woody	55	After a 13-yr. bout with Huntington's chorea (in Queens, NY)
1968	# GUY-BLACHE, Alice	95	Natural causes (at her daughter's home in Mahwah, NJ)
1991	GUZMAN, Pato	57	After a brief illness (in Santiago, Chile)
1959	#+ GWENN, Edmund ★	83	Died in Woodland Hills, CA
1976	GWYNN, Michael	59	Heart attack (in London, England)
1993	# GWYNNE, Fred "Herman Munster"	66	Pancreatic cancer (in Taneytown, MD)
	H		
1966	HAADE, William	63	Died in Los Angeles, CA
1968	HAAS, Hugo	65	Asthmatic attack (in Vienna, Austria)
1967	HACK, Herman	68	Heart attack (in Hollywood, CA)
1973	HACK, Signe	73	Leukemia (in Hollywood, CA)
1940	HACKATHORNE, George	44	After a long illness (in Hollywood, CA)
1959	HACKEL, A. W.	76	Heart attack (in Hollywood, CA)
1994	HACKES, Peter	69	Heart attack (in Washington, D.C.)
1995	HACKETT, Albert	95	Pneumonia (at St. Lukes-Roosevelt Hosp. in Manhattan, NY)
1976	#+ HACKETT, Bobby	61	Died in Chatham, MA
1954	HACKETT, Florence	72	Died in New York, NY
1967	HACKETT, Hal	44	After a long illness (in New York, NY)
1983	#+ HACKETT, Joan	49	Cancer (in Encino, CA)
1948	# HACKETT, Karl	55	After a long illness (in Sawtelle, CA)
1973	HACKETT, Lillian	76	Cerebral hemorrhage (in Hollywood, CA)
1958	HACKETT, Raymond	55	Cerebral hemorrhage (in Hollywood, CA)
1981	# HADEN, Sara	82	Died in Woodland Hills, CA
1974	# HADLEY, Reed	63	Heart attack (in Los Angeles, CA)

Deaths of Movie and Television Personalities — by Name

YEAR	NAME		AGE	CAUSE and/or PLACE OF DEATH
1958	HAGEN, Charles F.		96	Died in Hollywood, CA
1977	# HAGEN, Jean	☆	54	Throat cancer (in Woodland Hills, CA)
1991	HAGERTY, Michael		39	A.I.D.S. (in New York, NY)
1973	# HAGNEY, Frank S.		79	Died in Los Angeles, CA
1988	HAHN, Paul		67	After a short illness (in Hollywood, CA)
1989	HAIG, Jack		76	Cancer (in London, England)
1942	HAINES, Donald		24	
1964	HAINES, Rhea		69	Died in Los Angeles, CA
1990	HAINES, Richard		43	After surgery for a brain tumor (in Johannesburg, South Africa)
1973	+ HAINES, William		73	Cancer (in Santa Monica, CA)
1990	HAKINS, Dick		87	Died in Sherman Oaks, CA
1990	+ HALE, Alan Jr.		71	Cancer of the thymus (in Los Angeles, CA)
1950	#+ HALE, Alan Sr.		57	Liver ailment — virus infection (in Hollywood, CA)
1965	# HALE, Creighton		83	Died in South Pasadena, CA
1985	# HALE, Georgia		79	Died in Hollywood, CA
1966	# HALE, Jonathan		74	Suicide (gunshot) in Woodland Hills, CA
1933	HALE, Louise Closser		60	Two strokes following an accident (in Los Angeles, CA)
1981	HALE, Richard		87	Cardiac arrest in his sleep (in Northridge, CA)
1959	# HALE, Sonnie		57	Myelofibrosis (a blood disease) in London, England
1992	HALEY, Alex		70	Heart attack
1979	#+ HALEY, Jack		80	Heart attack (in Los Angeles, CA)
• 1996	HALIDAY, Bryant		68	Stroke (in Paris, France)
1968	HALL, Alexander	☆	74	Stroke (in San Francisco, CA)
1959	#+ HALL, Charlie		60	Died in North Hollywood, CA
1991	HALL, Ed		60	Cancer (in Providence, RI)
1981	HALL, Ella		85	Died in Canoga Park, CA
1970	HALL, Geraldine		65	Heart attack while hospitalized (in Woodland Hills, CA)
1985	HALL, Grayson	☆	58	Cancer (in New York, NY)
1940	# HALL, James		39	Cirrhosis of the liver (in Jersey City, NJ)
1979	#+ HALL, Jon		64	Suicide after bladder cancer surgery (gunshot) in Sherman Oaks, CA
1968	HALL, Juanita		66	Diabetic complications (in Bay Shore, NY)
1991	HALL, Kevin Peter		35	Pneumonia (in Hollywood, CA)
• 1959	HALL, Lillian		63	Suicide (barbituate overdose) Do not confuse with L. Hall-Davis
1953	# HALL, Porter		65	Heart attack (in Los Angeles, CA)
1990	HALL, Stuart		86	Complications from lung surgery (in Woodland Hills, CA)
1958	HALL, Thurston		75	Heart attack (in Beverly Hills, CA)
1947	HALL, Winter		68	Died in London, England
1933	HALL-DAVIS, Lilian		32	Suicide (gas) in London, England
• 1997	HALLAHAN, Charles		54	Died of a heart attack driving his car in Los Angeles, CA
1942	# HALLARD, C. M.		75	Died in Surrey, England
1966	HALLIDAY, Gardner		56	Suicide (sleeping pills) after suffering with cancer (in Hollywood, CA)
1947	HALLIDAY, John		67	Heart ailment (in Honolulu, HI)
1957	HALLIGAN, William		72	After a lingering illness (in Woodland Hills, CA)
1989	HALLIWELL, Leslie		59	Abdominal cancer
1944	HALLOR, Ray		44	Automobile accident (near Palm Springs, CA)
1967	HALLS, Ethel May		85	Died in Hollywood, CA
1976	#+ HALOP, Billy		56	Heart attack in his sleep (in Brentwood, CA)
1986	HALOP, Florence		63	Cancer (in Los Angeles, CA)
1989	HALSTED, Fred		47	Overdose of barbiturates
1959	+ HALTON, Charles		83	Hepatitis (in Los Angeles, CA)
1989	HAMBLEN, Stuart		80	Brain cancer (in Santa Monica, CA)
1990	# HAMER, Rusty		42	Suicide (gunshot) in De Ridder, LA
1995	HAMILTON, Anthony		42	A.I.D.S. pneumonia

Deaths of Movie and Television Personalities — by Name

YEAR	NAME	AGE	CAUSE and/or PLACE OF DEATH
1991	HAMILTON, Frank	66	Prostate cancer (in Los Angeles, CA)
1942	+ HAMILTON, Hale R.	62	Cerebral hemorrhage (in Los Angeles, CA)
1925	HAMILTON, Jack "Shorty"	37	Crushed after his car hit a steam shovel (in Hollywood, CA)
1958	HAMILTON, John	71	Heart condition (in Hollywood) Do not confuse with J. H., d. 1985
1985	HAMILTON, John	?	Heart attack (Do not confuse with John Hamilton, d. 1958)
1935	HAMILTON, Lloyd	43	Following an operation for a stomach disorder (in Hollywood, CA)
1960	HAMILTON, Mahlon	77	Cancer (in Woodland Hills, CA)
1985	+ HAMILTON, Margaret	83	Heart attack (in Salisbury, CO)
1986	HAMILTON, Murray	63	Lung cancer (in Washington, D.C.)
1984	# HAMILTON, Neil	85	Complications from asthma (in Escondido, CA)
1993	HAMMER, Alvin	78	Died in New York, NY
1990	+ HAMMER, Armand	92	
1987	HAMMER, Irene Wicker	86	
1993	HAMMER, Peter	54	Cancer (in New York)
1960	+ HAMMERSTEIN II, Oscar	65	Stomach cancer (in Doylestown, PA)
1948	HAMMERSTEIN, Elaine	50	Automobile collision (in Tijuana, Mexico)
1980	# HAMMOND, Kay	71	Following a heart attack (in Brighton, England)
1992	HAMMOND, Ruth	96	Cardiac arrest in her sleep (in Englewood, NJ)
1972	HAMMOND, Virginia	78	Died in Washington, D.C.
1955	#+ HAMPDEN, Walter	75	Stroke (in Hollywood, CA)
1963	# HAMPTON, Grace	87	Died in Woodland Hills, CA
1982	HAMPTON, Hope	84	Heart attack (in New York, NY)
1954	HAMPTON, Louise	72	Bronchial trouble (in London, England)
• 1996	HAN-HSIANG, Li	70	Heart problems (at a hospital in Beijing, China)
1992	+ HANCOCK, John	51	Found dead of a heart attack (in Los Angeles, CA)
1968	# HANCOCK, Tony	44	Suicide (overdose of sleeping pills) in Sydney, Australia
1987	HANDL, Irene	85	Died in London, England
1978	# HANDWORTH, Octavia	90	Died in Hemet, CA
1964	HANEY, Carol	30	Pneumonia and diabetes (in Saddle River, NJ)
1985	HANEY, David	44	Heart attack (in Studio City, CA)
• 1997	HANLEY, Eddie	91	After a long illness (in Los Angeles, CA)
1970	HANLEY, Jimmy	51	Cancer (in England)
1972	HANNEN, Nicholas	91	Died in London, England
1992	HANNES, Art	72	Respiratory failure
1947	HANRAY, Lawrence	73	Died in London, England
1961	HANSEN, Juanita	64	Heart attack (in Hollywood, CA)
• 1995	HANSEN, Larry	42	A.I.D.S.
1975	HANSEN, William	64	After a lengthy illness (in Woodland Hills, CA)
1965	HANSON, Lars	78	Died in Stockholm, Sweden
1960	HARBAUGH, Carl	73	Died in Hollywood, CA
1941	HARBEN, Hubert	63	Died in London, England
1981	+ HARBURG, E. Y.	84	Killed in an automobile crash (in Hollywood, CA)
1951	HARCOURT, James	77	Died in London, England
1973	HARDIE, Russell	69	Cancer (in Clarence, NY)
1991	HARDIN, Ken	62	Cancer
1981	#+ HARDING, Ann ☆	79	After an illness of several months (in Sherman Oaks, CA)
1952	# HARDING, Lyn	85	Died in London, England
1962	HARDTMUTH, Paul	72	Fall from his apartment building (in London, England)
1964	HARDWICKE, Cedric	71	Throat and lung cancer (in New York, NY)
1990	HARDY, Ian Dudley	79	Killed in a storm (in London, England)
1990	HARDY, Joseph	71	Died in New York, NY
1957	#+ HARDY, Oliver	65	Following a paralytic stroke (in North Hollywood, CA)
1935	+ HARDY, Sam B.	52	After intestinal surgery (in Hollywood, CA)

Deaths of Movie and Television Personalities — by Name

YEAR	NAME	AGE	CAUSE and/or PLACE OF DEATH
1964	HARE, F. Lumsden	89	Died in Hollywood, CA
1979	HARE, J. Robertson	87	Died in London, England
• 1997	HARE, Will	81	Heart attack in NY
1996	HAREN, Christian	61	A.I.D.S. (in San Francisco, CA)
1984	HARGREAVES, Christine	43	Brain hemorrhage (in London, England)
1996	HARGREAVES, John	50	After a long illness (in Sydney, Australia)
1967	HARKER, Gordon	81	After a long illness (in London, England)
1967	HARLAN, Kenneth D.	71	Aneurysm (in Sacramento, CA)
1940	HARLAN, Otis	75	Stroke (in Martinsville, IN)
1974	HARLAN, Russell B.	70	Died in Newport Beach, CA
1937 #+	HARLOW, Jean	26	Cerebral edema following uremic poisoning (in Hollywood, CA)
1958	HARMON, Pat	70	Died in Riverside, CA
1990	HARMON, Tom	70	Heart attack (in Los Angeles, CA)
1974 #	HAROLDE, Ralf	75	Pneumonia (in Santa Monica, CA)
1994	HARP, Bill	70	Heart attack (in Hollywood, CA)
1994	HARPER, Pat (TV anchor)	59	Heart attack at her home (in Capiliera, Spain)
1989	HARRIGAN, Nedda	89	Lung cancer (in New York, NY)
1966 +	HARRIGAN, William	72	Following surgery (in New York, NY)
1978	HARRINGTON, Kate	74	Following a stroke (in New York, NY)
• 1976	HARRIS, Arlene	77	
1991	HARRIS, Cassandra	39	Ovarian cancer (in Los Angeles, CA)
1994	HARRIS, Chris	51	Apparent heart attack at his home (in Newbury Park, CA)
1988	HARRIS, Fox	52	Lung cancer (in Los Angeles, CA)
1991	HARRIS, Lou	85	Heart attack (in Woodland Hills, CA)
1944	HARRIS, Marion	38	Burns in bed from a cigarette fire (in Hollywood, CA)
1944	HARRIS, Mildred	42	Pneumonia after an abdominal operation (in Hollywood, CA)
1974 #	HARRIS, Morris	59	Died in Syracuse, NY
1995 +	HARRIS, Phil	91	Heart failure (at his home in Rancho Mirage, CA)
1995	HARRIS, Robert	95	After a brief illness (in Denville Hall, England)
1981	HARRIS, Robert H.	72	Died in Brentwood, CA (Do not confuse with British actor)
1990 +	HARRIS, Robin	36	Found dead in his hotel room (in Chicago, IL)
1973	HARRIS, Stacy B.	54	Heart attack (in Los Angeles, CA)
1991	HARRIS, Ted	52	Cancer (in Los Angeles, CA)
1992	HARRIS, William E.	37	Stabbed when he interrupted a burglary (in Playa Del Rey, CA)
1995	HARRISON, Henry M. Jr. (Rev.)	67	Stroke (in Pineville, N.C.)
1994	HARRISON, Joan	83	Died in London, England
1990	HARRISON, Rex	82	Pancreatic cancer (in Manhattan, NY)
1920 #	HARRON, Bobby	27	Accidentally shot (in New York, NY)
1939	HARRON, John	36	Heart attack (in Seattle, WA)
1918 #	HARRON, Tessie	22	Spanish Influenza (in Los Angeles, CA)
1940	HART, Albert S.	65	After a long illness (in Hollywood, CA)
1943 +	HART, Lorenz	47	Pneumonia
1961 +	HART, Moss	57	Heart attack (in Palm Springs, CA)
1949 #	HART, Neal	70	Died in Woodland Hills, CA
1951	HART, Richard	35	Heart attack (in New York, NY)
1946 #+	HART, William S.	83	Stroke (in Los Angeles, CA)
1965 #	HARTE, Betty	81	Died in Sunland, CA
1951 #	HARTIGAN, Pat	69	Coronary attack (in Los Angeles, CA)
1994	HARTLEY, Neil	78	Heart failure (at his home in Los Angeles, CA)
1958	HARTMAN, Don	57	Died in his sleep of apparent heart attack (in Palm Springs, CA)
1987 +	HARTMAN, Elizabeth ☆	45	Suicide (jumped from her 5th-floor apartment) in Pittsburgh, PA
• 1997	HARTMAN, Maureen	53	Cancer at home in Harrison, NY
1973	HARTMAN, Paul	69	Heart attack (in Los Angeles, CA)

• New entry. # Original name (Pt. 7). + Interment (Pt. 5).   238   ☆ Oscar nominee, ★ Oscar winner (Pt. 10)

Deaths of Movie and Television Personalities — by Name

YEAR	NAME		AGE	CAUSE and/or PLACE OF DEATH
1998	+ HARTMAN, Phil		49	Murdered by his wife at his home in Encino, CA
1975	HARTNELL, William "Billy"		67	Died in London, England
1992	HARTOG, Simon		52	Leukemia (in London, England)
1963	HARVEY, Don C.		51	Heart attack (in Studio City, CA)
1945	HARVEY, Forrester		65	Stroke (in Laguna Beach, CA)
1929	# HARVEY, Hank		80	Died at his home in Culver City, CA
1996	HARVEY, Harold A. "Herk"		71	Died in Lawrence, Kansas
1985	HARVEY, Harry Sr.		84	Died in Sylmar, CA
1973	# HARVEY, Laurence	☆	45	Stomach cancer (in London, England)
1968	# HARVEY, Lilian		61	Died in Antibes, France
1955	+ HARVEY, Paul (actor)		72	Coronary thrombosis (Do not confuse with radio commentator)
1993	HARVEY, Rick		43	Kidney failure (in Memphis, TN)
1997	HARVEY, Rita Morley		69	Died of cancer in Simsbury, Conn
1992	HARVEY, Rudy		60	Kidney failure after a series of strokes
1990	HARVUOT, Clifford		77	Pancreatic cancer (in The Netherlands)
1984	HASKIN, Byron	☆	84	Lung cancer (in Santa Barbara, CA)
1978	# HASSE, O. E.		75	Died in a hospital (in West Berlin, Germany)
1937	HASSELL, George		55	Heart attack (in Chatsworth, CA)
1985	+ HATHAWAY, Henry	☆	86	Heart attack after pneumonia (in Los Angeles, CA)
1986	+ HATLEY, T. Marvin	☆	81	Cancer
1971	# HATTON, Raymond		84	Heart attack (in Palmdale, CA)
1931	# HATTON, Richard "Dick"		40	Traffic accident (in Los Angeles, CA)
1946	+ HATTON, Rondo		51	Heart attack (in Beverly Hills, CA)
1991	HAULMAN, Bob		49	Apparent heart attack
1931	HAUPT, Ullrich		43	Accidentally shot on a deer hunting trip (near Santa Maria, CA)
1985	HAUSER, Gayelord		89	Complications from pneumonia
1960	HAVER, Phyllis		61	Suicide (despondent over Mack Sennett's death) in Falls Village, CT
1994	HAWKINS, Corwin		29	Pneumonia (in Los Angeles, CA)
1973	HAWKINS, Jack		62	After cancer surgery (in London, England)
1977	+ HAWKS, Howard	☆	81	Died in his sleep following a fall and concussion (in Hollywood, CA)
1963	# HAWLEY, Wanda		67	Died in Los Angeles, CA
1993	HAWORTH, Ted	★	76	Heart failure (in Sundance, UT)
1942	HAWTHORNE, David		54	Died in London, England
1988	HAWTREY, Charles		72	Heart attack caused by arterial disease (in Walmer, England)
1957	HAY, Mary		55	Prolonged heart ailment (in Inverness, CA)
1949	HAY, Will		60	Died in London, England
1973	# HAYAKAWA, Sessue	☆	84	Cerebral thrombosis and pneumonia (in Tokyo, Japan)
1955	+ HAYDEN, Harry		72	After a long illness (in West Los Angeles, CA)
1981	#+ HAYDEN, Russell "Lucky"		68	Viral pneumonia (in Palm Springs, Ca.)
1986	# HAYDEN, Sterling		70	Cancer (in Sanjalito, CA)
1985	HAYDN, Richard		80	Heart attack (in Los Angeles, CA)
1994	HAYDON, Julie		84	Abdominal cancer (in LaCrosse, WI)
1991	HAYDON, Tom		53	Cancer (in Sydney, Australia)
1957	# HAYE, Helen		83	Died in London, England
1977	# HAYES, Allison		47	Blood poisoning (in La Jolla, CA)
1987	HAYES, Bernadine		75	Heart attack (in Los Angeles, CA)
1991	HAYES, Christopher		?	Heart attack (in Hollywood, CA)
1969	+ HAYES, George "Gabby"		83	Heart ailment (in Burbank, CA)
1989	HAYES, Grace		93	Heart attack (in Las Vegas, NV)
1993	+ HAYES, Helen	★	92	Congestive heart failure (in Nyack, NY)
1977	# HAYES, Margaret		61	Cancer complicated by hepatitis (in Miami Beach, FL)
1958	# HAYES, Sam		53	Heart attack preparing his morning news program (in San Diego, CA)
1988	HAYES, William S.		29	A.I.D.S. (in Wayland, MA)

• New entry.   # Original name (Pt. 7).   + Interment (Pt. 5).   239   ☆ Oscar nominee, ★ Oscar winner (Pt. 10)

Deaths of Movie and Television Personalities — by Name

YEAR		NAME		AGE	CAUSE and/or PLACE OF DEATH
1963		HAYLE, Grace		73	Died in Los Angeles, CA
1994		HAYMAN, Lillian		72	Heart attack at her home (in Hollis, NY)
1989		HAYMER, Johnny		69	Cancer (in Los Angeles, CA)
1980	#+	HAYMES, Dick		64	Lung cancer (in Los Angeles, CA)
1966		HAYNES, Arthur		52	Heart attack (in London, England)
1986		HAYNES, Hilda		72	Died in New York, NY
• 1998		HAYNES, Joy Hatton		64	Cancer at her home in Manhattan, NY
1987		HAYNES, Lloyd		52	Lung cancer (in Coronado, CA)
1994		HAYNES, Tiger		79	Cardiac arrest (at St. Vincent's Hospital in New York, NY)
1992		HAYS, Mickey		20	Progeria (a rare aging disorder)
1954		HAYS, Will H.		74	Died in Sullivan, IN
1983		HAYTER, James		75	Died in Spain
1985	#	HAYWARD, Louis		76	Lung cancer (in Palm Springs, CA)
1975	#+	HAYWARD, Susan	★	57	Brain tumor (in Beverly Hills, CA)
1987	#+	HAYWORTH, Rita		68	Alzheimer's disease (in New York, NY)
1994		HAZEN, Joseph		96	Died in his sleep at home (in Boca Raton, FL)
1981	+	HEAD, Edith		82	Undisclosed causes (in Los Angeles, CA)
1995		HEALY, David		64	Following a heart operation (in London, England)
1937	#+	HEALY, Ted		41	From injuries after a bar room fight in Los Angeles, CA
1963	#	HEARN, Edward "Eddie"		74	Died in Woodland Hills, CA
1964	+	HEARN, Sam		75	Heart attack (in Los Angeles, CA)
1993		HEARST, William Randolph Jr.		85	Heart attack (in New York)
1991		HEATH, Gordon		72	After a long illness (in Paris, France)
1937		HEATHERLEY, Clifford		48	Died in London, England
1972	+	HEATTER, Gabriel		82	Pneumonia (in Miami Beach, FL)
1964	+	HECHT, Ben		70	Cerebral thrombosis (in New York, NY)
1985	+	HECHT, Harold		77	Cancer (in Beverly Hills, CA)
1994		HEFLIN, Frances		71	Lung cancer (in New York, NY)
1971	#+	HEFLIN, Van	★	60	After a massive stroke while swimming (in Hollywood, CA)
1936	#	HEGGIE, O. P.		59	Pneumonia (in Los Angeles, CA)
1992		HEIDER, Frederick		75	
1986	+	HEIDT, Horace		85	Pneumonia and heart trouble (in Los Angeles, CA)
1987		HEIFETZ, Jascha		86	Following brain surgery after a fall (in Los Angeles, CA)
• 1996		HEINEMAN, George		78	Natural causes (in New York, NY)
1972	#	HEINZ, Gerard		68	Died in England
1979	+	HEISLER, Stuart R.		82	Died in San Diego, CA
1918	+	HELD, Anna		45	Pernicious anemia and bronchial pneumonia (in New York, NY)
1992		HELD, Martin		83	
• 1997		HELLER, Franklin M.		86	Emphysema in North Branford, Conn.
1947	+	HELLINGER, Mark		44	Heart attack (in Hollywood, CA)
1984	+	HELLMAN, Lillian		79	Heart disease (in Martha's Vineyard, MA)
• 1996	#	HELM, Brigitte		88	Heart failure (in Ascona, Switzerland)
1995		HELMORE, Tom		91	Died in Longboat Key, FL
1986		HELPMANN, Robert		76	After a long illness (in Sydney, Australia)
1971	+	HELTON, Percy		76	Died in Hollywood, CA
1981	#	HEMING, Violet		86	Died in New York, NY
• 1996		HEMINGWAY, Margaux		41	Suicide (phenobarbital overdose) in her Santa Monica, CA, apartment
1968		HEMSLEY, Estelle		70	After a brief illness (in Hollywood, CA)
1976		HENABERY, Joseph E.		88	Died in Woodland Hills, CA
1967		HENCKLES, Paul		81	Died in Dusseldorf, Germany
1956	#	HENDERSON, Del		73	Died in Woodland Hills, CA
1985	#	HENDERSON, Dickie		62	Cancer (in London, England)
1978		HENDERSON, Douglas "Doug"		58	Suicide (carbon monoxide) in Studio City, CA

• New entry. # Original name (Pt. 7). + Interment (Pt. 5).　　　　240　　　　☆ Oscar nominee, ★ Oscar winner (Pt. 10)

YEAR	NAME	AGE	CAUSE and/or PLACE OF DEATH
1952	#+ HENDERSON, Fletch	54	Stroke (in New York, NY)
1983	HENDERSON, Jack E.	88	Died in Woodland Hills, CA
1988	HENDERSON, Jo	54	Automobile accident (in Pamona, NY)
1988	HENDLEY, Janet Stover	55	Cancer (in Vorhees, NJ)
1938	HENDRICKS, Ben Jr.	44	Died in Los Angeles, CA
1930	# HENDRICKS, Ben Sr.	67	Died in Hollywood, CA
1965	HENDRIKSON, Anders	69	Died in Sweden
1970	#+ HENDRIX, Jimi	27	Inhalation of vomit after barbiturate intoxication (in London, England)
1981	#+ HENDRIX, Wanda	52	Double pneumonia (in Burbank, CA)
1984	HENDRY, Ian	53	Heart attack (in London, England)
1969	+ HENIE, Sonja	57	Leukemia (on a private plane bound for Oslo, Norway)
1964	HENLEY, Hobart	72	After a long illness (in Beverly Hills, CA)
1969	HENNECKE, Clarence R.	74	After a brief illness (in Santa Monica, CA)
1973	HENNING, Pat	62	Died in Miami Beach, FL
1992	#+ HENREID, Paul	84	Pneumonia after a stroke (in Santa Monica, CA)
1980	# HENRY, Charlotte	65	Brain tumor (in La Jolla, CA)
1971	HENRY, Robert "Buzz"	40	Motorcycle accident (in Los Angeles, CA)
1980	# HENRY, Tom	?	Died in Los Angeles, CA
1989	HENSHAW, Wandalie	54	Parkinson's disease (in Petoskey, MI)
1990	HENSON, Basil	71	Stroke (in Sevenoaks, England)
1990	HENSON, Jim	53	Streptococcus pneumonia and heart attack (in New York, NY)
1993	#+ HEPBURN, Audrey ★	63	Colon cancer (in Tolochenaz, Switzerland)
1953	HEPWORTH, Cecil M.	78	Died in Greenford, Middlesex, England
1956	#+ HERBERT, Holmes	74	Died in Hollywood, CA
1952	+ HERBERT, Hugh	64	Heart attack (in North Hollywood, CA)
1992	HERBERT, Percy	72	Heart attack
1989	HERBERT, Pitt	74	Amyotrophic lateral sclerosis
1927	HERBERT, Sidney	?	Died in Los Angeles, CA
1986	HERBERT, Tim	71	Heart attack (in Los Angeles, CA)
1924	+ HERBERT, Victor	65	Heart attack (in Ireland)
1987	#+ HERMAN, Woody	74	Congestive heart failure and emphysema (in Los Angeles, CA)
1945	# HERNANDEZ, Anna	77	Pneumonia (in Los Angeles, CA)
1922	HERNANDEZ, George F.	59	Died in Los Angeles, CA
1970	HERNANDEZ, Juan "Juano"	74	Cerebral hemorrhage (in San Juan, Puerto Rico)
1990	# HERNDON, Bill	54	A.I.D.S. (in New York, NY)
• 1998	HERRING, Sue	49	Cancer at Tarzana Medical Center
1995	# HERRIOT, James	78	Prostate cancer (at his home in Thirsk, England)
1975	+ HERRMANN, Bernard	64	Heart attack (in Hollywood, CA)
1941	HERSHELL, Mayall	78	Cerebral hemorrhage
1995	HERSHMAN, Robert	41	A.I.D.S. (in Santa Monica, CA)
1956	+ HERSHOLT, Jean ★	69	Cancer (in Beverly Hills, CA)
• 1998	HERTHUM, Harold	69	Heart attack in Baton Rouge, LA
1992	HERZBERGER, Jack L.	75	Following heart surgery (in Downey, CA)
1989	HESLER, G. Christian	33	A.I.D.S. (in Carmel, IN)
1982	HESSEL, Edith Bell	58	Alzheimer's disease and exposure
1967	HESTERBERG, Trude	70	Died in Munich, Germany
1986	HEWITT, Alan	71	Cancer (in New York, NY)
1947	# HEWSTON, Alfred H.	66	Died in Los Angeles, CA
1984	HEXUM, Jon-Erik	26	Accidentally shot himself (in Beverly Hills, CA)
1951	HEYBURN, Weldon	46	Died in Hollywood, CA
1960	HEYDT, Louis Jean	54	Heart attack (in Boston, MA)
1993	HEYES, Douglas	73	Congestive heart failure (in Beverly Hills, CA)
1958	HEYES, Herbert	68	Died in North Hollywood, CA

Deaths of Movie and Television Personalities — by Name

YEAR	NAME		AGE	CAUSE and/or PLACE OF DEATH
1996	HEYMAN, Barton		59	Heart failure (at his home in Manhattan, NY)
1989	HEYWOOD, Eddie		73	Parkinson's and Alzheimer's disease (in North Miami, FL)
1964	HEYWOOD, Herbert		83	Coronary thrombosis (in Van Nuys, CA)
1994	# HIATT, Ruth		88	Congestive heart failure (in Montrose, CA)
1993	HIBBERT, Dora		77	Following a brief illness (in New York, NY)
1985	HIBBS, Jesse		79	Alzheimer's disease (in Ojai, CA)
1997	HICKEY, William	☆	69	Died in New York, NY from complications of emphysema
1986	HICKMAN, Bill		65	Cancer (in Indio, CA)
1950	HICKMAN, Howard C.		69	Following a heart attack (in Los Angeles, CA)
1994	HICKS, Bill		32	Pancreatic cancer (in Little Rock, AR)
1957	# HICKS, Russell		61	Heart attack after a traffic accident (in Hollywood, CA)
1933	HIERS, Walter		39	Pneumonia (in Los Angeles, CA)
1986	HIGBE, Mary Jane		70	Stroke
1988	HIGGINS, Colin		47	A.I.D.S. (in Beverly Hills, CA)
1976	# HILDEBRAND, Hilde		78	Died in Berlin, Germany
1954	HILL, Al		62	(Do not confuse with stage actor of same name)
1992	#+ HILL, Benny		67	Heart ailment (in London, England)
1918	HILL, Dale P.		?	Spanish influenza
1996	# HILL, Dana		32	Following a diabetic coma and stroke (in Burbank, CA)
1934	# HILL, George W.		40	Suicide (gunshot) in Venice, CA
1993	HILL, Jacqueline		68	Cancer (in London, England)
1994	HILL, James		75	Undisclosed causes (in London, England)
1990	HILL, Ken		49	A.I.D.S. (in Los Angeles, CA)
1993	HILL, Martin		80	Cancer (in Sherman Oaks, CA)
1996	HILL, Ralston		69	While in rehearsal at the Paper Mill Playhouse (in NJ)
1966	HILL, Robert F.		79	After a long illness (in Los Angeles, CA)
1938	HILL, Thelma		32	Following a 3-month illness (in Culver City, CA)
1988	HILLAIRE, Marcel		79	Complications following surgery (in Los Angeles, CA)
1947	HILLIARD, Ernest		57	Following a heart attack (in Santa Monica, CA)
1966	HILLIARD, Harry S.		?	Complications after a fall (in St. Petersburg, FL)
1985	HILLPOT, William A.		79	Pneumonia (in New York, NY)
1979	# Hilo Hattie		78	Cancer following a stroke (in Honolulu, HI)
1954	HILTON, James		54	Cancer of the liver (in Long Beach, CA)
1947	HILYARD, Norman		74	
1948	HINDS, Samuel S.		73	Pneumonia (in Pasadena, CA)
1983	HINES, Earl		77	Heart attack
1967	HINES, Harry		78	After suffering from emphysema (in Hollywood, CA)
1970	HINES, Johnny		73	Heart attack (in Los Angeles, CA)
1988	HINTERMANN, Carlo		64	Automobile accident (in Catania, Italy)
1958	HINTON, Ed		30	Airplane crash (on Catalina Island, CA)
1980	+ HITCHCOCK, Alfred	☆	80	Heart attack (in Beverly Hills, CA)
1929	HITCHCOCK, Raymond		58	Heart trouble (in Beverly Hills, CA)
1995	HIVELY, Jack B.		85	After a brief illness (at his home in Hollywood, CA)
1962	HOBBES, Halliwell		84	Heart attack (in Santa Monica, CA)
1968	HOBBS, Jack		74	Died in Brighton, England
1979	HOCH, Winton C.		73	Effects of a stroke
1979	+ HODGE, Al		66	Heart failure from chronic bronchitis and emphysema (in New York)
1995	HODGES, Gill		80	
1961	HODGES, William C.		85	Died in Chardon, OH
1964	HODGINS, Earle		65	Heart attack (in Hollywood, CA)
1949	# HODGSON, Leland		55	Heart attack at his home (in Hollywood, CA)
1955	+ HODIAK, John		41	Coronary thrombosis (in Tarzana, CA)
1956	# HOEFLICH, Lucie		73	Heart attack (in Berlin, Germany)

Deaths of Movie and Television Personalities — by Name

YEAR	NAME		AGE	CAUSE and/or PLACE OF DEATH
1981	HOERBIGER, Paul		87	Died in Vienna, Austria
1960	# HOEY, Dennis		67	Died in Palm Beach, FL
1992	HOFF, Louise		69	After a brief illness (in Bethlehem, PA)
1989	HOFFMAN, Abbie		52	Suicide (massive drug overdose)
1986	HOFFMAN, Beth Webb		89	Died in Studio City, CA
1961	HOFFMAN, David		57	Died in Seattle, WA
• 1997	HOFFMAN, Joseph		88	Heart disease in Los Angeles, CA
1944	# HOFFMAN, Otto		65	Lung cancer (in Woodland Hills, CA)
1993	HOGAN, Paul (of WMAQ-TV)		48	Apparent heart attack (Do not confuse with the actor)
1964	HOHL, Arthur		74	Died in Los Angeles, CA
1987	HOLCOMBE, Harry		80	Died in Valencia, CA
1973	#+ HOLDEN, Fay		77	Cancer (in Woodland Hills, CA)
• 1991	HOLDEN, Gloria		82	
• 1996	HOLDEN, Gloria (Hoyt)		73	Cardiac arrest (in Redlands, CA)
1981	#+ HOLDEN, William	★	63	Blood loss after head was cut in a fall (in Santa Monica, CA)
1929	HOLDING, Thomas		49	Heart disease (in New York, NY)
1974	# HOLDREN, Judd		58	Suicide (gunshot) in West Los Angeles, CA
1990	HOLE, William J. Jr.		71	Respiratory failure (in Woodland Hills, CA)
1959	#+ HOLIDAY, Billie		44	Liver ailment and cardiac failure (in New York, NY)
1988	HOLLAND, Anthony		60	Suicide (after suffering from A.I.D.S.) in New York, NY
1993	HOLLAND, John		85	Respiratory failure and pneumonia (in Woodland Hills, CA)
1994	HOLLAND, Joseph		84	Heart failure (in Santa Fe, N.M.)
1984	HOLLANDER, Adam		19	Struck by car while riding a bicycle (in Albuquerque, NM)
1950	# HOLLES, Antony		49	Died in London, England
1984	HOLLIDAY, Bill		49	Apparent heart attack (in Sidell, CA)
1948	HOLLIDAY, Frank Jr.		35	Suicide (hanged himself with a belt while in jail) in Hollywood, CA
1965	#+ HOLLIDAY, Judy	★	41	Throat cancer (in New York, NY)
1969	HOLLIDAY, Marjorie		49	Brain hemorrhage (in Hollywood, CA)
1926	HOLLINGSWORTH, Alfred		52	After a brief illness (in Glendale, CA)
1973	HOLLISTER, Alice		86	Died in Costa Mesa, CA
1982	HOLLOWAY, Stanley	☆	91	Died in Little Hampton, England
1992	HOLLOWAY, Sterling		87	Cardiac arrest (in Los Angeles, CA)
1959	#+ HOLLY, Buddy		22	Airplane crash (northwest of Mason City, IA)
• 1996	HOLLYWOOD, Daniel Lawrence		82	Kidney failure (at his home in Orlando, FL)
1947	HOLMAN, Harry		73	After a heart attack at his home (in Hollywood, CA)
1971	#+ HOLMAN, Libby "Peaches"		65	Died in North Stamford, CT
1984	HOLMES, Billy		56	Cancer
1958	HOLMES, Burton		88	Died in Hollywood, CA
1950	HOLMES, Helen		58	Heart attack (in Burbank, CA)
1988	HOLMES, John C.		43	Encephalitis as a result of A.I.D.S. (in Los Angeles, CA)
1942	HOLMES, Phillips		33	Air collision of two RCAF planes (near Armstrong, Ont., Canada)
1945	HOLMES, Ralph		56	Natural causes (in New York, NY)
1971	HOLMES, Stuart		84	Ruptured abdominal aortic (in Hollywood, CA)
1959	HOLMES, Taylor		87	Died in Hollywood, CA
1951	#+ HOLT, Jack		62	Coronary thrombosis (in Los Angeles, CA)
1989	HOLT, Jason		39	A.I.D.S. (in New York, NY)
1973	# HOLT, Tim		54	Brain cancer (in Shawnee, OK)
1980	HOLTZ, Lou		87	Following open-heart surgery (in Los Angeles, CA)
1947	HOMANS, Robert E.		72	Heart attack (in Los Angeles, CA)
1978	HOMOLKA, Oscar	☆	79	Died in Sussex, England
1993	HONDA, Ishiro		81	Died in Tokyo, Japan
1955	# HONEGGER, Arthur		63	Heart disease (in Paris, France)
1987	HONRI, Baynham		83	

• New entry.   # Original name (Pt. 7).   + Interment (Pt. 5).   243   ☆ Oscar nominee, ★ Oscar winner (Pt. 10)

YEAR	NAME		AGE	CAUSE and/or PLACE OF DEATH
1979	#+ HOOD, Darla		47	Died in North Hollywood, CA
1965	HOOD, Joseph B. Sr.		69	Died in Philadelphia, PA
1995	# HOON, Shannon		28	Drug overdose (on a tour bus in New Orleans, LA)
1972	#+ HOOVER, J. Edgar		77	Heart disease (in Washington, D.C.)
1988	HOPE, Harry		62	Heart attack after playing in a basketball game (in Hollywood, CA)
1963	HOPE, Vida		45	Automobile accident (in Chelmsford, England)
1950	HOPKINS, Arthur		71	Heart ailment (in New York, NY)
1998	HOPKINS, John		67	Died in Woodland Hills, CA
1972	# HOPKINS, Miriam	☆	69	Heart attack (in New York, NY)
1946	HOPKINS, Sis			(See Rose Melville)
1993	HOPKINS, Speed	☆	44	Viral infection (in Sparks, MD)
1935	#+ HOPPER, De Wolf		77	Shortly after a radio broadcast (in Kansas City, MO)
1967	HOPPER, E. Mason		82	Died in Woodland Hills, CA
1966	#+ HOPPER, Hedda		75	Double pneumonia and heart complications (in Los Angeles, CA)
1988	HOPPER, Jerry		81	After suffering from heart problems (in San Clemente, CA)
1970	#+ HOPPER, William		55	Pneumonia (in Palm Springs, CA)
1945	# HOPTON, Russell "Russ"		45	Found dead of an overdose of sleeping pills (in N. Hollywood, CA)
1995	HORDERN, Michael		83	After a long illness (at an Oxford, England, hospital)
1994	HOREN, Robert		68	Cancer (in New York)
1996	HORN, Camilla		93	Died at a home for senior citizens (in Gilching, Germany)
1997	HORNBERGER, H. Richard		73	Died in Portland, Maine of leukemia
1970	HORNE, David		71	Died in London, England
1942	HORNE, James W.		60	Cerebral hemorrhage (in Hollywood, CA)
1994	HORNER, Harry	★	84	Pneumonia (at his home in Pacific Palisades, CA)
1989	HORNEZ, André		84	Died in Le-Perreux-sur-Marne, France
1995	HORNUNG, Richard		45	Complications from A.I.D.S. (in Los Angeles, CA)
1989	#+ HOROWITZ, Vladimir		85	Heart attack (in New York, NY)
1991	HORRALL, Craig		?	A.I.D.S. (in New York, NY)
1970	+ HORTON, Edward Everett		84	Cancer (in Encino, CA)
1978	# HORVATH, Charles		57	Died in Woodland Hills, CA
1980	# HOSKINS, Allen "Farina"		59	Cancer (in Oakland, CA)
1954	HOTELY, Mae		81	Died in Coronado, CA
1926	#+ HOUDINI, Harry		52	Peritonitis from a ruptured appendix (in Detroit, MI)
1989	HOULE, Daniel		41	A.I.D.S. (in Los Angeles, CA)
1961	HOUSE, Billy		71	Heart attack (in Hollywood, CA)
1988	# HOUSEMAN, John	★	86	Spinal cancer (in Los Angeles, CA)
1942	#+ HOUSMAN, Arthur		52	Pneumonia (in Los Angeles, CA)
1993	HOUSTON, David		57	Brain aneurysm
1991	HOUSTON, Donald		67	Undisclosed causes (in Coimbra, Portugal)
1944	HOUSTON, George F.		46	Heart attack (in Los Angeles, CA)
1980	# HOUSTON, Renée		77	Died in London, England
1981	HOVEN, Adrian		57	Heart attack (in Tegernsee, West Germany)
1989	HOVEY, Tim		44	Drug overdose
1992	HOVING, Jane Pickens		83	Heart failure
1936	HOWARD, Booth		47	Run down by a car (in Los Angeles, CA)
1993	HOWARD, Cy		77	Heart failure (in Los Angeles, CA)
1941	HOWARD, David		45	Heart ailment (in Hollywood, CA)
1965	HOWARD, Esther		72	Heart attack (in Hollywood, CA)
1965	HOWARD, Eugene		84	Died in New York, NY
1976	HOWARD, Frances		73	Heart attack after a lengthy illness (in Beverly Hills, CA)
1927	HOWARD, Helen		28	
1952	#+ HOWARD, Jerome "Curly"		48	Following several strokes (in San Gabriel, CA)
1995	HOWARD, John		82	Heart failure (at his home in Santa Rosa, CA)

Deaths of Movie and Television Personalities — by Name

YEAR	NAME		AGE	CAUSE and/or PLACE OF DEATH
1956	+ HOWARD, Kathleen		75	Died in Hollywood, CA
1943	#+ HOWARD, Leslie	☆	50	In a passenger plane shot down by a Nazi fighter (in Bay of Biscay)
1989	# HOWARD, Mary		76	After a brief illness (in Santa Monica, CA)
1975	#+ HOWARD, Moe		77	Lung cancer (in Hollywood, CA)
1996	HOWARD, Ronald		78	
1955	#+ HOWARD, Shemp		60	Coronary occlusion (in Hollywood, CA)
1939	HOWARD, Sidney	★	48	Died in a tractor accident on his farm
1946	HOWARD, Sydney		61	Died in London, England
1988	HOWARD, Trevor	☆	71	Influenza, bronchitis and jaundice (in Bushey, England)
1954	HOWARD, William K.		54	Throat cancer (in Hollywood, CA)
1949	#+ HOWARD, Willie		61	Pneumonia (in New York, NY)
1991	HOWDEN, Victoria		27	Suicide (gunshot)
1976	+ HOWE, James Wong		76	Cancer (in West Hollywood, CA)
1961	HOWELL, Alice		72	Died in Los Angeles, CA
1982	HOWELL, Lottice		84	Died in Greensboro, AL
1993	# HOWELL, Wayne		72	Unreported causes (in Pompano Beach, FL)
1992	HOWERD, Frankie		70	Apparent heart attack (in London, England)
1964	# HOWES, Reed		64	Died in Woodland Hills, CA
1936	+ HOWLAND, Jobyna		56	Heart attack (in Los Angeles, CA)
1984	HOWLETT, Noel		82	Died in London, England
1959	# HOWLIN, Olin		63	Died in Hollywood, CA
1982	HOXIE, Al		80	Died in Redlands, CA
1965	HOXIE, Jack		75	Died in Keyes, OK
1983	HOYOS, Rudolfo Jr.		68	Cerebral hemorrhage (in Los Angeles, CA)
1980	HOYOS, Rudolfo Sr.		83	Results of a fall (in Los Angeles, CA)
1953	HOYT, Arthur		79	After a long illness (in Woodland Hills, CA)
1991	# HOYT, John		86	Lung cancer (in Santa Cruz, CA)
1997	HU, King		65	After heart surgery (in Taipei, Taiwan)
1988	HUBBARD, John		65	Died in Camarillo, CA
1993	HUBER, Gusti		78	Heart failure (in Mount Kisco, NY)
1959	HUBER, Harold		49	Died in New York, NY
1963	HUDD, Walter		64	Died in London, England
1991	HUDDLESTON, Floyd	☆	73	Following a heart attack (in Los Angeles, CA)
1964	HUDMAN, Wesley		47	Murdered (in Williams, AZ)
1992	#+ HUDNET, Bill		47	Liver disease
1972	HUDSON, Rochelle		57	Found dead at her home (in Palm Desert, CA)
1985	#+ HUDSON, Rock	☆	59	Complications from A.I.D.S. (in Beverly Hills, CA)
1974	#+ HUDSON, William		49	Laennec's cirrhosis (in Woodland Hills, CA)
1973	HUFF, Louise		77	Died in New York, NY
1985	HUFFMAN, David		40	Murdered (stabbed to death) at his home in Balboa Island, CA
1988	HUFFMAN, Gregory		35	A.I.D.S.
1983	HUGHES, Arthur		89	Pneumonia (in New York, NY)
1965	HUGHES, Gareth		71	Died in Woodland Hills, CA
1976	+ HUGHES, Howard		70	Stroke (on a chartered airplane from Acapulco to Texas)
1970	HUGHES, Joseph Anthony		65	Acute alcohol and barbiturate mixture (in Pasadena, CA)
1995	HUGHES, Lillian H.		73	Cancer (at her Charlestown Retire. Ctr. home in Balt., MD)
1958	+ HUGHES, Lloyd		60	Died in Los Angeles, CA
1994	HUGO, Laurence		76	Alzheimer's disease (in Charlottesville, VA)
1974	HUGO, Mauritz		65	Heart ailment (in Woodland Hills, CA)
1964	# HULBERT, Claude		63	Bronchial pneumonia (in Sydney, Australia)
1978	HULBERT, Jack		69	Died in London, England
1977	HULL, Henry		86	Died in Cornwall, England
1957	#+ HULL, Josephine	★	71	Cerebral hemorrhage (in New York, NY)

• New entry.   # Original name (Pt. 7).   + Interment (Pt. 5).   245   ☆ Oscar nominee, ★ Oscar winner (Pt. 10)

YEAR		NAME		AGE	CAUSE and/or PLACE OF DEATH
1974	#	HULL, Warren		71	Heart failure (in Waterbury, CT)
1994	+	HUMANN, Helena Enize		52	After a long illness (in Dallas, Texas)
1984	+	HUMBERSTONE, Bruce H.		80	Stomach cancer and pneumonia (in Hollywood, CA)
1963		HUMBERT, George		81	
1967		HUME, Benita		61	Died in Egerton, England
1926		HUMPHREY, Paul		22	Premature explosion of dynamite while filming (in San Diego, CA)
1942	#	HUMPHREY, William		68	Coronary thrombosis (in Woodland Hills, CA)
1979		HUNNICUTT, Arthur	☆	68	Cancer (in Woodland Hills, CA)
1993		HUNT, Frances		77	Complications following a stroke
1969		HUNT, Martita		68	Acute asthmatic bronchitis (in London, England)
1992		HUNT, Richard		40	A.I.D.S. (in New York, NY)
1975		HUNTER, Ian		75	Died in Northwood, England
1969	#+	HUNTER, Jeffrey		42	Head injuries from a fall at his home (in Van Nuys, CA)
1996	#+	HUNTER, Ross	☆	75	Cancer (in Century City, CA)
1974	+	HUNTLEY, Chet		61	Lung cancer (in Bozeman, MT)
1990		HUNTLEY, Raymond		86	Undisclosed causes (in Westminster, England)
1995		HURD, Hugh		70	Complications of hypertension and kidney failure (in NY)
1989		HURLOCK, Madeline (Sherwood)		89	Died in Los Angeles, CA
1974	#+	HUROK, Sol		85	Apparent heart attack
1986		HURST, B. D.		91	
1947		HURST, Brandon		80	Arteriosclerosis (in Burbank, CA)
1994		HURST, Margaret		75	Heart failure (at Sherman Oaks Med. Ctr., CA)
1953		HURST, Paul C.		64	Suicide (in Hollywood, CA)
1946	+	HURT, Marlin		40	Heart attack
1995		HURWITZ, Harry		57	Heart failure (in Los Angeles, CA)
1991		HURWITZ, Leo		81	
1987	+	HUSTON, John	★	81	Complications from emphysema and pneumonia (in Middletown, RI)
1950	#+	HUSTON, Walter	★	66	Aneurysm (in Beverly Hills, CA)
1991		HUTCHENRIDER, C. B.		83	
1976		HUTCHESON, David		71	Died in Scotland
1945		HUTCHINS, Robert "Wheezer"		20	Killed in an Army training camp accident during World War 2
• 1998		HUTCHINSON, Josephine		94	Died in New York
1967		HUTH, Harold		75	After a long illness (in London, England)
• 1996		HUTIN, Jean-Pierre		64	Died in Paris, France
1984		HUTTON, Ina Ray		65	
1979	#+	HUTTON, Jim		45	Cancer of the liver (in Los Angeles, CA)
1987	#	HUTTON, Marion		67	Cancer (in Kirkland, WA)
1994	#	HUTTON, Robert		73	Died in Kingston, NY
1977		HYAMS, Leila		72	After a brief illness (in Bel Air, CA)
1992		HYDE, Jacquelyn		61	Died in Woodland Hills, CA
1991		HYDE-WHITE, Wilfrid		87	Congestive heart failure (in Woodland Hills, CA)
1977		HYLAND, Diana		41	Cancer (in Westwood, CA)
1995	+	HYMAN, Phyllis		45	Suicide (pills) found unconscious in her NYC apt.
1948		HYMER, Warren		42	After a long illness (alcoholism) in Los Angeles, CA
• 1996		HYSON, Dorothy		81	Died in London, England
1955		HYTTEN, Olaf		67	After a heart attack (on the set of "Sir Walter Raleigh") in L.A.
1990		IBBS, Ronald		74	Cancer (in San Antonio, TX)
1990		IDEN, Rosalind		82	
1972	+	IHNAT, Steve		37	Heart attack (in Cannes, France)
1987		ILINSKY, Igor		85	Died in Moscow, Russia
1991		IMAI, Tadashi		79	Cerebral hemorrhage (in Tokyo, Japan)
1974		IMBODEN, David C.		87	Cardiac arrest in his sleep (in Kansas City, MO)

YEAR	NAME		AGE	CAUSE and/or PLACE OF DEATH
1958	IMHOF, Roger		83	Died in Hollywood, CA
1989	# IMMEDIATO, Al		72	Cancer
1947	# INCE, John E.		68	Pneumonia (in Hollywood, CA)
1937	# INCE, Ralph W.		49	Automobile accident (in London, England)
1938	INCE, Richard		23	Died in Oakland, CA
1924	INCE, Thomas H.		42	Congestive heart failure (in Beverly Hills, CA)
1968	INDRISANO, John "Johnny"		62	Apparent suicide (hanging) at his home in San Fernando Valley, CA
1976	# INESCORT, Frieda		74	Multiple sclerosis (in Woodland Hills, CA)
1973	# INGE, William		60	Suicide (in Hollywood, CA)
1936	INGERSOLL, William		75	Acute indigestion (in Los Angeles, CA)
1993	INGLIS, Brian		76	Died in London, England
1956	INGRAHAM, Lloyd		81	Pneumonia (in Woodland Hills, CA)
1989	INGRAM, Bill		69	
1969	INGRAM, Jack		66	Heart attack (in Canoga Park, CA)
1969	+ INGRAM, Rex		73	Heart attack (in L.A.) — Do not confuse with Rex Ingram (Hitchcock)
1950	#+ INGRAM, Rex (Hitchcock)		57	Cerebral hemorrhage (in North Hollywood, CA)
1993	INNOCENT, Harold		60	After a short illness (in London, England)
1995	IPPOLITO, Joseph A.		39	Kidney failure (in Santa Monica, CA)
1990	+ IRELAND, Jill		54	Breast and lung cancer (in Malibu, CA)
1992	IRELAND, John	☆	78	Leukemia (in Santa Barbara, CA)
1990	IRVING, Richard		73	After heart surgery (in San Diego, CA)
1943	IRVING, William J.		50	Died in Los Angeles, CA
1961	IRVING. George		87	Heart attack (in Hollywood, CA)
1956	IRWIN, Bobby		42	Died in Los Angeles, CA
1957	IRWIN, Boyd		76	Died in Woodland Hills, CA
1969	# IRWIN, Charles W.		81	Cancer (in Woodland Hills, CA)
1938	IRWIN, May		76	Bronchial pneumonia (in New York, NY)
1992	ISING, Rudolf "Rudy"	★	88	Died in Newport Beach, CA
• 1997	ITAMI, Juzo		64	Suicide (jumped from 8 story roof top) in Tokyo, Japan
1969	ITURBI, Amparo		70	Died in Beverly Hills, CA
1980	+ ITURBI, José		84	Heart attack (in Hollywood, CA)
1959	IVAN, Rosalind		75	After a brief illness (in New York, NY)
1989	IVENS, Joris		90	Heart attack (in Paris, France)
• 1996	IVERS, Irving		57	Complications following surgery to remove his spleen (in Toronto)
1995	#+ IVES, Burl		85	Mouth cancer and congestive heart failure (in Anacortes, WA)
	J			
1992	JABARA, Paul	★	44	Lymphoma from A.I.D.S. (in Los Angeles, CA)
1995	# JACK, Wolfman		57	Heart attack (at his home in Belvidere, N.C.)
• 1997	JACKSON, Enid		43	Brain aneurysm in Las Vegas, NV
1992	JACKSON, Felix		90	Congestive heart failure
1990	JACKSON, Freda		82	Undisclosed causes (in London, England)
1990	JACKSON, Gordon		66	Cancer (in London, England)
1972	+ JACKSON, Mahalia		60	Heart disease (in Evergreen Park, IL)
1991	#+ JACKSON, Mary Ann		68	
1971	# JACKSON, Selmer		82	Heart disease (in Burbank, CA)
1967	JACKSON, Thomas E.		81	Heart attack (in Hollywood, CA)
1950	JACKSON, Warren		57	After his car collided with a truck (in Hollywood, CA)
1973	JACOBS, Arthur P.		51	Massive heart attack in his sleep (in Beverly Hills, CA)
1992	JACOBS, Everett "Jake"		68	Cancer
1993	JACOBSON, Arthur		92	Died in Woodland Hills, CA
1988	JACOBSON, Henrietta		82	Died in New York, NY
1980	# JACQUES, Hattie		56	Heart attack (in London, England)
• 1997	JAECKEL, Richard	☆	70	Died of cancer in Woodland Hills, CA

Deaths of Movie and Television Personalities — by Name

YEAR	NAME		AGE	CAUSE and/or PLACE OF DEATH
1991	JAFFA, Max		79	
1989	JAFFE, Allen		60	*After a long illness (in Woodland Hills, CA)*
1974	# JAFFE, Carl		71	*Died in London, England*
1992	JAFFE, Henry		85	*Died in Beverly Hills, CA*
• 1997	JAFFE, Leo		88	*After a long illness at home in New York City, NY*
1984	+ JAFFE, Sam	☆	93	*Cancer and heart attack (in Beverly Hills, CA)*
1991	JAGGER, Dean	★	87	*Influenza and heart attack (in Los Angeles, CA)*
1986	JAMES, Claire		65	
• 1997	JAMES, Dennis		79	*Cancer in Palm Springs, CA*
1995	JAMES, Edward		86	*Heart failure (in Escondido, CA)*
1948	JAMES, Gladden		56	*Leukemia (in Hollywood, CA)*
1983	JAMES, Harry		67	*Lymphatic cancer (in Las Vegas, NV)*
1925	JAMES, Horace B.		72	*After a long illness (in Orange, NJ)*
1990	JAMES, Jessica		60	*Cancer (in Los Angeles, CA)*
1992	JAMES, Ralph		67	*Died in Los Angeles, CA*
1976	JAMES, Sidney "Sid"		62	*Cerebral hemorrhage (in Sunderland, England)*
1946	JAMES, Walter		60	*Heart attack (in Gardena, CA)*
1987	JAMESON, Joyce		55	*Undisclosed causes (in Burbank, CA)*
1944	# JAMISON, Bud		50	*Heart attack (in Hollywood, CA)*
1980	JANNEY, Leon		63	*Cancer (in Guadalajara, Mexico)*
1938	JANNEY, William "Bill"		34	*After a short, serious setback while hospitalized (in New York, NY)*
1950	# JANNINGS, Emil	★	63	*Cancer (in Wolfgangsee, Austria)*
1980	#+ JANSSEN, David		48	*Died of a massive heart attack at his home (in Malibu, CA)*
1990	JANSSEN, Werner		91	
1958	# JAQUET, Frank		73	*Heart attack (in Los Angeles, CA)*
1990	JARAY, Hans		83	*Heart failure (in Vienna, Austria)*
1994	JARMAN, Derek		52	*Complications of A.I.D.S. (in London, England)*
1987	# JARRETT, Art		81	*Pneumonia*
• 1997	JARRICO, Paul	☆	82	*Died in a car accident in Los Angeles, CA*
1970	JARVIS, Al		60	*Heart attack (in Newport Beach, CA)*
1933	JARVIS, Jean		30	*After a lingering illness (in Hollywood, CA)*
1933	JARVIS, Laura E.		67	*Injuries from a hit-and-run driver (in Downey, CA)*
1993	JARVIS, Patience		56	*Melanoma*
1971	JARVIS, Robert C.		79	*Died in Bloomsbury, NJ*
1990	JARVIS, Scott		48	*A.I.D.S. (in New York, NY)*
1939	JARVIS, Sydney		58	*Died in Hollywood, CA*
1979	# JASON, Leigh		74	*After a long illness (in Woodland Hills, CA)*
• 1913	JASSET, Victorin		50	
1940	JAUBERT, Maurice		40	*Killed in action during World War 2 (in Azerailles, France)*
1995	JEAKINS, Dorothy	☆	81	*Alzheimer's and Parkinson's diseases (in Santa Barbara, CA)*
1985	JEANS, Isabel		93	*Died in London, England*
1973	# JEANS, Ursula		66	*Died near London, England*
1963	JEAVES, Allan		78	*Heart attack (in London, England)*
1932	JEFFERSON, Thomas		76	*Following a brief illness (in Hollywood, CA)*
1988	JEFFREY, Howard		53	*A.I.D.S. (in Los Angeles, CA)*
1987	JEFFRIES, Lang		55	*Cancer (in Huntington Beach, CA)*
1991	JEFFRIES, Peter		62	*Following open-heart surgery (in San Francisco, CA)*
1974	# JENKINS, Allen		74	*Complications following surgery (in Santa Monica, CA)*
1984	JENKINS, Gordon		73	*Amyotrophic lateral sclerosis (in Los Angeles, CA)*
1962	JENKS, Frank		60	*Cancer (in Hollywood, CA)*
1970	# JENKS, Si		93	*Heart disease (in Woodland Hills, CA)*
1961	JENNINGS, Al		97	*Died in Tarzana, CA*
1979	# JENNINGS, Claudia		29	*Head-on collision with a truck on Pacific Coast Hwy. (in Malibu, CA)*

• New entry. # Original name (Pt. 7). + Interment (Pt. 5).   248   ☆ Oscar nominee, ★ Oscar winner (Pt. 10)

Deaths of Movie and Television Personalities — by Name

YEAR	NAME		AGE	CAUSE and/or PLACE OF DEATH
1937	JENNINGS, De Witt		57	*Heart attack (in Hollywood, CA)*
• 1950	+ JENNINGS, Humphrey		43	*Accidentally fell off a cliff (on the greek island of Poros)*
1932	# JENNINGS, S. E.		51	*Died in Hollywood, CA*
1993	JENSEN, Lenore Kingston		79	*Cancer (in Van Nuys, CA)*
1986	# JEROME, Suzie		26	*Cut wrists and exposure (in Cornwall, England)*
1955	# JERROLD, Mary		77	*Pneumonia (in London, England)*
1981	+ JESSEL, George		83	*Heart attack (in Los Angeles, CA)*
1972	JEWELL, Isabel		61	*Heart attack (in Hollywood, CA)*
• 1997	JEWELL, Stuart		84	*Died of colon cancer in Costa Mesa, CA*
1966	JIMINEZ, Soledad		92	*Following a stroke (in Woodland Hills, CA)*
1994	JOBIM, Antonio Carlos		67	*Heart failure after minor surgery (in New York City)*
• 1996	JOELSON, Ben		70	*Died in Los Angeles, CA*
1993	JOHANN, Zita		89	*Pneumonia (in Nyack Hospital, Nyack, NY)*
1991	JOHANSEN, Gunnar		85	*Liver cancer*
1916	JOHNSON, Arthur V.		39	*Died in Philadelphia, PA*
1996	+ JOHNSON, Ben ★		77	*Apparent heart attack (in Mesa, AZ)*
1981	JOHNSON, Brad		56	*Died in Burbank, CA*
1982	JOHNSON, Celia		73	*Stroke (in Nettlebed, England)*
1962	#+ JOHNSON, Chic		70	*Kidney ailment (in Las Vegas, NV)*
1974	# JOHNSON, Chubby		71	*Died in Hollywood, CA*
1982	JOHNSON, Dan		38	*Undisclosed causes (in New York, NY)*
1984	JOHNSON, E. Lamont		29	*Died in Marina Del Rey, CA*
1960	JOHNSON, Emory		66	*Critically burned when his bed caught fire (in San Mateo, CA)*
1957	# JOHNSON, Katie		79	*Died in Elham, England*
1975	# JOHNSON, Kay		71	*Died in Waterford, CT*
1937	JOHNSON, Martin		52	*Airplane crash (in Los Angeles, CA)*
1977	+ JOHNSON, Nunnally		80	*Pneumonia (in Los Angeles, CA)*
1953	JOHNSON, Osa		58	*Heart attack (in New York, NY)*
1965	JOHNSON, Rita		52	*Brain hemorrhage (in West Hollywood, CA)*
1984	JOHNSON, Sunny		30	*Cerebral hemorrhage (in Los Angeles, CA)*
1971	#+ JOHNSON, Tor		67	*Heart condition (in San Fernando, CA)*
1996	JOHNSTON, Johnny		80	*Heart failure (in Cape Coral, FL)*
1966	JOHNSTON, Oliver		78	*Died in London, England*
1978	JOLLEY, L. Stanford		78	*Died in Woodland Hills, CA*
1950	#+ JOLSON, Al		64	*Heart attack (in San Francisco, CA)*
1983	JONAH, Dolly		53	*After a long illness*
1992	JONES, Allan		84	*Lung cancer (in New York, NY)*
1976	+ JONES, Anissa "Buffy"		18	*Lethal mix of Quaaludes and alcohol (in Oceanside, CA)*
1981	JONES, Barry		87	*Died in England*
1971	#+ JONES, Bobby		69	*Died in Atlanta, GA*
1969	#+ JONES, Brian		25	*Drowned while under the influence of liquor and drugs (in London)*
1942	#+ JONES, Buck		52	*Burned to death while trying to save others in a fire (in Boston, MA)*
1990	# JONES, Candy		64	*Cancer*
1983	+ JONES, Carolyn ☆		54	*Cancer (in Los Angeles, CA)*
1992	# JONES, Charlotte		76	*Heart disease*
1986	JONES, Darby		76	*Cancer (in Los Angeles, CA)*
1988	JONES, Duane		51	*Undisclosed causes (in Mineola, NY)*
1972	# JONES, Emrys		57	*Heart attack (in Johannesburg, South Africa)*
1930	JONES, F. Richard "Dick"		36	*Bronchial pneumonia (in Hollywood, CA)*
1963	JONES, Gordon		52	*Heart attack (in Tarzana, CA)*
• 1998	# JONES, Grandpa		84	*Died after a series of strokes in Nashville, Tenn.*
1993	+ JONES, Ken		54	*Cancer (in Los Angeles, CA)*
1989	JONES, Reed		35	*Liver cancer (in Sherman Oaks, CA)*

Deaths of Movie and Television Personalities — by Name

YEAR	NAME	AGE	CAUSE and/or PLACE OF DEATH
1965	#+ JONES, Spike	53	*Emphysema (in Beverly Hills, CA)*
1971	# JONES, T. C.	50	*Cancer (in Duarte, CA)*
1985	JONES, Tyrone	29	*Automobile accident (in Los Angeles, CA)*
1992	JONSON, Kevin Joe	74	*Cancer*
1970	+ JOPLIN, Janis	27	*Accidental drug overdose (heroin morphine) in Hollywood, CA*
1988	JORDAN, Dorothy (Cooper)	82	*Died in Los Angeles, CA*
1991	JORDAN, Gerry	45	*A.I.D.S.*
1988	+ JORDAN, Jim "Fibber McGee"	91	*Blood clot in brain (from a fall) in Los Angeles, CA*
1984	JORDAN, John Duffield	81	
1961	#+ JORDAN, Marion "Molly McGee"	64	*Cancer (in Encino, CA)*
1993	# JORDAN, Richard	56	*Brain tumor (at his home in Los Angles, CA)*
1965	JORDAN, Robert "Bobby"	42	*Liver ailment (in Los Angeles, CA)*
1989	JORGENSEN, Christine (George)	62	*Cancer of the bladder*
1982	+ JORY, Victor	79	*Apparent heart attack (in Santa Monica, CA)*
1981	JOSLYN, Allyn	75	*Cardiac failure (in Woodland Hills, CA)*
1951	# JOUVET, Louis	63	*Heart attack (in Paris, France)*
1985	# JOY, Leatrice	91	*Pernicious anemia (in Riverdale, NY)*
1964	JOY, Nicholas	79	*After a long illness (in Philadelphia, PA)*
1955	JOYCE, Alice "Vitagraph Girl"	65	*Heart ailment (in Hollywood, CA)*
1986	JOYCE, Anna	74	*Died in Hialeah, FL*
1957	JOYCE, Peggy Hopkins	63	*Died in New York, NY*
1980	JOYCE, Yootha	53	*Cirrhosis of the liver (in London, England)*
1969	JUDELS, Charles	86	*Died in Amsterdam, Netherlands*
1974	JUDGE, Arline	62	*Heart attack at her home (in West Hollywood, CA)*
1994	#+ JULIA, Raul	54	*Complications of a stroke (at a hospital in Manhasset, NY)*
1943	+ JULIAN, Rupert	54	*Cerebral thrombosis (in Hollywood, CA)*
1943	# JUNKERMANN, Hans	70	*Died in Berlin, Germany*
1982	+ JURGENS, Curt	69	*Heart attack (in Vienna, Austria)*
1995	JURGENS, Dick	85	*Cancer (in Sacramento, CA)*
1993	JURIST, Ed	76	*Died in Los Angeles, CA*
1975	JUSTICE, James Robertson	70	*Found dead in bed of apoplexy (in Winchester, Hampshire, England)*
• 1986	JUTRA, Claude	56	*Suicide after Alzheimer's (drowned himself in the St. Lawrence River)*

K

YEAR	NAME	AGE	CAUSE and/or PLACE OF DEATH
1994	# KABIBBLE, Ish	86	*Respiratory failure due to emphysema (Joshua Tree, CA)*
1979	KADAR, Jan	61	*Heart attack after being hospitalized (in Los Angeles, CA)*
1984	KADLER, Karen (Hartford)	50	*Cancer (in Los Angeles, CA)*
1968	KAHANAMOKU, Duke	77	*After a heart attack at the Waikiki Yacht Club (in Honolulu, HI)*
1995	KAIDANOVSKY, Alexander	49	*Heart attack (in Moscow)*
• 1998	KAISER, Sharon Lee	56	*Cancer in California*
• 1997	KAJITA, Alvin T.	55	*Lung cancer at Good Samaritan Hospital in Los Angeles, CA*
1975	KALICH, Jacob	82	*Cancer (in Lake Mahopac, NY)*
1941	KALIZ, Armand	48	*Heart attack (in Beverly Hills, CA)*
1995	KALKIN, Gary	44	*Complications from A.I.D.S. (at his home in L.A., CA)*
1980	# KALLMAN, Dick	46	*Murdered (in his Manhattan, NY, apartment)*
1980	KAMINSKA, Ida ☆	80	*Heart attack (in New York, NY)*
• 1998	KAMPEN, Irene	75	*Breast cancer at her Oceanside, CA home*
1950	# KAMPERS, Fritz	59	*Died in Garmisch-Partenkirchen, Germany*
1992	KANE, Dennis	69	*Cancer (in Great Neck, NY)*
1969	KANE, Eddie	79	*Heart attack (in Hollywood, CA)*
1966	+ KANE, Helen	58	*After a 10-year bout with liver cancer (in Jackson Heights, NY)*
1975	KANE, Joseph	81	*Heart attack (in Santa Monica, CA)*
1992	KANE, Paul	?	*Heart attack*
1993	KANIN, Michael	83	*Died in Los Angeles, CA*

Deaths of Movie and Television Personalities — by Name

YEAR	NAME	AGE	CAUSE and/or PLACE OF DEATH
1983	+ KAPER, Bronislau	81	Cancer (in Hollywood, CA)
1984	KARAS, Anton	78	Cancer (in Vienna, Austria)
1993	KARAS, Barry	49	Leukemia (in Boston, MA)
• 1996	KARAYN, Jim	64	Died in Washington, D.C.
1993	KARIN, Rita	73	Following a bout with pneumonia (in New York)
1969	#+ KARLOFF, Boris	81	Respiratory ailment (in Midhurst, England)
1985	# KARLSON, Phil	77	Cancer (in Los Angeles, CA)
1979	KARNES, Robert	62	Heart failure (in Sherman Oaks, CA)
1970	+ KARNS, Roscoe	76	After being hospitalized (in Los Angeles, CA)
1995	KAROL, Darcie	37	Breast cancer (in Boston, MA)
1990	KASHA, Lawrence	57	Brain cancer (in Los Angeles, CA)
1965	+ KASSEL, Art	69	
1984	KAST, Pierre	63	Heart attack (on an airplane from Rome to Paris)
1979	# KASZNAR, Kurt	65	Cancer (in Santa Monica, CA)
1958	# KATCH, Kurt	62	During surgery for lung cancer (in Los Angeles, CA)
1985	+ KATZ, Mickey	75	Natural causes
1996	KATZ, Oscar	82	After a bout with pneumonia (at his home in Los Angeles, CA)
1990	KATZKA, Gabriel	58	Heart attack (in Los Angeles, CA)
• 1996	KATZMAN, Leonard	69	Apparent heart attack (at his home in Malibu, CA)
1984	+ KAUFMAN, Andy	35	Lung cancer (in Los Angeles, CA)
• 1980	KAUFMAN, Boris ★	74	Cancer (at Hollywood Presbyterian Hospital in Hollywood, CA)
1915	KAUFMAN, Joseph	35	Pneumonia (in New York, NY)
1991	KAUFMAN, Robert ☆	60	Heart attack (in Beverly Hills, CA)
1986	# KAY, Beatrice	79	After suffering several strokes (in North Hollywood, CA)
1987	#+ KAYE, Danny	74	Heart failure due to hepatitis (in Los Angeles, CA)
1987	+ KAYE, Nora (Ross)	67	Cancer (in Santa Monica, CA)
1987	KAYE, Sammy	77	
• 1997	KAYE, Stubby	79	Died at his home in Los Rancho Mirage, CA of lung cancer
1991	KAYE, Sylvia Fine	78	Emphysema (in New York, NY)
1995	KAYE, Toni	49	Cancer (in Los Angeles, CA)
1989	KAYE-MARTIN, Edward	50	Lymphoma
1945	KAYSSLER, Friedrich	71	Died in Leinmachnow, Germany
1986	KEAN, Betty	69	After a brief illness (in Hollywood, CA)
1959	KEANE, Edward	75	Died in Los Angeles, CA
1993	KEANE, Joe	69	Cancer (in Woodland Hills, CA)
1981	KEANE, Robert Emmett	96	Died in Hollywood, CA
• 1997	KEAREY, Antony	77	
1956	KEARNS, Allen B.	61	Died in Albany, NY
1962	KEARNS, Joseph	55	Died in Los Angeles, CA
1961	KEATING, Fred	64	Heart attack (in New York, NY)
1964	KEATING, Larry	67	Leukemia (in Hollywood, CA)
1966	#+ KEATON, Buster	70	Lung cancer (in Woodland Hills, CA)
1946	# KEATON, Joseph Sr.	78	Died in Hollywood, CA
1981	KEATON, Louise	78	Cancer (in Van Nuys, CA)
1955	KEATON, Myra	?	
1994	KEATS, Steven	48	Suicide (found dead in his apartment) in Manhattan, NY
1993	KEEGAN, Terry	59	Suicide (near Kingman, Arizona)
1993	+ KEELER, Ruby	83	Cancer (in Rancho Mirage, CA)
1970	# KEEN, Malcolm	82	Died in England
1986	KEENAN, Paul	30	A.I.D.S. (in Boston, MA)
1971	KEENE, Richard	80	
1963	# KEENE, Tom	67	Died in Woodland Hills, CA
1984	+ KEIGHLEY, William	94	Pulmonary embolism (in New York, NY)

Deaths of Movie and Television Personalities — by Name

YEAR	NAME	AGE	CAUSE and/or PLACE OF DEATH
• 1997	KEITH, Brian	75	*Died at his home in Malibu, CA of a self-inflicted gun shot wound*
1960	# KEITH, Ian	61	*Died in New York, NY*
1966	KEITH, Robert	68	*Died in Los Angeles, CA*
1973	+ KELLAWAY, Cecil ☆	79	*Arteriosclerosis (in Beverly Hills, CA)*
1987	KELLER, Harry	73	*Heart complications (in Los Angeles, CA)*
1968	KELLER, Helen	86	*Died in Westport, CT*
1975	KELLERMAN, Annette	87	*Died in Southport, Australia*
1991	KELLEY, Edward (Barry)	82	*Congestive heart failure (in Woodland Hills, CA)*
1983	KELLIN, Mike	61	*Lung cancer (in Nyack, NY)*
1995	KELLIN, Sally Moffet	63	*Lung cancer (in Nyack, NY)*
1982	# KELLJAN, Robert	52	*After a long bout with cancer (in Los Angeles, CA)*
1976	KELLOGG, Ray	70	*Cancer (in Ontario, CA)*
1966	# KELLY, Dorothy	51	*Died in a fire at her home in La Jolla, CA*
1979	+ KELLY, Emmett	80	*Heart attack (in Sarasota, FL)*
1996	#+ KELLY, Gene ★	83	*Died in his sleep after suffering 2 strokes in 2 yrs. (in Beverly Hills)*
1982	+ KELLY, Grace ★	52	*Brain hemorrhage after a car crash (in Monaco)*
1992	KELLY, Jack	65	*After suffering a stroke (in Huntington Beach, CA)*
1964	KELLY, James "Tiny"	49	*Heart ailment (in Hollywood) Do not confuse with James T. Kelly*
1933	KELLY, James T.	79	*Do not confuse with James "Tiny" Kelly, d. 1964 (in New York, NY)*
1959	KELLY, Joe	57	*Heart attack (in Los Angeles, CA)*
1947	KELLY, John	46	
1968	KELLY, Kitty	66	*Cancer (in Hollywood, CA)*
1944	KELLY, Lew	65	*Died in Los Angeles, CA*
1995	+ KELLY, Nancy ☆	73	*Complications of diabetes (at her home in Bel Air, CA)*
1981	#+ KELLY, Patsy	71	*Cancer (in Woodland Hills, CA)*
1956	#+ KELLY, Paul	57	*Heart attack (in Los Angeles, CA)*
1992	KELLY, Paula	72	*After a long illness (in Costa Mesa, CA)*
1961	KELSEY, Fred A.	77	*Died in Hollywood, CA*
1946	KELSO, Mayme	79	*Heart attack (in South Pasadena, CA)*
1968	KELTON, Pert	60	*Stroke*
1940	KEMP, Hal	36	*Pneumonia after auto injuries (in Madera, CA)*
1953	KEMP, Paul	54	*Died in Bad Godesburg, West Germany*
1950	KEMPER, Charles	49	*Injuries from an automobile crash (in Burbank, CA)*
1991	KEMPFF, Wilhelm	95	*Parkinson's disease*
• 1984	KENDAL, Jennifer	50	
1953	# KENDALL, Cy	55	*Died in Woodland Hills, CA*
1959	#+ KENDALL, Kay (Harrison)	32	*Leukemia (in London, England)*
1990	KENDRICK, Henry	56	*Emphysema and pneumonia (in AZ)*
1992	KENDRICKS, Eddie	52	*Lung cancer*
1985	KENIN, Alexa	23	*Undisclosed causes (in New York)*
• 1997	KENNEDY, Adam	75	*Heart attack at home in Kent, Conn.*
1990	KENNEDY, Arthur ☆	75	*Brain tumor (in Branford, CT)*
1973	# KENNEDY, Douglas	58	*Cancer (in Kailua, Hawaii)*
1948	+ KENNEDY, Edgar	58	*Throat cancer (in Woodland Hills, CA)*
1958	# KENNEDY, Fred	48	*A broken neck after falling from his horse during filming (in Louisiana)*
1987	KENNEDY, Madge	96	*Respiratory failure (in Woodland Hills, CA)*
1944	KENNEDY, Merna	35	*Following a heart attack (in Los Angeles, CA)*
1965	KENNEDY, Tom	81	*Bone cancer (in Woodland Hills, CA)*
1989	KENNER, Warren	64	*Heart attack (in New Orleans, LA)*
1992	#+ KENNY, Herbert C.	77	*Cancer*
1923	KENT, Charles	70	*After being hospitalized (in Brooklyn, NY)*
1953	KENT, Craufurd	72	*After a short illness (in Los Angeles, CA)*
1955	# KENT, Robert	46	

• New entry. # Original name (Pt. 7). + Interment (Pt. 5). 252 ☆ Oscar nominee, ★ Oscar winner (Pt. 10)

Deaths of Movie and Television Personalities — by Name

YEAR		NAME		AGE	CAUSE and/or PLACE OF DEATH
1980		KENTON, Erle C.		83	Parkinson's disease and emphysema (in Glendale, CA)
1979	#+	KENTON, Stan		66	Stroke (in Hollywood, CA)
1979		KENYON, Doris		81	Cardiac arrest in her sleep (in Beverly Hills, CA)
1990	#	KERMACK, Paul		57	Heart attack (in Glasgow, Scotland)
1991		KERMAN, Sheppard		62	Lung cancer (in Manhasset, NY)
1966		KERN, James V.		57	Pneumonia, after a short illness (in Encino, CA)
1945	#+	KERN, Jerome		60	Cerebral hemorrhage (in New York, NY)
1968		KERR, Lorence "Larry"		?	
1994	#	KERR, Stu		66	After 8-yr. battle with bone marrow cancer (in Balt., MD)
1947	#+	KERRIGAN, J. Warren		67	Bronchial pneumonia (in Balboa Island, CA)
1964		KERRIGAN, Joseph M.		76	Died in Hollywood, CA
1956	#	KERRY, Norman		66	Died in Hollywood, CA
1991	+	KERT, Larry		60	A.I.D.S. (in New York, NY)
1995		KETCHUM, Larry		49	Heart attack (in Sierra Vista, AZ)
1954	#	KEY, Kathleen		47	Died in Woodland Hills, CA
1985		KEYSER, Andy		33	Cancer (in Santa Monica, CA)
1987		KEZER, Glenn B.		63	Cancer (in Okemah, OK)
• 1998		KHAMBATTA, Persis		49	Heart attack in Bombay, India
1995		KHEIFITS, Iosif		89	Died in St. Petersburg, Russia
• 1918		KHOLODNAYA, Vera		?	Spanish influenza
1956	#+	KIBBEE, Guy		70	Parkinson's disease (in East Islip, NY)
1993		KIBBEE, Lois		71	Brain tumor (at Sloane-Kettering Cancer Ctr., NY)
1970		KIBBEE, Milton		73	Died in Simi Valley, CA
1987		KIDD, Jonathan (Kurt Richards)		73	After surgery for an aorta aneurysm (in Los Angeles, CA)
1990		KIELY, Pat		59	After a long illness
1966		KIEPURA, Jan		64	Heart ailment (in Harrison, NY)
1996		KIESLOWSKI, Krzysztof	☆	54	Heart attack after suffering with A.I.D.S. (in Warsaw, Poland)
1991		KIKER, Douglas		61	Heart attack
1953	#+	Kiki		52	Natural causes (in Paris, France)
1972		KIKUME, Al		78	Heart attack (in Hollywood, CA)
1964	+	KILBRIDE, Percy		76	Brain injury from auto accident (in Los Angeles, CA)
1965	+	KILGALLEN, Dorothy		52	Accidental death? (Seconal and alcohol) in New York, NY
1991	#	KILIAN, Pauline		83	Complications from diabetes (in Peacham, VT)
1979	+	KILIAN, Victor		81	Killed by burglars (in his Hollywood, CA, apartment)
1938		KIMBALL, Edward M.		78	Died in Hollywood, CA
• 1996		KIMBROUGH, Clinton		63	Pneumonia (in Ada, OK)
1996		KINDLE, Tom		47	Complications of A.I.D.S. (in Los Angeles, CA)
• 1996		KING, Alyce (Clarke)		80	Chronic bronchial asthma (in Los Angeles, CA)
1963		KING, Anita		74	Heart attack (in Hollywood, CA)
1944		KING, Charles E.		54	Pneumonia (in London, England)
1957		KING, Charles L. Sr.		58	Died in Hollywood, CA
1941	#	KING, Claude E.		62	Died in Los Angeles, CA
1986		KING, Dennis Jr.		?	Heart attack
1971	#	KING, Dennis Sr.		73	Heart condition (in New York, NY)
1982	+	KING, Henry	☆	86	Died in his sleep at home (in Toluca Lake, CA)
1993		KING, Jean		76	Heart attack (in North Hollywood, CA)
1951		KING, Joe		68	Died in Woodland Hills, CA
1947		KING, Leslie		71	Died in Amityville, NY
1968	+	KING, Martin Luther Jr.		39	Murdered (shot)
1992	#	KING, Michael		69	Died in Tarzana, CA
1982		KING, Mollie		86	Following a stroke (in Fort Lauderdale, FL)
• 1996		KING, Paul Donaldson	☆	69	Cancer (at his home in Newport Beach, CA)
1984		KING, Walter Woolf		84	Heart attack (in Beverly Hills, CA)

• New entry.   # Original name (Pt. 7).   + Interment (Pt. 5).   253   ☆ Oscar nominee, ★ Oscar winner (Pt. 10)

Deaths of Movie and Television Personalities — by Name

	YEAR	NAME		AGE	CAUSE and/or PLACE OF DEATH
	1985	KING, Wayne		84	
	1991	KINGHAM, Bernard		65	A stroke related to spinal cancer (in Amersham, England)
	1958	KINGSFORD, Walter		75	Heart attack (in North Hollywood, CA)
•	1997	KINGSLEY, Dorothy		87	Died of a heart ailment in Monterey, CA
	1995	# KINGSLEY, Sidney		88	Stroke (at his home in Oakland, N.J.)
	1984	KINGSLEY, Susan		37	Died when her car was struck head-on by another (in Athens, Greece)
	1993	KINGSTON, Lenore (Jensen)		79	Cancer (in Van Nuys, CA)
	1967	KINGSTON, Winifred		73	Died in La Jolla, CA
	1992	KINISON, Sam		38	Internal injuries following a car crash (in Needles, CA)
•	1998	# KINLEY, Edwin		82	Heart failure in New York City, NY
	1988	KINNEAR, Roy		54	After falling from his horse during filming (in Madrid, Spain)
	1954	KINNELL, Murray		65	Died in Santa Barbara, CA
	1992	KINNEY, Jack		82	Died in Glendale, CA
	1983	KINSER, Patrick		30	Pulmonary failure (in Los Angeles, CA)
	1991	KINSKI, Klaus		65	Found dead of a heart attack (at his home in Lagunitas, CA)
	1974	KINSOLVING, Lee		36	Died in Palm Beach, FL
	1995	+ KIRBY, George		71	Parkinson's disease (at a nursing home in Las Vegas, NV)
	1948	# KIRK, Jack "Pappy"		53	Heart attack (in Alaska)
	1948	KIRK, John		86	After a heart attack
	1990	KIRK, Lisa		62	Lung cancer (in New York, NY)
	1971	KIRKLAND, Muriel		68	Emphysema and complications (in New York, NY)
	1989	KIRKWOOD, James Jr.		64	Cancer (in Manhattan, NY)
	1963	KIRKWOOD, James Sr.		80	Died in Woodland Hills, CA
	1992	KIRSTEN, Dorothy		82	Complications from a stroke and Alzheimer's disease (in L.A., CA)
•	1996	KITCHELL, Alma		103	Died at her home in Sarasota, FL
	1988	KJELLIN, Alf		68	Heart attack (in Los Angeles, CA)
•	1997	KLAP, Hans		52	Heart attack (at International Film Festival in Rotterdam, Netherlands)
	1983	KLEIN, Adelaide		82	Brain tumor (in New York, NY)
	1973	KLEMPERER, Otto		88	Died in his sleep
	1982	KLINGER, Ruth S.		59	Heart attack in her sleep (in Great Neck, NY)
	1950	KLOPFER, Eugen		64	Died in Wiesbaden, Germany
	1993	KLOS, Elmar	★	83	Cause unreported (in Prague, Czechoslovakia)
•	1955	+ KNAGGS, Skelton		43	Heart attack
	1981	KNAPP, Evelyn		72	Died in West Hollywood, CA
	1993	# KNIGHT, Bob		72	Heart attack (in New York)
	1987	KNIGHT, Esmond		80	Died in Egypt
	1976	# KNIGHT, Fuzzy		74	Heart attack (in Hollywood, CA)
	1987	# KNIGHT, June		74	Complications after a stroke (in Los Angeles, CA)
	1986	#+ KNIGHT, Ted		62	After surgery for a urinary tract growth (in Pacific Palisades, CA)
	1981	KNOPF, Edwin H.		82	Apoplexy attack (in Brentwood, CA)
	1955	KNOTT, Lydia		88	Died in Woodland Hills, CA
	1995	# KNOWLES, Patric		84	Cerebral hemorrhage (in Los Angeles, CA)
	1995	KNOX, Alexander		88	Bone cancer (at an infirmary in Northumberland, Eng.)
	1974	KNOX, Teddy		78	Died in England
	1991	KOBAL, John		51	Pneumonia
•	1996	KOBAYASHI, Masaki		80	Cardiac arrest (at his home in Tokyo, Japan)
	1995	KOCH, Howard	★	93	Pneumonia (in Kingston, NY) Do not confuse with producer
	1938	KOHLER, Fred Sr.		49	Heart attack (in Los Angeles, CA)
	1964	KOLB, Clarence		89	Stroke (in Los Angeles, CA)
	1991	KOLB, Glenn		39	A.I.D.S.
	1947	+ KOLKER, Henry		72	Injuries from a fall (in Los Angeles, CA)
•	1997	KOMACK, James		67	Died of heart failure in Los Angeles, CA
	1992	KOPLIN, Merton Y.		71	

Deaths of Movie and Television Personalities — by Name

YEAR	NAME	AGE	CAUSE and/or PLACE OF DEATH
1956	KORDA, Alexander	62	*Heart attack (in South Kensington, England)*
1961	KORDA, Zoltan	66	*After a long illness (in Hollywood, CA)*
• 1996	KOREMIN, Walter Michael	69	*Following an embolism (at Johns Hopkins Hosp. in Baltimore, MD)*
1944	KORFF, Arnold	73	*Heart ailment (in New York, NY)*
1980	+ KORJUS, Miliza ☆	73	*Heart attack (in Culver City, CA)*
1957	+ KORNGOLD, Erich Wolfgang	60	*The aftermath of a cerebral thrombosis (in North Hollywood, CA)*
1973	KORNMAN, Mary	56	*Cancer (in Glendale, CA)*
1967	KORTMAN, Robert F.	79	*Cancer (in Long Beach, CA)*
1970	KORTNER, Fritz	78	*Leukemia (in Munich, Germany)*
• 1998	# KORVIN, Charles	90	*Died at Lenox Hill Hospital in Manhattan, NY*
1994	KOSCINA, Sylva	61	*Cancer complicated by heart problems (in Rome, Italy)*
1994	KOSLECK, Martin	89	*After abdominal surgery (in Santa Monica, CA)*
1956	KOSLOFF, Theodore	74	*Died in Los Angeles, CA*
1994	KOSTAL, Irwin ★	83	*Heart attack (in Studio City, CA)*
1980	+ KOSTELANETZ, Andre	79	*Heart attack after pneumonia (in Haiti)*
1988	KOSTER, Henry	83	*After a long illness (in Camarillo, CA)*
1962	+ KOVACS, Ernie	42	*Automobile accident (in Beverly Hills, CA)*
1993	KRAFT, David	35	*Crohn's disease (in Los Angeles, CA)*
1950	# KRAHLY, Hanns	65	*After a long illness (in Hollywood, CA)*
1989	KRAMER, Mandel J.	72	*Died in Delray Beach, FL*
1992	KRAMER, Sy	59	*Cancer (in Los Angeles, CA)*
1992	KRAMER, Tim	34	*A.I.D.S.*
1995	KRAMEROV, Savelly	60	*Cancer (in San Francisco, CA)*
1981	KRASKER, Robert	67	*Died in London, England*
1984	KRASNA, Norman ★	74	*Heart attack*
1959	KRAUSS, Werner	75	*Died in Vienna, Austria*
1991	KREBS, Nita	85	*Apparent heart attack*
1989	KREEL, Kenneth	48	*A.I.D.S.*
1962	+ KREISLER, Fritz	86	*Following a heart attack*
1994	KRIM, Arthur	84	*After a long illness (at his home in New York City)*
1991	KROEGER, Berry	78	*Kidney failure (in Los Angeles, CA)*
1990	KRUEGER, Michael	39	*Cancer (in Milwaukee, WI)*
1960	KRUGER, Alma	91	*After a long illness (in Seattle, WA)*
1974	+ KRUGER, Otto	89	*Stroke and cerebral vascular complications (in Woodland Hills, CA)*
1992	KRUGMAN, Lou	78	*Cancer (in Burbank, CA)*
1973	+ KRUPA, Gene	64	*Heart problems and leukemia (in Yonkers, NY)*
1976	+ KUHLMAN, Kathryn	63	*Pulmonary hypertension after open-heart surgery*
1965	# KULKY, Henry "Hank"	53	*Heart attack (in Oceanside, CA)*
• 1997	KULLE, Jarl	70	*Died of bone cancer at his home in Stockholm, Sweden*
1993	KULLER, Sid Charles	83	*Colon cancer (in Sherman Oaks, CA)*
1983	KULLMAN, Charles	80	*Heart attack (in New Haven, CT)*
1991	KULP, Nancy	69	*Cancer of the jaw (in Palm Desert, CA)*
1990	KULUVA, Will	78	*Pulmonary embolism*
1963	KUPCINET, Karyn	22	*Murdered (bound and strangled) in West Los Angeles, CA*
• 1997	KURALT, Charles	62	*Died in NY Hospital-Cornell Medical Ctr. of heart failure*
1992	KUSELL, Maurice L.	89	*Pneumonia (in Los Angeles, CA)*
1931	# KUWA, George K.	46	*Died in Japan*
1982	KYDD, Sam	67	*Respiratory ailment (in London, England)*
1985	+ KYSER, Kay	79	*Heart attack (in Chapel Hill, NC)*
	L		
• 1988	L'AMOUR, Louis	80	*Died in Los Angeles, CA*
1963	# L'ESTRANGE, Dick	73	*Died in Burbank, CA*
1918	L'ESTRANGE, Julian	38	*Spanish influenza (in New York, NY)*

Deaths of Movie and Television Personalities — by Name

YEAR	NAME		AGE	CAUSE and/or PLACE OF DEATH
1978	L'HERBIER, Marcel		91	Cardiac arrest in his sleep (in Paris, France)
1917	LaBADIE, Florence		29	Blood poisoning after being crushed when her car overturned (in NY)
1952	LaCAVA, Gregory	☆	59	Heart attack at his home (in Malibu Beach, CA)
• 1996	# LaCENTRA, Peg		86	Heart attack (at her home in Los Angeles, CA)
1979	LACEY, Catherine		75	Died in London, England
1991	LACEY, Ronald		55	Cancer (in London, England)
1975	LACHMAN, Harry		88	Heart attack (in Beverly Hills, CA)
1968	LACKTEEN, Frank		73	Cerebral and respiratory illness (in Woodland Hills, CA)
1964	+ LADD, Alan		50	Accidental death (alcohol/drug mix) in Palm Springs, CA
1982	+ LADD, Sue Carol		73	Complications of heart attack (in Hollywood, CA)
1979	LAEMMLE, Carl Jr.		71	Stroke after a 16-yr. battle with multiple sclerosis (in Beverly Hills)
1939	+ LAEMMLE, Carl Sr.		72	Heart attack (in Hollywood, CA)
1967	#+ LAHR, Bert		72	Internal hemorrhage after pneumonia (in New York, NY)
1963	LAIDLAW, Ethan		63	
1936	LAIDLAW, Roy		52	Heart attack (in Hollywood, CA)
1991	+ LAIRD, Jack		69	Cancer (in Los Angeles, CA)
1967	LAKE, Alice		71	Heart attack (in Paradise, CA)
1987	#+ LAKE, Arthur "Dagwood"		81	Heart attack (in Indian Wells, CA)
1980	LAKE, Florence		75	Died in Woodland Hills, CA
1973	#+ LAKE, Veronica		51	Acute hepatitis (in Burlington, VT)
1985	LALLY, Michael Sr.		82	Died in Woodland Hills, CA
1926	#+ LaMARR, Barbara		29	Over-dieting (in Altadena, CA)
1982	+ LAMAS, Fernando		67	Cancer (in Los Angeles, CA)
1921	LAMBERT, Clara		?	
1986	LAMBERT, Douglas		50	A.I.D.S. (in London, England)
• 1997	LAMBERT, Paul		74	Cancer at St. John's Hospital in Santa Monica, CA
1950	# LAMBERTI, Professor		58	After a long illness (in Hollywood, CA)
• 1996	LAMMERS, Paul		74	Cancer (at his home in Washington, CT)
1993	LAMONT, Charles		98	Pneumonia (in Woodland Hills, CA)
1991	LAMONT, Deni		59	Lung cancer
1990	LAMONT, Estelle		82	Respiratory failure (in Woodland Hills, CA)
• 1996	#+ LAMOUR, Dorothy (Howard)		81	Died at her home in Los Angeles, CA
1989	LAMPKIN, Charles		76	Heart attack (in San José, CA)
1919	LAMPTON, Dee		21	Appendicitis (in New York, NY)
1994	#+ LANCASTER, Burt		80	Heart attack after suffering a stroke (at his condo in Los Angeles, CA)
1983	LANCASTER, Robert		70	Died in Lancaster, CA
1986	#+ LANCHESTER, Elsa	☆	84	Bronchial pneumonia (in Woodland Hills, CA)
1935	LANDAU, David		57	After a lingering illness (in Hollywood, CA)
1993	LANDAU, Ely A.		73	Complications following a stroke (in Los Angeles, CA)
1993	LANDAU, Richard		79	Complications after surgery (in Century City, CA)
1991	LANDERS, Hal		63	After being hospitalized for cancer treatment (in Los Angeles, CA)
1962	LANDERS, Lew		61	Heart attack (in Palm Desert, CA)
1948	# LANDI, Elissa		43	Cancer (in Kingston, NY)
1973	LANDIN, Hope		79	After a short illness (in Hollywood, CA)
1948	#+ LANDIS, Carole		29	Suicide (sleeping pills) in Brentwood Heights, CA
1975	LANDIS, Cullen		77	Died in Bloomfield Hills, MI
1992	# LANDIS, David		42	A.I.D.S. (in Los Angeles, CA)
1972	LANDIS, Jessie Royce		67	Cancer (in Danbury, CT)
1986	LANDIS, Joseph P.		67	Cancer
1992	LANDIS, Walter James		65	After a long illness (in Glendale, CA)
1991	#+ LANDON, Michael		54	Cancer of the liver and pancreas (in Malibu, CA)
1959	LANDOWSKA, Wanda		80	Died at her home in Lakeville, CT
1973	#+ LANE, Allan "Rocky"		69	Bone marrow cancer (in Woodland Hills, CA)

• New entry. # Original name (Pt. 7). + Interment (Pt. 5). 256 ☆ Oscar nominee, ★ Oscar winner (Pt. 10)

Deaths of Movie and Television Personalities — by Name

YEAR		NAME		AGE	CAUSE and/or PLACE OF DEATH
•	1997	LANE, Burton		84	*Died in New York, N.Y.*
	1945	# LANE, Charles		76	*Cancer (in Van Nuys, CA)*
	1993	LANE, David T.		52	*Brain cancer (in Dallas, TX)*
	1981	#+ LANE, Lola		75	*Inflammation of the arteries (in Santa Barbara, CA)*
	1959	# LANE, Lupino "Nipper"		67	*Died in London, England*
	1953	LANE, Pat		53	*Heart attack (in Beverly Hills, CA)*
	1995	# LANE, Priscilla		76	*After a brief illness (in an Andover, MA, nursing home)*
	1982	LANE, Richard		83	*Died in Newport Beach, CA*
	1974	#+ LANE, Rosemary		60	*Diabetes and pulmonary obstruction (in Woodland Hills, CA)*
	1995	LANE, Ziggy		75	*Congestive heart failure (at his home in Miami, FL)*
	1972	+ LANFIELD, Sidney		74	*Heart attack (in Marina Del Rey, CA)*
•	1998	LANG, Charles	★	96	*Pneumonia in Santa Monica, CA*
	1976	+ LANG, Fritz		85	*After a long illness (in Hollywood, CA)*
	1941	LANG, Howard		64	*Died in Hollywood, CA*
•	1996	LANG, Jennings		81	*Pneumonia (at Manor Care nursing home in Palm Desert, CA)*
	1948	LANG, Matheson		68	*Died in Bridgeton, Barbados*
	1972	LANG, Walter	☆	73	*Kidney failure (in Palm Springs, CA)*
	1991	LANGAN, Glenn		73	*Complications from cancer (in Los Angeles, CA)*
	1944	LANGDON, Harry		60	*Cerebral hemorrhage (in Los Angeles, CA)*
	1943	LANGDON, Lillian		82	*Died in Santa Monica, CA*
	1972	LANGLEY, Faith		43	*Died in New York, NY*
	1994	LANGTON, David		82	*Heart attack (at Stratford-on-Avon, England)*
	1980	LANGTON, Paul		66	*Heart attack (in Burbank, CA)*
	1991	LANHAM, Roy		68	*Cancer*
	1991	LANIN, Howard		93	*Pneumonia*
	1972	# LANSING, Joi		42	*Cancer (in Santa Monica, CA)*
	1994	# LANSING, Robert		66	*Cancer (at Calgary Hospice in the Bronx, NY)*
	1990	LANSON, Snooky		76	
	1993	# LANTEAU, William		70	*Complications after heart surgery (in Los Angeles, CA)*
	1992	# LANTZ, Gracie		88	*Spinal cancer (in Burbank, CA)*
	1994	+ LANTZ, Walter	★	93	*Heart attack (in Burbank, CA)*
	1959	#+ LANZA, Mario		38	*Heart attack after suffering pneumonia and phlebitis (in Rome, Italy)*
	1979	LaPLANCHE, Rosemary		54	*Cancer (in Glendale, CA)*
•	1996	LaPLANTE, Laura		91	*Died at the Motion Picture Country Home in Woodland Hills, CA*
	1945	LaRENO, Richard "Dick"		71	*Died in Hollywood, CA*
	1974	LARGAY, Raymond J. "Ray"		88	*Pulmonary embolism (in Woodland Hills, CA)*
	1946	# LARKIN, George		57	*Died in New York, NY*
	1936	LARKIN, John		62	*Pneumonia (in Los Angeles, CA)*
	1969	#+ LaROCQUE, Rod		70	*Died in Beverly Hills, CA*
	1975	LARRIMORE, Francine		77	*Pneumonia (in New York, NY)*
•	1996	+ LARSEN, William		67	*Heart attack (found dead at his home in Houston, TX)*
	1988	LARSON, Eric		83	*After a lengthy illness (in Flintridge, CA)*
	1990	LaRUE, Bart		57	*Heart failure (in Sweetwater, TX)*
	1960	# LaRUE, Frank H.		81	*Died in Woodland Hills, CA*
	1984	#+ LaRUE, Jack		83	*Heart attack (in Santa Monica, CA)*
•	1996	# LaRUE, Lash		78	*Died at Providence St. Joseph Med. Ctr. in Burbank, CA*
	1988	+ LASKY, Jesse L. Jr.		77	*Cancer (in London, England)*
	1958	+ LASKY, Jesse L. Sr.		77	*Heart attack (in Beverly Hills, CA)*
	1959	Lassie (original dog)		18	
	1985	LATCHAW, Paul		38	*Complications from A.I.D.S. (in New York, NY)*
	1967	# LATELL, Lyle		62	*Heart attack (in Hollywood, CA)*
•	1997	LATTANZI, Tina		99	*After a brief illness at home in Milan, Italy*
	1988	# LATZ, Elaine		71	

• New entry. # Original name (Pt. 7). + Interment (Pt. 5).

☆ Oscar nominee, ★ Oscar winner (Pt. 10)

Deaths of Movie and Television Personalities — by Name

YEAR	NAME	AGE	CAUSE and/or PLACE OF DEATH
1984	LAU, Wesley	63	Heart failure (in Los Angeles, CA)
1980	+ LAUCK, Chester H. "Lum"	79	After a brief illness (in Hot Springs, AR)
1950	LAUDER, Harry	79	Uremia (in Lenarkshire, Scotland)
1948	#+ LAUGHLIN, Billy "Froggy"	16	Motor scooter—truck accident (in Corvina, CA)
1962	+ LAUGHTON, Charles ★	63	Following surgery for spinal cancer (in Hollywood, CA)
1952	LAUGHTON, Edward "Eddie"	49	Pneumonia (in Hollywood, CA)
• 1997	LAUNDER, Frank	91	Cause unreported (at Princess Grace Hospital in Monaco)
1965	#+ LAUREL, Stan	74	Cerebral thrombosis (in Santa Monica, CA)
1980	LAURIE, John	83	Emphysema and a lung ailment (in Chalfont St. Peter, England)
1990	LAUTER, Harry	76	Heart failure (in Ojai, CA)
• 1997	LAUZON, Jean-Claude	43	Plane crash in Northern Quebec, Canada
1971	LAVA, William B.	59	Died in Los Angeles, CA
1991	LaVERE, Jane	87	Heart problems (in Woodland Hills, CA)
1945	#+ LAVERNE, Lucille	72	After being hospitalized for a broken hip (in Culver City, CA)
1940	LAW, Walter	64	Died in Hollywood, CA
1972	# LAWFORD, (Lady) May	?	Died in Monterey Park, CA
1960	LAWFORD, Betty	50	After a long illness (in New York, NY)
1940	LAWFORD, Ernest	69	Died in New York, NY
1984	+ LAWFORD, Peter	61	Cardiac arrest, liver and kidney disease (in Los Angeles, CA)
1995	# LAWRENCE, Bruno	54	Lung cancer (at his home on New Zealand's North Island)
1931	LAWRENCE, Eddy	?	Suicide (gas) in San Diego, CA
1938	+ LAWRENCE, Florence	50	Suicide (mixture of cough syrup and ant paste) in Beverly Hills, CA
1957	LAWRENCE, Gerald	84	Died in England
1952	#+ LAWRENCE, Gertrude	54	Cancer of the liver (in New York, NY)
1992	LAWRENCE, John	60	Heart attack (in Los Angeles, CA)
1990	LAWRENCE, Keith	39	Pneumonia (in Los Angeles, CA)
1926	+ LAWRENCE, Lillian	66	Heart attack at the home of her daughter (in Beverly Hills, CA)
1991	LAWRENCE, Mark (producer)	70	Prostate cancer (in Boston) Do not confuse with actor Marc Lawrence
1991	LAWRENCE, Mary	73	Respiratory failure following pneumonia (in Santa Monica, CA)
1995	# LAWRENCE, Rhoda	71	Pulmonary fibrosis (in Sherman Oaks, CA)
• 1997	LAWRENCE, Rosina	84	Died at Mt. Sinai Hospital Ctr. in New York City, NY
1961	+ LAWRENCE, Walter Smith	59	Died in Palm Dale, CA
1947	#+ LAWRENCE, William E. "Babe"	51	Died in Hollywood, CA
1966	# LAWSON, Wilfrid	66	Heart attack (in London, England)
1969	# LAWTON, Frank	64	Died in London, England
1994	LAYTON, Joe	64	After an extended illness (in Key West, FL)
1993	LAZARUS, Irma	80	Cancer (in Cincinnati, OH)
1990	LEACOCK, Philip	73	Collapsed lungs (in London, England)
1992	LEAMING, Chet	66	After a brief illness (in New York, NY)
1991	LEAMING, Jim	72	After a long illness
1991	LEAN, David	83	After a long illness (in London, England)
1981	# LEANDER, Zarah	74	Died near Stockholm, Sweden
1987	LEARN, Betsy	98	Died in Burbank, CA
1966	LEASE, Rex	64	Found dead of a heart attack at his home (in Hollywood, CA)
1953	+ LEBEDEFF, Ivan	53	Heart attack (in Hollywood, CA)
1990	LEBERMAN, Joseph	85	Cancer (in New York, NY)
1989	LeBORG, Reginald	86	Heart attack (in Los Angeles, CA)
1983	LeBOUVIER, Jean	62	Died in Van Nuys, CA
1984	LeCLAIR, Lucille	62	Diabetic infection (in Miami, FL)
1992	LECLERC, Ginette	79	Cancer (in Paris, France)
1949	+ LEDBETTER, Huddie "Leadbelly"	60	Amyotrophic lateral sclerosis
• 1996	LEDER, Paul	70	Lung cancer (at his home in Los Angeles, CA)
1976	LEDERER, Charles	65	After a long illness (at UCLA Med. Ctr., CA)

Deaths of Movie and Television Personalities — by Name

YEAR	NAME	AGE	CAUSE and/or PLACE OF DEATH
1955	LEDERER, Gretchen	64	Died in Anaheim, CA
1972	LEDERMAN, D. Ross	76	Kidney and heart condition (in Hollywood, CA)
1992	LEDERMAN, Victoria Kellem	52	Amyloidosis
1993	LEDOUX, Fernand	96	Unreported causes (in Villerville, France)
1941	LEE, Auriol	?	Automobile accident (in Hutchison, KS)
1961	LEE, Belinda	25	Automobile accident (in San Bernardino, CA)
1981	LEE, Bernard	73	Cancer (in London, England)
1989	# LEE, Billy	60	Heart failure (in Beaumont, CA)
1993	+ LEE, Brandon	27	Hit with a .44-caliber bullet in a filming accident (in Wilmington, NC)
1989	LEE, Brian	36	Pneumonia (in Los Angeles, CA)
1973	#+ LEE, Bruce	32	Acute cerebral edema after taking prescribed pain-killer (Hong Kong)
1952	#+ LEE, Canada	45	Heart attack (in New York, NY)
1986	LEE, Carl	52	Died in New York, NY
1980	LEE, Chingwah	78	Died in San Francisco, CA
1952	# LEE, Dixie	40	Cancer (in Holmby Hills, CA)
1959	LEE, Duke R.	78	Died in Los Angeles, CA
1962	LEE, Florence	74	Died in Hollywood, CA
1961	# LEE, Gwen	55	Died in Los Angeles, CA
1970	#+ LEE, Gypsy Rose	56	Cancer (in Los Angeles, CA)
1992	LEE, Irving Allen	43	A.I.D.S. (in New York, NY)
1965	# LEE, Johnny "Calhoun"	67	Heart attack (in Los Angeles, CA)
1990	LEE, Larry	48	A.I.D.S.
1973	# LEE, Lila	71	Stroke (in Saranac Lake, NY)
1982	LEE, My-ca Dinh	7	Killed by helicopter rotor while filming
1993	# LEE, Pinky	85	Heart attack (in Viejo, CA)
1974	LEE, Raymond	64	Cancer (in Canoga Park, CA)
1975	LEE, Rowland V.	84	Apparent heart attack at his home (in Palm Desert, CA)
1975	# LEE, Ruth	79	Cancer (in Woodland Hills, CA)
• 1997	LEE, Terry H.	75	Natural causes at home in Naples, FL
1992	# LEE, Vanessa	71	Causes unreported (in London, England)
1982	LEE, Will	74	Heart attack (in New York, NY)
1984	# LEEDS, Andrea ☆	70	Cancer (in Palm Springs, CA)
• 1996	LEEDS, Peter	79	Cancer
• 1998	LEEDS, Phil	82	Pneumonia at Cedars-Sinai Medical Center in Los Angeles, CA
1993	LEETCH, Thomas	60	Leukemia (in Sherman Oaks, CA)
• 1996	#+ LeFEVRE, Bill	75	Congestive heart failure (at his home in Shrewsbury, PA)
1991	LEFÈVRE, René	93	Cancer (in Poissy, France)
1991	LeGALLIENNE, Eva	92	Heart failure
1990	LEGATT, Alison	86	
1948	LEHAR, Franz	78	Stomach cancer (in Austria)
1993	LEHMAN, Gladys Collins	101	Pneumonia (in Newport Beach, CA)
1979	LEHMANN, Beatrix	76	Died in London, England
1990	LEHMANN, Carla	73	Died in England
1950	LEHR, Lew	54	Died at a sanitarium in Brookline, MA
1946	+ LEHRMAN, Henry	60	Following a heart attack (in Hollywood, CA)
1992	+ LEHRMAN, Oscar S.	73	Prostate cancer
• 1996	LEI, Chao	68	Pneumonia (in Hong Kong, China)
1949	+ LEIBER, Fritz	67	Heart attack (in Pacific Palisades, CA)
1976	LEIBERT, Richard "Dick"	73	
1948	LEIGH, Frank	69	Died in Hollywood, CA
1988	LEIGH, George	78	Heart disease and diabetes (in Culver City, CA)
1990	LEIGH, Megan	26	Apparent suicide
• 1996	LEIGH, Norman	66	Cancer (in New York, NY)

Deaths of Movie and Television Personalities — by Name

YEAR	NAME		AGE	CAUSE and/or PLACE OF DEATH
1967	#+ LEIGH, Vivien	★	53	Tuberculosis (in London, England)
1956	LEIGHTON, Lillian		81	Died in Woodland Hills, CA
1976	LEIGHTON, Margaret	☆	53	Multiple sclerosis (in Chichester, England)
1991	LEIGHTON, Merrill		51	Automobile accident
1972	LEISEN, Mitchell		74	Coronary complications (in Woodland Hills, CA)
• 1996	LEISER, Erwin		73	Died in Zurich, Switzerland
• 1985	LEMAIRE, Charles	★	87	Died in his sleep
1993	LeMASSENA, William		76	Lung cancer
1982	+ LEMBECK, Harvey		59	Heart attack (in Los Angeles, CA)
1983	LeMESURIER, John		71	Abdominal illness (in Ramsgate, England)
1956	# LeMOYNE, Charles		76	Died in Hollywood, CA
• 1997	LENARD, Kay		?	Natural causes (in Portland, OR)
• 1996	LENARD, Mark		68	Multiple myeloma (at NYU Hospital in Manhattan, NY)
1929	LENI, Paul		44	Blood poisoning from a neglected ulcerated tooth (in Hollywood, CA)
• 1971	LENNART, Isobel	☆	56	Automobile accident
1980	+ LENNON, John		40	Murdered (shot) in New York, NY
• 1996	LENOX, John Thomas		50	Massive heart attack (at his home in Los Angeles, CA)
1991	LENSKY, Leib		82	Liver cancer (in New York, NY)
1981	# LENYA, Lotte	☆	83	Died in New York, NY
1994	LEONARD, Bill		78	Stroke (at Laurel Regional Hospital in Laurel, MD)
1939	# LEONARD, Gus		83	After a long illness (in Los Angeles, CA)
1973	# LEONARD, Jack E.		62	Diabetic complications after open-heart surgery (in New York, NY)
1956	LEONARD, Marion		75	Died in Woodland Hills, CA
1968	#+ LEONARD, Robert Z.	☆	78	Aneurysm (in Beverly Hills, CA)
• 1997	# LEONARD, Sheldon		89	Natural causes (at his home in Beverly Hills, CA)
1986	LEONE, Johnny		71	Cerebral thrombosis (in Rome, Italy)
1989	LEONE, Sergio		60	Heart attack (in Rome, Italy)
1979	# LEONETTI, Tommy		50	Cancer (in Houston, TX)
1993	LEONTOVICH, Eugenie		93	Cardiac arrest and pneumonia (in Los Angeles, CA)
1993	LEOPOLD, Douglas		49	A.I.D.S.
1986	LERNER, Alan Jay		67	Lung cancer (in New York, NY)
1976	LERNER, Irving		67	Heart attack (in New York, NY)
1989	+ LERNER, Sam		86	Cancer (in Los Angeles, CA)
1985	# LeROY, Hal		71	Following heart surgery (in Hackensack, NJ)
1987	+ LeROY, Mervyn	☆	86	Heart failure and Alzheimer's disease (in Beverly Hills, CA)
1940	LeSAINT, Edward J.		69	After a long illness (in Hollywood, CA)
1987	LESCOULIE, Jack		75	Colon cancer (in Los Angeles, CA)
1974	# LESLEY, Carole		38	Overdose of barbiturates (in New Barnet, England)
1991	LESLIE, Bob		64	Undisclosed causes (in Los Angeles, CA)
1953	# LESLIE, Gene		48	Died in Los Angeles, CA
1976	LESLIE, Gladys		77	Died in Boynton Beach, FL
1940	LESLIE, Lilie "Lila"		48	Died in Los Angeles, CA
1980	LESSER, Sol	★	90	Cardiac arrest in his sleep (in Hollywood, CA)
1947	LESSEY, George A.		?	Died in Westbrook, CT
1995	LESTER, Jerry		85	Complications of Alzheimer's disease (in Miami, FL)
1924	# LESTER, Kate		65	Burned as studio dressing room gas stove exploded (in England)
1955	LETONDAL, Henri		52	Heart attack (in Burbank, CA)
1975	LETTIERI, Al		47	After being hospitalized (in New York, NY)
1972	+ LEVANT, Oscar		65	Heart attack (in Beverly Hills, CA)
1980	# LEVENE, Sam		74	Heart attack (in New York, NY)
1980	#+ LEVENSON, Sam		68	
1989	LeVEQUE, Edward		92	Died in Los Angeles, CA
1955	LEVEY, Ethel		73	Heart attack (in New York, NY)

• New entry.   # Original name (Pt. 7).   + Interment (Pt. 5).

☆ Oscar nominee, ★ Oscar winner (Pt. 10)

Deaths of Movie and Television Personalities — by Name

YEAR	NAME	AGE	CAUSE and/or PLACE OF DEATH
1975	LEVEY, Jules	78	Apparent heart attack (on a street in Manhattan, NY)
1980	LEVIN, Henry	70	Heart attack on the final day of filming (in Glendale, CA)
1996	LEVIN, Irving H.	74	Cancer (at his home in Brentwood, CA)
1987	LEVINE, Joseph E.	81	After a brief illness (in Greenwich, CT)
1989	LEVINE, Nathan	89	Heart attack (in Woodland Hills, CA)
1992	LEVY, Franklin R.	43	Pulmonary embolism (in Southington, CT)
• 1997	LEWENSTEIN, Oscar	80	Died in Brighton, England
1968	LEWIN, Albert	73	Pneumonia (in New York, NY)
• 1996	LEWIN, Albert E.	79	Heart failure (at USC Health Center, CA)
• 1997	LEWIS, Abby	87	Died of natural causes in her Greenwich Village Apt. NY City, NY
1986	LEWIS, Buddy	62	Apparent heart attack
1968	LEWIS, Cathy	50	Cancer (in Hollywood Hills, CA)
1992	LEWIS, David	83	After a short illness (in New York, NY)
1993	# LEWIS, Edwina	42	Heart attack (in Augusta, MI)
1990	LEWIS, Elliott	73	Cardiac arrest (in Newport Beach, CA)
1977	LEWIS, Forrest	77	Heart attack (in Burbank, CA)
1996	# LEWIS, Henry	63	Heart attack (at his home in Manhattan)
1985	LEWIS, Jarma	54	Heart attack in her sleep (in Los Angeles, CA)
1971	+ LEWIS, Joe E.	69	Liver and kidney ailments (in NYC) Do not confuse with the boxer
1993	LEWIS, Marlo	77	Heart failure (in Los Angeles, CA)
1956	+ LEWIS, Mitchell J.	76	After a lengthy illness (in Woodland Hills, CA)
1937	LEWIS, Ralph	65	Injuries from an automobile accident (in Los Angeles, CA)
• 1997	LEWIS, Robert	88	Heart Attack
1991	# LEWIS, Robert Q.	71	Emphysema (in Los Angeles, CA)
1982	LEWIS, Ronald	54	Suicide (sleeping pills) Do not confuse with R. "Raan" Lewis, d. 1995
1995	#+ LEWIS, Ronald "Raan"	39	Complications from A.I.D.S. (Do not confuse with R. Lewis, d. 1982)
• 1998	LEWIS, Shari	65	Cancer at Cedars-Sinai Medical Center in Los Angeles, CA
1958	LEWIS, Sheldon	89	Died in San Gabriel, CA
1971	#+ LEWIS, Ted	80	Heart attack (in New York, NY)
1927	+ LEWIS, Tom	63	Following an operation for cancer (in New York, NY)
1956	LEWIS, Vera	72	Died at the Motion Picture Country Hospital near Los Angeles, CA
1932	# LEWIS, Walter P.	60	Died in New York, NY
1948	LEYTON, George	84	Died in London, England
1983	+ LIBERACE, George	71	Leukemia and heart disease
1987	#+ LIBERACE, Walter "Lee"	67	Complications from A.I.D.S. (in Palm Springs, CA)
1992	LIDDELL, Laura	83	Following a series of heart problems (in London, England)
• 1996	LIDINGTON, Bruce Howard	46	
1945	LIEDTKE, Harry	64	Died in Bad-Sarrow-Pieskow, Germany
1988	LIGHT, Ann Rork	79	
1971	LIGHTNER, Winnie	69	Heart attack (in Sherman Oaks, CA)
1965	# LIGON, Grover G.	79	Died in Hollywood, CA
1989	# LILLIE, Beatrice	94	Died in Henley-On-Thames, England
1952	#+ LINCOLN, Elmo	63	Heart attack (in Hollywood, CA)
1957	# LINDER, Alfred	?	Died in Hollywood, CA
1925	# LINDER, Max	45	Suicided with his wife (cut wrists and took poison) in Paris, France
1995	# LINDFORS, Viveca	74	Complications from rheumatoid arthritis (in Uppsala, Sweden)
• 1997	LINDLEY, Audra	79	Died of complicatins from leukemia in Los Angeles, CA
1968	LINDO, Olga	68	Died in London, England
1993	LINDQUIST, Dan	65	Pneumonia (in Burbank, CA)
1968	+ LINDSAY, Howard	78	Died in New York, NY
1928	LINDSAY, James	59	Died in London, England
1981	#+ LINDSAY, Margaret	70	Emphysema (in Los Angeles, CA)
1988	LINDSAY, Phillip	64	Pneumonia (in New York, NY)

• New entry. # Original name (Pt. 7). + Interment (Pt. 5).   ☆ Oscar nominee, ★ Oscar winner (Pt. 10)

Deaths of Movie and Television Personalities — by Name

YEAR	NAME		AGE	CAUSE and/or PLACE OF DEATH
1978	# LINGEN, Theo		75	Died in Vienna, Austria
1950	LINGHAM, Thomas J.		75	Died in Woodland Hills, CA
1985	LINTON, Mark		28	Heart failure and pneumonia (in New York, NY)
1989	LION, Margo		90	Died in Annecy-Le-Vieux, France
1950	LIPATTI, Dinu		33	
1992	LISS, Ted		72	Heart attack (in Chicago, IL)
1985	LIST, Eugene		66	Found dead at home (in New York, NY)
• 1996	LIST, Shelly		55	Cancer (at her apartment in Manhattan, NY)
• 1997	LISTER, Eve		83	Died in England
1951	LISTER, Francis		52	Died in London, England
1970	#+ LISTON, Sonny		38	Died in Las Vegas, NV
1995	LISTYEV, Vladislav		?	Assassinated (at his home in Moscow)
1972	# LITEL, John		77	Died in Woodland Hills, CA
1984	LITTLE, Ann		93	Died in Los Angeles, CA
1967	# LITTLE, Billy		72	Stroke (in Hollywood, CA)
1952	# LITTLE, Bozo		45	Heart ailment (in Los Angeles, CA)
1992	LITTLE, Cleavon		53	Colon cancer (in Sherman Oaks, CA)
1965	#+ LITTLE, Malcolm "Malcolm X"		39	Assassinated (shot) in the Audubon Ballroom in Harlem, NY
1959	+ LITTLEFIELD, Lucien		64	Died in Hollywood, CA
1982	LITTLER, Susan		33	Cancer (in London, England)
1974	# LITVAK, Anatole	☆	72	Died in Neuilly-sur-Seine, France
1961	LIVESEY, Jack		60	Aneurysm (in Burbank, CA)
1976	LIVESEY, Roger		69	Died in Watford, England
1936	LIVESEY, Sam		63	Complications following surgery (in London, England)
1985	LIVINGSTON, Margaret		89	Died in Warrington, PA
1988	# LIVINGSTON, Robert (Bob)		79	Emphysema (in Tarzana, CA)
1983	#+ LIVINGSTONE, Mary		77	Heart attack in her sleep (in Los Angeles, CA)
1941	LLEWELLYN, Fewlass		55	Died in England
1983	LLEWELLYN, Richard		76	Heart attack
1954	LLOYD, Art		58	Paralytic stroke (after filming the Bikini Atoll atom bomb test)
1948	LLOYD, Charles M.		78	Heart attack (in Hollywood, CA)
1968	LLOYD, Doris		68	"Strained" heart (in Santa Barbara, CA)
1960	+ LLOYD, Frank	★	74	Died in Santa Monica, CA
1949	LLOYD, Frederick W.		69	Died in Hove, England
1971	LLOYD, Gladys		74	Stroke (in Culver City, CA)
1971	LLOYD, Harold Jr. "Duke"		39	Cerebral hemorrhage (in a sanitarium in North Hollywood, CA)
1971	#+ LLOYD, Harold Sr.		77	Cancer (in Glendale, CA)
1988	LLOYD, Paul Francis (Jimmy)		69	Liver disease (in Medford, OR)
1938	LLOYD, Rollo		55	Died in Los Angeles, CA
1994	LOCCHI, Pino		69	After suffering two strokes (in Rome, Italy)
1977	LOCHARY, David		30	Drug overdose (in New York, NY)
1969	#+ LOCHER, Felix		86	Died in Sherman Oaks, CA
1995	LOCKE, Katherine		85	Brain tumor (at her home in Thousand Oaks, CA)
1990	+ LOCKER, Frances		79	
1957	#+ LOCKHART, Gene	☆	65	Coronary thrombosis (in Santa Monica, CA)
1978	# LOCKHART, Kathleen		83	After a long illness (in Los Angeles, CA)
1920	+ LOCKLEAR, Omer		28	A plane crash filming accident (in Los Angeles, CA)
1990	# LOCKWOOD, Alexander		88	Died in Los Angeles, CA
1918	LOCKWOOD, Harold A.		29	Spanish influenza (in New York, NY)
1971	LOCKWOOD, King		73	Massive stroke (in Hollywood, CA)
1990	LOCKWOOD, Margaret		73	Complications of obesity (in London, England)
1990	LOCKWOOD, Paul		51	Heart disease
1980	LODEN, Barbara		48	Cancer (in New York, NY)

• New entry. # Original name (Pt. 7). + Interment (Pt. 5).   ☆ Oscar nominee, ★ Oscar winner (Pt. 10)

YEAR	NAME		AGE	CAUSE and/or PLACE OF DEATH
1988	# LODER, John		90	Died in Selbourne, England
1985	LODGE, John Davis		82	Heart attack (in New York, NY)
1984	LOEB, Tony		76	Cancer
1969	+ LOESSER, Frank		59	Lung cancer (in New York, NY)
1927	+ LOEW, Marcus		57	Died in his sleep of heart failure (in Glen Cove, NY)
1988	LOEWE, Frederick		86	Heart failure (in Palm Springs, CA)
1957	LOFGREN, Marianne		47	Died in Sweden
1947	+ LOFT, Arthur		49	Died in Los Angeles, CA
1943	+ LOFTUS, Cecilia "Cissie"		66	Heart attack (in her New York City hotel room)
1969	+ LOGAN, Ella		56	Cancer (in San Mateo, CA)
1983	LOGAN, Jacqueline		78	Died in Melbourne, FL
1988	LOGAN, Joshua	☆	79	Supranuclear palsy (in New York, NY)
1953	LOGAN, Stanley		67	Died in New York, NY
• 1997	LOHMANN, Dietrick		54	Leukemia at City of Hope Medical Ctr. in Duarte, CA
1975	LOHR, Marie		84	Died in Brighton, England
1961	LOMAS, Herbert		73	Died in Devonshire, England
1942	#+ LOMBARD, Carole	☆	33	Airplane crash (southeast of Las Vegas, NV)
• 1997	LOMBARDI, Joe		74	Bronchial pneumonia in London
1991	LOMBARDI, Paul Michael		31	A.I.D.S. (in Los Angeles, CA)
1970	#+ LOMBARDI, Vince		57	Cancer
1971	+ LOMBARDO, Carmen		67	Cancer (in North Miami, FL)
1977	#+ LOMBARDO, Guy		75	Respiratory, kidney and heart failure (in Houston, TX)
1993	LOMBARDO, Lebert J.		88	Emphysema (in Fort Meyers, FL)
• 1993	LOMBARDO, Victor		82	Asthma
1985	LONDON, George		64	Following a heart attack
1980	LONDON, Jean "Babe"		79	
1993	LONDON, Roy		50	Lymphoma (in Los Angeles, CA)
1963	#+ LONDON, Tom		70	Died in North Hollywood, CA
1987	LONERGAN, Lenore		59	Cancer (in Stuart, FL)
1959	LONERGAN, Lester Jr.		65	After a long illness (in New York, NY)
1984	LONG, Avon		73	Cancer (in New York, NY)
1938	LONG, Jack		?	Motorcycle accident (in Los Angeles, CA)
1949	LONG, Nick Jr.		43	Results of an automobile accident (in New York, NY)
1974	+ LONG, Richard		47	Heart ailment (in Los Angeles, CA)
1952	LONG, Walter		73	Heart attack (in Hollywood, CA)
1971	LONGDEN, John		70	Died in London, England
1923	LONSDALE, Harry G.		?	Died in England
1974	LONTOC, Leon		64	Died in Los Angeles, CA
1983	LOO, Richard		80	Died in Los Angeles, CA
1981	LOOS, Anita		93	Heart attack (in Manhattan, NY)
1986	LOOS, Anne		70	After a long illness (in Los Angeles, CA)
1954	# LOOS, Theodor		70	Died in Stuttgart, West Germany
1986	LOPEZ, J. Victor		39	A.I.D.S. (in Los Angeles, CA)
1975	#+ LOPEZ, Vincent		76	Liver and pancreas failure (in Miami Beach, FL)
1947	LORCH, Theodore A.		74	After a long illness (in Hollywood, CA)
• 1998	LORD, Jack		77	At his home in Honolulu, Hawaii of heart failure
1942	LORD, Marion		59	After a long illness (in Hollywood, CA)
1950	+ LORD, Pauline		60	Heart trouble (in Alamogordo, NM)
1973	LORDE, Athena		58	Cancer (in Van Nuys, CA)
1992	LORENTZ, Pare		86	Heart failure (in Armonk, NY)
1995	LORIMER, Louise		97	Following an extended illness (in Newton, MA)
1986	LORMER, Jon		80	Died in Burbank, CA
1968	# LORNE, Marion		80	Heart attack (in New York, NY)

Deaths of Movie and Television Personalities — by Name

YEAR	NAME	AGE	CAUSE and/or PLACE OF DEATH
1934	# LORRAINE, Harry	54	Died in London, England
1955	# LORRAINE, Lillian	63	Died in New York, NY
1981	# LORRAINE, Louise	79	After a long illness (in New York, NY)
1964	#+ LORRE, Peter	59	Stroke (in Hollywood, CA)
1975	# LOSCH, Tilly	70	Cancer (in Manhattan, NY)
1937	LOSEE, Frank	81	Pulmonary embolism after an attack of arthritis (in Yonkers, NY)
1984	# LOSEY, Joseph	75	Died in London, England
1990	# LOSS, Joe	80	Kidney failure
1991	LOTT, Lawrence	40	A.I.D.S.
1948	LOUDEN, Thomas	73	After a stroke (in Hollywood, CA)
• 1997	LOUIS, Jean ★	89	Natural causes at his Palm Springs, CA home
1981	#+ LOUIS, Joe "Brown Bomber"	66	Cardiac arrest (in Las Vegas, NV)
1926	LOUIS, Willard	40	After being ill with typhoid fever and pneumonia (in Glendale, CA)
1970	#+ LOUISE, Anita	55	Massive stroke (in West Los Angeles, CA)
1991	LOURIE, Eugene	89	Heart failure and complications from strokes (in Woodland Hills, CA)
1986	# LOVE, Bessie ☆	87	Undisclosed causes (in London, England)
1991	LOVE, Edward M.	43	A.I.D.S. (in New York, NY)
1991	LOVE, Geoff	73	Undisclosed causes (in London, England)
1943	# LOVE, Montagu	62	Died in Beverly Hills, CA
1948	LOVE, Robert	34	Suicide (5-story leap from his doctor's office) in Hollywood, CA
1962	+ LOVEJOY, Frank	48	Heart attack (in New York, NY)
1953	LOVELL, Raymond	53	Died in London, England
1980	# LOVELY, Louise	83	Died in Hobart, Australia
1988	LOW, Carl	71	Cancer (in Nyack, NY)
1958	LOW, Jack	60	After a 2-year illness (in Hollywood, CA)
1989	LOW, Warren	83	Following a long illness (in Woodland Hills, CA)
1982	LOWE, Arthur	67	Following a stroke (in Birmingham, England)
1971	+ LOWE, Edmund	81	Lung cancer (in Woodland Hills, CA)
1937	LOWELL, Helen	71	After a lingering illness (in Hollywood, CA)
1992	LOWENSTEIN, Cary Scott	30	A.I.D.S. (in Boca Raton, FL)
1991	LOWENSTEIN, Lynn Gendron	30	An inoperable brain tumor
1971	# LOWERY, Robert	57	Heart attack (in Hollywood, CA)
1976	# LOWRY, Judith	86	Apparent heart attack (in Greenwich Village, NY)
1988	LOWRY, Margerie Bonner	83	After suffering a stroke
1993	#+ LOY, Myrna ★	88	During surgery, after a lengthy illness (in New York)
1995	# LOY, Nanni	69	Heart attack (while vacationing in Fregene nr. Rome, Italy)
1995	LUBIN, Arthur	96	Six months after a stroke (in a Glendale, CA, nursing home)
• 1923	LUBIN, Sigmund "Pop"	72	
1947	+ LUBITSCH, Ernst ☆	55	Heart attack (in Los Angeles, CA)
1987	LUBOFF, Norman	70	Cancer (in Bynam, NC)
1954	# LUCAN, Arthur	67	Heart attack (in Hull, England)
1990	LUCAS, Gail	37	Viral hemorrhagic pneumonia (in Cleveland, OH)
• 1997	LUCAS, Isabelle Harriet	69	
1982	LUCAS, Nick	84	Following a stroke
1940	LUCAS, Wilfred	69	After an illness of 6-weeks (in Los Angeles, CA)
1989	LUCE, Claire	88	Died in New York (Do not confuse with Clare Booth Luce, d. 1987)
1987	# LUCE, Clare Boothe	84	Cancer (Do not confuse with Claire Luce, d. 1989)
1989	LUCKHAM, Cyril	81	Died in London, England
1945	LUCY, Arnold	80	Died in London, England
1981	LUDDEN, Allen	63	Cancer (in Los Angeles, CA)
1987	LUDLAM, Charles	44	Pneumonia complicated by A.I.D.S. (in New York, NY)
1996	LUDMIR, Joseph (Pepe)	64	Heart attack (in Woodland Hills, CA)
1982	LUDWIG, Edward	83	Stroke while hospitalized (in Santa Monica, CA)

• New entry. # Original name (Pt. 7). + Interment (Pt. 5).   264   ☆ Oscar nominee, ★ Oscar winner (Pt. 10)

Deaths of Movie and Television Personalities — by Name

YEAR	NAME		AGE	CAUSE and/or PLACE OF DEATH
1975	LUEDERS, Guenther		69	Cancer (in Duesseldorf, Germany)
1952	# LUFKIN, Sam		59	Uremia (in Los Angeles, CA)
1956	#+ LUGOSI, Bela		73	Heart attack from an overdose of drugs (in Hollywood, CA)
1995	LUKAS, Karl		75	Died in Agoura Hills, CA
1971	# LUKAS, Paul	★	76	Heart attack (in Tangier, Morocco)
1991	+ LUKE, Keye		86	After a stroke (in Hollywood, CA)
1970	LULLI, Folco		58	Heart attack (in Rome, Italy)
1988	LUMMIS, Dayton		84	Died in Santa Monica, CA
1947	#+ LUNCEFORD, Jimmy		45	Died in Seaside, OR
1990	LUND, Art		75	Liver cancer (in Salt Lake City, UT)
1992	LUND, John		81	Found dead in his home; heart trouble (in Coldwater Canyon, CA)
1960	LUND, Richard		75	Died in Sweden
1975	+ LUNDIGAN, William "Bill"		61	Lung and heart congestion (in Duarte, CA)
1977	+ LUNT, Alfred	☆	84	Cancer (in Chicago, IL)
1995	LUPINO, Ida		77	Colon cancer following a stroke (at her home in Burbank, CA)
1942	LUPINO, Stanley		48	Died in London, England
1961	# LUPINO, Wallace		63	After a long illness (in Ashford, England)
1960	# LUTHER, Ann		67	Heart condition (in Hollywood, CA)
1960	LUTHER, Johnny		51	Drowned in a boating accident (in San Pedro, CA)
1962	LUTHER, Lester		73	Stroke (in Hollywood, CA)
1953	# LUTTRINGER, Al		74	Died in Hollywood, CA
1994	LUXFORD, Nola (Dolberg)		99	Died at a convalescent home in Pasadena, CA
1969	LYDECKER, Howard		58	
1972	# LYEL, Viola		71	Died in England
1925	LYELL, Lottie		33	Died in Sydney, Australia
1957	+ LYMAN, Abe		59	Died in Los Angeles, CA
1994	LYNCH, Christopher		73	Heart attack (at his home in Worchestershire, England)
1965	LYNCH, Helen		64	Died in Miami Beach, FL
1990	LYNCH, Ken		79	Viral infection (in Burbank, CA)
1982	+ LYNDE, Paul		55	Prostate cancer and heart attack (in Beverly Hills, CA)
1971	#+ LYNN, Diana		45	Brain hemorrhage (in Los Angeles, CA)
1994	LYNN, Donald		54	A.I.D.S. complications (at his home in Manhattan, NY)
1958	LYNN, Emmett		61	Heart attack (in Hollywood, CA)
1967	LYNN, George M.		61	Died in Los Angeles, CA
1993	LYNN, Jack		67	Leukemia (in Albuquerque, NM)
1995	# LYNN, Jeffrey		89	Stroke (at St. Joseph's Hospital in Burbank, CA)
1988	LYNN, Mara		60	Cancer (in The Bahamas)
1962	LYNN, Ralph		81	Died in London, England
1963	# LYNN, Sharon		58	Died in Hollywood, CA
1979	+ LYON, Ben		78	Heart attack (aboard "Queen Elizabeth 2" in the Pacific Ocean)
1961	LYON, Frank		59	Died in Gardner, MA
1995	LYON, Milton		72	Natural causes (at his home in Princeton, NJ)
1974	# LYONS, Cliff "Tex"		71	Died in Los Angeles, CA
1926	LYONS, Eddie		39	Died in Pasadena, CA
1921	# LYONS, Fred		?	After his car skidded and overturned
1986	# LYS, Lya		78	Heart ailment (in Newport Beach, CA)
1954	LYTELL, Bert		69	Following surgery (in New York, NY)
1954	LYTELL, Wilfred		62	After an illness of several weeks (in Salem, NY)
1924	# LYTTON, L. Rogers		57	Died in New York, NY
	M			
1975	#+ MABLEY, Jackie "Moms"		78	Heart attack (in White Plains, NY)
1956	+ MacARTHUR, Charles		60	Internal hemorrhage after nephritis (in New York, NY)
1957	MacBRIDE, Donald		67	After a long illness (in Los Angeles, CA)

• New entry.   # Original name (Pt. 7).   + Interment (Pt. 5).   ☆ Oscar nominee, ★ Oscar winner (Pt. 10)

Deaths of Movie and Television Personalities — by Name

YEAR	NAME	AGE	CAUSE and/or PLACE OF DEATH
1989	MACCARI, Ruggero	70	*Died in Rome, Italy*
1959	MacDONALD, Donald	61	*Died in New York, NY*
1951	MacDONALD, Edmund	43	*Cerebral hemorrhage (in Los Angeles, CA)*
1952	#+ MacDONALD, J. Farrell	77	*Died in Hollywood, CA*
1991	MacDONALD, James	84	*Heart failure (in Glendale, CA)*
1965	+ MacDONALD, Jeanette Raymond	57	*Heart attack (in Houston, TX)*
1956	MacDONALD, Katherine	62	*After a 30-month illness (in Santa Barbara, CA)*
1978	MacDONALD, Wallace	87	*Died in Santa Barbara, CA*
1941	MacDOWELL, Melbourne	84	*Blood clot on the brain (in Decoto, CA)*
1917	# MACE, Fred	38	*Apoplexy (found dead in his room at the Hotel Astor in NYC)*
1983	MACE, Paul	33	*Killed in a traffic accident (in Los Angeles, CA)*
1967	MacFADDEN, Gertrude "Mickey"	67	*Heart attack (in Hollywood, CA)*
1987	MacGIBBON, Harriet	81	*After suffering from pulmonary and heart problems (in Beverly Hills)*
1973	MacGOWRAN, Jack	54	*After a bout with the flu (in his New York City hotel room)*
1992	MacGRATH, Leueen	77	*Complications after a stroke (in London, England)*
1948	MacGREGOR, Harman	70	*Died in Marblehead, MA*
1963	MACHATY, Gustav	63	*After a lengthy illness (in Munich, Germany)*
• 1997	MACINTOSH, Alex	71	
1962	# MACK, Cactus	62	*Heart attack (in Hollywood, CA)*
1934	#+ MACK, Charles E.	46	*Automobile accident (near Mesa, AZ) d.n.c. with C. Emmett Mack*
1927	MACK, Charles Emmett	27	*When another car struck and overturned his car (in Riverside, CA)*
1986	# MACK, Helen	72	*Cancer (in Beverly Hills, CA)*
1927	# MACK, Hughie	42	*Heart disease (in Santa Monica, CA)*
1948	MACK, James T.	77	*Died in Hollywood, CA*
1989	# MACK, Marion	86	*Heart failure (in Costa Mesa, CA)*
1927	+ MACK, Rose	61	*Died in the Lenox Hill hospital in New York, NY*
1972	MACK, Russell	79	*Stroke (in New York, NY)*
1976	MACK, Ted	71	
1993	MACK, Wayne	68	*Cancer (in New Orleans, LA)*
1964	MACK, Wilbur	91	*Died in Hollywood, CA*
1990	MACKAILL, Dorothy	87	*Kidney failure (in Honolulu, HI)*
1987	MACKAY, Fulton	64	*Undisclosed causes (in London, England)*
1940	MACKAYE, Dorothy	41	*Injuries from an automobile accident (in San Fernando Valley, CA)*
1968	MacKAYE, Norman	62	*After a brief illness*
1993	MACKENDRICK, Alexander	81	*Pneumonia (in Los Angeles, CA)*
1962	# MacKENNA, Kenneth	63	*After a long bout with cancer (in Hollywood, CA)*
1966	MacKENZIE, Mary	44	*Automobile accident (in London, England)*
1973	MACKIN, Clara	?	*Died in Santa Monica, CA*
1969	+ MacLANE, Barton	68	*Double pneumonia (in Santa Monica, CA)*
1985	MacLAREN, Mary	85	*Double pneumonia (in Los Angeles, CA)*
1986	MacLAUGHLIN, Don	79	*After a brief illnes (in Goshen, CT)*
1967	MacLEAN, Douglas	70	*Following a cerebral thrombosis (in Beverly Hills, CA)*
1991	MacMAHON, Aline ☆	92	*Pneumonia (in New York, NY)*
1954	MacMILLAN, Violet	66	*Died in Grand Rapids, MI*
1991	#+ MacMURRAY, Fred	83	*Pneumonia and cancer (in Santa Monica, CA)*
1944	+ MacPHERSON, Aimee Semple	53	*Heart attack in her sleep*
1946	MacPHERSON, Jeanie	59	*After a long illness (in Hollywood, CA)*
1942	MacQUARRIE, Murdock	63	*Died in Los Angeles, CA*
1967	# MACRAE, Duncan	61	*Died in Glasgow, Scotland (Do not confuse with Duncan McRae)*
1986	MacRAE, Gordon	65	*Cancer of the mouth and jaw (in Lincoln, NE)*
1973	+ MACREADY, George	63	*Emphysema (in Los Angeles, CA)*
1985	MacVEIGH, Earle	74	*Cancer (in Los Angeles, CA)*
1956	MACY, Jack	70	*Heart attack (in Wyoming)*

Deaths of Movie and Television Personalities — by Name

YEAR		NAME		AGE	CAUSE and/or PLACE OF DEATH
1983		MADDEN, Donald		49	*Died in Central Islip, NY*
1989		MADDEN, Jeanne		73	*Heart trouble*
1976		MADDEN, Peter		71	*Died in England*
1964		MADISON, Cleo		81	*Heart attack (in Burbank, CA)*
1996	#+	MADISON, Guy		74	*Emphysema (at Desert Hospital Hospice in Palm Springs, CA)*
1975	#	MADISON, Noel		77	*Died in Fort Lauderdale, FL*
1967	#	MAERTENS, Willy		74	*Died in Hamburg, Germany*
1993		MAGALOFF, Nikita		80	*After a long illness*
1982		MAGEE, Patrick		58	*Heart attack (in London, England)*
1992		MAGERMAN, Les		46	*A.I.D.S.*
1973		MAGNANI, Anna	★	64	*Pancreatic cancer (in Rome, Italy)*
1987		MAGNOTTA, Vic		43	*Drowned during filming of a car stunt (in Hoboken, NJ)*
1952		MAGRILL, George		52	*Died in Los Angeles, CA*
1989		MAGUIRE, Kathleen		64	*Cancer (in New York, NY)*
• 1998		MAHER, Joseph		64	*Brain tumor at his home in Los Angeles, CA*
1989	#	MAHONEY, Jock		70	*Heart attack following an auto accident (in Washington, D.C.)*
1991		MAIBAUM, Richard		81	*After a short illness (in Santa Monica, CA)*
1937	#	MAILES, Charles H.		66	*Died in Los Angeles, CA*
1975	#+	MAIN, Marjorie	☆	85	*Cancer (in Los Angeles, CA)*
1929		MAITLAND, Lauderdale		51	
1961	#	MAITLAND, Ruth		81	*Died in Dorking, England*
1956		MAKEHAM, Eliot		73	*Died in London, England*
1952		MALA, Ray		46	*Heart attack (in Hollywood, CA)*
1952		MALATESTA, Fred		62	*After a surgical operation (in Burbank, CA)*
1995		MALEY, Alan	★	64	*Heart attack (at his Belvedere, CA, home)*
1948		MALLALIEU, Aubrey		74	*Died in England*
1995	#	MALLE, Louis		63	*Lymphoma complications (at his home in Beverly Hills, CA)*
1969		MALLESON, Miles		80	*Died in London, England*
1958		MALLORY, Boots		45	*Died in Santa Monica, CA*
1978		MALONEY, James J. "Jim"		63	*Died in Los Angeles, CA*
1929		MALONEY, Leo D.		41	*Heart disease aggravated by alcoholism (in New York, NY)*
1963	#	MALTBY, H. F.		82	*Died in London, England*
1993		MALVERN, Paul		91	*Died in Los Angeles, CA*
1961	#	MALYON, Eily		81	*Cancer (in South Pasadena, CA)*
1987	+	MAMOULIAN, Rouben		90	*Cardiac arrest in his sleep (in Woodland Hills, CA)*
1994		MANCINI, Henry	★	70	*Complications from liver and pancreatic cancer (in Los Angeles, CA)*
1946	#	MANDER, Miles		57	*Heart attack (in Hollywood, CA)*
1945		MANDY, Jerry		52	*Following a heart attack (in Hollywood, CA)*
1989		MANES, Gina		96	*Died in Toulouse, France*
1989		MANGANO, Silvano		59	*Heart attack following a tumor operation (in Madrid, Spain)*
1987		MANGER, Winifred Brison		94	*Following a long illness*
1993		MANKIEWICZ, Francis		69	*Cancer (in Montreal, Canada)*
1953		MANKIEWICZ, Herman J.		55	*Uremic poisoning (in Hollywood, CA)*
1993	#	MANKIEWICZ, Joseph L.	★	83	*Heart failure (in Bedford, NY)*
1958		MANKIEWICZ, Rose Stradner		45	*Found dead at the family summer home (in Bedford Village, NY)*
• 1998		MANKOWITZ, Wolf		73	*Died in Dublin, Ireland of cancer*
1996		MANLEY, Walter		?	*Apparent asthma attack (in New York)*
1967	#	MANN, Anthony		60	*Heart attack (in Berlin, Germany)*
1974	#	MANN, Billy		?	*Died in New York, NY*
1991	#	MANN, Daniel		79	*Heart failure (in Los Angeles, CA)*
1977		MANN, George Kline		72	*Cancer (in Santa Monica, CA)*
1971	#	MANN, Hank		84	*Died in South Pasadena, CA*
1987		MANN, Jerry		77	*After a series of strokes that left him an invalid (in Los Angeles, CA)*

• New entry. # Original name (Pt. 7). + Interment (Pt. 5).   267   ☆ Oscar nominee, ★ Oscar winner (Pt. 10)

Deaths of Movie and Television Personalities — by Name

YEAR		NAME		AGE	CAUSE and/or PLACE OF DEATH
1941		MANN, Margaret		72	Cancer (in Los Angeles, CA)
1976		MANNHEIM, Lucie		81	Died in Braunlage, West Germany
1979		MANNI, Ettore		52	Accidental gun shot (in Rome, Italy)
1946		MANNING, Aileen		60	Died in Hollywood, CA
1980		MANNING, Knox		76	Died in Woodland Hills, CA
• 1997		MANNIX, Daniel Pratt		85	After a long illness (at his home in Malvern, PA)
1993		MANOS, Gloria		69	Cancer (in Reno, NV)
1967	#+	MANSFIELD, Jayne		35	Automobile accident (in New Orleans, LA)
1988		MANSFIELD, Marian		83	Emphysema (in La Jolla, CA)
1923	#	MANSFIELD, Martha		23	Burns when her dress accidentally ignited on location (San Antonio)
• 1996		MANSON, Eddy Lawrence		77	Congestive heart failure (in Los Angeles, CA)
1995	+	MANTLE, Mickey		63	Cancer following a liver transplant (in Dallas, TX)
1965	#	MANTZ, Paul		61	When a makeshift aircraft crashed enroute to film set (in CA)
1983		MANULIS, Katherine Bard		66	
1984		MAPES, Ted		82	After a brief illness (in Burbank, CA)
1988	+	MARAVICH, Pete		40	
1989		MARCH, Alex		68	Heart failure (in Los Angeles, CA)
1995		MARCH, Donald		53	Complications from A.I.D.S.
1974		MARCH, Eve		?	Cancer (in Hollywood, CA)
1975	#+	MARCH, Fredric	★	77	Cancer (in Los Angeles, CA)
1970	+	MARCH, Hal		49	Pneumonia and lung cancer (in Los Angeles, CA)
• 1997	#	MARCHAL, Georges		77	In Maurens, France
1969	#+	MARCIANO, Rocky		44	Airplane crash (near Des Moines, IA)
1937		MARCUS, James A.		69	Heart attack (in Hollywood, CA)
1967		MARCUSE, Theodore		47	When his car struck a truck on a Hollywood freeway
1978		MARDEN, Adrienne		69	Massive heart attack (in Los Angeles, CA)
1990		MARGLISS, Frances		76	Heart attack
1985	#+	Margo (Margo Albert)		68	After a long illness (in Pacific Palisades, CA)
1993		MARGOLIN, Janet		50	Ovarian cancer (in Los Angeles, CA)
1946		MARIAN, Ferdinand		44	Automobile accident (near Durneck, Germany)
1988		MARICLE, Leona		81	Apparent heart attack (in New York, NY)
1951		MARIN, Edwin L.		50	After a 3-week illness (in Hollywood, CA)
1973		MARION, Frances		85	Died in Los Angeles, CA
1945	+	MARION, George F. Sr.		85	Following a heart attack (in Carmel, CA)
1965		MARION, Sid		65	Heart attack (in Hollywood, CA)
1985	+	MARIS, Roger		51	Lymphatic cancer
1975		MARK, Michael		85	Heart failure (in Woodland Hills, CA)
1981		MARKEY, Enid		83	Heart attack (in Bay Shore, NY)
1981		MARKHAM, Dewey "Pigmeat"		77	Stroke (in New York, NY)
1991		MARKHAM, Marcella		68	Breast cancer (in New York, NY)
1991		MARKLE, Fletcher		70	Heart failure (in Los Angeles, CA)
1952		MARKS, Willis		87	Died in Los Angeles, CA
1993		MARLAND, Douglas		58	Complications following abdominal surgery (in Norwalk, CT)
1970		MARLE, Arnold		81	Died in London, England
1984		MARLEY, John	☆	77	Following open-heart surgery (in Los Angeles, CA)
1975		MARLOWE, Alan		40	Airplane crash
1964		MARLOWE, Frank		60	Heart attack (in Hollywood, CA)
1982	#+	MARLOWE, Hugh		71	Heart attack (in Manhattan, NY)
1984	+	MARLOWE, June		81	Died in Burbank, CA
1991		MARLOWE, Louis J.		85	Kidney failure (in Laguna Hills, CA)
1977		MARLOWE, Nora		62	After a long illness (in Los Angeles, CA)
1978	#	MARLY, Florence		59	Heart attack (in Glendale, CA)
1977		MARMONT, Percy		93	Died in Denville Hall, England

• New entry. # Original name (Pt. 7). + Interment (Pt. 5).　　268　　☆ Oscar nominee, ★ Oscar winner (Pt. 10)

Deaths of Movie and Television Personalities — by Name

YEAR	NAME	AGE	CAUSE and/or PLACE OF DEATH
1991	MAROFF, Robert	57	
1987	MARQUAND, Richard	49	Stroke (in London, England)
1990	MARQUARD, Yvonne Peattie	73	Heart attack in her sleep (in Los Angeles, CA)
1979	# MARQUET, Mary	84	Heart attack resulting from a fall (in Paris, France)
1989	MARQUISS, Ralph E. Jr.	34	Adrenal cancer
1990	MARR, Alice	89	Died in Woodland Hills, CA
1991	MARRERO, Ralph	33	Automobile accident (in Albuquerque, NM)
1949	# MARRIOTT, Moore	64	Died in England
1962	MARRIOTT, Sandee	63	Heart attack (in Hollywood, CA)
1981	# MARSH, Garry	78	Heart attack (in London, England)
1990	MARSH, Lois R.	74	After a long illness
1968	# MARSH, Mae	72	Heart attack (in Hermosa Beach, CA)
1925	# MARSH, Marguerite	33	Bronchial pneumonia (in New York, NY)
1989	# MARSH, Tiger Joe	78	Heart attack (in Chicago, IL)
1961	MARSHAL, Alan	52	Heart attack during live performance of "Sextette" (in Chicago, IL)
1989	MARSHALL, Andrew 3rd	52	Cancer (in Los Angeles, CA)
1950	MARSHALL, Boyd	65	Died in Jackson Heights, NY
1992	# MARSHALL, Brenda	77	Throat cancer (in Palm Springs, CA)
• 1998	MARSHALL, Everett G.	88	After a brief illness at his home in Mount Kisco
1975	+ MARSHALL, George E.	84	Pneumonia (in Hollywood, CA)
1966	+ MARSHALL, Herbert	75	Heart attack (in Beverly Hills, CA)
1991	MARSHALL, Robert H.	67	After a brief illness
1943	#+ MARSHALL, Tully	78	Heart and lung ailment (in Encino, CA)
1939	# MARSON, Aileen	26	Childbirth (in London, England)
1990	MARSTON, Merlin	45	Non-Hodgkins lymphoma (in Los Angeles, CA)
1976	MARTEL, Alphonse	85	
1953	# MARTIN, Chris-Pin	59	Heart attack (in Montebello, CA)
1984	MARTIN, D'urville	45	Heart attack (in Los Angeles, CA)
1995	#+ MARTIN, Dean	78	Acute respiratory failure (at his home in Beverly Hills, CA)
1987	+ MARTIN, Dean Paul Jr.	35	Crash of his F-4C Phantom-II jet on a training flight (in CA)
1964	MARTIN, Edie	83	Died in London, England
1995	# MARTIN, Ernest H.	75	Liver cancer (at his home in Los Angeles, CA)
1983	MARTIN, Freddy	76	After a series of strokes
1990	MARTIN, Kiel	46	Cardiovascular collapse caused by lung cancer (in Rancho Mirage)
1959	MARTIN, Lock	?	
1985	+ MARTIN, Marion	76	Cardiac arrest in her sleep (in Santa Monica, CA)
1990	+ MARTIN, Mary	76	Cancer (in Rancho Mirage, CA)
1994	MARTIN, Richard	75	Leukemia (at Hoag Mem. Hospital, Newport Beach, CA)
1981	#+ MARTIN, Ross	61	Heart attack playing tennis (in Poway, CA)
1980	+ MARTIN, Strother	61	Heart attack (in Thousand Oaks, CA)
1987	MARTIN, Vivian	95	After a long illness (in New York, NY)
1988	MARTIN-HARVEY, Muriel	97	Died in Northwood, England
1955	MARTINDEL, Edward B.	78	Heart attack (in Woodland Hills, CA)
• 1997	MARTINELLI, Enzo	89	Natural causes (in Jackson, TN)
1993	MARTINEZ, José "Tun Tun"	61	Following surgery for intestinal blockage (in Mexico)
1976	MARTINI, Nino	72	Heart attack (in Verone, Italy)
1992	# MARTON, Andrew	87	Pneumonia (in Santa Monica, CA)
1987	+ MARVIN, Lee ★	63	Heart attack (in Tucson, AZ)
1961	#+ MARX, "Chico"	74	Heart attack (in Beverly Hills, CA)
1977	#+ MARX, "Groucho"	86	Pneumonia (in West Hollywood, CA)
1977	#+ MARX, "Gummo"	84	Lung cancer (in Palm Springs, CA)
1964	#+ MARX, "Harpo"	75	During heart surgery (in Hollywood, CA)
1979	#+ MARX, "Zeppo"	78	Cancer (in Palm Springs, CA)

Deaths of Movie and Television Personalities — by Name

YEAR	NAME		AGE	CAUSE and/or PLACE OF DEATH
1992	+ MARX, Samuel		90	Congestive heart failure (Do not confuse with Samuel Marx, d. 1933)
1933	#+ MARX, Samuel "Frenchie"		72	Heart and kidney failure (in Hollywood, CA)
1969	# MASCHWITZ, Eric		68	Died in London, England
1994	+ MASINA, Giulietta (Fellini)		74	Lung cancer (at the Columbus Clinic in Rome, Italy)
1968	MASKELL, Virginia		31	Exposure and overdose of drugs (in Stoke Mandeville, England)
1975	# MASON, Buddy		71	Died in Woodland Hills, CA
1929	# MASON, Dan		76	Following an attack of pneumonia (in Baersville, NY)
1966	MASON, Haddon		68	Died in London, England
1984	MASON, James	☆	75	Massive heart attack (in Vevey, Switzerland)
1947	MASON, LeRoy		44	After a heart attack (while filming "California Firebrand") in L.A.
1959	MASON, Louis		71	After a long illness (in Hollywood, CA)
1980	# MASON, Mary		69	Cancer (in New York, NY)
• 1996	MASON, Pamela		80	Heart failure in her sleep (at her home in Beverly Hills, CA)
1962	MASON, Reginald		80	Died in Hermosa Beach, CA
• 1997	MASON, Richard		78	Throat cancer in Rome
1979	#+ MASON, Shirley (Lanfield)		78	Cancer (in Los Angeles, CA)
1976	MASON, Sydney		70	Heart attack (in Los Angeles, CA)
1941	MASON, William C. "Smiling Billy"		52	After a lengthy illness (in Orange, NJ)
1985	MASONER, Gene		41	A.I.D.S. (in New York, NY)
1983	MASSENGALE, Joseph		66	Suicide (gunshot) in Burbank, CA
1991	+ MASSEY, Curt		81	Undisclosed causes (in Rancho Mirage, CA)
• 1998	MASSEY, Daniel		64	After a long illness at a London Hospital
1984	+ MASSEY, Edith		65	Cancer (in Los Angeles, CA)
1974	#+ MASSEY, Ilona		63	Cancer (in Bethesda, MD)
1983	+ MASSEY, Raymond	☆	86	Pneumonia (in Los Angeles, CA)
• 1998	MASTERS, George		61	Heart failure in Los Angeles, CA
1969	MASTERS, Ruth		75	After a long illness (in Stamford, CT)
• 1996	MASTERSON, Paul C.		78	Cancer (at South Coast Med. Ctr. in Laguna Beach, CA)
• 1996	MASTROIANNI, Marcello	☆	72	Pancreatic cancer (at his home in Paris, France)
• 1996	MASTROIANNI, Ruggero		67	Heart attack (at his summer home in Torvaianica, Italy)
• 1996	MATAS, Alfredo		76	Lung cancer (in Barcelona, Spain)
1964	MATE, Rudolph		66	Following several heart attacks (in Hollywood, CA)
• 1997	MATEOS, Gabriel Figueroa	☆	90	Stroke in Mexico City, Mexico
• 1996	MATEOS, Julian		57	Lung cancer (in Madrid, Spain)
• 1997	MATEOS, Julian		57	Lung cancer in Madrid, Spain
1958	MATHER, Aubrey		72	After a long illness (in London, England)
• 1997	MATHER, George E.		77	Heart attack at home in North Hollywood, CA
1966	MATHER, Jack		58	Heart attack (in Wauconda, IL)
1985	MATHESON, Murray		73	Heart failure (in Woodland Hills, CA)
• 1986	MATHEWS, Beau		29	A.I.D.S.
1995	MATHEWS, Carmen Sylva		84	Natural causes (at her farm in W. Redding, CT)
1975	MATHIESON, Muir		64	Died in Oxford, England
• 1996	MATHIS, Lee		44	Complications of A.I.D.S. (in New York, NY)
1932	MATIESEN, Otto		58	Automobile accident (in Safford, AZ)
1978	MATRAY, Ernst		87	Heart attack (in Los Angeles, CA)
1989	MATSUDA, Yusaku		40	Bladder cancer (in Tokyo, Japan)
1960	# MATTHEWS, A. E. "Matty"		90	Heart attack in his sleep (in Bushey Heath, England)
• 1996	MATTHEWS, Billy		76	Aortal aneurysm (in London, England)
1977	+ MATTHEWS, Dorothy		54	Stroke (in Los Angeles, CA)
1984	MATTHEWS, George		73	Heart disease
1981	MATTHEWS, Jessie		74	Cancer (in London, England)
1975	MATTHEWS, Lester		74	Died in England
• 1998	MATTINGLY, Hedley		83	Cancer in Encino, CA

• New entry.   # Original name (Pt. 7).   + Interment (Pt. 5).

☆ Oscar nominee,   ★ Oscar winner (Pt. 10)

Deaths of Movie and Television Personalities — by Name

YEAR	NAME		AGE	CAUSE and/or PLACE OF DEATH
1934	# MATTO, Sisto		39	Automobile accident (in Los Angeles, CA)
1933	MATTOX, Martha		54	Heart ailment (in Sidney, NY)
1946	MATTRAW, Scott		61	After a long illness (in Hollywood, CA)
1989	MATUSZAK, John		38	Heart failure from drug overdose (in Burbank, CA)
1951	MAUDE, Cyril		88	Died in Torquay, England
1979	MAUDE, Margery		90	Died in Cleveland, OH
1965	# MAUGHAM, W. Somerset		91	Died in Nice, France
1964	MAUR, Meinhart		73	
1988	MAURA, Luis		38	A.I.D.S. (in Los Angeles, CA)
1918	# MAURICE, Mary "Mother"		73	Died in Port Carson, PA
1980	MAX, Edwin "Ed"		71	Died in Los Angeles, CA
1963	MAXEY, Paul		54	Heart attack (in Pasadena, CA)
1948	MAXWELL, Edwin		62	Cerebral hemorrhage (in Falmouth, MA)
1963	+ MAXWELL, Elsa		80	Died in New York, NY
1990	MAXWELL, James		33	A.I.D.S.
1981	MAXWELL, Jenny		39	Shot to death outside her condo by possible robbers (in Los Angeles)
1996	MAXWELL, Larry		43	Leukemia (at his home in Laurelville, OH)
1972	#+ MAXWELL, Marilyn		49	High blood pressure and pulmonary ailment (in Beverly Hills, CA)
1992	MAXWELL, Paul		70	Undisclosed causes (in London, England)
1980	MAY, Alyce		65	Heart attack (in Rosa Rito Beach, Baja, Mexico)
• 1997	MAY, Brian		63	Heart attack in Australia
1984	MAY, Doris		82	Heart failure (in Camarillo, CA)
• 1997	MAY, Jack		75	
1954	MAY, Joe		73	After a long illness (in Hollywood, CA)
1980	# MAY, Mia		96	After a brief illness (in Los Angeles, CA)
1995	MAYA, Frank		45	Heart failure due to complications of A.I.D.S. (in NYC)
1941	MAYALL, Hershell		78	Cerebral hemorrhage (in Detroit, MI)
1985	MAYER, Kenneth M. "Ken"		66	Died in North Hollywood, CA
1957	#+ MAYER, Louis B.		72	Leukemia (in Los Angeles, CA)
1948	MAYER, Ray		47	Heart attack (in Salt Lake City, UT)
1995	MAYER, Seymour R.		86	Heart failure (in New York City)
1973	+ MAYNARD, Ken		77	Died alone in his trailer of malnutrition (in Woodland Hills, CA)
1971	MAYNARD, Kermit		68	Heart attack (in North Hollywood, CA)
1947	MAYNE, Eric		80	Died in Hollywood, CA
• 1998	# MAYNE, Ferdinand (Ferdy)		81	Parkinson's disease in London
1968	+ MAYO, Archie		77	Cancer (in Guadalajara, Mexico)
1970	# MAYO, Edna		76	Died in San Francisco, CA
1963	+ MAYO, Frank		77	Heart attack (in Laguna Beach, CA)
1994	MAYS, Joe		45	A.I.D.S. complications (in Little Rock, AR)
1992	MAYS, Wendell		72	Cancer (in Santa Monica, CA)
1990	# MAZURKI, Mike		82	After a long illness (in Glendale, CA)
1989	McANALLY, Ray		63	Died in County Wicklow, Ireland
1984	McAVOY, May		82	Died in Sherman Oaks, CA
1992	McBATH, James H.		69	Heart attack
1990	McBEAN, Angus		86	
1993	McBEE, Keith W.		66	Cancer complicated by other illnesses
• 1997	MCBRIDE, Elizabeth	☆	42	Cancer at home in Santa Fe, NM
1976	McBRIDE, Mary Margaret		77	Died in Los Angeles, CA
1925	McCABE, Harry		44	After two operations (in Los Angeles, CA)
1994	McCALL, Barbara "Bobbie"		50	After a 3-yr. bout with cancer (in Beverly Hills, CA)
1938	McCALL, William		58	Died in Hollywood, CA
1991	McCALLION, James		72	Heart attack (in Van Nuys, CA)
1976	McCALLUM, Neil		45	Brain hemorrhage (in Reading, England)

Deaths of Movie and Television Personalities — by Name

YEAR	NAME	AGE	CAUSE and/or PLACE OF DEATH
1969	+ McCAREY, Leo ★	70	Emphysema (in Santa Monica, CA)
1948	McCAREY, Ray	50	Died alone in his apartment (in Los Angeles, CA)
1986	McCARTHY, Frank	74	Cancer (in Woodland Hills, CA)
1962	McCARTHY, John P.	78	Coronary thrombosis (in Pasadena, CA)
1992	McCARTHY, Julia	64	Cancer (in London, England)
1980	McCARTY, Mary	56	Died in Westwood, CA
1919	McCAULEY, Edna	?	Typhoid fever (in Rome, Italy)
1993	McCLEOD, Mercer	86	Heart failure (in New York)
1995	+ McCLURE, Doug	59	Lung cancer (at his home in Sherman Oaks, CA)
1959	McCOMB, Kate	87	Died in New York, NY
1979	McCONNELL, Gladys	71	Died in Los Angeles, CA
1962	McCONNELL, Lulu	80	Cancer (in Hollywood, CA)
1945	+ McCORMACK, John	61	Died at his home in Booterstown, Ireland
1953	McCORMACK, William M.	62	Following a heart attack (in Hollywood, CA)
1953	# McCORMICK, Merrill	61	Heart attack (in Hollywood, CA)
1962	McCORMICK, Myron	54	Cancer (in New York, NY)
1995	McCOY, Dan	37	Complications of A.I.D.S. (at Roosevelt Hosp. in Manhattan)
1967	# McCOY, Gertrude	77	Died in Atlanta, GA
1937	McCOY, Harry	43	Heart attack (in Hollywood, CA)
1991	McCOY, Jack	72	
1978	#+ McCOY, Tim	86	Heart attack (in Fort Huachuca, AZ)
• 1979	McCOY, Van	38	Heart attack
1988	McCRACKEN, James	61	Following two strokes
1990	# McCRAY, Helen Mary "Honey"	83	
1996	McCREA, Dusty Iron Wing	55	Diabetes (in Hondo, N.M.)
1990	McCREA, Joel	84	Pulmonary complications (in Woodland Hills, CA)
1992	McCULLERS, Edward	64	Heart attack
• 1936	McCULLOUGH, Paul	52	Suicide after suffering a nervous breakdown (slit throat w/razor)
1981	McCULLOUGH, Philo	90	Died in Burbank, CA
1991	McCULLOUGH, Stephen N.	48	Pulmonary hypertension
1946	McDANIEL, Etta	55	Died in Los Angeles, CA
1952	+ McDANIEL, Hattie ★	57	Breast cancer (in San Fernando Valley, CA)
1995	McDANIEL, Keith	38	Complications of A.I.D.S. (in Los Angeles, CA)
1962	# McDANIEL, Sam "Deacon"	76	Throat cancer (in Woodland Hills, CA)
1972	# McDERMOTT, Hugh	63	Died in London, England
1929	McDERMOTT, Marc	47	During gall bladder surgery (in Glendale, CA)
1996	McDERMOTT, Tom	83	Complications of prostate cancer (at Beth Israel hosp. in NY)
1976	# McDEVITT, Ruth	80	Died in Hollywood, CA
1968	McDONALD, Francis J.	77	After a lengthy illness (in Hollywood, CA)
1980	McDONALD, Frank	80	Died in Oxnard, CA
1965	#+ McDONALD, Marie	41	Accidental drug overdose (in Hidden Hills, CA)
1959	McDONALD, Ray	34	Died in New York, NY
1966	# McDOWELL, Claire	88	After a long illness (in Woodland Hills, CA)
1992	McEDWARD, Jack	94	Died in Los Angeles, CA
1942	McFADDEN, Charles Ivor	55	Cerebral hemorrhage (in Los Angeles, CA)
1993	+ McFARLAND, George "Spanky"	64	Unknown causes (at a hospital in Grapevine, TX)
1975	McFARLAND, Nan	58	Cancer (in Stamford, CT)
1977	McGANN, William H.	84	Heart attack in his sleep (in Woodland Hills, CA)
1975	# McGILL, Moyna	80	
1992	McGILL, Shaun	30	A.I.D.S.
1977	McGINN, Walter	38	After his car crashed into a parked truck (in Los Angeles, CA)
1990	McGIVENEY, Maura	51	Liver disease (in Sherman Oaks, CA)
1975	# McGIVER, John	61	Heart attack (in West Fulton, NY)

Deaths of Movie and Television Personalities — by Name

YEAR	NAME	AGE	CAUSE and/or PLACE OF DEATH
1951	McGLYNN, Frank Sr.	84	Died in Newburgh, NY
1977	# McGOWAN, J. P. "Jack"	81	(Screenplay writer) Died in Manhattan, NY
1952	# McGOWAN, John P.	72	(Silent star/producer) Died in Hollywood, CA
1971	McGOWAN, Oliver F.	64	Heart attack in his sleep (in Hollywood, CA)
1955	McGOWAN, Robert F.	72	Died in Santa Monica, CA
1970	McGRAIL, Walter B.	70	Died in San Francisco, CA
1967	McGRATH, Frank	64	Heart attack (in Beverly Hills, CA)
1978	McGRATH, Paul	74	Cardiac arrest in his sleep (in London, England)
1980	# McGRAW, Charles	66	After falling thru a glass shower door at home (in Studio City, CA)
1945	# McGREGOR, Malcolm	52	Burns from smoking in bed (in Los Angeles, CA)
1971	McGUINN, Joseph Ford "Joe"	67	Heart attack one week after surgery (in Hollywood, CA)
1989	McGUIRE, Jon Brandon	34	Liver failure (in North Hollywood, CA)
1978	McGUIRE, Kathryn	73	Pancreatic cancer (in Los Angeles, CA)
1954	McGUIRE, Tom	80	Died in Hollywood, CA
1988	McGUIRE, Tucker	75	Died in London, Canada
1994	McHUGH, Burke	77	Heart failure and pnemonia (at Falmouth Hosp., MA)
1995	McHUGH, Dorothy	87	Stroke
1981	McHUGH, Frank	82	After a brief illness (in Greenwich, CT)
1983	# McHUGH, Jack	69	Heart attack (in Las Vegas, NV)
1969	#+ McHUGH, Jimmy	74	Heart attack (in Beverly Hills, CA)
1971	# McHUGH, Matt	76	Heart attack (in Northridge, CA)
1991	McINTIRE, John Herrick	83	Emphysema and cancer (in Pasadena, CA)
1986	McINTIRE, Tim	42	Heart failure (in Los Angeles, CA)
1942	McINTOSH, Burr	79	Following a heart attack (in Hollywood, CA)
1984	McINTYRE, Christine	69	After a brief illness (in Northridge, CA)
1959	McINTYRE, Hal	44	Burns after falling asleep while smoking
1953	# McINTYRE, Leila	70	After a long illness (in West Los Angeles, CA)
1945	# McKAY, George W. "Red"	60	Died in Hollywood, CA
1987	McKAY, Scott	71	Kidney failure (in New York, NY)
1959	# McKEE, Lafe	87	Arteriosclerosis (in Temple City, CA)
1933	McKEEN, Snookums	8	Blood poisoning (in Los Angeles, CA)
1967	McKEEVER, Mike	27	Brain injuries from an automobile accident (in Hollywood, CA)
1958	McKENNA, Henry T.	64	Heart attack (in Hollywood, CA)
1986	McKENNA, Siobhan	63	Heart attack and lung cancer (in Dublin, Ireland)
1987	McKENZIE, Ella	82	Died in Hollywood, CA
1967	McKENZIE, Eva B.	78	Died in Hollywood, CA
1986	McKENZIE, Ida Mae	75	Died in Los Angeles, CA
1949	McKENZIE, Robert B.	65	Heart attack (in Manunuck, RI)
1927	McKIM, Robert	39	Cerebral hemorrhage (in Hollywood, CA)
1975	McKINNEY, Florine	62	Died in Woodland Hills, CA
1978	McKINNEY, Mira	?	
1967	McKINNEY, Nina Mae	54	Died in New York, NY
1978	McLAGLEN, Clifford	86	Undisclosed causes (in Huddersfield, Yorkshire, England)
1959	+ McLAGLEN, Victor ★	72	Congestive heart failure (in Newport Beach, CA)
1986	McLAUGHLIN, Don	79	After a brief illness
1991	McLAUGHLIN, Emily	61	Cancer (in Los Angeles, CA)
1960	McLAUGHLIN, Gibb	76	Died in Los Angeles, CA
1996	McLEAN, Barbara ★	92	Died in Newport Beach, CA
1995	McLEAN, David	73	Lung cancer (at UCLA Med. Ctr. in Los Angeles, CA)
1997	McLEOD, Catherine	75	Pneumonia (at Encino-Tarzana Medical Center in CA)
1961	McLEOD, Gordon	71	
1964	# McLEOD, Norman Z.	65	After suffering a stroke (in Hollywood, CA)
1973	# McLEOD, Tex	76	Heart attack (in Brighton, England)

Deaths of Movie and Television Personalities — by Name

YEAR		NAME		AGE	CAUSE and/or PLACE OF DEATH
1994		McLIAM, John		76	*Chronic bronchitis, Parkinson's disease and melanoma (in L.A.)*
1971		McMAHON, Horace		65	*Heart ailment*
1994		McMANUS, Mark		59	*Pneumonia (in Glasgow, Scotland)*
1989		McMILLAN, Kenneth		56	*Liver disease (in Santa Monica, CA)*
1984		McMURRAY, Richard		68	*Lung cancer (in Burbank, CA)*
1994	#+	McNALLY, Stephen		82	*Heart failure (at his home in Beverly Hills, CA)*
1944		McNAMARA, Edward C.		57	*Heart attack (on a Hollywood-bound train near Boston)*
1978		McNAMARA, Maggie		48	*Suicide (overdose of pills) in New York, NY*
1928		McNAMARA, Ted		36	*Pneumonia (in Ventura, CA)*
1955		McNAUGHTON, Charles		77	*Died in London, England*
1969	#	McNAUGHTON, Gus		85	*Died in Castor, England*
1967		McNAUGHTON, Harry		70	*Died in Amityville, NY*
1969	+	McNEAR, Howard		63	*After a long illness (in San Fernando Valley, CA)*
1993		McNEIL, Claudia		77	*Complications from diabetes (in Englewood, NJ)*
1944		McPHAIL, Douglas		30	*From the effects of poison (in Los Angeles, CA)*
1940		McPHERSON, Quinton		68	*Died in London, England*
1990		McPHILLIPS, Hugh		70	*Injuries from an automobile accident (in Sherman Oaks, CA)*
1995	#+	McQUEEN, "Butterfly"		84	*Burns (while lighting a kerosene heater at her home in Augusta, GA)*
1980	#+	McQUEEN, Steve	☆	50	*Heart attack after cancer surgery (in Juarez, Mexico)*
1994		McRAE, Carmen		74	*Following a stroke (at her home in Beverly Hills, CA)*
1931		McRAE, Duncan		49	*Died in London, England (Do not confuse with Duncan Macrae)*
1944		McRAE, Henry		68	*Heart attack (in Beverly Hills, CA)*
1964		McSHANE, Kitty		65	*Died in London, England*
1961		McTURK, Joe		62	*Heart attack (in Hollywood, CA)*
1925	#	McVEY, Lucille		35	*Respiratory illness (at her home in Hollywood, CA)*
1973		McVEY, Patrick		63	*After being hospitalized (in New York, NY)*
1943	+	McWADE, Edward		78	*After a brief illness (in Hollywood, CA)*
1956	+	McWADE, Margaret		83	*Died in Los Angeles, CA*
1938	+	McWADE, Robert Jr.		55	*Heart attack (in Culver City, CA)*
1941		MEADE, Bill		?	*Fell from a horse onto his sword while filming (in Hollywood, CA)*
1968	#	MEADE, Claire		84	*Pneumonia (in Encino, CA)*
1963		MEADER, George		75	
1996	+	MEADOWS, Audrey		71	*Lung cancer (at Cedars-Sinai Med. Ctr. in Los Angeles, CA)*
• 1986		MEADOWS, Robert		29	*After a brief illness*
1986		MEARS, Martha		78	*Complications from Alzheimer's disease*
1980	#	MEDFORD, Kay	☆	59	*Heart attack (in Manhattan, NY)*
• 1995		MEDINA, James		33	*A.I.D.S.*
1946	+	MEEK, Donald		66	*Acute leukemia and heart attack (in Los Angeles, CA)*
1988	#	MEEKER, Ralph		67	*Heart attack (in Los Angeles, CA)*
• 1996		MEES, Tom		46	*Accidentally drowned in his neighbor's pool (in Southington, CT)*
1988		MEGLIN, Ethel		98	
1995		MEGNA, John		42	*A.I.D.S. (in Los Angeles, CA)*
1981	#	MEGOWAN, Don		59	*Throat cancer (in Panorama City, CA)*
1968		MEHAFFEY, Blanche		60	*Died in Los Angeles, CA*
1995		MEIGHAN, Howard S.		88	*Cardiac arrest (at New York Hospital in Manhattan)*
1936		MEIGHAN, Thomas		57	*Lung cancer (in Great Neck, NY)*
1989		MEILLON, John		55	*Died in Sydney, Australia*
1940	#	MEINS, Gus		45	*Suicide (after arrest on morals charges) in La Crescenta, CA*
1993		MEISER, Edith		95	*Heart attack (at Roosevelt Hospital in New York)*
1994		MEISNER, Gunter		66	*Heart failure (in Berlin, Germany)*
• 1997		MEISNER, Sanford		91	*Natural causes (at his home in Sherman Oaks, CA)*
1973	#	MELCHIOR, Lauritz		82	*After gall bladder operation (in Santa Monica, CA)*
1949	#	MELESH, Alex		58	*Died in Hollywood, CA*

Deaths of Movie and Television Personalities — by Name

YEAR	NAME		AGE	CAUSE and/or PLACE OF DEATH
1961	MELFORD, George		84	Heart attack (in Hollywood, CA)
1938	# MELIES, Georges		77	After a long illness (in Orly, France)
1977	MELL, Joseph "Joe"		62	Heart condition (in Los Angeles, CA)
1992	# MELL, Marisa		53	Cancer of the thyroid (in Vienna, Austria)
1962	MELLER, Raquel		74	
1930	MELLISH, Fuller Jr.		35	Cerebral hemorrhage (in Forest Hills, NY)
1936	MELLISH, Fuller Sr.		71	Heart attack (in New York, NY)
1951	MELTON, Frank		43	After a heart attack (in Hollywood, CA)
1961	MELTON, James		57	Pneumonia (in New York, NY)
1995	MELTZER, Lewis		84	Pneumonia (at his home in Albuquerque, N.M.)
1946	MELVILLE, Rose "Sis Hopkins"		73	Died at her home in Lake George, NY
1989	MELVILLE, Sam		52	Heart attack
1985	MEMMOLI, George T.		46	Heart failure (in Los Angeles, CA)
1963	MENAHAN, Jean		58	
1990	MENDENHALL, Jim		62	Brain cancer
1963	#+ MENJOU, Adolphe ☆		73	Chronic hepatitis (in Beverly Hills, CA)
1956	# MENJOU, Henri		64	Died in Sawtelle, CA
1966	MENKEN, Helen		63	Heart attack (in New York, NY)
1957	# MENZIES, William C. ★		60	Died in Hollywood, CA
1975	# MERANDE, Doro		?	Following a massive stroke (in Miami Beach, FL)
1939	+ MERCER, Beryl		56	Following a major operation (in Santa Monica, CA)
1984	MERCER, Jack		74	After a brief illness (in New York, NY)
1976	#+ MERCER, Johnny		66	After surgery for a brain tumor (in Bel Air, CA)
1982	MERCHANT, Vivien ☆		53	Jaundice and hemorrhage caused by alcoholism (in London, Eng.)
1994	# MERCOURI, Melina		68	Complications of lung cancer (at a New York hospital)
1991	# MERCURY, Freddie		45	A.I.D.S.
• 1997	# MEREDITH, Burgess ☆		88	At his home in Malibu, CA
1964	+ MEREDITH, Charles		70	After a long illness (in Los Angeles, CA)
1964	MEREDITH, Cheerio		74	Died in Woodland Hills, CA
1980	# MEREDITH, Iris		64	Died in Los Angeles, CA
1969	# MEREDYTH, Bess		?	After a long illness (in Woodland Hills, CA)
1990	MERIVALE, John		72	Pneumonia (in London, England)
1946	MERIVALE, Philip		65	Heart ailment (in Los Angeles, CA)
1986	+ MERKEL, Una ☆		82	Died in Los Angeles, CA
1976	MERLO, Anthony "Tony"		88	Died in Woodland Hills, CA
1984	# MERMAN, Ethel		75	Results of a brain tumor (in Manhattan, NY)
• 1998	MERRILL, Bob ☆		77	Suicide in front of his Beverly Hills, CA home
1966	MERRILL, Frank		71	Died in Hollywood, CA
1990	MERRILL, Gary		74	Cancer (in Falmouth, ME)
1992	MERRILL, Joan		74	Stroke and Alzheimer's disease (in New York, NY)
1977	MERRITT, George		86	Died in London, England
• 1998	MERRITT, Theresa		75	Skin cancer in the Bronx, NY
1947	# MERSON, Billy		66	Died in London, England
1959	# MERTON, John		58	Heart attack (in Los Angeles, CA)
1976	# MERVYN, William		64	Died in London, England
1965	# MESSENGER, Buddy		55	Died in Hollywood, CA
1950	METAXA, Georges		51	Heart ailment (in Monroe, LA)
1990	METCALFE, Gordon		43	A.I.D.S. (in Los Angeles, CA)
1960	METCALFE, James J.		53	Heart attack (in Northridge, CA)
1951	METHOT, Mayo		47	Died in Portland, OR
1987	MEYER, Dorothy		62	Cancer (in Los Angeles, CA)
1987	+ MEYER, Emile G.		76	Alzheimer's disease (in Covington, LA)
1965	MEYER, Greta		82	Died in Los Angeles, CA

Deaths of Movie and Television Personalities — by Name

YEAR	NAME	AGE	CAUSE and/or PLACE OF DEATH
1975	MEYER, Torben	90	*Bronchial pneumonia (in Hollywood, CA)*
1939	MEYERHOLD, Vsevolod	65	*Tortured by Stalin's secret police on false charges of treason*
1969	MEYERS, Sidney	63	*Died in New York, NY*
1989	MEYERS, Timothy	44	*A.I.D.S. (in New York, NY)*
1964	MICHAEL, Gertrude	53	*Died in Beverly Hills, CA*
1985	MICHAELIDES, George	66	*Complications after heart surgery (in Los Angeles, CA)*
1983	MICHAELS, Loretta R.	45	*Cancer (in Boston, MA)*
• 1997	MICHENER, James A.	90	*Renal failure at home in Austin, TX from kidney problems*
1949	MIDDLEMASS, Robert M.	64	*Died in Los Angeles, CA*
1949	MIDDLETON, Charles B.	69	*Heart attack (in Los Angeles, CA)*
1973	# MIDDLETON, Guy	64	*Cancer (near London, England)*
1971	MIDDLETON, Josephine	87	*Died in England*
1984	MIDDLETON, Ray	77	*Heart attack (in Panorama City, CA)*
1977	# MIDDLETON, Robert	66	*Heart failure (in Encino, CA)*
1932	MIDGLEY, Fannie	54	*Died in Hollywood, CA*
1949	MIDGLEY, Florence	59	*Died in Hollywood, CA*
• 1997	MIFUNE, Toshiro	77	*Died of organ failure at a Tokyo hospital*
1948	MIKHOELS, Solomon	58	*Murdered (run over by a truck) presumably on Stalin's orders*
1989	MILANOV, Zinka	83	*Stroke*
1991	MILES, Bernard	83	*Died in Knaresborough, England*
1980	#+ MILESTONE, Lewis ★	84	*Following abdominal surgery (in Los Angeles, CA)*
1991	# MILFORD, Gene ★	89	*Pneumonia (in Santa Monica, CA)*
• 1998	MILHAUPT, Charles	48	*AIDS at his home in Manhattan, NY*
1960	MILJAN, John	66	*Died in Hollywood, CA*
1986	# MILLAND, Ray ★	81	*Cancer (in Torrance, CA)*
1966	MILLAR, Marjie	36	*Died in Los Angeles, CA*
1931	MILLARDE, Harry	45	*Heart attack (in Queens, NY)*
1990	MILLER, Barbara	68	*After a brain tumor operation (in London, England)*
1979	# MILLER, Carl	85	*Died in Honolulu, Hawaii*
1955	MILLER, Charles B.	64	*Suicide (gunshot) due to unemployment and ill health (Hollywood)*
1986	MILLER, Court	34	*Complications from A.I.D.S. (in Portland, ME)*
1992	MILLER, David	82	*Cancer (in Los Angeles, CA)*
1948	MILLER, Edward G.	65	*Died in Los Angeles, CA*
1971	# MILLER, Flournoy E.	82	*Heart failure (in Hollywood, CA)*
1944	# MILLER, Glenn	40	*Lost when his RAF plane disappeared while bound for Paris*
1992	MILLER, Hope	63	*Breast cancer (in New York, NY)*
1988	MILLER, Joan	78	*Died in London, England*
1978	# MILLER, Lorraine	49	*Died in Los Angeles, CA*
1936	#+ MILLER, Marilyn	37	*Toxemia from a sinus infection (in New York, NY)*
1969	# MILLER, Martin	70	*Heart attack (in Innsbruck, Austria)*
1985	+ MILLER, Marvin	72	*Heart attack (in Santa Monica, CA)*
1963	# MILLER, Max	68	*Died in Brighton, England*
1995	MILLER, Patsy Ruth	91	*Heart failure (at her home in Palm Desert, CA)*
1939	MILLER, Ranger Bill	61	*Died in Los Angeles, CA*
1992	MILLER, Roger	56	*Cancer (in Los Angeles, CA)*
1976	MILLER, Ruby	86	*Died in Chichester, England*
1981	MILLER, Ruth	78	*Died in Santa Monica, CA*
1922	# MILLER, W. Christy	79	*Died in Staten Island, NY*
1940	#+ MILLER, Walter C.	48	*After collapsing on a Republic Pictures set (in Los Angeles, CA)*
1993	MILLHOLLIN, James	77	*Cancer (in Biloxi, MS)*
1955	MILLICAN, James	45	*After a brief illness (in Los Angeles, CA)*
1991	MILLIGAN, Andy	62	*A.I.D.S. (in Los Angeles, CA)*
1973	MILLS, Frank	82	*Arteriosclerosis (in Los Angeles, CA)*

• New entry. # Original name (Pt. 7). + Interment (Pt. 5).

276

☆ Oscar nominee, ★ Oscar winner (Pt. 10)

Deaths of Movie and Television Personalities — by Name

YEAR	NAME		AGE	CAUSE and/or PLACE OF DEATH
1982	+ MILLS, Harry F.		68	*Following a tumor operation*
1989	MILLS, Herbert		77	
1936	MILLS, John Jr.		25	*Tuberculosis (in Bellefontaine, OH)*
1967	MILLS, John Sr.		78	*Died in Bellefontaine, OH*
1997	MILMO, Emilio Azcarraga		66	*Cancer in Miami, FL*
1966	# MILOS, Milos		24	*Suicide (gunshot) in Los Angeles, CA*
1992	MILSTEIN, Nathan		88	*Heart attack*
1989	MILTON, Billy		83	*Cardiac arrest in his sleep (in Northwood, England)*
1956	MILTON, Robert D.		70	*After a long illness and hospitalization (in Woodland Hills, CA)*
1962	MINCIOTTI, Esther		74	*Died in New York, NY*
1976	#+ MINEO, Sal ☆		37	*Murdered (stabbed to death) in West Hollywood, CA*
1982	# MINER, Tony		82	*Heart attack (in New York, NY)*
1964	MING, Moy Luke		101	*Died in Grenada Hills, CA*
1986	+ MINNELLI, Vincente ★		83	*Emphysema and pneumonia (in Beverly Hills, CA)*
1969	MINNER, Kathryn		77	*Heart attack (in Van Nuys, CA)*
1987	MINOR, Michael		46	*A.I.D.S.*
1990	MINOTIS, Alexis		90	*Stroke (in Athens, Greece)*
1984	#+ MINTER, Mary Miles		82	*Heart failure (in Santa Monica, CA)*
1988	# MINTZ, Eli		83	*Pneumonia (in Point Pleasant, NJ)*
1955	#+ MIRANDA, Carmen		51	*Heart attack (in Beverly Hills, CA)*
1982	MIRANDA, Isa		77	*Infected bone fracture (in Rome, Italy)*
1996	#+ MIRANDA, Willy		70	*Lung cancer (at Good Samaritan Hosp. in Baltimore, MD)*
1997	MIRO, Pilar		57	*Heart attack at home in Madrid, Spain*
1955	# Miroslava		29	*Suicide (poison) in Mexico City, Mexico*
1973	MISHIMA, Masao		67	*Heart ailment (in Tokyo, Japan)*
1979	MITCHELL, Belle		90	*After a long illness (in Woodland Hills, CA)*
1952	MITCHELL, Bruce		68	*Anemia (in Hollywood, CA)*
1994	+ MITCHELL, Cameron		75	*Lung cancer (at his home in Pacific Palisades, CA)*
1992	MITCHELL, Chuck		64	*Cirrhosis of the liver (in Hollywood, CA)*
1992	MITCHELL, Coleman		48	*After a sudden illness*
1988	MITCHELL, Ewing Young		77	*Following a stroke (in La Jolla, CA)*
1991	MITCHELL, Frank		84	*Cardiac arrest (in North Hollywood, CA)*
1949	MITCHELL, Geneva		42	*Died in California*
1957	MITCHELL, Grant		82	*Following a stroke (in Los Angeles, CA)*
1954	MITCHELL, Julien		65	*Died in London, England*
1949	+ MITCHELL, Margaret		46	*Struck by a speeding automobile (in Atlanta, GA)*
1953	MITCHELL, Millard		53	*Lung cancer (in Santa Monica, CA)*
1957	MITCHELL, Rhea "Ginger"		52	*Found strangled to death (at her home in Los Angeles, CA)*
1962	+ MITCHELL, Thomas ★		70	*Cancer (in Beverly Hills, CA)*
1979	MITCHELL, Yvonne		53	*Cancer (in London, England)*
1997	MITCHUM, Robert ☆		79	*Died at his home in CA from emphysema and lung cancer*
1988	MITRY, Jean		83	*Cancer (in La Garenne-Colombes, France)*
1994	MITTY, Nomi		54	*Cancer (at her home in Los Angeles, CA)*
1940	#+ MIX, Tom		60	*A broken neck after his car overturned (in Florence, AZ)*
1988	MOBERLY, Robert		49	*A.I.D.S. (in Los Angeles, CA)*
1970	MODOT, Gaston		82	*Died in Le Raincy, France*
1942	MOFFAT, Margaret		49	*Pneumonia (in Los Angeles, CA)*
1965	MOFFATT, Graham		46	*Heart attack (in Bath, England)*
1995	MOFFET, Sally		63	*Lung cancer (in Nyack, NY)*
1968	MOHR, Gerald		54	*Heart attack (in Stockholm, Sweden)*
1974	MOJICA, Don José		75	*Complications after open-heart surgery (in Lima, Peru)*
1992	MOLINARI, Antoinette		63	*Kidney failure (in Burbank, CA)*
1986	MOLLISON, Clifford		89	*Undisclosed causes (in Cyprus)*

Deaths of Movie and Television Personalities — by Name

YEAR	NAME	AGE	CAUSE and/or PLACE OF DEATH
• 1998	MONAHAN, John Paul 'Jay'	42	Cancer
1938	# MONCRIES, Edward	78	Heart attack (in Hollywood, CA)
1991	MONDO, Peggy	50	Heart attack (in Los Angeles, CA)
1940	MONG, William V.	65	After a 2-years' illness (in Studio City, CA)
1991	MONICA, Maria A. G.	92	Died in Las Vegas, NV
1982	+ MONK, Thelonius	64	Following a stroke (in Weehawken, NJ)
1994	MONKS, James	81	Cancer (at St. Luke's-Roosevelt Hospital in New York City)
• 1996	MONROE, Bill	84	After suffering a stroke (in Springfield, TN)
1962	#+ MONROE, Marilyn	36	Suicide? (drug overdose) in Brentwood, CA
1973	+ MONROE, Vaughn	62	Died in Stuart, FL
1919	MONTAGUE, Frederick	55	Acute intestinal obstruction (in Los Angeles, CA)
1959	# MONTAGUE, Walter "Monte"	67	Died in Burbank, CA
1991	MONTALBAN, Carlos	87	Heart failure (in New York, NY)
1950	# MONTANA, Lewis "Bull"	62	Coronary thrombosis (in Los Angeles, CA)
• 1998	# MONTANA, Montie	87	After a series of strokes in Los Angeles, CA
1991	#+ MONTAND, Yves	70	Heart attack following a stroke (in Senlis, France)
1964	+ MONTEUX, Pierre	89	Died in Hancock, MI
1951	# MONTEZ, Maria	33	Heart seizure while bathing in her home (in Suresnes, France)
1966	# MONTGOMERY, Douglass	57	Died in Norwalk, CT
1987	MONTGOMERY, Earl	65	Heart attack and leukemia (in Los Angeles, CA)
1995	+ MONTGOMERY, Elizabeth	62	Cancer after surgery to remove a tumor (Beverly Hills, CA)
1978	MONTGOMERY, Goodee	72	After a brief illness (in Hollywood, CA)
1981	#+ MONTGOMERY, Robert ☆	77	Cancer (in New York, NY)
1993	MONTI, Carlotta	86	After a long illness (in Woodland Hills, CA)
1980	MONTOVANI, Annunzio	75	
1970	MONTOYA, Alex P.	62	Congestive heart failure (in Los Angeles, CA)
1971	MOODY, Ralph	83	Heart attack following surgery (in Burbank, CA)
1967	MOON, George	80	Died in London, England
1978	MOON, Keith	31	Found dead from an overdose of heminevrin (in London, England)
1991	MOORCROFT, Judy	58	
1992	MOORE, Brian	59	Congestive heart failure (in Hollywood, CA)
1977	MOORE, Carlyle Jr.	67	Died in Sun Valley, ID
1924	MOORE, Carlyle Sr.	49	Suicide (in his Milford, NJ, home)
1959	# MOORE, Clara	?	Murdered
1973	MOORE, Cleo	44	Died in Inglewood, CA
1988	# MOORE, Colleen	87	Following a long illness (in Paso Robles, CA)
1970	MOORE, Del	53	Apparent heart attack (at his home in Encino, CA)
1964	MOORE, Dennis	49	Died in New York, NY
1991	# MOORE, Eleanor	84	Complications from emphysema (in Santa Monica, CA)
1955	MOORE, Eva	85	Died in Maidenhead, England
1993	# MOORE, Garry	78	Emphysema (at his home on Hilton Head Island, SC)
1947	+ MOORE, Grace ☆	45	Airplane crash (in Kastrup, Denmark
1964	MOORE, Ida	81	
1993	MOORE, Irving	74	Heart attack (in Sherman Oaks, CA)
• 1997	+ MOORE, Jack "Alvy"	75	Heart failure at his home in Palm Desert, CA
• 1997	MOORE, Joanna	63	Died of lung cancer in Indian Wells, CA
1983	MOORE, Kathryn	96	Died in Woodland Hills, CA
1960	MOORE, Matt	72	Died in Hollywood, CA
1939	MOORE, Owen	52	Heart attack (in Beverly Hills, CA)
1972	# MOORE, Patti	71	Cancer (in Los Angeles, CA)
1984	MOORE, Robert (director)	56	After a brief illness (in New York, NY)
1955	MOORE, Tom	70	Cancer (in Santa Monica, CA)
1962	+ MOORE, Victor	86	Heart attack (in East Islip, L.I., NY)

Deaths of Movie and Television Personalities — by Name

YEAR	NAME	AGE	CAUSE and/or PLACE OF DEATH
1974	#+ MOOREHEAD, Agnes ☆	67	*Lung cancer (in Rochester, MN)*
1991	MORALI, Jacques	44	*A.I.D.S.*
1982	MORAN, Dolores	56	*Died in Woodland Hills, CA*
1967	# MORAN, Frank	80	*Heart attack (in Hollywood, CA)*
1949	# MORAN, George	67	*After suffering a stroke (in Oakland, CA)*
1997	MORAN, Grace E.	79	*Died in her sleep at her son's home in Catonsville, MD*
1990	# MORAN, Jackie	67	*Cancer (in Greenfield, MA)*
1961	MORAN, Lee	70	*Heart ailment (in Woodland Hills, CA)*
1990	# MORAN, Lois	81	*Cancer (in Sedona, AZ)*
1968	MORAN, Patsy	63	*Died in Hollywood, CA*
1968	MORAN, Percy	?	*Died in England*
1952	# MORAN, Polly	68	*Heart ailment (in Los Angeles, CA)*
1964	# MORANTE, Milburn	76	*Heart disease (in Pacoima, CA)*
1982	MORE, Kenneth	67	*Parkinson's disease (in London, England)*
1981	MORE, Unity	86	*Died in London, England*
1984	# MORECAMBE, Eric	58	*Heart disease (in Cheltenham, England)*
1973	+ MORELAND, Mantan	72	*Died in Hollywood, CA*
1978	# MORELL, André	69	*After a long illness (in London, England)*
1967	+ MORENO, Antonio	78	*After a long illness (in Beverly Hills, CA)*
1968	# MORENO, Dario	47	*Cerebral hemorrhage (in Istanbul, Turkey)*
1948	# MORENO, Marguerite	77	*Died in Touzac, France*
1938	MORENO, Thomas "Sky Ball"	43	*Died in West Los Angeles, CA*
1988	MORGAN, Boyd F. "Red"	72	*Heart attack (in Tarzana, CA)*
1994	# MORGAN, Dennis	85	*Heart failure (at a hospital in Fresno, CA)*
1993	MORGAN, Edward P.	82	*Cancer*
1987	MORGAN, Elizabeth	84	*After a stroke (in New York, NY)*
1949	#+ MORGAN, Frank ☆	59	*Died at his home in Beverly Hills, CA*
1940	# MORGAN, Gene	48	*Heart attack (in Santa Monica, CA)*
1991	MORGAN, George J.	77	*Cancer (in Canoga Park, CA)*
1941	+ MORGAN, Helen	41	*Kidney and liver ailments (in Chicago, IL)*
1994	# MORGAN, Henry	79	*Lung cancer (at his home in Manhattan, NY)*
1967	# MORGAN, Lee	64	*Heart disease (in Los Angeles, CA)*
1989	MORGAN, Mary	81	
1956	#+ MORGAN, Ralph	72	*After a 3-yr. illness (in New York, NY)*
1975	MORGAN, Ray	?	*Cancer (in Englewood, NJ)*
1989	MORGAN, Rex	67	*Parkinson's disease (in Fairfax, VA)*
1969	+ MORGAN, Russ	65	*Cerebral hemorrhage (in Las Vegas, NV)*
1989	MORIN, Alberto	86	*Stroke (in Burbank, CA)*
1993	MORK, Erik	67	*Died in Copenhagen, Denmark*
1964	# MORLAY, Gaby	67	*Cancer (in Nice, France)*
1992	MORLEY, Robert	84	*After suffering a stroke (Do not confuse with Robert Morley, d. 1952)*
1952	MORLEY, Robert James ☆	60	*Died in Hollywood, CA (Do not confuse with Robert Morley, d. 1992)*
1948	MOROSCO, Walter	49	*Stroke (in Coronado, CA)*
1955	MORRELL, George	82	*After a long illness (in Hollywood, CA)*
1994	MORRILL, Priscilla	67	*Kidney infection (in Los Angeles, CA)*
1978	Morris (the original TV cat)	17	
1941	MORRIS, Adrian	38	*Died in Los Angeles, CA*
1994	MORRIS, Anita	50	*Cancer (at her home in Los Angeles, CA)*
1995	MORRIS, Charlotte	75	*Multiple medical problems (at NY Hosp.—Cornell Med. Ctr.)*
1970	# MORRIS, Chester ☆	69	*Overdose of barbiturates (in New Hope, PA)*
1974	MORRIS, Glenn	62	*Cancer (in Palo Alto, CA)*
1996	MORRIS, Greg	61	*After a 2-yr. battle with brain cancer (at his home in Las Vegas, NV)*
1990	MORRIS, Jack Julius	87	*Cardiac arrest in his sleep (in Sherman Oaks, CA)*

Deaths of Movie and Television Personalities — by Name

YEAR	NAME	AGE	CAUSE and/or PLACE OF DEATH
1969	# MORRIS, Johnny	83	Died in Hollywood, CA
1933	MORRIS, Lee	69	Died in Los Angeles, CA
1968	MORRIS, Margaret	64	(Do not confuse with choreographer of same name)
1988	MORRIS, Mary	72	Undisclosed causes (in Aigle, Switzerland)
1949	# MORRIS, Philip	56	Died in Los Angeles, CA
1996	MORRIS, Richard	72	Cancer (in Los Angeles, CA)
1986	MORRIS, Rolland "Rusty"	63	Cancer (in Los Angeles, CA)
1959	#+ MORRIS, Wayne	45	Heart attack (aboard an aircraft carrier in the Pacific Ocean)
1996	MORRIS, Wolfe	71	
1978	MORRISON, Ann	62	Cancer (in Woodland Hills, CA)
1950	MORRISON, Arthur	71	Died in Los Angeles, CA
1992	MORRISON, Barbara	84	Heart failure (in Woodland Hills, CA)
1975	MORRISON, Chester A.	52	Died in Portland, OR
1989	# MORRISON, Ernie	76	Cancer (in Lynwood, CA)
1973	MORRISON, George "Pete"	81	Died in Los Angeles, CA
1993	MORRISON, Harold	62	Died in Springfield, MO
1974	# MORRISON, James	86	Died in New York, NY
1971	+ MORRISON, Jim	27	Heart attack in his bath tub (after heavy drinking) in Paris, France
1946	MORRISON, Louis "Lou"	80	Died in CA
1993	MORRISON, Michael D.	33	Accidental overdose of alcohol and illegal drugs
1944	# MORRISSEY, Betty	37	Died in New York, NY
1968	# MORROW, Doretta	41	Cancer (in London, England)
1993	MORROW, Jeff	86	After a long illness (in Canoga Park, CA)
1982	+ MORROW, Vic	50	Killed in a filming accident (in Sangus Desert, CA)
1993	MORSE, Carleton	91	Died in Sacramento, CA
1964	MORTIMER, Charles	78	Died in London, England
1969	MORTON, Charles J.	70	Heart attack
1966	MORTON, Charles S.	59	Heart disease (in North Hollywood, CA)
1975	MORTON, Clive	71	Died in London, England
1997	MORTON, Howard	71	Stroke at St. Joseph's Hospital in Burbank, CA
1942	MORTON, James C.	58	After a long illness (in Reseda, CA)
1940	# MOSCOVITCH, Maurice	68	Following abdominal surgery (in Los Angeles, CA)
1964	# MOSER, Hans	83	Cancer (in Vienna, Austria)
1995	MOSES, Gilbert	52	Multiple myeloma (in New York)
1983	MOSQUINI, Marie	84	Died in Los Angeles, CA
1989	MOSS, Arnold	80	Lung cancer (in New York, NY)
1997	MOSS, Carlton	88	Died in Los Angeles, CA
1977	# MOSTEL, Zero	62	Cardiac disorder (in Philadelphia, PA)
1969	+ MOWBRAY, Alan	72	Heart attack (in Hollywood, CA)
1965	MOWER, Jack	74	Died in Hollywood, CA
1989	MOWER, Margaret	93	
1965	# MUDIE, Leonard	81	Heart ailment (in Hollywood, CA)
1989	# MUELLER, Cookie	40	A.I.D.S. (in New York, NY)
1992	MUELLER, William A. ☆	92	Natural causes
1960	# MUELLER, Wolfgang	36	Airplane crash (in Lostallo, Switzerland)
1995	MUIR, Esther	92	Natural causes (in Mount Kisco, NY)
1972	MUIR, Gavin	64	After a brief illness (in Fort Lauderdale, FL)
1996	MUIR, Jean	85	Natural causes (at a nursing home in Mesa, AZ)
1964	MULCASTER, George H.	72	Died in England
1979	MULHALL, Jack	87	Congestive heart failure (in Woodland Hills, CA)
1997	MULHARE, Edward	74	Lung Cancer in Los Angeles, CA
1982	MULLANEY, Jack	51	Stroke (in Hollywood, CA)
1979	MULLEN, Barbara	64	Heart attack (in London, England)

Deaths of Movie and Television Personalities — by Name

YEAR	NAME		AGE	CAUSE and/or PLACE OF DEATH
1937	# MULLER, Renate		30	Suicide (in Berlin, Germany)
1990	MULLINS, Ted		50	Heart attack
1974	MUMBY, Diana		51	Died in Westlake, CA
1939	MUNDIN, Herbert		40	Fractured skull from auto accident (in Van Nuys, CA)
1967	#+ MUNI, Paul	★	71	Heart trouble (in Montecito, CA)
1945	MUNIER, Ferdinand		55	After a heart attack (in Hollywood, CA)
1924	MUNRO, Douglas		?	Double pneumonia (in Birmingham, England)
1972	MUNRO, Janet		38	Choked to death while drinking tea (in London, England)
1992	MUNRO, Nan		87	Died in London, England
1970	MUNSHIN, Jules		54	Heart attack (in New York, NY)
1955	#+ MUNSON, Ona		51	Suicide (sleeping pills) in New York, NY
1968	# MURAT, Jean		79	Coronary thrombosis (in Aix-en-Provence, France)
1990	MURDOCH, Richard B.		83	Apparent heart attack (in Walton Heath, England)
1939	# MURDOCK, Ann		48	Died in Lucerne, Switzerland
1931	MURNAU, F. W.		42	Automobile accident (in Santa Barbara, CA)
1971	#+ MURPHY, Audie		46	Airplane crash (near Roanoke, VA)
1974	# MURPHY, Edna		69	Died in Santa Monica, CA
1992	MURPHY, George		89	Leukemia (in Palm Beach, FL)
1961	MURPHY, Joseph J.		84	Died in San Jose, CA
1978	MURPHY, Maurice		65	Died in Los Angeles, CA
1993	MURPHY, Richard		81	Stroke (in Los Angeles, CA)
1988	MURPHY, Timothy Patrick		29	A.I.D.S. (in Sherman Oaks, CA)
1991	# MURRAY, Arthur		95	Pneumonia
1979	# MURRAY, Bobby		80	Died in Nashua, NH
1941	MURRAY, Charlie		69	Pneumonia (in Hollywood, CA)
1940	+ MURRAY, J. Harold		49	After treatment for a kidney ailment (in Killingworth, CT)
1936	MURRAY, James		35	Drowned when he fell off a pier (in New York, NY)
1957	MURRAY, John T.		71	Following a stroke (in Woodland Hills, CA)
1988	MURRAY, Ken		85	Died in Burbank, CA
1965	#+ MURRAY, Mae		75	Heart condition (in North Hollywood, CA)
1990	MURRAY, Mary Phillips		68	Cancer
1935	MURRAY, Tom		60	After a 1-year illness (in Hollywood, CA)
1989	# MURRAY-MAZWI, Mark		52	Heart attack (in Los Angeles, CA)
1965	+ MURROW, Edward R.		57	Lung cancer (in Pawling, NY)
1979	MUSE, Clarence		90	Cerebral hemorrhage (in Perris, CA)
1957	# Musidora		68	Died in Paris, France
1991	MUSILLI, John		55	Cancer (in Kinnelon, NJ)
1996	MUSTARD, Jim		51	Bone cancer and A.I.D.S. (in Baltimore, MD)
1977	+ MUSTIN, Burt		94	Died in Glendale, CA
1990	MYDLAND, Brent		37	Overdose of morphine and cocaine
1996	MYEROVICH, Alvin		89	Heart failure (at a retirement home in Manchester Township, NJ)
1980	+ MYERS, Carmel		79	After a heart attack (in Los Angeles, CA)
1938	+ MYERS, Harry C.		52	Pneumonia (in Los Angeles, CA)
1993	MYERS, Stanley		63	Cancer (in London, England)
1995	MYERS, William		74	Pneumonia (in New York City)
1992	MYHERS, John		70	Pneumonia (in Los Angeles, CA)
1984	MYLES, Mary		93	Congestive heart failure (in Los Angeles, CA)
1975	MYLONG, John		82	After a long illness (in Beverly Hills, CA)
1978	MYRTILE, Odette		80	Stroke (at a hospital in Doylestown, PA)
	N			
1992	NABBIE, Jim		72	After double bypass heart surgery
1990	NADEL, Arthur H.		68	Diabetes (in Los Angeles, CA)
1966	# NAGEL, Anne		53	Cancer (in Los Angeles, CA)

YEAR	NAME	AGE	CAUSE and/or PLACE OF DEATH
1970	NAGEL, Conrad	72	Found dead in his apartment (in New York, NY)
1973	#+ NAISH, J. Carrol ☆	73	Died in La Jolla, CA
1992	# NAISMITH, Laurence	83	After a short illness (in Southport, Australia)
1991	# NALDER, Reggie	80	Bone cancer (in Santa Monica, CA)
1961	#+ NALDI, Nita	61	Died in New York, NY
1988	# NAPIER, Alan	85	After a stroke (in Santa Monica, CA)
• 1983	NAPIER, Diana	76	
1974	NAPIER, Russell	64	Died in London, England
1990	NAPOLEAN, Phil	89	
• 1998	NARDINO, Gary	62	Stroke at Cedars-Sinai Medical Center in Los Angeles, CA
1943	# NARES, Owen	54	Died in Brecon, Wales
1985	NASH, Clarence "Donald Duck"	80	Leukemia (in Burbank, CA)
1950	NASH, Florence	60	Heart ailment (in Los Angeles, CA)
1979	NASH, June	68	Died in Hampton Bays, L.I., NY
1976	# NASH, Mary	91	Died in Brentwood, CA
1942	NATHEAUX, Louis	44	Died in Los Angeles, CA
1990	NATWICK, Grim	100	Pneumonia and heart disease (in Santa Monica, CA)
1994	+ NATWICK, Mildred ☆	89	Cancer (at her home in Manhattan, NY)
1992	NAUGHTON, Bill	81	Died in England
1976	NAUGHTON, Charlie	88	Died in London, England
1986	NAZARRO, Ray	83	Died in Los Angeles, CA
1945	#+ NAZIMOVA, Alla	66	Coronary thrombosis (in Los Angeles, CA)
1979	# NAZZARI, Amedeo	71	Cardiac arrest (in Rome, Italy)
1986	# NEAGLE, Anna	81	Exhaustion (in England)
1972	NEAL, Tom	58	Lung cancer (in North Hollywood, CA)
1972	# NEDELL, Bernard	74	Died in Hollywood, CA
1947	+ NEGIN, Koliz	60	Died in San Francisco, CA
1987	#+ NEGRI, Pola	87	Brain tumor, complicated by pneumonia (in San Antonio, TX)
1993	+ NEGULESCO, Jean	93	Heart failure (in Marbella, Spain)
1989	NEIDORF, Ross Lee	34	A.I.D.S. (in Miami, FL)
1958	NEILAN, Marshall	67	Cancer (in Woodland Hills, CA)
1931	+ NEILL, James	70	Heart trouble (in Glendale, CA)
1970	NEILL, Richard R.	94	Died at Motion Picture Country Hospital, Woodland Hills, CA
1946	NEILL, Roy William	59	After a heart attack (in London, England)
• 1996	NEISE, George N.	79	Natural causes (at his home in Hollywood, CA)
1948	NELSON, Anne	37	Died in Torrance, CA
1979	NELSON, Billy	75	Following a heart attack (in Los Angeles, CA)
1988	NELSON, Christine	60	Lung cancer (in Los Angeles, CA)
1986	+ NELSON, Frank	75	Cancer
• 1996	NELSON, Gene	76	Cancer (in Los Angeles, CA)
1994	#+ NELSON, Harriet	85	Congestive heart failure (at her home in Laguna Beach, CA)
1990	NELSON, Herbert	76	Heart attack (in Englewood, NJ)
1993	NELSON, Kenneth	60	An A.I.D.S.-related illness (in London, England)
• 1994	+ NELSON, Nels P.	76	
1975	#+ NELSON, Ozzie	69	Cancer of the liver (in Hollywood, CA)
1987	NELSON, Ralph	71	Cancer (in Santa Monica, CA)
1985	#+ NELSON, Rick	45	Airplane crash (near DeKalb, TX) traces of cocaine found in his body
1992	NELSON, Ruth	87	Cancer complicated by a stroke and pneumonia (in Manhattan, NY)
1975	# NERVO, Jimmy	85	Died in London, England
1967	NESBIT, Evelyn (Thaw)	82	Died at a nursing home in a Santa Monica, CA
1982	NESBITT, Cathleen	93	Cardiac arrest in her sleep (in Chelsea, England)
1990	# NESBITT, Frank M.	48	Cancer (in Upper Marlboro, MD)
1960	NESBITT, John	49	Heart attack (in Carmel, CA)

Deaths of Movie and Television Personalities — by Name

YEAR	NAME		AGE	CAUSE and/or PLACE OF DEATH
1954	# NESBITT, Miriam		80	*Died in Hollywood, CA*
1972	NESMITH, Ottola		83	*Died in Hollywood, CA*
1958	+ NEUMANN, Kurt		50	*After emergency hospitalization (in Hollywood, CA)*
1995	NEVAREZ, Aramando		44	*Complications of A.I.D.S. (in Los Angeles, CA)*
1932	NEVILLE, George		66	*Died in New York, NY*
1937	NEWALL, Guy		51	*After a brief illness (in Hampstead, England)*
1969	NEWBURG, Frank		83	*Died at Motion Picture Country Hospital, Woodland Hills, CA*
1980	NEWELL, David (actor)		75	*Died in Los Angeles, CA*
1967	+ NEWELL, William "Billy"		72	*Died in Hollywood, CA*
• 1998	NEWEY, Murray		45	*Suicide at his home in Auckland, New Zealand*
1964	NEWFIELD, Sam		64	*Cancer (in Hollywood, CA)*
• 1997	NEWI, George		62	*Heart attack while on vacation in Norway*
1994	NEWINGTON, Peter		71	
1970	+ NEWMAN, Alfred	★	68	*Emphysema and complications (in Hollywood, CA)*
1995	NEWMAN, Joseph		86	*Lymphoma (in Washington, D.C.)*
1989	+ NEWMAN, Lionel		73	*Cardiac arrest (in Los Angeles, CA)*
1978	# NEWMAN, Scott		28	*Apparent accidental overdose of Valium and alcohol*
1991	NEWMAN, Thomas		60	*Heart attack (in Los Angeles, CA)*
1993	NEWMAN, Walter Brown	☆	77	*Cancer (at his home in Sherman Oaks, CA)*
1926	NEWTON, Charles		?	
1965	+ NEWTON, Robert		50	*Heart attack (in Beverly Hills, CA)*
1981	# NEY, Marie		86	*Died in London, England*
1996	NGOR, Dr. Haing S.	★	55	*Murdered (shot) outside his home in Los Angeles, CA*
1948	#+ NIBLO, Fred Sr.		74	*Pneumonia (in New Orleans, LA)*
1977	NICHOLLS, Anthony		69	*Died in London, England*
1976	#+ NICHOLS, Barbara		47	*Cancer of the liver (at Cedar Sinai Hospital in Los Angeles, CA)*
1986	# NICHOLS, Dandy		78	*Arthritis complications (in London, England)*
1960	NICHOLS, Dudley		64	*While hospitalized for cancer (in Hollywood, CA)*
1939	+ NICHOLS, George Jr.		42	*Automobile accident (in Los Angeles, CA)*
1927	NICHOLS, George Sr.		62	*Died at his home in Hollywood, CA*
1965	#+ NICHOLS, Red		60	*Heart attack (in Las Vegas, NV)*
1991	NICHOLSON, Thomas D.		68	*Cancer*
1988	#+ Nico		49	*Cerebral hemorrhage from a bicycle fall (in Ibiza, Spain)*
1972	# NIELSEN, Asta		89	*Died in Copenhagen, Denmark*
1967	NIELSEN, Hans		56	*Paralysis illness (in Berlin, Germany)*
1975	NIESEN, Gertrude		62	*Died in Kaiser-Permanente Hospital, Glendale, CA*
1993	NIGH, Jane		68	*Stroke (in Los Angeles, CA)*
1989	NIGHTINGALE, Earl		68	*After heart surgery*
1992	NIGRO, Robert		45	*A.I.D.S.*
1995	NIJHOFF, Loudi		94	*Died in Amsterdam, Holland*
1950	+ NIJINSKY, Vaslav		62	*Nephritis (in London, England)*
1988	NILES, Ken		82	
1974	# NILSSON, Anna Q.		85	*Heart attack (in Hemet, CA)*
1994	#+ NILSSON, Harry		52	*Following a heart attack (in Agoura Hills, CA)*
• 1997	NINCHI, Ave		83	*Died at her home in Trieste, Italy of diabetes*
1988	NISSEN, Greta		82	*Parkinson's disease (in Montecito, CA)*
1983	+ NIVEN, David	★	73	*Amyotrophic lateral sclerosis (in Chateau d'Oex, Switzerland)*
1983	NIXON, Marion		78	*Complications following open-heart surgery (in Los Angeles, CA)*
1993	#+ NIXON, Pat		81	*Lung cancer*
1994	NOBLE, Leighton		82	*Died in Victoria, Canada*
1978	# NOBLE, Ray		70	*Cancer (in London, England)*
1980	+ NOLAN, Bob		72	*Heart attack (in Newport Beach, CA)*
1985	NOLAN, James		69	*Lung cancer (in Woodland Hills, CA)*

YEAR	NAME	AGE	CAUSE and/or PLACE OF DEATH
• 1998	NOLAN, Jeanette ☆	86	Stroke in Los Angeles, CA
1985	+ NOLAN, Lloyd	83	Lung cancer (in Los Angeles, CA)
1948	#+ NOLAN, Mary	42	Found dead at home (in Los Angeles, CA)
1968	# NOONAN, Tommy	45	After an operation for a malignant brain tumor (in Woodland Hills)
1988	NORDEN, Christine	63	Chest infection after heart surgery (in London, England)
1949	NORDEN, Cliff	26	Suicide (pills) in Hollywood, CA
• 1998	NORDEN, Joseph	84	Long illness, Motion Picture & T.V. Hosp., Woodland Hills, CA
• 1998	NORIS, Assia	85	After a brief illness at a hospital in San Remo, Italy
• 1996	NORMAN, Connie	47	Complications of A.I.D.S.
1951	# NORMAN, Josephine	46	Died in Roslyn, NY
1993	NORMAN, Lester	81	Heart failure (in London, England)
• 1998	NORMAN, Maidie	85	Lung cancer in San Jose, CA
1930	#+ NORMAND, Mabel	35	Tuberculosis and pneumonia (in Monrovia, CA)
1983	NORRIS, Kenneth	34	Injuries from a fall (in New York, NY)
1991	NORTH, Alex ☆	81	Pancreatic cancer (in Pacific Palisades, CA)
1990	NORTH, Edmund	79	Complications after surgery (in Santa Monica, CA)
1945	# NORTH, Joe	71	Died in Woodland Hills, CA
1935	NORTH, Wilfrid	82	After a brief illness (in Hollywood, CA)
1936	NORTHRUP, Harry S.	58	Died in Los Angeles, CA
1956	# NORTON, Barry	51	Heart attack (in Hollywood, CA)
1953	# NORTON, Edgar	84	Died in Woodland Hills, CA
1958	# NORTON, Jack	69	Respiratory ailment (in Saranac Lake, NY)
1948	# NORWOOD, Eille	87	
1959	NORWORTH, Jack	80	Stroke and heart ailment (in Laguna Beach, CA)
1979	NOVAES, Guiomar	84	
1988	NOVAK, Eva	90	Pneumonia (in Woodland Hills, CA)
1990	NOVAK, Jane	94	Complications caused by a stroke (in Woodland Hills, CA)
1968	#+ NOVARRO, Ramon	69	Murdered (bludgeoned) at his home in Hollywood Hills, CA
1990	NOVELLI, Santo Alex	73	Died in Philadelphia, PA
1951	# NOVELLO, Ivor	58	Coronary thrombosis (in London, England)
1982	NOVELLO, Jay	78	Died in North Hollywood, CA
1992	NOVELLO, Roselle	95	Died in Los Angeles, CA
• 1966	NOVIS, Donald	60	After a brief illness
1994	NOVOTNA, Jarmila	86	Natural causes (at her home in Manhattan, NY)
1980	NUGENT, Elliott	80	Died in his sleep (in New York, NY)
1947	NUGENT, J. C.	72	Coronary thrombosis (at the Lambs Club in New York City)
1993	+ NUREYEV, Rudolph	54	Cardiac complications from A.I.D.S. (in Paris, France)
1993	NUSSBAUM, Raphael	61	Cancer (in Burbank, CA)
1991	NUTE, Don	56	A.I.D.S. (in New York, NY)
1982	NUTT, Rev. Grady	47	Airplane crash
1993	NYBY, Christian ☆	80	Cardiac arrest in his sleep (in Temecula, CA)
1974	NYE, Carroll	72	Heart attack and kidney failure (in North Hollywood, CA)
	◑		
1969	# O'BRIEN, David "Dave"	57	Heart attack (on Catalina Island, CA)
1985	+ O'BRIEN, Edmond ★	69	Alzheimer's disease after suffering heart problems (in Inglewood, CA)
1987	O'BRIEN, Eloise Taylor	84	
1966	O'BRIEN, Eugene	83	Bronchial pneumonia (in Los Angeles, CA)
1985	O'BRIEN, George	85	Following a stroke (in Broken Arrow, CA)
1985	O'BRIEN, Kenneth	49	Cancer (in Los Angeles, CA)
1996	O'BRIEN, Liam ☆	83	Heart failure (at his home in Los Angeles, CA)
1983	#+ O'BRIEN, Pat	83	Massive heart attack
1983	O'BRIEN, Richard	65	Cancer
• 1997	O'BRIEN, Robert H.	93	

Deaths of Movie and Television Personalities — by Name

YEAR	NAME		AGE	CAUSE and/or PLACE OF DEATH
1947	#+ O'BRIEN, Tom		55	Died in Los Angeles, CA
1979	O'BRIEN-MOORE, Erin		77	Cancer (in Woodland Hills, CA)
1981	O'CONNELL, Arthur	☆	73	Alzheimer's disease (in Woodland Hills, CA)
1996	O'CONNELL, David J.		79	Chronic lung disease (in Santa Monica, CA)
1993	+ O'CONNELL, Helen (Devol)		73	Cancer (at a hospice in San Diego, CA)
1943	O'CONNELL, Hugh		44	After a heart attack (in Hollywood, CA)
1932	O'CONNER, Edward		70	Died in New York, NY
1959	O'CONNOR, Frank (director/actor)		71	After a long illness (in Hollywood, CA)
1971	O'CONNOR, Harry M.		98	Pneumonia, complicated by cardiac trouble (in Woodland Hills, CA)
1995	O'CONNOR, Hugh		33	Suicide (gunshot) after 16 yrs. of drug abuse (in Los Angeles)
• 1998	O'CONNOR, Kendall		90	Natural causes at his home in Burbank, CA
1991	O'CONNOR, Kevin		56	Cancer (in New York, NY)
1962	O'CONNOR, Robert Emmett		77	Burns after his cigarette ignited his clothing (in Hollywood, CA)
1959	+ O'CONNOR, Una		78	After a long illness (in New York, NY)
1989	O'DAVOREN, Vesey		100	Died in Los Angeles, CA
1987	# O'DAY, Molly		64	Cancer
1989	O'DAY, Nell		79	Cardiac arrest in her sleep (in Los Angeles, CA)
1970	# O'DONNELL, Cathy		44	Following a stroke (in Los Angeles, CA)
1992	O'DONNELL, Gene		81	Lung cancer (in Woodland Hills, CA)
1996	O'DONNELL, Lynn		43	Ovarian cancer (in San Francisco, CA)
1989	# O'HANLON, George		76	Stroke (in Burbank, CA)
1979	+ O'HARA, Barry J.		53	Injuries from a car accident (in Woodland Hills, CA)
• 1996	O'HARA, Jack		39	Airplane crash (TWA Flight 800, off Long Island, NY)
1993	O'HARA, Patrick J.		55	After a lengthy illness (in Burbank, CA)
1979	# O'HARA, Shirley		68	Cancer (in Hollywood, CA)
1994	# O'HARE, Brad		43	Complications of A.I.D.S. (in Manhattan, NY)
• 1997	O'HERLIHY, Michael		69	Died in his sleep in Ireland
1968	#+ O'KEEFE, Dennis		60	Lung cancer (in Santa Monica, CA)
1951	O'MADIGAN, Isabel		78	Died in Los Angeles, CA
1985	O'MALLEY, J. Pat		80	Heart condition (in CA) Do not confuse with Pat O'Malley, d. 1966
1966	# O'MALLEY, Pat		75	Died while eating dinner at home (in Van Nuys, CA)
1976	O'MALLEY, Rex		75	After a long illness (at the Mary Manning Walsh Home, NY)
1983	O'MOORE, Patrick		74	Following surgery (in Van Nuys, CA)
1971	# O'NEAL, Anne		77	Pancreatitis (in Woodland Hills, CA)
1992	# O'NEAL, Frederick		86	After a long illness (in New York, NY)
1994	O'NEAL, Patrick		66	Respiratory failure, tuberculosis and cancer (in Manhattan, NY)
1980	O'NEIL, Barbara	☆	69	Died in Cos Cob, CT
1968	# O'NEIL, Sally		57	Pneumonia (in Galesburg, IL)
• 1998	O'NEIL, Thomas F.		82	Heart failure at his home in Greenwich, Conn.
1961	O'NEILL, Henry		69	Died in Hollywood, CA
1957	O'NEILL, Jack		74	Died in Hollywood, CA
1945	O'NEILL, Peggy		21	Suicide after a lover's quarrel (sleeping pills) in Beverly Hills, CA
1987	O'PHELAN, Sean		33	Cancer (in Minneapolis, MN)
1946	# O'ROURKE, Brefni		57	Died in Ireland
1988	+ O'ROURKE, Heather		12	Septic shock, congenital bowel narrowing (in San Diego, CA)
1980	O'SHEA, Daniel T.		75	
1973	# O'SHEA, Michael		67	Heart attack (in Dallas, TX)
1960	O'SHEA, Oscar		78	Died in Hollywood, CA
1995	O'SHEA, Tessie		82	Congestive heart failure (in Leesburg, FL)
• 1998	+ O'SULLIVAN, Maureen		87	Heart attack in Scottsdale Memorial Hospital In Phoenix, AZ
1992	O'TOOLE, Ollie		79	After a long illness (in Los Angeles, CA)
1978	#+ OAKIE, Jack	☆	74	Aortic aneurysm (in Northridge, CA)
1983	OAKLAND, Simon		61	After a long illness (in Cathedral City, CA)

• New entry.   # Original name (Pt. 7).   + Interment (Pt. 5).

285

☆ Oscar nominee, ★ Oscar winner (Pt. 10)

Deaths of Movie and Television Personalities — by Name

YEAR	NAME	AGE	CAUSE and/or PLACE OF DEATH
1958	# OAKLAND, Vivien	63	Died in Hollywood, CA
1949	OAKMAN, Wheeler	59	Died in Van Nuys, CA
1982	OATES, Warren	53	Heart attack (in Los Angeles, CA)
1982	+ OBER, Philip	80	Heart failure (in Mexico City, Mexico)
1950	OBER, Robert	68	Died in New York
1979	#+ OBERON, Merle ☆	68	Stroke (in Los Angeles, CA)
1987	OBOLER, Arch	78	Stroke (in Westlake Village, CA)
1993	OCHS, Saul P.	82	Unreported causes (in North Hollywood, CA)
1991	OCKO, Daniel	78	Respiratory failure (in Argentina)
1955	ODEMAR, Fritz	65	Cancer (in Munich, Germany)
1963	+ ODETS, Clifford	57	Cancer (in Los Angeles, CA)
1963	OFFERMAN, George Jr.	45	Died in New York, NY
1992	OGAWA, Shinsuke	56	
1940	#+ OGLE, Charles	75	Died in Long Beach, CA
1995	OKADA, Eiji	75	Died in Japan
1938	#+ OLAND, Warner	57	Bronchial pneumonia (in Stockholm, Sweden)
1949	OLCOTT, Sidney	76	After a long illness (in Hollywood, CA)
1946	# OLDFIELD, Barney	68	Cerebral hemorrhage
1992	OLIVER, David	30	A.I.D.S. (in Los Angeles, CA)
1942	#+ OLIVER, Edna May ☆	59	Intestinal disorder (in Hollywood, CA)
1995	OLIVER, Gordon	84	Emphysema (at Cedars-Sinai Med. Ctr. in Los Angeles)
1932	OLIVER, Guy	54	After a long bout with cancer (in the Hollywood Hospital, CA)
• 1997	OLIVER, Maurine	93	Natural causes at Marycrest Manor Culver City
1990	# OLIVER, Susan	53	Cancer (in Woodland Hills, CA)
1988	# OLIVER, Sy	77	Died in New York, NY
1964	# OLIVER, Vic	66	Died in Johannesburg, South Africa
1988	OLIVER, Virgil	72	Died in Baton Rouge, LA
1989	+ OLIVIER, Laurence ★	82	Died in his sleep (in London, England)
1995	OLLE, Andrew	47	Brain tumor (after collapsing in his Sydney, Australia home)
1975	# OLMSTEAD, Gertrude	70	Died at her home in Beverly Hills, CA
1954	+ OLSEN, Moroni	65	Found dead at home of a probable heart attack (in Los Angeles, CA)
1963	#+ OLSEN, Ole	71	Kidney ailment (in Albuquerque, NM)
1985	OLSON, Johnny ("Come on down")	75	Brain hemorrhage
1987	ONDRA, Anny	84	Cerebral thrombosis (in Hamburg, Germany)
1996	# OPATOSHU, David	78	After a long illness (in Los Angeles, CA)
1957	# OPHULS, Max	54	Two-months after a heart attack (in Hamburg, Germany)
1988	+ ORBISON, Roy	52	Heart attack (in Hendersonville, TN)
1979	ORCHARD, Julian	49	After a brief illness (in London, England)
1957	ORLAMOND, William	89	Died in Copenhagen, Denmark
1987	# ORLANDO, Don	75	Heart attack while playing golf (in Glendale, CA)
1992	# ORLOFF, Thelma	76	Kidney failure (in Los Angeles, CA)
1985	ORMANDY, Eugene	85	
1994	ORMONT, David	79	Heart attack (at his home in West Hollywood, CA)
1948	# ORTES, Armand F.	68	Died in San Francisco, CA
1962	ORTH, Frank	82	Died in Hollywood, CA
• 1973	+ ORY, Edward "Kid"	?	
1956	ORZAZEWSKI, Kasia	67	Rheumatic heart disease (in Los Angeles, CA)
1958	#+ OSBORN, Lyn	32	Following brain surgery (in Los Angeles, CA)
1988	OSBORN, Paul	86	Died in New York, NY
1994	# OSBORNE, John ★	65	Heart attack (at a hospital in Shropshire, England)
1961	OSBORNE, Vivienne	64	Died in Los Angeles, CA
1932	# OSBOURNE, Jefferson	61	Cerebral hemorrhage (in Hondo, CA)
1964	# OSBOURNE, Lennie "Bud"	82	Died in Hollywood, CA

Deaths of Movie and Television Personalities — by Name

YEAR	NAME	AGE	CAUSE and/or PLACE OF DEATH
1969	# OSCAR, Henry	78	Died in London, England
1994	OSIRIS, Wanda "Wandissima"	89	Cardiac arrest (at her home in Milan, Italy)
1959	OSMOND, Hal	40	
1989	OSTRICHE, Muriel	93	Cardiac arrest in her sleep (in St. Petersburg, FL)
1989	OSWALD, Gerd	72	Cancer (in Los Angeles, CA)
1948	# OSWALDA, Ossi	49	Died in Prague, Czechoslovakia
1994	OTT, Dennis C.	36	A.I.D.S. (in Los Angeles, CA)
1942	OTTIANO, Rafaela	48	Heart attack (in Boston, MA)
1992	OULTON, Brian	84	Died in London, England
1949	+ OUSPENSKAYA, Maria ☆	73	Burned to death from a cigarette fire (in her Hollywood apartment)
1950	OVERMAN, Jack	34	Following a heart attack (in Hollywood, CA)
1943	OVERMAN, Lynne	55	Following two heart attacks (in Santa Monica, CA)
1967	OVERTON, Frank	49	Heart attack (in Pacific Palisades, CA)
1951	# OVEY, George	80	Died in Hollywood, CA
1965	OWEN, Catherine Dale	62	Died in New York, NY
1951	OWEN, Garry	48	Heart attack (in Hollywood, CA)
1980	OWEN, Malcolm	24	Overdose of heroin
1972	#+ OWEN, Reginald	85	Heart attack (in Boise, ID)
1966	#+ OWEN, Seena	71	After a brief illness (in Hollywood, CA)
1980	#+ OWENS, Jesse	66	Lung cancer (in Tucson, AZ)
1937	+ OWSLEY, Monroe	35	Heart attack (in Belmont, CA)
1989	OZERAY, Madeleine	78	Cancer (in Paris, France)

P

YEAR	NAME	AGE	CAUSE and/or PLACE OF DEATH
1967	PADDEN, Sarah	?	Died in London, England
1943	PADDOCK, Charles	42	Airplane crash (near Sitaka, Alaska)
1941	+ PADEREWSKI, Ignace	80	Pneumonia (in New York, NY)
1991	PADILLA, Ruben Dario Sr.	81	Cancer (in San Diego, CA)
1967	# PADULA, Vincent	66	Peritonitis (in Glendale, CA)
1991	PAGANO, Ronald F.	37	After a long illness (in Los Angeles, CA)
1983	# PAGE, Gale	72	Lung cancer (in Santa Monica, CA)
1987	PAGE, Geraldine ★	62	Heart attack (in New York, NY)
1990	# PAGE, Jean	95	Died in Los Angeles, CA
• 1998	PAGE, Ken	69	Cancer in Toronto, Canada
1974	# PAGE, Paul	70	Heart attack (in Hermosa Beach, CA)
1925	PAGET, Alfred	45	
1980	# PAGLIERO, Marcello	73	Cancer (in Paris, France)
1995	PAICH, Martin "Marty" Louis	70	Cancer (at his Santa Ynez, CA, home)
1954	PAIGE, Mabel	74	Died in Van Nuys, CA
1987	# PAIGE, Robert	76	Heart attack (in San Clemente, CA)
1966	PAIVA, Nestor	61	Cancer (in Sherman Oaks, CA)
1980	+ PAL, George	72	Heart attack (in Beverly Hills, CA)
1962	PALANGE, Inez	73	Died in Los Angeles, CA
• 1998	PALCA, Alfred	78	Cancer in New York
1993	PALEY, Irving	77	Heart attack (in Los Angeles, CA)
1990	PALEY, William S.	89	Apparent heart attack brought on by pneumonia
1990	PALK, Anna	48	Cancer (in London, England)
1934	PALLENBERG, Max	57	Airplane crash (near Karlovy Vary, Czechoslovakia)
1954	PALLETTE, Eugene	65	Throat cancer (in Los Angeles, CA)
• 1923	PALMER, Inda	70	Skeleton found five months after her mysterious death
1991	PALMER, John	75	After a short illness
1986	#+ PALMER, Lilli	71	Cancer and heart attack (in Los Angeles, CA)
1981	PALMER, Maria	57	Cancer (in Los Angeles, CA)
1986	PALMER, Norman	65	After a long illness (in Duarte, CA)

Deaths of Movie and Television Personalities — by Name

YEAR	NAME	AGE	CAUSE and/or PLACE OF DEATH
1964	# PALMER, Patricia	69	Died in Hollywood, CA
• 1998	PALMIERI, Dominic	58	Cancer at his home in Florida
1987	#+ PAM, Anita	77	Died in Los Angeles, CA
1990	PAN, Hermes	80	Apparent stroke (in Beverly Hills, CA)
1958	+ PANGBORN, Franklin	65	Died in Santa Monica, CA
• 1996	PANOZZO, John	47	Gastrointestinal hemorrhage
1937	PANZER, Paul	70	Heart trouble (in NYC) Do not confuse with Paul Wolfgang Panzer
1958	#+ PANZER, Paul Wolfgang	86	Died in Hollywood, CA (Do not confuse with Paul Panzer, d. 1937)
1944	PAPE, Edward Lionel	77	After a long illness (in Woodland Hills, CA)
• 1996	PAPP, Frank	?	Cancer (in New York, NY)
1990	PARADJANOV, Sergei	66	Cancer (in Yerevan, Armenia)
1955	PARDAVE, Joaquin	54	Died in Mexico City, Mexico
1984	PARFREY, Woodrow	61	Heart attack (in Los Angeles, CA)
1993	# PARHAM, Ernie	64	After a long illness (in Glen Falls, NY)
1991	# PARIS, Freddie	63	Cancer (in Sydney, Australia)
1986	PARIS, Jerry	60	Complications from a brain tumor (in Los Angeles, CA)
1959	# PARIS, Manuel	65	Congestive heart failure (in Woodland Hills, CA)
1960	PARKE, Macdonald	68	Died in London, England
1992	PARKER, Al	40	A.I.D.S. (Do not confuse with Albert Parker, d. 1974)
1974	PARKER, Albert	87	Died in London, England (Do not confuse with Al Parker, d. 1992)
1941	# PARKER, Barnett	54	Died in Los Angeles, CA
1971	# PARKER, Cecil	73	Died in Brighton, England
1993	PARKER, Cecilia	79	Died in Ventura, CA
1955	+ PARKER, Charlie "Bird"	34	Heart attack (in the New York apartment of a female friend)
1985	PARKER, Dennis	38	After a brief illness (in New York, NY)
1990	PARKER, Ed	59	Following a heart attack
1960	PARKER, Edwin	59	Heart attack (in Sherman Oaks, CA)
1962	# PARKER, Frank "Pinky"	70	Heart attack (in Hollywood, CA)
1972	PARKER, Lew	64	Cancer (in New York, NY)
1993	PARKIN, Leonard	64	Cancer of the spine (in England)
1992	PARKS, Bert	77	Lung cancer (in La Jolla, CA)
1975	#+ PARKS, Larry ☆	60	Heart attack (in Studio City, CA)
1958	# Parkyakarkus	54	Heart attack (in Los Angeles, CA)
1979	PARNELL, Emory	85	Heart attack (in Woodland Hills, CA)
1961	PARNELL, James	38	Found dead in his automobile (in Hollywood, CA)
1959	PARRISH, Helen	34	Cancer (in Hollywood, CA)
1995	PARRISH, Robert ★	79	Died at Southampton Hospital on Long Island, NY
1939	#+ PARROTT, James	46	Heart attack (in Hollywood, CA)
1985	PARRY, Harvey	85	Heart attack (in Sherman Oaks, CA)
1992	PARSONS, Lindsley Sr.	87	Heart failure (in Burbank, CA)
1972	#+ PARSONS, Louella (Martin)	91	Arteriosclerosis (in Santa Monica, CA)
1980	PARSONS, Milton	75	
1944	PARSONS, Percy	66	Died in England
• 1996	PASCAL, Christine	42	Suicide after suffering depression (jumped out window in Paris)
1954	PASCAL, Gabriel	60	After an illness of 3-weeks (in New York, NY)
1992	PASCAL, Jean-Claude	64	Following surgery for stomach cancer (in Paris, France)
1933	PASHA, Kalla	56	Died in Talmage, CA
1975	PASOLINI, Pier Paolo	53	Murdered (beaten) near Ostia, Italy
1989	PASS, Lenny	37	Died in New York, NY
1991	PASTERNAK, Joe	89	Parkinson's disease and other ailments (in Beverly Hills, CA)
1992	PASTOR, Guy	55	Heart attack
1970	# PATCH, Wally	82	Died in London, England
1978	+ PATERSON, Pat	67	Cancer (in Phoenix, AZ)

• New entry. # Original name (Pt. 7). + Interment (Pt. 5).   288   ☆ Oscar nominee, ★ Oscar winner (Pt. 10)

Deaths of Movie and Television Personalities — by Name

YEAR	NAME	AGE	CAUSE and/or PLACE OF DEATH
1957	PATHE, Charles	93	Died in Monte Carlo, Monaco
1950	PATON, Charles	64	
1944	PATON, Stuart	59	Died in Woodland Hills, CA
1987	PATRICK, Dorothy	65	Cancer and heart attack (in Los Angeles, CA)
1980	# PATRICK, Gail	69	Leukemia (in Hollywood, CA)
1923	PATRICK, Jerome	40	Heart disease (in New York)
1982	+ PATRICK, Lee (Wood)	76	Heart seizure (in Laguna Hills, CA)
1981	# PATRICK, Nigel	68	Cancer (at a hospital in London, England)
1950	PATRICOLA, Tom	55	Following brain surgery (in Pasadena, CA)
1996	PATTEN, Luana	57	Lung cancer (in Long Beach, CA)
1966	PATTERSON, Elizabeth	91	Died in Los Angeles, CA
1975	# PATTERSON, Hank	86	Bronchial pneumonia (in Woodland Hills, CA)
1991	PATTISON, Arthur	60	Cancer
1982	PATTON, Mary	66	Cancer (in Santa Monica, CA)
1951	PATTON, William "Bill"	57	Died in Los Angeles, CA
1962	# PAUL, Val	75	Died in Hollywood, CA
1933	PAULIG, Albert	60	Heart trouble (in Berlin, Germany)
1954	PAULSEN, Harald	59	Heart attack (in Hamburg, Germany)
1997	PAULSEN, Pat	69	Colon and Brain cancer in Mexico
1989	PAULSON, Al	67	Heart failure
1931	PAVLOVA, Anna	46	Pleurisy (in The Hague, Netherlands)
1936	PAWLE, Lennox	63	Cerebral hemorrhage (at a hospital in Hollywood, CA)
1988	PAWLEY, Edward	84	Died in Charlottesville, VA
1952	PAWLEY, William	46	Died in New York
1973	# PAXINOU, Katina ★	72	Cancer (in Athens, Greece)
1965	PAYNE, Douglas	90	Died in England
1953	PAYNE, Edna	61	Liver ailment (in Los Angeles, CA)
1989	PAYNE, John	77	Congestive heart failure (in Malibu, CA)
1953	# PAYNE, Lou	77	Died in Woodland Hills, CA
1964	PAYSON, Blanche	83	Died in Hollywood, CA
1967	PAYTON, Barbara	39	Heart attack (in San Diego, CA)
1955	# PAYTON, Claude	72	Died in Los Angeles, CA
1970	PEABODY, Eddie	58	Cerebral thrombosis (in Covington, KY)
1966	PEACOCK, Kim	65	Heart attack (in Emsworth, England)
1918	PEACOCK, Lillian	27	From previous filming injuries (in Los Angeles, CA)
1993	PEALE, (Rev.) Norman Vincent	95	Following a stroke (at his farm in Pawling, NY)
1961	PEARCE, Al	62	Complications from an ulcer operation
1966	PEARCE, Alice	46	Cancer (in Los Angeles, CA)
1940	# PEARCE, George C.	75	Died in Los Angeles, CA
1984	PEARCE, Muriel	85	After a long illness (in Natick, MA)
1964	# PEARCE, Peggy	69	Died in Hollywood, CA
1966	PEARCE, Vera	69	Died in London, England
1993	PEARDON, Patricia	69	Pneumonia (at St. Luke's Hospital in Manhattan, NY)
1996	# PEARL, Minnie	83	Following a stroke (in Nashville, TN)
1969	#+ PEARSON, Drew	71	Died in Washington, D.C.
1966	PEARSON, Lloyd	68	Heart attack (in London, England)
1958	PEARSON, Virginia	70	Uremic poisoning (in Los Angeles, CA)
1985	PEARY, Harold "Gildersleeve"	76	Heart attack (in Torrance, CA)
1992	PECK, Ed	75	Heart attack (in Los Angeles, CA)
1959	+ PECKHAM, Francis Miles	66	Died in New York, NY
1984	PECKINPAH, Sam	59	Following several heart attacks (in Inglewood, CA)
1984	PEEPLES, Dennis	50	Heart attack
1984	PEERCE, Jan	80	Pneumonia and coma (in New York, NY)

• New entry. # Original name (Pt. 7). + Interment (Pt. 5).

☆ Oscar nominee, ★ Oscar winner (Pt. 10)

Deaths of Movie and Television Personalities — by Name

YEAR	NAME	AGE	CAUSE and/or PLACE OF DEATH
1975	PEERS, Joan	64	
1962	# PEIL, Edward Jr.	54	After a 2-year illness
1958	# PEIL, Edward Sr.	70	Died in Hollywood, CA
1983	PELISH, Thelma	55	Died in Woodland Hills, CA
1987	+ PELLER, Clara	86	Died in her sleep (at her home in Chicago, IL)
1977	PELT, Timothy "Tim"	39	Automobile accident (in Pacific Palisades, CA)
1950	PEMBERTON, Brock	64	After a heart attack at his home (in New York, NY)
1972	# PENA, Julio	60	Heart attack (in Marbella, Spain)
1986	PENDER, Stephen	35	Complications from A.I.D.S. (in Los Angeles, CA)
1967	PENDLETON, Nat	68	Heart attack (in San Diego, CA)
1992	PENDRELL, Ernest	?	Cancer (in New York, NY)
1975	# PENN, Leonard	68	Heart attack (in Los Angeles, CA)
1941	#+ PENNER, Joe	35	Heart attack (in Philadelphia, PA)
1964	PENNICK, Jack	68	After a year's illness (in Hollywood, CA)
1971	+ PENNINGTON, Ann	78	Died in Manhattan, NY
1931	PENROD, Alexander G.	?	Killed in a ship explosion while on location in the Antarctic
1930	PENWARDEN, Duncan	50	Died in Jackson Heights, NY
1994	+ PEPPARD, George	65	Pneumonia (at UCLA Medical Center, CA)
1969	PEPPER, Barbara	53	Coronary thrombosis (in Panorama City, CA)
1993	# PEPPER, Buddy	70	Heart failure
1993	+ PEPPLE, Sydney Chester	83	Died at Scripps Ocean View Hospital, Encinitas, CA
1934	# PERCIVAL, Walter C.	46	Died of complications from an illness (in Hollywood, CA)
1973	PERCY, Eileen	72	After a long bout with cancer (in Beverly Hills, CA)
1957	# PERCY, Esme	69	Died in Brighton, England
1993	PEREDES, Daniel	46	A.I.D.S. (in Los Angeles, CA)
1983	+ PEREIRA, Hal	78	Died in Los Angeles, CA
1978	+ PERFECT, Rose	82	Died in Hollywood, CA
1994	PERILLI, Ivo	92	After suffering a stroke (in Rome, Italy)
1965	PERINAL, Georges	68	Died in London, England
1940	PERIOLAT, George	63	Suicide (arsenic) at his home in Los Angeles, CA
1992	+ PERKINS, Anthony ☆	60	Complications from A.I.D.S. (at his home in Hollywood, CA)
1986	# PERKINS, Marlin	81	Lymphatic cancer
1937	PERKINS, Osgood	45	Apparent heart attack after tonsilitis (in Washington, D.C.)
1977	PERKINS, Voltaire	80	Apparent heart attack (in Los Angeles, CA)
1967	PERRIN, Jack	71	Heart attack (in Hollywood, CA)
1989	PERRIN, Vic	73	Cancer (in Los Angeles, CA)
1962	PERRINS, Leslie	60	Died in Esher, England
1946	#+ PERRY, Antoinette	58	Heart attack (in New York, NY)
1995	PERRY, Frank	65	Prostate cancer (at Mem. Sloan-Kettering Cancer Ctr. in NY)
• 1996	PERRY, Joan (Cohn)	85	Emphysema (at her home in Montecito, CA)
1962	PERRY, Robert E. "Bob"	82	Died in Hollywood, CA
1954	PERRY, Walter	85	Died in Los Angeles, CA
• 1996	PERTWEE, Jon	76	Undisclosed causes (in New York, NY)
1991	PERTWEE, Michael	74	Undisclosed causes (in London, England)
1994	PETERKOCH, Lydia	29	Automobile accident (in Los Angeles, CA)
1965	PETERS, Ann	45	Heart attack (in Paris, France)
1967	# PETERS, House Sr.	87	Died at M.P.C. Hospital, Woodland Hills, CA
1992	PETERS, Lennie	59	
1994	PETERS, Michael	46	Complications from A.I.D.S. (in Los Angeles, CA) (not orchestra leader)
1916	PETERS, Page E.	?	Drowned (at Hermosa Beach, CA)
1959	PETERS, Ralph	56	Died in Hollywood, CA
1952	#+ PETERS, Susan ☆	31	Bronchial pneumonia and chronic kidney infection (in Visalia, CA)
1971	PETERS, Werner	51	Heart attack (in Wiesbaden, West Germany)

Deaths of Movie and Television Personalities — by Name

YEAR	NAME	AGE	CAUSE and/or PLACE OF DEATH
• 1998	PETERSEN, Don	70	*Lung and liver disease in Pittsfield, MA*
• 1996	PETERSON, Arthur	83	*Alzheimer's disease (in Pasadena, CA)*
1979	# PETERSON, Dorothy	78	*Died in Los Angeles, CA*
• 1998	PETERSON, Louis	76	*Lung cancer at his home in Manhattan, NY*
1930	Petey ("Our Gang" dog)	7	*Arsenic poisoning (in Los Angeles, CA)*
• 1997	PETRIE, George O.	85	*Lymphoma in Los Angeles, CA*
1948	# PETRIE, Hay	53	*Died in London, England*
1968	PETRIE, Howard A.	61	*After a long illness (at a hospital in Keene, NH)*
1977	# PETROVA, Olga	91	*Died in Clearwater, FL*
1966	PETTINGELL, Frank	75	*Died in London, England*
1995	PETTIT, Tom	64	*Complications after surgery to repair a ruptured aorta (in NYC)*
1992	# PETTYJOHN, Angelique	48	*Cancer (in Las Vegas, NV)*
1918	PEYTON, Lawrence R. "Larry"	23	*Killed in action in France during World War I*
1992	PEYTON, Rev. Patrick	83	*Renal failure*
1993	PHELPS, Donald	61	*A.I.D.S. (in West Hollywood, CA)*
1953	PHELPS, Lee	58	*Died in Culver City, CA*
1993	+ PHILBIN, Mary	90	*Complications from Alzheimer's disease (in Huntington Beach, CA)*
1982	PHILBROOK, James	58	*Died in Los Angeles, CA*
1959	PHILIPE, Gerard	36	*Heart attack and liver cancer (in Paris, France)*
1975	PHILIPS, Mary	74	*Cancer (in Santa Monica, CA)*
1982	# PHILLIPS, Barney	68	*After a brief illness (in Los Angeles, CA)*
1980	PHILLIPS, Dorothy	90	*Pneumonia (in Woodland Hills, CA)*
1965	PHILLIPS, Edward N.	65	*Killed by a car while crossing the street (in North Hollywood, CA)*
1915	# PHILLIPS, Edwin R.	?	*Pneumonia and other complications (in Coney Island Hospital, NY)*
1993	PHILLIPS, Linn III	45	*Heart attack (in Denver, Colorado)*
1963	PHILLIPS, Mina	77	*Heart ailment (in New Orleans, LA)*
• 1997	PHILLIPS, Mirian	98	*Died at Actors' Equity Home in NJ of Alzheimer's disease*
1931	PHILLIPS, Norman Sr.	38	*Heart attack (in Culver City, CA)*
1930	PHILLIPS, Tubby	45	*Automobile accident (in London, England)*
• 1998	PHILLIPS, Webster	83	*Cancer at Cedars-Sinai Medical Center in Los Angeles, CA*
1980	PHILLPOTTS, Ambrosine	68	*Died in Ascot, England*
1980	PHIPPS, Nicholas	66	*Died in London, England*
1978	# PHIPPS, Sally	67	*Died at Long Island College Hospital, NY*
1986	# PHOENIX, Pat	62	*Lung cancer (in Manchester, England)*
1993	+ PHOENIX, River	23	*Acute multiple drug intoxication (at a niteclub in West Hollywood, CA)*
1963	#+ PIAF, Edith	47	*Internal hemorrhage (in Plascassier, France)*
1976	+ PIATIGORSKY, Gregor	73	*Died in Los Angeles, CA*
1991	PIAZZA, Ben	58	*Cancer (in Sherman Oaks, CA)*
1973	PICASSO, Pablo	91	*Died in Mougins, France*
• 1970	+ PICCOLO, Brian	27	*Cancer*
1954	PICHEL, Irving	63	*Following a heart attack (in Hollywood, CA)*
1931	PICK, Lupu	45	*Food poisoning (in Berlin, Germany)*
1959	PICKARD, Helena	59	*Died in Oxfordshire, England*
1983	# PICKENS, Slim	64	*Pneumonia and brain tumor (in Modesto, CA)*
1933	#+ PICKFORD, Jack	36	*Multiple neuritis (in Paris, France)*
1936	#+ PICKFORD, Lottie	41	*Heart attack (in Brentwood, CA)*
1979	#+ PICKFORD, Mary ★	86	*Cerebral hemorrhage (in Santa Monica, CA)*
1978	PICKLES, Wilfrid	73	*Died in Brighton, England*
1982	PICKMAN, Kathryn	60	*Cancer*
1992	PICON, Molly	94	*Died in her sleep following Alzheimer's disease (in Lancaster, PA)*
1984	+ PIDGEON, Walter ☆	87	*Series of strokes (in Santa Monica, CA)*
1963	PIEL, Harry	71	*Died in Munich, Germany*
1993	PIERCE, Edward	77	*Natural causes (in Jamesport, NY)*

YEAR	NAME	AGE	CAUSE and/or PLACE OF DEATH
1968	+ PIERCE, Jack P.	79	Died in Hollywood, CA
1991	PIERCE, Webb	69	Pancreatic cancer
1955	+ PIERLOT, Francis	78	Heart ailment (in Hollywood, CA)
1975	PIERSON, Arthur	73	Died at St. John's Hospital in Santa Monica, CA
1962	PIGOTT, Tempe	78	Died in Hollywood, CA
1963	PILOTTO, Camillo	73	Died in Rome, Italy
1938	PINCHOT, Rosamond	33	Suicide (carbon monoxide poisoning) in Old Brookfield, NY
1950	PINE, Ed	46	Died at the Motion Picture Country Home, Woodland Hills, CA
1934	PINERO, Arthur Wing	79	Died in London, England
1988	PINERO, Miguel	41	Cirrhosis of the liver (in New York, NY)
1957	#+ PINZA, Ezio	65	Following a series of strokes (in Stamford, CT)
1979	PIOUS, Minerva	75	
1979	PIPER, Frederick	77	Died in London, England
1990	PIPPIN, Nick	35	A.I.D.S. (in New York, NY)
1996	PISTILLI, Luigi	66	Suicide at his home before appearing on stage (in Milan, Italy)
1976	PISU, Mario	66	Cerebral hemorrhage (in Castelli Romani, Italy)
1990	PITOEFF, Sacha	70	Heart failure (in Paris, France)
1963	+ PITTS, Zazu (Woodall)	65	Cancer (in Hollywood, CA)
• 1996	PIVNICK, Marlene	59	Cancer (at her home in Encino, CA)
1993	PLAGE, Dieter	57	Died in an airplane filming accident in the Sumatra rain forest
1974	PLATT, Edward C. "Ed"	58	Heart attack (in Santa Monica, CA)
1934	PLAYFAIR, Nigel	60	Died in London, England
1937	PLAYTER, Wellington	57	Died in Oakland, CA
1995	PLEASENCE, Donald	75	After surgery to replace a heart valve (at home in France)
1960	# PLUMB, E. Hay	77	Died in England
1928	PLUMER, Lincoln	51	Heart disease (in Hollywood, CA)
1980	POE, James ★	58	Heart attack (at his home in Malibu, CA)
1952	# POFF, Lon	82	Died in Los Angeles, CA
1979	# POHLMANN, Eric	66	Died in Bad Reichenhall, Germany
1992	POIRET, Jean	65	Heart attack (in Suresnes, France)
1976	POLANSKI, Goury	83	Cancer (in Hollywood, CA)
• 1997	POLIER, Dan A.	78	Heart failure (in Palm Desert, CA)
1987	POLK, David	55	Cancer (in Los Angeles, CA)
1993	POLK, Lee	69	Leukemia
1971	POLLACK, Ben	67	Suicide (hanged himself in his bathroom) in Palm Springs, CA
1978	# POLLARD, Daphne	87	Died in Los Angeles, CA
1934	+ POLLARD, Harry	55	Cancer (in Pasadena, CA) Do not confuse with Harry "Snub" Pollard
1962	#+ POLLARD, Harry "Snub"	75	Heart attack (in Burbank, CA) Do not confuse with Harry Pollard
1961	# POLO, Eddie	86	Heart attack at a restaurant (in Hollywood, CA)
1966	POMMER, Erich	77	Died in Hollywood, CA
1989	POMPEII, James S.	51	After a long illness (in New York, NY)
1990	POND, Barbara	?	Lung cancer
1976	# PONS, Lily	77	Pancreatic cancer (in Dallas, TX)
1981	PONSELLE, Rosa	84	
1957	# PONTO, Erich	71	Died in Stuttgart, Germany
1986	POOLE, Roy	62	Died in Mount Kisco, NY
1991	POPKIN, Harry M.	85	Cancer (in Santa Monica, CA)
1992	+ PORCARO, Jeff	38	After an apparent allergic reaction to pesticides
1946	PORCASI, Paul	66	After a long illness (in Hollywood, CA)
1960	# PORTEN, Henny	70	After a long illness (in Berlin, Germany)
1964	+ PORTER, Cole	71	Following surgery for a kidney stone (in Santa Monica, CA)
1978	PORTER, Dick	45	Heart attack (in Sedalia, MO)
• 1997	PORTER, Don	84	Natural causes in Los Angeles, CA

Deaths of Movie and Television Personalities — by Name

YEAR	NAME	AGE	CAUSE and/or PLACE OF DEATH
1941	+ PORTER, Edwin S.	71	After a long illness (in New York, NY)
1995	PORTER, Eric	67	Colon cancer (at a hospital in north London, England)
1969	PORTMAN, Eric	66	Heart ailment (in St. Veep, England)
1952	POST, Charles A. "Buddy"	55	Died in Los Angeles, CA
• 1971	+ POST, Edith Sedqwick	28	
1968	POST, Guy Bates	92	Died in Hollywood, CA
1935	+ POST, Wiley	50	Airplane crash (near Barrow, Alaska)
1989	POST, William Jr.	88	Pulmonary embolism (in Oklahoma City, OK)
1994	# POTAMKIN, Luba	73	Alzheimer's disease (at her home in Miami, FL)
1947	+ POTEL, Victor "Vic"	57	Died in Hollywood, CA
1995	POTTER, Allan M.	75	Cancer (in Stuart, FL)
1994	POTTER, Dennis	59	Pancreatic and liver cancer (in Gloucestershire, England)
1977	# POTTER, H. C.	73	After a brief illness (in New York, NY)
1925	POWELL, David	39	Pneumonia after a nervous breakdown (in a NY Sanitarium)
1963	#+ POWELL, Dick	58	Cancer (in Hollywood, CA)
1982	+ POWELL, Eleanor	69	Cancer (in Beverly Hills, CA)
1944	#+ POWELL, Lee B.	36	Killed in action in the S. Pacific, during W.W.II
1990	POWELL, Michael	84	Cancer (in Avening, England)
1937	+ POWELL, Richard	39	Fractured skull from an auto accident (in Hollywood, CA)
1950	# POWELL, Russ	75	Arteriosclerosis (in Woodland Hills, CA)
1984	+ POWELL, William ☆	91	Cardiac arrest in his sleep (in Palm Springs, CA)
1931	# POWER, F. Tyrone	62	Heart attack (in Hollywood, CA)
1966	POWER, Hartley	71	After a long illness (in London, England)
1968	# POWER, Paul	65	Died in Hollywood, CA
1958	#+ POWER, Tyrone	44	Heart attack (in Madrid, Spain)
1991	POWERS, Tim	34	A.I.D.S. (in New York, NY)
1955	POWERS, Tom	65	Heart ailment (in Hollywood, CA)
1994	POZZI, Moana	33	Liver cancer (in Lyon, France)
1981	PRACK, Rudolf	77	Died in Vienna, Austria
1972	PRAGER, Stanley	55	While on a business trip (in Hollywood, CA)
1958	# PRATHER, Lee	67	During surgery (in Los Angeles, CA)
1991	PRATT, James C.	86	Pneumonia (in Los Angeles, CA)
1941	PRATT, Purnell B.	54	Died in Hollywood, CA
1995	PRECHT, Andrew	34	Cause unreported (in Grenada)
1984	PREISSER, June	61	Automobile collision (in Boca Raton, FL)
1979	PREJEAN, Albert	85	Heart attack (in Paris, France)
1986	PREMINGER, Otto ☆	79	Cancer (in Manhattan, NY)
1992	PRENTICE, Keith	52	Cancer (in Kettering, OH)
1979	PRENTISS, Eleanor	67	Died in New York, NY
• 1997	PRESCOTT, Eleanor	50	Heart failure (in Bayside, NY)
1977	#+ PRESLEY, Elvis	42	Cardiac arrhythmia (possibly due to drug abuse) in Memphis, TN
1988	PRESSBURGER, Emeric	85	Bronchial pneumonia (in England)
1987	# PRESTON, Robert	68	Lung cancer (in Santa Barbara, CA)
1992	PRESTON, Wayde	62	Cancer (in Lovelock, NV)
• 1998	PRESTON, William	77	After a brief illness in New York
1978	PRETTY, Arline	84	Died in Hollywood, CA
1993	PREVIN, Steve	68	Unreported causes (in Palm Desert, CA)
1937	# PREVOST, Marie	38	Acute alcoholism (in Los Angeles, CA)
1973	# PRICE, Dennis	58	Died in Guernsey, Channel Islands
1991	PRICE, Gilbert	48	Found dead of diabetic coma (in Vienna, Austria)
1964	# PRICE, Hal	77	
1943	# PRICE, Kate	70	After a long illness (in Woodland Hills, CA)
1987	PRICE, Kenny	?	

• New entry. # Original name (Pt. 7). + Interment (Pt. 5).   293   ☆ Oscar nominee, ★ Oscar winner (Pt. 10)

Deaths of Movie and Television Personalities — by Name

	YEAR	NAME	AGE	CAUSE and/or PLACE OF DEATH
	1970	# PRICE, Nancy	90	*Died in Worthing, England*
	1955	PRICE, Stanley L.	55	*Heart attack (in Hollywood, CA)*
	1993	+ PRICE, Vincent	82	*Lung cancer (at his home in Hollywood Hills, CA)*
	1976	PRICKETT, Maudie	63	*Uremic poisoning (in Pasadena, CA)*
	1993	PRIESTLY, Jack	66	*Unreported causes (at his home in Los Angeles, CA)*
	1991	PRIM, Suzy	95	*Suicide (in Boulogne-Billancourt, France)*
	1978	+ PRIMA, Louis	66	*Pneumonia (in New Orleans, LA)*
•	1996	PRINCE, William	83	*Unreported causes (at Phelps Memorial Hosp. in Tarrytown, NY)*
	1989	# PRINGLE, Aileen	94	*Died in New York, NY*
	1977	# PRINTEMPS, Yvonne	81	*Complications after fracturing her thighbone (in Paris, France)*
	1977	#+ PRINZE, Freddie	22	*Suicide (gunshot) in Hollywood, CA*
	1954	# PRIOR, Herbert	87	*Died in London, England*
	1986	PROACH, Henry	66	
	1974	+ PROHASKA, Janos	52	*Airplane crash (in Inyo County, CA)*
	1953	+ PROKOFIEV, Sergei	62	*Cerebral hemorrhage (in Moscow, Russia)*
	1952	PROSSER, Hugh	46	*Automobile crash (near Gallup, NM)*
	1956	PROUTY, Jed	77	*After a brief illness (in New York, NY)*
	1991	# PROVENZA, Sal	45	*Lymphoma (in New York, NY)*
•	1996	PROWSE, Juliet	59	*Pancreatic cancer (at her home in Holmby Hills, CA)*
	1967	PRUD'HOMME, Cameron	75	*After a long illness (at a hospital in Pompton Plains, NJ)*
	1972	# PRUD'HOMME, George	71	*Brain tumor (in Los Angeles, CA)*
	1974	PRYOR, Roger	72	*Heart attack (while visiting in Puerta Vallarta, Mexico)*
	1953	PUDOVKIN, Vsevolod	60	*Natural causes (in Moscow, Russia)*
	1975	PUGLIA, Frank	83	*Died in South Pasadena, CA*
	1968	PUIG, Eva G.	74	*Diabetes and heart failure (in Panorama City, CA)*
	1983	+ PULEO, Johnny	75	*Respiratory failure (in Washington, D.C.)*
	1972	PURCELL, Irene	70	*Died at her home in Racine, WI*
	1985	PURCELL, Noel	84	*Died in Dublin, Ireland*
	1944	PURCELL, Richard "Dick"	35	*Heart attack playing golf (in Hollywood, CA)*
	1953	# PURDELL, Reginald	56	*After a long illness (in London, England)*
	1960	PURDY, Constance	75	*Arteriosclerosis (in Los Angeles, CA)*
	1982	PURSELL, Robert	26	*Apparent suicide (hung himself from a tree) in Levittown, PA*
	1958	+ PURVIANCE, Edna	63	*After a long illness (in Woodland Hills, CA)*
•	1996	PUTTERMAN, William Zev	67	*Cancer (in Tucson, AZ)*
•	1997	+ PYLE, Denver	77	*Lung cancer at Providence St. Joseph Medical Ctr., Burbank, CA*
	1970	PYNE, Joe	45	*Lung cancer (in Los Angeles, CA)*
		Q		
	1987	# QUALEN, John	87	*Heart failure (in Torrance, CA)*
	1958	QUARTERMAINE, Charles	80	*Died in England*
	1989	QUAYLE, Anthony ☆	76	*Cancer (in London, England)*
	1989	QUERTERMOUS, Charlie	41	*Cancer (in Hollywood, CA)*
•	1998	QUESTEL, Mae	89	*At her home in Manhattan, NY*
	1964	QUIGLEY, Charles	58	*Cirrhosis of the liver (in Los Angeles, CA)*
	1990	QUILLAN, Eddie	83	*Cancer (in Burbank, CA)*
•	1965	QUIMBY, Fred ★	79	*Natural causes*
	1989	QUINE, Richard	68	*Suicide (shot himself) at his home in Los Angeles, CA*
	1919	QUINN, James	35	*Accidental (?) asphyxiation (gas) Do not confuse with Jimmie Quinn*
	1988	QUINN, Louis	73	*After a brief illness (in Los Angeles, CA)*
	1967	QUINN, Tony	67	*Died in London, England (Do not confuse with Anthony Quinn)*
	1926	QUIRK, William "Billy"	45	*After a 2-yr. illness (at a rest home in Hollywood, CA)*
		R		
	1993	# RA, Sun	79	*Circulatory problems after a series of strokes*
	1988	RAAB, Kurt	46	*A.I.D.S. (in Hamburg, Germany)*

Deaths of Movie and Television Personalities — by Name

YEAR	NAME	AGE	CAUSE and/or PLACE OF DEATH
1974	# RABAGLIATI, Alberto	67	Cerebral thrombosis (in Rome, Italy)
1998	RABB, Ellis	67	Heart failure in Tennessee
1943	+ RACHMANINOFF, Sergei	69	Cancer and pneumonia (in Beverly Hills, CA)
1992	RACKMIL, Milton R.	89	Stroke
1996	RADASKY, Michael J.	43	Automobile accident (in Texas)
1976	RADD, Ronald	47	Brain hemorrhage (in Toronto, Canada)
1952	RADFORD, Basil	55	Heart attack (in London, England)
1989	+ RADNER, Gilda	42	Ovarian cancer (in Los Angeles, CA)
1957	RAE, Jack	58	Heart attack (in Hollywood, CA)
1976	# RAEBURN, Frances	?	Heart failure (in Hollywood, CA)
1971	# RAFFERTY, Chips	62	Heart attack (in Sydney, Australia)
1990	# RAFFETTO, Michael	91	Natural causes (in Berkeley, CA)
1980	#+ RAFT, George	85	Leukemia (in Los Angeles, CA)
1946	# RAGLAND, John "Rags"	40	Uremia (in Los Angeles, CA)
1991	RAGNI, Gerome	48	Cancer (in New York, NY)
1957	# RAHM, Knute	81	Heart disease (in Los Angeles, CA)
1946	# RAIMU, Jules	62	Heart attack (in Neuilly-sur-Seine, France)
1979	RAINE, Jack	82	Died in South Laguna, CA
1988	RAINES, Ella	66	Throat cancer (in Sherman Oaks, CA)
1967	+ RAINS, Claude ☆	77	Intestinal hemorrhage (in Laconia, NH)
1984	RAISCH, William	79	Lung cancer (in Santa Monica, CA)
1959	# RAKER, Lorin	68	Cancer (in Woodland Hills, CA)
1923	# RALEIGH, Saba	57	
1944	# RALPH, Jessie	79	After a lingering illness (in Gloucester, MA)
1994	RALSTON, Esther	91	After a short illness (in Ventura, CA)
1992	RALSTON, Howard	?	After a brief illness (in Los Angeles, CA)
1967	RALSTON, Jobyna	62	After a long illness (in Woodland Hills, CA)
1988	# RAMAGE, Cecil	93	Cardiac arrest in his sleep (in Scotland)
1970	+ RAMBEAU, Marjorie ☆	80	Died in Palm Springs, CA
1994	RAMBO, Dack	53	A.I.D.S. (in Delano, CA)
1967	# RAMBO, Dirk	25	Burned to death in a car accident (in Los Angeles, CA)
1966	# RAMBOVA, Natacha	69	Dietary complications (in Pasadena, CA)
1992	RAMOS, Lou	51	After a brief illness (in New York, NY)
1988	RAMSEY, Anne ☆	59	Throat cancer (in Los Angeles, CA)
1993	RAMSEY, Gordon	63	Cancer (at his home in New York, NY)
1929	# RAMSEY, John Nelson	65	Heart disease (in London, England)
1976	# RAMSEY-HILL, C. S.	84	Died in Van Nuys, CA
1940	RAND, John F.	67	Died in Hollywood, CA
1979	#+ RAND, Sally	75	Heart failure (in Glendora, CA)
1945	#+ RANDALL, Addison "Jack"	38	Fell to his death from a horse, while filming (in Canoga Park, CA)
1996	RANDALL, Dick	70	Heart failure after a series of strokes (in London, England)
1984	RANDALL, Sue	49	Cancer of the lungs and larynx (in Philadelphia, PA)
1967	+ RANDOLPH, Amanda	65	Cerebral hemorrhage (in Durate, CA)
1930	# RANDOLPH, Anders	60	Following a relapse after a recent operation (in Hollywood, CA)
1993	RANDOLPH, Donald	87	Pneumonia (in Los Angeles, CA)
1973	RANDOLPH, Isabel	82	Cancer (in Burbank, CA)
1980	+ RANDOLPH, Lillian	65	Cancer (in Arcadia, CA)
1972	RANK, J. Arthur	83	Died in Winchester, England
1947	#+ RANKIN, Arthur	46	After a cerebral hemorrhage (in Hollywood, CA)
1946	RANKIN, Doris	66	Died in Washington, D.C.
1949	+ RAPF, Harry	67	Heart attack (in Manhattan, NY)
1991	RAPF, Matthew	71	After an attack of the flu
1983	RAPHAELSON, Samson	87	Died in Manhattan, NY

YEAR	NAME		AGE	CAUSE and/or PLACE OF DEATH
1990	RAPPAPORT, David		38	Apparent suicide (gunshot) in Laurel Canyon, CA
1921	+ RAPPE, Virginia		25	Ruptured bladder (in San Francisco, CA)
1991	RASCEL, Renato		78	Heart failure (in Rome, Italy)
1976	# RASP, Fritz		85	Cancer (in Graefelfing, Germany)
1991	RASULALA, Thalmus		55	Heart attack after suffering from leukemia (in Albuquerque, NM)
1956	RASUMNY, Mikhail		65	Died in Los Angeles, CA
1948	# RATCLIFFE, E. J.		85	Died in Los Angeles, CA
1967	#+ RATHBONE, Basil	☆	75	Heart attack (in New York, NY)
1960	RATOFF, Gregory		63	Circulatory problems (in Solothurn, Switzerland)
1925	# RATTENBERRY, Harry		65	Died at his home in Hollywood, CA
1977	RATTIGAN, Terence		66	Bone marrow cancer (in London, England)
1992	RAWLINGS, Richard Sr.		75	After a brief illness (in Los Angeles, CA)
1947	RAWLINS, Herbert		?	
• 1997	RAWLINS, John		94	Pneumonia in Arcadia, CA
1988	RAWLINS, Lester		63	Heart attack (in New York, NY)
1953	RAWLINSON, Herbert		67	Lung cancer (in Woodland Hills, CA)
1994	RAWSON, Ron		76	Cancer (at his home in Cohasset, MA)
1991	# RAY, Aldo		64	Complications from throat cancer and pneumonia (in San Francisco)
1955	RAY, Barbara		40	Leukemia (in Los Angeles, CA)
1943	#+ RAY, Charles		52	Throat infection from an infected tooth (in Hollywood, CA)
1992	RAY, Harry Milton		45	Stroke
1975	RAY, Jack		58	Died in Montclair, CA
1990	RAY, Johnnie (pop singer)		63	Liver failure (Do not confuse with actor Johnny Ray, d. 1927)
1979	# RAY, Nicholas		67	Lung cancer (in New York, NY)
1993	# RAY, René		81	Unreported causes (in Jersey, the Channel Islands)
1992	RAY, Satyajit	★	70	Heart ailment (in Calcutta, India)
1977	# RAY, Ted		67	Died in London, England
1994	#+ RAYE, Martha		78	After a stroke and circulatory problems (in Los Angeles, CA)
1973	RAYMOND, Cyril		76	Died in England
1961	RAYMOND, Frances "Frankie"		92	Died in Hollywood, CA
• 1998	RAYMOND, Gene		89	Pneumonia in Los Angeles, CA
1951	# RAYMOND, Jack		49	Heart attack (in Santa Monica, CA) Do not confuse with British actor
1953	# RAYMOND, Jack		66	Died in London, England (Do not confuse with U.S. actor)
1949	# RAYMOND, Royal		33	Cancer (in Van Nuys, CA)
1941	RAYNER, Minnie		72	Died in London, England
1948	# RAZETTO, Stella		67	Died in Malibu, CA
1968	REA, Mabel Lillian		36	Automobile accident (in Charlotte, NC)
1963	READ, Barbara		45	
1992	READE, Charles A.		82	After a 2-year hospitalization for a stroke (in Sangus, MA)
1985	READICK, Robert		59	Automobile accident (in Trenton, NJ)
1991	READING, Bertice		58	Stroke (in London, England)
1988	REARDON, John		58	Pneumonia
1991	REASONER, Harry		68	Complications and pneumonia after brain clot surgery
1994	RECTOR, Richard		69	After a brief illness (in San Rafael, CA)
1967	REDDING, Otis		26	Airplane crash (near Madison, WI)
1995	REDENBACHER, Orville		88	Drowned in his whirlpool spa after heart attack (Coronado, CA)
1976	REDFIELD, William "Billy"		49	Respiratory ailment complicated by leukemia (in New York, NY)
1985	REDGRAVE, Michael	☆	77	Parkinson's disease (in Denham, England)
1971	# REDWING, Rodd		66	Heart attack (while enroute by plane from London to Los Angeles)
1962	REECE, Brian		48	Bone disease (in London, England)
1977	#+ REED, Alan		69	After a long illness (in St. Vincent's hosp., West Los Angeles, CA)
1952	REED, Barbara		85	
1974	REED, Billy		59	Heart attack (in New York, NY)

Deaths of Movie and Television Personalities — by Name

YEAR	NAME		AGE	CAUSE and/or PLACE OF DEATH
1970	# REED, Carol		44	Cancer (Do not confuse with Carol Reed, d. 1976)
1976	REED, Carol	★	69	Heart attack (in London) Do not confuse with Carol Reed, d. 1970
1973	REED, Donald		70	Died in Los Angeles, CA
1986	#+ REED, Donna	★	64	Pancreatic cancer (in Beverly Hills, CA)
1967	+ REED, Florence		86	Died in East Islip, NY
1990	REED, Gavin		59	Respiratory failure (in Portland, ME)
1952	# REED, George H.		85	Arteriosclerosis (in Woodland Hills, CA)
1959	REED, J. Theodore "Ted"		72	Died in San Diego, CA
1961	REED, Luther		73	After a long illness (in New York, NY)
1980	REED, Marshall J.		62	Massive hemorrhage after suffering a brain tumor (in Los Angeles)
1974	REED, Maxwell		55	Died in England
1992	#+ REED, Robert		59	Colon lymphoma and A.I.D.S. (in Pasadena, CA)
1987	REED, T. Michael		42	Complications from A.I.D.S.
1993	REED, Taylor		60	Heart attack (in New York)
1992	REED, Vernon William Sr.		73	After a long illness (in Burlington, VT)
1992	REESE, Robert		66	Heart attack (in Los Angeles, CA)
1985	REESE, Sammy Pharr		55	Massive stroke (in Montgomery, AL)
1966	REEVE, Ada		91	Cardiac arrest in her sleep (in London, England)
1990	REEVE, Scott		38	A.I.D.S.
1959	#+ REEVES, George "Superman"		45	Apparent suicide (gunshot) in Beverly Hills, CA
1964	#+ REEVES, Jim		40	Airplane crash (near Nashville, TN)
1971	REEVES, Kynaston		78	Died in London, England
1969	REEVES, Michael		25	Suicide (sleeping pills) in London, England
1967	#+ REEVES, Richard J.		54	Cirrhosis of the liver (in Northridge, CA)
1996	# REGAN, Phil		89	Died in Santa Barbara, CA
1940	REGAS, George		50	Following an operation for a throat infection (in Los Angeles, CA)
1974	# REGAS, Pedro		92	Heart attack in his sleep (in Hollywood, CA)
• 1998	REGEN, Stuart		39	Cancer, U. of Southern CA/Kenneth Norris, Jr. Cancer Center
1965	REICHER, Frank		89	Died in Playa del Rey, CA
• 1996	REID, Beryl		76	In London, England
1973	+ REID, Carl Benton		79	Died in Studio City, CA
• 1996	REID, Don		85	Lymphoma (at his home in Harrison, NY)
1920	# REID, Hal		46	
1993	REID, Kate		62	Cancer (in Stratford, Ontario)
1965	REID, Trevor		55	Died in London, England
1989	REID, Vivian		95	Natural causes
1923	+ REID, Wallace		31	Drug addiction (in Los Angeles, CA)
1991	REILLY, Howard		79	After a coronary bypass operation
1994	REINHARDT, Gottfried		80	Pancreatic cancer (in Los Angeles, CA)
1943	+ REINHARDT, Max		70	Pneumonia following paralysis (in New York, NY)
1993	REINHEART, Alice		83	Died in Avon, CT
1953	REIS, Irving		47	Following a cancer operation (in Woodland Hills, CA)
1962	REISNER, Charles F. "Chuck"		75	Following a heart attack (in La Jolla, CA)
1991	Rellys		85	Died in Marseille, France
1960	RELPH, George		72	Died in London, England
1970	REMARQUE, Erich Maria		72	Heart collapse (in Locarno, Switzerland)
1991	REMICK, Lee		55	Kidney and lung cancer (in Brentwood, CA)
1992	REMME, John		56	A.I.D.S. (in New York, NY)
1967	# REMY, Albert		54	Heart attack (in Paris, France)
1980	# RENALDO, Duncan "Cisco Kid"		76	Lung cancer (in Goleta, CA)
• 1996	RENE, Norman		45	Complications from A.I.D.S. (in Manhattan, NY)
1969	RENEVANT, George		74	After a long illness (in Guadalajara, Mexico)
• 1998	RENFRO, V. Buddy		61	Cancer at his farm near Shepherdstown, W.VA

Deaths of Movie and Television Personalities — by Name

YEAR	NAME	AGE	CAUSE and/or PLACE OF DEATH
1991	RENICK, Ralph	62	Hepatitis and liver cancer
1984	+ RENICK, Ruth	91	Died in Hollywood, CA
1992	# Renie ★	90	Natural causes
1965	RENNIE, James	76	Died in New York, NY
1971	RENNIE, Michael	61	Heart attack (in Harrogate, Yorkshire, England)
1979	RENOIR, Jean ☆	84	Parkinson's disease (in Beverly Hills, CA)
1952	RENOIR, Pierre	67	Uremic poisoning (in Paris, France)
1974	# REPP, Stafford	56	Heart attack (in Inglewood, CA)
1996	# RETTIG, Tommy	54	Cancer (at his home in Marina Del Rey, CA)
1990	REVERE, Anne ★	87	Pneumonia (in Locust Valley, NY)
1993	REVIER, Dorothy	89	Died at Queen of Angels–Hollywood Pres. Med. Ctr., CA
1982	REVILLE, Alma (Hitchcock)	82	After a long illness (in Bel Air, CA)
1996	REVUELTAS, Rosaura	85	Lung cancer (at her home in Cuernavaca, Mexico)
1987	+ REY, Alejandro	57	Cancer (in Los Angeles, CA)
1994	# REY, Fernando	76	Bladder cancer (in Madrid, Spain)
1961	+ REYNOLDS, Adeline De Walt	98	Died in Los Angeles, CA
1949	# REYNOLDS, Craig	42	Motorcycle/car crash (in Los Angeles, CA)
1983	+ REYNOLDS, Frank	59	Viral hepatitis
1990	REYNOLDS, Helen Fortescu	65	
1990	REYNOLDS, Jack	83	Heart attack in his sleep (in Escondido, CA)
1927	+ REYNOLDS, Lynn	37	Suicide (gunshot) during a cocktail party in Los Angeles, CA
1997	# REYNOLDS, Marjorie	76	Congestive heart failure (in Manhattam Beach, CA)
1975	# REYNOLDS, Peter	48	Died in Australia
1965	+ REYNOLDS, Quentin	62	Cancer (in Los Angeles, CA)
1962	# REYNOLDS, Vera	62	Died in Woodland Hills, CA
1988	# RHODES, Billie	93	Died in Los Angeles, CA
1967	RHODES, Billy "Little Billy"	72	Stroke (in Hollywood, CA)
1990	+ RHODES, Erik	84	Pneumonia (in Oklahoma City, OK)
1987	RHODES, Grandon	82	After a long illness (in Encino, CA)
1979	RHODES, Marjorie	76	Died in Hove, Sussex, England
1971	RIANO, Renie	71	After a long illness (in Woodland Hills, CA)
1976	# RICCI, Nora	50	Liver cancer (in Rome, Italy)
1987	+ RICE, Adnia	64	Cancer
1990	RICE, Felix	46	A.I.D.S. (in Key West, FL)
1974	RICE, Florence	63	Lung cancer (in Honolulu, HI)
1936	# RICE, Frank	43	Nephritis and hepatitis (in Los Angeles, CA)
1954	+ RICE, Grantland ★	73	Following a heart attack (in New York)
1968	# RICE, Jack	75	Cancer (in Woodland Hills, CA)
1997	RICE, Joan	66	
1987	#+ RICH, Buddy	69	Heart attack (during brain tumor surgery)
1995	RICH, Charlie	62	Acute pulmonary embolism (in Hammond, LA)
1956	# RICH, Freddie	58	Paralysis after an accident (in Beverly Hills, CA)
1988	# RICH, Irene	96	Heart failure (in Santa Barbara, CA)
1954	RICH, Lillian	53	Died at the Motion Picture Country Home, in Woodland Hills, CA
1957	RICH, Vivian	64	Automobile accident (in Hollywood, CA)
1964	#+ RICHARDS, Addison	61	Heart attack (in Los Angeles, CA)
1978	RICHARDS, Cully	68	Cancer (in Los Angeles, CA)
1996	RICHARDS, E. Claude	72	Leukemia (at the VA Hospital in The Bronx, NY)
1964	RICHARDS, Gordon	70	Died in Hollywood, CA
1963	RICHARDS, Grant	47	Leukemia (in Hollywood, CA)
1992	RICHARDS, Lloyd	89	Pneumonia (in Wales)
1974	RICHARDS, Paul E.	50	Cancer (in Los Angeles, CA)
1996	RICHARDSON, Don	77	Heart failure (in Los Angeles, CA)

Deaths of Movie and Television Personalities — by Name

YEAR	NAME		AGE	CAUSE and/or PLACE OF DEATH
1962	RICHARDSON, Frankie		63	Following a heart attack (in Philadelphia, PA)
1983	RICHARDSON, James G.		37	Injuries from a fall while skiing (in Rock Creek, CA)
1959	#+ RICHARDSON, Jiles "Big Bopper"		28	Airplane crash (along with Buddy Holly, near Mason City, IA)
1983	+ RICHARDSON, Ralph	☆	80	
1995	# RICHARDSON, Ron		43	Complications from A.I.D.S. (in a Bronxville, NY, hospital)
1991	RICHARDSON, Tony	★	63	A.I.D.S. (in Los Angeles, CA)
1940	RICHMAN, Charles		75	After a brief illness (in a Bronx, NY nursing home)
1972	+ RICHMAN, Harry		77	Died in North Hollywood, CA
1973	# RICHMOND, Kane		66	Died in Corona Del Mar, CA
1948	RICHMOND, Warner		53	Coronary thrombosis (in Los Angeles, CA)
1976	RICHTER, Hans		87	Died in Locarno, Switzerland
1961	# RICHTER, Paul		65	Died in Vienna, Austria
1929	# RICKARD, Tex		59	Peritonitis following appendectomy (in Miami Beach, FL)
1939	RICKETTS, Thomas "Tom"		85	Pneumonia (in Hollywood, CA)
1958	RICKSON, Joe		77	Died in Los Angeles, CA
1985	+ RIDDLE, Nelson		64	Cardiac and kidney failure (in Los Angeles, CA)
1962	RIDGELY, Cleo		68	Died in Glendale, CA
1968	# RIDGELY, John		58	Heart ailment (in New York, NY)
1997	RIDGELY, Robert		65	Cancer at his home in Toluca Lake, CA
1951	# RIDGES, Stanley		59	Died in Westbrook, CT
1959	RIEMANN, Johannes		72	After a long illness (in Konstanz, West Germany)
1963	RIETTI, Victor		75	Heart ailment (in London, England)
1968	RIGA, Nadine		59	Cerebral hemorrhage (in Hollywood, CA)
1951	# RIGBY, Edward		71	Died in London, England
1995	RIGGS, Bobby		77	Prostate cancer (at his home in Leucadia, CA)
1994	RIGGS, Marlon		37	A.I.D.S. complications (in Oakland, CA)
1981	RIGON, Paolo		22	Injuries from a filming accident (in Cortina d'Ampezzo, Italy)
1992	RILEY, Alice Mary		51	Cancer (in Concord, CA)
1988	RILEY, Jay Flash		72	Died in Los Angeles, CA
1992	RILEY, Larry		39	A.I.D.S. complications (in Burbank, CA)
1932	Rin Tin Tin (original dog)		16	
1992	# RINALDO, Fred		78	Complications after an operation for a broken hip (in Los Angeles)
1970	# RINDT, Jochen		28	Injuries from automobile crash (near Monza, Italy)
1961	RING, Blanche		84	Died in Santa Monica, CA
1967	RING, Cyril		74	Died in Hollywood, CA
1992	RINI, David		40	Brain cancer (in Cleveland, OH)
1992	RIO, Joan Maloney		57	Cancer
1984	+ RIORDAN, Marjorie (Schlaff)		63	
1961	RIPLEY, Arthur		66	Cancer (in Los Angeles, CA)
1949	#+ RIPLEY, Robert L.		55	Heart attack (in New York, NY)
1979	+ RIPPERTON, Minnie		31	Cancer
1958	RISDON, Elisabeth		71	Brain hemorrhage (in Santa Monica, CA)
1955	RISKIN, Robert		58	After a long illness (in Beverly Hills, CA)
1970	RISS, Dan		60	Heart attack (at his home in Hollywood, CA)
1977	RISSONI, Giuditta		80	Died in Rome, Italy
1977	#+ RITCHARD, Cyril		80	Cardiac arrest (in Chicago, IL)
1921	RITCHIE, Billie		42	After a 2-yr. illness caused by a filming injury (in Los Angeles, CA)
1918	RITCHIE, Franklin		52	Crushed beneath his overturned automobile (in Los Angeles, CA)
1918	RITCHIE, Perry V.		30	Suicide (in Los Angeles, CA)
1990	RITT, Martin	☆	76	Cardiac disease (in Santa Monica, CA)
1974	#+ RITTER, Tex		67	Heart attack (in Nashville, TN)
1969	RITTER, Thelma	☆	63	Heart attack (in Forrest Hills, NY)
1965	#+ RITZ, Al		64	Heart attack (in New Orleans, LA)

YEAR	NAME	AGE	CAUSE and/or PLACE OF DEATH
1986	#+ RITZ, Harry	78	Cancer (in San Diego, CA)
1985	#+ RITZ, Jimmy	81	Heart failure (in Los Angeles, CA)
1976	RIVERO, Julian	84	Died in Hollywood, CA
1993	RIVERS, Al	65	Cancer
1996	RIVERS, Jerry	68	Cancer (at a hospital in Hermitage, TN)
1977	RIVERS, Victor	29	Injuries from performing a stunt (in Los Angeles, CA)
1971	ROACH, Bert	79	Died in Los Angeles, CA
1972	+ ROACH, Hal Jr.	53	Pneumonia (in Santa Monica, CA)
1992	+ ROACH, Hal Sr. ★	100	Pneumonia (in Bel Air, CA)
1996	# ROARKE, Adam	58	Heart attack (at his home in Euless, TX)
1963	+ ROBARDS, Jason Sr.	70	Heart attack (in Sherman Oaks, CA)
1992	ROBBINS, Duke	71	Pneumonia (in Duarte, CA)
1992	+ ROBBINS, Fred	73 ·	Lymphoma
1980	ROBBINS, Gale	57	Lung cancer (in Tarzana, CA)
1997	ROBBINS, Harold	81	Respiratory failure at Desert Hospital in Palm Springs, CA
1998	# ROBBINS, Jerome ★	79	Stroke at his home in Manhattan, NY
1982	+ ROBBINS, Marty	57	Heart attack (in Nashville, TN)
1992	ROBBINS, Michael	62	Died in London, England
1985	ROBBINS, Randall	45	After a long illness (in New York, NY)
1933	ROBBINS, Roy "Skeeter Bill"	36	Killed by a truck while wiping snow from his car (in CA)
1952	ROBER, Richard	46	Killed when his car went down an embankment due to fog (in CA)
1988	+ ROBERSON, Chuck	69	Cancer (in Bakersfield, CA)
1938	ROBERTI, Lyda	29	Heart ailment (in Los Angeles, CA)
1993	ROBERTS, Davis	76	Emphysema (in Chicago, IL)
1935	# ROBERTS, Edith	36	Died following the birth of a son (in Los Angeles, CA)
1962	ROBERTS, Evelyn	76	
1940	+ ROBERTS, Florence	79	After a brief illness (in Hollywood) Do not confuse with F.R., d. 1927
1992	ROBERTS, Howard	62	Prostate cancer
1961	ROBERTS, John H.	76	Died in London, England
1978	ROBERTS, Lenore	47	Cancer (in Los Angeles, CA)
1954	ROBERTS, Leona	73	Died in Santa Monica, CA
1978	#+ ROBERTS, Lynne (Mary Hart)	58	An intracranial hemorrhage
1992	ROBERTS, Meade	61	Congestive heart failure (in New York, NY)
1980	+ ROBERTS, Rachel ☆	53	Suicide (acute barbiturate intoxication) in Los Angeles, CA
1940	# ROBERTS, Ralph Arthur	55	Died in Berlin, Germany
1975	+ ROBERTS, Roy (actor)	69	Died suddenly after complaining of back pain (in Los Angeles, CA)
1936	ROBERTS, Stephen R.	41	Heart attack (in Beverly Hills, CA)
1928	+ ROBERTS, Theodore	67	Uremic poisoning after a flu attack (in Los Angeles, CA)
1941	ROBERTSHAW, Jerrold	74	Died in England
1988	ROBERTSON, Hugh A.	55	Cancer (in Los Angeles, CA)
1964	ROBERTSON, John Stuart	86	Died in Escondida, CA
1948	ROBERTSON, Willard	62	Died in Hollywood, CA
1976	#+ ROBESON, Paul	77	Cerebral vascular disorder (stroke) in Philadelphia, PA
1954	# ROBEY, George	85	Died in Saltdean, Sussex, England
1995	# ROBIN, Dany	68	Died in a fire (at her home in Paris, France)
1986	ROBINS, Barry	41	After a long illness (in Los Angeles, CA)
1986	ROBINSON, Bartlett "Bart"	73	After a long bout with cancer (in Fallbrook, CA)
1949	+ ROBINSON, Bill "Bojangles"	71	Heart ailment (in New York, NY)
1992	ROBINSON, Cardew	75	Following a bowel infection (in Boethampton, England)
1988	+ ROBINSON, Dar Allen	39	Motorcycle accident (in Page, AZ)
1995	ROBINSON, Darren	28	Cardiac arrest during a bout with the flu
1950	ROBINSON, Dewey	52	After a heart attack (in Las Vegas, NV)
1973	#+ ROBINSON, Edward G. ★	79	Cancer (in Hollywood, CA)

Deaths of Movie and Television Personalities — by Name

YEAR	NAME		AGE	CAUSE and/or PLACE OF DEATH
1974	+ ROBINSON, Edward G. Jr.		40	Heart attack (found unconscious at his home in West Hollywood, CA)
1971	# ROBINSON, Frances		55	Heart attack (in Hollywood, CA)
1962	ROBINSON, Gertrude R.		70	Died in Hollywood, CA
1957	ROBINSON, Inez Buck		67	
1972	#+ ROBINSON, Jackie		53	Heart disease (in Stamford, CT)
1988	ROBINSON, Max		49	A.I.D.S.
1989	+ ROBINSON, Sugar Ray		67	Heart and Alzheimer's disease and diabetes
1970	ROBLES, Rudy		60	Died in Manila, Philippine Islands
1984	+ ROBSON, Flora	☆	82	Undisclosed causes (in Brighton, England)
1978	ROBSON, Mark		64	Heart attack (in London, England)
1942	#+ ROBSON, May	☆	84	Neuritis (in Beverly Hills, CA)
1995	ROCCA, Daniela		57	Heart failure (at a rest home in Milo, Sicily)
1934	ROCCARDI, Albert		70	Died in Paris, France
1952	ROCHE, John C.		56	Cerebral thrombosis (in Hollywood, CA)
1981	ROCHELLE, Claire		72	Cancer (in La Jolla, CA)
1919	ROCK, Charles		53	Died in London, England
1984	# ROCK, Joe		93	After a brief illness (in Sherman Oaks, CA)
1996	ROCKETT, Norman		84	Heart failure (in Los Angeles, CA)
1931	#+ ROCKNE, Knute		43	Airplane crash (near Bazaar, KS)
1991	RODDENBERRY, Gene		70	Cardiac arrest from a massive blood clot (in Santa Monica, CA)
1979	+ RODGERS, Richard		77	
1951	RODGERS, Walter		64	Following a stroke (in Los Angeles, CA)
1994	RODNEY, Red		66	Lung cancer (in Boynton Beach, FL)
1966	RODRIGUEZ, Estelita		52	Died in Van Nuys, CA
1958	RODZINSKI, Artur		64	Heart ailment
1994	ROEBLING, Paul		60	While vacationing on a Navajo Indian reservation in Arizona
1988	ROGELL, Albert S.		86	Cancer and diabetes (in Los Angeles, CA)
1919	ROGERS, Eugene		51	Found dead in bed of myocarditis and alcoholism (in Los Angeles)
1995	#+ ROGERS, Ginger		83	Diabetic coma (at her home in Rancho Mirage, CA)
1991	# ROGERS, Jean		74	Following surgery (in Sherman Oaks, CA)
1994	ROGERS, Milton "Shorty"		70	Undisclosed causes (in Van Nuys, CA)
1966	ROGERS, Rena		64	Died in Santa Monica, CA
• 1998	ROGERS, Roy		86	Congestive heart failur in his sleep in Apple Valley, CA
1935	#+ ROGERS, Will		55	Airplane crash (near Barrow, Alaska)
1993	ROGERS, Will Jr.		81	Apparent suicide (gunshot) in Tubac, AZ
1991	ROGOT, Peter		37	Apparent heart attack
1995	ROKER, Roxie		66	Undisclosed causes (in Brooklyn, NY)
• 1997	ROKER, Roxie		66	Died in Los Angeles, CA
1994	# ROLAND, Gilbert "Cisco Kid"		88	Cancer (at his home in Beverly Hills, CA)
1937	+ ROLAND, Ruth		45	Cancer (in Los Angeles, CA)
1957	ROLF, Erik		46	
1993	ROLFE, Sam	☆	69	Heart attack while playing tennis (in Los Angeles, CA)
1990	ROLFING, Tom		40	An A.I.D.S.-related illness (in New York, NY)
• 1996	ROLLINS, Howard E. Jr.	☆	46	Complications from lymphoma (in New York, NY)
1995	# ROMAGNOLI, Margaret		73	Died in Mount Auburn hospital in Cambridge, MA
1991	ROMAN, Paul Reid		55	Cancer (in Los Angeles, CA)
1991	ROMANCE, Viviane		82	Cancer (in Nice, France)
1971	# ROMANOFF, Michael		81	Heart failure (in Los Angeles, CA)
1951	+ ROMBERG, Sigmund		64	Cerebral hemorrhage (in New York, NY)
1965	# ROME, Stewart		79	Died in Newbury, England
1994	+ ROMERO, Cesar		86	Complications from bronchitis and pneumonia (Santa Monica, CA)
1983	RONET, Maurice		55	Cancer (in Paris, France)
1958	ROOKE, Irene		?	Died in England

YEAR	NAME	AGE	CAUSE and/or PLACE OF DEATH
1962	+ ROONEY, Pat, II	82	*Died in New York, NY*
1979	ROONEY, Pat, III	70	*Died in Lake Blaisdell, NH*
1961	ROOPE, Fay	68	*Died in Port Jefferson, L.I., NY*
1989	ROOS, Joanna	88	*Ruptured aorta (in Princeton, NJ)*
1973	# ROOSEVELT, Buddy	75	*Died in Meeker, CO*
1991	ROOSEVELT, James	83	*Complications from a stroke and Parkinson's disease (in CA)*
1966	#+ ROPER, Jack	62	*Throat cancer (in Woodland Hills, CA)*
1943	ROQUEMORE, Henry	55	*Heart attack (at his home in Beverly Hills, CA)*
1973	# ROQUEVERT, Noel	81	*Heart attack (in Douarmenez, France)*
1987	+ RORKE, Hayden	76	*Cancer (in Toluka Lake, CA)*
1938	RORKE, Mary	80	*Died in London, England*
1996	ROSATTI, Gregory Joseph	43	*Complications of A.I.D.S. (in Sherman Oaks, CA)*
1974	# ROSAY, Françoise	82	*Complications after surgery (in Paris, France)*
1933	# ROSCOE, Alan	45	*Cancer (at a hospital in Hollywood, CA)*
1966	+ ROSE, Billy	67	
1953	# ROSE, Blanche	74	*Died at her home in Hollywood, CA*
1990	+ ROSE, David (pianist/composer)	80	*Heart disease (in Burbank, CA) Do not confuse with David E. Rose*
1992	ROSE, David E. (producer)	96	*Died in Phoenix, AZ (Do not confuse with the pianist/composer)*
1988	ROSE, George	68	*Murdered by his son (in Rio Plata, Dominican Republic)*
1979	ROSE, Jane	66	*Cancer (in Studio City, CA)*
1987	ROSE, William	67	*After a lengthy illness (in Jersey, England)*
1966	ROSEMOND, Clinton C.	82	*Pneumonia and stroke (in Los Angeles, CA)*
1990	ROSEN, Al	80	
1951	# ROSEN, Phil	63	*Died in Hollywood, CA*
1992	ROSENBERG, Mark	44	*Heart attack (in Stanton, TX)*
1992	ROSENBERGER, James	84	*Pneumonia*
1991	ROSENBLATT, Martin	74	*Heart attack (in New York, NY)*
1976	#+ ROSENBLOOM, "Slapsie" Maxie	71	*Paget's disease (in South Pasadena, CA)*
1995	ROSENBLUM, Ralph	69	*Heart failure (at his home in Manhattan)*
1953	ROSENTHAL, Harry	52	*Heart attack (in Hollywood, CA)*
1942	#+ ROSING, Bodil	63	*Heart attack (in Hollywood, CA)*
1937	ROSLEY, Adrian	47	*Following a heart attack (in Hollywood, CA)*
1971	# ROSMER, Milton	90	*Died in Chesham, England*
1991	ROSQUI, Tom	62	*Cancer (in Los Angeles, CA)*
1955	ROSS, Anthony	46	*Died in New York*
1990	ROSS, Betsy King	66	
1947	ROSS, Betty	67	*Died at her home in Hollywood, CA*
1995	ROSS, Bob	52	*Cancer (at his home in Orlando, FL)*
• 1961	ROSS, Earle	73	
1990	ROSS, Frank	85	*After brain surgery (in Los Angeles, CA)*
1995	ROSS, Gordon	65	*Cancer (at his home in Studio City, CA)*
1985	ROSS, Jane	50	*During surgery for cancer (in Los Angeles, CA)*
1982	+ ROSS, Joe E.	67	*Apparent heart attack (in Burbank, CA)*
1988	# ROSS, Lanny	82	*Following two strokes (in New York, NY)*
1976	# ROSS, Lenny	71	*Cancer (in Los Angeles, CA)*
• 1992	+ ROSS, Margery Jane	72	
• 1998	ROSS, Sam	86	*Heart failure in Laguna Beach, CA*
1975	# ROSS, Shirley	62	*Cancer (at a hospital in Menlo Park, CA)*
1959	ROSS, Thomas W.	86	*Died in Torrington, CT*
1977	ROSSELLINI, Roberto	71	*Heart attack (in Rome, Italy)*
1966	ROSSEN, Robert ☆	57	*After a long illness (in New York, NY)*
1990	ROSSIF, Frédéric	67	*Heart attack (in Paris, France)*
1984	ROSSITER, Leonard	57	*Apparent heart attack (in London, England)*

Deaths of Movie and Television Personalities — by Name

YEAR	NAME	AGE	CAUSE and/or PLACE OF DEATH
1991	# ROSSITTO, Angelo	83	Complications from surgery (in Los Angeles, CA)
1960	ROSSON, Arthur H.	73	Died in Los Angeles, CA
1988	ROSSON, Harold "Hal"	93	Cardiac arrest in his sleep (in Palm Beach, FL)
1953	+ ROSSON, Richard "Dick"	60	Suicide (carbon monoxide poisoning) in Los Angeles, CA
1979	ROTA, Nino	68	Cerebral thrombosis (in Rome, Italy)
1995	ROTH, David	72	Leukemia (in Leonia, NJ)
1976	# ROTH, Gene	73	Struck by a car (in Los Angeles, CA)
1980	#+ ROTH, Lillian	69	Stroke (in New York, NY)
1984	ROTHA, Paul	76	Died in Wallingford, England
1989	ROUD, Richard	59	Heart attack
1981	ROULEAU, Raymond	77	Died in Paris, France
1983	ROUNDS, David	53	Cancer (in Lomontville, NY)
1974	# ROUNESVILLE, Robert	60	Heart attack (in New York, NY)
1987	ROUSE, Russell	74	Heart failure after a cerebral thrombosis (in Santa Monica, CA)
• 1996	ROVERE, Luigi	88	Heart attack (in Rome, Italy)
1987	ROWAN, Dan	65	Lymphatic cancer (in Englewood, FL)
1966	ROWAN, Donald W. "Don"	60	Cerebral hemorrhage (in Rocky Hill, CT)
• 1998	ROWAN, Roy	78	Heart failure in Los Angeles, CA
1988	# ROWE, Fanny	75	Died in London, England
1971	ROWLAND, Adele	88	Died in Los Angeles, CA
1984	ROWLAND, Henry	70	Died in Northridge, CA
1944	ROWLANDS, Art	46	Died in Hollywood, CA
1946	# ROYCE, Julian	76	Died in England
1946	ROYCE, Lionel	55	Heart attack in Manilla while entertaining troops with the U.S.O.
1971	ROYCE, Ruth	78	Died in Los Angeles, CA
1983	ROYLE, Selena	78	After a brief illness (in Guadalajara, Mexico)
1989	ROZAKIS, Gregory	46	A.I.D.S. (in Brooklyn, NY)
• 1996	ROZELLE, Pete	70	Brain cancer
1995	ROZSA, Miklos ★	88	Pneumonia following a stroke (at Good Sam. Hosp. in L.A.)
1956	RUB, Christian	69	Died in Germany
1942	RUBEN, J. Walter	43	Heart ailment (in Hollywood, CA)
1931	# RUBENS, Alma	33	Pneumonia (in Los Angeles, CA)
1992	RUBENSTEIN, Phil	51	Heart attack (in Los Angeles, CA)
1986	RUBIN, Benny	86	Heart attack after surgery (in Los Angeles, CA)
1982	+ RUBINSTEIN, Artur	95	Cardiac arrest in his sleep (in Geneva, Switzerland)
1991	RUDOLPH, Oscar	79	Following a stroke (in Encino, CA)
1994	RUEHMANN, Heinz	92	Died in Berg, Germany
1991	RUFFIN, David	50	Apparent drug overdose
1970	+ RUGGLES, Charles	84	Cancer (in Santa Monica, CA)
1972	+ RUGGLES, Wesley ☆	82	After a stroke (in Santa Monica, CA)
1974	RUICK, Barbara	41	Natural causes (in Reno, NV)
1967	# RUMANN, Sig	82	Heart attack (in Julian, NE)
1946	#+ RUNYON, Damon	62	After a long bout with throat cancer (in New York, NY)
1995	RUSHTON, Donald	70	Died in Indianapolis, IN
1995	RUSHTON, Matthew	43	Complications of A.I.D.S. (in Los Angeles, CA)
• 1996	RUSHTON, Willie	59	Complications from diabetes and heart surgery (in London, Eng.)
1990	RUSINOW, Irving	75	Cancer (in Washington, D.C.)
1976	RUSKIN, Shimen	69	Cancer (in Los Angeles, CA)
1929	RUSSELL, Albert	37	Pneumonia (in Beverly Hills, CA)
1992	# RUSSELL, Andy	72	Complications from a stroke
• 1998	RUSSELL, Bob	90	In a Hospital near his Sarasota, Fla. home
1963	RUSSELL, Byron	79	After a brief illness (in New York)
1990	RUSSELL, Craig	42	A.I.D.S. (in Toronto, Canada)

• New entry.   # Original name (Pt. 7).   + Interment (Pt. 5).   ☆ Oscar nominee, ★ Oscar winner (Pt. 10)

Deaths of Movie and Television Personalities — by Name

YEAR		NAME		AGE	CAUSE and/or PLACE OF DEATH
1981	#	RUSSELL, Don		54	Heart attack (in Miami Beach, FL)
1961	+	RUSSELL, Gail (Moseley)		36	Found dead from alcohol overindulgence (in Los Angeles, CA)
1935		RUSSELL, J. Gordon		52	Heart attack (in Los Angeles, CA)
1991		RUSSELL, John		70	Died in Los Angeles, CA
1922	#+	RUSSELL, Lillian		61	Complications after a fall onboard ship (in Pittsburgh, PA)
1976	+	RUSSELL, Rosalind (Brisson)	☆	65	Cancer complicated by arthritis (in Beverly Hills, CA)
1915		RUSSELL, William		?	(Do not confuse with William Russell, d. 1929)
1929		RUSSELL, William		42	Pneumonia (in Beverly Hills) Do not confuse with W. Russell d. 1915
1948	#+	RUTH, Babe		53	Cancerous tumor (in New York, NY)
1982		RUTHERFORD, Jack "Buffalo Bill"		89	Died in Tucson, AZ
1972		RUTHERFORD, Margaret	★	80	After breaking a hip in a fall (in Chalfont St. Peter, England)
1983		RUTTENBERG, Joseph		93	Died in Los Angeles, CA
1941		RUTTMAN, Walther		54	Killed while filming a newsreel of the Eastern Front during W.W.2
1960		RUYSDAEL, Basil		72	Died in Hollywood, CA
1969		RYAN, Dick		72	Cancer (in Burbank, CA)
1984	+	RYAN, Edmond		79	Heart attack (in Louisville, KY)
1973	#+	RYAN, Irene		70	Stroke (in Santa Monica, CA)
1944		RYAN, Joe		57	Died in Los Angeles, CA
1985		RYAN, Kathleen		63	Died in Dublin, Ireland
1973		RYAN, Robert	☆	63	Lymphatic cancer (in New York, NY)
1975	#	RYAN, Sheila		54	Lung ailment (in Woodland Hills, CA)
1956		RYAN, Tim		57	Heart attack (in Hollywood, CA)
• 1997		RYAN, William Emmett III		70	After a long illness (in Point Marion, PA)
1918		RYCKMAN, Chester		21	Spanish influenza (in Fort Rosecrans, CA)
• 1995		RYDER, Richard		53	A.I.D.S.
• 1998		RYSANEK, Leonie		71	Bone cancer in Vienna
1985		RYSKIND, Morrie		89	Apparent stroke (in Washington, D.C.)
1993		RYU, Chishu		88	Cancer (in Yokohama, Japan)
1993		SABATINO, Anthony		48	A.I.D.S. (in Los Angeles, CA)
1994		SABLON, Jean		87	After a 3-yr. illness (at Clinica Hosp. in Cannes-la-Bocca, France)
1963	#+	Sabu		39	Heart attack (in Chatsworth, CA)
1992		SACHA, Kenny		39	A.I.D.S. (in Hollywood, CA)
1990		SACHS, Leonard		82	Kidney failure (in London, England)
1992		SACHS, Scotty		39	Murdered (multiple gunshot wounds) in Los Angeles, CA
1994		SACKS, Amy Jill		39	Complications from lupus (in Philadelphia, PA)
• 1996		SACKS, David Michael		79	Heart failure (in Pleasanton, CA)
1964		SADO, Keiji		38	Automobile accident (in Japan)
1994		SADOFF, Fred		68	A.I.D.S. complications (in Los Angeles, CA)
1981	+	SAGAL, Boris		58	Injuries from a helicopter crash (in Portland, OR)
• 1996		SAGAN, Carl		62	Pneumonia after a 2-yr. bout with bone marrow disease (in Seattle)
1974	#	SAGE, Willard		51	Died in Sherman Oaks, CA
• 1921		SAINT-SAENS, Camille		86	Died in his sleep (in Algiers, Algeria)
1971		SAIS, Marin		81	Cerebral arteriosclerosis (in Woodland Hills, CA)
1955	#+	SAKALL, S. Z. "Cuddles"		71	Heart attack (in Beverly Hills, CA)
1982		SAKATA, Harold		56	Cancer (in Honolulu, HI)
1993		SALANT, Richard "Dick"		78	Heart failure (while giving a speech)
1990		SALCIDO, Michael A.		39	Liver failure (in Van Nuys, CA)
1936	#+	SALE, Chic		51	Pneumonia (in Los Angeles, CA)
1993		SALE, Richard		80	After suffering two strokes (in Los Angeles, CA)
1992		SALE, Virginia (Wren)		92	Heart failure (in Woodland Hills, CA)
1935		SALISBURY, Monroe		59	Skull fracture from a fall (in San Bernardino, CA)
1993		SALKIN, Leo	☆	80	Congestive heart failure (in Burbank, CA)

Deaths of Movie and Television Personalities — by Name

YEAR	NAME	AGE	CAUSE and/or PLACE OF DEATH
1997	SALKIND, Alexander	76	Leukemia (at the American Hospital in Paris, France)
1990	SALMI, Albert	62	Suicide after murdering his wife (gunshot) in Spokane, WA
1993	SALMON, Scott	51	After an auto accident (in Northridge, CA)
1968	SALMONOVA, Lyda	79	Died in Prague, Czeckoslovakia
1987	SALT, Waldo	72	Cancer (in Los Angeles, CA)
1994	SALTER, Hans J.	98	Cardiac arrest in his sleep (in Los Angeles, CA)
1920	SALTER, Harry	?	Natural causes (in a New Jersey hospital)
1953	SALTER, Thelma	44	After a lingering illness (in Hollywood, CA)
1994	SALTZMAN, Harry	78	Died at the American Hospital in Neuilly-Sur-Seine, France
1984	SALVIO, Robert	45	Complications from A.I.D.S. (in New York, NY)
1983	#+ SAMPLES, Junior	56	Heart attack (in Cummings, GA)
1987	SAMPSON, Will	53	Following a heart-lung transplant (in Houston, TX)
1963	SAMSON, Ivan	67	Died in London, England
1992	SAMUEL, Andrew	82	Died in Colton, CA
1972	SANDE, Walter	65	Heart attack (while waiting for cab at O'Hare Airport in Chicago, IL)
1980	+ SANDERS, (Col.) Harland	90	Leukemia and pneumonia (in Louisville, KY)
1995	#+ SANDERS, Al	54	Lung cancer (at Johns Hopkins Hosp., Baltimore, MD)
1987	SANDERS, Denis	58	Heart attack in his sleep (in San Diego, CA)
1972	SANDERS, George ★	65	Suicide (overdose of barbiturates) in Casteldelfels, Spain
1998	SANDERS, Steve	45	Self-inflicted gunshot wound to the head in Cape Coral, FLA
1992	SANDERSON, Joan	79	After a lengthy illness (in Norwich, England)
1961	# SANDFORD, Tiny	67	Died in Los Angeles, CA
1925	SANDOW, Eugene	58	After a blood vessel in his brain burst (in London, England)
1945	SANDRICH, Mark	44	Heart disease (at his home in Hollywood, CA)
1980	SANDRINI, Luis "Felipe"	75	Cerebral hemorrhage (in Buenos Aires, Argentina)
1937	SANDROCK, Adele	73	Died in Berlin, Germany
1984	+ SANDS, Billy	73	Lung cancer (in Los Angeles, CA)
1973	+ SANDS, Diana	39	Cancer (in New York, NY)
1990	Sandy (original "Annie" dog)	16	Died in his sleep
1963	SANFORD, Ralph	64	Heart ailment (in Van Nuys, CA)
1969	SANGER, Bert	75	Died in Blackpool, England
1978	SANO, Shuji	66	Died in Japan
1990	SANSBERRY, Hope	94	Heart attack in her sleep (in Laguna Hills, CA)
1981	# SANTELL, Alfred	86	After a lengthy illness and several strokes (in Salinas, CA)
1995	SANTI, Lionello "Nello"	77	After a long illness (in Rome, Italy)
1953	# SANTLEY, Fred	64	Died in Hollywood, CA
1971	# SANTLEY, Joseph	81	Died in his West Los Angeles home
1987	SANTORO, Dean	49	Undisclosed causes (in Sherman Oaks, CA)
1931	SANTSCHI, Tom	51	High blood pressure (in Hollywood, CA)
1998	SAPERSTEIN, Henry G.	80	Cancer in Beverly Hills, CA
1985	# SAPPINGTON, Fay	78	After a long illness (in New York, NY)
1994	# SARGENT, Dick	64	Prostate cancer (at Cedars-Sinai Med. Ctr. in Los Angeles, CA)
1993	SARGENT, Thornton	90	Died in Rancho Palos Verdes, CA
1953	SARNO, Hector V.	73	After a long illness (in Pasadena, CA)
1997	SARNOFF, Robert W.	78	Cancer (in New York, NY)
1985	# SARONY, Leslie	88	Died in London, England
1925	+ SATIE, Erik	59	Cirrhosis of the liver (in Paris, France)
1992	SATZ, Wayne	47	Found dead in his home
1997	SAUDEK, Robert	85	Heart ailment (at Johns Hopkins Hospital in Baltimore, MD)
1989	SAUERS, Patricia	49	Complications from diabetes (in CA)
1943	SAUM, Clifford	60	Died in Glendale, CA
1954	SAUNDERS, Jackie	61	Died in Palm Springs, CA
1993	SAUTER, Carl	44	Undisclosed causes (in Los Angeles, CA)

YEAR	NAME		AGE	CAUSE and/or PLACE OF DEATH
1985	+ SAVALAS, George		60	Leukemia (in Westwood, CA)
1994	#+ SAVALAS, Telly "Kojak"	☆	70	Died in his sleep of prostate cancer (in Universal City, CA)
1985	SAVILLE, Ruth		92	Died in Los Angeles, CA
1979	SAVILLE, Victor		82	Died in London, England
1983	SAVITCH, Jessica		35	Automobile accident
1982	# SAWYER, Joe		80	Liver cancer (in Ashland, OR)
1970	SAWYER, Laura		85	Died at a nursing home in a Matawan, NJ
1935	# SAXE, Templar		69	Died in Cincinnati, OH
1945	SAXON, Hugh A.		76	Died at his home in Beverly Hills, CA
1989	SAYER, Philip		42	Abdominal cancer (in London, England)
1963	# SAYLOR, Syd		67	Heart attack (in Hollywood, CA)
1974	SAYRE, Jeffrey		73	Murdered (shot) in Los Angeles, CA
1972	#+ SCALA, Gia		38	Overdose of alcohol and medication (in Hollywood, CA)
1995	SCALI, John A.		77	Heart failure (in Washington, D.C.)
1994	SCANLAN, John		73	Congestive heart failure (at his home in Closter, NJ)
1954	SCARDON, Paul		75	Heart attack (in Fontana, CA)
1994	SCARFIOTTI, Ferdinando	★	53	After a brief illness (in Los Angeles, CA)
1968	SCARFIOTTI, Lodovico		34	Automobile crash (in Berchtesgaden, Germany)
1947	SCHABLE, Robert		74	Died in Hollywood, CA
1957	SCHAEFER, Ann		87	Died in Los Angeles, CA
1967	SCHAEFER, Armand L.		69	Died in Bridgeport, CA
• 1997	SCHAEFER, George		76	After a long illness
1991	SCHAEFFER, Elizabeth		42	Cerebral hemorrhage
1989	+ SCHAEFFER, Rebecca		21	Murdered (shot) in Los Angeles, CA
1991	SCHAFER, Natalie		90	Cancer (in Los Angeles, CA)
1993	SCHAFFEL, Hal		78	Undisclosed causes
1989	+ SCHAFFNER, Franklin J.	★	69	Cancer (in Santa Monica, CA)
1989	SCHAKNE, Robert		63	Cancer
• 1998	SCHAMONI, Ulrich		58	Died in Berlin, Germany
1963	# SCHARF, Herman "Boo-Boo"		61	Heart attack (in Hollywood, CA)
1980	SCHARY, Dore		74	Cancer (in New York, NY)
1941	+ SCHERTZINGER, Victor	☆	52	Heart attack (in Hollywood, CA)
1964	+ SCHILDKRAUT, Joseph	★	67	Heart attack (in New York, NY)
1930	SCHILDKRAUT, Rudolf		65	Heart disease (in Los Angeles, CA)
1957	# SCHILLING, Gus		48	Heart attack (in Hollywood, CA)
1948	# SCHINDELL, Cy		41	After a long illness (in Van Nuys, CA)
1965	SCHIPA, Tito		76	Heart attack (in New York, NY)
1949	+ SCHLESINGER, Leon		66	Viral infection (in Hollywood, CA)
1945	# SCHLETTOW, Hans Adelbert		57	Died in Berlin, Germany
1993	SCHMIECHEN, Richard		45	A.I.D.S. (in Los Angeles, CA)
1955	# SCHMITZ, Sybille		42	Suicide (pills) in Munich, Germany
1993	SCHNEIDER, Abe		87	Pneumonia and Alzheimer's disease complications
1993	SCHNEIDER, Alexander		84	Heart disease (in New York)
1994	SCHNEIDER, Harold		55	Heart attack
1967	SCHNEIDER, James		85	Died in Hollywood, CA
• 1996	SCHNEIDER, Magda		87	Heart disease (in Schoenau, Germany)
1982	#+ SCHNEIDER, Romy		43	Found dead of cardiac arrest (at her apartment in Paris, France)
1975	SCHNEIDER, Stanley		45	Heart attack in his hotel room (in New York, NY)
1990	SCHNUR, Jerome		66	Melanoma (skin cancer)
• 1985	SCHOEN, Margarethe		89	
1993	SCHOENBRUN, Michael		54	Pancreatic cancer (in Tarzana, CA)
1978	# SCHOENHALS, Albrecht		90	Died in Baden-Baden, West Germany
1961	SCHOFIELD, Johnnie		71	Died in England

Deaths of Movie and Television Personalities — by Name

YEAR	NAME	AGE	CAUSE and/or PLACE OF DEATH
1989	SCHORR, William W.	88	Respiratory failure (in Los Angeles, CA)
1980	SCHRAMM, Karla	88	Died in Los Angeles, CA
1936	# SCHRECK, Max	57	Died in Munich, Germany
1982	SCHREIBER, Elsa (Shdanoff)	81	Heart failure (in Los Angeles, CA)
1995	SCHULMAN, Edward L.	79	Heart disease (at his daughter's home in Detroit, MI)
1935	# SCHULTZ, Harry	52	After a lengthy illness (in Hollywood, CA)
1972	SCHULZ, Fritz	75	Died in Zurich, Switzerland
1936	+ SCHUMANN-HEINK, Ernestine	75	Leukemia (in Hollywood, CA)
1958	SCHUMANN-HEINK, Ferdinand	65	Heart attack (in Los Angeles, CA)
1990	SCHUMM, Hans	93	Heart failure (in Los Angeles, CA)
1954	SCHUNZEL, Reinhold	68	Heart ailment (in Munich, Germany)
1986	SCHUSTER, Harold D.	83	Died in Westlake Village, CA
1960	+ SCHWARTZ, Maurice	69	Heart attack (near Tel Aviv, Israel)
1992	SCHWARTZ, Sammy	86	Heart attack
1968	SCOBIE, James	?	
• 1997	SCORSESE, Catherine	84	Complications from Alzheimer's disease (in New York, NY)
1993	SCORSESE, Luciano Charles	80	After a long illness (in New York)
1991	# SCOTT, Daniel Simon	71	Alzheimer's disease (in Alamitos, CA)
1991	SCOTT, Dennis	51	After a long illness
1964	SCOTT, Harold	72	Died in London, England
1981	#+ SCOTT, Hazel	61	Cancer (in New York, NY)
1986	SCOTT, Ken	58	Emphysema and heart failure (in Los Angeles, CA)
1976	SCOTT, Mabel Julienne	82	Died at the Burlington Convalescent Hospital in Los Angeles, CA
1960	SCOTT, Mark	45	Heart attack (in Burbank, CA)
1987	#+ SCOTT, Randolph	89	Cardiac arrest in his sleep (in Los Angeles, CA)
1994	SCOTT, Terry	67	Cancer (in Godalming, England)
1988	SCOTT, Timothy	32	Complications from A.I.D.S. (Do not confuse with T. Scott, d. 1995)
1995	SCOTT, Timothy	57	Lung cancer (in Los Angeles) Do not confuse with T. Scott, d. 1988
1965	#+ SCOTT, Zachary	51	Brain tumor (in Austin, TX)
• 1996	SCOTTI, Vito	78	Died at the Motion Picture and TV Hosp. in Woodland Hills, CA
1985	SCOURBY, Alexander	71	Died in Boston, MA
1973	SEABURY, Ynez	64	Internal complications (at her home in Sherman Oaks, CA)
1990	SEALES, Franklyn	37	A.I.D.S. (in Brooklyn, NY)
1921	# SEARLE, Kamuela C.	33	From injuries while filming "The Son of Tarzan" (in Los Angeles, CA)
1942	SEARS, Allan	55	After a long illness (in Los Angeles, CA)
1957	SEARS, Fred	44	Heart attack (in Hollywood, CA)
1960	# SEASTROM, Victor	80	Died in Stockholm, Sweden
1979	SEATON, George ☆	68	Cancer (in Beverly Hills, CA)
1968	SEATON, Scott	90	After a lengthy illness (in Hollywood, CA)
1992	SEAY, James	78	Died in Capitol Beach, CA
1957	+ SEBASTIAN, Dorothy	54	Colon cancer (at the MPCH in Woodland Hills, CA)
1979	#+ SEBERG, Jean	40	Suicide (drug overdose) found dead in her car in Paris, France
1969	# SEBRING, Jay	35	Murdered (in Los Angeles, CA)
• 1996	SECOLSKY, Herman	73	Complications from lung cancer (in Palm Beach, FL)
1987	SECREST, James	51	Lymphoma of the brain (in New York, NY)
1982	SEDAN, Rolfe	86	Died in Santa Monica, CA
1968	#+ SEDDON, Margaret	95	Died in Philadelphia, PA
1971	#+ SEDGWICK, Edie	28	Acute barbiturate intoxication (in Santa Barbara, CA)
1953	SEDGWICK, Edward Jr.	60	Following a heart attack (in North Hollywood, CA)
1991	SEDGWICK, Eileen	93	Died in Hollywood, CA
1973	SEDGWICK, Josie	75	Stroke (in Santa Monica, CA)
1990	SEEGAR, Sara	76	Cerebral hemorrhage (in Langhome, PA)
1918	SEELOS, Annette	27	Spanish influenza (in New York, NY)

Deaths of Movie and Television Personalities — by Name

YEAR	NAME	AGE	CAUSE and/or PLACE OF DEATH
1992	SEGAL, Vivienne	95	Heart failure (in Beverly Hills, CA)
1962	# SEGAR, Lucia	77	Died in New York, NY
1987	SEGOVIA, Andres	94	Heart failure
1964	SEITER, William A.	72	Heart attack (at his home in Beverly Hills, CA)
1944	+ SEITZ, George B.	56	Died in Hollywood, CA
1982	SEKA, Ron	48	Heart attack (in Hollywood, CA)
1950	SELBIE, Evelyn	68	Heart ailment (in Hollywood, CA)
1940	SELBY, Norman "Kid McCoy"	66	Suicide (at a downtown hotel in Detroit, MI)
1980	SELBY, Sarah	73	Died in Los Angeles, CA
1948	# SELIG, William N.	84	Died in Hollywood, CA
• 1998	SELINGER, Dennis	77	Cancer in London
1980	+ SELLERS, Peter ☆	54	Heart attack (in London, England)
1937	SELLON, Charles	58	Cancer (in La Crescenta, CA)
1939	# SELTEN, Morton	79	Died in London, England
1980	SELTZER, Daniel	47	Heart attack (in New York, NY)
1948	# SELWYN, Clarissa	62	Died in West Hollywood, CA
1944	+ SELWYN, Edgar	68	After a cerebral hemorrhage (in Hollywood, CA)
1954	#+ SELWYN, Ruth	49	After a long illness (in Hollywood, CA)
1965	#+ SELZNICK, David O.	63	Acute coronary (in Hollywood, CA)
1990	SELZNICK, Irene	83	Breast cancer
• 1997	SELZNICK, L. Jeffery	64	Heart attack during a business meeting in Los Angeles, CA
1944	+ SELZNICK, Myron	45	Following an attack of portal thrombosis (in Santa Monica, CA)
1946	SEMELS, Harry	58	Died in Los Angeles, CA
1928	SEMON, Larry	39	Pneumonia (near Victorville, CA)
1980	SEN YUNG, Victor	65	Apparent victim of a gas leak at his home in North Hollywood, CA
• 1996	+ SENECA, Joe	82	Asthma and heart attack (in New York, NY)
1960	#+ SENNETT, Mack	80	Heart attack (in Hollywood, CA)
1989	# SERATO, Massimo	73	Heart attack (in Rome, Italy)
1965	SERDA, Julia	90	Died in Dresden, East Germany
1991	SERKIN, Rudolph	88	Cancer
1975	+ SERLING, Rod	50	Complications after heart surgery (in Rochester, NY)
1992	SERPE, Ralph B.	81	Cancer (in Tarzana, CA)
1976	SERVAIS, Jean	65	Heart failure following surgery (in Paris, France)
1968	SERVOSS, Mary	80	Heart ailment (at her home in Los Angeles, CA)
• 1998	SESSA, Alejandro	60	Heart failure in Buenos Aires, Argentine
1974	SESSIONS, Almira	86	From injuries after a fall (in Los Angeles, CA)
1969	SETON, Bruce	60	After a long illness (in London, England)
1991	# SEUSS, Dr.	87	Respiratory and kidney problems
1992	SEVAREID, Eric	79	Stomach cancer
• 1921	Severin-Mars	?	Heart ailment (in France)
1990	SEYLER, Athene	101	Died in London, England
1988	SEYMOUR, Anne	79	Heart failure and respiratory complications (in Los Angeles, CA)
1920	SEYMOUR, Clarine	19	Surgical complications and pneumonia (in New York, NY)
1993	+ SEYMOUR, Dan	78	Following a stroke (in Santa Monica, CA)
1967	SEYMOUR, Harry	77	Heart attack (in Hollywood, CA)
1956	# SEYMOUR, Jane	56	Died in New York, NY
• 1997	SEYMOUR, John D.	?	
1990	SEYRIG, Delphine	58	Lung cancer (in Paris, France)
1956	SHADE, Jamesson	60	Heart attack (in Hollywood, CA)
• 1996	SHAFTEL, Josef	76	After a 3-yr. battle with multiple myeloma (in London, England)
1967	# SHAIFFER, Howard "Tiny"	48	Died in Burbank, CA
• 1996	+ SHAKUR, Tupac "2-Pac"	25	Cardiopulmonary arrest from a drive-by shooting (in Las Vegas, NV)
• 1996	SHANLEY, Lila	86	Heart failure (at St. John's Hosp. in Santa Monica, CA)

Deaths of Movie and Television Personalities — by Name

YEAR	NAME		AGE	CAUSE and/or PLACE OF DEATH
1957	SHANNON, Cora		88	*Cancer (in Woodland Hills, CA)*
1990	SHANNON, Del		50	*Suicide (in Santa Clarita, CA)*
1954	SHANNON, Effie		87	*Died in Bay Shore, L.I., NY*
1951	SHANNON, Ethel		53	*Died in Hollywood, CA*
1959	SHANNON, Frank Connolly		83	*Died in Hollywood, CA*
1964	SHANNON, Harry		74	*Died in Hollywood, CA*
1990	SHANNON, Paul		80	*Cancer*
1941	#+ SHANNON, Peggy		32	*Acute alcoholism and heart attack (in North Hollywood, CA)*
1993	SHARAFF, Irene	★	83	*Congestive heart failure (in New York)*
1993	SHARITS, Paul		50	*Heart attack (in Buffalo, NY)*
1994	# SHARKEY, Jack		91	*Respiratory arrest (at a hospital in Beverly, MA)*
1993	SHARKEY, Ray		40	*A.I.D.S. (at a hospital in Brooklyn, NY)*
1944	SHARLAND, Reginald		57	*Died in Loma Linda, CA*
1984	SHARP, Anthony		69	*Died in London, England*
1964	# SHARP, Henry		76	*Died in Brooklyn, NY*
1980	+ SHARPE, David H.		70	*Parkinson's disease (in Altadena, CA)*
1985	# SHAUGHNESSY, Mickey		64	*Lung cancer (in Cape May Courthouse, NJ)*
1968	# SHAW, C. Montague		83	*Died in Woodland Hills, CA*
1971	SHAW, Denis		49	*Heart attack (in London, England)*
1950	+ SHAW, George Bernard		94	*Bladder ailment and injuries from a fall (in Ayot St. Lawrence, Eng.)*
1926	SHAW, Harold M.		47	*Automobile accident (in Los Angeles, CA)*
1967	SHAW, Oscar		76	
1982	+ SHAW, Reta		69	*Died in Encino, CA*
1978	SHAW, Robert	☆	53	*Heart attack (near Tourmakeady, Ireland)*
1990	SHAW, Steve		25	*Injuries from an automobile accident (in Los Angeles, CA)*
1978	# SHAW, Susan		49	*Died in Middlesex, England*
1988	# SHAW, Victoria		53	*Asthma (in Sydney, Australia)*
1982	# SHAW, Wini		72	*Died in New York, NY*
1987	# SHAWLEE, Joan		61	*Cancer (in Hollywood, CA)*
1990	SHAWLEY, Robert		63	*Pneumonia (in Westwood, CA)*
1987	#+ SHAWN, Dick		63	*Apparent heart attack (while appearing on stage) in San Diego, CA*
1978	#+ SHAY, Dorothy		57	*Following a massive stroke (in Santa Monica, CA)*
1992	# SHAYNE, Robert		92	*Lung cancer (in Woodland Hills, CA)*
1983	SHAYNE, Tamara		80	*Following a heart attack (in Los Angeles, CA)*
1969	+ SHEA, Donald J. "Shorty"		36	*Murdered (in Chatsworth, CA)*
1953	# SHEA, Mervin		52	*Died in Sacramento, CA*
1918	# SHEA, William J.		?	*Heart attack (in Brooklyn, NY)*
1949	#+ SHEAN, Al		81	*Died in New York, NY*
1979	SHEAR, Barry		56	*Cancer (in New York, NY)*
1971	SHEARER, Douglas		71	
1993	SHEARER, Jacqueline		46	*Colon cancer (at her home in Cambridge, MA)*
1983	#+ SHEARER, Norma	★	82	*Bronchial pneumonia (in Woodland Hills, CA)*
1952	SHEEHAN, John J., Jr.		61	*Died in Hollywood, CA*
1945	SHEEHAN, Winfield		62	*Following abdominal surgery (in Hollywood, CA)*
1979	+ SHEEN, (Bishop) Fulton J.		84	*Heart trouble (in New York, NY)*
1957	# SHEFFIELD, Reginald		56	*Died in Pacific Palisades, CA*
1939	SHELBY, Margaret (Fillmore)		39	*Chronic alcoholism*
1982	SHELDON, Gene		75	*Heart attack*
1962	SHELDON, Jerome		71	*Died in Hollywood, CA (Do not confuse with Jerry Sheldon)*
1962	# SHELDON, Jerry		60	*Died in Hollywood, CA (Do not confuse with Jerome Sheldon)*
1992	SHELDON, Richard		59	*Cancer (in Montecito, CA)*
1989	SHELLEY, Dave		58	*Lung complications after heart surgery (in Woodland Hills, CA)*
1994	SHELTON, Anne		66	*Apparent heart attack (at her home in Herstmonceux, Eng.)*

Deaths of Movie and Television Personalities — by Name

YEAR	NAME	AGE	CAUSE and/or PLACE OF DEATH
1976	SHELTON, Don	64	*Died in Los Angeles, CA*
1971	SHELTON, George	86	*Burns (in New York, NY)*
1972	SHELTON, John	54	*Heart attack (in Sri Lanka, Ceylon)*
• 1997	SHELTON, Reid	72	*Died of a Stroke in Protland, Ore.*
1989	SHENAR, Paul	53	*A.I.D.S. (in West Hollywood, CA)*
1993	SHEPARD, Bob	76	*Heart attack (on a visit to Manhattan, NY)*
1961	# SHEPLEY, Michael	53	*Died in London, England*
1988	SHER, Jack	75	*After a brief illness (in Beverly Hills, CA)*
1967	#+ SHERIDAN, Ann	51	*Cancer (in San Fernando Valley, CA)*
1963	# SHERIDAN, Dan	46	*Suicide (overdose of barbiturates) in Encino, CA*
1943	SHERIDAN, Frank	74	*After a brief illness (in Hollywood, CA)*
1973	#+ SHERMAN, Allan	48	*Respiratory failure caused by emphysema (in Los Angeles, CA)*
1989	SHERMAN, Connie	72	*Respiratory failure (in Pittsburgh, PA)*
1969	SHERMAN, Fred E.	64	*After suffering a stroke in 1962 (in Woodland Hills, CA)*
1991	SHERMAN, George	82	*Heart and kidney failure (in Los Angeles, CA)*
1952	SHERMAN, Harry	67	*After two surgical operations*
1989	SHERMAN, Hiram	81	*Following a stroke (in Springfield, IL)*
1934	+ SHERMAN, Lowell J.	49	*Pneumonia (in Hollywood, CA)*
1980	# SHERMAN, Mary	93	*Died in Santa Monica, CA*
1985	SHERMAN, Ransom	87	*Died in Henderson, NV*
1944	# SHERRY, J. Barney	71	*Died in Philadelphia, PA*
1990	SHERWOOD, Bill	38	*A.I.D.S. (in New York, NY)*
1981	# SHERWOOD, Bobby	65	*Cancer (in Auburn, MA)*
1989	SHERWOOD, Lydia	82	*Died in London, England*
1962	SHIELD, Leroy	68	*Died in Fort Lauderdale, FL*
1970	SHIELDS, Arthur	74	*Emphysema (in Santa Barbara, CA)*
1975	# SHIELDS, Frank	64	*Died in Los Angeles, CA*
1984	SHIELDS, John Webster	34	*Cancer (in Modesto, CA)*
1993	SHIELDS, Pat	70	*Found dead in his car (in Death Valley)*
1994	SHILTS, Randy	42	*A.I.D.S. (in Guerneville, CA)*
• 1996	SHIMA, Keiji	68	*Acute respiratory failure (in Japan)*
1981	SHIMODA, Yuki	58	*Emphysema (in Los Angeles, CA)*
1982	SHIMURA, Takashi	76	*Emphysema (in Tokyo, Japan)*
1977	# SHINDO, Eitaro	78	*Heart failure (in Tokyo, Japan)*
1939	SHINE, Wilfred	75	*Died in Kingston, England*
1966	SHINER, Ronald	63	*Died in London, England*
1993	# SHIRLEY, Anne ☆	74	*Lung cancer after a long illness (in Los Angeles, CA)*
1989	SHIRLEY, Bill	68	*Lung cancer (in Los Angeles, CA)*
1978	SHOEMAKER, Ann	87	*Cancer (in Hollywood, CA)*
1988	SHOLOMIR, Jack	57	*Heart attack (in Miami Beach, FL)*
1966	Shooting Star	76	*Stroke (in Hollywood, CA)*
1994	#+ SHORE, Dinah	76	*Cancer (at her home in Beverly Hills, CA)*
1957	SHORES, Byron L.	50	*Multiple sclerosis (in Kansas City, KS)*
1992	SHORR, Lester ★	85	*Cancer (in Los Angeles, CA)*
1972	SHORT, Antrim	72	*Emphysema (in Woodland Hills, CA)*
1968	SHORT, Gertrude	66	*After a brief illness (in Hollywood, CA)*
1958	SHORT, Lewis W.	83	*Died in Hollywood, CA*
1975	+ SHOSTAKOVICH, Dmitri	68	*After a 9-yr. battle with heart disease*
1934	SHOTWELL, Marie	54	*Died in L.I., NY*
1970	# SHRINER, Herb	51	*Killed with his wife in a car crash (in Delray Beach, FL)*
1937	SHUBERT, Eddie	38	*Heart attack watching a golf tournament (in Los Angeles, CA)*
1985	SHUE, Larry	38	*Airplane crash (in Weyers Cave, VA)*
1995	SHULMAN, Irving	82	*Alzheimer's disease (in Sherman Oaks, CA)*

YEAR	NAME	AGE	CAUSE and/or PLACE OF DEATH
1991	SHUMAN, Mort	52	Cancer of the liver (in London, England)
1973	+ SHUMAN, Roy	49	Heart attack (in New York, NY)
1979	SHUMLIN, Herman E.	80	Heart failure complicated by emphysema (in New York, NY)
1959	# SHUMWAY, Lee	75	
1965	# SHUMWAY, Walter	80	Heart disease (in Woodland Hills, CA)
1976	SHUTTA, Ethel	79	Died at St. Clare's Hospital in New York
1945	SHY, Gus	51	After a long illness (in Hollywood, CA)
1945	# SIDNEY, George (actor)	69	After a long illness (in Hollywood, CA)
1993	SIDNEY, Sid	?	Parkinson's disease
1976	SIEBER, Rudolf	77	Following a long illness
1940	# SIEGEL, Bernard	72	Heart attack (in Hollywood, CA)
1991	SIEGEL, Don	78	After a long bout with cancer (in Nipoma, CA)
1928	SIEGMANN, George A.	45	Pernicious anemia (in Hollywood, CA)
1993	SIEGRIST, Jeremy	20	Killed in a hiking accident (in Topanga Canyon Mountains, CA)
1963	SIERRA, Margarita	27	Following heart surgery (in Hollywood, CA)
1985	#+ SIGNORET, Simone ★	64	Pancreatic cancer (in Auteuil-Anthouillet, France)
1964	SILETTI, Mario G.	59	Automobile accident (in Los Angeles, CA)
1996	SILLIPHANT, Stirling ★	78	Prostate cancer (in Bangkok, Thailand)
1930	+ SILLS, Milton	48	Heart attack while playing tennis (in Santa Monica, CA)
1976	SILVA, David	58	Thrombosis (in Mexico City, Mexico)
1980	# SILVA, Mario	79	
1957	# SILVA, Simone	29	Suicide (in London, England)
1988	SILVA, Trinidad Jr.	38	Traffic accident (in Whittier, CA)
1964	SILVANI, Aldo	73	After a long illness (in Milan, Italy)
1994	SILVANI, Jole	84	Died in her hometown of Trieste, Italy
1991	SILVER, Dave	72	Heart attack
1989	SILVER, Joe	66	Liver cancer
1970	SILVERA, Frank	56	Accidentally electrocuted in his home (in Pasadena, CA)
1980	#+ SILVERHEELS, Jay "Tonto"	62	Complications from pneumonia (in Woodland Hills, CA)
1989	SILVERMAN, Mark	36	A.I.D.S. (in New York, NY)
1985	#+ SILVERS, Phil	73	Heart attack (in Century City, CA)
1976	SILVERS, Sid	72	Died in Los Angeles, CA
1976	SIM, Alastair	75	Cancer (in London, England)
1994	SIMEK, Vasek	66	Heart attack while playing at the Croatian Nat. Theatre (in Zagreb)
• 1998	SIMMONS, Ed	78	Cardiac arrest at Cedars-Sinai Med. Ctr. in Los Angeles, CA
1994	SIMMS, Ginny	81	Heart attack (at Desert Hosp. in Palm Springs, CA)
1994	# SIMMS, Hilda	75	Pancreatic cancer (in Buffalo, NY)
1969	SIMON, Abe	56	Died in Queens, NY
1975	# SIMON, Michel	80	Pulmonary embolism (in Bry-sur-Marne, France)
1992	SIMON, Robert F.	83	Heart attack (in Tarzana, CA)
1951	+ SIMON, S. Sylvan	41	Heart attack (in Beverly Hills, CA)
1986	# SIMPSON, Bill	54	After a long illness (in Mauchline, Scotland)
1996	# SIMPSON, Don	52	Heart failure due to drug abuse (at his home in Bel-Air, CA)
1951	SIMPSON, Ivan	76	Died in New York, NY
1985	SIMPSON, Mickey	72	Heart attack (in Northridge, CA)
1959	SIMPSON, Russell	79	Died in Hollywood, CA
• 1996	SIMPSON, Sloan	80	After an illness (in Dallas, TX)
• 1998	SINATRA, Frank		Heart attack at Cedars-Sinai Med. Ctr. in Los Angeles, CA
1980	# SINATRA, Ray	76	Intestinal problems (in Las Vegas, NV)
1951	# SINCLAIR, Arthur	68	Died in Belfast, Northern Ireland
• 1984	SINCLAIR, Gordon	83	Died in Toronto, Canada
1962	SINCLAIR, Hugh	59	Died in Slapton, England
1995	# SINCLAIR, Madge	57	Leukemia (in Los Angeles, CA)

• New entry.   # Original name (Pt. 7).   + Interment (Pt. 5).   311   ☆ Oscar nominee, ★ Oscar winner (Pt. 10)

Deaths of Movie and Television Personalities — by Name

YEAR	NAME	AGE	CAUSE and/or PLACE OF DEATH
1970	SINCLAIR, Robert B.	65	Stabbed to death by a burglar (in his California home)
1992	SINCLAIR, Ronald	68	Respiratory failure (in Woodland Hills, CA)
1969	#+ SINGLETON, Catherine	65	Died in Fort Worth, TX
1973	# SIODMAK, Robert ☆	73	Heart attack (in Locarno, Switzerland)
1928	SIPPERLY, Ralph	37	Died in Bangor, ME
1987	# SIRK, Douglas	86	Cancer (in Lugano, Switzerland)
1975	# SISSLE, Noble	86	Died in Tampa, FL
1954	SISSON, Vera	63	Overdose of barbiturates (in Carmel, CA)
• 1998	+ SITKA, Emil	83	Following a stroke in Camarillo, CA
1994	SKALA, Lilia ☆	90s	Died at her home in Bay Shore, NY
1934	# SKELLY, Hal	42	Killed by a train in a grade crossing accident (in West Cornwall, CT)
1976	# SKELTON, Georgia	54	Suicide (gunshot) in Rancho Mirage, CA
• 1997	+ SKELTON, Red	84	After a long illness at Eisenhower Med. Ctr. Rancho Mirage, CA
1979	+ SKINNER, Cornelia Otis	78	Cerebral hemorrhage (in New York, NY)
1968	SKINNER, Frank	69	Cancer (in Los Angeles, CA)
1942	SKINNER, Otis	83	Uremic poisoning (at his home in New York, NY)
1952	# SKIPWORTH, Alison	88	Died in New York, NY
1983	SKOLSKY, Sidney	78	Parkinson's disease (in Hollywood, CA)
1971	+ SKOURAS, Spyros	78	Died in Mamouroneck, NY
1965	# SLACK, Freddie	55	Heart attack (in Hollywood, CA)
1989	SLATE, Jack	80	Heart attack (in Los Angeles, CA)
1975	SLATER, John	58	Heart attack (in London, England)
1987	SLATER, Patrick Scott	42	A.I.D.S. (in New York, NY)
• 1997	SLATTERY, Richard X.	72	Following a stroke (in Woodland Hills, CA)
1956	# SLAUGHTER, Tod	70	Died in Derby, England
1983	SLEEPER, Martha	72	Heart attack (in Beaufort, NC)
1946	SLEZAK, Leo	71	Died in Rottach-Ergen, Germany
1983	SLEZAK, Walter	80	Suicide (gunshot) in Flower Hill, NY
1990	SLOANE, Doreen	56	Cancer (in Liverpool, England)
1965	+ SLOANE, Everett	55	Suicide (sleeping pills) in Brentwood, CA
1963	SLOANE, Olive	66	Died in London, England
1972	SLOMAN, Edward "Ted"	87	Died in Calabasas Park, CA
1992	SLYTER, Fred	56	After a long illness (in Los Angeles, CA)
1939	#+ SMALLEY, Phillips	63	Died in Hollywood, CA
1993	SMANEY, June	71	An apparent suicide (in Los Angeles, CA)
1960	SMART, J. Scott	57	Died in Springfield, IL
1945	SMILEY, Joseph W.	64	Died in New York
• 1998	# SMITH, "Buffalo Bob"	80	Lung cancer in a Hospital in Hendersonville, N.C.
1950	SMITH, "Whispering" Jack	51	Heart attack (in New York) Do not confuse with Jack Smith, d. 1989
1939	# SMITH, Albert J.	44	Died in Hollywood, CA
1993	# SMITH, Alexis	72	Cancer (at Cedars-Sinai Med. Ctr. in Los Angeles, CA)
1973	# SMITH, Art	73	Heart attack (in West Babylon, NY)
1991	SMITH, Burleigh	70	Cancer
1948	#+ SMITH, C. Aubrey	85	Double pneumonia (in Beverly Hills, CA)
1988	SMITH, Charles "Dizzy"	67	Apparent heart attack (in Burbank, CA)
1937	SMITH, Clifford S.	51	Peritonitis following a ruptured appendix (in Hollywood, CA)
1963	# SMITH, Cyril	70	Died in London, England
1959	SMITH, G. Albert	61	After a brief illness (in New York, NY)
1974	# SMITH, Gerald	77	After a short illness (in Woodland Hills, CA)
1994	+ SMITH, Hal	77	Apparent heart attack (at his home in Santa Monica, CA)
1968	SMITH, Howard I.	74	Heart attack (in Hollywood, Ca.)
1989	SMITH, Jack	57	A.I.D.S. (Do not confuse with "Whispering" Jack Smith, d. 1950)
1992	SMITH, Jacqueline	?	After a lengthy illness

• New entry. # Original name (Pt. 7). + Interment (Pt. 5).   312   ☆ Oscar nominee, ★ Oscar winner (Pt. 10)

Deaths of Movie and Television Personalities — by Name

YEAR	NAME		AGE	CAUSE and/or PLACE OF DEATH
1995	# SMITH, John		63	Cirrhosis and heart problems (at his home in L.A., CA)
1981	#+ SMITH, Joseph		96	Died in Englewood, NJ
1986	SMITH, Justin		66	Complications from A.I.D.S. (in Santa Monica, CA)
1986	#+ SMITH, Kate		79	After a long bout with diabetes and heart problems (in Raleigh, NC)
1985	SMITH, Kent		78	Congestive heart failure (in Woodland Hills, CA)
1995	SMITH, Michael C.		34	Died in Stoughton, MA)
1985	SMITH, Muriel		61	Died in Richmond, VA
1979	SMITH, Pete	★	86	Suicide (jumped from the roof of a nursing home) in Santa Monica
1978	SMITH, Queenie		70	Cancer (in Burbank, CA)
1991	SMITH, Ray		55	
1985	SMITH, Samantha		13	Airplane crash after filming in England (in Auburn-Lewiston, ME)
1988	SMITH, Tucker		52	Cancer of the neck and jaw (in Los Angeles, CA)
1974	SNEGOFF, Leonid		90	Heart failure and arteriosclerosis (in Los Angeles, CA)
1958	SNOW, Marguerite		68	Kidney complications (in Hollywood, CA)
1982	SNOWDEN, Leigh		51	Cancer (in Los Angeles, CA)
1996	SNYDER, Jimmy "The Greek"		76	Heart failure (at a hospital in Las Vegas, NV)
1991	SOBEK, Allan		46	A.I.D.S. (in New York, NY)
1948	SODERLING, Walter		75	Died in Los Angeles, CA
1988	SOFAER, Abraham		91	Congestive heart failure (in Woodland Hills, CA)
1954	# Sojin		63	Died in Tokyo, Japan
1962	+ SOKOLOFF, Vladimir		72	Stroke (in Hollywood, CA)
1997	SOLARES, Gilberto Martinez		90	Heart attack (in Mexico City, Mexico)
1961	# SOLER, Domingo Jr.		59	Heart attack (in Acapulco, Mexico)
1985	SOLON, Ewen		62	Died in Addlestone, England
1983	SOMACK, Jack		64	Heart attack (in Hollywood, CA)
1974	# SOMERSET, Pat		77	Arterial hemorrhage (in Apple Valley, CA)
1994	SOMES, Michael		77	Brain tumor (in London, England)
1990	SOMMER, Bert		42	Liver failure (in Albany, NY)
1995	SONBERT, Warren		46	Complications of A.I.D.S. (in Los Angeles, CA)
1985	# SONDERGAARD, Gale	★	86	After a long illness (in Woodland Hills, CA)
1991	SONNTAG, Jack		77	After a long illness (in Santa Barbara, CA)
1979	#+ SOO, Jack		63	Cancer of the esophagus (in Los Angeles, CA)
1948	SOREL, George S.		48	Died in Hollywood, CA
1989	SORM, Evald		57	
1996	SOSNICK, Harry		89	After a long illness (at Calvary Hospital in New York)
1947	# SOTHERN, Hugh		65	After an illness of 2 years (in Hollywood, CA)
1992	# SOUEZ, Ina		89	Stroke
1994	SOULE, Olan		84	Lung cancer (at his daughter's home in Corona, CA)
1932	+ SOUSA, John Philip		77	Heart attack (in Reading, PA)
1975	SOUSSANIN, Nicholas		66	Cardiac arrest (in New York, NY)
1990	SOUTHARD, Stephen		30	A.I.D.S. (in Sherman Oaks, CA)
1991	# SOUTHERN, Jeri		64	Pneumonia
1995	SOUTHERN, Terry		71	Emphysema (in New York, NY)
1983	SPACE, Arthur		74	Cancer (in Hollywood, CA)
1940	SPACEY, John Graham		44	Heart attack after attending a party (in Hollywood, CA)
1981	SPADARO, Umberto		77	Cancer (in Rome, Italy)
1983	SPAIN, Fay		50	Cancer (in Los Angeles, CA)
1957	#+ SPARKS, Ned		73	Intestinal block (in Victorville, CA)
1969	SPEAR, Harry		47	Died in Hollywood, CA
1995	SPENCE, Irven "Irv"		86	Heart attack (in Dallas, TX)
1949	SPENCE, Ralph		60	Heart attack (in Woodland Hills, CA)
1960	SPENCER, Douglas		50	Diabetic condition (in Hollywood, Ca.)
1992	SPENCER, Herbert	☆	87	Died in Culver City, CA

Deaths of Movie and Television Personalities — by Name

YEAR	NAME	AGE	CAUSE and/or PLACE OF DEATH
1988	+ SPERLING, Milton	76	After a long illness (in Beverly Hills, CA)
1990	SPEWACK, Bella	91	Died in New York, NY
1985	SPIEGEL, Sam	84	After surgery (while vacationing in Ile-Saint-Martin, Antilles)
• 1997	SPIELMANN, Fritz (Fred)	90	Natural causes in NY
• 1997	SPILLER, Cyreld	89	Brookline, Mass following a brief illness
1989	SPINELL, Joe	51	Heart attack (in New York, NY)
1990	# SPITALNY, Evelyn	79	
1970	SPITALNY, Phil	80	Cancer (in Miami Beach, FL)
1989	SPITZ, Hank	84	
1994	SPIVAK, Laurence	93	Congestive heart failure (in Washington, D.C.)
1971	# Spivy	64	Died at the Motion Picture Country Home in Woodland Hills, CA
1985	SPOLIANSKY, Mischa	86	Died in London, England
1953	SPOOR, George K.	81	Died in Chicago, IL
1958	# SQUIRE, Ronald	72	Died in London, England
1989	SQUIRE, William	72	Undisclosed causes (in London, England)
• 1998	# SQUIRES, Dorothy	83	Cancer in Llwynpia, Wales
1952	ST. CLAIR, Malcolm	55	Died in Pasadena, CA.
1974	ST. CYR, Lillian "Red Wing"	100	Died in New York, NY
1968	#+ ST. DENIS, Ruth	90	Heart attack (in Hollywood, CA)
1990	# ST. JACQUES, Raymond	60	Lymphatic cancer (in Los Angeles, CA)
1988	ST. JOHN, Adela Rogers	94	Died in Arroyo Grande, CA
1963	# ST. JOHN, Al "Fuzzy"	69	Heart attack (in Vidalia, GA)
1974	ST. JOHN, Howard	68	Heart attack (in New York, NY)
1957	ST. JOHN, Jane Lee	45	After a long illness
1993	ST. JOSEPH, Ellis	82	Cancer (in Beverly Hills, CA)
1994	ST. JUST, Maria	?	Heart failure from severe rheumatoid arthritis (in London, England)
1959	ST. MAUR, Adele	70	Leukemia (in Sunnydale, CA)
1946	# ST. POLIS, John	72	Died in Los Angeles, CA
1992	STAFFORD, Grace	88	
1968	#+ STAFFORD, Hanley	69	Heart attack (in Hollywood, Ca.)
1950	+ STAHL, John M.	63	Heart attack (in Hollywood, CA)
1961	STAINTON, Philip	53	Died in London, England
1990	STALKER, John	67	
1996	STAMENKOVIC, Stan	39	Head injuries from a fall in his home (in Titova Uzice, Serbia)
1946	STAMP-TAYLOR, Enid	41	Injuries from a fall (in London, England)
1994	+ STANDER, Lionel	86	Lung cancer (at his home in Brentwood, CA)
1937	STANDING, Guy	63	Following a heart attack (in Apple Valley, CA)
1955	STANDING, Herbert Jr.	71	Died in New York, NY
1917	STANDING, Jack	31	Died in Los Angeles, CA
1979	STANDING, Joan	75	Cancer (in Houston, TX)
1963	# STANDING, Wyndham	82	Died in Los Angeles, CA
• 1998	STANGERUP, Henrik	60	
1935	# STANHOPE, Adeline	82	Died in Los Angeles, CA
• 1937	STANLEY, Aileen	85	Died in Los Angeles, CA
• 1996	STANLEY, Alvah W., Jr.	56	Heart attack (at his home in Los Angeles, CA)
1994	STANLEY, Anita	88	
1944	STANLEY, Edwin	64	Died in Hollywood, CA
1969	STANLEY, Forrest	80	Results of a fall (in Los Angeles, CA)
1990	# STANLEY, Helene	62	Died in Los Angeles, CA
1982	STANLEY, Louise	66	Died in Cocoa Beach, FL
1943	# STANMORE, Frank	65	Died in England
1978	# STANTON, Harry	76	Heart disease (in Los Angeles, CA)
1955	STANTON, Paul	70	Died in Los Angeles, CA

Deaths of Movie and Television Personalities — by Name

YEAR	NAME	AGE	CAUSE and/or PLACE OF DEATH
1969	# STANTON, Will	84	Bronchial pneumonia (in Santa Monica, CA)
1990	#+ STANWYCK, Barbara ☆	82	Congestive heart failure (in Santa Monica, CA)
1977	# STARK, Pauline	76	Died in Santa Monica, CA
1995	STARK, Wilbur	83	Cancer (at New York Hospital in Manhattan)
1990	STARR, Jimmy	86	Died in Phoenix, AZ
1950	STARR, Muriel	62	Heart attack (in New York, NY)
1970	# STARR, Randy	39	Died in Los Angeles, CA
1986	STARRETT, Charles	82	Cancer (in Borrego Springs, CA)
1989	STARRETT, Jack	52	Kidney failure (in Sherman Oaks, CA)
1984	STAUDTE, Wolfgang	77	Heart attack (in Zigarski, Slovenia)
1988	STAVRIDIS, Nicos	77	Heart failure (in Greece)
1993	STEADMAN, John	83	Pneumonia (in Montrose, CA)
• 1996	STEADMAN, Kenneth Keith	27	Killed in a dune buggy accident on the set (40 mi. east of L.A.)
1966	STEADMAN, Vera	66	Died in Long Beach, CA
1990	STEBER, Eleanor	76	Congestive heart failure (in Langhome, PA)
1948	STEDMAN, Lincoln	41	Died in Los Angeles, CA
1938	STEDMAN, Myrtle	48	Heart trouble (in Los Angeles, CA)
1992	STEEL, Pippa	44	Cancer (in London, England)
1988	#+ STEELE, Bob	82	Heart failure after a long illness (in Burbank, CA)
• 1997	STEELE, Daron	51	Died of a brain tumor in Los Angeles, CA
1955	STEELE, Vernon	72	Heart attack (in Los Angeles, Ca.)
1966	# STEELE, William "Bill"	76	Died in Los Angeles, CA
1983	STEEN, Malcolm H. "Mike"	55	After a brief illness (in New York, NY)
1951	# STEERS, Larry	69	Died in Woodland Hills, CA
• 1995	STEFANO, Joey	27	Drug overdose
1991	STEIN, Robert M.	40	Lung cancer (in Los Angeles, CA)
• 1997	# STEINER, Arthur H.	82	Heart failure
1965	STEINER, Elio	60	Died in Rome, Italy
1971	+ STEINER, Max	83	Died in Hollywood, CA
1929	# STEINRUCK, Albert	57	Died in Berlin, Germany
1993	# STEN, Anna	85	Cardiac arrest (at her home in Manhattan, NY)
1980	STEPANEK, Karel	80	Died in Los Angeles, CA
1986	STEPHENS, Harvey	85	Died in Laguna Hills, CA
• 1996	STEPHENS, Phil	89	Cardiac arrest at his home
1995	STEPHENS, Robert	64	After a liver and kidney transplant (in London, England)
1956	#+ STEPHENSON, Henry	85	After a brief illness (in San Francisco, CA)
1941	+ STEPHENSON, James ☆	53	Heart attack (in Pacific Palisades, CA)
1992	STEPHENSON, Skip	54	Following an apparent heart attack
1969	# STEPPAT, Ilse	52	Heart attack (in West Berlin, Germany)
1932	STEPPLING, John C.	62	After an extended illness (in Hollywood, CA)
1939	# STERLING, Ford	58	Thrombosis of veins and heart attack (in Los Angeles, CA)
1958	STERLING, Larry	23	A water-skiing accident (in Clear Lake, CA)
1959	STERLING, Richard	78	Heart attack (in Douglaston, NY)
1971	STERN, Bill	64	Heart attack (in Rye, NY)
1964	STEVENS, Bert	59	Heart attack (in Hollywood, CA)
1964	STEVENS, Charles	71	Died in Hollywood, CA
1996	STEVENS, Chuck	64	Massive heart attack (in Las Vegas, NV)
1993	STEVENS, Dudley	57	A.I.D.S. (in Hove, England)
1923	STEVENS, Edwin	62	Pleurisy (in Los Angeles, CA)
1991	STEVENS, Fran	72	Cancer (in The Bronx, NY)
1975	+ STEVENS, George Sr. ★	70	Heart attack (in Lancaster, CA)
1970	#+ STEVENS, Inger	35	After an overdose of barbiturates (enroute to a Hollywood hospital)
1994	# STEVENS, K. T.	74	Lung cancer (at her home in Brentwood, CA)

YEAR	NAME	AGE	CAUSE and/or PLACE OF DEATH
1940	#+ STEVENS, Landers	63	*Heart attack following appendectomy (in Hollywood, CA)*
• 1998	STEVENS, Leslie	74	*After emergency angioplasty in Los Angeles, CA*
1991	STEVENS, Mort	62	*Pancreatic cancer (in Encino, CA)*
1977	# STEVENS, Onslow	74	*Murdered (while in a convalescent home) in Van Nuys, CA*
1986	STEVENS, Paul	65	*Pneumonia (in New York, NY)*
1989	STEVENS, Robert	68	*Heart attack (in Westport, CT)*
1953	STEVENSON, Houseley	74	*Died at City of Hope Sanitarium, near Los Angeles, CA*
1996	STEVENSON, McLean	66	*Heart attack (at a hospital in Los Angeles, CA)*
1986	STEVENSON, Robert (director)	81	*After a long illness (in Santa Barbara, CA)*
1961	+ STEWART, Anita	66	*Heart attack (in Beverly Hills, CA)*
1940	STEWART, Athole	61	*Died in Buckinghamshire, England*
1993	STEWART, Bill	67	*Heart attack (at a London airport, after filming in Madeira)*
1952	STEWART, Blanche	?	*Died in Los Angeles, CA*
1994	STEWART, Dennis	46	*Heart problems and swelling of the brain*
1966	# STEWART, Donald	54	*After a long illness (in Chertsey, England)*
1970	STEWART, Fred	63	*Died at the Actors Studio in New York*
1966	STEWART, Jack	51	*Died in London, England*
• 1997	+ STEWART, James (Jimmy) ★	89	*Died at his home in Beverly Hills, CA from a lung blood clot*
• 1997	STEWART, Larry	67	*Bacterial Infection and heart failure (in Van Nuys, CA)*
1986	STEWART, Paul	77	*Heart attack (in Los Angeles, CA)*
1938	STEWART, Richard	?	
1933	STEWART, Roy	43	*Heart attack (in Los Angeles, Ca.)*
1995	STEWART, Samuel Douglas	75	*Parkinson's disease (at the Motion Picture Hospital)*
1977	STEWART, Sophie	69	*Died in London, England*
• 1998	STICKNEY, Dorothy	101	*At her home in New York City, NY*
1991	STIERLE, Edward	23	*A.I.D.S.*
• 1997	STILL, Frank	79	*Heart attack (at his home in Laguna Beach, CA)*
1928	STILLER, Mauritz	45	*Pleurisy (in Stockholm, Sweden)*
1986	STOCK, Nigel	66	*Heart attack (in London, England)*
1953	# STOCKDALE, Carl	79	*Heart attack (in Woodland Hills, CA)*
1966	# STOCKFIELD, Betty	61	*Leukemia (in London, England)*
1959	STOECKEL, Joe	65	*Circulatory ailment (in Munich, Germany)*
1966	# STOKER, H. G.	81	*Died in England*
1977	#+ STOKOWSKI, Leopold	95	*Coronary attack (in Nether Wallop, Hampshire, England)*
1985	STOLL, George	79	*After a brief illness (in Monterey, CA)*
1980	STOLOFF, Morris W. ★	85	*Died in Woodland Hills, CA*
1940	STONE, Arthur	56	*After a brief illness (in Hollywood, CA)*
1995	STONE, Christopher	55	*Heart attack*
1994	STONE, Ezra "Henry Aldrich"	76	*Automobile accident (near Perth Amboy, NJ)*
1959	+ STONE, Fred	85	*Heart attack after a 2-year illness (in North Hollywood, CA)*
1967	# STONE, George E.	63	*Following a paralytic stroke (in Woodland Hills, CA)*
• 1997	STONE, Jon	65	*Amyotrophic lateral sclerosis (in New York, NY)*
1953	#+ STONE, Lewis ☆	74	*Heart attack (while chasing 3 teen-aged vandals) in Los Angeles, CA*
• 1998	STONE, Martin	83	*Heart attack in Washington, DC*
1980	+ STONE, Milburn	75	*Heart attack (in La Jolla, CA)*
1986	STONE, Sidney	83	*Heart failure (in New York, NY)*
1995	STONEBURNER, Sam	66	*Esophageal cancer (at his Manhattan home)*
1941	STONEHOUSE, Ruth	47	*Died in Hollywood, CA*
1950	# STOOPNAGLE, Col. Lemuel Q.	52	*Died in Encino, CA*
1988	STOPPA, Paolo	81	*Leukemia (in Rome, Italy)*
1985	STORER, Conrad L.	55	*Cancer (in Burbank, CA)*
1992	# STOREY, June	73	*Cancer (in Vista, CA)*
• 1996	STORKE, William F.	73	*Cancer (at his home in Manhattan, NY)*

Deaths of Movie and Television Personalities — by Name

YEAR	NAME		AGE	CAUSE and/or PLACE OF DEATH
1993	STORRS, Tim		43	*Found dead in his apartment after a fall*
1973	STOSSEL, Ludwig		89	*Died in Beverly Hills, CA*
1949	STOTHART, Herbert		64	*After an illness of several months (in Hollywood, CA)*
• 1998	STOTTER, Don		69	*Heart failure at his home in Hollywood, Fla.*
1989	STOUT, Bill		62	*Cardiac arrest (in Los Angeles, CA)*
1919	STOWELL, William H.		34	*Killed in a train wreck (in Elizabethville, South Africa)*
1958	STRADNER, Rose		45	*Found dead in her summer house (in Bedford Village, NY)*
1992	STRAIT, Ralph		56	*Heart attack (in New York, NY)*
1963	STRANDMARK, Erik		44	*Died in Trinidad, West Indies*
1992	STRANGE, Bill		62	*Cancer*
1973	#+ STRANGE, Glenn		74	*Cancer (in Burbank, CA)*
1952	STRANGE, Robert		70	*Died in Hollywood, CA*
1982	#+ STRASBERG, Lee ☆		80	*Heart attack (in New York, NY)*
1974	STRASSBERG, Morris		75	*Died in South Laguna Beach, CA*
1980	#+ STRATTEN, Dorothy		20	*Murdered (shot by her husband) in West Los Angeles, CA*
1970	STRATTON, Chester		57	*Died at his home in Los Angeles, CA*
1975	STRAUSS, Robert ☆		61	*Complications following a stroke (in New York, NY)*
1943	STRAUSS, William H.		58	*After a heart attack (in Hollywood, Ca.)*
1964	STRAYER, Frank R.		72	*Cancer (in Hollywood, CA)*
1971	STREET, David		54	*Died in Los Angeles, CA*
• 1997	STREHLER, Giorgio		76	*Died of a heart attact in Lugano, Switzerland*
1985	STRETTON, Ellen		71	*Pneumonia (in New York, NY)*
1938	STRICKLAND, Helen		74	*Died at Mt. Sinai Hospital in New York, NY*
1974	STRIKER, Joseph		74	*Died in St. Barnabas Hospital, Livingston, NJ*
1993	STRIVELLI, Jerry		61	*Heart attack (in New York)*
1994	STRODE, Woody		80	*Died in his sleep after long bout with cancer (Glendora, CA)*
1991	STROHM, Walter Clarence		86	*Heart failure*
• 1997	STROKA, Michael		58	*Cancer in West Hollywood, CA*
1968	+ STROMBERG, Hunt		74	*Massive stroke (in Santa Monica, CA)*
1980	# STRONG, Leonard		71	*Died in Glendale, CA*
1980	STRONG, Michael		55	*Cancer (in Los Angeles, CA)*
1923	STRONG, Porter		44	*Heart attack in his hotel room (in New York City)*
1993	STRONG, Robert B.		87	*Cardiac arrest in his sleep (in Burbank, CA)*
1985	STROUD, Claude		78	*Throat cancer (in Santa Monica, CA)*
1983	STRUDWICK, Shepperd		75	*Cancer (in Manhattan, NY)*
1987	STRYKER, Christopher		27	*A.I.D.S. (in New York, NY)*
1944	STUART, Donald		45	*Following a heart attack (in Hollywood, CA)*
1936	STUART, Iris		33	
1978	# STUART, John		81	*Cardiac arrest in his sleep (in London, England)*
1973	# STUART, Nick		68	*Cancer (in Biloxi, MS)*
1950	# STUBBS, Harry		75	*Heart attack (in Woodland Hills, CA)*
1986	STUCKER, Stephen		36	*Complications from A.I.D.S. (in Hollywood, CA)*
1976	# STUEWE, Hans		75	*Died in Berlin, Germany*
1992	STURGES, John ☆		82	*Heart attack and emphysema (at his home in San Luis Obispo, CA)*
1959	#+ STURGES, Preston		60	*Heart attack (at the Algonquin Hotel in New York, NY)*
1947	# STURGIS, Eddie		66	*Heart disease (in Los Angeles, CA)*
1990	STUSSY, Jan		68	*Cancer*
1994	STYNE, Jule		88	*After open-heart surgery (at Mt. Sinai Med. Ctr., NY)*
1991	SUBOTSKY, Milton		70	*Heart disease (in London, England)*
1970	SUDLOW, Joan		78	*Results of a fall in back of her hillside home (in Laurel Canyon, CA)*
1995	SUGHRUE, John		67	*Lung cancer (in New York)*
• 1997	SUGIMURA, Haruko		91	*Cancer at a Tokyo, Japan hospital*
1957	# SULKY, Leo		82	*Died in CA*

• New entry.   # Original name (Pt. 7).   + Interment (Pt. 5).   317   ☆ Oscar nominee, ★ Oscar winner (Pt. 10)

Deaths of Movie and Television Personalities — by Name

YEAR	NAME	AGE	CAUSE and/or PLACE OF DEATH
1960	#+ SULLAVAN, Margaret ☆	48	Suicide (sleeping pills) in New Haven, CT
1994	SULLIVAN, Barry	81	After a chronic respiratory ailment (Sherman Oaks, CA)
1969	# SULLIVAN, Brian	49	Died in Lake Geneva, Switzerland
1996	SULLIVAN, Daniel Webster	65	Cancer (at his Amelia Island, FL)
1974	#+ SULLIVAN, Ed	72	Cancer of the esophagus (in New York, NY)
1974	SULLIVAN, Elliott (Elliot)	66	Heart attack (while visiting in Los Angeles, CA)
1956	#+ SULLIVAN, Francis L.	53	Died in New York, NY
1996	SULLIVAN, Fred G. Jr.	50	Heart failure (in Saranac Lake, NY)
1993	SULLIVAN, Jeremiah	58	An A.I.D.S.-related illness (in Hollywood, CA)
1995	SULLIVAN, Joseph H.	67	After suffering a heart attack (at his Baltimore, MD, home)
1992	SULLIVAN, Larry	46	Stroke
1991	SULLIVAN, Marie Madeline	80	After a brief illness (in Ojai, CA)
1987	SULLIVAN, Maxine	75	A seizure brought on by pneumonia (in The Bronx, NY)
1933	# SULLIVAN, Pat	46	Pneumonia brought on by alcoholism (in New York, NY)
1946	SULLIVAN, William A. "Billy"	54	Died in Great Neck, NY
1975	# SULLY, Frank	67	Died in Woodland Hills, CA
1979	SUMMERS, Hope	78	Heart failure (in Woodland Hills, CA)
1997	SUMMERS, Jill	86	
1946	#+ SUMMERVILLE, Slim	53	Stroke (in Laguna Beach, CA)
1976	# SUNBEAUTY, Olga	78	Died in Italy
1987	SUNDBERG, Clinton	81	Heart failure (in Santa Monica, CA)
1989	SUNDIN, Michael	28	Undisclosed causes (in Newcastle, England)
1959	# SUNDMARK, Betty	45	Died in New York
1993	SUNDSTROM, Mark	36	A.I.D.S.
1963	# SUNSHINE, Marion	65	Died in New York, NY
1992	# Superman	54	Slain in combat with "Doomsday"
1962	SURATT, Valeska	79	Died in Los Angeles, CA
1987	SUSSKIND, David	66	Heart attack (in New York, NY)
1934	SUTHERLAND, Dick	51	Kidney disease (in Hollywood, CA)
1973	# SUTHERLAND, Eddie	78	Cancer (in Palm Springs, CA)
1987	SUTHERLAND, Esther	54	Heart attack (in Los Angeles, CA)
1968	SUTHERLAND, Victor	79	Died in Los Angeles, CA
1995	SUTTER, Linda	54	Brain cancer (in Cambridge, MA)
1974	+ SUTTON, Frank	50	Heart attack (in Shreveport, LA)
1995	# SUTTON, Grady	89	Natural causes (in Woodland Hills, CA)
1963	SUTTON, John	54	Died in Cannes, France
1970	SUTTON, Paul	58	Muscular dystrophy (in Ferndale, MI)
1994	SWACKHAMER, E. W.	67	Ruptured aortic aneurysm (in Berlin, Germany)
1935	SWAIN, Mack	59	Apparent heart attack (in Tacoma, WA)
1983	# SWANSON, Gloria ☆	84	Following heart surgery (in New York, NY)
1968	SWANWICK, Peter	56	Died in London, England
1969	SWARTHOUT, Gladys	64	Heart disease (at her villa in Florence, Italy)
1957	SWASEY, Bill	29	Automobile accident
1995	SWAYZE, John Cameron	89	Natural causes (at his home in Sarasota, FL)
1992	SWEENEY, Bob	73	Cancer (in Westlake Village, CA)
1950	SWEENEY, Jack	61	Died in Hollywood, CA
1986	SWEET, Blanche	90	Stroke (in Manhattan, NY)
1985	SWEET, Dolph	64	Cancer (in Tarzana, CA)
1978	SWENSON, Karl	70	Apparent heart attack (while visiting relatives in Torrington, CT)
1993	SWENSON, Swen	63	A.I.D.S.
1940	SWICKARD, Joseph	74	After a long illness (in Hollywood, CA)
1994	+ SWIFT, Paul "Eggman"	60	A.I.D.S. (at Francis Scott Key Med. Ctr., Baltimore, MD)
1959	+ SWITZER, Carl "Alfalfa"	32	Murdered (shot over a $50. debt) in Sepulveda, CA

• New entry.   # Original name (Pt. 7).   + Interment (Pt. 5).   318   ☆ Oscar nominee, ★ Oscar winner (Pt. 10)

Deaths of Movie and Television Personalities — by Name

YEAR	NAME		AGE	CAUSE and/or PLACE OF DEATH
1943	SWOR, Bert		65	Found dead in his Tulsa, Oklahoma hotel room
1965	SWOR, John		82	Died in Dallas, Texas
1968	# SYDNEY, Basil		73	Pleurisy (in London, England)
1989	SYDNOR, Earl L.		81	Lung cancer (in New York, NY)
1953	# SYLVANI, Gladys		68	After a long illness (in Alexandria, VA)
1980	# SYLVIA, Gaby		60	Cerebral hemorrhage (in Chamalieres, France)
1970	# Sylvie		87	Died in Complegne, France
1992	SYMS, Sylvia		74	Apparent heart attack (while performing on stage in London, England)
1993	SYRON, Brian		58	Leukemia (in Sydney, Australia)
	T			
1974	TABBERT, William		53	Apparent heart attack
1957	TABER, Richard		72	Died in New York, NY
1953	# TABLER, P. Dempsey		79	Died in San Francisco, CA
1979	TAFLER, Sydney		63	Cancer (in London, England)
1989	TAFOYA, Alfonso		60	Massive heart attack (in Pasadena, CA)
1973	TAFT, Sara		80	Heart attack (in Los Angeles, CA)
1947	TAGGART, Ben L.		58	Died in Santa Monica, CA
1995	TAGLIAVINI, Ferruccio		81	Respiratory problems after a long illness (in Reggio Emilia, Italy)
• 1996	TAK-HING, Kwan		91	Pancreatic cancer (in Hong Kong, China)
1996	TAKEMITSU, Toru		65	Pneumonia while undergoing cancer treatments (in Tokyo, Japan)
1996	# TALBOT, Lyle		94	Natural causes (at his home in San Francisco, CA)
1979	TALIAFERRO, Mabel		89	Died in Honolulu, Hawaii
1991	TALLICHET, Margaret (Wyler)		77	Cancer (in Indio, CA)
1973	+ TALMADGE, Constance		75	Pneumonia (in Los Angeles, CA)
1969	+ TALMADGE, Natalie		70	Died in Santa Monica, CA
1957	+ TALMADGE, Norma		64	Cerebral stroke and pneumonia (in Las Vegas, NV)
1981	# TALMADGE, Richard		88	Cancer (in Carmel, CA)
1968	+ TALMAN, William		53	Cancer (in Encino, CA)
1992	TALTON, Alix		72	After a long battle with lung cancer (in Burbank, CA)
1943	# Tamara		?	Airplane crash (near Lisbon, Portugal)
1980	# TAMBERLANI, Carlo		81	Died in Subiaco, Italy
1972	TAMIROFF, Akim	☆	72	Died in Palm Springs, CA
1977	TANAKA, Kinuyo		67	Cerebral tumor (in Tokyo, Japan)
• 1997	TANAKA, Tomoyuki		86	Stroke (at a hospital in Tokyo, Japan)
1994	TANDY, Jessica	★	85	Ovarian cancer (at her home in Easton, CT)
1947	+ TANGUAY, Eva		68	Heart attack and cerebral hemorrhage (in Hollywood, CA)
1980	TANNEN, Charles D.		65	Heart attack (while vacationing in San Bernardino, CA)
1965	TANNEN, Julius		84	After suffering a stroke (in Hollywood, CA)
1976	TANNEN, William		65	After a 2-month hospitalization (in Woodland Hills, CA)
1956	TAPLEY, Rose		72	Died at the Motion Picture Country Hospital in Woodland Hills, CA
• 1997	TAPPS, Georgie		85	Died at Providence St. Joseph Medical Center in Burbank, CA
• 1997	TAPS, Jonie		89	Natural causes in Santa Fe, NM
1986	TARKOVSKY, Andrei		54	Lung cancer (in Neilly-sur-Seine, France)
1993	TARLETON, Diane R.		51	Breast cancer (at her home in Manhattan, NY)
1992	TARLOW, Florence		70	Cancer (in New York, NY)
1990	TARRON, Elsie		87	Heart failure
• 1997	TARTIKOFF, Brandon		48	UCLA Medical Ctr. after Treatment for Hodgkins disease
1972	TASHLIN, Frank		59	Heart attack (in Beverly Hills, CA)
1934	TASHMAN, Lilyan		33	Tumorous condition and/or cancer (in New York, NY)
1955	TATE, Reginald		58	Heart attack (in London, England)
1969	+ TATE, Sharon (Polanski)		26	Murdered by members of the Charles Manson cult (in Bel Air, CA)
• 1997	TATELMAN, Harry		82	After a brief illness in Los Angeles, CA
1982	# TATI, Jacques		74	Pulmonary embolism (in Paris, France)

• New entry. # Original name (Pt. 7). + Interment (Pt. 5).   319   ☆ Oscar nominee, ★ Oscar winner (Pt. 10)

Deaths of Movie and Television Personalities — by Name

YEAR	NAME		AGE	CAUSE and/or PLACE OF DEATH
1956	+ TATUM, Art		46	Uremia (in Los Angeles, CA)
1967	+ TATUM, Reese "Goose"		45	
1948	#+ TAUBER, Richard		56	Complications after laryngitis (in a nursing home in London, England)
1981	TAUROG, Norman	★	82	After a long illness (in Rancho Mirage, CA)
1992	TAVARES, Albert		39	A.I.D.S.
1990	+ TAYBACK, Vic "Mel"		60	Heart attack (in Glendale, CA)
1974	TAYLOR, Alma		79	Died in London, England
1966	TAYLOR, Deems		67	Stroke (in New York, NY)
1966	TAYLOR, Donald F.		47	Found dead at home from an overdose of seconal (in Hollywood, CA)
1994	# TAYLOR, Dub		87	Congestive heart failure (at Westlake Med. Ctr., L.A., CA)
1958	+ TAYLOR, Estelle		58	Cancer (in Los Angeles, CA)
1961	TAYLOR, Ferris		68	Heart attack (in Hollywood, Ca.)
1965	TAYLOR, Forrest		80	Died in Garden Grove, CA
1982	TAYLOR, John		61	Heart attack (in Geneva, Switzerland)
1987	#+ TAYLOR, Kent		80	Following several heart operations (in Woodland Hills, CA)
1984	TAYLOR, Lance Sr.		69	Heart attack (in Los Angeles, CA)
1946	#+ TAYLOR, Laurette (Cooney)		62	Coronary thrombosis after several weeks of illness (in New York, NY)
1952	TAYLOR, Ray		63	Died in Hollywood, CA
1969	#+ TAYLOR, Robert		57	Lung cancer (in Santa Monica, CA)
1958	TAYLOR, Sam		62	Heart attack (in Santa Monica, CA)
1983	TAYLOR, Vaughn		72	Massive cerebral hemorrhage (in Los Angeles, CA)
1922	#+ TAYLOR, William Desmond		45	Murdered (shot) in Los Angeles, CA
1930	TAYLOR, William H. "Billy"		101	Died in Hollywood, CA
1964	+ TEAGARDEN, Jack		57	Pneumonia (in New Orleans, LA)
1976	TEAL, Ray		74	After a long illness (in Santa Monica, CA)
1994	TEALE, Leonard		72	Heart attack (in Sydney, Australia)
1938	# TEARLE, Conway		60	Heart attack (in Los Angeles, CA)
1953	TEARLE, Godfrey		68	Died in London, England
1994	TEAS, William Ellis		80	Died at Fort Miley Veterans Hospital in San Francisco, CA
1987	TEASDALE, Verree		80	Died in Beverly Hills, CA
1925	Teddy (dog)		14	(In Mack Sennett comedies)
• 1997	TEDESCO, Tommy		67	Lung cancer at home in Northridge, CA
1986	TEITEL, Carol		62	Complications after a car accident (in Camden, NJ)
1951	TELL, Olive		56	Died in New York, NY
1934	# TELLEGEN, Lou		52	Suicide (stabbed himself with a pair of scissors) in Los Angeles, CA
1942	# TEMPEST, Marie		78	After a long illness (in London, England)
1939	+ TEMPLETON, Fay		74	Died in San Francisco, CA
1979	TEMPLETON, Olive		96	Died in Manhattan, NY
1960	# TENBROOK, Harry		72	Lung cancer (in Woodland Hills, CA)
1973	TERHUNE, Max "Abibe"		82	Heart attack and stroke (in Cottonwood, AZ)
1966	#+ TERRELL, Kenneth		61	Arteriosclerosis (in Sherman Oaks, CA)
1971	# TERRIS, Ellaline		100	Died in London, England
1989	TERRIS, Norma		87	After a brief illness (in Lyme, CT)
1987	# TERRY, Alice (Alice Ingram)		88	Pneumonia (in Burbank, CA)
1988	# TERRY, Don		86	Stroke (in Oceanside, CA)
1931	TERRY, Ethel Grey		48	After a year's illness (in Hollywood, CA)
• 1971	TERRY, Paul		83	Cancer (in Rye, NY)
1957	# TERRY, Sheila		46	Died in Los Angeles, CA
1985	# TERRY, Tex		82	Died in Terre Haute, IN
1990	# Terry-Thomas		78	Parkinson's disease (in Godalming, England)
• 1996	TESICH, Steve	★	53	Heart attack (while vacationing in Nova Scotia, Canada)
1994	TESSARI, Duccio		67	Cancer (in Rome, Italy)
1990	TESSIER, Robert		56	Cancer (in Lowell, MA)

• New entry. # Original name (Pt. 7). + Interment (Pt. 5). ☆ Oscar nominee, ★ Oscar winner (Pt. 10)

Deaths of Movie and Television Personalities — by Name

YEAR	NAME	AGE	CAUSE and/or PLACE OF DEATH
1975	# TETLEY, Walter	60	Died in Los Angeles, CA
1977	TETZEL, Joan	56	Cancer (in Sussex, England)
1992	THACKER, Jim	64	Stroke
1936	#+ THALBERG, Irving	37	Lobar pneumonia (in Santa Monica, CA)
1942	# THATCHER, Eva	80	Died in Los Angeles, CA
1987	THATCHER, Heather	90	Died in Hiddington, England
1981	# THATCHER, Torin	76	Cancer (in Thousand Oaks, CA)
1982	THEARD, Sam	78	Died in Los Angeles, CA
1961	THESIGER, Ernest	81	Died in London, England
1975	# THIELE, William J.	85	Died at the Motion Picture Country Home in Woodland Hills, CA
1982	THOMA, Michael	55	Cancer (in Hollywood, CA)
1989	THOMAS, Ann	75	Lung cancer (in New Rochelle, NY)
1980	#+ THOMAS, Billy "Buckwheat"	49	Heart attack (in Los Angeles, CA)
1991	# THOMAS, Danny	79	After a heart attack (in Los Angeles, CA)
1981	THOMAS, David	73	Died in New York, NY
1989	THOMAS, Frank M.	100	Cardiac arrest in his sleep
1993	THOMAS, Gerald	72	Died in Beaconsfield, England
1939	THOMAS, Jameson	49	Tuberculosis (in Sierra Madre, CA)
1960	THOMAS, John Charles	68	Intestinal cancer (in Apple Valley, CA)
1981	+ THOMAS, Lowell	89	Heart attack (in Pawling, NY)
1989	THOMAS, Madoline	99	Cardiac arrest in her sleep (in Weston-Super-Mare, England)
1920	THOMAS, Olive	35	Suicide (mercury poisoning) in Paris, France
1995	# THOMAS, Rachel	90	After a fall and long illness (at Cardiff Hosp. in London, Eng.)
1992	# THOMAS, Ted	88	Heart attack (in Van Nuys, CA)
1991	THOMAS, Wilfrid	87	
1988	THOMPKINS, Toney	33	A.I.D.S. (in Los Angeles, CA)
1971	THOMPSON, Bill	58	
1990	# THOMPSON, Carlos	67	Suicide (gunshot) in Buenos Aires, Argentina
1925	THOMPSON, Frederick A.	55	Heart disease (in Hollywood, CA)
1992	# THOMPSON, Marshall	66	Congestive heart failure (in Royal Oak, MI)
1928	+ THOMSON, Fred	38	After an operation for gall stones (in Los Angeles, CA)
1967	THOMSON, Kenneth	68	Pulmonary emphysema and fibrosis (in Los Angeles, CA)
1989	THOR, Dan	34	A.I.D.S. (in Los Angeles, CA)
1993	THOR, Jerome	69	Cardiac arrest (in Westwood, CA)
1976	THOR, Larry	58	Aneurysm (in Santa Monica, CA)
1967	THORBURN, June	36	Airplane crash (in Fernhurst, Sussex, England)
1978	THORDSEN, Kelly	61	Cancer (in Sun Valley, CA)
1972	# THORNDIKE, Russell	87	Died in London, England
1976	+ THORNDIKE, Sybil	93	Heart attack (in London, England)
1953	+ THORPE, Jim	64	Heart attack (in Lomita, CA)
1991	# THORPE, Richard	95	Died in Palm Springs, CA
1989	THORPE-BATES, Peggy	75	Undisclosed causes (in London, England)
1994	THRING, Frank Jr.	68	Cancer (in Melbourne, Australia)
1955	#+ THUNDERCLOUD, Chief (1st)	66	Cancer (Do not confuse with 2nd Chief Thundercloud, d. 1967)
1967	# THUNDERCLOUD, Chief (2nd)	68	(Do not confuse with 1st Chief Thundercloud, d. 1955)
1925	THURMAN, Mary	31	Bronchial pneumonia (in New York, NY)
1977	THURSBY, David	88	Died in Hollywood, CA
1994	THURSTON, Ted	77	Stomach cancer (in East Hampton, NY)
1960	+ TIBBETT, Lawrence ☆	63	Following surgery for an old head injury (in New York, NY)
1960	# TIEDTKE, Jakob	85	Died in Berlin, Germany
1991	+ TIERNEY, Gene ☆	70	Emphysema (in Houston, TX)
1950	TILBURY, Zeffie	86	After a long illness (in Los Angeles, CA)
1998	TILLMAN, Harrel Gordon	73	Cancer in Houston, TX

• New entry. # Original name (Pt. 7). + Interment (Pt. 5).   321   ☆ Oscar nominee, ★ Oscar winner (Pt. 10)

Deaths of Movie and Television Personalities — by Name

YEAR	NAME		AGE	CAUSE and/or PLACE OF DEATH
1983	+ TINCHER, Fay		99	Natural causes (in Brooklyn, NY)
1992	TINDALL, Hilary		54	Cancer (in Selbourne, England)
1973	+ TINDALL, Loren		51	Heart attack (in Hollywood, CA)
1996	# Tiny Tim		66	Heart attack while singing on stage (in Minneapolis, MN)
1979	+ TIOMKIN, Dimitri	★	80	Cardiac arrest in his sleep (in London, England)
1992	TIPPET, Clark		37	A.I.D.S.
1993	TIPPING, Tim "Tip"		34	While re-enacting a sky-diving accident for TV (in Alnwick, England)
1989	TIRELLI, Teresa		81	Brain tumor (in Northridge, CA)
1973	TISSIER, Jean		76	Died in Granville, France
1929	TITUS, Lydia Yeamans		63	2 yrs. after a paralytic stroke (in a hospital in Glendale, CA)
1980	TOBIAS, George		78	Cancer (in Los Angeles, CA)
1982	TOBIN, Dan		72	After a lengthy illness (in Santa Monica, CA)
1995	TOBIN, Genevieve		93	Died at Las Encinas Hospital in Pasadena, CA
1993	TODD, Ann		82	After a stroke (at a hospital in London, England)
1992	# TODD, Christopher		30	A.I.D.S. (in New York, NY)
1958	#+ TODD, Mike		49	Airplane crash (in Mount Zuni, NM)
1935	+ TODD, Thelma		30	Suicide? Murder? Accident? (carbon monoxide) in Santa Monica, CA
1996	+ TODISCO, Mario		46	Cancer
1990	TOGNAZZI, Ugo		68	Cerebral hemorrhage (in Rome, Italy)
1997	TOKATYAN, LEON		73	Natural causes in Los Angeles, CA
1948	+ TOLAND, Gregg		44	Coronary thrombosis (in Hollywood, CA)
1947	+ TOLER, Sidney		73	Died at his home in Beverly Hills, CA
1962	#+ TOMACK, Sid		55	Heart ailment (in Palm Springs, CA)
1987	TOMLIN, Pinky		80	Heart attack
1993	TOMLINSON, Kate		96	Died in New Jersey, cause unreported
1968	# TONE, Franchot	☆	63	Lung cancer (in New York, NY)
1969	TONG, Kam		62	Died in Costa Mesa, CA
1964	TONG, Sammee		63	Suicide at his home (in Culver City, CA)
1942	# Tony (Tom Mix's horse)		33	
1991	TOOMEY, Regis		93	Heart attack (in Woodland Hills, CA)
1997	TOPOR, Roland		59	Cerebral hemorrhage/aneurysm in Paris
1957	TOREN, Marta		30	Rare brain disease (in Stockholm, Sweden)
1995	TORNBERG, Jeff		43	Complications of A.I.D.S. (in Los Angeles, CA)
1951	# TORRENCE, David		87	Died in Scotland
1933	#+ TORRENCE, Ernest		54	After an operation for gall stones (in New York, NY)
1987	+ TORRES, Raquel		78	Heart attack (in Malibu, CA)
1983	TORS, Ivan		67	Massive heart attack (in Matto Grosso, Brazil)
1957	+ TOSCANINI, Arturo		89	Following a stroke (in Riverdale, NY)
1967	# Toto		69	Died in Rome, Italy (Do not confuse with Toto the Clown, d. 1938)
1938	# Toto the Clown		50	Died in New York, NY (Do not confuse with Toto, d. 1967)
1995	TOTTEN, Robert		57	Heart attack (at his home in Sherman Oaks, CA)
1992	TOUCHSTONE, John		59	Cirrhosis of the liver (in Sherman Oaks, CA)
1996	TOUMANOVA, Tamara		77	After a brief illness (at Santa Monica Hospital, CA)
1977	TOURNEUR, Jacques		73	Died in Bergerac, France
1961	# TOURNEUR, Maurice		85	Injuries from a car accident (in Paris, France)
1923	TOWNSEND, Anna		39	After a brief illness (in Los Angeles, CA)
1995	# TOWNSEND, Claire		43	Cancer (at her parents' home in Los Angeles, CA)
1995	TOWNSEND, Dallas		76	Injuries from a fall (at Montclair, N.J., Community Hospital)
1972	TOZERE, Frederic		71	Died in his New York apartment
1978	TOZZI, Fausto		57	Emphysema (in Rome, Italy)
1992	TRACE, Christopher		59	Cancer (in London, England)
1968	#+ TRACY, Lee	☆	70	Cancer of the liver (in Santa Monica, CA)
1967	+ TRACY, Spencer	★	67	Heart attack (in Beverly Hills, CA)

Deaths of Movie and Television Personalities — by Name

YEAR	NAME	AGE	CAUSE and/or PLACE OF DEATH
1986	TRACY, Steve	34	Complications from A.I.D.S. (in Tampa, FL)
1967	TRACY, William	49	Died in Hollywood, CA
1987	TRAEGER, Kim Patrick	36	Heart attack (in Lakewood, CA)
1987	# TRAEGER, Rick	74	Apparent heart attack two days after his son died (in Lakewood, CA)
1940	+ TRAINOR, Leonard	61	Heart attack (in Los Angeles, CA)
1918	TRASK, Wayland	31	Spanish influenza (in Los Angeles, CA)
1983	TRAUBE, Shepard	76	Cancer (in Manhattan, NY)
1972	+ TRAUBEL, Helen	69	Heart attack (in Santa Monica, CA)
1990	TRAUBERG, Leonid	88	Died in Moscow, Russia
1994	TRAVERS, Bill	72	Died in his sleep (at his home in Dorking, England)
1965	#+ TRAVERS, Henry ☆	91	Arteriosclerosis (in Hollywood, CA)
1935	TRAVERS, Richard C.	45	Pneumonia (in San Pedro, CA)
1964	TRAVERSE, Madlaine	88	Died in Cleveland, OH
1989	TRAVIS, Richard	76	
1989	TRAYLOR, William	60	After a long illness (in Los Angeles, CA)
1975	# TREACHER, Arthur	81	Heart ailment (in Manhasset, NY)
1967	TREACY, Emerson	61	Injuries from a fall (in Woodland Hills, CA)
1960	TREADWELL, Laura	81	Died in Hollywood, CA
1992	# TREE, Dorothy	85	Heart failure (in Englewood, NJ)
1997	# TREE, Joanne	73	After a long illness in New York City, NY
1937	# TREE, Lady	72	After an operation from which she did not rally
1989	TREEN, Mary	82	Cancer (in Newport Beach, CA)
1989	TREGOE, William L.	67	Cardiac arrest (in Los Angeles, CA)
1990	TRENKER, Luis	97	After a long illness (in Bolzano, Italy)
1988	TREVELYAN, John	83	
1978	# TREVOR, Austin	80	Died in London, England
1933	TREVOR, Hugh	30	Three-weeks after an appendectomy (in Los Angeles, CA)
1980	TRIESAULT, Ivan	79	Heart failure (in Los Angeles, CA)
1965	+ Trigger (Roy Rogers' horse)	33	Natural causes
1954	TRIMBLE, Lawrence	69	Died at the Motion Picture Country House in Ca.
1994	TROISI, Massimo	41	Heart attack (in Ostia, near Rome, Italy)
1998	TROMBERG, Sheldon	68	Heart attack in Richmond, CA
1992	TROP, Jack Dunn	92	Respiratory infection (in Miami, FL)
1975	+ TROTTER, John Scott	67	Cancer (in Los Angeles, CA)
1987	TROUGHTON, Patrick	67	Heart attack (in Columbus, GA)
1967	+ TROWBRIDGE, Charles	85	Died in Los Angeles, CA
1994	TROY, Louise	60	Breast cancer (at her home in Manhattan, NY)
1985	TRUBSHAWE, Michael	80	Died in England
1994	TRUEMAN, Paula	96	Died in New York Hospital
1941	TRUESDALE, Howard	80	Heart attack (in Los Angeles, CA)
1973	+ TRUEX, Ernest	83	Heart attack (in Fallbrook, CA)
1998	TRUEX, Sylvia Field	97	Died at a nursing home in Falbrook-San Diego, CA
1984	+ TRUFFAUT, François	52	Brain cancer (in Neuilly-sur-Seine, France)
1977	TRUMAN, Ralph	77	Died in Ipswich, England
1993	TRUSCOTT, John ★	57	During emergency heart surgery (in Melbourne, Australia)
1970	TRYON, Glenn	70	Died in Los Angeles, CA
1991	# TRYON, Tom	65	Stomach cancer (in Los Angeles, CA)
1980	# TSCHECHOWA, Olga	83	Died in Munich, Germany
1971	TSIANG, H. T.	71	Died in Hollywood, CA
1984	+ TUBB, Ernest	70	Emphysema (in Nashville, TN)
1986	+ TUCKER, Forrest	71	Throat cancer
1921	# TUCKER, George Loane	49	After a years' illness (in Los Angeles, CA)
1949	# TUCKER, Harland	?	Heart attack (in Los Angeles, CA)

YEAR	NAME		AGE	CAUSE and/or PLACE OF DEATH
1989	TUCKER, Julius L.		92	
1991	TUCKER, Lem		52	Liver failure
1986	TUCKER, Lorenzo		79	Cancer (in Hollywood, CA)
1942	# TUCKER, Richard (actor)		58	Heart attack (in Woodland Hills, CA) Do not confuse with singer
1975	+ TUCKER, Richard (singer)		60	Heart attack (Do not confuse with actor, d. 1942)
1966	#+ TUCKER, Sophie		82	Lung and kidney ailment (in New York, NY)
1989	TUCKER, Tommy		86	
• 1998	TUERCK, George N.		91	In Weymouth, MA
1970	#+ TUFTS, Sonny		57	Pneumonia (in Santa Monica, CA)
1991	TULLY, Lee		61	Cancer (in Englewood, NJ)
1982	TULLY, Tom	☆	74	Complications after a long bout with cancer (in Newport Beach, CA)
1992	TUNBERG, Karl		83	Died in London, England
1978	#+ TUNNEY, Gene		80	Blood poisoning (in Greenwich, CT)
1990	TUPPER, Loretta		84	Cancer (in New York, NY)
1956	TURNBULL, John		75	Died in London, England
1946	TURNER, Florence		61	After a long illness (in Woodland Hills, CA)
1923	TURNER, Fred A.		64	
1987	TURNER, Jerry		60	Throat cancer (in Baltimore, MD)
1995	# TURNER, Lana		75	After a long battle with throat cancer (in Century City, CA)
1918	TURNER, Otis "Daddy"		55	Heart attack (in Hollywood, CA)
1992	TURNER, Teddy		75	Died in Horsforth, England
1940	#+ TURPIN, Ben		65	Heart disease (in Santa Monica, CA)
1963	#+ TUTTLE, Frank		70	Heart attack (in Hollywood, CA)
1986	+ TUTTLE, Lurene		79	Died in Encino, CA
1958	#+ TWELVETREES, Helen		49	Overdose of sleeping pills (in Harrisburg, PA)
1957	# TWITCHELL, A. R. "Archie"		50	Killed in a midair collision over Pacoima, CA
1993	# TWITTY, Conway		59	Surgery complications after a stomach aneurysm (Springfield, MO)
1961	TYLER, Harry		73	Cancer (in Hollywood, CA)
1957	#+ TYLER, Judy		24	Killed in an automobile crash (in Billy the Kid, WY)
1954	# TYLER, Tom		50	Heart attack after suffering crippling arthritis (in Hamtramck, MI)
1967	TYNAN, Brandon		91	Died at Lynwood Nursing Home in New York, NY
1949	TYRELL, John E.		46	Died in Los Angeles, CA
	U			
1972	ULMER, Edgar G.		68	After a long illness (in Woodland Hills, CA)
1971	ULRIC, Lenore		78	After several years of hospitalization (in Orangeburg, NY)
1966	UNDERWOOD, Loyal		73	Died in Los Angeles, CA
1990	UNGER, Bertil		69	Liver disease (in Hollywood, CA)
1978	UNSWORTH, Geoffrey	★	64	Heart attack (in London, England)
1975	URE, Mary	☆	42	Accidental mix of alcohol and tranquilizers (in London, England)
1966	# URECAL, Minerva		71	Heart attack (in Glendale, CA)
1979	# URZI, Saro		66	Heart attack (in San Giuseppe Vesuviano, Italy)
1944	USHER, Guy		69	After a brief illness (at his ranch in San Diego, CA)
• 1997	USHIYAMA, Junichi		67	Liver disease in Tokyo, Japan
• 1997	UTTAL, Ivan E.		66	Died of complications from AIDS at his home in New Orleans, LA
1996	# UYS, Jamie		74	Heart attack (at his home in Johannesburg, South Africa)
	V			
1974	# VAGUE, Vera		70	Died in Santa Barbara, CA
1954	VAJDA, Ernest		67	Heart attack (in Woodland Hills, CA)
1962	VAL, Paul		75	Died in Hollywood, CA
• 1997	VALE, Eugene		81	Natural causes at home in Los Angeles, CA
1918	VALE, Louise		?	Influenza (in Madison, WI)
1959	#+ VALENS, Ritchie		17	Airplane crash (along with Buddy Holly, near Mason City, IA)
1926	#+ VALENTINO, Rudolph		31	Peritonitis from a perforated ulcer and ruptured appendix (in N.Y.)

Deaths of Movie and Television Personalities — by Name

YEAR	NAME	AGE	CAUSE and/or PLACE OF DEATH
1987	VALENTY, Lili	86	Died in Hollywood, CA
1983	VALERIE, Joan	68	Automobile accident (in Long Beach, CA)
1956	# VALK, Frederick	55	Died in London, England
1986	#+ VALLEE, Rudy	84	Heart attack and cancer (in North Hollywood, CA)
1993	VALLI, June	64	Cancer
1980	VALLI, Romolo	54	Automobile accident (in Rome, Italy)
1968	#+ VALLI, Virginia (Farrell)	68	Following a stroke (in Palm Springs, CA)
1977	VALLIN, Richard "Rick"	57	Died in Los Angeles, CA
1932	VALLIS, Robert "Bob"	?	After a long illness (in Brighton, England)
1993	VALVANO, Jim	45	After a 1-year bout with cancer (in Durham, NC)
1980	#+ VAN, Bobby	49	After surgery to remove a brain tumor (in Los Angeles, CA)
1968	VAN, Gus	80	After two brain operations when hit by a car in Miami Beach, FL
1974	# VAN, Wally	93	Died in Englewood, NJ
1949	# VANBRUGH, Irene	76	Died in London, England
1947	VanBUREN, Mabel	69	Pneumonia (in Hollywood, CA)
1994	VANCE, Danitra	35	Breast cancer (at her grandfather's home in Markham, IL)
1979	+ VANCE, Vivian	66	Cancer (in Belvedere, CA)
1989	+ VanCLEEF, Lee	64	Heart attack (in Oxnard, CA)
1984	VanDYKE, Truman	86	Heart failure (in Los Angeles, CA)
1944	#+ VanDYKE, W. S. "Woody" ☆	53	After a 6-months' illness (in Brentwood, CA)
1986	VanDYKE, Willard	79	Heart attack (while driving from N.M. to MA.) in Jackson, TN
1940	VANE, Denton	50	Heart attack (while walking in Union Hill, NJ)
1989	VANEL, Charles	96	Heart attack (in Cannes, France)
1969	VanEYCK, Peter	55	Died in Zurich, Switzerland
1995	VanEYSSEN, John	73	Cancer (at a hospital in London, England)
1996	VanFLEET, Jo ★	76	Died at Jamaica Hosp. in Queens, NY
1990	VanHEUSEN, Jimmy	77	After a long illness (in Rancho Mirage, CA)
1991	VANOFF, Nick	61	Cardiac arrest
1973	VanROOTEN, Luis	66	Died in Chatham, MA
1998	VANSELOW, Robert A.	79	Heart related illness in Los Angeles, CA
1977	VanSICKEL, Dale	69	After a lengthy illness (at his home in Newport Beach, CA)
1964	VanSLOAN, Edward	81	Died in San Francisco, CA
1946	VanTASSELL, Marie	72	Died in Oakland, CA
1958	VanZANDT, Philip	53	Overdose of sleeping pills (in Hollywood, CA)
1977	+ VanZANT, Ronnie	28	Airplane crash (in Mississippi)
1976	# VARCONI, Victor	85	Heart attack (in Santa Barbara, CA)
1958	VARDEN, Evelyn	65	Died in New York, NY
1989	VARDEN, Norma	90	Heart failure (in Santa Barbara, CA)
1982	VARELA, Nina	83	Died in Hollywood, CA
1969	VARLEY, Beatrice	73	Died in England
1996	VARNO, Roland	88	Heart attack after a brief illness (in Lancaster, CA)
1992	VARSI, Diane ☆	54	Respiratory problems and Lyme disease (in Los Angeles, CA)
1955	VAUGHAN, Dorothy	65	Cerebral hemorrhage (in Hollywood, CA)
1990	VAUGHAN, Sarah	66	Lung cancer (in Los Angeles, CA)
1989	VAUGHAN, Skeeter	66	Heart attack
1990	+ VAUGHAN, Stevie Ray	35	Helicopter crash
1991	+ VAUGHN, Billy	72	Cancer
1957	VAUGHN, Hilda	60	Died in Baltimore, MD
1994	VAWTER, Ron	45	A.I.D.S.-related heart attack (on a plane bound to NY)
1984	VEAZIE, Carol Eberts	89	Cardiac arrest in her sleep (in Carmel, CA)
1988	VEHR, Bill	48	A.I.D.S. (in New York, NY)
1943	+ VEIDT, Conrad	50	Heart attack while playing golf (in Hollywood, CA)
1943	VEILLER, Bayard	74	After an illness of 2-months

Deaths of Movie and Television Personalities — by Name

YEAR	NAME	AGE	CAUSE and/or PLACE OF DEATH
1990	VEJAR, Rudolph L.	57	Respiratory failure (in Burbank, CA)
1944	#+ VELEZ, Lupe	36	Suicide (sleeping pills) in Beverly Hills, CA
1993	+ VENABLE, Evelyn	80	Cancer (in Post Falls, Idaho)
1974	VENABLE, Reginald	48	Heart attack (in Hollywood, Ca.)
1960	VENESS, Amy	84	Died in Saltdean, England
1992	VENTURA, Charlie	75	Lung cancer
1995	VENUTA, Benay	84	Lung cancer (at her home in Manhattan)
1978	VENUTI, Joe	81	Died in Seattle, WA
1981	#+ Vera-Ellen	55	Cancer (in Los Angeles, CA)
1958	VERMILYEA, Harold	68	Died in New York, NY
1984	VERNAC, Denise	66	Died in Paris, France
1967	# VERNE, Kaaren	49	Heart attack (in Hollywood, CA)
1975	VERNO, Jerry	79	Died in London, England
1939	+ VERNON, Bobby	42	Heart attack (in Hollywood, CA)
1970	# VERNON, Dorothy	94	Heart disease (in Grenada Hills, CA)
• 1996	VERNON, Harvey	69	Heart failure (at his home in Sun Valley, CA)
1987	VERNON, Jackie	62	Apparent heart attack (in Hollywood, CA)
• 1997	VERNON, Richard	72	Parkinsons disease in London, England
1970	VERNON, Wally	65	Killed by a hit-and-run driver (at a crosswalk in Van Nuys, CA)
• 1997	VERSACE, Gianni	50	Murdered at his home in South Miami Beach, FL
• 1954	# VERTOV, Dziga	58	Cancer
1976	# VESOTA, Bruno	54	Heart attack (in Culver City, CA)
1982	VESTOFF, Virginia	42	After a long illness (in New York, NY)
1939	VIBART, Henry	75	Died in England
1979	VICIOUS, Sid	21	Overdose of heroin
1971	# VICKERS, Martha	46	After a long illness (in Van Nuys, CA)
1965	# VICTOR, Charles	69	Died in London, England
1983	VICTOR, Dee	57	After a long illness (in Greenwich Village, NY)
1945	VICTOR, Henry	46	Brain tumor (in Hollywood, CA)
1959	# VIDAL, Henri	40	Heart attack (in Paris, France)
1959	+ VIDOR, Charles	58	Apparent heart attack (in Vienna, Austria)
1977	# VIDOR, Florence	82	Died in Pacific Palisades, CA
1982	VIDOR, King ☆	89	Heart ailment (in Pablo Robles, CA)
1953	VIERTEL, Berthold	68	Heart ailment (in Vienna, Austria)
1953	VIGNOLA, Robert G.	71	Died in Hollywood, CA
1934	#+ VIGO, Jean	29	Rheumatic septicemia
1986	VIGRAN, Herbert	76	Cancer (in Los Angeles, CA)
1994	VILLARD, Tom	40	Pneumonia complicated by A.I.D.S. (at a hosp. in Los Angeles, CA)
1958	VILLARREAL, Julio	73	Died in Mexico City, Mexico
1993	VILLECHAIZE, Herve "Tatoo"	50	Suicide (gunshot) at his home in North Hollywood, CA
1991	# VINCENT, Chuck	51	Heart attack after a bout with pneumonia (in Key West, FL)
1957	VINCENT, James	74	After a long illness (in New York)
1989	+ VINCENT, Romo	80	Died in Los Angeles, CA
1966	# VINCENT, Sailor Billy	70	Heart attack (in Toluca Lake, CA)
1992	VINE, Sam	69	Cancer
1963	# VINTON, Arthur	65	Died in Guadalajara, Mexico
1951	VISAROFF, Michael	58	Pneumonia (in Hollywood, CA)
1976	VISCONTI, Luchino	69	Influenza/cardiac ailment (in Rome, Italy)
1983	# VITTE, Ray	33	Stopped breathing after forcible police arrest (in Los Angeles, CA)
1991	# VITTO, G. L.	69	Heart attack
1961	VIVIAN, Percival	70	Arteriosclerosis (in Burbank, CA)
1983	+ VIVYAN, John	67	Heart failure (in Santa Monica, CA)
1969	# VOGAN, Emmett	76	Septicemia and pneumonia (in Woodland Hills, CA)

• New entry. # Original name (Pt. 7). + Interment (Pt. 5).

☆ Oscar nominee, ★ Oscar winner (Pt. 10)

Deaths of Movie and Television Personalities — by Name

YEAR	NAME		AGE	CAUSE and/or PLACE OF DEATH
1942	VOGEDING, Fredrik		52	*Following a heart attack (in Los Angeles, CA)*
1925	VOGEL, Henry		60	*Heart disease (in New York, NY)*
1967	VOGEL, Rudolf		67	*Died in Munich, Germany*
1994	VOLONTE, Gian Maria		61	*Heart attack (in Florina, Greece)*
• 1997	VOLPI, Franco		75	*Cancer (at a clinic in Rome, Italy)*
1962	VonBLOCK, Bela		73	*Died in Hollywood, CA*
1946	# VonBRINCKEN, Wilhelm		54	*Following a ruptured artery (in Los Angeles, CA)*
1989	VonCZIFFRA, Geza		88	*Died in Diessen, Germany*
1964	VonELTZ, Theodore		70	*After a long illness (in Woodland Hills, CA)*
1991	#+ VonERICH, Chris		21	
1984	#+ VonERICH, David		25	
1993	#+ VonERICH, Kerry		33	
1987	#+ VonERICH, Michael		23	
1989	VonKARAJAN, Herbert		81	*Heart failure (in Anif, Austria)*
1956	# VonMETER, Harry		85	*Died in Los Angeles, CA*
1943	VonSEYFFERTITZ, Gustav		80	*Died in Woodland Hills, CA*
1969	#+ VonSTERNBERG, Josef	☆	75	*Heart attack (in Hollywood, CA)*
1968	VonSTROHEIM, Erich Jr.		52	*Cancer (in Woodland Hills, CA)*
1957	# VonSTROHEIM, Erich Sr.	☆	71	*Spinal cancer (in Maurepas, France)*
1988	VonSTROHEIM, Valerie		91	
1947	VonTRAPP, Baron Georg		57	
1987	VonTRAPP, Marie Augusta		82	*Congestive heart failure*
1958	# VonTWARDOWSKI, Hans		60	*Died in New York, NY*
1961	# VonWINTERSTEIN, Eduard		90	*Died in East Berlin, Germany*
1981	VonZELL, Harry		75	*Cancer (in Woodland Hills, CA)*
1992	VonZERNECK, Peter		84	*Complications after surgery (in Burbank, CA)*
1989	VOORHEES, Donald		85	*Pneumonia*
1981	VOSKOVEC, George		76	*Died in Pear Blossom, CA*
• 1996	VOUYOUKLAKI, Aliki		63	*Cancer (in Athens, Greece)*
1976	# VYE, Murvyn		62	*Heart attack (while vacationing in Pompano Beach, FL)*

W

YEAR	NAME	AGE	CAUSE and/or PLACE OF DEATH
1974	+ WADSWORTH, Henry	72	*Died in New York, NY*
1950	WADSWORTH, William	77	*Died at Queens General Hospital in New York*
1979	+ WAGENHEIM, Charles	83	*Murdered (bludgeoned) in Hollywood, CA*
1984	WAGGNER, George	90	*Natural causes (in Hollywood, CA)*
1963	+ WAGNER, "Gorgeous" George	48	*Heart attack*
• 1958	WAGNER, Fritz Arno	68	*Automobile accident*
1965	WAGNER, Jack	68	*Died in Hollywood, CA*
1975	WAGNER, Max	73	*Heart attack (in West Los Angeles, CA)*
1992	WAGNER, Roger	78	*Cancer*
1964	WAGNER, William	79	*Died in Hollywood, CA*
1949	# WAITE, Malcolm	56	*Died in Los Angeles, CA*
1951	WAKEFIELD, Douglas	51	*Died in London, England*
1971	WAKEFIELD, Hugh	83	*Died in London, England*
1982	WAKELY, Jimmy	68	*Heart failure (in Mission Hills, CA)*
1969	WALBURN, Raymond	81	*After a long illness (in New York, NY)*
1962	+ WALD, Jerry	51	*After three heart attacks (in Beverly Hills, CA)*
1974	WALDIS, Otto	68	*Heart attack (in Hollywood, CA)*
1945	WALDMULLER, Lizzi	41	*Killed during an air raid (in Vienna, Austria)*
1957	WALDRIGE, Harold	50	*Died in New York, NY*
1946	+ WALDRON, Charles D.	71	*After a long illness (in Hollywood, CA)*
1952	# WALDRON, Charles K.	37	*Airplane crash (in Los Angeles, CA)*
1952	WALES, Ethel	71	*Died in Hollywood, CA*

Deaths of Movie and Television Personalities — by Name

YEAR	NAME	AGE	CAUSE and/or PLACE OF DEATH
1980	# WALES, Wally	83	Pneumonia, after suffering a stroke (in Sheridan, WY)
1982	WALKER, Betty	54	Cancer (in Manhattan, NY)
1992	WALKER, Bill	95	Cancer (in Woodland Hills, CA)
1958	WALKER, Charlotte	80	Died in Kerville, TX
1971	WALKER, Cheryl	49	Cancer (in Los Angeles, CA)
1956	WALKER, Hal	60	Died in Tracy, CA
1968	WALKER, Helen	47	Cancer (in North Hollywood, CA)
1949	WALKER, Johnnie	53	Coronary thrombosis (in New York, NY)
1966	+ WALKER, June	61	After a 5-yr. illness (in Sherman Oaks, CA)
1995	WALKER, Junior	57	Cancer
• 1996	WALKER, Keith A.	61	Following a short battle with cancer (in Franklin, TN)
1975	WALKER, Lillian "Dimples"	87	Died in Trinidad, West Indies (where she had a home)
1992	# WALKER, Nancy	69	Following a 2-year battle with lung cancer (in Studio City, CA)
1971	WALKER, Nella	85	Heart disease (in Los Angeles, CA)
1980	WALKER, Ray W.	76	Heart failure (in Los Angeles, CA)
1951	WALKER, Robert	32	Respiratory failure (Do not confuse with R. "Bob" Walker, d. 1954)
1954	WALKER, Robert "Bob"	65	(Do not confuse with actor Robert Walker, d. 1951)
1941	WALKER, Stuart	53	After a heart attack (at his home in Hollywood, CA)
1994	WALKER, Sydney	73	After a brief bout with cancer (in San Francisco, CA)
1975	WALKER, Walter "Wally"	74	Stroke (in Woodland Hills, CA)
1992	WALKER, William Arlen	74	Died in Lancaster, CA
1990	WALL, Max	82	Died in Westminster, England
1990	# WALLACE, Jean	66	After an internal hemorrhage (in Hollywood, CA)
1938	# WALLACE, May	61	Heart disease (in Los Angeles, CA)
1953	WALLACE, Morgan	65	Died in Tarzana, CA
1978	# WALLACE, Regina	86	Stroke (in Englewood, N.J.)
1951	WALLACE, Richard	57	Heart attack (in Los Angeles, CA)
1995	WALLACH, Ira ☆	83	Complications following a stroke (in New York City)
1992	WALLACK, Roy Homer	64	Pneumonia (in Van Nuys, CA)
1977	+ WALLER, Eddy C.	88	Stroke (in Los Angeles, CA)
1943	+ WALLER, Thomas "Fats"	39	Influenza and bronchial pneumonia (in Kansas City, MO)
1983	WALLGREN, Gunn	69	After a long illness (in Stockholm, Sweden)
1961	+ WALLING, Effie B.	81	Died in Berkeley, CA
1932	WALLING, William "Will"	59	Died in Hollywood, CA
• 1972	WALLINGTON, Jimmy	65	Died in Arlington, VA
1986	+ WALLIS, Hal B.	88	Cardiac arrest in his sleep (in Rancho Mirage, CA)
1949	WALLS, Tom	66	Died in Edwell, England
1981	WALSH, George	92	Complications from pneumonia (in Pomona, CA)
• 1998	WALSH, J.T.	54	Died of a heart attack in La Mesa, CA
1981	# WALSH, Raoul	93	Apparent heart attack (in Simi Valley, CA)
1991	WALTERS, Casey	75	After an illness brought on by a stroke
1982	WALTERS, Charles ☆	70	Lung cancer (in Malibu, CA)
1940	WALTERS, Hal	48	Killed by a German bomb during a WW2 air raid (in England)
1991	WALTERS, Thorley	78	Undisclosed causes (in London, England)
1936	+ WALTHALL, Henry B.	58	Chronic illness (near Monrovia, CA)
1971	#+ WALTHALL, Wallace	89	
1961	# WALTON, Douglas	52	Died in New York
1936	# WALTON, Fred	71	Pneumonia (in Los Angeles, CA)
1993	WALTON, Gladys (Herbel)	90	Cancer (at a nursing home in Morro Bay, CA)
• 1983	+ WALTON, William	80	Heart failure (at his home on the Italian island of Ischia)
1993	WANAMAKER, Sam	74	After a 5-yr. bout with cancer (in London, England)
• 1997	WARBECK, David	55	Cancer in London
1981	WARBURTON, John	78	Cancer (in Sherman Oaks, CA)

Deaths of Movie and Television Personalities — by Name

YEAR	NAME	AGE	CAUSE and/or PLACE OF DEATH
• 1997	WARCICK, Richard	52	AIDS
1926	# WARD, Carrie	63	After a long illness (in Hollywood, CA)
1952	WARD, Fannie	80	After suffering a cerebral hemorrhage (in Lennox Hill, NY)
1995	WARD, Janet	70	Comp. from a heart attack (at Mt. Sinai Med. Ctr. in NYC)
1952	WARD, Lucille	72	Died in Dayton, OH
• 1983	WARD, Penelope Dudley	67	
1967	# WARD, Warwick	76	Died in London, England
1975	WARDE, Anthony	66	Died in Hollywood, CA
• 1935	WARDE, Frederick	84	
1980	WARDE, Harlan	63	
1939	WARE, Helen	61	Throat infection (in Carmel, CA)
1951	+ WARFIELD, David	84	Died in New York
1991	# WARFIELD, Marjorie	88	Pneumonia (in Los Angeles, CA)
1987	+ WARHOL, Andy	59	Cardiac arrest during gall bladder surgery (in New York, NY)
1984	WARING, Fred	84	Stroke
1993	WARING, Richard	82	Natural causes
1986	WARNER, Gertrude	68	Cancer (in Los Angeles, CA)
1958	#+ WARNER, H. B. ☆	82	Died in Los Angeles, CA
1958	+ WARNER, Harry M.	76	Cerebral occlusion (in Bel Air, CA)
1978	+ WARNER, Jack L.	86	Pulmonary edema (in Los Angeles, CA)
1995	+ WARNER, Jack M.	79	Cancer (at Cedars-Sinai Med. Ctr. in Los Angeles, CA)
1927	+ WARNER, Sam	40	Sinus infection/brain abscess/pneumonia (in Los Angeles, CA)
1986	WARNERS, Robert	29	After a long illness (in New York, NY)
1990	WARREN, Betty	83	Died in London, England
1971	# WARREN, C. Denier	82	Died in Torquay, England
1990	WARREN, Charles Marquis	77	Following surgery for a heart aneurysm (in West Hills, CA)
1940	WARREN, E. Alyn	64	Died in Los Angeles, CA
1983	WARREN, Flip	69	Died in Hollywood, CA
1940	WARREN, Fred H.	60	Ruptured ulcer (in Hollywood, CA)
1981	#+ WARREN, Harry (songwriter) ★	87	Lung cancer (at Cedars-Sinai Med. Ctr. in Los Angeles, CA)
1988	WARREN, Jerry	65	Lung cancer (in Escondito, CA)
1993	WARREN, Joseph	77	Respiratory failure (at Village Nursing Home, NY)
1995	WARRILOW, David	60	Complications of A.I.D.S. (in New York City)
1993	WARRISS, Ben	83	Died in Twickenham, England
1972	# WARWICK, John	67	Heart attack (in Sydney, Australia)
1964	# WARWICK, Robert	85	Pulmonary embolism (in Hollywood, CA)
1988	WASHBOURNE, Mona	84	Undisclosed causes (in London, England)
1929	WASHBURN, Alice	68	Heart attack after an illness of several years (in Oshkosh, WI)
1960	WASHBURN, Bryant Jr.	?	
1963	WASHBURN, Bryant Sr.	74	Heart attack (in Hollywood, CA)
1963	#+ WASHINGTON, Dinah	39	Overdose of sleeping pills (in Detroit, MI)
1994	WASHINGTON, Fredi	91	
1919	WASHINGTON, Jesse	?	Drowned during a filming accident (in Newport, RI)
1988	WASHINGTON, Vernon	64	Died in Woodland Hills, CA
• 1998	WASSERMAN, Steven M.	45	Killed in a sailing accident off Los Angeles, CA
1995	WATERMAN, Willard	80	Bone marrow disease (at his home in Burlingame, CA)
1993	WATERS, Chuck	70	Died in Saginaw, Michigan
1990	WATERS, Elsie	95	Died in London, England
1977	+ WATERS, Ethel ☆	80	Heart ailment (in Chatsworth, CA)
1960	WATKIN, Pierre	70	After a brief illness (in Hollywood, CA)
1968	WATSON, Benjamin T. "Ben"	?	
1965	# WATSON, Bobby	77	Died in Hollywood, CA
1989	WATSON, Douglass	68	Heart attack (in AZ)

Deaths of Movie and Television Personalities — by Name

YEAR	NAME		AGE	CAUSE and/or PLACE OF DEATH
1962	WATSON, Lucile	☆	83	Died in New York, NY
1965	+ WATSON, Minor		75	Died in Alton, IL
1937	WATSON, Roy		61	Died in Hollywood, CA
1966	# WATSON, Wylie		67	Died in Scotland
1987	WATT, Harry		80	Died in London, England
1975	WATTIS, Richard		62	Heart attack (in London, England)
1966	WATTS, Charles		?	Cancer (in Nashville, TN)
1990	WATTS, Jr., Leroy		72	Died in Northfield, NJ
1980	WATTS, Queenie		52	Cancer (in London, England)
1967	#+ WAXMAN, Franz		60	Cancer (in Los Angeles, CA)
1985	WAYNE, Carol		42	Drowned (in Nanzanillo, Mexico)
1995	# WAYNE, David		81	After a long bout with lung cancer (in Los Angeles, CA)
• 1998	WAYNE, Gus		77	Heart failure at a Lakeland, Fla. Hospital
1979	#+ WAYNE, John	★	72	Lung and stomach cancer (in Santa Monica, CA)
1990	WAYNE, Johnny		72	Cancer
1970	WAYNE, Naunton		69	Died in Surbiton, England
• 1998	WAYNE, Olive Brasno		80	Heart failure at a Lakeland, Fla. Hospital
1959	WAYNE, Robert "Duke"		55	Following a heart attack (in San Antonio, TX)
1989	WEAVER, Carl Earl		36	A.I.D.S. (in New York, NY)
1983	#+ WEAVER, Doodles		71	Apparent suicide (gunshot) in Burbank, CA
1992	WEAVER, Jackson		72	Heart and kidney failure
1982	WEBB, Alan		75	Died in Sussex, England
1966	#+ WEBB, Clifton	☆	72	Heart attack (in Beverly Hills, CA)
1959	WEBB, Harry		63	Heart attack (in Hollywood, CA)
1982	+ WEBB, Jack		62	Heart attack (in West Hollywood, CA)
1935	WEBB, Millard		42	Intestinal ailment (in Los Angeles, CA)
1993	WEBB, Richard		77	Suicide (gunshot) after suffering a long illness (in Van Nuys, CA)
• 1983	WEBB, Rita		77	
1990	WEBB, Robert D.		87	Following a long illness
1982	WEBB, Roy		94	Heart attack
1989	WEBBER, Robert		64	Amyotrophic lateral sclerosis
1942	#+ WEBER, Joe		74	After an illness of 2-months (in Van Nuys, CA)
1990	WEBER, Karl		74	Congestive feart failure (in Boston, MA)
1939	WEBER, Lois		56	After a long illness (in Los Angeles, CA)
1918	# WEBER, Rex		29	Spanish influenza (in Chicago, IL)
1947	WEBSTER, Ben		82	Following an operation (in Hollywood, CA)
1991	WEBSTER, Byron		58	A.I.D.S. (in Sherman Oaks, CA)
• 1997	WEBSTER, Charles D.		73	Died at his home in Ashland, OR after a prolonged illness
1984	WEBSTER, Paul Francis		77	Parkinson's disease (in Beverly Hills, CA)
• 1997	WECHSLER, Bert		64	Died of cancer in New York
1975	WEED, Leland T.		74	Stroke (in Prescott, AZ)
1972	#+ WEEDE, Robert		69	After several months in a hospital
1993	WEEDIN, Harfield		77	Undisclosed causes (in Boise, ID)
1954	WEEKS, Barbara		47	Died in Los Angeles, CA
• 1996	WEEKS, Clair		84	Cancer (in Los Angeles, CA)
1968	WEEKS, Marion		81	Died in New York
1963	WEEMS, Ted		62	Emphysema (in Tulsa, OK)
1948	# WEGENER, Paul		74	Died in Berlin, Germany
1996	WEI, Lo		76	Heart failure (in a Hong Kong hospital)
1968	WEIDLER, Virginia		41	Heart attack (in Los Angeles, CA)
1951	WEIGEL, Paul		83	Died in Germany
1967	WEISBART, David		52	Stroke while playing golf (in Hollywood, CA)
1987	WEISENBORN, Gordon		64	Died in Chicago, IL

Deaths of Movie and Television Personalities — by Name

YEAR	NAME		AGE	CAUSE and/or PLACE OF DEATH
1984	#+ WEISSMULLER, Johnny		79	Heart disease and cerebral thrombosis (in Acapulco, Mexico)
1991	WEIST, Dwight		81	Heart attack (in Block Island, RI)
1960	WELCH, Joseph L.		69	Died in Hyannis, MA
1976	WELCH, Niles		81	Died in Laguna Nigel, CA
1992	+ WELK, Lawrence		89	Pneumonia
1993	WELLES, Gwen		42	Cancer (at her home in Santa Monica, CA)
1985	# WELLES, Orson	☆	70	Heart attack (in Los Angeles, CA)
1946	WELLESLEY, Charles		71	Died at the Brunswick Home, Amityville, L.I., NY
1993	WELLINGTON, Valerie		33	Brain aneurysm (in Maywood, IL)
1975	#+ WELLMAN, William A.	☆	79	Leukemia (in Los Angeles, CA)
1994	WELLS, Frank		62	Helicopter crash (in central Nevada)
1946	#+ WELLS, H. G.		80	Liver cancer (in London, England)
1949	WELLS, Marie		55	Suicide (sleeping pills) in Hollywood, CA
1992	+ WELLS, Mary		49	After a long bout with cancer
1947	WELLS, Ted		48	Heart attack
• 1996	WELLS, William G.		73	Aortic disection due to artherosclerosis (in Sydney, Australia)
1985	WELSH, John		70	Cancer (in London, England)
1995	WELSH, Patricia		79	Pneumonia (in Green Valley, AZ)
1993	# WELSH, Ronnie		52	Brain cancer (in New York)
1946	# WELSH, William		76	Died in Los Angeles, CA
1974	# WENGRAF, John E.		76	Died in Santa Barbara, CA
1974	# WENTWORTH, Martha		84	Died in Sherman Oaks, CA
1956	# WERBISECK, Gisela		81	After a 3-year illness (in Hollywood, CA)
1984	# WERNER, Oskar	☆	61	Heart attack (in Marbourg, Germany)
1965	# WERNICKE, Otto		72	Died in Munich, Germany
1965	# WESSEL, Dick		51	Heart attack (in Studio City, CA)
1945	# WESSELHOEFT, Eleanor		72	After a long illness (in Hollywood, CA)
1979	# WESSON, Dick		59	Suicide (gunshot) in Costa Mesa, CA
1975	# WEST, Billy		82	Heart attack (leaving Hollywood Park racetrack, CA)
1984	+ WEST, Brooks		67	Cerebral hemorrhage (in Los Angeles, CA)
1943	WEST, Charles H.		57	Died in Los Angeles, CA
1943	WEST, Claudine		59	After a long illness (in Beverly Hills, CA)
1991	# WEST, Dottie		58	Complications after an automobile accident
1989	WEST, Lockwood		83	Cancer (in Brighton, England)
1985	WEST, Madge		93	Cardiac arrest in her sleep (in Memphis, TN)
1980	#+ WEST, Mae		88	Complications following a stroke (in Hollywood, CA)
1944	# WEST, Pat		55	Died in Hollywood, CA
• 1998	WEST, Paul		86	Pneumonia at his home in San Anselmo, CA
1952	WEST, Roland		65	Heart ailment (in Santa Monica, CA)
1918	WEST, William		?	Injuries from a fall (in New York, NY)
1935	WESTCOTT, Gordon		31	After falling from his horse in a polo game (in Hollywood, CA)
• 1998	WESTCOTT, Helen		70	Cancer at Stevens Hospital in Edmunds, WA
1971	WESTERFIELD, James		59	Heart attack (in Woodland Hills, CA)
1942	# WESTLEY, Helen		67	After a long illness (in Middlebush, NJ)
1970	WESTMAN, Nydia		68	Cancer (in Burbank, CA)
1973	# WESTMORE, Bud		55	Heart attack (in New York, NY)
1967	+ WESTMORE, Ernest		63	After a heart attack
1985	WESTMORE, Frank		62	After treatment for a cardiac condition
• 1931	WESTMORE, George		52	Suicide (bichloride of mercury—which took 3 days to kill him)
1940	WESTMORE, Monte		39	Heart condition after a tonsilectomy
1970	#+ WESTMORE, Perc		65	Coronary occlusion
1973	# WESTMORE, Wally		67	Stroke
1960	WESTON, Doris		42	Cancer (in New York, NY)

• New entry.   # Original name (Pt. 7).   + Interment (Pt. 5).   331   ☆ Oscar nominee, ★ Oscar winner (Pt. 10)

Deaths of Movie and Television Personalities — by Name

YEAR	NAME	AGE	CAUSE and/or PLACE OF DEATH
1996	# WESTON, Jack	71	After a 6 yr. bout with lymphoma (at Lenox Hill Hosp. in New York)
1996	WESTON, Paul	84	Natural causes (at St. John's Hospital in Santa Monica, CA)
1985	WESTON, Steve	45	Results of a fall from the roof of his home (in Toronto, Canada)
1989	WETMORE, Joan	77	Cancer (in New York, NY)
1957	+ WHALE, James	60	After a fall in his empty swimming pool (in Hollywood, CA)
1974	# WHALEN, Michael	72	Bronchial pneumonia (in Woodland Hills, CA)
1992	WHALEY, Jim	44	Heart attack
1963	# WHEAT, Lawrence "Larry"	87	Died in Los Angeles, CA
1966	# WHEATCROFT, Stanhope	77	Heart attack (in Woodland Hills, CA)
1991	WHEATLEY, Alan	84	Heart attack (in London, England)
1991	WHEDON, John Ogden	86	Pneumonia (in Redford, OR)
1986	WHEEL, Patricia	61	After a long illness (in New York, NY)
1968	#+ WHEELER, Bert	72	Emphysema (in New York, NY)
1990	WHEELER, Jerry B.	44	A.I.D.S. (in Los Angeles, CA)
1993	+ WHELAN, Arleen (Cagney)	78	Following a stroke (in Orange County, CA)
1993	WHELAN, Kenneth	72	Died in New York
1957	WHELAN, Tim	63	Died in Beverly Hills, CA
1975	WHIPPER, Leigh	97	Cardiac arrest in her sleep (in Harlem, NY)
1960	WHITAKER, Charles "Slim"	66	Heart attack (in Los Angeles, CA)
1983	WHITE, Alice	78	Stroke (in Los Angeles, CA)
1991	WHITE, Carol	47	Overdose of drugs and alcohol (in London, England)
1989	WHITE, Chrissie	94	Died in London, England
1990	WHITE, David	74	Heart attack after being run over by an auto (in Hollywood, CA)
1992	WHITE, Glenn	42	A.I.D.S.
1945	WHITE, J. Fisher	79	Died in England
1997	#+ WHITE, Jesse	79	Heart attack after surgery (at Cedars Sinai Med. Ctr. in Los Angeles, CA)
1988	WHITE, John Sylvester	68	Pancreatic cancer (in Waikiki, HI)
1985	WHITE, Jules J.	84	Alzheimer's disease (in Van Nuys, CA)
1990	WHITE, Larry	74	Heart attack
1949	# WHITE, Lee Roy "Lasses"	61	Died in Hollywood, CA
1948	WHITE, Leo	68	Died in Hollywood, CA
1955	WHITE, Lew	52	Died in New York
1935	WHITE, Marjorie	27	Automobile accident (in Los Angeles, CA)
1938	+ WHITE, Pearl	49	Cirrhosis of the liver (in Neuilly-Sur-Seine, France)
1969	WHITE, Ruth	55	Cancer (in Perth Amboy, NJ)
1995	# WHITE, Slappy	74	Heart attack (at his home in Brigantine, N.J.)
1987	WHITE, Ward	60	Cancer (in West Palm Beach, FL)
1962	WHITEHEAD, John	89	Died in Hollywood, CA
1967	+ WHITEMAN, Paul	77	Heart attack (in Doylestown, PA)
1961	WHITING, Jack	59	Died in New York
1984	WHITING, Napoleon	75	Heart attack (in Los Angeles, CA)
1957	# WHITLEY, Crane	57	Died in Los Angeles, CA
1989	WHITLEY, Keith	33	Alcohol poisoning
1979	WHITLEY, Ray	77	While on a fishing trip (in Mexico)
1966	WHITLOCK, T. Lloyd	75	Died in Los Angeles, CA
1954	WHITMAN, Ernest	61	Following a heart attack (in Hollywood, CA)
1958	#+ WHITMAN, Gayne	68	Heart attack (in Hollywood, CA)
1969	WHITNEY, Claire	79	Died in Sylmar, CA
1982	WHITNEY, John Hay "Jock"	77	After a long illness (in Manhasset, NY)
1983	WHITNEY, Michael	52	After a heart attack in a restaurant (in New York, NY)
1972	# WHITNEY, Peter	55	Heart attack (in Santa Barbara, CA)
1928	WHITNEY, Ralph	54	Injuries from a fall (in Los Angeles, CA)
1961	WHITTELL, Josephine	73	After a long illness (in Hollywood, CA)

YEAR	NAME		AGE	CAUSE and/or PLACE OF DEATH
1948	WHITTY, May	☆	82	Heart attack (in Beverly Hills, CA)
1966	+ WHORF, Richard		60	Heart attack after hospitalization for an ulcer (in Santa Monica, CA)
1987	WIARD, William		59	Lung cancer (in Pacific Palisades, CA)
1995	#+ WICKES, Mary		85	Complications from surgery (at UCLA Med. Ctr. in Los Angeles)
1994	WICKS, Mark Randall		43	A.I.D.S. complications (in Los Angeles, CA)
• 1997	WIDERBERG, Bo		66	Unspecified long illness (at a hospital in Angelholm, Sweden)
1986	WIECK, Dorothea		78	Died in Berlin, Germany
1938	WIENE, Robert		57	Cancer (in Paris, France)
1970	+ WIERE, Sylvester		60	Kidney ailment (in Hidden Hills, CA)
1968	WIFSTRAND, Naima		78	Died in Stockholm, Sweden
1994	WIGGINS, James		30	A.I.D.S. (in Goldsboro, NC)
• 1998	WILBER, Carey		81	Cancer in Seattle, WA
1993	WILBERN, George E.		77	Emphysema (in Los Angeles, CA)
1973	WILBUR, Crane		83	Following a stroke (in North Hollywood, CA)
1974	WILCOX, Frank		66	Died in Granada Hills, CA
1964	WILCOX, Fred M.		59	Died at his home in Beverly Hills, CA
• 1960	WILCOX, Harlow		60	
1977	WILCOX, Herbert		85	Following a long illness (in London, England)
1955	WILCOX, Robert		45	Heart attack (on a train near Rochester, NY)
• 1998	WILCOX-SMITH, Tamara		57	Heart failure in Los Angeles, CA
1984	WILCOXON, Henry		78	Congestive heart failure (in Los Angeles, CA)
1989	#+ WILDE, Cornel	☆	74	Leukemia (in Los Angeles, CA)
1995	# WILDER, Honeychile		76	Cancer (at Mem. Sloan-Kettering Cancer Ctr., NY)
1983	WILDER, Marie		53	
1915	WILDER, Marshall P.		56	Heart disease, aggravated by pneumonia (in St. Paul, MN)
• 1997	WILDERBERG, Bo	☆	66	After a long illness in Angelholm, Sweden
1979	WILDING, Michael		66	Injuries from a fall (at his home in Chichester, England)
1993	WILEY, Jan (Greene)		82	Cancer (in Rancho Palos Verdes, CA)
1971	WILKERSON, Guy		72	Cancer (in Hollywood, CA)
1993	WILKINSON, Kate		76	Bone cancer (in New York)
1968	+ WILLARD, Jess		86	Cerebral hemorrhage (in Los Angeles, CA)
1988	WILLES, Jean		65	Liver cancer (in Van Nuys, CA)
1948	# WILLIAM, Warren		52	Multiple myeloma and blood disease (in Encino, CA)
1922	# WILLIAMS, Bert		49	Pneumonia (in New York, NY)
1992	# WILLIAMS, Bill		77	Complications of a brain tumor (in Burbank, CA)
1961	# WILLIAMS, Bramsby		91	Died in London, England
1990	WILLIAMS, Brenda		43	Cancer
1958	WILLIAMS, Charles B.		59	After a long illness (in Hollywood, CA)
1928	WILLIAMS, Clara		40	Following an operation (at her home in Los Angeles, CA)
1989	WILLIAMS, Clark		83	Died in Carmel, CA
1927	WILLIAMS, Cora		56	Heart trouble (in Los Angeles, CA)
1927	#+ WILLIAMS, Earle		47	Bronchial pneumonia (in Los Angeles, CA)
1987	WILLIAMS, Emlyn		81	Following cancer surgery (in London, England)
1995	WILLIAMS, Frances E.		89	Complications from a stroke (in Los Angeles, CA)
1985	WILLIAMS, Grant		54	Peritonitis (in Los Angeles, CA)
1962	WILLIAMS, Guinn "Big Boy"		63	Uremic poisoning (in Hollywood, CA)
1989	#+ WILLIAMS, Guy		65	Heart attack (in Buenos Aires, Argentina)
1953	+ WILLIAMS, Hank Sr.		29	Heart attack from excessive drinking (in Oak Hill, WV)
1957	WILLIAMS, Harcourt		77	Died in London, England
• 1997	#+ WILLIAMS, Harriette "Hedy" (Carr)		91	Heart failure (at her son's home in New Orleans, LA)
1969	# WILLIAMS, Hugh		65	Heart attack (in London, England)
1983	WILLIAMS, John		80	Following an aneurysm (Do not confuse with John J. Williams)
1918	WILLIAMS, John J.		62	Heart failure (in New York) Do not confuse w/John Williams, d. 1983

Deaths of Movie and Television Personalities — by Name

YEAR	NAME		AGE	CAUSE and/or PLACE OF DEATH
1960	WILLIAMS, Kathlyn		72	*Died in Hollywood, CA*
1988	WILLIAMS, Kenneth		62	*Heart attack (in London, England)*
1965	WILLIAMS, Mack		58	*Heart attack (in Hollywood, CA)*
1994	WILLIAMS, Marion		66	*Vascular disease (in Philadelphia, PA)*
• 1998	WILLIAMS, Mark		38	*Respiratory failure at Kaiser Hosp. in Panorama City, CA*
1996	WILLIAMS, Palmer		79	*Prostate cancer*
1973	# WILLIAMS, Paul		33	*Suicide (sang with "The Temptations")*
1969	+ WILLIAMS, Rhys		76	*After a brief illness (in Santa Monica, CA)*
1931	WILLIAMS, Robert		31	*Peritonitis after an operation for appendicitis (in Hollywood, CA)*
• 1997	WILLIAMS, Ronald Clive		68	
1969	WILLIAMS, Spencer "Andy"		76	*Kidney ailment (in Los Angeles, CA)*
1983	+ WILLIAMS, Tennessee		71	*After choking on a plastic bottle cap (in Manhattan, NY)*
1985	WILLIAMS, Tex		68	*Cancer (in Newhall, CA)*
1992	WILLIAMS, Tony		64	
• 1997	WILLIAMS, Vince		39	*Cancer (in Englewood, NJ)*
• 1996	WILLIMAN, Earl		80	*Natural causes (at his home in Santa Maria, CA)*
1989	WILLINGER, Laszlo		80	
1995	WILLINGHAM, Calder		72	*Lung cancer (at a hospital in Laconia, N.H.)*
1989	# WILLIS, Matt		75	*Died in Fredericksburg, VA*
1988	WILLMAN, Noel		70	*Heart attack (in New York, NY)*
1990	WILLOCK, Dave		81	*Complications following a stroke (in Woodland Hills, CA)*
1963	WILLS, Beverly		29	*Killed in a fire (in Palm Springs, CA)*
1975	+ WILLS, Bob		70	*Bronchial pneumonia (in Ft. Worth, TX)*
1978	WILLS, Chill	☆	75	*Cancer (in Encino, CA)*
1951	WILLS, Drusilla		66	*Died in London, England*
• 1997	WILLS, Mary Lillain	☆	82	*Died in Sedona, AZ*
1984	# WILLSON, Meredith		82	*Heart failure (in Santa Monica, CA)*
1991	WILSHIN, Sunday		86	*Undisclosed causes (in Chemsford, England)*
1930	WILSON, Benjamin F.		54	*Heart ailment (in Glendale, CA)*
1994	WILSON, Billy		59	*Complications from A.I.D.S. (in New York)*
• 1998	WILSON, Carl D.		51	*Lung cancer in Los Angeles, CA*
1948	WILSON, Charles Cahill		53	*Esophagal hemorrhage*
1941	# WILSON, Clarence H.		64	*Died in Hollywood, CA*
1983	+ WILSON, Dennis		39	*Drowned (in Marina Del Rey, CA)*
• 1997	WILSON, Dennis Main		73	
1982	WILSON, Don		81	*Stroke*
1953	WILSON, Dooley		59	*Died in Los Angeles, CA*
1987	WILSON, Earl		79	*After a long illness (in Los Angeles, CA)*
1981	#+ WILSON, Edith		83	*Cerebral hemorrhage (in Chcago, IL)*
1966	WILSON, Jack		49	*Cerebral hemorrhage (in Los Angeles, CA)*
1990	WILSON, Josephine		86	*Heart attack (in London, England)*
1993	WILSON, Lester		51	*Heart attack (in Los Angeles, CA)*
1988	WILSON, Lois		93	*Pneumonia (in Reno, NV)*
1986	WILSON, Margery		89	*Cardiac arrest in her sleep (in Alhambra, CA)*
1972	#+ WILSON, Marie		56	*Cancer (in Hollywood Hills, CA)*
1991	WILSON, Richard		75	*Pancreatic cancer (in Santa Monica, CA)*
1991	WILSON, Stu		87	*Died in Los Angeles, CA*
1986	WILSON, Teddy		73	*Following intestinal surgery (in New Britain, CT)*
1991	WILSON, Theodore R.		47	*Stroke (in Los Angeles, CA)*
1965	# WILSON, Tom		84	*Died in Los Angeles, CA*
1989	WILSON, Trey		40	*Cerebral hemorrhage (in New York, NY)*
1964	WILSON, Whip		49	*Heart attack (in Hollywood, CA)*
1957	WILTON, Eric		73	*Died in England*

Deaths of Movie and Television Personalities — by Name

	YEAR	NAME		AGE	CAUSE and/or PLACE OF DEATH
•	1997	WINBLAD, Marjorie King		86	Heart failure at Mercy Medical Center in Baltimore, MD
	1972	+ WINCHELL, Walter		74	Died in Los Angeles, CA
	1989	WINCKLER, Robert		62	Stomach cancer (in Woodland Hills, CA)
	1972	# WINDSOR, Claire		75	Heart attack (in Los Angeles, CA)
	1986	WINDSOR, Marie		64	
	1960	WINDUST, Brctaigne		54	Died in New York
	1969	WING, Dan		46	Heart attack (in Fresno, CA)
	1957	WING, Paul R.		65	Following a heart attack (in Portsmouth, VA)
	1974	# WING, Red		90	Cardiac arrest in her sleep (in New York, NY)
	1969	# WINNINGER, Charles		84	Died in Palm Springs, CA
	1991	WINSLOW, Dick		75	Complications from diabetes (in Los Angeles, CA)
	1991	WINTERS, Bernie		58	Cancer (in London, England)
	1989	WINTERS, Roland		84	Stroke (in Englewood, NJ)
	1950	# WINTHROP, Joy		86	Died in Hollywood, CA
	1980	WINTLE, Julian		67	Stroke (in Brighton, England)
	1958	WINTON, Jane		53	Died in New York
	1984	#+ WINWOOD, Estelle		101	Heart failure (in Woodland Hills, CA)
	1959	#+ WITHERS, Grant		54	Suicide (sleeping pills) in North Hollywood, CA
	1968	# WITHERS, Isabel		72	Died in Hollywood, CA
	1957	WITHERSPOON, Cora		67	Died in Las Crusas, NM
	1990	WITTENBERG, Marguerite N.		77	Cancer (in Culver City, CA)
	1990	WITTENBERG, Paul B.		63	Cancer (in Mission Hills, CA)
	1956	WIX, Florence E.		73	Cancer (in Woodland Hills, CA)
	1993	WOLF, Harry L.		85	Died at Cedars-Sinai Hospital in Los Angeles, CA
	1994	WOLFBERG, Dennis		48	After a 2-yr. battle with melanoma (in Culver City, CA)
	1992	WOLFE, Ian		95	Cardiac arrest in his sleep (in Los Angeles, CA)
•	1998	WOLFF, Albert H.		95	Died in Mason, Ohio
	1971	# WOLFF, Frank		43	Suicide (slashed his throat with a safety razor) in Rome, Italy
	1931	+ WOLHEIM, Louis		50	Stomach cancer (in Los Angeles, CA)
	1993	WONDER, Tommy		78	Complications from an ulcer (in New York City)
	1961	#+ WONG, Anna May		54	Heart attack (in Santa Monica, CA)
	1989	WONG, Iris		68	Died in Honolulu, HI
	1978	WONG, Joe		75	Heart condition (in Los Angeles, CA)
	1940	# WONG, Mary		25	Suicide (hanging) in Los Angeles, CA
	1960	WONTNER, Arthur		85	Died in London, England
	1965	WOOD, Britt		70	After a 6-month illness (in Hollywood, CA)
	1983	WOOD, Cindi		52	After a long illness (in Malibu, CA)
	1966	WOOD, Douglas		85	Died in Woodland Hills, CA
•	1997	WOOD, Duncan		71	
	1978	#+ WOOD, Ed		54	Heart attack brought on by acute alcoholism (in Los Angeles, CA)
•	1996	WOOD, Forrest Benjamin		76	Unreported causes (in Los Angeles, CA)
	1956	WOOD, Freeman N.		59	After a short illness (in Hollywood, CA)
	1990	WOOD, George		56	Diabetes (in New Orleans, LA)
	1981	#+ WOOD, Natalie	☆	43	Accidental drowning (off Catalina Island, CA)
	1978	WOOD, Peggy	☆	86	Cerebral hemorrhage (in Stamford, CT)
	1949	+ WOOD, Sam	☆	66	Heart attack (in Hollywood, CA)
	1958	WOOD, Victor		44	Died in London, England
	1973	WOODBRIDGE, George		66	Died in London, England
	1989	WOODBURY, Joan		73	Respiratory failure (in Desert Hot Springs, CA)
	1995	WOODMAN, William		63	Cardiac arrest (in New York)
	1980	WOODRUFF, Eleanor		89	Cardiac arrest in her sleep
	1942	WOODS, Arthur		38	Killed in action during World War 2
	1968	# WOODS, Harry L. Sr.		79	Uremia (in Los Angeles, CA)

Deaths of Movie and Television Personalities — by Name

YEAR	NAME		AGE	CAUSE and/or PLACE OF DEATH
1983	WOODS, Maurice		45	Cancer (in New York, NY)
1972	WOODWARD, Robert "Bob"		63	Heart attack (in Hollywood, CA)
1989	WOOLAND, Norman		83	Following several strokes (in Staplehurst, England)
1992	# WOOLERY, Ade		82	Cancer (in Santa Monica, CA)
1994	WOOLF, Charles		67	Cancer (in Sherman Oaks, CA)
1943	+ WOOLLCOTT, Alexander		56	Heart attack (while broadcasting at CBS in New York, NY)
1963	#+ WOOLLEY, Monty	☆	74	Kidney and heart ailment (in Albany, NY)
1938	+ WOOLSEY, Robert		48	Kidney ailment (in Malibu Beach, CA)
1992	#+ WORDEN, Hank		91	Died in his sleep of natural causes (at his Brentwood, CA, home)
1973	WORLOCK, Frederick		87	Cerebral ischemia after a long illness (in Woodland Hills, CA)
1985	WORMS, Robert A. III		52	Heart failure (in Hollywood, CA)
1991	WORSLEY, Wallace Jr.		82	Heart failure
1963	# WORTH, Constance		48	Died in Australia
1998	WORTH, Marvin		72	Complications frome Bronchioloalar carcinoma
1956	# WORTH, Peggy		64	Died in New York, NY
1941	WORTHINGTON, William J.		68	Died in Beverly Hills, CA
1968	WRAY, Aloha		39	Died in Hollywood, CA
1940	# WRAY, John		52	After a long illness (in Hollywood, CA)
1950	WRAY, Ted		41	Following a heart attack (in Big Bear City, CA)
1962	WREN, Sam		65	Died in Hollywood, CA
1989	WRIGHT, Ben		74	Heart failure after heart surgery (in Burbank, CA)
1995	WRIGHT, Eric "Easy-E"		31	A.I.D.S.
1998	WRIGHT, George		77	Died in California
1943	WRIGHT, Haidee		44	Died in London, England
1940	WRIGHT, Hugh E.		60	Died in Windsor, England
1965	WRIGHT, Mack V.		69	Died in Boulder City, NV
1962	WRIGHT, Will		71	Cancer (in Hollywood) Do not confuse with William Wright d. 1949
1949	WRIGHT, William		37	Cancer (in Ensenada, Mex.) Do not confuse with Will Wright d. 1962
1993	WRIGHTSON, Earl		77	Heart failure (in E. Norwich, CT)
1945	WU, Honorable		42	Died in Hollywood, CA
1958	WUEST, Ida		74	Died in Berlin, Germany
1925	WUNDERLEE, Frank		50	Apoplexy attack (while dining at the Green Room Club in NYC)
1990	WURSCHMIDT, Sigrid		37	Metastasized breast cancer (in San Francisco, CA)
1992	WYATT, Allan Sr.		72	Cancer (in Burbank, CA)
1956	+ WYCHERLY, Margaret	☆	74	Died in New York, NY
1988	WYCKOFF, Michael		69	After a stroke (in Madrid, Spain)
1992	WYLER, Jorie		61	After a brief illness (in New York, NY)
1981	+ WYLER, William	★	79	Heart attack (in Beverly Hills, CA)
1970	+ WYMARK, Patrick		44	Heart attack in his hotel room (in Melbourne, Australia)
1998	WYNETTE, Tammy		55	Blood clot in her lungs at her Nashville, Tenn. home
1966	#+ WYNN, Ed	☆	79	Cancer (in Los Angeles, CA)
1936	WYNN, Hugh		46	Heart attack
1986	#+ WYNN, Keenan		70	Cancer (in Brentwood, CA)
1971	WYNN, Nan		55	Cancer (in Santa Monica, CA)
1990	WYNNE, Paul		47	A.I.D.S.
1964	# WYNYARD, Diana	☆	58	Kidney ailment (in London, England)
	X			
1965	#+ X, Malcolm		39	(See Malcolm Little)
	Y			
1965	YACONELLI, Frank		67	Lung cancer (in Los Angeles, CA)
1986	YALE, Joseph		36	Complications from A.I.D.S. (in Palm Springs, CA)
1951	YARBOROUGH, Barton		51	Died in Hollywood, CA
1944	YARDE, Margaret		65	Died in London, England

• New entry. # Original name (Pt. 7). + Interment (Pt. 5).   336   ☆ Oscar nominee, ★ Oscar winner (Pt. 10)

Deaths of Movie and Television Personalities — by Name

YEAR	NAME	AGE	CAUSE and/or PLACE OF DEATH
1992	YARMY, Dick	59	Lung cancer (in Studio City, CA)
1991	YATES, Sterling	65	Cerebral hemorrhage
1928	YEARSLEY, Ralph	31	Suicide (at his home in Hollywood, CA)
1991	YELLEN, Jack	98	Died in Springville, NY
1992	YEVSTIGNEEV, Yevgeny	66	Cardio-vascular problems (in London, England)
• 1996	YODER, Alma Kitchell	103	Died in Sarasota, FL
1969	YORK, Chick	83	
1992	+ YORK, Dick	63	Emphysema and degenerative spinal condition (Grand Rapids, MI)
1952	YORK, Duke	49	Suicide (found shot to death at his home) in Hollywood, CA
1934	# YORKE, Edith	66	Died in London, England
1945	# YOST, Herbert A.	65	Died in New York, NY
1946	+ YOUMANS, Vincent	47	Tuberculosis (in Denver, CO)
1971	YOUNG, Carleton G.	64	Cancer (in Hollywood, CA)
1960	YOUNG, Clara Kimball	69	Died in Woodland Hills, CA
1951	YOUNG, Clifton	34	Asphyxiation after falling asleep while smoking (in Los Angeles, CA)
1995	YOUNG, Donald Jr.	63	Coronary artery disease (at his home in Los Angeles, CA)
• 1996	YOUNG, Faron	64	Suicide (gunshot) after prostate surgery (in Nashville, TN)
1978	#+ YOUNG, Gig ★	64	Suicide (gunshot) after shooting his 5th wife (in New York, NY)
1992	YOUNG, Jack Haydn	81	Neurological illness
1993	YOUNG, Marvin	90	Natural causes (in Los Angeles, CA)
1934	+ YOUNG, Mary	77	Following a 3-month illness (in Los Angeles, CA)
1958	YOUNG, Noah	71	Died in Los Angeles, CA
1940	YOUNG, Olive	33	Internal hemorrhages (in Bayonne, NJ)
• 1998	YOUNG, Robert	91	Respiratory failure at his home in Westlake Village, CA
1953	YOUNG, Roland ☆	65	Died at his home in New York, NY
1993	# YOUNG, Skip "Wally"	63	Found dead of a heart attack (at his CA home)
1936	YOUNG, Tammany	49	Died in his sleep of a heart attack (in Hollywood, CA)
1994	YOUNG, Terence	79	Heart attack (at a hospital in Cannes, France)
1956	+ YOUNG, Victor ★	55	Pneumonia (in Palm Springs, CA)
1957	YOUNG, Walter	79	Pneumonia (in New York, NY)
1995	YOUNGERMAN, Joseph C.	89	Complications from a stroke (at Cedars-Sinai Med. Ctr. in L.A.)
• 1998	YOUNGMAN, Henny	91	Complications from flu at Mt. Sinai Hosp. in New York City, NY
1974	YOUNGSON, Robert	56	Died at St. Vincent's Hospital in New York
• 1997	YOUNGSTEIN, Max E.	84	Died in Los Angeles, CA
1966	# YOWLACHIE, Chief	74	Pneumonia (in Los Angeles, CA)
1950	+ YULE, Joe	55	Heart attack (in Hollywood, CA)
1974	#+ YURKA, Blanche	87	Arteriosclerosis (in New York, NY)
	Z		
1947	ZAHLER, Lee	53	
1994	ZAMORA, Pedro	22	Neurological complications from A.I.D.S. (in Miami, FL)
1991	ZAMPA, Luigi	86	After a long illness (in Rome, Italy)
1994	# ZANE, Bartine	96	Heart attack (in Burbank, CA)
1979	#+ ZANUCK, Darryl F.	77	Pulmonary embolism aggravated by pneumonia (in Hollywood, CA)
1982	+ ZANUCK, Virginia Fox	83	Emphysema and stroke (in Santa Monica, CA)
1993	#+ ZAPPA, Frank	52	Prostate cancer (in Los Angeles, CA)
1986	# ZAREMBA, Jack	77	Heart attack (in Newport Beach, CA)
1989	ZAVATTINA, Cesare	86	Cerebral hemorrhage (in Rome, Italy)
1952	# ZEARS, Marjorie	41	Murdered in her bathroom (in Hollywood, CA)
1989	ZEMAN, Karel	78	Died in Gottwaldov, Czechoslovakia
1994	# ZETTERLING, Mai	68	Cancer (in London, England)
1932	+ ZIEGFELD, Florenz	63	Pleurisy and pneumonia (in Los Angeles, CA)
1975	# ZIMBALIST, Al	59	Heart attack (in Beverly Hills, CA)
1985	ZIMBALIST, Efrem Sr.	95	

Deaths of Movie and Television Personalities — by Name

YEAR	NAME	AGE	CAUSE and/or PLACE OF DEATH
1958	ZIMBALIST, Sam	57	Heart attack (in Rome, Italy)
• 1997	ZINNEMANN, Fred ★	89	Natural causes (at his home in London, England)
• 1997	ZINNEMANN, Renee Bartlett	88	Natural causes in London
1991	ZORNOW, Edith	72	Cancer (in New York, NY)
1962	+ ZUCCO, Frances	30	Throat cancer after an overdose of radiation therapy (in Los Angeles)
1960	+ ZUCCO, George	74	Pneumonia (at Monterey Sanitarium, S. San Gabriel, CA)
• 1997	ZUCKERT, Bill	76	Pneunonia in Woodland Hills, CA
1976	+ ZUKOR, Adolph	103	Died in Hollywood, CA
1994	ZUKOR, Eugene	97	Died at his home in Beverly Hills, CA
1991	ZWICKLER, Phil	36	Complications from A.I.D.S. (in New York, NY)

3

Statistical
Summary
of Deaths

Statistical Summary of Deaths

TOTAL NUMBER OF DEATHS LISTED
8,728

TOTAL NUMBER OF DEATHS LISTED — BY SEX			
Males	6,491	Females	2,237

TOTAL NUMBER OF DEATHS LISTED — BY YEAR			
1912	1	1956	85
1913	2	1957	98
1915	6	1958	101
1916	5	1959	114
1917	8	1960	91
1918	31	1961	105
1919	15	1962	94
1920	7	1963	99
1921	11	1964	109
1922	10	1965	119
1923	13	1966	118
1924	9	1967	130
1925	24	1968	126
1926	15	1969	129
1927	17	1970	109
1928	20	1971	137
1929	21	1972	117
1930	18	1973	147
1931	35	1974	139
1932	22	1975	133
1933	38	1976	122
1934	34	1977	112
1935	30	1978	126
1936	43	1979	133
1937	51	1980	150
1938	43	1981	123
1939	45	1982	150
1940	73	1983	150
1941	49	1984	146
1942	45	1985	173
1943	57	1986	177
1944	58	1987	191
1945	62	1988	216
1946	67	1989	274
1947	69	1990	316
1948	86	1991	349
1949	66	1992	363
1950	86	1993	327
1951	72	1994	251
1952	75	1995	264
1953	79	1996	273
1954	68	1997	235
1955	87	1998	134

Statistical Summary of Deaths

Age	Count	Age	Count
Age 1	1	Age 58	143
Age 6	1	Age 59	150
Age 7	2	Age 60	175
Age 8	1	Age 61	144
Age 10	1	Age 62	163
Age 12	1	Age 63	167
Age 13	2	Age 64	202
Age 14	1	Age 65	201
Age 16	3	Age 66	194
Age 17	2	Age 67	210
Age 18	3	Age 68	214
Age 19	5	Age 69	222
Age 20	8	Age 70	207
Age 21	7	Age 71	216
Age 22	12	Age 72	223
Age 23	10	Age 73	228
Age 24	9	Age 74	209
Age 25	17	Age 75	230
Age 26	15	Age 76	200
Age 27	24	Age 77	235
Age 28	19	Age 78	205
Age 29	31	Age 79	196
Age 30	32	Age 80	199
Age 31	23	Age 81	187
Age 32	27	Age 82	204
Age 33	48	Age 83	192
Age 34	33	Age 84	169
Age 35	43	Age 85	147
Age 36	41	Age 86	153
Age 37	45	Age 87	120
Age 38	54	Age 88	98
Age 39	56	Age 89	99
Age 40	52	Age 90	81
Age 41	51	Age 91	62
Age 42	79	Age 92	42
Age 43	68	Age 93	49
Age 44	75	Age 94	33
Age 45	97	Age 95	33
Age 46	76	Age 96	32
Age 47	86	Age 97	14
Age 48	88	Age 98	14
Age 49	104	Age 99	7
Age 50	91	Age 100	9
Age 51	97	Age 101	8
Age 52	126	Age 102	1
Age 53	119	Age 103	4
Age 54	137	Age 104	1
Age 55	127	Age 107	1
Age 56	110	Age ?	125
Age 57	150		

Statistical Summary of Deaths

Cause	Number	Percent
Heart Problems, including:	2,015	30.90%
• Heart attack		
• Heart failure		
• Heart disease, etc.		
Cancer, including:	1,362	20.89%
• Leukemia		
• Lung, breast, throat, brain, ovarian, etc.		
Respiratory Problems, including:	537	8.24%
• Asthma		
• Emphysema		
• Influenza		
• Pneumonia		
• Tuberculosis, etc.		
Following a Long Illness	374	5.74%
Accidents	345	5.29%
Stroke	290	4.45%
A.I.D.S.	237	3.63%
Suicide	174	2.67%
After a Brief Illness	137	2.10%
During or after surgery	134	2.06%
Hemorrhage	122	1.87%
Liver Ailments, including:	89	1.37%
• Hepatitis		
• Cirrhosis		
• Jaundice, etc.		
Kidney Ailments	85	1.30%
Natural Causes	82	1.26%
Murdered	76	1.17%
Drug Overdose	66	1.01%
Blood Disorders, including:	44	0.67%
• Anemia, etc.		
Tumor	43	0.66%
Sclerosis, including:	39	0.60%
• Amyotrophic lateral sclerosis, etc.		
Pancreatic diseases, including:	37	0.57%
• Diabetes, etc.		
Parkinson's Disease	27	0.41%
Alzheimer's Disease	25	0.38%
Aneurysm	22	0.34%
Other infections	16	0.25%
Intestinal Disorders	15	0.23%
Edema	9	0.14%
Spinal Diseases	8	0.12%
Ulcers	8	0.12%
Arthritis	7	0.11%
Gall Bladder Ailments	6	0.09%
Stomach Disorders	5	0.08%
Lymphatic Diseases	4	0.06%
All Other Causes	80	1.23%
	6,520	100%

Graphical Summary of Most Frequently Listed Causes of Death
(1912 - 1998)

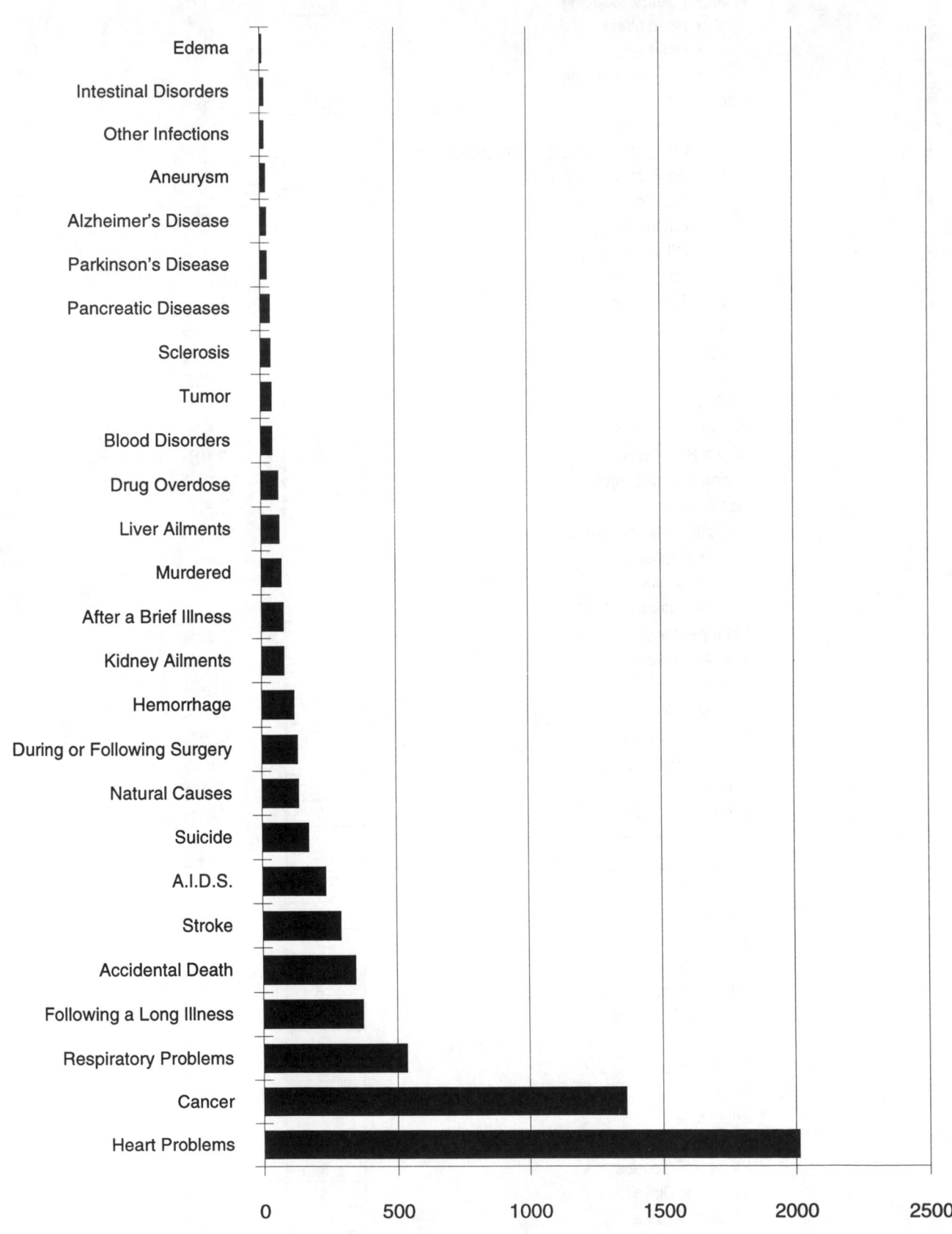

Statistical Summary of Deaths

Cemetery	Count	Percent
Arlington National Cemetery, Arlington, VA	9	1.00%
Calvary Cemetery, Los Angeles, CA	15	1.67%
Calvary Cemetery, Woodside (Queens), NY	6	0.67%
Cem. of the Gate of Heaven, Hawthorne, NY	7	0.78%
Chapel of the Pines Crematory, Los Angeles, CA	24	2.67%
Cypress Hills Cemetery, Brooklyn, NY	3	0.33%
Desert Memorial Park, Palm Springs, CA	5	0.56%
Eden Memorial Park, San Fernando, CA	5	0.56%
Ferncliff Cemetery and Maus., Hartsdale, NY	27	3.01%
Flushing Cemetery, Flushing (Queens), NY	4	0.45%
Forest Lawn—Cypress, Cypress, CA	4	0.45%
Forest Lawn—Glendale, Glendale, CA	252	28.06%
Forest Lawn—Hollywood Hills, Los Angeles, CA	107	11.92%
Grand View Memorial Park, Glendale, CA	3	0.33%
Green-Wood Cemetery, Brooklyn, NY	5	0.56%
Grove Hill Memorial Park, Dallas, TX	5	0.56%
Hillside Memorial Park, Los Angeles, CA	29	3.23%
Hollywood Memorial Park, Hollywood, CA	81	9.02%
Holy Cross Cem. and Maus., Culver City, CA	81	9.02%
Home of Peace Mem. Park, Los Angeles, CA	12	1.34%
Inglewood Park Cemetery, Inglewood, CA	13	1.45%
Kensico Cemetery, Valhalla, NY	20	2.23%
Los Angeles National Cemetery, L.A., CA	4	0.45%
Mount Hope Cem., Hastings-on-Hudson, NY	4	0.45%
Mount Sinai Memorial-Park, Los Angeles, CA	12	1.34%
Oakwood Memorial Park, Chatsworth, CA	8	0.89%
Palm Mortuary Mausoleum, Las Vegas, NV	3	0.33%
Père Lachaise Cemetery, Paris, France	6	0.67%
Restland Memorial Park, Dallas, TX	3	0.33%
Rose Dale Cemetery, Los Angeles, CA	4	0.45%
Rose Hills Memorial Park, Whittier, CA	4	0.45%
San Fernando Mission Cem., San Fernando, CA	11	1.22%
Valhalla Memorial Park, N. Hollywood, CA	13	1.45%
Westchester Hills Cem, Hastings-on-Hudson, NY	5	0.56%
Westwood Village Mem. Park, Los Angeles, CA	83	9.24%
Woodlawn Cemetery, Santa Monica, CA	8	0.89%
Woodlawn Cemetery, The Bronx, NY	13	1.45%

898

SPENCER TRACY

4

*Directory of
Cemeteries*

Directory of Cemeteries - by State and City

STATE/CITY	CEMETERY	STREET	ZIP	PHONE
A				
ARKANSAS				
Hot Springs	Greenwood Cemetery			
C				
CALIFORNIA				
Altadena	Mountain View Cemetery	2400 N. Fair Oaks Ave.	91001	(818) 794-7133
Benecia	Catholic Cemetery			
Burbank	Restland Memorial Park			
Chatsworth	Oakwood Memorial Park	22601 Lassen	91311	(818) 341-0344
Coachella	Coachella Valley Cemetery	82925 Avenue 52	92238	(619) 398-3221
Compton	Woodlawn Memorial Park	1715 W. Greenleaf Blvd.	90220	(213) 636-1696
Covina	Forest Lawn—Covina Hills	21300 E. Via Verde Dr.	91724	(714) 599-1236
"	"	"	"	(818) 966-3671
Culver City	Holy Cross Cemetery and Maus.	5835 W. Slauson Ave.	90230	(213) 776-1855
Cypress	Forest Lawn Mem. Park, Cypress	4471 Lincoln Ave.	90630	(213) 431-2517
"	"	.	"	(714) 828-3131
Escondido	Oak Hill Cemetery	2640 Glen Ridge Rd.	92027	(619) 745-1781
Glendale	Forest Lawn Mem. Park, Glendale	1712 S. Glendale Ave.	91205	(213) 254-3131
"	"	"	"	(818) 241-4151
Glendale	Grand View Memorial Park	1341 Glenwood Rd.	91201	(818) 242-2697
Hollywood	Beth-Olam Cemetery and Maus.	900 Gower	90038	(213) 469-2322
Hollywood	Hollywood Memorial Park	6000 Santa Monica Blvd.	90038	(213) 469-1181
Inglewood	Inglewood Park Cemetery	720 E. Florence Ave.	90301	(310) 412-6500
Lafayette	Queen of Heaven Cemetery			
La Jolla	El Camino Memorial Park	5600 Carroll Canyon Rd.	92037	(619) 453-2121
Long Beach	Forest Lawn—Sunnyside	1500 E. San Antonio Dr.	90807	(310) 424-1631
Los Angeles	Calvary Cemetery	4201 Whittier Blvd.	90023	(213) 261-3106
Los Angeles	Chapel of the Pines Crematory	1605 S. Catalina	90006	(Unpublished)
Los Angeles	Evergreen Cem. and Crematory	204 N. Evergreen Ave.	90033	(213) 268-6714
Los Angeles	Forest Lawn—Hollywood Hills	6300 Forest Lawn Dr.	90068	(213) 254-7251
"	"	"	"	(818) 984-1711
Los Angeles	Hillside Memorial Park	6001 W. Centinela Ave.	90045	(818) 502-8649
Los Angeles	Home of Peace Memorial Park	4334 Whittier Blvd.	90023	(213) 261-6135
Los Angeles	Los Angeles National Cemetery	950 Sepulveda Blvd.	90049	(310) 824-4311
Los Angeles	Mount Sinai Memorial-Park	5950 Forest Lawn Dr.	90068	(213) 469-6000
Los Angeles	Odd Fellows Cemetery	3640 Whittier Blvd.	90023	(213) 261-6156
Los Angeles	Rose Dale Cemetery	1831 W. Washington Blvd.	90007	(213) 734-3155
Los Angeles	Westwood Village Memorial Park	1218 Glendon Ave.	90024	(213) 474-1579
Newhall	Eternal Valley Memorial Park	23287 Sierra Hwy.	91321	(805) 259-0800
Newport Beach	Pacific View Memorial Park	3500 Pacific View Drive	92663	(714) 644-2700
North Hollywood	Valhalla Memorial Park	10621 Victory Blvd.	91606	(818) 763-9121
Oceanside	Eternal Hills Memorial Park	1999 El Camino Real	92054	(619) 757-2020
Palm Springs	Desert Memorial Park	69920 Ramon Rd.	92264	(619) 328-3316
Palm Springs	Welwood Murray Cemetery	100 S. Palm Canyon Dr.	92262	(619)323-8296
Red Bluff	Los Molinas Cemetery	Hwy 99-E at Taft St.	96055	(916) 384-1864
Sacramento	East Lawn Sierra Hills Mem. Park	5757 Greenback Lane	95841	(916) 732-2020
Sacramento	St. Mary's Mausoleum			
San Bruno	San Bruno/Golden Gate National	Sneath Lane (off Route 101)	94066	(415) 716-4616
San Diego	Catalina-Ft. Rose Crans Nat'l.	P.O. Box 6237	92166	(619) 553-2084
San Diego	Greenwood Memorial Park	Interstate 805 at Imperial Av.	92112	(619) 264-3131
San Fernando	Eden Memorial Park	11500 Sepulveda Blvd.	91345	(818) 361-7161
San Fernando	Glen Haven Memorial Park	13017 N. Lopez Canyon Rd.	91342	(818) 899-5211
San Fernando	San Fernando Mission Cemetery	11160 Stranwood Ave.	91345	(818) 361-7387
San Mateo	Holy Cross Cemetery	Menlo Park	94014	(415) 323-6375
Santa Barbara	Calvary Cemetery	199 Hope Ave.	93110	(805) 687-8811
Santa Barbara	Santa Barbara Cemetery	E. Cabrillo Blvd.	93108	(805) 969-3231
Santa Monica	Woodlawn Cemetery	1847 14th St.	90404	(310) 450-0781
Santa Rosa	Rural Cemetery			
Victorville	Roy Rogers-Dale Evans Museum	15650 Seneca Rd.	92392	(619) 243-4547

Directory of Cemeteries - by State and City

STATE/CITY	CEMETERY	STREET	ZIP	PHONE
Victorville	Victor Valley Memorial Park			
Westlake Village	Valley Oaks Memorial Park	5600 N. Lindero Canyon Rd.	91362	(818) 889-0902
Whittier	Rose Hills Memorial Park	3900 S. Workman Mill Rd.	90601	(213) 699-0921
◆ COLORADO				
Colorado Springs	Evergreen Cemetery	1005 S. Hancock Ave.	80903	(719) 578-6646
Denver	Fairmount Cemetery	430 S. Quebec St.	80231	(303) 399-0692
Lakewood	Crown Hill Cemetery and Mortuary	W. 29th Av. at Wadsworth Bl.	80218	(303) 233-4611
◆ CONNECTICUT				
Bridgeport	Mountain Grove Cemetery	2675 North Ave.	06604	(203) 336-3579
Greenwich	Putnam Cemetery	35 Parsonage Rd.	06830	(203) 869-4828
Killingworth	Evergreen Cemetery			
New Haven	Beaverdale Memorial Park	90 Pine Rock Ave.	06515	(203) 387-6601
Ridgefield	St. Mary's Cemetery			(Unpublished)
Stamford	Long Ridge Congregational Church			(203) 322-6975
Wethersfield	Emanuel Cemetery	1361 Berlin Turnpike	06109	(203) 236-1275
D				
◆ D.C.				
Washington	Congressional Cemetery, The	1801 East Street, S.E.	20003	(202) 543-0539
F				
◆ FLORIDA				
Ft. Lauderdale	Lauderdale Memorial Park	400 N.W. 27th Ave.	33310	(305) 761-5434
Gainesville	Evergreen Cemetery	Box 490 (1800 S.E. 4th St.)	32602	(904) 334-2160
Jacksonville	Jacksonville Memorial Gardens			
Miami	Mount Nebo Cemetery			
Miami	Southern Memorial Park	15000 W. Dixie Hwy.	33181	(305) 947-3543
Stuart	Fernhill Memorial Gardens	1501 SE Kanner Hwy.	34997	(407) 283-6246
Tampa	American Legion Cemetery			
G				
◆ GEORGIA				
Atlanta	Martin Luther King Memorial Center			
Atlanta	Oakland Cemetery			
Carrollton	Our Lady of Perpetual Help Church	Center Point Rd.	30117	(404) 832-8977
Cumming	Sawnee View Memorial Garden			
Cuthbert	Old Cemetery			
Royston	Royston Cemetery			
Savannah	Bonaventure Cemetery	Bonaventure Rd.	31404	(912) 651-6843
I				
◆ IDAHO				
Boise	Morris Hill Cemetery	317 N. Latah	83706	(208) 384-4391
◆ ILLINOIS				
Alsip	Burr Oak Cemetery			
Alton	Alton City Cemetery			
Calumet City	Holy Cross Cemetery	Burnham at Michigan City Rd	60409	(312) 862-5398
Chicago	Graceland Cemetery	4001 N. Clark St.	60613	(708) 525-1105
Chicago	Mount Glenwood Cemetery			
Chicago	Oak Woods Cemetery			
Chicago	Rosehill Cemetery			
Danville	Spring Hill Cemetery			
Evanston	Calvary Cemetery			
Evanston	Memorial Park Cemetery	9900 Gross Point Rd.	60076	
Evergreen Park	St. Mary's Cemetery			
Forest Park	Waldheim/Forest Home Cemetery	863 S. Desplaines St.	60607	(708) 366-4541

STATE/CITY	CEMETERY	STREET	ZIP	PHONE
Hillside	Queen of Heaven Cemetery			
Newton	Mound Cemetery			
Shiloh	Shiloh Memorial Park			
Worth	Holy Sepulchre Cemetery	6001 W. 111th St.	60482	(708) 422-3020
◆ INDIANA				
Bloomington	Rosehill Cemetery and Mausoleum	5800 N. Ravenswood Ave.	46401	(317) 561-5940
Fairmount	Park Cemetery	111 W. Washington	46928	(317) 948-4040
Lafayette	Rest Haven Memorial Park	1200 Sagamore Pkwy., N.	47904	(317) 447-1797
Noblesville	Oak Lawn Memorial Gardens	9700 Allisonville Rd.	46250	(317) 849-3616
Peru	Mount Hope Cemetery	W. 12th Street	46970	(317) 472-2493
South Bend	Highland Cemetery			
◆ IOWA				
Davenport	Oakdale Cemetery	2501 Eastern Avenue	52803	(319) 324-5121
Ft. Dodge	Oakland Cemetery	15th Street		
K				
◆ KENTUCKY				
Crestwood	Mt. Tabor United Methodist Church	3301 W. Highway 22	40014	(502) 241-8811
Louisville	Cave Hill Cemetery			
L				
◆ LOUISIANA				
Baton Rouge	Resthaven Gardens of Memory			
Metairie	Providence Memorial Park	8200 Airline Highway	70003	(504) 464-0541
New Orleans	Christ Church Cathedral	2919 St. Charles Ave.		
New Orleans	Greenwood Cemetery	120 City Park Ave.	70119	(504) 482-3232
New Orleans	Metairie Cemetery	5100 Pontchartrain Blvd.	70179	(504) 486-6331
M				
◆ MAINE				
Hancock	Riverside Cemetery			
Westbrook	St. Hyacinth's Church Cemetery	Stroudwater St.		(207) 854-2003
◆ MARYLAND				
Baltimore	Arbutus Memorial Park	1101 Sulphur Spring Rd.	21227	(410) 242-2700
Baltimore	Druid Ridge Cemetery	Park Hts. Ave. at Old Court Rd.	21208	(410) 486-5300
Baltimore	Garden of Faith Memorial Gardens	5598 Trumps Mill Rd.	21206	(410) 668-1086
Baltimore	Greek Orthodox Cemetery	Windsor Mill Rd.	21207	(410) 298-7296
Baltimore	Hebrew Friendship Cemetery	3600 E. Baltimore, St.	21224	(410) 276-8025
Baltimore	Hebrew Young Men's Cemetery	5800 Windsor Mill Rd.	21207	(410) 764-6393
Baltimore	Holy Cross Cemetery and Mausoleum	6020 Gov. Ritchie Hwy.	21225	(410) 789-5400
Baltimore	Lorraine Park Cemetery and Maus.	5608 Dogwood Rd.	21207	(410) 298-8118
Baltimore	New Cathedral Cemetery	4300 Old Frederick Rd.	21229	(410) 566-7770
Cockeysville	Dulaney Valley Mem. Gardens	200 Padonia Road, East	21030	(410) 666-0490
Columbia	St. John the Evangelist RC Church	Wilde Lake	21044	(410) 964-1425
nr. Chestertown	Old St. Paul's Episcopal Church	Sandy Bottom Rd (off Rt. 20)	21620	(410) 778-1540
Silver Spring	Gate of Heaven Cemetery	13801 Georgia Ave.	20906	(301) 871-6500
Towson	Prospect Hill Cemetery	York Rd. at Joppa Rd.	21204	(410) 252-8462
◆ MASSACHUSETTS				
Becket	Becket Cemetery	Rt. 8, west of Rt. 20	01223	(413) 623-5236
Chatham	Seaside Cemetery			
Chilmark (M.V.)	Abel's Hill Cemetery	South Rd.	02535	(No phone)
Fall River	Oak Grove Cemetery			
Malden	Holy Cross Cemetery			
Medford	Oak Grove Cemetery	165 Mystic Ave.	02155	(617) 396-7773
Nantucket	Prospect Hill Cemetery			
Newton	Newton Cemetery and Crematory	791 Walnut	02158	(617) 332-0047

STATE/CITY	CEMETERY	STREET	ZIP	PHONE
Quincy	Mount Wollaston Cemetery	20 Sea St.	02169	(617) 376-1295
Southborough	Southborough Cemetery	Rt. 85, Cordaville Rd.	01772	(508) 485-1618
Tisbury (M.V.)	Village Cemetery	Franklin St. (Town Hall)	02568	(508) 696-4200
Upton	Upton Cemetery			
West Roxbury	St. Joseph Cemetery	990 La Grange St.	02132	(617) 327-1010
◆MICHIGAN				
Dearborn	Northview Cemetery	600 Kensington St.	48128	(313) 565-0005
Saginaw	Mt. Olivet Cemetery and Mausoleum	3440 S. Washington	48601	(517) 752-7159
◆MISSOURI				
Kansas City	Calvary Catholic Cemetery	6901 Troost	64131	(816) 523-2114
Kansas City	Mount Carmel Cemetery			
◆MONTANA				
Helena	Forestdale Cemetery	490 Forestdale Rd, Box 5448	59604	(406) 458-5313
N				
◆NEVADA				
Las Vegas	Palm Mortuary Mausoleum	1325 N. Main St.	89101	(702) 382-1340
Las Vegas	Paradise Memorial Gardens			
◆NEW HAMPSHIRE				
Moultonborough	Red Hill Cemetery	Bean Rd.	03254	(Unpublished)
◆NEW JERSEY				
Orange	St. John's Cemetery			
Paramus	Cedar Park Cemetery			
Red Bank	Mount Olivet Cemetery			
Trenton	Ewing Church Cemetery			
Westwood	Cedar Park Cemetery	P. O. Box 329	07675	(201) 262-1100
◆NEW MEXICO				
Carlsbad	Carlsbad Cemetery	1506 Boyd Drive at Juarez St.	88220	(505) 887-1191
◆NEW YORK				
Bronxville	Kensico Cemetery (Lawrence Park)			
Brooklyn	Cypress Hills Cemetery	833 Jamaica Ave.	11208	(718) 277-2900
Brooklyn	Evergreen Cemetery	Bushwick at Conway Aves.	11207	(718) 455-5300
Brooklyn	Friends (Quaker) Cemetery	Prospect Park	11215	(718) 768-8298
Brooklyn	Green-Wood Cemetery	5th Ave. at 25th St.	11232	(718) 768-7300
Brooklyn	Holy Cross Cemetery			
Brooklyn	Salem Field Cemetery			
Clinton	Hamilton College			
Clovesville	Clovesville Cemetery	Rt. 28		(914) 254-5305
Cold Spring Harbor	St. John's Church Mem. Cemetery	P.O. Box 114	11724	(516) 692-6748
Elmira	Woodlawn Cemetery	1200 Walnut St.	14905	(607) 732-0151
Elmont (L.I.)	Beth David Cemetery	Elmont Road	11003	(516) 328-1300
Farmingdale (L.I.)	Long Island National Cemetery	Wellwood Ave.	11735	(516) 454-4949
Farmingdale (L.I.)	Pinelawn Memorial Park	Pinelawn Rd., P.O. Box 420	11735	(516) 249-6100
Flushing (Queens)	Flushing Cemetery	163-06 46th Ave.	11385	(718) 359-0100
Flushing (Queens)	Mount Hebron Cemetery	130-04 Horace Harding Exp.	11367	(718) 939-9405
Glendale (Queens)	Mt. Lebanon Cemetery	7800 Myrtle Ave.	11385	(718) 821-0200
Hartsdale	Ferncliff Cemetery and Mausoleum	Secor Road	10530	(914) 693-4700
Hastings-on-Hudson	Mount Hope Cemetery	Saw Mill River Rd at Jackson	10706	(914) 478-1855
Hastings-on-Hudson	Temple Israel Cemetery	Saw Mill River Rd at Jackson	10706	(914) 478-1343
Hastings-on-Hudson	Westchester Hills Cemetery	400 Saw Mill River Rd.	10706	(914) 478-1767
Hawthorne	Cemetery of the Gate of Heaven	Stevens Ave.	10532	(914) 769-3672
Hawthorne	Mount Pleasant Cemetery	80 Commerce St.	10532	(914) 769-0397
Horsehead	Maple Grove Cemetery			

STATE/CITY	CEMETERY	STREET	ZIP	PHONE
Johnstown	Ferndale Cemetery	545 N. Perry	13452	(518) 762-3922
Lake Ronkonkoma	Cenacle Convent (Retreat House)	310 Cenacle Rd. (L.I.)	11779	(516) 588-8366
Maspeth (Queens)	Mt. Zion Cemetery	59-63 54th Ave.	11378	(718) 335-2500
New Rochelle	Holy Sepulchre Cemetery	Shea Place	10801	(914) 636-6343
New York	St. Bartholomew's Episcopal Church	109 E. 50th St.	10022	(212) 751-1616
New York	St. Patrick's Cathedral	Fifth Ave. at 50th St.	10022	(212) 753-2261
N. Tarrytown	Sleepy Hollow Cemetery	540 N. Broadway	10591	(914) 631-0081
Nyack	Oak Hill Cemetery			
Pawling	Quaker Hill Christ Church Cemetery			
Penfield	Penfield Cemetery			
Port Jervis	Laurel Grove Cemetery		12771	(No phone)
(Queens)	Mount Carmel Cemetery			
Ridgewood (Queens)	Beth-El Cemetery	80-12 Cypress Hills St.	11385	(718) 366-3558
Ridgewood (Queens)	Machpelah Cemetery	82-30 Cypress Hills St.	11385	(718) 366-5959
Ridgewood (Queens)	Union Field Cemetery	8211 Cypress Ave.	11385	(718) 366-3748
Sag Harbor (L.I.)	Oakland Cemetery	Jermain Ave.	11963	(No phone)
Saratoga Springs	Greenridge Cemetery	17 Greenridge Place, S.W.	12866	(518) 584-5572
Southampton (L.I.)	Sacred Heart Cemetery	156 Hill St.	11968	(516) 283-0097
Southampton (L.I.)	Southampton Cemetery			
Staten Island	Silver Mount Cemetery	918 Victory Blvd.	10301	(718) 727-7020
The Bronx	St. Raymond's Cemetery	1140 Balcom Ave.	10465	(212) 792-1451
The Bronx	Woodlawn Cem. and Crematory	E. 233rd St. at Webster Ave.	10470	(212) 920-0500
Valhalla	Kensico Cemetery	Commerce at Lakeview Ave.	10595	(914) 949-0347
West Point	National Cemetery			(Unpublished)
Woodside (Queens)	Calvary Cemetery	4902 Laurel Hill Blvd.	11377	(718) 786-8000
◆ **NORTH CAROLINA**				
Chapel Hill	Old Cemetery			(919) 968-2738
Smithfield	Sunset Memorial Park	State Highway 70	27577	(919) 934-0139
Waynesville	Green Hills Cemetery	315 S. Welsh St.	28786	(704) 452-4227
◆ **NORTH DAKOTA**				
Fargo	Holy Cross Cemetery			
O				
◆ **OHIO**				
Circleville	Forest Cemetery	905 N. Court	43113	(614) 474-4401
Cleveland	Lake View Cemetery	12316 Euclid Ave.	44106	(216) 421-2665
Dayton	Dayton Memorial Park	8135 N. Dixie Dr.	45414	(513) 890-1831
◆ **OKLAHOMA**				
Claremore	Will Rogers Memorial	P. O. Box 157	74018	(918) 341-0719
El Reno	El Reno Cemetery	E. Elm at Heritage Dr.	73036	(405) 422-2146
Oklahoma City	Memorial Park	13400 N. Kelley	73131	(405) 478-0556
Tulsa	Memorial Park Burial Park			
P				
◆ **PENNSYLVANIA**				
Altoona	Rose Hill Cemetery	1207 12th Ave.	16601	(814) 942-1152
Berwick	SS. Cyril and Methodius Cemetery	706 N. Warren St.	18603	(717) 752-3172
Frazer	Haym Salomon Memorial Park	200 Moores Rd.	19355	(215) 877-1142
Jim Thorpe	Thorpe Mausoleum			
Kennett Square	Union Hill Cemetery	424 N. Union (Rt. 82)	19348	(215) 444-4554
Lackawaxen	Union Cemetery			
Middletown	Middletown Cemetery			
Pen Argyl	Fairview Cemetery	U.S. Rt. 22	18072	
Philadelphia	Mt. Vernon Cemetery	Ridge at Lehigh Ave.	19132	(215) 229-6038
Pittsburgh	Allegheny Cemetery	4734 Butler St.	15201	(412) 682-1624
Pittsburgh	Homewood Cemetery			
Shavertown	Evergreen Cemetery			

Directory of Cemeteries - by State and City

STATE/CITY	CEMETERY	STREET	ZIP	PHONE
T				
◆ TENNESSEE				
Chattanooga	Forest Hills Cemetery	4016 Tennessee Ave.	37409	(615) 821-4161
Goodlettsville	Forest Lawn Memorial Park	1150 Dickerson Rd.	37072	(615) 859-5279
Hendersonville	Woodlawn Memorial Park East	353 Johnny Cash Pkwy.	37075	(615) 824-3855
Hermitage	Hermitage Memorial Gardens			
Madison	Spring Hill Cemetery and Mausoleum	5110 Gallatin Pike	37115	(615) 865-1101
Memphis	Elmwood Cemetery			
Memphis	Graceland	3765 Elvis Presley Blvd.	38116	(901) 332-3322
Nashville	Woodlawn Memorial Park	660 Thompson Lane	37211	(615) 383-4754
Sparta	Crestlawn Cemetery	P.O. Box 825	38503	(615) 526-6384
◆ TEXAS				
Austin	Austin Memorial Park	2800 Hancock Drive	78731	(512) 453-2320
Beaumont	Forest Lawn Memorial Park	4955 Pine St.	77703	(409) 892-5912
Beeville	Glenwood Cemetery	Rt. 3, Box 120 (Lee Archer)		(512) 358-7238
Carthage	Jim Reeves Memorial Park	US Hwy 79, NE of Carthage	75633	(903) 693-6634
Dallas	Grove Hill Memorial Park	4118 Samuell Blvd.	75228	(214) 381-7118
Dallas	Hillcrest Memorial Park	7403 Northwest Hwy.	75225	(214) 363-5401
Dallas	Laurel Land Memorial Park	6000 S. R. L. Thornton Fwy.	75232	(214) 371-1336
Dallas	Restland Memorial Park	13005 Greenville Ave	75243	(214) 238-7111
DeKalb	Woodmen Cemetery	646 Front St. (US 82)	75559	(903) 667-3706
El Paso	Ft. Bliss National Cemetery	5200 Fred Wilson Hwy.	79906	(915) 564-0201
Fort Worth	Greenwood Memorial Park	3100 White Settlement Rd.	76107	(817) 336-0584
Fort Worth	Mount Olivet Cemetery	2301 N. Sylvania Ave.	76111	(817) 831-0511
Fort Worth	Oakwood Cemetery	701 Grand Ave.	76106	(817) 624-3531
Houston	Glenwood Cemetery			
Longview	Rosewood Park	Rt. 1844 (Seven Pines Rd.)	75601	(903) 757-0544
Lubbock	City of Lubbock Cemetery	2011 E. 31st St. at M.L.K. Blvd.	79404	(806) 767-2270
Port Neches	Oak Bluff Memorial Park	101 Block St.	77651	(409) 722-2114
V				
◆ VIRGINIA				
Arlington	Arlington National Cemetery	Fort Myer	22211	(703) 545-6700
Lancaster	St. Mary's Whitechapel Trinity Church	Rt. 201 at Rt. 354	22507	(804) 462-7457
Petersburg	Blanford Cemetery			(804) 733-2397
Richmond	Woodland Cemetery	2300 Magnolia Rd.	23223	(804) 643-4702
Winchester	Shenandoah Memorial Park	1270 Front Royal Pike	22602	(703) 667-2012
W				
◆ WASHINGTON				
Renton	Greenwood Memorial Cemetery	350 Monroe, N.E.	98057	(206) 255-1511
Seattle	Lake View Cemetery	1554 15th Avenue, East	98112	(206) 322-1582
◆ WISCONSIN				
Milwaukee	Forest Home Cemetery	2405 W. Forest Home Ave.	53215	(414) 645-2632

...Other Countries...

COUNTRY/CITY	CEMETERY	STREET	ZIP	PHONE
B				
◆ BRAZIL				
Rio de Janeiro	Sao Joao Baptista Cemetery			
C				
◆ CANADA				
Toronto (Ontario)	Mount Pleasant Cem. and Mausoleum	375 Mount Pleasant		

STATE/CITY	CEMETERY	STREET	ZIP	PHONE
E				
◆ **ENGLAND**				
Brighton	St. Nicholas Churchyard			
Cheltenham (Glou.)	Priory Road Cemetery	(In township of Prestbury)		
Guildford (Surrey)	Garden of Remembrance			
Harrogate (Yorkshire)	Harlow Hill Cemetery			
London	Brompton Cemetery	Old Brompton Rd.		
London (North)	Golders Green Cemetery	Hoop Rd.		
London (North)	Hampstead Cemetery	Fortune Green Rd. nr. Finchley		
London (North)	Highgate Cemetery (West and East)	Swains Lane		
London (North)	St. John-at-Hampstead Cemetery	Church Row		
London (North)	St. Marylebone Cemetery	East End and North Circular Rd.		
London	Westminster Abbey	Victoria St.		
Shirley (Southampton)	Hollybrook Cemetery			
F				
◆ **FRANCE**				
nr. Paris	Boissy-Sans-Avoir			
Paris	Arcueil Cemetery			
Paris	Bagneux Cemetery			
Paris	Batignolles Cemetery	Avenue du Cimetière		
Paris	Montmartre Cemetery	Rue Rachel off Blvd. de Clichy		
Paris	Montparnasse Cemetery	Boulevard Edgar Quinet		
Paris	Passy Cemetery	Rue du Commandant Schloesing		
Paris	Père Lachaise Cemetery	Boulevard de Ménilmontant		
G				
◆ **GERMANY**				
Berlin	Friedenau Cemetery			
I				
◆ **IRELAND**				
Booterstown	Dean's Grange Cemetery			
◆ **ITALY**				
Milan	Cimitero Monumentale	Via Carlo Farini at Garibaldi Sta.		
Naples	Cimitero di Santa Maria del Pianto	Nuovo del Campo		
Rimini	Civico Cimitero	Via Popilia, on road to Ravenna		
◆ **ISRAEL**				
Jerusalem	(In a forest just outside the city)			
J				
◆ **JAMAICA**				
Grant's Town	"Firefly" (a private estate)			
M				
◆ **MEXICO**				
Mexico City	Pateon Dolores Cemetery			
P				
◆ **POLAND**				
Warsaw	St. John the Baptist Cathedral			
R				
◆ **RUSSIA**				
Moscow	Novodevichy Cemetery			
Moscow	Vagankovskoya Cemetery			

STATE/CITY	CEMETERY	STREET	ZIP	PHONE
◆ **SWITZERLAND** Vaud Vevey	Tolochenaz Corsier-Sur-Vevey			

5

Specific
Interment Locations
— by Name

NAME	YEAR	CEMETERY	INTERMENT SITE*
A			
ABBOTT, Bud	1974	(Cremated—not interred)	Ashes scattered in the Pacific Ocean
• ACE, Goodman	1982	Mount Carmel Cemetery, Kansas City, MO	
• ACE, Jane	1974	Mount Carmel Cemetery, Kansas City, MO	
ACKER, Jean (Valentino)	1978	Holy Cross Cem. and Maus., Culver City, CA	Section N, "Mother of Sorrows," Plot 542
ACKERMAN, Harry	1991	Forest Lawn—Hollywood Hills, Los Angeles, CA	Garden of Heritage, Plot #3019
ACORD, Art	1931	Forest Lawn Memorial-Park, Glendale, CA	
ACUFF, Roy	1992	Spring Hill Cemetery, Madison, TN	
ADAMS, Constance (DeMille)	1960	Hollywood Memorial Park, Hollywood, CA	Section 8, in twin marble sarcophagi
ADAMS, Maude	1953	Cenacle Convent, Lake Ronkonkoma (L.I.), NY	
ADAMS, Nick (Adamshock)	1968	SS. Cyril and Methodius Cemetery, Berwick, PA	
• ADDINGTON, John	1997	Grove Hill Memorial Park, Dallas, TX	
ADLER, Buddy	1960	Forest Lawn Memorial-Park, Glendale, CA	Garden of Memory
• ADLER, Jacob	1926	Mount Carmel Cemetery. Flushing, NY	
ADOREE, Renée	1933	Hollywood Memorial Park, Hollywood, CA	Abbey of the Psalms, Foyer, Crypt 219
Adrian	1959	Hollywood Memorial Park, Hollywood, CA	Section 8, Lot 193
• AGEE, James	1955	(Private Property), Hillsdale, NY	Buried on his farm
AIDMAN, Charles	1993	Westwood Village Mem. Park, Los Angeles, CA	Room of Prayer
AKEMAN, David	1973	Forest Lawn Memorial Park, Goodlettsville, TN	
AKINS, Claude	1994	(Cremated—not interred)	Ashes scattered
ALBERTSON, Frank	1964	Holy Cross Cem. and Maus., Culver City, CA	Section P, Grave 1, Lot 309
ALBERTSON, Jack	1981	(Cremated—not interred)	Ashes scattered at sea
ALDA, Robert	1986	Forest Lawn Memorial-Park, Glendale, CA	Ascension Garden
ALEXANDER, John	1982	Kensico Cemetery, Valhalla, NY	Actors Fund Plot
ALEXANDER, Ross	1937	Forest Lawn Memorial-Park, Glendale, CA	Sunrise Slope
ALLEN, Fred	1956	Cem. of the Gate of Heaven, Hawthorne, NY	
ALLEN, Gracie (Burns)	1964	Forest Lawn Memorial-Park, Glendale, CA	Freedom Maus., Sanctuary of Heritage
ALLEN, Irwin	1991	Mount Sinai Memorial-Park, Los Angeles, CA	In Maus. behind the Garden of Heritage
ALLGOOD, Sara	1950	Holy Cross Cem. and Maus., Culver City, CA	Section D, Sacred Heart
ALLWYN, Astrid	1978	Forest Lawn Memorial-Park, Glendale, CA	Outside Freedom Mausoleum
AMECHE, Don	1993	(Cremated)	
AMES, Adrienne	1947	Oakwood Cemetery, Fort Worth, TX	Block 31, Lot 44 (nr. Avenue IX & B Street)
AMES, Leon	1993	Forest Lawn—Hollywood Hills, Los Angeles, CA	Col. of Valor, G-64429
• AMSTERDAM, Morey	1996	Forest Lawn—Hollywood Hills, Los Angeles, CA	Garden of Remembrance, wall crypt #3632
ANDERS, Glenn	1981	Kensico Cemetery, Valhalla, NY	Actors Fund Plot
ANDERSON, Eddie	1977	Evergreen Cemetery, Los Angeles, CA	Section A, Lot 2504
ANDERSON, G. M.	1971	Chapel of the Pines Crematory, Los Angeles, CA	
ANDRE, Gwili	1959	(Cremated)	Ashes in an urn in Copenhagen, Denmark
ANDREWS, Edward	1985	(Cremated—not interred)	Ashes scattered at sea
ANDREWS, LaVerne	1967	Forest Lawn Memorial-Park, Glendale, CA	Great Maus., Col. of Memory
• ANDREWS, Maxine	1995	Forest Lawn Memorial-Park, Glendale, CA	Great Maus., Col. of Memory
ANGEL, Heather	1986	Santa Barbara Cemetery, Santa Barbara, CA	
• ANKRUM, Morris	1964	Spring Hill Cemetery, Danville, IL	
ARBUCKLE, Roscoe "Fatty"	1933	(Cremated—not interred)	Ashes scattered at sea
ARDEN, Eve (West)	1990	Westwood Village Mem. Park, Los Angeles, CA	Section D, #81 (ashes interred)
ARLEN, Richard	1976	Holy Cross Cem. and Maus., Culver City, CA	Section T, Tier 57, Grave 130
ARMETTA, Henry	1945	Holy Cross Cem. and Maus., Culver City, CA	Section D
ARMSTRONG, Herbert W.	1986	Mountain View Cemetery, Altadena, CA	
ARMSTRONG, Louis	1971	Flushing Cemetery, Flushing (Queens), NY	Sect. 8
ARMSTRONG, Robert	1973	Forest Lawn—Hollywood Hills, Los Angeles, CA	Murmuring Trees, Plot #7318, Space 1
ARNAZ, Desi	1986	(Cremated—not interred)	Ashes scattered
ARNOLD, Edward	1956	San Fernando Mission Cem., San Fernando, CA	Section D, Block 9, Lot 132
ARQUETTE, Cliff	1974	(Cremated—not interred)	Ashes scattered by the Telophase Society
ARTHUR, Jean	1991	(Cremated—not interred)	Ashes scattered at sea off Point Lobos, CA
ASHE, Arthur	1993	Woodland Cemetery, Richmond, VA	
ASTAIRE, Adele (Douglas)	1981	Oakwood Memorial Park, Chatsworth, CA	Section G, Lot 77, Space 2
ASTAIRE, Fred	1987	Oakwood Memorial Park, Chatsworth, CA	Section G, Lot 82, Space 4
ASTOR, Mary	1987	Holy Cross Cem. and Maus., Culver City, CA	Section N, Lot 523, Grave 5
ATES, Roscoe	1962	Forest Lawn Memorial-Park, Glendale, CA	
ATWILL, Lionel	1946	Chapel of the Pines Crematory, Los Angeles, CA	Not available for public viewing
• AUBREY, James T.	1994	Westwood Village Mem. Park, Los Angeles, CA	
• AUDLEY, Eleanor	1991	Forest Lawn—Hollywood Hills, Los Angeles, CA	Mt. Sinai - Kedron

NAME	YEAR	CEMETERY	INTERMENT SITE*
AUSTIN, Gene	1972	Forest Lawn Memorial-Park, Glendale, CA	Great Maus., Sanctuary of Sacred Promise
AVERY, Frederick B. "Tex"	1980	Forest Lawn—Hollywood Hills, Los Angeles, CA	Gentleness
AYRES, Agnes	1940	Hollywood Memorial Park, Hollywood, CA	Columbarium, Niche 3, T.3, Lower S. Wall
B			
BACKUS, James "Jim"	1989	Westwood Village Mem. Park, Los Angeles, CA	Section D, #203
BACON, Irving	1965	Catalina-Ft. Rose Crans Cem., San Diego, CA	
BACON, Lloyd	1955	Forest Lawn—Hollywood Hills, Los Angeles, CA	
BAER, Jacob "Buddy"	1986	E. Lawn Sierra Hills Mem. Pk., Sacramento, CA	
• BAER, Max	1959	St. Mary's Mausoleum, Sacramento, CA	
• BAGDASARIAN, Ross	1972	Chapel of the Pines Crematory, Los Angeles, CA	
BAILEY, Pearl	1990	Rolling Green Memorial Park, Westchester, PA	
BAINTER, Fay	1968	Arlington National Cemetery, Arlington, VA	
BAKER, Art	1966	Forest Lawn Memorial-Park, Glendale, CA	Great Maus., Col. of Memory
BAKER, Kenny	1985	Solvang, CA	Priv. inter. in Santa Barbara Co. nr. Solvang
BALANCHINE, George	1983	Oakland Cemetery, Sag Harbor (L.I.), NY	
BALL, Lucille (Morton)	1989	Forest Lawn—Hollywood Hills, Los Angeles, CA	Courts of Remem., Col. of Radiant Dawn
BALL, Suzan (Long)	1955	Forest Lawn Memorial-Park, Glendale, CA	Eventide, Plot #2922
BANCROFT, George	1956	Woodlawn Cemetery, Santa Monica, CA	In Mausoleum, 147-P-3
BANKHEAD, Tallulah	1968	Old St. Paul's Epis. Ch., nr. Chestertown, MD	Buried near woods, 100 yds. behind church
BANKY, Vilma	1991	(Cremated—not interred)	Ashes scattered at sea
BARA, Theda	1955	Forest Lawn Memorial-Park, Glendale, CA	Great Maus., Col. of Memory, Niche #19566
• BARNES, George S.	1953	Hollywood Memorial Park, Hollywood, CA	Abbey of the Psalms, Crypt 2087, Corr G-2
BARRIE, Wendy	1978	Kensico Cemetery, Valhalla, NY	Actors Fund Plot
BARRIER, Edgar	1964	Westwood Village Mem. Park, Los Angeles, CA	
BARRIS, Harry	1962	Forest Lawn—Hollywood Hills, Los Angeles, CA	
BARRY, Don "Red"	1980	Forest Lawn—Hollywood Hills, Los Angeles, CA	Court of Liberty, Plot #5442 (under tree)
BARRYMORE, Diana	1960	Woodlawn Cemetery, The Bronx, NY	Div. 20, bet. E. Border Ave and Chapel Hill
BARRYMORE, Ethel (Colt)	1959	Calvary Cemetery, Los Angeles, CA	Main Mausoleum, Block 60, Crypt 3F
BARRYMORE, John	1942	Mt. Vernon Cemetery, Philadelphia, PA	Cremated 1980, reburied from Calvary Cem.
BARRYMORE, Lionel	1954	Calvary Cemetery, Los Angeles, CA	Main Mausoleum, Block 352
BARSI, Judith	1988	Forest Lawn—Hollywood Hills, Los Angeles, CA	
BARTHELMESS, Richard	1963	Ferncliff Cemetery and Maus., Hartsdale, NY	Maus., Unit 8, Alcove BB, Col. B, Niche 1
BARTON, James	1962	St. John's Ch. Cem., Cold Spring Harbor, NY	
BASEHART, Richard	1984	Westwood Village Mem. Park, Los Angeles, CA	Urn Garden (3 down from top, on right)
BASIE, William "Count"	1984	Pinelawn Mem. Park, Farmingdale (L.I.), NY	
• BASKETT, James	1948	Crown Hill Cemetery, Indianapolis, IN	
BATES, Barbara	1969	Crown Hill Cemetery and Mort., Lakewood, CO	Section 2, Block 69, Lot 144, Unit A
BATES, Granville	1940	Graceland Cemetery, Chicago, IL	
• BAVIER, Frances	1989	Oakwood Cemetery, Siler City, N.C.	
BAXTER, Warner	1951	Forest Lawn Memorial-Park, Glendale, CA	Garden of Memory
BAYLIS, Peter	1973	St. John-at-Hampstead Cem., London, England	At back of cemetery
BEARD, Matthew "Stymie"	1981	Evergreen Cemetery, Los Angeles, CA	
BEATTY, Clyde	1965	Forest Lawn—Hollywood Hills, Los Angeles, CA	Courts of Remem., 2175
BEAUDINE, William	1970	Hollywood Memorial Park, Hollywood, CA	
BEERY, Noah Sr.	1946	Forest Lawn—Hollywood Hills, Los Angeles, CA	Sheltering Hills
BEERY, Wallace	1949	Forest Lawn Memorial-Park, Glendale, CA	Vale of Memory - 2157-9808
BEGLEY, Ed Sr.	1970	San Fernando Mission Cem., San Fernando, CA	Section C, Block 8, Lot 401
BEIDERBECKE, Leon "Bix"	1931	Oakdale Cemetery, Davenport, IA	
BELL, Monta	1958	Hollywood Memorial Park, Hollywood, CA	Section 8, grave near Nelson Eddy
BELL, Rex	1962	Forest Lawn Memorial-Park, Glendale, CA	Freedom Maus., Sanctuary of Heritage
BELLAMY, Ralph	1991	Forest Lawn—Hollywood Hills, Los Angeles, CA	God's Acre, Plot #8687
BELUSHI, John	1982	Abel's Hill Cemetery, Chilmark (M.V.), MA	
BENADERET, Bea	1968	Valhalla Memorial Park, N. Hollywood, CA	Mausoleum of Hope, Row C, Crypt 34
• BENCHLEY, Robert	1945	Prospect Hill Cemetery, Nantucket, MA	
BENDIX, William	1964	San Fernando Mission Cem., San Fernando, CA	Section D, at Curb No. 241, 14 rows in
BENNETT, Constance	1965	Arlington National Cemetery, Arlington, VA	Section3, Lot 2231-A, Grid P-13
BENNETT, Richard	1944	Forest Lawn Memorial-Park, Glendale, CA	
BENNY, Jack	1974	Hillside Memorial Park, Los Angeles, CA	Mausoleum, Graciousness-Sarcophagus F
• BERADINO, John	1996	Holy Cross Cem. and Maus., Culver City, CA	
BERG, Gertrude	1966	Clovesville Cemetery, Clovesville, NY	In Jewish section
BERGEN, Edgar	1978	Inglewood Park Cemetery, Inglewood, CA	131 Miramar Plot, Grave #2
BERGERE, Ramona R.	1941	Forest Lawn Memorial-Park, Glendale, CA	

• New entry.

360

* Some cemeteries refuse to reveal specific locations.

NAME	YEAR	CEMETERY	INTERMENT SITE*
BERGMAN, Ingrid	1982	(Cremated—not interred)	Ashes scattered off the coast of Sweden
BERKELEY, Busby	1976	Desert Memorial Park, Palm Springs, CA	Section A-14, Lot 74
BERLIN, Irving	1989	Woodlawn Cemetery, The Bronx, NY	F-4, Columbine
BERN, Paul	1932	Inglewood Park Cemetery, Inglewood, CA	Golden West Maus., ashes in Niche F96
BERNARDI, Herschel	1986	Mount Sinai Memorial-Park, Los Angeles, CA	Courts of Tanach, Crypt 52250
BERNHARDT, Sarah	1923	Père Lachaise Cemetery, Paris, France	Division 44
• BERNIE, Ben	1943	Mount Hebron Cemetery, Flushing (Queens), NY	
BERNSTEIN, Leonard	1990	Green-Wood Cemetery, Brooklyn, NY	
BERTRAND, Mary (Rall)	1955	Forest Lawn Memorial-Park, Glendale, CA	
• BESSELL, Ted	1996	Woodlawn Cemetery, Santa Monica, CA	Section 13-S, Lot D, Grave 19
BESSER, Joe	1988	Forest Lawn Memorial-Park, Glendale, CA	
BICKFORD, Charles	1967	Woodlawn Cemetery, Santa Monica, CA	Cremated
BING, Herman	1947	Hollywood Memorial Park, Hollywood, CA	Section 8, 20 ft. east of John Huston
• BISSEL, Whit	1996	Westwood Village Mem. Park, Los Angeles, CA	
BIXBY, Bill	1993	(Cremated—not interred)	Ashes scattered on his Hana, Maui estate
BLANC, Mel	1989	Hollywood Memorial Park, Hollywood, CA	Pineland, near curb
BLANDICK, Clara	1962	Forest Lawn Memorial-Park, Glendale, CA	Great Mausoleum
BLOCH, Ray	1982	Ferncliff Cemetery and Maus., Hartsdale, NY	St. Paul, Plot 184, Grave 2
BLOCKER, Dan	1972	Woodmen Cemetery, DeKalb, TX	
BLONDELL, Joan	1979	Forest Lawn Memorial-Park, Glendale, CA	Garden of Honor, Col. of the Evening Star
BLUE, Ben	1975	Hillside Memorial Park, Los Angeles, CA	Mausoleum, Col. of Graciousness-810
BLUE, Monte	1963	Forest Lawn Memorial-Park, Glendale, CA	
BOCK-LEADER, Deborah Lyn	1990	Dulaney Valley Mem. Gdns., Cockeysville, MD	Eternal Light Section
BOGART, Humphrey	1957	Forest Lawn Memorial-Park, Glendale, CA	Garden of Memory, Col. of Eternal Light
BOLAND, Mary	1965	Forest Lawn Memorial-Park, Glendale, CA	Great Maus., Sanctuary of Vespers
BOLES, John	1969	Westwood Village Mem. Park, Los Angeles, CA	Sanctuary of Serenity
BOLESLAWSKI, Richard	1937	Calvary Cemetery, Los Angeles, CA	Main Mausoleum
BOLEY, May	1963	Forest Lawn Memorial-Park, Glendale, CA	
BOLGER, Ray	1987	Holy Cross Cem. and Maus., Culver City, CA	Mausoleum, Block 35, Crypt F-2
BOND, Ward	1960	Forest Lawn Memorial-Park, Glendale, CA	
• BONHAM, John	1980	(Cremated)	
BOOKE, Sorrell	1994	Hillside Memorial Park, Los Angeles, CA	Garden of Memories, Dedication-272-4B
BOONE, Richard	1981	(Cremated—not interred)	Ashes scattered in the Hawaiian Islands
BORDEN, Olive	1947	Forest Lawn Memorial-Park, Glendale, CA	
• BORDONI, Irene	1953	Ferncliff Cemetery, Hartsdale, NY	
BORZAGE, Frank	1962	Forest Lawn Memorial-Park, Glendale, CA	Garden of Everlasting Peace
BOSWELL, Connee	1976	Ferncliff Cemetery and Maus., Hartsdale, NY	Hillcrest J, Grave 227
BOSWORTH, Hobart	1943	Forest Lawn Memorial-Park, Glendale, CA	
BOW, Clara (Bell)	1965	Forest Lawn Memorial-Park, Glendale, CA	Freedom Maus., Sanctuary of Heritage
BOWES, Major Edward	1946	Sleepy Hollow Cemetery, N. Tarrytown, NY	Off Vernon Ave.
BOWLING, Alice	1981	Rosewood Park, Longview, TX	Chapel Mausoleum
BOYD, Jim	1973	Restland Memorial Park, Dallas, TX	
BOYD, Stephen (Millar)	1977	Oakwood Memorial Park, Chatsworth, CA	Mausoleum #1, North Wall, Niche #257
BOYD, William	1972	Forest Lawn Memorial-Park, Glendale, CA	Great Maus., Sanctuary of Sacred Promise
BOYER, Charles	1978	Holy Cross Cem. and Maus., Culver City, CA	St. Ann's Garden, Tier 186, Grave 5
BRABIN, Charles J.	1957	Forest Lawn Memorial-Park, Glendale, CA	
BRADLEY, Truman	1974	Forest Lawn—Hollywood Hills, Los Angeles, CA	Enduring Faith, Plot #3718
BRADY, Alice	1939	Sleepy Hollow Cemetery, N. Tarrytown, NY	
BRADY, Scott	1985	Holy Cross Cem. and Maus., Culver City, CA	Mausoleum, Block 156, Crypt B-7 upper flr.
BRAND, Neville	1992	E. Lawn Sierra Hills Mem. Pk., Sacramento, CA	#1327 Section L-L Morning Glory Rm.
BRASSELLE, Keefe	1980	Holy Cross Cem. and Maus., Culver City, CA	Section R, Tier 29, Grave 168
BREESE, Edmund	1936	Forest Lawn Memorial-Park, Glendale, CA	
BRENNAN, Walter	1974	Holy Cross Cem. and Maus., Culver City, CA	Section "Grotto," next to Rieta statue
BRESSART, Felix	1949	Hollywood Memorial Park, Hollywood, CA	Section 14, Row J, Grave 89
BRICE, Fanny	1951	Home of Peace Mem. Park, Los Angeles, CA	Chapel Maus., Har. and Benev., 57E #1109
BRISSON, Frederick	1984	Holy Cross Cem. and Maus., Culver City, CA	Section M, Lot 536, Grave 1
BRITTON, Pamela	1974	Forest Lawn—Hollywood Hills, Los Angeles, CA	Col. of Radiant Dawn, G61685
BRODERICK, James	1982	Holy Cross Cem. and Maus., Culver City, CA	Mausoleum, lower floor, top level
• BROOKS, Louise	1985	Holy Sepulchre Cemetery, Rochester, NY	
BROPHY, Ed	1960	Woodlawn Cemetery, Santa Monica, CA	
BROWN, Clarence	1987	Forest Lawn Memorial-Park, Glendale, CA	Court of Freedom, Col. of Honor
BROWN, Joe E.	1973	Forest Lawn Memorial-Park, Glendale, CA	Sunrise Slope

NAME	YEAR	CEMETERY	INTERMENT SITE*
BROWN, John H.	1957	Eden Memorial Park, San Fernando, CA	Akiba 17-55
BROWN, Johnny Mack	1974	Forest Lawn Memorial-Park, Glendale, CA	Court of Freedom, Col. of Heavenly Peace
BROWNE, Coral	1991	Hollywood Memorial Park, Hollywood, CA	Ashes scattered in the rose garden.
BROWNING, Tod	1962	Rose Dale Cemetery, Los Angeles, CA	Ashes interred in mausoleum
BRUCE, Lenny	1966	Eden Memorial Park, San Fernando, CA	Mt. Nebo. Section 298C
BRUCE, Nigel	1953	Chapel of the Pines Crematory, Los Angeles, CA	Vault #35167
BRUCKMAN, Clyde	1955		Body donated to L.A. County Med. Asso.
• BRYNNER, Yul	1985	Abbey de Bois Aubry, nr. Tours, France	(Cremated — ashes interred here)
BUCHANAN, Edgar	1979	Forest Lawn—Hollywood Hills, Los Angeles, CA	Morning Light, Plot #7780
• BUCK, Pearl S.	1973	Perkasie, PA	Buried on her farm
BUNNY, John	1915	Evergreen Cemetery, Brooklyn, NY	
BUONO, Victor	1981	Greenwood Memorial Park, San Diego, CA	Unmarked grave nr. pond, next to his mom
BURGESS, Helen M.	1937	Forest Lawn Memorial-Park, Glendale, CA	
BURKE, Billie	1970	Kensico Cemetery, Valhalla, NY	
BURNETTE, Smiley	1967	Forest Lawn—Hollywood Hills, Los Angeles, CA	Sheltering Hills, Plot #266
BURNS, Bob	1956	Forest Lawn Memorial-Park, Glendale, CA	Great Maus., Col. of Adoration
BURNS, George	1996	Forest Lawn Memorial-Park, Glendale, CA	Freedom Maus., Sanctuary of Heritage
BURR, Raymond	1993	Frasier Cemetery, New Westminister, B.C.	
BURROUGHS, Edgar Rice	1950	18354 Ventura Blvd., Tarzana, CA	Ashes buried under walnut tree in front yd
BURTON, Richard	1984	Protestant Churchyard, Celigny, Switzerland	
BUSH, Mae	1946	Chapel of the Pines Crematory, Los Angeles, CA	Near front door, on left, at eye-level
BUSHMAN, Francis X.	1966	Forest Lawn Memorial-Park, Glendale, CA	Freedom Maus., Sanctuary of Gratitude
BYINGTON, Spring	1971		Body donated for medical research
BYRD, Ralph M.	1952	Forest Lawn Memorial-Park, Glendale, CA	Eventide (under the olive tree)
BYRON, Arthur William	1943	(Cremated at Forest Lawn, Glendale, CA)	Ashes sent back to Maine
C			
CABOT, Bruce	1972	Carlsbad Cemetery, Carlsbad, NM	Division A, Block 48, Space 5 (E. Bujac, Jr.)
CABOT, Sebastian	1977	Westwood Village Mem. Park, Los Angeles, CA	Urn Garden East (top row, 9 from right)
CAGNEY, James	1986	Cem. of the Gate of Heaven, Hawthorne, NY	St. Francis of Assissi Mausoleum
CAHN, Sammy	1993	Westwood Village Mem. Park, Los Angeles, CA	Section D (near Donna Reed)
CALHERN, Louis	1956	Hollywood Memorial Park, Hollywood, CA	Abbey of Psalms, Foyer, Niche 308, Tier 3
CALLAS, Maria	1977	Pere Lachaise Cemetery, Paris, France	
CALVIN, Henry	1975	Grove Hill Memorial Park, Dallas, TX	60-3-16
CAMBRIDGE, Godfrey	1976	Forest Lawn—Hollywood Hills, Los Angeles, CA	Enduring Faith
CAMPANELLA, Roy	1993	Forest Lawn—Hollywood Hills, Los Angeles, CA	
CANDY, John	1994	Holy Cross Cem. and Maus., Culver City, CA	Mausoleum, Room 7, Crypt B-1
CANOVA, Judy	1983	Forest Lawn Memorial-Park, Glendale, CA	Garden of Memory, Col. of Eternal Light
CANTOR, Eddie	1964	Hillside Memorial Park, Los Angeles, CA	Mausoleum, Graciousness-207
• CANTY, Marietta	1986	Northwood Cemetery, Windsor, Conn.	Wilson Section
CAPOTE, Truman	1984	Westwood Village Mem. Park, Los Angeles, CA	New Mausoleum, 1st column, bottom
CAPRA, Frank	1991	Coachella Valley Cemetery, Coachella, CA	(near Indio)
CAREY, Harry	1947	Forest Lawn Memorial-Park, Glendale, CA	
CAREY, Macdonald	1994	Holy Cross Cem. and Maus., Culver City, CA	Section "Grotto," Lot 196, Grave 19
CAREY, Timothy	1994	Rose Hills Memorial Park, Whittier, CA	
CARLETON, William P.	1947	Chapel of the Pines Crematory, Los Angeles, CA	Permanent storage vault
CARLSON, Richard	1977	Chapel of the Pines Crematory, Los Angeles, CA	Section 17A C-3
CARMICHAEL, Hoagy	1981	Rosehill Cemetery, Bloomington, IN	
CARPENTER, Karen	1983	Forest Lawn Memorial-Park, Cypress, CA	Ascension M. Maus., Sanct. of Compassion
CARPENTER, Ken	1984	Westwood Village Mem. Park, Los Angeles, CA	Sanctuary of Tenderness, on rear wall
CARR, Nathan C. "Nat"	1944	Forest Lawn Memorial-Park, Glendale, CA	
CARRADINE, John	1988		Buried at sea, in the Catalina Channel, CA
CARRILLO, Leo	1961	Woodlawn Cemetery, Santa Monica, CA	Section 2, (near 14th Street)
CARROLL, Earl	1948	Forest Lawn Memorial-Park, Glendale, CA	Garden of Memory
CARROLL, John	1979	Forest Lawn Memorial-Park, Glendale, CA	
• CARROLL, Leo G.	1972	Woodlawn Cemetery, Santa Monica, CA	
CARSON, Jack	1963	Forest Lawn Memorial-Park, Glendale, CA	Great Maus., Col. of Memory
CARTER, Maybelle	1978	Woodlawn Mem. Park East, Hendersonville, TN	
CARUSO, Enrico	1921	Cimitero di Santa Maria del Pianto, Naples, Italy	Down the hill on the left, in sarcophagus
CASSAVETES, John	1989	Westwood Village Mem. Park, Los Angeles, CA	Lot 308
CASSIDY, Jack	1976	(Cremated—not interred)	Ashes scattered at sea
CASSIDY, Ted "Lurch"	1979	(Cremated)	Ashes buried in the front lawn of his home
CASTLE, Irene	1969	Woodlawn Cemetery, The Bronx, NY	Division 29, off Park View & Spruce Ave.

NAME	YEAR	CEMETERY	INTERMENT SITE*
CASTLE, Nick	1968	Holy Cross Cem. and Maus., Culver City, CA	Section "Grotto," Lot 187, Grave 2
CASTLE, Vernon	1918	Woodlawn Cemetery, The Bronx, NY	Division 29, off Park View & Spruce Ave.
CAULFIELD, Joan	1991	Forest Lawn—Hollywood Hills, Los Angeles, CA	
CERF, Bennett	1971	(Cremated—not interred)	Ashes scattered at his Mt. Kisco, NY, home
CHALIAPIN, Feodor	1938	Batignolles Cemetery, Paris, France	Div. 25, rose granite mon. topped w/cross
CHANDLER, Helen	1965	(Cremated—not interred)	Ashes have never been claimed
CHANDLER, Jeff (Ira Grossel)	1961	Hillside Memorial Park, Los Angeles, CA	Mausoleum, Graciousness (2nd. Fl.) #4015
CHANEY, Lon F. Sr.	1930	Forest Lawn Memorial Park, Glendale, CA	Great Mausoleum
CHAPLIN, Charles	1977	Corsier-Sur-Vevey, Switzerland	
CHAPLIN, Charles Jr. (son)	1968	Hollywood Memorial Park, Hollywood, CA	Abbey of the Psalms, Crypt 1065, Corr E-2
• CHARLES, Lewis	1979	Home of Peace Mem. Park, Los Angeles, CA	
CHARTERS, Spencer H.	1943	Forest Lawn Memorial-Park, Glendale, CA	
CHASE, Charley	1940	Forest Lawn Memorial-Park, Glendale, CA	Sunrise Slope, Lot 72, Grave 147
CHATTERTON, Ruth	1961	Mountain Grove Cemetery, Bridgeport, CT	
CHAYEFSKY, Paddy	1981	Kensico Cemetery, Valhalla, NY	Sharon Gardens section
CHESHIRE, Harry "Pappy"	1968	Forest Lawn—Hollywood Hills, Los Angeles, CA	Remembrance, Plot #323
CHEVALIER, Maurice	1972	Marnes-La-Coquette, France	(France)
CHRISTIANS, Mady	1951	Ferncliff Cemetery and Maus., Hartsdale, NY	
CLARK, Bobby	1960	Woodlawn Cemetery, The Bronx, NY	
CLARK, Buddy	1949	Forest Lawn Memorial-Park, Glendale, CA	
CLARK, Fred	1968	(Cremated—not interred)	Ashes scattered at sea
CLARK, Marguerite	1940	Metairie Cemetery, New Orleans, LA	Section 97 (Frank Williams property)
• CLEMENTE, Roberto	1972		His body has never been found
CLEVELAND, George	1957	Forest Lawn Memorial-Park, Glendale, CA	
CLIFT, Montgomery	1966	Friends Cemetery, Brooklyn, NY	
CLIFTON, Elmer	1949	Forest Lawn Memorial-Park, Glendale, CA	Tranquility
CLINE, Patsy	1963	Shenandoah Memorial Park, Winchester, VA	
CLIVE, Colin	1937	(Cremated in Los Angeles, CA)	Ashes unclaimed
CLYDE, Andy	1967	Forest Lawn Memorial-Park, Glendale, CA	Whispering Pines
COBAIN, Kurt	1994	(Cremated—not interred)	Ashes given to his wife, Courtney Love
COBB, Irvin S.	1944	(Cremated—not interred)	Ashes under a sapling in Paducah, KY
COBB, Lee J. (Leo Jacoby)	1976	Mount Sinai Memorial-Park, Los Angeles, CA	Garden of Sherrot, Lot 421
• COBB, Ty	1961	Royston Cemetery, Royston, GA	
COBURN, Charles	1961	(Cremated—not interred)	Ashes scattered in Georgia, Mass. & N.Y.
COCHRAN, Eddie (singer)	1960	Forest Lawn Memorial-Park, Cypress, CA	Abiding Faith, Plot #2996
COCTEAU, Jean	1963	Milly La Foret Cemetery, Milly La Foret, France	
COHAN, George M.	1942	Woodlawn Cemetery, The Bronx, NY	Division 31, off Park Ave.
COHN, Harry	1958	Hollywood Memorial Park, Hollywood, CA	Section 8, Lot 86
• COLASANTO, Nicholas	1985	Saint Anne's Cemetery, Cranston, RI	Section 31, Lot 217
COLE, Edwin "Buddy"	1964	Forest Lawn—Hollywood Hills, Los Angeles, CA	Enduring Faith, Plot #3999
COLE, Nat "King"	1965	Forest Lawn Memorial-Park, Glendale, CA	Freedom Maus., Sanctuary of Heritage
COLLIER, William Sr.	1944	Forest Lawn Memorial-Park, Glendale, CA	Great Mausoleum-Col. of Inspiration
COLLINS, Ray	1965	Forest Lawn—Hollywood Hills, Los Angeles, CA	Garden of Heritage, Plot #909
COLLYER, Bud	1969	Putnam Cemetery, Greenwich, CT	
COLMAN, Ronald	1958	Santa Barbara Cemetery, Santa Barbara, CA	Ridge Oval Section, Lot 663
COLUMBO, Russ	1934	Forest Lawn Memorial-Park, Glendale, CA	Great Maus., Sanctuary of Vespers
• COMPSON, Betty	1974	San Fernando Mission Cem., San Fernando, CA	
• CONIGLIARO, Tony	1990	Holy Cross Cemetery, Malden, MA	
CONNORS, Chuck	1992	San Fernando Mission Cem., San Fernando, CA	
CONRAD, William	1994	Forest Lawn—Hollywood Hills, Los Angeles, CA	Lincoln Terrace, Plot #4448
CONTE, Richard	1975	Westwood Village Mem. Park, Los Angeles, CA	Section D, #62
CONVY, Bert	1991	Forest Lawn—Hollywood Hills, Los Angeles, CA	Court of Liberty, left of sidewalk
CONWAY, Tom	1967	Chapel of the Pines Crematory, Los Angeles, CA	
COOGAN, Jackie	1984	Holy Cross Cem. and Maus., Culver City, CA	Section F, Tier 56, Grave 47
COOKE, Sam	1964	Forest Lawn Memorial-Park, Glendale, CA	Garden of Honor
COOPER, (Dame) Gladys	1971	Hampstead Cemetery, London, England	Nr. Public Footpath and 3rd path on right
COOPER, Gary	1961	Sacred Heart Cemetery, Southampton (L.I.), NY	Reburied from L.A., under a 3-ton boulder
COOPER, Melville	1973	Valhalla Memorial Park, N. Hollywood, CA	
COREY, Wendell	1968	Beckett Cemetery, Beckett, MA	
CORNELL, Katharine	1974	Village Cemetery, Tisbury (M.V.), MA	(Martha's Vineyard)
CORRELL, Charles "Andy"	1972	Holy Cross Cem. and Maus., Culver City, CA	St. Ann's Garden, Tier 144
CORTHELL, Herbert	1947	Forest Lawn Memorial-Park, Glendale, CA	

• New entry.

* Some cemeteries refuse to reveal specific locations.

NAME	YEAR	CEMETERY	INTERMENT SITE*
COSTELLO, Lou	1959	Calvary Cemetery, Los Angeles, CA	Main Mausoleum, Block 354, Crypt B-1
COTTON, Joseph	1994	Blanford Cemetery, Petersburg, VA	
• COUSTEAU,Jacques	1997	Saint-Andre-de-cuzbac, France	
COWAN, Jerome	1972	Forest Lawn—Hollywood Hills, Los Angeles, CA	Col. of Remembrance
COWARD, Noel	1973	"Firefly Hill", Grant's Town, Jamaica	(his private estate)
COWL, Jane	1950	Valhalla Memorial Park, N. Hollywood, CA	
COX, Wally	1973	(Cremated—not interred)	Ashes scattered in the Atlantic Ocean
CRAIG, James	1985	Forest Lawn Memorial-Park, Glendale, CA	Only cremated here - Ashes unkown
CRANE, Norma	1973	Westwood Village Mem. Park, Los Angeles, CA	Section D, #62
CRANE, Richard	1969	Valhalla Memorial Park, N. Hollywood, CA	
CRANE, Robert "Bob"	1978	Oakwood Memorial Park, Chatsworth, CA	Oak Knoll Section, Lot 34B, Space 8
CRAVEN, Frank	1945	Kensico Cemetery, Valhalla, NY	
CRAWFORD, Broderick	1986	Ferndale Cemetery, Johnstown, NY	
CRAWFORD, Jesse	1962	Ferncliff Cemetery and Maus., Hartsdale, NY	Maus., Unit 3, Alcove 4, Niche Arc.#21
CRAWFORD, Joan (Steele)	1977	Ferncliff Cemetery and Maus., Hartsdale, NY	Maus., Unit 8, Alcove E, Crypt 42
CREGAR, (Samuel) Laird	1944	Forest Lawn Memorial-Park, Glendale, CA	Eventide, Lot 37, Space 2
CREWS, Laura Hope	1942	Cypress Lawn Cemetery, Colma, CA	Rose Mound
CRISP, Donald	1974	Forest Lawn Memorial-Park, Glendale, CA	
CROCE, Jim	1973	Haym Salomon Memorial Park, Frazer, PA	
CROGHAN, Joe	1995	New Cathedral Cemetery, Baltimore, MD	
CROMWELL, Richard	1960	Chapel of the Pines Crematory, Los Angeles, CA	
CROSBY, Dennis	1991	(Cremated—not interred)	Ashes strewn in the north CA Novato area
• CROSBY, Gary	1995	Forest Lawn—Hollywood Hills, Los Angeles, CA	Tribute Section (at top of hill)
CROSBY, Harry "Bing"	1977	Holy Cross Cem. and Maus., Culver City, CA	Section "Grotto," Lot 119, Grave 1
CROSBY, Wilma "Dixie Lee"	1952	Holy Cross Cem. and Maus., Culver City, CA	Section "Grotto," Lot 119, Grave 2
• CROSS, Milton	1975	Kensico Cemetery, Valhalla, NY	
CROTHERS, Ben "Scatman"	1986	Forest Lawn—Hollywood Hills, Los Angeles, CA	Lincoln Terrace, Plot #4545
CRUZE, James	1942	Hollywood Memorial Park, Hollywood, CA	Abbey of Psalms, Foyer, Niche 211, Tier 2
CUKOR, George	1983	Forest Lawn Memorial-Park, Glendale, CA	Court of Freedom
• CULLY, Zara	1978	Forest Lawn Memorial-Park, Glendale, CA	Freedom Maus., Col. of Victory
CUMMINGS, Robert	1990	Forest Lawn Memorial-Park, Glendale, CA	Great Maus., Col. of Sanctity
CURTIZ, Michael	1962	Forest Lawn Memorial-Park, Glendale, CA	Whispering Pines
D			
D'ORSAY, Fifi	1983	Forest Lawn Memorial-Park, Glendale, CA	Devotion
DAILEY, Dan	1978	Forest Lawn Memorial-Park, Glendale, CA	Court of Freedom, marker 7065, L. of statue
DALEY, Cass (Katherine)	1975	Hollywood Memorial Park, Hollywood, CA	Section 8, near curb ("Williamson")
DAMITA, Lili (Loomis)	1994	Oakland Cemetery, Ft. Dodge, IA	
• DAMROSCH, Walter	1950	Woodlawn Cem. and Crematory, The Bronx, NY	
DANDRIDGE, Dorothy	1965	Forest Lawn Memorial-Park, Glendale, CA	Freedom Maus., Col. of Victory
DANE, Karl	1934	Hollywood Memorial Park, Hollywood, CA	Pineland, Plot 303 (next to road)
DANIELS, Bebe	1971	Hollywood Memorial Park, Hollywood, CA	Columbarium, Niche 7-8, T.3, Upper N. Wall
DANIELS, Victor	1955	Forest Lawn Memorial-Park, Glendale, CA	
DANTINE, Helmut	1982	Westwood Village Mem. Park, Los Angeles, CA	Section D, #130
DARBY, Ken	1992	Forest Lawn—Hollywood Hills, Los Angeles, CA	Lincoln Terrace, Plot #4246
DARIN, Bobby	1973	(No funeral)	Body donated to UCLA for med. research
DARNELL, Linda	1965	Union Hill Cemetery, Kennett Square, PA	
DARRELL, J. Stevan	1970	Westwood Village Mem. Park, Los Angeles, CA	
DARWELL, Jane	1967	Forest Lawn Memorial-Park, Glendale, CA	Whispering Pines, Plot #1817
DASSIN, Joe	1980	Hollywood Memorial Park, Hollywood, CA	Section 14, Grave 79, Row I
DASTAGIR, Sabu	1963	Forest Lawn—Hollywood Hills, Los Angeles, CA	Sheltering Hills, Plot #402
DASTAGIR, Sheik	1960	Forest Lawn—Hollywood Hills, Los Angeles, CA	Sheltering Hills, Plot #490
DAVENPORT, Alice	1936	Forest Lawn Memorial-Park, Glendale, CA	
DAVES, Delmar	1977	Forest Lawn Memorial-Park, Glendale, CA	Great Maus., Col. of Memory
DAVIES, Marion	1961	Hollywood Memorial Park, Hollywood, CA	Douras Mausoleum, Section 8, Lot 261-264
DAVIS, Bette	1989	Forest Lawn—Hollywood Hills, Los Angeles, CA	Courts of Remem., in sarc. left of entrance
DAVIS, Brad	1991	Forest Lawn—Hollywood Hills, Los Angeles, CA	Col. of Valor, G64054
DAVIS, Jim	1981	Forest Lawn Memorial-Park, Glendale, CA	Great Maus., 3rd floor (cremated)
DAVIS, Joan (Williams)	1961	Holy Cross Cem. and Maus., Culver City, CA	Mausoleum, Block 46, Crypt D-1, rt. of altar
DAVIS, Miles	1991	Woodlawn Cemetery, The Bronx, NY	D-4, Alpine Hill
• DAVIS, Philip K.	1996	Greek Orthodox Cemetery, Baltimore, MD	
DAVIS, Sammy Jr.	1990	Forest Lawn Memorial-Park, Glendale, CA	Garden of Honor
DAY, Dennis	1988	Holy Cross Cem. and Maus., Culver City, CA	Section W, Tier 53, Grave 37

• New entry.

* Some cemeteries refuse to reveal specific locations.

NAME	YEAR	CEMETERY	INTERMENT SITE*
DEAN, James	1955	Park Cemetery, Fairmount, IN	
DeCORDOBA, Pedro	1950	Holy Cross Cem. and Maus., Culver City, CA	Section G, Lot 258, Grave 1
DeFORE, Don	1993	Westwood Village Mem. Park, Los Angeles, CA	Rose Garden
DELMAR, Kenny	1984	Long Ridge Congregational Ch., Stamford, CT	
DeMILLE, Cecil B.	1959	Hollywood Memorial Park, Hollywood, CA	Section 8, in twin marble sarcophagi
DeMILLE, William C.	1955	Hollywood Memorial Park, Hollywood, CA	Abbey of the Psalms, Niche 2, T.6, Corr E-3
• DEMPSEY, Jack	1983	Southampton Cemetery, Southampton (L.I.), NY	
• DENNIS, Sandy	1992	Lincoln Memorial Park, Lincoln Neb.	Mauseleum #3, Wall A, Col. 1C
DENNY, Reginald	1967	Forest Lawn—Hollywood Hills, Los Angeles, CA	Morning Light, Plot #7451
DePUTTI, Lya	1931	Ferncliff Cemetery and Maus., Hartsdale, NY	Maus., Unit 1, Alcove E, Crypt 31
DeRITA, Joe	1993	Valhalla Memorial Park, N. Hollywood, CA	
DESMOND, Johnny	1985	Holy Cross Cem. and Maus., Culver City, CA	Section F, Tier 44, Grave 30
DEVINE, Andy	1977	(Cremated—not interred)	Ashes scattered at sea
DeWOLFE, Billy	1974	Mount Wollaston Cemetery, Quincy, MA	
DIAMOND, Selma	1985	Hillside Memorial Park, Los Angeles, CA	Courts of the Book, Jacob-I-4004
DIETRICH, Marlene	1992	Friedenau Cemetery, Berlin, Germany	Near her mother, Josefine von Losch
DIGGES, Dudley	1947	Cem. of the Gate of Heaven, Hawthorne, NY	
DINEHART, Mason Alan	1944	Forest Lawn Memorial-Park, Glendale, CA	Great Mausoleum
DISNEY, Roy	1971	Forest Lawn—Hollywood Hills, Los Angeles, CA	Sheltering Hills
DISNEY, Walt	1966	Forest Lawn Memorial-Park, Glendale, CA	Court of Freedom
Divine (Harris Glenn Milstead)	1988	Prospect Hill Cemetery, Towson, MD	
DIX, Richard	1949	Forest Lawn Memorial-Park, Glendale, CA	Whispering Pines, nr. "Finding of Moses"
DOLLY, Roszika "Rosie"	1970	Forest Lawn Memorial-Park, Glendale, CA	Great Maus., hall right side
DOLLY, Yansci "Jenny"	1941	Forest Lawn Memorial-Park, Glendale, CA	Great Maus., hall right side
• DONAT, Robert	1958	St. Marylebone Churchyard, London, England	Cremated—ashes interred here
DONLEVY, Brian	1972	(Cremated—not interred)	Ashes scattered at sea nr. Santa Monica, CA
DORN, Philip	1975	Westwood Village Mem. Park, Los Angeles, CA	Sanctuary of Tranquility, rear wall
DORSEY, Jimmy	1957	Annunciation Cemetery, Shenandoah, PA	
DORSEY, Tommy	1956	Kensico Cemetery, Valhalla, NY	On Cherokee Ave.
DOUGLAS, Paul	1959	Chapel of the Pines Crematory, Los Angeles, CA	
DOWLING, Constance (Tors)	1969	Holy Cross Cem. and Maus., Culver City, CA	Section P, Grave 4, Lot 421
• DOZIER, William	1991	Holy Cross Cem. and Maus., Culver City, CA	Section G, Tier 25, Grave 179
DRAKE, Tom	1982	Holy Cross Cem. and Maus., Culver City, CA	Section R, Tier 26, Grave 188
DRESSLER, Marie	1934	Forest Lawn Memorial-Park, Glendale, CA	Great Maus., Sanctuary of Benediction
• DREW, Sidney	1919	Mount Vernon Cemetery, Philadelphia, PA	
DUCHIN, Eddie	1951	(Cremated—not interred)	Ashes scattered in the Atlantic Ocean
• DUEL, Peter	1971	Penfield Cemetery, Penfield, NY	
DUMONT, Margaret	1965	Chapel of the Pines Crematory, Los Angeles, CA	
DUNCAN, Isadora	1927	Père Lachaise Cemetery, Paris, France	Div. 87, ashes interred in the Columbarium
DUNCAN, Rosetta	1959	Forest Lawn Memorial-Park, Glendale, CA	
DUNCAN, Vivian	1986	Forest Lawn Memorial-Park, Glendale, CA	
DUNN, James	1967	(Cremated—not interred)	Ashes scattered at sea
DUNNE, Dominique	1982	Westwood Village Mem. Park, Los Angeles, CA	Section D, #189
DUNNE, Irene (Griffin)	1990	Calvary Cemetery, Los Angeles, CA	Main Maus., left of altar in church area
DURANTE, Jimmy	1980	Holy Cross Cem. and Maus., Culver City, CA	Section F, Tier 96, Grave 6
DURFEE, Minta (Arbuckle)	1975	Forest Lawn Memorial-Park, Glendale, CA	Great Maus., Col. of Constancy #17743
DURKIN, Junior	1935	Forest Lawn Memorial-Park, Glendale, CA	
DUROCHER, Leo	1991	Forest Lawn—Hollywood Hills, Los Angeles, CA	Hillside, Plot #3211
DURYEA, Dan	1968	Forest Lawn—Hollywood Hills, Los Angeles, CA	Revelation, Plot #7347
DVORAK, Ann	1979	(Cremated—not interred)	Ashes scattered
DWAN, Allan	1981	San Fernando Mission Cem., San Fernando, CA	
E			
EAGELS, Jeanne	1929	Calvary Catholic Cemetery, Kansas City, MO	
EDDY, Nelson	1967	Hollywood Memorial Park, Hollywood, CA	Section 8, Lot 89
EDENS, Roger	1970	Westwood Village Mem. Park, Los Angeles, CA	Sanctuary of Remembrance
EDWARDS, Cliff	1971	Valhalla Memorial Park, N. Hollywood, CA	Section D, near Heritage Fountain
• EDWARDS, Gus	1945	Woodlawn Cem. and Crematory, The Bronx, NY	
EDWARDS, Snitz	1937		Cremated
EDWARDS, Vince (Zoine)	1996	Holy Cross Cem. and Maus., Culver City, CA	Section CC, Tier 64, Grave 29
EGAN, Richard	1987	Holy Cross Cem. and Maus., Culver City, CA	Section AA, Tier 37, Grave 139 (unmarked)
EILERS, Sally	1978	Forest Lawn Memorial-Park, Glendale, CA	Freedom Maus., Columbarium
• EISENSTEIN, Sergei	1948	Novodevichy Cemetery, Moscow, Russia	

• New entry.

* Some cemeteries refuse to reveal specific locations.

NAME	YEAR	CEMETERY	INTERMENT SITE*
ELGART, Les	1995	Hillcrest Memorial Park, Dallas, TX	Garden of Prayer, Block 10, Lot 27, Sp 2
ELLINGTON, Duke	1974	Woodlawn Cemetery, The Bronx, NY	Division 49, at Fir & Knollwood Aves.
ELLIOT, Cass (Cohen)	1974	Mount Sinai Memorial-Park, Los Angeles, CA	Court of Tanach, Lot 5000, Grave 2F
EMERSON, Hope	1960	Grace Hills Cemetery, Hawarden, PA	
EMMETT, Fern (Roquemore)	1946	Forest Lawn Memorial-Park, Glendale, CA	Masonic Section
ERROL, Leon	1951	Forest Lawn Memorial-Park, Glendale, CA	
ERWIN, Stuart	1967	Chapel of the Pines Crematory, Los Angeles, CA	
ETTING, Ruth	1978	Evergreen Cemetery, Colorado Springs, CO	Shrine of Rest Mausoleum

F

NAME	YEAR	CEMETERY	INTERMENT SITE*
FACTOR, Max	1938	Hillside Memorial Park, Los Angeles, CA	Courts of the Book, Isaiah-U-314
FAIRBANKS, Douglas Sr.	1939	Hollywood Memorial Park, Hollywood, CA	Section 11 (R. of Cathedral Mausoleum)
FAITH, Percy	1976	Hillside Memorial Park, Los Angeles, CA	Garden of Memories, Honor, Lawn Crypt 407
FARMER, Frances	1970	Oak Lawn Memorial Gardens, Noblesville, IN	Main Maus., in Chapel, Rt. side bottom row
FARNUM, Franklyn	1961	Chapel of the Pines Crematory, Los Angeles, CA	
FARNUM, William	1953	Forest Lawn Memorial-Park, Glendale, CA	
FARRELL, Charles	1990	Welwood Murray Cemetery, Palm Springs, CA	Section 10-3, Lot G
FARRELL, Glenda	1971	National Cemetery, West Point, NY	
FARRELL, Virginia Valli	1968	Welwood Murray Cemetery, Palm Springs, CA	Section 10-3, Lot F
FARROW, John	1963	Holy Cross Cem. and Maus., Culver City, CA	Section P, Holy Redeemer, Plot #342
FAY, Frank	1961	Calvary Cemetery, Los Angeles, CA	
FAYLEN, Frank	1985	San Fernando Mission Cem., San Fernando, CA	
FAZENDA, Louise	1962	Inglewood Park Cemetery, Inglewood, CA	
• FELD, Fritz	1993	Forest Lawn—Hollywood Hills, Los Angeles, CA	Mt. Sinai
FELDMAN, Marty	1982	Forest Lawn—Hollywood Hills, Los Angeles, CA	Garden of Heritage, Plot #5420
FELLINI, Federico	1993	Civico Cimitero, Rimini, Italy	Section O, in a brown brick-like family vault
Fernandel	1971	Passy Cemetery, Paris, France	Black stone tomb with a raised cross
FIEDLER, Arthur	1979	St. Joseph Cemetery, West Roxbury, MA	
FIELDS, Totie (Johnson)	1978	Mount Sinai Memorial-Park, Los Angeles, CA	Heritage Section, Crypt 60C
FIELDS, W. C.	1946	Forest Lawn Memorial-Park, Glendale, CA	Great Maus., Hall of Inspiration
FINCH, Flora	1940	Hollywood Memorial Park, Hollywood, CA	Section 1, Grave 416
FINCH, Peter	1977	Hollywood Memorial Park, Hollywood, CA	H'wood Cath. Maus., Crypt 1224, off Corr A
FINE, Larry	1975	Forest Lawn Memorial-Park, Glendale, CA	Freedom Maus., Sanctuary of Liberation
• FITZGERALD, Ella	1996	Inglewood Park Cemetery, Inglewood, CA	Main Mausoleum
FITZMAURICE, George F.	1940	Forest Lawn Memorial-Park, Glendale, CA	
FIX, Paul	1983	Woodlawn Cemetery, Santa Monica, CA	Block 17
FLATT, Lester	1979	Crestlawn Cemetery, Sparta, TN	
• FLAVIN, James	1976	Holy Cross Cem. and Maus., Culver City, CA	Section W
FLEMING, Eric	1966	University of San Marcos, Lima, Peru	Body donated for medical research
FLEMING, Victor	1949	Hollywood Memorial Park, Hollywood, CA	Abbey of the Psalms, Crypt 2081, Corr G-2
FLIPPEN, Jay C.	1971	Westwood Village Mem. Park, Los Angeles, CA	Corridor of Memories
FLYNN, Errol	1959	Forest Lawn Memorial-Park, Glendale, CA	Garden of Everlasting Peace
FLYNN, Joseph A. "Joe"	1974	Holy Cross Cem. and Maus., Culver City, CA	Section W, Tier 20, Grave 75
• FLYNT, Althea Leasure	1987	Lakeville, KY	Buried in family plot of husband Larry Flynt
FOLEY, Red	1968	Woodlawn Memorial Park, Nashville, TN	
FONDA, Henry	1982	Grand View Memorial Park, Glendale, CA	Cremated (Ashes given to his family)
FONTAINE, Frank	1978	Oak Grove Cemetery, Medford, MA	
FONTANE, Tony	1974	Forest Lawn—Hollywood Hills, Los Angeles, CA	Courts of Remem., 409
FONTANNE, Lynn	1983	Forest Home Cemetery, Milwaukee, WI	
FORD, John	1973	Holy Cross Cem. and Maus., Culver City, CA	Section M, Lot 304, Grave 5
FORD, Mary	1977	Forest Lawn—Covina Hills, Covina, CA	Churchyard Section, Lot 1498, Space 2
FORD, Paul	1976	Forest Lawn Memorial-Park, Cypress, CA	
FOSTER, Preston	1970	El Camino Memorial Park, La Jolla, CA	Sanctuary of Love (3), Crypt 4, Tier F
FOWLER, Gene	1960	Holy Cross Cem. and Maus., Culver City, CA	Section M, Lot 792, Grave 3
FOX, Wallace W.	1958	Forest Lawn Memorial-Park, Glendale, CA	
• FOXX, Redd	1991	Palm Desert Cemetery, Las Vegas, NV	
FOY, Bryan	1977	Calvary Cemetery, Los Angeles, CA	
FOY, Eddie Sr.	1928	Holy Sepulchre Cemetery, New Rochelle, NY	
FRANCIS, Robert	1955	Forest Lawn—Hollywood Hills, Los Angeles, CA	Hillside, Plot #4535
FRANKLIN, Rupert	1939	Forest Lawn Memorial-Park, Glendale, CA	
FRANKLIN, Sidney (actor)	1931	Hollywood Memorial Park, Hollywood, CA	Pineland, Lot #321
FRANKLIN, Sidney (director)	1972	Hollywood Memorial Park, Hollywood, CA	Section 8, grave next to palm tree
FRAWLEY, William	1966	San Fernando Mission Cem., San Fernando, CA	Section C, at Curb No. 64, 5 rows in

NAME	YEAR	CEMETERY	INTERMENT SITE*
FREDERICK, Fred Burke	1986	Chapel of the Pines Crematory, Los Angeles, CA	Cremated
FREDERICK, Pauline	1938	Grand View Memorial Park, Glendale, CA	
FREED, Arthur	1973	Hillside Memorial Park, Los Angeles, CA	Garden of Memories, Honor, Lawn Crypt 418
FREEMAN, Young Frank	1969	Westview Cemetery, Atlanta, GA	Section 10, Lot 277, Grave 10
FRELENG, Isadore "Friz"	1995	Hillside Memorial Park, Los Angeles, CA	Canaan, Block E-249
FRENCH, George B.	1961	Forest Lawn Memorial-Park, Glendale, CA	
FRIML, Rudolph	1972	Forest Lawn Memorial-Park, Glendale, CA	Great Maus., beneath Last Supper window
• FRISCO, Joe	1958	Hollywood Memorial Park, Hollywood, CA	
FRIZZELL, Lefty	1975	Forest Lawn Cemetery, Nashville, TN	
FRYE, Dwight	1943	Forest Lawn Memorial-Park, Glendale, CA	
FULLER, Mary	1973	Congressional Cemetery, Washington, D.C.	
FULTON, Maude	1950	Forest Lawn Memorial-Park, Glendale, CA	
G			
GABLE, Clark	1960	Forest Lawn Memorial-Park, Glendale, CA	Great Maus., Sanctuary of Trust
GABOR, Eva	1995	Westwood Village Mem. Park, Los Angeles, CA	Nr. Armand Hammer's Maus. (Right front)
• GALENTO, Tony "Two Ton"	1979	St. John's Cemetery, Orange, NJ	
GANZHORN, John W.	1956	Forest Lawn Memorial-Park, Glendale, CA	
GARBO, Greta	1990	(Cremated—not interred)	Ashes given to her niece, Gray Reisfield
GARCIA, Jerry	1995	(Cremated)	Ashes scattered in the Ganges River, India
GARDINER, Reginald	1980	Forest Lawn—Hollywood Hills, Los Angeles, CA	Courts of Remem., Sanc. of Reflection, 3322
GARDNER, Ava	1990	Sunset Memorial Park, Smithfield, NC	
GARFIELD, John	1952	Westchester Hills Cem, Hastings-on-Hudson, NY	
GARLAND, Judy	1969	Ferncliff Cemetery and Maus., Hartsdale, NY	Maus., Unit 9, Section HH, Crypt 31
• GARNER, Erroll	1977	Homewood Cemetery, Pittsburgh, PA	
• GARSON, Greer	1996	Hillcrest Memorial Park, Dallas, TX	
GAYE, Marvin	1984	(Cremated—not interred)	Ashes scattered from a ship at sea
GAYNOR, Janet (Gregory)	1984	Hollywood Memorial Park, Hollywood, CA	Section 8, Lot 193
• GAZZO, Michael Vincente	1995	Westwood Memorial Park, Los Angeles, CA	Room of Prayer
GEER, Will	1978	(Cremated—not interred)	Ashes scattered in San Fernando Valley, CA
GEHRIG, Lou	1941	Kensico Cemetery, Valhalla, NY	Ashes in family vault
GELLER, Bruce	1978	Mount Sinai Memorial-Park, Los Angeles, CA	
GEORGE, Christopher	1983	Westwood Village Mem. Park, Los Angeles, CA	Sanctuary of Tranquility
GEORGE, Gorgeous	1963	(See WAGNER, "Gorgeous" George)	
GERSHWIN, George	1937	Mount Hope Cem., Hastings-on-Hudson, NY	
GERSHWIN, Ira	1983	Mount Hope Cem., Hastings-on-Hudson, NY	
GIBB, Andy	1988	Forest Lawn—Hollywood Hills, Los Angeles, CA	Courts of Remem., 2534
GIBSON, Hoot	1962	Inglewood Park Cemetery, Inglewood, CA	Magnolia Plot, Lot 92, Grave 6
GILBERT, Billy	1971	Odd Fellows Cemetery, Los Angeles, CA	
GILBERT, John	1936	Forest Lawn Memorial-Park, Glendale, CA	Whispering Pines
GILLETT, King	1932	Forest Lawn Memorial-Park, Glendale, CA	Great Maus., Begonia Corridor
GINGOLD, Hermione	1987	Forest Lawn Memorial-Park, Glendale, CA	Great Maus., Sanctuary of the Holy Spirit
GISH, Dorothy	1968	St. Bartholomew's Epis. Ch., New York, NY	
• GISH, Lillian	1993	St. Bartholomew's Episcopal Church, New York, NY	
GLEASON, Jackie	1987	Our Lady of Mercies Cemetery, Miami, FL	
GLEASON, James	1959	Holy Cross Cem. and Maus., Culver City, CA	Section D, Sacred Heart
• GOBEL, George	1991	San Fernando Mission Cem., San Fernando, CA	
GODOWSKY, Dagmar	1975	Mount Hope Cem., Hastings-on-Hudson, NY	
GOETZ, William	1969	Hillside Memorial Park, Los Angeles, CA	Garden of Memories, Devotion, Sarcoph. B
GOLDWYN, Frances Howard	1976	Forest Lawn Memorial-Park, Glendale, CA	
GOLDWYN, Samuel	1973	Forest Lawn Memorial-Park, Glendale, CA	Garden of Honor, first garden on right
GOMEZ, Thomas	1971	Westwood Village Mem. Park, Los Angeles, CA	
GOODMAN, Benny	1986	Long Ridge Cemetery, Stamford, CT	
GOODSON, Mark	1992	Hillside Memorial Park, Los Angeles, CA	Mausoleum, Gdn. of Abraham-Sarcoph. B
GOODWIN, Bill	1958	Desert Memorial Park, Palm Springs, CA	Section B-1, Lot 17
GORCEY, Leo	1969	Los Molinas Cemetery, Red Bluff, CA	
• GORDON, Gale	1995	(Cremated—not interred)	Ashes sent to his sister in Arizona
GORDON, Huntly	1956	Forest Lawn Memorial-Park, Glendale, CA	
GORDON, Leon	1960	Forest Lawn Memorial-Park, Glendale, CA	
GOSDEN, Freeman	1982	Forest Lawn—Hollywood Hills, Los Angeles, CA	
GOTTLIEB, Conrad I.	1995	Hebrew Young Men's Cem., Baltimore, MD	
• GOUDAL, Jetta	1985	Forest Lawn—Hollywood Hills, Los Angeles, CA	Great Maus., Sanctuary of the Holy Spirit
GOULD, Glenn	1982	Mount Pleasant Cem., Toronto (Ont.), Canada	

* Some cemeteries refuse to reveal specific locations.

NAME	YEAR	CEMETERY	INTERMENT SITE*
GRABLE, Betty (James)	1973	Inglewood Park Cemetery, Inglewood, CA	Golden West Maus., A78, Sanc. of Dawn
• GRAHAME, Gloria	1981	Oakwood Memorial Park, Chatsworth, CA	Pioneer Section, Lot 242, Space 8
• GRAHAME, Gloria	1981	Oakwood Memorial Park, Chatsworth, CA	
GRANT, Cary	1986	(Cremated)	
GRANT, Earl	1970	Forest Lawn—Hollywood Hills, Los Angeles, CA	Lincoln Terrace, Plot #226
GRANVILLE, Bonita (Wrather)	1988	Holy Cross Cem. and Maus., Culver City, CA	Section "Grotto," Lot 196, Grave 12
GRAPEWIN, Charles	1956	Forest Lawn Memorial-Park, Glendale, CA	Great Maus., Col. of Inspiration
GRAY, Gilda	1959	Holy Cross Cem. and Maus., Culver City, CA	
GREEN, Alfred E.	1960	Forest Lawn Memorial-Park, Glendale, CA	Great Maus., Sanc. of Refuge, Crypt #5089
GREENE, Lorne	1987	Hillside Memorial Park, Los Angeles, CA	Courts of the Book, Lawn Crypt-5-800-8B
GREENSTREET, Sydney	1954	Forest Lawn Memorial-Park, Glendale, CA	Ashes in a utility room (not open to public)
• GREY, Zane	1939	Union Cemetery, Lackawaxen, PA	
GRIFFITH, David Wark	1948	Mt. Tabor United Meth. Ch., Crestwood, KY	
GRINKOV, Sergei	1995	Vagankovskoye Cem., Moscow, Russia	
• GRUNDGENS, Gustav	1963	Olsdorf Cemetery, Hamburg, Germany	
GUINAN, Mary L. "Texas"	1933	Calvary Cemetery, Woodside (Queens), NY	Section 47
GUTHRIE, Woody	1967	(Cremated—not interred)	Ashes cast into the ocean at Coney Is., NY
GWENN, Edmund	1959	Chapel of the Pines Crematory, Los Angeles, CA	In basement holding vault, not on view

H

NAME	YEAR	CEMETERY	INTERMENT SITE*
• HACKETT, Bobby	1976	Seaside Cemetery, Chatham, MA	
HACKETT, Joan	1983	Hollywood Memorial Park, Hollywood, CA	Abbey of the Psalms, Crypt 2314, Corr D-3
HAINES, William	1973	Woodlawn Cemetery, Santa Monica, CA	
• HALE, Alan Jr.	1990	(Cremated—not interred)	Ashes scattered at sea
HALE, Alan Sr.	1950	Forest Lawn Memorial-Park, Glendale, CA	Whispering Pines
HALEY, Jack	1979	Holy Cross Cem. and Maus., Culver City, CA	Section "Grotto," Lot 100, Grave 2
HALL, Charlie	1959	Forest Lawn Memorial-Park, Glendale, CA	Eventide, Lot 1928
HALL, Jon	1979	Forest Lawn—Hollywood Hills, Los Angeles, CA	Court of Liberty, same row w/Buster Keaton
HALOP, Billy	1976	Mount Sinai Memorial-Park, Los Angeles, CA	Garden of Sherrot, Crypt 64181 along wall
HALTON, Charles	1959	Forest Lawn Memorial-Park, Glendale, CA	
HAMILTON, Hale Rice	1942	Forest Lawn Memorial-Park, Glendale, CA	
• HAMILTON, Margaret	1985	Cremated	Ashes scattered over her home, Amenia, NY
HAMMER, Armand	1990	Westwood Village Mem. Park, Los Angeles, CA	In family mausoleum, near entrance
HAMMERSTEIN, Oscar II	1960	Ferncliff Cemetery and Maus., Hartsdale, NY	Ashes buried
HAMPDEN, Walter	1955	Restland Memorial Park, Burbank, CA	
HANCOCK, John	1992	Forest Lawn—Hollywood Hills, Los Angeles, CA	Devotion, Plot #8018
• HARBURG, E. Y.	1981	Grand View Memorial Park, Glendale, CA	Cremated
HARDING, Ann	1981	Forest Lawn Memorial-Park, Glendale, CA	Cremated
HARDY, Oliver	1957	Valhalla Memorial Park, N. Hollywood, CA	Gdn. of Hope, 2nd wall to rt. of Her. Fount.
HARDY, Sam	1935	Forest Lawn Memorial-Park, Glendale, CA	
HARLOW, Jean	1937	Forest Lawn Memorial-Park, Glendale, CA	Great Maus., Sanctuary of Benediction
HARRIGAN, William	1966	Arlington National Cemetery, Arlington, VA	
• HARRIS, Phil	1995	Forest Lawn—Hollywood Hills, Los Angeles, CA	Palm Springs Mausoleum
HARRIS, Robin	1990	Inglewood Park Cemetery, Inglewood, CA	Chap. of Freedom, Manchester Maus. #D5
HART, Lorenz	1943	Mt. Zion Cemetery, Maspeth, NY	
HART, Moss	1961	Ferncliff Cemetery and Maus., Hartsdale, NY	Maus., Unit 8 Alcove EE-FF, Col. D Niche 4
HART, William S.	1946	Green-Wood Cemetery, Brooklyn, NY	Section 191, Plot 29116
• HARTMAN, Elizabeth	1987	Boardman, Ohio	
• HARTMAN, Phil	1998	Cremated	Ashes Scattered over Emerald Bay, CA
HARVEY, Paul (actor)	1955	Forest Lawn Memorial-Park, Glendale, CA	
HATHAWAY, Henry	1985	Holy Cross Cem. and Maus., Culver City, CA	Mausoleum, left of the altar
• HATLEY, T. Marvin	1986	Forest Lawn—Hollywood Hills, Los Angeles, CA	Court of Remembrance
HATTON, Rondo	1946	American Legion Cemetery, Tampa, FL	
HAWKS, Howard	1977	(Cremated—not interred)	Ashes scattered
HAYDEN, Harry	1955	Forest Lawn Memorial-Park, Glendale, CA	
HAYDEN, Russell	1981	Oakwood Memorial Park, Chatsworth, CA	
HAYES, George "Gabby"	1969	Forest Lawn—Hollywood Hills, Los Angeles, CA	Hillside, Plot #4972
HAYES, Helen (MacArthur)	1993	Oak Hill Cemetery, Nyack, NY	Next to her husband, Charles MacArthur
HAYMES, Dick	1980	(Cremated—not interred)	Ashes given to family
HAYWARD, Susan	1975	Our Lady of Perpetual Help Ch., Carrollton, GA	
HAYWORTH, Rita	1987	Holy Cross Cem. and Maus., Culver City, CA	Section "Grotto", Lot 196, Grave 6
HEAD, Edith	1981	Forest Lawn Memorial-Park, Glendale, CA	Cathedral slope, Plot 1675, at the top of hill
HEALY, Ted	1937	Calvary Cemetery, Los Angeles, CA	Section F, Lot 1693, Grave 14

Specific Interment Locations — by Name

NAME	YEAR	CEMETERY	INTERMENT SITE*
HEARN, Sam	1964	Forest Lawn Memorial-Park, Glendale, CA	
• HEATTER, Gabriel	1972	Mount Nebo Cemetery, Miami, FL	
• HECHT, Ben	1964	Oak Hill Cemetery, Nyack, NY	
• HECHT, Harold	1985	Westwood Village Memorial Park, Los Angeles, CA	Section D in front of #81 (Eve Arden)
HEFLIN, Van	1971	Chapel of the Pines Crematory, Los Angeles, CA	
HEIDT, Horace	1986	Forest Lawn—Hollywood Hills, Los Angeles, CA	Enduring Faith
HEISLER, Stuart	1979	Eternal Hills Memorial Park, Oceanside, CA	
HELD, Anna	1918	Cem. of the Gate of Heaven, Hawthorne, NY	Div. 42
HELLINGER, Mark	1947	Kensico Cemetery, Valhalla, NY	
HELLMAN, Lillian	1984	Abels Hill Cemetery, Chilmark (M.V.), MA	
HELTON, Percy	1971	Westwood Village Mem. Park, Los Angeles, CA	Sanctuary of Remembrance
• HENDERSON, Fletch	1952	Old Cemetery, Cuthbert, GA	
HENDRIX, Jimi	1970	Greenwood Memorial Cemetery, Renton, WA	
HENDRIX, Wanda	1981	Forest Lawn—Hollywood Hills, Los Angeles, CA	Courts of Remem., 4349
HENIE, Sonja	1969	Henie-Onstad Art Center, Oslo, Norway	
• HENREID, Paul	1992	Woodlawn Cemetery, Santa Monica, CA	
HEPBURN, Audrey	1993	Tolochenaz, Vaud, Switzerland	
HERBERT, Holmes	1956	Forest Lawn Memorial-Park, Glendale, CA	
HERBERT, Hugh	1952	Holy Cross Cem. and Maus., Culver City, CA	Section D, Lot 267, Grave 11
HERBERT, Victor	1924	Woodlawn Cemetery, The Bronx, NY	Div. 42, in maus. at Border and Linden Ave.
HERMAN, Woody	1987	Hollywood Memorial Park, Hollywood, CA	Court of the Apostles, Crypt 6689, Unit 10
• HERRMANN, Bernard	1975	Cedar Park Cemetery, Paramus, NJ	
HERSHOLT, Jean	1956	Forest Lawn Memorial-Park, Glendale, CA	Great Maus., monument opp. entrance
HILL, Benny	1992	Hollybrook Cem., Shirley, Southampton, Eng.	
HITCHCOCK, (Sir) Alfred	1980	(Cremated—not interred)	Ashes scattered
• HODGE, Al	1979	Kensico Cemetery, Valhalla, NY	
HODIAK, John	1955	Calvary Cemetery, Los Angeles, CA	Main Mausoleum, next to Mabel Normand
HOLDEN, Fay	1973	Forest Lawn Memorial-Park, Glendale, CA	Whispering Pines
HOLDEN, William	1981	(Cremated—not interred)	Ashes scattered in the Pacific Ocean
HOLIDAY, Billie	1959	St. Raymond's Cemetery, The Bronx, NY	
HOLLIDAY, Judy	1965	Westchester Hills Cem, Hastings-on-Hudson, NY	
HOLLY, Buddy	1959	City of Lubbock Cemetery, Lubbock, TX	Block 44 at Azalea Ave. (nr. path)
• HOLMAN, Libby "Peaches"	1971	(Cremated—not interred)	Ashes scattered on her estate nr. Greenwich, CT
HOLT, Jack	1951	Los Angeles National Cemetery, Los Angeles, CA	Section 107
HOOD, Darla	1979	Hollywood Memorial Park, Hollywood, CA	Abbey of the Psalms, Crypt 7213, Corr G-4
• HOOVER, J. Edgar	1972	Congressional Cemetery, Washington, D.C.	
• HOPPER, De Wolf	1935	Green-Wood Cemetery, Brooklyn, NY	
HOPPER, Hedda	1966	Rose Hill Cemetery, Altoona, PA	Ashes buried
HOPPER, William	1970	Rose Hills Memorial Park, Whittier, CA	Memorial Urn Garden, Space 210
HOROWITZ, Vladimir	1989	Cimitero Monumentale, Milan, Italy	Toscanini family mausoleum
HORTON, Edward Everett	1970	Forest Lawn Memorial-Park, Glendale, CA	Whispering Pines
HOUDINI, Harry	1926	Machpelah Cemetery, Ridgewood, (Queens), NY	
HOUSMAN, Arthur	1942	Los Angeles National Cemetery, Los Angeles, CA	
HOWARD, Jerome "Curly"	1952	Home of Peace Mem. Park, Los Angeles, CA	Western Jewish Institute, SW Corner, Plot 1
• HOWARD, Kathleen	1956	Restland Memorial Park, Burbank, CA	
HOWARD, Leslie	1943		Body never recovered from Atlantic Ocean
HOWARD, Moe	1975	Hillside Memorial Park, Los Angeles, CA	Garden of Memories, Alcove of Love C233
HOWARD, Shemp	1955	Home of Peace Mem. Park, Los Angeles, CA	Chapel Maus., Eternal Life Corr., EW215
HOWARD, Willie	1949	Cedar Park Cemetery, Westwood, NJ	
HOWE, James Wong	1976	Westwood Village Mem. Park, Los Angeles, CA	Sanctuary of Tranquility, rear wall
HOWLAND, Jobyna	1936	Forest Lawn Memorial-Park, Glendale, CA	
HUDNET, William H. "Bill"	1992	Holy Cross Cemetery, Baltimore, MD	
HUDSON, Rock	1985	(Cremated—not interred)	Ashes scattered at sea
HUDSON, William Woodson Jr.	1974	Westwood Village Mem. Park, Los Angeles, CA	
HUGHES, Howard	1976	Glenwood Cemetery, Houston, TX	
HUGHES, Lloyd	1958	Forest Lawn Memorial-Park, Glendale, CA	
HULL, Josephine	1957	Newton Cemetery, Newton, MA	
HUMANN, Helena	1994	Restland Memorial Park, Dallas, TX	Chapel Gardens, Crypt 5 S-130
HUMBERSTONE, Bruce H.	1984	Hollywood Memorial Park, Hollywood, CA	
HUNTER, Jeffrey	1969	Glen Haven Memorial Park, San Fernando, CA	
• HUNTER, Ross	1996	Westwood Village Mem. Park, Los Angeles, CA	
HUNTLEY, Chet	1974	Sunset Hills Cemetery, Bozeman, ID	

NAME	YEAR	CEMETERY	INTERMENT SITE*
HUROK, Sol	1974	Mount Hope Cem., Hastings-on-Hudson, NY	
HURT, Marlin	1946	Forest Lawn Memorial-Park, Glendale, CA	
HUSTON, John	1987	Hollywood Memorial Park, Hollywood, CA	Section 8, Lot 8
HUSTON, Walter	1950	(Cremated at Chapel of the Pines, L. A., CA)	Ashes given to his family
HUTTON, Jim	1979	Westwood Village Mem. Park, Los Angeles, CA	
HYMAN, Phyllis	1995	(Cremated)	Ashes sent to her family in Pittsburgh, PA
I			
IHNAT, Steve	1972	Westwood Village Mem. Park, Los Angeles, CA	Corridor of Memories
INGRAM, Rex (actor)	1969	Forest Lawn—Hollywood Hills, Los Angeles, CA	Court of Liberty, Plot #822
INGRAM, Rex (director)	1950	Forest Lawn Memorial-Park, Glendale, CA	Great Maus., Col. of Memory, under window
IRELAND, Jill	1990	Forest Lawn Memorial-Park, Glendale, CA	Only cremated here
ITURBI, José	1980	Holy Cross Cem. and Maus., Culver City, CA	Mausoleum, Block 16, Crypt E-1
• IVES, Burl	1995	Mound Cemetery, Newton, IL	
J			
JACKSON, Mahalia	1972	Providence Memorial Park, Metairie, LA	Section E, on east side of Mausoleum
JACKSON, Mary Ann	1991	Lake View Cemetery, Cleveland, OH.	Section 43, Lot 678
JAFFE. Sam	1984	Eden Memorial Park, San Fernando, CA	Top of outside wall, at top of hill
JANSSEN, David	1980	Hillside Memorial Park, Los Angeles, CA	Mausoleum, Memorial Court-516
• JENNINGS, Humphrey	1950	Buried in Athens, Greece	
JESSEL, George	1981	Hillside Memorial Park, Los Angeles, CA	Mausoleum, Memorial Court-516
• JOHNSON, Ben	1996	Pawhuska, Oklahoma	
JOHNSON, Chic	1962	Palm Mortuary Mausoleum, Las Vegas, NV	Ground burial
JOHNSON, Nunnally	1977	Westwood Village Mem. Park, Los Angeles, CA	Sanctuary of Tranquility, rear wall
JOHNSON, Tor	1971	Eternal Valley Memorial Park, Newhall, CA	
JOLSON, Al	1950	Hillside Memorial Park, Los Angeles, CA	In Al Jolson Memorial (at top of waterfall)
• JONES, Anissa "Buffy"	1976	(Cremated—not interred)	Ashes scattered at sea
• JONES, Bobby	1971	Oakland Cemetery, Atlanta, GA	
JONES, Brian	1969	Priory Road Cemetery, Cheltenham, England	(In Prestbury)
JONES, Buck	1942	(Cremated—not interred)	Ashes scattered at sea
JONES, Carolyn	1983	Forest Lawn Memorial-Park, Glendale, CA	Great Maus., Col. of Memory
JONES, Ken	1993	Inglewood Park Cemetery, Inglewood, CA	Pineview Plot, Lot 932, Grave E
JONES, Lindley "Spike"	1965	Holy Cross Cem. and Maus., Culver City, CA	Mausoleum, Block 70, Crypt A-7
JOPLIN, Janis	1970	(Cremated—not interred)	Ashes strewn along coast of Northern CA
JORDAN, James "Jim"	1988	Holy Cross Cem. and Maus., Culver City, CA	St. Ann's Garden, Tier 153, Grave 1
JORDAN, Marion	1961	Holy Cross Cem. and Maus., Culver City, CA	St. Ann's Garden, Tier 153, Grave 2
JORY, Victor	1982	Westwood Village Mem. Park, Los Angeles, CA	
JULIA, Raul	1994	San Juan, Puerto Rico	
JULIAN, Rupert	1943	Forest Lawn Memorial-Park, Glendale, CA	
• JURGENS, Curt	1982	Zentralfriedhof Cemetery, Vienna, Austria	
K			
KANE, Helen	1966	Long Island Nat'l Cem., Farmingdale (L.I.), NY	
• KAPER, Bronislau	1983	Hollywood Memorial Park, Hollywood, CA	
• KARLOFF, Boris	1969	(Cremated)	Garden. of Remem., Guildford, Surrey, Eng.
KARNS, Roscoe	1970	Hollywood Memorial Park, Hollywood, CA	
KASSEL, Art	1965	Forest Lawn—Hollywood Hills, Los Angeles, CA	Col. of Remembrance, 6098
KATZ, Mickey	1985	Hillside Memorial Park, Los Angeles, CA	Valley of Remembrance, Block 1, Gr. 196-2
KAUFMAN, Andy	1984	Beth David Cemetery, Elmont (L.I.), NY	
KAYE, Danny	1987	Kensico Cemetery, Valhalla, NY	Valhalla Plot
KAYE, Nora (Ross)	1987	Westwood Village Mem. Park, Los Angeles, CA	Section D, #36
KEATON, Buster	1966	Forest Lawn—Hollywood Hills, Los Angeles, CA	Court of Liberty, nr. G. Washington statue
KEELER, Ruby	1993	Holy Sepulchre Cemetery, Orange, CA	"Ruby K. Lowe," Sect. N, Tier 21, Grave 46
KEIGHLEY, William	1984	Forest Lawn Memorial-Park, Glendale, CA	Great Maus., Col. of Memory
KELLAWAY, Cecil	1973	Westwood Village Mem. Park, Los Angeles, CA	Sanctuary of Remembrance
KELLY, Emmett	1979	Rest Haven Memorial Park, Lafayette, IN	Sunset Terr. sect., bet. entr. and exit drives
• KELLY, Gene	1996	(Cremated—not interred)	Ashes given to his family
KELLY, Grace	1982	Cathedral of St. Nicholas, Monte Carlo, Monaco	Grimaldi family vault
• KELLY, Nancy	1995	Westwood Village Mem. Park, Los Angeles, CA	
KELLY, Patsy	1981	Calvary Cemetery, Woodside (Queens), NY	
KELLY, Paul	1956	Holy Cross Cem. and Maus., Culver City, CA	Sect. D, Sacred Heart, 1 row above Plot 61
KENDALL, Kay (Harrison)	1959	St. John-at-Hampstead Cem., London, England	Near front fence
KENNEDY, Edgar	1948	Holy Cross Cem. and Maus., Culver City, CA	Section D, Sacred Heart, Grave 7, Lot 193
KENNY, Herbert C.	1992	St. John the Evangelist RC Ch., Columbia, MD	

• New entry.

* Some cemeteries refuse to reveal specific locations.

NAME	YEAR	CEMETERY	INTERMENT SITE*
KENTON, Stan	1979	Westwood Village Mem. Park, Los Angeles, CA	Rose Garden
KERN, Jerome	1945	Ferncliff Cemetery and Maus., Hartsdale, NY	Maus., Unit 4 Alcove C, Pvt. Niche Mem. 1
KERRIGAN, J. Warren	1947	Forest Lawn Memorial-Park, Glendale, CA	
KERT, Larry	1991	(Cremated—not interred)	
KIBBEE, Guy	1956	Kensico Cemetery, Valhalla, NY	Actors Fund Plot
Kiki	1953	Montparnasse Cemetery, Paris, France	
KILBRIDE, Percy	1964	San B./Golden Gate Nat'l Cem., San Bruno, CA	Section 2-B, nr. chain link fence by freeway
KILGALLEN, Dorothy	1965	Cem. of the Gate of Heaven, Hawthorne, NY	Div. 23
KILIAN, Victor	1979	Westwood Village Mem. Park, Los Angeles, CA	Ashes scattered in the Rose Garden
KING, Henry	1982	Holy Cross Cem. and Maus., Culver City, CA	
• KING, Martin Luther Jr.	1968	Martin L. King Memorial Center, Atlanta, GA	
• KIRBY, George	1995	Queen of Heaven Cemetery, Hillside, IL	Crucifixion Garden Mausoleum
• KNAGGS, Skelton	1955	Hollywood Memorial Park, Hollywood, CA	Section 8, 3 rows behind Tyrone Power
KNIGHT, Ted	1986	Forest Lawn Memorial-Park, Glendale, CA	Ascension Garden (left side)
KOLKER, Joseph Henry	1947	Forest Lawn Memorial-Park, Glendale, CA	Eventide
KORJUS, Miliza	1980	Westwood Village Mem. Park, Los Angeles, CA	Sanctuary of Tranquility, rear wall
KORNGOLD, Erich Wolfgang	1957	Hollywood Memorial Park, Hollywood, CA	Section 8, Lot 15
KOSTELANETZ, Andre	1980	(Cremated—not interred)	Ashes scattered at sea, off Kauai, Hawaii
KOVACS, Ernie	1962	Forest Lawn—Hollywood Hills, Los Angeles, CA	Across Vista Ln., facing Courts of Remem.
KREISLER, Fritz	1962	Woodlawn Cemetery, The Bronx, NY	Division 31, in mausoleum off Filbert Ave.
KRUGER, Otto	1974	Forest Lawn—Hollywood Hills, Los Angeles, CA	Churchyard, Plot #4266
KRUPA, Gene	1973	Holy Cross Cemetery, Calumet City, IL	Immaculata Section
KUHLMAN, Kathryn	1976	Forest Lawn Memorial-Park, Glendale, CA	Garden of Memory
• KURALT, Charles	1997	Old Chapel Hill Cemetery at University of NC	
KYSER, Kay	1985	Old Cemetery, Chapel Hill, NC	
L			
LADD, Alan	1964	Forest Lawn Memorial-Park, Glendale, CA	Freedom Maus., Sanctuary of Heritage
LADD, Sue Carol	1982	Forest Lawn Memorial-Park, Glendale, CA	Freedom Maus., Sanctuary of Heritage
LAEMMLE, Carl	1939	Home of Peace Mem. Park, Los Angeles, CA	Chapel Maus., in the Laemmle family room
LAHR, Bert	1967	Union Field Cem., Ridgewood (Queens), NY	
LAIRD, Jack	1991	Hollywood Memorial Park, Hollywood, CA	Section 8
LAKE, Arthur	1987	Hollywood Memorial Park, Hollywood, CA	Douras Mausoleum, Section 8, Lot 261-264
LAKE, Veronica	1973	(Cremated—not interred)	Ashes scattered at sea in Virgin Islands
LaMARR, Barbara	1926	Hollywood Memorial Park, Hollywood, CA	H'wood Cath. Maus.
LAMAS, Fernando	1982	Rose Dale Cemetery, Los Angeles, CA	
• LAMOUR, Dorothy	1996	Forest Lawn—Hollywood Hills, Los Angeles, CA	
• LANCASTER, Burt	1994	Westwood Village Mem. Park, Los Angeles, CA	Section D, near the curb
LANCHESTER, Elsa	1986	(Cremated—not interred)	Ashes scattered at sea
LANDIS, Carole	1948	Forest Lawn Memorial-Park, Glendale, CA	Everlasting Love, Lot 968, Gr. 8 next to curb
LANDON, Michael	1991	Hillside Memorial Park, Los Angeles, CA	Mausoleum, ashes in a private room
LANE, Allan "Rocky"	1973	Inglewood Park Cemetery, Inglewood, CA	Rosehill Plot, Lot 70, Grave A
LANE, Lola	1981	Calvary Cemetery, Santa Barbara, CA	Sect. M, Tier 17, Gr 97 (Lola Lane Hanlon)
LANE, Rosemary	1974	Forest Lawn Memorial-Park, Glendale, CA	No headstone
LANFIELD, Sidney	1972	Westwood Village Mem. Park, Los Angeles, CA	Sanctuary of Remembrance
LANG, Fritz	1976	Forest Lawn—Hollywood Hills, Los Angeles, CA	Murmuring Trees, Plot #3818
LANTZ, Walter	1994	Forest Lawn—Hollywood Hills, Los Angeles, CA	Col. of Radiant Light
LANZA, Mario	1959	Holy Cross Cem. and Maus., Culver City, CA	Mausoleum, Crypt D-2, Block 46
LaROCQUE, Rod	1969	(Cremated—not interred)	Ashes scattered at sea
• LARSEN, William	1996	(Cremated)	
LaRUE, Jack	1984	Holy Cross Cem. and Maus., Culver City, CA	Mausoleum, Block 69, Crypt E-3
• LASKY, Jesse L. Jr.	1988	Hollywood Memorial Park, Hollywood, CA	Columbarium, upper east wall, T.3 at window
• LASKY, Jesse L. Sr.	1958	Hollywood Memorial Park, Hollywood, CA	Abbey of the Psalms, Crypt 2196, Corr G-3
• LAUCK, Chester H. "Lum"	1980	Greenwood Cemtery, Hot Springs, AR	
LAUGHLIN, Billy "Froggy"	1948	Rose Hills Memorial Park, Whittier, CA	Older section
LAUGHTON, Charles	1962	Forest Lawn—Hollywood Hills, Los Angeles, CA	Courts of Remem., in black marble vault
LAUREL, Stanley	1965	Forest Lawn—Hollywood Hills, Los Angeles, CA	Ashes in Garden of Heritage at garden wall
LAVERNE, Lucille	1945	Inglewood Park Cemetery, Inglewood, CA	Center Grave D, Lot 236, Palm Plot
LAWFORD, Peter	1984	(Cremated—not interred)	Ashes scattered at sea
LAWRENCE, Florence	1938	Hollywood Memorial Park, Hollywood, CA	Grave300, Section 2-W, bronze marker
LAWRENCE, Gertrude	1952	Upton Cemetery, Upton, MA	
LAWRENCE, Lillian	1926	Hollywood Memorial Park, Hollywood, CA	H'wood Cath. Maus.
LAWRENCE, Walter Smith	1961	Glenwood Cemetery, Beeville, TX	

• New entry.

* Some cemeteries refuse to reveal specific locations.

NAME	YEAR	CEMETERY	INTERMENT SITE*
LAWRENCE, William E.	1947	Maple Grove Cemetery, Horsehead, NY	
LEBEDEFF, Ivan	1953	Forest Lawn Memorial-Park, Glendale, CA	Gardens of Memory
LEDBETTER, Huddie	1949	Shiloh Church Cemetery, Shreveport, LA	
LEE, Brandon	1993	Lake View Cemetery, Seattle, WA	Buried next to his father, Bruce Lee
LEE, Bruce	1973	Lake View Cemetery, Seattle, WA	
LEE, Canada	1952	Woodlawn Cemetery, The Bronx, NY	
LEE, Gypsy Rose	1970	Inglewood Park Cemetery, Inglewood, CA	Pinecrest Plot, Lot 1087, Grave 8
• LeFEVRE, Bill	1996	New Cathedral Cemetery, Baltimore, MD	Section SSS, Lot #179
LEHRMAN, Henry	1946	Hollywood Memorial Park, Hollywood, CA	Section 8, Lot 257 (next to Virginia Rappe)
LEHRMAN, Oscar S.	1992	Westwood Village Mem. Park, Los Angeles, CA	Section D, #81
LEIBER, Fritz	1949	Forest Lawn—Hollywood Hills, Los Angeles, CA	Everlasting Love, Plot #864, Grave 13
• LEIGH, Vivien	1967	Golders Green Crematorium, London, England	
LEMBECK, Harvey	1982	Eden Memorial Park, San Fernando, CA	
LENNON, John	1980	(Cremated—not interred)	Ashes given to his wife, Yoko Ono
LEONARD, Robert Z.	1968	Forest Lawn Memorial-Park, Glendale, CA	Great Maus., Sanctuary of Vespers
LERNER, Sam	1989	Hillside Memorial Park, Los Angeles, CA	Laurel Gardens, Block 18-177-3A
LeROY, Mervyn	1987	Forest Lawn Memorial-Park, Glendale, CA	Garden of Memory
LEVANT, Oscar	1972	Westwood Village Mem. Park, Los Angeles, CA	Sanctuary of Love, bottom right
• LEVENSON, Sam	1980	Beth David Cemetery, Elmont, NY	
• LEWIS, Joe E.	1971	Cedar Park Cemetery, Paramus, NJ	
LEWIS, Mitchell	1956	Forest Lawn Memorial-Park, Glendale, CA	
LEWIS, Ronald "Raan"	1995	Laurel Land Memorial Park, Dallas, TX	Field of Honor, Lot 125 B/C
LEWIS, Ted	1971	Forest Cemetery, Circleville, OH	
LEWIS, Tom	1927	Calvary Cemetery, Woodside (Queens), NY	
Liberace	1987	Forest Lawn—Hollywood Hills, Los Angeles, CA	Courts of Remem., in white sarcophagus
LIBERACE, George	1983	Forest Lawn—Hollywood Hills, Los Angeles, CA	Courts of Remem., in white sarcophagus
LINCOLN, Elmo	1952	Hollywood Memorial Park, Hollywood, CA	
• LINDSAY, Howard	1968	(Cremated—not interred)	Ashes scattered
LINDSAY, Margaret	1981	Holy Cross Cem. and Maus., Culver City, CA	Section P, Holy Redeemer, rt. of Plot 432
• LISTON, Sonny	1970	Paradise Memorial Gardens, Las Vegas, NV	
LITTLE, Malcolm "Malcolm X"	1965	Ferncliff Cemetery and Maus., Hartsdale, NY	Pinewood B, Grave 150
LITTLEFIELD, Lucien	1959	Forest Lawn Memorial-Park, Glendale, CA	Whispering Pines, Plot #1720
LIVINGSTONE, Mary (Benny)	1983	Hillside Memorial Park, Los Angeles, CA	Mausoleum, Graciousness, Sarcophagus F
LLOYD, Frank	1960	Forest Lawn Memorial-Park, Glendale, CA	Ascension
LLOYD, Harold Sr.	1971	Forest Lawn Memorial-Park, Glendale, CA	Great Maus., Begonia corridor #771
LOCHER, Felix	1969	Forest Lawn—Hollywood Hills, Los Angeles, CA	Court of Liberty
LOCKER, Frances	1990	Hollywood Memorial Park, Hollywood, CA	Abbey of the Psalms
LOCKHART, Gene	1957	Holy Cross Cem. and Maus., Culver City, CA	Section D, Lot 279, Grave 6
LOCKLEAR, Omer	1920	Greenwood Cemetery, Fort Worth, TX	89 - 9E
LOESSER, Frank	1969	(Cremated—not interred)	Ashes scattered at sea
LOEW, Marcus	1927	Cypress Hills Cemetery, Brooklyn, NY	
LOFT, Arthur	1947	Forest Lawn Memorial-Park, Glendale, CA	
• LOFTUS, Cecilia "Cissie"	1943	Kensico Cemetery, Valhalla, NY	
LOGAN, Ella	1969	Holy Cross Cemetery, San Mateo, CA	
LOMBARD, Carole (Gable)	1942	Forest Lawn Memorial-Park, Glendale, CA	Great Maus., Sanctuary of Trust
• LOMBARDI, Vince	1970	Mount Olivet Cemetery, Red Bank, NJ	
• LOMBARDO, Carmen	1971	Pinelawn Mem. Park, Farmingdale (L.I.), NY	
LOMBARDO, Guy	1977	Pinelawn Mem. Park, Farmingdale (L.I.), NY	
LONDON, Tom	1963	Forest Lawn Memorial-Park, Glendale, CA	
LONG, Richard	1974	Grand View Memorial Park, Glendale, CA	
LOPEZ, Vincent	1975	Southern Memorial Park, Miami, FL	
LORD, Pauline	1950	Kensico Cemetery, Valhalla, NY	
LORRE, Peter	1964	Hollywood Memorial Park, Hollywood, CA	H'wood Cath. Maus., Niche 5, T-1, Corr C
LOUIS, Joe	1981	Arlington National Cemetery, Arlington, VA	
LOUISE, Anita (Marks)	1970	Forest Lawn Memorial-Park, Glendale, CA	Next to her husband, Buddy Adler
LOVEJOY, Frank	1962	Holy Cross Cem. and Maus., Culver City, CA	Section P, Lot 306, Grave 5
LOWE, Edmund	1971	San Fernando Mission Cem., San Fernando, CA	Section B, Block 7, Lot 1113
LOY, Myrna	1993	Forestdale Cemetery, Helena, MT	Ashes buried alongside her parents
LUBITSCH, Ernst	1947	Forest Lawn Memorial-Park, Glendale, CA	
LUGOSI, Bela	1956	Holy Cross Cem. and Maus., Culver City, CA	Section "Grotto," Tier 120, Grave 1
LUKE, Keye	1991	Rose Hills Memorial Park, Whittier, CA	
• LUNCEFORD, Jimmy	1947	Elmwood Cemetery, Memphis, TN	

NAME	YEAR	CEMETERY	INTERMENT SITE*
LUNDIGAN, William	1975	Holy Cross Cem. and Maus., Culver City, CA	Section D, Lot 269, Grave 3
LUNT, Alfred	1977	Forest Home Cemetery, Milwaukee, WI	
LYMAN, Abe	1957	Forest Lawn Memorial-Park, Glendale, CA	
LYNDE, Paul	1982	(Cremated)	Ashes buried in Mount Vernon, Ohio
LYNN, Diana	1971	Chapel of the Pines Crematory, Los Angeles, CA	
LYON, Ben	1979	Hollywood Memorial Park, Hollywood, CA	Columbarium, Niche 7-8, T.3, Upper N. Wall
M			
MABLEY, Jackie "Moms"	1975	Ferncliff Cemetery and Maus., Hartsdale, NY	Knollwood Garden I, Row 14, Grave 4
• MacARTHUR, Charles	1956	Oak Hill Cemetery, Nyack, NY	
MacDONALD, Jeanette	1965	Forest Lawn Memorial-Park, Glendale, CA	Freedom Maus., Sanctuary of Heritage
MacDONALD, Joseph Farrell	1952	Chapel of the Pines Crematory, Los Angeles, CA	Memory Hall, Section K, B-2
MACK, Charles E.	1934	Forest Lawn Memorial-Park, Glendale, CA	
MACK, Rose	1927	In the family plot in Holyoke, MA	Buried with her husband, Joseph Lester
MacLANE, Barton	1969	Valhalla Memorial Park, N. Hollywood, CA	
MacMURRAY, Fred	1991	Holy Cross Cem. and Maus., Culver City, CA	Mausoleum, Room 7, Crypt D-1
• MacPHERSON, Aimee Semple	1944	Forest Lawn Memorial-Park, Glendale, CA	
MACREADY, George	1973		Body given to UCLA Medical School
• MADISON, Guy	1996	Forest Lawn—Hollywood Hills, Los Angeles, CA	Palm Springs Mausoleum
MAIN, Marjorie	1975	Forest Lawn—Hollywood Hills, Los Angeles, CA	Enduring Faith, Plot #2083
MAMOULIAN, Rouben	1987	Forest Lawn Memorial-Park, Glendale, CA	Ascension Garden
MANSFIELD, Jayne	1967	Fairview Cemetery, Pen Argyl, PA	Grave is near entrance
MANTLE, Mickey	1995	Hillcrest Memorial Park, Dallas, TX	Mausoleum St. Mark NE-N-C-13
• MARAVICH, Pete	1988	Resthaven Gardens of Memory, Baton Rouge, LA	
MARCH, Fredric	1975	New Milford, CT	Buried on his farm
MARCH, Hal	1970	Hillside Memorial Park, Los Angeles, CA	Mount Sholom, Block 4, Gr. 144-6
MARCIANO, "Rocky"	1969	Lauderdale Memorial Park, Ft. Lauderdale, FL	
Margo (Albert)	1985	Westwood Village Mem. Park, Los Angeles, CA	Section D, #61
• MARION, George F. Sr.	1945	Catholic Cemetery, Benecia, CA	
• MARIS, Roger	1985	Holy Cross Cemetery, Fargo, ND	
MARLOWE, Hugh	1982	Ferncliff Cemetery and Maus., Hartsdale, NY	Maus., Unit 10, Alcove BB-CC, Niche 9A
• MARLOWE, June	1984	San Fernando Mission Cem., San Fernando, CA	
• MARLOWE, June	1984	San Fernando Mission Cemetery, Mission Hills, CA	
MARSHALL, George E.	1975	Holy Cross Cem. and Maus., Culver City, CA	Mausoleum, Block 78, bottom row
• MARSHALL, Herbert	1966	Chapel of the Pines Crematory, Los Angeles, CA	
MARSHALL, Tully	1943	Hollywood Memorial Park, Hollywood, CA	Section 8, grave is beneath a tree
MARTIN, Dean	1995	Westwood Village Mem. Park, Los Angeles, CA	Sanctuary of Love
MARTIN, Dean Paul Jr.	1987	Los Angeles National Cemetery, Los Angeles, CA	
MARTIN, Marion	1985	Holy Cross Cem. and Maus., Culver City, CA	
MARTIN, Mary	1990	Old Greenwood Cemetery, Weatherford, TX	Unmarked, ashes buried with her husband
MARTIN, Ross	1981	Mount Sinai Memorial-Park, Los Angeles, CA	Temple Beth Hillel, Plot #3628
MARTIN, Strother	1980	Forest Lawn—Hollywood Hills, Los Angeles, CA	Courts of Remem., G62420
MARVIN, Lee	1987	Arlington National Cemetery, Arlington, VA	Section 7A, Grave 176
MARX, Arthur "Harpo"	1964	Forest Lawn Memorial-Park, Glendale, CA	
MARX, Herbert "Zeppo"	1979	(Cremated—not interred)	Ashes scattered at sea
MARX, Julius "Groucho"	1977	Eden Memorial Park, San Fernando, CA	In the Mausoleum, across from entrance
MARX, Leonard "Chico"	1961	Forest Lawn Memorial-Park, Glendale, CA	Freedom Maus., Sanctuary of Worship
MARX, Milton "Gummo"	1977	Forest Lawn Memorial-Park, Glendale, CA	Freedom Maus., Sanct. of Brotherhood
MARX, Samuel	1992	Westwood Village Mem. Park, Los Angeles, CA	Urn Garden (southeast)
• MARX, Samuel "Frenchie"	1933	Mount Carmel Cemetery, Queens, NY	
MASINA, Giulietta (Fellini)	1994	Civico Cimitero, Rimini, Italy	Section O, in the brown Fellini family vault
MASON, Shirley (Lanfield)	1979	Westwood Village Mem. Park, Los Angeles, CA	Sanctuary of Remembrance
MASSEY, Curt	1991	Westwood Village Mem. Park, Los Angeles, CA	Room of Prayer
MASSEY, Edith	1984	Westwood Village Mem. Park, Los Angeles, CA	Ashes scattered in the Rose Garden
MASSEY, Ilona (Dawson)	1974	Arlington National Cemetery, Arlington, VA	
MASSEY, Raymond	1983	Beaverdale Memorial Park, New Haven, CT	
MATHIS, June	1927	Hollywood Memorial Park, Hollywood, CA	H'wood Cath. Maus., Crypt 1199, Corr A
MATTHEWS, Dorothy (Davis)	1977	Westwood Village Mem. Park, Los Angeles, CA	
MAXWELL, Elsa	1963	Ferncliff Cemetery and Maus., Hartsdale, NY	Rosewood 2, Grave 1132
MAXWELL, Marilyn	1972	(Cremated at Chapel of the Pines, L.A., CA)	Ashes scattered at sea
MAYER, Louis B.	1957	Home of Peace Mem. Park, Los Angeles, CA	Chapel Maus., Corr. of Immortality, SW 405
MAYNARD, Ken	1973	Forest Lawn Memorial-Park, Cypress, CA	
MAYO, Archie	1968	Beth-Olam Cemetery, Hollywood, CA	Mausoleum

• New entry.

* Some cemeteries refuse to reveal specific locations.

. NAME	YEAR	CEMETERY	INTERMENT SITE*
MAYO, Frank	1963	Forest Lawn—Hollywood Hills, Los Angeles, CA	Col. of Remembrance, on left, 60450
McCAREY, Leo	1969	Holy Cross Cem. and Maus., Culver City, CA	
McCORMACK, John	1945	Dean's Grange Cemetery, Booterstown, Ireland	
McCOY, Tim	1978	Mt. Olivet Cemetery, Saginaw, MI	
• McCREA, Joel	1990	(Cremated—not interred)	Ashes scattered at sea north of Ventura, CA
McDANIEL, Hattie	1952	Rose Dale Cemetery, Los Angeles, CA	Section D, across from the office
McDONALD, Marie	1965	Forest Lawn Memorial-Park, Glendale, CA	Freedom Maus., Sanctuary of Heritage
McFARLAND, George	1993	(Cremated)	Ashes given to his family
• McHUGH, Jimmy	1969	Calvary Cemetery, Los Angeles, CA	
McLAGLEN, Victor	1959	Forest Lawn Memorial-Park, Glendale, CA	Garden of Memory, Col. of Eternal Light
• McMCLURE, Doug	1995	Woodlawn Cemetery, Santa Monica, CA	
McNALLY, Stephen	1994	Holy Cross Cem. and Maus., Culver City, CA	Section Y, St. Francis, Plot 35
McNEAR, Howard	1969	Los Angeles National Cemetery, L.A., CA	Columbarium
McQUEEN, "Butterfly"	1995	Body willed to the Medical College of Georgia	
McQUEEN, Steve	1980	(Cremated—not interred)	Ashes scattered in Santa Paula Valley, CA
• McWADE, Edward	1943	Rosehill Cemetery, Chicago, IL	Section 106, Lot 47
• McWADE, Margaret	1956	Rosehill Cemetery, Chicago, IL	Section 106, Lot 47
• McWADE, Robert Jr.	1938	Rosehill Cemetery, Chicago, IL	Section 106, Lot 47
MEADOWS, Audrey (Six)	1996	Holy Cross Cem. and Maus., Culver City, CA	Section F, Tier 29, Grave 57
MEEK, Donald	1946	Fairmount Cemetery, Denver, CO	In Maus., Sect. 392, Tier BB, Main floor
MENJOU, Adolphe	1963	Hollywood Memorial Park, Hollywood, CA	Section 8, Lot 11
MERCER, Beryl	1939	Forest Lawn Memorial-Park, Glendale, CA	Sunrise Slope 337
MERCER, Johnny	1976	Bonaventure Cemetery, Savannah, GA	Section H, Lot 48
MEREDITH, Charles	1964	Westwood Village Mem. Park, Los Angeles, CA	
• MERKEL, Una	1986	Highland Cemetery, Ft. Mitchell, KY	
MEYER, Emile G.	1987	Greenwood Cemetery, New Orleans, LA	
MILESTONE, Lewis	1980	Westwood Village Mem. Park, Los Angeles, CA	Sanctuary of Tranquility
MILLER, Marilyn	1936	Woodlawn Cemetery, The Bronx, NY	Division 50, Heather and Whitewood Ave
MILLER, Marvin E.	1985	Westwood Village Mem. Park, Los Angeles, CA	Sanctuary of Tenderness
• MILLER, Walter C.	1940	Calvary Cemetery, Evanston, IL	
MILLS, Harry F.	1982	Forest Lawn—Hollywood Hills, Los Angeles, CA	Courts of Remem., 3446
MINEO, Sal	1976	Cem. of the Gate of Heaven, Hawthorne, NY	Division 2
MINNELLI, Vincente	1986	Forest Lawn Memorial-Park, Glendale, CA	Small priv. garden in Triumphant Faith Terr.
MINTER, Mary Miles	1984	(Cremated—not interred)	Ashes scattered
MIRANDA, Carmen	1955	Sao Joao Baptista Cem., Rio de Janeiro, Brazil	
• MIRANDA, Willy	1996	Garden of Faith Mem. Gardens, Baltimore, MD	Entombed
• MITCHELL, Cameron	1994	Desert Memorial Park, Cathedral City, CA	
MITCHELL, Margaret	1949	Oakland Cemetery, Atlanta, GA	
MITCHELL, Thomas	1962	Chapel of the Pines Crematory, Los Angeles, CA	
• MITCHUM, Robert	1997	(Cremated)	Ashes scattered at sea off Calif. coast
MIX, Tom	1940	Forest Lawn Memorial-Park, Glendale, CA	Whispering Pines, Grave 986
MONK, Thelonius	1982	Ferncliff Cemetery and Maus., Hartsdale, NY	Hillcrest I, Grave 405
MONROE, Marilyn	1962	Westwood Village Mem. Park, Los Angeles, CA	Corridor of Memories, #24
MONROE, Vaughn	1973	Fernhill Memorial Gardens, Stuart, FL	
• MONTAND, Yves	1991	Pere Lachaise Cemetery, Paris, France	
MONTEAUX, Pierre	1964	Riverside Cemetery, Hancock, ME	
• MONTGOMERY, Elizabeth	1995	Cremated	
• MONTGOMERY, Robert	1981	(Cremated—not interred)	Ashes given to family
MOORE, Grace	1947	Forest Hills Cemetery, Chattanooga, TN	
• MOORE, Jack "Alvy"	1997	Cremated	
MOORE, Victor	1962	Cypress Hills Cemetery, Brooklyn, NY	
MOOREHEAD, Agnes	1974	Dayton Memorial Park, Dayton, OH	
MORELAND, Mantan	1973	Valhalla Memorial Park, N. Hollywood, CA	
• MORENO, Antonio	1967	Forest Lawn—Hollywood Hills, Los Angeles, CA	Great Maus., Sanc. of Valor
MORGAN, Frank	1949	Green-Wood Cemetery, Brooklyn, NY	
MORGAN, Helen	1941	Holy Sepulchre Cemetery, Worth, IL	Section 14, Block 2, Lot 10
MORGAN, Ralph	1956	Green-Wood Cemetery, Brooklyn, NY	The Wupperman lot
MORGAN, Russ	1969	Palm Mortuary Mausoleum, Las Vegas, NV	
MORRIS, Wayne	1959	Arlington National Cemetery, Arlington, VA	
MORRISON, Jim	1971	Père Lachaise Cemetery, Paris, France	Division 6
MORROW, Vic	1982	Hillside Memorial Park, Los Angeles, CA	Mount of Olives, Block 5-80-1
MOWBRAY, Alan	1969	Holy Cross Cem. and Maus., Culver City, CA	

• New entry.

374

* Some cemeteries refuse to reveal specific locations.

NAME	YEAR	CEMETERY	INTERMENT SITE*
MUNI, Paul	1967	Hollywood Memorial Park, Hollywood, CA	Section 14, Row 00, Grave 57
MUNSON, Ona	1955	Ferncliff Cemetery and Maus., Hartsdale, NY	Maus., Unit 8, Tier Y, Col. G, Niche 5
• MURPHY, Audie	1971	Arlington National Cemetery, Arlington, VA	Near the Battleship Maine memorial
MURRAY, J. Harold	1940	Evergreen Cemetery, Killingworth, CT	
MURRAY, Mae	1965	Valhalla Memorial Park, N. Hollywood, CA	Section G, Block 6328, Lot 6
MURROW, Edward R.	1965	Green-Wood Cemetery, Brooklyn, NY	Ashes buried
MUSTIN, Burt	1977	Forest Lawn—Hollywood Hills, Los Angeles, CA	Loving Kindness, Plot #7844
• MYERS, Carmel	1980	(Cremated—not interred)	Ashes strewn in Rose Garden at Pickfair
MYERS, Harry C.	1938	Forest Lawn Memorial-Park, Glendale, CA	Whispering Pines
N			
NAISH, J. Carrol	1973	Calvary Cemetery, Los Angeles, CA	Section G, Lot 1098, Grave 22
NALDI, Nita	1961	Calvary Cemetery, Woodside (Queens), NY	Section 1W, Range AA, Plot 13/14, Grave 5
NATWICK, Mildred	1994	Lorraine Park Cemetery, Baltimore, MD	
NAZIMOVA, Madame Alla	1945	Forest Lawn Memorial-Park, Glendale, CA	Whispering Pines
NEGIN, Koliz	1947	Forest Lawn Memorial-Park, Glendale, CA	
NEGRI, Pola	1987	Calvary Cemetery, Los Angeles, CA	Main Maus., St. Paul Corr, Blk 56, Crypt E19
NEGULESCO, Jean	1993	Marbella, Spain	
NEILL, James	1931	Bonaventure Cemetery, Savannah, GA	Section E, Lot 171
NELSON, Frank	1986	Forest Lawn Memorial-Park, Glendale, CA	Garden of Honor
NELSON, Harriet	1994	Forest Lawn—Hollywood Hills, Los Angeles, CA	Revelation
• NELSON, Nels P.	1994	Valhalla Memorial Park, N. Hollywood, CA	
NELSON, Ozzie	1975	Forest Lawn—Hollywood Hills, Los Angeles, CA	Revelation
NELSON, Rick	1985	Forest Lawn—Hollywood Hills, Los Angeles, CA	Revelation
NEUMANN, Kurt	1958	Home of Peace Mem. Park, Los Angeles, CA	Chapel Maus., Corr. of Eternal Life
NEWELL, William Most	1967	Westwood Village Mem. Park, Los Angeles, CA	
NEWMAN, Alfred	1970	Forest Lawn Memorial-Park, Glendale, CA	Great Maus., Sanctuary of Eternal Prayer
NEWMAN, Lionel	1989	Westwood Village Mem. Park, Los Angeles, CA	
NEWTON, Robert	1965	Chapel of the Pines Crematory, Los Angeles, CA	
• NIBLO, Fred L. Sr.	1948	Forest Lawn Memorial-Park, Glendale, CA	Great Mausoleum
NICHOLS, Barbara	1976	Pinelawn Memorial Park, Farmingdale, L.I., NY	Plot P, Row 3, Grave 34
NICHOLS, Ernest "Red"	1965	Forest Lawn—Hollywood Hills, Los Angeles, CA	Col. of Remembrance, on right, 60780
NICHOLS, George Jr.	1942	Forest Lawn Memorial-Park, Glendale, CA	
Nico (Christa Paffgen)	1988	Grunewald-Forst Cemetery, Berlin, Germany	
NIJINSKY, Vaslav	1950	Montmartre Cemetery, Paris, France	Division 22
NILSSON, Harry	1994	Valley Oaks Mem. Park, Westlake Village, CA	
NIVEN, David	1983	Village Churchyard, Chateau DOex, Switzerland	
NIXON, Pat	1993	Nixon Presidential Library, Yorba Linda, CA	Interred in the garden of the library
NOLAN, Bob	1980	(Cremated)	
NOLAN, Lloyd	1985	Westwood Village Mem. Park, Los Angeles, CA	Section D, #84
NOLAN, Mary	1948	Hollywood Memorial Park, Hollywood, CA	
NORMAND, Mabel (Cody)	1930	Calvary Cemetery, Los Angeles, CA	Main Mausoleum, in a main hallway
NOVARRO, Ramon	1968	Calvary Cemetery, Los Angeles, CA	Section C, Lot 586, Grave 5
NUREYEV, Rudolph	1993	Ste. Genevieve-Des-Bois, Paris, France	(Essone District)
O			
O'BRIEN, Edmond	1985	Holy Cross Cem. and Maus., Culver City, CA	Section F, Tier 54, Grave 50
O'BRIEN, Pat	1983	Holy Cross Cem. and Maus., Culver City, CA	Section F, Tier 56, Grave 62
O'BRIEN, Thomas Everett	1947	Forest Lawn Memorial-Park, Glendale, CA	
O'CONNELL, Helen (Devol)	1993	Holy Cross Cem. and Maus., Culver City, CA	Section CC, Tier 56, Grave 55
O'CONNOR, Una	1959	Calvary Cemetery, Woodside (Queens), NY	
O'HARA, Barry J.	1979	Cremated	Ashes given to his wife, Helen
O'KEEFE, Dennis	1968	(Cremated—not interred)	Ashes scattered at sea
• O'ROURKE, Heather	1988	Westwood Village Mem. Park, Los Angeles, CA	New Mausoleum, 1st column, bottom
• O'SULLIVAN, Maureen	1998	Most Holy Redeemer Cemetery, Niskayuna, NY	
OAKIE, Jack	1978	Forest Lawn Memorial-Park, Glendale, CA	Whispering Pines #1066 hilltop nr Cath. Dr.
OBER, Philip	1982	Chapel of the Pines Crematory, Los Angeles, CA	
OBERON, Merle (Wolders)	1979	Forest Lawn Memorial-Park, Glendale, CA	Garden of Remembrance
ODETS, Clifford	1963	Forest Lawn Memorial-Park, Glendale, CA	Court of Freedom, Col. of Honor
• OGLE, Charles	1940	Forest Lawn Memorial Park, Glendale, CA	
OLAND, Warner	1938	Southborough Cemetery, Southborough, MA	
OLIVER, David	1992	Forest Lawn—Hollywood Hills, Los Angeles, CA	
OLIVER, Edna May	1942	Forest Lawn Memorial-Park, Glendale, CA	Great Maus. - Col. of Security
OLIVIER, Laurence	1989	Westminster Abbey, London, England	Poets' Corner

NAME	YEAR	CEMETERY	INTERMENT SITE*
OLSEN, Moroni	1954	Forest Lawn Memorial-Park, Glendale, CA	
OLSEN, Ole	1963	Palm Mortuary Mausoleum, Las Vegas, NV	Ground burial
ORBISON, Roy	1988	Westwood Village Mem. Park, Los Angeles, CA	Section D, #97 (unmarked) nr. water spigot
ORY, Edward "Kid"	1973	Hollywood Memorial Park, Hollywood, CA	Section "Grotto," Lot 59, Grave 4
OSBORN, Lyn	1958	Forest Lawn Memorial-Park, Glendale, CA	
OUSPENSKAYA, Maria	1949	Chapel of the Pines Crematory, Los Angeles, CA	
• OWEN, Reginald	1972	Morris Hill Cemetery, Boise, ID	
• OWEN, Seena	1966	Hollywood Memorial Park, Hollywood, CA	Abbey of the Psalms, Crypt 2130, Corr G-2
OWENS, Jesse	1980	Oak Woods Cemetery, Chicago, IL	
OWSLEY, Monroe Righter	1937	Forest Lawn Memorial-Park, Glendale, CA	
P			
PADEREWSKI, Ignace Jan	1941	St. John the Baptist Cathedral, Warsaw, Poland	Originally buried in Arlington Nat'l. Cem.
"			His heart is entombed at the Shrine of
"			Our Lady of Czestochowa, Doylestown, PA
"			Reburied in free Poland in 1992.
PAL, George	1980	Holy Cross Cem. and Maus., Culver City, CA	
PALMER, Lilli (Thompson)	1986	Forest Lawn Memorial-Park, Glendale, CA	Court of Freedom
PAM, Anita	1987	Greenwood Memorial Park, Fort Worth, TX	Maus.-Westminster area (Valutage) (NM)
PAN, Hermes	1990	Holy Cross Cem. and Maus., Culver City, CA	Mausoleum, Block 127, Crypt D-5
PANGBORN, Franklin	1958	Forest Lawn Memorial-Park, Glendale, CA	Great Maus. - Col. of Security
PANZER, Paul	1958	Forest Lawn—Hollywood Hills, Los Angeles, CA	
PARKER, Charlie "Bird"	1955	Lincoln Cemetery, Kansas City, KS	
PARKS, Larry	1975	(Cremated)	Ashes buried at his Studio City, CA, home
PARROTT, James	1939	Forest Lawn Memorial-Park, Glendale, CA	Devotion
PARSONS, Louella (Martin)	1972	Holy Cross Cem. and Maus., Culver City, CA	Section D, Lot 235, Grave 8
PATERSON, Pat (Boyer)	1978	Holy Cross Cem. and Maus., Culver City, CA	St. Ann's Garden, Grave 6, Tier 186
• PATRICK, Lee (Wood)	1982	Westwood Village Mem. Park, Los Angeles, CA	Room of Prayer
• PEARSON, Drew	1969		
PEARSON, Drew	1969	(Cremated)	Ashes interred on his farm in Potomac, MD
• PECKHAM, Francis Miles	1959	Lake View Cemetery, Cleveland, OH	
PELLER, Clara	1987	Waldheim Jewish Cemetery, Forest Park, IL	nr. Gate 54
• PENNER, Joe	1941	Forest Lawn Memorial-Park, Glendale, CA	Great Mausoleum
PENNINGTON, Ann	1971	Kensico Cemetery, Valhalla, NY	
PEPPARD, George	1994	Northview Cemetery, Dearborn, MI	
PEPPLE, Sydney Chester	1993	All Saints Episcopal Cemetery, San Luis Rey, CA	Cremated—ashes interred
PEREIRA, Hal	1983	Westwood Village Mem. Park, Los Angeles, CA	
• PERFECT, Rose	1978	Westwood Village Mem. Park, Los Angeles, CA	
• PERKINS, Anthony	1992	Cremated	
• PERKINS, Anthony	1992	Cremated	
PERRY, Antoinette	1946	Woodlawn Cem. and Crematory, The Bronx, NY	
• PETERS, Susan	1952	Forest Lawn Memorial-Park, Glendale, CA	Whispering Pines, at "Finding of Moses"
PHILBIN, Mary	1993	Calvary Cemetery, Los Angeles, CA	
PHOENIX, River	1993	Evergreen Cemetery, Gainesville, FL	
PIAF, Edith	1963	Père Lachaise Cemetery, Paris, France	Black tomb in Division 97
• PIATIGORSKY, Gregor	1976	Westwood Village Mem. Park, Los Angeles, CA	Section D, #154
PICCOLO, Brian	1970	St. Mary's Cemetery, Evergreen Park, IL	
PICKFORD, Jack	1933	Forest Lawn Memorial-Park, Glendale, CA	Garden of Memory
PICKFORD, Lottie	1936	Forest Lawn Memorial-Park, Glendale, CA	Garden of Memory
PICKFORD, Mary	1979	Forest Lawn Memorial-Park, Glendale, CA	Garden of Memory
PIDGEON, Walter	1984	(No funeral)	Body donated to UCLA for med. research
PIERCE, Jack P.	1968	Forest Lawn Memorial-Park, Glendale, CA	Whispering Pines, nr. "Finding of Moses"
PIERLOT, Francis	1955	Forest Lawn Memorial-Park, Glendale, CA	
PINZA, Ezio	1957	Putnam Cemetery, Greenwich, CT	Section L-1
PITTS, Zazu (Woodall)	1963	Holy Cross Cem. and Maus., Culver City, CA	Section "Grotto," Lot 195, Grave 1
POLLARD, Harry "Snub"	1962	Forest Lawn—Hollywood Hills, Los Angeles, CA	Sheltering Hills
POLLARD, Harry A.	1934	Forest Lawn Memorial-Park, Glendale, CA	
PORCARO, Jeff	1992	Forest Lawn—Hollywood Hills, Los Angeles, CA	Lincoln Terrace, Plot #120
PORTER, Cole	1964	Mount Hope Cemetery, Peru, IN	
• PORTER, Edwin S.	1941	Kensico Cemetery, Valhalla, NY	
• POST, Edith	1971	Oak Hill Cemetery, Ballard, CA	
• POST, Wiley	1935	Memorial Park Cemetery, Oklahoma City, OK	
POTEL, Victor	1947	Rosehill Cemetery, Chicago, IL	

NAME	YEAR	CEMETERY	INTERMENT SITE*
POWELL, Dick	1963	Forest Lawn Memorial-Park, Glendale, CA	Garden of Memory, Col. of Honor
POWELL, Eleanor	1982	Hollywood Memorial Park, Hollywood, CA	H. C. Maus., Niche 432, T3, Foyer E/W
POWELL, Lee	1944		Missing in action in the Marianas Islands
POWELL, Richard	1937	Forest Lawn Memorial-Park, Glendale, CA	
POWELL, William	1984	Desert Memorial Park, Palm Springs, CA	Ashes interred in Section B-10, Lot 20
POWER, Tyrone	1958	Hollywood Memorial Park, Hollywood, CA	Section 8, near the Marion Davies Maus.
PRESLEY, Elvis	1977	Graceland, Memphis, TN	
PRICE, Vincent	1993	(Cremated—not interred)	
PRIMA, Louis	1978	Metairie Cemetery, New Orleans, LA	Section 88
• PRINZE, Freddie (Preutzel)	1977	Forest Lawn—Hollywood Hills, Los Angeles, CA	Courts of Remem., Sanctuary of Light
PROHASKA, Janos	1974	Woodlawn Cemetery, Santa Monica, CA	
PROKOFIEV, Sergei	1953	Novodevichy Cemetery, Moscow, Russia	
PULEO, Johnny	1983	Gate of Heaven Cemetery, Silver Spring, MD	
PURVIANCE, Edna	1958	Forest Lawn Memorial-Park, Glendale, CA	
• PYLE, Denver Dell	1997	Forreston Cemetery, Forreston, TX	
R			
RACHMANINOFF, Sergei	1943	Kensico Cemetery, Valhalla, NY	
RADNER, Gilda	1989	Long Ridge Cemetery, Stamford, CT	
RAFT, George	1980	Forest Lawn—Hollywood Hills, Los Angeles, CA	Courts of Remem., Sanctuary of Light
• RAGLAND, John "Rags"	1946	Louisville Evergreen Cemetery, Louisville, KY	
RAINS, Claude	1967	Red Hill Cemetery, Moultonborough, NH	Black marble headstone
RAMBEAU, Marjorie	1970	Desert Memorial Park, Palm Springs, CA	
RAND, Sally	1979	Oakdale Cemetery, Glendora, CA	ELM, Lot 34, Space 10
RANDALL, Addison Owen	1945	Forest Lawn Memorial-Park, Glendale, CA	Gardens of Memory
RANDOLPH, Amanda	1967	Forest Lawn—Hollywood Hills, Los Angeles, CA	Gentleness, under a tree
• RANDOLPH, Lillian	1980	Forest Lawn—Hollywood Hills, Los Angeles, CA	Gentleness, under a tree
RANKIN, Arthur	1947	Forest Lawn Memorial-Park, Glendale, CA	
RAPF, Harry	1949	Home of Peace Mem. Park, Los Angeles, CA	Chapel Maus., Corr. of Immortality
RAPPE, Virginia	1921	Hollywood Memorial Park, Hollywood, CA	Section 8, Lot 257
RATHBONE, Basil	1967	Ferncliff Cemetery and Maus., Hartsdale, NY	Shrine of Mem. Maus., Unit 1, T-K, #117
RAY, Charles	1943	Forest Lawn Memorial-Park, Glendale, CA	
• RAYE, Martha	1994	Fort Bragg Military Cemetery, NC	
REED, Alan	1977		Body donated to Loma Linda Univ. Med. Sch.
REED, Donna	1986	Westwood Village Mem. Park, Los Angeles, CA	Section D, #142
• REED, Florence	1967	Kensico Cemetery, Valhalla, NY	Actors Fund Plot
REED, Robert (Rietz)	1992	Memorial Park Cemetery, Evanston, IL	Section 6, Lot 21, Grave 4
REEVES, George	1959	Mountain View Cemetery, Altadena, CA	Ashes, Pasadena Maus. Sunrise Cor. #3555
REEVES, Jim	1964	Jim Reeves Memorial Park, Carthage, TX	On US Highway 79, 4 miles NE of Carthage
REEVES, Richard J.	1967	Oakwood Memorial Park, Chatsworth, CA	Section Elm, Lot 209, Grave 4
REID, Carl Benton	1973	Forest Lawn—Hollywood Hills, Los Angeles, CA	Enduring Faith, Plot #3722
REID, Wallace	1923	Forest Lawn Memorial-Park, Glendale, CA	Great Maus., Azalea Columbarium
• REINHARDT, Max	1943	Westchester Hills Cem, Hastings-on-Hudson, NY	
RENICK, Ruth	1984	Hollywood Memorial Park, Hollywood, CA	Columbarium, upper north wall, T.4
• REY, Alejandro	1987	Holy Cross Cem. and Maus., Culver City, CA	Section L, Lot 403, Grave 1
REYNOLDS, Adeline De Walt	1961	Westwood Village Mem. Park, Los Angeles, CA	
REYNOLDS, Frank	1983	Arlington National Cemetery, Arlington, VA	
• REYNOLDS, Lynn	1927	Hollywood Memorial Park, Hollywood, CA	Section 8
REYNOLDS, Quentin	1965	Holy Cross Cemetery, Brooklyn, NY	
RHODES, Erik	1990	El Reno Cemetery, El Reno, OK	Ashes buried New Add., Blk 14, Lot 24-A
• RICE, Adnia	1987	Rose Hill Cemetery, Fayetteville, TN	
RICE, Grantland	1954	Woodlawn Cem. and Crematory, The Bronx, NY	
RICH, Buddy	1987	Westwood Village Mem. Park, Los Angeles, CA	Sanc. of Tranquility, 2nd column, bottom
RICHARDS, Addison	1964	Forest Lawn Memorial-Park, Glendale, CA	
RICHARDSON, (Sir) Ralph	1983	Highgate East Cemetery, London, England	Near Main Road
RICHARDSON, Jiles	1959	Forest Lawn Memorial Park, Beaumont, TX	Block C, Lot 31, Space 3
RICHMAN, Harry	1972	Hillside Memorial Park, Los Angeles, CA	Garden of Memories, Alcove of Love B319
RIDDLE, Nelson	1985	Westwood Village Mem. Park, Los Angeles, CA	In the main "grassy" section
• RIORDAN, Marjorie (Schlaff)	1984	Westwood Village Mem. Park, Los Angeles, CA	Section D, #1
RIPLEY, Robert L.	1949	Rural Cemetery, Santa Rosa, CA	
RIPPERTON, Minnie	1979	Westwood Village Mem. Park, Los Angeles, CA	Section D (a few ft. east of Dorothy Stratten)
RITCHARD, Cyril	1977	St. Mary's Cemetery, Ridgefield, CT	
RITCHIE, Billie	1921	Forest Lawn—Hollywood Hills, Los Angeles, CA	

• New entry.

* Some cemeteries refuse to reveal specific locations.

NAME	YEAR	CEMETERY	INTERMENT SITE*
RITTER, Tex	1974	Oak Bluff Memorial Park, Port Neches, TX	Section 8
RITZ, Al	1965	Hollywood Memorial Park, Hollywood, CA	T-Bldg., T-4, Bottom row, right side
RITZ, Harry	1986	Hollywood Memorial Park, Hollywood, CA	T-Bldg., 3rd floor
RITZ, Jimmy	1985	Hollywood Memorial Park, Hollywood, CA	T-Bldg., T-5 (left side)
ROACH, Hal Jr.	1972	Calvary Cemetery, Los Angeles, CA	Block 14, Crypt 11 (at top)
ROACH, Hal Sr.	1992	Woodlawn Cemetery, Elmira, NY	Just inside the Walnut St. gate, 1st turn rt.
ROBARDS, Jason Sr.	1963	Forest Lawn—Hollywood Hills, Los Angeles, CA	Remembrance, Grave 975 (at curb)
ROBBINS, Fred	1992	Hebrew Friendship Cemetery, Baltimore, MD	
ROBBINS, Marty	1982	Woodlawn Memorial Park, Nashville, TN	
ROBERSON, C. H. "Chuck"	1988	Forest Lawn—Hollywood Hills, Los Angeles, CA	
ROBERTS, Florence	1940	Forest Lawn Memorial-Park, Glendale, CA	
• ROBERTS, Lynne (Mary Hart)	1978	Forest Lawn—Hollywood Hills, Los Angeles, CA	Buried beside her mother
ROBERTS, Rachel	1980	Chapel of the Pines Crematory, Los Angeles, CA	
ROBERTS, Roy	1975	Greenwood Memorial Park, Fort Worth, TX	314 - 42
ROBERTS, Theodore	1928	Hollywood Memorial Park, Hollywood, CA	Pineland
ROBESON, Paul	1976	Ferncliff Cemetery and Maus., Hartsdale, NY	Hillcrest A, Grave 1511
ROBINSON, Bill "Bojangles"	1949	Evergreen Cemetery, Brooklyn, NY	
ROBINSON, Dar Allen	1988	Forest Lawn—Hollywood Hills, Los Angeles, CA	
ROBINSON, Edward G.	1973	Beth-El Cemetery, Ridgewood (Queens), NY	
• ROBINSON, Edward G. Jr.	1973	Hollywood Memorial Park, Hollywood, CA	Abbey of the Psalms, Crypt 4386, Corr E-4
ROBINSON, Jackie	1972	Cypress Hills Cemetery, Brooklyn, NY	
ROBINSON, Sugar Ray	1989	Inglewood Park Cemetery, Inglewood, CA	Pinecrest Addition (top of hill), Lot 24
ROBSON, (Dame) Flora	1984	St. Nicholas Churchyard, Brighton, England	
• ROBSON, May	1942	Flushing Cemetery, Flushing (Queens), NY	Sect. 9, plain stone has fam. name 'Brown'
ROCKNE, Knute	1931	Highland Cemetery, South Bend, IN	
RODGERS, Richard	1979	(Cremated—not interred)	Ashes scattered
ROGERS, Ginger	1995	Oakwood Memorial Park, Chatsworth, CA	Section E, Lot 303, Space 1
ROGERS, Will	1935	Will Rogers Memorial, Claremore, OK	Reinterred in 1944 from Forest Lawn, CA
ROLAND, Ruth M.	1937	Forest Lawn Memorial-Park, Glendale, CA	Great Mausoleum, Azalea Columbarium
ROMBERG, Sigmund	1951	Ferncliff Cemetery and Maus., Hartsdale, NY	Maus., Unit 1, Sect. BC-1, Crypt 5
• ROMERO, Cesar	1994	Inglewood Park Cemetery, Inglewood, CA	Golden West Maus., Alcove of Music, Cr. 408
ROONEY, Pat II	1962	Evergreen Cemetery, Brooklyn, NY	
ROPER, Jack	1966	Cremated	Ashes given to his wife
RORKE, Hayden	1987	Holy Cross Cem. and Maus., Culver City, CA	
ROSE, Billy	1966	Westchester Hills Cem, Hastings-on-Hudson, NY	
ROSE, David	1990	Mount Sinai Memorial-Park, Los Angeles, CA	In Maus. behind the Garden of Heritage
ROSENBLOOM, Maxie	1976	Valhalla Memorial Park, N. Hollywood, CA	Section J, Block 9820, Space 3
ROSING, Bodil Ann	1942	Forest Lawn Memorial-Park, Glendale, CA	
ROSS, Joe E.	1982	Forest Lawn—Hollywood Hills, Los Angeles, CA	SummerLand, Plot #148
• ROSS, Margery J.	1992	East Lawn Memorial Park, Sacramento, CA	
ROSSON, Richard	1953	Hollywood Memorial Park, Hollywood, CA	Section 8, near Cecil B. DeMille
ROTH, Lillian	1980	Mount Pleasant Cemetery, Hawthorne, NY	
RUBENSTEIN, Artur	1982	Jerusalem, Israel	Buried in a special plot in forest outside city
RUGGLES, Charlie	1970	Forest Lawn Memorial-Park, Glendale, CA	Garden of Memory
• RUGGLES, Wesley	1972	Forest Lawn Memorial-Park, Glendale, CA	Garden of Memory
RUNYON, Damon	1946	(Cremated—not interred)	Ashes scattered by air over New York City
RUSSELL, Gail (Moseley)	1961	Valhalla Memorial Park, N. Hollywood, CA	Evergreen Section, Curb #4795
RUSSELL, Lillian	1922	Allegheny Cemetery, Pittsburgh, PA	In Mausoleum, Section 40, Space 5
RUSSELL, Rosalind (Brisson)	1976	Holy Cross Cem. and Maus., Culver City, CA	Section M, Lot 536, Grave 2
RUTH, George Herman "Babe"	1948	Cem. of the Gate of Heaven, Hawthorne, NY	Sect. 25 (at 10-ft. tall gray granite marker)
• RYAN, Edmon	1984	Cave Hill Cemetery, Louisville, KY	
RYAN, Irene	1973	Woodlawn Cemetery, Santa Monica, CA	In Mausoleum, 109-C-1
Sabu	1963	(See DASTAGIR, Sabu)	
SAGAL, Boris	1981	Forest Lawn—Hollywood Hills, Los Angeles, CA	Sheltering Hills
SAKALL, S. Z. "Cuddles"	1955	Forest Lawn Memorial-Park, Glendale, CA	Garden of Memory, as 'Szoke Szakall'
• SALE, Charles P. "Chic"	1936	Forest Lawn Memorial-Park, Glendale, CA	Great Mausoleum - Unity Col.
SAMPLES, Junior	1983	Sawnee View Mem. Garden, Cumming, GA	
SANDERS, (Col.) Harland	1980	Cave Hill Cemetery, Louisville, KY	
• SANDERS, Al	1995	Arbutus Memorial Park, Baltimore, MD	
SANDS, Billy	1984	Hillside Memorial Park, Los Angeles, CA	Courts of the Books, Sec. Jacob, bottom row
• SANDS, Diana	1973	Ferncliff Cemetery and Maus., Hartsdale, NY	Ashewood, Grave 545

• New entry.

* Some cemeteries refuse to reveal specific locations.

NAME	YEAR	CEMETERY	INTERMENT SITE*
SATIE, Erik	1925	Arcueil Cemetery, Paris, France	
SAVALAS, George	1985	Forest Lawn—Hollywood Hills, Los Angeles, CA	Lincoln Terrace, Plot #4596
SAVALAS, Telly	1994	Forest Lawn—Hollywood Hills, Los Angeles, CA	Garden of Heritage, Plot #1281
SCALA, Gia	1972	Holy Cross Cem. and Maus., Culver City, CA	Section M, 3 spaces left of Plot 581
SCHAEFFER, Rebecca	1989	Ahavai Sholom Cemetery, Portland, OR	
SCHAFFNER, Franklin J.	1989	Westwood Village Mem. Park, Los Angeles, CA	Lot 236
SCHERTZINGER, Victor	1941	Forest Lawn Memorial-Park, Glendale, CA	
SCHILDKRAUT, Joseph	1964	Hollywood Memorial Park, Hollywood, CA	Beth Olam Mausoleum, Niche 43
SCHLESINGER, Leon	1949	Beth-Olam Cemetery, Hollywood, CA	Mausoleum, ashes in vault
SCHNEIDER, Romy	1982	Boissy-Sans-Avoir (nr. Paris), France	
SCHUMANN-HEINK, Ernestine	1936	Greenwood Memorial Park, San Diego, CA	Cathedral Mausoleum, Corr. of Sunshine
SCHWARTZ, Maurice	1960	Mount Hebron Cem., Flushing (Queens), NY	
• SCOTT, Hazel	1981	Flushing Cemetery, Flushing (Queens), NY	Sect. 9, next to ex-husb. Adam C. Powell Sr.
SCOTT, Randolph	1987	Charlotte, NC	Buried in the family plot
• SCOTT, Randolph	1987	Ellmwood Cemetery, Charlotte, N.C.	
SCOTT, Zachary	1965	Austin Memorial Park, Austin, TX	Block 4, Lot 187A, Space 12
SEBASTIAN, Dorothy	1957	Holy Cross Cem. and Maus., Culver City, CA	
SEBERG, Jean	1979	Montparnasse Cemetery, Paris, France	Division 13
SEDDON, Margaret	1968	Greenmount Cemetery, Baltimore, MD	
• SEDGWICK, Edie	1971	Oak Hill Cemetery, Ballard, CA	
SEITZ, George B.	1944	Forest Lawn Memorial-Park, Glendale, CA	
• SELLERS, Peter	1980	Golders Green Cemetery, London, England	
SELWYN, Edgar	1944	Salem Field Cemetery, Brooklyn, NY	
SELWYN, Ruth (Warburton)	1954	Forest Lawn Memorial-Park, Glendale, CA	Gardens of Memory
SELZNICK, David O.	1965	Forest Lawn Memorial-Park, Glendale, CA	Great Maus., Sanctuary of Trust
• SELZNICK, Myron	1944	Forest Lawn Memorial-Park, Glendale, CA	
SENECA, Joe	1996	Cleveland, OH	
SENNETT, Mack	1960	Holy Cross Cem. and Maus., Culver City, CA	Section N, Lot 490, Grave 1
SERLING, Rod	1975	Interlaken Cemetery, Interlaken, NY	
• SEYMOUR, Dan	1993	Hillside Memorial Park, Los Angeles, CA	Mount of Olives, Block 7, Gr. 175-1
SHAKUR, Tupac	1996	(Cremated)	
SHANNON, Peggy	1941	Hollywood Memorial Park, Hollywood, CA	Section 5, Plot 43 (two rows in from road)
• SHARPE, David H.	1980	(Cremated)	
SHAW, George Bernard	1950	(Cremated—not interred)	Ashes scattered in his garden
SHAW, Reta	1982	Forest Lawn—Hollywood Hills, Los Angeles, CA	Col. of Remembrance, on left, 60402
SHAWN, Dick	1987	Hillside Memorial Park, Los Angeles, CA	Mausoleum, Memorial Court-734
• SHAY, Dorothy	1978	Westwood Village Mem. Park, Los Angeles, CA	
• SHEA, Donald J. "Shorty"	1969		His body has never been found
SHEAN, Al	1949	Mount Pleasant Cemetery, Hawthorne, NY	
SHEARER, Norma (Thalberg)	1983	Forest Lawn Memorial-Park, Glendale, CA	Great Maus., Sanctuary of Benediction
SHEEN, (Bishop) Fulton J.	1979	St. Patrick's Cathedral, New York, NY	In a crypt below the altar
SHERIDAN, Ann	1967	Chapel of the Pines Crematory, Los Angeles, CA	In vault #57542, not avail. for viewing
SHERMAN, Allan	1973	Hillside Memorial Park, Los Angeles, CA	Mausoleum, Columbarium of Hope, #513
SHERMAN, Lowell	1934	Forest Lawn Memorial-Park, Glendale, CA	Great Maus., Sanctuary of Trust
SHORE, Dinah	1994	Hillside Memorial Park, Los Angeles, CA	Courts of the Book, Isaiah-V-247
SHOSTAKOVICH, Dimitri	1975	Novodevichy Cemetery, Moscow, Russia	
• SHUMAN, Roy	1973	Kensico Cemetery, Valhalla, NY	Actors Fund Plot
• SIGNORET, Simone	1985	Le Pere Lachaise, Paris, France	
SILLS, Milton	1930	Rosehill Cemetery, Chicago, IL	
SILVERHEELS, Jay	1980	(Cremated at Chapel of the Pines, L.A., CA)	Ashes returned to his native Ontario, Can.
SILVERS, Phil	1985	Mount Sinai Memorial-Park, Los Angeles, CA	Garden of Heritage, Vault 1004
SIMON, S. Sylvan	1951	Forest Lawn Memorial-Park, Glendale, CA	Great Maus., Col. of Memory, Niche #20174
• SINGLETON, Catherine M.	1969	Mount Olivet Cemetery, Fort Worth, TX	Garden of Our Lady of Peace D, 136-B
• SKELTON, Red	1997	Forest Lawn Memorial-Park, Glendale, CA	Great Mausoleum
• STIKA, Emil	1998	Conejo Mountain Memorial Park, Camarillo, CA	Site #139
• SKINNER, Cornelia Otis	1979	Oak Grove Cemetery, Fall River, MA	
• SKOURAS, Spyros	1971	Cem. of the Gate of Heaven, Hawthorne, NY	
SLOANE, Everett	1965	Rose Dale Cemetery, Los Angeles, CA	
• SMALLEY, W. Phillips	1939	Forest Lawn—Hollywood Hills, Los Angeles, CA	Col. of Remembrance, on right, 60750
SMITH, C. Aubrey	1948	Chapel of the Pines Cemetery, Los Angeles, CA	
• SMITH, Hal	1994	Woodlawn Cemetery, Santa Monica, CA	
SMITH, Joseph	1981	Woodlawn Cem. and Crematory, The Bronx, NY	

• New entry.	379	* Some cemeteries refuse to reveal specific locations.

Specific Interment Locations — by Name

NAME	YEAR	CEMETERY	INTERMENT SITE*
• SMITH, Kate	1986	St. Agnes Cemetery, Lake Placid, NY	In a small private mausoleum
SOKOLOFF, Vladimir	1962	Hollywood Memorial Park, Hollywood, CA	
SOO, Jack	1979	Forest Lawn—Hollywood Hills, Los Angeles, CA	Eternal Love, Plot #3980
• SOUSA, John Philip	1932	Congressional Cemetery, Washington, D.C.	Range 77, Site 163-S
SPARKS, Ned	1957	Victor Valley Memorial Park, Victorville, CA	
SPERLING, Milton	1988	Mount Sinai Memorial-Park, Los Angeles, CA	
ST. DENIS, Ruth	1968	Forest Lawn—Hollywood Hills, Los Angeles, CA	Courts of Remem.
STAFFORD, Hanley	1968	Forest Lawn Memorial-Park, Glendale, CA	
STAHL, John M.	1950	Forest Lawn Memorial-Park, Glendale, CA	Great Mausoleum - Begonia Corridor
STANDER, Lionel	1994	Forest Lawn Memorial-Park, Glendale, CA	Court of Freedom, left of Maus. entrance
• STANISLAVSKY, Konstantin S.	1938	Novo-Devichy Cemetery, Moscow	
STANWYCK, Barbara	1990	(Cremated—not interred)	Ashes scattered over Lone Pine, CA
STEELE, Bob	1988	Forest Lawn—Hollywood Hills, Los Angeles, CA	Col. of Remembrance, on right, 60722
STEINER, Max	1971	Forest Lawn Memorial-Park, Glendale, CA	Great Maus., Sanctuary of Sacred Promise
STEPHENSON, Henry	1956	Kensico Cemetery, Valhalla, NY	Actors Fund Plot
STEPHENSON, James	1941	Forest Lawn Memorial-Park, Glendale, CA	
• STEVENS, George	1975	Forest Lawn—Hollywood Hills, Los Angeles, CA	Morning Light, Space 3, Plot 8034
STEVENS, Inger	1970	(Cremated—not interred)	Ashes scattered at sea
• STEVENS, Inger	1970	Cremated	Ashes scattered at sea
STEVENS, John Landers	1940	Forest Lawn Memorial-Park, Glendale, CA	
STEWART, Anita (Converse)	1961	Forest Lawn Memorial-Park, Glendale, CA	
• STEWART, James	1998	Forest Lawn Memorial-Park, Glendale, CA	Wee Kirk Churchyard, Space 2, Lot 8
STOKOWSKI, Leopold	1977	St. Marylebone Cemetery, London, England	East Avenue at Rosemary
• STONE, Fred	1959	Forest Lawn—Hollywood Hills, Los Angeles, CA	
STONE, Lewis	1953	Kensico Cemetery, Lawrence Park, Bronxville, NY	
STONE, Milburn	1980	El Camino Memorial Park, La Jolla, CA	Vista del Lago, 401-D
STRANGE, Glenn	1973	Forest Lawn—Hollywood Hills, Los Angeles, CA	Churchyard, Plot #4295
STRASBERG, Lee	1982	Westchester Hills Cem, Hastings-on-Hudson, NY	
STRATTEN, Dorothy	1980	Westwood Village Mem. Park, Los Angeles, CA	Section D, #170
STROMBERG, Hunt	1968	Calvary Cemetery, Los Angeles, CA	Section H, Lot 416 (by tree)
STURGES, Preston	1959	Ferncliff Cemetery and Maus., Hartsdale, NY	Maplewood R, Garden Grave 74
SULLAVAN, Margaret	1960	St. Mary's Whitechapel Church, Lancaster, PA	In churchyard, near curve in path
• SULLIVAN, Ed	1974	Ferncliff Cemetery and Maus., Hartsdale, NY	Maus., Unit 8, Alcove G, Side Comp. 122
• SULLIVAN, Francis L.	1956	Calvary Cemetery, Woodside (Queens), NY	
SUMMERVILLE, Slim	1946	Inglewood Park Cemetery, Inglewood, CA	
• SUTTON, Frank	1974	Greenwood Cemetery, Clarksville, TN	
SWIFT, Paul "Eggman"	1994	New Cathedral Cemetery, Baltimore, MD	
SWITZER, Carl "Alfalfa"	1959	Hollywood Memorial Park, Hollywood, CA	Section 6, Lot 26, Grave 6
T			
TALMADGE, Constance	1973	Hollywood Memorial Park, Hollywood, CA	Abbey of the Psalms, Family Rm, Corr G-7
TALMADGE, Natalie	1969	Hollywood Memorial Park, Hollywood, CA	Abbey of the Psalms, Family Rm, Corr G-7
TALMADGE, Norma	1957	Hollywood Memorial Park, Hollywood, CA	Abbey of the Psalms, Family Rm, Corr G-7
TALMAN, William	1968	Forest Lawn—Hollywood Hills, Los Angeles, CA	Garden of Heritage, Garden Crypt 633
TANGUAY, Eva	1947	Hollywood Memorial Park, Hollywood, CA	Abbey of the Psalms, Crypt 0558, Corr. D-1
TATE, Sharon (Polanski)	1969	Holy Cross Cem. and Maus., Culver City, CA	St. Ann's Garden, Grave 6, Tier 152
TATUM, Art	1956	Rose Dale Cemetery, Los Angeles, CA	Section 5, in Row 178
TATUM, Reece "Goose"	1967	Ft. Bliss National Cemetery, El Paso, TX	Section D, Grave 2668
TAUBER, Richard	1948	Brompton Cemetery, London, England	First sect. left of center path (nr. entrance)
• TAYBACK, Victor	1990	Forest Lawn—Hollywood Hills, Los Angeles, CA	Sheltering Hills, Plot #3813
TAYLOR, Estelle	1958	Hollywood Memorial Park, Hollywood, CA	
TAYLOR, Kent	1987	Westwood Village Mem. Park, Los Angeles, CA	Sanctuary of Remembrance
TAYLOR, Laurette (Cooney)	1946	Woodlawn Cemetery, The Bronx, NY	
TAYLOR, Robert	1969	Forest Lawn Memorial-Park, Glendale, CA	Garden of Honor, Col. of the Evening Star
TAYLOR, William Desmond	1922	Hollywood Memorial Park, Hollywood, CA	H'wood Cath. Maus. Crypt 594 (W.D.Tanner)
TEAGARDEN, Jack	1964	Forest Lawn—Hollywood Hills, Los Angeles, CA	
TEMPLETON, Fay	1939	Kensico Cemetery, Valhalla, NY	Actors Fund Plot
TERRELL, Kenneth	1966	Oakwood Memorial Park, Chatsworth, CA	Section Hollypoint, Lot 327
• THALBERG, Irving Grant	1936	Forest Lawn Memorial-Park, Glendale, CA	Great Maus., Sanctuary of Benediction
THOMAS, Lowell	1981	Quaker Hill Christ Church Cem., Pawling NY	
• THOMAS, William "Buckwheat"	1980	Inglewood Park Cemetery, Inglewood, CA	777 Acacia Slope, Grave 1
• THOMSON, Fred	1928	Forest Lawn Memorial-Park, Glendale, CA	
• THORNDYKE, Sybil	1976	Westminster Abbey, London, England	

• New entry. * Some cemeteries refuse to reveal specific locations.

NAME	YEAR	CEMETERY	INTERMENT SITE*
THORPE, Jim	1953	Thorpe Mausoleum, Jim Thorpe, PA	
THUNDERCLOUD, Chief	1955	Forest Lawn Memorial-Park, Glendale, CA	Great Maus., Corridor of Mercy, Crypt 7355
TIBBETT, Lawrence	1960	Forest Lawn Memorial-Park, Glendale, CA	Whispering Pines
• TIERNEY, Gene	1991	Glenwood Cemetery, Houston, TX	
TINCHER, Fay	1983	Silver Mount Cemetery, Staten Island, NY	
TINDALL, Loren	1973	Memorial Park, Oklahoma City, OK	Section 18, Lot 61, Space 6
TIOMKIN, Dimitri	1979	Forest Lawn Memorial-Park, Glendale, CA	Great Maus., Col. of Memory, Niche #19425
TODD, Mike (Goldbogen)	1958	Waldheim Jewish Cemetery, Forest Park, IL	S.W. nr. Gate 63
• TODD, Thelma	1935	Forest Lawn Memorial-Park, Glendale, CA	Section 19, Lot 5548
• TODISCO, Mario	1996	St. Raymond's Cemetery, The Bronx, NY	
• TOLAND, Gregg	1948	Hollywood Memorial Park, Hollywood, CA	Chapel of the Pines Mausoleum
• TOLER, Sidney	1947	Highland Cemetery, Wichita, KA	
TOMACK, Sid	1962	Desert Memorial Park, Palm Springs, CA	Section A-9, Lot 14
TORRENCE, Ernest	1933	Forest Lawn Memorial-Park, Glendale, CA	Great Maus., Col. of Prayer, Niche #10677
TORRES, Raquel	1987	Forest Lawn Memorial-Park, Glendale, CA	Great Maus., Hall of Celestial Peace
• TOSCANINI, Arturo	1957	Cimitero Monumentale, Milan, Italy	In the family's white marble mausoleum
TRACY, Lee	1968	Evergreen Cemetery, Shavertown, PA	
TRACY, Spencer	1967	Forest Lawn Memorial-Park, Glendale, CA	Garden of Everlasting Peace
TRAINOR, Leonard E.	1940	Forest Lawn Memorial-Park, Glendale, CA	
TRAUBEL, Helen (Bass)	1972	Westwood Village Mem. Park, Los Angeles, CA	Sanctuary of Remembrance
TRAVERS, Henry	1965	Forest Lawn Memorial-Park, Glendale, CA	Great Maus., Hall of Inspiration
Trigger	1965	Roy Rogers–Dale Evans Museum, Victorville, CA	On display in the museum
TROTTER, John Scott	1975	Sharon Cemetery, Charlotte, NC	
TROWBRIDGE, Charles	1967	Forest Lawn—Hollywood Hills, Los Angeles, CA	Remembrance, Plot #233
TRUEX, Ernest	1973	Flushing Cemetery, Flushing (Queens), NY	
• TRUFFAUT, François	1984	Montmartre Cemetery, Paris, France	Div. 21, near entrance, on Ave. Berlioz
TUBB, Ernest	1984	Hermitage Memorial Gardens, Hermitage, TN	
TUCKER, Forrest	1986	Forest Lawn—Hollywood Hills, Los Angeles, CA	Courts of Remem., Col. of Radiant Dawn
TUCKER, Richard	1975	Mt. Lebanon Cemetery, Glendale (Queens), NY	
• TUCKER, Sophie	1966	Emanuel Cemetery, Wethersfield, CT	
• TUFTS, Sonny	1970	Chapel of the Pines Cemetery, Los Angeles, CA	
TUNNEY, Gene	1978	Long Ridge Cemetery, Stamford, CT	
TURPIN, Ben	1940	Forest Lawn Memorial-Park, Glendale, CA	Great Mausoleum, Azalea Columbarium
TUTTLE, Frank W.	1963	Westwood Village Mem. Park, Los Angeles, CA	Section D, #105
• TUTTLE, Lurene	1986	Forest Lawn Memorial-Park, Glendale, CA	Whispering Pines, Lot #1570
• TWELVETREES, Helen	1958	Middletown Cemetery, Middletown, PA	
TYLER, Judy	1957	Ferncliff Cemetery, Hartsdale, NY	
U			
• UTTAL, Ivan	1997	Elmhurst Cemetery, Joliet, ILL	
V			
VALENS, Ritchie	1959	San Fernando Mission Cem., San Fernando, CA	Section C, at Curb No. 247, 3 rows in
VALENTINO, Rudolph	1926	Hollywood Memorial Park, Hollywood, CA	H'wood Cath. Maus., #1205, off Corr A
VALLEE, Rudy	1986	St. Hyacinth's Church Cemetery, Westbrook, ME	
VAN, Bobby	1980	Mount Sinai Memorial-Park, Los Angeles, CA	Maimonides, Plot #5728
VANCE, Vivian	1979	(Cremated)	
VanCLEEF, Lee	1989	Forest Lawn—Hollywood Hills, Los Angeles, CA	Serenity, Lot #156
• VanDYKE, Woody S. II	1944	Forest Lawn Memorial-Park, Glendale, CA	
VanZANT, Ronnie	1977	Jacksonville Memorial Gardens, Jacksonville, FL	
VAUGHAN, Stevie Ray	1990	Laurel Land Memorial Park, Dallas, TX	Private estate nr. Section 11
VAUGHN, Billy	1991	Oak Hill Cemetery, Escondido, CA	
VEIDT, Conrad	1943	Ferncliff Cemetery and Maus., Hartsdale, NY	
• VELEZ, Lupe	1944	Pateon Delores Cemetery, Mexico City, Mexico	
• VENABLE, Evelyn	1993	Cremated	
Vera-Ellen	1981	Glen Haven Memorial Park, San Fernando, CA	
VERNON, Bobby	1939	Forest Lawn Memorial-Park, Glendale, CA	
• VIDOR, Charles	1959	Home of Peace Mem. Park, Los Angeles, CA	Warner Maus. (was Harry's son-in-law)
VIGO, Jean	1934	Bagneux Cemetery, Paris, France	
VINCENT, Romo	1989	Westwood Village Mem. Park, Los Angeles, CA	Sanc. of Tranquility, on right, 4 bays up
VIVYAN, John	1983	Westwood Village Mem. Park, Los Angeles, CA	Room of Prayer, at wall EE, #175
VonERICH, Chris	1991	Grove Hill Memorial Park, Dallas, TX	Hilltop Lot 535, Space 4
VonERICH, David	1984	Grove Hill Memorial Park, Dallas, TX	Hilltop Lot 535
VonERICH, Kerry	1993	Grove Hill Memorial Park, Dallas, TX	Hilltop near Lot 535

• New entry.

* Some cemeteries refuse to reveal specific locations.

NAME	YEAR	CEMETERY	INTERMENT SITE*
VonERICH, Michael	1987	Grove Hill Memorial Park, Dallas, TX	Hilltop Lot 535
VonSTERNBERG, Josef	1969	Westwood Village Mem. Park, Los Angeles, CA	Sanctuary of Remembrance
W			
• WADSWORTH, Henry	1974	Maysville Cemetery, Maysville, KY	
WAGENHEIM, Charles	1979	Westwood Village Mem. Park, Los Angeles, CA	
• WAGNER, "Gorgeous" George	1963	Valhalla Memorial Park, N. Hollywood, CA	Section G, Block 6659, Sp. 2, next to mother
WALD, Jerry	1962	Forest Lawn Memorial-Park, Glendale, CA	
WALDRON, Charles D.	1946	Forest Lawn Memorial-Park, Glendale, CA	
WALKER, June	1966	Westwood Village Mem. Park, Los Angeles, CA	
WALLER, Eddy	1977	Forest Lawn—Hollywood Hills, Los Angeles, CA	Col. of Remembrance, on left, #60409
WALLER, Thomas "Fats"	1943	(Cremated—not interred)	Ashes scattered over Harlem, NY
WALLING, Effie Bond	1961	Forest Lawn Memorial-Park, Glendale, CA	
WALLIS, Hal	1986	Forest Lawn Memorial-Park, Glendale, CA	Great Mausoleum
WALTHALL, Henry B.	1936	Hollywood Memorial Park, Hollywood, CA	Abbey of the Psalms
• WALTHALL, Wallace	1971	Restland Memorial Park, Dallas, TX	Acacia 288, Grave 2-3
WALTON, William	1983	(Cremated)	Ashes buried at his home on Ischia Island
WARFIELD, David	1951	Ferncliff Cemetery and Maus., Hartsdale, NY	St. Paul, Plot 180, Grave 1
WARHOL, Andy	1987	St, John the Baptist Byzantine Cem, Bethel, PA	
WARNER, Harry B.	1958	Home of Peace Mem. Park, Los Angeles, CA	Warner Maus., Section D, Plot 16
WARNER, Harry M.	1958	Home of Peace Mem. Park, Los Angeles, CA	
WARNER, Jack L.	1978	Home of Peace Mem. Park, Los Angeles, CA	Section "Joshua," look for sm. sparrow statue
WARNER, Jack M.	1995	Hillside Memorial Park, Los Angeles, CA	
WARNER, Sam	1927	Home of Peace Mem. Park, Los Angeles, CA	In Mausoleum
• WARREN, Harry	1981	Westwood Village Mem. Park, Los Angeles, CA	Sanctuary of Tenderness, 5th col. bottom
WASHINGTON, Dinah	1963	Burr Oak Cemetery, Alsip, IL	Elmgrove section, Lot 155
• WATERS, Ethel	1977	Forest Lawn Memorial-Park, Glendale, CA	Ascension Garden (center)
WATSON, Minor	1965	Alton City Cemetery, Alton, IL	Nr. Mausoleum, Block 13, Lot 2
WAXMAN, Franz	1967	Beth-Olam Cemetery, Hollywood, CA	Mausoleum, ashes in urn at 2nd entrance
WAYNE, John	1979	Pacific View Mem. Park, Newport Beach, CA	Top of hill, grave unmarked, L. of C. Iversons
• WEAVER, Winstead 'Doodles"	1983	Avalon Cemetery, Santa Catalina Island, CA	
WEBB, Clifton	1966	Hollywood Memorial Park, Hollywood, CA	Abbey of the Psalms, Crypt 2350, Corr G-6
WEBB, Jack	1982	Forest Lawn—Hollywood Hills, Los Angeles, CA	Sheltering Hills, Plot #1999
• WEBER, Joe	1942	Hollywood Memorial Park, Hollywood, CA	Cremated; remains placed in a vault
WEEDE, Robert	1972	Queen of Heaven Cemetery, Lafayette, CA	
WEISSMULLER, Johnny	1984	Valley of Light Cemetery, Acapulco, Mexico	
WELK, Lawrence	1992	Holy Cross Cem. and Maus., Culver City, CA	Section Y, Tier 9, Grave 110
• WELLMAN, William A.	1975	(Cremated—not interred)	Ashes scattered from a WWI fighter plane
WELLS, H. G.	1946	(Cremated—not interred)	Ashes tossed into the English Channel
WELLS, Mary	1992	Forest Lawn Memorial-Park, Glendale, CA	Freedom Maus., Columbarium of Patriots
WEST, Brooks	1984	Westwood Village Mem. Park, Los Angeles, CA	Section D, #81
WEST, Mae	1980	Cypress Hills Cemetery, Brooklyn, NY	In a family Crypt, 3rd floor
WESTMORE, Ernest	1967	Hollywood Memorial Park, Hollywood, CA	Section 8, three-in from the road
WESTMORE, Perc	1970	Forest Lawn Memorial-Park, Glendale, CA	Garden of Remem., #1751, 3-in from walk
WHALE, James	1957	Forest Lawn Memorial-Park, Glendale, CA	Great Maus., Col. of Memory, Niche #20076
WHEELER, Bert	1968	Calvary Cemetery, Woodside (Queens), NY	Sect. 47, Catholic Actors Guild of America
• WHELAN, Arleen (Cagney)	1993	Holy Cross Cem. and Maus., Culver City, CA	
• WHITE, Jesse	1997	Mount Sinai Memorial Park, Los Angeles, CA	
• WHITE, Pearl	1938	Passy Cemetery, Paris, France	
WHITEMAN, Paul	1967	Ewing Church Cemetery, Trenton, NJ	
• WHITMAN, Gayne	1958	Forest Lawn Memorial-Park, Glendale, CA	
• WHORF, Richard	1966	Forest Lawn—Hollywood Hills, Los Angeles, CA	
WICKES, Mary (Wickenhauser)	1995	Shiloh Memorial Park, Shiloh, IL	Block 14, Lot 25
WIERE, Sylvester	1970	Westwood Village Mem. Park, Los Angeles, CA	
• WILDE, Cornel	1989	Westwood Village Mem. Park, Los Angeles, CA	Urn Garden
• WILLARD, Jess	1968	Forest Lawn—Hollywood Hills, Los Angeles, CA	
WILLIAMS, Earle	1927	Forest Lawn Memorial-Park, Glendale, CA	
• WILLIAMS, Guy	1989	Cremated	Ashes scattered at sea (Malibu, CA)
WILLIAMS, Hank Sr.	1953	Oakwood Cemetery Annex, Montgomery, AL	
WILLIAMS, Harriette "Hedy"	1997	Christ Church Cathedral, New Orleans, LA	in the church columbarium
WILLIAMS, Rhys	1969	Forest Lawn—Hollywood Hills, Los Angeles, CA	Col. of Remembrance, on right, #60467
• WILLIAMS, Tennessee	1983	Calvary Cemetery, St. Louis, MO	

• New entry.

* Some cemeteries refuse to reveal specific locations.

NAME	YEAR	CEMETERY	INTERMENT SITE*
• WILLS, Bob	1975	Memorial Park Burial Park, Tulsa, OK	
• WILSON, Dennis	1983		Buried at sea
WILSON, Edith	1981	Mount Glenwood Cemetery, Chicago, IL	
WILSON, Marie	1972	Forest Lawn—Hollywood Hills, Los Angeles, CA	Col. of Remembrance, Vault 61274
WINCHELL, Walter	1972	Greenwood Memorial Park, Phoenix, AZ	
WINWOOD, Estelle	1984	Westwood Village Mem. Park, Los Angeles, CA	
• WITHERS, Grant	1959	Forest Lawn Memorial-Park, Glendale, CA	Great Mausoleum - Sanc. of Springtime
WOLHEIM, Louis	1931	Hollywood Memorial Park, Hollywood, CA	Columbarium, Niche 5, T.2, Lower col. D
WONG, Anna May	1961	Rose Dale Cemetery, Los Angeles, CA	Section 5 (Pink marble monument)
WOOD, Ed	1978	(Cremated—not interred)	Ashes scattered at sea
WOOD, Natalie (Wagner)	1981	Westwood Village Mem. Park, Los Angeles, CA	Section D, #60
• WOOD, Sam	1949	Forest Lawn Memorial-Park, Glendale, CA	Gardens of Memory
• WOODS, Edward	1989	Salt Lake City Cemetery, Salt Lake City, UT	West Scetion 7-132-1-East
WOOLLCOTT, Alexander	1943	Hamilton College, Clinton, NY	
WOOLLEY, Monty	1963	Greenridge Cemetery, Saratoga Springs, NY	
WOOLSEY, Robert R.	1938	Forest Lawn Memorial-Park, Glendale, CA	
WORDEN, Hank	1994	Forest Lawn Memorial-Park, Glendale, CA	
WRATHER, Jack	1984	Holy Cross Cem. and Maus., Culver City, CA	Section "Grotto," Lot 196
WYCHERLY, Margaret	1956	Bepton Mid-Hurst Cemetery, Bepton, England	(Margaret Wycherly Veiller)
WYLER, William	1981	Forest Lawn Memorial-Park, Glendale, CA	Eventide, Plot #2998
WYMARK, Patrick	1970	Highgate West Cemetery, London, England	Near Chapel and Swains Lane
WYNN, Ed	1966	Forest Lawn Memorial-Park, Glendale, CA	Great Maus., Col. of Dawn
WYNN, Keenan	1986	Forest Lawn Memorial-Park, Glendale, CA	Great Maus., Col. of Dawn
X			
X, Malcolm	1965	(See LITTLE, Malcolm)	
• **Y**			
• YORK, Dick	1992	Plainfield Township Cemetery, Rochester, MI	
YOUMANS, Vincent	1946	(Cremated—not interred)	Ashes scattered at sea
YOUNG, Gig	1978	Green Hills Cemetery, Waynesville, NC	Ashes interred under the name "Byron Barr"
YOUNG, Mary	1934	Forest Lawn Memorial-Park, Glendale, CA	
• YOUNG, Robert	1998	Forest Lawn Memorial-Park, Glendale, CA	
YOUNG, Victor	1956	Beth-Olam Cemetery, Hollywood, CA	Mausoleum, main foyer
YULE, Joe	1950	Forest Lawn Memorial-Park, Glendale, CA	
YURKA, Blanche	1974	Kensico Cemetery, Valhalla, NY	Actors Fund Plot
Z			
ZANUCK, Darryl F.	1979	Westwood Village Mem. Park, Los Angeles, CA	Section D, #41
ZANUCK, Virginia Fox	1982	Westwood Village Mem. Park, Los Angeles, CA	Section D, #41
ZAPPA, Frank	1993	Westwood Village Mem. Park, Los Angeles, CA	Section D, #100 (unmarked) Next to Guild
ZIEGFELD, Florenz	1932	Kensico Cemetery, Valhalla, NY	
ZUCCO, Frances	1962	Forest Lawn—Hollywood Hills, Los Angeles, CA	
• ZUCCO, George	1960	Forest Lawn—Hollywood Hills, Los Angeles, CA	Cremated
ZUKOR, Adolph	1976	Temple Israel Cemetery, Hastings-on-Hudson, NY	

JOHNNY WEISSMULLER

6

Specific
Interment Locations
— by Cemetery

Specific Interment Locations — by Cemetery

CEMETERY	YEAR	NAME	INTERMENT SITE*
A			
Abel's Hill Cemetery, Chilmark (M.V.), MA	1982	BELUSHI, John	
"	1984	HELLMAN, Lillian	
Ahavai Sholom Cemetery, Portland, OR	1989	SCHAEFFER, Rebecca	
Allegheny Cemetery, Pittsburgh, PA	1922	RUSSELL, Lillian	In Mausoleum, Section 40, Space 5
All Saints Episcopal Cemetery, San Luis Rey, CA	1993	PEPPLE, Sydney Chester	Cremated—ashes interred
American Legion Cemetery, Tampa, FL	1946	HATTON, Rondo	
Annunciation Cemetery, Shenandoah, PA	1957	DORSEY, Jimmy	
Arbutus Memorial Park, Baltimore, MD	1995	SANDERS, Al	
Arlington National Cemetery, Arlington, VA	1971	MURPHY, Audie	Near the Battleship Maine memorial
"	1987	MARVIN, Lee	Section 7A, Grave 176
"	1968	BAINTER, Fay	
"	1965	BENNETT, Constance	Section 3, Lot 2231-A, Grid P-13
"	1966	HARRIGAN, William	
"	1981	LOUIS, Joe	
"	1974	MASSEY, Ilona (Dawson)	
"	1959	MORRIS, Wayne	
"	1983	REYNOLDS, Frank	
Austin Memorial Park, Austin, TX	1965	SCOTT, Zachary	Block 4, Lot 187A, Space 12
• Avalon Cemetery, Santa Catalina Island, CA	1947	WEAVER, Winstead 'Doodles'	
B			
Batignolles Cemetery, Paris, France	1938	CHALIAPIN, Feodor	Div. 25, rose granite mon. topped w/cross
Beaverdale Memorial Park, New Haven, CT	1983	MASSEY, Raymond	
Beckett Cemetery, Beckett, MA	1968	COREY, Wendell	
Bepton Mid-Hurst Cemetery, Bepton, England	1956	WYCHERLY, Margaret	(Margaret Wycherly Veiller)
Beth David Cemetery, Elmont (L.I.), NY	1984	KAUFMAN, Andy	
Beth-El Cemetery, Ridgewood (Queens), NY	1973	ROBINSON, Edward G.	
Blanford Cemetery, Petersburg, VA	1994	COTTON, Joseph	
Boissy-Sans-Avoir (nr. Paris), France	1982	SCHNEIDER, Romy	
Bonaventure Cemetery, Savannah, GA	1931	NEILL, James	Section E, Lot 171
"	1976	MERCER, Johnny	
Brompton Cemetery, London, England	1948	TAUBER, Richard	First sect. left of center path, near entrance
C			
Calvary Catholic Cemetery, Kansas City, MO	1929	EAGELS, Jeanne	
Calvary Cemetery, Los Angeles, CA	1972	ROACH, Hal Jr.	Block 14, Crypt 11 (at top)
"	1937	BOLESLAWSKI, Richard	Main Mausoleum
"	1990	DUNNE, Irene (Griffin)	Main Maus., left of altar in the church area
"	1987	NEGRI, Pola	Main Maus., St. Paul Corr, Blk 56, Crypt E19
"	1959	BARRYMORE, Ethel (Colt)	Main Mausoleum, Block 60, Crypt 3F
"	1954	BARRYMORE, Lionel	Main Mausoleum, Block 352
"	1959	COSTELLO, Lou	Main Mausoleum, Block 354, Crypt B-1
"	1930	NORMAND, Mabel (Cody)	Main Mausoleum, in a main hallway
"	1955	HODIAK, John	Main Mausoleum, next to Mabel Normand
"	1968	NOVARRO, Ramon	Section C, Lot 586, Grave 5
"	1937	HEALY, Ted	Section F, Lot 1693, Grave 14
"	1973	NAISH, J. Carrol	Section G, Lot 1098, Grave 22
"	1968	STROMBERG, Hunt	Section H, Lot 416 (by tree)
"	1961	FAY, Frank	
"	1977	FOY, Bryan	
Calvary Cemetery, Santa Barbara, CA	1981	LANE, Lola	Sect. M, Tier 17, Gr 97 (Lola Lane Hanlon)
Calvary Cemetery, St. Louis, MO	1983	WILLIAMS, Tennessee	
Calvary Cemetery, Woodside (Queens), NY	1968	WHEELER, Bert	Sect. 47, Catholic Actors Guild of America
"	1961	NALDI, Nita	Section 1W, Range AA, Plot 13/14, Grave 5
"	1933	GUINAN, Mary L. "Texas"	Section 47
"	1981	KELLY, Patsy	
"	1927	LEWIS, Tom	
"	1959	O'CONNOR, Una	
Carlsbad Cemetery, Carlsbad, NM	1972	CABOT, Bruce	Division A, Block 48, Space 5 (E. Bujac, Jr.)
Catalina-Ft. Rose Crans Cem., San Diego, CA	1965	BACON, Irving	
Cathedral of St. Nicholas, Monte Carlo, Monaco	1982	KELLY, Grace	Grimaldi family vault
• Cave Hill Cemetery, Louisville, KY	1984	RYAN, Edmon	
Cedar Park Cemetery, Westwood, NJ	1949	HOWARD, Willie	

• New entry.

387

* Some cemeteries refuse to reveal specific locations.

CEMETERY	YEAR	NAME	INTERMENT SITE*
Cem. of the Gate of Heaven, Hawthorne, NY	1976	MINEO, Sal	Division 2
"	1965	KILGALLEN, Dorothy	Division 23
"	1918	HELD, Anna	Division 42
"	1948	RUTH, George Herman "Babe"	Sect. 25 (at 10-ft. tall gray granite marker)
"	1986	CAGNEY, James	St. Francis of Assissi Mausoleum
"	1956	ALLEN, Fred	
"	1947	DIGGES, Dudley	
Cenacle Convent, Lake Ronkonkoma (L.I.), NY	1953	ADAMS, Maude	
Chapel of the Pines Crematory, Los Angeles, CA	1986	FREDERICK, Fred Burke	Cremated
"	1959	GWENN, Edmund	In basement holding vault, not on view
"	1947	CARLETON, William P.	Permanent storage vault
"	1967	SHERIDAN, Ann	In vault #57542, not avail. for viewing
"	1952	MacDONALD, Joseph Farrell	Memory Hall, Section K, B-2
"	1946	BUSH, Mae	Near front door, on left, at eye-level
"	1953	BRUCE, Nigel	Vault #35167
"	1971	ANDERSON, G. M.	
"	1946	ATWILL, Lionel	
"	1962	BROWNING, Tod	
"	1977	CARLSON, Richard	
"	1968	CLARK, Fred	
"	1967	CONWAY, Tom	
"	1960	CROMWELL, Richard	
"	1959	DOUGLAS, Paul	
"	1965	DUMONT, Margaret	
"	1967	ERWIN, Stuart	
"	1961	FARNUM, Franklyn	
"	1971	HEFLIN, Van	
"	1971	LYNN, Diana	
"	1962	MITCHELL, Thomas	
"	1965	NEWTON, Robert	
"	1982	OBER, Philip	
"	1949	OUSPENSKAYA, Maria	
Cimitero di Santa Maria del Pianto, Naples, Italy	1921	CARUSO, Enrico	Down the hill on the left, in sarcophagus
Cimitero Monumentale, Milan, Italy	1989	HOROWITZ, Vladimir	Toscanini family mausoleum
"	1957	TOSCANINI, Arturo	In the family's white marble mausoleum
City of Lubbock Cemetery, Lubbock, TX	1959	HOLLY, Buddy	Block 44 at Azalea Ave. (nr. path)
Civico Cimitero, Rimini, Italy	1993	FELLINI, Federico	Section O, in brown brick-like family vault
"	1994	MASINA, Giulietta (Fellini)	Section O, in the brown Fellini family vault
Clovesville Cemetery, Clovesville, NY	1966	BERG, Gertrude	In Jewish section
Coachella Valley Cemetery, Coachella, CA	1991	CAPRA, Frank	(near Indio)
• Conejo Mountain Memorial Park, Camarillo, CA	1998	SITKA, Emil	Site #139
Congressional Cemetery, Washington, D.C.	1973	FULLER, Mary	
"	1932	SOUSA, John Philip	
Corsier-Sur-Vevey, Switzerland	1977	CHAPLIN, Charles	
Crestlawn Cemetery, Sparta, TN	1979	FLATT, Lester	
Crown Hill Cemetery and Mort., Lakewood, CO	1969	BATES, Barbara	Section 2, Block 69, Lot 144, Unit A
• Crown Hill Cemetery, Indianapolis, IN	1948	BASKETT, James	
Cypress Hills Cemetery, Brooklyn, NY	1927	LOEW, Marcus	
"	1962	MOORE, Victor	
"	1980	WEST, Mae	Family Crypt, 3rd Floor
Cypress Lawn Cemetery, Colma, CA	1942	CREWS, Laura Hope	Rose Mound
D			
Dayton Memorial Park, Dayton, OH	1974	MOOREHEAD, Agnes	
Dean's Grange Cemetery, Booterstown, Ireland	1945	McCORMACK, John	
Desert Memorial Park, Palm Springs, CA	1984	POWELL, William	Ashes interred in Section B-10, Lot 20
"	1962	TOMACK, Sid	Section A-9, Lot 14
"	1976	BERKELEY, Busby	Section A-14, Lot 74
"	1958	GOODWIN, Bill	Section B-1, Lot 17
• "	1996	MADISON, Guy	
• "	1994	MITCHELL, Cameron	
"	1970	RAMBEAU, Marjorie	
Dulaney Valley Mem. Gdns., Cockeysville, MD	1990	BOCK-LEADER, Deborah Lyn	Eternal Light Section

Specific Interment Locations — by Cemetery

CEMETERY	YEAR	NAME	INTERMENT SITE*
E			
• East Lawn Memorial Park, Sacramento, CA	1992	BRAND, Nevill	Niche #1327, Section L-L, Morning Glory Rm.
"	1992	ROSS, Margery J.	
Eden Memorial Park, San Fernando, CA	1957	BROWN, John H.	Akiba 17-55
"	1977	MARX, Julius "Groucho"	In the Mausoleum, across from entrance
"	1966	BRUCE, Lenny	Mt. Nebo., Section 298C
"	1984	JAFFE. Sam	Top of outside wall, at top of hill
"	1902	LEMBECK, Harvey	
E. Lawn Sierra Hills Mem. Pk., Sacramento, CA	1986	BAER, Jacob "Buddy"	
"	1992	BRAND, Neville	
El Camino Memorial Park, La Jolla, CA	1970	FOSTER, Preston	Sanctuary of Love (3), Crypt 4, Tier F
"	1980	STONE, Milburn	Vista del Lago, 401-D
• Elmhurst Cemetery, Joliet, ILL	1997	UTTAL, Ivan	
• Elmwood Cemetery, Charlotte, N.C.	1987	SCOTT, Randolph	
• Elmwood Cemetery, River Grove, ILL	1982	BELUSHI, John	
El Reno Cemetery, El Reno, OK	1990	RHODES, Erik	Ashes buried New Add., Blk 14, Lot 24-A
Emanuel Cemetery, Wethersfield, CT	1966	TUCKER, Sophie	
Eternal Hills Memorial Park, Oceanside, CA	1979	HEISLER, Stuart	
Eternal Valley Memorial Park, Newhall, CA	1971	JOHNSON, Tor	
Evergreen Cemetery, Brooklyn, NY	1915	BUNNY, John	
"	1949	ROBINSON, Bill "Bojangles"	
Evergreen Cemetery, Colorado Springs, CO	1978	ETTING, Ruth	Shrine of Rest Mausoleum
Evergreen Cemetery, Gainesville, FL	1993	PHOENIX, River	
Evergreen Cemetery, Los Angeles, CA	1977	ANDERSON, Eddie	Section A, Lot 2504
"	1981	BEARD, Matthew "Stymie"	
F			
Fairmount Cemetery, Denver, CO	1946	MEEK, Donald	In Maus., Sect. 392, Tier BB, Main floor
Fairview Cemetery, Pen Argyl, PA	1967	MANSFIELD, Jayne	Grave is near entrance
Ferncliff Cemetery and Maus., Hartsdale, NY	1960	HAMMERSTEIN, Oscar II	Ashes buried
"	1973	SANDS, Diana	Ashewood, Grave 545
"	1955	ARLEN, Harold	Hickory, Grave 1666
"	1976	ROBESON, Paul	Hillcrest A, Grave 1511
"	1982	MONK, Thelonius	Hillcrest I, Grave 405
"	1976	BOSWELL, Connee	Hillcrest J, Grave 227
"	1975	MABLEY, Jackie "Moms"	Knollwood Garden I, Row 14, Grave 4
"	1959	STURGES, Preston	Maplewood R, Garden Grave 74
"	1931	De PUTTI, Lya	Maus., Unit 1, Alcove E, Crypt 31
"	1951	ROMBERG, Sigmund	Maus., Unit 1, Sect. BC-1, Crypt 5
"	1962	CRAWFORD, Jesse	Maus., Unit 3, Alcove 4, Niche Arc.#21
"	1945	KERN, Jerome	Maus., Unit 4 Alcove C, Pvt. Niche Mem. 1
"	1963	BARTHELMESS, Richard	Maus., Unit 8, Alcove BB, Col. B, Niche 1
"	1977	CRAWFORD, Joan (Steele)	Maus., Unit 8, Alcove E, Crypt 42
"	1961	HART, Moss	Maus., Unit 8 Alcove EE-FF, Col. D Niche 4
"	1974	SULLIVAN, Ed	Maus., Unit 8, Alcove G, Side Comp. 122
"	1955	MUNSON, Ona	Maus., Unit 8, Tier Y, Col. G, Niche 5
"	1969	GARLAND, Judy	Maus., Unit 9, Section HH, Crypt 31
"	1982	MARLOWE, Hugh	Maus., Unit 10, Alcove BB-CC, Niche 9A
"	1965	LITTLE, Malcom	Pinewood B, Grave 150
"	1965	Malcolm X.	Pinewood B, Grave 150
"	1963	MAXWELL, Elsa	Rosewood 2, Grave 1132
"	1967	RATHBONE, Basil	Shrine of Mem. Maus., Unit 1, T-K, #117
"	1951	WARFIELD, David	St. Paul, Plot 180, Grave 1
"	1982	BLOCH, Ray	St. Paul, Plot 184, Grave 2
"	1951	CHRISTIANS, Mady	
"	1943	VEIDT, Conrad	
Ferndale Cemetery, Johnstown, NY	1986	CRAWFORD, Broderick	
Fernhill Memorial Gardens, Stuart, FL	1973	MONROE, Vaughn	
"Firefly Hill", Grant's Town, Jamaica	1973	COWARD, Noel	(his private estate)
Flushing Cemetery, Flushing (Queens), NY	1971	ARMSTRONG, Louis	Sect. 8
"	1981	SCOTT, Hazel	Sect. 9, next to ex-husb. Adam C. Powell Sr.
"	1942	ROBSON, May	Sect. 9, plain stone has fam. name 'Brown'
"	1973	TRUEX, Ernest	

• New entry.   * Some cemeteries refuse to reveal specific locations.

CEMETERY	YEAR	NAME	INTERMENT SITE*
Forest Cemetery, Circleville, OH	1971	LEWIS, Ted	
Forestdale Cemetery, Helena, MT	1993	LOY, Myrna	Ashes buried alongside her parents
Forest Home Cemetery, Milwaukee, WI	1983	FONTANNE, Lynn	
"	1977	LUNT, Alfred	
Forest Lawn Cemetery, Nashville, TN	1975	FRIZZELL, Lefty	
Forest Lawn—Covina Hills, Covina, CA	1977	FORD, Mary	
Forest Lawn—Cypress, Cypress, CA	1983	CARPENTER, Karen	Ascension M. Maus., Sanct. of Compassion
"	1960	COCHRAN, Eddie (singer)	Abiding Faith, Plot #2996
Forest Lawn—Glendale, Glendale, CA	1976	FORD, Paul	
"	1973	MAYNARD, Ken	
"	1960	LLOYD, Frank	Ascension
"	1986	ALDA, Robert	Ascension Garden
"	1987	MAMOULIAN, Rouben	Ascension Garden
"	1977	WATERS, Ethel	Ascension Garden (center)
"	1986	KNIGHT, Ted	Ascension Garden (left side)
"	1954	GREENSTREET, Sydney	Ashes in a utility room (not open to public)
"	1981	HEAD, Edith	Cathedral slope, Plot 1675, at the top of hill
"	1962	BORZAGE, Frank	Court of Freedom
"	1983	CUKOR, George	Court of Freedom
"	1966	DISNEY, Walt	Court of Freedom
"	1986	PALMER, Lilli (Thompson)	Court of Freedom
"	1974	BROWN, Johnny Mack	Court of Freedom, Col. of Heavenly Peace
"	1987	BROWN, Clarence	Court of Freedom, Col. of Honor
"	1963	ODETS, Clifford	Court of Freedom, Col. of Honor
"	1978	DAILEY, Dan	Court of Freedom, marker 7065, L. of statue
"	1981	HARDING, Ann	Cremated
"	1983	D'ORSAY, Fifi	Devotion
"	1939	PARROTT, James	Devotion
"	1947	KOLKER, Joseph Henry	Eventide
"	1952	BYRD, Ralph M.	Eventide (under the olive tree)
"	1959	HALL, Charlie	Eventide, Lot 1928
"	1944	CREGAR, (Samuel) Laird	Eventide, Lot 37, Space 2
"	1955	BALL, Suzan (Long)	Eventide, Plot #2922
"	1981	WYLER, William	Eventide, Plot #2998
"	1948	LANDIS, Carole	Everlasting Love, Lot 968, Gr. 8 next to curb
"	1965	DANDRIDGE, Dorothy	Freedom Maus., Col. of Victory
"	1978	EILERS, Sally	Freedom Maus., Columbarium
"	1992	WELLS, Mary	Freedom Maus., Columbarium of Patriots
"	1977	MARX, Milton "Gummo"	Freedom Maus., Sanct. of Brotherhood
"	1966	BUSHMAN, Francis X.	Freedom Maus., Sanctuary of Gratitude
"	1964	ALLEN, Gracie (Burns)	Freedom Maus., Sanctuary of Heritage
"	1962	BELL, Rex	Freedom Maus., Sanctuary of Heritage
"	1965	BOW, Clara (Bell)	Freedom Maus., Sanctuary of Heritage
"	1996	BURNS, George	Freedom Maus., Sanctuary of Heritage
"	1965	COLE, Nat "King"	Freedom Maus., Sanctuary of Heritage
"	1964	LADD, Alan	Freedom Maus., Sanctuary of Heritage
"	1982	LADD, Sue Carol	Freedom Maus., Sanctuary of Heritage
"	1965	MacDONALD, Jeanette	Freedom Maus., Sanctuary of Heritage
"	1965	McDONALD, Marie	Freedom Maus., Sanctuary of Heritage
"	1975	FINE, Larry	Freedom Maus., Sanctuary of Liberation
"	1961	MARX, Leonard "Chico"	Freedom Maus., Sanctuary of Worship
"	1962	BORZAGE, Frank	Garden of Everlasting Peace
"	1959	FLYNN, Errol	Garden of Everlasting Peace
"	1967	TRACY, Spencer	Garden of Everlasting Peace
"	1964	COOKE, Sam	Garden of Honor
"	1990	DAVIS, Sammy Jr.	Garden of Honor
"	1986	NELSON, Frank	Garden of Honor
"	1979	BLONDELL, Joan	Garden of Honor, Col. of the Evening Star
"	1969	TAYLOR, Robert	Garden of Honor, Col. of the Evening Star
"	1973	GOLDWYN, Samuel	Garden of Honor, first garden on right
"	1960	ADLER, Buddy	Garden of Memory
"	1951	BAXTER, Warner	Garden of Memory

CEMETERY	YEAR	NAME	INTERMENT SITE*
Forest Lawn—Glendale, Glendale, CA	1948	CARROLL, Earl	Garden of Memory
"	1976	KUHLMAN, Kathryn	Garden of Memory
"	1987	LeROY, Mervyn	Garden of Memory
"	1933	PICKFORD, Jack	Garden of Memory
"	1936	PICKFORD, Lottie	Garden of Memory
"	1979	PICKFORD, Mary	Garden of Memory
"	1970	RUGGLES, Charlie	Garden of Memory
"	1972	RUGGLES, Wesley	Garden of Memory
"	1949	WOOD, Sam	Garden of Memory
"	1955	SAKALL, S. Z. "Cuddles"	Garden of Memory, as 'Szoke Szakall'
"	1957	BOGART, Humphrey	Garden of Memory, Col. of Eternal Light
"	1983	CANOVA, Judy	Garden of Memory, Col. of Eternal Light
"	1959	McLAGLEN, Victor	Garden of Memory, Col. of Eternal Light
"	1963	POWELL, Dick	Garden of Memory, Col. of Honor
"	1970	WESTMORE, Perc	Garden of Remem., #1751, 3-in from walk
"	1979	OBERON, Merle (Wolders)	Garden of Remembrance
"	1953	LEBEDEFF, Ivan	Gardens of Memory
"	1945	RANDALL, Addison Owen	Gardens of Memory
"	1954	SELWYN, Ruth (Warburton)	Gardens of Memory
"	1981	DAVIS, Jim	Great Maus., 3rd floor (cremated)
"	1923	REID, Wallace	Great Maus., Azalea Columbarium
"	1937	ROLAND, Ruth M.	Great Maus., Azalea Columbarium
"	1940	TURPIN, Ben	Great Maus., Azalea Columbarium
"	1932	GILLETT, King	Great Maus., Begonia Corridor
"	1950	STAHL, John M.	Great Maus., Begonia Corridor
"	1971	LLOYD, Harold Sr.	Great Maus., Begonia corridor #771
"	1972	FRIML, Rudolph	Great Maus., beneath Last Supper window
"	1942	OLIVER, Edna May	Great Maus., Col of Security
"	1958	PANGBORN, Franklin	Great Maus., Col of Security
"	1956	BURNS, Bob	Great Maus., Col. of Adoration
"	1975	DURFEE, Minta (Arbuckle)	Great Maus., Col. of Constancy #17743
"	1966	WYNN, Ed	Great Maus., Col. of Dawn
"	1986	WYNN, Keenan	Great Maus., Col. of Dawn
"	1944	COLLIER, William Sr.	Great Maus., Col. of Inspiration
"	1956	GRAPEWIN, Charles	Great Maus., Col. of Inspiration
"	1967	ANDREWS, LaVerne	Great Maus., Col. of Memory
"	1966	BAKER, Art	Great Maus., Col. of Memory
"	1963	CARSON, Jack	Great Maus., Col. of Memory
"	1977	DAVES, Delmar	Great Maus., Col. of Memory
"	1983	JONES, Carolyn	Great Maus., Col. of Memory
"	1984	KEIGHLEY, William	Great Maus., Col. of Memory
"	1979	TIOMKIN, Dimitri	Great Maus., Col. of Memory, Niche #19425
"	1955	BARA, Theda	Great Maus., Col. of Memory, Niche #19566
"	1957	WHALE, James	Great Maus., Col. of Memory, Niche #20076
"	1951	SIMON, S. Sylvan	Great Maus., Col. of Memory, Niche #20174
"	1950	INGRAM, Rex (director)	Great Maus., Col. of Memory, under window
"	1933	TORRENCE, Ernest	Great Maus., Col. of Prayer, Niche #10677
"	1990	CUMMINGS, Robert	Great Maus., Col. of Sanctity
"	1936	SALE, Charles P. "Chic"	Great Maus., Col. of Unity
"	1955	THUNDERCLOUD, Chief	Great Maus., Corridor of Mercy, Crypt 7355
"	1987	TORRES, Raquel	Great Maus., Hall of Celestial Peace
"	1946	FIELDS, W. C.	Great Maus., Hall of Inspiration
"	1965	TRAVERS, Henry	Great Maus., Hall of Inspiration
"	1970	DOLLY, Roszika "Rosie"	Great Maus., hall right side
"	1941	DOLLY, Yansci "Jenny"	Great Maus., hall right side
"	1956	HERSHOLT, Jean	Great Maus., monument opp. entrance
"	1960	GREEN, Alfred E.	Great Maus., Sanc. of Refuge, Crypt #5089
"	1934	DRESSLER, Marie	Great Maus., Sanctuary of Benediction
"	1937	HARLOW, Jean	Great Maus., Sanctuary of Benediction
"	1983	SHEARER, Norma (Thalberg)	Great Maus., Sanctuary of Benediction
"	1936	THALBERG, Irving Grant	Great Maus., Sanctuary of Benediction
"	1970	NEWMAN, Alfred	Great Maus., Sanctuary of Eternal Prayer

• New entry.

391

* Some cemeteries refuse to reveal specific locations.

CEMETERY	YEAR	NAME	INTERMENT SITE*
Forest Lawn—Glendale, Glendale, CA	1972	AUSTIN, Gene	Great Maus., Sanctuary of Sacred Promise
"	1972	BOYD, William	Great Maus., Sanctuary of Sacred Promise
"	1971	STEINER, Max	Great Maus., Sanctuary of Sacred Promise
"	1959	WITHERS, Grant	Great Maus., Sanctuary of Springtime
"	1987	GINGOLD, Hermione	Great Maus., Sanctuary of the Holy Spirit
"	1985	GOUDAL, Jetta	Great Maus., Sanctuary of the Holy Spirit
"	1960	GABLE, Clark	Great Maus., Sanctuary of Trust
"	1942	LOMBARD, Carole (Gable)	Great Maus., Sanctuary of Trust
"	1965	SELZNICK, David O.	Great Maus., Sanctuary of Trust
"	1934	SHERMAN, Lowell	Great Maus., Sanctuary of Trust
"	1967	CONWAY, Jack	Great Maus., Sanctuary of Valor
"	1965	BOLAND, Mary	Great Maus., Sanctuary of Vespers
"	1934	COLUMBO, Russ	Great Maus., Sanctuary of Vespers
"	1968	LEONARD, Robert Z.	Great Maus., Sanctuary of Vespers
"	1962	BLANDICK, Clara	Great Mausoleum
"	1930	CHANEY, Lon F. Sr.	Great Mausoleum
"	1944	DINEHART, Mason Alan	Great Mausoleum
"	1948	NIBLO, Fred L. Sr.	Great Mausoleum
"	1941	PENNER, Joe	Great Mausoleum
"	1997	SKELTON, Red	Great Mausoleum
"	1986	WALLIS, Hal	Great Mausoleum
"	1946	EMMETT, Fern (Roquemore)	Masonic Section
"	1970	LOUISE, Anita (Marks)	Next to her husband, Buddy Adler
"	1974	LANE, Rosemary	No headstone
"	1994	STANDER, Lionel	Outside Freedom Maus. (front)
"	1935	TODD, Thelma	Re-interned at Bellevue Cemetery
"	1986	MINNELLI, Vincente	Small priv. garden in Triumphant Faith Terr.
"	1937	ALEXANDER, Ross	Sunrise Slope
"	1973	BROWN, Joe E.	Sunrise Slope
"	1939	MERCER, Beryl	Sunrise Slope 337
"	1940	CHASE, Charley	Sunrise Slope, Lot 72, Grave 147
"	1949	CLIFTON, Elmer	Tranquility
"	1949	BEERY, Wallace	Vale of Memory, 2157-9808
"	1974	CRISP, Donald	Wee Kirk Churchyard
"	1997	STEWART, James 'Jimmy'	Wee Kirk Churchyard, Space2, Lot 8
"	1967	CLYDE, Andy	Whispering Pines
"	1962	CURTIZ, Michael	Whispering Pines
"	1936	GILBERT, John	Whispering Pines
"	1950	HALE, Alan Sr.	Whispering Pines
"	1973	HOLDEN, Fay	Whispering Pines
"	1970	HORTON, Edward Everett	Whispering Pines
"	1938	MYERS, Harry C.	Whispering Pines
"	1945	NAZIMOVA, Alla	Whispering Pines
"	1960	TIBBETT, Lawrence	Whispering Pines
"	1978	OAKIE, Jack	Whispering Pines #1066 hilltop nr Cath. Dr.
"	1952	PETERS, Susan	Whispering Pines, at "Finding of Moses"
"	1940	MIX, Tom	Whispering Pines, Grave 986
"	1986	TUTTLE, Lurene	Whispering Pines, Lot #1570
"	1949	DIX, Richard	Whispering Pines, nr. "Finding of Moses"
"	1968	PIERCE, Jack P.	Whispering Pines, nr. "Finding of Moses"
"	1959	LITTLEFIELD, Lucien	Whispering Pines, Plot #1720
"	1967	DARWELL, Jane	Whispering Pines, Plot #1817
"	1931	ACORD, Art	
"	1978	ALLWYN, Astrid	
"	1962	ATES, Roscoe	
"	1944	BENNETT, Richard	
"	1941	BERGERE, Ramona R.	
"	1955	BERTRAND, Mary (Rall)	
"	1988	BESSER, Joe	
"	1963	BLUE, Monte	
"	1963	BOLEY, May	
"	1960	BOND, Ward	

• New entry.

* Some cemeteries refuse to reveal specific locations.

Specific Interment Locations — by Cemetery

CEMETERY	YEAR	NAME	INTERMENT SITE*
Forest Lawn—Glendale, Glendale, CA	1947	BORDEN, Olive	
"	1943	BOSWORTH, Hobart	
"	1957	BRABIN, Charles J.	
"	1936	BREESE, Edmund	
"	1937	BURGESS, Helen M.	
"	1947	CAREY, Harry	
"	1944	CARR, Nathan C. "Nat"	
"	1979	CARROLL, John	
"	1943	CHARTERS, Spencer H.	
"	1949	CLARK, Buddy	
"	1957	CLEVELAND, George	
"	1947	CORTHELL, Herbert	
"	1985	CRAIG, James	
"	1955	DANIELS, Victor	
"	1936	DAVENPORT, Alice	
"	1959	DUNCAN, Rosetta	
"	1986	DUNCAN, Vivian	
"	1935	DURKIN, Junior	
"	1951	ERROL, Leon	
"	1953	FARNUM, William	
"	1940	FITZMAURICE, George F.	
"	1958	FOX, Wallace W.	
"	1939	FRANKLIN, Rupert	
"	1961	FRENCH, George B.	
"	1943	FRYE, Dwight	
"	1950	FULTON, Maude	
"	1956	GANZHORN, John W.	
"	1976	GOLDWYN, Frances Howard	
"	1956	GORDON, Huntly	
"	1960	GORDON, Leon	
"	1959	HALTON, Charles	
"	1942	HAMILTON, Hale Rice	
"	1935	HARDY, Sam	
"	1955	HARVEY, Paul (actor)	
"	1955	HAYDEN, Harry	
"	1964	HEARN, Sam	
"	1956	HERBERT, Holmes	
"	1936	HOWLAND, Jobyna	
"	1958	HUGHES, Lloyd	
"	1946	HURT, Marlin	
"	1990	IRELAND, Jill	
"	1943	JULIAN, Rupert	
"	1947	KERRIGAN, J. Warren	
"	1956	LEWIS, Mitchell	
"	1947	LOFT, Arthur	
"	1963	LONDON, Tom	
"	1947	LUBITSCH, Ernst	
"	1957	LYMAN, Abe	
"	1934	MACK, Charles E.	
"	1964	MARX, Arthur "Harpo"	
"	1947	NEGIN, Koliz	
"	1942	NICHOLS, George Jr.	
"	1947	O'BRIEN, Thomas Everett	
"	1940	OGLE, Charles	
"	1954	OLSEN, Moroni	
"	1958	OSBORN, Lyn	
"	1937	OWSLEY, Monroe Righter	
"	1955	PIERLOT, Francis	
"	1934	POLLARD, Harry A.	
"	1937	POWELL, Richard	
"	1958	PURVIANCE, Edna	
"	1943	RAY, Charles	

• New entry.

* Some cemeteries refuse to reveal specific locations.

CEMETERY	YEAR	NAME	INTERMENT SITE*
Forest Lawn—Glendale, Glendale, CA	1964	RICHARDS, Addison	
"	1940	ROBERTS, Florence	
"	1942	ROSING, Bodil Ann	
"	1941	SCHERTZINGER, Victor	
"	1944	SELZNICK, Myron	
"	1968	STAFFORD, Hanley	
"	1941	STEPHENSON, James	
"	1940	STEVENS, John Landers	
"	1961	STEWART, Anita (Converse)	
"	1940	TRAINOR, Leonard E.	
"	1944	Van DYKE, Woody S. II	
"	1939	VERNON, Bobby	
"	1946	WALDRON, Charles D.	
"	1961	WALLING, Effie Bond	
"	1958	WHITMAN, Gayne	
"	1927	WILLIAMS, Earle	
"	1938	WOOLSEY, Robert R.	
"	1994	WORDEN, Hank	
"	1934	YOUNG, Mary	
"	1998	YOUNG, Robert	
"	1950	YULE, Joe	
Forest Lawn—Hollywood Hills, Los Angeles, CA	1965	LAUREL, Stanley	Ashes in Garden of Heritage at garden wall
"	1978	ROBERTS, Lynne (Mary Hart)	Buried beside her mother
"	1974	KRUGER, Otto	Churchyard, Plot #4266
"	1973	STRANGE, Glenn	Churchyard, Plot #4295
"	1974	BRITTON, Pamela	Col. of Radiant Dawn, G61685
"	1994	LANTZ, Walter	Col. of Radiant Light
"	1972	COWAN, Jerome	Col. of Remembrance
"	1965	KASSEL, Art	Col. of Remembrance, #6098
"	1977	WALLER, Eddy	Col. of Remembrance, on left, #60409
"	1982	SHAW, Reta	Col. of Remembrance, on left, #60402
"	1963	MAYO, Frank	Col. of Remembrance, on left, #60450
"	1969	WILLIAMS, Rhys	Col. of Remembrance, on right, #60467
"	1988	STEELE, Bob	Col. of Remembrance, on right, #60722
"	1939	SMALLEY, W. Phillips	Col. of Remembrance, on right, #60750
"	1965	NICHOLS, Ernest "Red"	Col. of Remembrance, on right, #60780
"	1972	WILSON, Marie	Col. of Remembrance, Vault #61274
"	1993	AMES, Leon	Col. of Valor, #G64429
"	1991	DAVIS, Brad	Col. of Valor, #G64054
"	1969	LOCHER, Felix	Court of Liberty
"	1991	CONVY, Bert	Court of Liberty, left of sidewalk
"	1980	BARRY, Don "Red"	Court of Liberty, Plot #5442 (under tree)
"	1969	INGRAM, Rex (actor)	Court of Liberty, Plot #822
"	1979	HALL, Jon	Court of Liberty, same row w/Buster Keaton
"	1966	KEATON, Buster	Court of Liberty, nr. G. Washington statue
"	1989	BALL, Lucille (Morton)	Courts of Remem., Col. of Radiant Dawn
"	1986	TUCKER, Forrest	Courts of Remem., Col. of Radiant Dawn
"	1962	LAUGHTON, Charles	Courts of Remem., in black marble vault
"	1987	Liberace	Courts of Remem., in white sarcophagus
"	1983	LIBERACE, George	Courts of Remem., in white sarcophagus
"	1980	GARDINER, Reginald	Courts of Remem., Sanc. of Reflection, 3322
"	1968	ST. DENIS, Ruth	Courts of Remem.
"	1974	FONTANE, Tony	Courts of Remem., #409
"	1965	BEATTY, Clyde	Courts of Remem., #2175
"	1988	GIBB, Andy	Courts of Remem., #2534
"	1982	MILLS, Harry F.	Courts of Remem., #3446
"	1981	HENDRIX, Wanda	Courts of Remem., #4349
"	1980	MARTIN, Strother	Courts of Remem., #G62420
"	1989	DAVIS, Bette	Courts of Remem., in sarc. left of entrance
"	1977	PRINZE, Freddie (Preutzel)	Courts of Remem., Sanctuary of Light
"	1980	RAFT, George	Courts of Remem., Sanctuary of Light
"	1992	HANCOCK, John	Devotion, Plot #8018

* Some cemeteries refuse to reveal specific locations.

CEMETERY	YEAR	NAME	INTERMENT SITE*
Forest Lawn—Hollywood Hills, Los Angeles, CA	1976	CAMBRIDGE, Godfrey	Enduring Faith
"	1986	HEIDT, Horace	Enduring Faith
"	1975	MAIN, Marjorie	Enduring Faith, Plot #2083
"	1974	BRADLEY, Truman	Enduring Faith, Plot #3718
"	1973	REID, Carl Benton	Enduring Faith, Plot #3722
"	1964	COLE, Edwin "Buddy"	Enduring Faith, Plot #3999
"	1979	SOO, Jack	Eternal Love, Plot #3980
"	1949	LEIBER, Fritz	Everlasting Love, Plot #864, Grave 13
"	1968	TALMAN, William	Garden of Heritage, Garden Crypt 633
"	1965	COLLINS, Ray	Garden of Heritage, Plot #909
"	1994	SAVALAS, Telly	Garden of Heritage, Plot #1281
"	1991	ACKERMAN, Harry	Garden of Heritage, Plot #3019
"	1982	FELDMAN, Marty	Garden of Heritage, Plot #5420
"	1980	AVERY, Frederick B. "Tex"	Gentleness
"	1967	RANDOLPH, Amanda	Gentleness, under a tree
"	1980	RANDOLPH, Lillian	Gentleness, under a tree
"	1991	BELLAMY, Ralph	God's Acre, Plot #8687
"	1991	DUROCHER, Leo	Hillside, Plot #3211
"	1955	FRANCIS, Robert	Hillside, Plot #4535
"	1969	HAYES, George "Gabby"	Hillside, Plot #4972
"	1992	PORCARO, Jeff	Lincoln Terrace, Plot #120
"	1970	GRANT, Earl	Lincoln Terrace, Plot #226
"	1992	DARBY, Ken	Lincoln Terrace, Plot #4246
"	1994	CONRAD, William	Lincoln Terrace, Plot #4448
"	1986	CROTHERS, Ben "Scatman"	Lincoln Terrace, Plot #4545
"	1985	SAVALAS, George	Lincoln Terrace, Plot #4596
"	1977	MUSTIN, Burt	Loving Kindness, Plot #7844
"	1975	STEVENS, George	Morning Light
"	1967	DENNY, Reginald	Morning Light, Plot #7451
"	1979	BUCHANAN, Edgar	Morning Light, Plot #7780
"	1976	LANG, Fritz	Murmuring Trees, Plot #3818
"	1973	ARMSTRONG, Robert	Murmuring Trees, Plot #7318, Space 1
"	1968	CHESHIRE, Harry "Pappy"	Remembrance, Plot #323
"	1962	KOVACS, Ernie	Remembrance
"	1963	ROBARDS, Jason Sr.	Remembrance, Grave 975 (at curb)
"	1967	TROWBRIDGE, Charles	Remembrance, Plot #233
"	1994	NELSON, Harriet	Revelation
"	1975	NELSON, Ozzie	Revelation
"	1985	NELSON, Rick	Revelation
"	1968	DURYEA, Dan	Revelation, Plot #7347
"	1989	VanCLEEF, Lee	Serenity, Lot 156
"	1946	BEERY, Noah Sr.	Sheltering Hills
"	1967	BURNETTE, Smiley	Sheltering Hills, Plot #266
"	1963	DASTAGIR, Sabu	Sheltering Hills, Plot #402
"	1960	DASTAGIR, Sheik	Sheltering Hills, Plot #490
"	1971	DISNEY, Roy	Sheltering Hills
"	1962	POLLARD, Harry "Snub"	Sheltering Hills
"	1981	SAGAL, Boris	Sheltering Hills
"	1990	TAYBACK, Victor	Sheltering Hills, Plot #3813
"	1982	WEBB, Jack	Sheltering Hills, Plot #1999
"	1982	ROSS, Joe E.	SummerLand, Plot #148
"	1955	BACON, Lloyd	
"	1962	BARRIS, Harry	
"	1988	BARSI, Judith	
"	1993	CAMPANELLA, Roy	
"	1991	CAULFIELD, Joan	
"	1982	GOSDEN, Freeman	
"	1992	OLIVER, David	
"	1958	PANZER, Paul	
"	1921	RITCHIE, Billie	
"	1988	ROBERSON, C. H. "Chuck"	
"	1988	ROBINSON, Dar Allen	

• New entry.

* Some cemeteries refuse to reveal specific locations.

CEMETERY	YEAR	NAME	INTERMENT SITE*
Forest Lawn—Hollywood Hills, Los Angeles, CA	1959	STONE, Fred	
"	1964	TEAGARDEN, Jack	
"	1962	ZUCCO, Frances	
"	1960	ZUCCO, George	Cremated
Forest Lawn Memorial Park, Beaumont, TX	1959	RICHARDSON, Jiles	Block C, Lot 31, Space 3
Forest Lawn Memorial Park, Goodlettsville, TN	1973	AKEMAN, David	
• Forreston Cemetery, Forreston, TX	1997	PYLE, Denver Dell	
Fort Bragg Military Cemetery, NC	1994	RAYE, Martha	
Frasier Cemetery, New Westminister, B.C.	1993	BURR, Raymond	
Friedenau Cemetery, Berlin, Germany	1992	DIETRICH, Marlene	Near her mother, Josefine von Losch
Friends Cemetery, Brooklyn, NY	1966	CLIFT, Montgomery	
Ft. Bliss National Cemetery, El Paso, TX	1967	TATUM, Reece "Goose"	Section D, Grave 2668
G			
Gate of Heaven Cemetery, Silver Spring, MD	1983	PULEO, Johnny	
Glen Haven Memorial Park, San Fernando, CA	1969	HUNTER, Jeffrey	
Glenwood Cemetery, Beeville, TX	1961	LAWRENCE, Walter Smith	
Glenwood Cemetery, Houston, TX	1976	HUGHES, Howard	
• "	1991	TIERNEY, Gene	
Golders Green Cemetery, London, England	1980	SELLERS, Peter	
• "	1967	LEIGH, Vivien	
Grace Hills Cemetery, Hawarden, PA	1960	EMERSON, Hope	
Graceland Cemetery, Chicago, IL	1940	BATES, Granville	
Graceland, Memphis, TN	1977	PRESLEY, Elvis	
Grand View Memorial Park, Glendale, CA	1982	FONDA, Henry	Cremated (Ashes given to his family)
"	1938	FREDERICK, Pauline	
"	1974	LONG, Richard	
Green Hills Cemetery, Asheville, NC	1978	YOUNG, Gig	Ashes interred under the name "Byron Barr"
Greenmount Cemetery, Baltimore, MD	1968	SEDDON, Margaret	
Greenridge Cemetery, Saratoga Springs, NY	1963	WOOLLEY, Monty	
Green-Wood Cemetery, Brooklyn, NY	1965	MURROW, Edward R.	Ashes buried
"	1956	MORGAN, Ralph	The Wupperman lot
"	1990	BERNSTEIN, Leonard	
"	1946	HART, William S.	
"	1949	MORGAN, Frank	
• Greenwood Cemetery, Clarksville, TN	1974	SUTTON, Frank	
Greenwood Cemetery, Fort Worth, TX	1975	ROBERTS, Roy	314 - 42
"	1920	LOCKLEAR, Omer	89 - 9E
• Greenwood Cemetery, Hot Sprpings, AR	1980	LAUCK, Chester A.	
Greenwood Cemetery, New Orleans, LA	1987	MEYER, Emile G.	
Greenwood Memorial Cemetery, Renton, WA	1970	HENDRIX, Jimi	
Greenwood Memorial Park, Fort Worth, TX	1987	PAM, Anita	Maus.-Westminster area (Valutage) (NM)
Greenwood Memorial Park, Phoenix, AZ	1972	WINCHELL, Walter	
Greenwood Memorial Park, San Diego, CA	1936	SCHUMANN-HEINK, Ernestine	Cathedral Mausoleum, Corr. of Sunshine
"	1981	BUONO, Victor	Unmarked grave nr. pond, next to his mom
Grove Hill Memorial Park, Dallas, TX	1975	CALVIN, Henry	60-3-16
"	1991	VonERICH, Chris	Hilltop Lot 535, Space 4
"	1984	VonERICH, David	Hilltop Lot 535
"	1993	VonERICH, Kerry	Hilltop near Lot 535
"	1987	VonERICH, Michael	Hilltop Lot 535
Grunewald-Forst Cemetery, Berlin, Germany	1988	Nico (Christa Paffgen)	
H			
Hampstead Cemetery, London, England	1971	COOPER, (Dame) Gladys	Near Public Footpath and 3rd path on right
Haym Salomon Memorial Park, Frazer, PA	1973	CROCE, Jim	
Hebrew Friendship Cemetery, Baltimore, MD	1992	ROBBINS, Fred	
Hebrew Young Men's Cem., Baltimore, MD	1995	GOTTLIEB, Conrad I.	
Henie-Onstad Art Center, Oslo, Norway	1969	HENIE, Sonja	
Highgate East Cemetery, London, England	1983	RICHARDSON, (Sir) Ralph	Near Main Rd.
Highgate West Cemetery, London, England	1970	WYMARK, Patrick	Near Chapel and Swains Lane
• Highland Cemetery, Ft. Mitchell, KY	1986	MERKEL, Una	
• Highland Cemetery, Wichita, KN	1947	TOLER, Sidney	
Hillcrest Memorial Park, Dallas, TX	1995	MANTLE, Mickey	Mausoleum St. Mark NE-N-C-13
"	1995	ELGART, Les	Garden of Prayer, Block 10, Lot 27, Sp 2

• New entry.

* Some cemeteries refuse to reveal specific locations.

CEMETERY	YEAR	NAME	INTERMENT SITE*
• Hillcrest Memorial Park, Dallas, TX	1996	GARSON, Greer	
Hillside Memorial Park, Los Angeles, CA	1995	FRELENG, Isadore "Friz"	Canaan, Block E-249
"	1938	FACTOR, Max	Courts of the Book, Isaiah, U-314
"	1994	SHORE, Dinah	Courts of the Book, Isaiah, V-247
"	1985	DIAMOND, Selma	Courts of the Book, Jacob, I-4004
"	1987	GREENE, Lorne	Courts of the Book, Lawn Crypt, 5-800-8B
"	1975	HOWARD, Moe	Garden of Memories, Alcove of Love C233
"	1972	RICHMAN, Harry	Garden of Memories, Alcove of Love B319
"	1994	BOOKE, Sorrell	Garden of Memories, Dedication, 272-4B
"	1969	GOETZ, William	Garden of Memories, Devotion, Sarcoph. B
"	1976	FAITH, Percy	Garden of Memories, Honor, Lawn Crypt 407
"	1973	FREED, Arthur	Garden of Memories, Honor, Lawn Crypt 418
"	1950	JOLSON, Al	In Al Jolson Memorial (at top of waterfall)
"	1989	LERNER, Sam	Laurel Gardens, Block 18-177-3A
"	1991	LANDON, Michael	Mausoleum, ashes in a private room
"	1975	BLUE, Ben	Mausoleum, Col. of Graciousness, 810
"	1973	SHERMAN, Allan	Mausoleum, Col. of Hope, 513
"	1992	GOODSON, Mark	Mausoleum, Gdn. of Abraham, Sarcoph. B
"	1974	BENNY, Jack	Mausoleum, Graciousness, Sarcophagus F
"	1983	LIVINGSTONE, Mary (Benny)	Mausoleum, Graciousness, Sarcophagus F
"	1961	CHANDLER, Jeff (Ira Grossel)	Mausoleum, Graciousness, 2nd Floor, 4015
"	1964	CANTOR, Eddie	Mausoleum, Graciousness, 207
"	1980	JANSSEN, David	Mausoleum, Memorial Court, 516
"	1981	JESSEL, George	Mausoleum, Memorial Court, 516
"	1987	SHAWN, Dick	Mausoleum, Memorial Court, 734
"	1982	MORROW, Vic	Mount of Olives, Block 5-80-1
"	1993	SEYMOUR, Dan	Mount of Olives, Block 7-175-1
"	1970	MARCH, Hal	Mount Sholom, Block 4-144-6
"	1985	KATZ, Mickey	Valley of Remembrance, Block 1-196-2
"	1995	WARNER, Jack M.	
Hollybrook Cem., Shirley, Southampton, Eng.	1992	HILL, Benny	
Hollywood Memorial Park, Hollywood, CA	1942	CRUZE, James	Abbey of Psalms, Foyer, Niche 211, Tier 2
"	1956	CALHERN, Louis	Abbey of Psalms, Foyer, Niche 308, Tier 3
"	1970	BEAUDINE, William	Abbey of the Psalms
"	1934	DILLON, John Francis	Abbey of the Psalms
"	1975	LACHMAN, Harry	Abbey of the Psalms
"	1990	LOCKER, Frances	Abbey of the Psalms
"	1936	WALTHALL, Henry B.	Abbey of the Psalms
"	1947	TANGUAY, Eva	Abbey of the Psalms, Crypt 0558, Corr. D-1
"	1968	CHAPLIN, Charles Jr. (son)	Abbey of the Psalms, Crypt 1065, Corr E-2
"	1949	FLEMING, Victor	Abbey of the Psalms, Crypt 2081, Corr G-2
"	1958	LASKY, Jesse L. Sr.	Abbey of the Psalms, Crypt 2196, Corr G-3
"	1983	HACKETT, Joan	Abbey of the Psalms, Crypt 2314, Corr D-3
"	1966	WEBB, Clifton	Abbey of the Psalms, Crypt 2350, Corr G-6
"	1973	ROBINSON, Edward G. Jr.	Abbey of the Psalms, Crypt 4386, Corr E-4
"	1979	HOOD, Darla	Abbey of the Psalms, Crypt 7213, Corr G-4
"	1973	TALMADGE, Constance	Abbey of the Psalms, Family Rm, Corr G-7
"	1969	TALMADGE, Natalie	Abbey of the Psalms, Family Rm, Corr G-7
"	1957	TALMADGE, Norma	Abbey of the Psalms, Family Rm, Corr G-7
"	1933	ADOREE, Renée	Abbey of the Psalms, Foyer, Crypt 219
"	1955	DeMILLE, William C.	Abbey of the Psalms, Niche 2, T.6, Corr E-3
"	1991	BROWNE, Coral	Ashes scattered in the rose garden.
"	1967	WAXMAN, Franz	Beth Olam Maus., ashes in urn at 2nd ent.
"	1968	MAYO, Archie	Beth Olam Mausoleum
"	1949	SCHLESINGER, Leon	Beth Olam Mausoleum, ashes in vault
"	1956	YOUNG, Victor	Beth Olam Mausoleum, main foyer
"	1964	SCHILDKRAUT, Joseph	Beth Olam Mausoleum, Niche 43
"	1948	TOLAND, Greg	Chapel of the Pines Mausoleum
"	1940	AYRES, Agnes	Columbarium, Niche 3, T.3, Lower S. Wall
"	1971	DANIELS, Bebe	Columbarium, Niche 7-8, T.3, Upper N. Wall
"	1979	LYON, Ben	Columbarium, Niche 7-8, T.3, Upper N. Wall
"	1987	HERMAN, Woody	Court of the Apostles, Crypt 6689, Unit 10

CEMETERY	YEAR	NAME	INTERMENT SITE*
Hollywood Memorial Park, Hollywood, CA	1942	WEBER, Joe	Cremated; remains placed in a vault
"	1961	DAVIES, Marion	Douras Mausoleum, Section 8, Lot 261-264
"	1987	LAKE, Arthur	Douras Mausoleum, Section 8, Lot 261-264
"	1926	LaMARR, Barbara	H'wood Cath. Maus.
"	1926	LAWRENCE, Lillian	H'wood Cath. Maus.
"	1922	TAYLOR, William Desmond	H'wood Cath. Maus. Crypt 594 (W.D.Tanner)
"	1926	VALENTINO, Rudolph	H'wood Cath. Maus., #1205, off Corr A
"	1927	MATHIS, June	H'wood Cath. Maus., Crypt 1199, Corr A
"	1977	FINCH, Peter	H'wood Cath. Maus., Crypt 1224, off Corr A
"	1964	LORRE, Peter	H'wood Cath. Maus., Niche 5, T-1, Corr C
"	1982	POWELL, Eleanor	H. C. Maus., Niche 432, T-3, Foyer E/W
"	1928	ROBERTS, Theodore	Pineland
"	1931	FRANKLIN, Sidney (actor)	Pineland, Lot #321
"	1989	BLANC, Mel	Pineland, near curb
"	1934	DANE, Karl	Pineland, Plot 303 (next to road)
"	1940	FINCH, Flora	Section 1, Grave 416
"	1939	FAIRBANKS, Douglas Sr.	Section 11 (R. of Cathedral Mausoleum)
"	1980	DASSIN, Joe	Section 14, Grave 79, Row I
"	1967	MUNI, Paul	Section 14, Row 00, Grave 57
"	1949	BRESSART, Felix	Section 14, Row J, Grave 89
"	1938	LAWRENCE, Florence	Section 2 (several yds. from the pump house)
"	1941	SHANNON, Peggy	Section 5, Plot 43 (two rows in from road)
"	1959	SWITZER, Carl "Alfalfa"	Section 6, Lot 26, Grave 6
"	1959	DeMILLE, Cecil B.	Section 8
"	1991	LAIRD, Jack	Section 8
"	1927	REYNOLDS, Lynn	Section 8
"	1947	BING, Herman	Section 8, 20 ft. east of John Huston
"	1943	MARSHALL, Tully	Section 8, grave beneath a tree
"	1972	FRANKLIN, Sidney (director)	Section 8, grave next to palm tree
"	1963	MENJOU, Adolphe	Section 8, Lot 11
"	1957	KORNGOLD, Erich Wolfgang	Section 8, Lot 15
"	1959	Adrian	Section 8, Lot 193
"	1984	GAYNOR, Janet (Gregory)	Section 8, Lot 193
"	1921	RAPPE, Virginia	Section 8, Lot 257
"	1946	LEHRMAN, Henry	Section 8, Lot 257 (next to Virginia Rappe)
"	1987	HUSTON, John	Section 8, Lot 8
"	1958	COHN, Harry	Section 8, Lot 86
"	1967	EDDY, Nelson	Section 8, Lot 89
"	1953	ROSSON, Richard	Section 8, near Cecil B. DeMille
"	1975	DALEY, Cass (Katherine)	Section 8, near curb ("Williamson")
"	1958	BELL, Monta	Section 8, near Nelson Eddy
"	1958	POWER, Tyrone	Section 8, near the Marion Davies Maus.
"	1967	WESTMORE, Ernest	Section 8, three-in from the road
"	1986	RITZ, Harry	T-Bldg., 3rd floor
"	1985	RIDDLE, Nelson	T-Bldg., Niche 702, Tier 7, Corr T-1
"	1965	RITZ, Al	T-Bldg., T-4, Bottom row, right side
"	1985	RITZ, Jimmy	T-Bldg., T-5
"	1984	HUMBERSTONE, Bruce H.	
"	1970	KARNS, Roscoe	
"	1952	LINCOLN, Elmo	
"	1948	NOLAN, Mary	
Holy Cross Cem. and Maus., Culver City, CA	1975	MARSHALL, George E.	Mausoleum
"	1984	SANDS, Billy	Mausoleum
"	1980	ITURBI, José	Mausoleum, Block 16, Crypt E-1
"	1987	BOLGER, Ray	Mausoleum, Block 35, Crypt F-2
"	1961	DAVIS, Joan (Williams)	Mausoleum, Block 46, Crypt D-1, rt. of altar
"	1959	LANZA, Mario	Mausoleum, Block 46, Crypt D-2
"	1984	LaRUE, Jack	Mausoleum, Block 69, Crypt E-3
"	1965	JONES, Lindley "Spike"	Mausoleum, Block 70, Crypt A-7
"	1990	PAN, Hermes	Mausoleum, Block 127, Crypt D-5
"	1985	BRADY, Scott	Mausoleum, Block 156, Crypt B-7 upper floor
"	1985	HATHAWAY, Henry	Mausoleum, left of the altar

CEMETERY	YEAR	NAME	INTERMENT SITE*
Holy Cross Cem. and Maus., Culver City, CA	1982	BRODERICK, James	Mausoleum, lower floor, top level
"	1994	CANDY, John	Mausoleum, Room 7, Crypt B-1
"	1991	MacMURRAY, Fred	Mausoleum, Room 7, Crypt D-1
• "	1973	ORY, Edward "Kid"	Section "Grotto," Lot 59, Grave 4
"	1979	HALEY, Jack	Section "Grotto," Lot 100, Grave 2
"	1977	CROSBY, Harry "Bing"	Section "Grotto," Lot 119, Grave 1
"	1952	CROSBY, Wilma "Dixie Lee"	Section "Grotto," Lot 119, Grave 2
"	1956	LUGOSI, Bela	Section "Grotto," Lot 120, Grave 1
"	1968	CASTLE, Nick	Section "Grotto," Lot 187, Grave 2
"	1963	PITTS, Zazu (Woodall)	Section "Grotto," Lot 195, Grave 1
"	1984	WRATHER, Jack	Section "Grotto," Lot 196
"	1988	GRANVILLE, Bonita (Wrather)	Section "Grotto," Lot 196, Grave 12
"	1994	CAREY, Macdonald	Section "Grotto," Lot 196, Grave 19
"	1987	HAYWORTH, Rita	Section "Grotto," Lot 196, Grave 6
"	1987	EGAN, Richard	Section AA, Tier 37, Grave 139 (unmarked)
"	1993	O'CONNELL, Helen (Devol)	Section CC, Tier 56, Grave 55
"	1996	EDWARDS, Vince (Zoine)	Section CC, Tier 64, Grave 29
"	1950	ALLGOOD, Sara	Section D "Sacred Heart"
"	1945	ARMETTA, Henry	Section D "Sacred Heart"
"	1959	GLEASON, James	Section D "Sacred Heart"
"	1956	KELLY, Paul	Section D, 1 row above Lot 61
"	1952	HERBERT, Hugh	Section D, Lot 267, Grave 11
"	1975	LUNDIGAN, William	Section D, Lot 269, Grave 3
"	1946	OLDFIELD, Barney	Section D, Lot 290, Grave 11
"	1948	KENNEDY, Edgar	Section D, Lot 193, Grave 7
"	1972	PARSONS, Louella (Martin)	Section D, Lot 235, Grave 8
"	1957	LOCKHART, Gene	Section D, Lot 279, Grave 6
"	1996	MEADOWS, Audrey (Six)	Section F, Tier 29, Grave 57
"	1985	DESMOND, Johnny	Section F, Tier 44, Grave 30
"	1985	O'BRIEN, Edmond	Section F, Tier 54, Grave 50
"	1984	COOGAN, Jackie	Section F, Tier 56, Grave 47
"	1983	O'BRIEN, Pat	Section F, Tier 56, Grave 62
"	1980	DURANTE, Jimmy	Section F, Tier 96, Grave 6
"	1950	DeCORDOBA, Pedro	Section G, Lot 258, Grave 1
"	1987	REY, Alejandro	Section L, Lot 403, Grave 1
"	1973	FORD, John	Section M, Lot 304, Grave 5
"	1984	BRISSON, Frederick	Section M, Lot 536 (below the big cross)
"	1976	RUSSELL, Rosalind (Brisson)	Section M, Lot 536, Grave 2
"	1972	SCALA, Gia	Section M, 3 spaces left of Lot 581
"	1960	FOWLER, Gene	Section M, Lot 792, Grave 3
"	1960	SENNETT, Mack	Section N, Lot 490, Grave 1
"	1987	ASTOR, Mary	Section N, Lot 523, Grave 5
"	1978	ACKER, Jean (Valentino)	Section N, Lot 542
"	1962	LOVEJOY, Frank	Section P, Lot 306, Grave 5
"	1964	ALBERTSON, Frank	Section P, Lot 309, Grave 1
"	1963	FARROW, John	Section P, Lot 342
"	1969	DOWLING, Constance (Tors)	Section P, Lot 421, Grave 4
"	1981	LINDSAY, Margaret	Section P, rt. of Lot 432
"	1982	DRAKE, Tom	Section R, Tier 26, Grave 188
"	1980	BRASSELLE, Keefe	Section R, Tier 29, Grave 168
"	1976	ARLEN, Richard	Section T, Tier 57, Grave 130
"	1988	DAY, Dennis	Section W, Tier 53, Grave 37
"	1974	FLYNN, Joseph A. "Joe"	Section W, Tier 20, Grave 75
"	1992	WELK, Lawrence	Section Y, Tier 9, Grave 110
"	1994	McNALLY, Stephen	Section Y, Lot 35
"	1969	TATE, Sharon (Polanski)	St. Ann's Garden, Tier 152, Grave 6
"	1988	JORDAN, Jim	St. Ann's Garden, Tier 153, Grave 1
"	1961	JORDAN, Marion	St. Ann's Garden, Tier 153, Grave 2
"	1978	BOYER, Charles	St. Ann's Garden, Tier 186, Grave 5
"	1978	PATERSON, Pat (Boyer)	St. Ann's Garden, Tier 186, Grave 6
"	1972	CORRELL, Charles "Andy"	
"	1959	GRAY, Gilda	

• New entry.

399

* Some cemeteries refuse to reveal specific locations.

CEMETERY	YEAR	NAME	INTERMENT SITE*
Holy Cross Cem. and Maus., Culver City, CA	1982	KING, Henry	
"	1985	MARTIN, Marion	
"	1969	McCAREY, Leo	
"	1969	MOWBRAY, Alan	
"	1980	PAL, George	
"	1987	RORKE, Hayden	
"	1957	SEBASTIAN, Dorothy	
"	1993	WHELAN, Arleen (Cagney)	
Holy Cross Cemetery, Baltimore, MD	1992	HUDNET, William H. "Bill"	
Holy Cross Cemetery, Calumet City, IL	1973	KRUPA, Gene	Immaculata Section
Holy Cross Cemetery, San Mateo, CA	1969	LOGAN, Ella	
Holy Sepulchre Cemetery, New Rochelle, NY	1928	FOY, Eddie Sr.	
Holy Sepulchre Cemetery, Orange, CA	1993	KEELER, Ruby	"Ruby K. Lowe," Sect. N, Tier 21, Grave 46
• Holy Sepulchre Cemetery, Rochester, NY	1985	BROOKS, Louise	
Holy Sepulchre Cemetery, Worth, IL	1941	MORGAN, Helen	
Home of Peace Mem. Park, Los Angeles, CA	1955	HOWARD, Shemp	Chapel Maus., Eternal Light Corr., EW215
"	1958	NEUMANN, Kurt	Chapel Maus., Corr. of Eternal Life
"	1957	MAYER, Louis B.	Chapel Maus., Corr. of Immortality, SW 405
"	1949	RAPF, Harry	Chapel Maus., Corr. of Immortality
"	1951	BRICE, Fanny	Chapel Maus., Har. and Benev., 57E #1109
"	1939	LAEMMLE, Carl	Chapel Maus., in the Laemmle family room
"	1927	WARNER, Sam	In Mausoleum
"	1978	WARNER, Jack L.	Undergrd crypt, 50 yd. from Warner Maus.
"	1959	VIDOR, Charles	Warner Maus. (was Harry's son-in-law)
"	1958	WARNER, Harry B.	Warner Maus., Section D, Plot 16
"	1952	HOWARD, Jerome "Curly"	Western Jewish Institute, SW Corner, Plot 1
"	1958	WARNER, Harry M.	
I			
Inglewood Park Cemetery, Inglewood, CA	1978	BERGEN, Edgar	131 Miramar Plot, Grave #2
"	1980	THOMAS, William "Buckwheat"	777 Acacia Slope, Grave 1
"	1945	LAVERNE, Lucille	Center Grave D, Lot 236, Palm Plot
"	1990	HARRIS, Robin	Chap. of Freedom, Manchester Maus. #D5
"	1973	GRABLE, Betty (James)	Golden West Maus., A78, Sanc. of Dawn
"	1994	ROMERO, Cesar	Golden West Maus., Alcove of Music, Cr 408
"	1932	BERN, Paul	Golden West Maus., ashes in Niche F96
"	1962	GIBSON, Hoot	Magnolia Plot, Lot 92, Grave 6
"	1989	ROBINSON, Sugar Ray	Pinecrest Addition (top of hill), Lot 24
"	1970	LEE, Gypsy Rose	Pinecrest Plot, Lot 1087, Grave 8
"	1993	JONES, Ken	Pineview Plot, Lot 932, Grave E
"	1973	LANE, Allan "Rocky"	Rosehill Plot, Lot 70, Grave A
"	1962	FAZENDA, Louise	
Interlaken Cemetery, Interlaken, NY	1975	SERLING, Rod	
J			
Jerusalem, Israel	1982	RUBENSTEIN, Artur	Buried in a special plot in forest outside city
Jim Reeves Memorial Park, Carthage, TX	1964	REEVES, Jim	On US Highway 79, 4 miles NE of Carthage
K			
Kensico Cemetery, Valhalla, NY	1982	ALEXANDER, John	Actors Fund Plot
"	1981	ANDERS, Glenn	Actors Fund Plot
"	1978	BARRIE, Wendy	Actors Fund Plot
"	1956	KIBBEE, Guy	Actors Fund Plot
"	1967	REED, Florence	Actors Fund Plot
"	1973	SHUMAN, Roy	Actors Fund Plot
"	1956	STEPHENSON, Henry	Actors Fund Plot
"	1939	TEMPLETON, Fay	Actors Fund Plot
"	1974	YURKA, Blanche	Actors Fund Plot
"	1941	GEHRIG, Lou	Ashes in family vault
"	1956	DORSEY, Tommy	On Cherokee Ave.
"	1981	CHAYEFSKY, Paddy	Sharon Gardens section
"	1970	BURKE, Billie	
"	1945	CRAVEN, Frank	
"	1947	HELLINGER, Mark	
"	1987	KAYE, Danny	

CEMETERY	YEAR	NAME	INTERMENT SITE*
Kensico Cemetery, Valhalla, NY	1950	LORD, Pauline	
"	1941	PORTER, Edwin S.	
"	1943	RACHMANINOFF, Sergei	
"	1932	ZIEGFELD, Florenz	
L			
Lake View Cemetery, Cleveland, OH	1959	PECKHAM, Francis Miles	
"	1991	JACKSON, Mary Ann	Section 43, Lot 678
Lake View Cemetery, Seattle, WA	1993	LEE, Brandon	Buried next to his father, Bruce Lee
	1973	LEE, Bruce	
Lauderdale Memorial Park, Ft. Lauderdale, FL	1969	MARCIANO, "Rocky"	
Laurel Grove Cemetery, Port Jervis, NY	1968	DEAN, Julia	Grave unmarked
Laurel Land Memorial Park, Dallas, TX	1995	LEWIS, Ronald "Raan"	Field of Honor, Lot 125 B/C
"	1990	VAUGHAN, Stevie Ray	Section 25, Lot 194, Space 4
• Le Pere Lachaise, Paris, France	1985	SIGNORET, Simone	
Lincoln Cemetery, Kansas City, KS	1955	PARKER, Charlie "Bird"	
• Lincoln Cemetery, Lincoln, NB	1992	DENNIS, Sandy	Mauseleum #3, Wall A, Col. 1C
Long Island Nat'l Cem., Farmingdale (L.I.), NY	1966	KANE, Helen	
Long Ridge Cemetery, Stamford, CT	1986	GOODMAN, Benny	
"	1989	RADNER, Gilda	
Long Ridge Congregational Ch., Stamford, CT	1984	DELMAR, Kenny	
Lorraine Park Cemetery, Baltimore, MD	1994	NATWICK, Mildred	
Los Angeles National Cemetery, L.A., CA	1987	MARTIN, Dean Paul Jr.	
"	1969	McNEAR, Howard	Columbarium
"	1951	HOLT, Jack	Section 107
"	1942	HOUSMAN, Arthur	
Los Molinas Cemetery, Red Bluff, CA	1969	GORCEY, Leo	
• Louisville Evergreen Cemetery, Louisville, KY	1946	RAGLAND, John 'Rags'	
M			
Machpelah Cemetery, Ridgewood (Queens), NY	1926	HOUDINI, Harry	
Maple Grove Cemetery, Horsehead, NY	1947	LAWRENCE, William E.	
Marbella, Spain	1993	NEGULESCO, Jean	
Marnes-La-Coquette, France	1972	CHEVALIER, Maurice	(France)
• Maysville Cemetery, Maysville, KY	1974	WADSWORTH, Henry	
Memorial Park, Oklahoma City, OK	1973	TINDALL, Loren	Section 18, Lot 61, Space 6
• Memorial Park Cemetery, Skokie, ILL	1992	REED, Robert	
Metairie Cemetery, New Orleans, LA	1978	PRIMA, Louis	Section 88
"	1940	CLARK, Marguerite	Section 97 (Frank Williams property)
Milly La Foret Cemetery, Milly La Foret, France	1963	COCTEAU, Jean	
Montmartre Cemetery, Paris, France	1984	TRUFFAUT, François	Division 21, near entrance, on Ave. Berlioz
"	1950	NIJINSKY, Vaslav	Division 22
Montparnasse Cemetery, Paris, France	1953	Kiki	
"	1979	SEBERG, Jean	Division 13
Morris Hill Cemetery, Boise, ID	1972	OWEN, Reginald	
Most Holy Redeemer Cemetery, Niskayuna, NY	1998	O'SULLIVAN, Maureen	
Mountain Grove Cemetery, Bridgeport, CT	1961	CHATTERTON, Ruth	
Mountain View Cemetery, Altadena, CA	1959	REEVES, George	Ashes, Pasadena Maus. Sunrise Cor. #3555
"	1986	ARMSTRONG, Herbert W.	
• Mount Carmel Cemetery, Flushing (Queens), NY	1926	ADLER, Jacob	
• Mount Cemetery, Surrey, United Kingdom	1969	KARLOFF, Boris	Garden of Remembrance
Mount Hebron Cem., Flushing (Queens), NY	1960	SCHWARTZ, Maurice	
Mount Hope Cem., Hastings-on-Hudson, NY	1937	GERSHWIN, George	
"	1983	GERSHWIN, Ira	
"	1975	GODOWSKY, Dagmar	
"	1974	HUROK, Sol	
Mount Hope Cemetery, Peru, IN	1964	PORTER, Cole	
Mount Olivet Cemetery, Fort Worth, TX	1969	SINGLETON, Catherine M.	Garden of Our Lady of Peace D, 136-B
Mount Pleasant Cem., Toronto (Ont.), Canada	1982	GOULD, Glenn	
Mount Pleasant Cemetery, Hawthorne, NY	1980	ROTH, Lillian	
Mount Sinai Memorial-Park, Los Angeles, CA	1986	BERNARDI, Herschel	Courts of Tanach, Crypt 52250
"	1985	SILVERS, Phil	Garden of Heritage, Vault 1004
"	1976	HALOP, Billy	Garden of Sherrot, Crypt 64181 along wall
"	1976	COBB, Lee J. (Leo Jacoby)	Garden of Sherrot, Lot 421

CEMETERY	YEAR	NAME	INTERMENT SITE*
Mount Sinai Memorial-Park, Los Angeles, CA	1991	ALLEN, Irwin	In Maus. behind the Garden of Heritage
"	1990	ROSE, David	In Maus. behind the Garden of Heritage
"	1980	VAN, Bobby	Maimonides, Plot #5728
"	1981	MARTIN, Ross	Temple Beth Hillel, Plot #3628
"	1974	ELLIOT, "Mama" Cass	Court of Tanach, Lot 5000, Grave 2F
"	1978	FIELDS, Totie (Johnson)	Reinterred here 2/96 (from Las Vegas, NV)
"	1978	GELLER, Bruce	
"	1988	SPERLING, Milton	
Mount Wollaston Cemetery, Quincy, MA	1974	DeWOLFE, Billy	
Mt. Lebanon Cemetery, Glendale (Queens), NY	1975	TUCKER, Richard	
Mt. Olivet Cemetery, Saginaw, MI	1978	McCOY, Tim	
Mt. Tabor United Meth. Ch., Crestwood, KY	1948	GRIFFITH, David Wark	
Mt. Vernon Cemetery, Philadelphia, PA	1942	BARRYMORE, John	Cremated 1980, reburied from Calvary Cem.
Mt. Zion Cemetery, Maspeth, NY	1943	HART, Lorenz	
N			
National Cemetery, West Point, NY	1971	FARRELL, Glenda	
New Cathedral Cemetery, Baltimore, MD	1995	CROGHAN, Joe	
"	1994	SWIFT, Paul "Eggman"	
New Milford, CT	1975	MARCH, Fredric	Buried on his farm
Newton Cemetery, Newton, MA	1957	HULL, Josephine	
Nixon Presidential Library, Yorba Linda, CA	1993	NIXON, Pat	Interred in the garden of the library
Northview Cemetery, Dearborn, MI	1994	PEPPARD, George	
• Northwood Cemetery, Windsor, CN	1986	CANTY, Marietta	Wilson Section
Novodevichy Cemetery, Moscow, Russia	1953	PROKOFIEV, Sergei	
"	1975	SHOSTAKOVICH, Dmitri	
O			
Oak Bluff Memorial Park, Port Neches, TX	1974	RITTER, Tex	Section 8
Oakdale Cemetery, Davenport, IA	1931	BEIDERBECKE, Leon "Bix"	
Oakdale Cemetery, Glendora, CA	1979	RAND, Sally	ELM, Lot 34, Space 10
Oak Grove Cemetery, Medford, MA	1978	FONTAINE, Frank	
Oak Hill Cememtry, Nyack, NY	1993	HAYES, Helen	
Oak Hill Cemetery, Ballard, CA	1971	SEDGWICK, Edie	
• "	1971	POST, Edith (Sedgwick)	
Oak Hill Cemetery, Escondido, CA	1991	VAUGHN, Billy	
Oakland Cemetery, Atlanta, GA	1949	MITCHELL, Margaret	
Oakland Cemetery, Ft. Dodge, IA	1994	DAMITA, Lili (Loomis)	
Oakland Cemetery, Sag Harbor (L.I.), NY	1983	BALANCHINE, George	
Oak Lawn Memorial Gardens, Noblesville, IN	1970	FARMER, Frances	
Oakwood Cemetery Annex, Montgomery, AL	1953	WILLIAMS, Hank Sr.	
Oakwood Cemetery, Fort Worth, TX	1947	AMES, Adrienne	Block 31, Lot 44 (nr. Avenue IX & B Street)
• Oakwood Cemetery, Siler City, NC	1989	BAVIER, Frances	
Oakwood Memorial Park, Chatsworth, CA	1967	REEVES, Richard J.	Section Elm, Lot 209, Grave 4
"	1995	ROGERS, Ginger	Section E, Lot 303
"	1966	TERRELL, Kenneth	Section Hollypoint, Lot 327
"	1981	ASTAIRE, Adele (Douglas)	
"	1987	ASTAIRE, Fred	
"	1977	BOYD, Stephen	Outside mausoleum
"	1978	CRANE, Bob	
"	1981	GRAHAME, Gloria	
"	1981	HAYDEN, Russell	
• "	1971	GILBERT, Billy	
Odd Fellows Cemetery, Los Angeles, CA	1985	KYSER, Kay	
Old Cemetery, Chapel Hill, NC	1997	KURALT, Charles	
• Old Chapel Hill Cemetery, University of NC	1990	MARTIN, Mary	Has iron fence surrounding gravesite
Old Greenwood Cemetery, Weatherford, TX	1968	BANKHEAD, Tallulah	Buried near woods, 100 yds. behind church
Old St. Paul's Epis. Ch., nr. Chestertown, MD	1963	GRUNDGENS, Gustav	
• Olsdorf Cemetery, Hamburg, Germany	1987	GLEASON, Jackie	
Our Lady of Mercies Cemetery, Miami, FL	1975	HAYWARD, Susan	
Our Lady of Perpetual Help Ch., Carrollton, GA			
P			
Pacific View Mem. Park, Newport Beach, CA	1979	WAYNE, John	On a hill in an unmarked grave
Palm Mortuary Mausoleum, Las Vegas, NV	1962	JOHNSON, Chic	Ground burial
"	1963	OLSEN, Ole	Ground burial

Specific Interment Locations — by Cemetery

CEMETERY	YEAR	NAME	INTERMENT SITE*
Palm Mortuary Mausoleum, Las Vegas, NV	1969	MORGAN, Russ	
Park Cemetery, Fairmount, IN	1955	DEAN, James	
Passy Cemetery, Paris, France	1971	Fernandel	Black stone tomb with a raised cross
Pateon Delores Cemetery, Mexico City, Mexico	1944	VELEZ, Lupe	
Père Lachaise Cemetery, Paris, France	1923	BERNHARDT, Sarah	Division 44
"	1977	CALLAS, Maria	
"	1927	DUNCAN, Isadora	Div. 87, ashes interred in the Columbarium
"	1991	MONTAND, Yves	
"	1971	MORRISON, Jim	Division 6
"	1963	PIAF, Edith	Black tomb in Division 97
• Pierce Bro's Valhalla Mem. Park, N. Hollywood, CA	1994	NELSON, Nels P.	
Pinelawn Mem. Park, Farmingdale (L.I.), NY	1977	LOMBARDO, Guy	
"	1984	BASIE, William "Count"	
• Plain field Township Cemetery, Rochester, MI	1992	YORK, Dick	
Priory Road Cemetery, Cheltenham, England	1969	JONES, Brian	(In Prestbury)
Prospect Hill Cemetery, Towson, MD	1988	Divine (Harris Glenn Milstead)	
Protestant Churchyard, Celigny, Switzerland	1984	BURTON, Richard	
Providence Memorial Park, Metairie, LA	1972	JACKSON, Mahalia	Section E, on east side of Mausoleum
Putnam Cemetery, Greenwich, CT	1957	PINZA, Ezio	Section L-1
"	1969	COLLYER, Bud	

R

Red Hill Cemetery, Moultonborough, NH	1967	RAINS, Claude	Black marble headstone
Rest Haven Memorial Park, Lafayette, IN	1979	KELLY, Emmett	Sunset Terr. sect., bet. entr. and exit drives
Restland Memorial Park, Burbank, CA	1955	HAMPDEN, Walter	
Restland Memorial Park, Dallas, TX	1971	WALTHALL, Wallace	Acacia 288, Grave 2-3
"	1994	HUMANN, Helena	Chapel Gardens, Crypt 5 S-130
"	1973	BOYD, Jim	
Rimini, Italy	1993	FELLINI, Federico	Buried in a family vault
Rolling Green Memorial Park, Westchester, PA	1990	BAILEY, Pearl	
Rose Dale Cemetery, Los Angeles, CA	1961	WONG, Anna May	Section 5 (Pink marble monument)
"	1956	TATUM, Art	Section 5, in Row 178
"	1952	McDANIEL, Hattie	Section D, across from the office
"	1982	LAMAS, Fernando	
Rose Hill Cemetery, Altoona, PA	1966	HOPPER, Hedda	Ashes buried
Rosehill Cemetery, Bloomington, IN	1981	CARMICHAEL, Hoagy	
Rose Hill Cemetery, Fayetteville, TN	1987	RICE, Adnia	
Rose Hills Memorial Park, Whittier, CA	1970	HOPPER, William	Memorial Urn Garden, Space 210
"	1948	LAUGHLIN, Billy "Froggy"	Older section
"	1994	CAREY, Timothy	
"	1991	LUKE, Keye	
Rosewood Park, Longview, TX	1981	BOWLING, Alice	Chapel Mausoleum
Roy Rogers–Dale Evans Museum, Victorville, CA	1965	Trigger	On display in the museum

S

Sacred Heart Cemetery, Southampton (L.I.), NY	1961	COOPER, Gary	Reburied from L.A., under a 3-ton boulder
• Salt Lake City Cemetery, Salt Lake City, UT	1989	WOODS, Edward	West Section 7-132-1 East
San B./Golden Gate Nat'l Cem., San Bruno, CA	1964	KILBRIDE, Percy	Section 2-B, nr. chain link fence by freeway
San Fernando Mission Cem., San Fernando, CA	1971	LOWE, Edmund	Section B, Block 7, Lot 1113
"	1959	VALENS, Ritchie	Section C, at Curb No. 247, 3 rows in
"	1966	FRAWLEY, William	Section C, at Curb No. 64, 5 rows in
"	1970	BEGLEY, Ed Sr.	Section C, Block 8, Lot 401
"	1974	BRENNAN, Walter	Section D at Curb 445, 8 rows in
"	1964	BENDIX, William	Section D, at Curb No. 241, 14 rows in
"	1956	ARNOLD, Edward	Section D, Block 9, Lot 132
"	1992	CONNORS, Chuck	
"	1981	DWAN, Allan	
"	1985	FAYLEN, Frank	
"	1991	GOBLE, George	
• "	1984	MARLOWE, June	
• San Juan, Puerto Rico	1994	JULIA, Raul	
Santa Barbara Cemetery, Santa Barbara, CA	1958	COLMAN, Ronald	Ridge Oval Section, Lot 663
"	1986	ANGEL, Heather	
Sao Joao Baptista Cem., Rio de Janeiro, Brazil	1955	MIRANDA, Carmen	

CEMETERY	YEAR	NAME	INTERMENT SITE*
Sharon Cemetery, Charlotte, NC	1975	TROTTER, John Scott	
Shenandoah Memorial Park, Winchester, VA	1963	CLINE, Patsy	
Shiloh Church Cemetery, Shreveport, LA	1949	LEDBETTER, Huddie	
Silver Mount Cemetery, Staten Island, NY	1983	TINCHER, Fay	
Sleepy Hollow Cemetery, N. Tarrytown, NY	1946	BOWES, Major Edward	Off Vernon Ave.
"	1939	BRADY, Alice	
Solvang, CA	1985	BAKER, Kenny	Priv. inter. in Santa Barbara Co. nr. Solvang
Southborough Cemetery, Southborough, MA	1938	OLAND, Warner	
Southern Memorial Park, Miami, FL	1975	LOPEZ, Vincent	
Spring Hill Cemetery, Madison, TN	1992	ACUFF, Roy	
SS. Cyril and Methodius Cemetery, Berwick, PA	1968	ADAMS, Nick (Adamshock)	
• St. Agnes Cemetery, Lake Placid, NY	1986	SMITH, Kate	Private Mausoleum
• St. Anne's Cemetery, Cranston RI	1985	COLASANTO, Nicholas	Section 31, Lot 217
• St. Bartholomew's Epis. Ch., New York, NY	1968	GISH, Dorothy	
• "	1993	GISH, Lillian	
St. Hyacinth's Church Cemetery, Westbrook, ME	1986	VALLEE, Rudy	
St. John-at-Hampstead Cem., London, England	1973	BAYLIS, Peter	At back of cemetery
"	1959	KENDALL, Kay (Harrison)	Near front fence
St. John the Baptist Byzantine Cem, Bethel, PA	1987	WARHOL, Andy	
St. John the Baptist Cathedral, Warsaw, Poland	1941	PADEREWSKI, Ignace Jan	Originally buried in Arlington Nat'l. Cem.
"		"	His heart is entombed at the Shrine of
"		"	Our Lady of Czestochowa, Doylestown, PA
"		"	Reburied in free Poland in 1992.
St. John the Evangelist RC Ch., Columbia, MD	1992	KENNY, Herbert C.	
St. John's Ch. Cem., Cold Spring Harbor, NY	1962	BARTON, James	
St. Joseph Cemetery, West Roxbury, MA	1979	FIEDLER, Arthur	
St. Marylebone Cemetery, London, England	1977	STOKOWSKI, Leopold	East Ave. at Rosemary
St. Mary's Cemetery, Ridgefield, CT	1977	RITCHARD, Cyril	
St. Mary's Whitechapel Church, Lancaster, PA	1960	SULLAVAN, Margaret	In churchyard, near curve in path
St. Nicholas Churchyard, Brighton, England	1984	ROBSON, (Dame) Flora	
St. Patrick's Cathedral, New York, NY	1979	SHEEN, (Bishop) Fulton J.	In a crypt below the altar
St. Raymond's Cemetery, The Bronx, NY	1959	HOLIDAY, Billie	
• St Robert Churchyard, La Tourraine, France	1985	BRYNNER, Yul	Monastery of Saint Michael
Ste. Genevieve-Des-Bois, Paris, France	1993	NUREYEV, Rudolph	(Essone District)
Sunset Hills Cemetery, Bozeman, ID	1974	HUNTLEY, Chet	
Sunset Memorial Park, Smithfield, NC	1990	GARDNER, Ava	
T			
Tolochenaz, Vaud, Switzerland	1993	HEPBURN, Audrey	
U			
Union Field Cem., Ridgewood (Queens), NY	1967	LAHR, Bert	
Union Hill Cemetery, Kennett Square, PA	1965	DARNELL, Linda	
Upton Cemetery, Upton, MA	1952	LAWRENCE, Gertrude	
V			
Vagankovskoye Cem., Moscow, Russia	1995	GRINKOV, Sergei	
Valhalla Memorial Park, N. Hollywood, CA	1961	RUSSELL, Gail (Moseley)	Evergreen Section, Curb #4795
"	1957	HARDY, Oliver	Gdn. of Hope, 2nd wall to rt. of Her. Fount.
"	1968	BENADERET, Bea	Mausoleum of Hope, Row C, Crypt 34
"	1971	EDWARDS, Cliff	Section D, near Heritage Fountain
"	1965	MURRAY, Mae	Section G, Block 6328, Lot 6
"	1963	WAGNER, "Gorgeous" George	Section G, Block 6659, Sp. 2, next to mother
"	1976	ROSENBLOOM, Maxie	Section J, Block 9820, Space 3
"	1973	COOPER, Melville	
"	1950	COWL, Jane	
"	1969	CRANE, Richard	
"	1993	DeRITA, Joe	
"	1969	MacLANE, Barton	
"	1973	MORELAND, Mantan	
Valley Oaks Mem. Park, Westlake Village, CA	1994	NILSSON, Harry	
Valley of Light Cemetery, Acapulco, Mexico	1984	WEISSMULLER, Johnny	
Village Cemetery, Tisbury (M.V.), MA	1974	CORNELL, Katharine	(Martha's Vineyard)
Village Churchyard, Chateau DOex, Switzerland	1983	NIVEN, David	

CEMETERY	YEAR	NAME	INTERMENT SITE*
Waldheim/Forest Home Cem., Chicago (F.P.), IL	1958	TODD, Mike	
Welwood Murray Cemetery, Palm Springs, CA	1968	FARRELL, Virginia Valli	Section 10-3, Lot F
"	1990	FARRELL, Charles	Section 10-3, Lot G
Westchester Hills Cem, Hastings-on-Hudson, NY	1952	GARFIELD, John	
"	1965	HOLLIDAY, Judy	
"	1943	REINHARDT, Max	
"	1966	ROSE, Billy	
"	1982	STRASBERG, Lee	
Westminster Abbey, London, England	1989	OLIVIER, Laurence	Poets' Corner
"	1976	THORNDYKE, Sybil	
Westview Cemetery, Atlanta, GA	1969	FREEMAN, Young Frank	Section 10, Lot 277, Grave 10
Westwood Village Mem. Park, Los Angeles, CA	1979	KILIAN, Victor	Ashes scattered in the Rose Garden
"	1984	MASSEY, Edith	Ashes scattered in the Rose Garden
"	1971	FLIPPEN, Jay C.	Corridor of Memories
"	1972	IHNAT, Steve	Corridor of Memories
"	1962	MONROE, Marilyn	Corridor of Memories, #24
"	1990	HAMMER, Armand	In family mausoleum, near entrance
"	1989	SCHAFFNER, Franklin J.	Lot 236
"	1989	CASSAVETES, John	Lot 308
"	1984	CAPOTE, Truman	New Mausoleum, 1st column, bottom
"	1988	O'ROURKE, Heather	New Mausoleum, 1st column, bottom
"	1995	GABOR, Eva	Nr. Armand Hammer's Maus. (Right front)
"	1993	AIDMAN, Charles	Room of Prayer
"	1995	GAZZO, Michael Vincente	Room of Prayer
"	1991	MASSEY, Curt	Room of Prayer
"	1982	PATRICK, Lee (Wood)	Room of Prayer
"	1983	VIVYAN, John	Room of Prayer
"	1993	DeFORE, Don	Rose Garden
"	1979	KENTON, Stan	Rose Garden
"	1995	MARTIN, Dean	Sanctuary of Love
"	1972	LEVANT, Oscar	Sanctuary of Love, bottom right
"	1970	EDENS, Roger	Sanctuary of Remembrance
"	1971	HELTON, Percy	Sanctuary of Remembrance
"	1973	KELLAWAY, Cecil	Sanctuary of Remembrance
"	1972	LANFIELD, Sidney	Sanctuary of Remembrance
"	1979	MASON, Shirley (Lanfield)	Sanctuary of Remembrance
"	1987	TAYLOR, Kent	Sanctuary of Remembrance
"	1972	TRAUBEL, Helen (Bass)	Sanctuary of Remembrance
"	1969	VonSTERNBERG, Josef	Sanctuary of Remembrance
"	1969	BOLES, John	Sanctuary of Serenity
"	1985	MILLER, Marvin E.	Sanctuary of Tenderness
"	1981	WARREN, Harry	Sanctuary of Tenderness, 5th col., bottom
"	1984	CARPENTER, Ken	Sanctuary of Tenderness, rear wall
"	1983	GEORGE, Christopher	Sanctuary of Tranquility
"	1980	MILESTONE, Lewis	Sanctuary of Tranquility
"	1987	RICH, Buddy	Sanctuary of Tranquility, 2nd col., bottom
"	1975	DORN, Philip	Sanctuary of Tranquility, rear wall
"	1976	HOWE, James Wong	Sanctuary of Tranquility, rear wall
"	1977	JOHNSON, Nunnally	Sanctuary of Tranquility, rear wall
"	1980	KORJUS, Miliza	Sanctuary of Tranquility, rear wall
"	1989	VINCENT, Romo	Sanctuary of Tranquility, right, 4 bays up
"	1993	CAHN, Sammy	Section D (near Donna Reed)
"	1984	RIORDAN, Marjorie (Schlaff)	Section D, #1
"	1993	ZAPPA, Frank	Section D, #100 (unmarked) Next to Guild
"	1963	TUTTLE, Frank W.	Section D, #105
"	1982	DANTINE, Helmut	Section D, #130
"	1986	REED, Donna	Section D, #142
"	1976	PIATIGORSKY, Gregor	Section D, #154
"	1980	STRATTEN, Dorothy	Section D, #170
"	1982	DUNNE, Dominique	Section D, #189
"	1989	BACKUS, Jim	Section D, #203

• New entry.

405

* Some cemeteries refuse to reveal specific locations.

CEMETERY	YEAR	NAME	INTERMENT SITE*
Westwood Village Mem. Park, Los Angeles, CA	1987	KAYE, Nora (Ross)	Section D, #36
"	1979	ZANUCK, Darryl F.	Section D, #41
"	1982	ZANUCK, Virginia Fox	Section D, #41
"	1981	WOOD, Natalie (Wagner)	Section D, #60
"	1985	Margo (Albert)	Section D, #61
"	1975	CONTE, Richard	Section D, #62
"	1973	CRANE, Norma	Section D, #62
"	1992	LEHRMAN, Oscar S.	Section D, #81
"	1984	WEST, Brooks	Section D, #81
"	1990	ARDEN, Eve (West)	Section D, #81 (ashes interred)
"	1985	NOLAN, Lloyd	Section D, #84
"	1988	ORBISON, Roy	Section D, #97 (unmarked) Nr. water spigot
"	1985	HECHT, Harold	Section D, in front of #81 (Eve Arden)
"	1994	LANCASTER, Burt	Section D, Near the curb
"	1989	WILDE, Cornel	Urn Garden
"	1984	BASEHART, Richard	Urn Garden (3 down from top, on right)
"	1992	MARX, Samuel	Urn Garden (southeast)
"	1977	CABOT, Sebastian	Urn Garden East (top row, 9 from right)
"	1964	BARRIER, Edgar	
"	1970	DARRELL, J. Stevan	
"	1971	GOMEZ, Thomas	
"	1974	HUDSON, William Woodson Jr.	
"	1979	HUTTON, Jim	
"	1982	JORY, Victor	
"	1977	MATTHEWS, Dorothy (Davis)	
"	1964	MEREDITH, Charles	
"	1967	NEWELL, William Most	
"	1989	NEWMAN, Lionel	
"	1983	PEREIRA, Hal	
"	1978	PERFECT, Rose	
"	1979	RIPPERTON, Minnie	
"	1978	SHAY, Dorothy	
"	1979	WAGENHEIM, Charles	
"	1966	WALKER, June	
"	1970	WIERE, Sylvester	
"	1984	WINWOOD, Estelle	
Will Rogers Memorial, Claremore, OK	1935	ROGERS, Will	Reinterred in 1944 from Forest Lawn, CA
Woodlawn Cemetery, Elmira, NY	1992	ROACH, Hal Sr.	Just inside the Walnut St. gate, 1st turn rt.
Woodlawn Cemetery, Santa Monica, CA	1983	FIX, Paul	Block 17
"	1967	BICKFORD, Charles	Cremated
"	1973	RYAN, Irene	In Mausoleum, 109-C-1
"	1956	BANCROFT, George	In Mausoleum, 147-P-3
"	1961	CARRILLO, Leo	Section 2, (near 14th Street)
"	1960	BROPHY, Ed	
"	1973	HAINES, William	
"	1992	HENREID, Paul	
"	1995	McCLURE, Doug	
"	1994	SMITH, Hal	
Woodlawn Cemetery, The Bronx, NY	1960	BARRYMORE, Diana	Div. 20, bet. E. Border Ave and Chapel Hill
"	1969	CASTLE, Irene	Division 29, off Park View & Spruce Ave.
"	1918	CASTLE, Vernon	Division 29, off Park View & Spruce Ave.
"	1962	KREISLER, Fritz	Division 31, in mausoleum off Filbert Ave.
"	1942	COHAN, George M.	Division 31, off Park Ave.
"	1924	HERBERT, Victor	Div. 42, in maus. at Border and Linden Ave.
"	1974	ELLINGTON, Duke	Division 49, at Fir & Knollwood Aves.
"	1936	MILLER, Marilyn	Division 50, Heather and Whitewood Ave
"	1989	BERLIN, Irving	
"	1960	CLARK, Bobby	
"	1991	DAVIS, Miles	
"	1952	LEE, Canada	
"	1946	TAYLOR, Laurette (Cooney)	
Woodlawn Mem. Park East, Hendersonville, TN	1978	CARTER, Maybelle	

CEMETERY	YEAR	NAME	INTERMENT SITE*
Woodlawn Memorial Park, Nashville, TN	1968	FOLEY, Red	
"	1982	ROBBINS, Marty	
Woodmen Cemetery, DeKalb, TX	1972	BLOCKER, Dan	
Z			
• Zentralfriedhof Central Cemetery, Vienna, Austria	1982	JURGENS, Curt	

CAROLE LOMBARD

7

Original Names
of the Stars

Original Names of the Stars

PROFESSIONAL NAME*	BIRTH, LEGAL or FORMER NAME**
A	
ABBOTT, Bud	William Alexander Abbott
ACKLES, Kenneth	Kenneth Vincent Ackles
Acromaniacs, The	Italo (Al) Immediato
"	Hugo Immediato
"	Nino (Nick) Immediato
ADAMS, Don	Donald James Yarmy
ADAMS, Edie	Elizabeth Edith Enkc
ADAMS, Jimmy	James B. Adams
ADAMS, Maude	Maude Kiskadden
ADAMS, Nick	Nicholas Aloysius Adamschock
ADAMSON, James	William James Adamson
ADAMSON, Victor	(aka Denver Dixon)
ADLER, Buddy	Maurice E. Adler
ADLER, Celia	Celia Feinman Adler
ADOREE, Renée	Jeanne de la Fonte
Adrian	Adrian Adolph Greenberg (aka Gilbert Adrian)
ADRIAN, Iris	Iris Adrian Hosletter
ADRIAN, Louis	Louis Methenitis
ADRIAN, Max	Max Bor (aka Max Cavendish)
AHERNE, Gladys	Gladys Reese
AINLEY, Richard	(aka Richard Riddle)
AINSWORTH, Sidney	Charles Sidney Ainsworth (aka Sydney Ainsworth)
Aladdin	Aladdin Abdullah Achmed Anthony Pallante
ALBERT, Eddie	Edward Albert Heimberger
ALBRIGHT, Hardie	Hardy Albrecht
ALBRIGHT, Wally	Walton Albright, Jr.
ALDA, Robert	Alphonso Giuseppe Giovanni Roberto d'Abruzzo
ALDEN, Mary	Mary Maguire Alden
ALDERSON, Floyd Taliaferro	(aka Hal Taliaferro and Wally Wales)
ALEXANDER, Ben	Nicholas Benton Alexander
ALEXANDER, Jane	Jane Quigley
Alfalfa (of "Our Gang")	Carl Switzer
ALLEN, Fred	John Florence Sullivan
ALLEN, Gracie	Grace Ethel Cecile Rosalie
ALLEN, Woody	Allen Stewart Konigsberg
ALLEY, Paul	Paul Richter Alley
ALLISTER, Claud	William Claud Michael Palmer
ALLYSON, June	Ella Geisman (aka Jan Allyson)
ALVARADO, Don	José Page
AMECHE, Don	Dominic Felix Amici
AMES, Adrienne	Ruth Adrienne Ames
AMES, Leon	Leon Wycoff
Amos (of "Amos & Andy")	Freeman F. Gosden
ANDERS, Laurie	Laurie Raddatz
ANDERSON, Claire	Claire Mathes Anderson
ANDERSON, (Dame) Judith	Frances Margaret Anderson
ANDERSON, G. M.	Max Aronson (aka Gilbert Maxwell Anderson)
ANDOR, Lotte Palfi	Lotte Mosbacher
ANDOR, Paul	Wolfgang Zilzer
ANDRE, Gwili	Gurli Andresen
Andrews Sisters, The	LaVerne Andrews
"	Maxine Andrews
"	Patricia "Patti" Andrews
ANDREWS, Dana	Carver Daniel Andrews
ANDREWS, Edward	Edward Bryan Andrews, Jr.
ANDREWS, Julie	Julia Elizabeth Wells
ANDREWS, Lois	Lorraine Gourley
Andy (of "Amos & Andy")	Charles J. Correll

Original Names of the Stars

PROFESSIONAL NAME*	BIRTH, LEGAL or FORMER NAME**
ANGELI, Pier	*Anna Maria Pierangeli*
ANKRUM, Morris	*Morris Nussbaum (aka Stephen Morris)*
Ann-Margret	*Ann-Margaret Olson*
Annabella	*Suzanne Charpentier*
ANTHONY, Rick	*Enrico Cipriani*
ARBUCKLE, Roscoe "Fatty"	*Roscoe Conklin Arbuckle*
ARCHER, John	*Ralph Bowman*
ARDEN, Eve	*Eunice Quedens*
ARLEDGE, John	*Johnson Lundy Arledge*
ARLEN, Richard	*Cornelius Richard van Mattimore*
Arletty	*Léonie Maria Julia Bathiat*
ARLISS, George	*George Augustus Andrews*
ARMSTRONG, Louis	*Louis Daniel Armstrong*
ARNAUD, Georges	*Henri Georges Charles Achille Girard*
ARNAZ, Desi	*Desiderio Alberto Arnaz y de Acma*
ARNE, Peter	*Peter Arne Albrecht*
ARNESS, James	*James King Aurness*
ARNO, Sig	*Siegfried Arno*
ARNOLD, Edward	*Guenther Edward Arnold Schneider*
ARNOLD, Jessie	*Jessie Gertrude Arnold*
ARQUETTE, Cliff	*aka Charley Weaver*
ARTHUR, Beatrice (Bea)	*Bernice Frankel*
ARTHUR, Jean	*Gladys Georgianna Greene*
ARTHUR, Johnny	*John Lennox Arthur Williams*
ARTHUR, Robert	*Robert Arthaud*
ARVIDSON, Linda	*Linda Johnson*
ASH, Russell	*Russell Harvey Ash*
ASHCROFT, (Dame) Peggy	*Edith Margaret Emily Hutchinson*
ASHLEY, (Lady) Sylvia	*Edith Louise Sylvia Hawkes*
ASLAN, Gregoire	*Krikor Aslanian*
ASTAIRE, Adele	*Adele Marie Austerlitz*
ASTAIRE, Fred	*Frederick Austerlitz*
ASTOR, Mary	*Lucile Vasconcellos Langhanke*
AUDLEY, Michael	*Michael Audley Keck*
AUER, Mischa	*Mischa Simonovich Ounskowsky*
AULT, Marie	*Marie Cragg*
AUMONT, Jean-Pierre	*Jean-Pierre Philippe Salomons*
AUSTIN, Gene	*Eugene Lucas*
AVALON, Frankie	*Francis Thomas Avallone*
AVERY, Charles	*Charles Bradford Avery*
AVERY, Tex	*Frederick B. Avery*
AYE, Maryon	*(aka Marion Aye)*
AYERS, Agnes	*Agnes Hinkle*
AYERS, Lew	*Lewis Ayer*
AYLMER, (Sir) Felix	*Felix Edward Aylmer Jones*
B	
BABBITT, Art	*Arthur Babitsky*
Baby Jane	*Juanita Quigley*
• Baby Lawrence	*Lawrence Jackson*
• Baby Le Roy	*Le Roy Winebrenner*
• Baby Peggy	*Marjorie Eleanor Keyes*
• Baby Ruth Jen	*Ruth Guenther*
Baby Sandy	*Sandra Lea Henville*
Baby Sunshine	*Pauline Flood*
BACALL, Lauren	*Betty Jean Perske*
• BACHMANN, John	*Jack George Bachmann*
• BACKUS, Jim	*James Gilmore Backus*
• BACLANOVA, Olga	*Olga Petrovna Baklano*
BACON, David	*David Gaspar Griswold Bacon*

• New entry.   * Includes both living & deceased persons.   412   ** Sources do not always agree on spelling.

Original Names of the Stars

PROFESSIONAL NAME*	BIRTH, LEGAL or FORMER NAME**
BADDELEY, Angela	Madeleine Angela Clinton-Baddeley
BADEL, Alan	Alan Fernand Badel
• BADET, Régina	Anne Régina Badet
• BADHAM, John	John MacDonald Badham
• BADRAKHAN, Ahmed	Ahmed Badr Khan
BAER, Buddy	Jacob Henry Baer
• BAER, Max	Maximilian Adelbert Baer
• BAEZ, Joan	Joan Chaudoz Baez
BAGDASARIAN, Ross	(aka David Seville)
• BAGLEY, Don	Donald Jeff Bagley
• BAGLEY, Sam	Samuel Borken
• BAILEY, Frankie	Francesca Walters
• BAILEY, Pearl	Pearl Mae Bailey
• BAILEY, William Norton	Gordon Reineck
• BAILLET, Georges	Georges Victor Jules Baillet
• BAINTER, Fay	Fay Okell Bainter
• BAIRD, Bill	William Britton Baird
• BAIRD, Cora	Cora Burbar Eisenberg
• BAKER, Art	Arthur Shank
• BAKER, Benny	Benjamin Zifkin
• BAKER, Blanche	Blanche Garfein
BAKER, Bob	Leland "Tumble" Weed
BAKER, Chet	Chesney H. Baker
BAKER, Eddie	Edward King
BAKER, Kenny	Kenneth Lawrence Baker
BAKER-BERGEN, Stuart	Stuart Bergen, Jr.
BALANCHINE, George	Georgi Melitonovich Balanchivadze
BALDWIN, Alec	Alexander Rae Baldwin. III
BALL, Lucille	Dianne Belmont
BALL, Susan	Suzan Ball
BALLARD, Kaye	Catherine Gloria Balotta
BANCROFT, Anne	Anna Maria Italiano
BANCROFT, Charles	Fred Bently
BANJAMIN, Gladys	Gladys Lanphere
BANKHEAD, Tallulah	Tallulah Brockman Bankhead
BANKS, Monty	Mario Bianchi (aka Montague Banks)
BANKY, Vilma	Vilma Lonchit
BANNER, John	Johann Banner
BARA, Theda	Theodosia Goodman
• BARBARA	Monique Serf
BARBER, Red	Walter Lanier Barber
BARBOUR, Dave	David Michael Barbour
BARCLAY, Don	Don Van Tassel Barclay
BARCROFT, Roy	Howard Ravenscroft
BARDOT, Brigitte	Camille Javal
BARI, Lynn	Marjorie Schuyler Fisher-Bitzer
BARKER, Lex	Alexander Crichlow Barker, Jr.
BARNETT, Vince	Vincent Barnett
BARR, Leonard	Leonard Barri
BARRIE, (Sir) James	James Matthew Barrie
BARRIE, Wendy	Margaret Wendy Jenkins
BARRY, Don "Red"	Donald Barry d'Acosta
BARRY, Gene	Eugene Klass
BARRY, Tom	Hal Donahue
BARRY, Viola	(aka Peggy Pearce)
BARRYMORE, Diana	Diana Blanche Barrymore Blythe
BARRYMORE, Ethel	Ethel Mae Blythe
BARRYMORE, John	John Sidney Blythe
BARRYMORE, John Jr.	John Drew Barrymore

• New entry. * Includes both living & deceased persons.   ** Sources do not always agree on spelling.

Original Names of the Stars

PROFESSIONAL NAME*	BIRTH, LEGAL or FORMER NAME**
BARRYMORE, Lionel	Lionel Blythe
BARTHOLOMEW, Freddie	Frederick Llewellyn (Bartholomew was aunt's name)
BARTLETT, Richard	Richard Norris
• BARTOK, Eva	Eva Ivanova Szoeke
BASIE, Count	William James Basie
BASQUETTE, Lina	Lina Baskette
BASS, Alfie	Alfred Bass
BATES, Barbara	Barbara Jane Bates
BATES, Florence	Florence Rabe
BATORS, Stiv	Steve Bator
BAUM, Vicki	Hedwig Baum
BEAL, John	James Alexander Bliedung
BEAN, Orson	Dallas Frederick Burroughs
Beatles, The	Ringo Starr (Richard Starkey)
"	John Lennon
"	Paul McCartney
"	George Harrison
BEATTY, Warren	Henry Warren Beaty
BECKETT, Scotty	Scott Hastings Beckett
BEDDOE, Don	Donald T. Beddoe
BEECHER, Janet	Janet Beecher Meysenburg
Bee Gees, The	Robin, Barry and Maurice Gibb
BEIDERBECKE, Bix	Leon Bismark Beiderbecke
BEL GEDDES, Barbara	Barbara Geddes Schrewer
Belita	Maria Belita Gladys Lyne Jepson-Turner
BELL, Rex	George Francis Beldam
BENATAR, Pat	Patricia Andrzejewski
BENDER, Russell "Russ"	Richard Bender Jr.
BENNETT, Billie	Emily Haynie
BENEDICT, Billy	William Benedict
BENNETT, Bruce	Herman Brix
BENNETT, Joe	Joseph Bennett Aldert
BENNETT, Tony	Anthony Dominick Benedetto
BENNY, Jack	Benjamin Kubelsky
BENSON, Court	Courtenay E. Benson
BENSON, Robbie	Robin David Segal
BENTLEY, Irene	Alexina Bentley
BERANGER, George	George Andre Beranger
BERGEN, Edgar	Edgar John Berggren
BERKELEY, Busby	William Berkeley Enos, Jr.
BERKES, John	John Patrick Berkes
BERLE, Milton	Milton Berlinger
BERLIN, Irving	Israel Isidore Baline
BERNHARDT, Sarah	Henrietta Rosine Bernard
BERRY, Chuck	Charles Edward Anderson Berry
BEST, Edna	Edna Hove
BETZ, Matthew	Matthew Von Betz
Beulah	Louise Beavers
BEVAN, William "Billy"	William Bevan Harris
BEVANS, Clem	Clem Blevins
BEY, Turhan	Turhan Selahattin Sahultavy Bey
Big Bopper	(See RICHARDSON, Jiles)
Big Boy	Guinn Williams
BIG TREE, Chief John	Isaac Johnny John
Biograph Girl	Florence Lawrence
BIRCH, Wyrley	Ernest Wyrley Birch
BISHOP, Joey	Joseph Abraham Gottlieb
BISHOP, Julie	Jacqueline Wells-Brown (aka Diane Duval)
BISSELL, Whit	Whitner Bissell

Original Names of the Stars

PROFESSIONAL NAME*	BIRTH, LEGAL or FORMER NAME**
BJÖRNSTRAND, Gunnar	Knut Gunnar Björnstrand
BLACKLEY, Douglas	(See Robert Kent)
BLACKTON, J. Stuart	James Stuart Blackton
BLACKTON, Violet	Violet Virginia Blackton
BLAINE, Vivian	Vivienne S. Stapleton
BLAIR, Betsy	Elizabeth Winifred Boger
• BLAIR, Joan	Lilian Wilck
BLAIR, Randy	William Randall Blair
BLAIRE, Sallie	Sara Hutchins (aka Sallie Blair)
BLAKE, Al	Alva D. Blake (aka A. D. Blake)
BLAKE, Amanda	Beverly Louise Neill
BLAKE, Arthur	Arthur Blakely Clark
BLAKE, Eubie	James Hubert Blake
BLAKE, Marie	Edith Blossom MacDonald
BLAKE, Robert	Michael James Vijencio Gubitosi (aka Mickey Gubitosi)
BLAKELY, Colin	Colin George Edward Blakely
BLANC, Mel	Melvin Jerome Blanc
BLETCHER, Billy	William Bletcher
BLONDELL, Joan	Rose Joan Blondell
Blondie (Bumstead)	(see SINGLETON, Penny)
BLOOM, Bobby	Robert Martin Bloom
BLUE, Ben	Benjamin Bernstein
BLYDEN, Larry	Ivan Lawrence Blieden
BLYSTONE, Stanley	William Stanley Blystone
BLYTHE, Betty	Elizabeth Blythe Slaughter
BOARDMAN, True	William True Boardman
BOARDMAN, Virginia True	Virginia Eames
BOGARDE, Dirk	Derek Jules Gaspard Ulric Niven van den Bogaerde
BOGART, Humphrey	Humphrey DeForest Bogart
BOLES, Jim	James Boles, Jr.
BOLGER, Ray	Raymond Wallace Bulcao
BOLGER, Robert	Robert Erin Bolger
BOLT, Robert	Robert Oxton Bolt
BOND, Jack	Alfred Welch
BONDI, Beulah	Beulah Bondy
BONELLI, Richard	Richard Bunn
Bono (U2 lead singer)	Paul Hewson
BONO, Sonny	Salvatore Philip Bono
BOONE, Pat	Charles Eugene Patrick Boone
BOOTH, Edwina	Josephine Constance Woodruff
BOOTH, Shirley	Thelma Booth Ford
BOOTS, Tubby	Charles Andrew Booth
BORDEAUX, Joe	(aka Joe Bordeau)
BORDEN, Olive	Sybil Trinkle
BORGE, Victor	Borge Rosenbaum
BOSTWICK, Dorothy Davis	Dorothy Gompert (aka Dorothy Royce)
BOSWELL, Vet	Helvetia Boswell
Bowery Boys, The	Leo Gorcey
"	Huntz Hall
"	Bobby Jordan
"	Gabriel Dell
"	Bernard Gorcey
Bowery Boys, The (cont'd)	David Gorcey
"	Billy Benedict
"	Bennie Bartlett
BOWIE, David	David Robert Hayward-Jones
BOWLING, Alice	Alice Lon Bowling
BOYD, Jim	James A. Boyd
BOYD, Stephen	William Stephen Millar

• New entry.   * Includes both living & deceased persons.   ** Sources do not always agree on spelling.

PROFESSIONAL NAME*	BIRTH, LEGAL or FORMER NAME**
BOYNE, Sunny	Hazel Boyne
BRADY, Fred	Frederick Kress
BRADY, Scott	Gerald Kenneth Tierney
BRANDON, Henry	Heinrich von Kleinbach
BRASSELLE, Keefe	Keefe B. Brasselli
BRAUER, Tiny	Harold G. Brauer
BRENDEL, El	Elmer Goodfellow Brendel
BRENT, Evelyn	Mary Elizabeth Riggs
BRENT, George	George Brendan Nolan
BRENT, Romney	Romulo Larralde
BRIAN, Mary	Louise Byrdie Dantzler
BRICE, Fanny	Fannie Borach
BRISSON, Carl	Carl Brisson Peterson
BRITT, Elton	James Britt Baker
BRITT, May	Maybritt Wilkens
BRITTANY, Morgan	Suzanne Cupito
BRITTON, Barbara	Barbara Brantingham Czukor
BRITTON, Milt	Milton Levy
BRODIE, Steve	John Stevens
BRODY, Ann	Ann Brody Goldstein
BROMFIELD, John	Farron Bromfield
Broncho Billy	Gilbert Maxwell Aronson (aka G. M. Anderson)
BRONSON, Betty	Elizabeth Ada Bronson
BRONSON, Charles	Charles Dennis Buchinsky
BROOK, Clive	Clifford Hardman Brook
BROOKE, Ralph	Ralph Tweer Brooks
BROOKE, Tyler	Victor Huge de Biere
BROOKE, Van Dyke	Stewart McKerrow
BROOKS, Albert	Albert Einstein
BROOKS, Beverley	Viscountess Beverley Rothermere
BROOKS, Geraldine	Geraldine Stroock
BROOKS, Mel	Melvin Kaminsky
BROPHY, Ed	Edward S. Brophy
Brown Bomber	Joseph Louis Barrow (aka Joe Louis)
BROWN, Georgia	Lillian Claire Laiger Getel Klot
BROWN, Joe E.	Joseph Evans Brown
BROWN, Reno	Ruth Clarke
BROWN, Tom	Thomas Edward Brown
BROWN, Vanessa	Smylla Brind
BRUCE, David	Marden McBroom
BRUCE, Lenny	Leonard Alfred Schneider
BRUCE, Nigel	William Nigel Bruce
BRUCE, Virginia	Helen Virginia Briggs
BRYNNER, Yul	Taidje Khan
BUBBLES, John W.	John W. Sublett
BUCHANAN, Edgar	William Edgar Buchanan
Buckwheat (of "Our Gang")	William (Billy) Henry Thomas, Jr.
Buffalo Bill	William Frederick Cody
Bull	Lewis Montana
BURKE, Billie	Mary William Ethelbert Appleton Burke
BURKE, Chris	Christopher Joseph Burke
BURNETTE, Smiley	Lester Alvin Burnette
BURNS, Bazooka	Robert Burns (aka Bob Burns)
BURNS, Edmund J.	(aka Edward Burns and Ed Burns)
BURNS, George	Nathan Birnbaum
BURR, Raymond	Raymond William Stacy Burr
BURROWS, Abe	Abram Solman Borowitz
BURSTYN, Ellen	Edna Rae Gilhooley
BURTON, LeVar	Levardis Robert Martyn Burton, Jr.

PROFESSIONAL NAME*	BIRTH, LEGAL or FORMER NAME**
BURTON, Richard	Richard Walter Jenkins, Jr.
BUSHMAN, Francis X.	Francis Xavier Bushman
BUSTER, Budd	Budd Leland Buster (aka Bud Buster and George Selk)
Butch (of "Our Gang")	Tommy Bond
BUTLER, David	David Wayne Butler
BUTLER, Fred	Alfred Joline Butler
BUTLER, Royal	Royal Edwin Butler
BUTTONS, Red	Aaron Chwatt
BUZZELL, Eddie	Edward Buzzell
C	
CABANNE, William	William Christy Cabanne
CABOT, Bruce	Jacques-Etienne de Pelessier de Bujac, Jr.
CAGE, Nicolas	Nicholas Coppola
CAINE, Michael	Maurice Joseph Micklewhite
CALHERN, Louis	Carl Henry Vogt
CALHOUN, Alice	Alice Calhoun Chotiner
CALHOUN, Rory	Francis Timothy Durgin
CALLAS, Maria	Maria Sophie Cecilia Calogeropoulos
CALLAWAY, Cab	Cabell Calloway III
CALLEIA, Joseph	Joseph Spurin-Calleja
CALLENDER, Red	George Sylvester Callender
CALLOWAY, Cab	Cabell Calloway
CALVERT, E. H.	Elisha Helm Calvert
CALVERT, Phyllis	Phyllis Bickle
CALVET, Corinne	Corinne Dibos
CALVIN, Henry	Wimberly Calvin Goodman, Jr.
CAMERON, Rod	Nathan Roderick Cox
CAMPBELL, Webster	William Webster Campbell
CANDY, John	John Franklin Candy
CANOVA, Judy	Juliet Canova
CANTINFLAS	Mario Moreno Reyes
CANTOR, Eddie	Edward Israel Iskowitz
CANTOR, Ida	Ida Tobias
CANUTT, Yakima	Enos Edward Canutt
Capucine	Germaine Lefebvre
CARDWELL, James	Albert James Cardwell
CAREWE, Edwin	Edwin Jay Fox
CAREWE, Ora	Ora Whytock
CAREY, Joyce	Joyce Lillian Lawrence
CARLE, Richard	Charles Nicholas Carleton
CARLISLE, Kitty	Catherine Holzman
CARMICHAEL, Hoagy	Hoaglund Howard Carmichael
CARMINATI, Tullio	Count Tullio Carminati de Brambilla
CARNEY, Alan	David Bougal
CARR, Jane	Rita Brunstrom
CARR, Joe "Fingers"	Louis Busch
CARR, Mary K.	Mary Kennevan
CARR, Nat	Nathan C. Carr
CARRADINE, John	Richmond Reed Carradine
CARROL, Regina	Regina Gelfan
CARROLL, Dee	Betty Jean Marsh
CARROLL, Diahann	Carol Diahann Johnson
CARROLL, John	Julian la Faye
CARROLL, Nancy	Ann Veronica LaHiff
CARSON, Sunset "Kit"	Michael James Harrison
CARTER, Helena	Helen Rickerts
CARTER, Janis	Janis Dremann
CARVER, Louise	Louise Spilger Murray
CARVER, Lynn	Virginia Reid Sampson

Original Names of the Stars

PROFESSIONAL NAME*	BIRTH, LEGAL or FORMER NAME**

CASEY, Dolores	Margaret Dolores Katherine Casey
CASSIDY, Hopalong	William Boyd (aka Bill Boyd)
CASSIDY, Jack	John Edward Joseph Cassidy
CASTLE, Irene	Irene Foote
CASTLE, William	William Schloss
CAVENS, Fred	Frederic Adolphe Cavens
CHAMPLIN, Irene	Irene Field
CHANDLER, Jeff	Ira Grossel
CHANDLER, Janet	Lillian Guenther (aka Lillian Barrett)
CHANDLER, Lane	Lane Robert Chandler Oakes
CHANEY, Frances	Frances Cleveland Bush (aka Cleva Creighton)
CHANEY, Lon (Jr.)	Creighton T. Chaney
CHANEY, Lon (Sr.)	Alonso Chaney
CHANEY, Norman "Chubby"	Norman Myers Chaney
CHAPLIN, Charlie	Charles Spencer Chaplin
CHAPLIN, Sydney	Sydney Hawkes (half-brother of Charles)
CHARISSE, Cyd	Tula Ellice Finklea (aka Lily Norwood)
CHARLES, Ray	Ray Charles Robinson
CHASE, Charley	Charles Parrott
CHASE, Chevy	Cornelius Crane Chase
CHASE, Colin	Colin Collings
CHASE, Stephen	Stephen Alden Chase
CHAYEFSKY, Paddy	Sidney Aaron Chayefsky
CHEATHAM, Jack	John Preston Cheatham
CHECKER, Chubby	Ernest Evans
CHEFEE, Jack	(aka Jack Chefe)
Cher	Cherilyn Sarkisian LePierre
CHESEBRO, George	George Newell Chesebro
CHEVALIER, Maurice	Maurice Auguste Chevalier
Chief Thundercloud (later)	Scott T. Williams
Chief Thundercloud (original)	Victor Daniels
Chief Yowlachie	Daniel Simmons
Christian-Jaque	Christian Albert François Maudet
CHRISTIAN, Linda	Blanca Rosa Welter
CHRISTY, June	Shirley Luter
CHRYSIS, International	Billy Schumacher (became a transexual)
Chubby (of "Our Gang")	Norman Myers Chaney
Cisco Kid	Duncan Renaldo
CLAIR, René	René-Lucien Chomette
CLAIRE, Ina	Ina Fagan
CLARENCE, O. B.	Oliver B. Clarence
CLARK, Bobby	Robert Edwin Clark
CLARK, Buddy	Samuel Goldberg (Do not confuse with B. Clarke, d. 1957)
CLARK, Dane	Bernard Zanville
CLARK, Fred	Frederic Leonard Clark
• CLARK, Garrett Cameron	Garrett Cameron Miller
CLARKE, Buddy	Robert Clarke (Do not confuse with Buddy Clark, d. 1949)
CLARKE, Mae	Mary Klotz
CLARKE-SMITH, D. A.	Douglas A. Clarke-Smith
• CLASTER, Nancy	Nancy Goldman (aka Nancy Rogers and Miss Nancy)
CLAYTON, Buck	Wilbur Dorsey Clayton
CLAYTON, Marguerite	(aka Marguerite Bitter)
CLEMENTE, Roberto	Roberto Walker Clemente
CLEMENTO, Steve	aka Steve Clemente and Steve Clements
CLIBURN, Van	Harvey Lavan Cliburn, Jr.
CLIFFORD, Jack	Virgil James Montani
CLIFTON, Emma Bell	Emma MacGrew
CLINE, Eddie	Edward Francis Cline
CLINE, Patsy	Virginia Patterson Hensley

Original Names of the Stars

PROFESSIONAL NAME*	BIRTH, LEGAL or FORMER NAME**
CLIVE, Colin	Colin Clive Greig
CLIVE, E. E.	Edward E. Clive
CLIVE, Henry	Henry Clive O'Hara
COBB, Lee J.	Leo Jacoby
COBB, Ty	Tyrus Raymond Cobb
COBURN, Charles	Charles Douville Coburn
COBURN, Doddie	Dorothy Coburn
COCHRAN, Steve	Robert Alexander Cochran
CODY, Bill Sr.	William Frederick Cody
CODY, Emmett	Emmett Francis Cody
CODY, Lew	Louis Joseph Coté
COGHLAN, Junior	Frank Coghlan, Jr.
COLBERT, Claudette	Lily Claudette Chauchoin
COLBY, Anita	Anita Counihan
COLE, Buddy	Edwin Lamar Cole
COLE, Nat King	Nathaniel Adams Coles
COLLIER, Constance	Laura Constance Hardie
COLLIER, Patience	Renée Ritcher
COLLINS, Dorothy	Marjorie Chandler
COLLINS, Monty	Monte Francis Collins, Jr.
COLONNA, Jerry	Geraldo Luigi Colonna
COLUMBO, Russ	Ruggerio Eugenio di Rudolpho Colombo
COMINGORE, Dorothy	Linda Winters
COMO, Perry	Pierino Roland Como
CONNELLY, Bobby	Robert J. Connelly
CONNORS, Chuck	Kevin Joseph Connor
CONNORS, Michael	Krekor Jay Ohanian-Koreniowski
CONRAD, Robert	Conrad Robert Falk
CONRIED, Hans	Frank Foster Conried
CONTE, Richard	Richard Nicholas Peter Conte
CONTI, Albert	Albert De Conti Cadassamare
CONWAY, Tom	Thomas Charles Sanders
COOGAN, Jack Sr.	John Coogan
COOK, Cookie	Charles Cook
COOK, Joe	Joseph Lopez
COOKE, Alistair	Alfred Alistair Cooke
COOLEY, Spade	Donell Clyde Cooley
COOMBE, Carol	Gwendoline Alice Coombe
COOPER, Albert	Albert Raymond Cooper
COOPER, Alice	Vincent Furnier
COOPER, Gary	Frank James Cooper
COOPER, Jackie	John Cooperman, Jr.
COPPERFIELD, David	David Seth Kotkin
CORDAY, Josephine	(aka Josie Rich)
CORDAY, Rita	Jeanne Paule Teipotemarga
"	(aka Paula Corday and Paula Croset)
CORDY, Henry	Henry Korn
COREY, Joseph	Joseph Martorano
• CORNETT, Barbara	(aka Barbara Allen and Barbara Woodell)
CORRIGAN, Ray "Crash"	Raymond Benard (aka Ray Benard)
CORTEZ, Ricardo	Jacob (Jake) Krantzko (Kranze)
COSELL, Howard	Howard William Cohen
COSTELLO, Elvis	Declan Patrick McManus
COSTELLO, Lou	Louis Francis Cristillo
COTTON, Billy	William Edward Cotton
COWAN, Jerome	Jerome Palmer Cowan
COWARD, (Sir) Noel	Noel Pierce Coward
COX, Wally	Wallace Maynard Cox
CRABBE, Larry "Buster"	Clarence Linden Crabbe

• New entry.   * Includes both living & deceased persons.   ** Sources do not always agree on spelling.

Original Names of the Stars

PROFESSIONAL NAME*	BIRTH, LEGAL or FORMER NAME**
CRAIG, Blanche	Blanche Sanderson
CRAIG, James	John Henry Meador
CRAIG, Michael	Michael Gregson
CRAMER, Rychard	Rychard Earl Cramer (aka Richard Cramer)
CRANE, Norma	Norma Anna Bella Zuckerman
• CRASH, Darby	Jan Paul Beahm
CRAVEN, Eddie	John Edward Craven
CRAVEN, John E.	John Edward Craven
CRAWFORD, Anne	Imelda Crawford
CRAWFORD, Broderick	William Broderick Crawford
CRAWFORD, Howard Marion	(aka Howard Marion)
CRAWFORD, Joan	Lucille Fay LeSueur
CREGAR, Laird	Samuel Laird Cregar
CRIMMONS, Daniel	Alexander M. Lyons
CRIPPS, Kernan	John Kernan Cripps
CROCKETT, Dick	Richard Crockett
CROGHAN, Joe	Joseph Michael Croghan
CROMWELL, John	Elwood Dager Cromwell
CROMWELL, Richard	LeRoy Melvin Radebaugh
CRONYN, Hume	Hume Cronyn Blake
CROSBY, Bing	Harry Lillis Crosby
CROSBY, Dixie Lee	Wilma Wyatt
CRUISE, Tom	Thomas Cruise Mapother, IV
CRUZE, James	Jens Cruz Bosen
Cuddles (S. Z. Sakall)	Eugene Gero Szakall (aka Szoke Szakall)
CUEVAS, Joey	José Luis Cuevas
CULVER, Cal	John Calvin Culver (aka Casey Donovan)
CUMMINGS, Constance	Constance Halverstadt
CUMMINGS, Robert	Charles Clarence Robert Orville Cummings
CUMMINGS, Sandy	Sanford B. Cummings
CUMMINS, Dorothy	Dorothy Louise Cassil (aka Dorothy Cassil)
CUNARD, Grace	Harriet Mildred Jefferies
CUNNINGHAM, Joe	Joseph A. Cunningham
Curly (of "3 Stooges")	Jerome Lester Howard (Horwitz)
CURRIE, Finlay	Finley Jefferson Currie
CURTIS, Alan	Harold Neberroth
CURTIS, Jackie	John Holder, Jr.
CURTIS, Ken	Curtis Gates
CURTIS, Tony	Bernard Schwartz
CURTIZ, Michael	Mihaly Kertesz
CUSTER, Bob	Raymond Anthony Glenn
CUTTING, Dick	Richard H. Cutting
D	
DAGOVER, Lil	Antonia Maria Siegelind e Martha Seubert
Dagwood (Bumstead)	(see LAKE, Arthur)
DAINTY, Billy	William Dainty
D'ALBROOK, Sidney	(aka Sidney Dalbrook)
DALE, Bobby	Robert Flatley
DALE, Charlie	Charlie Marks
DALE, Virginia	Virginia Paxton
DALEY, Cass	Catherine Dailey
DALIO, Marcel	Marcel Benoit Blauschild
DALL, John	John Jenner Thompson
DALY, John	John Charles Daly
DAMITA, Lili	Liliane Marie Madeleine Carré (aka Liliane Loomis)
DAMONE, Vic	Vito Farinola
DAMPIER, Claude	Claude Cowan
DANA, Viola	Virginia Flugrath
DANGERFIELD, Rodney	Jacob Cohen

• New entry.   * Includes both living & deceased persons.   ** Sources do not always agree on spelling.

Original Names of the Stars

PROFESSIONAL NAME*	BIRTH, LEGAL or FORMER NAME**
DANIEL, Billy	William Baker
DANIELL, Henry	Charles Henry Daniell
DANIELS, Bebe	Phyllis Daniels
DANIELS, Mickey	Richard Daniels, Jr.
DANIELS, Victor	(aka Chief Thundercloud)
D'ARCY, Roy	Roy F. Guisti
DARIN, Bobby	Robert Walden Cassotto
Darla (of "Our Gang")	Darla Jean Hood
DARLING, Candy	James Slattery
DARLING, Jean	Dorothy Jean LeVake
DARNELL, Linda	Manetta Eloisa Darnell
DARREN, James	James William Ercolani
DARRO, Frankie	Frank Johnson
DARVI, Bella	Bayla Wegier
DARWELL, Jane	Patti Woodward
DASH, Pauly	Paul Walter Dashiff
DAUBE, Belle	(aka Harda Daube)
DAUPHIN, Claude	Claude Legrand
DAVENPORT, Alice	Alice Shepard
DAVES, Delmar	Delmar Lawrence Daves
DAVID, Thayer	David Thayer Hersey
DAVIES, Marion	Marion Cecilia Douras
DAVIS, Battle	Thomas Battle Davis
DAVIS, Bette	Ruth Elizabeth Davis
DAVIS, Jackie	John Harold Davis
DAVIS, Jim	James Davis
DAVIS, Miles	Miles Dewey Davis III
• DAVIS, Philip K.	Philip Kenneth Davis
DAVIS, Rufe	Rufus Eldon Davidson
DAW, Evelyn	Evelyn Daw Smith
DAY, Dennis	Eugene Dennis McNulty
DAY, Doris	Doris Mary Anne von Kappelhoff
DAY, Laraine	Laraine Johnson
Dead End Kids, The	Leo Gorcey
"	Huntz Hall
"	Billy Halop
"	Bobby Jordan
"	Bernard Punsley
DEAN, Eddie	Edgar Dean Glossup
DEAN, James	James Byron Dean
DEANE, Palmer	Palmer Deane Whitted, Jr.
DeCARLO, Yvonne	Peggy Yvonne Middleton
DeCASALIS, Jeanne	Jeanne de Casalis de Pury
DeCORDOVA, Arturo	Arturo Garcia Rodriguez
DEE, Frances	Jean Frances Dee
DEE, Sandra	Alexandra Cymboliak Zuck (or Sandra Douvain)
DeGREY, Sydney	Sidney de Gray
DEHNER, John	John Forkum
DEKKER, Albert	Albert Ecke
DEL MAR, Claire	Clara Eloise Mohr (married name)
DEL RIO, Dolores	Lolita Dolores de Martinez
DEL VAL, Jean	Jean Gauthier
DEMAIN, Gordon	(aka Gordon D. Wood)
DeMILLE, Cecil B.	Cecil Blount DeMille
DENNING, Richard	Louis A. Denninger
DENNIS, Sandy	Sandra Dale Dennis
DENNY, Reginald	Reginald Leigh Daymore
DENVER, John	Henry John Deutschendorf, Jr.
DEREK, Bo	Mary Cathleen Collins

• New entry.   * Includes both living & deceased persons.   ** Sources do not always agree on spelling.

Original Names of the Stars

PROFESSIONAL NAME*	BIRTH, LEGAL or FORMER NAME**
DEREK, John	*Derek Sullivan Harris*
• DeRITA, Joe	*Joseph Wardell*
DeROACH, Charles	*Charles d'Authier de Rochefort*
DESMOND, Florence	*Florence Dawson*
DEVEAU, Jack	*John R. Deveau*
DEVINE, Andy	*Andrew Devine*
DeVITO, Danny	*Daniel Michael DeVito*
DEVLIN, J. G.	*James G. Devlin*
DEVORE, Dorothy	*Alma Inez Williams*
DeWILDE, Brandon	*Andre Brandon de Wilde*
DeWOLFE, Billy	*William Andrew Jones*
DEXTER, Anthony	*Walter Reinhold Alfred Frederick Fleischmann*
DIAMOND, I. A. L.	*Itek Dommnici (aka Isadore Diamond)*
DICKERSON, Henry	*Dudley Henry Dickerson*
DICKINSON, Angie	*Angeline Brown*
DIETERLE, William	*Wilhelm Doerr (aka Wilhelm Dieterle)*
DIETRICH, Marlene	*Maria Magdalene von Losch*
DILLER, Phyllis	*Phyllis Driver*
DILLON, Jack	*John T. Dillon*
DILLON, Tom	*Thomas Patrick Dillon*
DINEHART, Alan Sr.	*Mason Alan Dinehart*
DISNEY, Walt	*Walter Elias Disney*
Divine	*Harris Glenn Milstead*
DIX, Richard	*Ernest Carlton Brimmer*
DIXON, Denver	*Victor Adamson*
DODSWORTH, John	*John Cecil Dodsworth*
DOLBERG, Nola	*Nola Luxford*
DOLLY, Jenny	*Janszieka Deutsch*
DOLLY, Rosie	*Roszicka Deutsch*
DOMINGUEZ, Joe	*José J. Dominguez*
DONAHUE, Troy	*Merle Johnson*
DONNELL, Jeff	*Jean Marie Donnell*
DONOVAN, Casey	*John Calvin Culver*
DORN, Philip	*Fritz van Dungen*
DORO, Marie	*Marie Kathleen Stewart*
DORR, Harry	*Harry Lester Dorr (aka Lester Dorr)*
DORS, Diana	*Diana Mary Fluck*
DORSEY, Jimmy	*James Francis Dorsey*
DORSEY, Tommy	*Thomas Francis Dorsey*
DOUGLAS, Donald	*Douglas Kinleyside*
DOUGLAS, Kirk	*Issur Danielovitch Demsky*
DOUGLAS, Melvyn	*Melvyn Hesselberg*
DOUGLAS, Robert	*Robert Douglas Finlayson*
DOUGLAS, Steve	*Steven Kreisman*
DOUGLASS, Kent	*Douglass Montgomery*
DOVE, Billie	*Lilian Bohney*
DOW, Peggy	*Peggy Varnadow*
DOWLING, Eddie	*Joseph Nelson Goucher*
DOWNS, Johnny	*John Morey Downs*
DRAKE, Alfred	*Alfred Capurro*
DRAKE, Charles	*Charles Ruppert*
DRAKE, Dona	*Rita Novella*
DRAKE, Tom	*Alfred Alderdice*
DRESSER, Louise	*Louise Josephine Kerlin*
DRESSLER, Marie	*Leila Maria von Koerber*
DREW, Ellen	*Terry Parker (aka Terry Ray and Sy Bartlett)*
Dr. Kildare	*Joel McCrea (1937)*
"	*Lew Ayres (1938-42)*
"	*Van Johnson (1942-44) — tried to replace Lew Ayres*

• New entry.   * Includes both living & deceased persons.   ** Sources do not always agree on spelling.

Original Names of the Stars

PROFESSIONAL NAME*	BIRTH, LEGAL or FORMER NAME**
Dr. Kildare (con't)	Philip Dorn (1942) — tried to replace Lew Ayres
"	Keye Luke (1942-47) — tried to replace Lew Ayres
"	Richard Quine (1942) — tried to replace Lew Ayres
"	James Craig (1947) — new protégé of Dr. Gillespie
"	Richard Chamberlain (1960-65) — Dr. Kildare on TV
DRU, Joanne	Joanne L. la Cock
DUEL, Peter	Peter Deuel
DUFF-GRIFFIN, William	William Joseph Duffy
DUGAN, Tom	Thomas J. Dugan
DUKE, Patty	Anna Marie Duke
DUMONT, Margaret	Daisy Margaret Baker
DUNBAR, Dixie	Christine Elizabeth Dunbar
DUNCAN, Kenne	Kenneth Duncan MacLachlan
Duncan Sisters, The	Rosetta Duncan ("Topsy")
"	Vivian Duncan ("Little Eva")
DUNFEE, Nora	Marjorie Dean Dunfee
DUNHAM, Phil	Phillip Gray Dunham
DUNN, Bobby	Robert V. Dunn
DUNN, James	James Howard Dunn
DUNN, Michael	Gary Neil Miller
DUNNE, Irene	Irene Marie Dunn
Durango Kid, The	Charles Starrett
DURANTE, Jimmy	James Francis Durante
DURBIN, Deanna	Edna Mae Durbin
DURKIN, Junior	James Trent Durkin
DURYEA, George	Richard Powers (aka Tom Keene)
DVORAK, Ann	Ann McKim
DWAN, Allan	Joseph Aloysius Dwan
DYLAN, Bob	Robert Allen Zimmerman
E	
EAGLE, Jimmy	James Eagle
EAMES, Virginia	(aka Virginia True Boardman)
EARLES, Harry	Kurt Schneider (aka Harry Doll)
EBSEN, Buddy	Christian Rudolf Ebsen
EDDY, Nelson	Nelson Ackerman Eddy
EDEN, Barbara	Barbara Jean Huffman
EDWARDS, Gus	Gus Simon
EDWARDS, Jimmy	James Keith O'Neill Edwards
EDWARDS, Neely	Cornelius Limbach
EDWARDS, Vince	Vincent Edward Zoine, III
EICHELBERGER, Ethyl	James Roy Eichelberger
EILERS, Sally	Dorothea Sally Eilers
ELDRIDGE, Florence	Florence McKechnie
ELDRIDGE, John	John Eldredge
ELLINGTON, Duke	Edward Kennedy Ellington
ELLIOT, Cass	Ellen Naomi Cohen (aka Mama Cass)
ELLIOTT, Dick	Richard Damon Elliott
ELLIOTT, William "Wild Bill"	Gordon Nance
ELLIOTT, William D.	William David Elliott
ELLIS, Patricia	Patricia Gene O'Brien
ELLISON, James	James Ellison Smith
ELMER, Billy	William Elmer Johns
ELSOM, Isobel	Isobel Jeanette Reed (aka Isobel Harbord)
ELY, Ron	Ronald Pierce
EMERSON, John	Clifton Paden
EMERTON, Roy	Hugh Fitzroy Emerton
EMERY, Gilbert	Gilbert Emery Bensley Pottle
ENDFIELD, Cy	Cyril Raker Endfield
ENGLISH, John W.	John Wilkinson English

Original Names of the Stars

PROFESSIONAL NAME*	BIRTH, LEGAL or FORMER NAME**
ENTWISTLE, Peg	Lillian Millicent Entwistle
EPSTEIN, David S.	David Schaffer Epstein
EPSTEIN, Jerry	Jerome Epstein
ERICKSON, Leif	William Wycliff Anderson
ERICSON, John	Joseph Alexander Meibes
ERGAS, Joseph	(aka Brutus Peck)
Esmeralda	Alma Graciela Haro Cabello (aka Haro Cabello)
ESMOND, Carl	Willy Eichberger
EVANS, Dale	Frances Octavia Smith
EVANS, Joan	Joan Eunson
EVERETT, Chad	Raymond Lee Cramton
EWELL, Tom	S. Yewell Tompkins
EYTHE, William	William John Joseph Eythe
F	
Fabian	Fabian Anthony Forte-Bonaparte
Fabio	Fabio Lanzoni
FABRAY, Nanette	Ruby Bernadette Nanette Theresa Fabares
FAIRBANKS, Douglas Jr.	Douglas Elton Ullman, Jr.
FAIRBANKS, Douglas Sr.	Douglas Elton Thomas Ullman
FAIRBROTHER, Sydney	Sydney Tapping
FAIRCHILD, Morgan	Patsy McClenny
FAITH, Adam	Terence Nelhams
FALK, Peter	Peter Michael Falk
FALKENBERG, Jinx	Euginia Falkenburg
FARENTINO, James	Ferdinand Anthony Ferrandino
Farina (of "Our Gang")	Allen Clayton Hoskins, Jr.
FARLEY, Dot	Dorothea Farley
FARLEY, Jim	James Lee Farley
FARMER, Frances	Frances Elena Farmer
FARMER, Virginia	Mary Virginia Farmer
FARROW, Mia	Maria de Lourdes Villiers
FAWCETT, Farrah	Mary Farrah Leni Fawcett
FAYE, Alice	Alice Jeanne Leppert
FAYLEN, Frank	Frank Ruf
FELDMAN, Marty	Martin Alan Feldman
FENTON, Frank	Frank Fenton-Morgan
FENTON, Leslie C.	Leslie Carter Fenton
Fernandel	Fernand Joseph Désiré Contandin
FERRER, José	José Vincente Ferrery de Otero y Cintron
FERRER, Mel	Melchior Gaston Ferrer
FETCHIT, Stepin	Lincoln Theodore Monroe Andrew Skeeter Perry
FETHERSTON, Eddie	(aka Eddie Featherstone)
Fibber McGee	Jim Jordan
FIELD, Virginia	Margaret Cynthia Field
FIELDS, Gracie	Grace Stansfield
FIELDS, Stanley	Walter L. Agnew
FIELDS, Totie	Sophie Feldman
FIELDS, W. C.	William Claude Dukenfield
FINCH, Peter	Peter George Frederick Ingle-Finch
FINE, Larry	Louis Feinberg
FINLAYSON, James	James Henderson Finlayson
• FINN, Lila	Lila Shanley
FISHER, Carrie	Carrie Frances Fisher
FISHER, Eddie	Edwin Jack Fisher
FISKE, Richard	Thomas Richard Potts
FISKE, Robert	Robert L. Fiske
FITZGERALD, Barry	William Joseph Shields
FITZGERALD, Walter	Walter Bond
FIX, Paul	Paul Fix Morrison

PROFESSIONAL NAME*	BIRTH, LEGAL or FORMER NAME**
FLATT, Lester	Lester Raymond Flatt
FLEISCHER, Max	Maximilian Fleischer
• FLEMING, Eric	Edward Heddy
FLEMING, Ian	Ian Mac Farlane
FLEMING, Rhonda	Marilyn Louis
FLOWERS, Wayland	Wayland Parrott Flowers, Jr.
FLYNN, Errol	Errol Leslie Thompson Flynn
FLYNN, Joe	Joseph Flynn
FLYNN, Sean	Sean Leslie Flynn
FOCH, Nina	Nina Consuelo Maud Fock
FOLEY, Red	Clyde Julian Foley
FONDA, Henry	Henri Jaynes Fonda
FONDA, Jane	Jane Seymour Fonda
FONDA, Peter	Peter Henry Fonda
FONTAINE, Joan	Joan de Beauvoir de Havilland (aka Joan Burfield)
FONTANNE, Lynn	Lillie Louise Fontanne
FONTEYN, (Dame) Margot	Peggy Hookham
FORAN, Dick	John Nicholas Foran
FORBES, Ralph	Ralph Taylor
FORD, Francis	Francis O'Fearna
FORD, Glenn	Gwyllyn Samuel Newton Ford (aka John Gover)
FORD, John	Sean Aloysius O'Fearna
FORD, Mary	Colleen Summers
FORD, Paul	Paul Ford Weaver
FORD, "Tennessee" Ernie	Ernest Jennings Ford
FORD, Wallace	Samuel Jones Grundy
FORMBY, George	(aka George Hoy)
FORREST, Mark	Lou Degni
FORREST, Sally	Katherine Sally Feeney
FORREST, Steve	William Forrest Andrews
FORSYTHE, John	John Lincoln Freund
FORTE, Joe	Josef Forte
FOSSE, Bob	Robert Louis Fosse
FOSTER, Dianne	Dianne Laruska
• FOSTER, Frances	Frances Brown
FOSTER, Jodie	Ariane Alicia Christian Foster
FOSTER, Norman	Norman Hoeffer
FOSTER, Phil	Fivel Feldman
FOSTER, Susanna	Suzanne DeLee Flanders Larsen
FOX, Harry	Arthur Carringford
FOX, Michael J.	Michael Andrew Fox
FOXX, Redd	John Elroy Sanford
FOY, Eddie Jr.	Edward Fitzgerald, Jr.
FOY, Eddie Sr.	Edward Fitzgerald
FRANCEN, Victor	Victor Franssen
FRANCHI, Franco	Francesco Benenato
FRANCIOSA, Anthony	Anthony George Papaleo
FRANCIS, Ann	Frances S. Roberts
FRANCIS, Arlene	Arlene Francis Kazanjian
FRANCIS, Connie	Concetta Maria Rosa Franconero
FRANCIS, Kay	Katherine Edwina Gibbs
FRANCIS, Robert	Robert Charles Francis
FRANCIS, Sandra	Sandra Francis Dian Bawdin (aka Sandra Donat)
FRANCIS, Wilma	Wilma Sareussen
FRANCISCUS, James	James Grover Franciscus
FRANEY, Billy	William Franey
FRANKLIN, Melvin	David English
FRANKLIN, Sidney	Sidney Arnold Franklin
FRANKOVICH, Mike	Mitchell J. Frankovich

Original Names of the Stars

PROFESSIONAL NAME*	BIRTH, LEGAL or FORMER NAME**

PROFESSIONAL NAME*	BIRTH, LEGAL or FORMER NAME**
FRASER, Bill	William Fraser
FRAZEE, Jane	Mary Jane Frahse
FREDERICI, Blanche	Blanche Friderici Campbell (aka Blanche Friderici)
FREDERICK, Pauline (actress)	Pauline Libbey
FREED, Arthur	Arthur Grossman
FREEMAN, Howard	Howard Schoppe Freeman
FREEMAN, Mona	Monica Elizabeth Freeman
FRELENG, Friz	Isadore Freleng
Frenchie	Samuel Marx
FRESNAY, Pierre	Pierre Jules Louis Laudenbach
FRIGANZA, Trixie	Brigid O'Callaghan
FRIML, Rudolf	Charles Rudolf Friml
FRISCO, Joe	Lewis W. Joseph
FRIZZELL, Lefty	William Orville Frizzell
FROEBE, Gert	Karl-Gerhard Frober
Froggy (of "Our Gang")	Billy McLaughlin
FURNESS, Betty	Elizabeth Mary Furness
FURST, Anton	Anthony Francis Furst
G	
GAAL, Franceska	Franziska Zilveritch
Gabby	George Francis Hayes
GABIN, Jean	Jean Gabin Alexis Moncorge
GABLE, Clark	William Clark Gable
GABOR, Zsa Zsa	Sari Gabor
GALLAGHER, Skeets	Richard Gallagher
GALVANI, Dino	(aka Dino Galvanoni)
GARBO, Greta	Greta Louisa Gustafsson
GARCIA, Andy	Andres Arturo Garcia-Menendez
GARCIA, Jerry	Jerome John Garcia
GARDENIA, Vincent	Vincenzio Scognamiglio
GARDINER, Reginald	William Reginald Gardiner
GARDNER, Ava	Ava Lavinia Gardner
• GARDNER, Ed	Edward Poggenberg
GARDNER, Helen	Helen Louise Gardner
GARFIELD, John	Jacob Julius Garfinkle
GARLAND, Beverly	Beverly Campbell
GARLAND, Judy	Frances Ethel Gumm
GARNER, James	James Scott Baumgarner
GARON, Pauline	Marie Pauline Garon
GARRALAGA, Martin	Martin Gorralaag
GAUDIO, Joe	Joseph E. Gaudio
GAYE, Marvin	Marvin Pentz Gay, Jr.
GAYLE, Crystal	Brenda Gayle Webb
GAYNOR, Janet	Laura Gainer
GAYNOR, Mitzi	Francesca Mitzi Marlene de Czanyi von Gerber
GAZZO, Michael	Michael Vincente Gazzo
GEARY, Bud	S. Maine Geary
GEER, Will	William Aughe Ghere
GEHRIG, Lou	Henry Louis Gehrig
GENTRY, Minnie L.	Minnie Lee Watson
GEORGE, Boy	George Alan O'Dowd
GEORGE, "Chief" Dan	Geswanouth Slahoot
GEORGE, Gladys	Gladys Anna Clare
GEORGE, Gorgeous	George Raymond Wagner
GEORGE, Heinrich	Heinz Georg Schulz
GERAY, Steve	Stefan Gyergay
GERRARD, Douglas	Douglas Gerrard McMurrogh-Kavanagh (aka Douglas Gerard)
GERRON, Kurt	Kurt Gerson
GERSHWIN, George	George Gershvin (Gershovitz or Gershwine)

Original Names of the Stars

PROFESSIONAL NAME*	BIRTH, LEGAL or FORMER NAME**
GERSON, Jeanne	Jeanne Aleshnick
GERSTLE, Frank	Frank Morris Gerstle
GIBSON, Helen	Rose August Wenger (aka Rose Gibson)
GIBSON, Hoot	Edmund Richard Gibson
GIBSON, Mel	Mel Columcille Gibson
GILBERT, John	John Pringle
GILFORD, Jack	Jacob Gellmann
GILLESPIE, Dizzy	John Birks Gillespie
GILLIS, Ann	Alma Mabel O'Connor
GIOVALE, Franco	Francesco Giovale
GISH, Dorothy	Dorothy Elizabeth de Guiche
GISH, Lillian	Lillian Diana de Guiche
GLAUDI, Hap	Lloyd Glaudi
GLEASON, James	James Austin Gleason
GLEASON, Lucille	Lucille Webster
GLENN, Raymond	Raymond Anthony Glenn Custer (aka Bob Custer)
GODDARD, Paulette	Pauline Marion Goddard (aka Marion Levy)
GOLDBERG, Whoopi	Karen Johnson
GOLDIN, Pat	(aka Pat Golden)
GOLDWYN, Frances Howard	Frances McLaughlin (aka Frances Howard)
GOLDWYN, Samuel	Samuel Goldfish
GOODE, Jack	Irwin Thomas Whittridge
GOODWIN, Bill	William Nettles Goodwin
GOODWIN, Ruby	Ruby Berkley Goodwin
• GORA, Claudio	Emilio Giordana
GORCEY, Leo	Leo Bernard Gorcey
GORDON, C. Henry	Henry Racke
GORDON, Robert	Robert Gordon Duncan
GORDON, Ruth	Ruth Gordon Jones
GORME, Eydie	Edith Gormezano
GRABLE, Betty	Ruth Elizabeth Grable
GRAHAM, Bill	Wolfgang Grajonca
GRAHAM, Morland	(aka Moreland Graham)
GRAHAME, Gloria	Gloria Grahame Hallward
GRANGER, Stewart	James Stewart-Lablache
GRANT, Cary	Archibald Alexander Leach
GRANT, Kathryn	Olive Katherine Grandstaff
GRANT, Kirby	Kirby Grant Horn
GRANT, Lee	Lyova Haskell Rosenthal
GRANT, Shauna	Colleen Marie Applegate
GRANT, Tiny	Ralph Grant Matthiessen
GRAPEWIN, Charley	Charles Grapewin
GRAVES, Peter	Peter Aurness-Graves
GRAVET, Fernand	Fernand Mertens (aka Fernand Gravey)
• GRAY, Barry	Bernard Yaroslaw
GRAY, Charles	Donald Marshall Gray
GRAY, Coleen	Doris Jensen
GRAY, Dulcie	Dulcie Bailey
GRAY, Gilda	Marianna Michalska
GRAY, Glen	Glen Gray Knoblaugh
GRAYSON, Kathryn	Zelma Kathryn Elizabeth Hedrick
GRAZIANO, Rocky	Thomas Rocco Barbella
Greatful Dead, The	Jerry Garcia
"	Mickey Hart
"	Bill Kreutzmann
"	Phil Lesh
"	Bob Weir
"	Vince Welnick
Great Gildersleeve, The	Harold José Pereira de Faria (aka Harold Peary)

• New entry.   * Includes both living & deceased persons.   ** Sources do not always agree on spelling.

Original Names of the Stars

PROFESSIONAL NAME*	BIRTH, LEGAL or FORMER NAME**

PROFESSIONAL NAME*	BIRTH, LEGAL or FORMER NAME**
GREAZA, Walter	*Walter Noel Greaza*
GREEN, Harry	*Harry Blitzer*
GREEN, Martyn	*William Martyn Green*
GREEN, Mitzi	*Elizabeth Keno*
GREENE, Herbert	*Herbert Stanton Greene*
GREENSTREET, Sydney	*Sydney Hughes Greenstreet*
GREENWOOD, Charlotte	*Frances Charlotte Greenwood*
GRENFELL, Joyce	*Joyce Irene Phipps*
GREY, Joel	*Joel Katz*
GREY, Nan	*Eschol Loleet Miller*
GREY, Olga	*Anna Zachak*
GREY, Robert H.	*Henry Virtue Goerner*
GRIBBON, Eddie	*Edward T. Gribbon*
GRIFFIES, Ethel	*Ethel Woods*
GRIFFIN, Carlton	*Carlton Elliott Griffin*
GRIFFITH, Corinne	*Corinne Scott*
GRIFFITH, D. W.	*David Llewelyn Wark Griffith*
GRIFFITH, Harry	*Harry Sutherland Griffith*
GRIFFITH, Katherine	*Katherine Kierman*
GUARD, Kit	*Christen Klitgaard*
GUBITOSI, Mickey	*(See Robert BLAKE)*
GUILFOYLE, James	*James Ancel Guilfoyle*
GUINAN, Texas	*Mary Louise Cecelie Guinan*
GURIE, Sigrid	*Sigrid Gurie Haukelid*
GUTHRIE, Woody	*Woodrow Wilson Guthrie*
GWENN, Edmund	*Edmund Kellaway, Jr.*
GWYNNE, Anne	*Marguerite Gwynne-Trice*
GWYNNE, Fred	*Frederick Hubbard Gwynne*
H	
HACKETT, Bobby	*Robert Leo Hackett*
HACKETT, Buddy	*Leonard Hacker*
HACKETT, Joan	*Joan Ann Hackett*
HACKETT, Karl	*Karl Ellsworth Germain*
HADEN, Sara	*Sara Hadden*
HADLEY, Reed	*Reed Bert Herring*
HAGEN, Jean	*Jean Shirley Verhagen*
HAGNEY, Frank S.	*(aka Frank Hagny)*
HALE, Alan	*Rufus Alan McKanan*
HALE, Creighton	*Patrick Fitzgerald*
HALE, Georgia	*Georgette Theodora Hale*
HALE, Jonathan	*Jonathan Hatley*
HALE, Sonnie	*John Robert Hale Munro*
HALEY, Jack	*Jonathan Joseph Haley*
HALL, Charlie	*Charles D. Hall*
HALL, Huntz	*Henry Hall*
HALL, James	*James Brown*
HALL, Jon	*Charles Hall Locher (aka Lloyd Crane)*
HALL, Porter	*Clifford Porter Hall*
HALOP, Billy	*William Halop*
HAMER, Rusty	*Russell Craig Hamer*
HAMILTON, Neil	*James Neal Hamilton*
Hammer	*Stanley Kirk Burrell*
HAMMOND, Kay	*Dorothy Katharine Standing*
HAMPDEN, Walter	*Walter Hampden Daugherty*
HAMPTON, Grace	*(aka Grayce Hampton)*
HANCOCK, Tony	*Anthony Hancock*
HANDWORTH, Octavia	*Octavia Boas*
HARDING, Ann	*Dorothy Walton Gatley*
HARDING, Lyn	*David Llewellyn Harding*

Original Names of the Stars

PROFESSIONAL NAME*	BIRTH, LEGAL or FORMER NAME**
HARDY, Oliver	Oliver Norvelle Hardy
HARLOW, Jean	Harlean Carpenter
HAROLDE, Ralf	Ralf Harolde Wigger
HARRELSON, Woody	Woodrow Tracy Harrelson
HARRIS, Morris	Morris Oliver Harris
HARRIS, Robert H.	Robert Harris Hurwitz
HARRISON, Rex	Reginald Carey Harrison
HARRON, Bobby	Robert Harron
HARRON, Tessie	Anna Theresa Harron
HART, Neal	Cornelius A. Hart, Jr.
HART, William S.	William Surrey Hart, Sr.
HARTIGAN, Pat	Patrick C. Hartigan
HARTLEY, Mariette	Mary Loretta Hartley
HARVEY, Hank	Herman Heacker
HARVEY, Laurence	Larushka Mischa Skikne
HARVEY, Lilian	Lilian Muriel Helen Harvey
HASSE, O. E.	Otto Eduard Hasse
HASSO, Signe	Signe Eleonora Cecilia Larsson
HATTON, Raymond	Raymond William Hatton
HAVER, June	June Stovenour
HAVOC, June	Ellen Evangeline Hovick
HAWLEY, Wanda	(aka Wanda Petit)
HAYAKAWA, Sessue	Sessue Kintaro Hayakawa
HAYDEN, Russell "Lucky"	Pate Lucid
HAYDEN, Sterling	Sterling Christian Relyea Walter
HAYES, Allison	Mary Jane Hayes
HAYES, Helen	Helen Hayes Brown
HAYES, Margaret "Maggie"	Lorette Ottenheimer
HAYES, Sam	Samuel Stewart Hayes
HAYMES, Dick	Richard Benjamin Haymes
HAYWARD, Louis	Louis Seafield-Grant
HAYWARD, Susan	Edythe Marreanner
HAYWORTH, Rita	Margarita Carmen Cansino
HEALY, Ted	Charles Earnest Lee Nash
HEARN, Eddie	Guy Edward Hearn
HEFLIN, Van	Emmett Evan Heflin, Jr.
HEGGIE, O. P.	Otto Peters Heggie
• HELM, Brigitte	Brigitte Eva Gisela Schittenhelm
HEMING, Violet	Violet Hemming
HENDERSON, Del	George Delbert Henderson
HENDERSON, Dickie	Richard Henderson
HENDERSON, Fletch	Fletcher Henderson
HENDRIX, Jimi	James Marshall Hendrix
HENDRIX, Wanda	Dixie Wanda Hendrix
HENRIED, Paul	Paulus Sergius Julius Henreid von Wasel Waldingau
HENRY, Charlotte	Charlotte Virginia Henry
HENRY, Tom	Thomas Browne Henry
HEPBURN, Audrey	Audrey Kathleen Ruston
HERBERT, Holmes	Edward Sanger
HERLIE, Eileen	Eileen O'Herlihy
HERMAN, Pee-wee	Paul Reubenfeld (aka Paul Reubens)
HERMAN, Woody	Woodrow Wilson Herman
HERNANDEZ, Anna	Anna Dodge
HERNDON, Bill	William E. Herndon
HERRIOT, James	James Alfred Wight
HERSHEY, Barbara	Barbara Herzstein (aka Barbara Seagull)
HERVEY, Irene	Irene Herwick
HEWSTON, Alfred H.	(aka Alfred Heuston)
HIATT, Ruth	Ruth Redfern

• New entry.   * Includes both living & deceased persons.   ** Sources do not always agree on spelling.

Original Names of the Stars

PROFESSIONAL NAME*	BIRTH, LEGAL or FORMER NAME**
HICKS, Russell	Edward Russell Hicks
HILDEBRAND, Hilde	Emma Minna Hildebrand
Hildegarde	Hildegarde Loretta Sell
HILL, Benny	Alfred Hawthorn Hill
• HILL, Dana	Dana Hill Goetz
HILL, George W.	George William Hill
Hilo Hattie	Clara Nelson
HOBART, Rose	Rose Keefer
HODGSON, Leland	(aka Leyland Hodgson)
HOEFLICH, Lucie	Helene Lucie von Holwede
HOEY, Dennis	Samuel David Hyams
HOFFMAN, Otto	Otto Frederick Hoffman
HOLDEN, Fay	Dorothy Fay Hammerton (aka Fay Gaby)
HOLDEN, William	William Franklin Beedle, Jr.
HOLDREN, Judd	Judd Clifton Holdren
HOLIDAY, Billie	Eleanor Gough McKay (aka Eleanor Fagan)
HOLLES, Antony	(aka Anthony Holles)
HOLLIDAY, Judy	Judith Tuvim
HOLLIMAN, Earl	Anthony Earl Numkena
HOLLY, Buddy	Charles Hardin Holly
HOLMAN, Libby "Peaches"	Elizabeth Holzman
HOLT, Jack	Charles John Holt
HOLT, Tim	John Charles Holt, III
HOLT, Ula	Ula Vale
HOMEIER, Skip	George Vincent Homeier
HOOD, Darla	Darla Jean Hood
HOON, Shannon	Richard Shannon Hoon
HOOVER, J. Edgar	John Edgar Hoover
Hopalong Cassidy	William Boyd
HOPE, Bob	Leslie Townes Hope
HOPKINS, Miriam	Ellen Miriam Hopkins
HOPPER, De Wolf	William DeWolf Hopper
HOPPER, Hedda	Elda Furry
HOPPER, William	William DeWolf Hopper, Jr.
HOPTON, Russell	Harry Russell Hopton
HOROWITZ, Vladimir	Vladimir Gorowicz
HORTON, Robert	Mead Howard Horton
HORVATH, Charles	Charles Frank Horvath
HOSKINS, Allen "Farina"	Allen Clayton Hoskins, Jr.
HOUDINI, Harry	Ehrich Weiss
HOUSEMAN, John	Jacques Haussmann
HOUSMAN, Arthur	(aka Arthur Houseman)
HOUSTON, Renée	Katherine Houston Gribbin
HOWARD, Jerome "Curly"	Jerome Lester Horwitz
HOWARD, John	John Cox
HOWARD, Leslie	Leslie Howard Stainer
HOWARD, Mary	Mary Rogers Brooks
HOWARD, Moe	Moses Harry Horwitz
HOWARD, Shemp	Samuel Horwitz
HOWARD, Willie	William Levkowitz
HOWE, James Wong	Wong Tung Jim
HOWELL, Wayne	Wayne Chappelle
HOWES, Reed	Herman Reed Howes
HOWLIN, Olin	(aka Olin Howland)
HOYT, John	John Hoysradt
HUDNET, Bill	William H. Hudnet
HUDSON, Rock	Roy Harold Scherer, Jr. (later Roy Harold Fitzgerald)
HUDSON, William	William Woodson Hudson, Jr.
HULL, Josephine	Josephine Sherwood

• New entry.   * Includes both living & deceased persons.   ** Sources do not always agree on spelling.

Original Names of the Stars

PROFESSIONAL NAME*	BIRTH, LEGAL or FORMER NAME**
HULL, Warren	John Warren Hull
HUMPERDINCK, Engelbert	Arnold George Dorsey
HUMPHREY, William	William Jonathan Humphrey
HUNT, Marsha	Marcia Virginia Hunt
HUNTER, Jeffrey	Henry Herman McKinnies, Jr.
HUNTER, Kim	Janet Cole
HUNTER, Ross	Martin Fuss
HUNTER, Tab	Arthur Gelien
HUNTLEY, Chet	Chester Robert Huntley
HUROK, Sol	Solomon Hurok
HURT, Mary Beth	Mary Beth Supinger
HUSTON, Walter	Walter Houghston
HUTTON, Betty	Elizabeth Jane Thornburg
HUTTON, Jim	Dana James Hutton
HUTTON, Marion	Marion Thornburg
HUTTON, Robert	Robert Bruce Winne

I

Ice-T	Tracy Marrow
ICE, Vanilla	Robert Van Winkle
IDOL, Billy	William Michael Broad
IMMEDIATO, Al	Italo Immediato
IMMEDIATO, Nick	Nino Immediato
INCE, John E.	John Edward Ince
INCE, Ralph W.	Ralph Waldo Ince
INESCORT, Frieda	Frieda Wightman
INGE, William	(aka Walter Gage)
INGRAM, Rex (Hitchcock)	Reginald Ingram Montgomery Hitchcock
"	(aka Rex Hitchcock)
"	(Do not confuse with the black actor named Rex Ingram)
Ink Spots, The	Herbert C. Kenny (replaced Orville "Hoppy" Jones in 1944)
"	Bill Kenny
"	Charlie Fuqua
"	Billy Bowen
IRWIN, Charles	Charles Wesley Irwin
"It" Girl, The	Clara Gorson Bow
IVES, Burl	Burl Icle Ivanhoe

J

JACK, Wolfman	Bob Smith
JACKSON, Mary Ann	Gloria Pressman (aka Mildred Jackson)
JACKSON, Selmer	Selmer Adolph Jackson
Jackson's, The	Maureen "Rebbie" Jackson (Eldest)
"	Sigmund Esco "Jackie" Jackson
"	Toriano Adaryll "Tito" Jackson
"	Jermaine LaJaune Jackson
"	LaToya Yvonne Jackson
"	Marion David Jackson
"	Michael Joe Jackson
"	Steven Randall "Randy" Jackson
"	Janet Dameta Jackson (Youngest)
JACQUES, Hattie	Josephine Edwina Jacques
JAMISON, Bud	William Jamison (or Jamieson)
JANNINGS, Emil	Theodor Friedrich Emil Janenz
JANSSEN, David	David Harold Meyer
JAQUET, Frank	Frank Garnier Jaquet
JARRETT, Art	Arthur Jarrett
JASON, Leigh	Leigh Jacobson
JEAN, Gloria	Gloria Jean Schoonover
JEANS, Ursula	Ursula McMinn
JENKINS, Allen	Alfred McGonegal

Original Names of the Stars

PROFESSIONAL NAME*	BIRTH, LEGAL or FORMER NAME**
JENKS, Si	Howard H. Jenkins
JENNINGS, Claudia	Mimi Chesterton
JENNINGS, S. E.	Sylvester Ennis Jennings
JEROME, Suzie	Susan Willis
JERROLD, Mary	Mary Allen
JOEL, Billy	William Martin Joel
JOHN, Elton	Reginald Kenneth Dwight
JOHNSON, Chic	Harold Ogden Johnson
JOHNSON, Chubby	Charles Randolph Johnson
JOHNSON, Don	Donald Wayne Johnson
JOHNSON, Katie	Katherine Johnson
JOHNSON, Kay	Catherine Townsend
JOHNSON, Tor	Tor Johansson
JOHNSON, Van	Charles Van Dell-Johnson
JOLSON, Al	Asa Yoelson
JONES, Bobby	Robert Tyre Jones, Jr.
JONES, Brian	Lewis Brian Hopkins-Jones
JONES, Buck	Charles Frederick Gebhardt
JONES, Candy	Jessica Arline Wilcox
JONES, Charlotte	Charlotte Nathanson
JONES, Emrys	Emrys Whittaker-Jones
• JONES, Grandpa	Louis Marshall Jones
JONES, Jennifer	Phyllis Isley
JONES, Spike	Lindley Armstrong Jones
JONES, T. C.	Thomas Craig Jones
JONES, Tom	Thomas Jones Woodward
JORDAN, Marion "Molly McGee"	Marion Driscoll
JORDAN, Richard	Robert Anson Jordan
JOSLYN, Allyn	Allyn Morgan Joslyn
JOURDAN, Louis	Louis Gendre
JOY, Leatrice	Leatrice Joy Zeidler
JOYCE, Brenda	Betty Graffina Leabo
JULIA, Raul	Raul Rafael Carlos Julia y Arcelay
JURADO, Katy	Maria Christina Estella Marcella Jurado Garcia
JUSTIN, John	Juan Ledesman
K	
KABIBBLE, Ish	Merwyn Bogue
KARINA, Anna	Hanne Karin Bayer
KARLOFF, Boris	William Henry Pratt
KARLSON, Phil	Philip Karlstein
KASZNAR, Kurt	Kurt Serwicher
KATCH, Kurt	Isser Kac
KAY, Beatrice	Hannah Beatrice Kuper
KAYE, Danny	David Daniel Kominski
KAYE, Darwood "Waldo"	Darwood Kenneth Smith
KAZAN, Elia	Elia Kazanjoglous
KEACH, Stacy	Walter Stacy Keach, Jr.
KEATON, Buster	Joseph Francis Keaton
KEATON, Diane	Diane Hall
KEATON, Michael	Michael Douglas
KEEL, Howard	Harold Leek
KEELER, Ruby	Ethel Keeler
KEENE, Tom	George Duryea (aka Richard Powers)
KEITH, Brian	Robert Brian Keith, Jr.
KEITH, Ian	Keith Ross
KELLJAN, Robert	Robert Kelljchian
KELLY, Dorothy	Dorothy Helen Kelly
KELLY, Gene	Eugene Curran Kelly
KELLY, Patsy	Sarah Kelly

PROFESSIONAL NAME*	BIRTH, LEGAL or FORMER NAME**
KELLY, Paul	Paul Michael Kelly
KENDALL, Cy	Cyrus W. Kendall
KENDALL, Kay	Justine Kendall McCarthy
KENNEDY, Arthur	John Arthur Kennedy
KENNEDY, Douglas	Douglas Richards Kennedy (aka Keith Douglas)
KENNEDY, Fred	Frederick O. Kennedy
KENNY, Herbert C.	Herbert Cornelius Kenny
KENT, Jean	Joan Summerfield (aka Jean Carr)
KENT, Robert	Douglas Blackley
KENTON, Stan	Stanley Newcombe Kenton
KERMACK, Paul	Stewart Auchinleck
KERN, Jerome	Jerome David Kern
KERR, Deborah	Deborah Kerr-Trimmer
KERR, Frederick	Frederick Keen
KERR, Stu	Thomas Stewart Kerr (aka Prof. Kool and Bozo the Clown)
KERRIGAN, J. Warren	Jack Warren Kerrigan
KERRY, Norman	Arnold Kaiser
Kettles, The	Marjorie Main (Ma)
"	Percy Kilbride (Pa)
KEY, Kathleen	Kitty Lanahan
Keystone Kops, The	Charles Avery
"	Eddie Baker
"	Bobby Dunn
"	Georgie Jesky
"	Edgar Kennedy
"	Grover Ligon
"	Hank Mann
"	Victor Potel
"	Mack Riley
"	Slim Summerville
KHAN, Chaka	Yvette Stevens
KIBBEE, Guy	Guy Bridges Kibbee
KIDDER, Margot	Margaret Kidder
Kiki	Alice Prin (aka Kiki du Montparnasse)
KILIAN, Pauline	(aka Pauline Hopkins and Pauline Stone)
KING, Andrea	Georgetta Barry
KING, Carole	Carole Klein
KING, Claude E.	Claude Ewart King
KING, Dennis	Dennis Pratt
KING, Michael	Richard C. Wegener
• King Sisters, The	Alyce King
• "	Donna King
• "	Louise King
• "	Yvonne King
KINGSLEY, Ben	Krishna Banji
KINGSLEY, Sidney	Sidney Kirshner
• KINLEY, Edwin	Edwin Kienle
KINSKI, Klaus	Nikolaus Gunther Nakszynski
KINSKI, Nastassja	Nastassja Nakszynski (aka Nastassia Kinski)
KIRK, Phyllis	Phyllis Kirkegaard
• K.I.S.S.	Peter Criss
• "	Ace Frehley
• "	Gene Simmons
• "	Paul Stanley
KNIEVEL, Evel	Robert Craig
KNIGHT, Bob	Robert Honold
KNIGHT, Fuzzy	J. Forrest Knight
KNIGHT, June	Margaret Rose Vallikett
KNIGHT, Ted	Tadeus Wladyslaw Konopka

Original Names of the Stars

PROFESSIONAL NAME*	BIRTH, LEGAL or FORMER NAME**

KNOWLES, Patric	*Reginald Lawrence Knowles*
"Kodak" Girl, The	*Eleanor Boardman*
KORVIN, Charles	*Geza Karpathi*
• KORVIN, Charles	*Geza Karpathi*
KOSLECK, Martin	*Nicolai Yoshkin*
KOSTER, Henry	*Hermann Kosterlitz*
KRAHLY, Hanns	*(aka Hans Kraly)*
KULKY, Henry	*(aka Bomber Kulkavich)*
• KUNEY, Francine	*Francine Ames*
L	
• LaCENTRA, Peg	*Margherita La Centra*
LADD, Cheryl	*Cheryl Stoppelmoor*
LAHR, Bert	*Irving Lahrheim*
LAINE, Frankie	*Frank Paul Lo Vecchio*
LAKE, Arthur	*Arthur Silverlake*
LAKE, Veronica	*Constance Ockleman*
LaMARR, Barbara	*Reatha Watson*
LAMARR, Hedy	*Hedwig Kiesler*
LAMBERTI, Professor	*Michael Lamberti*
LAMOUR, Dorothy	*Mary Leta Dorothy Stanton*
LANCASTER, Burt	*Burton Stephen Lancaster*
LANCHESTER, Elsa	*Elizabeth Sullivan*
LANDERS, Ann	*Esther "Eppie" Pauline Friedman*
LANDI, Elissa	*Elisabeth-Marie-Christine Kuhnelt*
LANDIS, Carole	*Frances Ridste*
LANDIS, David	*David Landis Fritz*
LANDON, Michael	*Eugene Maurice Orowitz*
LANE, Allan "Rocky"	*Harry L. Albershart*
LANE, Charles	*Charles Willis Lane*
LANE, Lola	*Lola Mullican*
LANE, Lupino	*Henry George Lupino*
LANE, Priscilla	*Priscilla Mullican*
LANE, Rosemary	*Rosemary Mullican*
LANG, June	*June Vlasek*
lang, k.d.	*Katherine Dawn Lang*
LANSING, Joi	*Joyce Wassmansdoff*
LANSING, Robert	*Robert Brown*
LANTEAU, William	*William Lanctot*
LANTZ, Gracie	*Grace Stafford*
LANZA, Mario	*Alfredo Arnold Cocozza*
LaROCQUE, Rod	*Rodrique la Rocque de la Rour*
LaRUE, Frank H.	*Frank Herman La Rue*
LaRUE, Jack	*Gaspare Biondolillo*
LATELL, Lyle	*Lyle Zeiem*
LATIMORE, Frank	*Frank Kline*
LATZ, Elaine	*Elaine Sandra Latz*
LAUGHLIN, Billy "Froggy"	*(aka Billy McLaughlin)*
LAUREL, Stan	*Arthur Stanley Jefferson*
LAURIE, Piper	*Rosetta Jacobs*
LAVERNE, Lucille	*(aka Lucille Q. Scott)*
LAWFORD, (Lady) May	*May Summerville*
LAWRENCE, Gertrude	*Alexandre Dagmar Lawrence-Klasen*
LAWRENCE, Jody	*Josephine Lawrence Goddard*
LAWRENCE, Steve	*Sidney Leibowitz*
LAWSON, Wilfrid	*Wilfred Worsnop*
LAWTON, Frank	*Frank Lawton Mokeley*
LEANDER, Zarah	*Zarah Stina Hedberg*
LEE, Anna	*Joanna Winnifrith*
LEE, Billy	*Billy Lee Schlensker*

Original Names of the Stars

PROFESSIONAL NAME*	BIRTH, LEGAL or FORMER NAME**
LEE, Brenda	Brenda Mae Tarpley
LEE, Bruce	Li Yuen Kam (aka Li Siu-lung)
LEE, Canada	Leonard Lionel Cornelius Canegata
LEE, Dixie	Wilma Wyatt
LEE, Gwen	Gwendolyn Le Pinski
LEE, Gypsy Rose	Rose Louise Hovick
LEE, Johnny "Calhoun"	John Dotson Lee, Jr.
LEE, Lila	Augusta Appel
LEE, Michelle	Michelle Dusiak
LEE, Peggy	Norma Egstrom
LEE, Ruth	Ruth Rhodes
LEE, Vanessa	Winifred Ruby Moule
LEEDS, Andrea	Antoinette Lees
• LeFEVRE, Bill	William F. LeFevre
LEIGH, Janet	Jeanette Morrison
LEIGH, Vivien	Vivien Mary Hartley
LeMOYNE, Charles	Charles J. Lemon
LENYA, Lotte	Karoline Blamauer
LEONARD, Gus	Gustav Lerond
LEONARD, Jack E.	Leonard Lebitsky
LEONARD, Robert Z.	Robert Zigler Leonard
LEONARD, Sheldon	Sheldon Leonard Bershad
LEONETTI, Tommy	Nicola Tomaso Leonetti
LE ROY, Baby	Le Roy Winnebrenner
LE ROY, Hal	John LeRoy Schotte
LESLEY, Carole	Maureen Rippingale
LESLIE, Gene	Leslie Eugene Halverson
LESLIE, Joan	Joan Brodell
LESTER, Bruce	Bruce Lister
LESTER, Kate	Sarah Cody
L'ESTRANGE, Dick	Gunther van Strensch
"	(aka Richard LaStrange and Dick LeStrange)
LEVENE, Sam	Samuel Levine
LEVENSON, Sam	Samuel Levenson
LEWIS, Buddy	Morgan Lewis, Jr.
LEWIS, Edwina	Margaret Klenck
LEWIS, Henry	Henry Jay Lewis
LEWIS, Huey	Hugh Cregg
LEWIS, Jerry	Joseph Levitch
LEWIS, Joe	Joe Lewis Barrow
LEWIS, Robert Q.	Robert Lewis (he added the "Q." at age 22)
LEWIS, Ronald "Raan"	Ronald Dean Lewis
LEWIS, Ted	Theodore Leopold Friedman
LEXY, Edward	Edward Gerald Little
Liberace	Wladziu Valentin Liberace (aka Walter "Lee" Liberace)
LIGHTNER, Winnie	Winifred Hanson
LIGON, Grover G.	(aka Grover Liggon and G. G. Ligon)
LILLIE, Beatrice	Constance Sylvia Munston (Lady Peel)
LINCOLN, Elmo	Otto Elmo Linkenhelt
LINDEN, Hal	Harold Lipshitz
LINDER, Max	Gabriel Louville
LINDFORS, Viveca	Elsa Viveca Tortensdotter
LINDSAY, Margaret	Margaret Kies
LINGEN, Theo	Franz Theodor Schmitz
LISTON, Sonny	Charles Liston
LITEL, John	John Beach Litel
LITTLE, Billy	Billy Rhodes
LITTLE, Bozo	John F. Pizzo
Little Rascals, The	(see "Our Gang")

PROFESSIONAL NAME*	BIRTH, LEGAL or FORMER NAME**
LITVAK, Anatole	*Michael Anatole Litvak*
LIVINGSTON, Robert (Bob)	*Robert Randall*
LIVINGSTONE, Mary	*Sadye Marks*
LLOYD, Harold	*Harold Clayton Lloyd*
LOCHER, Felix	*Felix Maurice Locher*
LOCKHART, Kathleen	*Kathleen Arthur*
LOCKWOOD, Alexander	*Aleksander Wyrwicz*
LOCKWOOD, Margaret	*Margaret Day*
LODER, John	*John Lowe*
LOM, Herbert	*Herbert Charles Angelo Kuchacevich ze Schluderpacheru*
LOMBARD, Carole	*Jane Alice Peters*
LOMBARDI, Vince	*Vincent Thomas Lombardi*
LOMBARDO, Guy	*Gaetano Albert Lombardo*
LONDON, Julie	*Julie Peck*
LONDON, Tom	*Leonard Clapham*
LOPEZ, Vincent	*Vincent Joseph Lopez*
LORD, Jack	*John Joseph Ryan*
LORDS, Traci	*Nora Louise Kuzma*
LOREN, Sophia	*Sofia Scicolone*
LORNE, Marion	*Marion Lorne MacDougal*
LORRAINE, Harry	*Harry Wolf*
LORRAINE, Lillian	*Mary Ann Brennan*
LORRAINE, Louise	*Louise Escovar*
LORRE, Peter	*Laszlo Loewenstein*
LORRING, Joan	*Magdalen Ellis*
LOSCH, Tilly	*Ottila Losch*
LOSEY, Joseph	*Joseph Walton Losey*
LOSS, Joe	*Joshua Alexander Loss*
LOUIS, Joe "Brown Bomber"	*Joseph Lewis Barrow*
LOUISE, Anita	*Anita Louise Fremault*
LOVE, Bessie	*Juanita Horton*
LOVE, Montagu	*(aka Montague Love)*
LOVELY, Louise	*Louise Corbasse*
LOWERY, Robert	*Robert Lowery Hanke*
LOWRY, Judith	*Judith Ives*
LOY, Myrna	*Myrna Williams*
LUCAN, Arthur	*Arthur Towle*
LUCE, Clare Boothe	*Ann Clare Boothe*
LUFKIN, Sam	*Samuel William Lufkin*
LUGOSI, Bela	*Bela Lugosi Blasko*
LUKAS, Paul	*Pal Lukacs*
LUNCEFORD, Jimmy	*James Melvin Lunceford*
LUPINO, Wallace	*(aka Wallace Lane)*
LUTHER, Ann	*(aka Anna Luther)*
LUTTRINGER, Al	*Alfonse Luttringer*
LYEL, Viola	*Violet Watson*
LYNN, Diana	*Dolly Loehr*
LYNN, Jeffrey	*Ragnar Godfrey Lind*
LYNN, Sharon	*D'Auvergne Sharon Lindsay*
LYNN, (Dame) Vera	*Vera Welch*
LYONS, Fred	*Fred F. Leyva*
LYS, Lya	*Natalia Lyecht*
M	
MABLEY, Jackie "Moms"	*Loretta Mary Aiken*
• MACDONALD, J. Farrell	*Joseph Farrell Macdonald*
MacGRAW, Ali	*Alice MacGraw*
MACK, Cactus	*Thomas McPheeters*
MACK, Charles E.	*Charles E. Sellers*
MACK, Helen	*Helen McDougall*

Original Names of the Stars

PROFESSIONAL NAME*	BIRTH, LEGAL or FORMER NAME**
MACK, Hughie	Hugh McGowan
MACK, Marion	Joey McCreery
MacKENNA, Kenneth	Leo Mielziner, Jr.
MacKENZIE, Gisele	Marie Marguerite Louise Gisele LaFleche
MacLAINE, Shirley	Shirley Maclean Beaty
MacMURRAY, Fred	Frederick Martin MacMurray
MACRAE, Duncan	John Duncan Graham Macrae
MADISON, Guy	Robert Ozell Moseley
MADISON, Noel	Nathaniel Moscovitch
Madonna	Madonna Louise Veronica Ciccone
MAHONEY, Jock	Jacques O'Mahoney
MAILES, Charles H.	Charles Hill Mailes
MAIN, Marjorie	Mary Tomlinson (Krebs)
MAITLAND, Ruth	Ruth Erskine
MAJORS, Lee	Harvey Lee Yeary, 2nd
MALDEN, Karl	Mladen Sekulovich
MALONE, Dorothy	Dorothy Maloney
MALTBY, H. F.	Henry F. Maltby
MALYON, Eily	Eily Sophie Lees-Craston
MANDER, Miles	Lionel Mander
MANKIEWICZ, Joseph L.	Joseph Leo Mankiewicz
MANN, Anthony	Emil Bundsmann
MANN, Billy	William B. Mann
MANN, Daniel	Daniel Chugerman
MANN, Hank	David W. Lieberman
MANNERS, David	Rauff de Ryther Duan Acklom
MANNING, Irene	Inez Harvet
MANSFIELD, Jayne	Vera Jane Palmer
MANSFIELD, Martha	Martha Ehrlich
MANTZ, Paul	Albert Paul Mantz
MARA, Adele	Adelaida Delgado
MARCH, Fredric	Ernest Frederick McIntyre Bickel
• MARCHAL, Georges	Georges Luois Lucot
MARCIANO, "Rocky"	Rocco Francis Marchegiano
Margo	Maria Marguerita Guadelupe Boldao y Castilla
MARLOWE, Hugh	Hugh Hipple
MARLY, Florence	Hana Smekalova
MARRIOTT, Moore	George Thomas Moore-Marriott
MARSH, Carol	Norma Simpson
MARSH, Garry	Leslie March Gerahty
MARSH, Mae	Mary Warne Marsh
MARSH, Marguerite	Margaret Marsh (aka Marguerite Loveridge)
MARSH, Marion	Violet Krauth
MARSH, Tiger Joe	Joseph Marusich
MARSHALL, Brenda	Ardis Ankerson Gaines
MARSHALL, E. G.	Everett G. Marshall
MARSHALL, Peter	Pierre LaCock
MARSHALL, Tully	Tully Marshall Phillips
MARSON, Aileen	Aileen Pitt Marson
MARTIN, Chris-Pin	Ysabel Chris-Pin Martin Piaz
MARTIN, Dean	Dino Paul Crocetti
MARTIN, Ernest H.	Ernest Markowitz
MARTIN, Ross	Martin Rosenblatt
MARTIN, Tony	Alvin Maris
MARTON, Andrew	Endre Marton
Marx Brothers, The	Leonard "Chico" Marx (eldest)
"	Adolph (aka Arthur) "Harpo" Marx
"	Milton "Gummo" Marx
"	Julius "Groucho" Marx

Original Names of the Stars

PROFESSIONAL NAME*	BIRTH, LEGAL or FORMER NAME**
"	*Herbert "Zeppo" Marx (youngest)*
MARX, Samuel "Frenchie"	*Simon Marrix*
MASCHWITZ, Eric	*Holt Marvell*
MASON, Dan	*Dan Grassman*
MASON, Mary	*Betty Ann Jenks*
MASON, Shirley	*Leonie Flugrath*
MASSEY, Ilona	*Ilona Hajmassy*
MATTHAU, Walter	*Walter Matuschanskayasky*
MATTHEWS, A. E.	*Alfred Edward Matthews*
MATTO, Sesto	*Sisto Mata*
MAUGHAM, W. Somerset	*William Somerset Maugham*
MAURICE, Mary "Mother"	*Mary Birch*
MAXWELL, Lois	*Lois Hooker*
MAXWELL, Marilyn	*Marvel Maxwell*
MAY, Joe	*Joseph Mandel*
MAYER, Louis B.	*Louis Burt Mayer*
• MAYNE, Ferdinand (Ferdy)	*Ferdinand Mayer-Horckel*
MAYO, Virginia	*Virginia Jones*
MAZURKI, Mike	*Mikhail Mazuruski (Mazurski)*
McCALLISTER, Lon	*Herbert Alonzo McCallister*
McCAMBRIDGE, Mercedes	*Carlotta Mercedes McCambridge*
McCLURE, Greg	*Dale Easton*
McCORMICK, Merrill	*William Merrill McCormick*
McCOY, Gertrude	*Gertrude Lyon*
McCOY, Tim	*Timothy J. McCoy*
McCRAY, Helen Mary	*Helen Mary Keating*
McDANIEL, Sam "Deacon"	*Samuel Rufus McDaniel*
McDEVITT, Ruth	*Ruth Thane Shoecraft*
McDONALD, Marie	*Marie Frye*
McDOWALL, Roddy	*Andrew Roderick McDowall*
McDOWELL, Claire	*(aka Claire MacDowell)*
McGEE, Fibber	*Jim Jordan*
McGEE, Molly	*Marion Jordan*
McGILL, Moyna	*Moyna McIldowie*
McGIVER, John	*George Morris*
McGOWAN, J. P. "Jack"	*John P. McGowan*
McGRAW, Charles	*Charles Butters*
McGREGOR, Malcolm	*(aka Malcolm MacGregor)*
McHUGH, Jack	*John McHugh*
McHUGH, Matt	*Mathew O. McHugh*
McKAY, George W.	*George W. Reuben*
McKEE, Lafe	*Lafayette Stocking McKee*
McLEOD, Norman Z.	*Norman Zenos McLeod*
McLEOD, Tex	*Alexander D'Avila McLeod*
McNALLY, Stephen	*Horace Vincent McNally*
McNAUGHTON, Gus	*Augustus Howard*
McQUEEN, "Butterfly"	*Thelma McQueen*
McQUEEN, Steve	*Terence Stephen McQueen*
McVEY, Lucille	*(aka Mrs. Sidney Drew and June Morrow)*
MEADE, Claire	*Marguerite Fields*
MEDFORD, Kay	*Kathleen Patricia Regan*
MEEKER, Ralph	*Ralph Rathgeber*
MEGOWAN, Don	*(aka Dan Megowan)*
MEINS, Gus	*Gustave Meins*
MELCHIOR, Lauritz	*Lebrecht Hommel*
MELESH, Alex	*Alexander Melesher*
MELL, Marisa	*Marlies Moitzi*
MENJOU, Henri	*Henry Arthur Menjou*
MENZIES, William	*William Cameron Menzies*

• New entry.   * Includes both living & deceased persons.   ** Sources do not always agree on spelling.

Original Names of the Stars

PROFESSIONAL NAME*	BIRTH, LEGAL or FORMER NAME**
MERANDE, Doro	Dora Matthews
MERCER, Johnny	John Herndon Mercer
MERCOURI, Melina	Maria Amalia Mercouri
MERCURY, Freddie	Frederick Bulsara
• MEREDITH, Burgess	Oliver Burgess
MEREDITH, Iris	Iris Meredith Berlin
MEREDYTH, Bess	Helen MacGlashan
MERLO, Tony	Anthony Merlo
MERMAN, Ethel	Ethel Zimmerman
MERRALL, Mary	Mary Lloyd
MERSON, Billy	William Henry Thompson
MERTON, John	John Merton La Varre
MERVYN, William	William Mervyn Pickwood
MESSENGER, Buddy	Melvin Joe Messinger
MICHAEL, Ralph	Ralph Champion Shotter
MIDDLETON, Guy	Guy Middleton-Powell
MIDDLETON, Robert	Samuel G. Messer
MILES, Vera	Vera Ralston
MILFORD, Gene	Arthur Eugene Milford
MILLAND, Ray	Reginald Truscott-Jones
MILLER, Ann	Lucille Ann Collier
MILLER, Carl	Carlton Miller
MILLER, Glenn	Alton Glenn Miller
MILLER, Lorraine	(aka Lorraine Young)
MILLER, Marilyn	Mary Lynn Reynolds
MILLER, Martin	Rudolph Muller
MILLER, Max	Thomas Sargent
MILLER, Walter C.	Walter Corwin Miller
MILLER, W. Christy	William Christy Miller
Mills Brothers, The	Herbert Mills
"	Harry Mills
"	Donald Mills
"	John Mills, Jr.
MILOS, Milos	Milos Milosevic
MINEO, Sal	Salvatore Mineo, Jr.
MINER, Tony	Worthington C. Miner
MINTER, Mary Miles	Juliet Shelby
MINTZ, Eli	Edward Satz
MIRANDA, Carmen	Maria de Carmo Miranda de Cunha
• MIRANDA, Willy	Guillermo Miranda
Miroslava	Miroslava Stern
MITCHELL, Joni	Roberta Joan Anderson
MIX, Tom	Thomas Edwin Mix
Moe (3 Stooges)	Moses Howard (Horowitz)
Molly McGee	Marion Jordan
Moms	Jackie Mabley
MONCRIES, Edward	(aka Edward Moncrief)
MONROE, Marilyn	Norma Jean Mortenson (later Baker)
MONTAGUE, Monte	Walter Montague
MONTANA, Lewis "Bull"	Luigi Montagna
• MONTANA, Montie	Owen Harlan Mickel
MONTAND, Yves	Yvo Livi (aka Ivo Livi)
MONTEZ, Lola	Eliza Gilbert
MONTEZ, Maria	Maria Africa Antonia Gracia Vidal da Santo Silas
MONTGOMERY, Douglass	Robert Douglass Montgomery
MONTGOMERY, George	George Montgomery Letz
MONTGOMERY, Robert	Henry Montgomery
MOODY, Ron	Ronald Moodnick
MOORE, Clara	Clara Eloise Moore

Original Names of the Stars

PROFESSIONAL NAME*	BIRTH, LEGAL or FORMER NAME**
MOORE, Colleen	Kathleen Morrison
MOORE, Demi	Demi Guynes
MOORE, Dickie	John Richard Moore
MOORE, Eleanor	(aka Eleanor Merry)
MOORE, Garry	Thomas Garrison Morfit
MOORE, Terry	Helen Koford
MOOREHEAD, Agnes	Agnes Robertson Moorehead
MORAN, Frank	Frank Charles Moran
MORAN, George	George Searcy
MORAN, Jackie	John E. Moran
MORAN, Lois	Lois Darlington Dowling
MORAN, Polly	Pauline Theresa Moran
MORECAMBE, Eric	John Eric Bartholemew
MORELL, André	André Mesritz
MORENO, Rita	Rosita Dolores Alverio
MORGAN, Dennis	Stanley Morner
MORGAN, Frank	Francis Wupperman
MORGAN, Gene	Eugene Schwartzkopf
MORGAN, Harry	Harry Bratsburg
MORGAN, Henry	Henry Lerner von Ost, Jr.
MORGAN, Lee	Raymond Lee Morgan
MORGAN, Ralph	Raphael Kuhner Wupperman
MORISON, Patricia	Eileen Morrison
MORLAY, Gaby	Blanche Fumoleau
MORLEY, Karen	Mildred Linton
MORRIS, Chester	John Chester Morris
MORRIS, Johnny	John Morris Erickson
MORRIS, Philip	Francis Charles Philip Morris
MORRIS, Wayne	Bert de Wayne Morris
MORRISON, Ernie	Frederic Ernest Morrison
MORRISON, James	James Woods Morrison
MORRISON, Lou	Louis Morrison
MORRISSEY, Betty	(aka Betty Morrisey)
MORROS, Boris	Boris Milhailovitch
MORROW, Doretta	Doretta Marano
MOSCOVITCH, Maurice	Morris Maaskoff
MOSER, Hans	Jean Juliet
MOSTEL, Zero	Samuel Joel Mostel
Mr. Green Jeans	Hugh Brannum
Mr. Magoo	voice by Jim Backus
MUDIE, Leonard	Leonard Mudie Cheetham
MUELLER, Cookie	Dorothy Mueller
MUELLER, Wolfgang	(aka Wolfgang Muller)
MULLER, Renate	(aka Renate Mueller)
MUNI, Paul	Muni Weisenfreund
MUNSON, Ona	Ona Wolcott
MURDOCK, Ann	Irene Coleman
MURPHY, Audie	Audie Leon Murphy
MURPHY, Edna	Elizabeth Edna Murphy
MURRAY, Arthur	Moses Teichman
MURRAY, Bobby	Robert Hayes Murray
MURRAY, Jan	Murray Janofsky
MURRAY, Mae	Marie Adrienne Koenig
MURRAY-MAZWI, Mark	Ralph Holland Murray
Musidora	Jeanne Roques

N

NAGEL, Anne	Ann Dolan
NAISH, J. Carrol	Joseph Carrol Naish
NAISMITH, Laurence	Laurence Johnson

• New entry.   * Includes both living & deceased persons.   ** Sources do not always agree on spelling.

Original Names of the Stars

PROFESSIONAL NAME*	BIRTH, LEGAL or FORMER NAME**
NALDER, Reggie	Alfred Reginald Natzler
NALDI, Nita	Anita Donna Dooley
NAPIER, Alan	Alan Napier-Clavering
NAPIER, Diana	Molly Ellis
NARES, Owen	Owen Nares Ramsay
NASH, Mary	Mary Ryan
NAZIMOVA, Alla	Alla Lavendera
NAZZARI, Amedeo	Salvatore Amedeo Buffa
NEAGLE, Anna	Marjorie Robertson
NEDELL, Bernard	Bernard Jay Nedell
NEFF, Hildegarde	Hildegarde Knef
NEGRI, Pola	Apolina Mathias-Chalupec
NELSON, Gene	Gene Berg
NELSON, Harriet	Harriet Louise Snyder
"	(aka Peggy Lou Snyder and Harriet Hilliard)
NELSON, Ozzie	Oswald Nelson
NELSON, Rick (Ricky)	Eric Hilliard Nelson
NERVO, Jimmy	James Nervo
NESBITT, Frank M.	Frank McCormick Nesbitt
New Kids On The Block	Jonathan Knight
"	Jordan Knight
"	Joe McIntyre
"	Donnie Wahlberg
"	Danny Wood
NEWMAN, Scott	Allan Scott Newman (aka William Scott)
NEY, Marie	Marie Fix
NIBLO, Fred	Federico Nobile
NICHOLS, Barbara	Barbara Marie Nickerauer
NICHOLS, Dandy	Daisy Nichols
NICHOLS, Mike	Michael Igor Peschowsky
NICHOLS, Red	Ernest Loring Nichols
Nico	Christa Paffgen (aka Christa Pavlovski and Nico Ozsak)
NIELSEN, Asta	(aka Die Asta)
NILSSON, Anna Q.	Anna Querentia Nilsson
NILSSON, Harry	Harry Edward Nelson, III
NIXON, Pat	Thelma Catherine Ryan
NOLAN, Mary	Mary Imogene Robertson
NOONAN, Tommy	Tommy Noon
NORMAN, Josephine	Josephine Arrich
NORMAND, Mabel	Mabel Fortescue
NORRIS, Chuck	Carlos Ray
NORTH, Joe	Joseph B. North
NORTH, Sheree	Dawn Bethel
NORTON, Barry	Alfredo Biraben
NORTON, Jack	Mortimer J. Naughton
NORWOOD, Eille	Anthony Brett
NOVAK, Kim	Marilyn Novak
NOVARRO, Ramon	Jose Ramon Samaniegos
NOVELLO, Ivor	David Ivor Novello
⬤	
OAKIE, Jack	Lewis Delaney Offield
OAKLAND, Vivien	Vivian Anderson
OBERON, Merle	Estelle Merle O'Brien Thompson
O'BRIAN, Hugh	Hugh Krampke
O'BRIEN, Dave	David Barclay
O'BRIEN, Margaret	Angela Maxine O'Brien
O'BRIEN, Pat	William Joseph O'Brien, Jr.
O'BRIEN, Tom	Thomas Everett O'Brien
O'DAY, Molly	Laverne Williamson

Original Names of the Stars

PROFESSIONAL NAME*	BIRTH, LEGAL or FORMER NAME**
O'DONNELL, Cathy	*Ann Steeley*
OGLE, Charles	*Charles Stanton Ogle*
O'HANLON, George	*George Rice*
O'HARA, Maureen	*Maureen Fitzsimons*
O'HARA, Shirley	*Shirley O'Hara-Nolan*
O'HARE, Brad	*Steven Bradford O'Hare*
O'KEEFE, Dennis	*Edward 'Bud' Flanagan*
O'KEEFE, Win	*James Winston O'Keefe*
OLAND, Werner	*Wernur Olund*
OLCOTT, Sidney	*John S. Alcott*
OLDFIELD, Barney	*Berna Eli*
OLIVER, Edna May	*Edna May Cox Nutter*
OLIVER, Susan	*Charlotte Gercke*
OLIVER, Sy	*Melvin James Oliver*
OLIVER, Vic	*Victor von Samek*
OLMSTEAD, Gertrude	*Gertrude Olmsted*
OLSEN, Ole	*John Sigvard Olsen*
O'MALLEY, Pat	*Patrick H. O'Malley, Jr.*
O'NEAL, Anne	*Patsy Ann Epperson*
O'NEAL, Frederick	*Frederick Douglass O'Neal*
O'NEAL, Ryan	*Patrick Ryan O'Neal*
O'NEIL, Sally	*Virginia Louise Noonan (aka Chotsie Noonan)*
O'NEILL, Maire	*Maire Allgood*
Oomph Girl, The	*Ann Sheridan*
OPHULS, Max	*Max Oppenheimer*
ORLANDO, Don	*Orlando Biogio Ferrara*
ORLANDO, Tony	*Michael Anthony Orlando Cassavitis*
ORLOFF, Thelma	*Thelma Joel*
O'ROURKE, Brefni	*(aka Brefni O'Rorke)*
ORTES, Armand	*Armand Francis Ortes*
OSBORN, Lyn	*Clair Lynn Osborn*
OSBORNE, John	*John James Osborne*
OSBOURNE, Jefferson	*Jefferson W. Schroeder*
OSBOURNE, Lennie "Bud"	*(aka Miles Osborne)*
OSCAR, Henry	*Henry Oscar Wale*
O'SHEA, Michael	*Edward Michael O'Shea*
Osmond Brothers	*Alan Osmond*
"	*Wayne Osmond*
"	*Merrill Osmond*
"	*Jay Osmond*
OSWALDA, Ossi	*Oswalda Staglich*
Our Gang (aka "The Little Rascals" on TV)	*Alfalfa (Carl Switzer)*
"	*Baby Patsy*
"	*Buckwheat (William Henry Thomas, Jr.)*
"	*Butch (Tommy Bond)*
"	*Chubby (Norman Chaney)*
"	*Darla Hood*
"	*Dickie Moore (John Richard Moore)*
"	*Echo (Dorothy Betty Jean DeBorba)*
"	*Farina (Allen Clayton Hoskins, Jr.)*
"	*Froggy (Billy Laughlin)*
"	*Harold Switzer*
"	*Harry Spear*
"	*Jackie Condon*
"	*Jackie Cooper*
"	*Jackie Davis (John H. Davis)*
"	*Jay R. Smith*
"	*Jean Darling (Dorothy Jean LeVake)*
"	*Joe Cobb (Joe Frank Cobb)*

PROFESSIONAL NAME*	BIRTH, LEGAL or FORMER NAME**
Our Gang (Cont'd)	*Johnny Downs (John Morey Downs)*
"	*Mary Ann Jackson*
"	*Mary Kornman*
"	*Mickey Daniels (Richard Daniels, Jr.)*
"	*Mickey Gubitosi (now Robert Blake)*
"	*Mildred Jean Kornman*
"	*Pete, the Pup*
"	*Porky Lee (Eugene Lee)*
"	*Scotty Beckett*
"	*Shirley Jean Rickert*
"	*Spanky (George McFarland)*
"	*Stymie (Matthew Beard, Jr.)*
"	*Sunshine Sammy (Ernie Morrison)*
"	*Waldo (Darwood Kenneth Smith)*
"	*Wally Albright (Walton Albright, Jr.)*
"	*Wheezer (Bobby Hutchins)*
OWEN, Bill	*Bill Rowbotham*
OWEN, Reginald	*John Reginald Owen*
OWEN, Seena	*Signe Auen*
OWENS, Jesse	*James Cleveland Owens*
P	
PACINO, Al	*Alfredo Pacino*
PADULA, Vincent	*Vincente Padula*
PAGE, Gale	*Sally Rutter*
PAGE, Jean	*Lucile Beatrice O'Hair*
PAGE, Patti	*Clara Ann Fowler*
PAGE, Paul	*Campbell U. Hicks*
PAGET, Debra	*Debralee Griffin*
PAGLIERO, Marcello	*(aka Marcel Pagliero)*
PAIGE, Janis	*Donna Mae Tjaden*
PAIGE, Robert	*John Arthur Page*
PALANCE, Jack	*Vladimir (later, Walter) Palaniuk*
PALMER, Gregg	*Palmer Lee*
PALMER, Lilli	*Lilli Peiser*
PALMER, Patricia	*(aka Margaret Gibson)*
PAM, Anita	*Anita Friedheim Davidson*
PANZER, Paul Wolfgang	*Paul Panzerbeiter*
PARHAM, Ernie	*Ernest R. Parham*
PARIS, Freddie	*Freddie Paris-Smith*
PARIS, Manuel	*Manuel R. Conesa*
PARKER, Barnett	*William Barnett Parker*
PARKER, Cecil	*Cecil Schwabe*
PARKER, Frank "Pinky"	*Franklin Parker*
PARKER, Jean	*Lois Mae Greene*
PARKER, Suzy	*Cecelia Parker*
PARKS, Bert	*Bert Jacobson*
PARKS, Larry	*Samuel Kleusman Lawrence Parks*
Parkyakarkus	*Harry Einstein*
PARROTT, James	*James Gibbons Parrott*
PARSONS, Louella	*Louella Oettinger*
PATCH, Wally	*Walter Vinicombe*
PATRICK, Gail	*Margaret Fitzpatrick*
PATRICK, Nigel	*Nigel Wemyss*
PATTERSON, Hank	*Elmer C. Patterson*
PAUL, Les	*Lester Polsfuss*
PAVAN, Marisa	*Marisa Pierangeli*
PAXINOU, Katina	*Katina Konstantopoulou*
PAYNE, Lou	*William Lou Payne*
PAYTON, Claude	*Claude Duval Payton (aka Claude Peyton)*

Original Names of the Stars

PROFESSIONAL NAME*	BIRTH, LEGAL or FORMER NAME**
Peaches	Libby Holman
PEARCE, George C.	(aka George Pierce)
PEARCE, Peggy	(aka Viola Barry)
PEARL, Minnie	Sarah Ophelia Colley Cannon
PEARSON, Drew	Andrew Russell Pearson
PECK, Gregory	Eldred Gregory Peck
PEIL, Edward Jr.	Charles Edward Peil, Jr. (aka Johnny Jones)
PEIL, Edward Sr.	Charles Edward Peil, Sr.
PENN, Leonard	Leonard Monson Penn
PENNER, Joe	Joe Pinter
PEPPER, Buddy	Jack R. Starkey
PERCIVAL, Walter C.	Charles David Lingenfelter
PERKINS, Marlin	Richard Marlin Perkins
PERKINS, Tony	Anthony Perkins
PERREAU, Gigi	Ghislaine Perreau-Saussine
PERRY, Antoinette	(aka Annette Perry)
PETERS, Bernadette	Bernadette Lazzaro
PETERS, Roberta	Roberta Peterman
PETERS, Susan	Suzanne Carnahan
PETRIE, Hay	David Hay Petrie
PETROVA, Olga	(aka Muriel Harding)
PETTYJOHN, Angelique	(aka Heaven St. John and Angelique)
PHILLIPS, Barney	Bernard Phillips
PHIPPS, Sally	Byrnece Beutler
PHOENIX, Pat	Patricia Mansfield
PIAF, Edith	Edith Gassion
PICKENS, Slim	Louis Bert Lindley
PICKFORD, Jack	Jack Smith
PICKFORD, Lottie	Lottie Smith
PICKFORD, Mary	Gladys Mary Smith
PIERCE, Big Jim	James H. Pierce
PINZA, Ezio	Fortunato Pinza
PLUMB, E. Hay	Edward Hay Plumb
POFF, Lon	Alonzo M. Poff
POHLMANN, Eric	Erich Pohlmann
POLLAR, Gene	Joseph C. Pohler
POLLARD, Daphne	Daphne Trott
POLLARD, Harry "Snub"	Harold Fraser
POLO, Eddie	Edward P. Polo
PONS, Lily	Alice Josephine Pons
Porky (of "Our Gang")	Eugene Lee
POTAMKIN, Luba	Luba Chaiken
POTTER, H. C.	Henry Codman Potter
POWELL, Dick	Richard E. Powell
POWELL, Jane	Suzanne Burce
POWELL, Lee B.	Lee Berrian Powell
POWELL, Russ	Russell J. Powell
POWER, F. Tyrone	Frederick Tyrone Power
POWER, Paul	Luther Vestergard
POWER, Tyrone	Tyrone Edmund Power
POWERS, Mala	Mary Ellen Powers
POWERS, Stefanie	Stefania Zofia Ferderkievicz
PRATHER, Lee	Oscar Lee Prather
PRENTISS, Paula	Paula Ragusa
PRESLEY, Elvis	Elvis Aron Presley
PRESTON, Robert	Robert Preston Meservey
PREVOST, Marie	Marie Bickford Dunn
PRICE, Dennis	Dennistoun Franklyn John Rose-Price
PRICE, Kate	Kate Duffy

Original Names of the Stars

PROFESSIONAL NAME*	BIRTH, LEGAL or FORMER NAME**
PRICE, Nancy	Lillian Nancy Maude
Prince	Prince Rogers Nelson
PRINGLE, Aileen	Aileen Bisbee
PRINTEMPS, Yvonne	Yvonne Wigniolle
PRINZE, Freddie	Freddie Preutzel
PRIOR, Herbert	(aka Herbert Pryor)
PROVENZA, Sal	Salvatore D. Provenza
PRUD'HOMME, George	(aka George Pembroke)
PURDELL, Reginald	Reginald Grasdorf
Q	
QUALEN, John	John Oleson
Queen:	Brian May (guitar)
"	Roger Taylor (drums)
"	John Deacon (bass)
"	Freddie Mercury (vocal)
R	
RA, Sun	(aka Herman "Sonny" Blount and Sonny Bourke)
RABAGLIATI, Alberto	Alberto Rabagliati-Vinata
RAEBURN, Frances	Frances Hedrick Kurstin
RAFFERTY, Chips	John Goffage
RAFFETTO, Michael	Elwyn Creighton Raffetto
RAFT, George	George Ranft
RAGLAND, Rags	John Ragland
RAIMU, Jules	Jules Muraire
RAKER, Lorin	(aka Lorrin Raker)
RALEIGH, Saba	(aka Isabel Ellissen)
RALPH, Jessie	Jessie Ralph Chambers
RAMAGE, Cecil	Cecil Beresford Ramage
RAMBO, Dirk	Orman Ray Rambo
RAMBOVA, Natacha	Winifred Shaunessy (aka Winifred Hudnut)
RAMSEY, John Nelson	(aka Neilson Ramsey)
RAMSEY-HILL, C. S.	(aka Ramsey Hill)
RAND, Sally	Helen Gould Beck
RANDALL, Addison "Jack"	Addison Owen Randall
RANDALL, Tony	Leonard Rosenberg
RANDLE, Frank	Arthur McEvoy
RANDOLPH, Anders	Anders Randolf
RANKIN, Arthur	Arthur Davenport
RASP, Fritz	Heinrich Rasp
RATCLIFFE, E. J.	(aka E. J. Radcliffe)
RATHBONE, Basil	Philip St. John Basil Rathbone
RATTENBERRY, Harry	(aka Harry Rattenbury)
RAY, Aldo	Aldo daRe
RAY, Charles	Charles Edgar Alfred Ray
RAY, Nicholas	Raymond N. Kienzle
RAY, Rene	Irene Creese
RAY, Ted	Charles Olden
RAYE, Carol	Kathleen Corkrey
RAYE, Martha	Margaret Yvonne Reed
RAYMOND, Gene	Raymond Guion
RAYMOND, Jack (d. 1951)	George Feder (U.S. actor/director)
RAYMOND, Jack (d. 1953)	John Caines (British actor/director/producer)
RAYMOND, Paula	Paula Ramona Wright
RAYMOND, Royal	Royal Aaron Raymond
RAZETTO, Stella	(aka Stella Le Saint)
Red	Boyd F. Morgan
REDFORD, Robert	Charles Robert Redford, Jr.
REDWING, Rodd	Roderick Redwing
REED, Alan	(aka Teddy Bergman)

• New entry.   * Includes both living & deceased persons.   ** Sources do not always agree on spelling.

Original Names of the Stars

PROFESSIONAL NAME*	BIRTH, LEGAL or FORMER NAME**
REED, Carol	*Mary Walther*
REED, Donna	*Donna Belle Mullenger*
REED, George H.	*George Henry Reed*
REED, Robert	*John Robert Rietz, Jr.*
REESE, Della	*Delloreese Patricia Early*
REEVES, George	*George Besselo*
REEVES, Jim	*James Travis Reeves*
REGAS, Pedro	*Panagiotis Regas*
RENALDO, Duncan	*Renault Renaldo Duncan*
Renie	*Irene Brouillet*
REPP, Stafford	*Stafford Alois Repp*
RETTIG, Tommy	*Thomas Noel Rettig*
REVIER, Dorothy	*Doris Velegra*
REY, Fernando	*Fernando Casado Arambillet*
REYNOLDS, Burt	*Burton M. Reynolds, Jr.*
REYNOLDS, Craig	*Hugh Enfield*
REYNOLDS, Debbie	*Marie Frances Reynolds*
REYNOLDS, Marjorie	*Marjorie Goodspeed*
REYNOLDS, Peter	*Peter Horrocks*
REYNOLDS, Vera	*Vera Norma Reynolds*
RHODES, Billie	*Levita Axlerod*
RICE, Frank	*Frank Thomas Rice*
RICE, Jack	*Jack Clifford Rice*
RICH, Buddy	*Bernard Rich*
RICH, Irene	*Irene Luther*
RICHARD, Cliff	*Harold Webb*
RICHARDS, Addison	*Addison Whitaker Richards, Jr.*
RICHARDS, Kurt	*Jonathan Kidd*
RICHARDSON, Jiles	*Jiles Perry Richardson (aka "The Big Bopper")*
RICHETTS, Tom	*Thomas Richetts*
RICHMOND, Kane	*Frederick W. Bowditch*
RICKARD, Tex	*George L. Rickard*
RIDGELEY, John	*John Huntingdon Rea*
RIDGES, Stanley	*Stanley Charles Ridges*
RIGBY, Edward	*Edward Coke*
RINALDO, Fred	*Frederic I. Rinaldo*
RINDT, Jochen	*Karl Jochen Rindt*
RIPLEY, Robert L.	*Robert LeRoy Ripley*
RISDON, Elizabeth	*Elizabeth Evans*
RITCHARD, Cyril	*Cyril Trimnell-Ritchard*
RITTER, John	*Jonathan Ritter*
RITTER, Tex	*Maurice Woodward Ritter*
Ritz Brothers, The	*Al Joachim (aka Al Ritz)*
"	*James Joachim (aka Jimmy Ritz)*
"	*Harry Joachim (aka Harry Ritz)*
RIVERA, Chita	*Delores Conchita Figuero del Rivero*
RIVERA, Geraldo	*Miguel Rivera*
RIVERS, Joan	*Joan Sandra Molinsky*
• ROBBINS, Jerome	*Jerome Rabinowitz*
ROBERTS, Edith	*Edith Josephine Roberts*
ROBERTS, Lynne	*Theda Mae Roberts (aka Mary Hart)*
ROBERTS, Oral	*Granville Oral Roberts*
ROBEY, George	*George Edward Wade*
ROBINSON, Edward G.	*Emmanuel Goldenberg*
ROBINSON, Frances	*Marion Frances Ladd*
ROBINSON, Jackie	*Jack Roosevelt Robinson*
ROBSON, May	*Mary Robison*
ROC, Patricia	*Felicia Riese*
Rochester	*Eddie Anderson*

Original Names of the Stars

PROFESSIONAL NAME*	BIRTH, LEGAL or FORMER NAME**
ROCKNE, Knute	Knute Kenneth Rockne
ROGERS, Buddy	Charles Rogers
ROGERS, Ginger	Virginia Katherine McMath
ROGERS, Jean	Eleanor Lovegren
ROGERS, Roy	Leonard Slye
ROGERS, Will	William Penn Adair Rogers
ROLAND, Gilbert	Luis Antonio Damaso de Alonso
ROMAGNOLI, Margaret	Margaret O'Neill
ROMANOFF, Michael	Prince Michael Alexandrovich Dimitri Oblensky
ROME, Stewart	Septimus William Ryott
ROMNEY, Edana	Edana Rubenstein
ROONEY, Mickey	Joe Yule, Jr.
ROOSEVELT, Buddy	Kenneth Sanderson
ROSAY, Françoise	Françoise Bandy de Naleche
ROSCOE, Alan	Albert Roscoe
ROSE, Blanche	Blanche Starr
ROSEN, Phil	Philip E. Rosen
ROSENBLOOM, Maxie	Maxie Rosenblum
ROSING, Bodil	Bodil Hammerich
ROSMER, Milton	Arthur Milton Lunt
ROSS, Lanny	Lancelot Patrick Ross
ROSS, Lenny	Leonardo Del Rossi
ROSS, Shirley	Shirley Dolan Blum
ROSSITTO, Angelo	Angelo Salvatore Rossitto
ROTH, Gene	(aka Gene Stutenroth)
ROTH, Lillian	Lillian Rustein
ROUNESVILLE, Robert	(aka Robert Field)
ROURKE, Mickey	Philip André Rourke
ROWE, Fanny	Frances Rowe
ROWLANDS, Gena	Virginia Rowlands
ROYCE, Julian	Julian Gardener
RUBENS, Alma	Alma Smith
RUGGLES, Charles	Charles Sherman Ruggles
RUMANN, Sig	Siegfried Albon Rumann
RUNYON, Damon	Alfred Damon Runyon
RUSSELL, Andy	Andres Rabago
RUSSELL, Don	Samuel H. Borgesi
RUSSELL, Jane	Ernestine Jane Russell
RUSSELL, Lillian	Helen Leonard
RUTH, Babe	George Herman Ruth
RYAN, Irene	Irene Nablett
RYAN, Sheila	Katherine Elizabeth McLaughlin
RYDER, Winona	Winona Laura Horowitz
☙	
Sabu	Sabu Dastagir
SAGE, Willard	James Willard Sage
SAKALL, S. Z.	Eugene Gero Szakall
SALE, Chic	Charles Sale
SALES, Soupy	Milton Hines
• SAMPLES, Junior	Alvin Samples, Jr.
SANDERS, Al	Albert W. Gay, Jr.
SANDFORD, Tiny	Stanley J. Sandford
SANTELL, Alfred	Alfred Allen Santell
SANTLEY, Fred	Frederic Santley
SANTLEY, Joseph	Joseph Mansfield
SAPPINGTON, Fay	Harriet Richardson
SARANDON, Susan	Susan Tomaling
SARGENT, Dick	Richard Cox
SARONY, Leslie	Leslie Frye

Original Names of the Stars

PROFESSIONAL NAME*	BIRTH, LEGAL or FORMER NAME**
Satchmo	*Louis Armstrong*
SAVALAS, Telly	*Aristotle Savalas*
SAWYER, Joe	*Joseph Sauer (aka Joseph Sawyer)*
SAXE, Templar	*Templer William Edward Edevein*
SAXON, John	*Carmen Orrico*
SAYLOR, Syd	*Leo Sailor*
SCALA, Gia	*Giovanna Scoglio*
Scat	*Johnny Davis*
Scatman	*Benjamin Crothers*
SCHARF, Herman	*(aka Herman Scharff)*
SCHILLING, Gus	*August E. Schilling*
SCHINDELL, Cy	*Seymore Schindell*
SCHLETTOW, Hans Adelbert	*(aka Hans von Schlettow)*
SCHNEIDER, Romy	*Rosemarie Magdalena Albach-Retty*
SCHULTZ, Harry	*Alexander Heinberg*
SCOTT, Daniel Simon	*Daniel Dale Simon*
SCOTT, Gordon	*Gordon M. Werschkull*
SCOTT, Hazel	*Dorothy Scott*
SCOTT, Lizabeth	*Emma Matzo*
SCOTT, Randolph	*George Randolph Crane Scott*
SCOTT, Zachary	*Zachary Thompson Scott, Jr.*
SEASTROM, Victor	*Victor Sjostrom*
SEBERG, Jean	*Jean Dorothy Seberg*
SEBRING, Jay	*Thomas Jay Kummer*
SEDDON, Margaret	*Marguerite Hungerford Whiteley*
SEDGWICK, Edie	*Edith Minturn Sedgwick*
SEGAR, Lucia	*(aka Lucia Seger and Lucia Bacus)*
SELIG, William N.	*William Nicholas Selig*
SELTEN, Morton	*Morton Stubbs*
SELWYN, Clarissa	*Clarissa Schultz*
SELWYN, Ruth	*Ruth Wilcox*
SELZNICK, David O.	*David Oliver Selznick*
SENNETT, Mack	*Mickall Sinott (aka Michael Sinnott)*
SERATO, Massimo	*Giuseppe Segato*
SEUSS, Dr.	*Theodor Seuss Geisel*
SEYMOUR, Jane	*Joyce Frankenberg*
SHAIFFER, Howard "Tiny"	*Howard Charles Shaiffer*
SHANNON, Peggy	*Winona Sammon*
SHARKEY, Jack	*Joseph Paul Cukoschay*
SHARIF, Omar	*Michel Shalhouz*
SHARP, Henry	*Henry Schacht*
SHAUGHNESSY, Mickey	*Joseph Shaughnessy*
SHAW, Artie	*Arthur Arshawsky*
SHAW, Susan	*Patsy Sloots*
SHAW, Victoria	*Jeanette Elphick*
SHAW, Wini	*Winifred Shaw*
SHAWLEE, Joan	*Joan Fulton*
SHAWN, Dick	*Richard Schulefand*
SHAY, Dorothy	*Dorothy Sims*
SHAYNE, Robert	*Robert Shaen Dawe*
SHEA, Mervin	*Mervin David John Shea*
SHEA, William	*William James Shea*
SHEAN, Al	*Alfred Schoenberg*
SHEARER, Moira	*Moira King*
SHEARER, Norma	*Edith Norma Fisher*
SHEEN, Charlie	*Carlos Irwin Estevez*
SHEEN, Martin	*Ramon Estevez*
SHEFFIELD, Reginald	*Reginald Sheffield Casson*
SHELDON, Jerry	*Charles H. Patton (Do not confuse with Jerome Sheldon)*

Original Names of the Stars

PROFESSIONAL NAME*	BIRTH, LEGAL or FORMER NAME**
Shemp (3 Stooges)	Samuel Howard (Horowitz)
SHEPARD, Sam	Samuel Shepard Rogers
SHEPLEY, Michael	Michael Shepley-Smith
SHERIDAN, Ann	Clara Lou Sheridan
SHERIDAN, Dan	Daniel Marvin Sheridan
SHERMAN, Mary	Ida Sherman
SHERRY, J. Barney	J. Barney Sherry Reeves
SHERWOOD, Bobby	Robert J. Sherwood, Jr.
SHIELDS, Frank	Francis X. Shields
SHIRE, Talia	Talia Coppola
SHIRLEY, Anne	Dawn Paris
SHORE, Dinah	Frances (Fanny) Rose Shore
SHRINER, Herb	Herbert Schiner
SHUMWAY, Lee	Leonard C. Shumway
SHUMWAY, Walter	Walter George Shumway
SIDNEY, George (actor)	Sammy Greenfield
SIDNEY, Sylvia	Sophia Kosow
SIEGEL, Bernard	(aka Bernard Segal)
SIGNORET, Simone	Simone Kaminker
SILLS, Beverly	Belle Silverman
SILVA, Mario	(aka Murray Smith)
SILVERHEELS, Jay	Harold J. Smith
SILVERS, Phil	Philip Silversmith
SIMMONS, Daniel	(aka Chief Yowlachie)
SIMMS, Hilda	Hilda Moses (aka Julie Riccardo)
SIMON, Michel	François Simon
SIMPSON, Bill	William Simpson
SINATRA, Frank	Francis Albert Sinatra
SINATRA, Ray	Raymond Dominic Sinatra
SINCLAIR, Arthur	Arthur McDonnell
SINGLETON, Catherine	Catherine Moylan Singleton
SINGLETON, Penny	Dorothy McNulty
SIODMAK, Robert	Robert Siodmark
SIRK, Douglas	Detlef Sierck
SKELLY, Hal	Joseph Harold Skelly
SKELTON, Georgia	Georgia Maureen Davis
SKELTON, Red	Richard Skelton
SKIPWORTH, Alison	Alison Groom
SLAUGHTER, Tod	N. Carter Slaughter
SMALLEY, Phillips	Wendell Phillips Smalley
SMITH, Alexis	Gladys Smith
SMITH, Art	Arthur Gordon Smith
• SMITH, 'Buffalo Bob'	Robert E. Smith
SMITH, Gerald	Gerland Oliver Smith
SMITH, John	Robert Earl Van Orden
SMITH, Joseph	Joseph Sultzer
SMITH, Kate	Kathryn Elizabeth Smith
SMITH, (Sir) C. Aubrey	Charles Aubrey Smith
Sojin	Sojin Kamiyama
SOMERS, Suzanne	Suzanne Mahoney
SOMERSET, Pat	Patrick Holme-Somerset
SOMMER, Elke	Elke Schletz
SONDERGAARD, Gale	Edith Holm Sondergaard
SOO, Jack	Goro Suzuki
SOTHERN, Ann	Harriette Lake
SOTHERN, Hugh	Roy Sutherland
SOUEZ, Ina	Ina Rains
SOUTHERN, Jeri	Genevieve Hering
SPACEK, Sissy	Mary Elizabeth Spacek

Original Names of the Stars

PROFESSIONAL NAME*	BIRTH, LEGAL or FORMER NAME**
Spanky (of "Our Gang")	George Robert Phillips McFarland
SPARKS, Ned	Edward A. Sparkman
SPITALNY, Evelyn	Evelyn Klein
Spivy	Spivy Le Voe
SQUIRE, Ronald	Ronald Squirl
• SQUIRES, Dorothy	Edna May Squires
STACY, James	Maurice Elias
STAFFORD, Hanley	John Austin
STANDING, Wyndham	Charles Wyndham Standing
STANLEY, Helene	Delores Diane Freymouth (aka Delores Diane)
STANMORE, Frank	Francis Henry Pink
STANTON, Harry	Harry Isaacs Stanton
STANTON, Will	William Sidney Stanton
STANWYCK, Barbara	Ruby Stevens
STAPLETON, Jean	Jeanne Murray
STARK, Pauline	Pauline Starke
STARR, Randy	Joseph Randall
STARR, Ringo	Richard Starkey
ST. DENIS, Ruth	Ruth Dennis
STEELE, Bob	Robert North Bradbury, Jr.
STEELE, Tommy	Tommy Hicks
STEERS, Larry	Lawrence Steers
• STEINER, Arthur H.	(aka Art Stanley Steiner)
STEN, Anna	Annel (or Anjuschka) Stenskaya Sudakevich
STEPHENSON, Henry	Henry S. Garroway
Stepin Fetchit	Lincoln Perry
STERLING, Ford	George F. Stitch
STERLING, Jan	Jane Sterling Adriance
STERLING, Robert	William Sterling Hart
STEVENS, Cat	Stephen Demetri Georgiou (aka Yusef Islam)
STEVENS, Connie	Concetta Ingolia
STEVENS, Craig	Gail Shikles
STEVENS, Inger	Inger Stensland
STEVENS, K. T.	Gloria Wood (aka Katherine Stevens)
STEVENS, Landers	John Landers Stevens
STEVENS, Onslow	Onslow Ford Stevenson
STEVENS, Risé	Risé Steenburg
STEVENS, Stella	Estelle Eggleston
STEWART, James	James Maitland Stewart
STEWART, Jon	Jon Stewart Liebowitz
Sting	Gordon Matthew Sumner
ST. JACQUES, Raymond	James Arthur Johnson
ST. JAMES, Susan	Susan Miller
ST. JOHN, Betta	Betty Streidler
ST. JOHN, Fuzzy	Al St. John
ST. JOHN, Jill	Jill Oppenheim
STOCKDALE, Carl	Carlton Stockdale
STOCKFIELD, Betty	(aka Betty Stockfeld)
STOCKWELL, Dean	Robert Dean Stockwell
STOKER, H. G.	Hew Gordon Dacre Stoker (aka Hew Gordon)
STOKOWSKI, Leopold	Leopold Stokes (or Boleslowowicz)
STONE, George E.	George Stein
STONE, Lewis	Louis Shepherd Stone
Stooges, The Three	Moses "Moe" Howard (Horowitz)
"	Larry Fine
"	Jerome "Curly" Howard (Horowitz)
" (after Curly's death):	Samuel "Shemp" Howard (Horowitz)
" (after June 1959):	Joe DeRita
" (after Shemp's death):	Joe Besser

Original Names of the Stars

PROFESSIONAL NAME*	BIRTH, LEGAL or FORMER NAME**

PROFESSIONAL NAME*	BIRTH, LEGAL or FORMER NAME**
STOOPNAGLE, Col. Lemuel Q.	F. Chase Taylor
STOREY, June	Mary June Storey
STORM, Gale	Josephine Cottle
ST. POLIS, John	(aka John Sainpolis)
STRANGE, Glenn	George Glenn Strange
STRASBERG, Lee	Israel Strassberg
STRATTEN, Dorothy R.	Dorothy Hoogstraten
STREEP, Meryl	Mary Louise Streep
STREISAND, Barbra	Barbara Streisand
STRONG, Leonard	Leonard Clarence Strong
STUART, Gloria	Gloria Stuart Finch
STUART, John	John Croall
STUART, Nick	Nicholas Pratza
STUBBS, Harry	Harry Oakes Stubbs
STUEWE, Hans	(aka Hans Stuwe)
STURGES, Preston	Edmond P. Biden
STURGIS, Eddie	Josef Edwin Sturgis
STYNE, Jule	Jules Styne
Sugar	Tanya Geise
SULLAVAN, Margaret	Margaret Brooke Sullavan
SULLIVAN, Barry	Patrick Barry
SULLIVAN, Brian	Harry Joseph Sullivan
SULLIVAN, Ed	Edward Vincent Sullivan
SULLIVAN, Francis L.	Francis Loftus Sullivan
SULLY, Frank	Frank Sullivan
SUMMERS, Donna	LaDonna Gaines
SUMMERVILLE, Slim	George J. Summerville
SUNBEAUTY, Olga	(aka Olga Solbelli)
SUNDMARK, Betty	Elizabeth S. Shannon
SUNSHINE, Baby	Pauline Flood
Sunshine Sammy (of "Our Gang")	Frederic Ernest Morrison
SUNSHINE, Marion	Mary Tunstall Ijames
Superman	(aka Clark Kent)
SUTHERLAND, Eddie	A. Edward Sutherland
SUTTON, Grady	Grady Harwell Sutton
SWANSON, Gloria	Gloria Swenson
Sylvie	Louise Sylvain
T	
TABLER, P. Dempsey	Perce Dempsey Tabler
TALBOT, Lyle	Lisle Henderson
TALMADGE, Richard	Sylvester Metzetti
Tamara	Tamara Swann
TAMBLYN, Russ	Russell Tamblyn
Tarzan (the Ape Man)	Elmo Lincoln (1918, 21)
"	Gene Pollar (1920)
"	P. Dempsey Tabler (1920-21)
"	Big Jim Pierce (1927)
"	Frank Merrill (1928, 30)
"	Johnny Weissmuller (1932, 34, 36, 39, 41-43, 45-48)
"	Buster Crabbe (1933)
"	Herman Brix (1935)
"	Glenn Morris (1938)
"	Lex Barker (1949-53)
"	Gordon Scott (1955, 57-60)
"	Dennis Miller (1959)
"	Jock Mahoney (1962-63)
"	Mike Henry (1966-68)
"	Ron Ely (1970)
"	Miles O'Keefe (1981)

Original Names of the Stars

PROFESSIONAL NAME*	BIRTH, LEGAL or FORMER NAME**
Tarzan (Cont'd)	Christopher Lambert (1984)
"	Joe Lara (1989 TV movie)
TATI, Jacques	Jacques Tatischeff
TAUBER, Richard	Ernst Seifert
TAYLOR, Billy	William H. Taylor
TAYLOR, Dub	Walter Clarence Taylor, 2nd
TAYLOR, Jackie Lynn	Jacqueline Lynn Taylor
TAYLOR, Kent	Louis Weiss
TAYLOR, Laurette	Laura Cooney (aka LaBelle Laurette)
TAYLOR, Robert	Spangler Arlington Brugh
TAYLOR, Rod	Robert Taylor
TAYLOR, William Desmond	William Deane-Tanner
TEARLE, Conway	Frederick Levy
TELLEGEN, Lou	Isidor Louis Bernard Von Dammeir
TEMPEST, (Dame) Marie	Marie Susan Etherington
TENBROOK, Harry	Henry Olaf Hansen
TERRISS, Ellaine	Ellaine Lewin
TERRY, Alice	Alice Frances Taafe
TERRY, Don	Don Loker
TERRY, Ruth	Ruth Mae McMahon
TERRY, Sheila	Kay Clark
TERRY, Tex	Edward Earl Terry
Terry-Thomas	Thomas Terry Hoar-Stevens
TETLEY, Walter	Walter Campbell Tetley
THALBERG, Irving	Irving Grant Thalberg
THATCHER, Eva	Evelyn Thatcher
THATCHER, Torin	Torren Thatcher
THIELE, William J.	Wilhelm J. Thiele
THOMAS, Billy "Buckwheat"	William Henry Thomas, Jr.
THOMAS, Danny	Muzyad Yaghoob (aka Amos Jacobs)
THOMAS, Ted	Theodore Hertzl Thomashefsky
THOMPSON, Carlos	Juan Carlos Mundin Schafter
THOMPSON, Marshall	James Marshall Thompson
THORPE, Richard	Rollo Smolt Thorpe
THUNDERCLOUD, Chief (later)	Scott T. Williams
THUNDERCLOUD, Chief (original)	Victor Daniels
TIM, Tiny	Herbert Khaury
TODD, Ann	Ann Todd Mayfield
TODD, Christopher	Todd Wangberg
TODD, Mike	Avrom Hirsh Goldenborgen (Goldbogen)
TOMACK, Sid	Sidney Tomack
TONE, Franchot	Stanislas Franchot Tone
Tonto	Jay Silverheels
Tony (Tom Mix's horse)	(aka Tony The Wonder Horse)
TORRENCE, David	David Thoyson
TORRENCE, Ernest	Ernest Thoyson
TORN, Rip	Elmore Torn
Toto	Antonio Furst de Curtis-Gagliardi
Toto the Clown	Armando Novello
TOURNEUR, Maurice	Maurice Thomas
TRACY, Lee	William Lee Tracy
TRAEGER, Rick	Richard A. Traeger
TRAVERS, Henry	Travers Heagerty
TRAVERS, Linden	Florence Lindon-Travers
TRAVIS, Richard	William Justice
TREACHER, Arthur	Arthur Veary
TREE, Dorothy	Dorothy Estelle Triebitz
TREE, Lady	Helen Maude Holt
TREVOR, Austin	Austin Schilsky

PROFESSIONAL NAME*	BIRTH, LEGAL or FORMER NAME**
TREVOR, Claire	Claire Wemlinger
TRYON, Tom	Thomas Tryon
TSCHECHOWA, Olga	Olga von Knipper-Dolling
TUCKER, George L.	George Loane Tucker
TUCKER, Harland	(aka Harlan Tucker)
TUCKER, Sophie	Sonia Kalish
TUFTS, Sonny	Bowen Charleton Tufts, III
TUNNEY, Gene	James Joseph Tunney
TURNER, Lana	Julia Jean Mildred Frances Turner
TURNER, Tina	Annie Mae Bullock
TURPIN, Ben	Bernard Turpin
TUTTLE, Frank	Frank Wright Tuttle
TWELVETREES, Helen	Helen Jurgens
Twiggy	Leslie Hornby
TWITCHELL, A. R. "Archie"	Michael Brandon
TWITTY, Conway	Harold Lloyd Jenkins
Twoton	Tony Galento
TYLER, Judy	Judith Mae Hess
TYLER, Tom	Vincent Markowski (aka Vincent Marko)
U	
URECAL, Minerva	Minerva Holzer
V	
VADIM, Roger	Roger Vadim Plemiannikow
VAGUE, Vera	Barbara Jo Allen
VALE, Jerry	Genaro Louis Vitaliano
VALENTINO, Rudolph	Rudolfo Alfonzo Raffaelo Pierre Filibert Guglielmi di Valentina d'Antonguolla
"	
VALK, Frederick	Fritz Valk
VALLEE, Rudy	Hubert Prior Vallee
VALLI, Alida	Alida Maria Altenburger
VALLI, Frankie	Frank Castelluccio
VALLI, Virginia	Virginia McSweeney
VALLIN, Rick	Richard Vallin
VAN, Bobby	Robert Jack Stein
VANBRUGH, (Dame) Irene	Irene Barnes
VanBUREN, Abigail	Pauline "Popo" Esther Friedman
VanDAMME, Jean-Claude	Jean-Claude Van Varenberg
VAN DOREN, Mamie	Joan Lucille Olander
Van DYKE, W. S.	Woodbridge Strong Van Dyke II
VARCONI, Victor	Mihaly Varkonyi
VELEZ, Lupe	Guadelupe Velez de Villalobos
Vera-Ellen	Vera-Ellen Westmeyr Rohe
VERNE, Kaaren	Ingaborg Katrina Marie Rose Klinckerfuss
VERNON, Anne	Edith Vignaud
VERNON, Dorothy	(aka Dorothy Baird and Dorothy Burns)
VERSOIS, Odile	Militza de Poliakoff-Baidarov
• VERTOV, Dziga	Denis Kaufman
VESOTA, Bruno	Bruno William VeSota
VICKERS, Martha	Martha MacVicar
VICTOR, Charles	Charles Victor Harvey
VIDOR, Florence	Florence Cobb
VIDOR, King	King Wallis Vidor
Village People, The	Victor Willis (1977-79) — cop and lead vocal
"	Ray Simpson (1979-present) — cop and lead vocal
"	Alex Briley — military man
"	David Hodo — construction worker
"	Glenn M. Hughes — biker
"	Randy Jones — cowboy
"	Felipe Rose — Indian chief

Original Names of the Stars

PROFESSIONAL NAME*	BIRTH, LEGAL or FORMER NAME**
VINCENT, Chuck	Charles Vincent Dingley
VINCENT, Sailor Billy	William J. Vincent
VINSON, Helen	Helen Rulfs
VINTON, Arthur	Arthur Rolfe Vinton
"Vitagraph" Girl, The	Alice Joyce
VITTE, Ray	Raymond Anthony Vitte
VITTO, G. L.	Lawrence Vitto
VLADY, Marina	Marina de Poliakoff-Baidarov
VOGAN, Emmett	Charles Emmet Vogan
Von BRINCKEN, Wilhelm	(aka Roger Beckwith)
Von ERICH, Chris	Chris Barton Adkisson
Von ERICH, David	David Adkisson
Von ERICH, Kerry	Kerry Gene Adkisson
Von ERICH, Michael	Michael Adkisson
Von METER, Harry	(aka Harry Van Meter)
Von STERNBERG, Josef	(aka Jo Sternberg and Joe Stern)
Von STROHEIM, Erich	Hans Erich Maria Stroheim von Nordenwall
Von SYDOW, Max	Carl Von Sydow
Von TWARDOWSKI, Hans	Hans Heinrich von Twardowski
VYE, Murvyn	Murvyn Wesley Vye, Jr.

W

PROFESSIONAL NAME*	BIRTH, LEGAL or FORMER NAME**
WAITE, Malcolm	Malcolm Ivan Waite
WALBROOK, Anton	Adolf Wohlbruck
Waldo (of "Our Gang")	Darwood Kenneth Smith
WALES, Wally	Floyd Taliaferro Alderson
WALKEN, Christopher	Ronald Walken
WALKER, Clint	Norman Walker
WALKER, Nancy	Anna Myrtle Swoyer
WALLACE, Jean	Jean Wallasek
WALLACE, May	May Maddox
WALLACE, Regina	Regina Katherine Wallace
WALSH, Raoul	Albert Edward Walsh
WALTHALL, Wallace	Wallace Wales Walthall
WALTON, Douglas	J. Douglas Duder
WALTON, Fred	Frederick Heming
WARD, Carrie	Carrie Clarke-Ward
WARD, Polly	Byno Poluski
WARD, Warwick	Warwick Mannon
WARFIELD, Marjorie	Marjorie Warfield Chase
WARNER, H. B.	Henry Bryan Warner Lickford
WARREN, C. Denier	Charles Denier Warren (aka Denier Warren)
WARREN, Harry	Salvatore Guaragna
WARWICK, John	John Beattie
WARWICK, Robert	Robert Taylor Bien
WASHINGTON, Dinah	Ruth Jones
WATSON, Bobby	Robert Watson Knucher
WATSON, Wylie	John Wylie Robertson
WAYNE, David	Wayne James McMeekan
WAXMAN, Franz	Franz Wachsmann
WAYNE, David	Wayne David McMeekan
WAYNE, John	Marion Michael Morrison
WEAVER, "Doodles"	Winstead Sheffield Glendenning Dixon Weaver
WEAVER, Charley	Cliff Arquette
WEAVER, Sigourney	Susan Alexandra Weaver
WEBB, Clifton	Webb Parmalee Hollenbeck
WEBER, Joe	Morris Weber
WEBER, Rex	Frederick Webber
WEIR, Peter	Peter Lindsay Weir
WEISSMULLER, Johnny	Peter John Weissmuller

• New entry.   * Includes both living & deceased persons.   ** Sources do not always agree on spelling.

Original Names of the Stars

PROFESSIONAL NAME*	BIRTH, LEGAL or FORMER NAME**
WELCH, Raquel	Teresa Jo Tejada
WELD, Tuesday	Susan Ker Weld
WELLES, Orson	George Orson Welles
WELLMAN, William A.	William Augustus Wellman
WELLS, H. G.	Herbert George Wells
WELLS, Jacqueline	(aka Julie Bishop)
WELSH, William	William Joseph Welsh (aka William Welch)
WENDELL, Howard D.	Howard David Wendell
WENGRAF, John E.	Johannes E. Wenngraft
WENTWORTH, Martha	Verna Martha Wentworth
WERBISECK, Gisela	Gisela Werbezirk
WERNER, Oskar	Oskar Josel Boschliessmayer
WESSEL, Dick	Richard Wessel
WESSELHOEFT, Eleanor	Elinor Wesselhoeft
WESSON, Dick	Richard Lewis Wesson
WEST, Billy	Roy B. Weisberg
WEST, Dottie	Dorothy Marie Marsh
WEST, Mae	Mae Cohen
WEST, Pat	Arthur Pat West
WESTCOTT, Helen	Myrthas Helen Hickman
WESTLEY, Helen	Henrietta Remson Meserole Manney
WESTMORE, Bud	Hamilton Adolph Westmore
"	(aka George Hamilton Westmore)
WESTMORE, Perc	Percy Westmore
WESTMORE, Wally	Walter J. Westmore
WHALEN, Michael	Joseph Kenneth Shovlin
WHEAT, Larry	Lawrence Wheat (aka Laurence Wheat)
WHEATCROFT, Stanhope	Stanhope Nelson Wheatcroft
WHEELER, Bert	Albert Jerome Wheeler
Wheezer (of "Our Gang")	Bobby Hutchins
WHITE, Jesse	Jesse Marc Wiedenfeld
WHITE, Lasses	Lee Roy White
WHITE, Slappy	Melvin White
WHITLEY, Crane	Clem Wilenchick
WHITMAN, Gayne	(aka Alfred Vosburgh)
WHITNEY, Peter	Peter King Engle
WICKES, Mary	Mary Isabelle Wickenhausen
Wild Bill	William Cody
WILDE, Cornel	Cornelius Louis Wilde
WILDER, Gene	Jerome Silberman
WILDER, Honeychile	Patricia Wilder (aka Princess Alexander Hohenlohe and
"	Princess Honeychile)
WILLES, Jean	Jean Donahue
WILLIAM, Warren	Warren William Krech
WILLIAMS, Bert	Egbert Austins Williams
WILLIAMS, Bill	William H. Katt, Sr.
WILLIAMS, Earle	Earle Rafael Williams
WILLIAMS, Guy	Armand Catalano
WILLIAMS, Hank Sr.	Hiram Williams
• WILLIAMS, Hedy	Harriette Antoinette Williams (Carr)
WILLIAMS, Hugh	Brian Williams
WILLIAMS, Scott T.	(aka Chief Thundercloud)
WILLIAMS, Treat	Richard Williams
WILLIS, Matt	Marion Willis, 3rd
WILLSON, Meredith	Robert Meredith Reiniger
WILSON, Clarence	Clarence Hummel Wilson
WILSON, Edith	Edith Woodall
WILSON, Marie	Katherine Elizabeth White
WINDSOR, Claire	Claire Viola Cronk

Original Names of the Stars

PROFESSIONAL NAME*	BIRTH, LEGAL or FORMER NAME**
WINDSOR, Marie	Emily Marie Bertelson
WING, Red	Princess Lillian Red Wing St. Cyr
WING, Toby	Martha Virginia Wing
WINNINGER, Charles	Karl Winninger
• WINSHIP, Joanne Tree	Joanne Tree
WINSLOW, George 'Foghorn'	George Wenzlaff
WINTERS, Shelly	Shirley Schrift
WINTHROP, Joy	Josephine Williams
WINWOOD, Estelle	Estelle Goodwin
WITHERS, Googie	Georgette Withers
WITHERS, Grant	Granville G. Withers
WOLFF, Frank	Frank Hermann
WONDER, Stevie	Stevland Morris
WONG, Anna May	Wong Liu Tsong
WONG, Mary	Mary Liu H. Wong
WOOD, Natalie	Natasha Gurdin
WOODS, Harry L. Sr.	Harry Lewis Woods
WOOLERY, Ade	Adrian Woolery
WOOLLEY, Monty	Edgar Montillion Woolley
WORDEN, Hank	Norton Earl Worden
WORTH, Constance	Jocelyn Howarth
WRAY, John	John Griffith Wray
WYMAN, Jane	Sarah Jane Fulks
WYNN, Ed	Isaiah Edwin Leopold
WYNN, Keenan	Francis Keenan Wynn
WYNTER, Dana	Dagmar Wynter
WYNYARD, Diana	Dorothy Isobel Cox
X	
X, Malcolm	Malcolm Little (Muslim name: Hajj-Malik El-Shabazz)
Y	
YORKE, Edith	Edithe Byard (aka Edithe Yorke)
YORKIN, Bud	Alan Yorkin
YOST, Herbert A.	(aka Barry O'Moore)
YOUNG, Alan	Angus Young
YOUNG, Bobby	(aka Clifton Young)
YOUNG, Gig	Byron Ellsworth Barr (aka Bryant Fleming)
YOUNG, Loretta	Gretchen Young
YOWLACHIE, Chief	Daniel Simmons
YURKA, Blanche	Blanche Jurka
Z	
ZANE, Bartine	(aka Bartine Burkette)
ZANUCK, Darryl F.	Darryl Frank Zanuck
ZANUCK, Richard D.	Richard Darryl Zanuck
ZAPPA, Frank	Francis Vincent Zappa
ZAREMBA, Jack	John C. Zaremba
ZEARS, Marjorie	Marjorie Page
ZETTERLING, Mai	Mai Elizabeth Zetterling
ZIMBALIST, Al	Alfred N. Zimbalist
ZORINA, Vera	Eva Brigitta Hartwig

8

Who is Related to Whom — Off Screen?

Who is Related to Whom — Off Screen? *

HUSBAND	SHOW-BIZ WIVES**	WIFE	SHOW-BIZ HUSBANDS**
A		**A**	
Harry Ackerman	Elinor Donahue	May Abbey	George Lessey
Art Acord	Louise Lorraine	Gypsy Abbott	Henry King
William Perry Adams	Eleanor Wells	Paula Abdul	Emilio Estevez
Al Adamson	Regina Carrol	Jean Acker	Rudolph Valentino
Wesley Addy	Celeste Holm	Constance Adams	Cecil B. DeMille
Buddy Adler	Anita Louise	Edie Adams	Ernie Kovacs
Luther Adler	Sylvia Sidney	Renee Adoree	Tom Moore
John Agar	Shirley Temple	Lola Albright	Jack Carson
Brian Aherne	Joan Fontaine	Mari Aldon	Tay Garnett
Eddie Albert	Margo	Elizabeth Allan	Robert Montgomery
Ross Alexander	Anne Nagel	Adrianne Allen	Raymond Massey
Peter Allen	Liza Minnelli	Gracie Allen	George Burns
Steve Allen	Jayne Meadows	Kirstie Alley	Parker Stevenson
Robert Ames	Vivienne Segal	Astrid Allwyn	Robert Kent
Paul Andor	Lotte Palfi Andor	June Allyson	Dick Powell
Fatty Arbuckle	Minta Durfee	Loni Anderson	Burt Reynolds
Richard Arlen	Jobyna Ralston	Pamela Anderson	Tommy Lee
George Arliss	Florence Arliss	Lotte Palfi Andor	Paul Andor
Tom Arnold	Roseanne Barr	Ursula Andress	John Derek
Desi Arnaz	Lucille Ball	Julie Andrews	Blake Edwards
William Asher	Elizabeth Montgomery	Lois Andrews	George Jessel
Nils Asther	Vivian Duncan	Pier Angeli	Vic Damone
Roscoe Ates	Barbara Ray	Annabella	Tyrone Power
James T. Aubrey	Phyllis Thaxter	Ann-Margret	Roger Smith
Jean Pierre Aumont	Maria Montez	Laura Anson	Philo McCullough
"	Marisa Pavan	Tsuru Aoki	Sessue Hayakawa
Dan Aykroyd	Donna Dixon	Zeudi Araya	Franco Cristaldi
Lew Ayres	Lola Lane	Eve Arden	Brooks West
"	Ginger Rogers	Florence Arliss	George Arliss
		Lucie Arnaz	Laurence Luckinbill
B		Patricia Arquette	Nicholas Cage
Kevin Bacon	Kyra Sedgwick	Jean Arthur	Frank Ross
Max Baer	Dorothy Dunbar	Linda Arvidson	David W. Griffith
Alec Baldwin	Kim Bassinger	Elizabeth Ashley	George Peppard (twice)
Lucien Ballard	Merle Oberon	Dorrit Ashton	Charles Newton
Antonio Banderas	Melanie Griffith	**B**	
Monty Banks	Gladys Frazin	Lauren Bacall	Humphrey Bogart
"	Gracie Fields	Barbara Bach	Ringo Starr
Harry Bannister	Ann Harding	Olga Baclanova	Nicholas Soussanin
Dave Barbour	Peggy Lee	Lynne Baggett	Sam Spiegel
Ben Bard	Ruth Roland	Lucille Ball	Desi Arnaz
Jess Barker	Susan Hayward	Suzan Ball	Richard Long
Lex Barker	Arlene Dahl	Anne Bancroft	Mel Brooks
"	Lana Turner	Tallulah Bankhead	John Emery
Reginald Barker	Clara Williams	Vilma Banky	Rod La Rocque
John Barrymore	Delores Costello	Theda Bara	Charles J. Brabin
Lionel Barrymore	Doris Rankin	Brigitte Bardot	Roger Vadim
Richard Barthelmess	Mary Hay	Binnie Barnes	Mike Frankovich
Frank Beal	Louise Lester	Roseanne Barr	Tom Arnold
Royal Beal	Edna Bennett	Edith Barrett	Vincent Price
Wallace Beery	Gloria Swanson	Linda Barrett	Victor Sutherland
Edward Begley	Martha Raye	Majel Barrett	Gene Roddenberry
Monta Bell	Betty Lawford	Dusty Bartlett	Jeffrey Hunter
Rex Bell	Clara Bow	Lina Basquette	Sam Warner
Ralph Bellamy	Catherine Willard	Kim Bassinger	Alec Baldwin
"	Ethel Smith (organist)	Anne Baxter	John Hodiak
Brian Benben	Madeleine Stowe	Meredith Baxter	David Birney
Charles J. Bennett	Boots Mallory	Jennifer Beals	Alexander Rockwell
Richard Bennett	Adrianne Morrison	Helen Beck	Peter Cushing
Jack Benny	Mary Livingstone		

* Includes only show-biz personalities.

HUSBAND	SHOW-BIZ WIVES**	WIFE	SHOW-BIZ HUSBANDS**
Jacques Bergerac	Ginger Rogers	Olga Bellin	Paul Roebling
Busby Berkeley	Esther Muir	Constance Bennett	Gilbert Roland
Paul Bern	Jean Harlow	Edna Bennett	Royal Beal
Herbert Biberman	Gale Sondergaard	Enid Bennett	Fred Niblo, Sr.
David Birney	Meredith Baxter	Joan Bennett	Walter Wanger
Bill Bixby	Brenda Benet	Candice Bergen	Louis Malle
Clint Black	Lisa Hartman	Ingrid Bergman	Roberto Rossellini
Larry Blyden	Carol Haney	Valerie Bertinelli	Eddie Van Halen
True Boardman	Virginia Eames	Edna Best	Herbert Marshall
Humphrey Bogart	Helen Menken	Josie Bissett	Rob Estes
"	Mary Philips	Betsy Blair	Gene Kelly
"	Mayo Methot	Janet Blair	Joe "Fingers" Carr
"	Lauren Bacall	Joan Blondell	Dick Powell
Robert Bolt	Sarah Miles (twice)	"	Mike Todd
Sonny Bono	Cher	Claire Bloom	Rod Steiger
Ernest Borgnine	Ethel Merman	Betty Blythe	Paul Scardon
Frank Borzage	Rena Rogers	Eleanor Boardman	King Vidor
Phillip Bourneuf	Frances Reid	"	Harry d'Abbadie d'Arrast
John Bowers	Marguerite de la Motte	Lillian Boardman	Howard I. Smith
Bruce Boxleitner	Melissa Gilbert	Adrian Booth	David Brian
William Boyd	Elinor Fair	Shirley Booth	Archie Gardner
"	Dorothy Sebastian	Veda Ann Borg	Andrew McLaglen
"	Grace Bradley	Hazel Bourne	David C. Imboden
Charles Boyer	Pat Paterson	Clara Bow	Rex Bell
Charles J. Brabin	Theda Bara	Grace Bradley	William Boyd
Kenneth Branagh	Emma Thompson	Evelyn Brent	Harry Fox
George Brent	Ruth Chatterton	Christie Brinkley	Billy Joel
"	Helen Nolan	May Britt	Sammy Davis, Jr.
"	Constance Worth	Helen Broderick	Lester Crawford
"	Ann Sheridan	Coral Browne	Vincent Price
Jeremy Brett	Anna Massey	Lucile Browne	James Flavin
"	Joan Wilson	Lorayne Brox	Henry Busse
David Brian	Adrian Booth	Virginia Bruce	John Gilbert
Jack Briggs	Giner Rogers	Billie Burke	Florenz Ziegfeld
Frederick Brisson	Rosalind Russell	Delta Burke	Gerald McRaney
Mel Brooks	Anne Bancroft	Olivia Burwell	John Gilbert
Charles Bronson	Jill Ireland	Pauline Bush	Alan Dwan
Pierce Brosnan	Cassandra Harris	**C**	
Georg Stanford Brown	Tyne Daly	Lily Cahill	Brandon Tynan
Yul Brynner	Virginia Gilmore	Dyan Cannon	Cary Grant
George Burns	Gracie Allen	Ida (Tobias) Cantor	Eddie Cantor
Richard Burton	Elizabeth Taylor (twice)	Claudia Cardinale	Franco Cristaldi
Niven Busch	Teresa Wright	Brenda Carlin	George Carlin
Henry Busse	Lorayne Brox	Judy Carne	Burt Reynolds
Eddie Buzzell	Ona Munson	Sue Carol	Nick Stuart
C		"	Alan Ladd
Nicholas Cage	Patricia Arquette	Regina Carrol	Al Adamson
Louis Calhern	Natalie Schafer	Diahann Carroll	Vic Damone
Kirk Cameron	Chelsea Noble	Madeleine Carroll	Sterling Hayden
Webster Campbell	Corinne Griffith	Dixie Carter	Hal Holbrook
Eddie Cantor	Ida (Tobias) Cantor	Irene Castle	Vernon Castle
George Carlin	Brenda Carlin	Phoebe Cates	Kevin Kline
Thomas A. Carlin	Frances Sternhagen	Joan Caulfield	Frank Ross
Joe "Fingers" Carr	Janet Blair	Helene Chadwick	William Wellman
"	Margaret Whiting	Marge (Belcher) Champion	Gower Champion
Keith Carradine	Sandra Will	Oona Chaplin	Charlie Chaplin
Jack Carson	Lola Albright	Cyd Charisse	Tony Martin
Johnny Cash	June Carter	Mary Charleson	Henry B. Walthall
Jack Cassidy	Shirley Jones	Charo	Xavier Cugat
Shaun Cassidy	Susan Diol	Ruth Chatterton	George Brent

Who is Related to Whom — Off Screen? *

HUSBAND	SHOW-BIZ WIVES**	WIFE	SHOW-BIZ HUSBANDS**
Oleg Cassini	Gene Tierney	Ruth Chatterton (con't)	Ralph Forbes
Vernon Castle	Irene Castle	Cher	Sonny Bono
William Chalee	Ruth Nelson	Virginia Cherrill	Cary Grant
Gower Champion	Marge (Belcher) Champion	Linda Christian	Tyrone Power
Charlie Chaplin	Mildred Harris	Connie Chung	Maury Povich
"	Paulette Goddard	Marguerite Churchill	George O'Brien
"	Oona Chaplin	Ina Claire	John Gilbert
Arthur Chesney	Estelle Winwood	Ludi Claire	John Claire
Donald Churchill	Pauline Yates	"	Lawrence Hugo
John Claire	Ludi Claire	Ethel Clayton	Ian Keith
Stanley Clements	Gloria Grahame	Rosemary Clooney	José Ferrer (twice)
Andy Clyde	Elsie Tarron	Imogene Coca	King Donovan
David Clyde	Fay Holden	Ann Codee	Frank Orth
Lew Cody	Mabel Normand	Claudette Colbert	Norman Foster
"	Dorothy Dalton	Natalie Cole	André Fischer
Harry Cohn	Joan Perry	Constance Collier	Julian L'Estrange
William A. Colleran	Lee Remick	Joan Collins	Maxwell Reed
Gary Collins	Mary Ann Mobley	"	Anthony Newley
G. Pat Collins	Billie Rhodes	Lisa Collins	Billy Zane
Ronald Colman	Benita Hume	June Collyer	Stuart Erwin
Nick Condos	Martha Raye	Betty Compson	James Cruze
Walter Connolly	Nedda Harrigan	Sheilah Connolly	Guy Madison
Jack Coogan Sr.	Lillian Dolliver	Peggy Converse	Don Porter
Jackie Coogan	Betty Grable	Mara Corday	Richard Long
Tom Corrigan	Mabel Taliaferro	Rita Corday	Harold Nebenzal
Norman Corwin	Katherine Locke	Delores Costello	John Barrymore
Joseph Cotten	Patricia Medina	Helen Costello	Lowell Sherman
William Courtleigh, Jr.	Ethel Flemming	Katie Couric	John Paul (Jay) Monahan
Richy Craig, Jr.	Edith Craig	Jeanne Coyne	Gene Kelly
Les Crane	Tina Louise	Edith Craig	Richey Craig, Jr.
Lester Crawford	Helen Broderick	Cindy Crawford	Richard Gere
Franco Cristaldi	Claudia Cardinale	Joan Crawford	Douglas Fairbanks Jr.
"	Zeudi Araya	"	Franchot Tone
John Cromwell	Ruth Nelson	"	Philip Terry
Richard Cromwell	Angela Lansbury	**D**	
Hume Cronyn	Jessica Tandy	Arlene Dahl	Fernando Lamas
Bing Crosby	Dixie Lee	"	Lex Barker
"	Kathryn Grant	Dorothy Dalton	Lew Cody
Beverley Cross	Dame Magie Smith	Tyne Daly	Georg Stanford Brown
Tom Cruise	Mimi Rogers	Lili Damita	Errol Flynn
"	Nicole Kidman	Bebe Daniels	Ben Lyon
James Cruze	Marguerite Snow	Kim Darby	James Stacy
"	Betty Compson	Dorothy Davenport	Wallace Reid
Xavier Cugat	Charo	Fanny Davenport	Melbourne MacDowell
Alan Curtis	Ilona Massey	Bette Davis	Gary Merrill
"	Betty Sundmark	Geena Davis	Jeff Goldblum
Dick Curtis	Ruth Sullivan	Mildred Davis	Harold Lloyd
Tony Curtis	Janet Leigh	Nancy Davis	Ronald Reagan
Peter Cushing	Helen Beck	Frances Dee	Joel McCrea
D		Sandra Dee	Bobby Darin
Grover Dale	Anita Morris	Gloria de Haven	John Payne
Vic Damone	Pier Angeli	Marguerite de la Motte	John Bowers
"	Diahann Carroll	Lorella De Luca	Duccio Tessari
Ted Danson	Mary Steenburgen	Katherine DeMille	Anthony Quinn
Bobby Darin	Sandra Dee	Bo Derek	John Derek
Frankie Darro	Aloha Wray	Colleen Dewhurst	James Vickery
Jules Dassin	Melina Mercouri	"	George C. Scott (twice)
Thayer David	Valerie French	Susan Diol	Shaun Cassidy
Miles Davis	Frances Taylor	Donna Dixon	Dan Aykroyd
"	Betty Mabry	Shannen Doherty	Ashley Hamilton

Who is Related to Whom — Off Screen? *

HUSBAND	SHOW-BIZ WIVES**	WIFE	SHOW-BIZ HUSBANDS**
Miles Davis (con't)	Cicely Tyson	Lillian Dolliver	Jack Coogan Sr.
Sammy Davis, Jr.	May Britt	Jenny Dolly	Harry Fox
Daniel Day-Lewis	Rebecca Miller	Faith Domergue	Hugo Fregonese
Roy Del Ruth	Winnie Lightner	Elinor Donahue	Harry Ackerman
Gordon Demain	Octavia Handworth	Jeff Donnell	Aldo Ray
Cecil B. DeMille	Constance Adams	Cathy Downs	Joe Kirkwood, Jr.
John Derek	Patti Behrs	Patricia Doyle	Robert Wise
"	Ursula Andress	Ethel Drew	Wilfrid Hyde-White
"	Linda Evans	Joanne Dru	Dick Haymes
"	Bo Derek	"	John Ireland
Bruce Dern	Dianne Ladd	Dorothy Dunbar	Max Baer
Vittorio de Sica	Giuditta Rissoni	Vivian Duncan	Nils Asther
Danny DeVito	Rhea Perlman	Deanna Durbin	Felix Jackson
Bradford Dillman	Suzy Parker	Minta Durfee	Fatty Arbuckle
Joe DiMaggio	Marilyn Monroe	Ann Dvorak	Leslie C. Fenton
Alan Dobie	Rachel Roberts	**E**	
Troy Donahue	Suzanne Pleshette	Virginia Eames	True Boardman
King Donovan	Imogene Coca	Dorothy Earle	George "Gabby" Hayes
Virgil Jack Dougherty	Barbara Lamar	Nora Eddington	Errol Flynn
Paul Douglas	Jan Sterling	Sally Eilers	Hoot Gibson
William Dozier	Ann Rutherford	Florence Eldridge	Fredric March
	Joan Fontaine	Vera Engels	Ivan Lebedeff
Sydney Drew	Lucille McVey	Jill Esmond	Laurence Olivier
Howard Duff	Ida Lupino	Dale Evans	Roy Rogers
Douglas Dumbrille	Patricia Mowbray	Linda Evans	John Derek
James Dunn	Frances Gifford	**F**	
Charles Dutton	Debbie Morgan	Shelley Fabares	Mike Farrell
Alan Dwan	Pauline Bush	Elinor Fair	William Boyd
E		Frances Farmer	Leif Erikson
Clint Eastwood	Dina Ruiz	Mia Farrow	Frank Sinatra
Herb Edelman	Louise Sorel	"	André Previn
Blake Edwards	Julie Andrews	Farrah Fawcett	Lee Majors
Neely Edwards	Marguerite Snow	Alice Faye	Tony Martin
Denholm Elliott	Virginia McKenna	"	Phil Harris
"	Susan Robinson	Elsie Ferguson	Frederick Worlock
William D. Elliott	Dionne Warwick	Helen Ferguson	William Russell (d. 1929)
Robert Ellis	Vera Reynolds	Debra Feuer	Mickey Rourke
John Emerson	Anita Loos	Gracie Fields	Monty Banks
John Emery	Tallulah Bankhead	Rhonda Fleming	Lang Jeffries
Leif Erikson	Frances Farmer	Ethel Flemming	William Courtleigh, Jr.
Stuart Erwin	June Collyer	Jane Fonda	Roger Vadim
Rob Estes	Josie Bissett	"	Ted Turner
Emilio Estevez	Paula Abdul	Joan Fontaine	Brian Aherne
Wilbur Evans	Susanna Foster	"	William Dozier
Charles Eyton	Kathlyn Williams	Lynn Fontanne	Alfred Lunt
F		Mary Ford	Les Paul
Douglas Fairbanks, Jr.	Joan Crawford	Susanna Foster	Wilbur Evans
Douglas Fairbanks, Sr.	Mary Pickford	Lynne Frederick	Peter Sellers
Dustin Farnum	Winifred Kingston	"	David Frost
Charles Farrell	Virginia Valli	Valerie French	Thayer David
Mike Farrell	Shelley Fabares	**G**	
John Farrow	Maureen O'Sullivan	Magda Gabor	George Sanders
Frank Fay	Barbara Stanwyck	Zsa Zsa Gabor	George Sanders
Federico Fellini	Giulietta Masina	Ava Gardner	Mickey Rooney
Leslie C. Fenton	Ann Dvorak	"	Artie Shaw
José Ferrer	Rosemary Clooney (twice)	"	Frank Sinatra
"	Uta Hagen	Judy Garland	David Rose
Mel Ferrer	Audrey Hepburn	"	Vincente Minnelli
André Fischer	Natalie Cole	Pauline Garon	Lowell Sherman

Who is Related to Whom — Off Screen? *

HUSBAND	SHOW-BIZ WIVES**	WIFE	SHOW-BIZ HUSBANDS**
Eddie Fisher	Debbie Reynolds	Greer Garson	Richard Ney
"	Elizabeth Taylor	Gladys George	Leonard Penn
James Flavin	Lucile Browne	Frances Gifford	James Dunn
Errol Flynn	Nora Eddington	Melissa Gilbert	Bruce Boxleitner
"	Lili Damita	Virginia Gilmore	Yul Brynner
"	Patrice Wymore	Dorothy Gish	James Rennie
Henry Fonda	Margaret Sullavan	Lucille (Webster) Gleason	James Gleason
Ralph Forbes	Ruth Chatterton	Paulette Goddard	Charlie Chaplin
Glenn Ford	Eleanor Powell	"	Burgess Meredith
Dudley Foster	Eileen Kenally	Dagmar Godowsky	Frank Mayo
Norman Foster	Claudette Colbert	Frances Goodrich	Albert Hackett
Harry Fox	Jenny Dolly	Yekaterina Gordeeva	Sergei Grinkov
"	Evelyn Brent	Betty Grable	Jackie Coogan
Robert Foxworth	Elizabeth Montgomery	"	Harry James
Anthony Franciosa	Shelley Winters	Gloria Grahame	Stanley Clements
Mike Frankovich	Binnie Barnes	"	Nicholas Ray
Hugo Fregonese	Faith Domergue	"	Cy Howard
Eugene Frenke	Anna Sten	Kathryn Grant	Bing Crosby
David Frost	Lynne Frederick	Mary Grant	Vincent Price
G		Bonita Granville	Jack Wrather
Clark Gable	Carole Lombard	Jane Greer	Rudy Vallee
"	Josephine Dillon	Mercedes Gregory	André Gregory
Ben Gage	Esther Williams	Nan Grey	Frankie Laine
Richard "Skeets" Gallagher	Pauline Mason	Corinne Griffith	Webster Campbell
Archie Gardner	Shirley Booth	Melanie Griffith	Antonio Banderas
Tay Garnett	Patsy Ruth Miller	**H**	
"	Mari Aldon	Florence Hackett	Arthur V. Johnson
Vittorio Gassman	Shelley Winters	Uta Hagen	José Ferrer
Richard Gere	Cindy Crawford	Barbara Hale	Bill Williams
Hoot Gibson	Sally Eilers	Geraldine Hall	Porter Hall
Frank Gifford	Kathie Lee	Octavia Handworth	Harry Handworth
Billy Gilbert	Lally McKenzie	"	Gordon Demain
John Gilbert	Olivia Burwell	Carol Haney	Larry Blyden
"	Leatrice Joy	Joan Harben	Clive Morton
"	Ina Claire	Ann Harding	Harry Bannister
"	Virginia Bruce	"	Werner Janssen
James Gleason	Lucille (Webster) Gleason	Jean Harlow	Paul Bern
Jeff Goldblum	Geena Davis	"	Harold Rosson
Samuel Goldwyn	Frances Howard	Nedda Harrigan	Walter Connolly
John Good	Louise Currie	"	Joshua Logan
James Gordon	Mabel Van Buren	Cassandra Harris	Pierce Brosnan
Kip Gowans	Lee Remick	Mildred Harris	Charles Chaplin
Stewart Granger	Elspeth March	Mary Hart	Burt Sugarman
"	Jean Simmons	Lisa Hartman	Clint Black
Cary Grant	Virginia Cherrill	Teri Hatcher	Jon Tenney
"	Betsy Drake	June Haver	Fred MacMurray
"	Dyan Cannon	Mary Hay	Richard Barthelmess
Peter Graves	Vanessa Lee	Helen Hayes	Charles MacArthur
Alfred E. Green	Vivian Reid	Susan Hayward	Jess Barker
André Gregory	Mercedes Gregory	Joy Hatton Haynes	Tiger Haynes
David W. Griffith	Linda Arvidson	Rita Hayworth	Dick Haymes
Raymond Griffith	Bertha Mann	"	Orson Welles
Sergei Grinkov	Yekaterina Gordeeva	"	James Hill
H		Amy Heckerling	Neal Israel
Albert Hackett	Frances Goodrich	Wanda Hendrix	Audie Murphy
Raymond Hackett	Myra Hampton	Audrey Hepburn	Mel Ferrer
"	Blanche Sweet	Anna (Dodge) Hernandez	George F. Hernandez
John Hall	Frances Langford	Harriet Hilliard	Ozzie Nelson
Porter Hall	Geraldine Hall	Alma Reville Hitchcock	(Sir) Alfred Hitchcock
Ashley Hamilton	Shannen Doherty	Lucie Hoeflich	Emil Jannings

Who is Related to Whom — Off Screen? *

HUSBAND	SHOW-BIZ WIVES**	WIFE	SHOW-BIZ HUSBANDS**
Harry Handworth	*Octavia (Boas) Handworth*	Fay Holden	*David Clyde*
Tom Hanks	*Rita Wilson*	Gladys Holland	*Bill Zuckert*
Mickey Hargitay	*Jayne Mansfield*	Marjorie Holliday	*Michael St. Angel*
Kenneth Harlan	*Marie Prevost*	Celeste Holm	*Wesley Addy*
Tom Harmon	*Elyse Knox*	Patty Hope	*George O. Petrie*
Ed Harris	*Amy Madigan*	Miriam Hopkins	*Anatole Litvak*
Phil Harris	*Alice Faye*	Hedda (Furry) Hopper	*De Wolf Hopper*
Gregory Harrison	*Randi Oakes*	Marilyn Horne	*Henry Lewis*
Rex Harrison	*Kay Kendall*	Frances Howard	*Samuel Goldwyn*
"	*Lilli Palmer*	Benita Hume	*Ronald Colman*
"	*Rachel Roberts*	Benita Hume	*Goerge Sanders*
Laurence Harvey	*Margaret Leighton*	Martha Hyer	*Hal Wallis*
Sessue Hayakawa	*Tsuru Aoki*	**I**	
Russell "Lucky" Hayden	*Lillian Porter*	Jill Ireland	*Charles Bronson*
Sterling Hayden	*Madeleine Carroll*	Amy Irving	*Steven Spielberg*
George "Gabby" Hayes	*Dorothy Earle*	Elaine Irwin	*John Mellencamp*
Dick Haymes	*Rita Hayworth*	**J**	
"	*Joanne Dru*	Anne Jackson	*Eli Wallach*
Tiger Haynes	*Joy Hatton Haynes*	Isabel Jeans	*Claude Rains*
Leland Hayward	*Margaret Sullavan*	Ursula Jeans	*Robin Irvine*
Louis Hayward	*Ida Lupino*	"	*Roger Livesey*
Jascha Heifetz	*Florence Vidor*	Anne Jeffries	*Robert Sterling*
Del Henderson	*Florence Lee*	Jennifer Jones	*Robert Walker*
Hugh Herbert	*Anita Pam*	"	*David O. Selznick*
George F. Hernandez	*Anna (Dodge) Hernandez*	Shirley Jones	*Jack Cassidy*
Weldon Heyburn	*Greta Nissen*	"	*Marty Ingels*
George F. Hill	*Frances Marion*	Marion Jordan	*Jim "Fibber McGee" Jordan*
(Sir) Alfred Hitchcock	*Alma Reville Hitchcock*	Leatrice Joy	*John Gilbert*
Henry M. Hobart	*Olive Tell*	Alice Joyce	*Tom Moore*
John Hodiak	*Anne Baxter*	Elaine Joyce	*Bobby Van*
Paul Hogan	*Linda Kozlowski*	Arlene Judge	*Wesley Ruggles*
Hal Holbrook	*Dixie Carter*	**K**	
William Holden	*Brenda Marshall*	Sylvia Fine Kaye	*Danny Kaye*
Oscar Homolka	*Joan Tetzel*	Myra Keaton	*Joseph Keaton, Sr.*
Arthur Hornblow, Jr.	*Myrna Loy*	Ruby Keeler	*Al Jolson*
James Horne	*Cleo Ridgely*	Nancy Kelly	*Edmond O'Brien*
De Wolf Hopper	*Hedda (Furry) Hopper*	Eileen Kenally	*Dudley Foster*
Peter Horton	*Michelle Pfeiffer*	Kay Kendall	*Rex Harrison*
Cy Howard	*Gloria Grahame*	Linda Kerridge	*Corey Parker*
Lawrence Hugo	*Ludi Claire*	Evelyn Keyes	*John Huston*
Jeffrey Hunter	*Barbara Rush*	"	*Artie Shaw*
"	*Dusty Bartlett*	Nicole Kidman	*Tom Cruise*
"	*Emily McLaughlin*	Winifred Kingston	*Dustin Farnum*
John Huston	*Evelyn Keyes*	Kathleen Kinmont	*Lorenzo Lamas*
Timothy Hutton	*Debra Winger*	Nastassja Kinski	*Ibraham Moussa*
Wilfrid Hyde-White	*Ethel Drew*	Patricia Knight	*Cornel Wilde*
I		Elyse Knox	*Tom Harmon*
David C. Imboden	*Hazel Bourne*	Linda Kozlowski	*Paul Hogan*
Marty Ingels	*Shirley Jones*	Lorraine Krueger	*Stu Wilson*
John Ireland	*Elaine Rosen*	**L**	
"	*Joanne Dru*	Dianne Ladd	*Bruce Dern*
Robin Irvine	*Ursula Jeans*	Barbara Lamar	*Virgil Jack Dougherty*
Neal Israel	*Amy Heckerling*	Hedy Lamarr	*John Loder*
J		Lillian La Monte	*Fred MacMurray*
Felix Jackson	*Deanna Durbin*	Elsa Lanchester	*Charles Laughton*
Henry Jaffe	*Jean Muir*	Diane Lane	*Christopher Lambert*
Harry James	*Betty Grable*	Lola Lane	*Lew Ayres*
Emil Jannings	*Lucie Hoeflich*	Hope Lange	*Don Murray*
Werner Janssen	*Ann Harding*	Frances Langford	*John Hall*
Lang Jeffries	*Rhonda Fleming*	Angela Lansbury	*Richard Cromwell*

Who is Related to Whom — Off Screen? *

HUSBAND	SHOW-BIZ WIVES**	WIFE	SHOW-BIZ HUSBANDS**
George Jessel	Norma Talmadge	Betty Lawford	Monta Bell
"	Lois Andrews	Evelyn Laye	Frank Lawton
Billy Joel	Christie Brinkley	Zarah Leander (Hedberg)	Nils Leander
Arthur V. Johnson	Florence Hackett	Kelly LeBrock	Steven Seagal
Al Jolson	Ruby Keeler	Gretchen Lederer	Otto Lederer
Jim "Fibber McGee" Jordan	Marion Jordan	Dixie Lee	Bing Crosby
Richard Jordan	Kathleen Widdoes	Florence Lee	Del Henderson
K		Kathie Lee	Frank Gifford
Jacob Kalich	Molly Picon	Peggy Lee	Dave Barbour
Edward Kaufman	Thelma Salter	Vanessa Lee	Peter Graves
Danny Kaye	Sylvia Fine Kaye	Janet Leigh	Tony Curtis
James Keach	Jane Seymour	Vivien Leigh	Laurence Olivier
Robert Emmett Keane	Claire Whitney	Margaret Leighton	Laurence Harvey
Buster Keaton	Natalie Talmadge	"	Michael Wilding
Joseph Keaton, Sr.	Myra Keaton	Louise Lester	Frank Beal
Don Keefer	Catherine McLeod	Diana Lewis	William Powell
Brian Keith	Victoria Young	Winnie Lightner	Roy Del Ruth
Ian Keith	Ethel Clayton	Viveca Lindfors	Don Siegel
David Kelley	Michelle Pfeiffer	Mary Livingstone	Jack Benny
Gene Kelly	Jeanne Coyne	Gladys Lloyd	Edward G. Robinson
"	Betsy Blair	Katherine Locke	Norman Corwin
Paul Kelly	Dorothy Mackaye	Kathleen (Arthur) Lockhart	Gene Lockhart
Robert Kent	Astrid Allwyn	Heather Locklear	Tommy Lee
Val Kilmer	Joanne Whalley	"	Richie Sambora
Henry King	Gypsy Abbott	Carole Lombard	William Powell
James Kirkwood	Gertrude R. Robinson	"	Clark Gable
Joe Kirkwood, Jr.	Cathy Downs	Anita Loos	John Emerson
Werner Klemperer	Louise Troy	Sophia Loren	Carlo Ponti
Kevin Kline	Phoebe Cates	Louise Lorraine	Art Acord
Alexander Korda	Merle Oberon	Anita Louise	Buddy Adler
Ernie Kovacs	Edie Adams	Tina Louise	Les Crane
L		Judith Lowry	Rudd Lowry
Alan Ladd	Sue Carol	Margerie Bonner Lowry	Malcolm Lowry
Frankie Laine	Nan Grey	Myrna Loy	Arthur Hornblow, Jr.
Fernando Lamas	Arlene Dahl	"	Gene Markey
"	Esther Williams	Ida Lupino	Louis Hayward
Lorenzo Lamas	Kathleen Kinmont	"	Howard Duff
Christopher Lambert	Diane Lane	**M**	
Sidney Lanfield	Shirley Mason	Jeanette MacDonald	Gene Raymond
David Lansbury	Ally Sheedy	Ali MacGraw	Steve McQueen
Rod La Rocque	Vilma Banky	Rose Mack	Joseph Lester
Matt Lattanzi	Olivia Newton-John	Dorothy Mackaye	Paul Kelly
Charles Laughton	Elsa Lanchester	Amy Madigan	Ed Harris
Frank Launder	Bernadette O'Farrell	Madonna	Sean Penn
Frank Lawton	Evelyn Laye	Boots Mallory	Charles J. Bennett
David Lean	Ann Todd	Bertha Mann	Raymond Griffith
Nils Leander	Zarah (Hedberg) Leander	Jayne Mansfield	Mickey Hargitay
Ivan Lebedeff	Vera Engels	Elspeth March	Stewart Granger
Otto Lederer	Gretchen Lederer	Margo	Eddie Albert
Tommy Lee	Heather Locklear	Frances Marion	Fred Thomson
"	Pamela Anderson	"	George F. Hill
Robert Z. Leonard	Gertrude Olmstead	Brenda Marshall	William Holden
Mervyn Le Roy	Edna Murphy	Giulietta Masina	Federico Fellini
Edward J. LeSaint	Stella Razetto	Pauline Mason	Richard "Skeets" Gallagher
George Lessey	May Abbey	Shirley Mason	Sidney Lanfield
Joseph Lester	Rose Mack	Anna Massey	Jeremy Brett
Julian L'Estrange	Constance Collier	Ilona Massey	Alan Curtis
Oscar Levant	Barbara Cornett	Virginia Mayo	Michael O'Shea
Henry Lewis	Marilyn Horne	Gertrude McCoy	Duncan McRae
Sheldon Lewis	Virginia Pearson	Marie McDonald	Donald F. Taylor

Who is Related to Whom — Off Screen? *

HUSBAND	SHOW-BIZ WIVES**	WIFE	SHOW-BIZ HUSBANDS**
Anatole Litvak	*Miriam Hopkins*	Claire McDowell	*Charles H. Mailes*
Roger Livesey	*Ursula Jeans*	Virginia McKenna	*Bill Travers*
Harold Lloyd	*Mildred Davis*	"	*Denholm Elliott*
Gene Lockhart	*Kathleen (Arthur) Lockhart*	Eva B. McKenzie	*Robert B. McKenzie*
John Loder	*Hedy Lamarr*	Lally McKenzie	*Billy Gilbert*
Joshua Logan	*Nedda Harrigan*	Emily McLaughlin	*Jeffrey Hunter*
Richard Long	*Suzan Ball*	Catherine McLeod	*Don Keefer*
"	*Mara Corday*	Lucille McVey	*Sydney Drew*
Jean Louis	*Loretta Young*	Margaret McWade	*Edward McWade*
Lyle Lovett	*Julia Roberts*	Jayne Meadows	*Steve Allen*
Edmund Lowe	*Lilyan Tashman*	Anne Meara	*Jerry Stiller*
Robert Lowery	*Jean Parker*	Patricia Medina	*Joseph Cotten*
Malcolm Lowry	*Margerie Bonner Lowry*	Helen Menken	*Humphrey Bogart*
Rudd Lowry	*Judith Lowry*	Melina Mercouri	*Jules Dassin*
Laurence Luckinbill	*Lucie Arnaz*	Ethel Merman	*Ernest Borgnine*
Allen Ludden	*Betty White*	Dina Merrill	*Cliff Robertson*
Alfred Lunt	*Lynn Fontanne*	Mayo Methot	*Humphrey Bogart*
Ben Lyon	*Bebe Daniels*	Sarah Miles	*Robert Bolt (twice)*
"	*Marion Nixon*	Patsy Ruth Miller	*Tay Garnett*
		Rebecca Miller	*Daniel Day-Lewis*
M		Liza Minnelli	*Peter Allen*
Charles MacArthur	*Helen Hayes*	Mary Ann Mobley	*Gary Collins*
Melbourne MacDowell	*Fanny Davenport*	Marilyn Monroe	*Joe DiMaggio*
Wilbur Mack	*Gertrude Purdy*	Maria Montez	*Jean Pierre Aumont*
Fred MacMurray	*Lillian La Monte*	Elizabeth Montgomery	*Gig Young*
"	*June Haver*	"	*William Asher*
Guy Madison	*Gail Russell*	"	*Robert Foxworth*
"	*Sheilah Connolly*	Goodee Montgomery	*Frank McDonald*
John Lee Mahin	*Patsy Ruth Miller*	Demi Moore	*Bruce Willis*
Charles H. Mailes	*Claire McDowell*	Eleanor Moore	*Thomas J. Moore*
Lee Majors	*Farrah Fawcett*	Debbie Morgan	*Charles Dutton*
Louis Malle	*Candice Bergen*	Anita Morris	*Grover Dale*
Henry Mancini	*Ginny O'Connor*	Adrianne Morrison	*Richard Bennett*
Fredric March	*Florence Eldridge*	Patricia Mowbray	*Douglas Dumbrille*
Gene Markey	*Myrna Loy*	Esther Muir	*Busby Berkeley*
Hugh Marlowe	*K. T. Stevens*	Jean Muir	*Henry Jaffe*
Herbert Marshall	*Edna Best*	Ona Munson	*Eddie Buzzell*
William Marshall	*Ginger Rogers*	Edna Murphy	*Mervyn Le Roy*
Steve Martin	*Victoria Tennant*	**N**	
Tony Martin	*Alice Faye*	Anne Nagel	*Ross Alexander*
"	*Cyd Charisse*	Diana Napier	*Richard Tauber*
Raymond Massey	*Adrianne Allen*	Ruth Nelson	*John Cromwell*
Frank Mayo	*Dagmar Godowsky*	"	*William Chalee*
John McCallum	*Googie Withers*	Olivia Newton-John	*Matt Lattanzi*
Joel McCrea	*Frances Dee*	Lisa Niemi	*Patrick Swayze*
Philo McCullough	*Laura Anson*	Greta Nissen	*Weldon Heyburn*
Frank McDonald	*Goodee Montgomery*	Marion Nixon	*Ben Lyon*
Malcolm McDowell	*Mary Steenburgen*	Chelsea Noble	*Kirk Cameron*
John McEnroe	*Tatum O'Neal*	Helen Nolan	*George Brent*
Paul McGrath	*Anne Sargent*	Jeanette Nolan	*John McIntire*
John McIntire	*Jeanette Nolan*	Josephine Norman	*Herbert Rawlins*
David McKay	*Joan Chandler*	Mabel Normand	*Lew Cody*
Scott McKay	*Ann Sheridan*	**O**	
Robert B. McKenzie	*Eva B. McKenzie*	Vivien Oakland	*John T. Murray*
Andrew McLaglen	*Veda Ann Borg*	Merle Oberon	*Alexander Korda*
Steve McQueen	*Ali MacGraw*	Eloise Taylor O'Brien	*Pat O'Brien*
Duncan McRae	*Gertrude McCoy*	Ginny O'Connor	*Henry Mancini*
Gerald McRaney	*Delta Burke*	Gertrude Olmstead	*Robert Z. Leonard*
Edward McWade	*Margaret McWade*	Tatum O'Neal	*John McEnroe*
John Mellencamp	*Elaine Irwin*	Maureen O'Sullivan	*John Farrow*
Adolphe Menjou	*Veree Teasdale*		

* Includes only show-biz personalities.

466

Who is Related to Whom — Off Screen? *

HUSBAND	SHOW-BIZ WIVES**	WIFE	SHOW-BIZ HUSBANDS**
Burgess Meredith	Paulette Goddard	Carré Otis	Mickey Rourke
Gary Merrill	Bette Davis	Seena Owen	George Walsh
Vincente Minnelli	Judy Garland	**P**	
John Paul (Jay) Monahan	Katie Couric	Geraldine Page	Rip Torn
Ricardo Montalban	Georgiana Young	Jean Page	Albert Edward Smith
Yves Montand	Simone Signoret	Debra Paget	David Street
George Montgomery	Dinah Shore	Lilli Palmer	Rex Harrison
Robert Montgomery	Elizabeth Allan	"	Carlos Thompson
Owen Moore	Mary Pickford	Anita Pam	Hugh Herbert
Thomas J. Moore	Eleanor Moore	Jean Parker	Robert Lowery
Tom Moore	Alice Joyce	Suzy Parker	Bradford Dillman
"	Renee Adoree	Pat Paterson	Charles Boyer
Clive Morton	Joan Harben	Marisa Pavan	Jean-Pierre Aumont
"	Fanny Rowe	Barbara Payton	Franchot Tone
Ibraham Moussa	Nastassja Kinski	Virginia Pearson	Sheldon Lewis
Audie Murphy	Wanda Hendrix	Barbara Pepper	Craig Reynolds
Don Murray	Hope Lange	Rhea Perlman	Danny DeVito
John T. Murray	Vivien Oakland	Joan Perry	Harry Cohn
N		Susan Peters	Richard Quine
Harold Nebenzal	Rita Corday	Michelle Pfeiffer	Peter Horton
Liam Neeson	Natasha Richardson	"	David Kelley
Ozzie Nelson	Harriet Hilliard	Mary Philips	Humphrey Bogart
Anthony Newley	Joan Collins	Mary Pickford	Owen Moore
Paul Newman	Joanne Woodward	"	Douglas Fairbanks, Sr.
Charles Newton	Dorrit Ashton	"	Buddy Rogers
Richard Ney	Greer Garson	Molly Picon	Jacob Kalich
Fred Niblo, Sr.	Enid Bennett	Suzanne Pleshette	Troy Donahue
Edward Norris	Ann Sheridan	Lillian Porter	Russell "Lucky" Hayden
O		Eleanor Powell	Glenn Ford
Philip Ober	Vivian Vance	Priscilla Presley	Elvis Presley
Robert Ober	Mabel Taliaferro	Kelly Preston	John Travolta
Edmond O'Brien	Nancy Kelly	Marie Prevost	Kenneth Harlan
"	Olga San Juan	Gertrude Purdy	Wilbur Mack
"	Anne Sargent	**R**	
George O'Brien	Marguerite Churchill	Gilda Radner	Gene Wilder
Pat O'Brien	Eloise Taylor O'Brien	Luise Rainer	Clifford Odets
Clifford Odets	Luise Rainer	Bonnie Raitt	Michael O'Keefe
Michael O'Keefe	Bonnie Raitt	Jobyna Ralston	Richard Arlen
Gary Oldman	Uma Thurman	Vera Hruba Ralston	Herbert Y. Yates
Laurence Olivier	Jill Esmond	Natacha Rambova	Rudolph Valentino
"	Vivien Leigh	Doris Rankin	Lionel Barrymore
Frank Orth	Ann Codee	Barbara Ray	Roscoe Ates
Michael O'Shea	Virginia Mayo	Martha Raye	Bud Westmore
P		"	David Rose
Corey Parker	Linda Kerridge	"	Nick Condos
Les Paul	Mary Ford	"	Ed Begley
John Payne	Gloria de Haven	"	Mark Harris
"	Anne Shirley	Stella Razetto	Edward J. LeSaint
Tony Peck	Cheryl Tiegs	Barbara Read	William Talman
Leonard Penn	Gladys George	Vanessa Redgrave	Tony Richardson
Sean Penn	Madonna	Frances Reid	Phillip Bourneuf
George Peppard	Elizabeth Ashley (twice)	Vivian Reid	Alfred E. Green
George O. Petrie	Patty Hope	Lee Remick	William A. Colleran
Jack Pickford	Olive Thomas	"	Kip Gowans
Roman Polanski	Sharon Tate	Dorothy (Velegra) Revier	Harry J. Revier
Carlo Ponti	Sophia Loren	Debbie Reynolds	Eddie Fisher
Don Porter	Peggy Converse	Vera Reynolds	Robert Ellis
Maury Povich	Connie Chung	Billie Rhodes	G. Pat Collins

* Includes only show-biz personalities.

Who is Related to Whom — Off Screen? *

HUSBAND	SHOW-BIZ WIVES**	WIFE	SHOW-BIZ HUSBANDS**
Dick Powell	Joan Blondell	Florence Rice	Robert Wilcox
"	June Allyson	Natasha Richardson	Liam Neeson
William Powell	Carole Lombard	Cleo Ridgely	James Horne
"	Diana Lewis	Blanche Ring	Charles Winninger
Tyrone Power	Annabella	Elisabeth Risdon	George Loane Tucker
"	Linda Christian	Giuditta Rissoni	Vittorio de Sica
Elvis Presley	Priscilla Presley	Julia Roberts	Lyle Lovett
André Previn	Mia Farrow	Rachel Roberts	Alan Dobie
Vincent Price	Edith Barrett	"	Rex Harrison
"	Mary Grant	Gertrude R. Robinson	James Kirkwood
"	Coral Browne	Susan Robinson	Denholm Elliott
Roger Pryor	Ann Sothern	Estelita Rodriguez	Grant Withers
Q		Ginger Rogers	Lew Ayres
Dennis Quaid	Meg Ryan	"	Jack Briggs
Richard Quine	Susan Peters	"	Jacques Bergerac
Anthony Quinn	Katherine DeMille	"	William Marshall
R		Mimi Rogers	Tom Cruise
Claude Rains	Isabel Jeans	Rena Rogers	Frank Borzage
Herbert Rawlins	Josephine Norman	Ruth Roland	Ben Bard
Aldo Ray	Jeff Donnell	Elaine Rosen	John Ireland
Nicholas Ray	Gloria Grahame	Fanny Rowe	Clive Morton
Gene Raymond	Jeanette MacDonald	Adele Rowland	Charles Ruggles
Ronald Reagan	Jane Wyman	"	Conway Tearle
	Nancy Davis	Dina Ruiz	Clint Eastwood
Maxwell Reed	Joan Collins	Barbara Rush	Jeffrey Hunter
Wallace Reid	Dorothy Davenport	Gail Russell	Guy Madison
James Rennie	Dorothy Gish	Rosalind Russell	Frederick Brisson
Harry J. Revier	Dorothy (Velegra) Revier	Ann Rutherford	William Dozier
Burt Reynolds	Judy Carne	Meg Ryan	Dennis Quaid
"	Loni Anderson	**S**	
Craig Reynolds	Barbara Pepper	Virginia Sale	Sam Wren
Tony Richardson	Vanessa Redgrave	Thelma Salter	Edward Kaufman
Tim Robbins	Susan Sarandon	Olga San Juan	Edmond O'Brien
Cliff Robertson	Dina Merrill	Susan Sarandon	Tim Robbins
Edward G. Robinson	Gladys Lloyd	Anne Sargent	Edmond O'Brien
Alexander Rockwell	Jennifer Beals	"	Paul McGrath
Gene Roddenberry	Majel Barrett	Natalie Schafer	Louis Calhern
Paul Roebling	Olga Bellin	Kim Schmidt	Gig Young
Buddy Rogers	Mary Pickford	Patti Scialfa	Bruce Springsteen
Roy Rogers	Dale Evans	Sydna Scott	Jerome Thor
Gilbert Roland	Constance Bennett	Dorothy Sebastian	William Boyd
Erik Rolf	Ruth Warwick	Kyra Sedgwick	Kevin Bacon
Mickey Rooney	Ava Gardner	Sara Seegar	Ezra Stone
"	Martha Vickers	Vivienne Segal	Robert Ames
David Rose	Judy Garland	Ruth Wilcox Selwyn	Edgar Selwyn
"	Martha Raye	Irene Mayer Selznick	David O. Selznick
Frank Ross	Jean Arthur	Jane Seymour	James Keach
"	Joan Caulfield	Norma Shearer	Irving Thalberg
Roberto Rossellini	Ingrid Bergman	Ally Sheedy	David Lansbury
Mickey Rourke	Carré Otis	Ann Sheridan	George Brent
"	Debra Feuer	"	Edward Norris
Charles Ruggles	Adele Rowland	"	Scott McKay
Wesley Ruggles	Arlene Judge	Talia Shire	Jack Swartzman
William Russell (d. 1929)	Helen Ferguson	Anne Shirley	John Payne
S		Ann Shoemaker	Henry Stephenson
Richie Sambora	Heather Locklear	Dinah Shore	George Montgomery
George Sanders	Benita Hume	Sylvia Sidney	Luther Adler
"	Magda Gabor	Simone Signoret	Yves Montand
"	Zsa Zsa Gabor	Jean Simmons	Stewart Granger
Tommy Sands	Nancy Sinatra	"	Richard Brooks

HUSBAND	SHOW-BIZ WIVES**	WIFE	SHOW-BIZ HUSBANDS**
Robert W. Sarnoff	Anna Moffo	Nancy Sinatra	Tommy Sands
Paul Scardon	Betty Blythe	Alexis Smith	Craig Stevens
George C. Scott	Colleen Dewhurst	Dame Maggie Smith	Beverley Cross
Steven Seagal	Kelly LeBrock	Ethel Smith	Ralph Bellamy
Douglas Seale	Louise Troy	Maggie Smith	(Sir) Robert Stephens
Peter Sellers	Lynne Frederick	Marguerite Snow	James Cruze
Edgar Selwyn	Ruth Wilcox Selwyn	"	Neely Edwards
David O. Selznick	Jennifer Jones	Gale Sondergaard	Herbert Biberman
"	Irene Mayer Selznick	Louise Sorel	Herb Edelman
Artie Shaw	Lana Turner	Ann Sothern	Roger Pryor
"	Ava Gardner	"	Robert Sterling
"	Evelyn Keyes	Evelyn Klein Spitalny	Phil Spitalny
Lowell Sherman	Pauline Garon	Jill St. John	Robert Wagner
"	Helen Costello	Barbara Stanwyck	Frank Fay
Don Siegel	Viveca Lindfors	"	Robert Taylor
Frank Sinatra	Ava Gardner	Myrtle Stedman	Marshall Stedman
"	Mia Farrow	Mary Steenburgen	Malcolm McDowell
Wendell Phillips Smalley	Lois Weber	"	Ted Danson
Albert Edward Smith	Jean Page	Anna Sten	Eugene Frenke
Howard I. Smith	Lillian Boardman	Jan Sterling	Paul Douglas
Roger Smith	Ann-Margret	Frances Sternhagen	Thomas A. Carlin
Nicholas Soussanin	Olga Baclanova	Connie Stevens	James Stacy
Sam Spiegel	Lynne Baggett	K. T. Stevens	Hugh Marlowe
Steven Spielberg	Amy Irving	Madeleine Stowe	Brian Benben
Phil Spitalny	Evelyn Klein Spitalny	Karen Jensen Stroka	Michael Stroka
Bruce Springsteen	Patti Scialfa	Margaret Sullavan	Henry Fonda
James Stacy	Connie Stevens	"	William Wyler
"	Kim Darby	"	Leland Hayward
Michael St. Angel	Marjorie Holliday	Ruth Sullivan	Dick Curtis
Ringo Starr	Barbara Bach	Betty Sundmark	Alan Curtis
Marshall Stedman	Myrtle Stedman	Gloria Swanson	Wallace Beery
Rod Steiger	Claire Bloom	**T**	
(Sir) Robert Stephens	Maggie Smith	Mabel Taliaferro	Tom Corrigan
Henry Stephenson	Ann Shoemaker	"	Robert Ober
Robert Sterling	Ann Sothern	Margaret Tallichet	William Wyler
"	Anne Jeffreys	Natalie Talmadge	Buster Keaton
Craig Stevens	Alexis Smith	Norma Talmadge	George Jessel
Parker Stevenson	Kirstie Alley	Jessica Tandy	Hume Cronyn
Jerry Stiller	Anne Meara	Elsie Tarron	Andy Clyde
Ezra Stone	Sara Seegar	Lilyan Tashman	Edmund Lowe
David Street	Debra Paget	Sharon Tate	Roman Polanski
Michael Stroka	Karen Jensen Stroka	Elizabeth Taylor	Michael Wilding
Nick Stuart	Sue Carol	"	Mike Todd
Burt Sugarman	Mary Hart	"	Eddie Fisher
Victor Sutherland	Pearl White	"	Richard Burton (twice)
"	Linda Barrett	Veree Teasdale	Adolphe Menjou
Jack Swartzman	Talia Shire	Olive Tell	Henry M. Hobart
Patrick Swayze	Lisa Niemi	Shirley Temple	John Agar
T		Victoria Tennant	Steve Martin
William Talman	Barbara Read	Joan Tetzel	Oscar Homolka
Richard Tauber	Diana Napier	Phyllis Thaxter	James T. Aubrey
Donald F. Taylor	Marie McDonald	Olive Thomas	Jack Pickford
Robert Taylor	Barbara Stanwyck	Emma Thompson	Kenneth Branagh
Conway Tearle	Adele Rowland	Uma Thurman	Gary Oldman
Jon Tenney	Teri Hatcher	Cheryl Tiegs	Tony Peck
Philip Terry	Joan Crawford	Gene Tierney	Oleg Cassini
Duccio Tessari	Lorella De Luca	Ann Todd	David Lean
Irving Thalberg	Norma Shearer	Louise Treadwell	Spencer Tracy
Carlos Thompson	Lilli Palmer	Dorothy Tree	Michael Uris
Fred Thomson	Frances Marion	Louise Troy	Werner Klemperer

HUSBAND	SHOW-BIZ WIVES**	WIFE	SHOW-BIZ HUSBANDS**
Jerome Thor	Sydna Scott	"	Douglas Seale
Mike Todd	Joan Blondell	Sylvia Field Truex	Ernest Truex
"	Elizabeth Taylor	Lana Turner	Artie Shaw
Franchot Tone	Joan Crawford	"	Lex Barker
"	Jean Wallace	"	Stephen Crane (twice)
"	Barbara Payton	Cicely Tyson	Miles Davis
Rip Torn	Geraldine Page	▼	
Spencer Tracy	Louise Treadwell	Virginia Valli	Charles Farrell
Bill Travers	Virginia McKenna	Mabel Van Buren	James Gordon
John Travolta	Kelly Preston	Vivian Vance	Philip Ober
Ernest Truex	Sylvia Field Truex	Lupe Velez	Johnny Weismuller
George Loane Tucker	Elisabeth Risdon	Martha Vickers	Mickey Rooney
Ted Turner	Jane Fonda	Florence (Cobb) Vidor	King Vidor
Brandon Tynan	Lily Cahill	"	Jascha Heifitz
U		**W**	
Michael Uris	Dorothy Tree	Marcy Walker	Billy Warlock
▼		Jean Wallace	Franchot Tone
Roger Vadim	Annette Vadim	"	Cornel Wilde
"	Brigitte Bardot	Dionne Warwick	William D. Elliott
"	Jane Fonda	Ruth Warwick	Erik Rolf
Rudolph Valentino	Jean Acker	Olive Brasno Wayne	Gus Wayne
"	Natacha Rambova	Lois Weber	Wendell Phillips Smalley
Rudy Vallee	Jane Greer	Eleanor Wells	William Perry Adams
Bobby Van	Elaine Joyce	Gwen Welles	Harris Yulin
Eddie Van Halen	Valerie Bertinelli	Joanne Whalley	Val Kilmer
King Vidor	Eleanor Boardman	Betty White	Allen Ludden
"	Florence (Cobb) Vidor	Pearl White	Victor Sutherland
W		Margaret Whiting	Joe "Fingers" Carr
Robert Wagner	Natalie Wood (twice)	Claire Whitney	Robert Emmett Keane
"	Jill St. John	Josephine Whittell	Robert Warwick
Keith A. Walker	Peggy Walton	(Dame) May Whitty	Ben Webster
Robert Walker	Jennifer Jones	Kathleen Widdoes	Richard Jordan
Eli Wallach	Anne Jackson	Sandra Will	Keith Carradine
Hal Wallis	Martha Hyer	Catherine Willard	Ralph Bellamy
George Walsh	Seena Owen	Clara Williams	Reginald Barker
Henry B. Walthall	Mary Charleson	Esther Williams	Ben Gage
Walter Wanger	Joan Bennett	"	Fernando Lamas
Billy Warlock	Marcy Walker	Kathlyn Williams	Charles Eyton
Sam Warner	Lina Basquette	Joan Wilson	Jeremy Brett
Robert Warwick	Josephine Whittell	Rita Wilson	Tom Hanks
Gus Wayne	Olive Brasno Wayne	Debra Winger	Timothy Hutton
Ben Webster	(Dame) May Whitty	Shelley Winters	Vittorio Gassman
Johnny Weismuller	Lupe Velez	"	Anthony Franciosa
Orson Welles	Rita Hayworth	Estelle Winwood	Arthur Chesney
William Wellman	Helene Chadwick	Googie Withers	John McCallum
Brooks West	Eve Arden	Natalie Wood	Robert Wagner
Bud Westmore	Martha Raye	Joanne Woodward	Paul Newman
Robert Wilcox	Florence Rice	Constance Worth	George Brent
Cornel Wilde	Patricia Knight	Aloha Wray	Frankie Darro
"	Jean Wallace	Teresa Wright	Niven Busch
Gene Wilder	Gilda Radner	Jane Wyman	Ronald Reagan
Michael Wilding	Elizabeth Taylor	Patrice Wymore	Errol Flynn
"	Margaret Leighton	**Y**	
Bill Williams	Barbara Hale	Pauline Yates	Donald Churchill
Bruce Willis	Demi Moore	Georgiana Young	Ricardo Montalban
Stu Wilson	Lorraine Krueger	Loretta Young	Grant Withers
Charles Winninger	Blanche Ring	"	Jean Louis
Robert Wise	Patricia Doyle	Victoria Young	Brian Keith
Grant Withers	Loretta Young	**Z**	
"	Estelita Rodriguez	Renee Bartlett Zinneman	Fred Zinneman
Frederick Worlock	Elsie Ferguson		

Who is Related to Whom — Off Screen? *

HUSBAND	SHOW-BIZ WIVES**	WIFE	SHOW-BIZ HUSBANDS**
Jack Wrather	Bonita Granville		
Sam Wren	Virginia Sale		
William Wyler	Margaret Sullavan		
	Margaret Tallichet		
Y			
Herbert Y. Yates	Vera Hruba Ralston		
Gig Young	Elizabeth Montgomery		
"	Kim Schmidt		
Harris Yulin	Gwen Welles		
Z			
Billy Zane	Lisa Collins		
Florenz Ziegfeld	Billie Burke		
Fred Zinneman	Renee Bartlett Zinneman		
Bill Zuckert	Gladys Holland		

FATHER	SHOW-BIZ SONS	FATHER	SHOW-BIZ DAUGHTERS
A		**A**	
Henry H. Ainley	Richard Ainley	Desi Arnaz	Lucie Arnaz
Eddie Albert	Edward Albert, Jr.	**B**	
Robert Alda	Alan Alda	Martin Balsam	Talia Balsam
"	Antony Alda	George Bancroft	Ann Bancroft
Alan Arkin	Adam Arkin	John Barrymore	Diana Barrymore
Pedro Armendariz	Pedro Armendariz, Jr.	Maurice Barrymore	Ethel Barrymore
Herbert W. Armstrong	Garner "Ted" Armstrong	Frank Beal	Dolly Beal
William Austin	Laurence Austin	Richard Bennett	Barbara Bennett
Felix Aylmer	David Aylmer	"	Constance Bennett
B		"	Joan Bennett
Philip Barry	Philip Barry, Jr.	Edgar Bergen	Candice Bergen
Maurice Barrymore	John Barrymore	Pat Boone	Debbie Boone
"	Lionel Barrymore		
Frank Beal	Scott Beal	**C**	
Noah Beery, Sr.	Noah Beery, Jr.	Charlie Chaplin	Geraldine Chaplin
Ed Begley	Ed Begley, Jr.	"	Josephine Chaplin
Jussi Bjorling	Rolf Bjorling	Nat "King" Cole	Natalie Cole
Dan Blocker	Dirk Blocker	Carmine Coppola	Talia Shire
Lloyd Bridges	Beau Bridges	Francis Ford Coppola	Sofia Coppola
"	Jeff Bridges	Ernest Cossart	Valerie Cossart Livingston
Carl Brisson	Frederick Brisson	Lou Costello	Carol Costello
James Broderick	Matthew Broderick	Maurice Costello	Dolores Costello
Joe E. Brown	Mike Frankovich (adopted)	"	Helene Costello
Francis X. Bushman	Francis X. Bushman, Jr.	Hume Cronyn	Tandy Cronyn
"	(aka Ralph Bushman)	Tony Curtis	Jamie Lee Curtis
Fred Butler	David Butler	**D**	
C		James Daly	Tyne Daly
Frank Capra	Tom Capra	Harry Davenport	Dorothy Davenport
John Carradine	David Carradine	Carter DeHaven, Sr.	Gloria DeHaven
"	Keith Carradine	Cecil B. DeMille	Katherine DeMille (adopted)
"	Robert Carradine	Bruce Dern	Laura Dern
Enrico Caruso	Enrico Caruso, Jr.	Oliva Dionne	Emelie Dionne
Jack Cassidy	David Cassidy	"	Marie Dionne
"	Shaun Cassidy	Maurice Dorléac	Catherine Deneuve
Lon Chaney	Lon Chaney, Jr.	"	Françoise Dorléac
Emile Chautard (step-father)	George Archainbaud	**F**	
Nick Clooney	George Clooney	John Farrow	Mia Farrow
Jack Coogan Sr.	Jackie Coogan	Eddie Fisher	Carrie Fisher
Carmine Coppola	Francis Ford Coppola	"	Joely Fisher
William Courtleigh, Sr.	William Courtleigh, Jr.	Henry Fonda	Jane Fonda
Frank Craven	John Craven	Peter Fonda	Bridget Fonda
Bing Crosby	Gary Crosby	**G**	
"	Dennis Crosby	Joel Gray	Jennifer Gray
"	Lindsay Crosby		

---

* Includes only show-biz personalities.

471

Who is Related to Whom — Off Screen? *

FATHER	SHOW-BIZ SONS	FATHER	SHOW-BIZ DAUGHTERS
Bing Crosby (con't)	Philip Crosby	**H**	
D		Jack Holt	Jennifer Holt
James Daly	Timothy Daly	John Huston	Anjelica Huston
Jules Dassin	Joe Dassin	**I**	
Harry Davenport	Arthur Rankin	Jules Irving	Amy Irving
Frank Davis	Battle Davis	**K**	
Carter DeHaven, Sr.	Carter DeHaven, Jr.	Edward M. Kimball	Clara Kimball Young
Dom DeLuise	Peter DeLuise	Klaus Kinski	Nastassja Kinski
"	Michael DeLuise	**L**	
Gerard Depardieu	Guillaume Depardieu	Michael Landon	Leslie Landon
Kirk Douglas	Michael Douglas	Ernest Lawford	Betty Lawford
Morton Downey	Morton Downey, Jr.	Gene Lockhart	June Lockhart
Eddie Duchin	Peter Duchin	**M**	
Franklin Dyall	Valentine Dyall	Raymond Massey	Anna Massey
E		Marcello Mastroianni	Chiara Mastroianni
Bob Elliott	Chris Elliott	Cyril Maude	Margery Maude
F		Robert B. McKenzie	Ida Mae McKenzie
Douglas Fairbanks	Douglas Fairbanks, Jr.	"	Lally McKenzie
Max Fleischer	Richard Fleischer	"	Fay McKenzie
Errol Flynn	Sean Flynn	John Mills	Hayley Mills
Henry Fonda	Peter Fonda	Vincente Minnelli	Liza Minnelli
Eddie Foy, Sr.	Eddie Foy, Jr.	Robert Montgomery	Elizabeth Montgomery
"	Bryan Foy	Vic Morrow	Jennifer Jason Leigh
G		Alan Mowbray	Patricia Mowbray
Clark Gable	John Clark Gable	**O**	
John Garfield	David Garfield	Ryan O'Neal	Tatum O'Neal
James Gleason	Russell Gleason	**P**	
Bernard Gorcey	Leo Gorcey	Sidney Poitier	Pam Poitier
"	David Gorcey	Don Porter	Melissa Converse
Woody Guthrie	Arlo Guthrie	Richard Pryor	Rain Pryor
H		**R**	
Alan Hale	Alan Hale, Jr.	John Raitt	Bonnie Raitt
George Hamilton	Ashley Hamilton	Michael Redgrave	Lynn Redgrave
Ben Henricks, Sr.	Ben Hendricks, Jr.	"	Vanessa Redgrave
Jim Henson	Brian Henson	Grantland Rice	Florence Rice
Taylor Holmes	Ralph Holmes	Tony Richardson	Natasha Richardson
"	Phillips Holmes	"	Joely Richardson
Jack Holt	Tim Holt	Roberto Rossellini	Isabella Rossellini
"	David Holt	**S**	
De Wolf Hopper	William Hopper	Boris Sagal	Katey Sagal
Rudolfo Hoyos, Sr.	Rudolfo Hoyos, Jr.	"	Jean Sagal
Jim Hutton	Timothy Hutton	"	Liz Sagal
I		Edward Sedgwick	Josie Sedgwick
Thomas H. Ince	Richard Ince	Martin Sheen	Renee Estevez
John Ireland	John Ireland, Jr.	Frank Sinatra	Nancy Sinatra
K		Otis Skinner	Cornelia Otis Skinner
Robert Kaufman	Christopher Kaufman	Paul Sorvino	Mira Sorvino
Mickey Katz	Joel Gray	(Sir) Guy Standing	Kay Hammond
Dennis King, Sr.	Dennis King, Jr.	"	(aka Dorothy Standing)
Sam Kydd	Jonathan Kydd	Houseley Stevenson, Sr.	Onslow Stevens
L		Jerry Stiller	Amy Stiller
Michael Landon	Michael Landon, Jr.	Lee Strasberg	Susan Strasberg
Bruce Lee	Brandon Lee	**T**	
Duke R. Lee	Duke Lee, Jr.	Danny Thomas	Marlo Thomas
"	John Lee	**W**	
Jack Lemmon	Chris Lemmon	Sam Wood	K. T. Stevens
John Lennon	Julian Lennon	"	(aka Gloria Wood)
Sam Livesey	Jack Livesey		
"	Roger Livesey		
Felix Locher	Jon Hall		

Who is Related to Whom — Off Screen? *

FATHER	SHOW-BIZ SONS		FATHER	SHOW-BIZ DAUGHTERS
M			**Z**	
Charles MacArthur	James MacArthur (adopted)		Efrem Zimbalist, Jr.	Stephanie Zimbalist
Bob Marley	Ziggy Marley		George Zucco	Frances Zucco
Dean Martin	Dean Paul Martin, Jr.		Bill Zuckert	Kymm
Samuel "Frenchie" Marx	"Chico" Marx			
"	"Harpo" Marx			
"	"Gummo" Marx			
"	"Groucho" Marx			
"	"Zeppo" Marx			
Raymond Massey	Daniel Massey			
John McIntire	Tim McIntire			
Steve McQueen	Chad McQueen			
Fuller Mellish, Sr.	Fuller Mellish, Jr.			
John Merton	Lane Bradford			
John Mills, Sr.	Herbert Mills			
"	Harry Mills			
"	Donald Mills			
"	John Mills, Jr.			
Maurice Moskovitch	Noel Madison			
N				
Tom Neal	Tom Neal, Jr.			
Ozzie Nelson	David Nelson			
"	Rick Nelson			
Rick Nelson	Matthew Nelson			
"	Gunnar Nelson			
Paul Newman	Scott Newman			
George Nichols, Sr.	George Nichols, Jr.			
Christian Nyby	Christian Nyby II			
O				
Carroll O'Connor	Hugh O'Connor			
Ryan O'Neal	Griffin O'Neal			
P				
Emory Parnell	James Parnell			
Tony Pastor	Guy Pastor			
Gregory Peck	Tony Peck			
Edward Peil, Sr.	Edward Peil, Jr.			
Osgood Perkins	Anthony Perkins			
Norman Phillips Sr.	Norman Phillips Jr.			
F. Tyrone Power	Tyrone Power			
Tyrone Power	Tyrone Power, Jr. (IV)			
R				
Hal Reid	Wallace Reid			
Wallace Reid	Wallace Reid, Jr.			
Carl Reiner	Rob Reiner			
Max Reinhardt	Gottfried Reinhardt			
George Relph	Michael Relph			
Jason Robards, Sr.	Jason Robards, Jr.			
Will Rogers	Will Rogers, Jr.			
Pat Rooney, II	Pat Rooney, III			
Oscar Rudolph	Alan Rudolph			
S				
Rudolph Schildkraut	Joseph Schildkraut			
George C. Scott	Campbell Scott			
Edward Sedgwick	Edward M. Sedgwick			
David O. Selznick	L. Jeffre Selznick			
"	Daniel Selznick			
Al Shean	Larry Shean			
Martin Sheen	Emilio Estevez			
"	Charlie Sheen			
Frank Sinatra	Frank Sinatra, Jr.			

* Includes only show-biz personalities.

FATHER	SHOW-BIZ SONS	FATHER	SHOW-BIZ DAUGHTERS
Jack Sonntag	Robert Sonntag		
Sylvester Stallone	Sage Stallone		
Marshall Stedman	Lincoln Stedman		
Houseley Stevenson	Onslow Stevenson		
Jerry Stiller	Ben Stiller		
Donald Sutherland	Kiefer Sutherland		
T			
Julius Tannen	Charles D. Tannen		
"	William Tannen		
Dub Taylor	Buck Taylor		
Maurice Tourneur	Jacques Tourneur		
V			
Roger Vadim	Christian Vadim		
Dick Van Patten	Nels Van Patten		
"	Jimmy Van Patten		
"	Vince Van Patten		
Melvin Van Peebles	Mario Van Peebles		
W			
Charles D. Waldron	Charles K. Waldron		
Robert Walker	Robert Walker, Jr.		
Jack L. Warner	Jack M. Warner		
Bryant Washburn Sr.	Bryant Washburn Jr.		
John Wayne	Patrick Wayne		
Bill Williams	William Katt		
Ed Wynn	Keenan Wynn		
Y			
Joe Yule	Mickey Rooney		
Z			
Darryl F. Zanuck	Richard D. Zanuck		
Fred Zinnemann	Tim Zinnemann		
Adolph Zukor	Eugene Zukor		

MOTHER	SHOW-BIZ SONS	MOTHER	SHOW-BIZ DAUGHTERS
B		**B**	
Fay Bainter	Reginald Venable	Dorothy Helen Baker	Diane Baker
Helen Broderick	Broderick Crawford	Lucille Ball	Lucie Arnaz
C		Ingrid Bergman	Isabella Rossellini
Jeanne Cooper	Corbin Bernsen	Adele Blood	Dawn Hope
Delores Costello	John Blythe Barrymore, Jr.	**C**	
Dixie Lee Crosby	Gary Crosby	Maybelle Carter	June Carter (Cash)
"	Dennis Crosby	Oona Chaplin	Geraldine Chaplin
"	Philip Crosby	"	Josephine Chaplin
"	Lindsay Crosby	Peggy Converse	Melissa Converse
D		**D**	
Arlene Dahl	Lorenzo Lamas	Abby Dalton	Kathleen Kinmont
Lili Damita	Sean Flynn	Ruby Dandridge	Dorothy Dandridge
Dorothy Davenport	Wallace Reid, Jr.	Alice Davenport	Dorothy Davenport
Mildred Davis	Harold Lloyd, Jr.	Joan Davis	Beverly Wills
Catherine Deneuve	Christian Vadim	Catherine Deneuve	Chiara Mastroianni
Julia De Vito	Danny De Vito	Renée Deneuve	Catherine Deneuve
Colleen Dewhurst	Campbell Scott	"	Françoise Dorléac
E		**G**	
Lillian Eliott	Lloyd Corrigan	Judy Garland	Liza Minnelli
F		"	Lorna Luft
Mary Forbes	Ralph Forbes	**J**	
G		Naomi Judd	Ashley Judd
Lucille Gleason	Russell Gleason	"	Wynonna Judd
H		**L**	
Florence Hackett	Raymond Hackett	Dianne Ladd	Laura Dern
Barbara Hale	William Katt	Lillian Lawrence	Ethel Grey Terry

* Includes only show-biz personalities.

474

Who is Related to Whom — Off Screen? *

MOTHER	SHOW-BIZ SONS
Kay Hammond	John Standing
Helen Hayes	James MacArthur
Harriet Hilliard	David Nelson
"	Rick Nelson
Hedda Hopper	William Hopper
J	
Shirley Jones	Shaun Cassidy
"	David Cassidy (stepson)
L	
Lady May Lawford	Peter Lawford
Louise Lester	Scott Beal
M	
Brenda Marshall	Scott Holden
Anne Meara	Ben Stiller
N	
Harriet Hilliard Nelson	David Nelson
"	Rick Nelson
O	
Peggy O'Neill	Michael Landon
S	
Irene Mayer Selznick	L. Jeffrey Selznick
"	Daniel Selznick
Myrtle Stedman	Lincoln Stedman
Fanny Schiller	Manolo Fabregas
Adeline Stanhope	Stanhope Wheatcroft
Stella Stevens	Andrew Stevens
Barbra Streisand	Jason Gould
V	
Dorothy Vernon	Bobby Vernon
W	
Joanne Woodward	Scott Newman (stepson)

MOTHER	SHOW-BIZ DAUGHTERS
Louise Lester	Dolly Beal
M	
Moyna McGill	Angela Lansbury
Leila McIntyre	Leila Hyams
Eva B. McKenzie	Lally McKenzie
"	Fay McKenzie
Anne Meara	Amy Stiller
Jean Menahan	Eileen Brennan
Elizabeth Allen Montgomery	Elizabeth Montgomery
Adrianne Morrison	Barbara Bennett
"	Constance Bennett
"	Joan Bennett
O	
Maureen O'Sullivan	Mia Farrow
P	
Priscilla Pointer	Amy Irving
R	
Vanessa Redgrave	Natasha Richardson
Debbie Reynolds	Carrie Fisher
Joan Rivers	Melissa Rivers
S	
Magda Schneider	Romy Schneider
Dorothy Hammond Standing	Kay Hammond
Connie Stevens	Joely Fisher
T	
Jessica Tandy	Tandy Cronyn

SHOW-BIZ BROTHERS

A	
Alan Alda	Antony Alda
Don Ameche	Jim Ameche
Dana Andrews	Steve Forrest
James Arness	Peter Graves
B	
Max Baer	Jacob "Buddy" Baer
Alec Baldwin	William Baldwin
"	Daniel Baldwin
"	Stephen Baldwin
John Barrymore	Lionel Barrymore
Wallace Beery	Noah Beery, Sr.
John Belushi	Jim Belushi
Herschel Bernardi	Jack Bernardi
Royce Blackburn	Ramon Blackburn (twins)
Frank Borzage	Daniel Borzage
Scott Brady	Lawrence Tierney
C	
Jack Carson	Robert Carson
Charlie Chaplin	Sydney Chaplin
Charley Chase	James Parrott
Andy Clyde	David Clyde
Gary Crosby	Dennis Crosby
"	Philip Crosby
"	Lindsay Crosby

SHOW-BIZ SISTERS

A	
LaVerne Andrews	Patti Andrews
"	Maxine Andrews
Pier Angeli	Marisa Pavan
B	
Hermione Baddeley	Angela Baddeley
Joan Bennett	Constance Bennett
C	
Dolores Costello	Helene Costello
D	
Catherine Deneuve	Françoise Dorléac
F	
Joan Fontaine	Olivia de Havilland
G	
Zsa Zsa Gabor	Magda Gabor
"	Eva Gabor
Lillian Gish	Dorothy Gish
Kathryn Grayson	Frances Raeburn
I	
May Irwin	Flo Irwin
J	
Ashley Judd	Wynonna Judd
K	
Jennifer Kendal	Felicity Kendal

* Includes only show-biz personalities.

475

Who is Related to Whom — Off Screen? *

SHOW-BIZ BROTHERS		SHOW-BIZ SISTERS	
D		**L**	
Sabu (Dastagir)	Sheik Dastagir	Priscilla Lane	Rosemary Lane
Dino DeLaurentiis	Luigi DeLaurentiis	"	Lola Lane
Peter DeLuise	Michael DeLuise	**M**	
Cecil B. DeMille	William C. DeMille	Jeanette MacDonald	Blossom Rock
Jack Dillon	Edward Dillon	Barbara Mandrell	Irlene Mandrell
Walt Disney	Roy O. Disney	"	Louise Mandrell
Jimmy Dorsey	Tommy Dorsey	Hattie McDaniel	Etta McDaniel
E		Audrey Meadows	Jayne Meadows
Les Elgart	Larry Elgart	Mary Miles Minter	Margaret Shelby
F		**N**	
William Farnum	Dustin Farnum	Florence Nash	Mary Nash
Barry Fitzgerald	Arthur Shields	**O**	
Dave Fleischer	Louis Fleischer	Ashley Olsen	Mary-Kate Olsen
"	Max Fleischer	Sally O'Neil	Molly O'Day
G		**P**	
William Gargan	Edward Gargan	Paula Prentiss	Ann Prentiss
George Gershwin	Ira Gershwin	Michelle Pfeiffer	DeDee Pfeiffer
Andy Gibb	Barry Gibb	**R**	
"	Robin Gibb	Lillian Randolph	Amanda Randolph
"	Maurice Gibb	Vanessa Redgrave	Lynn Redgrave
Leo Gorcey	David Gorcey	**S**	
Eddie Gribbon	Harry Gribbon	Katey Sagal	Jean Sagal
Edmund Gwenn	Arthur Chesney	"	Liz Sagal
H		Marguerite Shaw	Reta Shaw
Bobby Harron	John Harron	**T**	
Phillips Holmes	Ralph Holmes	Norma Talmadge	Constance Talmadge
Donald Houston	Glyn Houston	"	Natalie Talmadge
Eugene Howard	Willie Howard	Nicholle Tom	Heather Tom
Jerome "Curly" Howard	Moe Howard	**V**	
"	Shemp Howard	Odile Versois	Marina Vlady
Al Hoxie	Jack Hoxie	Marina Vlady	Odile Versois
Jack Hulbert	Claude Hulbert	**Y**	
I		Loretta Young	Georgianna Young
Al Immediato	Hugo Immediato	"	Sally Young
"	Nino "Nick" Immediato	"	Polly Ann Young
John E. Ince	Ralph W. Ince	"	Sally Blane
"	Richard Ince		
J			
Michael Jackson	Sigmund "Jackie" Jackson		
"	Toriano "Tito" Jackson		
"	Marion David Jackson		
"	Michael Joe Jackson		
"	Jermaine Jackson		
"	Steven "Randy" Jackson		
K			
Lawrence Kasha	Al Kasha		
Stacy Keach	James Keach		
Edgar Kennedy	Tom Kennedy		
Zoltan Korda	(Sir) Alexander Korda		
L			
Walter "Lee" Liberace	George Liberace		
Jack Livesey	Roger Livesey		
Guy Lombardo	Carmen Lombardo		
"	Lebert Lombardo		
"	Victor Lombardo		
Bert Lytell	Wilfred Lytell		
M			
"Groucho" Marx	"Chico" Marx		
"	"Harpo" Marx		

SHOW-BIZ BROTHERS

"Groucho" Marx (con't)	"Zeppo" Marx
"	"Gummo" Marx
Ken Maynard	Kermit Maynard
Frank McHugh	Matt McHugh
Lewis Meltzer	Sid Melton
Adolphe Menjou	Henri Menjou
Ricardo Montalban	Carlos Montalban
Tom Moore	Matt Moore
	Owen Moore
Frank Morgan	Ralph Morgan
Chester Morris	Adrian Morris
N	
Tommy Noonan	Michael Noon
"	John Ireland (half-brother)
P	
House Peters	Page E. Peters
River Phoenix	Joaquin "Leaf" Phoenix
Jeff Porcaro	Steve Porcaro
"	Mike Porcaro
André Previn	Steve Previn
R	
Pedro Regas	George Regas
Jean Renoir	Pierre Renoir
Al Ritz	Harry Ritz
"	Jimmy Ritz
Mark Rosenberg	Alan Rosenberg
Charles Ruggles	Wesley Ruggles
William Russell (d. 1929)	Albert Russell
S	
Terry Sanders	Denis Sanders
Fred Santley	Joseph Santley
David O. Selznick	Myron Selznick
"	Howard Selznick
L. Jeffrey Selznick	Daniel Selznick
Charlie Sheen	Emilio Estevez
Rider Strong	Shiloh Strong
Patrick Swayze	Don Swayze
T	
Charles D. Tannen	William Tannen
(Sir) Godfrey Tearle	Conway Tearle (half-brother)
David Torrence	Ernest Torrence
V	
Dick Van Dyke	Jerry Van Dyke
W	
Raoul Walsh	George Walsh
Henry B. Walthall	Wallace W. Walthall
Jack L. Warner	Harry M. Warner
James Woolf	John Woolf

SHOW-BIZ SISTERS

BROTHER	SHOW-BIZ SISTERS	BROTHER	SHOW-BIZ SISTERS
A		**I**	
Fred Astaire	Adele Astaire	David Irving	Amy Irving
B		José Iturbi	Amparo Iturbi
Bill Bailey	Pearl Bailey	**J**	
John Barrymore	Ethel Barrymore	Michael Jackson	La Toya Jackson
Lionel Barrymore	Ethel Barrymore	"	Maureen Jackson
Jason Bateman	Justine Bateman	"	Janet Jackson
Warren Beatty	Shirley MacLaine		
Billy Bletcher	Arline Bletcher		

* Includes only show-biz personalities.

477

Who is Related to Whom — Off Screen? *

BROTHER	SHOW-BIZ SISTERS
Marlon Brando	Jocelyn Brando
Lew Brice	Fanny Brice
C	
James Cagney	Jeanne Cagney
Kirk Cameron	Candace Cameron
Richard Carpenter	Karen Carpenter
Andy Clyde	Jean Clyde
David Clyde	"
Bud Collyer	June Collyer
Francis Ford Coppola	Talia Shire
D	
Timothy Daly	Tyne Daly
Carter DeHaven, Jr.	Gloria DeHaven
F	
Peter Fonda	Jane Fonda
Ralph Forbes	Brenda Forbes
Mick Fleetwood	Susan Fleetwood
G	
Maurice Geraghty	Carmelita Geraghty
H	
Billy Halop	Florence Halop
Bobby Harron	Tessie Harron
John Harron	"

BROTHER	SHOW-BIZ SISTERS
K	
James Keach	Stacy Keach
Jack Kelly	Nancy Kelly
L	
Arthur Lake	Florence Lake
M	
Louis J. Marlowe	June Marlowe
Sam "Deacon" McDaniel	Hattie McDaniel
"	Etta McDaniel
John Megna	Connie Stevens (half-sister)
P	
Jack Pickford	Mary Pickford
"	Lottie Pickford
R	
Howard Ralston	Esther Ralston
Cyril Ring	Blanche Ring
Eric Roberts	Julia Roberts
S	
Douglas Shearer	Norma Shearer
Andrew Shue	Elisabeth Shue
Chuck Stevens	Connie Stevens

UNCLE	SHOW-BIZ NEPHEWS
B	
Wallace Beery	Noah Beery, Jr.
C	
Francis Ford Coppola	Nicolas Cage
Frank Craven	Eddie Craven
S	
Al Shean	The 5 Marx Brothers

AUNT	SHOW-BIZ NEPHEWS
C	
Rosemary Clooney	George Clooney
Olive Cooper	George Stevens
L	
Angela Lansbury	David Lansbury
S	
Talia Shire	Nicholas Cage

UNCLE	SHOW-BIZ NIECES
Cecil B. De Mille	Agnes De Mille
Alfred Winslow	Sally Ann Kaufman Caton

AUNT	SHOW-BIZ NIECES
Nanette Fabray	Shelley Fabares

SHOW-BIZ COUSINS	
L	
Lupino Lane	Ida Lupino
Peter Lawford	Betty Lawford
M	
Henry Morgan	Alan Jay Lerner
R	
Bonnie Raitt	James Raitt
S	
Edie Sedgwick	Kyra Sedgwick
V	
Dee Victor	James Arness, Peter Graves

BROTHER-IN-LAW	SHOW-BIZ SISTER-IN-LAW
Dick Foran	Mary Foran

GRANDMOTHER	SHOW-BIZ GRANDSONS
Virginia Fabregas	Manolo Fabregas

GRANDFATHER	SHOW-BIZ GRANDSONS
Carmine Coppola	Nicholas Cage

FATHER-IN-LAW	SON-IN-LAW
Arturo Toscanini	Vladimir Horowitz

9

Studios
of the Stars

COLUMBIA

Robert Allen	Jack Holt*
Jean Arthur*	Victor Jory*
Lucille Ball*	Fred Keating*
James Blakeley	Peter Lorre*
Johnny Mack Brown*	Marian Marsh
Jack Buckler*	Tim McCoy*
Nancy Carroll*	Geneva Mitchell*
Walter Connolly*	Grace Moore*
Donald Cook*	George Murphy*
Inez Courtney*	Gene Raymond
Richard Cromwell*	Florence Rice*
Allyn Drake	Billie Seward
Douglas Dumbrille*	Ann Sothern
Wallace Ford*	Raymond Walburn*
John Gilbert*	Fay Wray
Arthur Hohl*	The 3 Stooges*

FOX

Frank Albertson*	Walter Johnson
Astrid Allwyn*	Walter Woolf King*
Rosemary Ames	June Lang
Lew Ayres*	Edmund Lowe*
Catalina Barcena*	Victor McLaglen*
Mona Barrie	Frank Melton*
Warner Baxter*	Frank Mitchell*
John Boles*	Conchita Montenegro
John Bradford	Rosita Moreno
Frances Carlon*	Herbert Mundin*
Madeleine Carroll*	Warner Oland*
Dave Chasen*	Valentin Parera
Tito Coral	Pat Paterson*
Jane Darwell*	Ruth Peterson
Alan Dinehart*	John Qualen*
James Dunn*	Will Rogers*
Jack Durant*	Gilbert Roland*
Alice Faye*	Raul Roulien
Peggy Fears	Siegfried Rumann*
Stepin Fetchit*	Albert Shean*
Dick Foran*	Berta Singerman
Norman Foster*	Shirley Temple
Ketti Gallian*	Spencer Tracy*
Janet Gaynor*	Claire Trevor
Harry Green*	Helen Twelvetrees*
Sterling Holloway*	Bianca Vischer
Rochelle Hudson*	Henry B. Walthall*
Roger Imhof*	Hugh Williams*

METRO-GOLDWYN-MAYER

Brian Aherne*	Virginia Bruce*
Katharine Alexander*	Ralph Bushman*
Elizabeth Allan*	Charles Butterworth*
Lionel Barrymore*	Mary Carlisle
Wallace Beery*	Leo Carrillo*
Constance Bennett*	Ruth Channing

Maurice Chevalier*	Jeanette MacDonald*
Mady Christians*	Una Merkel*
Constance Collier*	Robert Montgomery*
Jackie Cooper	Frank Morgan*
Joan Crawford*	Karen Morley
Jimmy Durante*	Ramon Novarro*
Nelson Eddy*	Maureen O'Sullivan*
Stuart Erwin*	Cecil Parker*
Madge Evans*	Jean Parker
Muriel Evans	Nat Pendleton*
Louise Fazenda*	Rosamond Pinchot*
Preston Foster*	William Powell*
Betty Furness*	May Robson*
Clark Gable*	Shirley Ross*
Greta Garbo*	Rosalind Russell*
Gladys George*	Maurice Schwartz*
C. Henry Gordon*	Norma Shearer*
Ruth Gordon*	Frank Shields*
Russell Hardie*	Sid Silvers*
Jean Harlow*	Martha Sleeper*
Helen Hayes*	Harvey Stephens*
Louise Henry	Lewis Stone*
William Henry	Gloria Swanson*
Jean Hersholt*	William Tannen*
Irene Hervey	Robert Taylor*
Isabel Jewell*	Franchot Tone*
Barbara Kent	Henry Wadsworth*
June Knight*	Lucile Watson*
Otto Kruger*	Johnny Weissmuller*
Elsa Lanchester*	Diana Wynyard*
Evelyn Laye	Robert Young*
Myrna Loy*	The Marx Brothers*

PARAMOUNT

Iris Adrian*	Marlene Dietrich*
Gracie Allen*	Frances Drake
Max Baer*	Mary Ellis
George Barbier*	W. C. Fields*
Ben Bernie*	William Frawley*
Douglas Blackley*	Paul Gerrits
Mary Boland*	Cary Grant*
Grace Bradley	David Holt
Lorraine Bridges	Dean Jagger*
Carl Brisson*	Roscoe Karns*
Mary Ellen Brown	Lois Kent
Kathleen Burke*	Elissa Landi*
George Burns*	Charles Laughton*
Alan Campbell*	Billy Lee*
Kitty Carlisle	Baby LeRoy
Dolores Casey*	Carole Lombard*
Claudette Colbert*	Pauline Lord*
Gary Cooper*	Ida Lupino*
Jack Cox	Helen Mack*
Buster Crabbe*	Fred MacMurray*
Eddie Craven*	Marian Mansfield*
Bing Crosby*	Herbert Marshall*
Katherine DeMille*	Gertrude Michael*

Ray Milland*
Joe Morrison
Lloyd Nolan*
Jack Oakie*
Lynne Overman*
Gail Patrick*
Joe Penner*
George Raft*
Lyda Roberti*
Lanny Ross*
Jean Rouverol
Charlie Ruggles*
Randolph Scott*

Ann Sheridan*
Sylvia Sidney
Alison Skipworth*
Queenie Smith*
Sir Guy Standing*
Colin Tapley
Kent Taylor*
Lee Tracy*
Virginia Weidler*
Mae West*
Henry Wilcoxon*
Howard Wilson
Toby Wing

RKO-RADIO PICTURES

Glenn Anders*
Fred Astaire*
John Beal*
Willie Best*
Eric Blore*
Alice Brady*
Helen Broderick*
Bruce Cabot*
Chic Chandler*
Richard Dix*
Steffi Duna
Irene Dunne*
Hazel Forbes
Skeets Gallagher*
Wynne Gibson*
Alan Hale*
Margaret Hamilton*
Ann Harding*

Katharine Hepburn
Pert Kelton*
Francis Lederer
Gene Lockhart*
Joel McCrea*
Raymond Middleton*
Polly Moran*
June Preston
Gregory Ratoff*
Virginia Reid
Erik Rhodes*
Barbara Robbins
Ginger Rogers*
Anne Shirley*
Frank Thomas, Jr.
Thelma Todd*
Bert Wheeler*
Robert Woolsey*

UNIVERSAL

Heather Angel*
Henry Armetta*
Binnie Barnes*
Noah Beery, Jr.*
Dean Benton
Mary Brooks
Willy Castello
June Clayworth*
Carol Coombe*
Philip Dakin
Ann Darling
Andy Devine*
Sally Eilers*
Valerie Hobson*
Henry Hull*
G. P. Huntley, Jr.
Baby Jane
Lois January
Buck Jones*

Boris Karloff*
Frank Lawton*
Bela Lugosi*
Paul Lukas*
Florine McKinney*
Douglass Montgomery*
Victor Moore*
Chester Morris*
Hugh O'Connell*
Roger Pryor*
Claude Rains*
Onslow Stevens*
Gloria Stuart
Margaret Sullavan*
Francis L. Sullivan*
Polly Walters
Alice White*
Clark Williams*
Jane Wyatt

HAL ROACH

Don Barclay*
Billy Bletcher*
Charley Chase*
Billy Gilbert*
Oliver Hardy*

Patsy Kelly*
Stan Laurel*
Billy Nelson*
Our Gang
Douglas Wakefield*

20th CENTURY

George Arliss*
Ronald Colman*

Fredric March*
Loretta Young

UNITED ARTISTS

Eddie Cantor*
Charles Chaplin*
Douglas Fairbanks*

Miriam Hopkins*
Mary Pickford*
Anna Sten*

WARNERS-FIRST NATIONAL

Ross Alexander*
Johnnie Allen
Mary Astor*
Arthur Aylesworth*
Robert Barrat*
Joan Blondell*
Glen Boles
George Brent*
Joe E. Brown*
James Cagney*
Enrico Caruso, Jr.*
Hobart Cavanaugh*
Joseph Cawthorn*
Colin Clive*
Ricardo Cortez*
Dorothy Dare
Marion Davies*
Bette Davis*
Dolores Del Rio*
Claire Dodd*
Ruth Donnelly*
Maxine Doyle*
Ann Dvorak*
John Eldredge*
Patricia Ellis*
Florence Fair
Glenda Farrell*
Errol Flynn*
Kay Francis*
William Gargan*
Hugh Herbert*
Russell Hicks*
Leslie Howard*
Ian Hunter*

Josephine Hutchinson
Allen Jenkins*
Al Jolson*
Olive Jones
Ruby Keeler*
Guy Kibbee*
Robert Light
Margaret Lindsay*
Anita Louise*
Helen Lowell*
Aline MacMahon*
Everett Marshall*
Frank McHugh*
James Melton*
Jean Muir
Paul Muni*
Pat O'Brien*
Henry O'Neill*
Dick Powell*
Phillip Reed
Philip Regan*
Edward G. Robinson*
Winifred Shaw*
Barbara Stanwyck*
Lyle Talbot*
Verree Teasdale*
Genevieve Tobin*
Dorothy Tree*
Mary Treen*
Harry Tyler*
Rudy Vallee*
Gordon Westcott*
Warren William*
Donald Woods

10

Major
Academy
Awards

Please Note

This section includes the names of Academy Award nominees and winners within only the following five categories:

- Best Actor
- Best Actress
- Best Supporting Actor
- Best Supporting Actress
- Best Director

If a person listed in Parts 1 and 2 is shown to be an Oscar winner but their name is missing from Part 10, it is because their category of award was other than one of the five identified above.

Annual Major Academy Awards

YEAR	BEST PICTURE	BEST ACTOR	BEST ACTRESS
1927-28	"Wings"	Emil Jannings, *"The Way of All Flesh"*	Janet Gaynor, *"Seventh Heaven"*
1928-29	"Broadway Melody"	Warner Baxter, *"In Old Arizona"*	Mary Pickford, *"Coquette"*
1929-30	"All Quiet On The Western Front"	George Arliss, *"Disraeli"*	Norma Shearer, *"The Divorcee"*
1930-31	"Cimarron"	Lionel Barrymore, *"Free Soul"*	Marie Dressler, *"Min and Bill"*
1931-32	"Grand Hotel"	Fredric March, *"Dr. Jekyll and Mr. Hyde"* (tie) Wallace Berry, *"The Champ"* (tie)	Helen Hayes, *"The Sin of Madelon Claudet"*
1932-33	"Cavalcade"	Charles Laughton, *"The Private Life of Henry VIII"*	Katharine Hepburn, *"Morning Glory"*
1934	"It Happened One Night"	Clark Gable, *"It Happened One Night"*	Claudette Colbert, *"It Happened One Night"*
1935	"Mutiny On The Bounty"	Victor McLaglen, *"The Informer"*	Bette Davis, *"Dangerous"*
1936	"The Great Ziegfeld"	Paul Muni, *"The Story of Louis Pasteur"*	Luise Rainer, *"The Great Ziegfeld"*
1937	"The Life Of Emile Zola"	Spencer Tracy, *"Captains Courageous"*	Luise Rainer, *"The Good Earth"*
1938	"You Can't Take It With You"	Spencer Tracy *"Boys Town"*	Bette Davis, *"Jezebel"*
1939	"Gone With The Wind"	Robert Donat, *"Goodbye, Mr. Chips"*	Vivien Leigh, *"Gone With the Wind"*
1940	"Rebecca"	James Stewart, *"The Philadelphia Story"*	Ginger Rogers, *"Kitty Foyle"*
1941	"How Green Was My Valley"	Gary Cooper, *"Sergeant York"*	Joan Fontaine, *"Suspicion"*
1942	"Mrs. Miniver"	James Cagney, *"Yankee Doodle Dandy"*	Greer Garson, *"Mrs. Miniver"*
1943	"Casablanca"	Paul Lucas, *"Watch On the Rhine"*	Jennifer Jones, *"The Song of Bernadette"*
1944	"Going My Way"	Bing Crosby, *"Going My Way"*	Ingrid Bergman, *"Gaslight"*
1945	"The Lost Weekend"	Ray Milland, *"The Lost Weekend"*	Joan Crawford, *"Mildred Pierce"*
1946	"The Best Years Of Our Lives"	Fredric March, *"The Best Years of Our Lives"*	Olivia de Havilland, *"To Each His Own"*
1947	"Gentlemen's Agreement"	Ronald Colman, *"A Double Life"*	Loretta Young, *"The Farmer's Daughter"*
1948	"Hamlet"	Laurence Olivier, *"Hamlet"*	Jane Wyman, *"Johnny Belinda"*
1949	"All The King's Men"	Broderick Crawford, *"All the King's Men"*	Olivia de Havilland, *"The Heiress"*
1950	"All About Eve"	José Ferrer, *"Cyrano de Bergerac"*	Judy Holliday, *"Born Yesterday"*
1951	"An American In Paris"	Humphrey Bogart, *"The African Queen"*	Vivien Leigh, *"A Streetcar Named Desire"*
1952	"The Greatest Show On Earth"	Gary Cooper, *"High Noon"*	Shirley Booth, *"Come Back, Little Sheba"*
1953	"From Here To Eternity"	William Holden, *"Stalag 17"*	Audrey Hepburn, *"Roman Holiday"*
1954	"On The Waterfront"	Marlon Brando, *"On the Waterfront"*	Grace Kelly, *"The Country Girl"*
1955	"Marty"	Ernest Borgnine, *"Marty"*	Anna Magnani, *"The Rose Tatoo"*
1956	"Around The World In 80 Days"	Yul Brynner, *"The King and I"*	Ingrid Bergman, *"Anastasia"*
1957	"The Bridge On The River Kwai"	Alec Guiness, *"The Bridge On the River Kwai"*	Joanne Woodward, *"The Three Faces of Eve"*
1958	"Gigi"	David Niven, *"Separate Tables"*	Susan Hayward, *"I Want to Live"*

Annual Major Academy Awards

YEAR	BEST PICTURE	BEST ACTOR	BEST ACTRESS
1959	"Ben-Hur"	Charlton Heston, *"Ben-Hur"*	Simone Signoret, *"Room At the Top"*
1960	"The Apartment"	Burt Lancaster, *"Elmer Gantry"*	Elizabeth Taylor, *"Butterfield 8"*
1961	"West Side Story"	Maximillian Schell, *"Judgment at Nuremberg"*	Sophia Loren, *"Two Women"*
1962	"Lawrence Of Arabia"	Gregory Peck, *"To Kill a Mockingbird"*	Anne Bancroft, *"The Miracle Worker"*
1963	"Tom Jones"	Sidney Poitier, *"Lillies of the Field"*	Patricia Neal, *"Hud"*
1964	"My Fair Lady"	Rex Harrison, *"My Fair Lady"*	Julie Andrews, *"Mary Poppins"*
1965	"The Sound Of Music"	Lee Marvin, *"Cat Ballou"*	Julie Christie, *"Darling"*
1966	"A Man For All Seasons"	Paul Scofield, *"A Man for All Seasons"*	Elizabeth Taylor, *"Who's Afraid of Virginia Woolf?"*
1967	"In The Heat Of The Night"	Rod Steiger, *"In the Heat of the Night"*	Katharine Hepburn, *"Guess Who's Coming to Dinner"*
1968	"Oliver"	Cliff Robertson, *"Charly"*	Katharine Hepburn, *"The Lion in Winter" (tie)* Barbra Streisand, *"Funny Girl" (tie)*
1969	"Midnight Cowboy"	John Wayne, *"True Grit"*	Maggie Smith, *"The Prime of Miss Jean Brodie"*
1970	"Patton"	George C. Scott, *"Patton" (refused)*	Glenda Jackson, *"Women in Love"*
1971	"The French Connection"	Gene Hackman, *"The French Connection"*	Jane Fonda, *"Klute"*
1972	"The Godfather"	Marlon Brando, *"The Godfather" (refused)*	Liza Minnelli, *"Cabaret"*
1973	"The Sting"	Jack Lemmon, *"Save the Tiger"*	Glenda Jackson, *"A Touch of Class"*
1974	"The Godfather Part II"	Art Carney, *"Harry and Tonto"*	Ellen Burstyn, *"Alice Doesn't Live Here Anymore"*
1975	"One Flew Over The Cuckoo's Nest"	Jack Nicholson, *"One Flew Over the Cuckoo's Nest"*	Louise Fletcher, *"One Flew Over the Cuckoo's Nest"*
1976	"Rocky"	Peter Finch, *"Network"*	Faye Dunaway, *"Network"*
1977	"Annie Hall"	Richard Dreyfuss, *"The Goodbye Girl"*	Diane Keaton, *"Annie Hall"*
1978	"The Deer Hunter"	Jon Voight, *"Coming Home"*	Jane Fonda, *"Coming Home"*
1979	"Kramer vs. Kramer"	Dustin Hoffman, *"Kramer vs. Kramer"*	Sally Field, *"Norma Rae"*
1980	"Ordinary People"	Robert De Niro, *"Raging Bull"*	Sissy Spacek, *"Coal Miner's Daughter"*
1981	"Chariots Of Fire"	Henry Fonda, *"On Golden Pond"*	Katharine Hepburn, *"On Golden Pond"*
1982	"Gandhi"	Ben Kingsley, *"Gandhi"*	Meryl Streep, *"Sophie's Choice"*
1983	"Terms Of Endearment"	Robert Duvall, *"Tender Mercies"*	Shirley MacLaine, *"Terms of Endearment"*
1984	"Amadeus"	F. Murray Abraham, *"Amadeus"*	Sally Field, *"Places in the Heart"*
1985	"Out Of Africa"	William Hurt, *"Kiss of the Spider Woman"*	Geraldine Page, *"The Trip to Bountiful"*
1986	"Platoon"	Paul Newman, *"The Color of Money"*	Marlee Matlin, *"Children of a Lesser God"*
1987	"The Last Emperor"	Michael Douglas, *"Wall Street"*	Cher, *"Moonstruck"*
1988	"Rain Man"	Dustin Hoffman, *"Rain Man"*	Jodie Foster, *"The Accused"*
1989	"Driving Miss Daisy"	Daniel Day-Lewis, *"My Left Foot"*	Jessica Tandy, *"Driving Miss Daisy"*

Annual Major Academy Awards

YEAR	BEST PICTURE	BEST ACTOR	BEST ACTRESS
1990	"Dances With Wolves"	Jeremy Irons, *"Reversal of Fortune"*	Kathy Bates, *"Misery"*
1991	"The Silence Of The Lambs"	Anthony Hopkins, *"The Silence of the Lambs"*	Jodie Foster, *"The Silence of the Lambs"*
1992	"Unforgiven"	Al Pacino, *"Scent of a Woman"*	Emma Thompson, *"Howards End"*
1993	"Schindler's List"	Tom Hanks, *"Philadelphia"*	Holly Hunter, *"The Piano"*
1994	"Forrest Gump"	Tom Hanks, *"Forrest Gump"*	Jessica Lange, *"Blue Sky"*
1995	"Braveheart"	Nicolas Cage, *"Leaving Las Vegas"*	Susan Sarandon, *"Dead Man Walking"*
1996	"The English Patient"	Geoffrey Rush, *"Shine"*	Frances McDormand, *"Fargo"*
1997	"Titanic"	Jack Nicholson, *"As Good As It Gets"*	Helen Hunt *"As Good As It Gets"*

YEAR	BEST SUPPORTING ACTOR	BEST SUPPORTING ACTRESS	BEST DIRECTOR
1927-28	*(No award)*	*(No award)*	Frank Borzage, *"Seventh Heaven"*
1928-29	*(No award)*	*(No award)*	Frank Lloyd, *"The Divine Lady"*
1929-30	*(No award)*	*(No award)*	Lewis Milestone, *"All Quiet On the Western Front"*
1930-31	*(No award)*	*(No award)*	Norman Taurog, *"Skippy"*
1931-32	*(No award)*	*(No award)*	Frank Borzage, *"Bad Girl"*
1932-33	*(No award)*	*(No award)*	Frank Lloyd, *"Cavalcade"*
1934	*(No award)*	*(No award)*	Frank Capra, *"It Happened One Night"*
1935	*(No award)*	*(No award)*	John Ford, *"The Informer"*
1936	Walter Brennan, *"Come and Get It"*	Gale Sondergaard, *"Anthony Adverse"*	Frank Capra, *"Mr. Deeds Goes to Town"*
1937	Joseph Schildkraut, *"The Life of Emile Zola"*	Alice Brady, *"In Old Chicago"*	Leo McCarey, *"The Awful Truth"*
1938	Walter Brennan, *"Kentucky"*	Fay Bainter, *"Jezebel"*	Frank Capra, *"You Can't Take It With You"*
1939	Thomas Mitchell, *"Stagecoach"*	Hattie McDaniel, *"Gone With the Wind"*	Victor Fleming, *"Gone With the Wind"*
1940	Walter Brennan, *"The Westerner"*	Jane Darwell, *"The Grapes of Wrath"*	John Ford, *"The Grapes of Wrath"*
1941	Donald Crisp, *"How Green Was My Valley"*	Mary Astor, *"The Great Lie"*	John Ford, *"How Green Was My Valley"*
1942	Van Heflin, *"Johnny Eager"*	Teresa Wright, *"Mrs. Miniver"*	William Wyler, *"Mrs. Miniver"*
1943	Charles Coburn, *"The More the Merrier"*	Katina Paxinou, *"For Whom the Bell Tolls"*	Michael Curtiz, *"Casablanca"*
1944	Barry Fitzgerald, *"Going My Way"*	Ethel Barrymore, *"None But the Lonely Heart"*	Leo McCarey, *"Going My Way"*
1945	James Dunn, *"A Tree Grows in Brooklyn"*	Anne Revere, *"National Velvet"*	Billy Wilder, *"The Lost Weekend"*
1946	Harold Russell, *"The Best Years of Our Lives"*	Anne Baxter, *"The Razor's Edge"*	William Wyler, *"The Best Years of Our Lives"*
1947	Edmund Gwenn, *"Miracle On 34th Street"*	Celeste Holm, *"Gentleman's Agreement"*	Elia Kazan, *"Gentleman's Agreement"*
1948	Walter Huston, *"Treasure of Sierra Madre"*	Claire Trevor, *"Key Largo"*	John Huston, *"Treasure of Sierra Madre"*
1949	Dean Jagger, *"Twelve O'Clock High"*	Mercedes McCambridge, *"All the King's Men"*	Joseph L. Mankiewicz, *"A Letter to Three Wives"*
1950	George Sanders, *"All About Eve"*	Josephine Hull, *"Harvey"*	Joseph L. Mankiewicz, *"All About Eve"*
1951	Karl Malden, *"A Streetcar Named Desire"*	Kim Hunter, *"A Streetcar Named Desire"*	George Stevens, *"A Place in the Sun"*
1952	Anthony Quinn, *"Viva Zapata"*	Gloria Grahame, *"The Bad and the Beautiful"*	John Ford, *"The Quiet Man"*
1953	Frank Sinatra, *"From Here to Eternity"*	Donna Reed, *"From Here to Eternity"*	Fred Zinnemann, *"From Here to Eternity"*
1954	Edmund O'Brien, *"The Barefoot Contessa"*	Eva Marie Saint, *"On the Waterfront"*	Elia Kazan, *"On the Waterfront"*
1955	Jack Lemmon, *"Mr. Roberts"*	Jo Van Fleet, *"East of Eden"*	Delbert Mann, *"Marty"*
1956	Anthony Quinn, *"Lust for Life"*	Dorothy Malone, *"Written On the Wind"*	George Stevens, *"Giant"*
1957	Red Buttons, *"Sayonara"*	Miyoshi Umeki, *"Sayonara"*	David Lean, *"The Bridge On the River Kwai"*
1958	Burl Ives, *"The Big Country"*	Wendy Hiller, *"Separate Tables"*	Vincente Minnelli, *"Gigi"*
1959	Hugh Griffith, *"Ben-Hur"*	Shelley Winters, *"The Diary of Anne Frank"*	William Wyler, *"Ben-Hur"*

Annual Major Academy Awards

YEAR	BEST SUPPORTING ACTOR	BEST SUPPORTING ACTRESS	BEST DIRECTOR
1960	Peter Ustinov, "Spartacus"	Shirley Jones, "Elmer Gantry"	Billy Wilder, "The Apartment"
1961	George Chakiris, "West Side Story"	Rita Moreno, "West Side Story"	Robert Wise & Jerome Robbins, "West Side Story"
1962	Ed Begley, "Sweet Bird of Youth"	Patty Duke, "The Miracle Worker"	David Lean, "Lawrence of Arabia"
1963	Melvyn Douglas, "Hud"	Margaret Rutherford, "The V.I.P.s"	Tony Richardson, "Tom Jones"
1964	Peter Ustinov, "Topkapi"	Lila Kedrova, "Zorba the Greek"	George Cukor, "My Fair Lady"
1965	Martin Balsam, "A Thousand Clowns"	Shelley Winters, "A Patch of Blue"	Robert Wise, "The Sound of Music"
1966	Walter Matthau, "The Fortune Cookie"	Sandy Dennis, "Who's Afraid of Virginia Woolf?"	Fred Zinnemann, "A Man For All Seasons"
1967	George Kennedy, "Cool Hand Luke"	Estelle Parsons, "Bonnie & Clyde"	Mike Nichols, "The Graduate"
1968	Jack Albertson, "The Subject Was Roses"	Ruth Gordon, "Rosemary's Baby"	Carol Reed, "Oliver!"
1969	Gig Young, "They Shoot Horses, Don't They?"	Goldie Hawn, "Cactus Flower"	John Schlesinger, "Midnight Cowboy"
1970	John Mills, "Ryan's Daughter"	Helen Hayes, "Airport"	Franklin J. Schaffner, "Patton"
1971	Ben Johnson, "The Last Picture Show"	Cloris Leachman, "The Last Picture Show"	William Friedkin, "The French Connection"
1972	Joel Grey, "Cabaret"	Eileen Heckart, "Butterflies Are Free"	Bob Fosse, "Cabaret"
1973	John Houseman, "The Paper Chase"	Tatum O'Neal, "Paper Moon"	George Roy Hill, "The Sting"
1974	Robert De Niro, "The Godfather, Part II"	Ingrid Bergman, "Murder On the Orient Express"	Francis Ford Coppola, "The Godfather, Part II"
1975	George Burns, "The Sunshine Boys"	Lee Grant, "Shampoo"	Milos Forman, "One Flew Over the Cuckoo's Nest"
1976	Jason Robards, "All the President's Men"	Beatrice Straight, "Network"	John Avildsen, "Rocky"
1977	Jason Robards, "Julia"	Vanessa Redgrave, "Julia"	Woody Allen, "Annie Hall"
1978	Christopher Walken, "The Deer Hunter"	Maggie Smith, "California Suite"	Michael Cimino, "The Deer Hunter"
1979	Melvyn Douglas, "Being There"	Meryl Streep, "Kramer vs. Kramer"	Robert Benton, "Kramer vs. Kramer"
1980	Timothy Hutton, "Ordinary People"	Mary Steenburgen, "Melvin and Howard"	Robert Redford, "Ordinary People"
1981	John Gielgud, "Arthur"	Maureen Stapleton, "Reds"	Warren Beatty, "Reds"
1982	Louis Gossett, Jr., "An Officer and a Gentleman"	Jessica Lange, "Tootsie"	Richard Attenborough, "Gandhi"
1983	Jack Nicholson, "Terms of Endearment"	Linda Hunt, "The Year of Living Dangerously"	James L. Brooks, "Terms of Endearment"
1984	Dr. Haing S. Ngor, "The Killing Fields"	Dame Peggy Ashcroft, "A Passage to India"	Milos Forman, "Amadeus"
1985	Don Ameche, "Cocoon"	Anjelica Huston, "Prizzi's Honor"	Sydney Pollack, "Out of Africa"
1986	Michael Caine, "Hannah and Her Sisters"	Dianne Wiest, "Hannah and Her Sisters"	Oliver Stone, "Platoon"
1987	Sean Connery, "The Untouchables"	Olympia Dukakis, "Moonstruck"	Bernardo Bertolucci, "The Last Emperor"
1988	Kevin Kline, "A Fish Called Wanda"	Geena Davis, "The Accidental Tourist"	Barry Levinson, "Rain Man"
1989	Denzel Washington, "Glory"	Brenda Fricker, "My Left Foot"	Oliver Stone, "Born On the Fourth of July"
1990	Joe Pesci, "GoodFellas"	Whoopi Goldberg, "Ghost"	Kevin Costner, "Dances With Wolves"
1991	Jack Palance, "City Slickers"	Mercedes Ruehl, "The Fisher King"	Jonathan Demme, "The Silence of the Lambs"

Annual Major Academy Awards

YEAR	BEST SUPPORTING ACTOR	BEST SUPPORTING ACTRESS	BEST DIRECTOR
1992	Gene Hackman, *"Unforgiven"*	Marisa Tomei, *"My Cousin Vinny"*	Clint Eastwood, *"Unforgiven"*
1993	Tommy Lee Jones, *"The Fugitive"*	Anna Paquin, *"The Piano"*	Steven Spielberg, *"Schindler's List"*
1994	Martin Landau, *"Ed Wood"*	Dianne Wiest, *"Bullets Over Broadway"*	Robert Zemeckis, *"Forrest Gump"*
1995	Kevin Spacey, *"The Usual Suspects"*	Mira Sorvino, *"Mighty Aphrodite"*	Mel Gibson *"Braveheart"*
1996	Cuba Gooding, Jr., *"Jerry Maguire"*	Juliette Binoche, *"The English Patient"*	Anthony Minghella, *"The English Patient"*
1997	Robin Williams, *"Good Will Hunting"*	Kim Basinger, *"L.A. Confidential"*	James Cameron, *"Titanic"*

Multible Oscar Winners

NAME	CATEGORY	YEARS WON
4 Oscars		
FORD, John	Best Director	1935, 1940, 1941, 1952
HEPBURN, Katharine	Best Actress	1932-33, 1967, 1968, 1981
3 Oscars		
BERGMAN, Ingrid	Best Actress	1944, 1956, 1974
BRENNAN, Walter	Best Supp. Actor	1936, 1938, 1940
CAPRA, Frank	Best Director	1934, 1936, 1938
NICHOLSON, Jack	Best Actor	1975, 1997
"	Best Supp. Actor	1983
WYLER, William	Best Director	1942, 1946, 1959
2 Oscars		
BORZAGE, Frank	Best Director	1927-28, 1931-32
BRANDO, Marlon	Best Actor	1954, 1972
COOPER, Gary	Best Actor	1941, 1952
DAVIS, Bette	Best Actress	1935, 1938
De HAVILLAND, Olivia	Best Actress	1946, 1949
De NIRO, Robert	Best Supp. Actor	1974
"	Best Actor	1980
DOUGLAS, Melvyn	Best Supp. Actor	1963, 1979
FIELD, Sally	Best Actress	1979, 1984
FONDA, Jane	Best Actress	1971, 1978
FORMAN, Milos	Best Director	1975, 1984
FOSTER, Jodie	Best Actress	1988, 1991
HACKMAN, Gene	Best Supp. Actor	1992
"	Best Actor	1971
HANKS, Tom	Best Actor	1993, 1994
HAYES, Helen	Best Actress	1931-32
"	Best Supp. Actress	1970
HOFFMAN, Dustin	Best Actor	1979, 1988
JACKSON, Glenda	Best Actress	1970, 1973
LEAN, David	Best Director	1957, 1962
LEIGH, Vivien	Best Actress	1939, 1951
LEMMON, Jack	Best Supp. Actor	1955
"	Best Actor	1973
LLOYD, Frank	Best Director	1928-29, 1932-33
MANKIEWICZ, Joseph L.	Best Director	1949, 1950
MARCH, Fredric	Best Actor	1931-32, 1946
McCAREY, Leo	Best Director	1937, 1944
QUINN, Anthony	Best Supp. Actor	1952, 1956
RAINER, Luise	Best Actress	1936, 1937
ROBARDS, Jr., Jason	Best Supp. Actor	1976, 1977
SMITH, Maggie	Best Supp. Actress	1978
"	Best Actress	1969
STEVENS, George	Best Director	1951, 1956
STONE, Oliver	Best Director	1986, 1989
STREEP, Meryl	Best Supp. Actress	1979
"	Best Actress	1982
TAYLOR, Elizabeth	Best Actress	1960, 1966
TRACY, Spencer	Best Actor	1937, 1938
USTINOV, Peter	Best Supp. Actor	1960, 1964
WIEST, Dianne	Best Supp. Actress	1986, 1994
WILDER, Billy	Best Director	1945, 1960
WINTERS, Shelley	Best Supp. Actress	1959, 1965
WISE, Robert	Best Director	1961, 1965
ZINNEMANN, Fred	Best Director	1953, 1966

NAME*	CATEGORY	YEARS WON	YEARS NOMINATED **
A			
ABRAHAM, F. Murray	Best Actor	1984	
ADAMS, Nick	Best Supp. Actor		1963
ADJANI, Isabelle	Best Actress		1975, 1989
AHERNE, Brian	Best Supp. Actor		1939
AIELLO, Danny	Best Supp. Actor		1989
AIMEE, Anouk	Best Actress		1966
ALBERT, Eddie	Best Supp. Actor		1953, 1972
ALBERTSON, Jack	Best Supp. Actor	1968	
ALEXANDER, Jane	Best Actress		1970, 1983
"	Best Supp. Actress		1976, 1979
ALEXANDRO, Norma	Best Supp. Actress		1987
ALLEN, Joan	Best Supp. Actress		1995
ALLEN, Woody	Best Actor		1977
"	Best Director	1977	1978, 1984, 1986, 1989, 1994
ALLGOOD, Sara	Best Supp. Actress		1941
ALTMAN, Robert	Best Director		1970, 1975, 1993
AMECHE, Don	Best Supp. Actor	1985	
ANDERSON, Judith	Best Supp. Actress		1940
ANDERSON, Michael	Best Director		1956
ANDREWS, Julie	Best Actress	1964	1965, 1982
Ann-Margret	Best Supp. Actress		1971
"	Best Actress		1975
ANTONIONI, Michelangelo	Best Director		1966
ARCHER, Anne	Best Supp. Actress		1987
ARDEN, Eve	Best Supp. Actress		1945
ARKIN, Alan	Best Actor		1966, 1968
ARLISS, George	Best Actor	1929-30	1929-30
ARTHUR, Jean	Best Actress		1943
ASHBY, Hal	Best Director		1978
ASHCROFT, Dame Peggy	Best Supp. Actress	1984	
ASTAIRE, Fred	Best Supp. Actor		1974
ASTOR, Mary	Best Supp. Actress	1941	
ATTENBOROUGH, Richard	Best Director	1982	
AUER, Mischa	Best Supp. Actor		1936
AVERY, Margaret	Best Supp. Actress		1985
AVILDSEN, John	Best Director	1976	
AYKROYD, Dan	Best Supp. Actor		1989
AYRES, Lew	Best Actor		1948
B			
BABENCO, Hector	Best Director		1985
BADDELEY, Hermione	Best Supp. Actress		1959
BADHAM, Mary	Best Supp. Actress		1962
BAINTER, Fay	Best Actress		1938
"	Best Supp. Actress	1938	1961
BAKER, Carroll	Best Actress		1956
BALSAM, Martin	Best Supp. Actor	1965	
BANCROFT, Anne	Best Actress	1962	1964, 1967, 1977, 1985
BANCROFT, George	Best Actor		1928-29
BANNEN, Ian	Best Supp. Actor		1965
BARRAULT, Marie-Christine	Best Actress		1976
BARRIE, Barbara	Best Supp. Actress		1979
BARRYMORE, Ethel	Best Supp. Actress	1944	1946, 1947, 1949
BARRYMORE, Lionel	Best Director		1928-29
"	Best Actor	1930-31	
BARTHELMESS, Richard	Best Actor		1927-28
BARYSHNIKOV, Mikhail	Best Supp. Actor		1977
BASINGER, Kim	Best Supp. Actress	1997	
BASSERMAN, Albert	Best Supp. Actor		1940
BASSETT, Angela	Best Actress		1993

* Includes only actors, actresses and directors.

** Other than years won.

Major Academy Award Winners and Nominees — by Name

NAME*	CATEGORY	YEARS WON	YEARS NOMINATED **
BATES, Alan	Best Actor		1968
BATES, Kathy	Best Actress	1990	
BATES, Alan	Best Actor		1968
BATES, Kathy	Best Actress	1990	
BAXTER, Anne	Best Actress		1950
"	Best Supp. Actress	1946	
BAXTER, Warner	Best Actor	1928-29	
BEATTY, Ned	Best Supp. Actor		1976
BEATTY, Warren	Best Actor	1981	1967, 1978
"	Best Director		1978, 1981
BEAUMONT, Harry	Best Director		1928-29
BEERY, Wallace	Best Actor	1931-32	1929-30
BEGLEY, Ed	Best Supp. Actor	1962	
BEL GEDDES, Barbara	Best Supp. Actress		1948
BENDIX, William	Best Supp. Actor		1942
BENING, Annette	Best Supp. Actress		1990
BENTON, Robert	Best Director	1979	1984
BERENGER, Tom	Best Supp. Actor		1986
BERESFORD, Bruce	Best Director		1983
BERGEN, Candice	Best Supp. Actress		1979
BERGMAN, Ingmar	Best Director		1973, 1976, 1983
BERGMAN, Ingrid	Best Actress	1944, 1956, 1974	1943, 1945, 1948, 1978
BERGNER, Elizabeth	Best Actress		1935
BERLIN, Jeannie	Best Supp. Actress		1972
BERTOLUCCI, Bernardo	Best Director	1987	1973
BICKFORD, Charles	Best Supp. Actor		1943, 1947, 1948
BIKEL, Theodore	Best Supp. Actor		1958
BINOCHE, Juliette	Best Supp. Actress	1996	
BLACK, Karen	Best Supp. Actress		1970
BLAIR, Betsy	Best Supp. Actress		1955
BLAIR, Linda	Best Supp. Actress		1973
BLAKELY, Ronee	Best Supp. Actress		1975
BLONDELL, Joan	Best Supp. Actress		1951
BLYTH, Ann	Best Supp. Actress		1945
BOGART, Humphrey	Best Actor	1951	1943, 1954
BOGDANOVICH, Peter	Best Director		1971
BONDI, Beulah	Best Supp. Actress		1936, 1938
BOORMAN, John	Best Director		1972, 1987
BOOTH, Shirley	Best Actress	1952	
BORGNINE, Ernest	Best Actor	1955	
BORZAGE, Frank	Best Director	1927-28, 1931-32	
BOYER, Charles	Best Actor		1937, 1938, 1944, 1961
BRACCO, Lorraine	Best Supp. Actress		1990
BRADY, Alice	Best Supp. Actress	1937	1936
BRANAGH, Kenneth	Best Actor		1989
BRANDAUER, Klaus Maria	Best Supp. Actor		1985
BRANDO, Marlon	Best Actor	1954, 1972	1951, 1952, 1953, 1957, 1973
"	Best Supp. Actor		1989
BRENNAN, Walter	Best Supp. Actor	1936, 1938, 1940	1941
BRENON, Herbert	Best Director		1927-28
BRIDGES, Jeff	Best Supp. Actor		1971, 1974
"	Best Actor		1984
BROOKS, Albert	Best Supp. Actor		1987
BROOKS, James L.	Best Director	1983	
BROOKS, Richard	Best Director		1958, 1966, 1967
BROWN, Clarence	Best Director		1929-30 (2), 1930-31, 1943, 1945, 1946
BROWNE, Leslie	Best Supp. Actress		1977
BRYNNER, Yul	Best Actor	1956	
BUJOLD, Genevieve	Best Actress		1969
BUONO, Victor	Best Supp. Actor		1962

* Includes only actors, actresses and directors.

493

** Other than years won.

Major Academy Award Winners and Nominees — by Name

NAME*	CATEGORY	YEARS WON	YEARS NOMINATED **
BURKE, Billie	Best Supp. Actress		1938
BURNS, Catherine	Best Supp. Actress		1969
BURNS, George	Best Supp. Actor	1975	
BURSTYN, Ellen	Best Supp. Actress		1971
"	Best Actress	1974	1973, 1978, 1980
BURTON, Richard	Best Supp. Actor		1952
"	Best Actor		1953, 1964, 1965, 1966, 1969, 1977
BUSEY, Gary	Best Actor		1978
BUTTONS, Red	Best Supp. Actor	1957	
BYINGTON, Spring	Best Supp. Actress		1938
● C			
CAAN, James	Best Supp. Actor		1972
CACOYANNIS, Michael	Best Director		1964
CAESAR, Adolph	Best Supp. Actor		1984
CAGE, Nicolas	Best Actor	1995	
CAGNEY, James	Best Actor	1942	1938, 1955
CAINE, Michael	Best Actor	1986	1966, 1972, 1983
CALHERN, Louis	Best Actor		1950
CAMERON, James	Best Director	1997	
CAMPION, Jane	Best Director		1993
CANNON, Dyan	Best Supp. Actress		1969, 1978
CAPRA, Frank	Best Director	1934, 1936, 1938	1932-33, 1939, 1946
CARDIFF, Jack	Best Director		1960
CAREY, Harry	Best Supp. Actor		1939
CARLIN, Lynn	Best Supp. Actress		1968
CARNEY, Art	Best Actor	1974	
CARON, Leslie	Best Actress		1953, 1963
CARROLL, Diahann	Best Actress		1974
CARROLL, Nancy	Best Actress		1929-30
CARTER, Helena Bonham	Best Actres		1997
CASS, Peggy	Best Supp. Actress		1958
CASSAVETES, John	Best Supp. Actor		1967
"	Best Director		1974
CASSEL, Seymour	Best Supp. Actor		1968
CASTELLANO, Richard	Best Supp. Actor		1970
CATTANEO, Peter	Best Director		1997
CHAKIRIS, George	Best Supp. Actor	1961	
CHANDLER, Jeff	Best Supp. Actor		1950
CHANNING, Carol	Best Supp. Actress		1967
CHANNING, Stockard	Best Actress		1993
CHAPLIN, Charles	Best Director		1927-28
"	Best Actor		1940
CHATTERTON, Ruth	Best Actress		1928-29, 1929-30
CHEKHOV, Michael	Best Supp. Actor		1945
Cher	Best Supp. Actress		1983
"	Best Actress	1987	
CHEVALIER, Maurice	Best Actor		1929-30
CHRISTIE, Julie	Best Actress	1965	1971, 1997
CILENTO, Diane	Best Supp. Actress		1963
CIMINO, Michael	Best Director	1978	
CLARK, Candy	Best Supp. Actress		1973
CLAYBURGH, Jill	Best Actress		1978, 1979
CLAYTON, Jack	Best Director		1959
CLIFT, Montgomery	Best Supp. Actor		1961
"	Best Actor		1948, 1951, 1953
CLOSE, Glenn	Best Supp. Actress		1983, 1984
"	Best Actress		1987, 1988
COBB, Lee J.	Best Supp. Actor		1954, 1958
COBURN, Charles	Best Supp. Actor	1943	1941, 1946
COLBERT, Claudette	Best Actress	1934	1935, 1944

Major Academy Award Winners and Nominees — by Name

NAME*	CATEGORY	YEARS WON	YEARS NOMINATED **
COLLINGE, Patricia	Best Supp. Actress		1941
COLLINS, Pauline	Best Actress		1989
COLMAN, Ronald	Best Actor	1947	1929-30, 1942
COMPSON, Betty	Best Actress		1928-29
CONNERY, Sean	Best Supp. Actor	1987	
CONTI, Tom	Best Actor		1983
COOPER, Gary	Best Actor	1941, 1952	1936, 1942, 1943
COOPER, Gladys	Best Supp. Actress		1942, 1943, 1964
COOPER, Jackie	Best Actor		1930-31
COPPOLA, Francis Ford	Best Director	1974	1972, 1979, 1990
CORBY, Ellen	Best Supp. Actress		1948
CORTESE, Valentina	Best Supp. Actress		1974
COSTA-GAVRAS	Best Director		1969
COSTNER, Kevin	Best Actor		1990
"	Best Director	1990	
COURTENAY, Tom	Best Supp. Actor		1965
"	Best Actor		1983
CRAIN, Jeanne	Best Actress		1949
CRAWFORD, Broderick	Best Actor	1949	
CRAWFORD, Joan	Best Actress	1945	1947, 1952
CRICHTON, Charles	Best Director		1988
CRISP, Donald	Best Supp. Actor	1941	
CROMWELL, James	Best Supp. Actor		1995
CRONYN, Hume	Best Supp. Actor		1944
CROSBY, Bing	Best Actor	1944	1945, 1954
CROSSE, Rupert	Best Supp. Actor		1969
CROUSE, Lindsay	Best Supp. Actress		1984
CRUISE, Tom	Best Actor		1989
CUKOR, George	Best Director	1964	1932-33, 1940, 1947, 1950
CUMMINGS, Irving	Best Director		1928-29
CUMMINGS, Quinn	Best Supp. Actress		1977
CURTIS, Tony	Best Actor		1958
CURTIZ, Michael	Best Director	1943	1938 (2), 1942
CUSACK, Joan	Best Supp. Actress		1988, 1997
D			
DAFOE, Willem	Best Supp. Actor		1986
DAILEY, Dan	Best Actor		1948
DALL, John	Best Supp. Actor		1945
DAMON, Matt	Best Actor		1997
DANDRIDGE, Dorothy	Best Actress		1954
DARIN, Bobby	Best Supp. Actor		1963
DARWELL, Jane	Best Supp. Actress	1940	
DASSIN, Jules	Best Director		1960
DAVIS, Bette	Best Actress	1935, 1938	1939, 1940, 1941, 1942, 1944, 1950, 1952, 1962
DAVIS, Geena	Best Supp. Actress	1988	
DAVIS, Judy	Best Actress		1984
DAVISON, Bruce	Best Supp. Actor		1990
DAY, Doris	Best Actress		1959
DAY-LEWIS, Daniel	Best Actor	1989	1993
DEAN, James	Best Actor		1955, 1956
De HAVILLAND, Olivia	Best Supp. Actress		1939
"	Best Actress	1946, 1949	1941, 1948
DEMAREST, William	Best Supp. Actor		1946
DeMILLE, Cecil B.	Best Director		1952
DEMME, Jonathan	Best Director	1991	
De NIRO, Robert	Best Supp. Actor	1974	
"	Best Actor	1980	1976, 1978, 1990
DENCH, Judi	Best Actress		1997
DENNIS, Sandy	Best Supp. Actress	1966	

Major Academy Award Winners and Nominees — by Name

NAME*	CATEGORY	YEARS WON	YEARS NOMINATED **
DEPARDIEU, Gerard	Best Actor		1990
DERN, Bruce	Best Supp. Actor		1978
De SICA, Vittorio	Best Supp. Actor		1957
De WILDE, Brandon	Best Supp. Actor		1953
DiCAPRIO, Leonardo	Best Supp. Actor		1993
DIETERLE, William	Best Director		1937
DIETRICH, Marlene	Best Actress		1930-31
DILLON, Melinda	Best Supp. Actress		1977
DIX, Richard	Best Actor		1930-31
DMYTRYK, Edward	Best Director		1947
DONAT, Robert	Best Actor	1939	1938
DONLEVY, Brian	Best Supp. Actor		1939
DOUGLAS, Kirk	Best Actor		1949, 1952, 1956
DOUGLAS, Melvyn	Best Supp. Actor	1963, 1979	
"	Best Actor		1970
DOUGLAS, Michael	Best Actor	1987	
DOURIF, Brad	Best Supp. Actor		1975
DRESSER, Louise	Best Actress		1927-28
DRESSLER, Marie	Best Actress	1930-31	1931-32
DREYFUSS, Richard	Best Actor	1977	1995
DRIVER, Minnie	Best Supp. Actress		1997
DUKAKIS, Olympia	Best Supp. Actress	1987	
DUKE, Patty	Best Supp. Actress	1962	
DUNAWAY, Faye	Best Actress	1976	1967, 1974
DUNN, James	Best Supp. Actor	1945	
DUNN, Michael	Best Supp. Actor		1965
DUNNE, Irene	Best Actress		1930-31, 1936, 1937, 1939, 1948
DUNNOCK, Mildred	Best Supp. Actress		1951, 1956
DURNING, Charles	Best Supp. Actor		1983
DUVALL, Robert	Best Supp. Actor		1972, 1979
"	Best Actor	1983	1980, 1997
E			
EAGELS, Jeanne	Best Actress		1928-29
EASTWOOD, Clint	Best Director	1992	
EGGAR, Samantha	Best Actress		1965
EGOYAN, Atom	Best Director		1997
ELLIOTT, Denholm	Best Supp. Actor		1986
EMERSON, Hope	Best Supp. Actress		1950
ERWIN, Stuart	Best Supp. Actor		1936
EVANS, Dame Edith	Best Supp. Actress		1963, 1964
"	Best Actress		1967
F			
FALK, Peter	Best Supp. Actor		1960, 1961
FARNSWORTH, Richard	Best Supp. Actor		1978
FARROW, John	Best Director		1942
FELLINI, Federico	Best Director		1961, 1963, 1970, 1975
FERRER, Jose	Best Actor	1950	1952
"	Best Supp. Actor		1948
FIELD, Sally	Best Actress	1979, 1984	
FIENNES, Ralph	Best Supp. Actor		1993
FIGGIS, Mike	Best Director		1995
FINCH, Peter	Best Actor	1976	1971
FINLAY, Frank	Best Supp. Actor		1965
FINNEY, Albert	Best Actor		1963, 1974, 1983, 1984
FIRTH, Peter	Best Supp. Actor		1977
FISHBURNE, Laurence	Best Actor		1993
FITZGERALD, Barry	Best Supp. Actor	1944	
"	Best Actor		1944
FITZGERALD, Geraldine	Best Supp. Actress		1939
FLEMING, Victor	Best Director	1939	

* Includes only actors, actresses and directors. ** Other than years won.

Major Academy Award Winners and Nominees — by Name

NAME*	CATEGORY	YEARS WON	YEARS NOMINATED **
FLETCHER, Louise	Best Actress	1975	
FOCH, Nina	Best Supp. Actress		1954
FONDA, Henry	Best Actor	1981	1940
FONDA, Jane	Best Actress	1971, 1978	1969, 1977, 1979, 1986
FONDA, Peter	Best Actor		1997
FONTAINE, Joan	Best Actress	1941	1940, 1943
FONTANNE, Lynne	Best Actress		1931-32
FORD, Harrison	Best Actor		1985
FORD, John	Best Director	1935, 1940, 1941, 1952	1939
FORMAN, Milos	Best Director	1975, 1984	
FORREST, Frederic	Best Supp. Actor		1979
FORSTER, Robert	Best Supp. Actor		1997
FOSSE, Bob	Best Director	1972	1974, 1979
FOSTER, Jodie	Best Supp. Actress		1976, 1994
"	Best Actress	1988, 1991	
FRANCIOSA, Anthony	Best Actor		1957
FRANKLIN, Sidney	Best Director		1937
FREARS, Stephen	Best Director		1990
FREEMAN, Morgan	Best Supp. Actor		1987
"	Best Actor		1989, 1994
FREY, Leonard	Best Supp. Actor		1971
FRICKER, Brenda	Best Supp. Actress	1989	
FRIEDKIN, William	Best Director	1971	1973

G

NAME*	CATEGORY	YEARS WON	YEARS NOMINATED **
GABLE, Clark	Best Actor	1934	1935, 1939
GARBO, Greta	Best Actress		1929-30, 1937, 1939
GARCIA, Andy	Best Supp. Actor		1990
GARDENIA, Vincent	Best Supp. Actor		1973, 1987
GARDNER, Ava	Best Actress		1953
GARFIELD, John	Best Supp. Actor		1938
"	Best Actor		1947
GARGAN, William	Best Supp. Actor		1940
GARLAND, Judy	Best Actress		1954
"	Best Supp. Actress		1961
GARNER, James	Best Actor		1985
GARSON, Greer	Best Actress	1942	1939, 1941, 1943, 1944, 1945, 1960
GAYNOR, Janet	Best Actress	1927-28	1937
GAZZO, Michael V.	Best Supp. Actor		1974
GENN, Leo	Best Supp. Actor		1951
GEORGE, Chief Dan	Best Supp. Actor		1970
GEORGE, Gladys	Best Actress		1936
GERMI, Pietro	Best Director		1962
GIANNINI, Giancarlo	Best Actor		1976
GIBSON, Mel	Best Director	1995	
GIELGUD, John	Best Supp. Actor	1981	1964
GILFORD, Jack	Best Supp. Actor		1973
GISH, Lillian	Best Supp. Actress		1946
GLEASON, Jackie	Best Supp. Actor		1961
GLEASON, James	Best Supp. Actor		1941
GLENVILLE, Peter	Best Director		1964
GODDARD, Paulette	Best Supp. Actress		1943
GOLDBERG, Whoopi	Best Actress		1985
"	Best Supp. Actress	1990	
GOMEZ, Thomas	Best Supp. Actor		1947
GOODING, Cuba Jr.	Best Supp. Actor	1996	
GORDON, Dexter	Best Actor		1986
GORDON, Ruth	Best Supp. Actress	1968	1965
GOSSETT, Louis Jr.	Best Supp. Actor	1982	
GOULD, Elliott	Best Supp. Actor		1969
GRAHAME, Gloria	Best Supp. Actress	1952	1947

* Includes only actors, actresses and directors.   ** Other than years won.

Major Academy Award Winners and Nominees — by Name

NAME*	CATEGORY	YEARS WON	YEARS NOMINATED **
GRANT, Cary	Best Actor		1941, 1944
GRANT, Lee	Best Supp. Actress	1975	1951, 1970, 1976
GRANVILLE, Bonita	Best Supp. Actress		1936
GREENE, Graham	Best Supp. Actor		1990
GREENSTREET, Sydney	Best Supp. Actor		1941
GREY, Joel	Best Supp. Actor	1972	
GRIFFITH, Hugh	Best Supp. Actor	1959	1963
GRIFFITH, Melanie	Best Actress		1988
GUINNESS, Alec	Best Actor	1957	1952
"	Best Supp. Actor		1977, 1988
GWENN, Edmund	Best Supp. Actor	1947	1950
H			
HACKMAN, Gene	Best Supp. Actor	1992	1967, 1970
"	Best Actor	1971	1988
HAGEN, Jean	Best Supp. Actress		1952
HALL, Alexander	Best Director		1941
HALL, Grayson	Best Supp. Actress		1964
HALLSTROM, Lasse	Best Director		1987
HANKS, Tom	Best Actor	1993, 1994	1988
HANSON, Curtis	Best Director		1997
HARDING, Ann	Best Actress		1930-31
HARPER, Tess	Best Supp. Actress		1986
HARRIS, Barbara	Best Supp. Actress		1971
HARRIS, Ed	Best Supp. Actor		1995
HARRIS, Julie	Best Actress		1952
HARRIS, Richard	Best Actor		1963, 1990
HARRIS, Rosemary	Best Supp. Actress		1994
HARRISON, Rex	Best Actor	1964	1963
HARTMAN, Elizabeth	Best Actress		1965
HARVEY, Anthony	Best Director		1968
HARVEY, Laurence	Best Actor		1959
HATHAWAY, Henry	Best Director		1935
HAWKS, Howard	Best Director		1941
HAWN, Goldie	Best Supp. Actress	1969	
"	Best Actress		1980
HAWTHORNE, Nigel	Best Actor		1994
HAYAKAWA, Sessue	Best Supp. Actor		1957
HAYES, Helen	Best Actress	1931-32	
"	Best Supp. Actress	1970	
HAYWARD, Susan	Best Actress	1958	1947, 1949, 1952, 1955
HECKART, Eileen	Best Supp. Actress	1972	1956
HEFLIN, Van	Best Supp. Actor	1942	
HEMINGWAY, Mariel	Best Supp. Actress		1979
HENRY, Buck	Best Director		1978
HENRY, Justin	Best Supp. Actor		1979
HEPBURN, Audrey	Best Actress	1953	1954, 1959, 1961, 1967
HEPBURN, Katharine	Best Actress	1932-33, 1967, 1968, 1981	1935, 1940, 1942, 1951, 1955, 1956, 1959, 1962
HESTON, Charlton	Best Actor	1959	
HICKEY, William	Best Supp. Actor		1985
HILL, George Roy	Best Director	1973	1969
HILLER, Arthur	Best Director		1970
HILLER, Wendy	Best Actress		1938
"	Best Supp. Actress	1958	1966
HITCHCOCK, Alfred	Best Director		1940, 1944, 1945, 1954, 1960
HOFFMAN, Dustin	Best Actor	1979, 1988	1967, 1969, 1974, 1982, 1997
HOLDEN, William	Best Actor	1953	1950, 1976
HOLLIDAY, Judy	Best Actress	1950	
HOLLOWAY, Stanley	Best Supp. Actor		1964
HOLM, Celeste	Best Supp. Actress	1947	1949, 1950

Major Academy Award Winners and Nominees — by Name

NAME*	CATEGORY	YEARS WON	YEARS NOMINATED **
HOMOLKA, Oscar	Best Supp. Actor		1948
HOPKINS, Anthony	Best Actor	1991	1993, 1995
"	Best Supp. Actor		1997
HOPKINS, Miriam	Best Actress		1935
HOPPER, Dennis	Best Supp. Actor		1986
HOSKINS, Bob	Best Actor		1986
HOUSEMAN, John	Best Supp. Actor	1973	
HOWARD, Leslie	Best Actor		1932-33, 1938
HOWARD, Trevor	Best Actor		1960
HUDSON, Rock	Best Actor		1956
HULCE, Tom	Best Actor		1984
HULL, Josephine	Best Supp. Actress	1950	
HUNNICUTT, Arthur	Best Supp. Actor		1952
HUNT, Helen	Best Actress	1997	
HUNT, Linda	Best Supp. Actress	1983	
HUNTER, Holly	Best Actress	1993	1987, 1993
HUNTER, Kim	Best Supp. Actress	1951	
HURT, John	Best Supp. Actor		1978
"	Best Actor		1980
HURT, William	Best Actor	1985	1986, 1987
HUSSEY, Ruth	Best Supp. Actress		1940
HUSTON, Anjelica	Best Supp. Actress	1985	1989
HUSTON, Anjelica	Best Actress		1990
HUSTON, John	Best Director	1948	1950, 1951, 1952, 1985
HUSTON, John	Best Supp. Actor		1963
HUSTON, Walter	Best Actor	1948	1936, 1941, 1942
HUTTON, Timothy	Best Supp. Actor	1980	
HYER, Martha	Best Supp. Actress		1958
I			
IRELAND, John	Best Supp. Actor		1949
IRONS, Jeremy	Best Actor	1990	
IRVING, Amy	Best Supp. Actress		1983
IVES, Burl	Best Supp. Actor	1958	
IVORY, James	Best Director		1986, 1993
J			
JACKSON, Glenda	Best Actress	1970, 1973	1971, 1975
JACKSON, Samuel L.	Best Supp. Actor		1994
JAECKEL, Richard	Best Supp. Actor		1971
JAFFE, Sam	Best Supp. Actor		1950
JAGGER, Dean	Best Supp. Actor	1949	
JANNINGS, Emil	Best Actor	1927-28	
JEWISON, Norman	Best Director		1967, 1971, 1987
JOFFE, Roland	Best Director		1984, 1986
JOHNS, Glynis	Best Supp. Actress		1960
JOHNSON, Ben	Best Supp. Actor	1971	
JOHNSON, Celia	Best Actress		1946
JONES, Carolyn	Best Supp. Actress		1957
JONES, James Earl	Best Actor		1970
JONES, Jennifer	Best Actress	1943	1945, 1946, 1955
"	Best Supp. Actress		1944
JONES, Shirley	Best Supp. Actress	1960	
JONES, Tommy Lee	Best Supp. Actor	1993	
JURADO, Katy	Best Supp. Actress		1954
K			
KAHN, Madeline	Best Supp. Actress		1973, 1974
KAMINSKA, Ida	Best Actress		1966
KANE, Carol	Best Actress		1975
KAZAN, Elia	Best Director	1947	1951, 1955, 1963
KEATON, Diane	Best Actress	1977	1981
KEDROVA, Lila	Best Supp. Actress	1964	

* Includes only actors, actresses and directors.

** Other than years won.

NAME*	CATEGORY	YEARS WON	YEARS NOMINATED **
KELLAWAY, Cecil	Best Supp. Actor		1948, 1967
KELLERMAN, Sally	Best Supp. Actress		1970
KELLY, Gene	Best Actor		1945
KELLY, Grace	Best Supp. Actress		1953
"	Best Actress	1954	
KELLY, Nancy	Best Actress		1956
KENNEDY, Arthur	Best Supp. Actor		1949, 1955, 1957, 1958
"	Best Actor		1951
KENNEDY, George	Best Supp. Actor	1967	
KERR, Deborah	Best Actress		1949, 1953, 1956, 1957, 1958, 1960
KIESLOWSKI, Krzysztof	Best Director		1994
KING, Henry	Best Director		1943, 1944
KINGSLEY, Ben	Best Actor	1982	
KINNEAR, Greg	Best Supp. Actor		1997
KIRKLAND, Sally	Best Actress		1987
KLINE, Kevin	Best Supp. Actor	1988	
KNIGHT, Shirley	Best Supp. Actress		1960, 1962
KNOX, Alexander	Best Actor		1944
KOHNER, Susan	Best Supp. Actress		1959
KORJUS, Miliza	Best Supp. Actress		1938
KOSTER, Henry	Best Director		1947
KRAMER, Stanley	Best Director		1958, 1961, 1967
KRUSCHEN, Jack	Best Supp. Actor		1960
KUBRICK, Stanley	Best Director		1964, 1968, 1971, 1975
KUROSAWA, Akira	Best Director		1985
L			
La CAVA, Gregory	Best Director		1936, 1937
LADD, Diane	Best Supp. Actress		1974, 1990
La GARDE, Jocelyne	Best Supp. Actress		1966
LAHTI, Christine	Best Supp. Actress		1984
LANCASTER, Burt	Best Actor	1960	1953, 1962, 1981
LANCHESTER, Elsa	Best Supp. Actress		1949, 1957
LANDAU, Martin	Best Supp. Actor	1994	1988, 1989
LANG, Walter	Best Director		1956
LANGE, Hope	Best Supp. Actress		1957
LANGE, Jessica	Best Supp. Actress	1982	
"	Best Actress	1994	1982, 1984, 1985, 1989
LANSBURY, Angela	Best Supp. Actress		1944, 1945, 1962
LAUGHTON, Charles	Best Actor	1932-33	1935, 1957
LAURIE, Piper	Best Actress		1961
"	Best Supp. Actress		1976, 1986
LEACHMAN, Cloris	Best Supp. Actress	1971	
LEAN, David	Best Director	1957, 1962	1946, 1947, 1955, 1965, 1984
LEE, Peggy	Best Supp. Actress		1955
LEEDS, Andrea	Best Supp. Actress		1937
LEIGH, Janet	Best Supp. Actress		1960
LEIGH, Vivien	Best Actress	1939, 1951	
LEIGHTON, Margaret	Best Supp. Actress		1971
Le LOUCH, Claude	Best Director		1966
LEMMON, Jack	Best Supp. Actor	1955	
"	Best Actor	1973	1959, 1960, 1962, 1979, 1980, 1982
LENYA, Lotte	Best Supp. Actress		1961
LEONARD, Robert Z.	Best Director		1929-30, 1936
Le ROY, Mervyn	Best Director		1942
LEVINSON, Barry	Best Director	1988	
LITHGOW, John	Best Supp. Actor		1983
LITVAK, Anatole	Best Director		1948
LLOYD, Frank	Best Director	1928-29, 1932-33	1928-29 (2), 1935
LOCKE, Sondra	Best Supp. Actress		1968
LOCKHART, Gene	Best Supp. Actor		1938

Major Academy Award Winners and Nominees — by Name

NAME*	CATEGORY	YEARS WON	YEARS NOMINATED **
LOGAN, Joshua	Best Director		1955, 1957
LOGGIA, Robert	Best Supp. Actor		1985
LOMBARD, Carole	Best Actress		1936
LOREN, Sophia	Best Actress	1961	1964
LORRING, Joan	Best Supp. Actress		1945
LOVE, Bessie	Best Actress		1928-29
LUBITSCH, Ernst	Best Director		1928-29, 1929-30, 1943
LUCAS, George	Best Director		1973, 1977
LUKAS, Paul	Best Actor	1943	
LUMET, Sidney	Best Director		1957, 1975, 1976
LUNT, Alfred	Best Actor		1931-32
LYNCH, David	Best Director		1986
LYNNE, Adrian	Best Director		1987
M			
MacGRAW, Ali	Best Actress		1970
MacLAINE, Shirley	Best Actress	1983	1958, 1960, 1963, 1977
MacMAHON, Aline	Best Supp. Actress		1944
MADIGAN, Amy	Best Supp. Actress		1985
MAGNANI, Anna	Best Actress	1955	1957
MAIN, Marjorie	Best Supp. Actress		1947
MAKO	Best Supp. Actor		1966
MALDEN, Karl	Best Supp. Actor	1951	1954
MALKOVICH, John	Best Supp. Actor		1984, 1993
MALONE, Dorothy	Best Supp. Actress	1956	
MANKIEWICZ, Joseph L.	Best Director	1949, 1950	1952, 1972
MANN, Delbert	Best Director	1955	
MANTELL, Joe	Best Supp. Actor		1955
MARCH, Fredric	Best Actor	1931-32, 1946	1930-31, 1937, 1951
MARCHAND, Colette	Best Supp. Actress		1952
MARLEY, John	Best Supp. Actor		1970
MARVIN, Lee	Best Actor	1965	
MASON, James	Best Actor		1954
"	Best Supp. Actor		1966
MASON, Marsha	Best Actress		1973, 1977, 1979, 1981
MASSEY, Daniel	Best Supp. Actor		1968
MASSEY, Raymond	Best Actor		1940
MASTRANTONIO, Mary Elizabeth	Best Supp. Actress		1986
MASTROIANNI, Marcello	Best Actor		1962, 1977, 1987
MATLIN, Marlee	Best Actress	1986	
MATTHAU, Walter	Best Supp. Actor	1966	
"	Best Actor		1971, 1975
McCAMBRIDGE, Mercedes	Best Supp. Actress	1949	1956
McCAREY, Leo	Best Director	1937, 1944	1945
McCARTHY, Kevin	Best Supp. Actor		1951
McCORMACK, Patty	Best Supp. Actress		1956
McDANIEL. Hattie	Best Supp. Actress	1939	
McDONNELL, Mary	Best Supp. Actress		1990
McDORMAND, Frances	Best Actress	1996	
"	Best Supp. Actress		1988
McGUIRE, Dorothy	Best Actress		1947
McLAGLEN, Victor	Best Actor	1935	1952
McNAMARA, Maggie	Best Actress		1953
McQUEEN, Steve	Best Actor		1966
MEDFORD, Kay	Best Supp. Actress		1968
MENJOU, Adolphe	Best Actor		1930-31
MERCHANT, Vivien	Best Supp. Actress		1966
MERCOURI, Melina	Best Actress		1960
MEREDITH, Burgess	Best Supp. Actor		1975, 1976
MERKEL, Una	Best Supp. Actress		1961
MIDLER, Bette	Best Actress		1979

* Includes only actors, actresses and directors.

** Other than years won.

NAME*	CATEGORY	YEARS WON	YEARS NOMINATED **
MILES, Sarah	Best Actress		1970
MILES, Sylvia	Best Supp. Actress		1969, 1975
MILESTONE, Lewis	Best Director	1929-30	1927-28, 1930-31
MILFORD, Penelope	Best Supp. Actress		1978
MILLAND, Ray	Best Actor	1945	
MILLER, Jason	Best Supp. Actor		1973
MILLS, John	Best Supp. Actor	1970	
MINEO, Sal	Best Supp. Actor		1955, 1960
MINGHELLA, Anthony	Best Director	1996	
MINNELLI, Liza	Best Actress	1972	1969
MINNELLI, Vincente	Best Director	1958	1951
MIRREN, Helen	Best Supp. Actress		1994
MITCHELL, Thomas	Best Supp. Actor	1939	1937
MITCHUM, Robert	Best Supp. Actor		1945
MOLINARO, Edouard	Best Director		1979
MONTGOMERY, Robert	Best Actor		1937, 1941
MOODY, Ron	Best Actor		1968
MOORE, Dudley	Best Actor		1981
MOORE, Grace	Best Actress		1934
MOORE, Juanita	Best Supp. Actress		1959
MOORE, Julianne	Best Supp. Actress		1997
MOORE, Mary Tyler	Best Actress		1980
MOORE, Terry	Best Supp. Actress		1952
MOOREHEAD, Agnes	Best Supp. Actress		1942, 1944, 1948, 1964
MORENO, Rita	Best Supp. Actress	1961	
MORGAN, Frank	Best Actor		1934
"	Best Supp. Actor		1942
MORITA, Noriyuki "Pat"	Best Supp. Actor		1984
MORLEY, Robert	Best Supp. Actor		1938
MORRIS, Chester	Best Actor		1928-29
MULLIGAN, Robert	Best Director		1962
MUNI, Paul	Best Actor	1936	1928-29, 1932-33, 1937, 1959
MURRAY, Don	Best Supp. Actor		1956
N			
NAISH, J. Carrol	Best Supp. Actor		1943, 1945
NATWICK, Mildred	Best Supp. Actress		1967
NEAL, Patricia	Best Actress	1963	1968
NEESON, Liam	Best Actor		1993
NEGULESCO, Jean	Best Director		1948
NEWMAN, Paul	Best Actor	1986	1958, 1961, 1963, 1967, 1981, 1982, 1994
NGOR, Dr. Haing S.	Best Supp. Actor	1984	
NICHOLS, Mike	Best Director	1967	1966, 1983, 1988
NICHOLSON, Jack	Best Supp. Actor	1983	1969
"	Best Actor	1975, 1997	1970, 1973, 1974, 1985, 1987
NIVEN, David	Best Actor	1958	
NOONAN, Chris	Best Director		1995
O			
OAKIE, Jack	Best Supp. Actor		1940
OBERON, Merle	Best Actress		1935
O'BRIEN, Edmond	Best Supp. Actor	1954	1964
O'CONNELL, Arthur	Best Supp. Actor		1955, 1959
O'HERLIHY, Dan	Best Actor		1954
OLIN, Lena	Best Supp. Actress		1989
OLIVER, Edna May	Best Supp. Actress		1939
OLIVIER, Laurence	Best Actor	1948	1939, 1940, 1946, 1956, 1960, 1965, 1972, 1976, 1978
"	Best Director		1948
OLMOS, Edward James	Best Actor		1988
OLSON, Nancy	Best Supp. Actress		1950

Major Academy Award Winners and Nominees — by Name

NAME*	CATEGORY	YEARS WON	YEARS NOMINATED **
O'NEAL, Ryan	Best Actor		1970
O'NEAL, Tatum	Best Supp. Actress	1973	
O'NEIL, Barbara	Best Supp. Actress		1940
O'TOOLE, Peter	Best Actor		1962, 1964, 1968, 1969, 1972, 1980, 1982
OUSPENSKAYA, Maria	Best Supp. Actress		1936, 1939
P			
PACINO, Al	Best Supp. Actor		1972, 1990
"	Best Actor	1992	1973, 1974, 1975, 1979
PAGE, Geraldine	Best Supp. Actress		1953, 1966, 1972, 1984
"	Best Actress	1985	1961, 1962, 1978
PAKULA, Alan J.	Best Director		1976
PALANCE, Jack	Best Supp. Actor	1991	1952, 1953
PALMINTERI, Chazz	Best Supp. Actor		1994
PAQUIN, Anna	Best Supp. Actress	1993	
PARKER, Alan	Best Director		1978, 1988
PARKER, Eleanor	Best Actress		1950, 1951, 1955
PARKS, Larry	Best Actor		1946
PARSONS, Estelle	Best Supp. Actress	1967	1968
PAVAN, Marisa	Best Supp. Actress		1955
PAXINOU, Katina	Best Supp. Actress	1943	
PECK, Gregory	Best Actor	1962	1945, 1946, 1947, 1949
PENN, Arthur	Best Director		1962, 1967, 1969
PENN, Sean	Best Actor		1995
PEREZ, Rosie	Best Supp. Actress		1993
PERKINS, Anthony	Best Supp. Actor		1956
PERRINE, Valerie	Best Actress		1974
PERRY, Frank	Best Director		1962
PESCI, Joe	Best Supp. Actor	1990	
PETERS, Susan	Best Supp. Actress		1942
PFEIFFER, Michelle	Best Supp. Actress		1988
"	Best Actress		1989
PHOENIX, River	Best Supp. Actor		1988
PICKFORD, Mary	Best Actress	1928-29	
PIDGEON, Walter	Best Actor		1942, 1943
PITT, Brad	Best Supp. Actor		1995
POITIER, Sidney	Best Actor	1963	1958
POLANSKI, Roman	Best Director		1974
POLLACK, Sydney	Best Director	1985	1969
POLLARD, Michael J.	Best Supp. Actor		1967
PONTECORVO, Gillo	Best Director		1968
POSTLETHWAITE, Pete	Best Supp. Actor		1993
POWELL, William	Best Actor		1934, 1936, 1947
PREMINGER, Otto	Best Director		1944, 1963
Q			
QUAID, Randy	Best Supp. Actor		1973
QUAYLE, Anthony	Best Supp. Actor		1969
QUINLAN, Kathleen	Best Supp. Actress		1995
QUINN, Anthony	Best Supp. Actor	1952, 1956	
"	Best Actor		1957, 1964
R			
RADFORD, Michael	Best Director		1995
RAINER, Luise	Best Actress	1936, 1937	
RAINS, Claude	Best Supp. Actor		1939, 1943, 1944, 1946
RAMBEAU, Marjorie	Best Supp. Actress		1940, 1953
RAMSEY, Anne	Best Supp. Actress		1987
RATHBONE, Basil	Best Supp. Actor		1936, 1938
REDFORD, Robert	Best Actor		1973
"	Best Director	1980	1994
REDGRAVE, Lynn	Best Actress		1966

* Includes only actors, actresses and directors.   ** Other than years won.

NAME*	CATEGORY	YEARS WON	YEARS NOMINATED **
REDGRAVE, Michael	Best Actor		1947
REDGRAVE, Vanessa	Best Actress		1966, 1968, 1971, 1984
"	Best Supp. Actress	1977	
REDMAN, Joyce	Best Supp. Actress		1963, 1965
REED, Carol	Best Director	1968	1949, 1950
REED, Donna	Best Supp. Actress	1953	
REMICK, Lee	Best Actress		1962
RENOIR, Jean	Best Director		1945
REVERE, Anne	Best Supp. Actress	1945	1943, 1947
REYNOLDS, Burt	Best Supp. Actor		1997
REYNOLDS, Debbie	Best Actress		1964
RICHARDS, Beah	Best Supp. Actress		1967
RICHARDSON, Miranda	Best Actress		1994
RICHARDSON, Ralph	Best Supp. Actor		1949, 1984
RICHARDSON, Tony	Best Director	1963	
RITT, Martin	Best Director		1963
RITTER, Thelma	Best Supp. Actress		1950, 1951, 1952, 1953, 1959, 1962
ROBARDS, Jr., Jason	Best Supp. Actor	1976, 1977	
ROBBINS, Jerome	Best Director	1961	
ROBBINS, Tim	Best Director		1995
ROBERTS, Eric	Best Supp. Actor		1985
ROBERTS, Julia	Best Supp. Actress		1989
"	Best Actress		1990
ROBERTS, Rachel	Best Actress		1963
ROBERTSON, Cliff	Best Actor	1968	
ROBSON, Flora	Best Supp. Actress		1946
ROBSON, Mark	Best Director		1957, 1958
ROBSON, May	Best Actress		1932-33
ROGERS, Ginger	Best Actress	1940	
ROONEY, Mickey	Best Actor		1939, 1943
"	Best Supp. Actor		1956, 1979
ROSS, Diana	Best Actress		1972
ROSS, Herbert	Best Director		1977
ROSS, Katharine	Best Supp. Actress		1967
ROSSEN, Robert	Best Director		1949, 1961
ROTH, Tim	Best Supp. Actor		1995
ROWLANDS, Gena	Best Actress		1974, 1980
RUEHL, Mercedes	Best Supp. Actress	1991	
RUGGLES, Wesley	Best Director		1930-31
RUSH, Geoffrey	Best Actor	1996	
RUSSELL, Harold	Best Supp. Actor	1946	
RUSSELL, Ken	Best Director		1970
RUSSELL, Rosalind	Best Actress		1942, 1946, 1947, 1958
RUTHERFORD, Margaret	Best Supp. Actress	1963	
RYAN, Robert	Best Supp. Actor		1947
RYDER, Winona	Best Supp. Actress		1993
RYDER, Winona	Best Actress		1994
SAINT, Eva Marie	Best Supp. Actress	1954	
SANDERS, George	Best Supp. Actor	1950	
SARANDON, Chris	Best Supp. Actor		1975
SARANDON, Susan	Best Actress	1995	1981, 1991, 1992, 1994
SAVALAS, Telly	Best Supp. Actor		1962
SCHAFFNER, Franklin J.	Best Director	1970	
SCHEIDER, Roy	Best Supp. Actor		1971
"	Best Actor		1979
SCHELL, Maximilian	Best Actor	1961	1975
SCHELL, Maximilian	Best Supp. Actor		1977
SCHERTZINGER, Victor	Best Director		1934
SCHILDKRAUT, Joseph	Best Supp. Actor	1937	

* Includes only actors, actresses and directors.

** Other than years won.

Major Academy Award Winners and Nominees — by Name

NAME*	CATEGORY	YEARS WON	YEARS NOMINATED **
SCHLESINGER, John	Best Director	1969	1965, 1971
SCHROEDER, Barbet	Best Director		1990
SCOFIELD, Paul	Best Actor	1966	
SCOFIELD, Paul	Best Supp. Actor		1994
SCORSESE, Martin	Best Director		1988, 1990
SCOTT, George C.	Best Supp. Actor		1959, 1961
"	Best Actor	1970	1971
SCOTT, Martha	Best Actress		1940
SEATON, George	Best Director		1954
SEGAL, George	Best Supp. Actor		1966
SELLERS, Peter	Best Actor		1964, 1979
SHARIF, Omar	Best Supp. Actor		1962
SHAW, Robert	Best Supp. Actor		1966
SHEARER, Norma	Best Actress	1929-30	1929-30, 1930-31, 1934, 1936, 1938
SHEPARD, Sam	Best Supp. Actor		1983
SHERIDAN, Jim	Best Director		1989, 1993
SHIRE, Talia	Best Supp. Actress		1974
"	Best Actress		1976
SHIRLEY, Anne	Best Supp. Actress		1937
SHUE, Elisabeth	Best Actress		1995
SIDNEY, Sylvia	Best Supp. Actress		1973
SIGNORET, Simone	Best Actress	1959	1965
SIMMONS, Jean	Best Supp. Actress		1948
"	Best Actress		1969
SINATRA, Frank	Best Supp. Actor	1953	
"	Best Actor		1955
SINISE, Gary	Best Supp. Actor		1994
SIODMAK, Robert	Best Director		1946
SKALA, Lilia	Best Supp. Actress		1963
SMITH, Maggie	Best Supp. Actress	1978	1965, 1986
"	Best Actress	1969	1972
SNODGRESS, Carrie	Best Actress		1970
SONDERGAARD, Gale	Best Supp. Actress	1936	1946
SORVINO, Mira	Best Supp. Actress	1995	
SOTHERN, Ann	Best Supp. Actress		1987
SPACEK, Sissy	Best Actress	1980	1976, 1982, 1984, 1986
SPACEY, Kevin	Best Supp. Actor	1995	
SPIELBERG, Steven	Best Director	1993	1977
STACK, Robert	Best Supp. Actor		1956
STALLONE, Sylvester	Best Actor		1976
STAMP, Terence	Best Supp. Actor		1962
STANLEY, Kim	Best Actress		1964
STANWYCK, Barbara	Best Actress		1937, 1941, 1944, 1948
STAPLETON, Maureen	Best Supp. Actress	1981	1958, 1970, 1978
STEENBURGEN, Mary	Best Supp. Actress	1980	
STEIGER, Rod	Best Supp. Actor		1954
"	Best Actor	1967	1965
STEPHENSON, James	Best Supp. Actor		1940
STERLING, Jan	Best Supp. Actress		1954
STEVENS, George	Best Director	1951, 1956	1943, 1953, 1959
STEVENSON, Robert	Best Director		1964
STEWART, James	Best Actor	1940	1939, 1946, 1950, 1959
STOCKWELL, Dean	Best Supp. Actor		1988
STONE, Lewis	Best Actor		1928-29
STONE, Oliver	Best Director	1986, 1989	
STONE, Sharon	Best Actress		1995
STRAIGHT, Beatrice	Best Supp. Actress	1976	
STRASBERG, Lee	Best Supp. Actor		1974
STRAUSS, Robert	Best Supp. Actor		1953

* Includes only actors, actresses and directors.   ** Other than years won.

NAME*	CATEGORY	YEARS WON	YEARS NOMINATED **
STREEP, Meryl	Best Supp. Actress	1979	1978
"	Best Actress	1982	1981, 1983, 1985, 1987, 1988, 1990, 1995
STREISAND, Barbra	Best Actress	1968	1973
STUART, Gloria	Best Supp. Actress		1997
STURGES, John	Best Director		1955
SULLAVAN, Margaret	Best Actress		1938
SUZMAN, Janet	Best Actress		1971
SWANSON, Gloria	Best Actress		1927-28, 1929-30, 1950
T			
TAMBLYN, Russ	Best Supp. Actor		1957
TAMIROFF, Akim	Best Supp. Actor		1936, 1943
TANDY, Jessica	Best Actress	1989	
TARANTINO, Quentin	Best Director		1994
TAUROG, Norman	Best Director	1930-31	1938
TAYLOR, Elizabeth	Best Actress	1960, 1966	1957, 1958, 1959
TESHIGAHARA, Hiroshi	Best Director		1965
THOMPSON, Emma	Best Actress	1992	1993, 1995
"	Best Supp. Actress		1993
THOMPSON, J. Lee	Best Director		1961
THURMAN, Uma	Best Supp. Actress		1994
TIBBETT, Lawrence	Best Actor		1929-30
TIERNEY, Gene	Best Actress		1945
TILLY, Jennifer	Best Supp. Actress		1994
TILLY, Meg	Best Supp. Actress		1985
TODD, Richard	Best Actor		1949
TOMEI, Marisa	Best Supp. Actress	1992	
TOMLIN, Lily	Best Supp. Actress		1975
TONE, Franchot	Best Actor		1935
TOPOL	Best Actor		1971
TORN, Rip	Best Supp. Actor		1983
TRACY, Lee	Best Supp. Actor		1964
TRACY, Spencer	Best Actor	1937, 1938	1936, 1950, 1955, 1958, 1960, 1961, 1967
TRAVERS, Henry	Best Supp. Actor		1942
TRAVOLTA, John	Best Actor		1977, 1994
TREVOR, Claire	Best Supp. Actress	1948	1937, 1954
TROELL, Jan	Best Director		1972
TROISI, Massimo	Best Actor		1995
TRUFFANT, Francois	Best Director		1974
TULLY, Tom	Best Supp. Actor		1954
TURNER, Kathleen	Best Actress		1986
TURNER, Lana	Best Actress		1957
TYRRELL, Susan	Best Supp. Actress		1972
TYSON, Cicely	Best Actress		1972
U			
ULLMANN, Liv	Best Actress		1972, 1976
UMEKI, Miyoshi	Best Supp. Actress	1957	
URE, Mary	Best Supp. Actress		1960
USTINOV, Peter	Best Supp. Actor	1960, 1964	1951
V			
VACCARO, Brenda	Best Supp. Actress		1975
Van DYKE, W. S.	Best Director		1934, 1936
Van FLEET, Jo	Best Supp. Actress	1955	
Van SANT, Gus Jr.	Best Director		1997
VARSI, Diane	Best Supp. Actress		1957
VAUGHN, Robert	Best Supp. Actor		1959
VIDOR, King	Best Director		1927-28, 1929-30, 1931-32, 1938, 1956
VOIGHT, Jon	Best Actor	1978	1969, 1985
Von STERNBERG, Josef	Best Director		1930-31, 1931-32
Von STROHEIM, Erich	Best Supp. Actor		1950

Major Academy Award Winners and Nominees — by Name

NAME*	CATEGORY	YEARS WON	YEARS NOMINATED **
Von SYDOW, Max	Best Actor		1988
W			
WALKEN, Christopher	Best Supp. Actor	1978	
WALTERS, Charles	Best Director		1953
WALTERS, Julie	Best Actress		1983
WARDEN, Jack	Best Supp. Actor		1975, 1978
WARNER, H. B.	Best Supp. Actor		1937
WASHINGTON, Denzel	Best Supp. Actor	1989	
WATERS, Ethel	Best Supp. Actress		1949
WATERSTON, Sam	Best Actor		1984
WATSON, Lucile	Best Supp. Actress		1943
WAYNE, John	Best Actor	1969	1949
WEAVER, Sigourney	Best Actress		1986, 1988
"	Best Supp. Actress		1988
WEBB, Clifton	Best Supp. Actor		1944, 1946
"	Best Actor		1948
WEIR, Peter	Best Director		1985, 1989
WELD, Tuesday	Best Supp. Actress		1977
WELLES, Orson	Best Actor		1941
"	Best Director		1941
WELLMAN, William A.	Best Director		1937, 1949, 1954
WERNER, Oskar	Best Actor		1965
WERTMULLER, Lina	Best Director		1976
WHITMAN, Stuart	Best Actor		1961
WHITMORE, James	Best Supp. Actor		1949
"	Best Actor		1975
WHITTY, Dame May	Best Supp. Actress		1937, 1942
WIDMARK, Richard	Best Supp. Actor		1947
WIEST, Dianne	Best Supp. Actress	1986, 1994	1989
WILD, Jack	Best Supp. Actor		1968
WILDE, Cornel	Best Actor		1945
WILDE, Ted	Best Director		1927-28
WILDER, Billy	Best Director	1945, 1960	1944, 1950, 1953, 1954, 1957, 1959
WILDER, Gene	Best Supp. Actor		1968
WILLIAMS, Cara	Best Supp. Actress		1958
WILLIAMS, Robin	Best Actor		1987, 1989
"	Best Supp. Actor	1997	
WILLS, Chill	Best Supp. Actor		1960
WINFIELD, Paul	Best Actor		1972
WINFREY, Oprah	Best Supp. Actress		1985
WINGER, Debra	Best Actress		1982, 1983, 1993
WINNINGHAM, Mare	Best Supp. Actress		1995
WINSLET, Kate	Best Supp. Actress		1995
"	Best Actress		1997
WINTERS, Shelley	Best Actress		1951
"	Best Supp. Actress	1959, 1965	1972
WISE, Robert	Best Director	1961, 1965	1958
WOOD, Natalie	Best Supp. Actress		1955
"	Best Actress		1961, 1963
WOOD, Peggy	Best Supp. Actress		1965
WOOD, Sam	Best Director		1939, 1940, 1942
WOODARD, Alfre	Best Supp. Actress		1983
WOODS, James	Best Actor		1986
WOODWARD, Joanne	Best Actress	1957	1968, 1973, 1990
WOOLLEY, Monty	Best Actor		1942
"	Best Supp. Actor		1944
WRIGHT, Teresa	Best Supp. Actress	1942	1941
"	Best Actress		1942
WYCHERLY, Margaret	Best Supp. Actress		1941
WYLER, William	Best Director	1942, 1946, 1959	1936, 1939, 1940, 1941, 1949, 1951,

* Includes only actors, actresses and directors.　　　　** Other than years won.

Major Academy Award Winners and Nominees — by Name

NAME*	CATEGORY	YEARS WON	YEARS NOMINATED **
WYLER, William	Best Director		1953, 1956, 1965
WYMAN, Jane	Best Actress	1948	1946, 1951, 1954
WYNN, Ed	Best Supp. Actor		1959
WYNYARD, Diana	Best Actress		1932-33
Y			
YATES, Peter	Best Director		1979, 1983
YORK, Susannah	Best Supp. Actress		1969
YOUNG, Burt	Best Supp. Actor		1976
YOUNG, Gig	Best Supp. Actor	1969	1951, 1958
YOUNG, Loretta	Best Actress	1947	1949
YOUNG, Roland	Best Supp. Actor		1937
Z			
ZEFFIRELLI, Franco	Best Director		1968
ZEMECKIS, Robert	Best Director	1994	
ZINNEMANN, Fred	Best Director	1953, 1966	1948, 1952, 1959, 1960, 1977

* Includes only actors, actresses and directors.

** Other than years won.

11

Who's Who
— A Photo Gallery
of Names and Faces

Gone...But Never Forgotten!

A **C**

FRANK ALBERTSON

ADRIENNE AMES

VILMA BANKY

LEX BARKER

CHARLES BICKFORD

JOAN BLONDELL

SCOTT BRADY

GEORGE BRENT

HELEN BRODERICK

CLIVE BROOK

BILLIE BURKE

JACK CARSON

LANE CHANDLER

DANE CLARK

RICHARD CONTE

DONALD CRISP

Gone…But Never Forgotten!

D   **H**

FRANCES DEE

BRIAN DONLEVY

RICHARD EGAN

FAYE EMERSON

MADGE EVANS

FRANCES FARMER

DICK FORAN

RALPH FORBES

JUDY GARLAND

JOHN GILBERT

CARY GRANT

RICHARD GREENE

CHARLOTTE GREENWOOD

WILLIAM HAINES

SESSUE HAYAKAWA

HELEN HAYES

Gone...But Never Forgotten!

J **O**

CAROLYN JONES

TOM KEENE

FERNANDO LAMAS

MARIO LANZA

JACK LA RUE

FLORENCE LAWRENCE

ROBERT LOWERY

JOHN LUND

IDA LUPINO

MARILYN MAXWELL

MARIA MONTEZ

DENNIS MORGAN

DAVID NIVEN

LLOYD NOLAN

MARY NOLAN

WARNER OLAND

Gone...But Never Forgotten!

P **W**

GAIL PATRICK

ELIZABETH PATTERSON

WALTER PIDGEON

DICK POWELL

MARTHA RAYE

THELMA RITTER

EDWARD G. ROBINSON

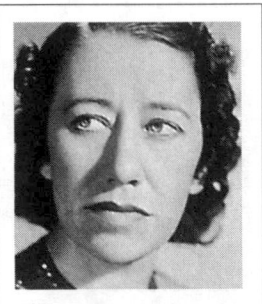

FLORA ROBSON

ANNE SHIRLEY

ALISON SKIPWORTH

LYLE TALBOT

MARSHALL THOMPSON

FRANCHOT TONE

VERA-ELLEN

ROBERT WALKER

CLIFTON WEBB

Suggested Bibliography

- CELEBRITY DIRECTORY, 6th Ed. 1996. Published by Axiom Information Resources, P. O. Box 8015, Ann Arbor, MI 48107 ($39.95)
- CEMETERIES OF THE UNITED STATES by Deborah M. Burek, 1994 (Published by Gale) $155.
- THE 1995 FAN CLUB DIRECTORY, Issue #19. Published annually by the National Association of Fan Clubs, P.O. Box 7487, Burbank, CA 91510, (Telephone: 1-818-763-3280); Printed by "Not Just Printing," 4532 Telephone Rd., #102, Ventura, CA 93003, (Telephone: 1-805-644-3245)
- THE ILLUSTRATED WHO'S WHO OF HOLLYWOOD DIRECTORS by Michael Barson (Published by The Noonday Press, 19 Union Square West, New York, NY 10003) $27.50
- PERMANENT CALIFORNIANS (An Illustrated Guide to the Cemeteries of California) by Judi Culbertson and Tom Randall, 1989 (Published by Chelsea Green Pub. Co., Chelsea, Vermont) $16.95
- PERMANENT ITALIANS (An Illustrated Guide to the Cemeteries of Italy) by Judi Culbertson and Tom Randall, 1989 (Published in U.S. by Walker Pub. Co., 435 Hudson St., New York, NY 10014) $16.95
- PERMANENT LONDONERS (An Illustrated Guide to the Cemeteries of London) by Judi Culbertson and Tom Randall, 1991 (Published in U.S. by Walker Pub. Co., 435 Hudson St., New York, NY 10014) $16.95
- PERMANENT NEW YORKERS (An Illustrated Guide to the Cemeteries of New York) by Judi Culbertson and Tom Randall, 1989 (Published by Chelsea Green Pub. Co., Chelsea, Vermont) $16.95
- PERMANENT PARISIANS (An Illustrated Guide to the Cemeteries of Paris) by Judi Culbertson and Tom Randall, 1986 (Published in U.S. by Walker Pub. Co., 435 Hudson St., New York, NY 10014) $16.95
- SILENT FILM NECROLOGY by Gene Vazzana, 1995 (Published by McFarland and Company, Inc., Box 611, Jefferson, NC 28640)
- STAR GUIDE (Movie Star Home Address Book), 1996-97 (Published by Axiom Information Resources, P. O. Box 8015, Ann Arbor, MI 48107) $12.95 + $1.95 S&H
- TOO YOUNG TO DIE by Patricia Fox-Sheinwold, 1991 (Published by Crescent Books, distributed by Outlet Book Co., Inc., a Random House Co., New York, NY)
- THE ULTIMATE DIRECTORY OF THE SILENT SCREEN PLAYERS by Billy Doyle, 1995 (Published by Scarecrow Press)
- VARIETY OBITUARIES (1905 to 1994) in 11 volumes + 4 Bi-annual Yearbooks (Garland Publishers, Inc., New York and London)
- VARIETY (Weekly) Newspaper (Subscription Dept., P.O. Box 6400, Torrance, CA 90504-9867)
- WHO WAS WHO ON SCREEN by Evelyn Mack Truitt, 3rd Ed. 1983 (Published by R. R. Bowker Co., 205 East 42nd St., New York, NY 10017). A condensed, softcover 1984 "Illustrated Edition" is available @ $29.95

Related Web Sites

■ BENEATH LOS ANGELES, by Ken Goldstein and Steve Goldstein.
   http://home.earthlink.net/~steve56

■ FIND A GRAVE, by Jim Tipton.
   http://www.findagrave.com

■ HOLLYWOOD UNDERGROUND, by Karen McHale.
   http://members.aol.com/karenhm/graves.htm